Your Class.
Their Career.
Everyone's Future.

Helping today's students become the teachers of tomorrow.

"Teacher educators who are developing pedagogies for the analysis of teaching and learning contend that analyzing teaching artifacts has three advantages: it enables new teachers time for reflection while still using the real materials of practice; it provides new teachers with experience thinking about and approaching the complexity of the classroom; and in some cases, it can help new teachers and teacher educators develop a shared understanding and common language about teaching. . . ."[1]

As Linda Darling-Hammond and her colleagues point out, grounding teacher education in real classrooms—among real teachers and students and among actual examples of students' and teachers' work—is an important,

PEARSON
myeducationlab™
Where the Classroom Comes to Life

and perhaps even an essential, part of training teachers for the complexities of teaching today's students in today's classrooms. For a number of years, we have heard the same message from many of you as we sat in your offices learning about the goals of your courses and the challenges you face in teaching the next generation of educators. Working with a number of our authors and with many of you, we have created a website that provides you and your students with the context of real classrooms and artifacts that research on teacher education tells us is so important. Through authentic in-class video footage, interactive simulations, rich case studies, examples of authentic teacher and student work, and more, **MyEducationLab** offers you and your students a uniquely valuable teacher education tool.

MyEducationLab is easy to use! Wherever the **MyEducationLab** logo appears in the margins or elsewhere in the text, you and your students can follow the simple link instructions to access the **MyEducationLab** resource that corresponds with the chapter content. These include:

VIDEO ■ Authentic classroom videos show how real teachers handle actual classroom situations.

HOMEWORK & EXERCISES ■ These assignable activities give students opportunities to understand content more deeply and to practice applying content.

BUILDING TEACHING SKILLS ■ These assignments help students practice and strengthen skills that are essential to quality teaching. By analyzing and responding to real student and teacher artifacts and/or authentic classroom videos, students practice important teaching skills they will need when they enter real classrooms.

CASE STUDIES ■ A diverse set of robust cases drawn from some of our best-selling books further expose students to the realities of teaching and offer valuable perspectives on common issues and challenges in education.

SIMULATIONS ■ Created by the IRIS Center at Vanderbilt University, these interactive simulations give hands-on practice at adapting instruction for a full spectrum of learners.

STUDENT & TEACHER ARTIFACTS ■ Authentic student and teacher classroom artifacts are tied to course topics and offer practice in working with the actual types of materials that teachers encounter every day.

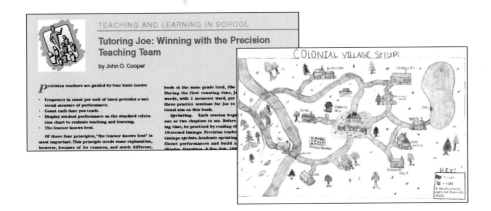

INDIVIDUALIZED STUDY PLAN ■ Your students have the opportunity to take pre- and post-tests before and after reading each chapter of the text. Their test results automatically generate a personalized study plan, identifying areas of the chapter they must reread to fully understand chapter concepts. They are also presented with interactive multimedia exercises to help ensure learning. The study plan is designed to help your students perform well on exams and to promote deep understanding of chapter content.

READINGS ▪ Specially selected, topically relevant articles from ASCD's renowned *Educational Leadership* journal expand and enrich students' perspectives on key issues and topics.

Other Resources

LESSON & PORTFOLIO BUILDERS ▪ With this effective and easy-to-use tool, you can create, update, and share standards-based lesson plans and portfolios.

MyEducationLab is easy to assign, which is essential to providing the greatest benefit to your students. Visit **www.myeducationlab.com** for a demonstration of this exciting new online teaching resource.

[1] Darling-Hammond, L., & Bransford, J., Eds. (2005). *Preparing Teachers for a Changing World.* San Francisco: John Wiley & Sons.

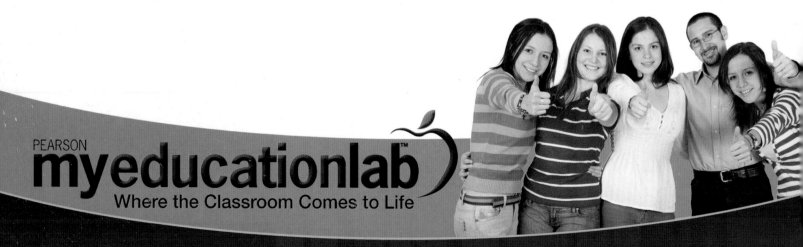

PEARSON
myeducationlab™
Where the Classroom Comes to Life

ESSENTIALS OF
EDUCATIONAL PSYCHOLOGY

ESSENTIALS OF EDUCATIONAL PSYCHOLOGY

Second Edition

Jeanne Ellis Ormrod

University of Northern Colorado (Emerita)
University of New Hampshire

Merrill
is an imprint of

Upper Saddle River, New Jersey
Columbus, Ohio

Library of Congress Cataloging-in-Publication Data

Ormrod, Jeanne Ellis.
    Essentials of educational psychology / Jeanne Ellis Ormrod.
      p. cm.
    Includes bibliographical references and index.
    ISBN-13: 978-0-13-501657-2 (pbk.)
    ISBN-10: 0-13-501657-6 (pbk.)
    1. Educational psychology—Textbooks.   I. Title
    LB1051.O663 2009
    370.15—dc22

                            2008007096

Vice President and Executive Publisher: Jeffery W. Johnston
Publisher: Kevin M. Davis
Development Editor: Christina Robb
Editorial Assistant: Lauren Reinkober
Senior Managing Editor: Pamela D. Bennett
Project Manager: Mary Harlan
Copy Editor: Lorretta Palagi
Production Coordinator: Bev Kraus
Design Coordinator: Diane C. Lorenzo
Photo Coordinator: Valerie Schultz
Text Design: Candace Rowley
Cover Design: Candace Rowley
Cover Image: SuperStock
Operations Specialist: Laura Messerly
Director of Marketing: Quinn Perkson
Marketing Manager: Erica M. DeLuca
Marketing Coordinator: Brian Mounts

This book was set in Minion by S4Carlisle Publishing Services. It was printed and bound by Courier/Kendallvillle. The cover was printed by Phoenix Color Corp.

Photo Credits: Billy E. Barnes/PhotoEdit Inc., p. 360; Robert Brenner/PhotoEdit Inc., p. 56; David Buffington/Getty Images, Inc.–Photodisc, p. 104; Susan Burger/www.naturephotohawaii.com, pp. 247, 263; Jim Carter/Photo Researchers, Inc., p. 93; Myrleen Ferguson Cate/PhotoEdit Inc., p. 354; Cindy Charles/PhotoEdit Inc., p. 249; Creatas/Dynamic Graphics, p. 196; Jim Cummins/Taxi/Getty Images, Inc., p. 26; Scott Cunningham/Merrill, pp. 8, 76, 224, 314, 320, 324, 394; Bob Daemmrich/The Image Works, p. 70; Mary Kate Denny/Getty Images Inc.–Stone Allstock, p. 166; Mary Kate Denny/PhotoEdit Inc., pp. 338, 346; Laura Dwight/Creative Eye/MIRA.com, p. 235; Tony Freeman/PhotoEdit Inc., p. 330; Jeff Greenberg/PhotoEdit Inc., pp. 138, 182, 275; Jeff Greenberg/Photolibrary.com, p. 98; Ken Hammond/USDA/NRCS/Natural Resources Conservation Service, p. 59; Will Hart/PhotoEdit Inc., pp. 204, 298, 316, 384; Li-Hua Lan/The Syracuse Newspapers/The Image Works, p. 43; Richard Lord/The Image Works, p. 143; David Mager/Pearson Learning Photo Studio, p. 39; Anthony Magnacca/Merrill, pp. 11, 109, 332, 335; Will & Deni McIntyre/Photo Researchers, Inc., pp. 4, 232; Ryan McVay/PhotoDisc/Getty Images, p. 227; Michael Newman/PhotoEdit Inc., pp. 1, 362, 369; Jonathan Nourok/PhotoEdit Inc., pp. 79, 107; F. Pedrick/The Image Works, p. 72; Jim Pickerell/The Stock Connection, p. 176; Mark Richards/PhotoEdit Inc., p. 148; © Ellen B. Senisi/Ellen Senisi, pp. 197, 278; Courtesy of Vanderbilt University, p. 128; Rudi Von Briel/PhotoEdit Inc., p. 67; Tom Watson/Merrill, pp. 119, 334; Yellow Dog Productions/Image Bank/Getty Images, p. 141; and David Young-Wolff/PhotoEdit Inc., pp. 16, 134, 156.

Pearson® is a registered trademark of Pearson plc
Merrill® is a registered trademark of Pearson Education, Inc.

Pearson Education Ltd., London
Pearson Education Singapore Pte. Ltd
Pearson Education Canada, Inc.
Pearson Education–Japan
Pearson Education Australia PTY, Limited

Pearson Education North Asia, Ltd., Hong Kong
Pearson Educación de Mexico, S.A. de C.V.
Pearson Education Malaysia Pte. Ltd.
Pearson Education Upper Saddle River, New Jersey

Merrill
is an imprint of

10 9 8 7 6 5 4 3 2 1
ISBN-13: 978-0-13-501657-2
ISBN-10:   0-13-501657-6

To my children, two who have become teachers themselves and one who, in his own way, continues to teach me many things about human potential and growth

JEANNE ELLIS ORMROD received her A.B. in psychology from Brown University and her M.S. and Ph.D. in educational psychology from The Pennsylvania State University. She earned licensure in school psychology through postdoctoral work at Temple University and the University of Colorado at Boulder and has worked as a middle school geography teacher and school psychologist. She taught educational psychology at the University of Northern Colorado from 1976 until 1998, when she moved east to return to her native New England. She is currently affiliated with the University of New Hampshire, where she occasionally teaches courses in educational psychology and research methods. She has published numerous research articles on cognition and memory, cognitive development, and giftedness, but she is probably best known for this textbook and four others: *Educational Psychology: Developing Learners* (currently in its sixth edition); *Human Learning* (currently in its fifth edition); *Child Development and Education* (co-authored with Teresa McDevitt, soon to appear in its fourth edition); and *Practical Research* (co-authored with Paul Leedy, soon to appear in its ninth edition). With her three children now grown and out on their own, she lives in New Hampshire with her husband Richard.

PREFACE

Ever since my first encounter with psychology as a college freshman many years ago, I have found psychological concepts and principles to be invaluable in helping me understand and work effectively with my fellow human beings. By the time I was a college senior, I was determined to apply psychology to an enterprise about which I care deeply: the education of children. And I have been doing so, in a variety of ways, ever since.

My undergraduate training in psychology in the late 1960s focused largely on theory and research in the behaviorist tradition. In contrast, my graduate training in educational psychology in the early 1970s had a strong information processing bent. Since then I've come to know (and love) not only behaviorism and information processing theory, but also a host of other theoretical perspectives. And as a teacher and school psychologist, I've found all of these perspectives to be useful in my work with children and adolescents.

> "The traditional approach to teaching and writing about educational psychology is to take one theory at a time, explaining its assumptions and principles and then identifying implications for educational practice. . . . I've started to teach my own educational psychology courses differently, focusing more on commonalities than differences among theories."

The traditional approach to teaching and writing about educational psychology is to take one theory at a time, explaining its assumptions and principles and then identifying implications for educational practice. I take this approach myself in my book *Educational Psychology: Developing Learners*, now in its sixth edition. But in recent years I've started to teach my own educational psychology courses differently, focusing more on commonalities than differences among theories. In fact, although researchers from different traditions have approached human cognition and behavior from many different angles, they sometimes arrive at more or less the same conclusions. The language they use to describe their observations is often different, to be sure, but beneath all the words are certain nuggets of "truth" that can be remarkably similar.

In this book I've tried to integrate ideas from many theoretical perspectives into what is, for me, a set of principles and guidelines that psychology as a whole can offer beginning teachers. These are, in essence, the Big Ideas I've spoken about—and increasingly heard others speak about as well—at professional meetings. After a short introduction to research and its importance (Chapter 1), I begin with the essence of the human experience: cognition (Chapter 2). From that foundation I go in five different directions—to learning in various contexts (Chapter 3), higher-level processes (Chapter 4), cognitive development (Chapter 5), motivation (Chapter 6), and personal and social development (Chapter 7)—but always returning to underlying cognitive processes. The last three chapters build on the earlier ones to offer recommendations in instruction (Chapter 8), classroom management (Chapter 9), and assessment (Chapter 10).

> In this book I've tried to integrate ideas from many theoretical perspectives into what is, for me, a set of principles and guidelines that psychology *as a whole* can offer beginning teachers . . . in essence, the Big ideas. . . .

Some of my colleagues will be surprised at my use of footnotes rather than APA style throughout the book. My decision was strictly a pedagogical one. Yes, students need to know that the principles and recommendations in this book are research-based. But I've found that APA style can be very distracting for someone who is reading about psychology for the first time and is trying to sort out what things are and are not important to learn and remember. Novice psychologists should be concerned more with the *ideas themselves* than with the people behind the ideas, and by putting most of the people in small print at the bottom of the page, I can help novices better focus their attention on what things truly are most important to know and understand.

FEATURES OF THE BOOK

The book's ten chapters have a variety of features that can help my readers better understand, remember, and apply what they're reading:

EACH CHAPTER BEGINS WITH A CASE STUDY that introduces some of the ideas and issues that the chapter addresses. Throughout each chapter I periodically revisit the case to offer new insights and interpretations.

I often put readers themselves in the position of "learner" and ask them to engage in a short learning or thinking activity. These SEE FOR YOURSELF exercises are similar to those that I use in my own educational psychology classes. My students have found them to be quite helpful in making concepts and principles more "real" to them—and hence more vivid, understandable, and memorable.

SEE FOR YOURSELF

Wooden Beads

To the right are 12 wooden beads. As you can see, some of them are brown and some of them are white. Are there more wooden beads or more brown beads?

If you flip through the pages of the book, you'll see many classroom artifacts—that is, EXAMPLES OF WORK CREATED BY ACTUAL STUDENTS AND TEACHERS. I use artifacts throughout the book to help readers connect concepts, principles, and strategies to students' behavior and classroom practice.

To a considerable degree, I talk about concepts and principles that apply to children and adolescents at all grade levels. Yet first graders often think and act very differently than sixth graders do, and sixth graders can, in turn, be quite different from eleventh graders. Chapters 2 through 10 each have one or more DEVELOPMENTAL TRENDS tables that highlight developmental differences that teachers are apt to see in grades K–2, 3–5, 6–8, and 9–12.

DEVELOPMENTAL TRENDS

TABLE 2.3   Typical Learning Strategies at Different Grade Levels

Grade Level	Age-Typical Characteristics	Suggested Strategies
K–2	• Organization of physical objects as a way to remember them • Appearance of rehearsal to remember verbal material; used infrequently and relatively ineffectively • Emerging ability to use visual imagery to enhance memory, especially if an adult suggests this strategy • Few if any intentional efforts to learn and remember verbal material; learning and memory are a by-product of other things children do (creating things, talking about events, listening to stories, etc.)	• Get students actively involved in topics, perhaps through hands-on activities, engaging reading materials, or fantasy play. • Relate new topics to students' prior experiences. • Model rehearsal as a strategy for remembering things over the short run. • Provide pictures that illustrate verbal material.
3–5	• Spontaneous, intentional, and increasingly effective use of rehearsal to remember things for a short time period • Increasing use of organization as an intentional learning strategy for verbal information • Increasing effectiveness in use of visual imagery as a learning strategy	• Emphasize the importance of making sense of, rather than memorizing, information. • Encourage students to organize what they are learning; suggest possible organizational structures for topics. • Provide a variety of visual aids to facilitate visual imagery, and suggest that students create their own drawings or visual images of things they need to remember.
6–8	• Predominance of rehearsal as a learning strategy • Greater abstractness and flexibility in categories used to organize information • Emergence of elaboration as an intentional learning strategy	• Suggest questions that students might ask themselves as they study; emphasize questions that promote elaboration (e.g., "Why would _____ do that?" "How is _____ different from _____?"). • Assess true understanding rather than rote memorization in assignments and quizzes.

Chapters 2 through 10 also each have two or more CLASSROOM STRATEGIES boxes that offer concrete suggestions and examples of how teachers might apply a particular concept or principle. These features should provide yet another mechanism to help my readers apply educational psychology to actual classroom practice.

CLASSROOM STRATEGIES

Encouraging Productive Interactions Among Diverse Groups

• Set up situations in which students can form new friendships.

   A junior high school science teacher decides how students will be paired for weekly lab activities. She changes the pairings every month and frequently pairs students from different ethnic backgrounds.

• Minimize or eliminate barriers to social interaction.

   Students in a third-grade class learn basic words and phrases in American Sign Language so that they can work and play with a classmate who is deaf.

• Conduct class discussions about the negative consequences of intergroup hostilities.

   A high school English teacher in a low-income, inner-city school district uses a lesson on Shakespeare's *Romeo and Juliet* to start a dis-

dominates in membership or leadership in any particular activity.

   When recruiting members for the scenery committee for the annual school play, the committee's teacher-adviser encourages both "popular" and "unpopular" students to participate. Later he divides the workload in such a way that students who don't know one another very well must work closely and cooperatively.

• Develop nondisabled students' understanding of students with special educational needs.

   In a widely publicized case, Ryan White, a boy who had contracted AIDS from a blood transfusion, met considerable resistance against his return to his neighborhood school because parents and students thought he might infect others. After Ryan's family moved to a differ-

In Chapter 3 I describe some of the ways in which culture influences children's learning and development. As a follow-up to that discussion, CULTURAL CONSIDERATIONS features describe cultural differences in specific areas—for instance, in behavior, reasoning, or motivation. These features appear in Chapters 3 through 10.

CULTURAL CONSIDERATIONS

Cultural and Ethnic Differences in Verbal Interaction

If you've grown up in mainstream Western culture, you've learned that there are certain ways of conversing with others that are socially acceptable and certain other ways that are definitely *not* acceptable. For instance, if you are having lunch with a friend, the two of you will probably try to keep a conversation going throughout the meal. And if someone else is speaking—especially if that someone else is an authority figure—you probably know not to interrupt until the speaker has finished what he or she is saying. Once the speaker *is* finished, however, you can ask a question if you are confused about the message or need further information.

Such social conventions are by no means universal. Here we look at cultural and eth-

dance tonight").[a] At one time researchers believed that an African American dialect represented a less complex form of speech than Standard English, and they urged educators to teach students to speak "properly" as quickly as possible. But researchers now realize that African American dialects are, in fact, very complex languages that have their own predictable idioms and grammatical rules and that these dialects promote communication and complex thought as readily as Standard English.[b]

   When a local dialect is the language preferred by residents of a community, it is often the means through which people can most effectively connect with one another in day-to-day interactions. Furthermore, many

culture is a chatty one. People often say things to one another even when they have very little to communicate, making small talk as a way of maintaining interpersonal relationships and filling awkward silences.[h] In some African American communities as well, people speak frequently—for instance, spontaneously shouting out during church services.[i]

   In certain other cultures, however, silence is golden. Brazilians and Peruvians often greet their guests silently, Arabs stop talking to indicate a desire for privacy, and many Native American communities value silence in general.[j] Many Chinese believe that effective learning is best accomplished through attentive listening rather than

Although my approach in this book is to integrate the concepts, principles, and educational strategies that diverse theoretical perspectives offer, it's also important for future teachers to have some familiarity with specific psychological theories and with a few prominent theorists (e.g., Jean Piaget, Lev Vygotsky, B. F. Skinner) who have had a significant influence on psychological thinking. I occasionally mention these theories and theorists in the text discussion, but I also highlight them in THEORETICAL PERSPECTIVES tables in Chapters 2, 5, and 6.

THEORETICAL PERSPECTIVES

TABLE 5.1	General Theoretical Approaches to the Study of Child and Adolescent Development		
Theoretical Perspective	General Description	Examples of Prominent Theorists	Where You Will See This Perspective in the Book
Cognitive-Developmental Theory	Cognitive-developmental theorists propose that one or more aspects of development can be characterized by a predictable sequence of stages. Each stage builds on acquisitions from any preceding stages and yet is qualitatively different from its predecessors. Many cognitive-developmentalists are *constructivists*, in that they portray children as actively trying to make sense of their world and constructing increasingly complex understandings to interpret and respond to experiences.	Jean Piaget Jerome Bruner Robbie Case Kurt Fischer Lawrence Kohlberg *Supplementary readings on Piaget's theory and Kohlberg's theory appear in the Homework and Exercises section in Chapters 5 and Chapter 7, respectively, of MyEducationLab.*	Piaget's ideas appear frequently in this chapter's discussions of developmental processes and trends (e.g., see the discussions of assimilation, accommodation, and equilibration, as well as Table 5.2 and some entries in Table 5.3). We will look at Kohlberg's theory in our discussion of moral development in Chapter 7.
Nativism	Some behaviors are biologically built in. A few behaviors (e.g., the reflex to suck on a nipple placed	Renee Baillargeon Elizabeth Spelke	The influence of nativism is most obvious in this chapter's discussions of heredity, matura-

In the United States, state teacher licensing requirements in many states include passing exams such as the Praxis tests published by the Educational Testing Service (ETS). Many items on these exams involve interpreting case studies. At the end of each chapter, then, I present a PRACTICE FOR YOUR LICENSURE EXAM exercise that includes a case study along with a constructed-response question (typically requiring a one- to two-paragraph response) and a multiple-choice question based on the case. By and large, these exercises draw on content from the chapters in which they're located, but occasionally they draw on material from earlier chapters as well.

PRACTICE FOR YOUR LICENSURE EXAM

Interview with Emily

In the 9th and 10th grades, Emily earns mostly Cs and Ds in her classes. When she reaches 11th grade, however, she begins to work more diligently on her schoolwork, and by the fall of 12th grade, she is earning As and Bs. Ms. Tillman, a preservice teacher, interviews Emily about her study strategies:

Ms. T.: How did you learn to study for a test?

Emily: I'm not really sure. I never learned the correct way to study for a test. I use my own methods, and they seem to be working because I'm now receiving the grades I want.

Ms. T.: How did you go about studying for a test when you were younger?

Emily: Honestly, I never really studied too hard. I never studied for math tests because I didn't know how to. For other subjects like history, I'd just skim over the text. Skimming the text never made the material stick in my head. I guess I never really had a strategy for studying.

Ms. T.: Now that you're receiving good grades, how do you study for a test?

Emily: Well, it's different for every subject. Now when I study for a math test, I do many practice problems. When I'm studying for a history or science test, I first review my notes. My favorite thing to do is make flash cards with the important facts. I then go through the flash cards many times and try to learn the facts on them.

Ms. T.: What do you mean, "learn" the facts on them?

Observe Kent's conservation of number in the "Cognitive Development: Middle Childhood" video in the Additional Resources section in Chapter 5 of MyEducationLab.

Accompanying the book are VIDEOS in an innovative online resource called MYEDUCATIONLAB. These videos depict numerous elementary, middle, and secondary school classrooms in action, as well as one-on-one interviews with children and adolescents.

CHANGES IN THE SECOND EDITION

Throughout the book I've made many small changes to reflect research findings and new ways of thinking that have been published or presented since I wrote the first edition. Occasionally I've also reorganized or revised sections in line with reviewers' suggestions. More obvious, however, are the following modifications and additions:

- A model of the interconnectedness of student characteristics and behaviors, planning, instruction, the classroom environment, and assessment—a model that previously appeared in Chapter 8—has been moved to Chapter 1 to emphasize that, ultimately, *student characteristics and behaviors* must underlie teacher decision making and classroom strategies. In other words, effective classroom practice must be learner-centered. Consistent with this change, I now introduce students with special needs and inclusion in Chapter 1. (Discussion of the Individuals with Disabilities Education Act remains in Chapter 3, where it was in the first edition.)

- The Theoretical Perspectives tables now have an additional column entitled "Where You Will See This Perspective in the Book." Furthermore, psychodynamic theory has been added to the developmental perspectives presented in Table 5.1, and behaviorism, humanism, and positive psychology have been added to the perspectives of motivation presented in Table 6.1. In keeping with the "Big Ideas" nature of the book, the ideas of specific theorists do not always appear in a single spot. However, readers who want focused discussions of several classic theories—those of B. F. Skinner, Jean Piaget, Lev Vygotsky, Abraham Maslow, Erik Erikson, and Lawrence Kohlberg—can find them in online supplementary readings in MyEducationLab.

- Some of the Cultural Considerations boxes that appear in Chapters 3 through 10 have been expanded. New topics in these boxes include cultural diversity in worldviews, epistemological beliefs, views and manifestations of intelligence, achieving a sense of self-worth, views about appropriate emotions, and cognitive dissonance. The discussion of dialect differences, formerly in Chapter 3, is now in Chapter 8.

- A new case study ("Ben and Sylvia") begins Chapter 3 to better illustrate the pervasive role of culture in students' lives.

- Chapter 5 includes new discussions about the role of children's own behaviors in their development, the importance of language as a facilitator of cognitive development, and cognitive styles and dispositions.

- Chapter 6 now begins with a discussion of four basic human needs—arousal, competence and self-worth, self-determination, and relatedness—with many subsequent topics being tied in one way or another to these needs.

- Chapter 7 includes expanded discussions of adolescent risk taking and bullying and a new section on communicating with peers via the Internet. It also has a new section on disabilities that affect social functioning; this section includes the discussion of autism (now expanded to include autism spectrum disorders) that previously appeared in Chapter 3.

- The discussion about working with parents, previously in Chapter 7, has been moved to Chapter 9, where it is now incorporated into a new section called "Expanding the Sense of Community Beyond the Classroom." The section "Reducing Unproductive Behaviors" now includes a discussion of functional analysis and positive behavioral support, topics that were previously addressed in Chapter 3. A new section on addressing gang-related violence appears near the end of the chapter.

- Another new case study ("Akeem") begins Chapter 10 to illustrate how sound, reasoned classroom assessment practices can enhance students' learning, development, and school success. A section on keeping parents in the loop regarding student assessments is also new. And, of course, the discussion of the No Child Left Behind Act has been updated to reflect current practices and recent research.

SUPPLEMENTARY MATERIALS

Many supplements to the textbook are available to enhance readers' learning and development as teachers.

"Teacher educators who are developing pedagogies for the analysis of teaching and learning contend that analyzing teaching artifacts has three advantages: it enables new teacher time for reflection while still using the real materials of practice; it provides new teachers with experience thinking about and approaching the complexity of the classroom; and in some cases, it can help new teachers and teacher educators develop a shared understanding and common language about teaching. . . ." [1]

As Linda Darling-Hammond and her colleagues point out, grounding teacher education in real classrooms—among real teachers and students and among actual examples of students' and teachers' work—is an important, and perhaps even an essential, part of training teachers for the complexities of teaching today's students in today's classrooms. A collaborative effort among numerous authors and editors at Merrill Education has led to the creation of a website that provides instructors and students with the context of real classrooms and artifacts that research on teacher education tells us is so important. Through authentic in-class video footage, interactive activities, examples of authentic teacher and student work, and more, MYEDUCATIONLAB offers a uniquely valuable teacher education tool.

MYEDUCATIONLAB is easy to use! Wherever the MyEducationLab logo appears in the margins or elsewhere in the text, readers can follow the simple link instructions to access the MyEducationLab resource that corresponds with the chapter content. For each chapter you'll find most or all of the following resources:

Study Plan

- **Chapter Objectives:** Give students targets to shoot for as they read and study.
- **Focus Questions:** Help students test themselves on specific ideas in each section of the chapter.
- **Self-Check Quizzes:** Allow students to test their mastery of each chapter objective. Not only do these quizzes provide overall scores for each objective, but they also explain *why* responses to particular items are correct or incorrect.
- **Review, Remediation, and Enrichment Exercises:** Deepen students' understanding of particular concepts and principles in the chapter.

Homework and Exercises

- *Educational Leadership* **Article Analyses:** Ask students to answer several questions related to one of the articles in the For Further Reading list at the end of the chapter.
- **Practice Essay Questions:** Give students practice in answering essay questions similar to those that they might find on a quiz or test.
- **Student Artifact Analyses:** Ask students to apply chapter concepts in analyzing children's written work or oral responses to interview questions.
- **Video Analyses:** Present video clips of children and/or teachers in action and ask students to apply chapter concepts in drawing inferences and conclusions.
- **Supplementary Readings:** Deepen students' knowledge of particular theorists or concepts.

Building Teaching Skills Provide practice in a particular aspect of teaching, perhaps in lesson planning, assessment, or sensitivity to diverse cultures.

Additional Resources

- **Video Examples:** Illustrate principles of cognition, development, motivation, and effective classroom practices. Each video is included in the chapter(s) to which it is relevant.
- **Chapter Glossary:** Provides definitions for all of the key terms.
- **Common Student Beliefs and Misconceptions:** Describe incorrect or only-partly-correct notions that are likely to interfere with students' understanding of educational psychology.

[1] Darling-Hammond, l., & Bransford, J., Eds.(2005). *Preparing Teachers for a Changing World.* San Francisco: John Wiley & Sons.

- **Classroom Observations:** Contain suggestions about chapter-relevant phenomena to look for during visits to elementary and secondary school classrooms.
- **For Further Reading:** Provides web links to all of the *Educational Leadership* articles in the For Further Reading list at the end of each chapter.

ONLINE INSTRUCTOR'S MANUAL Available to instructors for download on www.pearsonhighered.com is an *Instructor's Manual* with suggestions for learning activities, supplementary lectures, group activities, and additional media resources. These have been carefully selected to provide opportunities to support, enrich, and expand on what students read in the textbook.

ONLINE POWERPOINT® SLIDES PowerPoint slides are available to instructors for download on www.pearsonhighered.com. These slides include key concept summarizations and other graphic aids to help students understand, organize, and remember core concepts and ideas.

ONLINE TEST BANK AND TESTGEN The *Test Bank* that accompanies this text contains both multiple-choice and essay questions. Some items (lower-level questions) simply ask students to identify or explain concepts and principles they have learned. But many others (higher-level questions) ask students to apply those same concepts and principles to specific classroom situations—that is, to actual student behaviors and teaching strategies. The lower-level questions assess basic knowledge of educational psychology. But ultimately it is the higher-level questions that can best assess students' ability to use principles of educational psychology in their own teaching practice. Along with the *Test Bank* is *TestGen* software that enables instructors to create and customize exams. This software is available in both Macintosh and PC/Windows versions. Both the *Test Bank* and *Test Gen* are available for instructors to download on www.pearsonhighered.com.

COMPUTER SIMULATION SOFTWARE *Simulations in Educational Psychology and Research*, version 2.1 (ISBN 0-13-113717-4), features five psychological/educational interactive experiments on a CD-ROM. Exercises and readings help students explore the research components and procedures connected to these experiments. Both qualitative and quantitative designs are included. Instructors should contact their local Prentice Hall sales representative to order a copy of these simulations.

ARTIFACT CASE STUDIES: INTERPRETING CHILDREN'S WORK AND TEACHERS' CLASSROOM STRATEGIES I have written *Artifact Case Studies* (ISBN 0-13-114671-8) as a supplement to the textbook. It is especially useful for helping students apply psychological concepts and principles related to learning, motivation, development, instruction, and assessment. The case studies, or *artifact cases*, within this text offer work samples and instructional materials that cover a broad range of topics, including literacy, mathematics, science, social studies, and art. Every artifact case includes background information and questions to consider as readers examine and interpret the artifact. Instructors should contact their local Prentice Hall sales representative to order a copy of this book.

ACKNOWLEDGMENTS

Although the title page lists me as the sole author of this book, I have hardly written it alone. I am greatly indebted to the innumerable psychologists, educators, and other scholars whose insights and research findings I have pulled together in these pages. Another key player has been my editor at Merrill Education, Kevin Davis, who has been enthusiastic about the book since its inception and devotedly guided its progress through two editions. Others at Merrill have also helped to turn my vision into reality. Autumn Benson and Christie Robb have always been available as sounding boards and counsel when I wanted to take the book in particular directions. Lorretta Palagi has found and addressed many little trouble spots I had overlooked, on several occasions going well beyond the call of duty, and Sue Kopp has meticulously checked the final pages to find additional flaws that needed fixing. Valerie Schultz has sorted through hundreds of possible photos to locate those that could effectively translate abstract ideas into concrete realities. Kay Banning has contributed her indexing talents to help my readers find the many topics that might otherwise be hard to locate. And, as always, Mary Harlan has generously accommodated the idiosyncrasies in my writing style and schedule and has expertly coordinated the gazillion "little" things that needed doing to turn my rough manuscript pages into a polished final product.

On the home front, I'm grateful to the many students and teachers whose examples, artifacts, and interviews illustrate some of the concepts, developmental trends, and classroom strategies I describe: Andrew Belcher, Katie Belcher, Don Burger, Noah Davis, Shea Davis, Barbara Dee, Amaryth Gass, Anthony Gass, Ben Geraud, Darcy Geraud, Macy Gotthardt, Colin Hedges, Erin Islo, Jesse Jensen, Sheila Johnson, Shelly Lamb, Carol Lincoln, Meghan Milligan, Michele Minichiello, Mark Nichols, Susan O'Byrne, Alex Ormrod, Jeff Ormrod, Tina Ormrod, Isabelle Peters, Ann Reilly, Corey Ross, Ashton Russo, Alex Sheehan, Connor Sheehan, Matt Shump, Melinda Shump, Emma Thompson, Melissa Tillman, Grace Tober, Grant Valentine, and Brian Zottoli. And special gratitude goes to Ann Shump, who continues to be on the lookout for treasure troves of artifacts among her friends, neighbors, and professional colleagues.

It is important, too, to recognize the invaluable contributions of my colleagues Jayne Downey (Montana State University) and Teresa McDevitt (University of Northern Colorado), who conceptualized and produced many of the videos that appear in MyEducationLab. I am delighted that Rhoda Cummings (University of Nevada at Reno) has agreed to write the *Instructor's Manual* and *PowerPoint Slides* for the book.

I must also acknowledge the contributions of my professional colleagues around the country who have reviewed various versions of the book and offered many suggestions that strengthened it. Reviewing early drafts of the first edition were Lynley H. Anderman, University of Kentucky; Bonnie Armbruster, University of Illinois at Urbana-Champaign; Ty Binfet, Loyola Marymount University; Rhoda Cummings, University of Nevada at Reno; Randi A. Engle, University of California, Berkeley; Robert B. Faux, University of Pittsburgh; Robert L. Hohn, University of Kansas; Julita G. Lambating, California State University at Sacramento; Frank R. Lilly, California State University at Sacramento; Jeffrey Miller, California State University at Dominguez Hills; Marla Reese-Weber, Illinois State University; Michelle Riconscente, University of Maryland at College Park; Cecil Robinson, University of Alabama; Beverly Snyder, University of Colorado at Colorado Springs; Michael P. Verdi, California State University at San Bernardino; Vickie Williams, University of Maryland, Baltimore County; and Steven R. Wininger, Western Kentucky University. Reviewers who helped shape this current, second edition were three previous reviewers—Rhoda Cummings, University of Nevada at Reno; Frank Lilly, California State University at Sacramento; and Cecil Robinson, University of Alabama—along with several new colleagues: Heidi Andrade, State University of New York at Albany; Emily de la Cruz, Portland State University; William M. Gray, University of Toledo; Donna Jurich, Knox College; Mark Szymanski, Pacific University; and John Woods, Grand Valley State University. I am deeply indebted to them all for their deep commitment to professional teacher education and to getting the word out about the many things that the field of educational psychology has to offer.

Finally, of course, I must thank my husband Richard and children Tina, Alex, and Jeff, who have all shaped my life—and so also this book—in ways too numerable to mention.

BRIEF CONTENTS

CONTENTS

CHAPTER 3   LEARNING IN CONTEXT   56

CHAPTER 5   COGNITIVE DEVELOPMENT   134

CHAPTER 6   MOTIVATION AND AFFECT   182

CHAPTER 10 ASSESSMENT STRATEGIES   354

Note: Every effort has been made to provide accurate and current Internet information in this book. However, the Internet and information posted on it are constantly changing, so it is inevitable that some of the Internet addresses listed in this text will change.

ESSENTIALS OF
EDUCATIONAL PSYCHOLOGY

CHAPTER 1

Introduction to Educational Psychology

CASE STUDY   Starting High School

In a research study described in the *American Educational Research Journal* in 1999, researchers Melissa Roderick and Eric Camburn tracked students' academic progress as they made the transition from relatively small elementary or middle schools to much larger high schools in the Chicago public school system. Roderick and Camburn discovered that many students showed a sharp decline in academic achievement in ninth grade, their first year of high school.

As an example, consider what happened to Anna, an intelligent Mexican American student. During her childhood and early adolescence, Anna certainly had more than her share of life's challenges. Her parents divorced. Several of her friends were victims of gang violence. During such traumatic times, teachers and other staff members at Anna's school were a source of considerable social and emotional support. Anna's mother described the school as "not a school . . . more like a second home, [like] the home of the grandparents of the kids."[1] The teachers also provided regular feedback and guidance to help Anna and her classmates improve their academic skills. By eighth grade, Anna's performance on a standardized achievement test placed her reading skills at a ninth-grade level—seemingly confirming that she was well equipped to tackle the high school years.

Anna initially looked forward to her first year at a large city high school. "Well, my sister tells me that it's gonna be more fun because you're involved in things. . . . And they don't really treat you like little kids anymore."[2] But despite the academic skills she acquired in the elementary and middle school grades, Anna quickly found herself floundering in her ninth-grade classes, and her first-semester final grades included several Ds and an F. Anna seemed overwhelmed by the new demands that high school placed on her, as reflected in the following explanations she gave during an interview with one of the researchers:

> In geography, "he said the reason why I got a lower grade is 'cause I missed one assignment and I had to do a report, and I forgot that one." In English, "I got a C . . . 'cause we were supposed to keep a journal, and I keep on forgetting it 'cause I don't have a locker. Well I do, but my locker partner she lets her cousins use it, and I lost my two books there. . . . I would forget to buy a notebook, and then I would have them on separate pieces of paper, and I would lose them." And, in biology, "the reason I failed was because I lost my folder . . . it had everything I needed, and I had to do it again, and, by the time I had to turn in the new folder, I did, but he said it was too late . . . 'cause I didn't have the folder, and the folder has everything, all the work. . . . That's why I got an F."[3]

Although Anna's math teacher offered to find tutors for students who were having difficulty, Anna perceived most of her teachers as being uncaring, unaware of how students were progressing, and inflexible in evaluating students' achievement. Twice she went to the school counselor's office—visits that got her in trouble for being late to her next class—but the counselor was not available to meet with her on either occasion.

[1] Roderick & Camburn, 1999, p. 304.
[2] Roderick & Camburn, 1999, p. 304.
[3] Roderick & Camburn, 1999, p. 305.

Despite her rocky start, Anna hoped to earn her high school diploma and go to college. But her first-semester performance was not a good sign. In their study of more than 27,000 students, Roderick and Camburn found that more than 40 percent of first-semester ninth graders (males especially) failed at least one course, and students who achieved at low levels early in their high school career were at higher-than-average risk for dropping out before graduation.

- Why did Anna's academic performance drop so dramatically in ninth grade? Drawing both from information presented in the case study and from your own experiences in middle school and high school, identify several factors that might have contributed to her academic decline.
- According to Anna's achievement test results, she seemingly had adequate reading skills to succeed in high school. What important skills did she apparently *not* have?
- What things might Anna's teachers have done to help her succeed in high school?

When students begin high school, they face many new challenges—more stringent course requirements, less individualized guidance and instruction, making new friends, and so on—while also dealing with the unsettling physiological changes of puberty.

The questions I've just posed have multiple possible answers. For instance, Anna's academic performance may have declined for any number of reasons. Perhaps the subject matter and assigned tasks in her high school classes were more challenging than those in middle school. Perhaps the high school teachers had such large classes that they had little time to give students one-on-one assistance. Given that Anna was now attending classes with many students she didn't know, perhaps she was more focused on making friends and fitting in with her new peer group than she was on mastering school subject matter. Furthermore, Anna apparently did not have the organizational skills she needed to keep track of class materials and assignments.

Many adolescents do quite well in high school, and under different circumstances Anna might also have done well. Although students themselves certainly play a key role in their academic success, teachers can do many things to make students' success more likely. For example, they can get students genuinely interested in and excited about classroom topics. They can present information in such a way that students truly understand—rather than simply memorize—it. They can give students opportunities to practice new skills within the context of real-life situations and problems. They can teach students how to keep track of assignments and due dates, organize study materials, take good class notes, and in other ways gain self-sufficiency in academic pursuits. And they can regularly monitor students' progress and provide ongoing feedback that helps students improve.

Teaching children and adolescents—whether in an elementary or secondary school classroom, in a preschool or after-school child care facility, on the playing field, or elsewhere—is one of the most rewarding activities on the planet. Yet to actually help young people *learn* what you want to teach them, you cannot be concerned only about your subject matter. You must consider how children and adolescents typically think and learn, what abilities youngsters in different age-groups are likely to have, and what conditions are apt to motivate them to master important knowledge and skills. And you must also have a large toolbox of strategies for planning and carrying out instruction, creating an environment that keeps students motivated and on task, and assessing their progress and achievement.

In this book we'll explore the field of **educational psychology**, which applies concepts and theories of psychology to instructional practice and offers a wide variety of classroom strategies that can help students of all ages succeed in the classroom. In particular, we'll look at the following:

Chapter 2: The nature of human learning, thinking, and memory. In this chapter we'll identify teaching strategies that can help students like Anna learn and remember new information and skills.

educational psychology Academic discipline that studies and applies concepts and theories of psychology relevant to instructional practice.

Chapter 3: Specific environmental conditions and more general social and cultural factors that foster learning and development. The chapter's discussion of one particular topic—socioeconomic status—can sensitize us to the many challenges that children in lower-income, inner-city school districts (such as many students in the Chicago public schools) are apt to face.

Chapter 4: Complex thinking processes that enable children to study and learn effectively, apply what they learn to new situations, and critically evaluate new ideas and perspectives. As we discuss self-regulation in this chapter, we'll identify strategies for helping students like Anna acquire better study habits.

Chapter 5: Trends in cognitive development that influence how children of different ages think about and learn academic subject matter. Here we'll discover how Anna, as a typical high school student, probably thinks about and understands classroom topics somewhat differently than her teachers and other adults do.

Chapter 6: Motives and emotions that turn students "on" or "off" to learning and academic achievement. As we explore various facets of human motivation and emotion, we'll identify strategies for getting students like Anna engaged in and excited about academic subject matter.

Chapter 7: Aspects of personal and social development that influence classroom success. As we look at the development of sense of self and peer relationships, we'll find that high school students are often preoccupied with defining themselves ("Who is the *real me*?"), making and keeping friends, and perhaps finding romantic partners—preoccupations that can distract them from their academic studies.

Chapter 8: Strategies for planning and carrying out effective instruction. In this chapter we'll find that instructional methods are not one-size-fits-all—that different methods are useful in different situations and for different kinds of students.

Chapter 9: Strategies for keeping students on task and minimizing unproductive classroom behaviors. Here we'll identify strategies for establishing productive teacher–student relationships and making students feel that they are important members of the school community—conditions that can greatly enhance students' desire to stay in school.

Chapter 10: Strategies for assessing students' progress and final achievement. Our exploration of standardized tests in this chapter will give us a sense of what large-scale achievement tests (such as the one Anna took in eighth grade) can and cannot tell us about what students know and can do.

BASIC ASSUMPTIONS OF EDUCATIONAL PSYCHOLOGY

As you can see from the preceding chapter descriptions, the field of educational psychology focuses on those aspects of psychology—thinking, learning, child and adolescent development, motivation, assessment of human characteristics, and so on—that have particular relevance for classroom practice. The "glue" that holds all of these topics together consists of the following general assumptions.

An in-depth knowledge of students must drive teacher decision making.

How children and adolescents think and learn, what knowledge and skills they have and have not mastered, where they are in their developmental journeys, what their interests and priorities are—all of these factors influence the effectiveness of various classroom strategies. Thus, the decisions that teachers make in the classroom—decisions about what topics and skills to teach (*planning*), how to teach those topics and skills (*instruction*), how to keep students on task and supportive of one another's learning efforts (creating an effective *classroom environment*), and how best to determine what students have learned (*assessment*)—must ultimately depend on students' existing characteristics and behaviors.

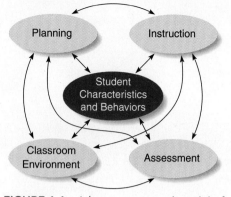

FIGURE 1.1   A learner-centered model of instruction

Of course, teachers' classroom strategies also *change* what students know, think, and do. Thus, the relationship between student characteristics and behaviors, on the one hand, and teacher strategies, on the other, is a two-way street. Furthermore, as you'll discover in Chapters 8 through 10, planning, instruction, the classroom environment, and assessment practices influence one another as well.

Figure 1.1 depicts how student characteristics and behaviors, planning, instruction, the classroom environment, and assessment mutually affect one another. Notice how student characteristics and behaviors are at the center of the figure, because these must drive almost everything that teachers do in the classroom. Such an approach to teaching is sometimes known as **learner-centered instruction**.[4]

In many cases teachers can accommodate students' unique characteristics within the context of typical classroom practices and activities. Yet some students, known as **students with special needs**, are different enough that they require specially adapted instructional materials or practices to help them maximize their learning and development. Now, more than ever before, many of these students are in general education classrooms, a practice called **inclusion**. Regardless of the grade level or subject matter, teachers should expect to have students with a wide variety of special needs in their classrooms at one time or another. At several points in the book, we will consider students with particular kinds of special needs and identify strategies that may be especially useful in working with them.

The effectiveness of various classroom practices can best be determined through systematic research.

You yourself have been a student for many years now, and in the process you have undoubtedly learned a great deal about how children learn and develop and about how teachers can foster their learning and development. But exactly how much *do* you know? To help you find out, I've developed a short pretest, Ormrod's Own Psychological Survey (OOPS).

Ormrod's Own Psychological Survey (OOPS)

Decide whether each of the following statements is *true* or *false*.

True/False

_____ 1. The best way to learn and remember a new fact is to repeat it over and over again.

_____ 2. Most children 5 years of age and older are natural learners: They know the best way to learn something without having to be taught how to learn it.

_____ 3. When a teacher rewards one student for appropriate behavior, the behavior of other students usually suffers as a result.

_____ 4. Students are often poor judges of how much they've learned.

_____ 5. Anxiety sometimes helps students learn and perform more successfully in the classroom.

_____ 6. When teachers have children tutor their classmates in academic subject matter, the tutors gain very little from the process.

_____ 7. The ways in which teachers assess students' learning influence what and how the students actually learn.

learner-centered instruction Approach to teaching in which instructional strategies are chosen largely on the basis of students' existing abilities, predispositions, and needs.

student with special needs Student who is different enough from peers that he or she requires specially adapted instructional materials and practices.

inclusion The practice of educating all students, including those with severe and multiple disabilities, in neighborhood schools and general education classrooms.

[4] For good general discussions of learner-centered instructional practices, see McCombs, 2005; National Research Council, 2000. You may also want to look at the American Psychological Association's (APA's) 14 *Learner-Centered Psychological Principles* on the APA Web site at http://www.apa.org. (Type "learner-centered principles" in the search box on APA's home page.)

Now let's see how well you did on the OOPS. The answers, along with an explanation for each one, are as follows:

1. The best way to learn and remember a new fact is to repeat it over and over again. FALSE—Although repeating information over and over again is better than doing nothing at all, repetition is a relatively *in*effective way to learn specific pieces of information. Students learn new information more easily and remember it longer when they connect it with things they already know and when they engage in **elaboration**—that is, when they embellish on the information in some way, perhaps by drawing inferences from a historical fact, identifying new examples of a mathematical concept, or thinking of possible ways they might apply a scientific principle. Chapter 2 describes several cognitive processes that effectively help students learn and remember school subject matter.

2. Most children 5 years of age and older are natural learners: They know the best way to learn something without having to be taught how to learn it. FALSE—Many students of all ages are relatively naive about how they can best learn something, and they often use inefficient strategies when they study. For example, most elementary students and a substantial number of high school students don't engage in elaboration as they study classroom material—that is, they don't analyze, interpret, or otherwise add their own ideas to the things they need to learn. We'll look at developmental trends in elaboration and other learning strategies in Chapter 2.

3. When a teacher rewards one student for appropriate behavior, the behavior of other students usually suffers as a result. FALSE—When teachers reward one student for behaving in a particular way, other students who have observed that student being rewarded sometimes begin to behave in a similar manner. We'll examine this phenomenon, known as *vicarious reinforcement*, in Chapter 3.

4. Students are often poor judges of how much they've learned. TRUE—Contrary to popular opinion, students are usually *not* the best judges of what they do and do not know. For example, many students think that if they've spent a long time studying a textbook chapter, they must know its contents very well. Yet if they have spent most of their study time inefficiently (perhaps by "reading" while thinking about something else altogether or by mindlessly copying definitions), they may know far less than they think they do. We'll consider this *illusion of knowing* further in Chapter 4.

5. Anxiety sometimes helps students learn and perform more successfully in the classroom. TRUE—Many people think that anxiety is always a bad thing. Yet for some classroom tasks, and especially for relatively easy tasks, a moderate level of anxiety actually *improves* students' learning and performance. We'll explore the effects of anxiety and other emotions in Chapter 6.

6. When teachers have children tutor their classmates in academic subject matter, the tutors gain very little from the process. FALSE—When students teach one another, the tutors often benefit as much as the students being tutored. For instance, in one research study,[5] when low-achieving fourth graders tutored first and second graders in basic arithmetic skills, the tutors themselves showed a substantial improvement in arithmetic. We'll look more closely at the effects of peer tutoring in Chapter 8.

7. The ways in which teachers assess students' learning influence what and how the students actually learn. TRUE—What and how students learn depend, in part, on how they expect their learning to be assessed. For example, students typically spend more time studying the things they think will be on a test than the things they think the test won't cover. And they are more likely to pull class material into an integrated, meaningful whole if they expect assessment activities to require such integration. Chapter 10 describes the effects of classroom assessment practices on students' learning.

How many of the OOPS items did you answer correctly? Did some of the false items seem convincing enough that you marked them true? Did some of the true items contradict

---

[5] Inglis & Biemiller, 1997.

elaboration Cognitive process in which learners embellish on new information based on what they already know.

When one student tutors another, the tutor often learns as much from the experience as the student being tutored.

certain beliefs you had? If either of these was the case, you're hardly alone. College students often agree with statements that seem obvious but are, in fact, partially or completely incorrect.[6] Furthermore, many students in teacher education classes reject research findings when those findings appear to contradict their own personal beliefs and experiences.[7]

It's easy to be persuaded by "common sense" and assume that what seems logical must be reality. Yet common sense and logic do not always give us the straight story about how people actually learn and develop, nor do they always give us accurate information about how best to help students succeed in the classroom. Educational psychologists believe that knowledge about teaching and learning should come from a more objective source of information—that is, from psychological and educational research.

When educational psychologists describe human learning, development, and motivation, and when they suggest particular instructional practices, classroom management strategies, and assessment techniques, they usually identify the particular research articles, books, conference presentations, and other sources on which they base their claims. Typically they follow **APA style**, guidelines prescribed by the American Psychological Association for identifying sources and preparing references. In APA style a source is cited by presenting the author(s) and date of publication in the body of the text. For example, let's return to the earlier paragraph that begins "How many of the OOPS items. . . ." If I had written that paragraph using APA style, it would have looked like this:[8]

> How many of the OOPS items did you answer correctly? Did some of the false items seem convincing enough that you marked them true? Did some of the true items contradict certain beliefs you had? If either of these was the case, you're hardly alone. College students often agree with statements that seem obvious but are, in fact, partially or completely incorrect (Gage, 1991; L. S. Goldstein & Lake, 2000; Woolfolk Hoy, Davis, & Pape, 2006). Furthermore, many students in teacher education classes reject research findings when those findings appear to contradict their own personal beliefs and experiences (Gregoire, 2003; Holt-Reynolds, 1992; Patrick & Pintrich, 2001; Wideen, Mayer-Smith, & Moon, 1998).

Notice how I've included initials for only one author, Lisa Goldstein. When two or more first authors listed in the references have the same surname (as is true for the surname Goldstein in this book), APA style dictates that initials be included to distinguish among those authors, making it easier for readers to find the relevant source(s) in the reference list.

Most books about educational psychology use the APA style of referencing, and in fact I've used it in the other textbooks I've written. I'm intentionally deviating from APA style in this book for pedagogical reasons. When I assign books that have citations sprinkled throughout the discussion, I find that some of the students in my classes focus too much on the names and dates and not enough on what's really important for them to learn and remember: the *ideas*. Rather than presenting my sources within the text, then, I'm presenting them in footnotes. When you find some of the book's ideas especially interesting, exciting, or perhaps even disturbing, I urge you to read my sources firsthand. You'll find the detailed citations for all of them in the reference list at the back of the book.

Different kinds of research studies lead to different kinds of conclusions.

Psychological and educational research studies take a variety of forms. For instance, in the study described at the beginning of the chapter, Roderick and Camburn tracked the academic progress of Chicago high school students over the course of their 9th- and 10th-grade years. Another study might compare the effects of different methods of teaching reading comprehension skills to middle school students.[9] Still another might explore how children's friendships change with age.[10]

An in-depth discussion of research methods is beyond the scope of this book. However, when drawing on research results to identify effective classroom practices, we must keep in

---

APA style Rules and guidelines on referencing, editorial style, and manuscript format prescribed by the American Psychological Association.

[6] Gage, 1991; L. S. Goldstein & Lake, 2000; Woolfolk Hoy, Davis, & Pape, 2006.

[7] Gregoire, 2003; Holt-Reynolds, 1992; Patrick & Pintrich, 2001; Wideen, Mayer-Smith, & Moon, 1998.

[8] For more information on APA style, see APA's *Publication Manual* (2001) or visit http://www.apastyle.org.

[9] For example, see Palincsar & Brown, 1984.

[10] For example, see Gottman, 1983.

TABLE 1.1 **Examples of Questions We Might Answer with Descriptive, Correlational, and Experimental Studies**		
Descriptive Studies	Correlational Studies	Experimental Studies
What percentage of high school students can think abstractly about classroom subject matter?	Are older students more capable of abstract thought than younger students?	Can abstract thinking skills be improved through specially designed educational programs?
What kinds of aggressive behaviors do we see in our schools, and with what frequencies do we see them?	Are students more likely to be aggressive at school if they often see violence at home or in their neighborhood?	Which method is most effective in reducing aggressive behavior—rewarding appropriate behavior, punishing aggressive behavior, or a combination of these two strategies?
How pervasive are gender stereotypes in books commonly used to teach reading in the elementary grades?	Are better readers also better spellers?	Which of two reading programs produces greater gains in reading comprehension?
How well have our nation's students performed on a recent standardized achievement test?	Do students who get the highest scores on multiple-choice tests also get the highest scores on essays dealing with the same material?	Do different kinds of tests (e.g., multiple-choice vs. essay tests) encourage students to study in different ways and therefore affect what students actually learn?

mind that different kinds of research yield different kinds of information and warrant different kinds of conclusions. Most research studies fall into one of three categories: descriptive, correlational, or experimental.

A **descriptive study** does exactly what its name implies: It *describes* a situation. Descriptive studies might give us information about the characteristics of students, teachers, or schools. They might also provide information about how frequently certain events or behaviors occur. Descriptive studies allow us to draw conclusions about the way things are—the current state of affairs. The left-hand column of Table 1.1 presents examples of questions we could answer with descriptive studies.

Some descriptive studies are primarily *quantitative* in nature: They yield numbers that reflect percentages, frequencies, or averages related to certain characteristics or phenomena. Other descriptive studies are more *qualitative*: They yield nonnumeric information— perhaps in the form of verbal reports, written documents, pictures, or maps—that captures a complex situation in a way that cannot be reduced to numbers. The study by Roderick and Camburn included both quantitative information (e.g., percentages of students who failed at least one course each semester) and qualitative information (e.g., students' reflections about their high school experiences).

A **correlational study** explores possible relationships among different things. For instance, it might tell us how closely two human characteristics are associated with each other, or it might give us information about the consistency with which certain human behaviors occur in conjunction with certain environmental conditions. In general, correlational studies enable us to draw conclusions about **correlation**: the extent to which two characteristics or phenomena tend to be found together or to change together. Two variables are correlated when one increases as the other increases (a *positive correlation*) or when one *decreases* as the other increases (a *negative correlation*) in a somewhat predictable manner. The middle column of Table 1.1 presents examples of questions we might answer with correlational studies. Notice how each of these questions asks about an association between two variables—between age and abstract thought, between student aggression and violence at home, between reading and spelling, or between multiple-choice and essay test scores.

When we determine that a correlation exists between two variables, knowing the status of one variable allows us to make *predictions* about the other variable. For example, if we find that older students are more capable of abstract thought than younger students, we can predict that 10th graders will benefit more from an abstract discussion of democratic government than 4th graders. If we find a correlation between multiple-choice and essay test scores, we can predict that students who have done well on essays in a biology class will probably also do well on a national test covering the same topics in a multiple-choice format. The study by Roderick and Camburn was correlational as well as descriptive, in that it revealed

descriptive study Research study that enables researchers to draw conclusions about the current state of affairs but not about correlational or cause-and-effect relationships.

correlational study Research study that explores possible relationships among variables.

correlation Extent to which two variables are associated, such that when one variable increases, the other either increases or decreases somewhat predictably.

that early failure in high school was associated with, and so predicted, later school failure and dropping out.

Descriptive and correlational studies describe things as they exist naturally in the environment. In contrast, an **experimental study**, or **experiment**, is a study in which the researcher somehow changes, or *manipulates*, one or more aspects of the environment (often called *independent variables*) and then measures the effects of such changes on something else. In educational research the "something else" being affected (often called the *dependent variable*) is usually some aspect of student behavior—perhaps end-of-semester grades, skill in executing a complex physical movement, persistence in tackling difficult math problems, or ability to interact appropriately with peers. In a good experiment a researcher *separates and controls variables*, testing the possible effects of one variable while holding all other potentially influential variables constant.

Often experimental studies involve two or more groups that are treated differently. Consider these examples:

- A researcher teaches reading comprehension skills to two different groups of students using two different instructional methods. (Instructional method is the independent variable.) The researcher then assesses students' reading ability (the dependent variable) and compares the average performances of the two groups.
- A researcher gives three different groups of students varying amounts of practice with woodworking skills. (Amount of practice is the independent variable.) The researcher subsequently scores the quality of each student's woodworking projects (the dependent variable) and compares the average scores of the three groups.
- A researcher gives one group of students an intensive training program designed to improve their study habits. The researcher gives another group either no training at all or, better still, gives the group the same amount of training as the first group, but in subject matter unrelated to study habits. (Presence or absence of training in study habits is the independent variable.) The researcher later assesses study habits and obtains students' grade point averages (these are both dependent variables) to see if the training program had an effect.

Each of these examples includes one or more **treatment groups** that are the recipients of an intervention. The third example also includes a **control group** that receives either no intervention or an intervention that is unlikely to affect the dependent variable(s) in question. In many experimental studies, participants are assigned to groups *randomly*—for instance, by drawing names out of a hat. Such random assignment to groups is apt to yield groups that are, on average, roughly equivalent on other variables (ability levels, personality characteristics, motivation, etc.) that might affect the dependent variable.

When carefully designed and conducted, experimental studies enable us to draw conclusions about *causation*—about what variables cause or influence certain other variables. The right-hand column of Table 1.1 lists examples of questions that might be answered through experimental studies. Notice how each question addresses a cause-and-effect relationship—the effect of educational programs on abstract thinking, the effect of rewards and punishment on aggressive behavior, the effect of a reading program on the development of reading comprehension, or the effect of test-question format on students' learning.

Drawing conclusions about cause-and-effect relationships requires that all other possible explanations for an outcome be eliminated.

When we look at the results of a research study, we can determine that a particular condition or intervention has led to a particular outcome—that is, there is a cause-and-effect relationship between them—only if we've eliminated all other possible explanations for the results we've observed. As an example, imagine that Hometown School District wants to find out which of two reading programs, *Reading Is Great* (RIG) or *Reading and You* (RAY), leads to better reading in third grade. The district asks each of its third-grade teachers to choose one of these two reading programs and use it throughout the school year. The district then compares the end-of-year achievement test scores of students in the RIG and RAY classrooms and finds that RIG students have gotten substantially higher reading comprehension scores than RAY students. We might quickly jump to the conclusion that RIG

experimental study (experiment) Research study that involves the manipulation of one variable to determine its possible effect on another variable.

treatment group Group of people in a research study who are given a particular experimental treatment (e.g., a particular method of instruction).

control group Group of people in a research study who are given either no treatment or a treatment that is unlikely to have an effect on the dependent variable.

promotes better reading comprehension than RAY—in other words, that a cause-and-effect relationship exists between instructional method and reading comprehension. But is this really so?

Not necessarily. The fact is, the school district hasn't eliminated all other possible explanations for the difference in students' reading comprehension scores. Remember, the third-grade teachers personally *selected* the instructional program they used. Why did some teachers choose RIG and others choose RAY? Were the teachers who chose RIG different in some way from the teachers who chose RAY? Had RIG teachers taken more graduate courses in reading instruction, were they more open minded and enthusiastic about using innovative methods, did they have higher expectations for their students, or did they devote more class time to reading instruction? If the RIG and RAY teacher groups were different from each other in any of these ways—or perhaps different in some other way we might not happen to think of—then the district hasn't eliminated alternative explanations for why the RIG students have developed better reading skills than the RAY students. A better way to study the causal influence of reading program on reading comprehension would be to *randomly assign* teachers to the RIG and RAY programs, thereby making the two groups of teachers roughly equivalent in such areas as graduate-level course work, personality, motivation, expectations for students, and class time devoted to reading instruction.

As implemented, the study just described can, at best, tell us only about correlation. In general, correlational studies, although they demonstrate that an association exists, can never tell us the specific factors that explain *why* it exists. In other words, *correlation does not necessarily indicate causation.*

Be careful that you don't jump too quickly to conclusions about what factors are affecting students' learning, development, and behavior in particular situations. Scrutinize descriptions of research carefully, always with these questions in mind: *Have the researchers separated and controlled variables that might have an influence on the outcome? Have they ruled out other possible explanations for their results?* Only when the answers to both of these questions are undeniably *yes* should you draw a conclusion about a cause-and-effect relationship.

Only systematic research—and ideally, experimental research—can tell us which instructional strategies truly enhance students' learning and development.

As we proceed through the book, we will draw largely from descriptive and correlational studies to identify characteristics and behaviors that are typical for various age-groups and grade levels. We will rely more heavily on experimental studies to identify effective teacher strategies. We must keep in mind, however, that for practical or ethical reasons, many important questions about classroom instruction and children's development do not easily lend themselves to carefully controlled experimental studies. For instance, although we might reasonably hypothesize that children can better master difficult math concepts if they receive individual tutoring, most public school systems cannot afford such a luxury, and it would be unfair to provide tutoring for some students and deny it to a control group of other, equally needy students. And, of course, it would be highly unethical to study the effects of aggression by intentionally placing some children in a violent environment. Some important educational and developmental questions, then, can be addressed only with descriptive or correlational studies, even though such studies cannot help us pin down specific cause-and-effect relationships.

Theories can help synthesize, explain, and apply research findings.

As researchers learn more and more about how things are (descriptive studies), what variables are associated with one another (correlational studies), and what events cause what outcomes (experimental studies), they begin to develop **theories** that integrate and explain their findings. In their theories, researchers typically speculate about the underlying (and often unobservable) mechanisms involved in thinking, learning, development, motivation, or some other aspect of human functioning.

By giving us ideas about such mechanisms, theories can ultimately help us create learning environments that facilitate students' learning and achievement to the greatest extent possible. Let's take an example. In Chapter 2 we'll discover that a particular theory of how people learn—information processing theory—proposes that attention is an essential ingredient in the learning process. More specifically, if a learner pays attention to new information, the information moves from the first component of memory (the sensory register)

theory Integrated set of concepts and principles developed to explain a particular phenomenon.

to the second component (working memory). If the learner *doesn't* pay attention, the information disappears from the memory system, essentially going "in one ear and out the other." The importance of attention in information processing theory suggests that strategies that capture and maintain students' attention—perhaps providing interesting reading materials, presenting intriguing problems, or praising good performance—are apt to enhance students' learning and achievement.

Psychological theories are rarely, if ever, set in stone. Instead, they are continually expanded and modified as additional data come to light, and in some cases one theory may be abandoned in favor of another that better explains many phenomena that researchers have observed. Furthermore, different theories often focus on different aspects of human functioning, and psychologists have not yet been able to pull them together into a single "megatheory" that adequately accounts for all of the diverse phenomena and experiences that comprise human existence.

Throughout the book we'll examine a number of theories related to thinking, learning, development, motivation, and behavior. Although these theories will inevitably change in the future, they can be quite useful even in their present, unfinished forms. They help us pull together thousands of research studies into concise, integrated understandings of how children typically learn and develop, and they allow us to make inferences and predictions about how students in classrooms are apt to perform and achieve in particular situations. In general, theories can help us both *explain* and *predict* human behavior, and so they will give us numerous ideas about how best to help children and adolescents achieve academic and social success at school.

STRATEGIES FOR LEARNING AND STUDYING EFFECTIVELY

As you read this book, you'll gain many insights about how you can help students more effectively learn the things you want to teach them. At the same time, I hope you will also gain insights about how *you yourself* can better learn and remember course material. But rather than wait until we begin our discussion of learning in Chapter 2, let's look briefly at four strategies you can use as you read and study this book.

Relate what you read to things you already know.

Try to connect the ideas you read in the book with things you already know and believe. For example, connect new concepts and principles with your past experiences, with your previous course work, or with your general knowledge about people and their behavior. I'll occasionally assist you in this process by asking you to reflect on your prior experience, knowledge, and beliefs related to a topic.

Be careful, however. As my earlier OOPS test may already have shown you, some of what you currently "know" and believe may be sort-of-but-not-quite accurate or even downright *in*accurate. As you read this book, then, think about how some ideas and research findings may actually contradict your prior "knowledge." In such instances I hope you'll revise your understanding of whatever topic we're discussing. That is, I hope you'll undergo *conceptual change*, a process we'll explore in Chapter 2.

Tie abstract concepts and principles to concrete examples.

As we'll discover in Chapter 5, children become increasingly able to think about abstract ideas as they get older, but people of *all* ages can more readily understand and remember abstract information when they tie it to concrete objects and events. Thus I will often illustrate new concepts and principles with opening case studies or brief vignettes that describe specific student and teacher behaviors in classroom settings. In addition, I will occasionally ask you to view certain video clips in MyEducationLab, the online course that accompanies the book. I'll signal such requests with an icon like the one shown in the margin. Seeing psychological concepts and principles in action in the video clips can enhance your understanding of them and help you recognize them when you see them in your own work with children and adolescents.

View video clips in the Additional Resources section of MyEducationLab to help you tie concepts and theories of educational psychology to real children, adolescents, and classroom practices.

Sometimes it is even better to see a concept or principle in action in *oneself.* Thus I will often ask you to relate a concept or principle to your own past experiences as a student. In some instances I will actually *give* you illustrative experiences in the form of *See for Yourself* exercises. You've completed one of these exercises—the OOPS test—already and will encounter many additional ones throughout the book.

Elaborate on what you read, going beyond it and adding to it.

Earlier we noted the benefits of elaboration—embellishing on new information in some way—for learning and memory. So try to think *beyond* the things you read. Draw inferences from the ideas presented. Generate new examples of concepts. Identify your own educational applications of various principles of learning, development, and motivation.

Periodically check yourself to make sure you remember and understand what you've read.

There are times when even the most diligent students don't concentrate on what they're reading—when they are actually thinking about something else as their eyes go down the page. So stop once in a while (perhaps once every two or three pages) to make sure you have really learned and understood the things you've been reading. Try to summarize the material. Ask yourself questions about it. Make sure everything makes logical sense to you. And when you've finished reading a chapter, tackle the Practice for Your Licensure Exam exercise that appears after the chapter summary. We'll explore the nature and advantages of such *comprehension monitoring* in Chapter 4.

Find additional suggestions in the supplementary reading "General Study Tips" in the Homework and Exercises section in Chapter 1 of MyEducationLab. Find chapter-specific focus questions, self-check quizzes and practice exercises in *every* chapter of this online course.

You can find these and other suggestions in the online MyEducationLab course. This course also has chapter-specific focus questions, self-check quizzes, and practice exercises that can help you check both your understanding and your ability to apply what you are learning to new situations.

SUMMARY

The field of educational psychology focuses on aspects of psychology (e.g., thinking, learning, human development, motivation, assessment) that have particular relevance to classroom practice. Educational psychologists tend to base their assertions and suggestions not on "common sense" and logic—things that are somewhat unreliable indicators of effective instructional strategies—but rather on bodies of research evidence. Different types of research studies—descriptive, correlational, and experimental—address different questions about children and their learning, but all can enhance classroom decision making. As researchers learn more and more about how things are (descriptive studies), what variables are associated with one another (correlational studies), and what events cause what outcomes (experimental studies), they gradually develop, expand on, and modify theories that integrate and explain their findings.

You can use what you learn about thinking and learning not only to help children and adolescents be successful in the classroom but also to help *you* learn successfully. Among other things, you should relate new information to what you already know, tie abstract ideas to concrete examples, embellish (elaborate) on what you're learning, and occasionally stop to test yourself on what you've read and studied.

PRACTICE FOR YOUR LICENSURE EXAM

New Software

Mr. Gualtieri, a high school mathematics teacher, begins his class one Monday with an important announcement: "Our school has just purchased a new instructional software program for our computer lab. This program, called 'Problem-Excel,' will give you practice in applying the concepts and procedures we'll be studying this year. I strongly encourage you to stay after school once

or twice a week to get extra practice with the software whenever you're having trouble with the assignments I give you."

Mr. Gualtieri is firmly convinced that the new instructional software will help his students better understand and apply mathematics. To test his hypothesis, he keeps a record of which students report to the computer lab after school and which students do not. Later, he looks at how well the two groups of students perform on his tests and quizzes. Much to his surprise, he discovers that, on average, the students who have stayed after school to use the computer software have gotten *lower* scores than those who have not used the software. "How can this be?" he puzzles. "Is the computer software actually doing more harm than good?"

1. **Constructed-response question**

   Mr. Gualtieri wonders if the computer software is actually hurting, rather than helping, his students. Assume that the software has been carefully designed by an experienced educator and that Mr. Gualtieri's tests and quizzes are good measures of how well his students have learned the material they've been studying. Then:

   A. Explain why Mr. Gualtieri cannot draw a conclusion about a cause-and-effect relationship from the evidence he has. Base your response on principles of psychological and educational research.

   B. Identify another plausible explanation for the results Mr. Gualtieri has obtained.

2. **Multiple-choice question**

   Which one of the following research findings would provide the most convincing evidence that the Problem-Excel software enhances students' mathematics achievement?

   a. Ten high schools in New York City purchase Problem-Excel and make it available to their students. Students at these high schools get higher mathematics achievement test scores than students at 10 other high schools that have *not* purchased the software.

   b. A high school purchases Problem-Excel, but only four of the eight math teachers at the school decide to have their students use it. Students of these four teachers score at higher levels on a mathematics achievement test than students of the other four teachers.

   c. All 10th graders at a large high school take a mathematics achievement test in September. At some point during the next two months, they each spend 20 hours working with Problem-Excel. The students all take the same math achievement test again in December and, on average, get substantially higher scores than they did in September.

   d. Students at a high school are randomly assigned to two groups. One group works with Problem-Excel, and the other group works with a software program called "Write-Away," designed to teach better writing skills. The Problem-Excel group scores higher than the Write-Away group on a subsequent mathematics achievement test.

Once you have answered these questions, compare your responses with those presented in Appendix A.

FOR FURTHER READING

The following articles from the journal *Educational Leadership* are especially relevant to this chapter. You can find these articles in Chapter 1 of MyEducationLab for this text.

Duck, L. (2000). The ongoing professional journey. *Educational Leadership, 57*(8), 42–45.

Flippo, R. F. (1999). Redefining the reading wars: The war against reading researchers. *Educational Leadership, 57*(2), 38–41.

Giangreco, M. F. (1996). What do I do now? A teacher's guide to including students with disabilities. *Educational Leadership, 53*(5), 56–59.

Villa, R. A., & Thousand, J. S. (2003). Making inclusive education work. *Educational Leadership, 61*(2), 19–23.

MYEDUCATIONLAB

Now go to Chapter 1 of MyEducationLab at **www.myeducationlab.com,** where you can:

- Find instructional objectives for the chapter, along with focus questions that can help you zero in on important ideas in the chapter.
- Take a self-check quiz on concepts and principles you've just read about.
- Complete exercises and assignments that can help you more deeply understand the chapter content.
- Read supplementary material that can broaden your knowledge of one or more of the chapter's topics.

CHAPTER 2

Learning, Cognition, and Memory

CASE STUDY   The New World

Rita attends fourth grade at a school in Michigan. Her class recently studied a unit on Michigan's state history. Rita still knows little about U.S. history; she will study that subject as a fifth grader next year. Despite her limited background in history, Rita willingly responds to an interviewer's questions about the New World.

Interviewer: Our country is in the part of the world called America. At one time, America was called the New World. Do you know why it was called the New World?

Rita: Yeah. We learned this in social studies.

Interviewer: What did you learn?

Rita: Because they used to live in England, the British, and they didn't know about . . . they wanted to get to China 'cause China had some things they wanted. They had some cups or whatever—no, they had furs. They had fur and stuff like that and they wanted to have a shorter way to get to China so they took it and they landed in Michigan, but it wasn't called Michigan. I think it was the British that landed in Michigan and they were there first and so they tried to claim that land, but it didn't work out for some reason so they took some furs and brought them back to Britain and they sold them, but they mostly wanted it for the furs. So then the English landed there and they claimed the land and they wanted to make it a state, and so they got it signed by the government or whoever, the big boss, then they were just starting to make it a state so the British just went up to the Upper Peninsula and they thought they could stay there for a little while. Then they had to fight a war, then the farmers, they were just volunteers, so the farmers went right back and tried to get their family put together back again.

Interviewer: Did you learn all this in state history this year?

Rita: Um hum.[1]

- Which parts of Rita's response accurately describe the history of the New World? Which parts are clearly *in*accurate?
- Michigan's Upper Peninsula is separated from the rest of the state by the Straits of Mackinac, a narrow waterway that connects Lake Michigan and Lake Huron. Why might Rita think that making Michigan a state caused the British to move to the Upper Peninsula?
- At the time that British colonists were first settling in Michigan, merchants back in England were seeking a new trade route to the Far East so they could more easily secure the tea, spices, and silk available there. Why might Rita initially suggest that the British wanted to get cups from China? Why might she then say that they wanted to get furs?

[1] VanSledright & Brophy, 1992, p. 849.

Rita has certainly learned some facts about her state and its history. For example, she is aware of a region called the Upper Peninsula, and she knows that many of the state's early European settlers were British. But she has taken what she knows to spin a tale that could give a historian heart failure.

To some extent, Rita's lack of information about certain things is limiting her ability to make sense of what she has learned about Michigan's history. More specifically, Rita doesn't know that the British and the English were the *same people*. Thinking of them as two different groups, she assumes that the arrival of the latter group drove the former group to the Upper Peninsula.

Yet occasionally what Rita *does* know is a source of difficulty as well. For instance, she associates *China* with dinnerware (including cups), and she has learned that some early European explorers sought exotic animal furs (especially beaver pelts) to send back to their homeland. She uses such information to draw logical but incorrect inferences about why the British were so eager to find a new route to China.

To understand how children and adolescents acquire understandings about their physical and social worlds, about academic subject matter, and about themselves as human beings, we must first understand the nature of learning. As Rita's depiction of Michigan's history clearly illustrates, learning is often a matter of creating, rather than absorbing, knowledge about the world. In other words, learning is a *constructive process*, as we shall see now.

LEARNING AS A CONSTRUCTIVE PROCESS

For purposes of our discussion, we will define **learning** as a long-term change in mental representations or associations due to experience. Let's divide this definition into its three parts. First, learning is a *long-term change* in that it isn't just a brief, transitory use of information—such as remembering a phone number long enough to dial it and then forgetting it—but it doesn't necessarily last forever. Second, learning involves *mental representations or associations* and so presumably has its basis in the brain. Third, learning is a change *due to experience*, rather than the result of physiological maturation, fatigue, alcohol or drugs, or onset of mental illness.

Psychologists have been studying the nature of learning for more than a century. In the process they have taken a variety of theoretical perspectives. Table 2.1 summarizes five diverse perspectives that will contribute considerably to our understanding of what learning involves. The table also lists examples of theorists associated with each perspective. You will find many of these theorists cited in footnotes in this and later chapters.

For the most part, diverse perspectives of learning complement rather than contradict one another, and together they can give us a rich, multifaceted picture of human learning. As we explore the nature of learning in this book, then, we will draw useful ideas from all five perspectives. In this chapter, however, we will be looking primarily at what goes on *inside* the learner, and so we will find the information processing and constructivist approaches most helpful.

A few basic principles, discussed in the following sections, underlie much of what theorists have learned about learning.

By the time they reach school age, young learners are usually actively involved in their own learning.

Sometimes children learn from an experience without really giving the experience much thought. For example, as infants and toddlers acquire the basic vocabulary and syntax of their first language, they seem to do so without consciously trying to acquire these things and without thinking about what they are learning. Much of the learning that occurs during infancy and toddlerhood is such *implicit learning*, and even older children and adults continue to learn some things about their environments in a nonintentional, "thoughtless" way.[2] But as children grow, they increasingly engage in intentional, *explicit learning:* They

learning Long-term change in mental representations or associations due to experience.

[2] See S. W. Kelly, Burton, Kato, & Akamatsu, 2001; Reber, 1993.

THEORETICAL PERSPECTIVES

TABLE 2.1 General Theoretical Approaches to the Study of Learning

Theoretical Perspective	General Description	Examples of Prominent Theorists	Where You Will See This Perspective in the Book
Behaviorism	Behaviorists argue that because thought processes cannot be directly observed and measured, it is difficult to study thinking objectively and scientifically. Instead, they focus on two things that researchers *can* observe and measure: people's behaviors *(responses)* and the environmental events *(stimuli, reinforcement)* that precede and follow those responses. Learning is viewed as a process of acquiring and modifying associations among stimuli and responses, largely through a learner's direct interactions with the environment.	B. F. Skinner Edward Thorndike Ivan Pavlov A supplementary reading on Skinner's theory appears in the Homework and Exercises section in Chapter 3 of MyEducationLab.	We will examine learning from a stimulus–response perspective early in Chapter 3 (see the first four principles in the section "The Immediate Environment as Context"). We will also draw from behaviorist ideas when we address classroom management in Chapter 9 (see the discussions of cueing, punishment, systematic interventions, functional analysis, and positive behavioral support in the section "Reducing Unproductive Behaviors").
Social Learning Theory	Social learning theorists focus on the ways in which people learn from observing one another. Environmental stimuli affect behavior, but cognitive processes (e.g., *awareness* of stimulus–response relationships, *expectations* about future events) also play a significant role. Oftentimes people learn through *modeling*: They watch and imitate what others do. Whether people learn and perform effectively is also a function of their *self-efficacy*, the extent to which they believe they can successfully accomplish a particular task or activity. Although the environment certainly influences people's behaviors, over time most people begin to engage in *self-regulation*; that is, they take charge of and direct their own actions. In recent years social learning theory has increasingly considered the role of thought processes in learning, and so it is sometimes called **social cognitive theory**.	Albert Bandura Dale Schunk Barry Zimmerman	The social learning perspective will come into play in our discussions of modeling, vicarious consequences, incentives, and reciprocal causation in Chapter 3, as well as in our discussion of self-regulation in Chapter 4. Later, we will sometimes draw from social learning theory as we examine motivation (and especially as we focus on self-efficacy and goals) in Chapter 6.
Information Processing Theory	While not denying that the environment plays a critical role in learning, information processing theorists investigate what goes on *inside* learners, focusing on the cognitive processes involved in learning, memory, and performance. From observations of how people execute various tasks and behave in various situations, these theorists draw inferences about how people may perceive, interpret, and mentally manipulate information they encounter in the environment. They speculate about what internal mechanisms underlie human cognition (e.g., *working memory* and *long-term memory*) and about how people mentally process information (e.g., through *elaboration* and *visual imagery*). Initially, some information processing theorists believed that human thinking is similar to how a computer works (hence, they borrowed terms such as *encoding, storage,* and *retrieval* from computer lingo), but in recent years most theorists have largely abandoned the computer analogy.	Richard Atkinson Richard Shiffrin John Anderson Alan Baddeley Elizabeth Loftus	Information processing theory is most evident in the model of human memory presented in Figure 2.4; this model provides the basis for much of the discussion of learning and memory in this chapter. Information processing theory will also help us understand the higher-level cognitive processes discussed in Chapter 4. It will be influential, too, in our discussions of cognitive development and intelligence in Chapter 5, cognitive factors in motivation in Chapter 6, and social cognition in Chapter 7. Furthermore, Table 8.3 in Chapter 8 draws largely from information processing theory.
Constructivism	Constructivists, like information processing theorists, concern themselves with internal aspects of learning. They propose that people create (rather than absorb) knowledge from their observations and experiences. They suggest that people combine much of what they learn into integrated bodies of knowledge and beliefs (e.g., these might take the form of *schemas* and *theories*) that may or may not be accurate and useful understandings of the world. Some constructivists focus on how individual learners create knowledge through their interactions with the environment; this approach is known as **individual constructivism**. Others emphasize that by working together, two or more people can often gain better understandings than anyone could gain alone; this approach is called **social constructivism**.	Jean Piaget Jerome Bruner John Bransford Giyoo Hatano A supplementary reading on Piaget's theory appears in the Homework and Exercises section in Chapter 5 of MyEducationLab.	Constructivist ideas are intermingled with information processing theory throughout this chapter; in fact, many contemporary information processing theorists have a constructivist bent. The ideas of one of the earliest constructivists, developmental theorist Jean Piaget, are presented in Chapter 5. Constructivism will also be evident in the discussions of knowledge co-construction, epistemological beliefs, attributions, and personal and social understandings in Chapters 3, 4, 6, and 7, respectively.

(continued)

Theoretical Perspective	General Description	Examples of Prominent Theorists	Where You Will See This Perspective in the Book
Sociocultural Theory	Sociocultural theorists emphasize that the social, cultural, and historical contexts in which children grow up have profound influences on thinking, learning, and effective instructional practice. In social interactions within their communities, young learners encounter culturally appropriate ways of thinking about and interpreting objects and events. With time and practice, these ways of thinking—which are first used in a social context—are gradually *internalized* into nonspoken, mental processes that learners use on their own. Because of their varying environments, historical circumstances, and needs, different cultures have developed somewhat different ways of thinking, learning, and teaching.	Lev Vygotsky Barbara Rogoff Mary Gauvain Jean Lave A supplementary reading on Vygotsky's theory appears in the Homework and Exercises section in Chapter 5 of MyEducationLab.	We will first make use of sociocultural theory in Chapter 3, especially in the sections "Social Interaction as Context" and "Culture and Society as Context" (e.g., see the discussions of mediated learning experiences and cognitive tools). In Chapter 5, Vygotsky's theory of cognitive development will help us understand how children's social environments are essential for their cognitive development (e.g., see the discussions of internalization, self-talk, and zone of proximal development). Furthermore, the "Cultural Considerations" boxes in Chapters 3 through 10 will continually remind us how students' cultural backgrounds are likely to influence their thoughts, perceptions, and behaviors.

actively think about, interpret, and reconfigure what they see and hear in their environment. As a simple example, try the following exercise.

SEE FOR YOURSELF
Remembering Words

Study the 12 words below. Then cover up the page, and write down the words in the order they come to mind.

daisy	apple	dandelion
hammer	pear	wrench
tulip	pliers	watermelon
banana	rose	screwdriver

In what order did you remember the words? Did you recall them in their original order, or did you rearrange them somehow? If you are like most people, you grouped the words into three categories—flowers, fruit, and tools—and remembered one category at a time. In other words, you *organized* the words. As children get older, they are more likely to organize what they learn, and learners of all ages learn more effectively when they organize the subject matter at hand.

Cognitive processes influence what is learned.

The various ways in which people think about what they are seeing, hearing, studying, and learning are collectively known as **cognition**, and the more specific things people do are often referred to as **cognitive processes**. As will become clear as we proceed through the chapter, the cognitive processes that learners use to understand and remember information can have a profound effect on what they specifically learn and on how well they can remember it over the long run.

An example of a cognitive process is **encoding**, in which a learner changes incoming information in some way in order to remember it more easily. Whenever people mentally change the information they are learning—whether they interpret it, organize it, or in some other way modify or add to it—they are encoding it. In the preceding "Remembering Words" exercise, chances are that you learned not only a list of words but also a categorical structure for the words. But let's consider some alternative strategies you might have used to encode and remember the list. For instance, you might have created a story or poem that included all 12 words (e.g., "As *Daisy* and *Tulip* were walking, they ran across *Dandy* and *Rose*. They stopped in dismay when they noticed that Dandy had *pliers* on her nose . . ."). Or you might have formed a mental image of the 12 items in an elaborate, if not entirely edible, fruit salad (see Figure 2.1). All of these approaches are forms of encoding the 12-word list.

cognition Various ways of thinking about information and events.

cognitive process Particular way of mentally responding to or thinking about information or an event.

encoding Changing the format of information being stored in memory in order to remember it more easily.

Learners must be selective about what they focus on and learn.

People are constantly bombarded with information. Consider the many stimuli you are encountering at this very moment. How many separate stimuli appear on the two open pages of your book? How many objects do you see in addition to the book? How many sounds are reaching your ears? How many objects—perhaps on your fingertips, on your toes, at your back, or around your waist—do you feel? I suspect that you have been ignoring most of these stimuli until just now; you were not actively processing them until I asked you to do so. People can handle only so much information at any one time, and so they must be selective. Effective learners focus on what they think is important and ignore almost everything else.

FIGURE 2.1 A visual image for encoding a list of 12 words

As an analogy, consider the hundreds of items a typical adult receives in the mail each year, including all the packages, letters, bills, brochures, catalogs, advertisements, and requests for donations. Do you open, examine, and respond to every piece of mail? Probably not. If you're like me, you "process" only a few key items (e.g., packages, letters, bills, and a few miscellaneous things that catch your eye). You may inspect other items long enough to know that you don't need them. You may discard some items without even opening them.

People don't always make good choices about what to attend to, of course. Just as they might overlook a small, inconspicuous rebate check while opening a colorful "You May Already Have Won . . ." sweepstakes announcement, so, too, might they fail to catch an important idea in a classroom lesson because they're focusing on trivial details in the lesson or on a classmate's attention-getting behavior across the room. An important job for teachers, then, is to help students understand what is most important to learn and what can reasonably be cast aside as "junk mail."

Learners create (rather than receive) knowledge.

As was apparent in Rita's depiction of Michigan's history, learning is not simply a process of absorbing information from the environment. Rather, it is a process of *making*—actively and intentionally constructing—knowledge and understandings.[3] As an example, try the following exercise.

SEE FOR YOURSELF
Rocky

Read the following passage *one time only:*

> Rocky slowly got up from the mat, planning his escape. He hesitated a moment and thought. Things were not going well. What bothered him most was being held, especially since the charge against him had been weak. He considered his present situation. The lock that held him was strong but he thought he could break it. He knew, however, that his timing would have to be perfect. Rocky was aware that it was because of his early roughness that he had been penalized so severely—much too severely from his point of view. The situation was becoming frustrating; the pressure had been grinding on him for too long. He was being ridden unmercifully. Rocky was getting angry now. He felt he was ready to make his move. He knew that his success or failure would depend on what he did in the next few seconds.[4]

Now summarize what you've just read in two or three sentences.

Were you able to make sense of the passage? What did you think it was about? A prison escape? A wrestling match? Or perhaps something else altogether? The passage about Rocky includes a number of facts but leaves a lot unsaid. For instance, it tells us nothing about where Rocky was, what kind of "lock" was holding him, or why timing was of the utmost importance. Yet you were probably able to use the information you were given to construct

---

[3] For example, see Segalowitz, 2007.

[4] R. C. Anderson, Reynolds, Schallert, & Goetz, 1977, p. 372.

an overall understanding of Rocky's situation. Most people do find meaning of one sort or another in the passage.

This active sense-making process—what theorists sometimes refer to as *constructing meaning*—is hardly limited to verbal material. For another example, try the following exercise.

SEE FOR YOURSELF
Three Faces

Figure 2.2 contains three pictures. What do you see in each one? Most people perceive the picture on the left as being that of a woman, even though many of her features are missing. Enough features are visible—an eye, parts of the nose, mouth, chin, and hair—that you can construct a meaningful perception from them. Is enough information available in the other two figures for you to construct two more faces? Constructing a face from the figure on the right may take you a while, but it can be done.

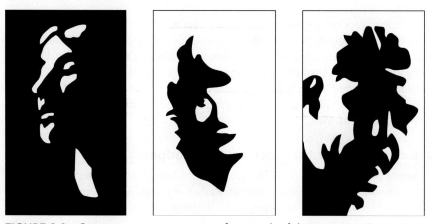

FIGURE 2.2 Can you construct a person from each of these pictures?

Source: From "Age in the Development of Closure Ability in Children," by C. M. Mooney, 1957, *Canadian Journal of Psychology, 11*, p. 220. Copyright 1957. Canadian Psychological Association. Reprinted with permission.

Objectively speaking, the three configurations of black splotches in Figure 2.2, and especially the two rightmost ones, leave a lot to the imagination. For example, the woman in the middle is missing half of her face, and the man on the right is missing the top of his head. Yet knowing how human faces typically appear is probably enough to enable you to add the missing features (mentally) and perceive complete pictures. Curiously, once you have constructed faces from the figures, they then seem obvious. If you were to close this book now and not pick it up again for a week or more, you would probably see the faces almost immediately, even if you had had considerable difficulty perceiving them originally.

Learners make sense of new experiences using what they already know and believe.

In the "Rocky" and "Three Faces" exercises you just did, you were able to make sense of situations even though a lot of information was missing. Your prior knowledge—perhaps about how prison escapes or wrestling matches typically proceed, and certainly about how human facial features are arranged—allowed you to fill in many missing details. Prior knowledge and beliefs usually play a major role in the meanings people construct.

On many occasions different people construct different meanings from the same situation, in part because they each bring unique prior experiences and knowledge to the situation. For example, when the "Rocky" passage was used in an experiment with college students, physical education majors frequently interpreted it as a wrestling match, but music education majors (most of whom had little or no knowledge of wrestling) were more likely to think it was about a prison break.[5] Not only do learners bring different areas of expertise to a learning task, they also bring different childhood experiences, cultural backgrounds, and assumptions about the world, and such differences are apt to have a significant impact on how they interpret new information.

The brain is, of course, the place where human beings think about, make sense of, and learn from their environment. We now look briefly at what the brain is like and how it functions.

THINKING AND LEARNING IN THE BRAIN

The brain is an incredibly complicated mechanism that includes somewhere in the neighborhood of *one hundred billion* nerve cells.[6] These nerve cells, known as **neurons**, are microscopic in size and interconnected in innumerable ways. Some neurons receive information from the rest of the body, others synthesize and interpret the information, and still others send messages that tell the body how to respond to its present circumstances. Curiously, neurons don't actually touch one another. Instead, using a variety of substances known as **neurotransmitters**, they send chemical messages to their neighbors across the tiny spaces—**synapses**—between them. Any single neuron may have synaptic connections with hundreds or even thousands of other neurons.[7]

As we'll discover in Chapter 5, the brain changes in important ways over the course of childhood and adolescence. Yet three basic points about the brain are important to keep in mind as we explore cognition and learning in this chapter.

The various parts of the brain work closely with one another.

Groups of neurons in different parts of the brain seem to specialize in different things. Structures in the lower and middle parts of the brain specialize in essential physiological processes (e.g., breathing, heart rate), bodily movements (e.g., walking, riding a bicycle), and basic perceptual skills (e.g., coordinating eye movements, diverting attention to potentially life-threatening stimuli). Complex thinking, learning, and knowledge are located primarily in the upper and outer parts of the brain collectively known as the **cortex,** which rests on the top and sides of the brain like a thick, bumpy toupee (see Figure 2.3). The portion of the cortex located near the forehead, known as the *prefrontal cortex,* is largely responsible for a wide variety of very "human" activities, including sustained attention, reasoning, planning, decision making, coordinating complex activities, and inhibiting nonproductive thoughts and behaviors. Other parts of the cortex are important as well, being actively involved in interpreting visual and auditory information, identifying the spatial characteristics of objects and events, and keeping track of general knowledge about the world.

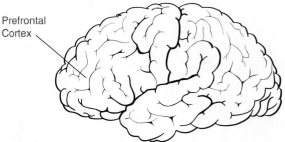

Prefrontal Cortex

FIGURE 2.3 Cortex of the human brain

To some degree, the left and right halves, or *hemispheres,* of the cortex have different specialties.[8] For most people, the left hemisphere has primary responsibility for speech, language comprehension, reading, and mathematical calculations. The right hemisphere is more dominant in visual and spatial processing, such as perceiving shapes and faces, mentally manipulating visual images, visually estimating and comparing quantities, drawing and painting, and interpreting another person's body language. In general, the left side is more apt to handle details, whereas the right side is better suited for looking at and synthesizing an overall whole.

Yet contrary to a popular belief, people rarely if ever think exclusively in one hemisphere. There is no such thing as "left-brain" or "right-brain" thinking: The two hemispheres typically collaborate in day-to-day tasks. In fact, the various parts of the brain *all* communicate constantly with one another. Recall a point made earlier: Neurons have synapses with many, many other neurons. As information travels through the brain, messages go across areas that handle very different sensory modalities or types of tasks. In essence, learning or

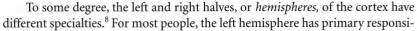

[5] R. C. Anderson et al., 1977.
[6] Goodman & Tessier-Lavigne, 1997.
[7] Goodman & Tessier-Lavigne, 1997; Lichtman, 2001; Mareschal et al., 2007.

[8] Byrnes, 2001; Ornstein, 1997; T. Roberts & Kraft, 1987.

neuron Cell in the brain or another part of the nervous system that transmits information to other cells.

neurotransmitter Chemical substance with which one neuron sends a message to another.

synapse Tiny space across which one neuron regularly communicates with another; reflects an ongoing but modifiable connection between the two neurons.

cortex Upper and outer parts of the human brain, which are largely responsible for conscious and higher-level human thought processes.

thinking about virtually anything tends to be *distributed* across many parts of the brain. A task as seemingly simple as identifying a particular word in speech or print involves numerous areas of the cortex.[9]

Most learning probably involves changes in neurons and synapses.

From a physiological standpoint, how and where does learning occur? Many theorists and researchers believe that the physiological basis for most learning lies in changes in the interconnections among neurons. In particular, learning may involve strengthening existing synapses or forming new ones.[10] In some instances, however, learning may actually involve *eliminating* synapses. Effective learning requires not only that people think and do certain things, but also that they *not* think or do other things—in other words, that they inhibit tendencies to think or behave in particular ways.[11]

Another biological phenomenon may be involved in learning as well. Until recently, it was common "knowledge" that all of the neurons a person would ever own are produced in the first few weeks after conception—that is, long before the person is born. Researchers are finding, however, that some formation of new neurons continues throughout life in the *hippocampus* (a small, seahorse-shaped structure in the middle of the brain) and possibly also in certain areas of the cortex.[12] Neuron formation appears to be stimulated by new learning experiences, but the precise role it plays in the learning process is still unclear.[13]

As for *where* learning occurs, the answer is: many places. The prefrontal cortex is active when people must pay attention to and think about new information and events, and all of the cortex may be active to a greater or lesser extent in interpreting new input in light of previously acquired knowledge.[14] The hippocampus also seems to be a central figure in learning, in that it pulls together the information it simultaneously receives from various parts of the brain.[15]

Knowing how the brain functions and develops tells us only so much about learning and instruction.

Even as researchers pin down how and where learning occurs, current knowledge of brain physiology doesn't begin to tell us everything we need to know about learning or how to foster it. For instance, brain research cannot tell us much about what information and skills are most important for people to have in a particular community and culture.[16] Nor does it provide many clues about how teachers can best help their students acquire important information and skills.[17] In fact, educators who speak of "using brain research" or "brain-based learning" are, in most instances, actually talking about what psychologists have learned from studies of human *behavior* rather than from studies of brain anatomy and physiology.

By and large, if we want to understand the nature of human cognition and identify effective ways of helping children and adolescents learn more effectively, we must look primarily at what psychologists, rather than neurologists, have discovered.[18] We begin our exploration of cognitive processes by looking at what psychologists have learned about human memory.

HOW HUMAN MEMORY OPERATES

The term **memory** refers to learners' ability to "save" things (mentally) that they have learned. In some cases we will use the term to refer to the actual process of saving knowledge or skills for a period of time. In other instances we will use it to talk about a particular

---

memory Ability to save something (mentally) that has been previously learned; also, the mental "location" where such information is saved.

[9] Bressler, 2002; Byrnes, 2001; Huey, Krueger, & Grafman, 2006; Rayner, Foorman, Perfetti, Pesetsky, & Seidenberg, 2001; Thelen & Smith, 1998.
[10] Byrnes & Fox, 1998; Greenough, Black, & Wallace, 1987; Merzenich, 2001; C. A. Nelson, Thomas, & de Haan, 2006.
[11] Bruer & Greenough, 2001; Byrnes, 2001; Dempster, 1992; Haier, 2001.
[12] Gould, Beylin, Tanapat, Reeves, & Shors, 1999; C. A. Nelson et al., 2006; Sapolsky, 1999.
[13] Most newly acquired information and skills seem to need some time to "firm up" in the brain—a process

called *consolidation*. An event that interferes with this consolidation (e.g., a serious brain injury) may cause a learner to forget things that happened several seconds, minutes, days, or months prior to the event; see Bauer, DeBoer, & Lukowski, 2007; Wixted, 2005.
[14] Byrnes, 2001; Huey et al., 2006.
[15] Bauer, 2002; Squire & Alvarez, 1998.
[16] L. Bloom & Tinker, 2001; Chalmers, 1996; Gardner, 2000b.
[17] Byrnes, 2001, 2007; R. E. Mayer, 1998.
[18] For a classic article on this topic, see Bruer, 1997.

"location" where knowledge is held. For instance, we will soon be talking about two components of the human memory system known as *working memory* and *long-term memory*.

The process of "putting" something into memory is called **storage**. Just as you might store groceries in a kitchen cabinet, so, too, do you store newly acquired knowledge in your memory. At some later time, you may find that you need to use what you've learned. The process of remembering previously stored information—that is, "finding" it in memory—is called **retrieval**. The following exercise illustrates the retrieval process.

SEE FOR YOURSELF
Retrieval Practice

See how quickly you can answer each of the following questions:

1. What is your name?
2. What is the capital of France?
3. In what year did Christopher Columbus first sail across the Atlantic Ocean to reach the New World?
4. What did you have for dinner three years ago today?
5. When talking about serving appetizers at a party, we sometimes use a French term instead of the word *appetizer*. What is that French term, and how is it spelled?

As you probably noticed when you tried to answer these questions, retrieving information from memory is sometimes an easy, effortless process. For example, you undoubtedly had little difficulty remembering your name. But other things can be retrieved only after some thought and effort. For example, it may have taken you a few seconds to recall that the capital of France is Paris and that Columbus first sailed across the Atlantic in 1492. Still other pieces of information, even though you may have stored them in memory at one time, may be almost impossible to retrieve. Perhaps a dinner menu three years ago and the correct spelling of *hors d'oeuvre* fall into this category.

Psychologists do not agree about the exact nature of human memory. But many have suggested that it has three components that hold information for different lengths of time.[19] A model of memory that includes these components is depicted in Figure 2.4. Working from the model and drawing from countless research studies of human memory, we can derive some general principles about how human memory operates.

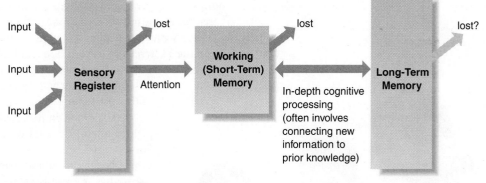

FIGURE 2.4 A model of human memory

Sensory input stays in a raw form only briefly.

If you have ever played with a lighted sparkler at night, then you've seen the tail of light that follows a sparkler as you wave it about. If you have ever daydreamed in class, then you may have noticed that when you tune back in to a lecture, you can still "hear" the three or four words that were spoken just *before* you started paying attention to your instructor again. The sparkler's tail and the words that linger are not "out there" in the environment. Instead, they are recorded in your sensory register.

The **sensory register** is the component of memory that holds the information you receive—*input*—in more or less its original, *un*encoded form. Much of what your body sees, hears, and otherwise senses is stored in the sensory register. In other words, the sensory register has a *large capacity*: It can hold a great deal of information at one time.

---

[19] For example, see R. C. Atkinson & Shiffrin, 1968; Reisberg, 1997; Willingham, 2004.

storage Process of "putting" new information into memory.

retrieval Process of "finding" information previously stored in memory.

sensory register Component of memory that holds incoming information in an unanalyzed form for a very brief time (perhaps one to two seconds).

That's the good news. The bad news is that information stored in the sensory register doesn't last very long.[20] Visual information (what you see) probably lasts for less than a second. As a child, I never could spell out my entire first name (Jeanne) with a sparkler; the *J* had always faded before I got to the first *n*, no matter how quickly I wrote. Auditory information (what you hear) probably lasts slightly longer, perhaps for two or three seconds. To keep information for any time at all, then, learners need to move it to *working memory*.

Attention is essential for most learning and memory.

Information taken directly from the environment, such as the light cast by a sparkler, doesn't last very long no matter what we do. But we can preserve a memory of it by encoding it in some minimal way—for instance, by interpreting a sparkler's curlicue tail as the letters *Jea*. The first step in this process is **attention**: *Whatever people pay attention to (mentally) moves into working memory*. Information in the sensory register that doesn't get a person's attention typically disappears from the memory system.[21]

Paying attention involves directing not only the appropriate sensory receptors (in the eyes, ears, fingertips, etc.) but also the *mind* toward whatever needs to be learned and remembered. Imagine yourself reading a textbook for one of your classes. Your eyes are moving down each page, but meanwhile you are thinking about something altogether different—a recent argument with a friend, a high-paying job advertised in the newspaper, or your growling stomach. What will you remember from the textbook? Absolutely nothing. Even though your eyes were focused on the words in your book, you weren't *mentally* paying attention to the words.

Children, too, often have trouble keeping their attention on a task at hand. We find an example in the "Memory and Metacognition: Middle Childhood" video in MyEducationLab. Ten-year-old David remembers only 3 of the 12 words that an interviewer reads to him. When he says, "My brain was turned off right now," he really means that his *attention* was turned off, or at least directed to something other than what the interviewer was saying.

Unfortunately, people can attend to only a very small amount of information at any one time. In other words, attention has a *limited capacity*.[22] For example, if you are in a room where several conversations are going on at once, you can usually attend to—and therefore can learn from—only one of those conversations. If you are sitting in front of the television with your textbook open in your lap, you can attend to the *Friends* rerun playing on the TV screen *or* to your book, but not to both simultaneously. If you are preoccupied in class with your instructor's ghastly taste in clothing and desperate need for a fashion makeover, you will have a hard time paying attention to the content of the instructor's lecture.

Exactly *how* limited is the limited capacity of human attention? People can often perform two or three well-learned, automatic tasks at once. For example, you can walk and chew gum simultaneously, and you can probably drive a car and drink a cup of coffee at the same time. But when a stimulus or event is detailed and complex (as is true for both textbooks and *Friends* reruns) or when a task requires considerable thought (understanding a lecture and driving a car on an icy mountain road are examples of tasks requiring one's utmost concentration), then people can usually attend to only *one* thing at a time.

Let's return to a point made earlier in the chapter: Learners must be selective about what they focus on and learn. Now we see the reason why: Attention has a limited capacity, allowing only a very small amount of information stored in the sensory register to move on to working memory. The vast majority of information that the body initially receives is quickly lost from the memory system, much as we might quickly discard most of that junk mail we receive every day.

Observe David's realization that attention affects memory in the "Memory and Metacognition: Middle Childhood" video in the Additional Resources section in Chapter 2 of MyEducationLab.

Children learn effectively only when they pay attention, both physically and mentally, to the subject matter.

attention   Focusing of mental processes on particular stimuli.

---

[20] Cowan, 1995; Darwin, Turvey, & Crowder, 1972; Sperling, 1960.
[21] Some nonattended-to information may remain, but without the learner's conscious awareness of it, it may be extremely difficult to recall, especially over the long run; see, for example, Cowan, 2007.
[22] J. R. Anderson, 1990; Cowan, 2007; Reisberg, 1997.

Working memory—where the action is in thinking and learning—has a short duration and limited capacity.

Working memory is the component of memory where attended-to information stays for a short while so that we can make better sense of it. It is also where much of our thinking, or cognitive processing, occurs. It is where we try to understand new concepts presented in a lecture, draw inferences from ideas encountered in a textbook passage, or solve a problem. Basically, this is the component that does most of the mental work of the memory system—hence its name *working* memory.[23]

Information stored in working memory doesn't last very long—perhaps five to twenty seconds at most—unless people do something else with it.[24] Accordingly, it is sometimes called *short-term memory*. For example, imagine that you need to call a friend, so you look up the friend's number in the telephone book. Because you've paid attention to the number, it is presumably in your working memory. But you discover that someone else is using the phone. You have no paper and pencil handy. What do you do to remember the number until the phone is available?

To keep the number in your memory until you can dial it, you might simply repeat it to yourself over and over again. This process, known as **rehearsal**, keeps information in working memory for as long as you're willing to continue talking to yourself. But once you stop, the number may disappear fairly quickly.

Put your working memory to work for a moment in the following exercise.

SEE FOR YOURSELF
A Divisive Situation

Try computing the answer to this division problem in your head:

$$59 \overline{)49{,}383}$$

Did you find yourself having trouble remembering some parts of the problem while you were dealing with other parts? Did you ever arrive at the correct answer of 837? Most people cannot solve a division problem with this many digits unless they write the problem on paper. The fact is, working memory just doesn't have enough space both to hold all that information and to perform mathematical calculations with it. Like attention, working memory has a *limited capacity,* perhaps just enough for a telephone number or very short grocery list.[25] In and of itself, it lets you hold and think about only a very small amount of material at once.

I sometimes hear students talking about putting class material in "short-term memory" so that they can do well on an upcoming exam. Such a statement reflects two common misconceptions: that (a) this component of memory lasts for several days, weeks, or months; and (b) it has a fair amount of "room." Now you know otherwise: Information stored in working memory lasts only a few seconds unless it is processed further, and only a few things can be stored there at one time. Working (short-term) memory is obviously *not* the "place" to leave information you will need for an exam later in the week, or even for information you'll need for a class later today. For such memory tasks, storage in long-term memory— the final component of the memory system—is in order.

Long-term memory has a long duration and virtually limitless capacity.

Long-term memory is where we store our general knowledge about the world (e.g., our names and frequently used telephone numbers), recollections of prior experiences, and

---

[23] Rather that being a single entity, working memory probably has several components for holding and working with different kinds of information—for example, for handling visual information, auditory information, and meanings—as well as a component that integrates multiple kinds of information; see

Baddeley, 2001; Cowan, Saults, & Morey, 2006; E. E. Smith, 2000; Willingham, 2004.

[24] For example, see Baddeley, 2001; L. R. Peterson & Peterson, 1959.

[25] Awh, Barton, & Vogel, 2007; Baddeley, 2001; Cowan, Chen, & Rouder, 2004; G. A. Miller, 1956; Simon, 1974.

working memory Component of memory that holds and actively thinks about and processes a limited amount of information.

rehearsal Cognitive process in which information is repeated over and over as a possible way of learning and remembering it.

long-term memory Component of memory that holds knowledge and skills for a relatively long time.

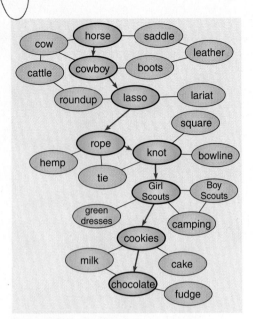

FIGURE 2.5 Related ideas are often associated with one another in long-term memory. Here you see the author's train of thought from *horse* to *chocolate*.

things we've learned in school (perhaps the capital of France or the correct spelling of *hors d'oeuvre*). Such knowledge about *what and how things are* is known as **declarative knowledge**. Long-term memory is also where we store knowledge about how to perform various behaviors, such as how to ride a bicycle, swing a baseball bat, or write a cursive letter *J*. Such knowledge about *how to do things* is known as **procedural knowledge**. When procedural knowledge includes knowing how to respond differently under different conditions, it is sometimes known as *conditional knowledge*.

As you might guess, information stored in long-term memory lasts much longer than information stored in working memory—perhaps a day, a week, a month, a year, or a lifetime (more on the "lifetime" point later in the chapter). Even when it's there, however, people cannot always find (retrieve) it when they need it. As we will see in upcoming sections, people's ability to retrieve previously learned information from long-term memory depends on both the way in which they initially stored it and the context in which they're trying to remember it.

Long-term memory seems to be able to hold as much information as a learner needs to store there. There is probably no such thing as someone "running out of room." In fact, for reasons we'll discover shortly, the more information already stored in long-term memory, the easier it is to learn new things.

Information in long-term memory is interconnected and organized to some extent.

To get a glimpse of how your own long-term memory is organized, try the following exercise.

SEE FOR YOURSELF
Horse

What is the first word that comes to your mind when you see the word *horse?* And what word does that second word remind you of? And what does that third word remind you of? Beginning with the word *horse,* follow your train of thought, letting each word remind you of another one, for a sequence of at least eight words. Write down your sequence of words as each word comes to mind.

You probably found yourself easily following a train of thought from the word *horse,* perhaps something like the route I followed:

horse → cowboy → lasso → rope → knot → Girl Scouts → cookies → chocolate

The last word in your sequence might be one with little or no obvious relationship to horses. Yet you can probably see a logical connection between each pair of words in your sequence. Related pieces of information are often associated with one another in long-term memory, perhaps in a network similar to the one depicted in Figure 2.5.

In the process of constructing knowledge, learners often create well-integrated entities that encompass particular ideas or groups of ideas. Beginning in infancy, they form **concepts** that enable them to categorize objects and events.[26] In Figure 2.6, 8-year-old Noah shows his knowledge about the concept *butterfly.* Some concepts, such as *butterfly, chair,* and *backstroke,* refer to a fairly narrow range of objects or events. Other concepts are fairly general ones that encompass numerous more specific concepts. For example, the concept *insect* includes ants, bees, and butterflies. The concept *furniture* includes chairs, tables, beds, and desks. The concept *swim* includes the backstroke, dog paddle, and butterfly. As you can see, the word *butterfly* can be associated with two very different, more general concepts (insects and swimming) and so might lead someone to follow a train of thought such as this one:

horse → cowboy → lasso → rope → knot → Girl Scouts → camping
→ outdoors → nature → insect → butterfly → swimming

declarative knowledge Knowledge related to "what is"—that is, to the nature of how things are, were, or will be.

procedural knowledge Knowledge concerning how to do something (e.g., a skill).

concept Mental grouping of objects or events that have something in common.

[26] Behl-Chadha, 1996; Eimas & Quinn, 1994; Quinn, 2002.

Learners pull some concepts together into general understandings of what things are typically like. Such understandings are sometimes called **schemas**.[27] For example, let's return to our friend the horse. You know what horses look like, of course, and you can recognize one when you see one. Hence, you have a concept for *horse*. But now think about the many things you know *about* horses. What do they eat? How do they spend their time? Where are you most likely to see them? You probably have little difficulty retrieving many facts about horses, perhaps including their fondness for oats and carrots, their love of grazing and running, and their frequent appearance in pastures and at racetracks. The various things you know about horses are closely interrelated in your long-term memory in the form of a "horse" schema.

People have schemas not only about objects but also about events. For example, read the following passage about John.

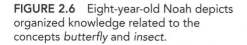

SEE FOR YOURSELF

John

Read the following passage *one time only:*

> John was feeling bad today so he decided to go see the family doctor. He checked in with the doctor's receptionist, and then looked through several medical magazines that were on the table by his chair. Finally the nurse came and asked him to take off his clothes. The doctor was very nice to him. He eventually prescribed some pills for John. Then John left the doctor's office and headed home.[28]

FIGURE 2.6 Eight-year-old Noah depicts organized knowledge related to the concepts *butterfly* and *insect.*

You probably had no trouble understanding the passage because you have been to a doctor's office yourself and have a schema for how those visits usually go. You can therefore fill in a number of details that the passage doesn't tell you. For example, you probably inferred that John must have *gone* to the doctor's office, although the story omits this essential step. Likewise, you probably concluded that John took off his clothes in the examination room, *not* in the waiting room, even though the story never makes it clear where John did his striptease. When a schema involves a predictable sequence of events related to a particular activity, as is the case in a visit to the doctor's office, it is sometimes called a **script**.

On a much larger scale, human beings—young children included—construct general understandings and belief systems, or **theories**, about how the world operates.[29] People's theories include many concepts and the relationships (e.g., frequent co-occurrence, cause-and-effect) among them. To see what some of your own theories are like, try the next exercise.

SEE FOR YOURSELF

Coffeepots and Raccoons

Consider each of the following situations:

1. People took a coffeepot that looked like Drawing A. They removed the handle, sealed the top, took off the top knob, sealed the opening to the spout, and removed the spout. They also sliced off the base and attached a flat piece of metal. They attached a little stick, cut out a window, and filled the metal container with birdseed. When they were done, it looked like Drawing B.

   After these changes, was this a coffeepot or a bird feeder?

A

B

schema General understanding of what an object or event is typically like.

script Schema that involves a predictable sequence of events related to a common activity.

theory Integrated set of concepts and principles developed to explain a particular phenomenon.

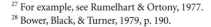

[27] For example, see Rumelhart & Ortony, 1977.
[28] Bower, Black, & Turner, 1979, p. 190.

[29] Gelman, 2003; Keil, 1989, 1994; Wellman & Gelman, 1998.

2. Doctors took the raccoon in Drawing C and shaved away some of its fur. They dyed what was left black. Then they bleached a single stripe all white down the center of the animal's back. Then, with surgery, they put in its body a sac of supersmelly odor, just like the smell a skunk has. After they were all done, the animal looked like Drawing D.

After the operation, was this a skunk or a raccoon?[30]

Chances are, you concluded that the coffeepot had been transformed into a bird feeder but that the raccoon was still a raccoon despite its cosmetic makeover and major surgery. Fourth graders come to these conclusions as well.[31] Now how is it possible that the coffeepot could be made into something entirely different, whereas the raccoon could not?

Even as infants, children seem to make a basic distinction between human-made objects (e.g., coffeepots, bird feeders) and biological entities (e.g., raccoons, skunks).[32] By the preschool years, children seem to conceptualize the two categories in fundamentally different ways: For instance, human-made objects are defined largely by the *functions* they serve (e.g., brewing coffee, feeding birds), whereas biological entities are defined primarily by their origins (e.g., the parents who brought them into being, their DNA).[33] Thus, when a coffeepot begins to hold birdseed rather than coffee, it becomes a bird feeder because its function has changed. But when a raccoon is cosmetically and surgically altered to look and smell like a skunk, it still has raccoon parents and raccoon DNA and so cannot possibly *be* a skunk.

By the time children reach school age, they have constructed basic theories about their physical, biological, and social worlds.[34] They have also constructed preliminary theories about the nature of their own and other people's thinking. For instance, they realize that people's inner thoughts are distinct from external reality, and they understand that the people in their lives have thoughts, emotions, and motives that drive much of what they do (see Chapter 7). In general, children's self-constructed theories facilitate their acquisition of new information, and they help children organize and make sense of personal experiences, classroom subject matter, and other new information.[35] Yet because children's theories often evolve with little or no guidance from more knowledgeable individuals, they sometimes include erroneous beliefs about the world that can wreak havoc with new learning (more about this point shortly).

How well long-term memory is integrated and in what ways it is integrated are to some degree the result of how learners first store information in long-term memory, as we shall see in our discussion of the next principle.

Some long-term memory storage processes are more effective than others.

In the memory model depicted in Figure 2.4, you will notice that the arrow between working memory and long-term memory points in both directions. The process of storing new information in long-term memory often involves drawing on "old" information already stored there—that is, it involves using prior knowledge.[36] To see what I mean, try the following exercise.

[30] Both scenarios based on Keil, 1989, p. 184.
[31] Keil, 1986, 1989.
[32] Gelman & Kalish, 2006; Inagaki & Hatano, 2006.
[33] Greif, Kemler Nelson, Keil, & Gutierrez, 2006; Inagaki & Hatano, 2006; Keil, 1987, 1989.
[34] Geary, 2005; Torney-Purta, 1994; Wellman & Gelman, 1998.

[35] Gelman, 2003; Reiner, Slotta, Chi, & Resnick, 2000; Wellman & Gelman, 1998.
[36] For a good discussion of this point, see Kirschner, Sweller, & Clark, 2006.

TABLE 2.2   Long-Term Memory Storage Processes

Process	Definition	Example	Effectiveness
Rote learning: Learning primarily through repetition and practice, with little or no attempt to make sense of what is being learned			
Rehearsal	Repeating information verbatim, either mentally or aloud	Word-for-word repetition of a formula or definition	Relatively ineffective: Storage is slow, and later retrieval is difficult.
Meaningful learning: Making connections between new information and prior knowledge			
Elaboration	Adding additional ideas to new information based on what one already knows	Thinking about possible reasons that historical figures made the decisions they did	Effective if associations and additions made are appropriate and productive.
Organization	Making connections among various pieces of new information	Studying how one's lines in a play relate to the play's overall story line	Effective if organizational structure is legitimate and consists of more than just a "list" of separate facts.
Visual imagery	Forming a mental picture of something, either by actually seeing it or by envisioning how it might look	Imagining how various characters and events in a novel might have looked	Individual differences in effectiveness; especially beneficial when used in combination with elaboration or organization.

SEE FOR YOURSELF
Two Letter Strings, Two Pictures

1. Study each of the following strings of letters until you can remember them perfectly:

   AIIRODFMLAWRS   FAMILIARWORDS

2. Study each of the two pictures in the margin until you can reproduce them accurately from memory.

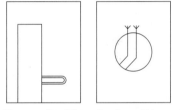

Source: Figures are from "Comprehension and Memory for Pictures" by G. H. Bower, M. B. Karlin, and A. Dueck, 1975, *Memory and Cognition, 3,* p. 217. Reprinted by permission of Psychonomic Society, Inc.

No doubt the second letter string was easier for you to learn because you could relate it to something you already knew: the words *familiar words.* How easily were you able to learn the two pictures? Do you think you could draw them from memory a week from now? Do you think you would be able to remember them more easily if they had titles such as "a very short man playing a trombone in a telephone booth" and "an early bird who caught a very strong worm"? The answer to the last question is almost certainly *yes,* because the titles help you relate the pictures to familiar shapes, such as those of trombones, telephone booths, and birds' feet.[37]

With the preceding exercise in mind, let's distinguish between two basic types of learning: rote learning and meaningful learning (e.g., see Table 2.2). People engage in **rote learning** when they try to learn and remember something without attaching much meaning to it. This would be the case, for instance, if you tried to remember the letter string AIIRODFMLAWRS without trying to find some kind of "sense"—patterns in the letters, perhaps, or similarities to words you know—in the sequence. You would also be engaging in rote learning if you tried to remember the shapes in the "telephone booth" and "early bird" figures simply by trying to memorize where each line and curve is on the page.

One common form of rote learning is *rehearsal,* repeating something over and over, perhaps by saying it aloud or perhaps by continuously thinking about it in a more or less unaltered, verbatim fashion. We have already seen how rehearsal can help learners keep information in working memory indefinitely. Unfortunately, however, rehearsal is *not* a very effective way of storing information in *long-term* memory. If learners repeat something often enough, it might eventually "sink in," but the process is slow, laborious, and not much fun. Furthermore, for reasons we will identify later, people who use rehearsal and other forms of rote learning often have trouble remembering what they've learned.[38]

---

[37] Bower, Karlin, & Dueck, 1975.
[38] J. R. Anderson, 1995; Ausubel, 1968; Craik & Watkins, 1973.

rote learning Learning information in a relatively uninterpreted form, without making sense of it or attaching much meaning to it.

In contrast to rote learning, **meaningful learning** involves recognizing a relationship between new information and something already stored in long-term memory. Seeing the words *familiar words* in the letter string FAMILIARWORDS and seeing meaningful shapes (a trombone, birds' feet, etc.) in simple line drawings are two examples. Here are some additional illustrations:

- Relating subtraction facts to previously learned addition facts (e.g., $5 - 3 = 2$ is just a backward version of $2 + 3 = 5$)
- Noticing how words in a foreign language are similar to, and have similar meanings as, words in English (e.g., the German word *buch* means "book," and the French word *le crayon* means "pencil")
- Seeing parallels among historical events (e.g., the rationale for the "ethnic cleansing" that occurred in Kosovo in the 1990s was in many ways similar to the Nazis' belief in white superiority in the 1930s and 1940s)

In the vast majority of cases, meaningful learning is more effective than rote learning for storing information in long-term memory.[39] It is especially effective when learners relate ideas to *themselves* as human beings.[40]

Meaningful learning can take a variety of forms, and in many cases it involves adding to or restructuring information in some way. For instance, in **elaboration**, learners use their prior knowledge to expand on a new idea, thereby storing *more* information than was actually presented. For example, a student who reads that allosaurs (a species of dinosaurs) had powerful jaws and sharp, pointed teeth might correctly deduce that allosaurs were meat eaters. Similarly, if a student learns that the crew on Columbus's first trip across the Atlantic threatened to revolt and turn the ships back toward Europe, the student might speculate, "I'll bet the men were really frightened when they continued to travel west day after day without ever seeing signs of land."[41]

Another form of meaningful learning is **organization**, in which learners arrange new information in a logical structure. For example, they might group information into categories, just as you probably categorized the 12 words (daisy, apple, hammer, etc.) in the "Remembering Words" exercise near the beginning of the chapter. An alternative way of organizing information is to identify interrelationships among its various parts. For example, when learning about *velocity, acceleration, force,* and *mass* in a physics class, a student might better understand these concepts by seeing how they're interconnected—for instance, by learning that velocity is the product of acceleration and time ($v = a \times t$) and that an object's force is determined by both the object's mass and its acceleration ($f = m \times a$). The trick is not simply to memorize the formulas (this would be rote learning), but rather to make sense of and understand the relationships that the formulas represent. In most instances, learners who learn an organized body of information remember it better, and they can use it more effectively later on, than would be the case if they tried to learn the same information as a list of separate, isolated facts.[42]

Still another effective long-term memory storage process is **visual imagery**, forming a mental picture of objects or ideas. To discover firsthand how effective visual imagery can be, try learning a bit of Mandarin Chinese in the next exercise.

meaningful learning Cognitive process in which learners relate new information to things they already know.

elaboration Cognitive process in which learners embellish on new information based on what they already know.

organization Cognitive process in which learners find connections (e.g., by forming categories, identifying hierarchies, determining cause-and-effect relationships) among various pieces of information they need to learn.

visual imagery Process of forming mental pictures of objects or ideas.

SEE FOR YOURSELF
Five Chinese Words

The top of page 33 presents five Chinese words. Try learning the words by forming the visual images I describe (don't worry about learning the marks over the words).

[39] J. R. Anderson, 1995; Ausubel, Novak, & Hanesian, 1978; Bransford & Johnson, 1972; R. E. Mayer, 1996.
[40] Heatherton, Macrae, & Kelley, 2004; T. B. Rogers, Kuiper, & Kirker, 1977.
[41] Notice that we are using the term *elaboration* to describe something that *learners* do, not something that teachers do. Elaboration as a *cognitive process* occurs inside rather than outside the learner. However, teachers can certainly *help* students engage in elaboration, as you'll discover later in the chapter.
[42] Bjorklund, Schneider, Cassel, & Ashley, 1994; Bower, Clark, Lesgold, & Winzenz, 1969; Mandler & Pearlstone, 1966; Tulving, 1962.

Chinese Word	English Meaning	Image
fáng	house	Picture a *house* with *fangs* growing on its roof and walls.
mén	door	Picture a restroom *door* with the word *MEN* painted on it.
ké	guest	Picture a person giving someone else (the *guest*) a *key* to the house.
fàn	food	Picture a plate of *food* being cooled by a *fan*.
shū	book	Picture a *shoe* with a *book* sticking out of it.

Now find something else to do for a couple of minutes. Stand up and stretch, get a glass of water, or use the restroom. But be sure to come back to your reading in just a minute or two. . . .

Now that you're back, cover the list of Chinese words, English meanings, and visual images. Try to remember what each word means:

ké   fàn   mén   fáng   shū

Did the Chinese words remind you of the visual images you stored? Did the images, in turn, help you remember the English meanings of the Chinese words? You may have remembered all five words easily, or you may have remembered only one or two. People differ in their ability to use visual imagery: Some form images quickly and easily, whereas others form them only slowly and with difficulty.[43] Especially for people in the former category, visual imagery can be a powerful means of storing information in long-term memory.[44]

The three forms of meaningful learning we've just examined—elaboration, organization, and visual imagery—are clearly *constructive* in nature: They all involve combining several pieces of information into a meaningful whole. When you elaborate on new information, you combine it with things you already know to help you make better sense of it. When you organize information, you give it a logical structure (categories, cause-and-effect relationships, etc.). And when you use visual imagery, you create mental pictures (perhaps a house with fangs or a restroom door labeled *MEN*) based on how certain objects typically look.

Practice makes knowledge more automatic and durable.

Storing something in long-term memory on one occasion is hardly the end of the story. When people continue to practice the information and skills they acquire—and especially when they do so in a variety of situations and contexts—they gradually become able to use what they've learned quickly, effortlessly, and automatically. In other words, people eventually achieve **automaticity** for well-practiced knowledge and skills.[45]

As we noted earlier, rehearsal—repeating information over and over within the course of a few seconds or minutes—is a relatively *in*effective way of getting information into long-term memory. But when we talk about acquiring automaticity, we're talking about repetition over the long run: reviewing and practicing information and procedures at periodic intervals over the course of a few weeks, months, or years. When practice is spread out in this manner, people of all ages (even young infants) learn something better and remember it longer.[46]

Practice is especially important for gaining procedural knowledge. As an example, think of driving a car, a complicated skill that you can probably perform easily. Your first attempts at driving years ago may have required a great deal of mental energy and effort.

[43] Behrmann, 2000; J. M. Clark & Paivio, 1991; Kosslyn, 1985.

[44] Dewhurst & Conway, 1994; Johnson-Glenberg, 2000; D. B. Mitchell, 2006; Sadoski, Goetz, & Fritz, 1993; Sadoski & Paivio, 2001.

[45] J. R. Anderson, 1983; P. W. Cheng, 1985; Graham, Harris, & Fink, 2000; Proctor & Dutta, 1995; Schneider & Shiffrin, 1977; Semb & Ellis, 1994.

[46] J. R. Anderson & Schooler, 1991; Belfiore, Skinner, & Ferkis, 1995; Dempster, 1991; Linton, 1986; Proctor & Dutta, 1995; Rovee-Collier, 1993; West & Stanovich, 1991.

automaticity Ability to respond quickly and efficiently while mentally processing or physically performing a task.

But now you can drive without having to pay much attention to what you are doing. Even if your car has a standard transmission, driving is, for you, an automatic activity.

Many complex procedures, such as driving a car, may begin largely as explicit, declarative knowledge—in other words, as *information* about how to execute a procedure rather than as the actual *ability* to execute it. When learners use declarative knowledge to guide them as they carry out a new procedure, their performance is slow and laborious, the activity consumes a great deal of mental effort, and they often talk themselves through their actions. As they continue to practice the activity, however, their declarative knowledge gradually evolves into procedural knowledge. This knowledge becomes fine-tuned over time and eventually allows learners to perform an activity quickly and easily—that is, with automaticity.[47]

With age and experience, children acquire more effective learning strategies.

Sometimes learners engage in effective long-term memory storage processes (elaboration, organization, visual imagery, etc.) without intentionally trying to do so. For example, if I tell you that *I used to live in Colorado,* you might immediately deduce that I lived in or near the Rocky Mountains. In this case you are automatically engaging in elaboration (my statement made no mention of the Rockies, so you supplied this information from your own long-term memory). If an image of pointy, snow-capped mountains comes to mind, then you are using visual imagery as well.

At other times learners deliberately use certain cognitive processes in their efforts to learn and remember information. For example, in the "Remembering Words" exercise near the beginning of the chapter, you may have quickly noticed the categorical nature of the 12 words in the list and intentionally used the categories *flowers, fruit,* and *tools* to organize them. Similarly, in the "Five Chinese Words" exercise, you intentionally formed visual images in accordance with my instructions. When learners *intentionally* engage in certain cognitive processes to help them learn and remember something, they are using a **learning strategy**.

Even infants show some ability to organize their experiences, and by age 4, children may intentionally organize a set of objects in an effort to remember them.[48] In the preschool years children elaborate on their experiences as well.[49] But for the most part, children don't intentionally choose particular learning strategies until they reach school age. Rehearsal typically appears first, perhaps between ages 5 and 7, and children use it with increasing frequency and effectiveness—at least for things they need to remember for only a few minutes—as they progress through the elementary and middle school grades.[50] The ability to use visual images effectively to encode and remember information also improves over the course of elementary and middle school.[51] By the upper elementary grades, children also begin to organize information to help them learn it, and their organizational structures become more hierarchical and abstract as they move into the middle and high school grades.[52] As an intentional learning strategy, elaboration appears fairly late in development (usually around puberty) and gradually increases during the teenage years.[53] Even so, many high school students rely largely on rehearsal, rather than on more effective strategies, to study and learn academic material.[54] Table 2.3 summarizes developmental trends in learning strategies across the grade levels.

Prior knowledge and beliefs affect new learning, usually for the better but sometimes for the worse.

What learners already know provides a **knowledge base** on which new learning builds. To engage in meaningful learning, learners must, of course, have prior knowledge that's relevant to what they're learning. For instance, when you read the passage about John's visit to the doctor's office earlier in the chapter, you could make sense of the passage—in which a lot of important information was missing—only if you yourself have visited a doctor many

Observe how organization improves with age in the early childhood, early adolescence, and late adolescence "Memory and Metacognition" videos in the Additional Resources section in Chapter 2 of MyEducationLab.

learning strategy Intentional use of one or more cognitive processes for a particular learning task.

knowledge base One's existing knowledge about specific topics and the world in general.

[47] J. R. Anderson, 1983, 1987; Beilock & Carr, 2003.
[48] Behl-Chadha, 1996; DeLoache & Todd, 1988; Quinn, 2002.
[49] Fivush, Haden, & Adam, 1995.
[50] Cowan et al., 2006; Gathercole & Hitch, 1993; Kunzinger, 1985; Lehmann & Hasselhorn, 2007; Pressley & Hilden, 2006.
[51] Kosslyn, Margolis, Barrett, Goldknopf, & Daly, 1990; Pressley & Hilden, 2006.
[52] Bjorklund & Jacobs, 1985; Bjorklund et al., 1994; DeLoache & Todd, 1988; Lucariello, Kyratzis, & Nelson, 1992; Plumert, 1994; Pressley & Hilden, 2006.
[53] Schneider & Pressley, 1989.
[54] Pressley, 1982; J. W. Thomas, 1993.

DEVELOPMENTAL TRENDS

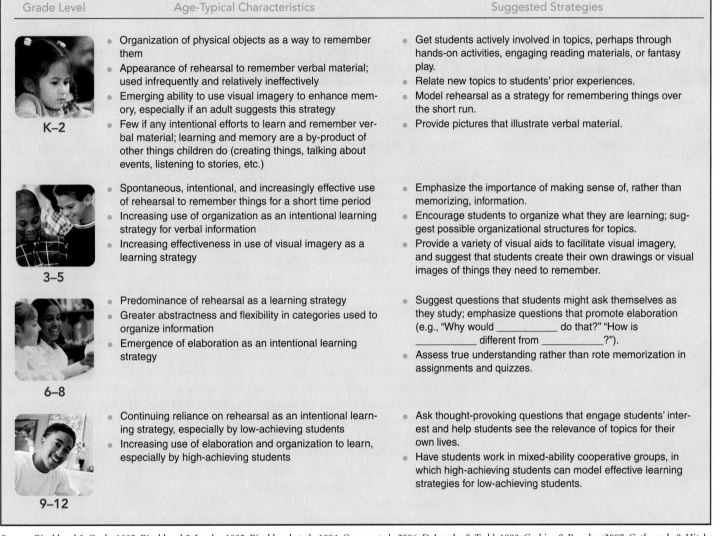

TABLE 2.3 Typical Learning Strategies at Different Grade Levels

Grade Level	Age-Typical Characteristics	Suggested Strategies
K–2	• Organization of physical objects as a way to remember them • Appearance of rehearsal to remember verbal material; used infrequently and relatively ineffectively • Emerging ability to use visual imagery to enhance memory, especially if an adult suggests this strategy • Few if any intentional efforts to learn and remember verbal material; learning and memory are a by-product of other things children do (creating things, talking about events, listening to stories, etc.)	• Get students actively involved in topics, perhaps through hands-on activities, engaging reading materials, or fantasy play. • Relate new topics to students' prior experiences. • Model rehearsal as a strategy for remembering things over the short run. • Provide pictures that illustrate verbal material.
3–5	• Spontaneous, intentional, and increasingly effective use of rehearsal to remember things for a short time period • Increasing use of organization as an intentional learning strategy for verbal information • Increasing effectiveness in use of visual imagery as a learning strategy	• Emphasize the importance of making sense of, rather than memorizing, information. • Encourage students to organize what they are learning; suggest possible organizational structures for topics. • Provide a variety of visual aids to facilitate visual imagery, and suggest that students create their own drawings or visual images of things they need to remember.
6–8	• Predominance of rehearsal as a learning strategy • Greater abstractness and flexibility in categories used to organize information • Emergence of elaboration as an intentional learning strategy	• Suggest questions that students might ask themselves as they study; emphasize questions that promote elaboration (e.g., "Why would _____ do that?" "How is _____ different from _____?"). • Assess true understanding rather than rote memorization in assignments and quizzes.
9–12	• Continuing reliance on rehearsal as an intentional learning strategy, especially by low-achieving students • Increasing use of elaboration and organization to learn, especially by high-achieving students	• Ask thought-provoking questions that engage students' interest and help students see the relevance of topics for their own lives. • Have students work in mixed-ability cooperative groups, in which high-achieving students can model effective learning strategies for low-achieving students.

Sources: Bjorklund & Coyle, 1995; Bjorklund & Jacobs, 1985; Bjorklund et al., 1994; Cowan et al., 2006; DeLoache & Todd, 1988; Gaskins & Pressley, 2007; Gathercole & Hitch, 1993; Kosslyn et al., 1990; Kunzinger, 1985; Lehmann & Hasselhorn, 2007; Lucariello et al., 1992; L. S. Newman, 1990; Plumert, 1994; Pressley, 1982; Pressley & Hilden, 2006; Schneider & Pressley, 1989.

times and so know how such visits typically go. Generally speaking, people who already know something about a topic learn new information about that topic more effectively than people who have little relevant background.[55] In other words, the rich (in knowledge) get richer, and the poor stay relatively poor.

Recall how in the case study at the beginning of the chapter, Rita misinterpreted what she learned about Michigan's history in part because she did not know that two words in her history lessons, *British* and *English,* were essentially synonyms. When learners have little relevant knowledge on which to build, they are apt to struggle in their efforts to make sense of new information.

Prior knowledge about a topic is not always helpful, however. Occasionally it *interferes* with new learning. In some instances, it may do so because a learner makes an inappropriate connection. Figure 2.7 provides an example: Calvin thinks that a *feudal* system is a *futile*

---

[55] P. A. Alexander, Kulikowich, & Schulze, 1994; Cromley & Azevedo, 2007; Schneider, 1993; Shapiro, 2004.

FIGURE 2.7   Learners benefit from their prior knowledge only when they make appropriate connections. Here Calvin is trying to learn new information meaningfully, but his efforts are in vain because he's unfamiliar with the word *feudal*.

Source: CALVIN AND HOBBES © 1990 Watterson. Dist. by UNIVERSAL PRESS SYNDICATE. Reprinted with permission. All rights reserved.

system. We see additional examples in the opening case study. Rita initially associates the word *China* with dinnerware and speculates that the Europeans wanted to import cups from the Far East. She also recalls that furs were an important commodity during the colonial period in the New World and so mistakenly reports that the furs came from China.

At other times things learned at an earlier time may interfere with new learning because that previous "knowledge" is incorrect. For instance, imagine a group of children who think that the earth is flat. Such an idea is consistent with their early experiences, especially if they live in, say, Illinois or Kansas. You now tell them that the world is actually round. Rather than replacing the *flat* idea with a *round* one, they might pull both ideas together and conclude that the earth is shaped something like a pancake, which is flat *and* round.[56]

Figure 2.8 presents examples of misconceptions that children and adolescents may bring with them to the classroom. Especially when such misconceptions are embedded in learners' general theories about the world, instruction intended to correct them may do little to change learners' minds.[57] Instead, thanks to the process of elaboration—a process that usually facilitates learning—learners may interpret or distort the new information to be consistent with what they already "know." As a result, they can spend a great deal of time learning the wrong thing! Consider the case of Barry, an 11th grader whose physics class was studying the idea that an object's mass and weight do *not*, in and of themselves, affect the speed at which the object falls. Students were asked to design and build an egg container that would keep an egg from breaking when dropped from a third-floor window. They were told that on the day of the egg drop, they would record the time it took for the eggs to reach the ground. Convinced that heavier objects fall faster, Barry added several nails to his egg's container. Yet when he dropped it, classmates timed its fall at 1.49 seconds, a time very similar to that for other students' lighter containers. He and his teacher had the following discussion about the result:

> **Teacher:** So what was your time?
> **Barry:** 1.49. I think it should be faster.
> **Teacher:** Why?
> **Barry:** Because it weighed more than anybody else's and it dropped slower.
> **Teacher:** Oh really? And what do you attribute that to?
> **Barry:** That the people weren't timing real good.[58]

This tendency to look for what one thinks is true and to ignore evidence to the contrary is known as **confirmation bias**. For instance, when students in a science lab observe results that contradict what they have expected will happen, many are apt to discredit the results, perhaps complaining that "our equipment isn't working right" or "I can never do science anyway."[59] Similarly, when students in a history class read accounts of a historical event that conflicts with prior, not-quite-accurate beliefs about the event—especially if those beliefs are widely held in their cultural group—they may stick with their initial understandings, perhaps saying, "it is not written here . . . but I think this is what happened."[60]

As you can see, then, although prior knowledge and beliefs about a topic are usually a blessing, they can sometimes be a curse. When we explore the topic of *conceptual change* later in the chapter, we'll identify strategies that may help learners replace their naive notions with more accurate understandings.

Now that we've explored basic principles related to *putting* information in long-term memory, let's turn our attention to retrieval, the process of *finding* that information later on.

confirmation bias Tendency to seek information that confirms rather than discredits current beliefs.

[56] Vosniadou, 1994.
[57] Derry, 1996; P. K. Murphy & Mason, 2006; Sinatra & Pintrich, 2003a; C. L. Smith, Maclin, Grosslight, & Davis, 1997.
[58] Hynd, 1998a, p. 34.
[59] Minstrell & Stimpson, 1996, p. 192.
[60] Porat, 2004, p. 989.

FIGURE 2.8 Common student misconceptions

ASTRONOMY

Fact: The earth revolves around the sun.

Misconception: The sun revolves around the earth. It "rises" in the morning and "sets" in the evening, at which point it "goes" to the other side of the earth.

Fact: The earth is shaped more or less like a sphere.

Misconception: The earth is shaped like a round, flat disk.

BIOLOGY

Fact: A living thing is something that carries on such life processes as metabolism, growth, and reproduction.

Misconception: A living thing is something that moves and/or grows. The sun, wind, clouds, and fire are living things.

Fact: A plant is a living thing that produces its own food.

Misconception: A plant grows in a garden and is relatively small. Carrots and cabbage are vegetables, not plants. Trees are plants only if they are small.

PHYSICS

Fact: An object remains in uniform motion until a force acts upon it; a force is needed only to *change* speed or direction.

Misconception: Any moving object has a force acting upon it. For example, a ball thrown in the air continues to be pushed upward by the force of the throw until it begins its descent.

Fact: Light objects and heavy objects fall at the same rate unless other forces (e.g., air resistance) differently affect the objects (e.g., feathers tend to fall slowly because they encounter significant air resistance relative to their mass).

Misconception: Heavy objects fall faster than light objects.

GEOGRAPHY

Fact: The Great Lakes contain freshwater.

Misconception: The Great Lakes contain salt water.

Fact: Rivers run from higher elevation to lower elevation.

Misconception: Rivers run from north to south (going "down" on a map). For example, rivers can run from Canada into the United States, but not vice versa.

Source: S. Carey, 1986; Kyle & Shymansky, 1989; Maria, 1998; Nussbaum, 1985; Sneider & Pulos, 1983; Vosniadou, 1994; Vosniadou & Brewer, 1987; geography misconceptions courtesy of R. K. Ormrod.

WHY LEARNERS MAY OR MAY NOT REMEMBER WHAT THEY'VE LEARNED

Retrieving information from long-term memory appears to involve following a pathway of associations. Almost literally, it's a process of going down Memory Lane. One idea reminds you of another idea—that is, one idea *activates* another—the second idea reminds you of a third idea, and so on, in a manner similar to what happened when you followed a train of thought from the word *horse* earlier in the chapter. If the pathway of associations eventually leads you to what you're trying to remember, you do indeed remember it. If the path takes you in other directions, you're out of luck.

How easily and accurately people remember what they've previously learned can be described using the following general principles.

How easily something is recalled depends on how it was initially learned.

People are more likely to remember something they've previously learned if, in the process of storing it, they connected it with something else in long-term memory. Ideally, the "new" and the "old" have a logical relationship. To illustrate this idea, let's return once again to all that mail that arrives in your mailbox. Imagine that, on average, you receive five important items—things you really want to save—every day. At six postal deliveries a week and 52 weeks a year, minus a dozen or so holidays, you save about 1,500 pieces of mail each year. If you save this much mail over the course of 15 years, you eventually have more than 22,000 important things stashed somewhere in your home.

One day you hear that stock in a clothing company (Mod Bod Jeans, Inc.) has tripled in value. You remember that your wealthy Uncle Fred sent you some Mod Bod stock certificates for your birthday several years ago, and you presumably decided they were important enough to save. But where in the world did you put them? How long will it take you to find them among all those important letters, bills, brochures, catalogs, advertisements, requests for donations, and sweepstakes announcements?

How easily you find the certificates and, in fact, whether you find them at all depend on how you have been storing your mail as you've accumulated it. If you've been storing it in a logical, organized fashion—for instance, by putting all paid bills on a closet shelf, all mail-order catalogs on the floor under your bedside table, and all items from relatives in a file cabinet (in alphabetical order by last name)—then you should be able to retrieve Uncle Fred's gift fairly quickly. But if you simply tossed each day's mail randomly around the house, you will be searching your home for a long, long time, possibly without ever finding a trace of that Mod Bod stock.

Like a home with 15 years' worth of mail, long-term memory contains a great deal of information. And like finding the Mod Bod certificates, the ease with which information is retrieved from long-term memory depends somewhat on whether the information is stored in a logical "place"—that is, whether it is connected with related ideas. Through making those important connections with existing knowledge—that is, through meaningful learning—people know where to "look" for information when they need it. In contrast, learning something by rote is like throwing Uncle Fred's gift randomly among thousands of pieces of unorganized mail: A person may never retrieve it again.

Learners are especially likely to retrieve information when they have *many* possible pathways to it—in other words, when they have associated the information with numerous other ideas in their existing knowledge. Making multiple connections is like using cross-references in your mail storage system. You may have filed the Mod Bod stock in the "items from relatives" file drawer, but you've also written the stock's location on notes left in many other places—perhaps with your birth certificate (after all, you received the stock on your birthday), with your income tax receipts, and in your safe deposit box. By looking in any one of these logical places, you will discover where to find your valuable stock.

Remembering depends on the context.

When I hear certain "oldies" songs (songs by the Beatles, Supremes, Mamas and Papas, Turtles, etc.), I immediately recall my college years, when those songs were played regularly at parties, in my dormitory, and on the beach. The songs send me down that Memory Lane of associations that leads me to my stored versions of the people, places, events, and ideas that were so important to me in college. You too may find that certain songs, smells, pictures, or words stir up memories of days gone by. Things in the environment that remind people of something they've learned in the past—those things that facilitate retrieval—are **retrieval cues**.

Retrieval cues clearly help learners recall what they've previously learned.[61] As an example, try the following exercise.

SEE FOR YOURSELF

The Great Lakes

1. If you were educated in North America, then at one time or another you probably learned the names of the five Great Lakes. While timing yourself with the second hand of a clock or watch, see if you can recall all of them within a 15-second period.
2. If you had trouble remembering all five lakes within that short time, here's a hint: The first letters of the Great Lakes spell the word *HOMES*. Now see if you can recall all five lakes within 15 seconds.

If you did poorly at step 1, the word *HOMES* probably helped you do better at step 2 because it gave you some idea about where to "look" in your long-term memory. Perhaps you couldn't initially remember Lake Michigan. If so, *HOMES* told you that one of the lakes begins with the letter *M*, and so you searched among the *M* words in your long-term memory until, possibly, you stumbled on "Michigan." The letters in *HOMES* acted as retrieval cues that started your search of long-term memory in the right directions.

Whether people remember something they've learned when they need it later depends on whether something in their environment sends them down the appropriate pathway in long-term memory. In some cases the retrieval cue might be something inherent in the task

---

retrieval cue Stimulus that provides guidance about where to "look" for a piece of information in long-term memory.

[61] Tulving, 1983; Tulving & Thomson, 1973.

to be done. For example, if I ask you to solve the problem $13 + 24 = ?$, the plus sign ($+$) tells you that you need to add, and so you retrieve what you know about addition. In other cases another person might give you a hint, just as I did when I suggested that you use *HOMES* to help you remember the Great Lakes. The presence or absence of such retrieval cues plays a critical role in people's ability to apply, or *transfer*, what they've learned to new situations, as you'll discover in Chapter 4.

How easily something is recalled and used depends on how often it has been recalled and used in the past.

Practice doesn't necessarily make perfect, but as we've seen, it does make knowledge more durable and automatic. Practice also makes knowledge easier to "find" when it's needed. When we use information and skills frequently, we essentially "pave" the pathways we must travel to find them, in some cases creating superhighways.

Knowledge that has been learned to automaticity has another advantage as well. Remember, working memory has a limited capacity: The active, "thinking" part of the human memory system can do only so much at a time. When much of its capacity must be used for recalling single facts or carrying out simple procedures, little room is left for addressing more complex situations or tasks. One key reason for learning some facts and procedures to automaticity, then, is to free up working memory capacity for tackling complex tasks and problems that require those facts and procedures.[62] For example, fourth graders faced with the multiplication problem

$$\begin{array}{r} 87 \\ \times\ 59 \end{array}$$

can solve it more easily if they can quickly retrieve such basic facts as $9 \times 8 = 72$ and $5 \times 7 = 35$. High school chemistry students can more easily interpret Na_2CO_3 (sodium carbonate) if they don't have to stop to think about what the symbols *Na*, *C*, and *O* represent.

Recall often involves reconstruction.

Have you ever remembered an event very differently than a friend did, even though the two of you had participated actively and equally in the event? Were you and your friend both certain of the accuracy of your own memories and therefore convinced that the other person remembered the situation incorrectly? Like storage, retrieval has a constructive side, which can explain your differing recollections.

Retrieving something from long-term memory isn't necessarily an all-or-none phenomenon. Sometimes people retrieve only certain parts of something they've previously learned. In such situations they may construct their "memory" of an event by combining the tidbits they can recall with their general knowledge and assumptions about the world.[63] The following exercise illustrates this point.

Frequent practice of basic skills, such as addition and subtraction, makes them more durable and automatic.

SEE FOR YOURSELF
Missing Letters

Fill in the missing letters of the following five words:

1. sep-rate
2. exist-nce
3. adole---nce
4. perc--ve
5. hors d'o-----

[62] D. Jones & Christensen, 1999; Proctor & Dutta, 1995; L. B. Resnick, 1989; Stanovich, 2000.
[63] Kolodner, 1985; Leichtman & Ceci, 1995; Loftus, 1991; Roediger & McDermott, 2000; Rumelhart & Ortony, 1977; Schacter, 1999.

Were you able to retrieve the missing letters from your long-term memory? If not, then you may have found yourself making reasonable guesses, using either your knowledge of how the words are pronounced or your knowledge of how words in the English language are typically spelled. For example, perhaps you used the "*i* before *e* except after *c*" rule for word 4. If so, you reconstructed the correct spelling of *perceive*. Perhaps you used your knowledge that *-ance* is a common word ending. Unfortunately, if you used this knowledge for word 2, then you spelled *existence* incorrectly. Neither pronunciation nor typical English spelling patterns would have helped you with *hors d'oeuvre*, a term borrowed from the French. (The correct spellings for words 1 and 3 are *separate* and *adolescence*.)

When people fill in gaps in what they've retrieved based on what seems "logical," they often make mistakes—a phenomenon known as **reconstruction error**. In the opening case study, Rita's version of what she learned in history is a prime example. Rita retrieved certain facts from her history lessons (e.g., the British wanted furs; some of them eventually settled in the Upper Peninsula) and constructed what was, to her, a reasonable scenario.

Long-term memory isn't necessarily forever.

People certainly don't need to remember everything. For example, you probably have no reason to remember the phone number of a florist you called yesterday, the plot of last week's rerun of *Friends*, or the due date of an assignment you turned in last semester. Much of the information you encounter is, like junk mail, not worth keeping. Forgetting enables you to get rid of needless clutter.[64]

Unfortunately, people sometimes forget important things as well as inconsequential ones. Some instances of forgetting may reflect **retrieval failure**: A person simply isn't looking in the right "place" in long-term memory.[65] Perhaps the forgetful person hasn't learned the information in a meaningful way, or perhaps the person doesn't have a good retrieval cue. But other instances of forgetting may be the result of **decay**: Knowledge stored in long-term memory may gradually weaken over time and perhaps disappear altogether, especially if it isn't used very often.[66] To some degree, then, the expression "Use it or lose it" may apply to human memory.

Regardless of whether forgetting is due to retrieval failure or to decay, human beings don't always remember the things they've learned. However, teachers can increase the odds that their students *do* remember academic subject matter. Let's switch gears and put theory into practice, identifying strategies for promoting effective learning and memory processes in the classroom.

PROMOTING EFFECTIVE COGNITIVE PROCESSES

As we've seen, learning is an active, constructive process, and what students learn is rarely a carbon copy of what a teacher or textbook has presented. A teacher's goal, then, should not, and in fact *cannot*, be that students absorb all the information they are given. Instead, a more achievable goal is that students construct appropriate and useful understandings of academic subject matter—that they make reasonable *sense* of it.

How effectively students make sense and meaning from what they are studying depends in large part on the cognitive processes in which they engage. Although students are ultimately the ones "in charge" of their own thinking and learning, a teacher can do many things to help them think and learn more effectively. We can organize these strategies into four general categories: remembering how the human memory system works, encouraging effective long-term memory storage, promoting retrieval, and monitoring students' progress.

Remembering How the Human Memory System Works

The model of memory depicted in Figure 2.4 and discussed at length in this chapter tells us several important things about human memory. First, attention is critical for moving information into working memory. Second, working memory has a short duration (less than

---

reconstruction error Construction of a logical but incorrect "memory" by using information retrieved from long-term memory in combination with general knowledge and beliefs about the world.

retrieval failure Inability to locate information that currently exists in long-term memory.

decay Weakening over time of information stored in long-term memory, especially if the information is used infrequently.

---

[64] Schacter, 1999.
[65] Loftus & Loftus, 1980.

[66] Altmann & Gray, 2002; J. R. Anderson, 1990; Reisberg, 1997; Schacter, 1999.

half a minute) and limited capacity. And third, effective long-term storage typically involves making connections between new information and prior knowledge. These points have several implications for classroom practice.

Grab and hold students' attention.

What teachers do in the classroom can have a huge impact on the extent to which students pay attention to the subject matter at hand. For example, teachers can pique students' interest in a topic, perhaps by building on students' existing interests and concerns, presenting unusual or puzzling phenomena, or modeling their own enthusiasm for a topic. Incorporating a wide variety of instructional methods (discovery learning sessions, debates about controversial issues, cooperative problem-solving activities, etc.) into the weekly schedule also helps keep students actively attentive to and engaged in mastering new information and skills. The Classroom Strategies box "Getting and Keeping Students' Attention" offers and illustrates several additional suggestions for teachers.

Hear 12-year-old Claudia describe things her teachers do that capture or lose her attention in the "Motivation: Early Adolescence" video in the Additional Resources section in Chapter 2 of MyEducationLab.

Keep the limited capacity of working memory in mind.

Like all human beings, students have only limited "space" in their working memories, imposing an upper limit on how much they can think about and learn within a given time interval. Teachers must keep this point in mind when planning classroom lessons and activities. Many new teachers make the mistake of presenting too much information too quickly, and their students' working memories simply can't keep up. Instead, teachers should introduce new information in such a way that students have time to process it all. In addition to maintaining a reasonable pace, teachers might repeat the same idea several times (perhaps rewording it each time), stop to write important points on the chalkboard, provide numerous examples and illustrations, and have students use the content in a variety of activities and assignments over a period of time.

Even so, the amount of new information presented in a typical classroom is much more than students can reasonably learn and remember, and students aren't always the best judges

CLASSROOM STRATEGIES

Getting and Keeping Students' Attention

- Create stimulating lessons in which students *want* to pay attention.

  In a unit on nutrition, a high school biology teacher has students determine the nutritional value of various menu items at a popular local fast-food restaurant.

- Get students physically involved with the subject matter.

  A middle school history teacher schedules a day late in the school year when all of his classes "go back in time" to the American Civil War. In preparation for the event, the students spend several weeks learning about the Battle of Gettysburg, researching typical dress and meals of the era, gathering appropriate clothing and equipment, and preparing snacks and lunches. On the day of the "battle," students assume various roles: Union and Confederate soldiers, government officials, journalists, merchants, housewives, doctors and nurses, and so on.

- Incorporate a variety of instructional methods into lessons.

  After explaining how to calculate the area of squares and rectangles, a fourth-grade teacher has her students practice calculating area in a series of increasingly challenging word problems. She then breaks the class into cooperative groups of three or four members each. Each group is given a tape measure and calculator and asked to determine the area of the classroom floor, excluding those parts of the floor covered by several built-in cabinets that extend into the room. To complete the task, the students must divide the room into several smaller rectangles, compute the area of each rectangle separately, and add the "subareas" together.

- Provide frequent breaks from quiet, sedentary activities, especially when working with students in the elementary grades.

  To provide practice with the alphabet, a kindergarten teacher occasionally has students make letters with their bodies: one child standing with arms extended up and out to make a Y, two children bending over and joining hands to form an M, and so on.

- In the middle school and high school grades, encourage students to take notes.

  In a middle school science class, different cooperative groups have been specializing in and researching various endangered species. As each group gives an oral report about its species to the rest of the class, the teacher asks students in the "audience" to jot down questions about things they would like to know about the animal. On completion of their prepared report, members of the presenting group answer their classmates' questions.

- Minimize distractions when students must work quietly and independently.

  The windows of several classrooms look out onto an area where a new parking lot is being created. Teachers in those rooms have noticed that many students are being distracted by the construction activity outside. The teachers ask the principal to arrange that the construction company work elsewhere on the day that an important statewide assessment is scheduled to be administered.

of what is most important.[67] Teachers can help students make the right choices by identifying main ideas, offering guidelines on how and what to study, and omitting unnecessary details from lessons.

Relate new ideas to students' prior knowledge and experiences.

Students can more effectively learn and remember classroom subject matter if they connect it to things they already know. Yet students don't always make such connections on their own, and as a result they often resort to rote learning. Teachers can encourage more meaningful learning by showing how new material relates to

- Concepts and ideas in the same subject area (e.g., showing how multiplication is related to addition)
- Concepts and ideas in other subject areas (e.g., talking about how scientific discoveries have affected historical events)
- Students' general knowledge of the world (e.g., relating the concept of *inertia* to how passengers are affected when an automobile quickly turns a sharp corner)
- Students' personal experiences (e.g., finding similarities between the family feud in *Romeo and Juliet* and students' own group conflicts)
- Students' current activities and needs outside of the classroom (e.g., showing how persuasive writing skills might be used to write a personal essay for a college application)

Ideally, teachers should use students' existing knowledge as a starting point whenever they introduce a new topic. For example, in a first-grade classroom, they might begin a unit on plants by asking students to describe what their parents do to keep flowers or vegetable gardens growing. Or, in a secondary English literature class, they might introduce Sir Walter Scott's *Ivanhoe* (in which Robin Hood is a major character) by asking students to tell the tale of Robin Hood as they know it. Having students bring relevant ideas to mind as they study a new topic is a strategy known as **prior knowledge activation**.

Accommodate diversity in students' background knowledge.

All students come to school with some common understandings about the world. For example, they all know that dogs and cats typically have four legs and that objects fall down (not up) when released. But in many ways students' prior knowledge and understandings are truly their own, because each one has been exposed to a unique set of experiences, interpersonal relationships, and cultural practices and beliefs. Thus students from diverse backgrounds may come to school with somewhat different knowledge—different concepts, schemas, scripts, self-constructed theories, and so on—that they will use to make sense of any new situation.[68] To see what I mean, try the next exercise.

SEE FOR YOURSELF
The War of the Ghosts

Read the following story *one time only:*

> One night two young men from Egulac went down to the river to hunt seals, and while they were there it became foggy and calm. Then they heard war-cries, and they thought, "Maybe this is a war-party." They escaped to the shore, and hid behind a log. Now canoes came up, and they heard the noise of paddles, and saw one canoe coming up to them. There were five men in the canoe, and they said:
>
> "What do you think? We wish to take you along. We are going up the river to make war on the people."
>
> One of the young men said: "I have no arrows."
>
> "Arrows are in the canoe," they said.

---

prior knowledge activation Process of reminding learners of things they have already learned relative to a new topic.

[67] Calfee, 1981; E. D. Gagné, 1985; Garner, Alexander, Gillingham, Kulikowich, & Brown, 1991; R. E. Reynolds & Shirey, 1988.

[68] Lipson, 1983; R. E. Reynolds, Taylor, Steffensen, Shirey, & Anderson, 1982; Steffensen, Joag-Dev, & Anderson, 1979.

"I will not go along. I might be killed. My relatives do not know where I have gone. But you," he said, turning to the other, "may go with them."

So one of the young men went, but the other returned home.

And the warriors went on up the river to a town on the other side of Kalama. The people came down to the water, and they began to fight, and many were killed. But presently the young man heard one of the warriors say, "Quick, let us go home: that Indian has been hit." Now he thought: "Oh, they are ghosts." He did not feel sick, but they said he had been shot.

So the canoes went back to Egulac, and the young man went ashore to his house, and made a fire. And he told everybody and said, "Behold I accompanied the ghosts, and we went to fight. Many of our fellows were killed, and many of those who attacked us were killed. They said I was hit, and I did not feel sick."

He told it all, and then he became quiet. When the sun rose he fell down. Something black came out of his mouth. His face became contorted. The people jumped up and cried.

He was dead.[69]

Now cover the story, and write down as much of it as you can remember.

Compare your own rendition of the story with the original. What differences do you notice? Your version is almost certainly the shorter of the two, and you probably left out many details. But did you also find yourself distorting certain parts of the story so that it made more sense to you?

A Native American ghost story, "The War of the Ghosts" may be inconsistent with some of the schemas and scripts you've acquired, especially if you were raised in a non–Native American culture. In an early study of long-term memory, students at England's Cambridge University were asked to read the story twice and then to recall it at various times later on. Students' recollections of the story often included additions and distortions that made the story more consistent with English culture. For example, people in England rarely go "to the river to hunt seals" because seals are saltwater animals and most rivers have freshwater. Students might therefore say that the men went to the river to *fish*. Similarly, the ghostly aspect of the story did not fit comfortably with the religious beliefs of most Cambridge students and so was often modified. When one student was asked to recall the story six months after he had read it, he provided the following account:

> Four men came down to the water. They were told to get into a boat and to take arms with them. They inquired, "What arms?" and were answered "Arms for battle." When they came to the battle-field they heard a great noise and shouting, and a voice said: "The black man is dead." And he was brought to the place where they were, and laid on the ground. And he foamed at the mouth.[70]

Notice how the student's version of the story leaves out many of its more puzzling aspects—puzzling, at least, from his own cultural perspective.

Some concepts, schemas, scripts, and theories are specific to particular cultures, and lessons that require them will cause difficulty for students from other cultural backgrounds. You probably discovered this principle firsthand when you did "The War of the Ghosts" exercise. As another example, consider how, in the opening case study, Rita focuses on what European settlers were doing as she explains events in the New World. In contrast, a Native American student might look at this time period from the perspective of those whose land was being occupied and ultimately taken away by self-serving foreigners. The latter student's description of events in Michigan might reflect a theme of *invasion* rather than settlement.[71]

All of this is not to say that some students have *less* knowledge than their peers, but rather that they have *different* knowledge. For example, some (but by no means all) students from low-income families lag behind their classmates in such basic academic skills as reading, writing, and

Even though these two students are working together on a science activity, their prior knowledge and beliefs may lead each one to derive a different understanding from the experience.

---

[69] From *Remembering: A Study in Experimental and Social Psychology* (p. 65), by F. C. Bartlett, 1932, Cambridge, England: Cambridge University Press. Copyright 1932, 1955 by Cambridge University Press. Reprinted with permission of Cambridge University Press.

[70] From *Remembering: A Study in Experimental and Social Psychology* (pp. 71–72), by F. C. Bartlett, 1932, Cambridge, England: Cambridge University Press. Copyright 1932, 1955 by Cambridge University Press. Reprinted with permission of Cambridge University Press.

[71] Banks, 1991.

computation.[72] Yet they are apt to bring many strengths to the classroom. They may have a wealth of knowledge about pop culture—rap music lyrics, dialogues from popular films, and so on.[73] They are often quite clever at improvising with everyday objects.[74] If they work part-time to help their families make ends meet, they may have a good understanding of the working world. If they are children of single, working parents, they may know far more than their classmates about cooking, cleaning house, and taking care of younger siblings. If financial resources have been particularly scarce, they may know firsthand what it is like to be hungry for days at a time or to live in an unheated apartment in the winter, and so they may have a special appreciation for basic human needs and true empathy for victims of war or famine around the world. In some domains, then, students who have grown up in poverty have more knowledge and skills than their economically advantaged peers.

Provide experiences on which students can build.

In some instances, of course, students simply do not have the background knowledge they need to understand a new topic. When students don't have such knowledge, teachers can provide concrete experiences that provide a foundation for classroom lessons. For example, students can better understand how large the dinosaurs were if they see a life-size dinosaur skeleton at a museum of natural history. Students can more easily understand the events of an important battle if they visit the battlefield. Often teachers can create foundational experiences in the classroom itself, perhaps by offering opportunities to work with physical objects and living creatures (e.g., timing the fall of light versus heavy objects, caring for a class pet), providing computer software that simulates complex activities (e.g., running a lemonade stand, dissecting a frog), or conducting in-class activities similar to those in the adult world (e.g., trying a mock courtroom case, conducting a political campaign).

Encouraging Effective Long-Term Memory Storage

Having prior knowledge relevant to a classroom topic is, of course, essential for meaningful learning. But it is equally important that students actively *think about* what they're studying—that they consciously and intentionally engage in effective learning strategies such as elaboration, organization, and visual imagery. The following suggestions should promote active, effective learning.

Present questions and tasks that encourage elaboration.

The more students elaborate on new material—the more they mentally expand on what they are learning—the more effectively they are apt to understand and remember it. For example, in the "Civil War" video clip in MyEducationLab, a fifth-grade teacher continually urges her students to step into the shoes of people living in America in the mid-1800s. Following are two examples:

> If you think of the way people lived [prior to the American Civil War] and what we didn't have in terms of stores, what's something that everybody did for his family in this time? What did they do to make a living? What do you think they would all have had to do? (A student responds, "Farm.") Good for you. They would have to have farmed, wouldn't they, because . . . they had to eat.

> We've talked about slavery. Now I want you to pretend inside your head that you are a slave. . . . One of the problems that the slaves had, of course, was that they wanted to be free. So they did things . . . and they were angry at their masters very many times, because they were beaten and they were not cared for as they should have been. If you were a slave, what are some things that you might have done? . . . How could you get back at a master? (A student responds, "Put rocks in the machines.") They broke the equipment; I think that's a little bit of what Jesse was saying. Yes, they would break the tools. Makes sense, doesn't it?

Observe a teacher promote meaningful learning in the "Civil War" video in the Additional Resources section in Chapter 2 of MyEducationLab.

[72] Goldenberg, 2001; Klibanoff, Levine, Huttenlocher, Vasilyeva, & Hedges, 2006; Serpell, Baker, & Sonnenschein, 2005.

[73] Freedom Writers, 1999.

[74] Torrance, 1995.

CLASSROOM STRATEGIES

Encouraging Elaboration of Classroom Topics

- **Communicate the belief that students can and should make sense of the things they study.**

    A junior high school language arts teacher tells his class that he does not expect students to memorize the definitions he gives them for new vocabulary words. "Always put definitions in your own words," he says, "and practice using your new words in sentences. For example, one of the new words in this week's list is *garish*. Look at the definition on the handout I gave you. In what situations might you use the word *garish*?"

- **Ask questions that require students to draw inferences from what they are learning.**

    Students in a high school first-aid class have learned that when people suffer from traumatic shock, many normal bodily functions are depressed because less blood is circulating through the body. The teacher asks, "Given what you have learned about traumatic shock, why do experts recommend that if we find a person in shock, we *have them lie down* and *keep them warm but not hot*?"

- **Have students apply what they've learned to new situations and problems.**

    To give her class practice in creating and interpreting bar graphs, a second-grade teacher asks children to write their favorite kind of pet on a self-stick note she has given each of them. "Let's make a graph that can tell us how many children like different kinds of pets," she says. On the chalkboard the teacher draws a horizontal line and a vertical line to make the graph's *x*-axis and *y*-axis. "Let's begin by making a column for dogs," she continues. "How many of you wrote *dog* as your favorite pet? Seven of you? OK, come on up here and put your sticky notes on the graph where I've written *dog*. We'll put them one above another to make a bar." After the dog lovers have attached their notes to the graph, the teacher follows the same procedure for cats, birds, fish, and so on.

- **Focus on an in-depth understanding of a few key ideas instead of covering many topics superficially.**

    In planning his geography curriculum for the coming school year, a fourth-grade teacher suspects that his students will gain little from studying facts and figures about numerous countries around the globe. Instead, he chooses six countries with very different cultures—Egypt, Italy, Japan, Peru, New Zealand, and Norway—that the class will focus on that year. Through an in-depth study of these countries, the teacher plans to help his students discover how different climates, topographies, cultures, and religions lead to different lifestyles and economies.

- **Create opportunities for small-group or whole-class discussions in which students can freely exchange their views.**

    In a unit on World War II, a high school history teacher has students meet in small groups to speculate about the problems the Japanese people must have faced after atomic bombs were dropped on Hiroshima and Nagasaki.

The Classroom Strategies box "Encouraging Elaboration of Classroom Topics" describes and illustrates several ways that teachers might help students embellish on what they have learned.

Show how new ideas are interrelated.

Let's look again at the opening case study. Rita has acquired a few tidbits about American history, but she has apparently learned them as separate, isolated facts and does not pull them together until an adult asks her to explain what she has learned. Unfortunately, such learning of isolated facts, without any true understanding of how they fit together, is all too common at both the elementary and secondary grade levels.[75]

The more interrelationships students form within the subject matter they are learning—in other words, the better they *organize* it—the more easily they can remember and apply it later on.[76] When students form many logical connections within the specific concepts and ideas of a topic, they gain a **conceptual understanding** of the topic. For example, rather than simply memorize basic mathematical computation procedures, students should learn how those procedures reflect underlying principles of mathematics. Rather than learn historical facts as a list of unrelated people, places, and dates, students should place those facts within the context of major social and religious trends, migration patterns, economic considerations, human personality characteristics, and so on.

One strategy for helping students find interrelationships within a content area is to organize instructional units around a few core ideas and themes, always relating specific ideas back to this core.[77] (For example, two core ideas in the chapter you are currently reading are

[75] J. Hiebert & Lefevre, 1986; Hollon, Roth, & Anderson, 1991; McCaslin & Good, 1996; McRobbie & Tobin, 1995; Paxton, 1999.

[76] L. M. Anderson, 1993; Bédard & Chi, 1992; J. J. White & Rumsey, 1994.

[77] Brophy & Alleman, 1992; Prawat, 1993; J. J. White & Rumsey, 1994.

conceptual understanding Knowledge about a topic acquired in an integrated and meaningful fashion.

the *constructive nature of learning and memory* and the *importance of meaningful learning.*) Another strategy is to ask students to teach what they have learned to others—a task that encourages them to focus on main ideas and pull these ideas together in a way that makes sense.[78] But ultimately, students are most likely to gain a conceptual understanding of what they are studying if they explore the topic in depth—for instance, by considering many examples, examining cause-and-effect relationships, and discovering how specific details relate to general principles. Accordingly, many educators advocate the principle "Less is more": *Less* material studied more thoroughly is learned *more* completely and with greater understanding.[79]

Facilitate visual imagery.

As we have discovered, visual imagery can be a highly effective way to learn and remember information. Teachers can promote students' use of visual imagery in several ways.[80] They can ask students to imagine how certain events in literature or history might have looked. They can provide visual materials (pictures, charts, graphs, three-dimensional models, etc.) that illustrate or graphically organize important ideas. And they can ask students to create their *own* pictures, diagrams, or models of things they are learning. You can find examples of such strategies in the "Scarlet Letter" and "Geometry Lesson" videos in MyEducationLab.

In many situations teachers better help students remember new ideas when they encourage students to encode classroom subject matter *both* verbally and visually.[81] In Figure 2.9, 9-year-old Nicholas uses both words and a picture to describe his findings from a third-grade science experiment, in which he observed what happened when he dropped small, heavy objects into a glass full of water. Nick has difficulties with written language that qualify him for special educational services. Notice how he misspells many words and writes *up* from the bottom of the page. Perhaps by writing upward rather than in the normal top-down fashion, Nick is thinking about how the water traveled up and out of the glass as blocks were dropped into it.

Give students time to think.

We've talked about the importance of having students find personal meaning in, elaborate on, organize, and visualize classroom subject matter. Such processes require thought, and thought requires time. Yet teachers don't always give students that time. For instance, when teachers ask students a question, they typically wait one second or less for a response. If students don't respond in that short time, teachers tend to speak again—sometimes by asking another student the same question, sometimes by rephrasing the question, sometimes by answering the question themselves. Teachers are equally reluctant to let much time lapse after students answer questions or make comments in class—once again, they typically allow one second or less of silence before responding to a statement or asking another question.[82] The problem here is one of insufficient **wait time**.

When teachers instead allow at least *three seconds* to elapse after their own questions and after students' comments, dramatic changes can occur in students' behaviors. More students (especially more females and minority students) participate in class, and students begin to respond to one another's comments and questions. Students are more likely to support their reasoning with evidence or logic and more likely to speculate when they don't know an answer. Furthermore, they are more motivated to learn classroom subject matter, behavior problems decrease, and learning increases. Such changes are in part due to the fact that with increased wait time, *teachers'* behaviors change as well. Teachers ask fewer "simple" questions (e.g., those requiring recall of facts) and more thought-provoking ones (e.g., those requiring elaboration). They modify the direction of discussion to accommodate students' comments and questions, and they allow their classes to pursue a topic in greater depth than they had originally anticipated. And their expectations for many students, especially previously low-achieving ones, begin to improve.[83]

Observe strategies for promoting visual imagery in the "Scarlet Letter" and "Geometry Lesson" videos in the Additional Resources section in Chapter 2 of MyEducationLab.

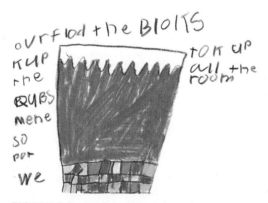

FIGURE 2.9 With both words and a picture, 9-year-old Nicholas describes his findings from a science experiment. The bottom sentence begins at the bottom and goes upward (Translation: "We poured so many cubes [that] the cup overflowed. The blocks took up all the room.")

wait time Length of time a teacher pauses, after either asking a question or hearing a student's comment, before saying something.

[78] Hatano & Inagaki, 2003; McCaslin & Good, 1996.
[79] Brophy & Alleman, 1992; Kyle & Shymansky, 1989; Marshall, 1992; Sizer, 1992.
[80] R. K. Atkinson et al., 1999; Carlson, Chandler, & Sweller, 2003; Edens & Potter, 2001; Sadoski & Paivio, 2001; Van Meter, 2001; Van Meter & Garner, 2005; Verdi, Kulhavy, Stock, Rittschof, & Johnson, 1996.

[81] Kulhavy, Lee, & Caterino, 1985; Moreno, 2006; Sadoski & Paivio, 2001; Winn, 1991.
[82] M. B. Rowe, 1974, 1987.
[83] Giaconia, 1988; Mohatt & Erickson, 1981; M. B. Rowe, 1974, 1987; Tharp, 1989; Tobin, 1987.

Suggest mnemonics for hard-to-remember facts.

As we have seen, meaningful learning—making sense of something—is far more effective than rote learning. Yet some things are hard to make sense of. For instance, why do bones in the human body have such names as *humerus, fibula,* and *ulna?* Why is *fáng* the Chinese word for house? Why is Augusta the capital of Maine? For all practical purposes, there is no rhyme or reason to such facts.

When students are apt to have trouble making connections between new material and their prior knowledge, or when a body of information has an organizational structure with no apparent logic behind it (e.g., as is true for many lists), special memory tricks known as **mnemonics** can help them learn classroom material more effectively.[84] Three commonly used mnemonics are described in Figure 2.10.

Several examples of mnemonics are shown in the video clips in MyEducationLab. In the "Memory and Metacognition: Middle Childhood" video, 10-year-old David describes a mnemonic he uses to remember the Hebrew letter *pay* (פ).

> *Pay,* it kind of goes like this, then this, then this, then this, then this, and then there's a little person right there. Well, not a little person, but a dot right there. . . . We pretend that in front of the dot is a counter and then the dot is a head, and then the head is "paying." So that's how we remember *pay.*

In the "Memory and Metacognition: Late Adolescence" video, 16-year-old Hilary remembers that Amendment 2 to the U.S. Constitution is the right to bear arms by thinking, "A bear has two arms." And in the "Group Work" video, a junior high school science teacher shows students how to develop a *superimposed meaningful structure*—in particular, a story—to help them remember the life cycle of a sheep liver fluke.

Observe mnemonics in the middle childhood and late adolescence "Memory and Metacognition" videos and in the "Group Work" video in the Additional Resources section in Chapter 2 of MyEducationLab.

Promoting Retrieval

Even when students engage in meaningful learning, they don't necessarily retrieve important information when they need it. Remember, retrieval involves following a pathway of mental associations, and students sometimes travel down the wrong path. The next two recommendations can enhance students' ability to retrieve what they've learned.

Provide many opportunities to practice important knowledge and skills.

Some information and skills are so fundamental that students must become able to retrieve and use them quickly and effortlessly—that is, with automaticity. For instance, to read well, students must be able to recognize most of the words on the page without having to sound them out or look them up in the dictionary. To solve mathematical word problems, students should have such number facts as $2 + 4 = 6$ and $5 \times 9 = 45$ on the tips of their tongues. And to write well, students should be able to form letters and words without having to stop and think about how to make an uppercase *G* or spell *the.* Unless such knowledge and skills are learned to automaticity, a student may use so much working memory capacity retrieving and using them that there is little "room" to do anything more complex.[85]

Ultimately, students can learn basic information and skills to automaticity only by using and practicing them repeatedly. This is *not* to say that teachers should fill each day with endless drill-and-practice exercises involving isolated facts and procedures. Automaticity can occur just as readily when the basics are embedded in a variety of stimulating and challenging activities. Furthermore, students should practice new skills within the context of instruction and guidance that help them *improve* those skills. The Classroom Strategies box "Helping Students Acquire New Skills" provides examples of instructional strategies that can help students more effectively acquire procedural knowledge.

At the same time, teachers must be aware that automaticity has a downside.[86] In particular, students may quickly recall certain ideas or perform certain procedures when other,

Observe engaging activities that encourage basic-skills practice in the "Teaching Basic Skills in Math" video in the Additional Resources section in Chapter 2 of MyEducationLab.

[84] Bower & Clark, 1969; Bulgren, Schumaker, & Deshler, 1994; M. S. Jones, Levin, Levin, & Beitzel, 2000; Pressley, Levin, & Delaney, 1982; Scruggs & Mastropieri, 1989.

[85] R. E. Mayer & Wittrock, 1996; McCutchen, 1996; Perfetti, 1983; Sweller, 1994.

[86] Killeen, 2001; E. J. Langer, 2000; LeFevre, Bisanz, & Mrkonjic, 1988.

mnemonic Memory aid or trick designed to help students learn and remember a specific piece of information.

FIGURE 2.10 Common mnemonic techniques

VERBAL MEDIATION

A **verbal mediator** is a word or phrase that creates a logical connection, or "bridge," between two pieces of information. Verbal mediators can be used for such paired pieces of information as foreign language words and their English meanings, countries and their capitals, chemical elements and their symbols, and words and their spellings. Following are examples:

Information to Be Learned	Verbal Mediator
Handschuh is German for "glove."	A glove is a *shoe* for the hand.
Quito is the capital of Ecuador.	Mos*quito*es are at the *equator*.
Au is the symbol for gold.	'*Ay, you* stole my *gold* watch!
The word *principal* ends with the letters *pal* (not *ple*).	The *principal* is my *pal*.
The *humerus* bone is the large arm bone above the elbow.	The *humorous* bone is just above the *funny* bone.

KEYWORD METHOD

Like verbal mediation, the **keyword method** aids memory by making a connection between two things. This technique is especially helpful when there is no logical verbal mediator to fill the gap—for example, when there is no obvious sentence or phrase to relate a foreign language word to its English meaning. The keyword method involves two steps, which I will illustrate using the Spanish word *amor* and its English meaning *love:*

1. Identify a concrete object to represent each piece of information. The object may be either a commonly used symbol (e.g., a heart to symbolize *love*) or a soundalike word (e.g., a suit of armor to represent *amor*). Such objects are *keywords.*
2. Form a mental picture of the two objects together. To remember that *amor* means *love,* you might picture a knight in a suit of armor with a huge red heart painted on his chest.

You used the keyword method when you learned the meanings of *fáng, mén, ké, fàn,* and *shū* in the "Five Chinese Words" exercise earlier in the chapter. Following are additional examples:

Information to Be Learned	Visual Image
Das Pferd is German for "horse."	Picture a *horse* driving a *Ford.*
Augusta is the capital of Maine.	Picture *a gust of* wind blowing through a horse's *mane.*
Tchaikovsky composed *Swan Lake.*	Picture a *swan* swimming on a *lake,* wearing a *tie* and *cough*ing.

SUPERIMPOSED MEANINGFUL STRUCTURE

A larger body of information, such as a list of items, can often be learned by superimposing a meaningful organization—a familiar shape, word, sentence, rhythm, poem, or story—on the information. Following are examples of such **superimposed meaningful structures**:

Information to Be Learned	Superimposed Meaningful Structure
The shape of Italy	A "boot"
The Great Lakes (Huron, Ontario, Michigan, Erie, Superior)	HOMES
Lines on the treble clef (E G B D F)	Elvis's guitar broke down Friday, *or* every good boy does fine.
The number of days in each month	Thirty days has September . . . .
How to turn a screw (clockwise to tighten it, counterclockwise to loosen it)	Righty, tighty; lefty, loosey.
How to multiply in a mathematical expression of the form $(ax + b)(cx + d)$	FOIL: multiply the *f*irst terms within each set of parentheses, then the two *o*uter terms, then the two *i*nner terms, and finally the *l*ast terms

---

verbal mediator Word or phrase that forms a logical connection or "bridge" between two pieces of information.

keyword method Mnemonic technique in which an association is made between two ideas by forming a visual image of one or more concrete objects (*keywords*) that either sound similar to, or symbolically represent, those ideas.

superimposed meaningful structure Familiar shape, word, sentence, poem, or story imposed on information in order to facilitate recall.

less automatic ideas or procedures are more useful. Students can be more flexible and, hence, more likely to identify unique approaches to situations or creative solutions to problems when they aren't automatically "locked in" to a particular response. We'll revisit this issue in our discussion of *mental set* in Chapter 4.

Give hints that help students recall or reconstruct what they've learned.

Sometimes forgetting is simply a matter of retrieval difficulty: Students either can't "find" knowledge that's in long-term memory or else neglect to "look" for it altogether. In such situations retrieval cues are often helpful and appropriate. For example, if a student asks how

CLASSROOM STRATEGIES

Helping Students Acquire New Skills

- Help students understand the logic behind the procedures they are learning.

    As a teacher demonstrates the correct way to swing a tennis racket, he asks his students, "Why is it important to have your feet apart rather than together? Why is it important to hold your arm straight as you swing?"

- When skills are especially complex, break them into simpler tasks that students can practice one at a time.

    Knowing how overwhelming the task of driving a car can initially be, a driver education teacher begins behind-the-wheel instruction by having students practice steering and braking in an empty school parking lot. Only later, after students have mastered these skills, does she have them drive in traffic on city streets.

- Provide mnemonics that can help students remember a sequence of steps.

    A math teacher presents this equation:

$$y = \frac{3\,(x + 6)^2}{2} + 5$$

"When x equals 4, what does y equal?" she asks. She gives students a mnemonic, *Please excuse my dear Aunt Sally*, that they can use to help them remember how to solve problems involving such complex algebraic expressions. First, you simplify things within parentheses (this is the *P* in *Please*). Then, you simplify anything with an exponent (this is the *e* in *excuse*). Then, you do any necessary multiplication and division (these are the *m* and *d* in *my dear*). Finally, you do any remaining addition and subtraction (these are the *A* and *S* in *Aunt Sally*).

- As students practice new skills, provide the feedback they need to help them improve.

    A science teacher asks his students to write lab reports after each week's lab activity. Many of his students have had little or no previous experience in scientific writing, so when he grades the reports, he writes numerous comments as well. Some comments describe the strengths that he sees, and others provide suggestions for making the reports more objective, precise, or clear.

the word *liquidation* is spelled, a teacher might say, "*Liquidation* means to make something liquid. How do you spell *liquid?*" Another example comes from one of my former teacher interns, Jesse Jensen. A student in her eighth-grade history class had been writing about the Battle of New Orleans, a decisive victory for the United States in the War of 1812. The following exchange took place:

Student: Why was the Battle of New Orleans important?
Jesse: Look at the map. Where is New Orleans?
(The student locates New Orleans.)
Jesse: Why is it important?
Student: Oh! It's near the mouth of the Mississippi. It was important for controlling transportation up and down the river.

In the early grades teachers typically provide many retrieval cues: They remind students about the tasks they need to do and when they need to do them ("I hear the fire alarm. Remember, we all walk quietly during a fire drill"; or "It's time to go home. Do you all have the field trip permission slip to take to your parents?"). But as students grow older, they must develop greater independence, relying more on themselves and less on their teachers for the things they need to remember. At all grade levels, teachers can teach students ways of providing retrieval cues for *themselves*. For example, if second-grade teachers expect children to bring signed permission slips to school the following day, they might ask the children to write a reminder on a piece of masking tape that they attach to their jackets or lunch boxes. If junior high school teachers give students a major assignment due several weeks later, they might suggest that students help themselves remember the due date by taping a note to the bedside table or making an entry on the kitchen calendar. In such instances teachers are fostering *self-regulation*, a topic we'll explore in Chapter 4.

Monitoring Students' Progress

As you'll learn in Chapter 10, some classroom assessments—listening to what students say in class, watching students' body language, and so on—are spontaneous, *informal* ones. Others—such as in-class quizzes and assigned projects—are more systematic, *formal* ones that require advance planning. Both informal and formal assessments are important for promoting effective cognitive processes, as the following recommendations reveal.

October 22nd

I went to a new school today. My teacher's name is Mrs. Whaley. I accidentally cracked an egg on my head. Mrs. Whaley told the nurse that I was a show off and a nuisance. I got really sad and wanted to run away from school, but I didn't leave.

. . .

October 27th

We presented our book reports today. I was the last one to present my book report. Whenever I did my book report, they laughed at me, but the teacher said they were laughing with me. I asked the teacher why she had called me a nuisance the first day. And she said, "Darcy, I didn't call you a nuisance. I was saying to Mrs. Larson that it was a nuisance to try to wash egg out of your hair." I was so happy. I decided to like Mrs. Whaley again.

FIGURE 2.11   As you can see from her journal entries, 8-year-old Darcy initially interpreted a casual remark to the school nurse in a way very different from the teacher's intended meaning. Fortunately, the teacher corrected the misunderstanding a few days later.

Regularly assess students' understandings.

As constructivist theorists tell us, human beings construct their own versions of "reality," and such constructions are not always accurate or productive. For example, the first day that 8-year-old Darcy attended third grade at a new school, she accidentally got egg in her hair. Her teacher, Mrs. Whaley, brought her to the nurse's office to have the egg washed out. In the journal entries in Figure 2.11, Darcy initially misinterpreted Mrs. Whaley's comment about the situation. Not until five days later did she gain a more accurate understanding of what Mrs. Whaley had said.

Darcy's misinterpretation of her teacher's comment got her off to a rocky start at her new school. In other situations students may misinterpret material in classroom lessons—for example, thinking that a "round" earth must be shaped like a pancake or (as Barry did) believing that heavy egg containers fall faster than light ones despite evidence to the contrary—and so learn things that their teachers never anticipated.

Teachers must continually keep in mind that students won't necessarily construct the meanings from classroom events and lessons that teachers intend for them to construct. Rather, students will each interpret classroom subject matter in their own, idiosyncratic ways. Accordingly, teachers should frequently monitor students' understandings by asking questions, encouraging dialogue, and listening carefully to students' ideas and explanations.

Identify and address students' misconceptions.

Teachers often present new information in class with the expectation that such information will replace students' erroneous beliefs. Yet students of all ages can hold quite stubbornly to their existing misconceptions about the world, even after considerable instruction that explicitly contradicts them.[87] In some cases students never make the connection between what they are learning and what they already believe, perhaps because they engage in rote learning as they study academic subject matter.[88] In other instances students truly try to make sense of classroom material, but thanks to the process of elaboration, they interpret new information in light of what they already "know" about the topic, and they may reject or discredit something that doesn't fit.[89] (Recall our earlier discussion of *confirmation bias*.)

When students hold scientifically inaccurate or in other ways counterproductive beliefs about the world, teachers must work actively and vigorously to help them revise their thinking. That is, teachers must encourage **conceptual change**. The Classroom Strategies box "Promoting Conceptual Change" presents and illustrates several potentially useful techniques.

Convincing students to replace long-held and well-engrained beliefs can be quite a challenge, and ultimately it may require addressing students' *epistemological beliefs* and *motivation* as well as their long-term memory storage processes. We'll explore these two topics in Chapters 4 and 6, respectively.

Focus assessments on meaningful learning rather than rote learning.

As students get older, they increasingly encounter assignments, exams, and other formal assessments that are used in determining final class grades. Unfortunately, many teachers' classroom assessment practices tend to encourage students to learn school subjects in a rote rather than meaningful manner. Think back to your own experiences in school. How many times were you allowed to define a word by repeating a dictionary definition, rather than being expected to explain it in your own words? In fact, how many times were you *required* to learn something word for word? And how many times did an exam assess your knowledge of facts

---

conceptual change Revision of one's understanding of a topic in response to new information.

[87] S. Carey, 1986; Chambliss, 1994; Chinn & Brewer, 1993; Eaton, Anderson, & Smith, 1984; Shuell, 1996.
[88] Chambliss, 1994; Keil & Silberstein, 1996; Strike & Posner, 1992.

[89] De Lisi & Golbeck, 1999; Gunstone & White, 1981; Hynd, 1998b; Kuhn, Amsel, & O'Loughlin, 1988.

CLASSROOM STRATEGIES

Promoting Conceptual Change

- **Probe for misconceptions that may lead students to interpret new information incorrectly.**

  When a third-grade teacher asks, "What is gravity?" one of his students replies that it's "something that pulls you down." The teacher points to Australia on a globe and asks, "What do you mean by *down*? What do you think would happen if we traveled to Australia? Would gravity pull us off the earth and make us fall into space?"

- **Provide information and experiences that explicitly contradict students' inaccurate beliefs.**

  In a lesson about air, a first-grade teacher wants to address the common misconception that air has no substance. She asks students to predict what will happen when she submerges an upside-down glass in a large bowl of water, and the children have differing opinions about whether the "empty" glass will fill with water. The teacher stuffs the glass with a crumpled paper towel, turns it upside-down, and pushes it straight down into the water. The paper towel remains dry, leading the class to a discussion of how air takes up space. (You can observe this lesson in the "Properties of Air" video in the Additional Resources section in Chapter 2 of MyEducationLab.)

- **Ask questions that challenge students' misconceptions.**

  A high school physics teacher has just begun a unit on inertia. Some students assert that when a baseball is thrown in the air, a force continues to act on the ball, pushing it upward for a short while. The teacher asks, "What force in the air could possibly be pushing that ball upward after it has left the thrower's hand?" The students offer several possibilities but acknowledge that none of them provide satisfactory explanations.

- **Show students how an alternative explanation is more plausible and useful—how it makes more sense—than their original belief.**

  The same physics teacher points out that the baseball continues to move upward even though no force pushes it in that direction. He brings in the concept of *inertia:* The ball needs a force only to get it *started* in a particular direction. Once the force has been exerted, other forces (gravity and air resistance) alter the ball's speed and direction.

- **Give students corrective feedback about responses that reflect misunderstanding.**

  Students in a fourth-grade class have just completed a small-group lab activity in which they observe the reactions of earthworms to varying conditions. Their teacher pulls the class back together and asks "What happens if an earthworm dries out?" One student responds, "They like water, they like to splash around in it . . . if they're in the hot sun they can die because they'll dry up . . . their cells will get hard." The teacher acknowledges that the student is right about the preference for moist conditions while also gently refining the student's explanation: "Absolutely right, good. I don't think they usually like to splash around in water so much, but they like to stay where it's moist." (You can observe this lesson in the "Earthworm Investigation" video in the Additional Resources section in Chapter 2 of MyEducationLab.)

- **Build on any kernels of truth in students' existing understandings.**

  In a sixth-grade lesson about rain, the following exchange occurs between the teacher and one of her students:

  Teacher: What is rain?
  Student: It's water that falls out of a cloud when the clouds evaporate.

  Teacher: What do you mean, "clouds evaporate"?
  Student: That means water goes up in the air and then it makes clouds and then, when it gets too heavy up there, then the water comes and they call it rain.
  Teacher: Does the water stay in the sky?
  Student: Yes, and then it comes down when it rains. It gets too heavy.
  Teacher: Why does it get too heavy?
  Student: 'Cause there's too much water up there.
  Teacher: Why does it rain?
  Student: 'Cause the water gets too heavy and then it comes down.
  Teacher: Why doesn't the whole thing come down?
  Student: Well, 'cause it comes down at little times like a salt shaker when you turn it upside down. It doesn't all come down at once 'cause there's little holes and it just comes out.
  Teacher: What are the little holes in the sky?
  Student: Umm, holes in the clouds, letting the water out.

  The teacher recognizes several accurate understandings in the student's explanation: (a) Clouds have water, (b) evaporation is involved in the water cycle, and (c) rain is the result of water being too heavy to remain suspended in air. She uses this knowledge as starting points for further instruction; for instance, she clarifies where in the water cycle evaporation is involved (i.e., in cloud formation) and how a cloud actually *is* water rather than a shaker-like water container.

- **When pointing out misconceptions that students have, do so in a way that maintains their self-esteem.**

  A fourth-grade teacher begins a lesson on plants by asking, "Where do plants get their food?" Various students suggest that plants get their food from dirt, water, or fertilizer. The teacher responds, "You know, many children think exactly what you think. It's a very logical way to think. But actually, plants *make* their food, using sunlight, water, and things in the soil." The teacher continues by introducing the concept of photosynthesis.

- **Engage students in discussions of the pros and cons of various explanations.**

  After students express the stereotypical belief that new immigrants to the country are "lazy," a middle school social studies teacher invites several recent immigrants to visit the class and describe their efforts to adjust to their new environment. The following day, he asks students to reflect on the guest speakers: "Several of you have told me that many immigrants are lazy. Do you think the people you met yesterday were lazy? Why or why not?" In the ensuing discussion the students begin to realize that most immigrants probably work very hard to adapt to and succeed in their new society and its culture.

- **Ask students to apply their revised understandings to new situations and problems.**

  When several students express the belief that rivers always run from north to south, a middle school geography teacher reminds them that water travels from higher elevations to lower elevations, not vice versa. She then pulls out a map of Africa. "Let's look at the Nile River," she says. "One end of the Nile is here [she points to a spot on Egypt's Mediterranean coast] and the other end is here [she points to a spot in Uganda]. In which direction must the Nile be flowing?"

Sources: Chan, Burtis, & Bereiter, 1997; Chinn & Brewer, 1993; D. B. Clark, 2006; diSessa, 2006; Hattie & Timperley, 2007; Hynd, 1998b; Murphy & Alexander, in press; Murphy & Mason, 2006; Pine & Messer, 2000; Pintrich, Marx, & Boyle, 1993; Posner, Strike, Hewson, & Gertzog, 1982; Prawat, 1989; Putnam, 1992; K. J. Roth, 1990; K. J. Roth & Anderson, 1988; Slusher & Anderson, 1996; Stepans, 1991, p. 94 (salt shaker dialogue); Vosniadou & Brewer, 1987.

1) One of the coolest things about dinosaurs is that of all the millions there were, we only know about a few _thousand_ of them.
2) The word "fossil" comes from the Latin word meaning _dug up_.
3) What four things can fossils tell us about dinosaurs?
   1. _ate_ 3. _what they did w/ young_
   2. _look like_ 4. _size/weight_
4) Two steps in the process of fossilization are:
   - _need to die_ - _then are covered in layers of sediment_
5) One of the processes which forms a fossil is _pre-mineralized_ This means that minerals replace the bones of the dinosaur.
6) The evidence that dinosaurs once lived is found in discovering _fossils_.
7) Scientists can learn about dinosaurs by observing _where_ their fossils are buried, how _deep_ the fossils are, and what is buried _nearby_ the dinosaur fossils.
8) Dinosaurs lived on earth for about _1400_ _million_ years.
9) Dinosaurs died out about _105_ _million_ years ago.
10) One reason dinosaurs may have become extinct is _a meteorite_.

FIGURE 2.12 Seventh-grade science students complete these and other fill-in-the-blank questions when they watch a video about dinosaurs. Although the questions probably help students pay attention to the video, they encourage rote rather than meaningful learning.

or principles without ever assessing your ability to relate those facts and principles to everyday life or to things you had learned in previous courses? Perhaps you had assignments and quizzes similar to the fill-in-the-blank questions shown in Figure 2.12. When students discover that assignments and exams focus on recall of unrelated facts—rather than on understanding and application of an integrated body of knowledge—many rely on rote learning, believing that this approach will yield a higher score and that meaningful learning would be counterproductive.[90] Ultimately, teachers must communicate in every way possible—including in their classroom assessments—that it is more important to *make sense* of classroom material than to memorize it. In Chapter 10, we will identify numerous strategies for assessing meaningful learning.

Be on the lookout for students who have unusual difficulty with certain cognitive processes.

Some students may show ongoing difficulties in processing and learning from academic (or in some cases social) situations. Students with **learning disabilities** have significant deficits in one or more specific cognitive processes. For instance, they may have trouble remembering verbal instructions, recognizing words in print *(dyslexia)*, or thinking about and remembering information involving numbers *(dyscalculia)*. Students with **attention-deficit hyperactivity disorder (ADHD)** may show marked deficits in attention, have trouble inhibiting inappropriate thoughts and behaviors, or both. Most experts believe that learning disabilities and ADHD have a biological basis and are often inherited.[91]

When students have been officially identified as having a learning disability or ADHD, specialists are often called on to assist them in their learning. Even so, most of these students are in general education classrooms for much or all of the school day. Strategies for working effectively with them include the following:[92]

- Identify and capitalize on the times of day when students learn best.
- Minimize distractions.
- Explicitly present the information that students need to learn; also be explicit about how various ideas are organized and interrelated.
- Use multiple modalities to present information (e.g., supplement verbal explanations with pictures or simple diagrams).
- Actively address students' areas of weakness (e.g., in reading or math).
- Teach mnemonics for specific facts.
- Help students organize and use their time effectively.
- Teach general learning and memory strategies.
- Provide a structure to guide students' learning efforts (e.g., present a partially filled-in outline for taking notes; suggest questions to answer while reading a textbook chapter; break large projects into small, manageable steps).
- Keep study sessions short; provide frequent breaks so that students can release pent-up energy.
- Regularly monitor students' recall and understanding of classroom material.

Some of these strategies should look familiar, as you've seen them at earlier points in the chapter. We'll revisit others in our discussion of metacognition and self-regulation in Chapter 4. By and large, the most effective strategies for students with special educational needs are the same ones that are effective with *all* learners.

learning disability Deficiency in one or more specific cognitive processes despite relatively normal cognitive functioning in other areas.

attention-deficit hyperactivity disorder (ADHD) Disorder marked by inattention, inability to inhibit inappropriate thoughts and behaviors, or both.

[90] Crooks, 1988.

[91] Barkley, 1998; Coch, Dawson, & Fischer, 2007; J. M. Fletcher, Lyon, Fuchs, & Barnes, 2007; Purdie, Hattie, & Carroll, 2002; Shaywitz, Mody, & Shaywitz, 2006.

[92] Barkley, 1998; Brigham & Scruggs, 1995; Eilam, 2001; E. S. Ellis & Friend, 1991; J. M. Fletcher et al., 2007; Meltzer, 2007; Pellegrini & Bohn, 2005; Wilder & Williams, 2001.

As you have discovered, effective instruction involves a lot more than simply telling students what they need to learn. In our discussion of cognitive processes and memory in this chapter, we've focused primarily on things that happen inside the learner when learning takes place. However, we can better understand how human beings learn when we look at *social processes* as well as internal, mental processes. We'll consider the social nature of learning as we address "Learning in Context" in Chapter 3.

SUMMARY

Learning is not simply a process of "absorbing" information from the environment. Rather, it is a process of actively *constructing* meaning from both informal experiences and formal instruction. In their attempts to make sense of the world, learners combine some (but not all) of what they observe with their existing knowledge and beliefs to create an ever-expanding and distinctly idiosyncratic understanding of the world.

At the most basic level, learning probably involves changes in neurons and synapses in the brain. Different parts of the brain specialize in different tasks, but many parts of the brain in both hemispheres tend to work closely together in everyday tasks.

The results of many psychological studies of human learning and behavior indicate that human memory may have three distinct components. One component, the *sensory register*, holds incoming sensory information for two or three seconds at the very most. What a learner pays attention to moves on to *working memory*, where it is held for a somewhat longer period while the learner actively thinks about, manipulates, and interprets it. Yet working memory can hold only a small amount of information at one time, and information that is not actively being thought about tends to disappear quickly (typically in less than half a minute) unless the learner processes it sufficiently that it is stored in long-term memory.

Long-term memory appears to have as much capacity as human beings could ever need. In fact, the more information learners already have there, the more easily they can store new material. Effective storage typically involves *meaningful learning*—that is, connecting new information with existing knowledge and beliefs. By making such connections, learners make better sense of their experiences, retrieve what they've learned more easily, and create an increasingly organized and integrated body of knowledge that helps them interpret new experiences. In some instances, however, meaningful learning leads learners to distort new information, such that they construct inaccurate and potentially counterproductive understandings.

Knowledge about the brain tells us little about how teachers can best help students learn. Fortunately, psychological and educational research provides considerable guidance. Teachers must continually emphasize the importance of *understanding* classroom subject matter—making sense of it, drawing inferences from it, seeing how it all ties together, and so on—rather than simply memorizing it in a rote, "thoughtless" manner. Such an emphasis must be reflected not only in teachers' words but also in their instructional activities, classroom assignments, and assessment practices. For instance, rather than just presenting important ideas in classroom lectures and asking students to take notes, teachers might ask thought-provoking questions that require students to evaluate, synthesize, or apply what they are learning. As an alternative to asking students to memorize procedures for adding two-digit numbers, teachers might ask them to suggest at least three different ways they might solve problems such as 15 + 45 or 29 + 68 and to justify their reasoning. Rather than assessing students' knowledge of history by asking them to recite names, places, and dates, teachers might ask them to explain why certain historical events happened and how those events altered the course of subsequent history. At the same time, teachers must also be alert to the misconceptions that students either bring with them to the classroom or acquire from instructional activities, and then make a concerted effort to convince and motivate them to change their beliefs.

PRACTICE FOR YOUR LICENSURE EXAM

Vision Unit

Ms. Kontos is teaching a unit on human vision to her fifth-grade class. She shows her students a diagram of the various parts of the human eye: lens, cornea, retina, and so on. She then explains that people can see objects because light from the sun or another light source bounces off those objects and into the eye. To illustrate this idea, she shows them the picture to the right.

"Do you all understand how our eyes work?" she asks. Her students nod that they do.

The next day Ms. Kontos gives her students this picture:

She asks them to draw how light travels so that the child can see the tree. More than half of the students draw lines something like this:[93]

1. Constructed-response question

Obviously, most of Ms. Kontos's students have not learned what she thought she had taught them about human vision.

A. Explain why many students believe the *opposite* of what Ms. Kontos has taught them. Base your response on contemporary principles and theories of learning and cognition.

B. Describe two different ways in which you might improve on the lesson to help students gain a more accurate understanding of human vision. Base your strategies on contemporary principles and theories of learning and cognition.

2. Multiple-choice question

Many elementary school children think of human vision in the way that Ms. Kontos's fifth graders do—that is, as a process that originates in the eye and goes outward toward objects that are seen. When students revise their thinking to be more consistent with commonly accepted scientific explanations, they are said to be:

a. Acquiring a new script
b. Developing automaticity
c. Undergoing conceptual change
d. Acquiring procedural knowledge

Once you have answered these questions, compare your responses with those presented in Appendix A.

FOR FURTHER READING

The following articles from the journal *Educational Leadership* are especially relevant to this chapter. You can find these articles in Chapter 2 of MyEducationLab for this text.

Ancess, J. (2004). Snapshots of meaning-making classrooms. *Educational Leadership, 62*(1), 36–41.

Jensen, E. (2000). Brain-based learning: A reality check. *Educational Leadership, 57*(7), 76–80.

Perkins, D. (1999). The many faces of constructivism. *Educational Leadership, 57*(3), 6–11.

Williams, B., & Woods, M. (1997). Building on urban learners' experiences. *Educational Leadership, 54*(7), 29–32.

MYEDUCATIONLAB

Now go to Chapter 2 of MyEducationLab at **www. myeducationlab.com,** where you can:

- Find instructional objectives for the chapter, along with focus questions that can help you zero in on important ideas in the chapter.
- Take a self-check quiz on concepts and principles you've just read about.

- Complete exercises and assignments that can help you more deeply understand the chapter content.
- Read supplementary material that can broaden your knowledge of one or more of the chapter's topics.
- Apply what you've learned to classroom contexts in Building Teaching Skills activities.

---

[93] The case presented in this exercise is based on a study by J. F. Eaton et al., 1984.

CHAPTER 3

Learning in Context

CASE STUDY   Ben and Sylvia

For many years, Frank McCourt taught English at Stuyvesant High School, a highly selective school in the New York City public school system that has long been noted for its strong academic curriculum. On one particular day Mr. McCourt announced that his class would be reading Charles Dickens's *A Tale of Two Cities*, a novel that depicts many people living in poverty during the French Revolution. Several students complained loudly, arguing that they would prefer to read science fiction, such as *Dune* or *The Lord of the Rings*. Having himself grown up in extreme poverty in Ireland, Mr. McCourt admonished his students for their apparent lack of concern about the needs of individuals less economically privileged than themselves: "You'll go home today to your comfortable apartments and houses, head for the refrigerator, open the door, survey contents, find nothing that will please you, ask Mom if you can send out for pizza even though you'll have dinner in an hour. She says, 'Sure, honey, because you have a hard life going to school every day and putting up with teachers who want you to read Dickens and why shouldn't you have a little reward?'"

Sylvia, a small, well-dressed African American student in the front row, teased him in response. "You're losing it, Mr. McCourt. Chill. Relax. Where's that big old Irish smile?" Her classmates laughed and applauded her remarks.

After class, a student named Ben, the son of Chinese immigrants, stayed behind. In his book *Teacher Man*, Mr. McCourt recounted Ben's comments:

> He knew what I was saying about poverty. The kids in this class didn't understand anything. But it wasn't their fault and I shouldn't get mad. He was twelve when he came to this country four years ago. He knew no English

but he studied hard and learned enough English and mathematics to pass the Stuyvesant High School entrance exam. He was happy to be here and his whole family was so proud of him. People back in China were proud of him. He competed against fourteen thousand kids to get into this school. His father worked six days a week, twelve hours a day, in a restaurant in Chinatown. His mother worked in a downtown sweatshop. Every night she cooked dinner for the whole family, five children, her husband, herself. Then she helped them get their clothes ready for the next day. . . . His mother made sure the children sat at the kitchen table and did their homework. He could never call his parents silly names like Mom or Dad. That would be so disrespectful. They learned English words every day so that they could talk to teachers and keep up with the children. Ben said everyone in his family respected everyone else and they'd never laugh at a teacher talking about the poor people of France because it could just as easily be China or even Chinatown right here in New York.

Mr. McCourt thanked Ben, who responded, "Thank you, Mr. McCourt, and don't worry about Sylvia. She really likes you."

The following day Sylvia stayed after class to confirm Ben's impression and clarify her remarks.

"Mr. McCourt, about yesterday, I didn't mean to be mean."

"I know, Sylvia. You were trying to help."

"The class didn't mean to be mean, either. They just hear grown-ups and teachers yelling at them all the time. But I knew what you were talking about. I have to go through all kinds of stuff when I go down my street every day in Brooklyn."

"What stuff?"

"Well, it's like this. I live in Bedford-Stuyvesant. You know Bed-Stuy?"

"Yes. Black neighborhood."

"So there is nobody on my street ever gonna go to college. Whoops."

"What's the matter?"

"I said 'gonna.' If my mom heard me say 'gonna' she'd make me write 'going to' a hundred times. Then she'd make me say it another hundred times. So, what I'm saying is, when I walk to my house there are kids out there jeering at me. 'Oh, here she come. Here come whitey. Hey, Doc, you scrape yourself an' you find that honky skin?' They call me Doc because I wanna, want to, be a doctor. 'Course I feel sorry for the poor French, but we have our own troubles in Bed-Stuy."

"What kind of doctor will you be?"

"Pediatrician or psychiatrist. I want to get the kids before the streets get to them and tell them they're no good because I see kids in my neighborhood afraid to show how smart they are and the next thing is they're acting stupid in vacant lots and burned-out buildings. You know there's a lotta, lot of, smart kids in poor neighborhoods."

- What factors in Ben's and Sylvia's school and home environments appear to have enhanced their ability to learn in the classroom?
- What factors may have *interfered* with their ability to learn?

Mr. McCourt obviously created a supportive classroom environment in which students felt comfortable voicing their opinions about topics of study and personal matters. Furthermore, both Ben and Sylvia had parents who encouraged academic success—Ben's by making sure that he did his homework and Sylvia's by insisting that she not take "shortcuts" ("gonna," "wanna," "lotta") in her speech. Yet the two students also faced obstacles that probably made their classroom learning more challenging than was true for their classmates: Ben had immigrated to the United States and learned English only four years earlier, and some of Sylvia's neighborhood peers derided her for her high aspirations.

Learning always takes place within particular *contexts*—for instance, within a particular classroom environment, social group, culture, and society. Such contexts are the subject of this chapter. We'll begin by looking at the effects of learners' immediate surroundings. As we do so, we'll draw largely from behaviorism and social learning theory (recall the descriptions of these perspectives in Table 2.1 in Chapter 2). Later in the chapter we'll expand our field of vision by examining more general effects that other people have in learners' lives, both through day-to-day social interactions and through the many influences of the larger culture and society. At that point, social constructivism and sociocultural theory (also described in Table 2.1) will guide much of our discussion.

THE IMMEDIATE ENVIRONMENT AS CONTEXT

To some degree, learners' behaviors (**responses**) are influenced by the objects and events (**stimuli**, plural for **stimulus**) they are currently encountering. For instance, in the opening case study Mr. McCourt's supportive demeanor (e.g., as reflected in statements such as "You were trying to help" and "What's the matter?") encouraged Sylvia to open up about life in her neighborhood. Several general principles sum up much of what researchers have learned about the effects that stimuli in the immediate environment have on learners' behavior and ultimately on their learning as well.

response Specific behavior that an individual exhibits.

stimulus (pl. stimuli) Specific object or event that influences an individual's learning or behavior.

Some stimuli tend to elicit certain kinds of behaviors.

Certain stimuli in our lives naturally lead us to behave in particular ways. A neighbor's smile might make us feel good and prompt a response such as "Hello, it's nice to see you." An ill-informed and highly biased newspaper editorial might make us angry and lead us to write a letter to the editor. Different pieces of music evoke different moods and behavioral states, perhaps exciting or agitating us, perhaps provoking us to tap our feet or take to the dance floor, or perhaps helping us relax and "mellow out." Stimuli that precede and evoke particular responses are known as **antecedent stimuli.**

A variety of environmental conditions have been shown to bring about particular behaviors, sometimes for the better and sometimes for the worse. For example, preschoolers are more likely to interact with their peers if they have a relatively small area in which to play and if the toys available to them (balls, puppets, toy housekeeping materials) encourage cooperation and group activity.[1] The kinds of games older children are asked to play influence their interpersonal behavior: Cooperative games promote cooperative behavior, whereas competitive games promote aggressive behavior.[2] The nature of classroom activities influences students' on-task behavior. For instance, students are much more likely to misbehave in class during independent seatwork or classmates' oral presentations than during lessons in which teachers are providing explanations or leading a discussion.[3]

Both physical stimuli (e.g., specimens to touch and books to read) and social stimuli (e.g., hugs from peers and explanations from teachers) can have a significant impact on children's learning.

Learners are more likely to acquire behaviors that lead to desired consequences.

Learners often learn and perform behaviors specifically because those behaviors lead to certain end results. Following are examples:

- Laura studies hard for her French vocabulary quiz. She gets an A on the quiz.
- Linda copies her answers to the French quiz from Laura's paper. She, too, gets an A.
- Julian changes the way he holds a basketball before shooting it toward the basket. He now gets more baskets than he used to.
- James throws paper clips at the girl beside him and discovers that this is one way he can get her attention.

Many appropriate and productive behaviors, such as studying for a French quiz or holding a basketball in a particular way, are acquired because of the consequences they bring. Many less productive behaviors, such as cheating on a quiz or throwing paper clips at a classmate, may be acquired for the same reason.

When we talk about the effects of desired consequences on learners' behaviors, we are talking about **operant conditioning**, a form of learning described by many behaviorists and most notably by B. F. Skinner.[4] The central principle of operant conditioning is a simple one:

A response that is followed by a reinforcing stimulus (a reinforcer) is more likely to occur again.

When behaviors are consistently followed by desired consequences, they tend to increase in frequency. When behaviors don't produce results, they typically decrease and may disappear altogether.

Teachers often talk about giving students rewards for academic achievement and appropriate classroom behavior. But as you may have noticed, I have not used the term *reward* in my description of operant conditioning, and for a very important reason. The word *reward* brings to mind things we would all agree are pleasant and desirable—perhaps praise, money, trophies, or special privileges. But some individuals increase their behavior for consequences that others would not find so appealing. A **reinforcer** is *any consequence that increases the frequency of a particular behavior*, whether or not other people would find that consequence appealing. The act of following a particular response with a reinforcer is known as **reinforcement.**

Reinforcers come in all shapes and sizes, and different ones are effective for different learners. We explore a few of the possibilities in the following exercise.

> Learn more about Skinner's ideas in a supplementary reading in the Homework and Exercises section in Chapter 3 of MyEducationLab.

antecedent stimulus Stimulus that increases the likelihood that a particular response will follow.

operant conditioning Form of learning in which a response increases in frequency as a result of its being followed by reinforcement.

reinforcer Consequence of a response that leads to increased frequency of the response.

reinforcement Act of following a response with a reinforcer.

---

[1] W. H. Brown, Fox, & Brady, 1987; Frost, Shin, & Jacobs, 1998; S. S. Martin, Brady, & Williams, 1991.
[2] Bay-Hinitz, Peterson, & Quilitch, 1994.
[3] W. Doyle, 1986a.

[4] For example, see Skinner, 1953, 1954, 1968. Some behaviorists instead use the term *instrumental conditioning.*

SEE FOR YOURSELF

SEE FOR YOURSELF
What Would It Take?

Imagine this scenario:

> You are currently enrolled in my educational psychology class. As your instructor, I ask you if you would be willing to spend an hour after class tutoring two classmates who are having difficulty understanding the course material. You have no other commitments for that hour, but you'd really like to spend the time at a nearby coffee shop where several friends are having lunch. What would it take for you to spend the hour tutoring your classmates instead of joining your friends? Would you do it to gain my approval? Would you do it for a candy bar? How about if I gave you five dollars? Would you do it simply because it made you feel good inside to be helping someone else? Write down a reward—perhaps one I have listed or perhaps a different one altogether—that would persuade you to help your classmates instead of meeting your friends.

Now imagine this second scenario:

> A few weeks later, I ask you to spend the weekend (eight hours a day on both Saturday and Sunday) tutoring the same two struggling classmates. What would it take this time to convince you to do the job? Would my approval do the trick? A candy bar? Five dollars? Five *hundred* dollars? Or would your internal sense of satisfaction be enough? Once again, write down what it would take for you to agree to help your classmates.

Obviously, there are no right answers to the exercise you just completed. Different people would agree to tutor classmates for different reasons. But you were probably able to identify at least one consequence in each situation that would entice you to spend time helping others.

Some reinforcers, such as a candy bar, are **primary reinforcers**, in that they serve a basic biological need. Food, water, sources of warmth, and oxygen are all primary reinforcers. To some extent, physical affection and cuddling may address built-in biological needs as well, and for an adolescent addicted to an illegal substance, the next "fix" is also a primary reinforcer.[5]

Other reinforcers, known as **secondary reinforcers**, don't satisfy any physiological need. Praise, money, good grades, and trophies are examples. Such stimuli may become reinforcing over time through their association with other reinforcers. For example, if praise is occasionally associated with a special candy treat from mother, and if money often comes with a hug from father, the praise and money eventually become reinforcing in and of themselves.

All of the examples we've discussed so far are instances of **positive reinforcement**. Whenever a particular stimulus is *presented* after a behavior and the behavior increases as a result, positive reinforcement has occurred. Don't be misled by the word *positive*, which in this case has nothing to do with the pleasantness or general desirability of the stimulus being presented. Positive reinforcement can occur even when the presented stimulus is one that others might think is *un*pleasant or *un*desirable. Instead, *positive* simply means *adding* something to the situation. Although many students will behave in ways that earn teacher praise, others may behave to get themselves *any* form of teacher attention, even a scolding.[6] Most students will work for As, but a few may actually prefer Cs or even Fs. (As a school psychologist, I once worked with a high school student who used Fs as a way to get revenge on his overbearing and overly controlling parents.) Depending on the individual, any one of these stimuli—praise, a scolding, an A, or an F—can be a positive reinforcer. Following are examples of the forms that positive reinforcement might take:

- A *concrete reinforcer* is an actual object—something that can be touched (e.g., a snack, sticker, or toy).
- A *social reinforcer* is a gesture or sign (e.g., a smile, attention, praise, or "thank you") that one person gives another, usually to communicate positive regard.

primary reinforcer Consequence that satisfies a biologically built-in need.

secondary reinforcer Consequence that becomes reinforcing over time through its association with another reinforcer.

positive reinforcement Phenomenon in which a response increases as a result of the presentation (rather than removal) of a stimulus.

[5] Harlow & Zimmerman, 1959; Lejuez, Schaal, & O'Donnell, 1998; Vollmer & Hackenberg, 2001.

[6] Flood, Wilder, Flood, & Masuda, 2002; McComas, Thompson, & Johnson, 2003.

- An *activity reinforcer* is an opportunity to engage in a favorite activity. Learners will often do one thing, even something they don't like to do, if completing the task enables them to do something they enjoy.[7]
- Sometimes the simple message that an answer is correct or that a task has been done well—*positive feedback*—is reinforcement enough. Positive feedback is most effective when it tells learners in explicit terms what they are doing well and what they can do to improve their performance even further.[8] (See Figure 3.1.)

The reinforcers just listed are **extrinsic reinforcers**, those provided by the external environment (often by other people). Yet some positive reinforcers are **intrinsic reinforcers**, those supplied by learners themselves or inherent in tasks being performed. Learners engage in some activities simply because they enjoy the activities or because they like to feel competent and successful. When people perform certain behaviors in the absence of any observable reinforcers—when they read *The Lord of the Rings* from cover to cover in a single weekend, practice on their electric guitars into the wee hours of the morning, or do extra classwork without being asked—they are probably working for the intrinsic reinforcement that such behaviors yield. If in the preceding "What Would It Take?" exercise, you agreed to help your classmates simply because doing so would make you feel good, then you would be working for an intrinsic reinforcer.

Children's preferences for various kinds of reinforcers tend to change as they grow older. For example, concrete reinforcers (e.g., scratch-and-sniff stickers, small trinkets) can be effective with young children, but teenagers are more likely to appreciate opportunities to spend time with friends. Table 3.1 presents forms of reinforcement that may be especially effective at various grade levels. An important developmental trend is evident in Table 3.1 as well: As children get older, they become better able to handle **delay of gratification**. That is, they can forego small, immediate reinforcers for the larger reinforcers that their long-term efforts may bring down the road.[9] Whereas a preschooler or kindergartner is apt to choose a small reinforcer she can have *now* over a larger and more attractive reinforcer she cannot get until tomorrow, an 8-year-old may be willing to wait a day or two for the more appealing item. Some adolescents can delay gratification for several weeks or even longer.

Learners are also likely to acquire behaviors that help them avoid or escape unpleasant circumstances.

Sometimes learners behave not to get something, but instead to get *rid of* something. On such occasions negative reinforcement rather than positive reinforcement is at work. Whereas positive reinforcement involves the presentation of a stimulus, **negative reinforcement** brings about the increase of a behavior through the *removal* of a stimulus (typically an unpleasant one, at least from the perspective of the learner). The word *negative* here is not a value judgment. It simply refers to the act of *taking away* (rather than adding) a stimulus. Following are examples:

- Reuben must read *A Tale of Two Cities* for his English literature class before the end of the month. He doesn't like having this assignment hanging over his head, so he finishes it early. When he's done, he no longer has to worry about it. In other words, the annoying *worry* feeling disappears.
- Rhonda is in the same literature class. Each time she sits down at home to read *A Tale of Two Cities*, she finds the novel confusing and difficult to understand. She quickly ends her study sessions by finding other things she "needs" to do instead—washing her hair, folding her laundry, playing basketball with the neighbors, and so on. In other words, the *difficult assignment* disappears, at least for the time being.
- When students complain about having to read *A Tale of Two Cities*, Mr. McCourt rants and raves about their lack of concern for people living in poverty. They quiet down, with only one student telling him to "chill" and "relax." Through his actions, Mr. McCourt terminates a *noisy and unpleasant situation*, even if only temporarily.

FIGURE 3.1 In commenting on Matt's book project, a middle school teacher is explicit about what Matt can do to improve but vague about what he has done well. Knowing what *specific* things made his summary and project description "very good" would help Matt repeat these things in the future.

extrinsic reinforcer Reinforcer that comes from the outside environment, rather than from within the learner.

intrinsic reinforcer Reinforcer provided by oneself or inherent in a task being performed.

delay of gratification Ability to forego small, immediate reinforcers to obtain larger ones later on.

negative reinforcement Phenomenon in which a response increases as a result of the removal (rather than presentation) of a stimulus.

---

[7] Premack, 1959, 1963.

[8] Bangert-Drowns, Kulik, Kulik, & Morgan, 1991; D. L. Butler & Winne, 1995; Feltz, Chase, Moritz, & Sullivan, 1999; Hattie & Timperley, 2007.

[9] Green et al., 1994; Rotenberg & Mayer, 1990.

DEVELOPMENTAL TRENDS

TABLE 3.1 Effective Reinforcers at Different Grade Levels

Grade Level	Age-Typical Characteristics	Suggested Strategies
K–2	• Preference for small, immediate rewards over larger, delayed ones • Examples of effective reinforcers: • Concrete reinforcers (e.g., stickers, crayons, small trinkets) • Teacher approval (e.g., smiles, praise) • Privileges (e.g., going to lunch first) • "Grown-up" responsibilities (e.g., taking absentee forms to the office)	• Give immediate praise for appropriate behavior. • Describe enjoyable consequences that may come later as a result of students' present behaviors. • Use colorful stickers to indicate a job well done; choose stickers that match students' interests (e.g., use favorite cartoon characters). • Have students line up for recess, lunch, or dismissal based on desired behaviors (e.g., "Table 2 is the quietest and can line up first"). • Rotate opportunities to perform classroom duties (e.g., feeding the goldfish, watering plants) among all students; make such duties contingent on appropriate behavior.
3–5	• Increasing ability to delay gratification (i.e., to put off small reinforcers in order to gain larger ones later on) • Examples of effective reinforcers: • Concrete reinforcers (e.g., snacks, pencils, small toys) • Teacher approval and positive feedback • "Good citizen" certificates • Free time (e.g., to draw or play games)	• Use concrete reinforcers only occasionally, perhaps to add novelty to a classroom activity. • Award a certificate to a "citizen of the week," explicitly identifying things the recipient has done especially well; be sure that every student gets at least one certificate during the school year. • Plan a trip to a local amusement park for students with good attendance records (especially useful for students at risk for academic failure).
6–8	• Increasing desire to have social time with peers • Examples of effective reinforcers: • Free time with friends • Acceptance and approval from peers • Teacher approval and support (becomes especially critical after the transition to middle school or junior high) • Specific positive feedback about academic performance (preferably given in private)	• Make short periods of free time with peers (e.g., five minutes) contingent on accomplishing assigned tasks. • Spend one-on-one time with students, especially those who appear to be socially isolated. • Provide explicit feedback about what things students have done well (e.g., pointing out their use of colorful language in an essay or commending them for helping classmates with challenging subject matter).
9–12	• Increasing ability to postpone immediate pleasures in order to gain long-term rewards • Concern about getting good grades (especially for students who are applying to selective colleges) • Examples of effective reinforcers: • Opportunities to interact with friends • Specific positive feedback about academic performance • Public recognition for group performance (e.g., newspaper articles about a club's public service work) • Positions of responsibility (e.g., being student representative to Faculty Senate)	• Acknowledge students' concern about earning good grades, but focus their attention on the value of learning school subject matter for its own sake (see the discussion of achievement goals in Chapter 6). • Be sure that good grades are contingent on students' own work; do not reinforce cheating or plagiarism. • Publicize accomplishments of extracurricular groups and athletic teams in local news media. • Provide opportunities for independent decision making and responsibility, especially when students show an ability to make wise decisions.

Sources: L. H. Anderman, Patrick, Hruda, & Linnenbrink, 2002; Cizek, 2003; Fowler & Baer, 1981; Green, Fry, & Myerson, 1994; Hine & Fraser, 2002; Krumboltz & Krumboltz, 1972; Rimm & Masters, 1974; Rotenberg & Mayer, 1990; M. G. Sanders, 1996.

In the examples just presented, notice how negative reinforcement sometimes promotes desirable behaviors (such as completing an assignment early) and at other times promotes undesirable behaviors (such as procrastination). Notice, as well, how students are not the only ones who respond to reinforcement in the classroom. After all, teachers are human beings too!

Negative reinforcement often comes into play when students face especially difficult—perhaps seemingly impossible—academic tasks.[10] The following explanation reveals what one student with a learning disability has learned to do:

> When it comes time for reading I do everything under the sun I can to get out of it because it's my worst nightmare to read. I'll say I have to go to the bathroom or that I'm sick and I have to go to the nurse right now. My teacher doesn't know that I'll be walking around campus. She thinks I am going to the bathroom or whatever my lame excuse is. All I really want to do is get out of having to read.[11]

Occasionally, learners' attempts to avoid seemingly impossible assignments lead them to engage in blatant misbehaviors, as this statement from another student with a learning disability reveals:

> They [his teachers] used to hand us all our homework on Mondays. One day my teacher handed me a stack about an inch thick and as I was walking out of class there was a big trash can right there and I'd, in front of everybody including the teacher, just drop it in the trash can and walk out. I did this because I couldn't read what she gave me. It was kind of a point that I wanted to get the teacher to realize. That while I'm doing it, inside it kind of like hurt because I really wanted to do it but I couldn't and just so it didn't look like I was goin' soft or anything like that I'd walk over to the trash and throw it in.[12]

Learners tend to steer clear of behaviors that lead to unpleasant consequences.

Over the years I've heard many people incorrectly use the term *negative reinforcement* when they intend to impose unpleasant consequences to reduce someone's inappropriate behavior. In reality, they are talking about administering punishment, *not* negative reinforcement. Whereas negative reinforcement increases the frequency of a response, **punishment** is a consequence that *decreases* the frequency of the response it follows.

All punishing consequences fall into one of two categories. **Presentation punishment** involves presenting a new stimulus, presumably something a learner finds unpleasant and doesn't want. Scoldings and teacher scowls, *if* they lead to a reduction in the behavior they follow, are instances of presentation punishment. **Removal punishment** involves removing an existing stimulus or state of affairs, presumably one a learner finds desirable and doesn't want to lose. Loss of a privilege, a fine or penalty (involving the loss of money or previously earned points), and "grounding" (when certain pleasurable outside activities are missed) are all examples of removal punishment. Table 3.2 should help you understand how positive reinforcement, negative reinforcement, presentation punishment, and removal punishment are distinctly different concepts.

We see one clear example of punishment in the opening case study. Sylvia mentioned that her mother "makes me write 'going to' a hundred times" and then "make[s] me say it another hundred times." Such a consequence clearly influenced her behavior, because she corrected herself not only when she said "gonna" but also after saying "wanna" and "lotta." Quite possibly the neighborhood children's derisive remarks also had a punishing effect. By asking "Hey, Doc, you scrape yourself an' you find that honky skin?," Sylvia's peers were essentially accusing her of "acting white," an epithet that some African American students find aversive (more on this point in Chapter 7). The neighbors clearly didn't dissuade Sylvia from becoming a doctor, but they probably discouraged her from walking in their direction if she saw them on the street.

Certain forms of punishment, especially those that are mild in nature and cause no physical or psychological harm, can be quite effective in helping children and adolescents acquire more effective behaviors.[13] But without proper precautions, the use of punishment in the classroom can be counterproductive. In our discussion of classroom

punishment Consequence that decreases the frequency of the response it follows.

presentation punishment Punishment involving presentation of a new stimulus, presumably one a learner finds unpleasant.

removal punishment Punishment involving removal of an existing stimulus, presumably one a learner finds desirable and doesn't want to lose.

[10] McComas et al., 2003; K. A. Meyer, 1999; Van Camp et al., 2000.
[11] Zambo & Brem, 2004, p. 5.
[12] Zambo & Brem, 2004, p. 6.
[13] Conyers et al., 2004; R. V. Hall et al., 1971; Landrum & Kauffman, 2006; Walters & Grusec, 1977.

TABLE 3.2 Distinguishing Among Positive Reinforcement, Negative Reinforcement, and Punishment

Consequence	Effect	Examples
Positive reinforcement	Response *increases* when a new stimulus (presumably one the learner finds desirable) is *presented*.	• A student *is praised* for writing an assignment in cursive. She begins to write other assignments in cursive as well. • A student *gets lunch money* by bullying a girl into surrendering hers. He begins bullying his classmates more frequently.
Negative reinforcement	Response *increases* when a previously existing stimulus (presumably one the learner finds undesirable) is *removed*.	• A student *no longer has to worry* about a research paper he has completed several days before the due date. He begins to do his assignments ahead of time whenever possible. • A student *escapes the principal's wrath* by lying about her role in a recent incident of school vandalism. She begins lying to school faculty whenever she finds herself in an uncomfortable situation.
Presentation punishment	Response *decreases* when a new stimulus (presumably one the learner finds undesirable) is *presented*.	• A student *is scolded* for taunting other students. She taunts others less frequently after that. • A student *is ridiculed by classmates* for asking a "stupid" question during a lecture. He stops asking questions in class.
Removal punishment	Response *decreases* when a previously existing stimulus (presumably one the learner finds desirable) is *removed*.	• A student *is removed from the softball team for a week* for showing poor sportsmanship. She rarely shows poor sportsmanship in future games. • A student *loses points on a test* for answering a question in a creative but unusual way. He takes fewer risks on future tests.

management strategies in Chapter 9, we'll look at effective punishments and guidelines for their use.

Learners acquire many behaviors by observing other people.

Sometimes learners acquire new behaviors on their own, perhaps by "experimenting" with various responses and seeing which ones lead to reinforcement and which ones lead to punishment. But they don't always learn in this trial-and-error manner. Learners also acquire many new responses simply by observing and imitating the behaviors of other individuals (**models**).

When one person demonstrates a behavior and another person imitates it, **modeling** is occurring. Consistent with how the term is used both in everyday speech and in social learning theory, I will sometimes use *modeling* to describe what the model does (i.e., demonstrate a behavior) and at other times to describe what the observer does (i.e., imitate that behavior). To minimize confusion, I will often use the verb *imitate* rather than *model* when referring to what the observer does.

Potential models are everywhere. Some are **live models**, people in learners' immediate environments. Others are **symbolic models**, real or fictional characters portrayed in books, in films, on television, and through various other media. For instance, children and adolescents can learn valuable lessons by studying the behaviors of important figures in history or by reading stories about people who accomplish great things in the face of adversity.

Learners acquire a wide variety of academic skills, at least in part, by observing what others do. For instance, they may learn how to solve long-division problems or write a cohesive composition partly by observing how their teachers and peers do these things.[14] Modeling of academic skills can be especially effective when the model demonstrates not only

model Person who demonstrates a behavior for someone else.

modeling Demonstrating a behavior for another; also, observing and imitating another's behavior.

live model Individual whose behavior is directly observed in one's immediate environment.

symbolic model Real or fictional character portrayed in the media that influences an observer's behavior.

---

[14] Braaksma, Rijlaarsdam, & van den Bergh, 2002; R. J. Sawyer, Graham, & Harris, 1992; Schunk & Hanson, 1985; Schunk & Swartz, 1993.

how to *do* a task, but also how to *think about* the task.[15] As an example, consider how a teacher might model the thinking processes involved in the long-division problem in the margin:

$$4\overline{)276}$$

> First I have to decide what number to divide 4 into. I take 276, start on the left and move toward the right until I have a number the same as or larger than 4. Is 2 larger than 4? No. Is 27 larger than 4? Yes. So my first division will be 4 into 27. Now I need to multiply 4 by a number that will give an answer the same as or slightly smaller than 27. How about 5? 5 × 4 = 20. No, too small. Let's try 6. 6 × 4 = 24. Maybe. Let's try 7. 7 × 4 = 28. No, too large. So 6 is correct.[16]

By observing and imitating others, learners acquire many interpersonal behaviors as well. For instance, they often learn **prosocial behaviors**—showing compassion, sharing possessions with others, and, in general, putting others' needs and well-being before their own—when they *see* models that exhibit prosocial behavior (e.g., by watching *Sesame Street* or *Barney and Friends*). In contrast, they are more likely to be aggressive and violent when they witness aggression and violence in their personal lives or in the media.[17] What about situations in which a model advocates certain behaviors and yet does the exact opposite? When children hear a model say one thing and do something else, they are more likely to imitate what the model *does* than what the model *says*.[18] To be truly effective, models must practice what they preach.

Of course, learners don't always imitate the people they see in their surroundings and in the media. When are they most likely to model others' behaviors? The next exercise should help you discover the answer.

"Don't cry, Megan. Remember, it's not whether Daddy wins the brawl in the stands that's important. It's how you played the game."

Models' actions often speak louder than their words.

SEE FOR YOURSELF
Five People

Write down the names of five people whom you admire and whose behaviors you would like to imitate in some way. Then, beside each name, write one or more reasons *why* you admire these people.

Chances are, the five people you chose have one or more of the following characteristics:[19]

- **Competence.** Learners typically try to imitate people who do something well, not those who do it poorly.
- **Prestige and power.** Learners often imitate people who are famous or powerful, either at a national or international level (e.g., a renowned athlete, a popular rock star) or on the local scene (e.g., a head cheerleader, the captain of the high school hockey team, a gang leader).
- **"Gender-appropriate" behavior.** Learners are more apt to adopt behaviors they believe are appropriate for their gender (with different learners defining *gender-appropriate* somewhat differently).
- **Behavior relevant to one's own situation.** Learners are most likely to imitate behaviors they believe will help them in their own lives and circumstances.

The last of these—behavior relevant to one's own situation—leads us to the next general principle.

Learners learn what behaviors are acceptable and effective by observing what happens to others.

When I was in third grade, I entered a neighborhood Halloween costume contest dressed as "Happy Tooth," a character in several toothpaste commercials at the time. I didn't win the

---

[15] R. J. Sawyer et al., 1992; Schunk, 1981, 1998; Schunk & Swartz, 1993.

[16] Schunk, 1998, p. 146.

[17] C. A. Anderson et al., 2003; Eron, 1980; N. E. Goldstein, Arnold, Rosenberg, Stowe, & Ortiz, 2001;

Guerra, Huesmann, & Spindler, 2003; Hearold, 1986; Rushton, 1980.

[18] Bryan, 1975.

[19] Bandura, 1986; Sasso & Rude, 1987; Schunk, 1987.

prosocial behavior Behavior directed toward promoting the well-being of another.

contest; a "witch" won first prize. So the following year I entered the same contest dressed as a witch, figuring I was a shoo-in for first place. My dressing-as-a-witch behavior increased not because I was reinforced for such behavior, but rather because I saw someone *else* being reinforced for it.

Learners sometimes experience reinforcement and punishment *vicariously*—that is, by observing the consequences of other people's behaviors. Learners who observe someone else being reinforced for a particular behavior tend to exhibit that behavior more frequently themselves—a phenomenon known as **vicarious reinforcement**. For example, by taking note of the consequences their classmates experience, students might learn that studying hard leads to good grades, that being elected to class office brings status and popularity, or that neatness counts.

Conversely, when learners see someone else get punished for a certain behavior, they are *less* likely to behave that way themselves—a phenomenon known as **vicarious punishment**. For example, when a coach benches a football player for poor sportsmanlike conduct, other players are unlikely to mimic such behavior. Unfortunately, vicarious punishment may suppress desirable behaviors as well as undesirable behaviors. For example, when a teacher belittles a student for asking a "silly" question, other students may be reluctant to ask questions of their own.

By seeing what happens to themselves and others, learners form expectations about the probable outcomes of various behaviors.

So far, we have been focusing largely on what learners *do*. But the consequences of their own and others' behaviors also affect what learners *think*. In particular, learners begin to see patterns in the consequences that follow various responses, and they form *expectations* that certain responses will lead to desirable results and other responses will not. These expectations, in turn, affect what learners do and don't do in future situations. To understand how this principle might play out in your own life, try the next exercise.

SEE FOR YOURSELF
Dr. X

How many of the following questions can you answer about your educational psychology instructor? For lack of a better name, I'm going to call your instructor "Dr. X."

1. Is Dr. X right-handed or left-handed?
2. Is Dr. X a flashy dresser or a more conservative one?
3. What kind of shoes does Dr. X wear to class?
4. Does Dr. X wear a wedding ring?
5. Does Dr. X bring a briefcase to class each day?

If you've been going to class regularly, you probably know the answers to at least two of the questions, and possibly you can answer all five. But I'm guessing that you've never mentioned what you've learned to anyone else, because you've had no reason to believe that demonstrating your knowledge about such matters would be reinforced. When learners *do* expect reinforcement for such knowledge, it suddenly surfaces. For example, every time I teach educational psychology, I take a minute sometime during the semester to hide my feet behind the podium and then ask my students to tell me what my shoes look like. Students first look at me as if I have two heads, but after a few seconds of awkward silence, at least a half dozen of them (usually those sitting in the first two rows) begin to describe my shoes, right down to the rippled soles, scuffed leather, and beige stitching.

People learn many things that they never demonstrate because there is little likelihood that they would be reinforced for doing so. At school, for instance, children learn facts and figures, they learn ways of getting their teacher's attention, and they may even learn such tiny details as which classmate stores Twinkies in his desk and what kind of shoes the teacher wears to class. Of all the things they learn, children will be most likely to demonstrate the

vicarious reinforcement Phenomenon in which a response increases in frequency when another (observed) person is reinforced for that response.

vicarious punishment Phenomenon in which a response decreases in frequency when another (observed) person is punished for that response.

ones they think will bring them reinforcement. The things they think will *not* be reinforced may remain hidden forever.

When people choose to behave in a way that may bring them future reinforcement, they are working for an **incentive**. Incentives are never guaranteed—for instance, people never know that they are going to get an A on a test when they study for it or that they are going to win a Halloween costume contest when they enter it. An incentive is an expected or hoped-for consequence, one that may or may not actually occur. It is apt to influence behavior only if it is obtainable and if a learner perceives it as such. For example, in a classroom of 30 children, a competition in which one prize will be awarded for the highest test score is apt to motivate just a handful of top achievers. (We'll look more closely at learners' perceptions about their chances for success in our discussion of *self-efficacy* in Chapter 6.)

What happens when learners' expectations aren't met—for instance, when an expected reinforcement never comes? When, as a fourth grader, I entered the Halloween costume contest as a witch, I lost once again. (First prize went to a girl with a metal colander on her head. She was dressed as *Sputnik*, the first satellite launched into space by what was then the Soviet Union.) That was the last time I entered a Halloween contest. I had expected reinforcement and felt cheated because I didn't get it. When learners think that a certain response is going to be reinforced, yet the response is *not* reinforced, they are less likely to exhibit that response in the future. In other words, the *non*occurrence of expected reinforcement is a form of punishment.[20]

Just as the nonoccurrence of reinforcement is a form of punishment, the nonoccurrence of punishment is a form of reinforcement.[21] Perhaps you can think of a time when you broke a rule, expecting to be punished, but got away with your crime. Or perhaps you can remember seeing someone else break a rule without being caught. When nothing bad happens after a forbidden behavior, people may actually feel as if they have been reinforced for the behavior.

Learned behavior and cognitive processes are sometimes situated in specific environmental contexts.

People often associate particular behaviors and ways of thinking with particular environments, and so those behaviors and ways of thinking are more frequent in such environments. This tendency for some responses and cognitive processes to be rooted in particular contexts is known as **situated learning** or **situated cognition**.[22]

Even at school, students may abandon the knowledge and skills they've learned in one class once they're in another class. A study with high school students[23] provides an illustration. Students were asked to figure out how much postage they should put on an envelope of a particular weight, and they were given a table of postage rates that would enable them to determine the correct amount. When students were given the task in a social studies class, most of them used the postage table to find the answer. But when students were given the task in a math class, most of them ignored the postage table and tried to *calculate* the postage in some manner, sometimes figuring it to several decimal places. Thus the

Learning sometimes remains limited to (*situated in*) specific environments. As often as possible, then, learners should practice new skills in real-world contexts.

students in the social studies class were more likely to solve the problem correctly—as a former social studies teacher myself, I suspect that, in that context, they were well accustomed to looking for information in tables and charts. In contrast, many of the students in the math class drew on strategies they associated with that class (using formulas and performing calculations) and so overlooked the more efficient and accurate approach.

incentive Hoped-for, but not guaranteed, future consequence of behavior.

situated learning and cognition Knowledge, behaviors, and thinking skills acquired and used primarily within certain contexts, with limited if any use in other contexts.

[20] Bandura, 1986.
[21] Bandura, 1986.
[22] Bassok & Holyoak, 1990, 1993; J. S. Brown, Collins, & Duguid, 1989; Greeno, Collins, & Resnick, 1996; Lave & Wenger, 1991; Light & Butterworth, 1993.
[23] Säljö & Wyndhamn, 1992.

Fortunately, not all school learning is "stuck" in a particular classroom. People use many of the skills they've learned at school—reading, writing, arithmetic, map interpretation, and so on—in a variety of everyday situations in the outside world.[24] Nevertheless, people don't use what they've learned in the classroom as often as they might. We'll explore this issue further in our discussion of *transfer* in Chapter 4.

SOCIAL INTERACTION AS CONTEXT

In the preceding section we discussed things that other people might do *to* or *in the presence of* a learner—providing reinforcement, modeling behavior, and so on. Yet many effective learning contexts involve active *interaction* among two or more individuals. In particular, learners may *co-construct* knowledge with others, as reflected in the following two principles.

Learners sometimes co-construct knowledge and understandings with more experienced individuals.

Adults and other more experienced individuals often help children and adolescents make sense of the world through joint discussion of a phenomenon or event they are experiencing or have recently experienced together.[25] Such an interaction, sometimes called a **mediated learning experience**, encourages a young learner to think about the phenomenon or event in particular ways: to attach labels to it, recognize concepts and principles that underlie it, draw certain inferences and conclusions from it, and so on.

As an example, consider the following exchange, in which a 5-year-old boy and his mother are talking about a prehistoric animal exhibit at a natural history museum:

Boy: Cool. Wow, look. Look giant teeth. Mom, look at his giant teeth.
Mom: He looks like a saber tooth. Do you think he eats meat or plants?
Boy: Mom, look at his giant little tooth, look at his teeth in his mouth, so big.
Mom: He looks like a saber tooth, doesn't he. Do you think he eats plants or meat?
Boy: Ouch, ouch, ouch, ouch. (referring to sharp tooth)
Mom: Do you think he eats plants or meat?
Boy: Meat.
Mom: How come?
Boy: Because he has sharp teeth. (growling noises)[26]

Even without his mother's assistance, the boy would almost certainly learn something about the characteristics of saber-toothed tigers from his museum visit. Yet Mom helps her son make better sense of the experience than he might have done on his own—for instance, by using the label *saber tooth* and helping him connect tooth characteristics to eating preferences. Notice how persistent Mom is in asking her son to make the tooth–food connection. She continues to ask her question about meat versus plants until the boy finally infers, correctly, that saber-toothed tigers must have been meat eaters.

As children discuss objects and events with adults and other knowledgeable individuals within the context of everyday activities, they gradually incorporate into their own thinking the ways in which the people around them talk about and interpret the world, and they begin to use many concepts, symbols, mental strategies, and problem-solving procedures that others use, model, and share.[27] In essence, they are developing a variety of **cognitive tools** that will enable them to think about and respond to situations and problems more effectively.

When children talk with parents, teachers, and other adults about past and present experiences, their memory for those experiences is better as a result.[28] Adults usually have more knowledge than children's peers do, and they tend to be more skillful teachers. Accordingly, they are often the partners of choice when children are trying to master complex new subject matter and skills.[29]

mediated learning experience Social interaction in which an adult helps a child interpret a phenomenon or event in particular (usually culturally appropriate) ways.

cognitive tool Concept, symbol, strategy, procedure, or other culturally constructed mechanism that helps people think about and respond to situations more effectively.

---

[24] J. R. Anderson, Reder, & Simon, 1996.
[25] Eacott, 1999; Feuerstein, 1990; Feuerstein, Klein, & Tannenbaum, 1991; John-Steiner & Mahn, 1996; Reese & Fivush, 1993.
[26] Ash, 2002, p. 378.

[27] Markus & Hamedani, 2007; K. Nelson, 1996; Vygotsky, 1962, 1978.
[28] Haden, Ornstein, Eckerman, & Didow, 2001; Hemphill & Snow, 1996; K. Nelson, 1993; Tessler & Nelson, 1994.
[29] Gauvain, 2001; Radziszewska & Rogoff, 1988.

In the eyes of sociocultural psychologists, mediated learning experiences and cognitive tools are not simply helpful—they are *essential* if children are to acquire the knowledge, skills, and beliefs appropriate for their culture. Accordingly, we will return to these concepts in our discussion of cognitive development in Chapter 5.

Learners also co-construct knowledge and understandings with peers who have ability levels similar to their own.

Flip back to Figure 2.2 (the three black-and-white faces) in Chapter 2. Did you initially have trouble seeing the man on the right side of the figure? If so, perhaps you enlisted the assistance of friends or classmates to help you identify the top of the man's head, locations of the eyes and an ear, and other details. Think, too, about times when you've worked cooperatively with classmates to make sense of a confusing topic in one of your classes. Quite possibly, by sharing various interpretations, your group jointly constructed a better understanding of the material than any one of you could have constructed on your own.

In addition to co-constructing meanings with more experienced individuals, learners often talk with one another to help them make better sense of their experiences—for instance, by exploring, discussing, explaining, and debating certain topics in study groups or classroom discussions. When learners work together in such a manner, they are, in essence, engaging in **distributed cognition**: They spread the learning task across many minds and can draw on multiple knowledge bases and ideas.[30] There is certainly some truth to the old adage "Two heads are better than one."

As an example of distributed cognition, let's look in on Ms. Lombard's fourth-grade class, which has been studying fractions. Ms. Lombard has never taught her students how to divide a number by a fraction. Nevertheless, she gives them the following problem, which can be solved by dividing 20 by ¾:[31]

> Mom makes small apple tarts, using three-quarters of an apple for each small tart. She has 20 apples. How many small apple tarts can she make?[32]

Ms. Lombard asks the students to work in small groups to figure out how they might solve the problem. One group of four girls—Jeanette, Liz, Kerri, and Nina—has been working on the problem for some time and so far has arrived at such answers as 15, 38, and 23. We join the girls midway through their discussion, when they've already agreed that they can use three-fourths of each apple to make a total of 20 tarts:

Jeanette: In each apple there is a quarter left. In each apple there is a quarter left, so you've used, you've made twenty tarts already and you've got a quarter of twenty see—

Liz: So you've got twenty quarters *left*.

Jeanette: Yes, … and twenty quarters is equal to five apples, … so five apples divided by—

Liz: Six, seven, eight.

Jeanette: But three-quarters equals three.

Kerri: But she can't make only three apple tarts!

Jeanette: No, you've still got twenty.

Liz: But you've got twenty quarters, if you've got twenty quarters you might be right.

Jeanette: I'll show you.

Liz: No, I've drawn them all here.

Kerri: How many quarters have you got? Twenty?

Liz: Yes, one quarter makes five apples and out of five apples she can make five tarts which will make that twenty-five tarts and then she will have, wait, one, two, three, four, five quarters, she'll have one, two, three, four, five quarters. …

Nina: I've got a better. …

Kerri: Yes?

Liz: Twenty-six quarters and a remainder of one quarter left.[33]

---

[30] Hewitt & Scardamalia, 1998; Kuhn, 2001b; Palincsar & Herrenkohl, 1999; Salomon, 1993; Wiley & Bailey, 2006.

[31] In case your memory of how to divide by a fraction is rusty, you can approach the problem 20 ÷ ¾ by inverting the fraction and multiplying, like so: $20 \times \frac{4}{3} = \frac{80}{3} = 26\frac{2}{3}$. In the problem Ms. Lombard presents, Mom can make 26 tarts and have enough apple to make two-thirds of another tart. If Mom has two-thirds of the three-fourths of an apple she needs to make another whole tart, then she has half an apple left over ($\frac{2}{3} \times \frac{3}{4} = \frac{1}{2}$).

[32] J. Hiebert et al., 1997, p. 118.

[33] J. Hiebert et al., 1997, p. 121.

distributed cognition Process in which two or more learners each contribute knowledge and ideas as they work collaboratively on an issue or problem.

When learners must explain their thinking to someone else, they usually organize and elaborate on what they've learned. These processes help them develop a more integrated and thorough understanding of the material.

The discussion and occasional disagreements continue, and the girls eventually arrive at the correct answer: Mom can make 26 tarts and then will have half an apple left over.

When learners share their ideas and perspectives with one another, they can enhance their understanding of a topic in several ways:[34]

- They must clarify and organize their ideas well enough to explain and justify them to others.
- They tend to elaborate on what they've learned—for example, by drawing inferences, generating hypotheses, and asking questions.
- They are exposed to the views of others, who may have a more accurate understanding of a topic.
- They can model effective ways of thinking about and studying academic subject matter for one another.
- They may detect flaws and inconsistencies in their own thinking, thereby helping them identify gaps in their understanding.
- They may discover how people from different cultural and ethnic backgrounds may interpret the topic in different, yet perhaps equally valid, ways.
- In the process of debating controversial material, they may gain a more sophisticated view of the nature of knowledge and learning. For example, they may begin to realize that acquiring "knowledge" involves acquiring an integrated set of ideas about a topic and that such knowledge is likely to evolve gradually over time (more on this point in the discussion of *epistemological beliefs* in Chapter 4).

Such joint meaning-making doesn't necessarily have to occur in a single learning session, however. Social construction of meaning may proceed gradually over the course of several days or weeks or even longer. In fact, if we look at human beings' interpretations of their experiences on a much grander scale, the evolution of such academic disciplines as mathematics, science, history, economics, and psychology reflects co-construction of knowledge and understandings stretched out over the course of many decades or centuries.

CULTURE AND SOCIETY AS CONTEXT

The term **culture** refers to the behaviors and beliefs that members of a long-standing social group tend to share and pass along to successive generations. Culture is a pervasive part of any learning environment—it permeates people's social interactions, as well as the books, toys, television shows, and other man-made objects and media that people encounter. But culture is an "inside-the-head" thing as well as an "out-there-in-the-world" thing, in that it provides an overall framework by which people determine what things are normal and abnormal, true and not true, rational and irrational, good and bad.[35] A learner's cultural background influences the perspectives and values the learner acquires, the skills the learner masters and finds important, and the long-term goals toward which the learner strives.

A concept related to, but somewhat distinct from, culture is **society**: a large, enduring social group that is socially and economically organized and has collective institutions and activities. For instance, virtually any nation is a society, in that it has a government that regulates some of its activities, a set of laws that identify acceptable and unacceptable behaviors, a monetary system that allows members to exchange goods and services, and so on.

Cultures and societies are not static entities. Instead, they continue to change over time as they incorporate new ideas, practices, and ways of thinking, and especially as they come into contact with other cultures and societies.[36] Furthermore, considerable variation exists

---

culture Behaviors and belief systems that members of a long-standing social group share and pass along to successive generations.

society Large, enduring social group that is socially and economically organized and has collective institutions and activities.

[34] L. M. Anderson, 1993; Banks, 1991; Barnes, 1976; M. Carr & Biddlecomb, 1998; Chinn, 2006; Fosnot, 1996; Hatano & Inagaki, 1993, 2003; E. H. Hiebert & Raphael, 1996; K. Hogan, Nastasi, & Pressley, 2000; A. King, 1999; Schwarz, Neuman, & Biezuner, 2000; Sinatra & Pintrich, 2003a; N. M. Webb & Palincsar, 1996.
[35] Different theorists define culture somewhat differently, but virtually all agree that it has both

physical and mental components; for instance, see M. Cole, 2006; Kağitçibaşi, 2007; Markus and Hamedani, 2007; Shweder et al., 1998; Smedley & Smedley, 2005.
[36] Kitayama, Duffy, & Uchida, 2007; O. Lee, 1999; Rogoff, 2003.

in attitudes and behaviors within a particular culture and society, in that individual members may adopt some cultural values and societal practices but reject others.[37] For example, in the opening case study Sylvia comments on how some of her neighborhood age-mates don't share her interest in academic endeavors: "I see kids in my neighborhood afraid to show how smart they are and the next thing is they're acting stupid in vacant lots and burned-out buildings."

Sometimes the word *culture* is used to refer to behaviors and beliefs that are widely shared over a large geographic area. As an example, *mainstream Western culture* encompasses behaviors, beliefs, and values shared by many people in many North American and western European societies. Among other things, members of this culture generally value self-reliance, democratic decision making, and academic achievement. Other cultures are more local and self-contained. For instance, a culture might be specific to a particular island in the South Pacific. Still others may be *subcultures* that reside within, but are in some ways different from, a more widespread and dominant culture.

Although countries in North America and western Europe share a common mainstream culture, most also have many distinct cultural groups within them. For example, the United States is a nation comprised largely of immigrants and their descendents; only Native Americans lived on U.S. soil before the 1500s. People with a heritage from a particular country or region often form an **ethnic group**—a group of individuals with a common culture and the following characteristics:[38]

- Its roots either precede the creation of or are external to the country in which it currently resides. For example, it may be composed of people of the same race, national origin, or religious background.
- Its members share a sense of interdependence—a sense that their lives are intertwined.

In his high school Spanish class, Ben created this burlap-and-yarn eagle inspired by Mexican designs. The true essence of a cultural group is not found in its art, music, clothing, holiday celebrations, and other observable customs, however. Rather, it comprises the assumptions, beliefs, and values that underlie its members' behaviors and interpretations of the world.

We cannot determine people's ethnicity strictly on the basis of physical characteristics (e.g., race) or birthplace, however. For instance, although my daughter Tina was born in Colombia and has Hispanic and Native American biological ancestors, she was raised by two European American parents. Ethnically, Tina is probably more European American than anything else. In general, we can get the best sense of students' cultural backgrounds and ethnic group memberships by learning the extent to which they have participated and continue to participate in various cultural and ethnic-group activities.[39] Furthermore, some individuals participate actively in two or more cultures or ethnic groups, perhaps because their parents came from distinctly different racial or ethnic backgrounds or perhaps because they encounter new perspectives and ways of doing things as they move from one community or country to another.[40]

The culture(s) and society in which learners participate have numerous effects on their learning and development. We can summarize many of these effects with the following general principles.

The behaviors that others encourage and model are usually compatible with the culture in which they live.

Culture is a phenomenon that is largely unique to the human species.[41] Through its culture a human social group ensures that each new generation benefits from the wisdom that preceding generations have accumulated. For instance, over the years members of any long-standing group have learned that some interpersonal behaviors increase social harmony and thus ensure the group's survival, whereas other behaviors create discord and reduce the group's productivity. Similarly, group members have acquired numerous strategies—for

---

[37] Markus & Hamedani, 2007; Serpell, Baker, & Sonnenschein, 2005; Tudge et al., 1999; Turiel, 2002.
[38] NCSS Task Force on Ethnic Studies Curriculum Guidelines, 1992.
[39] Gutiérrez & Rogoff, 2003.
[40] A. M. Lopez, 2003; Root, 1999.
[41] For a discussion of culture in other primates, see M. Cole, 2006.

ethnic group People who have common historical roots, values, beliefs, and behaviors and who share a sense of interdependence.

preparing a healthful meal, building an energy-efficient home, transporting goods from one place to another, and so on—that enhance the quality and longevity of life, and they have abandoned many other, less effective strategies. By passing along this collective knowledge about what works and what does not, a cultural group increases the chances that it will endure over the long run.

Most members of a cultural group work hard to help growing children adopt the behaviors and beliefs that the group holds dear. Beginning early in life, children learn that there are some things they can or should do and other things they definitely should *not* do, and they acquire a cultural "lens" for viewing social situations and tasks. This process of molding behavior and beliefs so that children fit in with their cultural group is called **socialization**.

Sometimes adults' socialization efforts are obvious. For instance, the message is clear when an adult tells Johnny, "You know that it's not nice to hit other children," and puts Johnny in a time-out room for his aggressive behavior. At other times socialization is more subtle. For example, adults communicate cultural values and beliefs by encouraging and modeling certain activities ("Let's give some of our clothes and toys to the homeless shelter") and discouraging others ("Stay away from that neighborhood; there are drug dealers on every corner").

Children typically learn their earliest lessons about their culture's standards and expectations from parents and other family members, who teach them personal hygiene, table manners, rudimentary interpersonal skills (e.g., saying "please" and "thank you"), and so on. Yet once children begin school, teachers become equally important socialization agents.[42] For instance, many first-grade teachers ask their students to sit quietly rather than interrupt when an adult is speaking, middle school teachers engage students in cooperative learning activities, and high school teachers expect students to turn in homework assignments on time. In doing

Teachers are important socialization agents for growing children. The children in this class have learned two behaviors that are highly valued in many Western classrooms: sitting quietly and paying attention to the speaker.

such things, these teachers communicate important cultural beliefs: that children should defer to and show respect for adults, that cooperation with peers can enhance learning and productivity, and that punctuality is essential for getting ahead in life.

To the extent that a society includes a variety of cultures and ethnic groups, different families will socialize different behaviors and ways of looking at the world. Throughout the book we will examine such diversity in *Cultural Considerations* boxes. The first of these, "Examples of Ethnic Differences" (page 74), gives you a taste of the diversity that teachers are apt to see in school-age children. But as you read the Cultural Considerations boxes in the book, please keep in mind a point made earlier: *Considerable variation exists in the behaviors and beliefs found within a single cultural group.*[43]

Concepts and other cognitive tools are also the products of a culture.

We see obvious effects of culture in many of children's everyday activities—in the books they read, the jokes they tell, the roles they enact in pretend play, the extracurricular activities they pursue, and so on. Yet culture permeates children's thinking processes as well. Earlier I introduced the idea of a *cognitive tool*, a word, concept, mental strategy, or problem-solving procedure that helps a learner interpret and address the situations and problems they face. Such cognitive tools are almost invariably the products of a learner's culture.

As an example of the kinds of cognitive tools that mainstream Western culture provides, try the following exercise.

---

[42] Helton & Oakland, 1977; R. D. Hess & Holloway, 1984; Wentzel & Looney, 2007.

[43] Markus and Hamedani (2007) point out that it is easier to use a label such as "East Asians" than to say "people participating in the ideas and practices that

are pervasive in East Asian cultural contexts" (p. 11). If we're not careful, however, such simple labels can lead us to inaccurately overgeneralize about people from any geographic location or cultural background.

socialization Process of molding a child's behavior and beliefs to be appropriate for the cultural group.

Building a Treehouse

Imagine that you are building a treehouse that has a floor four feet across, a side wall three feet high, and an opposite wall six feet high. You need to buy planks for a slanted roof that will reach from the taller wall to the shorter one. How long must the roof planks be to reach from one wall to the other? Try to solve this problem before you read further.

One way to address the problem is to measure the side walls and floor (which have known dimensions) and determine whether the drawing has been created using a particular scale. In this case the scale is one-fourth of an inch per foot. You could then apply the same scale in estimating the length of the necessary roof planks: Because the roof in the diagram is 1¼ inches long, the actual roof must be five feet long. Another approach involves geometry and algebra. If you have studied geometry, then you've probably learned the *Pythagorean theorem*: In any right triangle, the square of the hypotenuse (the longest side) equals the sum of the squares of the other two sides. Looking at the top part of the treehouse (from the dotted line upward) as a triangle, we can find the length for the roof planks (x) this way:

$$(\text{slanted side})^2 = (\text{horizontal side})^2 + (\text{vertical side})^2$$

$$x^2 = 4^2 + (6 - 3)^2$$

$$x^2 = 16 + 9$$

$$x^2 = 25$$

$$x = 5$$

Regardless of which approach you took, you used several cognitive tools to solve the problem, perhaps the concepts of *measurement*, *inches*, *feet*, and *scale*, or perhaps the *Pythagorean theorem*, the concept of *variable* (x), and algebraic procedures. Mathematics provides innumerable cognitive tools that help people solve a wide variety of problems. In fact, mathematics as a discipline—even such basic elements as numbers and counting—does not exist in the physical, "out there" world. Instead, it is a cultural construction.

Other academic disciplines, too, provide cognitive tools that help people think more effectively about various aspects of their lives. For instance, learners often become better musicians when they can interpret musical notation, understand what *chords* and *thirds* are, and think about particular musical pieces using such concepts. Learners can more easily understand scientific phenomena when they understand and apply concepts such as *force*,

CULTURAL CONSIDERATIONS

Examples of Ethnic Differences

Tremendous cultural variation exists within African American, Asian American, European American, Hispanic, and Native American groups. Thus we must be careful not to form stereotypes about *any* group. At the same time, knowledge of frequently observed differences among ethnic groups can sometimes help us better understand why learners from different backgrounds behave as they do. The following examples illustrate the kinds of cultural and ethnic diversity teachers might see in their classrooms.

Individual versus cooperative efforts.   In a traditional classroom, learning is often a solitary, individual endeavor: Students receive praise, stickers, and good grades when they perform at high levels, regardless of how their classmates perform. Sometimes individual school achievement is even quite competitive, in that students' performance is evaluated by comparing it with the performance of classmates (e.g., teachers grade "on a curve" or post "best" papers on the bulletin board). Yet in some cultures (e.g., in many Native American, Mexican American, African, Southeast Asian, and Pacific Island communities), it is *group* achievement, rather than individual achievement, that is recognized: The success of the village or community is valued over personal success. Students from such cultures are often more accustomed to working cooperatively and for the benefit of the community, rather than for themselves.[a] The Zulu

word *ubuntu*,[b] reflecting the belief that people attain their "humanness" largely through relationships with others and have a responsibility to work for the common good, epitomizes this cooperative spirit.

Eye contact.   For many of us, looking someone in the eye is a way to show that we are trying to communicate or are listening intently to what another person is saying. But in many Native American, African American, Mexican American, and Puerto Rican communities, a child who looks an adult in the eye is showing disrespect. In these communities children are taught to look down in the presence of adults.[c]

Personal space.   In some cultures, such as in some African American and Hispanic communities, people stand close together when they talk and may touch one another frequently.[d] In contrast, European Americans and Japanese Americans tend to keep a fair distance from one another—they maintain some **personal space**—especially if they don't know one another very well.[e]

Public versus private performance.   In many classrooms learning is a very public enterprise: Individual students are often expected to answer questions or demonstrate skills in full view of their classmates, and they are encouraged to ask questions themselves when they don't understand. Such practices, which many teachers take for granted, may

confuse or even alienate the students of some ethnic groups.[f] Many Native American children are accustomed to practicing a skill privately at first, and then performing in front of a group only after they have attained a reasonable level of mastery.[g] And children in some Native American and Hawaiian communities may feel more comfortable responding to an adult's questions as a group rather than interacting with an adult one-on-one.[h]

Family relationships and expectations.   In some groups—for example, in many Hispanic, Native American, and Asian communities, as well as in some rural European American communities—family bonds and relationships are especially important, and extended family members often live nearby. Children raised in these cultures are likely to feel responsibility for their family's well-being and a strong sense of loyalty to other family members. They may exhibit considerable respect for, and also go to great efforts to please, their parents. In some communities it is not unusual for students to leave school when their help is needed at home.[i]

In the opening case study, Ben's refusal to call his parents "silly names like Mom or Dad" showed his high regard for his parents as authority figures. Furthermore, Ben's relatives in New York and China were quite proud that Ben had earned entrance into a very prestigious and selective high school.

gravity, and *chemical reaction*. They can more easily find their way around their community and society when they can read street signs and interpret maps. All of these tools are social inventions that one or more cultures have created to make human endeavors easier or better in some way.

One of the most universal and basic cultural creations—language—provides many cognitive tools that shape growing children's thinking processes. For instance, preschoolers learn to categorize some people as "girls" and others as "boys," and they begin to associate certain behaviors with one sex or the other. Over time, the many words and concepts children acquire—for instance, *snow, yucky, birthday party, bully*—help them interpret and respond to their physical and social experiences in generally adaptive ways.

personal space Personally or culturally preferred distance between two people during social interaction.

In most cultures school achievement is valued highly, and parents encourage their children to do well in school.[j] But in a few groups school achievement may be less valued than achievement in other areas. For example, in some very traditional Native American and Polynesian communities, children are expected to excel in art, dance, and other aspects of their culture rather than in more academic pursuits such as reading or mathematics.[k] And in some African American and Native American families, early pregnancies are cause for joy even if the mothers-to-be have not yet completed high school.[l]

Conceptions of time. Many people regulate their lives by the clock: Being on time to appointments, social engagements, and the dinner table is important. This emphasis on punctuality is not characteristic of all cultures, however. For example, many Hispanic and Native American communities don't observe strict schedules and timelines.[m] Not surprisingly, children from these communities may often be late for school and may have trouble understanding the need to complete school tasks within a certain time frame.

Worldviews. The cultural and ethnic differences we've identified so far reveal themselves, in one way or another, in students' behaviors. Yet recall how our earlier definition of culture included beliefs as well as behaviors. When people's beliefs are related to specific physical, biological, social, or men-

tal phenomena, they are known as *theories* (see Chapter 2). In contrast, a **worldview** is a general set of beliefs and assumptions about reality—about "how things are and should be"—that influences learners' interpretations and understandings of a wide variety of phenomena.[n] Following are examples of beliefs that are apt to be components of a person's worldview:[o]

- Life and the universe came into being through random acts of nature *or* as part of a divine plan and purpose.
- Human beings are at the mercy of the forces of nature *or* must learn to live in harmony with nature *or* should strive to master the forces of nature.
- People's successes and failures in life are the result of their own actions *or* divine intervention *or* fate *or* random occurrences.
- People are most likely to enhance their well-being by relying on scientific principles and logical reasoning processes *or* by seeking guidance from authority figures.

To a considerable degree, such beliefs and assumptions are culturally transmitted, with different cultures communicating somewhat different beliefs and assumptions through adults' day-to-day interactions with children.[p]

Worldviews are often such an integral part of everyday thinking that learners take them for granted and usually aren't consciously aware of them. In many cases, then, worldviews reflect *implicit* rather than explicit learning. Nevertheless they influence learn-

ers' interpretations of current events and classroom subject matter. For instance, students might interpret a hurricane not as the unfortunate result of natural meteorological forces, but instead as divine punishment for their own or other people's wrongdoings.[q] And they may struggle with a science curriculum that explores how human beings can manipulate and gain control over natural events, rather than how people might strive to accept and live in harmony with nature as it is.[r]

[a] Lomawaima, 1995; Mejía-Arauz, Rogoff, Dexter, & Najafi, 2007; Tharp, 1994.
[b] In a professional trip to South Africa in 2005, I was struck by how often this word was used in daily conversation.
[c] Gilliland, 1988; Irujo, 1988; Torres-Guzmán, 1998.
[d] Hale-Benson, 1986; Slonim, 1991; D. W. Sue, 1990.
[e] Irujo, 1988; Trawick-Smith, 2003.
[f] Eriks-Brophy & Crago, 1994; Garcia, 1994; Lomawaima, 1995.
[g] Garcia, 1994; S. Sanders, 1987; Suina & Smolkin, 1994.
[h] K. H. Au, 1980; L. S. Miller, 1995.
[i] Banks & Banks, 1995; Fuligni, 1998; Kağıtçıbaşı, 2007; Timm & Borman, 1997.
[j] Duran & Weffer, 1992; Goldenberg, Gallimore, Reese, & Garnier, 2001; Hossler & Stage, 1992; Okagaki, 2006.
[k] Kirschenbaum, 1989; Reid, 1989.
[l] Deyhle & Margonis, 1995; Stack & Burton, 1993.
[m] H. G. Burger, 1973; Garrison, 1989; Gilliland, 1988.
[n] Koltko-Rivera, 2004.
[o] Kelemen, 2004; Koltko-Rivera, 2004; Losh, 2003; Medin, 2005.
[p] Astuti, Solomon, & Carey, 2004; Koltko-Rivera, 2004; Losh, 2003.
[q] O. Lee, 1999.
[r] Atran, Medin, & Ross, 2005; Medin, 2005.

Inconsistencies between the cultures at home and at school can interfere with maximum learning and performance.

For most children, expectations for behavior are different at school than they are at home. For instance, at home children may be accustomed to speaking whenever they have something to say, but at school there are certain times when silence is golden. Or at home children may be able to choose what they want to do and when to do it, but the school day typically involves a series of tasks that all children must complete within certain time frames. To the extent that behaviors expected at school differ from those allowed or expected at home, children may experience some confusion, or **culture shock**, when they begin school.

worldview General, culturally based set of assumptions about reality that influence understandings of a wide variety of phenomena.

culture shock Sense of confusion when a student encounters a culture with behavioral expectations very different from those previously learned.

Children may experience some culture shock when they begin school, especially if behaviors expected at school are very different from those expected at home.

Culture shock is more intense for some children than for others.[44] Most schools in North America and western Europe are based largely on mainstream Western culture, and so children with this cultural background often adjust fairly quickly to the school environment. But students who come from other cultural backgrounds, especially those with very different views about acceptable behavior, may initially find school a confusing and unsettling place. For example, recent immigrants from other parts of the world may not know what to expect from other people in their new country or what behaviors other people expect of them.[45] Children raised in a culture where gender roles are clearly differentiated—where males and females are socialized to behave very differently—may have difficulty adjusting to a school in which similar expectations are held for both sexes.[46] Any such **cultural mismatch** between home and school cultures can interfere with students' adjustment to the school setting and ultimately with their academic achievement as well.[47] Often children from diverse cultural backgrounds try desperately to fit in at school yet find the inconsistencies between home and school difficult to resolve, as a teacher who has worked with immigrant Muslim children from Pakistan and Afghanistan reports:

> During the days of preparation for Ramadan Feast, the children fasted with the adults. They were awakened by their parents before dawn. They had breakfast and then went back to sleep until it was time to get themselves ready for school. In school they refrained from food or drink—even a drop of water—until sunset. By noon, especially on warm days, they were a bit listless. I had observed that they refrained from praying in a public school even though prayer was a part of their cultural attitude. They spoke about their obligation to pray five times daily. In their writing they expressed the conflict within:
>
> > *I always think about my country. I think about going there one day, seeing it and practicing my religion with no problems. Here we don't have enough priests. We call them mullah. Here we have only the mosque. The mullah is important because we learn the Koran from him. I can't practice my religion. Before sunrise, I can pray with my family. But at school we can't say to my teacher, "Please, teacher, I need to pray."*[48]

As students gain experience with the culture of their school, they become increasingly aware of their teachers' and peers' expectations for behavior and ways of thinking. Many eventually become adept at switching their cultural vantage point as they move from home to school and back again.[49] One Mexican American student's recollection provides an example:

> At home with my parents and grandparents the only acceptable language was Spanish; actually that's all they really understood. Everything was really Mexican, but at the same time they wanted me to speak good English. . . . But at school, I felt really different because everyone was American, including me. Then I would go home in the afternoon and be Mexican again.[50]

Not all students make an easy adjustment, however. Some students actively resist adapting to the existing school culture, perhaps because they view it as being inconsistent with—even contradictory to—their own cultural background and identity.[51] And let's face it: Traditional classrooms don't always encourage behaviors that are in students' long-term best interests. For instance, a classroom that encourages students to compete with one another for grades—rather than fostering the cooperation that many cultural groups value—may engender an unhealthy one-upmanship that interferes with congenial peer relationships both in and outside the classroom.

cultural mismatch Situation in which a child's home culture and the school culture hold conflicting expectations for the child's behavior.

[44] P. M. Cole & Tan, 2007; Kağitçibaşi, 2007; Phalet, Andriessen, & Lens, 2004; Pearce, 2006.

[45] C. R. Harris, 1991; Igoa, 1995.

[46] Kirschenbaum, 1989; Vasquez, 1988.

[47] A. S. Cole & Ibarra, 2005; García, 1995; C. D. Lee & Slaughter-Defoe, 1995; Ogbu, 1992; Phelan, Yu, & Davidson, 1994.

[48] Igoa, 1995, p. 135.

[49] Y. Hong, Morris, Chiu, & Benet-Martínez, 2000; LaFromboise, Coleman, & Gerton, 1993; Phalet et al., 2004; Phelan et al., 1994.

[50] Padilla, 1994, p. 30.

[51] Cross, Strauss, & Fhagen-Smith, 1999; Kumar, Gheen, & Kaplan, 2002; Ogbu, 1999; Phelan et al., 1994.

The problems associated with cultural mismatch can be compounded when teachers misinterpret the behaviors of students from ethnic minority groups. The following exercise provides an example.

Ruckus in the Lunchroom

In the following passage, a young adolescent named Sam is describing an incident in the school cafeteria to his friend Joe:

> I got in line behind Bubba. As usual the line was moving pretty slow and we were all getting pretty restless. For a little action Bubba turned around and said, "Hey Sam! What you doin' man? You so ugly that when the doctor delivered you he slapped your face!" Everyone laughed, but they laughed even harder when I shot back, "Oh yeah? Well, you so ugly the doctor turned around and slapped your momma!" It got even wilder when Bubba said, "Well, man, at least my daddy ain't no girl scout!" We really got into it then. After a while more people got involved—4, 5, then 6. It was a riot! People helping out anyone who seemed to be getting the worst of the deal. All of a sudden Mr. Reynolds the gym teacher came over to try to quiet things down. The next thing we knew we were all in the office. The principal made us stay after school for a week; he's so straight! On top of that, he sent word home that he wanted to talk to our folks in his office Monday afternoon. Boy! Did I get it when I got home. That's the third notice I've gotten this semester. As we were leaving the principal's office, I ran into Bubba again. We decided we'd finish where we left off, but this time we would wait until we were off the school grounds.[52]

- Exactly what happened in the school cafeteria? Were the boys fighting? Or were they simply having a good time?

The story you just read is actually about *playing the dozens*, a friendly exchange of insults common among male youth in some African American communities.[53] Some boys engage in such exchanges to achieve status among their peers—those hurling the most outlandish insults are the winners—whereas others do it simply for amusement. If you interpreted the cafeteria incident as a knock-down-drag-out fight, you're hardly alone, as many eighth graders in a research study did likewise.[54] But put yourself in the place of Sam, the narrator of the story. If you were punished simply for what was, in your mind, an enjoyable verbal competition, you might understandably feel angry and alienated.

Many groups and institutions within a society influence children's learning and development either directly or indirectly.

Any large society, such as a state, province, or nation, provides many "layers" of context that all affect children's learning and development in one way or another.[55] At the most basic level for most children is the *family*, which can potentially support learning in a variety of ways—for instance, by providing a place for children to study, helping with homework assignments, being a "cheerleader" for academic success, and working cooperatively with teachers to address learning and behavior problems. Surrounding the family is another layer, the neighborhood and community, which can offer additional support, perhaps in the form of preschools, after-school homework assistance programs, libraries, museums, zoos, and internships in local businesses. At a still broader level, the state (or province) and country in which children reside influence learning through legislation that governs school policy, tax dollars that flow back to local schools, agencies and professional groups that offer

[52] R. E. Reynolds, Taylor, Steffensen, Shirey, & Anderson, 1982, p. 358.
[53] DeLain, Pearson, & Anderson, 1985; R. E. Reynolds et al., 1982; you may also see the terms *joaning, sounding, signifying,* or *snapping.*
[54] R. E. Reynolds et al., 1982.
[55] Much of the discussion in this section is based on Urie Bronfenbrenner's ecological systems theory and bioecological model; for instance, see Bronfenbrenner, 1989, 2005; Bronfenbrenner & Morris, 1998.

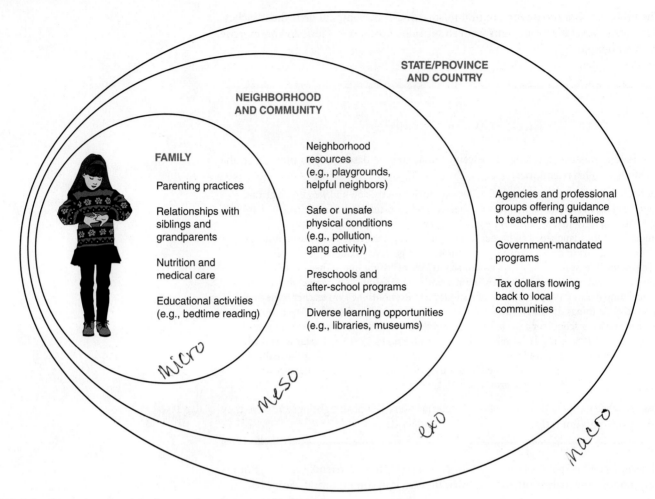

FIGURE 3.2 Examples of various layers of environmental influences

Source: ORMROD, JEANNE E., EDUCATIONAL PSYCHOLOGY: DEVELOPING LEARNERS, 6th, © 2008. Electronically reproduced by permission of Pearson Education, Inc., Upper Saddle River, New Jersey.

information and training in new teaching strategies, and so on. Figure 3.2 illustrates the kinds of environmental influences that the different layers might involve.

In the United States the **Individuals with Disabilities Education Act (IDEA)** provides an example of how national policy can indirectly affect learning. This legislation guarantees that children with disabilities have access to appropriate interventions and services designed to enhance their physical and cognitive development. It also mandates that once these children reach school age, they be educated in their neighborhood schools and with their nondisabled peers to the fullest extent possible—a practice known as *inclusion*. Early intervention clearly *is* effective in enhancing the development of children with a wide variety of special educational needs.[56] Furthermore, many children with disabilities achieve at higher levels when they remain in general education classrooms rather than being segregated into "special" classrooms or schools—something that often happened prior to the legislation's initial enactment in 1975. Placement in regular classes is most successful when instructional materials and practices are tailored to students' specific educational needs and academic levels.[57]

Access to resources at home and in the community also affects learning.

In virtually any society, different learners have access to different resources. For instance, some, but not all, have a quiet place to study and parents who can help them with challenging homework assignments. Some, but not all, have a home computer that provides a vari-

Learn more about IDEA in the supplementary reading "The Individuals with Disabilities Education Act" in the Homework and Exercises section in Chapter 3 of MyEducationLab.

Individuals with Disabilities Education Act (IDEA) U.S. legislation granting educational rights to people with cognitive, emotional, or physical disabilities from birth until age 21; initially passed in 1975, it has been amended and reauthorized several times.

[56] J. M. Fletcher, Lyon, Fuchs, & Barnes, 2007; Kağitçibaşi, 2007; Pelphrey & Carter, 2007.
[57] Halvorsen & Sailor, 1990; Hunt & Goetz, 1997;

Scruggs & Mastropieri, 1994; Slavin, 1987; Stainback & Stainback, 1992.

ety of tools (e.g., word processing programs, electronic encyclopedias, access to the Internet) that can enhance learning and classroom performance. Some, but not all, live near or can easily travel to public libraries, museums, and zoos.

One important factor affecting learners' access to resources is their **socioeconomic status**, often abbreviated as **SES**. This concept encompasses a number of variables, including family income, parents' education levels, and parents' occupations (e.g., whether parents are business executives, teachers, assembly line workers, etc.). Students' school performance is correlated with their socioeconomic status: Higher-SES students tend to have higher academic achievement, and lower-SES students tend to be at greater risk for dropping out of school. As students from lower-SES families move through the grade levels, they fall further and further behind their higher-SES peers. When researchers find achievement differences among students from different ethnic groups, the differences in the students' socioeconomic status, *not* their cultural differences per se, seem to be largely to blame.[58]

Children and adolescents from low-SES families are a diverse group.[59] Many live in inner-city neighborhoods, others live in rural areas, and some live in modest apartments or homes in wealthy suburban towns. Regardless of where they live, these learners may face one or more of the following challenges:

- **Poor nutrition**. Poor nutrition in early childhood is associated with poorer attention and memory and impaired learning ability. Poor nutrition can influence school achievement both directly—for instance, by hampering early brain development— and indirectly—for instance, by leaving children listless and inattentive in class.[60]

- **Inadequate housing.** Many low-SES families live in tight quarters, perhaps sharing only one or two rooms with other family members. In old, poorly maintained apartment buildings, children may be exposed to lead in the dust from deteriorating paint, and such lead can cause brain damage. In addition, if children move frequently from one rental apartment to another, they must often change schools as well. In the process they lose existing social support networks and may miss lessons on important academic skills.[61]

- **Gaps in background knowledge**. Some children from low-SES families lack basic knowledge and skills (e.g., familiarity with letters and numbers) on which successful school learning so often depends.[62] Access to early educational opportunities that might help develop such skills—books, educational toys, trips to zoos and museums, and so on—is always somewhat dependent on a family's financial resources. Furthermore, if parents are preoccupied with providing such basic necessities as food and clothing, they may have little time or energy to consider how they might promote their children's intellectual development. In addition, some parents have few literacy skills to share with their children. We must be careful not to overgeneralize, however. Some low-income parents have considerable education (sometimes they have college degrees) and are in other ways well equipped to read to their children and provide other enriching educational experiences.[63] And as noted in Chapter 2, children from low-income homes are apt to bring other useful knowledge and skills (e.g., more experience with cooking and child care, an ability to improvise with everyday objects) to the classroom.

Visits to museums, zoos, farms, and other local places of interest may be especially beneficial for children from low-income families, who often don't have the financial resources to make such visits on their own.

---

[58] Byrnes, 2003; N. E. Hill, Bush, & Roosa, 2003; Jimerson, Egeland, & Teo, 1999; McLoyd, 1998; L. S. Miller, 1995; Murdock, 2000; Sirin, 2005; Stevenson, Chen, & Uttal, 1990.
[59] Sidel, 1996.
[60] Byrnes, 2001; D'Amato, Chitooran, & Whitten, 1992; L. S. Miller, 1995; Sigman & Whaley, 1998; R. A. Thompson & Nelson, 2001.

[61] Dilworth & Moore, 2006; Hubbs-Tait, Nation, Krebs, & Bellinger, 2005; Knutson & Mantzicopoulos, 1999; Schoon, 2006.
[62] Goldenberg, 2001; Klibanoff, Levine, Huttenlocher, Vasilyeva, & Hedges, 2006; Serpell et al., 2005.
[63] Goldenberg, 2001; Gutman & McLoyd, 2000; Hauser-Cram, Sirin, & Stipek, 2003; McLoyd, 1998; Raikes et al., 2006; Sidel, 1996.

socioeconomic status (SES) One's general social and economic standing in society (encompasses family income, educational level, occupational status, and related factors).

- **Neighborhood influences**. The neighborhoods in which children live can have a significant impact on their academic achievement and emotional well-being. Higher frequencies of community violence, greater prevalence of alcoholism and drug abuse, greater numbers of low-achieving or antisocial peers, fewer academically oriented and prosocial adult role models—all of these make growing up all the more challenging for children and adolescents in low-income neighborhoods.[64] Such problems are compounded when children live near factories or power plants that emit toxic substances negatively impacting their physical health and brain development.[65] And, of course, the dreary physical environments that characterize many low-income inner-city neighborhoods (Sylvia spoke of "vacant lots and burned-out buildings") can be downright depressing.

- **Lower-quality schools**. Unfortunately, children who are in most need of a good education are those least likely to have access to it. Schools in low-SES neighborhoods and communities tend to receive less funding than those in higher-SES areas and, as a result, are often poorly maintained and equipped. Teacher turnover rates are high. Furthermore, some teachers at these schools have lower expectations for students—and so offer a less engaging and challenging curriculum, assign less homework, and provide fewer opportunities to develop advanced thinking skills—than tends to be true for teachers in wealthier school districts.[66]

Children who face only one or two of these challenges often do quite well in school—Ben and Sylvia in the opening case study are two good examples—but those who face most or all of them are at high risk for academic failure.[67] Especially when poverty is an ongoing way of life rather than a temporary state of affairs, children may feel considerable emotional stress about their life circumstances,[68] and as you will discover in Chapter 6, students learn and perform less effectively when they are highly anxious. Not all low-SES children live in chronically stressful conditions, of course, and those whose families provide consistent support, guidance, and discipline (as Ben's and Sylvia's did) generally enjoy good mental health.[69]

HOW LEARNERS AFFECT THEIR ENVIRONMENT

We've examined a variety of ways in which learners' environments—both those that are specific and local and those that are more general and global—can affect learning and behavior. But the reverse is true as well: Learners can have a profound influence on the environments they encounter. The following two principles describe the kinds of influences that learners can have.

Learners alter their environment both through their behaviors and through their internal traits and mental processes.

To some degree learners influence their environments through their behaviors. The responses students make (e.g., the academic classes they choose, the extracurricular activities they pursue, the company they keep) determine the learning opportunities they have and the consequences (e.g., reinforcements and punishments) they experience. But internal cognitive processes and other things that in some way "reside" inside learners come into play as well. For instance, learners are apt to focus their attention on (and so learn from) only certain aspects of their environment (see Chapter 2), and they are more likely to choose activities for which they have expectations of doing well rather than poorly. In fact, all three of these—*environment, behavior*, and learner characteristics (which some theorists call *person* variables)—influence one another. This interdependence among environment, behavior,

---

[64] Cook, Herman, Phillips, & Settersten, 2002; Duncan & Magnuson, 2005; Leventhal & Brooks-Gunn, 2000; Ogbu, 2003; R. J. Rose et al., 2003.

[65] Hemmings, 2004; Hubbs-Tait et al., 2005; Koger, Schettler, & Weiss, 2005.

[66] Becker & Luthar, 2002; Eccles, Wigfield, & Schiefele, 1998; Hemmings, 2004; McLoyd, 1998; Portes, 1996.

[67] Gerard & Buehler, 2004; Grissmer, Williamson, Kirby, & Berends, 1998.

[68] Caspi, Taylor, Moffitt, & Plomin, 2000; McLoyd, 1998.

[69] N. E. Hill et al., 2003.

TABLE 3.3   Mutual Influences (Reciprocal Causation) Among Environment, Behavior, and Person

		General Examples	Examples in Lorraine's Case (Scene One)	Examples in Lorraine's Case (Scene Two)
Effect of Environment	On Behavior	Reinforcement and punishment affect the learner's future behavior.	The teacher's decision to spend most of his time with other students leads to Lorraine's continuing classroom failure.	The teacher's new instructional methods lead to Lorraine's improved academic performance.
	On Person	Feedback from others affects the learner's expectations (either positively or negatively) about future performance.	The teacher's lack of time and effort with Lorraine perpetuates her low self-confidence about classroom tasks.	The teacher's new instructional methods capture Lorraine's interest and attention.
Effect of Behavior	On Environment	Specific behaviors affect the amount of reinforcement and punishment the learner receives.	Lorraine's poor classroom performance initially leads her teacher to meet privately with her, then eventually to ignore her.	Lorraine's improved learning strategies and academic performance lead to more reinforcement from her teacher.
	On Person	Current successes and failures affect the learner's expectations for future performance.	Lorraine's current poor classroom performance leads to her low expectations about future performance.	Lorraine's improved learning strategies and academic performance boost her self-confidence about future classroom performance.
Effect of Person	On Environment	Expectations about future performance in various domains affect the specific activities the learner chooses to engage in and therefore also affect the learning opportunities the learner encounters.	Lorraine's attention to classmates during instructional activities causes her peers to be more influential stimuli than her teacher.	Lorraine's greater attention to classroom activities results in instruction having a stronger impact than it did previously.
	On Behavior	Attention, learning strategies, and other cognitive processes affect the learner's classroom performance.	Lorraine's attention to classmates rather than to instruction leads to her academic failure.	Lorraine's greater self-confidence and increased motivation lead to more regular and effective study habits.

and personal factors is known as **reciprocal causation**.[70] Figure 3.3 illustrates this concept, and several examples of the interplay among the three kinds of variables are presented in the "General Examples" column in Table 3.3.

As a concrete illustration of how environment, behavior, and personal factors are continually intertwined, let's consider "Scene One" in the case of Lorraine:

Scene One

Lorraine often comes late to Mr. Broderick's seventh-grade social studies class, and she is usually ill prepared for the day's activities. In class she spends more time interacting with her friends (e.g., whispering, passing notes) than getting involved in classroom activities. Lorraine's performance on most exams and assignments (when she turns the latter in at all) is unsatisfactory.

One day in mid-October, Mr. Broderick takes Lorraine aside to express his concern about her lack of classroom effort. He suggests that Lorraine could do better if she paid more attention in class. He also offers to work with her twice a week after school to help her understand class material. Lorraine is less optimistic, describing herself as "not smart enough to learn this stuff."

For a week or so after her meeting with Mr. Broderick, Lorraine seems to buckle down and exert more effort, but she never does stay after school for extra help. And before long, Lorraine is back to her old habits. Mr. Broderick eventually concludes that Lorraine is a lost cause and decides to devote his time and effort to helping more motivated students.

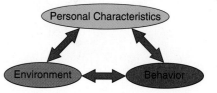

FIGURE 3.3 Environmental, behavioral, and person variables mutually influence one another.

reciprocal causation Mutual cause-and-effect relationships among environment, behavior, and personal variables as these three factors influence learning and development.

[70] Bandura, 1989, 2006.

Lorraine's low expectations for her classroom performance (a *person* factor) may partly explain why she spends so much class time engaged in task-irrelevant activities (*behaviors*). The fact that she devotes her attention (another *person* factor) to her classmates, rather than to her teacher, affects the particular stimuli she experiences (her *environment*). Lorraine's poor study habits and resulting poor performance on assignments and exams (*behaviors*) adversely affect both her expectations for future academic success (*person*) and Mr. Broderick's treatment of her (*environment*). By eventually concluding that Lorraine is a lost cause, Mr. Broderick begins to ignore Lorraine (*environment*), contributing to her further failure (*behavior*) and even lower self-confidence (*person*). (See the "Scene One" column in Table 3.3 for examples of such interactive effects.) Clearly, Lorraine is showing signs of being at risk for long-term academic failure.

But now imagine that after reading several research articles about how to work with students at risk, Mr. Broderick develops greater optimism that he can break the vicious cycle of environment/behavior/person for students such as Lorraine. Midway through the school year, he makes the following changes in his classroom:

- He communicates clearly and consistently that he expects all students to succeed in his classroom.
- He incorporates students' personal experiences and interests into the study of social studies.
- He identifies specific, concrete tasks that students will accomplish each week.
- He provides guidance and structure for how each task should be accomplished.
- After consulting with the school's reading specialist and school psychologist, he helps students develop more effective reading and learning strategies.
- He gives a quiz every Friday so that students can see that they're making progress each week.

Let's see what happens next, as we consider "Scene Two":

Scene Two

By incorporating students' personal experiences and interests into his daily lesson plans, Mr. Broderick starts to capture Lorraine's interest and attention. She begins to realize that social studies has implications for her own life and thus she becomes more involved in classroom activities. With the more structured assignments, better guidance about how to study class material, and frequent quizzes, Lorraine finds herself succeeding in a subject at which she has previously experienced only failure. Mr. Broderick is equally pleased with her performance, something he tells her frequently through his facial expressions, his verbal feedback, and his willingness to provide help whenever she needs it.

By the end of the school year, Lorraine is studying course material more effectively and completing her assignments regularly. She is eagerly looking forward to next year's social studies class, confident that she will continue to do well.

Once again, we see the interplay among environment, behavior, and person. Mr. Broderick's new instructional methods (*environment*) engage Lorraine's attention (*person*), foster better study habits, and enhance academic performance (*behaviors*). Lorraine's improved classroom performance, in turn, influences Mr. Broderick's treatment of her (*environment*) and her own self-confidence (*person*). And her improved self-confidence, her greater attention to classroom activities, and her increased motivation to succeed (all *person* variables) affect her ability to benefit from Mr. Broderick's instruction (*environment*) and thus also affect her classroom success (*behavior*). (See the "Scene Two" column in Table 3.3 for examples of such interactive effects.)

Learners actively seek out environments that are a good fit with their existing characteristics and behaviors.

As children get older, they can increasingly *choose* and thereby control their environments. With such choice and control, they are apt to seek out situations in which they feel comfortable—situations that match their existing abilities, interests, and needs and that allow them to engage in preferred activities. This tendency to seek out environmental conditions that are a good match with existing characteristics and behaviors, a phenomenon known as **niche-picking**, tends to increase existing differences among learners.[71]

For example, as children move through the grade levels, they gain a wider choice of peers with whom they can spend time, and they increasingly affiliate with peers who share their interests and activities. As they reach middle school or junior high, and even more so as they reach high school, they select some of the courses they take—thus, they begin to focus on subject matter that they find appealing and may steer clear of subject matter with which they have previously struggled. As they master public transportation systems or learn how to drive, they have increasing access to environments beyond home and the immediate neighborhood. Some of these environments, such as a library, gymnasium, music studio, or (as in the case of Ben and Sylvia) prestigious high school, can help them acquire valuable new knowledge and skills. Others, such as a gathering place for antisocial peers or an all-night dance party ("rave") where illegal drugs are readily available, can be harmful to their cognitive and social development.

Although children and adolescents influence and control their own environments to some degree, teachers, too, have considerable control over an environment that is a big part of youngsters' daily lives: school. In the following, final section of the chapter we consider strategies for creating a classroom environment that fosters young people's learning, academic achievement, and social success.

PROVIDING SUPPORTIVE CONTEXTS FOR LEARNING

The various "layers" of the environment—from the specific stimuli that learners encounter in their immediate circumstances to the general cultures and societies in which learners live—have numerous implications for classroom practice. The strategies offered in this section fall into three general categories: encouraging productive behaviors, providing physical and social support for effective cognitive processes, and taking into account the broader contexts in which students live.

Encouraging Productive Behaviors

Applying the concepts of *antecedent stimulus*, *reinforcement*, and *modeling* can be quite helpful in encouraging productive behaviors, as the following recommendations reveal.

Create conditions that elicit desired responses.

Early in the chapter we learned that certain stimulus conditions—cooperative toys and games, appropriately guided instruction, and so on—tend to evoke productive behaviors. Furthermore, as we'll discover in Chapter 9, a general classroom climate in which students feel accepted and appreciated by teacher and classmates alike tends to bring out the best in almost everyone.

Sometimes teachers provide explicit reminders about desirable and undesirable behaviors. In the classroom, providing such reminders is known as **cueing**. On some occasions cueing involves a nonverbal signal, such as ringing a bell or flicking an overhead light switch to remind children to talk quietly rather than loudly. At other times it involves a verbal reminder, either direct or indirect, about what children should be doing. In the "Reading Group" video clip in MyEducationLab, a second-grade teacher provides many cues about appropriate behavior, including the following:

- "I called the Tigers. Someone wasn't listening."
- "It's not time to open our books yet."
- "Back on task, Chris. Remember your English work. . . ."

Such statements are examples of the *retrieval cues* we discussed in Chapter 2, although in this case they remind students about appropriate classroom behavior rather than about academic subject matter.

Observe cueing in the "Reading Group" video in the Additional Resources section in Chapter 3 of MyEducationLab.

niche-picking Tendency for a learner to seek out environmental conditions that are a good match with his or her existing characteristics and behaviors.

cueing Use of simple signals to indicate that a certain behavior is desired or that a certain behavior should stop.

[71] Bandura, 2006; Halpern & LaMay, 2000; Petrill & Wilkerson, 2000; Scarr & McCartney, 1983.

Make sure productive behaviors are reinforced and unproductive behaviors are *not* reinforced.

Teachers should be sure that desirable behaviors—reading frequently, constructing a well-researched science fair poster, working cooperatively with classmates, and so on—are regularly reinforced in some way. For reasons we'll explore in our discussion of motivation in Chapter 6, the best reinforcers are intrinsic ones, such as the pleasure one gets from reading, the pride one feels after accomplishing a challenging task, or the internal satisfaction one gains from helping others. But not all classroom tasks and activities can be intrinsically enjoyable and satisfying, and in such cases extrinsic reinforcers—praise, colorful stickers, free time to engage in favorite activities, and so on—can keep students on task as they work to master important information and skills.

Regardless of the form that reinforcement takes, *some* kind of reinforcer should follow desired behaviors. Otherwise, those behaviors might decrease and eventually disappear—a phenomenon known as **extinction**. Initially, to increase the frequency of a desired response, reinforcement should be *continuous*, occurring every time the response occurs. Once a student makes the response frequently, reinforcement can be *intermittent*—that is, given on some occasions but not others—so that the response doesn't extinguish.

At the same time, teachers must not inadvertently reinforce behaviors that will interfere with learners' success over the long run. For example, if a teacher repeatedly allows Carol to turn in assignments late because she says she forgot her homework, and if that teacher often lets Colin get his way by bullying classmates on the playground, the teacher is reinforcing (and hence increasing) Carol's excuse making and Colin's aggressiveness.

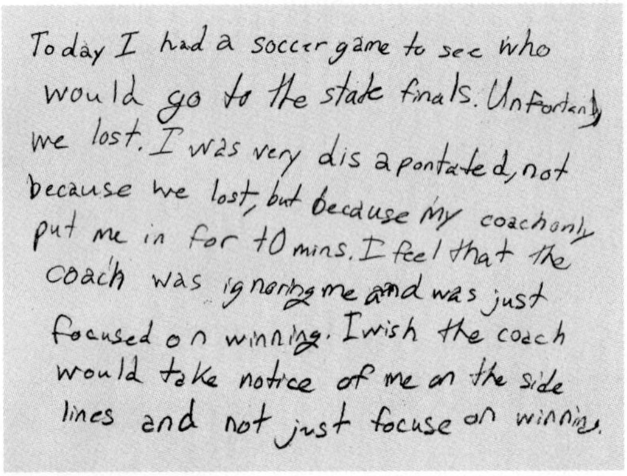

The use of reinforcement is far more effective when reinforcers are tailored to students' developmental levels and individual interests and preferences. How can teachers determine which reinforcers are likely to be effective with particular students? One approach is to ask students themselves (or perhaps ask their parents) about the consequences students find especially appealing. When taking this approach, however, teachers must keep in mind that children do not always have a good sense of which consequences are or will be truly reinforcing for them.[72] Another approach is to observe students' behaviors, keeping a lookout for consequences that students seem to appreciate. Still another is to draw inferences from the things students say and write. For example, in the journal entry in Figure 3.4, it is clear that playing soccer is intrinsically reinforcing for 11-year-old Amie. It appears, too, that Amie appreciates attention from her coach, perhaps in part because it might allow her to gain entry onto the playing field and in part because she would like feedback about what she is doing well and how she might improve her skills. Although Amie might appreciate winning and advancing to the state finals under other circumstances, these things have little appeal if she sits on the sidelines for most of a game.

In some cases teachers can let students choose their own reinforcers and perhaps even choose different reinforcers on different occasions.[73] One useful strategy is a **token economy**, in which students who exhibit desired behaviors receive *tokens* (poker chips, specially marked pieces of colored paper, etc.) that they can later use to "purchase" a variety of *backup reinforcers*—perhaps small treats, free time in the reading center, or a prime position in the lunch line. By and large, however, teachers should stay away from concrete reinforcers such as small toys and trinkets, which can distract students' attention away from their schoolwork. Fortunately, many nontangible reinforcers—for instance, positive feedback, special privileges, or favorite activities—and reinforcement at home for school behaviors can be quite effective with school-age children and adolescents.[74]

Make response-reinforcement contingencies clear.

Whenever teachers use reinforcement in the classroom, they should explicitly describe the cause-and-effect relationships, or **contingencies**, between responses and reinforcers. For example, kindergarten students are more likely to respond appropriately if they are told,

Today I had a soccer game to see who would go to the state finals. Unfortantly we lost. I was very disapontated, not because we lost, but becduse my coach only put me in for 10 mins. I feel that the coach was ignoring me and was just focused on winning. I wish the coach would take notice of me on the side lines and not just focuse on winning.

FIGURE 3.4 In this journal entry, 11-year-old Amie reveals some of the consequences that are reinforcing and punishing for her.

extinction Gradual disappearance of an acquired response; in the case of a response acquired through operant conditioning, it results from repeated lack of reinforcement for the response.

token economy Classroom strategy in which desired behaviors are reinforced by tokens that the learner can use to "purchase" a variety of other, backup reinforcers.

contingency Situation in which one event (e.g., reinforcement) happens only after another event (e.g., a specific response) has already occurred (one event is *contingent* on the other's occurrence).

---

[72] Atance & Meltzoff, 2006; Northup, 2000.
[73] Bowman, Piazza, Fisher, Hagopian, & Kogan, 1997; Fisher & Mazur, 1997.

[74] Feltz et al., 1999; Homme, deBaca, Devine, Steinhorst, & Rickert, 1963; Kelley & Carper, 1988.

"The quietest group will be first to get in line for lunch." Ninth graders are likely to complete their Spanish assignments if they know that by doing so they will be able to take a field trip to a local Cinco de Mayo festival. In the "Reading Group" video clip in MyEducationLab, a second-grade teacher is quite explicit in the behaviors she praises. For example, she says, "I like the way you're working quietly" and "You should see Ricky being so polite. Thank you, Ricky, for not disturbing the rest of the class."

One way of explicitly communicating expectations for behavior and response-reinforcement contingencies is a **contingency contract**. To develop such a contract, the teacher meets with a student to discuss a problem behavior (e.g., talking to friends during independent seatwork or making rude comments to classmates). The teacher and student then identify and agree on desired behaviors that the student will demonstrate (e.g., completing seatwork assignments within a certain time frame or speaking with classmates in a friendly, respectful manner). The two also agree on one or more reinforcers for those behaviors (e.g., a certain amount of free time, or points earned toward a particular privilege or prize) that the student values. Together the teacher and student write and sign a contract that describes the behaviors the student will perform and the reinforcers that will result. Contingency contracts can be a highly effective means of improving a wide variety of academic and social behaviors.[75]

Observe explicit praise in the "Reading Group" video in the Additional Resources section in Chapter 3 of MyEducationLab.

As an alternative to punishment, reinforce productive behaviors that are incompatible with unproductive ones.

As mentioned earlier, certain forms of punishment can be effective in reducing inappropriate behaviors, and in some instances punishment may be a teacher's only alternative (we'll look at the use of punishment more closely in Chapter 9). Oftentimes, however, rather than using punishment, a teacher can reduce the frequency of an unproductive behavior simply by reinforcing a *different* behavior. Ideally, the two behaviors are **incompatible behaviors**, in that they cannot be performed simultaneously. To discover examples of incompatible behaviors in your own life, try the following exercise.

SEE FOR YOURSELF
Asleep on Your Feet

Have you ever tried to sleep while standing up? Horses can do it, but most of us humans really can't. In fact, there are many pairs of responses that we can't possibly perform simultaneously. Take a minute to identify something you cannot possibly do when you perform each of these activities:

When you:	You cannot simultaneously:
Sit down	_____
Eat crackers	_____
Take a walk	_____

Obviously, there are no single "right" answers in this exercise. As one possibility, you might have said that sitting is incompatible with standing. Eating crackers is incompatible with singing, or at least with singing *well*. Taking a walk is incompatible with taking a nap. In each case it is physically impossible to perform both activities at exactly the same time.

To apply the concept of incompatible behaviors in the classroom, a teacher might, for example, reinforce a hyperactive student for sitting down, because sitting is incompatible with getting-out-of-seat and roaming-around-the-room behaviors. Similarly, a teacher might discourage off-task responses by reinforcing *on*-task responses or discourage verbally

contingency contract Formal agreement between teacher and student that identifies behaviors the student will exhibit and the reinforcers that will follow.

incompatible behaviors Two or more behaviors that cannot be performed simultaneously.

[75] Brooke & Ruthren, 1984; D. L. Miller & Kelley, 1994; Rueger & Liberman, 1984; Welch, 1985.

aggressive behavior by reinforcing socially appropriate actions. And consider how one school dealt with a chronic litterbug:

> Walt was a junior high school student who consistently left garbage (banana peels, sunflower seed shells, etc.) on the lunchroom floor, in school corridors, and on the playground. When the school faculty established an "anti-litter" committee, it decided to put Walt on the committee, and the committee eventually elected Walt as its chairman. Under Walt's leadership, the committee instituted a massive anti-litter campaign, complete with posters and lunchroom monitors, and Walt received considerable recognition for the campaign's success. Curiously (or perhaps not), school personnel no longer found Walt's garbage littering the school grounds.[76]

Model desired behaviors.

As we've seen, teachers "teach" not only by what they say but also by what they do. It is critical that teachers model appropriate behaviors and *not* model inappropriate ones. Do they model enthusiasm and excitement about the subject matter or merely tolerance for a dreary topic the class must somehow muddle through? Do they model fairness to all students or favoritism to a small few? Do they expound on the virtues of innovation and creativity yet use the same curriculum materials year after year? Their actions often speak louder than their words.

Four conditions help students learn effectively from models:[77]

"Chicken"   "Airplane"   "Soldier"

FIGURE 3.5 Students can often more easily remember a complex behavior, such as the arm movements for the elementary backstroke, when those behaviors have verbal labels.

- **Attention**. As we discovered in Chapter 2, attention is critical for getting information into working memory. To learn effectively, then, a learner must pay attention to the model and especially to critical aspects of the modeled behavior.

- **Retention**. To learn from a model, the learner must retain (remember) what the model does—in particular, by storing it in long-term memory. As noted in Chapter 2, students are more likely to remember information when they encode it in more than one way, perhaps as both a visual image and a verbal message. For instance, teachers may want to talk about what they're doing while they demonstrate a particular skill. Teachers may also want to give descriptive labels to complex behaviors that might otherwise be difficult to remember.[78] For example, when teaching swimming, an easy way to help students remember the sequence of arm positions in the elementary backstroke is to teach them the labels *chicken*, *airplane*, and *soldier* (see Figure 3.5).

- **Motor reproduction**. In addition to attending and remembering, the learner must be physically capable of reproducing the modeled behavior. When a student lacks the ability to reproduce an observed behavior, motor reproduction obviously cannot occur. For example, kindergartners who watch a high school student throw a softball do not possess the muscular coordination to mimic the throw. It is often useful to have students imitate a desired behavior immediately after they see it modeled. When they do so, their teachers can give them the feedback they need to improve their performance. Yet teachers must keep in mind a point made in the earlier Cultural Considerations box: Students from some ethnic groups may prefer to practice new behaviors in private at first and to demonstrate what they've learned only after they've achieved some degree of competence.

- **Motivation**. Finally, the learner must be motivated to demonstrate the modeled behavior. In Chapter 6 we'll identify numerous strategies for increasing students' motivation to exhibit the academic and social skills they learn in the classroom.

Provide a variety of role models.

In addition to modeling desired behaviors themselves, teachers should expose students to other models whom students are apt to perceive as competent and prestigious. For example, teachers might invite respected professionals (e.g., police officers, nurses, newspaper re-

[76] Krumboltz & Krumboltz, 1972.
[77] Bandura, 1986.
[78] Gerst, 1971; T. L. Rosenthal, Alford, & Rasp, 1972.

porters) to demonstrate skills within particular areas of expertise. They might also have students read about or observe positive role models through such media as books and films. For instance, students might read Helen Keller's autobiography or watch news clips of Martin Luther King, Jr.

Furthermore, students can benefit from observing the final products of a model's efforts. Art students might gain useful strategies by studying the works of such masters as Vincent Van Gogh and Paul Gauguin, and music students can acquire new strategies by listening to skillful musicians with diverse musical styles. In one seventh-grade language arts class, students found examples of figurative writing in favorite books (see Figure 3.6), and such examples served as models for their own writing efforts.

Recall that one of the characteristics of effective models listed earlier in the chapter was *behavior relevant to one's own situation*. Students are less likely to perceive a model's behaviors as relevant to their own circumstances if the model is different from them in some obvious way. For instance, students from a lower socioeconomic neighborhood or ethnic minority group won't necessarily see the actions of a middle-income European American as being useful for themselves. Similarly, students with disabilities may believe that they are incapable of accomplishing the things a nondisabled teacher demonstrates. So it's important that teachers include individuals from lower-SES backgrounds and minority-group cultures, as well as individuals with disabilities, in the models they present to students. Minority-group students benefit from observing successful minority-group adults, and students with disabilities become more optimistic about their own futures when they meet adults successfully coping with and overcoming their own disabilities.[79]

The blackness of the night came in, like snakes around the ankles."
—Caroline Cooney, *Wanted*, p. 176

"Flirtatious waves made passes at the primly pebbled beach."
—Lilian Jackson Braun, *The Cat Who Saw Stars*, p. 120

"Water boiled up white and frothy, like a milkshake."
—Lurlene McDaniel, *For Better, for Worse, Forever*, p. 60

"Solid rocket boosters suddenly belched forty-four million horsepower."
—Ben Mikaelsen, *Countdown*, p. 148

"I try to swallow the snowball in my throat."
—Laurie Halse Anderson, *Speak*, p. 72

FIGURE 3.6 Students in Barbara Dee's seventh-grade language arts class chose these models of effective figurative writing from books they were reading.

Shape complex behaviors gradually over time.

When dramatic changes are necessary, it's unreasonable to expect students to make them overnight. A teacher who wants students to exhibit behavior radically different from what they're currently doing may need to use a process called **shaping**. To shape a desired behavior, the teacher takes the following steps:

1. First, reinforce any response that in some way resembles the desired behavior.
2. Then reinforce a response that more closely approximates the desired behavior (no longer reinforcing the previously reinforced response).
3. Then reinforce a response that resembles the desired behavior even more closely.
4. Continue reinforcing closer and closer approximations to the desired behavior.
5. Finally reinforce only the desired behavior.

Each response in the sequence is reinforced every time it occurs until the student exhibits it regularly. Only at that point does the teacher begin reinforcing a behavior that more closely approaches the desired behavior.

For example, imagine that a student, Bernadette, can't seem to sit still long enough to get much of anything done. Her teacher would ultimately like her to sit still for 20-minute periods. However, the teacher may first have to reinforce her for staying in her seat for just 2 minutes. The teacher can gradually increase the "sitting" time required for reinforcement as Bernadette makes progress.

Shaping is often used to teach academic skills as well as appropriate classroom behaviors. For instance, kindergartners and first graders are taught to write their letters on wide-lined paper, and they are praised for well-formed letters whose bottoms rest on one line and whose tops touch a higher line. As children progress through the grade levels, the spaces between the lines become smaller, and teachers become fussier about how letters are formed. Most children begin to write consistently sized and carefully shaped letters with the benefit of only a lower line, and eventually they need no line at all. In Figure 3.7 you can see how my son Jeff's handwriting was gradually shaped from first to fourth grade. (The changing nature of the lines is an example of *scaffolding*, a concept we'll discuss in Chapter 5.)

---

[79] Pang, 1995; Powers, Sowers, & Stevens, 1995.

shaping Process of reinforcing successively closer and closer approximations to a desired behavior.

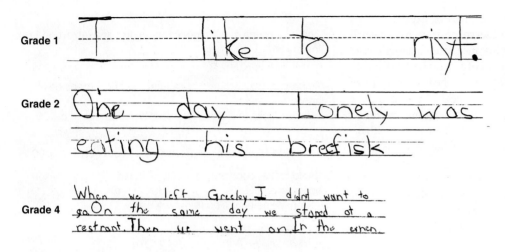

Grade 1

Grade 2

Grade 4

FIGURE 3.7   As Jeff moved through the elementary grades, gradual changes in his writing paper required him to write smaller and, eventually, with only a single line to guide him.

In much the same way, teachers can (and often do) gradually shape students' ability to work independently on academic assignments. They begin by giving first graders structured tasks that may take only 5 to 10 minutes to complete. As students move through the elementary school years, their teachers expect them to work independently for longer periods and begin to give them short assignments to do at home. By the time students reach high school, they have extended study halls and complete lengthy assignments on their own after school hours. In the college years, student assignments require a great deal of independence and self-direction.

Have students practice new behaviors and skills in a variety of contexts.

As noted earlier in the chapter, learning and cognition are sometimes *situated* in particular contexts. For instance, students may recall the Pythagorean theory *only* in a math class, rather than also using it to determine the length of a treehouse roof. And they may apply what they've learned about persuasive writing only in writing essays in a language arts class, rather than also using it to evaluate political campaign brochures and newspaper editorials. If teachers want students to use what they've learned in many situations both in and out of school, they should give students practice using the subject matter with a variety of stimulus materials and in many different contexts. We'll explore this idea further in our discussions of *transfer* and *authentic activities* in Chapter 4.

The Classroom Strategies box "Capitalizing on Stimulus–Response Relationships to Encourage Productive Behaviors" illustrates some of the preceding recommendations and offers additional ones as well.

Providing Physical and Social Support for Effective Cognitive Processes

Environmental contexts, both past and present, affect not only students' behaviors but also their thinking processes, as reflected in the next three recommendations.

Provide physical and cognitive tools that can help students work and think more effectively.

No other species can compare to the human race in its use of tools to facilitate daily living. Some tools—such as paper, pencils, and scissors—are strictly physical objects. Others—such as concepts, mathematical formulas, and study strategies—are entirely cognitive in nature. Still others—such as dictionaries, maps, flowcharts, and computers—are *both* physical and cognitive, in that they are physical manifestations of concepts, formulas, thought processes, and other forms of human cognition. Virtually all of the tools that students learn to use are the cultural legacies of previous generations. And all of them can greatly enhance students' ability to solve problems, communicate with one another, and, more generally, thrive and prosper.

Encourage student dialogue and collaboration.

We have already identified numerous advantages to having learners talk with one another about classroom topics. And, in fact, students *do* seem to remember new ideas and experiences more effectively and accurately when they talk about these things with others.[80] Accordingly,

---

[80] Hacker, 1998; Schank & Abelson, 1995; Tessler & Nelson, 1994; Wasik, Karweit, Burns, & Brodsky, 1998.

CLASSROOM STRATEGIES

Capitalizing on Stimulus–Response Relationships to Encourage Productive Behaviors

- **Cue appropriate behaviors.**

  As students are busily working on cooperative small-group projects, their teacher notices that one group's discussion is being dominated by a single student. She announces to the class, "Please remember a point I made earlier: You are more likely to create a good product if *all* group members contribute their ideas."

- **Reinforce desired behaviors.**

  To a student who has just completed an excellent oral book report, a teacher says, "Nice job, Monica. You made the book sound so interesting. *I* certainly want to read it now, and I suspect that many of your classmates do as well."

- **Remember that students differ in the consequences they find reinforcing.**

  A teacher allows students to engage in favorite activities during the free time they earn each day. Some students work on the classroom computer, others work on art projects, and still others quietly converse with friends.

- **Follow through with the reinforcements you have promised for desirable student behaviors. Also follow through with the adverse consequences students expect for undesirable behaviors.**

  When announcing tryouts for an upcoming holiday play, a teacher tells students that only those who sign up ahead of time may try out. Although she later regrets making this statement—some of the most talented students don't sign up in time—she sticks to her word during tryout sessions and gently turns away anyone whose name does not appear on her sign-up sheet.

- **Describe the specific behaviors you are reinforcing, so that students are aware of the response-reinforcement contingencies operating in the classroom.**

  A teacher tells his class, "Because everyone remained on task throughout the cooperative group activity this morning, we'll have ten minutes of free time just before lunch."

- **Give feedback about specific behaviors rather than general areas of performance.**

  As his students are cleaning up after a class art project, a teacher says, "I like how everyone is remembering to pick up the scraps of paper around their desks. And look at how LaMarr and Julia are collecting every group's paintbrushes and glue bottles without my having to ask them!"

- **Keep in mind that students can experience consequences not only directly but also vicariously—that is, by watching what happens to their peers.**

  The student council president, even though she is well liked and highly respected by both students and teachers, is nevertheless punished in accordance with school policy when she is caught cheating on an exam.

- **Provide opportunities for students to practice desired behaviors in a variety of contexts.**

  When teaching social skills to a group of students who have difficulty getting along with peers, a school counselor conducts role-playing activities in which the students practice giving compliments, listening to others' perspectives, resolving social conflicts, and so on. The counselor discreetly observes the students as they practice their new skills in the classroom, lunchroom, and school yard and gives them feedback and suggestions in later group meetings.

- **Once students are exhibiting a desired behavior frequently, continue to reinforce it intermittently to prevent extinction.**

  Over a three-month period, a teacher has taught a distractible second grade student to stay on task for longer and longer time periods. The student can now stay on task for 20 to 30 minutes at a stretch, which is quite sufficient for most independent seatwork assignments in the class. Throughout the rest of the year, the teacher continues to praise the student at least once a week for his on-task behavior.

---

many theorists recommend that classroom dialogues be a regular feature of classroom instruction. For example, in the "Scarlet Letter" video clip in MyEducationLab, you can see how high school English teacher Sue Southam encourages students to construct a better understanding of the character Arthur Dimmesdale in Nathaniel Hawthorne's *The Scarlet Letter*. She reads a paragraph in the novel that describes Dimmesdale's character and then says:

> Jot down some of the important characteristics of that description. What's the diction that strikes you as being essential to understanding Dimmesdale's character? How do you see him? If you were going to draw a portrait of him, what would you make sure he had? . . . Just write some things, or draw a picture if you'd like.

Ms. Southam walks around the room, monitoring what students are doing until they appear to have finished writing. She then promotes the following discussion:

Ms. Southam: What pictures do you have in your minds of this man . . . if you were directing a film of *The Scarlet Letter*?

Mike: I don't have a person in mind, just characteristics. About five-foot-ten, short, well-groomed hair, well dressed. He looks really nervous and inexperienced. Guilty look on his face. Always nervous, shaking a lot. . . .

Mrs. Southam: He's got a guilty look on his face. His lips always trembling, always shaking.

Mike: He's very unsure about himself.

Observe a teacher encourage student dialogue in the "Scarlet Letter" video in the Additional Resources section in Chapter 3 of MyEducationLab.

Matt: Sweating really bad. Always going like this. (He shows how Dimmesdale might be wiping his forehead.) He does . . . he has his hanky. . . .

Ms. Southam: Actually, we don't see him mopping his brow, but we do see him doing what? What's the action? Do you remember? If you go to the text, he's holding his hand over his heart, as though he's somehow suffering some pain.

Student: Wire-framed glasses. . . . I don't know why. He's like. . . .

Mike: He's kind of like a nerd-type guy. . . . Short pants. Michael J. Fox's dad. . . . (Mike is referring to a nerdish character in the film *Back to the Future.*)

Ms. Southam: With the short pants and everything.

Student: Yeah, George McFly. (Student identifies the nerdish character's name in the film.)

Ms. Southam: George McFly in his younger years. But at the same time . . . I don't know if it was somebody in this class or somebody in another class when we had all these pictures up here on the wall that characterize this woman. I guess it was one of the guys in fourth period. . . . He said, "Well, she was sure *worth* it." Worth risking your immortal soul for, you know? . . . Obviously she's sinned, but so has he, right? And if she was worth it, don't we also have to see him as somehow having been worthy of her risking *her* soul for this?

By hearing such diverse ideas, students can gain an increasingly complex, multifaceted understanding of Dimmesdale that probably includes both verbal concepts (e.g., *unsure, nerd*) and visual images. (We'll revisit this dialogue in a Practice for Your Licensure Exam exercise in Chapter 7, but at that point we'll look at it from a very different angle.)

In the *Scarlet Letter* lesson, the teacher is actively involved in facilitating student discussion. Yet students can also co-construct understandings without teacher assistance, as we saw earlier in a small-group discussion of a math problem involving apple tarts. With or without teacher assistance, classroom dialogues can help students master classroom subject matter, perhaps by acquiring more sophisticated interpretations of literature or developing greater conceptual understanding of what it means to divide by a fraction.[81] Classroom dialogues have an important benefit for teachers as well: By carefully monitoring students' comments and questions, teachers can identify and address any misconceptions that might interfere with students' ability to acquire further knowledge and skills.[82]

Create a community of learners.

With the benefits of student dialogue in mind, and with the goal of promoting social co-construction of meaning, some psychologists and educators suggest that teachers create a **community of learners**, a classroom in which teachers and students collaborate to build a body of knowledge and consistently work to help one another learn.[83] A classroom that operates as a community of learners is likely to have characteristics such as the following:

- All students are active participants in classroom activities.
- The primary goal is to acquire a body of knowledge on a specific topic, with students contributing to and building on one another's efforts.
- Discussion and collaboration among two or more students are common occurrences and play a key role in learning.
- Diversity in students' interests and rates of progress is expected and respected.
- Students and teacher coordinate their efforts at helping one another learn. No one has exclusive responsibility for teaching others.
- Everyone is a potential resource for the others. Different individuals are likely to serve as resources on different occasions, depending on the topics and tasks at hand. In some cases students may "major" in a particular topic and become local "experts" on it.
- The teacher provides some guidance and direction for classroom activities, but students may also contribute to such guidance and direction.
- Students regularly critique one another's work.
- The process of learning is emphasized as much as, and sometimes more than, the finished product.

community of learners Class in which teacher and students actively and collaboratively work to create a body of knowledge and help one another learn.

[81] Eeds & Wells, 1989; E. H. Hiebert & Raphael, 1996; J. Hiebert et al., 1997; Keefer, Zeitz, & Resnick, 2000; Lampert, Rittenhouse, & Crumbaugh, 1996.
[82] Presseisen & Beyer, 1994; Sosniak & Stodolsky, 1994.
[83] Bielaczyc & Collins, 2006; A. L. Brown & Campione, 1994; Campione, Shapiro, & Brown, 1995; A. Collins, 2006; Engle, 2006; Hewitt & Scardamalia, 1998; Prawat, 1992; Rogoff, 1994; Rogoff, Matusov, & White, 1996.

As one example of how a community of learners might be structured, students are divided into small groups to study different subtopics falling within a general theme. For instance, subtopics for the theme *changing populations* might be *extinct, endangered, artificial, assisted,* and *urbanized.* Each group conducts research and prepares teaching materials related to its subtopic. The class then reassembles into new groups that include at least one representative from each of the previous groups, and within these groups the students teach one another what they have learned.[84]

Some teachers use a computer network to create a community of learners.[85] In such an electronic environment, students post their work (notes, short stories, reports, problem solutions, diagrams and flowcharts related to scientific phenomena, etc.) as computer files that their classmates can read, react to, and possibly modify or build on. Students also interact in an ongoing computer-based "chat room" in which they present questions or issues to which their classmates respond. As an example, consider three students' online responses to another student's question, "How does heat affect solids?"; note that they use the headings "My theory" and "I need to understand" to structure their discussion:

JA: *My theory:* I think that heat makes solids burn or melt. I think that my prediction is right because I've seen solids melt and burn.

AR: *My theory:* I think that if a solid comes in contact with heat, it becomes hot. I also think it might change colour. Generally if any solid comes in contact with heat then it becomes hot. I think that the solid would become hot faster if it could conduct energy well. If an object didn't conduct energy well then it would heat up, but take a longer time than an object that conducts energy well. It might change colour because we think that if something is very hot it is white or red and sort of hot it is orange or yellow. There might be some truth to this.

AD: *My theory:* I think that it depends on how much heat there is. I also think that it depends on what sort of solid it is. For instance, the heat that might melt rubber might not melt metal. (This last sentence might be wrong, I'm just using it as an example.)

I need to understand: What makes wood burn instead of melt?

My theory: I think that it might have something to do with wood being organic, because I can't think of anything that is organic, and would melt.[86]

Such online discussions may be particularly beneficial for students who are shy or for other reasons feel uncomfortable communicating with their classmates in a more public fashion.[87]

A classroom organized as a community of learners tends to be highly motivating for students, and it can promote fairly complex thinking processes for extended time periods.[88] In addition to its motivational and cognitive benefits, a community of learners can foster productive peer relationships and create a *sense of community* in the classroom—a sense that teachers and students have shared goals, are mutually respectful and supportive of one another's efforts, and believe that everyone makes an important contribution to classroom learning. We'll look at this idea more closely in Chapter 9.

A community of learners can be especially worthwhile when a classroom includes students from diverse cultural and socioeconomic backgrounds.[89] Such a community values the contributions of all students, using everyone's individual backgrounds, cultural perspectives, and unique abilities to enhance the overall performance of the class. It also provides a context in which students can form friendships across the lines of ethnicity, gender, socioeconomic status, and disability.

Yet we should note a couple of potential weaknesses that communities of learners, and peer-group discussions more generally, may have.[90] For one thing, what students learn will inevitably be limited to the knowledge that they themselves acquire and share with one another. Second, students may occasionally pass their misconceptions along to their classmates.

[84] A. L. Brown & Campione, 1994.

[85] Bereiter & Scardamalia, 2006; Hewitt & Scardamalia, 1998; Scardamalia & Bereiter, 2006; Stahl, Koschmann, & Suthers, 2006.

[86] Dialogue from Hewitt & Scardamalia, 1998, p. 85.

[87] Hewitt & Scardamalia, 1998.

[88] A. L. Brown & Campione, 1994; Rogoff, 1994.

[89] Garcia, 1994; Ladson-Billings, 1995.

[90] A. L. Brown & Campione, 1994; Hynd, 1998b.

Obviously, then, when teachers conduct classroom discussions or structure classrooms as communities of learners, they must carefully monitor student discussions to make sure that students ultimately acquire *accurate* understandings of the subject matter they are studying.

Taking into Account the Broader Contexts in Which Students Live

Students' learning and classroom achievement is influenced by what goes on *outside* as well as inside the classroom—by students' cultural groups, neighborhoods, and so on. The last set of recommendations reflects this idea.

Learn as much as you can about students' cultural backgrounds, and come to grips with your own cultural lens.

As people who grow up within a particular culture, we often interpret others' behaviors within the context of what our own culture deems to be appropriate and inappropriate. As an example, try one final exercise.

SEE FOR YOURSELF
Jack

Imagine that you are working as a seventh-grade teacher in a Navajo school district in the American Southwest. One of your students, Jack, is a good-natured young man who seems to enjoy school, works hard in his studies, and gets along well with his classmates. But Jack has been absent from school all week. In fact, he hasn't even been home all week. His family (which doesn't have a telephone) isn't sure exactly where he is but doesn't seem to be in any rush to find him.

A few days later, Jack's sister explains that her parents are now looking for Jack. "He went to see *Rambo II* with friends and never came home," she says. "If he was in trouble we would know. But now the family needs him to herd sheep tomorrow."[91] It is spring—time for the family to plant crops and shear the sheep—and all family members need to help out.

The parents soon locate Jack but keep him home for several days to help irrigate the family's corn field. It's another week before he returns to school.[92]

- With this information in mind, what might you conclude about Jack and his parents?

If you are a product of mainstream Western culture, you may have concluded that Jack and his parents don't place much value on formal education. If so, your conclusion was based on two widely held beliefs in your culture: (a) School should take priority over activities at home and elsewhere, and (b) responsible parents insist that their children attend school. In reality, most Navajo children and adults fully recognize the importance of a good education. To truly understand what has transpired in Jack's family, we need to know a couple of things about Navajo culture. First, Navajos place high value on individual autonomy: People must respect others' right (even children's right) to make their own decisions.[93] From this perspective, good parenting does not mean demanding that children do certain things or behave in certain ways—thus, Jack's parents do not insist that Jack come home after the movie. Instead, Navajo parents offer suggestions and guidance that nudge children toward productive choices. If children make poor decisions despite their parents' guidance, they often learn a great deal from the consequences.

But in addition to individual autonomy, Navajos value cooperation and interdependence, believing that community members should work together for the common good. Even though Jack enjoys school, when he returns home his highest priority must be to help

---

[91] Deyhle & LeCompte, 1999, p. 127.
[92] Case of Jack described by Deyhle & LeCompte, 1999, pp. 127–128.

[93] Deyhle & LeCompte, 1999.

his family. In the Navajo view, people must cooperate of their own free will; being forced to help others is not true cooperation at all. Such respect for both individual autonomy and cooperative interdependence is seen in certain other Native American cultures as well.[94]

When people act in accordance with beliefs, values, and social conventions very different from our own, it is all too easy for us to write them off as being "odd," "unmotivated," or "negligent." The assumptions and beliefs we have acquired in our own culture—perhaps including an assumption that good parents "control" their children—are often integral parts of our own culturally based worldviews. As such, they are apt to be so pervasive in our lives that we tend to treat them as common sense, or even as facts, rather than as the beliefs they really are. These beliefs become a *cultural lens* through which we view events, and they may lead us to conclude that other groups' practices are somehow irrational and inferior to our own. As one sociocultural theorist has put it, "Like the fish that is unaware of water until it has left the water, people often take their own community's ways of doing things for granted."[95] Only when we find ourselves in a very different cultural environment can we truly begin to understand how we, too, are very much a product of our own culture.

Teachers can most effectively work with students when they understand the fundamental assumptions and beliefs that underlie students' behavior and recognize that their *own* assumptions and beliefs are not necessarily the only "right" ones. To some degree, teachers can learn about their students' cultures by reading about various cultures in books and journals and on Internet Web sites. But perhaps even more helpful is immersing oneself directly in another culture, perhaps by participating in local community activities and conversing regularly with community members.[96]

Remember that membership in a particular cultural or ethnic group is not an either-or situation; rather, it is a more-or-less phenomenon.

As noted earlier in the chapter, individuals vary considerably in how much they *participate* in various cultural and ethnic-group activities. The extent of their participation inevitably affects the strengths of their culture-specific behaviors and beliefs. For instance, some Mexican American students live in small, close-knit communities where Spanish is spoken and traditional Mexican practices and beliefs permeate everyday life, but others live in more culturally heterogeneous communities in which Mexican traditions are often cast aside. Likewise, some students who have recently emigrated from another country hold steadfastly to the customs and values of their homeland, whereas others eagerly adopt some of the customs and habits of their new school and community.[97]

Be sensitive to cultural differences, and accommodate them as much as possible.

If students are to be successful at school and in mainstream Western culture, their teachers must foster certain behaviors—being punctual, working independently, and so on—that will make success possible. At the same time, teachers must recognize that not all cultures place the same premium on such behaviors that mainstream Western culture does. Accordingly, teachers must be patient and supportive if students sometimes change their work habits only slowly over time.

Yet many cultural differences in behavior are simply that—*differences*—and have no adverse effect on learning and school performance. For instance, whether students look a teacher in the eye and whether they tend to keep more or less personal space between themselves and others are largely matters of personal preference. Teachers can readily accommodate such differences in their interactions with students. The following anecdote shows how a teacher's sensitivity to one student's cultural background had considerable impact:

> A teacher [described a Native American] student who would never say a word, nor even answer when she greeted him. Then one day when he came in she looked in the other direction and said, "Hello, Jimmy." He answered enthusiastically, "Why hello Miss Jacobs." She found

In some cultures (e.g., in many Native American communities), children are taught to look down as a sign of respect to an adult who speaks to them.

[94] Chisholm, 1996; Rogoff, 2003.

[95] Rogoff, 2003, p. 13.

[96] McCarty & Watahomigie, 1998; Rogoff, 2003; H. L. Smith, 1998.

[97] McBrien, 2005; S. M. Quintana et al., 2006.

that he would always talk if she looked at a book or at the wall, but when she looked at him, he appeared frightened.[98]

To maximize students' learning, cultural differences in worldviews must be accommodated as well. For example, underlying the traditional European American approach to teaching American history is a subtle message of "increasing progress and freedom" from the 1500s to the present time. A more balanced, multicultural approach would involve taking the perspectives of Native Americans and African Americans into account—perspectives that might include themes related to invasion, oppression, and inequality.[99] Students' worldviews may also include strong religious beliefs that impact their receptiveness to particular classroom topics. For instance, students who strongly believe in the divine creation of humankind may readily dismiss any suggestion that the human race has evolved from more primitive species. In discussing the topic of evolution in a science class, then, teachers might strive to help students *understand* (rather than *accept*) scientists' explanations and lines of reasoning.[100]

In some instances teachers might actually take advantage of the behaviors and beliefs that certain cultures nurture. For instance, when students show a noticeable preference for cooperation rather than competition, cooperative group activities often facilitate their learning and school achievement.[101] And a concern about the need to live in harmony with nature rather than to control it—a belief held by people in some Native American groups— provides a nice foundation for discussions about ecology and global climate change.[102]

Foster an appreciation for cultural diversity.

Not only must teachers be sensitive to the ways in which students of various cultural groups are likely to act and think differently, but they should also help *students* develop such sensitivity, as illustrated in Figure 3.8. True **multicultural education** is not limited to cooking ethnic foods, celebrating Cinco de Mayo, or studying famous African Americans during Black History Month. Rather, it integrates the perspectives and experiences of numerous cultural groups throughout the curriculum and gives all students reason for pride in their own cultural heritage.[103] Following are examples of how teachers can incorporate content from diverse cultures into many aspects of the school curriculum:

- In literature, read the work of authors and poets from a variety of ethnic groups.
- In history, look at wars from diverse perspectives (e.g., the Spanish perspective of the Spanish-American War, the Japanese perspective of World War II).
- In current events, address issues related to racism and discrimination.
- In mathematics, use mathematical principles to address multicultural tasks and problems (e.g., use graph paper and specific geometric patterns to design and order materials for a Navajo rug).
- In art, consider the creations and techniques of artists from around the world.

As students explore various cultures, teachers should help them discover that diverse cultural groups have much to learn from one another. For example, students may be surprised to learn that several key practices underlying many democratic governments in Western nations—for instance, sending delegates to a central location to represent various groups, allowing only one person in a governing council to speak at a time, keeping government and military bodies separate—were adopted from Native American governing practices (those of the Iroquois League) in the 1700s.[104] Fostering appreciation for diverse perspectives does not necessarily mean portraying all cultural practices as equally acceptable, however. Rather, it means that teachers and students should try to understand another cultural group's behaviors within the context of that group's beliefs and assumptions. Teachers must certainly not embrace a culture that blatantly violates some people's basic human rights.

> To me, diversity is not only a fact of life, but it is life. To be different and unique is what allows people to live a fulfilling life. To learn and admire other people's differences is perhaps one of the keys to life and without that key, there will be too many doors that will be locked, keeping you out and not allowing you to succeed. To learn that a majority of one kind in one place may be a minority of another kind in another place can help to initiate an outlook on life that promotes perspective and reason of any situation.

FIGURE 3.8 Despite growing up in a culturally homogeneous, predominantly European American community in rural New Hampshire, 16-year-old Randy revealed his appreciation for cultural diversity in this essay for his American history class. Following high school graduation, Randy moved to Brazil, where he lived for two years before returning home to attend college.

multicultural education Instruction that integrates perspectives and experiences of numerous cultural groups throughout the curriculum.

[98] Gilliland, 1988, p. 26.
[99] Banks, 1991; T. Epstein, 2000.
[100] E. M. Evans, 2001; Southerland & Sinatra, 2003.
[101] García, 1995; Losey, 1995; McAlpine & Taylor, 1993; L. S. Miller, 1995.
[102] Atran, Medin, & Ross, 2005.
[103] Banks, 1995; García, 1995; Hollins, 1996; NCSS Task Force on Ethnic Studies Curriculum Guidelines, 1992.
[104] Rogoff, 2003; Weatherford, 1988.

CLASSROOM STRATEGIES

Creating a Multicultural Environment

- **Educate yourself about the cultures in which students have been raised.**

  A teacher accepts an invitation to have dinner with several of his students and their families, all of whom are dining together one evening at one family's home on the Navajo Nation in western New Mexico. During his visit the teacher discovers why his students are always interrupting one another and completing one another's sentences: Their parents converse with one another in a similar manner.

- **Build on students' cultural backgrounds.**

  A language arts teacher asks a classroom of inner-city African American students to vote on their favorite rap song. She puts the words to the song on an overhead transparency and asks students to translate each line for her. In doing so, she shows students how their local dialect and Standard English are related, and she gives them a sense of pride in being bilingual.

- **Use curriculum materials that represent all ethnic groups in a positive and competent light.**

  A history teacher peruses a history textbook to make sure that it portrays members of all ethnic groups in a nonstereotypical manner. He supplements the text with readings that highlight the important roles that members of various ethnic groups have played in history.

- **Expose students to successful models from various ethnic backgrounds.**

  A teacher invites several successful professionals from ethnic minority groups to speak with her class about their careers. When some students seem especially interested in one or more of these careers, she arranges for the students to spend time with the professionals in their workplaces.

- **Provide opportunities for students of different backgrounds to get to know one another better.**

  A school in Alabama with a majority of African American students and a school in Massachusetts with a majority of European American students initiate a "sister schools program" in which students regularly communicate through the mail or the Internet, exchanging news, stories, photographs, art projects, and other artifacts from their local environments.

- **Get students involved in community action projects that provide services to a particular ethnic group.**

  A middle school community service club spends one afternoon a month conducting a variety of activities (concerts, plays, craft projects, etc.) at a senior center in a Mexican American neighborhood.

Sources: Banks, 1994; Koeppel & Mulrooney, 1992; Ladson-Billings, 1994a (rap song example), 1994b; Ormrod & McGuire, 2007 (Navajo dinner example).

Multicultural understanding also comes from interacting regularly and productively with people from diverse cultural, ethnic, and racial groups. When students from diverse groups interact regularly—and especially when they come together as equals, work toward a common goal, and see themselves as members of the same "team"—they are more apt to accept and possibly even value one another's differences.[105]

Several strategies for promoting multicultural understanding are described in the Classroom Strategies box "Creating a Multicultural Environment." (Additional strategies are presented in a discussion of facilitating cross-group social interactions in Chapter 7.) Ultimately, acquiring true cross-cultural understandings must involve discovering commonalities as well as differences. For example, a class might study how various cultural groups celebrate the beginning of a new year, discovering that "out with the old and in with the new" is a common theme among many such celebrations.[106] In the secondary grades it can be beneficial to explore issues that adolescents of all cultures face: gaining the respect of elders, forming trusting relationships with peers, and finding a meaningful place in society.[107] One important goal of multicultural education should be to communicate that, underneath it all, people are more alike than different.

Identify and, if possible, provide missing resources and experiences important for successful learning.

Some students from very poor families may lack basic essentials—nutritious meals, warm clothing, adequate health care, school supplies, and so on—that will be important for their school success. Many government programs and community agencies can help to provide such essentials. School districts offer free and reduced-cost meal programs for children from low-income families. Charitable organizations often distribute warm winter jackets gathered from annual clothing drives. Many communities have low-cost health clinics. And some office supply stores and large discount chains donate notebooks, pens, and other

---

[105] Dovidio & Gaertner, 1999; Oskamp, 2000; J. H. Pfeifer, Brown, & Juvonen, 2007.

[106] Ramsey, 1987.

[107] Ulichny, 1996.

school supplies to children who need them. Indeed, most communities provide a variety of resources for children and adolescents with limited financial means.

In addition to connecting low-income students and families with community resources, teachers should identify any basic experiences that students may not have had. Field trips to zoos, aquariums, natural history museums, farms, the mountains, or the ocean may be in order. And of course, teachers should identify and teach any basic skills that, for whatever reason, students have not yet acquired. When teachers do so, they are likely to see significant improvements in students' classroom performance.[108]

Yet teachers must also remember that students who have grown up in poverty may, in some respects, have more knowledge and skills than their more economically advantaged peers (see Chapter 2). Such knowledge and skills can often provide a basis for teaching classroom subject matter. Furthermore, students who are willing to talk about the challenges they've faced can sensitize their classmates to the serious inequities that currently exist in their society. In general, research gives us cause for optimism that students from low-income backgrounds can achieve at high levels if their teachers are committed to helping them do so and give them a strong academic program that supports their learning efforts.[109]

SUMMARY

Learning takes places within many contexts that operate at a variety of levels. A learner's most local and immediate learning context consists of the stimuli that are present in the here and now, both those that elicit certain behaviors and those that serve as consequences of learners' behaviors. Some especially influential stimuli are the people in learners' lives who model various ways of performing and thinking about everyday tasks.

Learners acquire knowledge and skills not only from the things that environmental events and other people do *to* or *for* them, but also from the things that other people do *with* them. Learners often co-construct knowledge with other people, sometimes with adults and other more experienced individuals and sometimes with peers whose ability levels equal their own. Social interaction has many benefits. For instance, it introduces learners to ways in which their culture interprets and responds to everyday experiences and problems, and it encourages learners to elaborate on prior knowledge and examine existing beliefs for possible gaps in understanding.

On a much broader scale, learners learn within the context of a particular culture. Culture is a largely human phenomenon that defines appropriate and inappropriate behaviors and beliefs and enables the transmission of knowledge and skills from one generation to the next. A learner's culture hands down innumerable tools, both physical and cognitive, that help learners survive and thrive in their physical and social worlds. Inconsistencies between cultures at home and at school can wreak havoc with school success, however, and teachers must bring the two contexts into alignment to the extent possible. The society within which a learner lives is yet another context that can affect learning either directly or indirectly—for instance, through government policies that mandate certain instructional practices and through community institutions and agencies that offer learning opportunities and support services.

Not only does the environment affect learners and their learning, but so, too, do learners influence their environment. Learners' characteristics and behaviors affect the consequences they experience, the ways in which other people treat them, and the resources to which they have access. And especially as they get older and more independent, learners may actively seek out environments that are a good match with their existing characteristics and behaviors. Such niche-picking tends to increase existing differences among learners.

Teachers can do many things to create supportive learning contexts for students. For instance, they can make sure that productive behaviors lead to desirable consequences (reinforcement) and that counterproductive ones do not. They can provide role models to illustrate effective ways of dealing with academic and social tasks. They can teach concepts, mental strategies, problem-solving procedures, and other cognitive tools that help students think about and respond to everyday situations and problems more effectively. They can encourage dialogues and cooperative activities that enable students to learn from one another. And they can foster an appreciation for the many ways in which diverse cultures all offer useful perspectives.

---

[108] S. A. Griffin, Case, & Capodilupo, 1995; McLoyd, 1998; G. Phillips, McNaughton, & MacDonald, 2004.

[109] Becker & Luthar, 2002; Goldenberg, 2001; G. Phillips et al., 2004.

PRACTICE FOR YOUR LICENSURE EXAM

Adam

Thirteen-year-old Adam seems to cause problems wherever he goes. In his sixth-grade classroom he is rude and defiant. On a typical school day, he comes to class late, slouches in his seat, rests his feet on his desk, yells obscenities at classmates and his teacher, and stubbornly refuses to participate in classroom activities. Not surprisingly, his grades are quite low, just as they have been for most of his school career.

Away from his teacher's watchful eye, Adam's behavior is even worse. He shoves and pushes students in the hall, steals lunches from smaller boys in the cafeteria, and frequently initiates physical fights on the school grounds.

For obvious reasons, no one at school likes Adam very much. His classmates say he's a bully, and their parents describe him as a "bad apple," rotten to the core. Even his teacher, who tries to find the best in all of her students, has seen few redeeming qualities in Adam and is beginning to write him off as a lost cause.

Adam doesn't seem to be bothered by the hostile feelings he generates. Already he's counting the days until he can legally drop out of school.

1. Constructed-response question

Adam is the type of student whom educators often refer to as a *student at risk*: He has a high probability of failing to acquire the minimal academic skills he will need to be successful in the adult world.

A. It is entirely possible that factors in his home and neighborhood are encouraging Adam's inappropriate behaviors. Yet factors at school may also be contributing to these behaviors. Drawing from concepts and principles of learning related to *operant conditioning*, identify two possible school-based causes for Adam's behaviors at school.

B. Again drawing on operant conditioning concepts and principles, describe two different strategies that you might use to help Adam develop more appropriate and productive behaviors.

2. Multiple-choice question

Social learning theorists suggest that learning environments are ultimately the result of *reciprocal causation*. Which one of the following alternatives best reflects this concept?

a. Adam's defiant behaviors may be his way of escaping assignments he doesn't think he can complete successfully.

b. Adam's behaviors alienate his teacher, whose subsequent actions reduce his learning opportunities and class performance.

c. One of Adam's classmates decides that aggression is appropriate classroom behavior and acts accordingly.

d. Many parents complain to the principal that Adam is adversely affecting the quality of their children's education.

Once you have answered these questions, compare your responses with those presented in Appendix A.

FOR FURTHER READING

The following articles from the journal *Educational Leadership* are especially relevant to this chapter. You can find these articles in Chapter 3 of MyEducationLab for this text.

Boaler, J. (2006). Promoting respectful learning. *Educational Leadership, 63*(5), 74–78.

Hartman, C. (2006). Students on the move. *Educational Leadership, 63*(5), 20–24.

Landesman, J. (2006). Bearers of hope. *Educational Leadership, 63*(5), 26–32.

Rothstein-Fisch, C., Greenfield, P. M., & Trumbull, E. (1999). Bridging cultures with classroom strategies. *Educational Leadership, 56*(7), 64–67.

Rubinstein-Ávila, E. (2006). Connecting with Latino learners. *Educational Leadership, 63*(5), 38–43.

Wardle, F. (1999). Children of mixed race—no longer invisible. *Educational Leadership, 57*(4), 68–71.

Zaslavsky, C. (2002). Exploring world cultures in math class. *Educational Leadership, 60*(2), 66–69.

MYEDUCATIONLAB

Now go to Chapter 3 of MyEducationLab at **www. myeducationlab.com,** where you can:

- Find instructional objectives for the chapter, along with focus questions that can help you zero in on important ideas in the chapter.
- Take a self-check quiz on concepts and principles you've just read about.

- Complete exercises and assignments that can help you more deeply understand the chapter content.
- Read supplementary material that can broaden your knowledge of one or more of the chapter's topics.
- Apply what you've learned to classroom contexts in Building Teaching Skills activities.

Higher-Level Cognitive Processes

CASE STUDY Taking Over

In March a ninth-grade math teacher goes on maternity leave, and substitute teacher Ms. Gaunt takes over her classes for the remainder of the school year. Ms. Gaunt has quite a challenge ahead of her. In accordance with Massachusetts state standards, the students need to master numerous mathematical concepts and procedures, including working with exponents and irrational numbers, graphing linear equations, and applying the Pythagorean theorem. Yet many of the students have not yet mastered more basic concepts and operations. Some think that any positive number less than one (e.g., a decimal such as 0.15) is a negative number. Some don't understand percentages. Some can't do long division. A few haven't even learned such number facts as $6 \times 3 = 18$ and $7 \times 8 = 56$.

As she begins to work with the students, Ms. Gaunt discovers that not only do they lack a solid foundation in basic mathematics, but they also have beliefs and attitudes that impede their progress. Many think that a teacher's job is to present material in such a way that they "get it" immediately and will remember it forever. Thus they neither work hard to understand the material nor take notes during her explanations. In fact, a few insist on individual tutoring during class time. On one occasion, when Ms. Gaunt is at Jason's desk demonstrating a procedure, she asks Mark, who is sitting beside Jason, to watch what she is doing and listen to what she is saying. "I don't need to," Mark responds. "After you're done explaining it to Jason, you can come and explain it to *me*."

Another problem is that most of the students are concerned only with getting the "right" answer as quickly as possible. They depend on calculators to do their mathematical thinking for them and complain when Ms. Gaunt insists that they solve a problem with pencil and paper rather than a calculator. Students rarely check to see if their solutions make logical sense. For instance, in a problem such as this one:

> Louis can type 35 words a minute. He needs to type a final copy of his English composition, which is 4,200 words long. How long will it take Louis to type his paper?

a student might submit an answer of 147,000 minutes—an answer that translates into more than 100 days of around-the-clock typing—and not give the outlandishness of the solution a second thought. (It would actually take Louis two hours to type the paper.)

By mid-April, with the statewide mathematics competency exam looming on the horizon, Ms. Gaunt begins moving through lessons more rapidly so that she can cover the mandated ninth-grade math curriculum by the end of the school year. "Students can't do well on the exam if they haven't even been exposed to some of the required concepts and procedures," she reasons. "Mastery probably isn't possible at this point, but I should at least *present* what students need to know. Maybe this will help a few of them with some of the test items." [1]

Why are the students having difficulty mastering what the state of Massachusetts considers to be a ninth-grade mathematics curriculum? Can you identify at least three different factors that appear to be interfering with students' learning?

[1] I thank a friend, who must remain anonymous, for sharing this case with me.

One factor, of course, is students' lack of prerequisite knowledge and skills on which the ninth-grade curriculum depends. Much of mathematics is hierarchical in nature—complex concepts and procedures build on more basic ones—and some of the students have little knowledge on which to build. A few students haven't learned basic number facts, let alone achieved automaticity for them, and so even fairly simple word problems may exceed their working memory capacity.

Students' beliefs about learning and problem solving are also playing a role. In their minds, learning should come quickly and easily if the teacher does her job. They seem not to understand that understanding classroom subject matter is a constructive process involving considerable effort on their part and that certain strategies (e.g., taking notes) can enhance their learning. And they view mathematical problem solving as a quick, mindless enterprise that involves plugging numbers into a calculator and writing down the result, rather than a step-by-step process that requires logical reasoning and frequent self-checking.[2]

Study skills and problem solving are examples of **higher-level cognitive processes**, processes in which learners go far beyond the specific information they are studying, perhaps to apply it to a new situation, use it to solve a problem or create a product, or critically evaluate it. Mastering basic facts and skills is important, to be sure. But learners gain little if they cannot also *do something* with what they've learned—for instance, by applying, analyzing, or evaluating it.

In this chapter we'll look at several higher-level processes, including self-regulation, transfer, problem solving, creativity, and critical thinking. But we'll begin with a particular form of higher-level thinking that in one way or another influences all of the others: metacognition.

⚚METACOGNITION

The term **metacognition** literally means "thinking about thinking." It includes learners' knowledge and beliefs about their own cognitive processes, as well as their conscious attempts to engage in behaviors and thought processes that increase learning and memory. For example, metacognition includes

- Reflecting on the general nature of thinking and learning
- Knowing the limits of one's own learning and memory capabilities
- Knowing what learning tasks can realistically be accomplished within a certain time period
- Planning a reasonable approach to a learning task
- Knowing which learning strategies are effective and which are not
- Applying effective strategies to learn and remember new material
- Reflecting on previous learning efforts—for instance, recognizing when one has or has not successfully learned something

As an illustration, you have undoubtedly learned by now that you can acquire only so much information so fast—you cannot possibly absorb the contents of an entire textbook in an hour. You have also discovered that you can learn information more quickly and recall it more easily if you put it into some sort of organizational framework. And perhaps you've taken to heart one of my recommendations in Chapter 1: You periodically check yourself to make sure you remember and understand what you've read. In general, you are metacognitively aware of some things you can do (mentally) to learn new information effectively.

The more learners know about thinking and learning—the greater their metacognitive awareness—the better their learning and academic achievement will be.[3] Here we'll look at four principles that characterize metacognition in children and adolescents.

Some effective study strategies are readily apparent in learners' behaviors.

Some study strategies are **overt strategies**—ones we can easily see in learners' behaviors. For instance, effective learners allocate specific times to study, and they find a quiet place to do their

---

higher-level cognitive process Cognitive process that involves going well beyond information specifically learned (e.g., by analyzing, applying, or evaluating it).

metacognition Knowledge and beliefs about one's own cognitive processes, as well as conscious attempts to engage in behaviors and thought processes that increase learning and memory.

overt strategy Learning strategy that is at least partially evident in the learner's behavior (e.g., taking notes during a lecture).

---

[2] Such beliefs about mathematics are common; see Muis, 2004.

[3] L. Baker, 1989; Hofer & Pintrich, 2002; Meltzer, 2007; D. N. Perkins, 1995.

work. When they have to learn and remember a large body of information—say, for a major exam—they may spread their study sessions over several days or weeks.

Another easily observable study strategy is taking notes. In general, learners who take more notes learn and remember more. The *quality* of the notes is equally important: Good notes reflect the main ideas of a lesson or reading assignment.[4] Figure 4.1 shows two sets of notes about King Midas taken during a seventh-grade language arts lesson on Greek mythology. Both sets were taken using a note-taking form the teacher provided. Neither set is complete, but the notes on the left should help the student recall the key characters and general plot of the King Midas story. In contrast, the notes on the right are so sketchy that the student who took them may have difficulty recalling or reconstructing the story.

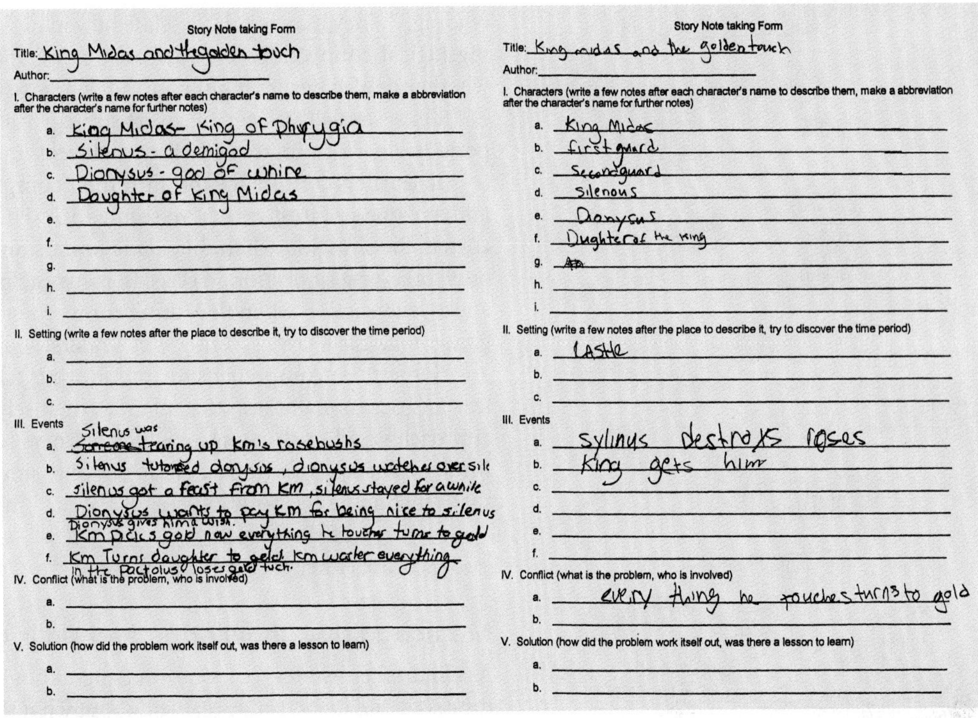

Story Note taking Form

Title: King Midas and the golden touch

Author:

I. Characters (write a few notes after each character's name to describe them, make a abbreviation after the character's name for further notes)

a. King Midas- King of Phyrygia
b. Silenus - a demigod
c. Dionysus - god of whine
d. Daughter of King Midas
e.
f.
g.
h.
i.

II. Setting (write a few notes after the place to describe it, try to discover the time period)

a.
b.
c.

III. Events

a. ~~Someone~~ Silenus was tearing up km's rosebushs
b. Silenus tutored dionysus, dionysus watches over silenus
c. Silenus got a feast from km, silenus stayed for a while
d. Dionysus wants to pay km for being nice to silenus Dionysus gives him a wish.
e. Km picks gold now everything he touches turns to gold
f. Km Turns daughter to gold. km washes everything in the Pactolus. loses gold tuch.

IV. Conflict (what is the problem, who is involved)

a.
b.

V. Solution (how did the problem work itself out, was there a lesson to learn)

a.
b.

Story Note taking Form

Title: King midas and the golden touch

Author:

I. Characters (write a few notes after each character's name to describe them, make a abbreviation after the character's name for further notes)

a. King Midas
b. first guard
c. Second guard
d. Silenous
e. Dionysus
f. Dughter of the king
g.
h.
i.

II. Setting (write a few notes after the place to describe it, try to discover the time period)

a. CAStle
b.
c.

III. Events

a. sylinus destroys roses
b. King gets him
c.
d.
e.
f.

IV. Conflict (what is the problem, who is involved)

a. every thing he touches turns to gold
b.

V. Solution (how did the problem work itself out, was there a lesson to learn)

a.
b.

FIGURE 4.1 Good class notes involve both quantity and quality, as seen in the notes on the left but not those on the right. Both sets were taken during a seventh-grade lesson on Greek mythology.

Still another effective study strategy is organizing information in an explicit, concrete manner. When students engage in activities that help them organize what they are studying, they learn more effectively.[5] One useful way of organizing information is *outlining* the material, which may be especially helpful for low-achieving students.[6] Another approach is to make a **concept map**, a diagram that depicts the concepts of a unit and their interrelationships.[7] Figure 4.2 shows concept maps constructed by two fifth graders after they watched a slide lecture on Australia. The concepts themselves are in circles, and interrelationships among them are indicated by lines with words or short phrases. As is true for class notes, both quantity and quality affect the usefulness of concept maps. The two maps in Figure 4.2 show considerable differences in depth and organization of knowledge about Australia. Furthermore, the top map has a few errors. For example, Adelaide is *not* part of Melbourne; it is a different city altogether. If geographic knowledge about Australia is an important instructional goal, then this student clearly needs further instruction to correct such misconceptions.

Even more important than observable study behaviors are the cognitive processes that underlie them.

Such strategies as taking notes and constructing concept maps are effective, in large part, because they require certain cognitive processes.[8] Many of these processes are those we previously examined in Chapter 2. For instance, to take notes, learners must *pay attention* to and *encode* information, thus facilitating effective storage in memory. To construct a concept map, learners must focus on how key concepts relate to one another and to things they already know, and so they must engage in *meaningful learning*. Both class notes and concept maps also provide a means through which learners encode information visually (i.e., forming *visual images*) as well as verbally. It is probably such **covert strategies**—mental strategies we can't directly see—that are ultimately responsible for successful learning.[9]

Oftentimes effective learners engage in study strategies that are not evident in their observable behaviors. For instance, they may try to identify main ideas in what they are

concept map Diagram of concepts and their interrelationships; used to enhance learning and memory of a topic.

covert strategy Learning strategy that is strictly mental (rather than behavioral) in nature and so cannot be observed by others.

[4] A. L. Brown, Campione, & Day, 1981; Kiewra, 1985; Peverly, Brobst, Graham, & Shaw, 2003.
[5] M. A. McDaniel & Einstein, 1989; Mintzes, Wandersee, & Novak, 1997; Nesbit & Adesope, 2006.
[6] L. Baker, 1989; M. A. McDaniel & Einstein, 1989; Wade, 1992.
[7] Nesbit & Adesope, 2006; Novak, 1998; Novak & Gowin, 1984.
[8] Di Vesta & Gray, 1972; Holley & Dansereau, 1984; Katayama & Robinson, 2000; Kiewra, 1989; Rawson & Kintsch, 2005.
[9] Kardash & Amlund, 1991.

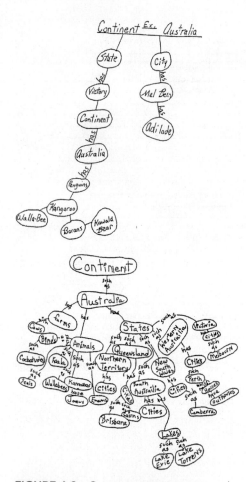

FIGURE 4.2 Concept maps constructed by two fifth graders after watching a slide lecture on Australia

Source: From *Learning How to Learn* (pp. 100–101), by J. D. Novak and D. B. Gowin, 1984, Cambridge, England: Cambridge University Press. Copyright 1984 by Cambridge University Press. Reprinted with the permission of Cambridge University Press.

Listen to Brent, David, Colin, and Hilary reflect on their thought processes in the four "Memory and Metacognition" videos in the Additional Resources section in Chapter 4 of MyEducationLab.

comprehension monitoring Process of checking oneself to be sure one understands and remembers newly acquired information.

reading.[10] They may regularly relate new material to what they already know, perhaps finding logical connections between the "new" and the "old," or perhaps asking themselves whether new material might contradict an existing belief.[11]

One especially powerful covert strategy is **comprehension monitoring**, the process of periodically checking oneself for recall and understanding that I mentioned earlier. Successful learners continually monitor their comprehension both *while* they study something and at some point *after* they've studied it.[12] Furthermore, successful learners take steps to correct the situation when they *don't* understand, perhaps by rereading a section of a textbook or asking a question in class. In contrast, low achievers rarely check themselves or take appropriate action when they don't comprehend. Poor readers, for instance, seldom reread paragraphs they haven't completely understood the first time around.[13]

Sometimes comprehension monitoring takes the form of *self-explanation*, in which learners occasionally stop to explain to themselves what they've learned.[14] Another, similar approach is *self-questioning*, in which learners regularly stop and ask themselves questions. Ideally, their self-questions include not only simple, fact-based questions but also questions that encourage elaboration (e.g., "What might happen if _____?" "How is _____ different from _____?").[15] Yet another strategy is *summarizing* a body of information, either mentally or on paper.[16]

Metacognitive knowledge and skills gradually improve with age.

As children grow older, they become increasingly aware of their own thinking and learning processes and increasingly realistic about what they can learn and remember in a given time period (see Table 4.1). You can get a general sense of how metacognitive awareness changes with age by listening to 6-year-old Brent, 10-year-old David, 12-year-old Colin, and 16-year-old Hilary talk about learning, memory, and studying in the "Memory and Metacognition" video clips in MyEducationLab. For instance, when 6-year-old Brent is asked to explain what kinds of things he did to remember a list of 12 words, he says only "Think" and "Holded it, hold it in my brain." As a 16-year-old, Hilary is much more introspective about why she's done well on the task: "Just 'cause they're things that I have in the house and that we use every day . . . and just thinking it over, I guess. It helps when I picture things, too."

With their growing awareness of their own thinking and learning processes, children gradually acquire study strategies that help them learn and remember academic subject matter more effectively. As we discovered in Chapter 2, children begin using rehearsal in the early elementary grades. More sophisticated strategies emerge quite slowly, however, especially if young learners must develop these strategies on their own.[17] For instance, unless they are specifically instructed to take notes, many young adolescents take few or no notes to help them remember class material (recall how infrequent note taking is in Ms. Gaunt's ninth-grade math class). Even when they do take notes, they often have trouble identifying the most important information to learn in a lesson or reading assignment. Typically, children and adolescents zero in on superficial characteristics, such as what a teacher writes on the chalkboard or what a textbook author puts in *italics* or **boldface**.[18] In the following excerpts from interviews conducted by students in my own educational psychology classes, Annie (a fifth grader) and Damon (an eighth grader) reveal their naiveté about how to identify the most important things to learn in a lesson:

> **Adult:** When you read, how do you know what the important things are?
>
> **Annie:** Most of my books have words that are written darker than all of the other words. Most of the time the "vocab" words are important. In my science books there

---

[10] Dee-Lucas & Larkin, 1991; Dole, Duffy, Roehler, & Pearson, 1991; R. E. Reynolds & Shirey, 1988.
[11] Ausubel, Novak, & Hanesian, 1978; Murphy & Mason, 2006; Sinatra & Pintrich, 2003a.
[12] Hacker, Bol, Horgan, & Rakow, 2000; T. O. Nelson & Dunlosky, 1991; Weaver & Kelemen, 1997.
[13] L. Baker & Brown, 1984; Hacker, 1998; Haller, Child, & Walberg, 1988; Stone, 2000.

[14] deLeeuw & Chi, 2003.
[15] De La Paz, 2005; A. King, 1992; Wong, 1985.
[16] Hidi & Anderson, 1986; A. King, 1992; Wade-Stein & Kintsch, 2004.
[17] Barnett, 2001; Pintrich & De Groot, 1990; Prawat, 1989; Rawson & Kintsch, 2005; Schommer, 1994a.
[18] Dee-Lucas & Larkin, 1991; Dole et al., 1991; R. E. Reynolds & Shirey, 1988.

DEVELOPMENTAL TRENDS

TABLE 4.1 Metacognition at Different Grade Levels

Grade Level	Age-Typical Characteristics	Suggested Strategies
K–2	• Awareness of thought in oneself and others, albeit in a simplistic form; limited ability to reflect on the specific nature of one's own thought processes • Considerable overestimation of what has been learned and how much can be remembered in the future • Belief that learning is a relatively passive activity • Belief that the absolute truth about any topic is "out there" somewhere, waiting to be discovered	• Talk often about thinking processes (e.g., "I *wonder* if . . ." "Do you *remember* when. . . ?"). • Provide opportunities for students to "experiment" with their memories (e.g., playing "I'm going on a trip and am going to pack ___," in which each student repeats items previously mentioned and then adds another item to the list). • Introduce simple learning strategies (e.g., rehearsal of spelling words, repeated practice of motor skills).
3–5	• Increasing ability to reflect on the nature of one's own thought processes • Some overestimation of memory capabilities • Emerging realization that learning is an active, constructive process and that people may misinterpret what they observe • Continuing belief in an absolute truth "out there"	• Provide simple techniques (e.g., self-test questions) that enable students to monitor their learning progress. • Examine scientific phenomena through hands-on activities and experimentation; ask students to make predictions for what will happen and to debate competing explanations for what they observe.
6–8	• Few and relatively ineffective study strategies (e.g., poor note-taking skills, little if any comprehension monitoring) • Belief that "knowledge" about a topic consists largely of a collection of discrete facts • Increasing realization that knowledge can be subjective and that conflicting perspectives may each have some validity (e.g., "people have a right to have their own opinions") • Increasing differentiation among different content domains (e.g., thinking that math involves right vs. wrong answers, whereas social studies allows for diverse opinions)	• Teach and model effective strategies within the context of various subject areas. • Provide tools to assist students in their studying efforts (e.g., provide a structure for note taking, give students questions to answer as they study). • Introduce multiple perspectives about topics (e.g., asking whether Christopher Columbus was a brave scientist in search of new knowledge or, instead, an entrepreneur in search of personal wealth). • Explicitly ask students to reflect on their beliefs about the nature of various academic disciplines (e.g., "Can a math problem sometimes have two *different* right answers?").
9–12	• Growing (but incomplete) knowledge of which study strategies are effective in different situations • Increasing recognition that knowledge involves understanding interrelationships among ideas • Increasing recognition that mastering a topic or skill takes time and practice (rather than happening quickly as a result of innate ability) • Emerging understanding that conflicting perspectives should be evaluated on the basis of evidence and logic (seen in a small minority of high school students)	• Continue to teach and model effective learning strategies; ask students to describe their strategies to one another. • Develop classroom assignments and assessments that emphasize understanding, integration, and application, rather than recall of discrete facts. • Present various subject areas as dynamic entities that continue to evolve with new discoveries and theories. • Have students weigh pros and cons of various explanations and documents using objective criteria (e.g., hard evidence, logical reasoning processes).

Sources: Andre & Windschitl, 2003; Astington & Pelletier, 1996; Barnett, 2001; Buehl & Alexander, 2006; Chandler, Hallett, & Sokol, 2002; Elder, 2002; Flavell, Friedrichs, & Hoyt, 1970; Flavell, Miller, & Miller, 2002; Hatano & Inagaki, 2003; P. M. King & Kitchener, 2002; Kuhn, Garcia-Mila, Zohar, & Andersen, 1995; Kuhn & Park, 2005; Kuhn & Weinstock, 2002; Lovett & Flavell, 1990; Markman, 1977; Meltzer, Pollica, & Barzillai, 2007; Muis, Bendixen, & Haerle, 2006; D. N. Perkins & Ritchhart, 2004; Schommer, 1994a, 1997; Short, Schatschneider, & Friebert, 1993; J. W. Thomas, 1993; vanSledright & Limón, 2006; Wellman, 1985, 1990.

are questions on the side of the page. You can tell that stuff is important because it is written twice.[19]

Adult: What do you think are the important things to remember when your teacher is talking?

Damon: The beginning sentences of their speech or if there's a formula or definition.[20]

---

[19] Interview excerpt courtesy of a student who wishes to remain anonymous.

[20] Interview excerpt courtesy of Jenny Bressler.

Furthermore, many children and adolescents engage in little if any comprehension monitoring.[21] When they don't monitor their learning and comprehension, they don't know what they know and what they don't know, and so they may think they have mastered something when they really haven't. This **illusion of knowing** is seen in learners at all levels, even college students.[22]

Comprehension monitoring is not just an important study strategy in its own right—it also plays a pivotal role in the development of *other* study strategies.[23] Learners will acquire and use new, more effective strategies only if they realize that their prior strategies have been *in*effective in helping them learn. If, instead, they mistakenly believe that they are successfully mastering school topics, they will have little reason to abandon ineffective strategies (such as rote memorization of isolated facts) for more sophisticated ones.

Learners' views about the nature of knowledge and learning influence their approaches to learning tasks.

I once had a conversation with my son Jeff, then an 11th grader, about the Canadian Studies program that a local university had just added to its curriculum. Jeff's comments revealed a very simplistic view of what "history" is:

Jeff: The Canadians don't have as much history as we [Americans] do.
Me: Of course they do.
Jeff: No, they don't. They haven't had as many wars.
Me: History's more than wars.
Jeff: Yeah, but the rest of that stuff is really boring.

Once Jeff reached college, he discovered that history is a lot more than wars and other, "really boring" stuff. In fact, he majored in history, with a minor in art history. But it's unfortunate that he had to wait until college to discover the true nature of history as an academic discipline.

Children and adolescents have many misconceptions about academic disciplines. For instance, in the opening case study, Ms. Gaunt's students think that mathematics consists of nothing more than a collection of procedures that yield "right" answers. Most young learners have misconceptions about the nature of learning as well. For instance, Ms. Gaunt's students think they should be able to learn mathematical concepts and procedures quickly and easily, with little or no effort on their part, as long as their teacher does her job.

Learners' beliefs about knowledge and learning are collectively known as **epistemological beliefs.** Such beliefs often influence studying and learning.[24] For example, when learners believe that learning happens quickly in an all-or-none fashion (as Ms. Gaunt's students apparently do), they are apt to believe they have mastered something before they really have. Furthermore, they tend to give up quickly in the face of failure and express discouragement or dislike regarding the topic they are studying. In contrast, when learners believe that learning is a gradual process that often takes time and effort, they are likely to use a wide variety of learning strategies as they study and to persist until they have made sense of the material.[25]

As another example, some learners believe that when they read a textbook, they are passively absorbing information—often in the form of isolated facts—directly from the page to their minds. In contrast, other learners believe that learning from reading requires them to construct their own meanings by actively interpreting, organizing, and applying the information. Learners who realize that reading is a constructive, integrative process are more likely to engage in meaningful learning as they read and more likely to undergo conceptual change when they encounter ideas that contradict their existing beliefs.[26]

Students often need help distinguishing important facts and concepts from more trivial information. Yet teachers should be careful that they don't portray academic learning as involving nothing more than *memorizing* those facts and concepts.

illusion of knowing Thinking that one knows something that one actually does *not* know.

epistemological belief Belief about the nature of knowledge or knowledge acquisition.

---

[21] Dole et al., 1991; Markman, 1979; J. W. Thomas, 1993.
[22] L. Baker, 1989; D. L. Butler & Winne, 1995; Hacker, 1998; Horgan, Hacker, & Huffman, 1997; Stone, 2000.
[23] Kuhn et al., 1995; Lodico, Ghatala, Levin, Pressley, & Bell, 1983; Loranger, 1994.
[24] Hofer & Pintrich, 1997; Purdie, Hattie, & Douglas, 1996; Schommer, 1994b, 1997.
[25] D. L. Butler & Winne, 1995; Kardash & Howell, 2000; Schommer, 1990, 1994b.
[26] Gunstone, 1994; Paxton, 1999; Purdie et al., 1996; Schommer, 1994b; Schommer-Aikins, 2001; Sinatra & Pintrich, 2003a; Wittrock, 1994.

Epistemological beliefs tend to evolve over the course of childhood and adolescence.[27] Children in the elementary grades typically believe in the certainty of knowledge: They think that for any topic there is an absolute truth "out there" somewhere. As they reach the high school grades, some (but by no means all) of them begin to realize that knowledge is a subjective entity and that different perspectives on a topic can sometimes be equally valid. Other changes may also occur at the high school level. For example, students in 12th grade are more likely than 9th graders to believe that knowledge consists of complex interrelationships rather than discrete facts and that learning happens slowly rather than quickly. And throughout adolescence students' epistemological beliefs become increasingly domain specific.[28] For instance, they may believe that in math answers are always "right" or "wrong" (recall the students in the opening case study), but that in social studies conflicting perspectives may all have some validity. Such developmental trends are reflected in some of the entries in Table 4.1.

Yet effective study strategies and sophisticated epistemological beliefs are not the only factors affecting learning success. Self-regulation is equally important, as we shall see now.

SELF-REGULATION

As we discovered in Chapter 3, the environment has some influence over people's learning and behavior, but it does not have complete control. Learners' actions influence the environments they experience; in fact, learners often seek out certain kinds of environments (recall our discussions of *reciprocal causation* and *niche-picking*). Yet learners take control in another way as well: They make decisions about, direct, monitor, and evaluate their own learning and behavior. In other words, they engage in some degree of *self-regulated learning*, *self-regulated behavior*, and, more generally, **self-regulation**.[29]

To better understand the nature of self-regulation, let's add another component, a **central executive**, to the model of human memory we considered in Chapter 2 (see Figure 4.3). In particular, this central executive (which is probably part of working memory) focuses attention and directs information processing throughout the memory system. It becomes increasingly sophisticated and effective—and perhaps most importantly, under voluntary control—as the brain continues to mature over the course of childhood and adolescence.[30]

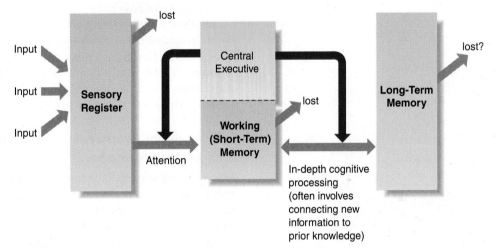

FIGURE 4.3 Adding a central executive to the model of human memory.

To get a sense of how self-regulating *you* are, test yourself in the following exercise.

Self-Reflection About Self-Regulation

In each of the following situations, choose the alternative that most accurately describes your attitudes, thoughts, and behaviors as a college student. No one will see your answers except you, so be honest!

1. In terms of my final course grades, I am trying very hard to:
   a. Earn all As.
   b. Earn all As and Bs.

[27] Astington & Pelletier, 1996; Kuhn & Park, 2005; Muis et al., 2006; Schommer, 1997.

[28] Buehl & Alexander, 2006; Muis et al., 2006.

[29] Good general references on this topic include Bandura, 1986, 1989; Schunk & Zimmerman, 1998; Zimmerman & Schunk, 2004.

[30] Baddeley, 2001; Demetriou, Christou, Spanoudis, & Platsidou, 2002; Fischer & Daley, 2007; Luciana, Conklin, Hooper, & Yarger, 2005; Zelazo, Müller, Frye, & Marcovitch, 2003.

self-regulation Process of taking control of and evaluating one's own learning and behavior.

central executive Component of the human information processing system that oversees the flow of information throughout the system.

c. Keep my overall grade point average at or above the minimally acceptable level at my college.
2. As I am reading or studying a textbook:
   a. I often notice when my attention is wandering, and I immediately get my mind back on my work.
   b. I sometimes notice when my attention is wandering, but not always.
   c. I often get so lost in daydreams that I waste a lot of time.
3. Whenever I finish a study session:
   a. I write down how much time I have spent on my schoolwork.
   b. I make a mental note of how much time I have spent on my schoolwork.
   c. I don't really think much about the time I have spent.
4. When I turn in an assignment:
   a. I usually have a good idea of the grade I will get on it.
   b. I am often surprised by the grade I get.
   c. I don't think much about the quality of what I have done.
5. When I do exceptionally well on an assignment:
   a. I feel good about my performance and might reward myself in some way.
   b. I feel good about my performance but don't do anything special for myself afterward.
   c. I don't feel much differently than I had before I received a grade on the assignment.

Regardless of how you answered Item 1, you could probably identify a particular goal toward which you are striving. Your response to Item 2 should give you an idea of how much you monitor and try to control your thoughts when you are studying. Your responses to Items 3 and 4 tell you something about how frequently and accurately you evaluate your performance. And your response to Item 5 indicates whether you are apt to impose your own reinforcements for desired behaviors. The following general principles illustrate these and other aspects of self-regulation.

Self-regulating learners establish goals and standards for their own performance.

Self-regulating learners know what they want to accomplish when they read or study. For instance, they may want to learn specific facts, gain a broad conceptual understanding of a topic, or simply acquire enough knowledge to do well on a classroom exam.[31] Effective learners often tie their goals for a particular activity to longer-term goals and aspirations—gaining admission to a particular university, exhibiting their work in a prestigious art show, becoming a veterinarian, and so on.[32] To a considerable degree, learners' goals reflect certain self-imposed general standards for performance, and these standards vary from one learner to the next. For example, some may perceive poor school performance to be unacceptable and therefore strive for straight-A report cards. Others may be less demanding of themselves and thus are quite content with Cs.

Learners' goals and standards are often modeled after those they see other people adopt.[33] For instance, at the high school I attended, many students wanted to go to the best college or university they possibly could. In such an environment, others began to share the same academic aspirations. But at a different high school, getting a job after graduation (or perhaps *instead* of graduation) might be the aspiration more commonly modeled by a student's classmates.

Self-regulating learners plan a course of action for a learning task.

Self-regulating learners determine ahead of time how best to use the time and resources they have available for a learning task.[34] They also choose different learning strategies

---

[31] Gaskins, Satlow, & Pressley, 2007; Nolen, 1996; Winne & Hadwin, 1998; Wolters, 1998.

[32] Bembenutty & Karabenick, 2004; R. B. Miller & Brickman, 2004; Zimmerman & Schunk, 2004.

[33] Bandura, 1986; Locke & Latham, 1990.

[34] Zimmerman, 1998; Zimmerman & Schunk, 2004.

depending on the specific goal they hope to accomplish. For example, how they read a magazine article depends on whether they are reading it for entertainment or studying for an exam.[35]

In the following interview, Shelly (a student in one of my educational psychology classes) asks her 17-year-old sister Becky about study habits. Notice how Becky chooses different study strategies for different topics. Notice, too, how she prioritizes her assignments and plans the best times for doing each one.

Shelly: When you have a test, how do you study for it and when?
Becky: I don't usually study; I just look over the notes. If I have to memorize something, I repeat it over and over or write it down, which is like repeating it. I sometimes use [word association], patterns, and oversimplification to remember. I will also look it over at night and then again in the morning. I derive math formulas, those I don't memorize. . . .
Shelly: What types of study skills do you practice on a regular basis?
Becky: Organize homework. I rewrite my assignments. I do smaller tasks first, then put the bigger ones in a pile. I do the easier ones first, then writing and studying I do last. Long-term projects I do last, or first if I want to force myself to do them. . . .
Shelly: If you have a lot of work for one subject and a few things in other subjects, in what kind of order do you attack the tasks?
Becky: I do the little ones first and then leave the big task till the end. I get more of a sense of accomplishment that way.
Shelly: At what time of day do you learn best? [At what time do you] best study on your own?
Becky: I learn better early in the day. I am in a better mood and I am not sick of school yet. At the end of the day, my brain is full. I study best in the morning; that's when I edit my essays from the night before.[36]

Becky is clearly a self-regulating learner. Although she sometimes resorts to rehearsal to learn facts verbatim, many of her strategies—review, organization (looking for patterns), elaboration (deriving formulas)—are probably quite effective. (She does not explain "over-simplification," but perhaps she means that she looks for key ideas or in some other way summarizes the material.) Given how well Becky takes charge of her learning, it may not surprise you to learn that at the time of the interview, she was a high-achieving high school student.

Self-regulating learners typically set one or more goals for a study session and plan a course of action that will enable them to meet their goals.

Self-regulating learners control and monitor their cognitive processes and progress during a learning task.

Self-regulating learners intentionally engage in processes that will enhance their learning. They try to focus their attention on the subject matter at hand and to clear their minds of potentially distracting thoughts.[37] They may also give themselves **self-instructions** that help them direct their efforts. As an example, one formerly impulsive child learned to talk himself through matching tasks in which he needed to find two identical pictures among several very similar ones:

> I have to remember to go slowly to get it right. Look carefully at this one, now look at these carefully. Is this one different? Yes, it has an extra leaf. Good, I can eliminate this one. Now, let's look at this one. I think it's this one, but let me first check the others. Good, I'm going slow and carefully. Okay, I think it's this one.[38]

Another important aspect of self-regulation is **self-monitoring**: Self-regulating learners continually check their progress toward their goals, and they change their learning strategies or modify their goals if necessary.[39] The process of *comprehension monitoring*, described earlier, is an example of such self-monitoring.

self-instructions Instructions that one gives oneself while executing a complex task.

self-monitoring Observing and recording one's own behavior to check progress toward a goal.

[35] Gaskins et al., 2007; Linderholm, Gustafson, van den Broek, & Lorch, 1997; Winne, 1995a.
[36] Interview excerpt courtesy of Shelly Lamb.
[37] Harnishfeger, 1995; Kuhl, 1985; Winne, 1995a.
[38] Meichenbaum & Goodman, 1971, p. 121.
[39] D. L. Butler & Winne, 1995; C. S. Carver & Scheier, 1990; Gaskins et al., 2007.

Self-regulating learners also monitor and try to control their motivation and emotions.

Self-regulating learners use a variety of strategies to keep themselves on task—perhaps embellishing on an assignment to make it more fun, reminding themselves of the importance of doing well, or promising themselves a reward after they finish.[40] They also try to keep in check any emotions (anxiety, anger, etc.) that might interfere with their performance.[41] (We'll identify strategies related to such *emotional self-regulation* in Chapter 6.)

Self-regulating learners seek assistance and support when they need it.

Truly self-regulating learners don't necessarily try to do everything on their own. On the contrary, they recognize when they need other people's help and seek out such assistance. They are especially likely to ask for the kind of help that will enable them to work more independently in the future.[42]

Self-regulating learners evaluate the final outcomes of their efforts.

Both at home and in school, children's and adolescents' behaviors and achievements are often judged by others—their parents, teachers, classmates, and so on. As they become increasingly self-regulating, however, youngsters also begin to judge their *own* behaviors and achievements in terms of the goals and standards they have set for themselves.[43] In other words, self-regulating learners engage in **self-evaluation**. Their ability to evaluate themselves with some degree of objectivity and accuracy will ultimately be critical for their learning and achievement over the long run.[44]

Self-regulating learners self-impose consequences for their performance.

How do you feel when you accomplish a difficult task—for instance, when you earn an A in a challenging course, get elected president of an organization, or make a three-point basket in a basketball game? How do you feel when you fail in your endeavors—for instance, when you get a D on an exam because you forgot to study, thoughtlessly hurt a friend's feelings, or miss an easy goal in a soccer game?

When you accomplish something you've set out to do, especially if the task is complex and challenging, you probably feel quite proud of yourself and give yourself a mental pat on the back. In contrast, when you fail to accomplish a task, you are probably unhappy with your performance, and you may also feel guilty, regretful, or ashamed.[45] Likewise, as children and adolescents become increasingly self-regulating, they begin to reinforce themselves (perhaps by feeling proud or telling themselves they did a good job) when they accomplish their goals. And they may punish themselves (perhaps by feeling sorry, guilty, or ashamed) when they do something that does not meet their own performance standards. Such self-reinforcement and self-punishment are **self-imposed contingencies**. A poem that 16-year-old Melinda wrote about horseback riding, presented in Figure 4.4, clearly shows both self-punishment ("Now I feel guilty because I'm making the horse work harder") and self-reinforcement ("Good job! . . . Now I feel warm inside and proud").

> Sit up,
>   shoulders back,
>   drop your right shoulder."
> Now I feel guilty because I'm making the horse work harder.
> "Heels down,
>   elbows at your sides,
>   lower leg back,
>   drop your right shoulder down and back."
> Now I feel like I have no talent and like I'm hurting the horse.
> "More impulsion from the left hind leg!
>   Send him into the rein more!"
> Now I'm thinking, "This is so complicated!"
> "Good job!
>   Walk when you're ready and give him the rein.
>   Did you feel that?"
> "Yeah!"
> "Good! That was really good!
>   You've accomplished so much with him and your position."
> Now I feel warm inside and proud. All this time has paid off
>   and I realize that's why I love horseback riding so much!

FIGURE 4.4 Sixteen-year-old Melinda expresses guilt and pride—two examples of self-imposed contingencies—in this piece about horseback riding.

self-evaluation Judgment of one's own performance or behavior.

self-imposed contingency Self-reinforcement or self-punishment that follows a particular behavior.

[40] Corno, 1993; Wolters, 2003.
[41] Bronson, 2000; Winne, 1995a.
[42] R. Butler, 1998b; A. M. Ryan, Pintrich, & Midgley, 2001.
[43] D. L. Butler & Winne, 1995; Gaskins et al., 2007; Schraw & Moshman, 1995; Zimmerman & Schunk, 2004.
[44] Dunning, Heath, & Suls, 2004; Vye et al., 1998.
[45] Harter, 1999; R. B. Miller & Brickman, 2004.

Yet self-imposed contingencies are not necessarily confined to emotional reactions. Many self-regulating individuals reinforce themselves in far more concrete ways when they do something well.[46] For example, I once had a colleague who went shopping every time she completed a research article or report (she had one of the best wardrobes in town). I myself am more frugal. When I finish each major section of a chapter, I either help myself to a piece of chocolate or take a half hour to watch one of my favorite quiz shows. (As a result, I am chubbier than my colleague, but I have a wealth of knowledge of game-show trivia and would almost certainly beat her in a game of Trivial Pursuit.)

Learners become increasingly self-regulating over the course of childhood and adolescence.

On average, children and adolescents become increasingly self-regulating as they grow older. As you can see in Table 4.2, a few elements of self-regulation (e.g., setting self-chosen goals, self-evaluation of behavior) are evident in the primary grades. Additional aspects (e.g., conscious attempts to focus attention, ability to complete short learning tasks at home) tend to appear in the upper elementary grades. Still others (e.g., planning, self-motivation) emerge in the middle school and high school years. One aspect of self-regulation—seeking help when needed—may actually *decline*, however, especially if students consistently struggle with their academic work but want to hide their difficulties and perceive their teachers to be aloof and nonsupportive.[47]

When children and adolescents are self-regulating, they set more ambitious academic goals for themselves, learn more effectively, and achieve at higher levels in the classroom.[48] Self-regulation becomes increasingly important in adolescence and adulthood, when many learning activities—reading, doing homework, finding information on the Internet, and so on—occur in isolation from other people and therefore require considerable self-direction.[49]

Unfortunately, not all adolescents acquire a high level of self-regulation, perhaps in part because traditional instructional practices do little to foster it.[50] Let's return to an incident in the opening case study in which Mark refuses to look on while Ms. Gaunt demonstrates a procedure for Jason. "I don't need to," Mark says. "After you're done explaining it to Jason, you can come and explain it to *me*." In Mark's eyes, making sure that he learns is his teacher's responsibility, not his own. We find another example of poor self-regulation in "Starting High School," the opening case study in Chapter 1. Anna was unable to keep track of her work and assignments, and she apparently had little idea about how to keep herself on task, monitor her progress, or get help when she needed it.

To some extent, self-regulated learning probably develops from opportunities to engage in age-appropriate independent learning activities.[51] But self-regulated learning also has roots in socially regulated learning.[52] At first, other people (e.g., teachers, parents) might help children learn by setting goals for a learning activity, keeping children's attention focused on the learning task, suggesting effective learning strategies, monitoring learning progress, and so on. Over time, children assume increasing responsibility for these processes. That is, they begin to set their *own* goals, stay on task with little prodding from others, identify potentially effective strategies, and evaluate their own learning. A reasonable bridge between other-regulated learning and self-regulated learning is **co-regulated learning**, in which an adult and one or more children share responsibility for directing various aspects of the learning process.[53] Initially, the adult (or perhaps a "virtual teacher" in the form of specially designed computer software) provides considerable structure for children's learning efforts, gradually

Self-regulated learning often emerges from *co-regulated learning*, in which teacher and learner share responsibility for directing various aspects of the learning process—setting goals, identifying effective strategies, evaluating progress, and so on.

[46] Bandura, 1977.

[47] Marchand & Skinner, 2007.

[48] D. L. Butler & Winne, 1995; Corno et al., 2002; Duckworth & Seligman, 2005; Zimmerman & Risemberg, 1997.

[49] Azevedo, 2005b; Meltzer et al., 2007; Winne, 1995a.

[50] Meltzer, 2007; Paris & Ayres, 1994; Zimmerman & Risemberg, 1997.

[51] Paris & Paris, 2001; Vye et al., 1998; Zimmerman, 1998.

[52] Stright, Neitzel, Sears, & Hoke-Sinex, 2001; Vygotsky, 1962; Zimmerman, 1998.

[53] Azevedo, 2005a; McCaslin & Good, 1996; N. E. Perry, 1998; C. Quintana, Zhang, & Krajcik, 2005.

co-regulated learning Process through which an adult and child share responsibility for directing various aspects of the child's learning.

DEVELOPMENTAL TRENDS

TABLE 4.2 Self-Regulation at Different Grade Levels

Grade Level	Age-Typical Characteristics	Suggested Strategies
K–2	• Some internalization of adults' standards for behavior • Emerging ability to set self-chosen goals for learning and achievement • Some use of self-talk (self-instructions) to guide behavior • Some self-evaluation of effectiveness and appropriateness of actions; feelings of guilt about wrongdoings • Individual differences in self-control of impulses, emotions, and attention; amount of self-control in these areas affects peer relationships and classroom performance	• Discuss rationales for class rules for behavior. • Show students how some behaviors can help them reach their goals and how other behaviors interfere with goal attainment. • Organize the classroom so that students can carry out some activities on their own (e.g., have reading centers where children can listen to storybooks on tape). • When students show impulsiveness or poor emotional control, provide consistent guidelines and consequences for behavior.
3–5	• Improving ability to assess own performance and progress • Guilt and shame about unsatisfactory performance and moral transgressions • Emerging self-regulated learning strategies (e.g., conscious attempts to focus attention, ability to do short assignments independently at home) • Difficulties with self-control for some students who have cognitive or behavioral disabilities	• Have students set specific, concrete goals for their learning. • Encourage students to assess their own performance; provide criteria they can use to evaluate their work. • Ask students to engage in simple, self-regulated learning tasks (e.g., small-group learning activities, homework assignments); provide some structure to guide students' efforts. • Encourage students to use their peers as resources. • If students have continuing difficulty with self-control, teach self-instructions that can help them control their behavior.
6–8	• Increasing ability to plan future actions, due in part to increased capacity for abstract thought • Increasing mastery of some self-regulated learning strategies, especially those that involve overt behaviors (e.g., keeping a calendar of assignments and due dates) • Self-motivational strategies (e.g., minimizing distractions, devising ways to make a boring task more interesting and enjoyable, reminding oneself about the importance of doing well) • Decrease in help-seeking behaviors during times of confusion, especially if teachers appear to be aloof and nonsupportive	• Assign homework and other tasks that require independent learning. • Provide concrete strategies for keeping track of learning tasks and assignments (e.g., provide monthly calendars in which students can write due dates). • Provide concrete guidance about how to learn and study effectively (e.g., give students questions they should answer as they complete reading assignments at home). • Give students frequent opportunities to assess their own learning; have them compare your evaluations with their own.
9–12	• More long-range goal setting • Increasing mastery of covert learning strategies (e.g., intentional elaboration, comprehension monitoring) • Increasing ability to accurately self-evaluate learning and achievement • Wide variation in ability to self-regulate learning (many low-achieving high school students have few if any self-regulating learning strategies)	• Relate classroom learning tasks to students' long-range personal and professional goals. • Don't assume that all students are metacognitively sophisticated; describe and model effective cognitive strategies for reading, learning, and studying. • Assign complex independent learning tasks, providing the necessary structure and guidance for students who are not yet self-regulating learners.

Sources: Blair, 2002; Bronson, 2000; Damon, 1988; Dunning et al., 2004; Eccles, Wigfield, & Schiefele, 1998; Kochanska, Gross, Lin, & Nichols, 2002; Marchand & Skinner, 2007; Meichenbaum & Goodman, 1971; Meltzer et al., 2007; S. D. Miller, Heafner, Massey, & Strahan, 2003; Paris & Paris, 2001; Wolters & Rosenthal, 2000.

removing it as children become more self-regulating. Co-regulated learning is an example of *scaffolding*, a concept we'll discuss in Chapter 5.

Once learners acquire specific self-regulation strategies, they are apt to apply them to a wide variety of situations. This process, called *transfer*, is our next topic.

TRANSFER

Consider these three students:

- Elena is bilingual: She speaks both English and Spanish fluently. She begins a French course in high school and immediately recognizes many similarities between French and Spanish. "Aha," she thinks, "what I know about Spanish will help me learn French."

- In her middle school history class, Stella discovers that she does better on exams when she takes more notes. She decides to take more notes in her geography class as well, and once again the strategy pays off.
- Ted's fifth-grade class has been working with decimals for several weeks. His teacher asks, "Which number is larger, 4.4 or 4.14?" Ted recalls something that he knows about whole numbers: Numbers with three digits are larger than numbers with only two digits. "The larger number is 4.14," he mistakenly concludes.

When knowledge and skills that learners have previously acquired affect how they learn or perform in another situation, **transfer** is occurring. In most cases, prior learning *helps* learning or performance in another situation. Such **positive transfer** takes place when Elena's Spanish helps her learn French and when Stella's experience with note taking in history class improves her performance in geography.

In some instances, however, existing knowledge or skills actually *hinder* later learning. Such **negative transfer** is the case for poor Ted: He transfers a principle related to whole numbers—one number is larger than another if it has more digits—to a situation where it doesn't apply: comparing decimals. We saw another example in "The New World," the opening case study in Chapter 2: When talking about *China*, Rita apparently retrieved multiple possible meanings of the word—including "dinnerware"—and erroneously concluded that Europeans wanted to import *cups* from the Far East.

Ideally, *positive* transfer should be a major objective for classrooms at all grade levels. When people cannot use their basic arithmetic skills to compute correct change or balance a checkbook, when they cannot use their knowledge of English grammar in a job application or business report, and when they cannot apply their knowledge of science to an understanding of personal health or environmental problems, then we have to wonder whether the time spent learning the arithmetic, the grammar, and the science might have been better spent doing something else.

Four general principles can help us predict when learners are likely to transfer what they learn in one situation to a new situation.

Transfer of knowledge and skills is most likely to occur when there is obvious similarity between the "old" and the "new."

Transfer from one situation to another often occurs when the two situations overlap in content.[54] Consider Elena, the student fluent in Spanish who is now taking French. Elena should have an easy time learning to count in French because the numbers (*un, deux, trois, quatre, cinq*) are very similar to the Spanish she already knows (*uno, dos, tres, cuatro, cinco*). When transfer occurs because the original learning task and the transfer task overlap in content, we have **specific transfer**.

The similarity of two situations usually promotes positive transfer from one to the other. But occasionally it can instead lead to negative transfer. As an example, try the following exercise.

SEE FOR YOURSELF

A Division Problem

Quickly estimate an answer to this division problem:

$$20 \div 0.38$$

Is your answer larger or smaller than 20?

---

[54] J. R. Anderson, Greeno, Reder, & Simon, 2000; Bassok, 1990; Blake & Clark, 1990; Di Vesta & Peverly, 1984.

transfer Phenomenon in which something a person has learned at one time affects how the person learns or performs in a later situation.

positive transfer Phenomenon in which something learned at one time facilitates learning or performance at a later time.

negative transfer Phenomenon in which something learned at one time interferes with learning or performance at a later time.

specific transfer Instance of transfer in which the original learning task and the transfer task overlap in content.

If you applied your knowledge of division by whole numbers here, you undoubtedly concluded that the answer is smaller than 20. In fact, the answer is approximately 52.63, a number *larger* than 20. Has this exercise reminded you of Ted's erroneous conclusion (that 4.14 is larger than 4.4) based on his knowledge of how whole numbers can be compared? Many students at all levels, even in college, show negative transfer of whole-number principles to situations involving decimals.[55] Working with decimals appears, on the surface, to be similar to working with whole numbers. The only difference—a very important one, as it turns out—is a tiny decimal point.

THE FAR SIDE® BY GARY LARSON

Brain aerobics

When transfer occurs, there is usually some similarity between the original learning situation and the transfer task. Engaging in activities simply for general mental "exercise" —for instance, memorizing poems or solving artificial "logic" problems—typically has little if any effect.

Learning strategies and general beliefs and attitudes may also transfer to new situations.

Consider Stella's strategy of taking more notes in geography because note taking has been beneficial in her history class. History and geography don't necessarily overlap in content, but she can apply a strategy she's acquired in one class to help her in the other. Here is an instance of **general transfer**: Learning in one situation affects learning and performance in a somewhat dissimilar situation.

We frequently see general transfer of learning and study strategies: When people acquire effective learning and study strategies within the context of one subject area, they often apply the strategies in a very different subject area.[56] In addition, the general beliefs and attitudes that learners acquire about learning and thinking—for instance, confidence in their ability to master school subject matter, recognition that learning often takes hard work, and willingness to consider multiple viewpoints on controversial issues—can have a profound impact on later learning and achievement across multiple domains and so clearly illustrate general transfer at work.[57]

When application of specific academic topics is involved, however, general transfer occurs far less often than specific transfer.[58] If transfer does occur, it typically involves *some* kind of similarity between the material involved in the two situations. Knowledge about one topic rarely transfers to a very different topic. For example, studying computer programming, though certainly a worthwhile activity in its own right, does not necessarily help a person with other kinds of logical thinking tasks.[59]

Context cues increase the probability of transfer.

Learners can apply something they've learned to a new situation only if they *retrieve* it in the new situation.[60] Here we see one reason why specific transfer is more common than general transfer. When two situations overlap in content, the second situation is apt to provide *retrieval cues* that remind learners of relevant things they have previously learned.[61]

In Chapter 3 we examined the phenomenon of *situated cognition*: People associate particular behaviors and ways of thinking with certain contexts and tend not to use them in—that is, they don't transfer them to—other contexts. We can now explain this phenomenon quite simply. When people initially acquire knowledge and skills in a particular setting, that setting may later provide retrieval cues that help them retrieve what they've learned. However, such cues may be missing in a dissimilar situation.

---

[55] Ni & Zhou, 2005; Tirosh & Graeber, 1990.

[56] J. M. Alexander, Johnson, Scott, & Meyer, 2008; Bransford et al., 2006; Brooks & Dansereau, 1987; D. N. Perkins, 1995.

[57] De Corte, 2003; Pugh, Bergin, & Rocks, 2003; Volet, 1999.

[58] Gray & Orasanu, 1987.

[59] R. E. Mayer & Wittrock, 1996; D. N. Perkins & Salomon, 1989.

[60] Cormier, 1987; Gick & Holyoak, 1987; Halpern, 1998.

[61] Gick & Holyoak, 1987; D. N. Perkins & Salomon, 1989; Sternberg & Frensch, 1993.

[62] Bereiter, 1995; Brooks & Dansereau, 1987; R. E. Mayer & Wittrock, 1996; Pugh & Bergin, 2006.

general transfer Instance of transfer in which the original learning task and the transfer task are different in content.

Meaningful learning and conceptual understanding increase the probability of transfer.

Learners are much more likely to apply new knowledge and skills when they engage in meaningful rather than rote learning.[62] Ideally, they should acquire *conceptual understanding* of a topic, such that many concepts and procedures are interrelated in a cohesive, logical whole (recall our discussion of this concept in Chapter 2). When numerous ideas are interconnected in memory, learners are more likely to retrieve them in appropriate situations.

One critical factor affecting meaningful learning and conceptual understanding is amount of instructional time. The more time learners spend studying a single topic, the more likely they are to transfer what they learn to a new situation, undoubtedly because they are better able to make the interconnections that meaningful, conceptual understanding involves.[63] In-depth instruction on a topic is especially effective when learners see many examples of concepts and have many opportunities to apply skills to diverse situations.[64] In such cases learners can connect their new knowledge to a wide variety of contexts, increasing the odds that they will later retrieve it when they need it.[65]

In general, then, the *less is more* principle introduced in Chapter 2 applies here: Learners are more likely to transfer new knowledge and skills to new situations, including those beyond the classroom, when they study a few things in depth and learn them *well*, rather than study many topics superficially.[66] The *less is more* principle is clearly being violated in the opening case study. Ms. Gaunt decides that she must move fairly quickly if she is to cover all of the ninth-grade math curriculum, even if it means that few students will master any particular topic or procedure. Given the upcoming statewide mathematics exam, she may have little alternative, but her students are unlikely to *use* what they're learning on future occasions.

Two activities in which learners regularly transfer what they've learned are problem solving and creativity, topics we turn to now.

PROBLEM SOLVING AND CREATIVITY

Both problem solving and creativity involve applying previously learned knowledge or skills to a new situation. In **problem solving**, we use what we know to address a previously unanswered question or troubling situation. Psychologists have varying opinions about the nature of **creativity**, but in general it involves new and original behavior yielding a product appropriate for, and in some way valuable to, one's culture.[67]

To successfully tackle a problem, we typically pull together two or more pieces of information into some sort of "whole" that resolves the problem. This combining of information into a single idea or product is known as **convergent thinking**. In contrast, when we engage in creativity, we often begin with a single idea and take it in a variety of directions, at least one of which leads to something that is new, original, and culturally appropriate. This process of generating many different ideas from a single starting point is known as **divergent thinking**.

Figure 4.5 illustrates the difference between convergent and divergent thinking. To see the difference firsthand, try the following exercise.

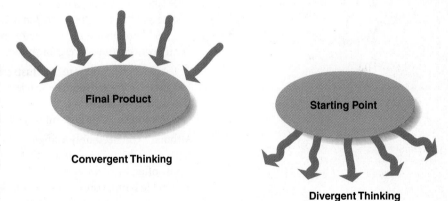

FIGURE 4.5 Convergent versus divergent thinking

problem solving Using existing knowledge or skills to address an unanswered question or troubling situation.

creativity New and original behavior that yields a productive and culturally appropriate result.

convergent thinking Process of pulling several pieces of information together to draw a conclusion or solve a problem.

divergent thinking Process of mentally moving in a variety of directions from a single idea.

---

[63] Gick & Holyoak, 1987; Schmidt & Bjork, 1992; Voss, 1987.

[64] Cox, 1997; Reimann & Schult, 1996; Ross, 1988; Schmidt & Bjork, 1992.

[65] D. N. Perkins & Salomon, 1987; Voss, 1987.

[66] Brophy, 1992; Porter, 1989.

[67] Plucker, Beghetto, & Dow, 2004; Ripple, 1989; Runco, 2004; R. K. Sawyer, 2003.

SEE FOR YOURSELF
Convergent and Divergent Thinking

On a sheet of paper, write your responses to each of the following:

1. You buy two apples for 25¢ each and one pear for 40¢. How much change will you get back from a dollar bill?
2. You have a rectangle with a width of 8 meters and a height of 6 meters, as shown to the right. What is the length of the diagonal line?
3. What are some possible uses of a brick? Try to think of as many different and unusual uses as you can.[68]
4. Add improvements to the wagon to make it more fun to play with.[69]

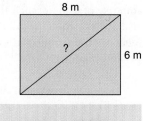

To answer Question 1, you must pull together at least four facts ($2 \times 25 = 50, 50 + 40 = 90$, one dollar = 100 cents, and $100 - 90 = 10$) to arrive at the solution 10¢. To answer Question 2, you must use the Pythagorean theorem (the square of the hypotenuse equals the sum of the squares of the other two sides) plus at least four number facts ($6^2 = 36, 8^2 = 64, 36 + 64 = 100$, $\sqrt{100} = 10$) to arrive at the solution 10 meters. Both Questions 1 and 2, then, involve convergent thinking. In contrast, Questions 3 and 4 require you to think in many different ways about a single object—you must consider how a brick might be used in different contexts and how different parts of the wagon might be embellished—with some of your responses being novel and unique. (For instance, perhaps you thought a brick might make an interesting base for a small table lamp, and perhaps you fastened a hobby horse to the wagon's handle to make it look like a horse and buggy.) Questions 3 and 4, then, involve divergent thinking.

Problem solving and creativity are not necessarily mutually exclusive.[70] Problem solving often involves some divergent thinking and creativity. For example, consider this problem:

> As a teacher, you want to illustrate the idea that metal battleships float even though metal is denser (and so heavier) than water. You don't have any toy boats made of metal. What can you use instead to show students that a metal object with a hollow interior can float on water?

Although you need only a single solution, you must consider a variety of options. Many objects might serve as a ship substitute, and some might work better than others. Similarly, creativity often involves some problem solving. For example, if you were to use a brick as a base for a table lamp, you would need to identify strategies for attaching the brick securely to a metal harness for the lampshade and for running an electrical wire through or around the brick to an electrical outlet.

As you can see, then, problem solving and creativity can be overlapping processes. Furthermore, several general principles apply to both of them.

The depth of learners' knowledge influences their ability to solve problems and think creatively.

Learners who are successful problem solvers and creative thinkers usually have considerable knowledge and conceptual understanding of the topic in question.[71] Especially in the case of creativity, such knowledge may also involve mental associations among very different ideas and subject areas.[72]

[68] Modeled after Torrance, 1970.
[69] Modeled after Torrance, 1970.
[70] Lubart & Mouchiroud, 2003; Simonton, 2000; Treffinger, 1995.
[71] Amabile & Hennessey, 1992; Heller & Hungate, 1985; Lubart & Mouchiroud, 2003; Simonton, 2000; Voss, Greene, Post, & Penner, 1983.
[72] Runco & Chand, 1995.

When learners have limited knowledge about a topic and little conceptual understanding of it, they are apt to choose problem-solving strategies on the basis of superficial problem characteristics.[73] For example, when I was in elementary school, I recall that some of my classmates were having trouble deciding how to attack word problems. Our teacher told us that the word *left* in a problem indicates that subtraction is called for. Encoding a "left" problem as a subtraction problem works well in some instances, such as this one:

Tim has 7 apples. He gives 3 apples to Sarah. How many apples does he have left?

But it is inappropriate in other instances, such as this one:

Tim goes shopping. He spends $4 and then counts his money when he gets home. He has $5 left. How much did Tim have when he started out?[74]

The latter problem requires addition, not subtraction. Obviously, words alone can be deceiving.

Both convergent and divergent thinking are constrained by working memory capacity.

You may recall from an exercise in Chapter 2 just how difficult it is to solve a long division problem in your head. Remember, working memory has a limited capacity: It can hold only a few pieces of information and can accommodate only so much cognitive processing at any one time. If a problem or task requires the learner to handle a great deal of information at once, to manipulate information in a very complex way, or to generate a wide variety of new ideas, working memory capacity may be insufficient for arriving at an accurate or creative result.[75]

Learners can overcome the limits of working memory in at least two ways. One obvious approach is to create an external record of needed information—for example, by writing it on a piece of paper. (This is typically our strategy when we do long division problems, so that we don't have to hold all the numbers in working memory at once.) Another approach is to learn some skills to automaticity—in other words, to learn them to a point where they can be retrieved quickly and easily.[76] Yet in the case of automaticity, it's possible to have too much of a good thing, as we'll see shortly.

How learners encode a problem or situation influences their strategies and eventual success.

Any particular problem or situation might be represented in working memory—that is, *encoded*—in a variety of ways. As an example, see whether you can solve the problem in the following exercise.

SEE FOR YOURSELF

Pigs and Chickens

Old MacDonald has a barnyard full of pigs and chickens. Altogether there are 21 heads and 60 legs in the barnyard (not counting MacDonald's own head and legs). How many pigs and how many chickens are running around the barnyard?

Can you figure out the answer? If you're having difficulty, try thinking about the problem this way:

Imagine that the pigs are standing in an upright position on only their two hind legs; their front two legs are raised over their heads. Therefore, all the animals—pigs and chickens alike—are standing on two legs. Figure out how many legs are on the ground and how many must be in the air. From this, can you determine the number of pigs and chickens Old MacDonald has?

Some ways of encoding a problem promote more successful problem solving than others.

---

[73] Chi, Feltovich, & Glaser, 1981; Schoenfeld & Hermann, 1982.

[74] Modeled after a similar problem in L. B. Resnick, 1989, p. 165.

[75] Hambrick & Engle, 2003; Johnstone & El-Banna, 1986; H. L. Swanson, 2006; Sweller, 1994.

[76] N. Frederiksen, 1984a; R. E. Mayer & Wittrock, 2006; Sweller, 1994.

In case you're still having trouble solving the problem, follow this logic:

- Obviously, because there are 21 heads, the total number of animals must be 21.
- Because each animal has 2 legs on the ground and because there must be twice as many legs on the ground as there are number of heads, there are 42 (21 × 2) legs on the ground.
- Because there are 42 legs on the ground, there must be 18 (60 − 42) pigs' legs in the air.
- Because each pig has 2 front legs, there must be 9 (18 ÷ 2) pigs.
- Because there are 9 pigs, there must be 12 (21 − 9) chickens.

If you're a proficient mathematician, you may simply have used algebra to encode and solve the problem, perhaps using x for the number of pigs and y for the number of chickens and then solving for these variables in the equations $x + y = 21$ and $4x + 2y = 60$. Algebra provides many helpful procedures for solving problems involving unknown quantities. In my own experience, however, I've found that most college students rarely use algebra to solve problems outside of a math class. (They are victims of the *situated cognition* we've spoken of previously.) And students at all grade levels often have trouble solving word problems because they don't know how to translate the problems into the mathematical procedures or operations they've learned at school.[77]

Sometimes learners encode a problem or situation in a seemingly logical way that nevertheless fails to yield a workable result. As an example, take a stab at the problem in the following exercise.

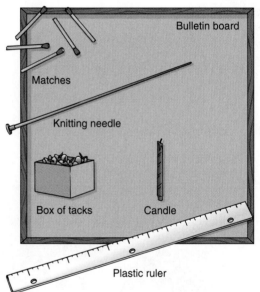

Bulletin board

Matches

Knitting needle

Box of tacks   Candle

Plastic ruler

The Candle Problem

You are in a room with a bulletin board firmly affixed to the wall about four feet above the floor. Your task is to *stand a candle upright* in front of the bulletin board. You do not want the candle touching the bulletin board, because the candle's flame must not singe the board. Instead, you need to place the candle about a centimeter away. How can you accomplish the task with the following materials?

- Small candle
- Metal knitting needle
- Matches
- Box of thumbtacks
- 12-inch plastic ruler

See whether you can solve the problem before you read further.[78]

As it turns out, the ruler and knitting needle are useless in solving the candle problem. If you try to pierce the candle with the knitting needle, you will probably break the candle. If you try to balance the ruler on a few tacks, it will probably fall down. (I speak from experience here, as my own students have unsuccessfully tried both strategies.) The easiest solution is to fasten the thumbtack box to the bulletin board with tacks and then attach the candle to the top of the box with either a tack or some melted wax. Many people don't consider this possibility, however, because they encode the box only as a *container of tacks* and so overlook its potential use as a candle stand. When people encode a problem or situation in a way that excludes potential solutions, they are the victims of a **mental set**.

Mental sets sometimes emerge when learners practice solving a particular kind of problem (e.g., doing subtraction problems in math or applying the formula $E = mc^2$ in physics) without also practicing other kinds of problems at the same time.[79] In general, repetitive

---

mental set Inclination to encode a problem or situation in a way that excludes potential solutions.

[77] R. E. Mayer & Wittrock, 2006; L. B. Resnick, 1989; Reusser, 1990.

[78] Candle problem based on one described by Duncker, 1945.

[79] E. J. Langer, 2000; Luchins, 1942.

practice can lead learners to encode problems and situations in a particular way without really thinking about them—that is, it can lead to automaticity in encoding. Although automaticity in the basic information and skills needed for problem solving and creative thinking is often an advantage (it frees up working memory capacity), automaticity in *encoding* problems and situations may yield incorrect solutions or inappropriate products,[80] in part because it leads learners down a counterproductive path of associations in long-term memory.

Problem solving and creativity often involve heuristics that facilitate, but do not guarantee, successful outcomes.

Some problems can be successfully solved by following specific, step-by-step instructions—that is, by using an **algorithm**. We can correctly assemble the pieces of a new bookcase by following the "Directions for Assembly" that come with the package. We can calculate the hypotenuse of a right triangle by using the Pythagorean theorem. We can solve for x and y when we apply algebraic procedures to combine and manipulate the equations $x + y = 21$ and $4x + 2y = 60$. When we follow an algorithm faithfully, we invariably arrive at a correct solution.

Some problems can be solved by an algorithm, a set of step-by-step instructions that guarantees a correct solution.

CALVIN AND HOBBES © 1990 Watterson. Dist. by UNIVERSAL PRESS SYNDICATE. Reprinted with permission. All rights reserved.

Yet the world presents many problems for which no algorithms exist. And creativity, by its very nature, requires original, nonalgorithmic approaches to situations. Furthermore, algorithms are few and far between outside the domains of mathematics and science. There are no rules we can follow to identify a substitute metal ship for a class demonstration, address ongoing ethnic and religious conflicts in the Middle East, or reduce global climate change—a problem that involves economics and political science as much as physics and meteorology.

In the absence of an algorithm, learners must instead use a **heuristic**, a general approach that may or may not yield a successful outcome. Some heuristics are specific to particular content domains. Others, such as the following, can be useful in a variety of contexts:[81]

- **Identify subgoals.** Break a large, complex task into two or more specific subtasks that can be more easily addressed.
- **Use paper and pencil.** Draw a diagram, list a problem's components, or jot down potential solutions or approaches.
- **Draw an analogy.** Identify a situation analogous to the problem situation, and derive potential solutions from the analogy.
- **Brainstorm.** Generate a wide variety of possible approaches or solutions—including some that might initially seem outlandish or absurd—without initially evaluating any of them. After creating a lengthy list, evaluate each item for its potential relevance and usefulness.
- **"Incubate" the situation.** Let a problem remain unresolved for a few hours or days, thereby allowing mental sets to dissipate and enabling other potential approaches to be retrieved and considered.

Effective problem solving and creativity are partly metacognitive activities.

Earlier in the chapter we discovered the importance of metacognition for effective learning and studying. Metacognitive processes play an important role in problem solving and

[80] E. J. Langer, 2000; Lubart & Mouchiroud, 2003.
[81] J. E. Davidson & Sternberg, 1998, 2003; Halpern, 1997; Meltzer et al., 2007; Zimmerman & Campillo, 2003.

algorithm Prescribed sequence of steps that guarantees a correct problem solution.

heuristic General strategy that facilitates problem solving or creativity but does not always yield a successful outcome.

creativity as well. For instance, effective problem solvers and creative thinkers tend to do the following:[82]

- Identify one or more goals toward which to strive.
- Break a complex problem or task into two or more simpler components.
- Plan a systematic, sequential approach to addressing these components.
- Continually monitor and evaluate their progress toward their goal(s).
- Identify and address obstacles that may be impeding their progress.
- Change to a new strategy if the current one isn't working.
- Evaluate accomplishments in accordance with high standards.

Such metacognitive processes enable learners to use problem-solving and creative strategies flexibly, to apply those strategies to more complex situations, and to know when particular strategies are and are not appropriate.

In the opening case study, many of Ms. Gaunt's students rarely critique their problem solutions for logical sense—for instance, recognizing that typing a 4,200-word paper is unlikely to take 100 days. Essentially, the students engage in little or no self-evaluation of their problem solutions. Truly successful learners evaluate not only their own work but also the ideas and work of others. In other words, they engage in critical thinking, our next topic.

CRITICAL THINKING

The process of **critical thinking** involves evaluating the accuracy and worth of information and lines of reasoning.[83] It can take a variety of forms, depending on the context. The following exercise presents four possibilities.

SEE FOR YOURSELF
Colds, Cars, Chance, and Cheer

Read and respond to each of the following situations:

1. It's autumn, and the days are becoming increasingly chilly. You see the following advertisement in the newspaper:

   > Aren't you tired of sniffles and runny noses all winter? Tired of always feeling less than your best? Get through a whole winter without colds. Take Eradicold Pills as directed.[84]

   Should you go out and buy a box of Eradicold Pills?

2. You have a beat-up old car and have invested several thousand dollars to get it in working order. You can sell the car in its present condition for $1,500, or you can invest a couple of thousand dollars more on repairs and then sell it for $3,000. What should you do?[85]

3. You have been rolling a typical six-sided die (i.e., one member of a pair of dice). You know for a fact that the die is not "loaded" (it's not heavier on one side than another), and yet in the past 30 rolls you have not rolled a number 4 even once. What are the odds that you will get a 4 on the next roll?

4. Here is a research finding presented by Dr. Edmund Emmer at an annual meeting of the American Educational Research Association:

   > Teachers who feel happy when they teach are more likely to have well-behaved students.[86]

   If you are a teacher, do such results suggest that you should try to feel happy when you enter the classroom each morning?

In each of these situations, you had to evaluate information and make some sort of judgment. In Item 1, I hope you weren't tempted to purchase Eradicold Pills, because the

---

critical thinking Process of evaluating the accuracy and worth of information and lines of reasoning.

[82] Csikszentmihalyi, 1996; J. E. Davidson & Sternberg, 1998; Dominowski, 1998; Glover, Ronning, & Reynolds, 1989; Minsky, 2006; Runco & Chand, 1995.
[83] Definition adapted from Beyer, 1985.
[84] R. J. Harris, 1977, p. 605.
[85] Modeled after Halpern, 1998.
[86] Emmer, 1994.

advertisement provided no proof that they reduce cold symptoms. It simply included the suggestion to "Take Eradicold Pills as directed" within the context of a discussion of undesirable symptoms—a common ploy in persuasive advertising.

As for Item 2, it makes more sense to sell the car now. If you sell the car for $3,000 after making $2,000 worth of repairs, you make $500 less than you would otherwise. Yet many people mistakenly believe that their past investments justify making additional ones, when in fact past investments are irrelevant to the present state of affairs.[87]

In Item 3 the chance of rolling a 4 on an evenly balanced die is—as it always is—one in six. The outcomes of previous rolls are irrelevant, because each roll is independent of the others. But when a 4 hasn't shown up even once in 30 rolls, many people believe that a 4 is long overdue and so greatly overestimate its probability.

Now what about making sure you're happy each time you enter the classroom (Item 4)? One common mistake people make in interpreting research results is to think that an association (*correlation*) between two things means that one of those things must definitely *cause* the other. As noted in Chapter 1, however, correlation does not necessarily show causation. Perhaps teacher happiness directly influences students' classroom behavior, but perhaps not. In fact, there are other possible explanations for the correlation. For instance, perhaps good student behavior makes teachers feel happy (rather than vice versa), or perhaps teachers who are feeling upbeat use more effective teaching techniques and keep students on task as a result of using those techniques.[88]

The four situations presented in the exercise illustrate several forms that critical thinking might take:[89]

- **Verbal reasoning:** Understanding and evaluating persuasive techniques found in oral and written language (e.g., deductive and inductive logic). You engaged in verbal reasoning when deciding whether to purchase Eradicold Pills.
- **Argument analysis:** Discriminating between reasons that do and do not support a conclusion. You engaged in argument analysis when you considered possible pros and cons of investing an additional $2,000 on car repairs.
- **Probabilistic reasoning:** Determining the likelihood and uncertainties associated with various events. You engaged in probabilistic reasoning when you determined the probability of rolling a 4 on the die.
- **Hypothesis testing:** Judging the value of data and research results in terms of the methods used to obtain them and their potential relevance to certain conclusions. When hypothesis testing includes critical thinking, it involves considering questions such as these:
  - Was an appropriate method used to measure a particular outcome?
  - Have other possible explanations or conclusions been eliminated?
  - Can the results obtained in one situation be reasonably generalized to other situations?
  You engaged in hypothesis testing when you evaluated Dr. Emmer's findings about teacher happiness.

The nature of critical thinking is, of course, different in various content domains. In writing, critical thinking may involve reading the first draft of a persuasive essay to look for errors in logical reasoning or for situations in which opinions have not been sufficiently justified. In science it may involve revising existing theories or beliefs to account for new evidence—that is, it may involve conceptual change. In history it may involve drawing inferences from historical documents, attempting to determine whether things *definitely* happened a particular way or only *maybe* happened that way.

As you might guess, critical thinking abilities emerge gradually over the course of childhood and adolescence.[90] Yet all too often, learners at all grade levels (even college students) take the information they see in textbooks, advertisements, media reports, and elsewhere at face value. In other words, they engage in little or no critical thinking as they consider the accuracy and worth of the information they encounter.

Critical thinking takes different forms in different content domains.

[87] Halpern, 1998.

[88] Emmer, 1994.

[89] Halpern, 1997, 1998.

[90] Amsterlaw, 2006; P. M. King & Kitchener, 2002; Kuhn & Franklin, 2006; D. N. Perkins & Ritchhart, 2004; Pillow, 2002.

CULTURAL CONSIDERATIONS

Influences of Culture and Community on Higher-Level Cognitive Processes

Learners' experiences at home and in their general community and culture can have a significant effect on the development of higher-level cognitive processes. Following are several areas in which cultural differences have been observed.

Epistemological beliefs. Researchers have observed some consistent differences in beliefs about what it means to *learn* something. From the perspective of mainstream Western culture, learning is largely a mental enterprise: People learn in order to understand the world and acquire new skills and abilities. But for many people in China, learning also has moral and social dimensions: It enables an individual to become increasingly virtuous and honorable and to contribute in significant ways to the betterment of society. From a traditional East Asian per-

spective, true learning is not a quick-and-easy process; rather, it comes only with a great deal of diligence, concentration, and perseverance.[a]

Learning strategies. Consistent with a belief that learning requires diligence and perseverance, many East Asian parents and teachers encourage frequent use of rehearsal and rote memorization as learning strategies.[b] Rehearsal and memorization are also common in cultures that value committing oral histories or verbatim passages of sacred text (e.g., the Koran, the Bible) to memory.[c] In contrast, many schools in mainstream Western culture are increasingly presenting lessons and encouraging strategies that foster meaningful learning. Even so, they typically insist that students learn certain things—such as

multiplication tables and word spellings—by heart.[d]

Self-regulated learning. Also consistent with the importance placed on diligence and persistence, East Asian parents and teachers are apt to encourage considerable self-discipline and stick-to-it-iveness as children tackle new projects. In doing so, they foster self-regulation.[e] Self-regulation is less common when youngsters have few role models for effective study habits and self-regulation skills. Such may be the case for some (but certainly not *all!*) children and adolescents attending schools in low-socioeconomic neighborhoods. Although these students may hope to graduate, go on to college, and eventually become successful professionals, they may have little idea about how to accomplish these things.[f] The

The following two principles can help us understand why critical thinking tends to be the exception rather than the rule.

Critical thinking requires sophisticated epistemological beliefs.

Learners are more likely to look analytically and critically at new information if they believe that even experts' understanding of a topic continues to evolve as new evidence accumulates. They are less likely to engage in critical thinking if they believe that "knowledge" is an absolute, unchanging entity.[91] In other words, learners' *epistemological beliefs* enter into the critical thinking process.

Critical thinking is a disposition as much as a cognitive process.

By **disposition,** I mean a general inclination to approach and think about learning and problem-solving situations in a particular way—perhaps in a thoughtful, analytical, evaluative manner, on the one hand, or in a thought*less*, unquestioning manner, on the other. Some learners clearly have a general disposition to think critically about the subject matter they read and study.[92] Those who do show more advanced reasoning capabilities and are more likely to undergo conceptual change when it's warranted.[93]

disposition General inclination to approach and think about learning and problem-solving tasks in a particular way.

[91] Kardash & Scholes, 1996; P. M. King & Kitchener, 2002; Kuhn, 2001a; Schommer-Aikins, 2001.
[92] Facione, Facione, & Giancarlo, 2000; Kardash & Scholes, 1996; P. M. King & Kitchener, 2002; D. N. Perkins, Tishman, Ritchhart, Donis, & Andrade, 2000.
[93] Southerland & Sinatra, 2003; Stanovich, 1999.

following interview with a middle school student in inner-city Philadelphia illustrates the problem:

Adult: Are you on track to meet your goals?

Student: No. I need to study more.

Adult: How do you know that?

Student: I just know by some of my grades. [mostly Cs]

Adult: Why do you think you will be more inclined to do it in high school?

Student: I don't want to get let back. I want to go to college.

Adult: What will you need to do to get better grades?

Student: Just do more and more work. I can rest when the school year is over.[g]

The student wants to get a college education, but to do so he understands only that he needs to "study more" and "do more and more work." Motivation and effort are important, to be sure, but so are planning, time management, regular self-monitoring and self-evaluation, and appropriate help-seeking—things this student seems to have little awareness of. Some learners, then, may need considerable guidance and support to acquire the learning and self-regulation strategies that will serve them well in college and the outside world.

Critical thinking. Critical thinking is another higher-level process that seems to depend somewhat on students' cultural backgrounds. Some cultures place high value on respecting one's elders or certain religious leaders; in doing so they may foster the epistemological belief that "truth" is a cut-and-dried entity that is best gained from authority figures.[h] In addition, a cultural emphasis on maintaining group harmony may discourage children from hashing out differences in perspective, which critical thinking often entails.[i] Perhaps as a result of such factors, critical thinking may be less common in some groups (e.g., in some traditional Asian communities and in some fundamentalist religious groups in the United States) than in others.[j] In some situations, then, teachers must walk a fine line between teaching students to critically evaluate persuasive arguments and scientific evidence, on the one hand, and to show appropriate respect and strive for group harmony in their community and culture, on the other.

[a] Dahlin & Watkins, 2000; H. Grant & Dweck, 2001; Li, 2005; Li & Fischer, 2004.
[b] Dahlin & Watkins, 2000; D. Y. F. Ho, 1994; Purdie & Hattie, 1996.
[c] MacDonald, Uesiliana, & Hayne, 2000; Rogoff et al., 2007; Q. Wang & Ross, 2007.
[d] Q. Wang & Ross, 2007.
[e] Morelli & Rothbaum, 2007.
[f] Belfiore & Hornyak, 1998; B. L. Wilson & Corbett, 2001.
[g] B. L. Wilson & Corbett, 2001, p. 23.
[h] Delgado-Gaitan, 1994; Losh, 2003; Qian & Pan, 2002.
[i] Kağıtçıbaşı, 2007; Kuhn & Park, 2005.
[j] Kuhn, Daniels, & Krishnan, 2003; Kuhn & Park, 2005.

Researchers do not yet have a good understanding of why some learners are more predisposed to think critically than others. The larger culture and society in which learners grow up certainly have an effect, as can be seen in the Cultural Considerations box "Influences of Culture and Community on Higher-Level Cognitive Processes." And quite possibly, teachers' actions in the classroom—for instance, whether they encourage exploration, risk taking, and critical thinking with respect to classroom topics—make a difference.[94] In the following classroom interaction, a teacher actually seems to *discourage* any disposition to think analytically and critically about classroom material:

Teacher: Write this on your paper . . . it's simply memorizing this pattern. We have meters, centimeters, and millimeters. Let's say . . . write millimeters, centimeters, and meters. We want to make sure that our metric measurement is the same. If I gave you this decimal, let's say .234 m (yes, write that). In order to come up with .234 m in centimeters, the only thing that is necessary is that you move the decimal. How do we move the decimal? You move it to the right two places. (Jason, sit up please.) If I move it to the right two places, what should .234 m look like, Daniel, in centimeters? What does it look like, Ashley?

Ashley: 23.4 cm.

Teacher: Twenty-three point four. Simple stuff. In order to find meters, we're still moving that decimal to the right, but this time, boys and girls, we're only going to move it one place. So, if I move this decimal one place, what is my answer for millimeters?[95]

[94] Flum & Kaplan, 2006; Kuhn, 2001b, 2006.   [95] Dialogue from J. C. Turner, Meyer, et al., 1998, p. 741.

Undoubtedly, this teacher means well: She wants her students to understand how to convert from one unit of measurement to another. But notice the attitude she engenders: "Write this . . . it's simply memorizing this pattern."

Critical thinking and other higher-level processes will obviously enhance learners' long-term success both in higher education and in the outside world. We now look at various ways in which teachers might encourage such processes.

PROMOTING HIGHER-LEVEL COGNITIVE PROCESSES

If teachers focus classroom activities on the learning of isolated facts, and if they also use assessment techniques that emphasize knowledge of those facts, students will naturally begin to believe that school learning is a process of absorbing information in a rote fashion and regurgitating it at a later time. But if they instead focus class time and activities on *doing things with* information—for instance, applying it to new situations, using it to solve problems, and critically evaluating it—then students should acquire the cognitive processes and skills that will serve them well in the world beyond the classroom.

Following are numerous suggestions for encouraging students to engage in higher-level thinking, both in the classroom and in the outside world. Some focus on the specific processes we've examined in this chapter, whereas others are relevant across the board.

Promoting Specific Higher-Level Processes

Research related to particular higher-level processes yields several recommendations.

Actively nurture students' metacognitive awareness and self-reflection.

As we have seen, children and adolescents become increasingly aware of their mental processes as they get older. Yet teachers shouldn't leave students' metacognitive development in the hands of fate. Instead, they can actively nurture students' self-reflection about mental activities. For example, a teacher might ask students to explain what they are doing, and also why they are doing it, while they work on a problem.[96] Alternatively, a teacher might give students questions to ask *themselves* as they work on a problem—questions such as "Are we getting closer to our goal?" and "Why is this strategy most appropriate?"[97] The right-hand column of Table 4.1 (p. 103) offers additional suggestions.

Explicitly teach effective learning strategies.

Many children and adolescents know little about how they can best learn and remember information. For example, many students at all grade levels (even many college students) erroneously believe that rote learning (rehearsal, use of flash cards, etc.) is an effective way to study.[98] Explicit training in study strategies—preferably integrated into ongoing instruction about academic topics—can definitely enhance students' learning and achievement.[99] Such instruction is especially important for students who have a history of academic difficulties and are at risk for dropping out before high school graduation.[100]

Ideally, students should learn many different learning strategies and the situations in which each one is appropriate.[101] For instance, meaningful learning is more important for learning general principles within a discipline, whereas mnemonics are often more useful in learning hard-to-remember pairs and lists. In addition, students should be encouraged to

[96] Dominowski, 1998; Johanning, D'Agostino, Steele, & Shumow, 1999.

[97] A. King, 1999, p. 101; Kramarski & Mevarech, 2003, p. 286.

[98] Barnett, 2001; Pintrich & De Groot, 1990; Prawat, 1989; Schommer, 1994a.

[99] Hattie, Biggs, & Purdie, 1996; Paris & Paris, 2001; Pressley, El-Dinary, Marks, Brown, & Stein, 1992; Pressley, Harris, & Marks, 1992.

[100] Alderman, 1990; Meltzer & Krishnan, 2007; Pressley & Hilden, 2006.

[101] R. E. Mayer & Wittrock, 1996; Nist, Simpson, Olejnik, & Mealey, 1991; Paris, 1988; Pressley, El-Dinary, et al., 1992; Pressley, Harris, & Marks, 1992.

practice each new strategy with a variety of learning tasks over a period of time.[102] Effective strategy instruction is clearly not a one-shot deal.

When teaching learning strategies, teachers must be sure that they include covert strategies—elaboration, comprehension monitoring, and so on—as well as overt ones.[103] One effective way to teach covert mental processes is to model them by thinking aloud about classroom topics.[104] For example, in a lecture on Napoleon in a world history class, a teacher might say, "Hmm . . . it seems to me that Napoleon's military tactics were quite similar to those of the ancient Assyrians. Let's briefly review the kinds of things the Assyrians did." When assigning a textbook chapter to be read at home, a teacher might say, "Whenever I read a textbook chapter, I begin by looking at the headings and subheadings in the chapter. I then think about questions that the chapter will probably address, and I try to find the answers as I read. Let me show you how *I* might tackle the chapter I've asked you to read tonight. . . ."

Yet students are likely to use new study strategies only if they discover for themselves that the strategies are actually helpful.[105] For instance, in my own classes I occasionally do little "experiments," presenting information that is difficult to learn and remember and giving some (but not all) students a specific strategy (e.g., a mnemonic) for learning the information. We find out how much students in the strategy and no-strategy groups can recall by writing students' "test" scores on the chalkboard. The performance of the two groups is usually so dramatically different that my students readily acknowledge the usefulness of the strategy I've taught them.

Teachers must keep in mind that students will often need considerable guidance and support in their early efforts to use new strategies. For example, to help students identify the most important information in a lesson, a teacher might provide a list of objectives for the lesson, write key concepts and principles on the chalkboard, or ask questions that focus students' attention on central ideas.[106] To help students elaborate on what they read, teachers can provide examples of questions for students to answer (e.g., "Explain why. . ." or "What is a new example of . . . ?").[107] And to help students in their early note-taking efforts, teachers might provide a structure to fill in during a lesson. An example of such a structure for a lesson on muscles is presented in Figure 4.6. You can find another example in the two sets of notes on King Midas presented earlier in Figure 4.1.

MUSCLES

A. *Number of Muscles*
   1. There are approximately _____ muscles in the human body.

B. *How Muscles Work*
   1. Muscles work in two ways:
      a. They _____ , or shorten.
      b. They _____, or lengthen.

C. *Kinds of Muscles*
   1. _____ muscles are attached to the bones by _____ .
      a. These muscles are _____ (voluntary/involuntary).
      b. The purpose of these muscles is to _____
         _____ .
   2. _____ muscles line some of the body's _____ .
      a. These muscles are _____ (voluntary/involuntary).
      b. The purpose of these muscles is to _____
         _____ .
   3. The _____ muscle is the only one of its kind.
      a. This muscle is _____ (voluntary/involuntary).
      b. The purpose of this muscle is to _____
         _____ .

FIGURE 4.6   Example of a partially filled-in outline that can guide students' note taking

Communicate that acquiring knowledge is a dynamic, ongoing process—that one never completely "knows" something.

Epistemological beliefs about particular academic disciplines, as well as about knowledge and learning more generally, have a significant impact on how students study, what they

[102] A. L. Brown & Palincsar, 1987; A. Collins, Brown, & Newman, 1989; Gaskins & Pressley, 2007; Pressley, El-Dinary, et al., 1992; Pressley, Harris, & Marks, 1992.
[103] Kardash & Amlund, 1991.
[104] A. L. Brown & Palincsar, 1987; Pressley, El-Dinary, et al., 1992; Pressley, Harris, & Marks, 1992.

[105] Hattie et al., 1996; Paris & Paris, 2001; Pressley & Hilden, 2006.
[106] Kiewra, 1989; R. E. Reynolds & Shirey, 1988; Schraw, Wade, & Kardash, 1993.
[107] Questions from A. King, 1992, p. 309.

learn, how readily they apply classroom subject matter, and how often they critically evaluate it. Instruction in study strategies alone will not necessarily change those beliefs.[108]

One possible way to change students' epistemological beliefs is to talk specifically about the nature of knowledge and learning—for instance, to describe learning as an active, ongoing process of finding interconnections among ideas and eventually constructing one's own understanding of the world.[109] But probably a more effective approach is to provide classroom experiences that lead students to discover that knowledge must necessarily be a dynamic, rather than static, entity and to realize that successful learning sometimes occurs only through effort and persistence. For example, teachers can have students address complex issues and problems that have no clear-cut right or wrong answers.[110] They can teach strategies for gathering data and testing competing hypotheses.[111] They can ask students to compare several explanations of a particular phenomenon or event and consider the validity and strength of evidence supporting each one.[112] And they can show students, perhaps by presenting puzzling phenomena, that their own current understandings, and in some cases even those of experts in the field, do not yet adequately explain all of human experience.[113]

First Quarter

Math Grade Log		Name Lea Demers		Total
				(as needed)
Assignment	Due Date	Points/Points Possible		
1 Anagram Name	8-27	5/5		5/5
2 1-1 #2-42 even	8/26	5/5		10/10
3 Your Life in Math	8/27	5/5		15/15
4 1-2 #2-52 evens	8/30	5/5		20/20
5 1-3 #2-46 even	8/31	5/5		25/25
6 1-5 #1-36	9/1	5/5		30/30
7 Quiz 1-1 to 1-3	9/2	20/25		50/55
8 4-4's Problem	9/1	6/5		56/60
9 TI Programming A	9/3	5/5		61/65
10 Quiz 1-5 to 1-8	9/10	23/25		84/90
11 1-7 #1-48	9/7	5/5		89/95

FIGURE 4.7 In this daily log sheet, 13-year-old Lea has kept track of her math assignments, their due dates, and her performance on them.

Observe Keenan's self-evaluation in the "Portfolio" video in the Additional Resources section in Chapter 4 of MyEducationLab.

Encourage and support self-regulated learning and behavior.

If they are to be productive and successful adults who work well independently, students must become increasingly self-regulating over the course of childhood and adolescence. Some students acquire self-regulation skills largely on their own, but many others need a great deal of guidance and support from teachers. For example, students with a history of academic failure acquire better study habits when they're given explicit instruction in self-regulation strategies.[114]

Consistent with the concept of *co-regulation* introduced earlier, teachers can probably best foster self-regulation skills by initially providing considerable structure and then gradually loosening the reins as students become more self-directed. The right-hand column in Table 4.2 (p. 110) offers suggestions that are apt to be appropriate at different grade levels. The Classroom Strategies box "Fostering Self-Regulation" presents several more specific ideas.

Of the many self-regulation strategies students might acquire, perhaps most important are strategies with which students can monitor their own learning and behavior. Following are several things teachers might do to encourage self-monitoring and self-evaluation:

- Have students set specific goals and objectives for themselves, and then describe achievements in relation to them.[115]
- Provide specific criteria that students can use to judge their performance.[116]
- On some occasions, delay teacher feedback so that students first have the opportunity to evaluate their own performance.[117]
- To check for long-term retention of reading material, suggest questions that students can ask themselves to assess their understanding after a significant time delay.[118]
- Ask students to keep ongoing records of their performance and to reflect on their learning in writing assignments, journals, or portfolios.[119] (For example, see the "Portfolio" video clip in MyEducationLab.)

One simple strategy is to provide blank forms that students can use to track their performance on classroom assessments. The daily log sheet presented in Figure 4.7 shows a

[108] Schraw & Moshman, 1995.

[109] Gaskins & Pressley, 2007; Muis et al., 2006; Schommer, 1994b.

[110] Kardash & Scholes, 1996; P. M. King & Kitchener, 2002; Schommer, 1994b.

[111] Andre & Windschitl, 2003; P. M. King & Kitchener, 2002; C. L. Smith, Maclin, Houghton, & Hennessy, 2000.

[112] Andre & Windschitl, 2003; P. M. King & Kitchener, 2002; vanSledright & Limón, 2006.

[113] Chan, Burtis, & Bereiter, 1997; Vosniadou, 1991.

[114] Cosden, Morrison, Albanese, & Macias, 2001; Eilam, 2001; Graham & Harris, 1996; Meltzer, 2007; N. E. Perry, 1998.

[115] Eilam, 2001; Meltzer, 2007; Morgan, 1985.

[116] Meltzer, 2007; Paris & Ayres, 1994; Winne, 1995b.

[117] D. L. Butler & Winne, 1995; Schroth, 1992.

[118] Dunning et al., 2004.

[119] Belfiore & Hornyak, 1998; Paris & Paris, 2001; N. E. Perry, 1998.

CLASSROOM STRATEGIES

Fostering Self-Regulation

- **Help students set challenging yet realistic goals and standards.**

  A teacher encourages a pregnant student to stay in school until she graduates. Together they discuss strategies for juggling motherhood and schoolwork.

- **Have students observe and record their own behavior.**

  A student with attention-deficit hyperactivity disorder frequently tips his chair back to the point where he is likely to topple over. Concerned for the student's safety, his teacher asks him to record each instance of such behavior on a sheet of graph paper. Both student and teacher notice how quickly the behavior disappears once the student has become aware of his bad habit.

- **Teach students instructions they can give themselves to remind them of what they need to do.**

  To help students remember the new dance steps they are learning, their teacher instructs them to say such things as "One, two, gallop, gallop" and "One leg, other leg, turn, and turn" while performing the steps.

- **Encourage students to evaluate their own performance.**

  A science teacher gives students a list of criteria to evaluate the lab reports they have written. In assigning grades, she considers not only what students have written in their reports but also how accurately students have evaluated their own reports.

- **Teach students to reinforce themselves for appropriate behavior.**

  A teacher helps students develop more regular study habits by encouraging them to make a favorite activity—for example, shooting baskets, watching television, or calling a friend on the telephone—contingent on completing their homework first.

- **Give students opportunities to engage in learning tasks with little or no help from their teacher.**

  A middle school social studies teacher distributes various magazine articles related to current events in the Middle East, making sure that each student receives an article appropriate for his or her reading level. He asks students to read their articles over the weekend and prepare a one-paragraph summary to share with other class members. He also provides guidelines about what information students should include in their summaries.

Source: Vintere, Hemmes, Brown, & Poulson, 2004, p. 309 (dancing self-instructions).

form that one middle school math teacher has used. The form has its limits, however, in that it focuses students' attention entirely on the number of points they are accumulating. It provides no place for students to record the types of problems they get wrong, the kinds of errors they make, or any other information that might help them improve. To help students evaluate the *quality* of their work, teachers can provide self-assessment instruments listing the criteria that students should look for. Another effective strategy is to have students compare their self-assessments with teacher assessments of their work.[120] Figure 4.8 presents a form a high school social studies teacher has used to help her students learn to evaluate their performance in a cooperative group activity.

To be successful over the long run, students must actively monitor their behavior as well as their academic performance. Yet children and adolescents aren't necessarily accurate observers of their own behavior. They aren't always aware of how frequently they do something incorrectly or ineffectively or of how *in*frequently they do something well. To help students attend to the things they do and don't do, teachers can have them observe and record their own behavior. For instance, if Raymond is speaking out of turn too often, his teacher can bring the seriousness of the problem to his attention by asking him to make a check mark on a sheet of paper every time he catches himself speaking out of turn. If Olivia has trouble staying on task during assigned activities, her teacher can ask her to stop and reflect on her behavior every few minutes (perhaps with the aid of an egg timer or electronic beeper) to determine whether she was staying on task during each interval. When teachers encourage such self-focused record keeping, students are more likely to stay on task and complete assignments, and they are less likely to engage in disruptive classroom behaviors.[121]

Even kindergartners and first graders can be encouraged to reflect on their performance and progress, perhaps through questions such as "What were we doing that we're proud of?" and "What can we do that we didn't do before?"[122] By engaging regularly in self-monitoring and self-evaluation of classroom assignments, students should eventually develop appropriate

[120] McCaslin & Good, 1996; Paris & Ayres, 1994; Schraw, Potenza, & Nebelsick-Gullet, 1993.

[121] K. D. Allen, 1998; Belfiore & Hornyak, 1998; K. R. Harris, 1986; Mace & Kratochwill, 1988; Webber, Scheuermann, McCall, & Coleman, 1993.

[122] N. E. Perry, VandeKamp, Mercer, & Nordby, 2002, p. 10.

Project description ___Travel Guide_____

Evaluate with a 1 for weak, a 2 for fair, a 3 for good, a 4 for very good, and a 5 for excellent.

Student	Teacher	
4	4	1. The task was a major amount of work in keeping with a whole month of effort.
5	4	2. We used class time quite well.
4	5	3. The workload was quite evenly divided. I did a fair proportion.
4	5	4. I showed commitment to the group and to a quality project.
5	4	5. My report went into depth; it didn't just give the obvious, commonly known information.
5	5	6. The project made a point: a reader (or viewer) could figure out how all of the details fitted together to help form a conclusion.
5	5	7. The project was neat, attractive, well assembled. I was proud of the outcome.
4	5	8. We kept our work organized; we made copies; we didn't lose things or end up having to redo work that was lost.
5	4	9. The work had a lot of original thinking or other creative work.
4	4	10. The project demonstrated mastery of basic language skills—composition, planning, oral communication, writing.
45	45	Total

Comments:

46 group average   (A)ᴳ   (A)

FIGURE 4.8 After a cooperative group activity with three classmates, Rochelle and her teacher used the same criteria to rate Rochelle's performance and that of her group. With the two sets of ratings side by side, Rochelle can evaluate the accuracy of her self-assessments.

authentic activity Approach to instruction similar to one students might encounter in the outside world.

problem-based learning Classroom activity in which students acquire new knowledge and skills while working on a complex problem similar to those in the outside world.

project-based learning Classroom activity in which students acquire new knowledge and skills while working on a complex, multifaceted project that yields a concrete end product.

standards for their performance and apply those standards regularly to the things they accomplish—true hallmarks of a self-regulating learner.

Provide numerous and varied opportunities to apply classroom subject matter to new situations and problems.

As we discovered earlier, learners can transfer what they've learned only if they *retrieve* it as they encounter a new task or problem. When teachers present material within a particular academic discipline, then, they should relate the material to other disciplines and to the outside world as often as possible.[123] In doing so, they help students mentally connect the concepts and procedures learned in any single classroom with situations outside that classroom. For example, a teacher might show students how human digestion relates to principles of good nutrition, how physics concepts apply to automobile engines and home construction, or how economic issues have an impact on global climate change.

Ideally, teachers should have students use what they learn in a wide variety of contexts. For example, students can study arithmetic operations by working on such diverse problems as calculating change, balancing a checkbook, or estimating profits and necessary supplies for a lemonade stand. They can apply the concept of *scale* in cartography by estimating distances on a variety of local, state, and country maps.

One widely recommended approach is to use **authentic activities**, activities similar to those that students are apt to encounter in real-world contexts. For example, students' writing skills may show greater improvement in both quality and quantity when students write stories, essays, and letters to real people, rather than when they complete short, artificial writing exercises[124] (e.g., see Figure 4.9). Students gain a more complete understanding of how to use and interpret maps effectively when they construct their own maps than when they engage in workbook exercises involving map interpretation[125] (e.g., see Figure 4.10). Students are more likely to check their solutions to mathematics problems—in particular, to make sure their solutions make logical sense—when they use math for real-life tasks.[126] And the motivational benefits of authentic activities can be considerable, as one high school student explains:

> In ninth grade, we did this moon-tracking activity. It was the first time I can remember in school doing something that wasn't in the textbook, that was real, like we were real scientists or something. We had to keep data sheets, measure the time and angle of the moonrise every day for a month. It drove my mom nuts because sometimes we'd be eating dinner, and I'd look at my watch and race out the door! We had to measure the river near us to see how it was affected by the moon. I spent a lot of time outside while I was doing that, and I went down to the river more than I have in my whole life, I think. Then we had to do the calculations, that was another step, and we had to chart our findings. The test was to analyze your findings and tell what they meant about the relationship of the tides and the moon. It was hard, and you had to know what you were talking about or you didn't get credit for it. . . . I felt that I did something real, and I could see the benefit of it.[127]

---

[123] Blake & Clark, 1990; A. Collins et al., 1989; D. N. Perkins, 1992.

[124] E. H. Hiebert & Fisher, 1992.

[125] Gregg & Leinhardt, 1994.

[126] Cognition and Technology Group at Vanderbilt, 1993; Rogoff, 2003.

[127] Wasley, Hampel, & Clark, 1997, pp. 117–118.

Authentic activities can be identified for virtually any area of the curriculum. For example, teachers might ask students to engage in one or more of the following activities:

- Give an oral report.
- Converse in a foreign language.
- Write an editorial.
- Play in an athletic event.
- Participate in a debate.
- Complete an art project.
- Find information in the library.
- Perform in a concert.
- Conduct an experiment.
- Tutor a classmate.
- Graph data.
- Make a videotape.
- Construct a chart or model.
- Perform a workplace routine.
- Create and distribute a class newsletter.
- Develop classroom Web pages to showcase special projects.

In some instances authentic activities take the form of **problem-based** or **project-based learning,** in which students acquire new knowledge and skills as they work on complex problems or projects similar to those they might find in the outside world.[128] To be effective in enhancing students' learning—rather than sources of frustration and failure—most complex authentic activities require considerable teacher guidance and support.[129]

We find a technology-based example of problem-based learning in the Adventures of Jasper Woodbury series,[130] a videodisc program in which middle school students encounter a number of realistic problem situations. In one episode, "Journey to Cedar Creek," Jasper has just purchased an old boat he is hoping to pilot home the same day. Because the boat has no running lights, he must figure out whether he can get home by sunset, and because he has spent all his cash and used his last check, he must figure out whether he has enough gas to make the trip. Throughout the video, all of the information students need to answer these questions is embedded in authentic contexts (e.g., a marine radio announces time of sunset, and mileage markers are posted at various landmarks along the river), but students must sift through a lot of irrelevant information to find it. In another episode, "The Right Angle," teenager Paige Littlefield searches for a cave in which her Native American grandfather left her a special gift before he died. Her grandfather gave her directions to the cave that require knowledge and use of geometric principles (e.g., "From the easternmost point of Black Hawk Bluff, travel at a bearing of 25 degrees until you are almost surrounded by rock towers. Go to Flat Top Tower. . . . You will know Flat Top Tower because at a distance of 250 feet from the northern side of its base, the angle of elevation of its top is 45 degrees"). Using the directions and a map of the region, students must locate the cave. There are numerous ways to approach each Jasper problem, and students work in small groups to brainstorm and carry out possible problem solutions. Students of all

Dear Bexley City Council,

I suggest that a law should be passed that say littering is not allowed. The law would help keep Bexley looking nice.

Everyday when I go outside to walk to school or to a friend's house, I find at least two pieces of litter someone else put in our yard.

No one in my family ever litters. I think it is because we feel so strongly about protecting the environment. This why I am writing this letter.

I always see signs on the lamp posts saying, "Keep Bexley Beautiful," and I think this would be the first step to keep Bexley beautiful.

I know I am only a fourth grade student, but I would like you to consider my idea. Thank you for your time.

Sincerely,

Cindy M.

FIGURE 4.9   In an authentic writing activity, 9-year-old Cindy wrote this letter to her town's city council.

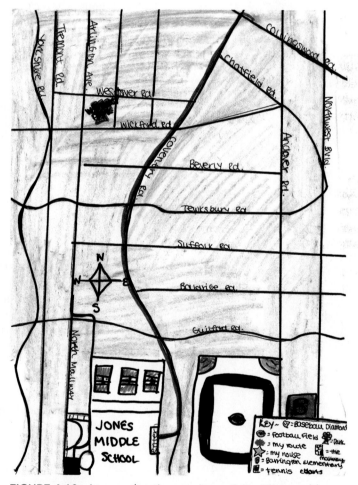

FIGURE 4.10   In an authentic mapping activity, 12-year-old Mary Lynn constructed this map of the area between her home and school.

---

[128] Hmelo-Silver, 2004, 2006; Krajcik & Blumenfeld, 2006; Mergendoller, Markham, Ravitz, & Larmer, 2006; Polman, 2004.

[129] Hmelo-Silver, Duncan, & Chinn, 2007; Krajcik & Blumenfeld, 2006; Mergendoller et al., 2006.

[130] For online information about the series, visit http://peabody.vanderbilt.edu and type "Jasper Woodbury" in the search box.

The Adventures of Jasper Woodbury series uses videodisc technology to present authentic problem-solving tasks. To assist Jasper in his decision making in "Journey to Cedar Creek," students must use information presented in real-world contexts to determine distance, speed, and gas mileage.

ability levels find the Jasper series highly motivating. Furthermore, they acquire new problem-solving skills and often transfer these skills to new problems.[131]

It is not necessarily desirable to fill the entire school day with complex, authentic tasks, however. For one thing, students can sometimes achieve automaticity for basic skills more quickly when they practice them in relative isolation from other activities. For example, when learning to play the violin, students need to master their fingering before they join an orchestra, and when learning to play soccer, they need to practice dribbling and passing before they can play effectively in a game.[132] Second, some authentic tasks may be too expensive and time consuming to warrant regular use in the classroom.[133] It is probably more important that classroom tasks encourage students to engage in learning processes that promote long-term retention and transfer of classroom subject matter—organization, elaboration, comprehension monitoring, and so on—than that tasks always be authentic.[134]

Create the conditions that creative thinking and problem solving require.

Students are more apt to think creatively when a teacher asks higher-level, thought-provoking questions that require them to use previously learned information in new and unusual ways. Questions that require divergent thinking may be especially helpful.[135] For example, during a unit on the Pony Express, a teacher might ask these questions:

- What are all the ways mail might have been transported across the United States at that time?
- Can you think of some very unusual way that no one else has thought of to transport mail today?[136]

It is important, too, to encourage students to encode situations and problems in multiple ways, so that they don't get locked into mental sets that exclude potentially effective approaches and solutions. For instance, a teacher might ask students to work in cooperative groups to identify several *different* ways of representing a single problem on paper—perhaps as a formula, a table, and a graph.[137] And certainly a teacher should mix the kinds of problems that students tackle in any single practice session, so that students must think carefully about which problem-solving procedures are appropriate for each one.[138]

If they are to think about tasks and problems creatively, students must also have the freedom and security they need to take risks, which they are unlikely to do if they are afraid of failing.[139] To encourage risk taking, teachers can allow students to engage in certain activities without evaluating their performance. They can also urge students to think of their mistakes and failures as an inevitable, but usually temporary, aspect of the creative process.[140] For example, when students are writing a creative short story, a teacher might give them several opportunities to get feedback before they turn in a final product.[141]

Finally, teachers must provide the *time* that creative thinking requires.[141] Students need time to experiment with new materials and ideas, to think in divergent directions, and occasionally to make mistakes. For example, when teaching a foreign language, a teacher might ask small groups of students to write and videotape a television commercial spoken entirely in that language. This is hardly a project that students can do in a day. They may need several weeks to brainstorm ideas, write and revise a script, find or develop the props they need, and rehearse their lines. Creative ideas and projects seldom emerge overnight.

[131] Cognition and Technology Group at Vanderbilt, 1990, 1997; Hickey, Moore, & Pellegrino, 2001; Learning Technology Center, Vanderbilt University, 1996.

[132] J. R. Anderson, Reder, & Simon, 1996; Bransford et al., 2006.

[133] M. M. Griffin & Griffin, 1994.

[134] J. R. Anderson et al., 1996.

[135] Feldhusen & Treffinger, 1980; Feldhusen, Treffinger, & Bahlke, 1970; D. N. Perkins, 1990; Torrance & Myers, 1970.

[136] Feldhusen & Treffinger, 1980, p. 36.

[137] Brenner et al., 1997; J. C. Turner, Meyer, et al., 1998.

[138] E. J. Langer, 2000; Mayfield & Chase, 2002.

[139] Houtz, 1990; Sternberg, 2003.

[140] Feldhusen & Treffinger, 1980; B. A. Hennessey & Amabile, 1987; Pruitt, 1989.

[141] Feldhusen & Treffinger, 1980; Pruitt, 1989; Sternberg, 2003.

CLASSROOM STRATEGIES

Fostering Critical Thinking

- **Teach elements of critical thinking.**

  In a unit on persuasion and argumentation, a junior high school language arts teacher explains that a sound argument meets three criteria: (a) The evidence presented to justify the argument is accurate and consistent; (b) the evidence is relevant to, and provides sufficient support for, the conclusion; and (c) there is little or no missing information that, if present, would lead to a contradictory conclusion. The teacher then has students practice applying these criteria to a variety of persuasive and argumentative essays.

- **Foster epistemological beliefs that encourage critical thinking.**

  Rather than teach history as a collection of facts to be memorized, a high school history teacher portrays the discipline as an attempt by informed but inevitably biased scholars to interpret and make sense of historical events. On several occasions he asks his students to read two or three different historians' accounts of the same incident and to look for evidence of personal bias in each one.

- **Embed critical thinking skills within the context of authentic activities.**

  In a unit on statistical and scientific reasoning, an eighth-grade science class studies concepts related to probability, correlation, and experimental control. Then, as part of a simulated "legislative hearing," the students work in small groups to develop arguments for or against a legislative bill concerning the marketing and use of vitamins and other dietary supplements. To find evidence to support their arguments, the students apply what they've learned about statistics and experimentation as they read and analyze journal articles and government reports about the possible benefits and drawbacks of nutritional supplements.

Sources: Derry, Levin, Osana, & Jones, 1998 (statistics example); Halpern, 1997 (criteria for sound argument); Paxton, 1999 (history example).

Encourage critical thinking.

Critical thinking encompasses a variety of skills, and so strategies for encouraging it are many and varied. Here are several suggestions:

- Encourage some intellectual skepticism—for instance, by urging students to question and challenge the ideas they read and hear—and communicate the message that people's knowledge and understanding of any single topic will continue to change over time.[142]
- Model critical thinking—for instance, by thinking aloud while analyzing a persuasive argument or scientific report.[143]
- Give students numerous opportunities to practice critical thinking—for instance, by identifying flaws in the arguments of persuasive essays, evaluating the quality and usefulness of scientific findings, and using evidence and logic to support particular viewpoints.[144]
- Ask questions such as these to encourage critical thinking:
  - What additional information do I need?
  - What information is relevant to this situation? What information is irrelevant?
  - What persuasive technique is the author using? Is it valid, or is it designed to mislead the reader?
  - What reasons support the conclusion? What reasons do *not* support the conclusion?
  - What actions might I take to improve the design of this study?[145]
- Have students debate controversial issues from several perspectives, and occasionally ask them to take a perspective quite different from their own.[146]
- Help students understand that critical thinking involves considerable mental effort but that its benefits make the effort worthwhile.[147]
- Embed critical thinking skills within the context of authentic activities as a way of helping students retrieve those skills later on, both in the workplace and in other aspects of adult life.[148]

The Classroom Strategies box "Fostering Critical Thinking" presents examples of what teachers might do in language arts, social studies, and science.

---

[142] Kardash & Scholes, 1996; Kuhn, 2001a; Onosko, 1989.

[143] Onosko & Newmann, 1994.

[144] Halpern, 1998; Kuhn & Weinstock, 2002.

[145] Questions based on Halpern, 1998, p. 454.

[146] Reiter, 1994.

[147] Halpern, 1998.

[148] Derry et al., 1998; Halpern, 1998.

Promoting Higher-Level Processes in General

Several especially important instructional practices are apt to promote a wide variety of sophisticated cognitive processes.

Teach higher-level thinking skills within the context of academic disciplines and subject matter.

Teachers occasionally run across packaged curricular programs designed to teach study skills, problem solving, creativity, or critical thinking. As a general rule, however, teachers should teach higher-level cognitive processes *not* as separate entities, but instead within the context of day-to-day academic topics. For example, they might teach critical thinking and problem-solving skills during science lessons or teach creative thinking during writing instruction.[149] And to help students become truly effective learners, teachers should teach study strategies in *every* academic discipline.[150] For example, when presenting new information in class, a teacher might (a) suggest how students can organize their notes, (b) describe mnemonics for facts and procedures that are hard to remember, and (c) ask various students to summarize the main points of a lesson. When assigning textbook pages to be read at home, a teacher might (a) suggest that students recall what they already know about a topic before they begin reading about it, (b) provide questions for students to ask themselves as they read, and (c) have students create concept maps interrelating key ideas.

Pursue topics in depth rather than superficially.

To apply classroom material to real-world situations and problems, use it flexibly and creatively, and think critically about it, students should not just study the material on one occasion. Instead, they must *master* it.[151] Ultimately, students should gain a thorough, conceptual understanding of topics that can help them make better sense of their world and function more effectively in adult society. This *less is more* principle applies across the board: Teaching a few topics in depth is almost invariably more effective than skimming over the surface of a great many.

In the "Charles's Law" video clip in MyEducationLab, a high school science teacher uses several strategies to promote a conceptual understanding of Charles's law, which describes the relationship between the temperature and volume of a gas. She activates students' prior knowledge relevant to the law, demonstrates the law "in action" with balloons and water of various temperatures, and presents examples of how students can use the law to make predictions and solve problems. In a later part of the class not depicted in the video, she gives students additional problems to solve on their own and monitors their progress and understanding.

Observe a teacher promote conceptual understanding in the "Charles's Law" video in the Additional Resources section in Chapter 4 of MyEducationLab.

Foster higher-level thinking through group discussions and projects.

In Chapter 3 we noted that learners can often gain a better understanding of a topic when they discuss it with peers. A rapidly growing body of research evidence indicates that group activities, especially when structured to some degree, can also promote higher-level processes.[152] When students talk with one another, they must verbalize (and therefore become more metacognitively aware of) what and how they themselves are thinking. They also hear other (possibly better) study strategies, problem-solving approaches, and critical analyses. And by working together, they can often accomplish more difficult tasks than they would accomplish on their own (e.g., students typically tackle the Jasper Woodbury problems in groups rather than alone). The last two sections of the "Group Work" video clip in MyEducationLab show a middle school science teacher teaching mnemonics and problem solving in small-group activities.

Observe groups developing mnemonics and addressing challenging problems in the "Group Work" video in the Additional Resources section in Chapter 4 of MyEducationLab.

---

[149] M. C. Linn, Clement, Pulos, & Sullivan, 1989; Porath, 1988; Pulos & Linn, 1981; Stanley, 1980.
[150] Hattie et al., 1996; Meltzer et al., 2007; Paris & Paris, 2001; Pressley, El-Dinary, et al., 1992; Pressley, Harris, & Marks, 1992.

[151] Amabile & Hennessey, 1992; N. Frederiksen, 1984a; D. N. Perkins, 1990; Prawat, 1989; Rittle-Johnson, Siegler, & Alibali, 2001.
[152] For example, see A. M. O'Donnell, Hmelo-Silver, & Erkens, 2006.

One effective approach is to teach students to ask one another, and then answer, higher-level questions about the material they are studying—for instance, "Why is it that such-and-such is true?"[153] In the following dialogue, fifth graders Katie and Janelle are working together to study class material about tide pools. Katie's job is to ask Janelle questions that encourage elaboration:

Katie: How are the upper tide zone and the lower tide zone different?

Janelle: They have different animals in them. Animals in the upper tide zone and splash zone can handle being exposed—have to be able to use the rain and sand and wind and sun—and they don't need that much water and the lower tide animals do.

Katie: And they can be softer 'cause they don't have to get hit on the rocks.

Janelle: Also predators. In the spray zone it's because there's predators like us people and all different kinds of stuff that can kill the animals and they won't survive, but the lower tide zone has not as many predators.

Katie: But wait! Why do the animals in the splash zone have to survive?[154]

Notice how the two girls are continually relating the animals' characteristics to survival in different tide zones, and eventually Katie asks why animals in the splash zone even *need* to survive—a question that clearly reflects critical thinking.

Create an overall classroom culture that values higher-level thinking.

Through both words and actions, teachers should communicate that sophisticated learning strategies, transfer, creative problem solving, and critical thinking must be commonplace in the classroom.[155] For example, teachers might

- Have students conduct "strategy share" discussions or create "strategy books" in which class members explain their techniques for learning and remembering specific classroom topics.[156]
- Regularly encourage students to think "How might I use this information?" as they listen, read, and study.[157]
- Consistently welcome creative ideas, even those that might occasionally fly in the face of conventional ways of thinking.[158]
- Conduct extended discussions of intriguing "Why?" questions and controversial issues and ask students to defend diverse perspectives with evidence and logic.[159]

Incorporate higher-level thinking into assessment activities.

As you will discover in Chapter 10, it is fairly easy to construct assignments and tests that assess knowledge of basic facts and procedures. But it is ultimately more important that teachers assess what students can *do* with that knowledge. As an illustration, Figure 4.11 presents an assessment task that asks students to apply their knowledge of geographic principles to several new problems. By consistently incorporating application of classroom topics into assessment tasks and problems, teachers clearly communicate that academic subject matter can and should be flexibly and creatively used in many different contexts.

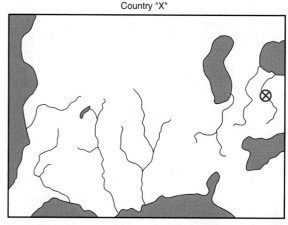

Country "X"

0 250 500   Major Rivers   Bodies of Water (Seas)
Scale (miles)

- If people living at the point marked "X" on the map began to migrate *or* expand, where would they go and what direction might they take?
- What would be the distribution of population in country "X"; that is, where would many people live, few, and so on?
- Where would large cities develop in country "X"?
- How would you judge the country's economic potential; that is, what areas might be best for development, which worst, and so on?

FIGURE 4.11 Example of an assessment activity that asks students to apply what they've learned in geography to new problems

Source: Problems and figure from Massialas, Byron G., and Zevin, Jack, *Teaching Creatively: Learning Through Discovery*, 1983, Krieger Publishing Company, Malabar, Florida, U.S.A. Reprinted with permission.

---

[153] Kahl & Woloshyn, 1994; A. King, 1994, 1999; V. L. Martin & Pressley, 1991; Palincsar & Herrenkohl, 1999; Rosenshine, Meister, & Chapman, 1996; Woloshyn, Pressley, & Schneider, 1992; E. Wood et al., 1999.

[154] A. King, 1999, p. 97.

[155] Engle, 2006; Haskell, 2001; Muis et al., 2006; Pea, 1987; D. N. Perkins & Ritchhart, 2004.

[156] Meltzer et al., 2007.

[157] D. N. Perkins, 1992; Stein, 1989; Sternberg & Frensch, 1993.

[158] Lubart & Mouchiroud, 2003.

[159] Chinn, 2006; D. N. Perkins & Ritchhart, 2004.

SUMMARY

Higher-level cognitive processes are processes in which learners go far beyond the information they have learned, perhaps to better remember it, apply it to a new situation, use it to solve a problem or create a product, or critically evaluate it. One form of higher-level thinking, which is often an element of other forms of higher-level thinking as well, is *metacognition*, literally "thinking about thinking." Metacognition includes knowledge and beliefs about one's own cognitive processes as well as conscious attempts to engage in behaviors and cognitive processes that maximize learning and memory. Learners' learning strategies include both overt strategies (e.g., taking notes, drawing concept maps) and covert strategies (e.g., identifying main ideas, monitoring comprehension), but ultimately it is the covert strategies that most influence learning and achievement. Although metacognitive awareness and effective learning strategies improve with age, even many high school students are quite naive about how they can best study and learn classroom subject matter. To some degree, learners' *epistemological beliefs* about the nature of knowledge and learning affect the study strategies they use. For example, students who realize that reading is a constructive process are more likely to engage in meaningful learning as they read and more likely to undergo conceptual change when they encounter ideas that contradict what they currently believe.

Self-regulation—the process of making decisions about, directing, monitoring, and evaluating one's own performance—affects learning success as well. Self-regulation includes establishing goals and standards for performance, planning a course of action, actively controlling both external behaviors and internal thoughts and emotions, monitoring progress, evaluating final outcomes, and self-imposing consequences (either internal or external) for success and failure. *Co-regulated learning*, in which an adult and child share responsibility for directing a learning task, helps young learners gradually assume control of their own learning processes.

When learners apply something they've learned in one context to a new context, *transfer* is occurring. Transfer is more common when a new situation is obviously similar to an earlier situation in which certain knowledge and skills have come into play (e.g., learning French should help someone learn Spanish because many words are similar in the two languages). But general study strategies, beliefs, and attitudes (e.g., knowing how to take good notes, realizing that mastering classroom topics takes hard work and persistence) often transfer from one content domain to a very different domain. Learners are most apt to apply school subject matter to outside tasks and problems when they learn it meaningfully and have a thorough, conceptual understanding of it.

Problem solving—addressing and resolving an unanswered question or troubling situation—and *creativity*—developing an original and culturally appropriate product—involve varying degrees of convergent and divergent thinking. Learners can usually solve problems more effectively and think more creatively when they have acquired considerable knowledge about a topic, have automatized basic skills but *not* automatized particular ways of encoding problems and situations, and can metacognitively reflect on and monitor their progress.

Critical thinking involves evaluating the accuracy and worth of information and lines of reasoning. It takes a variety of forms, such as analyzing persuasive arguments, identifying statements that do and don't support a particular conclusion, and judging the value of data collected through different research methods. When learners have sophisticated epistemological beliefs (e.g., recognizing that an understanding of a topic continues to evolve over time) and are predisposed to question and evaluate new information, they are more likely to think critically about what they read and hear.

A variety of classroom practices can promote higher-level cognitive processes. Some are specific to particular processes, but several are applicable across the board. For instance, teachers are more likely to foster higher-level thinking skills within the context of teaching everyday classroom subject matter, rather than as separate curriculum units on, say, "study skills" or "creativity." Group discussions that enable students to critique and build on one another's ideas as they tackle challenging topics, tasks, and issues should be commonplace. And ultimately, higher-level processes—transfer, creative problem solving, critical thinking, and so on—should be the expectation and norm in the classroom, not only in lessons but also in assessment activities.

PRACTICE FOR YOUR LICENSURE EXAM

Interview with Emily

In the 9th and 10th grades, Emily earns mostly Cs and Ds in her classes. When she reaches 11th grade, however, she begins to work more diligently on her schoolwork, and by the fall of 12th grade, she is earning As and Bs. Ms. Tillman, a preservice teacher, interviews Emily about her study strategies:

Ms. T.: How did you learn to study for a test?

Emily: I'm not really sure. I never learned the correct way to study for a test. I use my own methods, and they seem to be working because I'm now receiving the grades I want.

Ms. T.: How did you go about studying for a test when you were younger?

Emily: Honestly, I never really studied too hard. I never studied for math tests because I didn't know how to. For other subjects like history, I'd just skim over the text. Skimming the text never made the material stick in my head. I guess I never really had a strategy for studying.

Ms. T.: Now that you're receiving good grades, how do you study for a test?

Emily: Well, it's different for every subject. Now when I study for a math test, I do many practice problems. When I'm studying for a history or science test, I first review my notes. My favorite thing to do is make flash cards with the important facts. I then go through the flash cards many times and try to learn the facts on them.

Ms. T.: What do you mean, "learn" the facts on them?

Emily: I guess I try to memorize the facts. I'll go through the flash cards many times and say them over and over in my head until I remember them.

Ms. T.: How do you know when a fact is memorized?

Emily: I'll repeat a fact over and over in my head until I think I've memorized it. Then I'll leave and do something else, like get a snack. I know I've memorized something if I still remember it after taking my break.

Ms. T.: Do you consider yourself a good textbook reader?

Emily: Not really. Textbooks are pretty boring. I'll try to read everything in the textbook, but at times I find myself looking for boldface print. Phrases in bold print are important.

Ms. T.: What are some good methods for studying for a test?

Emily: I really like the flash card method because it helps me to memorize facts. I also like to reread the text and my notes. Another good method is outlining the text, but this method takes too long so I rarely use it.[160]

1. **Constructed-response question**

   In the interview Emily reveals several strategies she uses to learn and remember school subject matter.

   A. Identify three specific strategies that Emily uses when she studies.

   B. For each of the strategies you've identified, describe the extent to which it is likely to help Emily remember and apply school subject matter over the long run. Base your explanation on contemporary principles and theories of learning, memory, metacognition, self-regulation, or a combination of these.

2. **Multiple-choice question**

   Emily says, "My favorite thing to do is make flash cards with the important facts. I then go through the flash cards many times and try to learn the facts on them." This statement suggests that Emily views academic subject matter as being primarily a collection of discrete facts. Such a perspective is an example of:

   a. A covert strategy
   b. Divergent thinking
   c. An illusion of knowing
   d. An epistemological belief

   Once you have answered these questions, compare your responses with those presented in Appendix A.

FOR FURTHER READING

The following articles from the journal *Educational Leadership* are especially relevant to this chapter. You can find these articles in Chapter 4 of MyEducationLab for this text.

Curtis, D. (2002). The power of projects. *Educational Leadership, 60*(1), 50–53.

Dong, Y. R. (2006). Learning to think in English. *Educational Leadership, 64*(2), 22–26.

Helm, J. H. (2004). Projects that power young minds. *Educational Leadership, 62*(1), 58.

Ivey, G., & Fisher, D. (2006). When thinking skills trump reading skills. *Educational Leadership, 64*(2), 16–21.

Krynock, K., & Robb, L. (1999). Problem solved: How to coach cognition. *Educational Leadership, 57*(3), 29–32.

Lent, R. (2006). In the company of critical thinkers. *Educational Leadership, 64*(2), 68–72.

McConachie, S., Hall, M., Resnick, L., Ravi, A. K., Bill, V. L., Bintz, J., & Taylor, J. A. (2006). Task, text, and talk: Literacy for all subjects. *Educational Leadership, 64*(2), 8–14.

Richetti, C., & Sheerin, J. (1999). Helping students ask the right questions. *Educational Leadership, 57*(3), 58–62.

Schack, G. D. (1993). Involving students in authentic research *Educational Leadership, 50*(7), 29–31.

MYEDUCATIONLAB

Now go to Chapter 4 of MyEducationLab at **www.myeducationlab.com,** where you can:

- Find instructional objectives for the chapter, along with focus questions that can help you zero in on important ideas in the chapter.

- Take a self-check quiz on concepts and principles you've just read about.
- Complete exercises and assignments that can help you more deeply understand the chapter content.
- Apply what you've learned to classroom contexts in Building Teaching Skills activities.

---

[160] Interview courtesy of Melissa Tillman.

What Shapes
Can You
Build?

CHAPTER 5

Cognitive Development

CASE STUDY   Hidden Treasure

Six-year-old Lupita has just enrolled in Ms. Padilla's kindergarten classroom. The daughter of migrant workers, Lupita has been raised in Mexico by her grandmother, who has limited financial resources and thus has not been able to provide very many playthings such as toys, puzzles, crayons, and scissors. Ms. Padilla rarely calls on Lupita in class because of her lack of academic skills. By midyear Ms. Padilla is thinking about holding Lupita back for a second year of kindergarten.

Lupita is always quiet and well behaved in class. In fact, she's so quiet that Ms. Padilla sometimes forgets she's there. Yet a researcher's video camera captures a different side of her. On one occasion Lupita is quick to finish her Spanish assignment and so starts to work on a puzzle during her free time. A classmate approaches, and he and Lupita begin playing with a box of toys. A teacher aide asks the boy whether he has finished his Spanish assignment, implying that he should return to complete it, but the boy does not understand the aide's subtle message. Lupita gently persuades him to go back and finish his work. She then returns to her puzzle and successfully fits most of it to-

gether. Two classmates having difficulty with their own puzzles request Lupita's assistance, and she competently and patiently shows them how to assemble puzzles and how to help each other.

Ms. Padilla is amazed when she views the videotape, which shows Lupita to be a competent girl with strong teaching and leadership skills. Ms. Padilla readily admits, "I had written her off . . . her and three others. They had met my expectations and I just wasn't looking for anything else." Ms. Padilla and her aides begin working closely with Lupita on academic skills, and they often allow her to take a leadership role in group activities. At the end of the school year, Lupita earns achievement test scores indicating exceptional competence in language skills and mathematics, and she is promoted to first grade.[1]

- Why might Ms. Padilla initially underestimate Lupita's academic potential?
- What clues in the case study suggest that Lupita is, in fact, quite bright?

---

[1] Case described by Carrasco, 1981.

Over the years Ms. Padilla has almost certainly had students who lacked basic knowledge and skills (color and shape names, counting, the alphabet, etc.), and many of them undoubtedly struggled with the kindergarten curriculum as a result. And in Ms. Padilla's experience, children who can answer questions and contribute to class discussions usually speak up or raise their hands, but Lupita is quiet and reserved. With such things in mind, it might be all too easy to conclude that Lupita needs a second year in kindergarten. Yet the speed with which Lupita finishes her assignment and her behavior during free time—her facility with puzzles despite little prior experience with them, her correct interpretation of an aide's subtle message, and her skill in guiding peers—suggest that she learns quickly and has considerable social know-how.

Children and adolescents gain many new abilities and skills as they progress through the school years. But as is clear in Lupita's case, cognitive development begins long before children enter kindergarten or first grade. For instance, by the time infants are 3 or 4 months old, they have some knowledge about their physical worlds, including rudimentary understandings of gravity and of the principle that no two objects can occupy the same space at the same time.[2] Many preschoolers know a fair amount about their fellow human beings and how to interact effectively with them.[3] And, of course, young children make considerable progress in the language of their culture, so that by age 6, English speakers understand 8,000 to 14,000 words.[4]

In previous chapters we've learned that as children get older, they acquire more effective learning and study strategies, greater metacognitive awareness, and an increasing ability to regulate their own learning. As we look in greater depth at cognitive development in this chapter, we'll draw from several theoretical perspectives, including two—information processing theory and sociocultural theory—that have also had a significant influence on the study of learning (see Table 2.1 in Chapter 2) and two others—cognitive-developmental theory and nativism—whose influence we'll be seeing for the first time. In Table 5.1, I describe these four perspectives in the order in which they'll enter the picture in this chapter. In the table I also describe a fifth perspective—psychodynamic theory—that will contribute to our discussion of personal and social development in Chapter 7.

Keep in mind, however, that the various perspectives of child and adolescent development are not always mutually exclusive. For example, some developmental theorists have drawn on *both* the cognitive-developmental and information processing perspectives in their work on cognitive processes (notice how theorists Robbie Case and Kurt Fischer appear in two places in Table 5.1). Keep in mind, too, that the perspectives presented in the table are not the *only* ones psychologists have used in studying child development. Behaviorism, social learning theory, and other perspectives, although not as dominant, have made significant contributions to developmental psychology as well.

Two early developmental theorists, Jean Piaget and Lev Vygotsky, have been especially influential and so will play key roles in our discussion in the upcoming pages. Piaget, who was Swiss, developed many ingenious tasks to probe children's and adolescents' thinking and reasoning.[5] He observed that young learners often have self-constructed understandings of physical and social phenomena and that these understandings change in qualitative ways over time. Hence Piaget was a cognitive-developmental theorist. Meanwhile, Vygotsky, who was Russian, proposed mechanisms through which children's social and cultural environments influence their development, and his work provided the groundwork for sociocultural theory.[6] Some of Vygotsky's ideas—especially mediated learning, cognitive tools, and the importance of culture—appeared in Chapter 3. However, because Vygotsky was, first and foremost, concerned about children's cognitive development, we will continue to look at his ideas in this chapter.

Our initial focus will be on general processes and trends that characterize the development of the great majority of children and adolescents. Later, we will look at the variability in cognitive abilities we are apt to see among children in any single group—variability that is often called *intelligence*.

Learn more about Piaget's and Vygotsky's theories of cognitive development in supplementary readings in the Homework and Exercises section in Chapter 5 of MyEducationLab.

---

[2] Baillargeon, 1994; Spelke, 1994.

[3] Birch & Bloom, 2002; Farver & Branstetter, 1994; Flavell, 2000.

[4] S. Carey, 1978.

[5] For example, see Piaget, 1928, 1952b, 1959, 1970, 1980; Inhelder & Piaget, 1958.

[6] For example, see Vygotsky, 1962, 1978, 1987, 1997. Vygotsky died in 1934, but many of his works were not translated into English until considerably later.

THEORETICAL PERSPECTIVES

TABLE 5.1 General Theoretical Approaches to the Study of Child and Adolescent Development

Theoretical Perspective	General Description	Examples of Prominent Theorists	Where You Will See This Perspective in the Book
Cognitive-Developmental Theory	Cognitive-developmental theorists propose that one or more aspects of development can be characterized by a predictable sequence of stages. Each stage builds on acquisitions from any preceding stages and yet is qualitatively different from its predecessors. Many cognitive-developmentalists are *constructivists*, in that they portray children as actively trying to make sense of their world and constructing increasingly complex understandings to interpret and respond to experiences.	Jean Piaget Jerome Bruner Robbie Case Kurt Fischer Lawrence Kohlberg *Supplementary readings on Piaget's theory and Kohlberg's theory appear in the Homework and Exercises section in Chapters 5 and Chapter 7, respectively, of MyEducationLab.*	Piaget's ideas appear frequently in this chapter's discussions of developmental processes and trends (e.g., see the discussions of assimilation, accommodation, and equilibration, as well as Table 5.2 and some entries in Table 5.3). We will look at Kohlberg's theory in our discussion of moral development in Chapter 7.
Nativism	Some behaviors are biologically built in. A few behaviors (e.g., the reflex to suck on a nipple placed in the mouth) are evident at birth. Others (e.g., walking) emerge gradually, and usually in a predictable order, as genetic instructions propel increasing physical *maturation* of the brain and body. Nativists suggest that in addition to genetically preprogrammed behaviors, some knowledge, skills, and predispositions—or at least the basic "seeds" from which such things will grow—are also biologically built in.	Renee Baillargeon Elizabeth Spelke Noam Chomsky	The influence of nativism is most obvious in this chapter's discussions of heredity, maturation, sensitive periods, brain development, and intelligence. It will also be reflected in our discussion of temperament both in this chapter and in Chapter 7.
Sociocultural Theory	Sociocultural theorists emphasize the role of social interaction and children's cultural heritage in directing the course of development. Parents, teachers, and peers are especially instrumental, in that they pass along culturally prescribed ways of thinking about and responding to objects and events. As children gain practice in certain behaviors and cognitive processes within the context of social interactions, they gradually adopt and adapt these behaviors and processes as their own.	Lev Vygotsky Barbara Rogoff Jean Lave Mary Gauvain *A supplementary reading on Vygotsky's theory appears in the Homework and Exercises section in Chapter 5 of MyEducationLab.*	Vygotsky's theory and other sociocultural perspectives come into play in this chapter whenever we discuss the influence of social interaction on cognitive development (e.g., see the discussions of internalization, zone of proximal development, cultural differences, and distributed intelligence). In addition, it underlies many of the chapter's recommendations for fostering cognitive development (e.g., see the discussions of play activities, reciprocal teaching, scaffolding, and apprenticeships). It will also help us understand the effectiveness of peer mediation in Chapter 7.
Information Processing Theory	Developmental psychologists who take an information processing approach focus on how memory capabilities and specific cognitive processes change with age. For example, some examine how an expanding working memory capacity enables more complex thought. Others consider how increasingly sophisticated metacognitive knowledge and beliefs spur more advanced and effective learning strategies. Still others explore the cognitive processes involved in children's social interactions with peers.	Robert Siegler Deanna Kuhn John Flavell Robbie Case Kurt Fischer Nicki Crick Kenneth Dodge	Some trends in cognitive development described in this chapter (e.g., changes in children's working memory and knowledge bases, as well as their impacts on children's reasoning) are based on information processing research. Discussions of the cognitive processes involved in intelligence and related abilities also draw largely from information processing theory. In Chapter 7, we'll draw on this perspective once again in our discussion of social information processing.
Psychodynamic Theory	By and large, psychodynamic theorists focus on personality development, and sometimes on abnormal development as well. They propose that a child's early experiences can have significant effects on a child's later development, even when those experiences are buried in a child's *unconscious* and so are unavailable for recall and self-reflection. Some theorists also propose that children go through qualitatively distinct stages in their development. One key concept in many psychodynamic theories is *identity*, one's self-constructed definition of who one is and hopes to become.	Sigmund Freud Erik Erikson *A supplementary reading on Erikson's theory appears in the Homework and Exercises section in Chapter 7 of MyEducationLab.*	Identity formation will be an important topic in our discussion of sense of self in Chapter 7. In that discussion, we'll draw on research by James Marcia (a psychologist who drew heavily from Erik Erikson's theory) to identify the various paths that adolescents might take in their search for identity.

GENERAL PRINCIPLES OF DEVELOPMENT

Virtually any aspect of development—whether physical, cognitive, personal, or social—is characterized by several general principles.

The sequence of development is somewhat predictable.

To some degree, human development is reflected in the acquisition of **developmental milestones**—new, developmentally more advanced behaviors—that appear in a predictable sequence. For example, children typically begin to walk only after they can sit up and crawl. Children begin to think logically about abstract ideas only after they have learned to think logically about concrete objects and observable events. They become concerned about what other people think of them only after they realize that other people *do* think about them. To some extent, then, we see **universals** in development: We see similar patterns in how children change over time regardless of the specific environment in which they grow up.

Research often tells us the *average* age at which various developmental milestones are reached. But we must remember that individual children develop at different rates.

Children develop at different rates.

Many descriptive studies in child and adolescent development tell us the average ages at which various developmental milestones are reached. For example, the average child can draw square and triangular shapes at age 3, starts using rehearsal as a way of remembering information at age 7 or 8, and begins puberty at age 10 (for girls) or 11½ (for boys).[7] But not all children reach developmental milestones at the average age. Some reach milestones earlier, some later. Accordingly, we are apt to see considerable variability in learners' developmental accomplishments at any single grade level, and so we must never jump to conclusions about what any individual learner can and cannot do on the basis of age alone.

Development is often marked by spurts and plateaus.

Development does not necessarily proceed at a constant rate. Instead, periods of relatively rapid growth (*spurts*) may appear between periods of slower growth (*plateaus*). For example, toddlers may speak with a limited vocabulary and one-word "sentences" for several months and then, sometime around their second birthday, display a virtual explosion in language development, with vocabulary expanding rapidly and sentences becoming longer and longer within just a few weeks. During the early elementary school years, children gain an average of two or three inches in height per year. In contrast, during their adolescent growth spurt, they may grow as much as five inches per year.[8]

Development involves both quantitative and qualitative changes.

In some cases development simply means acquiring *more* of something. For example, whereas English-speaking children know about 8,000 to 14,000 words by first grade, they know about 50,000 words by sixth grade and about 80,000 words by high school.[9] Yet in many respects children also tend to think and behave in qualitatively different ways at different ages. For example, as we discovered in Chapter 2, children in the elementary grades depend heavily on rehearsal when they study and try to remember classroom subject matter. Strategies such as organization and elaboration appear later, and high-achieving adolescents increasingly rely on these strategies rather than on rehearsal. We see qualitative changes in epistemological beliefs as well. For instance, as we learned in Chapter 4, views about the nature of knowledge often change in the high school years. Ninth graders frequently think of "knowledge" as being little more than mastery of a collection of isolated facts. By 12th grade, many students realize that knowledge includes not only knowing specific facts but also understanding interrelationships among ideas.

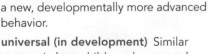

developmental milestone Appearance of a new, developmentally more advanced behavior.

universal (in development) Similar pattern in how children change and progress over time regardless of their specific environment.

---

[7] T. M. McDevitt & Ormrod, 2007.
[8] Berk, 2003; A. C. Harris, 1986.

[9] G. A. Miller & Gildea, 1987; Nippold, 1988; Owens, 1996.

Some theorists, especially those taking the cognitive-developmental approach described in Table 5.1, believe that patterns of uneven growth and qualitative change reflect distinctly different periods in children's development. In a **stage theory**, development is characterized as progressing through a predictable sequence of stages, with earlier stages providing a foundation on which later, more advanced ones build. For example, as we'll discover shortly, Piaget characterized the development of logical reasoning skills as having four distinct stages. Other theorists have identified stages in the development of expertise (more about these stages later in the chapter), morality (more about these stages in Chapter 7), and such domains as reading and personality development.[10]

In recent years many developmental psychologists have begun to believe that most aspects of development can be better characterized as reflecting general *trends*—for instance, a gradual transition from rehearsal to elaboration over a period of many years—rather than discrete stages.[11] Even so, developmental changes often do occur in a predictable sequence, with some acquisitions occurring before, and possibly being prerequisites for, later ones.

Heredity and environment interact in their effects on development.

As nativist theorists point out, virtually all aspects of development are affected either directly or indirectly by a child's genetic makeup. Not all inherited characteristics appear at birth, however. Heredity continues to control a child's growth through the process of **maturation**, an unfolding of genetically directed changes as the child develops. For example, basic motor skills such as walking, running, and jumping emerge primarily as a result of neurological (brain) development, increased strength, and increased muscular control—changes that are largely determined by inherited biological "instructions." Children are also genetically endowed with particular ways of responding to their physical and social environments, and such **temperaments** influence their tendencies to be calm or irritable, outgoing or shy, adventuresome or cautious, cheerful or fearful.[12]

Yet the environment plays an equally critical role in most aspects of development. For example, genes require certain "supplies" and outside influences—in the forms of oxygen, nutrients, and environmental stimulation—to carry out their work. Thus, as we learned in Chapter 3, poor nutrition can hamper brain development. Although basic motor skills appear only after brain and muscle maturation make them possible, exercise and practice affect how fast children can run and how far they can jump. And although children's behaviors are partly the result of inherited temperaments, the ways in which their local environment and broader culture socialize them to behave—through reinforcement, punishment, modeling, and so on—are just as influential.

The effects of both heredity and environment are well documented, but psychologists disagree about how *much* each contributes to development—an issue known as *nature versus nurture*. In fact, heredity and environment typically *interact* in their effects, such that we can probably never disentangle their unique influences on development.[13] In some cases the interaction between heredity and environment takes the form of a **sensitive period**, a biologically predetermined point in development during which a child is especially susceptible to environmental conditions. For example, the quality of nutrition has a greater impact on cognitive development in the early years, when children's brains are rapidly maturing, than in middle childhood or adolescence.[14] There may also be sensitive periods for some aspects of language development. In particular, children have an easier time mastering a language's grammatical subtleties and learning how to pronounce words flawlessly if they are immersed in the language within the first 5 to 10 years of life.[15] However, there is *no* evidence

stage theory Theory that depicts development as a series of relatively discrete periods (*stages*).

maturation Unfolding of genetically controlled changes as a child develops.

temperament Genetic predisposition to respond in particular ways to one's physical and social environments.

sensitive period Genetically determined age range during which a certain aspect of a child's development is especially susceptible to environmental conditions.

[10] For examples of stage theories in reading and personality development, see Chall, 1996, and Erikson, 1963, 1972, respectively. You can also find details of Erikson's theory in a supplementary reading in the Homework and Exercises section in Chapter 7 of MyEducationLab.

[11] For example, see Flavell, 1994; Rest, Narvaez, Bebeau, & Thoma, 1999; Siegler & Alibali, 2005.

[12] Kagan, 1998; Keogh, 2003.

[13] W. A. Collins, 2005; Gottlieb, 2000; Halpern, 2006; Kolb, Gibb, & Robinson, 2003; Petrill & Wilkerson, 2000.

[14] Sigman & Whaley, 1998.

[15] Bialystok, 1994; Bortfeld & Whitehurst, 2001; Bruer, 1999.

to indicate that sensitive periods exist for traditional academic subjects such as reading, writing, or mathematics.[16]

Children's own behaviors also influence their development.

Not only does heredity interact with environment, but so, too, do children's day-to-day behaviors interact with environmental factors. Furthermore, some of their behaviors are a result of inherited characteristics. Ultimately, then, we have a three-way interplay among behavior, heredity, and environment.[17] We saw manifestations of this interplay in two principles presented in Chapter 3:

- **Learners alter their environment both through their behaviors and through their internal traits and mental processes.** For example, in the opening case study, Lupita behaves in a quiet, reserved, manner, possibly reflecting inherited temperaments to be calm and shy. Because she is so easy to overlook, Ms. Padilla gives her very little attention in class. Had a researcher's video camera not captured some of her strengths, Lupita might very well have spent a second year in kindergarten.
- **Learners actively seek out environments that are a good fit with their existing characteristics and behaviors** (recall our discussion of *niche-picking*). In the opening case study, Lupita voluntarily chooses to work on a puzzle during her free time. Thus she actively seeks out an activity that will nurture an existing interest and talent.

DEVELOPMENTAL PROCESSES

Heredity, environment, and children's own behaviors all nudge children toward increasingly complex and sophisticated ways of thinking and behaving. The means by which they do so are reflected in the following principles.

The brain continues to develop throughout childhood, adolescence, and adulthood.

At birth the human brain is about one-fourth the size it will be in adulthood. By age 2 or 3, it has reached at least three-fourths of its adult size.[18] The cortex is the least mature part of the brain at birth, and changes in the cortex that occur in infancy and childhood probably account for many advancements in young children's ability to think and reason.

Neurons in the brain begin to form synapses with one another long before a child is born. But shortly after birth the rate of synapse formation increases dramatically. Much of this early **synaptogenesis** appears to be driven primarily by genetic programming rather than by learning experiences. Thanks to synaptogenesis, children in the elementary grades have many more synapses than adults do. As children encounter a wide variety of stimuli and experiences in their daily lives, some synapses come in quite handy and are used repeatedly. Other synapses are largely irrelevant and useless, and these gradually fade away through a process known as **synaptic pruning**. In some parts of the brain, intensive synaptic pruning occurs fairly early (e.g., in the preschool or early elementary years). In other parts, it begins later and continues until well into adolescence.[19]

Why do growing brains create a great many synapses, only to eliminate a sizable proportion of them later on? In the case of synapses, more is not necessarily better.[20] Experts speculate that by generating more synapses than will ever be needed, human beings have the potential to adapt to a wide variety of conditions and circumstances. As children encounter certain regularities in their environment, some synapses are actually a nuisance because they are inconsistent with typical environmental events and typical behavior patterns. Synaptic pruning, then, may be Mother Nature's way of making the brain more efficient.

---

synaptogenesis Universal process in early brain development in which many new synapses form spontaneously.

synaptic pruning Universal process in brain development in which many previously formed synapses wither away.

[16] Bruer, 1999; Geary, 1998; Greenough, Black, & Wallace, 1987.

[17] Flavell, 1994; Mareschal et al., 2007; Plomin & Spinath, 2004; Scarr & McCartney, 1983.

[18] M. H. Johnson & de Haan, 2001; Lenroot & Giedd, 2007; Kolb & Whishaw, 1990.

[19] Bruer, 1999; Huttenlocher & Dabholkar, 1997; M. H. Johnson & de Haan, 2001.

[20] Bruer & Greenough, 2001; Byrnes, 2001; Spear, 2007.

Another developmental process that enhances the brain's efficiency over time is **myelination**: Many (but not all) neurons gradually acquire a white, fatty coating known as *myelin*. A discussion of the precise nature and effects of myelin is beyond the scope of this book, but we should note that its arrival means that neurons can transmit messages much faster than they could previously. A few neurons (especially those involved in basic survival skills) become myelinated before birth, but most of them don't acquire myelin until well after birth, with different areas becoming myelinated in a predictable sequence. Myelination accounts for a sizable proportion of the brain's increase in volume after birth.[21]

In the cortex, synaptic pruning continues into the middle childhood and adolescent years, and myelination continues into early adulthood.[22] Several parts of the brain, especially those that are heavily involved in thinking and learning, continue to increase in size and interconnections until late adolescence or early adulthood.[23] In addition, the beginning of puberty is marked by significant changes in hormone levels, which affect the continuing maturation of brain structures and possibly also affect the production and effectiveness of neurotransmitters.[24] Theorists have speculated that this combination of changes may affect—and, for a short time, possibly limit—adolescents' functioning in a variety of areas, including attention, planning, and impulse control.[25]

One widespread myth about the brain is that it does all of its "maturing" within the first few years of life and that its development can best be nurtured by bombarding it with as much stimulation as possible—reading instruction, violin lessons, art classes, and so on—before its owner ever reaches kindergarten. As you can see, nothing could be further from the truth. In fact, young brains may not be capable of benefiting from some kinds of experiences, especially those that are fairly complex and multifaceted.[26] Ultimately, learning and development are, and must be, long-term endeavors.[27] People continue to form new synapses—and thus continue to be able to learn quite effectively—throughout their lives. In other words, the brain retains considerable **plasticity**—a capacity to learn from and adapt itself to new circumstances—not only in childhood and adolescence but also in adulthood and old age.[28] For most topics and skills, there is not necessarily a single "best" or "only" time to learn.

Although a high school student's brain has made great strides over the course of childhood and adolescence, it will still change in important ways in later adolescence and early adulthood.

Children have a natural tendency to organize their experiences.

Children appear to have a genetic predisposition to detect patterns in and organize what they see and hear, and they begin to categorize aspects of their world almost from day one.[29] According to Piaget, the things that children learn and do are organized as **schemes**—groups of similar actions or thoughts that are used repeatedly in response to the environment. (Do not confuse these with the *schemas* we discussed in Chapter 2.[30]) Initially, Piaget suggested, schemes are based largely on sensory and behavioral responses to objects. To illustrate, an infant may have a scheme for putting things in her mouth, and she may call on this scheme when dealing with a variety of objects, including her thumb, her toys, and her blanket. Over time, however, mental schemes—which other theorists might call *categories* or *concepts*—emerge as well. For example, a 7-year-old may have a scheme for identifying snakes that includes their long, thin bodies, their lack of legs, and their slithery nature. A 13-year-old may have a scheme for what constitutes *fashion*, allowing her to classify her peers as being either "totally awesome" or "complete dorks."

[21] Byrnes, 2001; M. Diamond & Hopson, 1998.

[22] M. H. Johnson & de Haan, 2001; Lenroot & Giedd, 2007; Merzenich, 2001; Paus et al., 1999.

[23] Giedd et al., 1999; Pribram, 1997; Sowell & Jernigan, 1998; Sowell, Thompson, Holmes, Jernigan, & Toga, 1999; E. F. Walker, 2002.

[24] Achenbach, 1974; N. Eisenberg, Martin, & Fabes, 1996; E. F. Walker, 2002.

[25] Benes, 2007; Kuhn & Franklin, 2006; L. Steinberg, 2007; Silveri et al., 2006; Spear, 2007.

[26] C. A. Nelson, Thomas, & de Haan, 2006.

[27] R. D. Brown & Bjorklund, 1998.

[28] Bruer, 1999; Kolb et al., 2003; C. A. Nelson et al., 2006.

[29] Behl-Chadha, 1996; Eimas & Quinn, 1994; Gelman, 2003; Quinn, 2002, 2003; Quinn, Bhatt, Brush, Grimes, & Sharpnack, 2002.

[30] Piaget distinguished between *schemes* and *schemas*, but neither concept is identical to the *schemas* about which contemporary theorists speak. By *scheme*, Piaget meant a particular way in which children repeatedly act or think about certain objects and events. By *schema*, he meant a simplified mental representation of a particular object or event, perhaps in the form of a visual image. For more information on the distinction, see Piaget, 1970, p. 705 (especially see the translator's note at the bottom of the page).

myelination Growth of a fatty coating (myelin) around neurons, enabling faster transmission of messages.

plasticity Capacity for the brain to learn and adapt to new circumstances.

scheme Organized group of similar actions or thoughts that are used repeatedly in response to the environment.

Observe Maddie's curiosity about a new object in the "Cognitive Development: Early Childhood" video in the Additional Resources section in Chapter 5 of MyEducationLab.

Children are naturally inclined to make sense of and adapt to their environment.

Although children have diverse temperaments that predispose them to behave in different ways, Mother Nature seems to endow all of them with a natural curiosity about their world. Accordingly, they actively seek out information to help them understand and make sense of it. They continually experiment with the objects they encounter, manipulating them and observing the effects of their actions. You can see an example of such curiosity and experimentation when 2-year-old Maddie discovers an intriguing new object in the "Cognitive Development: Early Childhood" video clip in MyEducationLab.

Piaget proposed that underlying children's curiosity is a desire to adapt to—and so be successful in—their environment. Such adaptation occurs through two complementary processes, assimilation and accommodation. **Assimilation** entails responding to and possibly interpreting an object or event in a way that is consistent with an existing scheme. For example, an infant may assimilate a new teddy bear into her putting-things-in-the-mouth scheme. A 7-year-old may quickly identify a new slithery object in the backyard as a snake. A 13-year-old may readily label a classmate's clothing as being either quite fashionable or "soooo yesterday."

But sometimes children cannot easily relate to a new object or event using existing schemes. In these situations one of two forms of **accommodation** will occur: Children will either modify an existing scheme to account for the new object or event or else form an entirely new scheme to deal with it. For example, the infant may have to open her mouth wider than usual to accommodate a teddy bear's fat paw. The 13-year-old may have to revise her existing scheme of fashion according to changes in what's hot and what's not. The 7-year-old may find a long, thin, slithery thing that cannot possibly be a snake because it has four legs. After some research, he will construct a new scheme—*salamander*—for this creature.

Assimilation and accommodation typically work hand in hand as children develop their knowledge and understanding of the world. Children interpret each new event within the context of their existing knowledge (assimilation) but at the same time may modify their knowledge as a result of the new event (accommodation). Accommodation rarely happens without assimilation. Young learners can benefit from (accommodate to) new experiences only when they can relate those experiences to their current knowledge and beliefs.

Development builds on prior acquisitions.

We've just seen how children can accommodate to new stimuli and events only when they can, to some degree, also assimilate those new stimuli and events into their existing knowledge and understandings. We saw the same idea in our discussion of *rote* versus *meaningful learning* in Chapter 2: Children learn more effectively when they can relate new information and experiences to what they already know. This idea also underlies the notion of *stage theory* I mentioned earlier: Later stages build on the accomplishments of earlier ones.

In general, then, children rarely start from scratch. Instead, virtually all aspects of their development involve a continual process of refining, building on, and occasionally reconfiguring previous abilities and achievements. In the opening case study, Ms. Padilla is concerned about Lupita's lack of basic academic skills. Although she mistakenly assumes that Lupita isn't capable of acquiring these skills in a single school year, she is on target in one respect: The skills will be essential for Lupita's success in first grade and beyond.

Interactions with, as well as observations of, the physical environment promote development.

Piaget believed that active experimentation with the physical world is essential for cognitive growth. By exploring and manipulating physical objects—for instance, by fiddling with sand and water, measuring things, playing games with balls and bats, and experimenting in a science lab—children learn the nature of such characteristics as volume and weight, discover principles related to force and gravity, acquire a better understanding of cause-and-effect relationships, and so on.

When interaction with the physical environment is not possible, however, children must at least be able to *observe* physical phenomena. For instance, children with significant

assimilation Responding to and possibly interpreting a new event in a way that is consistent with an existing scheme.

accommodation Responding to a new object or event by either modifying an existing scheme or forming a new one.

physical disabilities, who cannot actively experiment with physical objects, learn a great deal about the world simply by watching what happens around them.[31]

Language development facilitates cognitive development.

Cognitive development is, of course, essential for the development of language: Children can talk only about things that they can in some way first *think* about. But language is equally important for children's cognitive development.[32] From Piaget's perspective, it provides a set of entities (*symbols*) through which human beings can mentally represent external events and internal schemes. We often think by using specific words that our language provides. For example, when we think about household pets, our thoughts are apt to contain words such as *dog* and *cat*.

Vygotsky proposed that thought and language are separate functions for infants and young toddlers. In these early years, thinking occurs independently of language, and when language appears, it is first used primarily as a means of communication rather than as a mechanism of thought. But sometime around age 2, thought and language become intertwined: Children begin to express their thoughts when they speak, and they begin to think in words. As we noted a bit earlier, children's language skills virtually explode at this age, and their rapidly increasing vocabularies enable them to represent and think about a wide variety of objects and events.

When thought and language first merge, children often talk to themselves—a phenomenon known as **self-talk**. Vygotsky suggested that self-talk plays an important role in cognitive development. By talking to themselves, children learn to guide and direct their own behaviors through difficult tasks and complex maneuvers in much the same way that adults may have previously guided them. Self-talk eventually evolves into **inner speech**, in which children "talk" to themselves mentally rather than aloud. They continue to direct themselves verbally through tasks and activities, but others can no longer see and hear them do it. Here we are essentially talking about *self-regulation*, a concept we explored in Chapter 4.

Recent research has supported Vygotsky's views regarding the progression and role of self-talk and inner speech. The frequency of children's audible self-talk decreases during the preschool and early elementary years, but this decrease is at first accompanied by an increase in whispered mumbling and silent lip movements, presumably reflecting a transition to inner speech.[33] Furthermore, self-talk increases when children are performing more challenging tasks, at which they must exert considerable effort to be successful.[34] As you undoubtedly know from your own experience, even adults occasionally talk to themselves when they face new challenges!

Interactions with other people promote development.

Language facilitates cognitive development in a very different way as well: It enables children to exchange ideas with adults and peers. Both Piaget and Vygotsky suggested that social interaction is critical for cognitive development. In Piaget's view, exchanging ideas with others helps children realize that different individuals see things differently than they themselves do and that their own perspectives are not necessarily completely accurate or logical ones. For example, a 9-year-old may recognize the logical inconsistencies in what she says and does only after someone else points them out. And through discussions with peers or adults about social and political issues, a high school student may modify some initially abstract and idealistic notions about how the world "should" be to reflect the constraints the real world imposes.

For Vygotsky, social interactions are even more important. In fact, they provide the very foundations for cognitive development. We initially encountered some of Vygotsky's ideas about social interaction in Chapter 3. For one

In part through sharing their thoughts with one another, children and adolescents discover that their own perspectives of the world may be different from those of others.

self-talk Process of talking to oneself as a way of guiding oneself through a task.

inner speech Process of "talking" to oneself mentally (usually to guide oneself through a task) rather than aloud.

---

[31] Bebko, Burke, Craven, & Sarlo, 1992; Brainerd, 2003.
[32] For contemporary discussions of language's roles in memory, see K. Nelson & Fivush, 2004; Q. Wang & Ross, 2007.
[33] Bivens & Berk, 1990; Winsler & Naglieri, 2003.
[34] Berk, 1994; Schimmoeller, 1998.

thing, as children and adults interact, the adults often share the meanings and interpretations they attach to objects, events, and, more generally, human experience. In the process adults transform, or *mediate*, the situations that children encounter (recall our discussion of *mediated learning experiences*). Not only do adults help children interpret experiences, but they also share concepts, procedures, strategies, and other *cognitive tools* that enable children to deal effectively with complex tasks and problems. To the extent that specific cultures pass along unique interpretations, beliefs, concepts, ideas, procedures, strategies, and so on, children in different cultures will acquire somewhat different knowledge, skills, and ways of thinking.

Vygotsky further proposed that social activities provide the seeds from which complex cognitive processes can grow. Essentially, children use complex processes first in interactions with other people and gradually become able to use them independently in their own thought processes. Vygotsky called this process **internalization**. The progression from self-talk to inner speech just described illustrates this process: Over time, children gradually internalize adults' directions so that they are eventually giving *themselves* directions. Yet keep in mind that children do not necessarily internalize *exactly* what they see and hear in a social context. Rather, internalization often involves transforming ideas and processes to make them uniquely one's own.[35]

Not all mental processes evolve as children interact with adults. Some also develop as children interact with peers. As an example, children frequently argue with one another about a variety of matters—how best to carry out an activity, what games to play, who did what to whom, and so on. Childhood arguments can help children discover that there are often several ways to view the same situation. Eventually, children internalize the "arguing" process, developing the ability to look at a situation from several different angles *on their own*.[36]

Formal schooling promotes development.

Informal conversations are one common method by which adults pass along culturally relevant ways of interpreting situations. But from the perspective of sociocultural theorists, contemporary cognitive-developmental theorists, and information processing theorists, formal education is just as important, perhaps even more so. (Recall how much progress Lupita makes once Ms. Padilla and her aides begin to work hard to help her master basic academic skills.) Through formal, preplanned lessons, teachers systematically impart the ideas, concepts, and procedures used in various academic disciplines. In this way, rather than having to reinvent the wheel (both literally and figuratively), each generation can benefit from the discoveries, understandings, and problem-solving strategies of previous generations.[37]

Inconsistencies between existing understandings and external events promote development.

Earlier we noted that children are naturally inclined to make sense of their environment. According to Piaget, when children can comfortably explain new events using what they already know and believe about the world, they are in a state of **equilibrium**. But this equilibrium doesn't continue indefinitely. As children have new experiences—for instance, in formal school lessons or informal discussions with peers—they sometimes encounter events they cannot adequately address with their existing knowledge and beliefs. Such inexplicable events create **disequilibrium**, a sort of mental "discomfort" that leads children to reexamine their current understandings. By replacing, reorganizing, or better integrating their schemes (in other words, through accommodation), children eventually are able to understand and explain previously puzzling events. The movement from equilibrium to disequilibrium and back to equilibrium again is known as **equilibration**. Piaget suggested that equilibration and children's intrinsic desire to achieve equilibrium promote the development of more complex levels of thought and knowledge.

To better understand how thinking changes with age, and to discover the circumstances under which children might revise their thinking in light of new experiences, Piaget devel-

---

internalization Process through which a learner gradually incorporates socially based activities into his or her internal cognitive processes.

equilibrium State of being able to explain new events with existing schemes.

disequilibrium Inability to explain new events with existing schemes; tends to be accompanied by a sense of discomfort.

equilibration Movement from equilibrium to disequilibrium and back to equilibrium, a process that promotes development of more complex thought and understandings.

---

[35] Thus, Vygotsky's theory, while primarily sociocultural in nature, also has a constructivist element to it.

[36] Vygotsky, 1978.
[37] Case & Okamoto, 1996; M. Cole, 2006; Karpov & Haywood, 1998; Klahr & Nigam, 2004; Vygotsky, 1962.

oped a variety of tasks that would reveal children's reasoning processes and in some cases create disequilibrium. As an example of such a task, try the following exercise.

SEE FOR YOURSELF

SEE FOR YOURSELF

Wooden Beads

To the right are 12 wooden beads. As you can see, some of them are brown and some of them are white. Are there more wooden beads or more brown beads?

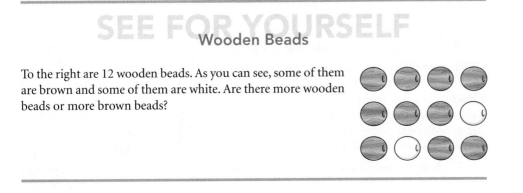

A ridiculously easy question, you might think. But in fact young children often answer incorrectly, responding that there are more *brown* beads than wooden ones. Consider the following dialogue between a 6-year-old, whom we'll call "Brian,"[38] and an adult about a set of beads similar to those I just showed you:

Adult: Are there more wooden beads or more brown beads?
Brian: More brown ones, because there are two white ones.
Adult: Are the white ones made of wood?
Brian: Yes.
Adult: And the brown ones?
Brian: Yes.
Adult: Then are there more brown ones or more wooden ones?
Brian: More brown ones.
Adult: What color would a necklace made of the wooden beads be?
Brian: Brown and white. (Here Brian shows that he understands that all the beads are wooden.)
Adult: And what color would a necklace made with the brown beads be?
Brian: Brown.
Adult: Then which would be longer, the one made with the wooden beads or the one made with the brown beads?
Brian: The one with the brown beads.
Adult: Draw the necklaces for me.

Brian draws a series of black rings for the necklace of brown beads; he then draws a series of black rings plus two white rings for the necklace of wooden beads.

Adult: Good. Now which will be longer, the one with the brown beads or the one with the wooden beads?
Brian: The one with the brown beads.[39]

Notice how the adult continues to probe Brian's reasoning to be sure he realizes that all of the beads are wooden but only some are brown. Even so, Brian responds that there are more brown beads than wooden ones. Piaget suggested that young children such as Brian have trouble with *class inclusion* tasks in which they must simultaneously think of an object as belonging to two categories—in this case, thinking of a bead as being both *brown* and *wooden* at the same time.

Notice, too, how the adult asks Brian to draw two necklaces, one made with the wooden beads and one made with the brown beads. The adult hopes that after Brian draws a brown-and-white necklace that is longer than an all-brown necklace, he will notice that his drawings are inconsistent with his statement that there are more brown beads. The inconsistency

---

[38] Piaget identified individuals in his studies by abbreviations. In this study he used the letters *BRI*, but I've given the child a name to allow for easier discussion.

[39] Dialogue from Piaget, 1952a, pp. 163–164.

might lead Brian to experience disequilibrium, perhaps to the point where he would reevaluate his conclusion and realize that the number of all the brown beads plus two white ones must necessarily be greater than the number of brown beads alone. In this case, however, Brian apparently is oblivious to the inconsistency, remains in equilibrium, and so has no need to revise his thinking.

Challenging tasks promote development.

Children can typically do more difficult things in collaboration with adults or other more advanced individuals than they can do on their own.[40] For instance, when learning how to swing a baseball bat, children are often more successful if adults initially guide their swing. In the opening case study, two of Lupita's classmates can assemble puzzles only when they have Lupita's assistance. And notice how a student who cannot independently solve division problems with remainders is more successful when her teacher helps her think through the process:

> **Teacher:** [writes 6)$\overline{44}$ on the board] 44 divided by 6. What number times 6 is close to 44?
> **Child:** 6.
> **Teacher:** What's 6 times 6? [writes 6]
> **Child:** 36.
> **Teacher:** 36. Can you get one that's any closer? [erasing the 6]
> **Child:** 8.
> **Teacher:** What's 6 times 8?
> **Child:** 64 . . . 48.
> **Teacher:** 48. Too big. Can you think of something . . .
> **Child:** 6 times 7 is 42.[41]

The range of tasks children cannot yet perform independently but *can* perform with the help and guidance of others is, in Vygotsky's terminology, the **zone of proximal development (ZPD)** (see Figure 5.1). A child's zone of proximal development includes learning and problem-solving abilities that are just beginning to develop—abilities that are in an immature, "embryonic" form. Naturally, any child's ZPD will change over time. As some tasks are mastered, other, more complex ones appear on the horizon to take their place.

Vygotsky proposed that children develop very little from performing tasks they can already do independently. Instead, they develop primarily by attempting tasks they can accomplish only in collaboration with a more competent individual—that is, when they attempt tasks within their zone of proximal development. In a nutshell, it is the challenges in life, not the easy successes, that promote development.

Although challenging tasks are beneficial, impossible tasks, which children cannot do even with considerable structure and guidance, are of no benefit whatsoever. Essentially, a child's ZPD sets an upper limit on what he or she is cognitively capable of learning.

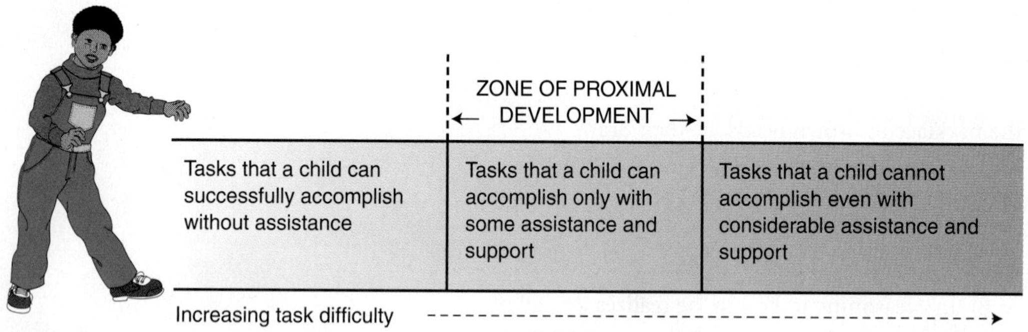

	ZONE OF PROXIMAL DEVELOPMENT	
Tasks that a child can successfully accomplish without assistance	Tasks that a child can accomplish only with some assistance and support	Tasks that a child cannot accomplish even with considerable assistance and support

Increasing task difficulty --->

FIGURE 5.1 Tasks in a child's zone of proximal development (ZPD) promote maximal cognitive growth.

TRENDS IN COGNITIVE DEVELOPMENT

In our discussions of learning and cognition in previous chapters, we've already identified several trends in cognitive development:

- With age and experience, children acquire more effective learning strategies (Chapter 2).

zone of proximal development (ZPD) Range of tasks that a child can perform with the help and guidance of others but cannot yet perform independently.

---

[40] Fischer & Immordino-Yang, 2006; Vygotsky, 1978.   [41] Pettito, 1985, p. 251.

- Metacognitive knowledge and skills improve gradually with age (Chapter 4).
- Learners become increasingly self-regulating over the course of childhood and adolescence (Chapter 4).

We now pull from the research of information processing theorists and cognitive-developmental theorists (including both Piaget and more contemporary researchers) to identify the following additional trends.

Children's growing working memory capacity enables them to handle increasingly complex cognitive tasks.

As you should recall, working memory—the component of the human memory system where active cognitive processing occurs—has a very limited capacity. It can think about only so much, and in fact not *very* much, at once. But as children grow older, their working memory capacity seems to increase a bit, in that they can gradually handle bigger and more complex thinking and learning tasks. A good deal of this increase in capacity is probably due to the fact that children's cognitive processes become faster and more efficient and so take up less "space" in working memory. But the available physical "space" of working memory may increase somewhat as well.[42]

Challenges, rather than easy successes, promote development.

Children's growing knowledge base enhances their ability to learn new things.

One reason children use increasingly effective learning strategies as they grow older is that they acquire an ever-expanding body of knowledge that they can use to interpret, organize, and elaborate on new experiences.[43] As an example, consider the case of an Inuit (Eskimo) man named Tor.

SEE FOR YOURSELF
Tor of the Targa

Tor, a young man of the Targa tribe, was out hunting in the ancient hunting territory of his people. He had been away from his village for many days. The weather was bad and he had not yet managed to locate his prey. Because of the extreme temperature he knew he must soon return but it was a matter of honor among his people to track and kill the prey single-handed. Only when this was achieved could a boy be considered a man. Those who failed were made to eat and keep company with the old men and the women until they could accomplish this task.

Suddenly, in the distance, Tor could make out the outline of a possible prey. It was alone and not too much bigger than Tor, who could take him single-handed. But as he drew nearer, a hunter from a neighboring tribe came into view, also stalking the prey. The intruder was older than Tor and had around his neck evidence of his past success at the hunt. "Yes," thought Tor, "he is truly a man." Tor was undecided. Should he challenge the intruder or

---

[42] Ben-Yehudah & Fiez, 2007; Fry & Hale, 1996; Kail, 2007; Luna, Garver, Urban, Lazar, & Sweeney, 2004; Van Leijenhorst, Crone, & Van der Molen, 2007.

[43] J. M. Alexander, Johnson, Albano, Freygang, & Scott, 2006; Flavell, Miller, & Miller, 2002; Halford, 1989; Kail, 1990.

return home empty handed? To return would mean bitter defeat. The other young men of the tribe would laugh at his failure. He decided to creep up on the intruder and wait his chance.44

- On what kind of terrain was Tor hunting?
- What was the weather like?
- What kind of prey might Tor have been stalking?

You may have used your knowledge about Inuit people to speculate that Tor was hunting polar bears or seals on snow and ice, possibly in freezing temperatures or a bad blizzard. But notice that the story itself didn't tell you any of these things. Instead, you had to *infer* them. Like you, many older children know a fair amount about the lifestyle of Inuits and other Native Americans who live in the northernmost regions of North America. They can use that information to help them elaborate on, and so better understand and remember, this very ambiguous story about Tor.

In cases where children have more knowledge than adults, the children are often the more effective learners.[45] For example, when my son Alex and I used to read books about lizards together, Alex always remembered more than I did, because he was a self-proclaimed "lizard expert" and I myself knew very little about reptiles of any sort.

As children grow older, they become increasingly able to draw inferences from what they see, in part because they have a larger and better integrated knowledge base to help them interpret their experiences.

Children's knowledge, beliefs, and thinking processes become increasingly integrated.

Through such processes as knowledge construction, organization, and elaboration, children increasingly pull together what they know and believe about the world into cohesive wholes (e.g., recall our discussion of children's *theories* in Chapter 2). The knowledge base of young children is apt to consist of many separate, isolated facts. In contrast, the knowledge base of older children and adolescents typically includes many associations and interrelationships among concepts and ideas.[46]

Piaget suggested that not only children's knowledge, but also their *thought processes*, become increasingly integrated over time. In particular, their many "thinking" schemes gradually combine into well-coordinated systems of mental processes. These systems—Piaget called them *operations*—allow children to think in increasingly logical ways, as will be evident in the next three developmental trends we consider.[47]

Thinking becomes increasingly logical during the elementary school years.

As noted earlier, Piaget proposed that cognitive development proceeds through four distinct stages. Table 5.2 summarizes these stages and presents examples of abilities acquired during each one. As you can see from the age ranges in the table, the preoperational, concrete operations, and formal operations stages are all evident in children's thinking during the school years, and so they will be relevant to our discussion here. Yet we must keep in mind that research studies conducted in recent decades suggest that children's reasoning abilities emerge more gradually than Piaget's stage theory might lead us to believe. Furthermore, many contemporary theorists believe—and Piaget himself acknowledged—that the four stages better describe how children and adolescents *can* think, rather than how they always *do* think, at any particular age.[48]

In Piaget's view, children passing through the **preoperational stage** (which typically occurs during the preschool and kindergarten years) think in somewhat illogical ways. As an example, recall 6-year-old Brian's insistence that in a set of 12 wooden beads, including

preoperational stage Piaget's second stage of cognitive development, in which children can think about objects beyond their immediate view but do not yet reason in logical, adult-like ways.

[44] A. L. Brown, Smiley, Day, Townsend, & Lawton, 1977, p. 1460.

[45] Chi, 1978; Rabinowitz & Glaser, 1985.

[46] J. M. Alexander et al., 2006; Bjorklund, 1987; Fischer & Immordino-Yang, 2006; Flavell et al., 2002.

[47] For a more recent, "neo-Piagetian" perspective on how thinking processes might become integrated, see

Kurt Fischer's discussions of *multiple, parallel strands*; for instance, see Fischer & Immordino-Yang, 2006; Fischer, Knight, & Van Parys, 1993.

[48] Flavell, 1994; Halford & Andrews, 2006; Klaczynski, 2001; Tanner & Inhelder, 1960.

TABLE 5.2   Piaget's Four Stages of Cognitive Development

Stage	Proposed Age Range[a]	General Description	Examples of Abilities Acquired
Sensorimotor	Birth to age 2	Schemes are based largely on behaviors and perceptions. Especially in the early part of this stage, children cannot think about things that are not immediately in front of them, and so they focus on what they are doing and seeing at the moment.	• *Trial-and-error experimentation with physical objects*: Exploration and manipulation of objects to determine their properties • *Object permanence*: Realization that objects continue to exist even when removed from view • *Symbolic thought*: Representation of physical objects and events as mental entities (*symbols*)
Preoperational	Age 2 through age 6 or 7	Thanks in part to their rapidly developing language and the symbolic thought it enables, children can now think and talk about things beyond their immediate experience. However, they do not yet reason in logical, adult-like ways.	• *Language*: Rapid expansion of vocabulary and grammatical structures • *Intuitive thought*: Some logical thinking based on "hunches" and "intuition" rather than on conscious awareness of logical principles (especially after age 4)
Concrete Operations	Age 6 or 7 through age 11 or 12	Adult-like logic appears but is limited to reasoning about concrete, real-life situations.	• *Class inclusion*: Ability to classify objects as belonging to two or more categories simultaneously • *Conservation*: Realization that amount stays the same if nothing is added or taken away, regardless of alterations in shape or arrangement
Formal Operations	Age 11 or 12 through adulthood[b]	Logical reasoning processes are applied to abstract ideas as well as to concrete objects and situations. Many capabilities essential for advanced reasoning in science and mathematics appear.	• *Reasoning about hypothetical ideas*: Ability to draw logical deductions about situations that have no basis in physical reality • *Proportional reasoning*: Conceptual understanding of fractions, percentages, decimals, and ratios • *Separation and control of variables*: Ability to test hypotheses by manipulating one variable while holding other variables constant

[a]The age ranges presented in the table are *averages*; some children reach more advanced stages a bit earlier, others a bit later. Also, some children may be in *transition* from one stage to the next, displaying characteristics of two adjacent stages at the same time.

[b]Recent researchers have found much variability in when adolescents begin to show reasoning processes consistent with Piaget's formal operations stage. Furthermore, not all cultures value or nurture formal operational logic, perhaps because it is largely irrelevant to people's daily lives and tasks (see the Cultural Considerations box later in this chapter).

10 brown ones and 2 white ones, there are more brown beads than wooden ones. And consider the following situation:

> We show 5-year-old Nathan the three glasses depicted at the top of Figure 5.2. We ask him whether Glasses A and B contain the same amount of water, and he replies confidently that they do. We then pour the water from Glass B into Glass C and ask him whether A and C have the same amount. Nathan replies, "No, that glass [pointing to Glass A] has more because it's taller."

Nathan's response reflects lack of **conservation**: He does not realize that because nothing has been added or taken away, the amount of water in the two glasses must be equivalent. Young children such as Nathan often confuse changes in appearance with changes in amount.

Piaget found that children as young as age 4 or 5 occasionally draw logically correct conclusions about classification and conservation problems. However, he suggested that their reasoning is based on hunches and intuition rather than on any conscious awareness of underlying logical principles, and so they cannot yet explain *why* their conclusions are correct. More recently, researchers have discovered that how logically young children think depends partly on situational factors, such as how task materials are presented, how questions are worded, and whether adults provide explicit guidance about how to think about a problem.[49]

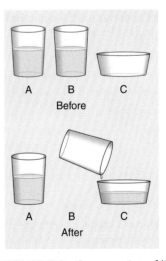

FIGURE 5.2 Conservation of liquid: Do Glasses A and C contain the same amount of water?

conservation Realization that if nothing is added or taken away, amount stays the same regardless of alterations in shape or arrangement.

---

[49] M. Donaldson, 1978; Gelman, 2003; Halford & Andrews, 2006; Siegler & Svetina, 2006.

In any event, most children have mastered simple logical tasks, such as those involving class inclusion and simple forms of conservation, by age 7—an age at which, in Piaget's view, they are now in the **concrete operations stage**. As an example, consider how an 8-year-old whom we'll call "Natalie" responded to the same wooden beads problem that Brian tackled:

> **Adult:** Are there more wooden beads or more brown beads?
>
> **Natalie:** More wooden ones.
>
> **Adult:** Why?
>
> **Natalie:** Because the two white ones are made of wood as well.
>
> **Adult:** Suppose we made two necklaces, one with all the wooden beads and one with all the brown ones. Which one would be longer?
>
> **Natalie:** Well, the wooden ones and the brown ones are the same, and it would be longer with the wooden ones because there are two white ones as well.[50]

Observe Kent's conservation of number in the "Cognitive Development: Middle Childhood" video in the Additional Resources section in Chapter 5 of MyEducationLab.

Notice how easily Natalie reaches her conclusion: Because the wooden beads include white ones as well as brown ones, there obviously must be more wooden ones. The "Cognitive Development: Middle Childhood" video clip in MyEducationLab presents another example of conservation, one that involves conservation of number rather than conservation of liquid. Ten-year-old Kent confidently concludes that two rows of M&Ms each have the same amount even though the M&Ms in one row are spaced farther apart than those in the other row.

Children continue to refine their newly acquired logical thinking capabilities throughout the elementary school years. For instance, some forms of conservation, such as conservation of liquid and conservation of number, appear at age 6 or 7. Others don't emerge until later. Consider the problem in Figure 5.3. Using a balance scale, an adult shows a child that two balls of clay have the same weight. One ball is removed from the scale and smashed into a pancake shape. Does the pancake weigh the same as the unsmashed ball, or are the weights different? Children typically do not achieve conservation of weight—they don't realize that the flattened pancake weighs the same as the round ball it was earlier—until sometime between ages 8 and 11.[51]

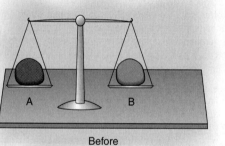

FIGURE 5.3   Conservation of weight: Ball A and Ball B initially weigh the same. When Ball B is flattened into a pancake shape, how does its weight now compare with that of Ball A?

Thinking becomes increasingly abstract in the middle school and secondary school years.

In Piaget's theory, children in the concrete operations stage can reason only about concrete objects and events, and especially about things they can actually see. Once they acquire abilities that characterize the **formal operations stage**—perhaps at around age 11 or 12, Piaget suggested—they are capable of abstract thought. That is, they can think about concepts and ideas that have little or no basis in everyday concrete reality. For example, in mathematics they should have an easier time understanding such concepts as *negative number*, *pi* (π), and *infinity*. In science they should be able to think about *molecules* and *atoms* and understand how it's possible for temperature to go below zero. In the poem in Figure 5.4, 11-year-old Erin uses several abstract ideas (e.g., *war darkens the day*, *honor is divine*) as she laments the pointlessness of war.

In Piaget's theory, formal operational thought also involves *hypothetical reasoning*, thinking logically about things that may or may not be true. In some instances, such reasoning involves things that definitely are *false*. As an example, try the following exercise.

concrete operations stage Piaget's third stage of cognitive development, in which adult-like logic appears but is limited to concrete reality.

formal operations stage Piaget's fourth and final stage of cognitive development, in which logical reasoning processes are applied to abstract ideas as well as to concrete objects, and more sophisticated scientific and mathematical reasoning processes emerge.

---

[50] Dialogue from Piaget, 1952a, p. 176.

[51] Sroufe, Cooper, DeHart, & Bronfenbrenner, 1992; Sund, 1976.

SEE FOR YOURSELF
Beings and Basketballs

Take a moment to answer these two questions:

1. If all children are human beings,
   And if all human beings are living creatures,
   Then must all children be living creatures?
2. If all children are basketballs,
   And if all basketballs are jellybeans,
   Then must all children be jellybeans?

When you read the first question, you were probably able to conclude fairly quickly that, yes, all children must be living creatures. The second question is a bit trickier. It follows the same line of reasoning as the first but the conclusion it leads to—all children must be jellybeans—contradicts what is true in reality.

Abstract and hypothetical reasoning seem to emerge earlier and more gradually than Piaget proposed. Children in the elementary grades occasionally show an ability to reason abstractly and hypothetically about certain topics.[52] And yet once children reach puberty, they may continue to struggle with some abstract subject matter. For instance, although many can understand some abstract scientific and mathematical concepts in early adolescence, they are apt to have trouble understanding abstract concepts in history and geography until well into the high school years.[53] In fact, some adolescents never do show much evidence of formal operational thinking, especially if their culture and schooling do little to encourage it.[54]

Erin
Poetry Class 5th Grade

Dear God, Help Us
The black of war
Darkens the day.
There is no point;
I say.
Why do all these poor men die
Fighting those
Who could be friends.
Gun shots sound through the air
Only to bring sadness and despair.
Why do leaders sit around,
While innocent men
Fall to the ground.
When the grass is painted red,
you know
Some man has lost his head.
When you're in a war
you're guarenteed to come out sore.
While you are lying in pain,
slowly,
You'll become insane.
The men you kill shouldn't die,
Their souls shouldn't float in the sky.
As a solider gasps
One more time,
He should know
His honor is
Divine.

FIGURE 5.4 As children reach puberty, they become increasingly able to reason about abstract ideas.

(Poetry by Erin, age 11)

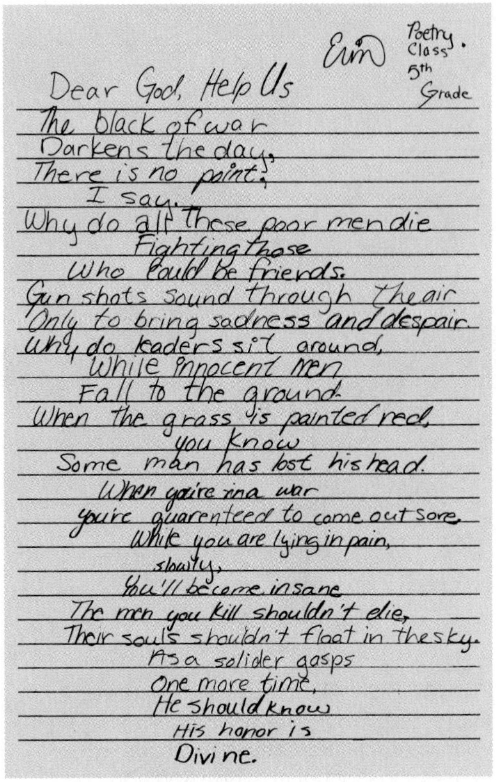

Once learners become capable of abstract thought, they are able to look beyond the literal meanings of messages.[55] Children in the early elementary grades often take the words they hear at face value—for instance, interpreting the expression "Your eyes are bigger than your stomach" quite literally (see Figure 5.5). And they have little success determining the underlying meaning of such proverbs as "Look before you leap" or "Don't put the cart before the horse." In the "Cognitive Development" video clips for middle childhood and late adolescence in MyEducationLab, you can observe how children's ability to understand proverbs improves with age. For example, whereas 10-year-old Kent seems baffled by the old adage "A rolling stone gathers no moss," 14-year-old Alicia offers a reasonable explanation: "Maybe when you go through things too fast, you don't . . . collect anything from it." Students' ability to interpret proverbs in a generalized, abstract fashion continues to improve even in the high school years.[56]

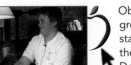

Observe the progression in understanding proverbs in the "Cognitive Development" videos for middle childhood and late adolescence in the Additional Resources section in Chapter 5 of MyEducationLab.

Another outgrowth of abstract and hypothetical thinking is the ability to envision how the world might be different from the way it actually is. In some cases adolescents envision a world that is much *better* than the one they live in, and they exhibit considerable concern and idealism about social and political issues. Some secondary school students devote a great deal of energy to local or global problems, such as water pollution or world hunger. However, they may offer recommendations for change that seem logical but aren't practical in today's world. For example, a teenager might argue that racism would disappear overnight if people would just begin to love one another, or suggest that a nation should eliminate its armed forces and weaponry as a way of moving toward world peace. Piaget proposed that adolescent idealism reflects an inability to separate one's own logical abstractions from the perspectives of others and from practical considerations. Only through experience do adolescents eventually begin to temper their optimism with some realism about what is possible in a given time frame and with limited resources.

[52] Beck, Robinson, Carroll, & Apperly, 2006; S. Carey, 1985; Metz, 1995.
[53] Kuhn & Franklin, 2006; Lovell, 1979; Tamburrini, 1982.
[54] Flieller, 1999; Lerner, 2002; Rogoff, 2003.
[55] Owens, 1996; Winner, 1988.
[56] Owens, 1996.

FIGURE 5.5 Adults typically use the expression "Your eyes are bigger than your stomach" figuratively, perhaps to describe a situation in which someone has ordered more food than can possibly be eaten. Here, however, 8-year-old Jeff interprets the expression quite literally.

Observe seventh graders' difficulty separating and controlling variables in the "Designing Experiments" video in the Additional Resources section in Chapter 5 of MyEducationLab.

Several logical thinking processes important for mathematical and scientific reasoning improve considerably during adolescence.

In Piaget's view, several additional abilities accompany the advancement to the formal operations stage. One is *proportional reasoning*, the ability to understand and think logically about such proportions as fractions, decimals, percentages, and ratios. For example, if you can quickly and easily recognize that the following statement is true

$$\frac{2}{8} = \frac{6}{24} = 0.25 = 25\%$$

then you have mastered some degree of proportional reasoning.

Scientific reasoning skills also improve in adolescence. Two of them—*formulating and testing hypotheses* and *separating and controlling variables*—together allow learners to use a scientific method, in which several possible explanations for an observed phenomenon are proposed and tested in a systematic manner. As an example, consider the pendulum problem in the exercise that follows.

SEE FOR YOURSELF

Pendulum Problem

In the absence of other forces, an object suspended by a rope or string—a pendulum—swings at a constant rate. (A playground swing and the pendulum of a grandfather clock are two everyday examples.) Some pendulums swing back and forth rather slowly, others more quickly. What characteristics of a pendulum determine how fast it swings? Write down at least three hypotheses about the variable(s) that might affect a pendulum's oscillation rate.

Now gather several small, heavy objects (e.g., an eraser, a large screw or bolt, a fishing sinker) and a piece of string. Tie one of the objects to one end of the string, and set your pendulum in motion. Conduct one or more experiments to test each of your hypotheses.

What can you conclude? What variable or variables affect the rate at which a pendulum swings?

What hypotheses did you generate? Perhaps you considered the weight of the object, the length of the string, the force with which the pendulum is pushed, and the height from which the object is first released. Did you then test each hypothesis in a systematic fashion? A person capable of formal operational thinking separates and controls variables, testing one at a time while holding all others constant. (This strategy should remind you of our discussion of *experimental studies* in Chapter 1.) For example, if you were testing the hypothesis that weight makes a difference, you might have tried objects of different weights while keeping constant the length of the string, the force with which you pushed each object, and the height from which you released or pushed it. Similarly, if you hypothesized that the length of the string was a critical factor, you might have varied the length while continuing to use the same object and setting the pendulum in motion in the same manner. If you carefully separated and controlled variables, then you would have come to the correct conclusion: Only length affects a pendulum's oscillation rate. The "Designing Experiments" video clip in MyEducationLab shows the difficulty that four seventh graders have with the pendulum problem: They repeatedly vary both length and weight until their teacher nudges them toward the realization that this approach prevents them from drawing a firm conclusion.

Children show signs that they can think about simple proportions as early as first or second grade.[57] And by the upper elementary grades, some can separate and control variables, es-

---

[57] Empson, 1999; Van Dooren, De Bock, Hessels, Janssens, & Verschaffel, 2005.

DEVELOPMENTAL TRENDS

TABLE 5.3   Logical Thinking Abilities at Different Grade Levels

Grade Level	Age-Typical Characteristics	Suggested Strategies
K–2	• Emergence of class inclusion • Emergence of conservation in simple tasks (e.g., conservation of liquid and number) • Increasing ability to explain and justify conclusions about logical reasoning tasks	• Use concrete manipulatives and experiences to illustrate concepts and ideas. • Provide practice in classifying objects in multiple ways—for instance, by shape, size, color, and texture. • In early arithmetic lessons, determine whether children have achieved conservation of number—for instance, by asking them whether a set of objects you have just rearranged has more or fewer objects than it had previously.
3–5	• Emergence of conservation in more challenging tasks (e.g., conservation of weight) • Occasional abstract and hypothetical thinking • Ability to understand simple fractions (e.g., 1/3, 1/5, 1/8) that can be related to concrete objects and everyday events	• Supplement verbal explanations with concrete examples, pictures, and hands-on activities. • Have students engage in simple scientific investigations, focusing on familiar objects and phenomena. • Introduce simple fractions by relating them to everyday objects (e.g., pizza slices, kitchen measuring cups).
6–8	• Increasing ability to reason logically about abstract, hypothetical, and contrary-to-fact situations • Some ability to test hypotheses and to separate and control variables, especially when an adult provides hints about how to proceed; conclusions sometimes affected by *confirmation bias* (see Chapter 2) • Increasing ability to understand and work with proportions • Some ability to interpret proverbs, figures of speech, and other forms of figurative language	• Present abstract concepts and principles central to various academic disciplines, but make them concrete in some way (e.g., relate *gravity* to everyday experiences, show a diagram of an *atom*). • Ask students to speculate on the meanings of well-known proverbs (e.g., "Two heads are better than one," "A stitch in time saves nine"). • Assign mathematics problems that require use of simple fractions, ratios, or decimals. • Have students conduct simple experiments to answer questions about cause-and-effect; encourage them to change only one variable at a time.
9–12	• Greater ability to think abstractly in math and science than in the social sciences • Increasing proficiency in aspects of the scientific method (e.g., formulation and testing of hypotheses, separation and control of variables); effects of confirmation bias still evident • Greater proficiency in interpreting figurative language • Idealistic (but not always realistic) views about how government, social policy, and other aspects of society should be changed	• Study particular topics in depth; introduce complex and abstract explanations and theories. • Ask students to speculate on the meanings of unfamiliar proverbs (e.g., "As you sow, so shall you reap," "Discretion is the better part of valor"). • Have students design some of their own experiments in science labs and science fair projects. • Encourage discussions about social, political, and ethical issues; elicit multiple perspectives on these issues.

Sources: Barchfeld et al., 2005; S. Carey, 1985; Danner & Day, 1977; M. Donaldson, 1978; Elkind, 1981; Empson, 1999; Flavell, 1963; Fujimura, 2001; Halford & Andrews, 2006; Hynd, 1998a; Inhelder & Piaget, 1958; Karplus, Pulos, & Stage, 1983; Kuhn & Dean, 2005; Kuhn & Franklin, 2006; Lovell, 1979; Metz, 1995; Newcombe & Huttenlocher, 1992; Owens, 1996; Piaget, 1928, 1952b, 1959; Rosser, 1994; Siegler & Alibali, 2005; Sroufe et al., 1992; Sund, 1976; Tamburrini, 1982; Van Dooren et al., 2005.

pecially if given hints about the importance of controlling all variables except the one they are testing.[58] But by and large, the mathematical and scientific reasoning abilities just described don't really take wing until puberty, and they continue to develop throughout adolescence.[59]

The progression of logical reasoning processes shown in Table 5.3 draws on both Piaget's early work and more recent research findings. It also presents examples of teaching strategies that take these processes into account.

[58] Barchfeld, Sodian, Thoermer, & Bullock, 2005;
Danner & Day, 1977; Kuhn & Dean, 2005; Metz, 1995.
[59] Barchfeld et al., 2005; Byrnes, 1988; Kuhn, Garcia-
Mila, Zohar, & Andersen, 1995; Tourniaire & Pulos,
1985; Van Dooren et al., 2005.

Children can think more logically and abstractly about tasks and topics they know well.

The ability to think logically about a situation or topic depends to some degree on learners' background knowledge and educational experiences. For example, even 4-year-olds sometimes show conservation after having practice with conservation tasks, especially if they can actively manipulate the task materials and discuss their reasoning with someone who already exhibits conservation.[60] Five-year-olds are more likely to solve class inclusion problems—for instance, they're more likely to conclude that a picture of three cats and six dogs has more animals than dogs—if an adult helps them think logically about such problems.[61] Children in the elementary grades can better understand fractions if they work with familiar concrete objects.[62] Young adolescents can solve logical problems involving hypothetical ideas if they are taught relevant problem-solving strategies, and they become increasingly able to separate and control variables if they have numerous experiences that require them to do so.[63] Junior high and high school students (and adults as well) often apply formal operational reasoning processes to topics about which they have a great deal of knowledge and yet think concretely about topics with which they are unfamiliar.[64]

As an illustration of how knowledge affects scientific reasoning processes, consider the fishing pond in Figure 5.6. In one study[65] 13-year-olds were shown a similar picture and told, "These four children go fishing every week, and one child, Herb, always catches the most fish. The other children wonder why." If you look at the picture, it is obvious that Herb differs from the other children in several ways, including the kind of bait he uses, the length of his fishing rod, and his location by the pond. Adolescents who were avid fishermen more effectively separated and controlled variables for this situation than they did for the pendulum problem described earlier, whereas the reverse was true for nonfishermen. In the "Cognitive Development" video clips for middle childhood and late adolescence in MyEducationLab, 10-year-old Kent and 14-year-old Alicia both look at the picture shown in Figure 5.6. Notice how Kent, who appears to have some experience with fishing, considers several potentially relevant variables and holds off judgment about which might be more influential. In contrast, Alicia, who is older but admittedly a nonfisherman, considers only two and almost immediately jumps to the conclusion that one of them—kind of bait—is the deciding factor:

Observe how experience with fishing affects Kent's and Alicia's ability to identify relevant variables in the "Cognitive Development" videos for middle childhood and late adolescence in the Additional Resources section in Chapter 5 of MyEducationLab.

Kent: He has live . . . live worms, I think. Fish like live worms more, I guess 'cause they're live and they'd rather have that than the lures, plastic worms. . . . Because he might be more patient or that might be a good side of the place. Or maybe since Bill has, like, a boombox thing (referring to the radio) . . . I don't think they would really like that because . . . and he doesn't have anything that's extra. . . . But he's the standing one. I don't get that. But Bill, that could scare the fish away to Herb because he's closer. . . .

Alicia: Because of the spot he's standing in, probably. . . . I don't know anything about fishing. Oh, OK! He actually has live worms for bait. The other girl's using saltine crackers (she misreads *crickets*). . . . She's using plastic worms, he's using lures, and she's using crackers and he's actually using live worms. So obviously the fish like the live worms best.

FIGURE 5.6   What are some possible reasons that Herb is catching more fish than the others?

Source: Based on Pulos & Linn, 1981.

[60] Field, 1987; Murray, 1978.
[61] Siegler & Svetina, 2006.
[62] Empson, 1999; Fujimura, 2001.
[63] S. Lee, 1985; Schauble, 1990.

[64] Girotto & Light, 1993; M. C. Linn, Clement, Pulos, & Sullivan, 1989; Schliemann & Carraher, 1993.
[65] Pulos & Linn, 1981.

True expertise comes only after many years of study and practice.

As noted earlier, learners acquire an increasing amount of information in their long-term memories over time. Some of them eventually acquire a great deal of information about a particular topic—say, lizards, World War II, auto mechanics, or photography—to the point where they are *experts*. Not only do experts know more than their peers, but their knowledge is also qualitatively different from that of others. In particular, their knowledge tends to be tightly organized, with many interrelationships among the things they know and with many abstract generalizations unifying more specific, concrete details.[66] Such qualities enable experts to retrieve the things they need more easily, to find parallels between seemingly diverse situations, and to solve problems effectively.[67]

There may be three somewhat distinct stages in the development of knowledge related to a particular topic.[68] At the first stage, *acclimation*, learners familiarize themselves with a new content domain, much as someone might do by taking an introductory course in biology, European history, or economics. At this point, learners pick up a lot of facts that they tend to store in relative isolation from one another. As a result of such "fragmented" learning, they are likely to hold on to many misconceptions that they may have acquired before they started studying the subject systematically.

At the second stage, *competence*, learners acquire considerably more information about the subject matter, and they also acquire some general principles that help tie the information together. Because learners at the competence stage make numerous interconnections among the things they learn, they are likely to correct many of the misconceptions they have previously developed. Those misconceptions that remain, however, are apt to intrude into many of learners' thoughts about the subject. At the competence stage, learners' entire approach to the subject matter begins to resemble that of experts. For example, they may engage in some of their own scientific research or start to "think like a historian." Competence is something that people acquire only after studying a particular subject in depth, perhaps by taking several biology courses or reading a great many books about World War II.

At the final stage, **expertise**, learners have truly mastered their field. They know a great deal about the subject matter, and they have pulled much of their knowledge together—including, perhaps, a few persistent misconceptions—into a tightly integrated whole. At this point, they are helping to lead the way in terms of conducting research, proposing new ways of looking at things, solving problems, and, in general, making new knowledge. Expertise comes only after many years of study and practice in a particular field.[69] As a result, few learners ever reach this stage, and we are unlikely to see it before late adolescence or adulthood.

To some extent, different cultures encourage different reasoning skills.

As noted earlier, children's developmental advancements are spurred, in part, by their desire to adapt successfully to their environment. That environment includes not only their physical surroundings but also the culture and society in which they live. Certain logical reasoning skills are more important—and so are more likely to be nurtured—in some cultures than in others. The Cultural Considerations box "Cultural Differences in Reasoning Skills and Views About Intelligence" describes some of the cross-cultural differences in reasoning skills that researchers have identified.

INTELLIGENCE

What kinds of behaviors lead you to believe that someone is "intelligent"? Do you think of intelligence as a general ability that contributes to success in many different areas? Or is it possible for a person to be intelligent in one area yet not in another? What exactly *is* intelligence?

---

[66] P. A. Alexander & Judy, 1988; Bédard & Chi, 1992; Proctor & Dutta, 1995; Zeitz, 1994.

[67] Chi, Glaser, & Rees, 1982; De Corte, Greer, & Verschaffel, 1996; Rabinowitz & Glaser, 1985; Voss, Greene, Post, & Penner, 1983.

[68] The stages described here are based on the work of P. A. Alexander, 1997, 1998, 2004.

[69] P. A. Alexander, 1997, 1998, 2004; Dai & Sternberg, 2004; Ericsson, 2003; Ericsson & Chalmers, 1994.

expertise Extensive and well-integrated knowledge of a topic that comes from many years of study and practice.

CULTURAL CONSIDERATIONS

Cultural Differences in Reasoning Skills and Views About Intelligence

Piaget proposed that his stages of cognitive development were universal, that they applied to children and adolescents around the globe. Researchers have found, however, that the acquisition of at least one key aspect of concrete operational thinking—conservation—and several aspects of formal operational thinking depend partly on whether a cultural group nurtures them. Furthermore, cultures differ in significant ways in their views of what it means to be an "intelligent" person.

Conservation. Imagine two balls of clay of the same size, as shown here.

You change the shape of one of these balls, perhaps flattening it into a pancake or rolling it into a sausage shape. Rather than asking a child if the two pieces of clay *weigh*

the same (this would be the conservation of weight task shown in Figure 5.3), you simply ask whether the two pieces have the same *amount*. On average, school children in Europe and North America master such *conservation of substance* with clay at around age 7. In contrast, Mexican children whose families make pottery for a living master this task a bit earlier, by age 6. Apparently, making pottery requires children to make frequent judgments about needed quantities of clay, and these judgments must be fairly accurate regardless of the specific shape of the clay.[a] Yet in other cultures, especially in some where children neither attend school nor work at activities that require keeping track of quantity, conservation may appear several years later than it does in mainstream Western societies.[b]

Formal operational reasoning skills. In some cultures, formal operational thinking skills have little relevance to people's daily

lives and activities.[c] For example, let's look once again at the second problem in the "Beings and Basketballs" exercise presented earlier in the chapter:

> If all children are basketballs,
> And if all basketballs are jellybeans,
> Then must all children be jellybeans?

Following rules of formal logic—that is, if we assume the first two premises to be true—the answer is *yes*. Such reasoning about hypothetical and perhaps contrary-to-fact ideas is taught and encouraged in many schools in mainstream Western societies, especially within the context of math and science instruction. But in numerous other cultures, including many modern Asian societies, logical reasoning tends to be rooted in people's everyday, concrete realities. Adults in these cultures may find little purpose in hypothetical and contrary-to-fact reasoning and so don't always nurture it in their schools or elsewhere.[d]

One component of intelligence is the ability to use prior knowledge to analyze new situations. These students are trying to calculate the volume of the large pyramid by applying geometric principles they've learned in their math class.

intelligence Ability to modify and adjust behaviors to accomplish new tasks successfully; involves many different mental processes and may vary in nature depending on one's culture.

Unfortunately, psychologists have not yet reached consensus on the answers to these questions. Virtually all of them agree, however, that children in any single age-group differ in how quickly they acquire new knowledge and skills, and most use the term **intelligence** to refer to this individual difference variable. Here are several components of what many psychologists construe *intelligence* to be:[70]

- It is *adaptive*. It involves modifying and adjusting one's behaviors to accomplish new tasks successfully.
- It is related to *learning ability*. Intelligent people learn information more quickly and easily than less intelligent people.
- It involves the *use of prior knowledge* to analyze and understand new situations effectively.
- It involves the complex interaction and coordination of *many different thinking and reasoning processes*.
- It is *culture specific*. What is "intelligent" behavior in one culture is not necessarily intelligent behavior in another culture.

Let's consider the culture-specific aspect of intelligence for a moment. Because intelligence is adaptive, it must, of course, help learners survive and thrive in their particular cul-

---

[70] Barnet & Ceci, 2002; Gardner, 1983; Neisser et al., 1996; Sternberg, 1997, 2004; Sternberg & Detterman, 1986.

In some cultures, aspects of formal operational thought are inconsistent with people's worldviews.[e] For instance, whereas most people in mainstream Western culture place great value on the scientific method—forming hypotheses, collecting evidence to test them, separating and controlling variables, and so on—people in certain other cultures tend to depend on other sources of information, perhaps authority figures, holy scriptures, or general cultural folklore as a more trusted means of determining what is "truth."

Views and manifestations of intelligence. In North America and western Europe, intelligence is largely thought of as an ability that influences children's academic achievement and adults' professional success. Such a view is hardly universal. Many Hispanic, African, Asian, and Native American cultures think of intelligence as involving social as well as academic skills—maintaining harmonious interpersonal relationships, working effectively together to accomplish challenging tasks, and so on.[f] And in Buddhist and Confucian societies in the Far East (e.g., China, Taiwan), intelligence also involves acquiring strong moral values and making meaningful contributions to society.[g]

Cultural groups differ, too, in the behaviors that they believe reflect intelligence. For instance, on many traditional intelligence tests, speed is valued: Children score higher if they answer questions quickly as well as correctly. Yet people in some cultures tend to value thoroughness over speed and may even be suspicious of tasks completed very quickly.[h] As another example, in mainstream Western culture, strong verbal skills are considered to be a sign of high intelligence. Not all cultures value chattiness, however. Among many Japanese and among the Inuit people of northern Quebec, talking a lot can be interpreted as a sign of immaturity or low intelligence.[i] One researcher working at an Inuit school in northern Quebec asked a teacher about a boy whose language seemed unusually advanced for his age-group. The teacher replied:

"Do you think he might have a learning problem? Some of these children who don't have such high intelligence have trouble stopping themselves. They don't know when to stop talking."[j]

As you will discover as you read the rest of the chapter, intelligence tests are at best only imperfect measures of children's intellectual abilities, and so teachers must be extremely cautious in interpreting the test results for *any* child. Clearly, extra caution is warranted when children come from diverse cultural backgrounds.

[a] Price-Williams, Gordon, & Ramirez, 1969.
[b] Berk, 2003; Fahrmeier, 1978; Trawick-Smith, 2003.
[c] M. Cole, 1990; J. G. Miller, 1997.
[d] Norenzayan, Choi, & Peng, 2007.
[e] Kağitçibaşi, 2007; Losh, 2003; Norenzayan et al., 2007.
[f] Greenfield et al., 2006; Li & Fischer, 2004; Sternberg, 2004, 2007.
[g] Li, 2004; Sternberg, 2003.
[h] Sternberg, 2007.
[i] Crago, 1988; Minami & McCabe, 1996; Sternberg, 2003.
[j] Crago, 1988, p. 219.

ture. And because cultures can differ from one another in significant ways, intelligence must take different forms depending on the culture in which learners live (see the Cultural Considerations box).[71] But regardless of the forms intelligence might take, most psychologists think of it as being somewhat distinct from what a child has actually learned (e.g., as reflected in school achievement). At the same time, intelligent thinking and intelligent behavior *depend* on prior learning. The more young learners know about their environment and about the tasks they need to perform, the more intelligently they can behave. Intelligence, then, is not necessarily a permanent, unchanging characteristic. As you will soon discover, it can be modified through experience and learning.

The following general principles describe the nature of intelligence.

Intelligence can be measured only imprecisely at best.

Curiously, although psychologists cannot pin down exactly what intelligence is, they have been trying to measure it for more than a century. In 1904 government officials in France asked Alfred Binet to develop a method of identifying students unlikely to benefit from regular school instruction and therefore in need of special educational services. To accomplish the task, Binet devised a test that measured general knowledge, vocabulary, perception, memory, and abstract thought. In doing so, he designed the earliest version of what we now call an **intelligence test**. To get a feel for what intelligence tests are like, try the following exercise.

intelligence test General measure of current cognitive functioning, used primarily to predict academic achievement over the short run.

[71] Gardner, 1983; Sternberg, 1997, 2004.

SEE FOR YOURSELF

Mock Intelligence Test

Answer each of these questions:

1. What does the word *penitence* mean?
2. How are a goat and a beetle alike?
3. What should you do if you get separated from your family in a large department store?
4. What do people mean when they say, "A rolling stone gathers no moss"?
5. Complete the following analogy:

These test items are modeled after items on many modern-day intelligence tests. Think, for a moment, about the capabilities you needed to answer them successfully. Does general knowledge about the world play a role? Is knowledge of vocabulary important? Is abstract thought involved? The answer to all three questions is *yes*. Although intelligence tests have evolved considerably since Binet's time, they continue to measure many of the same abilities that Binet's original test did.

The nature of intelligence changes somewhat as children get older. For example, in the early elementary grades it is apt to include children's ability to manipulate and work successfully with concrete objects (recall Lupita's facility with puzzles in the opening case study). In adolescence, however, it is more likely to involve reasoning about abstract ideas. Because intelligence itself changes with age, how it is measured must also change. Table 5.4 describes some of the ways in which intelligence is measured at different grade levels. It also includes several grade-specific considerations in the measurement of intelligence.

Scores on intelligence tests were originally calculated using a formula that involves division. Hence they were called "intelligence quotient," or **IQ**, scores. Even though we still use the term *IQ*, intelligence test scores are no longer based on the old formula. Instead, they are determined by comparing a child's performance on the test with the performance of others in the same age-group. A score of 100 indicates average performance: Children with this score have performed better than half of their age-mates on the test and not as well as the other half. Scores well below 100 indicate below-average performance on the test. Scores well above 100 indicate above-average performance.

Figure 5.7 shows the percentage of individuals getting scores at different points along the scale (e.g., 12.9% get scores between 100 and 105).[72] Notice how the curve is high in the middle and low at both ends. This tells us that we have many more children obtaining scores close to 100 than we have children scoring very much higher or lower than 100. For example, if we add up the percentages in different parts of Figure 5.7, we find that approximately two-thirds (68 percent) of children score within 15 points of 100 (i.e., between 85 and 115). In contrast, only 2 percent of children score as low as 70, and only 2 percent score as high as 130. This symmetric and predictable distribution of scores happens by design rather than by chance: Psychologists have created a method of scoring intelligence test performance that intentionally yields such a distribution. You can learn more about the nature of IQ scores in the discussion of *standard scores* in Appendix B, "Interpreting Standardized Test Scores."

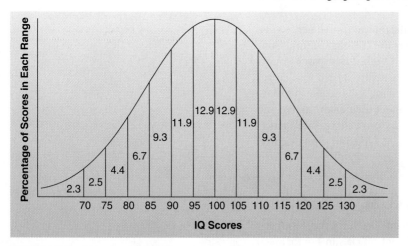

FIGURE 5.7   Percentage of IQ scores in different ranges

IQ score Score on an intelligence test; determined by comparing a person's performance with that of others in the same age-group.

[72] If you have some knowledge of descriptive statistics, it may help you to know that most intelligence tests have a mean of 100 and a standard deviation of 15.

DEVELOPMENTAL TRENDS

TABLE 5.4   Intelligence and Its Measurement at Different Grade Levels

Grade Level	Age-Typical Characteristics	Suggested Strategies
K–2	• Success on test items that involve defining commonly used concrete words, copying geometric figures (e.g., squares, diamonds), remembering short lists, identifying similarities and differences • Tendency to define words in an overly simplistic manner • Short attention span, influencing test performance • Variability in test scores from one occasion to the next	• Use IQ tests primarily to identify significant delays in cognitive development; follow up by seeking appropriate interventions for students with such delays. • Do *not* use test scores to make long-term predictions about students' ability to learn and achieve.
3–5	• Success on test items that involve defining concrete words, assembling puzzles, remembering sentences and short sequences of digits, recognizing concrete analogies, and identifying absurdities in illogical statements • Emerging ability to define common abstract words • Some consistency in overall test scores from one occasion to the next • Tendency for some cognitive abilities to be more developed than others	• Individualize instruction to accommodate students' varying abilities to learn classroom topics. • Do *not* assume that poor performance in some domains necessarily indicates limited ability to learn in other areas. • When students show dramatic differences in performance in different domains (e.g., when fourth graders understand fractions but cannot read simple words), consult with specialists about possible learning disabilities.
6–8	• Success on test items that involve defining commonly used abstract words, drawing logical inferences from verbal descriptions, and identifying similarities across dissimilar concepts • Considerable individual differences in the ability to understand abstract material • Tendency for some students from minority backgrounds to hide their high ability, perhaps for fear of being perceived by peers as conforming to mainstream Western culture	• Expect considerable diversity in students' ability to master abstract classroom material, and individualize instruction accordingly. • Recognize that intelligence may take different forms in different cultures; for instance, it may be reflected in exceptional communication and "people" skills or in originality and resourcefulness in problem solving.
9–12	• Success on test items that involve defining infrequently encountered vocabulary words, identifying differences between similar abstract words, interpreting proverbs, and breaking down complex geometric figures into component parts • Relative stability in most students' IQ scores from one occasion to the next • Continuing tendency for some students to hide high ability levels to maintain popularity with peers • Increasing independence (e.g., obtaining driver's licenses), enabling students to seek out opportunities that enhance talents in particular areas	• Remember that all students can think more "intelligently" when they have appropriate physical and social support (see the discussion of *distributed intelligence* later in this chapter). • Provide challenging activities for students who show exceptional ability in particular areas. • Encourage bright adolescents from lower-income families to pursue postsecondary education, and help them with the logistics of college applications (e.g., applying for financial aid).

Sources: N. Brody, 1992; G. A. Davis & Rimm, 1998; Maker & Schiever, 1989; McLoyd, 1998; Neisser et al., 1996; Ogbu, 1994; Roid, 2003; Salomon, 1993; Sattler, 2001; Terman & Merrill, 1972; Thorndike, Hagen, & Sattler, 1986; Wechsler, 2003.

Modern intelligence tests have been designed with Binet's original purpose in mind: to predict how well students are likely to perform in the classroom and similar situations. Studies repeatedly show that performance on intelligence tests is correlated with school achievement.[73] On average, children with higher IQ scores do better on standardized achievement tests, have higher school grades, and complete more years of education. In other words, IQ scores often *do* predict school achievement, albeit imprecisely. As a result, intelligence tests are frequently used by school psychologists and other specialists in their efforts to identify students with disabilities and other special needs who might require individualized educational programs.

[73] N. Brody, 1997; Gustafsson & Undheim, 1996; Sattler, 2001.

While recognizing the relationship between intelligence test scores and school achievement, we must also keep three points in mind about this relationship. First, intelligence does not necessarily *cause* achievement; it is simply correlated with it. Even though students with high IQs typically perform well in school, we cannot say conclusively that their high achievement is actually the result of their intelligence. Intelligence probably does play an important role in school achievement, but many other factors—motivation, quality of instruction, family resources, parental support, peer group expectations, and so on—are also involved. Second, the relationship between IQ scores and achievement is an imperfect one, with many exceptions to the rule. For a variety of reasons, some students with high IQ scores don't perform well in the classroom, and others achieve at higher levels than we would predict from their IQ scores alone. Third and most important, we must remember that an IQ score simply reflects a child's performance on a particular test at a particular time—it is *not* a permanent characteristic etched in stone—and that some change is to be expected over time.

To some degree, intelligence reflects general speed and efficiency of cognitive processing.

Whenever we use a single IQ score as an estimate of a learner's cognitive ability, we are to some extent buying into the notion that intelligence is a single, general ability that affects performance on many different tasks. Historically, considerable evidence has supported this idea. Although different intelligence tests yield somewhat different scores, people who score high on one test tend to score high on others as well.[74] One early psychologist, Charles Spearman, called this single "intelligence" entity a *general factor*, or *g*.[75] (You may sometimes see the term *Spearman's g*.)

Recall how, in the opening case study, Lupita finishes an assignment more quickly than many of her classmates. Some contemporary information processing theorists believe that underlying *g* may be a general ability to process information quickly and efficiently.[76] For example, children who, as infants, quickly learn and remember new objects and patterns tend to have substantially higher IQ scores in childhood and adolescence.[77]

Intelligence also involves numerous specific processes and abilities.

Certainly intelligence is not just a matter of doing something quickly. Most psychologists realize that any particular task probably involves more specific cognitive processes and abilities that are helpful in *that* task but irrelevant in dissimilar ones.[78] For example, let's return to the "Mock Intelligence Test" presented in a See for Yourself exercise earlier in this chapter. Defining words such as *penitence* (Item 1) requires considerable knowledge of English vocabulary plus sufficient verbal skills to explain a word's meaning with some precision. In contrast, finding analogies among geometric figures (Item 5) involves reasoning about nonverbal, visual entities.

Drawing on findings from research in human information processing, Robert Sternberg has proposed that intelligent behavior involves an interplay of three factors, all of which may vary from one occasion to the next:[79]

- **Environmental context for a task.** As previously noted, intelligent behavior involves adaptation, and different behaviors may be more or less adaptive in different cultures. In Sternberg's view, adaptation can take one of three forms: Learners can (a) adapt their behaviors to deal successfully with specific environmental conditions, (b) modify the environment to better fit their own needs, or (c) select an alternative environment more conducive to success.
- **Prior experiences related to the task.** When learners encounter a new task or problem, they must draw on past experience and consider the kinds of responses that

---

g Theoretical general factor in intelligence that influences one's ability to learn in a wide variety of contexts.

[74] McGrew, Flanagan, Zeith, & Vanderwood, 1997; Neisser et al., 1996; Spearman, 1927.

[75] Spearman, 1904, 1927.

[76] N. Brody, 1992; Bornstein et al., 2006; Haier, 2003; Vernon, 1993.

[77] Dougherty & Haith, 1997; Kavsek, 2004; McCall & Mash, 1995; S. A. Rose & Feldman, 1995.

[78] P. L. Ackerman & Lohman, 2006; Carroll, 2003; McGrew et al., 1997; Neisser et al., 1996; Spearman, 1927; Thurstone, 1938.

[79] Sternberg, 1984, 1985, 1997, 2003.

have been effective in similar circumstances. When they deal with more familiar tasks, basic knowledge and skills related to the task must be sufficiently automatic that the task can be completed quickly and effortlessly. As noted in Chapter 2, automaticity results from experience—from retrieving certain information and using certain skills over and over again.

- **Cognitive processes required by the task.** In Sternberg's view, numerous cognitive and metacognitive processes are involved in intelligent behavior: separating important and relevant information from unimportant and irrelevant details, encoding useful information to make it more memorable, identifying and executing possible strategies for solving a problem, evaluating progress toward a goal, and so on. Different cognitive and metacognitive processes are likely to be relevant to different situations, and thus an individual may behave more or less "intelligently" depending on the specific processes needed at the time.

These three dimensions of intelligence are summarized in Figure 5.8.

To date, research neither supports nor refutes the notion that intelligence has the three-dimensional nature that Sternberg suggests.[80] Nevertheless, Sternberg's perspective helps us understand intelligence in terms of the specific information processing mechanisms that may underlie it. Furthermore, it reminds us that a child's ability to behave intelligently may vary considerably, depending on the particular context and specific knowledge, skills, and cognitive processes that a task requires.

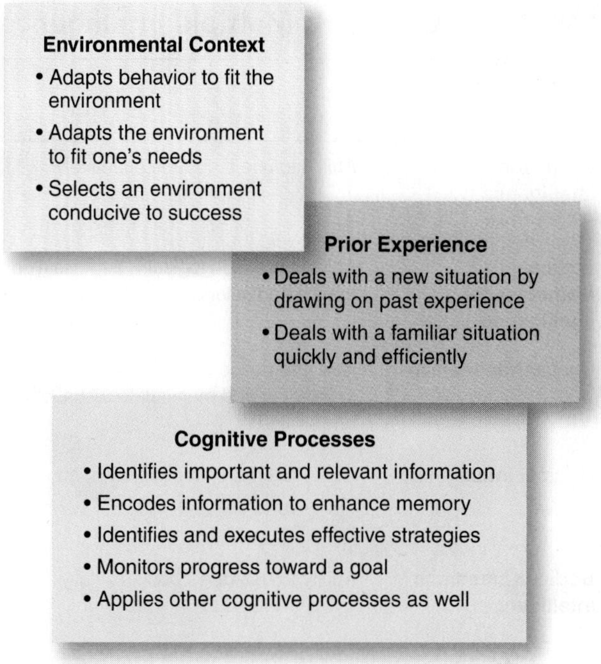

Environmental Context
- Adapts behavior to fit the environment
- Adapts the environment to fit one's needs
- Selects an environment conducive to success

Prior Experience
- Deals with a new situation by drawing on past experience
- Deals with a familiar situation quickly and efficiently

Cognitive Processes
- Identifies important and relevant information
- Encodes information to enhance memory
- Identifies and executes effective strategies
- Monitors progress toward a goal
- Applies other cognitive processes as well

FIGURE 5.8 Sternberg's three dimensions of intelligence

Learners may be more intelligent in some domains than in others.

Although learners who perform well on one intelligence test also tend to perform well on others, a single high score certainly does not *guarantee* that a learner will perform well on other measures. For instance, some children score higher on tests that assess verbal abilities than on tests that assess nonverbal, spatial skills (e.g., assembling puzzles, analyzing complex geometric designs). Other children's test scores show the opposite pattern.

In response to such findings, some psychologists have suggested that children may develop two or more different "intelligences" that are somewhat independent of one another. For example, Sternberg suggests that people may be more or less intelligent in three different domains.[81] *Analytical intelligence* involves making sense of, analyzing, contrasting, and evaluating the kinds of information and problems that are often seen in academic settings and on traditional intelligence tests. *Creative intelligence* involves imagination, invention, and synthesis of ideas within the context of new situations, and so it encompasses the creativity we spoke of in Chapter 4. *Practical intelligence* involves applying knowledge and skills effectively to manage and respond to everyday problems and social situations.[82]

Another psychologist, Howard Gardner, suggests that there are at least eight different, relatively independent abilities.[83] These *multiple intelligences* are described in Table 5.5. (He suggests that there may also be a ninth intelligence, which he calls *existential intelligence*. However, he acknowledges that evidence for it is weaker than that for the other eight intelligences,[84] and so I have omitted it from the table.) Gardner's multiple-intelligences perspective offers the possibility that most learners have the potential to be fairly intelligent in one way or another, perhaps showing exceptional promise in language, mathematics, music, or athletics. In the opening case study, Lupita reveals an ability that Gardner calls *interpersonal intelligence*: She correctly interprets an adult's subtle message, persuades one classmate to finish his work, and skillfully assists two others as they struggle with puzzles.

---

[80] Sattler, 2001; Siegler & Alibali, 2005.
[81] Sternberg calls his theory of intelligence a *triarchic model* of intelligence, in part because of the three dimensions depicted in Figure 5.8 and in part because of the three domains described here.

[82] Sternberg, 1998, 2004; Sternberg et al., 2000.
[83] Gardner, 1983, 1998, 1999.
[84] Gardner, 2000a, 2003.

TABLE 5.5 Gardner's Multiple Intelligences

Type of Intelligence	General Description	Examples of Relevant Behaviors
Linguistic Intelligence	Ability to use language effectively	• Making persuasive arguments • Writing poetry • Noticing subtle nuances in word meanings
Logical-Mathematical Intelligence	Ability to reason logically, especially in mathematics and science	• Solving mathematical problems quickly • Generating mathematical proofs • Formulating and testing hypotheses about observed phenomena[a]
Spatial Intelligence	Ability to notice details of what one sees and to imagine and manipulate visual objects in one's mind	• Conjuring up mental images • Drawing a visual likeness of an object • Making fine discriminations among very similar objects
Musical Intelligence	Ability to create, comprehend, and appreciate music	• Playing a musical instrument • Composing a musical work • Showing a keen awareness of the underlying structure of music
Bodily-Kinesthetic Intelligence	Ability to use one's body skillfully	• Dancing • Playing basketball • Performing pantomime
Interpersonal Intelligence	Ability to notice subtle aspects of other people's behaviors	• Reading another person's mood • Detecting another person's underlying intentions and desires • Using knowledge of others to influence their thoughts and behaviors
Intrapersonal Intelligence	Awareness of one's own feelings, motives, and desires	• Discriminating among such similar emotions as sadness and regret • Identifying the motives guiding one's own behavior • Using self-knowledge to relate more effectively with others
Naturalist Intelligence	Ability to recognize patterns in nature and differences among various life-forms and natural objects	• Identifying members of particular plant or animal species • Classifying natural forms (e.g., rocks, types of mountains) • Applying one's knowledge of nature in such activities as farming, landscaping, or animal training

[a]This example may remind you of Piaget's theory of cognitive development. Many of the stage-specific characteristics that Piaget described fall within the realm of logical-mathematical intelligence.

Gardner presents some evidence to support the existence of multiple intelligences. For example, he describes people who are quite skilled in one area (perhaps in composing music) and yet have seemingly average abilities in other areas. He also points out that people who suffer brain damage sometimes lose abilities that are restricted primarily to one intelligence (e.g., they may show deficits only in verbal skills). However, many psychologists do not believe that Gardner's evidence is sufficiently compelling to support the notion of eight distinctly different abilities.[85] Others disagree that abilities in specific domains, such as in music or bodily movement, are really "intelligence" per se.[86] Still others are taking a wait-and-see attitude about Gardner's theory until more research is conducted.

Intelligence is a product of both heredity and environment.

Children probably don't inherit a single "IQ gene" that determines their intellectual ability. However, they *do* inherit a variety of characteristics that in one way or another affect their cognitive development and intellectual abilities.[87] Thus, children who share common genes (e.g., identical twins) tend to have more similar IQ scores than children who do not.[88]

[85] N. Brody, 1992; Corno et al., 2002; Kail, 1998; Waterhouse, 2006.
[86] Bracken, McCallum, & Shaughnessy, 1999; Sattler, 2001.
[87] Kovas, Petrill, & Plomin, 2007; Shaw et al., 2006; Simonton, 2001.
[88] Bouchard, 1997; Plomin, 1994.

Environmental factors influence intelligence as well, sometimes for the better and sometimes for the worse. Poor nutrition in the early years of development (including the nine months before birth) leads to lower IQ scores, as does a mother's excessive use of alcohol during pregnancy.[89] Attending school has a consistently positive effect on IQ scores.[90] Moving a child from a neglectful, impoverished home environment to a more nurturing, stimulating one (e.g., through adoption) can result in IQ gains of 15 points or more.[91] Furthermore, researchers are finding that, worldwide, there is a slow but steady increase in people's performance on intelligence tests—a trend that is probably due to better nutrition, smaller family sizes, better schooling, increasing cognitive stimulation (through increased access to television, reading materials, etc.), and other improvements in people's environments.[92]

How *much* of a role do nature and nurture each play in the development of intelligence? This question has been a source of considerable controversy over the years, especially when IQ differences are found among various racial or ethnic groups. Increasingly, however, researchers are concluding that any *group* differences in IQ are probably due to differences in environment, and more specifically to economic circumstances that affect the quality of prenatal and postnatal nutrition, availability of stimulating books and toys, access to educational opportunities, and so on.[93] Furthermore, various groups have become increasingly *similar* in average IQ score in recent years—a trend that can be attributed only to more equitable environmental conditions.[94]

Close attention to detail in 10-year-old Luther's drawing of a plant suggests some talent in what Gardner calls *naturalist* intelligence.

Learners may have specific cognitive styles and dispositions that predispose them to think and act in more or less intelligent ways.

Most measures of intelligence focus on specific things that a person *can* do, with little consideration of what a person is *likely* to do. For instance, intelligence tests don't evaluate the extent to which learners are willing to view a situation from multiple perspectives, examine data with a critical eye, or actively take charge of and self-regulate their own learning. Yet such inclinations are sometimes just as important as intellectual ability in determining success in academic and real-world tasks.[95]

Students with the same intelligence levels often approach classroom tasks and think about classroom topics differently. Some of these individual differences are **cognitive styles** over which students don't necessarily have much conscious control. Others are **dispositions** that students intentionally bring to bear on their efforts to master school subject matter. I urge you not to agonize over the distinction between the two concepts, because their meanings overlap considerably. Both involve not only specific cognitive tendencies but also personality characteristics. Dispositions have a motivational component—an I-*want*-to-do-it-this-way quality—as well.[96]

Over the years psychologists and educators have examined a variety of cognitive styles (some have used the term *learning styles*) and dispositions. The traits they've identified and the instruments they've developed to assess these traits don't always hold up under the scrutiny of other researchers.[97] Furthermore, matching students' self-reported "styles" to particular learning environments doesn't necessarily make a difference in academic achievement.[98] Some cognitive styles and dispositions *do* seem to influence how and what students learn, however. For instance, at least two dimensions of cognitive style appear to have an impact:

- **Analytic versus holistic processing:** Some learners tend to break new stimuli and tasks into their subordinate parts (an *analytic* approach), whereas others tend to perceive them primarily as integrated, indivisible wholes (a *holistic* approach). Overall, an analytic approach appears to be more beneficial in school learning,

cognitive style Characteristic way in which a learner tends to think about a task and process new information; typically comes into play automatically rather than by choice.

disposition General inclination to approach and think about learning and problem-solving tasks in a particular way; typically has a motivational component in addition to cognitive components.

[89] D'Amato, Chitooran, & Whitten, 1992; Neisser et al., 1996; Ricciuti, 1993.
[90] Ceci, 2003; Ramey, 1992.
[91] Capron & Duyme, 1989; Scarr & Weinberg, 1976; van IJzendoorn & Juffer, 2005; Zigler & Seitz, 1982.
[92] Daley, Whaley, Sigman, Espinosa, & Neumann, 2003; Flynn, 1987, 2003; Neisser, 1998b.
[93] Brooks-Gunn, Klebanov, & Duncan, 1996; Byrnes, 2003; Dickens & Flynn, 2006; McLoyd, 1998.
[94] Dickens & Flynn, 2006; Neisser et al., 1996.

[95] Duckworth & Seligman, 2005; Kuhn, 2006; Luciana, Conklin, Hooper, & Yarger, 2005; D. N. Perkins, Tishman, Ritchhart, Donis, & Andrade, 2000.
[96] Kuhn, 2001a; Messick, 1994b; D. N. Perkins & Ritchhart, 2004; Stanovich, 1999; Zhang & Sternberg, 2006.
[97] Irvine & York, 1995; Krätzig & Arbuthnott, 2006; Messick, 1994b.
[98] Curry, 1990; Snider, 1990.

although research is not entirely consistent on this point. Most students become increasingly analytical as they grow older.[99]

- **Verbal versus visual learning:** Some learners seem to learn better when information is presented through words (*verbal* learners), whereas others seem to learn better when it's presented through pictures (*visual* learners). There isn't necessarily a "good" or "bad" style here. Rather, learning success probably depends on which modality is used more extensively in classroom activities and instructional materials.[100]

Whereas psychologists have often been reluctant to identify some cognitive styles as being more adaptive than others, certain kinds of dispositions are clearly beneficial in the classroom. Researchers have identified several productive dispositions:[101]

- **Stimulation seeking:** Eagerly interacting with one's physical and social environment
- **Need for cognition:** Regularly seeking and engaging in challenging cognitive tasks
- **Conscientiousness:** Consistently addressing assigned tasks in a careful, focused, and responsible manner
- **Critical thinking:** Consistently evaluating information or arguments in terms of their accuracy, logic, and credibility, rather than accepting them at face value (recall the Chapter 4 discussion about critical thinking being a disposition as well as a cognitive process)
- **Open-mindedness:** Being willing to consider alternative perspectives and multiple sources of evidence, and to suspend judgment rather than leap to an immediate conclusion

Such dispositions are often positively correlated with students' learning and achievement, and many theorists have suggested that they play a causal role in what and how much students learn. In fact, they sometimes "overrule" intelligence in their influence on long-term achievement.[102] For instance, learners with a high need for cognition learn more from what they read, are more likely to base conclusions on sound evidence and logical reasoning, and are more likely to undergo conceptual change when it's warranted.[103] And learners who critically evaluate new evidence and are receptive to and open-minded about diverse perspectives show more advanced reasoning capabilities and achieve at higher levels.[104]

Researchers do not yet have a good understanding of where various cognitive styles and dispositions come from. Perhaps inherited characteristics (e.g., a strong aptitude for remembering visual information or an inquisitive temperament) play a role. Perhaps parents or cultural groups encourage certain ways of looking at and dealing with the world.[105] And quite possibly, teachers' actions in the classroom—for instance, whether they encourage exploration, risk taking, and critical thinking with respect to classroom topics—make a difference.[106]

Learners act more intelligently when they have physical, symbolic, or social support.

Implicit in our discussion so far has been the assumption that intelligent behavior is something people engage in with little if any help from the objects or people around them. Yet people are far more likely to think and behave intelligently when they have assistance from their physical, cultural, or social environment—an idea that is sometimes referred to as **distributed intelligence**.[107] Learners can "distribute" a challenging task—that is, they can pass some of the cognitive burden onto something or someone else—in at least three ways. First, they can use physical objects, especially technology (e.g., calculators, computers), to

distributed intelligence Idea that people act more "intelligently" when they have physical, symbolic, or social assistance.

---

[99] Bagley & Mallick, 1998; Irvine & York, 1995; Jonassen & Grabowski, 1993; A. Miller, 1987; Norenzayan et al., 2007; Riding & Cheema, 1991; Shipman & Shipman, 1985.

[100] R. E. Mayer & Massa, 2003; Riding & Cheema, 1991; Robinson & Sloutsky, 2004.

[101] Cacioppo, Petty, Feinstein, & Jarvis, 1996; Facione, Facione, & Giancarlo, 2000; Halpern, 1997; Kardash & Scholes, 1996; P. M. King & Kitchener, 2002; Matthews, Zeidner, & Roberts, 2006; Raine, Reynolds, & Venables, 2002; Southerland & Sinatra, 2003; Stanovich, 1999; Trautwein, Lüdtke, Schnyder, & Niggli, 2006.

[102] Dai & Sternberg, 2004; Kuhn & Franklin, 2006; D. N. Perkins & Ritchhart, 2004.

[103] Cacioppo et al., 1996; Dai, 2002; Murphy & Mason, 2006.

[104] Matthews et al., 2006; Stanovich, 1999.

[105] Irvine & York, 1995; Kuhn, Daniels, & Krishnan, 2003.

[106] Flum & Kaplan, 2006; Kuhn, 2001b, 2006.

[107] Barab & Plucker, 2002; Pea, 1993; D. N. Perkins, 1992, 1995; Salomon, 1993; Sternberg & Wagner, 1994.

handle and manipulate large amounts of information. Second, they can encode and mentally manipulate the situations they encounter using various symbolic systems—words, charts, diagrams, mathematical equations, and so on—and other cognitive tools their culture provides. And third, they can work with other people to explore ideas and solve problems.

For illustrations of the forms that distributed intelligence might take, consider the problem in the following exercise.

SEE FOR YOURSELF
How Many Reams?

Imagine you are a middle school social studies teacher. At the beginning of the school year, the school secretary sends the following e-mail message to you and the other three social studies teachers at your school:

> How much paper will the Social Studies Department need for all its handouts, assignments, quizzes, and so on this year? For the 483 students who took social studies last year, the four of you used 160 reams of paper. As you know, enrollments are up, and so you'll have a total of 526 students in your classes this year.
>
> I order paper by the ream. A ream contains 500 sheets of paper. How many reams of paper should I order for you? Please don't order more reams than you're likely to use, as the school budget is *very* tight this year.

Obviously you and your fellow social studies teachers don't have a crystal ball and so have no way of knowing *exactly* how much paper you will need. Can you make a fairly accurate estimate based on the information the secretary has given you?

Perhaps you're a whiz at math. If so, you might immediately realize that you can set up the problem as two equivalent ratios with one unknown variable. Using the proportional reasoning of which Piaget spoke, you create the following equation:

$$\frac{483}{526} = \frac{160}{x}$$

You don't solve for x in your head, of course. Rather, you use pencil and paper to write the problem down and keep track of the various numbers involved, and you use a calculator to do the necessary multiplication and division. You determine that x equals approximately 174.24 and, rounding up, conclude that you will need 175 reams of paper for the coming school year. Using both a symbolic system your culture has passed along to you (algebra) and several physical tools (pencil, paper, calculator), you solve a difficult problem fairly easily.

But perhaps, instead, you initially have no idea how to tackle such a problem. This is where your fellow teachers might come in. Imagine that the four of you take up the problem at a department meeting. The following dialogue ensues:

Teacher A: Let's go on the assumption that we'll use the same amount of paper per student this year as we did last year.

Teacher B: That seems reasonable. But rather than dealing with reams, how about if we figure out how many *sheets of paper* we used for each student last year? We can then use that figure to estimate how many sheets of paper we'll need for all of our students this year.

Teacher C: OK. We used 160 reams last year. If we multiply that by 500—because there are 500 sheets of paper in a ream—then we used (Teacher C pauses as she does some quick mental math) 80,000 sheets of paper.

You: So with 483 students, that's . . . let's see (you pull out a calculator and divide 80,000 by 483) . . . that's about 166 sheets of paper per student last year.

Teacher B: This year we'll have 526 students, so multiplying that by 166, we'll use . . . can I borrow your calculator? (you slide your calculator across the table to him) . . . we'll use about 87,316 sheets.

You: OK, so if we divide that figure by 500, we get the number of reams we'll need.

Teacher B: (after doing the division on your calculator) I get 174.632.

You: So we need to round up to 175 reams.

The concept of *distributed intelligence* suggests that learners can often think more intelligently by using technology to manipulate large bodies of data, using culturally based symbolic systems to simplify complex ideas and processes, and brainstorming possible problem solutions with peers.

During the discussion you and your colleagues take advantage of both a symbolic system (in this case, arithmetic rather than algebra) and a physical tool (a calculator). Furthermore, you share various parts of the task among the four of you, reflecting the *distributed cognition* I spoke of in Chapter 3. When learners work together on complex, challenging tasks and problems, they often think more intelligently than any one of them could think alone. In fact, they sometimes teach one another strategies and ways of thinking that can help each of them to think even *more* intelligently on future occasions.[108]

ADDRESSING STUDENTS' DEVELOPMENTAL NEEDS

In our exploration of principles of cognitive development and intelligence, we've discovered that learners of different ages, and to some extent learners of the *same* age, have different thinking and reasoning capabilities. We've also discovered that environmental factors can definitely impact learners' thinking and reasoning capabilities for the better. In this final section of the chapter, we look at (a) how to accommodate developmental differences and diversity in the classroom and (b) how to foster cognitive development in *all* children and adolescents.

Accommodating Developmental Differences and Diversity

Think, for a moment, about your own experiences in the early elementary grades. What topics did you study, and what instructional strategies did your teachers use to teach those topics? Now think about your high school years. In what ways were the subject matter and instructional methods different from those in elementary school? Certainly many differences come to mind. For instance, in the early elementary grades you probably focused on basic knowledge and skills: learning letter–sound correspondences, reading simple prose, using correct capitalization and punctuation, adding and subtracting two-digit numbers, and so on. Your teachers probably provided a great deal of structure and guidance, giving you small, concrete tasks that would enable you to practice and eventually master certain information and procedures. By high school, however, you were studying complex topics—biological classification systems, historical events, symbolism in literature and poetry, manipulation of algebraic equations, and so on—that were abstract and multifaceted, and your teachers put much of the burden of mastering those topics on *you*.

Such differences reflect the fact that classroom instruction must be *developmentally appropriate*. That is, it must take into account the characteristics and abilities that learners of a particular age-group are likely to have. Yet as we've discovered, learners develop at different rates, and so instruction must also allow for considerable *diversity* in the characteristics and abilities of any single age-group. The following recommendations can help teachers in their efforts to accommodate developmental differences and student diversity in the classroom.

Explore students' reasoning with problem-solving tasks and probing questions.

In his work with children and adolescents, Piaget pioneered a technique known as the **clinical method**. In particular, he would give a child a problem and probe the child's reasoning about the problem through a series of individually tailored follow-up questions. We saw an example of the clinical method in the interview with 6-year-old Brian presented earlier. An adult asked Brian whether a set of 12 wooden beads—some brown, some white—had more wooden beads or more brown beads. When Brian responded, "More brown ones," the adult continued to press Brian (e.g., "Which would be longer, [a necklace] made with the wooden beads or . . . one made with the brown beads?") to be sure Brian truly believed there were more brown beads and possibly also to create disequilibrium.

By presenting a variety of Piagetian tasks involving either concrete or formal operational thinking skills—tasks involving class inclusion, conservation, separation and control

clinical method Procedure in which an adult probes a child's reasoning about a task or problem, tailoring follow-up questions to the child's earlier responses.

[108] Salomon, 1993.

Materials
2 glasses containing equal amounts of water
2 balls of clay equal in size and smaller in
diameter than the water glasses
2 rubber bands
1 plastic knife

Procedure
1. Show the child the two glasses of water. Put one rubber band around each glass at the level of the waters surface. Ask, "Do both glasses have the same amount of water?" If the child says no, say, "Then please make them the same." Allow the child to pour water from one glass to the other until satisfied that both glasses have equal amounts. Adjust the rubber bands if necessary, or have the child adjust them.
2. Show the child the two balls of clay. Ask, "Are these balls of clay the same size?" If the child says no, say, "Then please make them the same size." Allow the child to add to or subtract from one or both of the balls until satisfied that the two are equal.
3. Being sure that the child is watching, place one ball of clay in one of the glasses of water. Say, "See how the water went up when I did that. Let's move the rubber band to the place where the surface of the water is." Move the rubber band appropriately.
4. Take the other ball of clay and other glass of water. Say, "I'm going to cut this ball of clay into several pieces." Use the plastic knife to cut the ball into four or five pieces. Ask, "How much do you think the water will rise when I drop all this clay into the glass? Move the rubber band to the level where you think the water's surface will be." Allow the child to adjust the rubber band until satisfied with its location. If the child moves the rubber band to the same level as the other rubber band, proceed with steps 5a–7a. If the child moves it to a higher or lower level than the other rubber band, proceed with steps 5b–6b.

If the child has predicted an equal rise in height:
5a. Say, "Tell me why you think the water will rise to that spot." Examples of possible responses are
   • "It's the same amount of clay."
   • "I don't know. I just guessed."
6a. Drop all the pieces of clay into the water. Say, "You were right. Are you surprised?" Examples of possible responses are
   • "Not surprised. Even though you cut the clay up, there's still the same amount."
   • "Surprised, because I wasn't really sure it would go there."
7a. If the child was surprised, ask, "Why do you think it rose to that level?" Listen to determine whether the child now understands the same amount of clay should, regardless of number of pieces, displace the same amount of water.

If the child has predicted an unequal rise in height:
5b. Say, "Tell me why you think the water will rise to that spot." Examples of possible responses are
   • "There's less clay."
   • "There are more pieces."
   • "I don't know. I just guessed."
6b. Drop all the pieces of clay into the water. Say, "You weren't quite right. Look, it rose the same amount of water as in the other glass. Why do you think it rose to that level?" Examples of possible responses are
   • "Even though you cut the clay up, there's still the same amount as in the other ball."
   • "It doesn't make sense, because the smaller pieces should take up less room in the glass."
   • "I don't know."

Interpretation
Children who have fully achieved conservation of displaced volume should (a) predict that the water in the second glass will rise to the same level at that in the first glass and (b) justify the prediction by saying that both the water and clay in the two glasses will be the same. Children who are on the verge of achieving conservation of displaced volume might either (a) predict the correct level without initially being able to justify it or (b) initially make an incorrect prediction. In either case, however, they should be able to explain the final result by acknowledging that, despite differences in appearance, the clay in the two glasses displaces the same amount of water. Children who can neither make a correct prediction nor explain the final result are not yet able to reason correctly about problems involving conservation of displaced volume.

FIGURE 5.9   Conservation of displaced volume: An example of how a teacher might probe a student's reasoning using Piaget's clinical method

of variables, proportional reasoning, and so on—and observing students' responses to such tasks, teachers can gain valuable insights into how their students think and reason. Formulating follow-up questions that effectively probe a child's reasoning often comes only with considerable experience, however. In Figure 5.9, I present a procedure that a novice interviewer might use in probing students' reasoning related to *conservation of displaced volume*, a fairly advanced form of conservation that, in Piaget's theory, emerges sometime around puberty.

Teachers need not stick to traditional Piagetian reasoning tasks, however. On the contrary, the clinical method is applicable to a wide variety of academic domains and subject matter. To illustrate, a teacher might present various kinds of maps (e.g., a road map of Pennsylvania, an aerial map of Chicago, a three-dimensional relief map of a mountainous area) and ask students to interpret what they see. Children in the primary grades (kindergarten, first grade, second grade) are apt to interpret many symbols on the maps in a concrete fashion. For instance, they might think that roads depicted in red are *actually* red. They might also have difficulty with the scale of a map, perhaps thinking that lines can't be roads because they're "too skinny for two cars to fit on" or that mountains depicted by bumps on a relief map aren't really mountains because "they aren't high enough."[109] Understanding the concept of *scale* of a map requires proportional reasoning—an ability that students don't fully master until adolescence—and so it is hardly surprising that young children would be confused by it.

Interpret intelligence test results cautiously.

As we've seen, intelligence tests are simply collections of questions and tasks that psychologists have developed and continue to revise over the years to get a handle on how well children and adolescents think, reason, and learn. These tests predict school achievement to some extent, but they are hardly magical instruments that can mysteriously determine a learner's true intelligence—if, in fact, such a thing as "true" intelligence even exists. When teachers are aware of students' IQ scores, they should keep the following points in mind:[110]

- Different kinds of intelligence tests may yield somewhat different scores.
- A student's performance on any test is inevitably affected by temporary factors present at the time the test is taken, including distracting events, general health, mood, fatigue, and time of day. Young children are especially susceptible to such factors. (Here we're talking about a test's *reliability*, a concept we'll consider in Chapter 10.)
- Test items typically focus on skills that are important in mainstream Western culture, and especially in school settings. They do not necessarily tap into skills that may be more highly valued in other contexts or other cultures.
- Some students may be unfamiliar with the content or types of tasks involved in particular test items and so perform poorly on those items.
- Students with limited English proficiency (e.g., recent immigrants) are at an obvious disadvantage when an intelligence test is administered in English.
- Some students (e.g., minority-group students who want to avoid being perceived as conforming to "white" culture) may not be motivated to perform at their best and so may obtain scores that underestimate their capabilities.
- IQ scores have a limited "shelf life." They predict school achievement over the short run (e.g., over the next two to three years) but not necessarily over the long run, especially when the scores are obtained during the preschool or early elementary years.

Used within the context of other information, IQ scores can, in many cases, give a general idea of a student's current cognitive functioning. But as you can see from the limitations just listed, teachers should always maintain a healthy degree of skepticism about the accuracy of IQ scores, especially when students come from diverse cultural backgrounds, have acquired only limited proficiency in English, or were fairly young when the scores were obtained.

Look for signs of exceptional abilities and talents.

Earlier we discovered that a learner benefits most from tasks that he or she can accomplish only with assistance—tasks that are in the learner's *zone of proximal development*. Because different students are at different points in their cognitive development, they are likely to have different ZPDs. Almost any classroom is apt to have one or more students whose ability levels far surpass those of their peers. Although experts disagree about how such **giftedness** should be defined and identified, it is probably the result of both genetic and environmental factors.[111]

Students who are gifted tend to be among our schools' greatest underachievers. When required to progress at the same rate as their nongifted peers, they achieve at levels far

giftedness Unusually high ability in one or more areas, to the point where students require special educational services to help them meet their full potential.

[109] Liben & Downs, 1989.
[110] Bartholomew, 2004; Dirks, 1982; Hayslip, 1994; Heath, 1989; Neisser et al., 1996; Ogbu, 1994; D. N. Perkins, 1995; Sattler, 2001; Sternberg, 1996, 2007; Zigler & Finn-Stevenson, 1992.

[111] K. R. Carter, 1991; Keogh & MacMillan, 1996; Renzulli, 2002; Simonton, 2001; Winner, 2000b.

short of their capabilities.[112] Furthermore, many students with special gifts and talents become bored or frustrated when their school experiences don't provide tasks and assignments that challenge them and help them develop their unique abilities.[113] In the "Motivation: Middle Childhood" video clip in MyEducationLab, 9-year-old Elena reveals her desire for challenge in her description of PEAK, a program at her school for students who are gifted:

> **Adult:** What do you like best about school?
>
> **Elena:** I like PEAK. . . . It's for smart kids who have, like, good ideas for stuff you could do. And so they make it more challenging for you in school. So instead of third-grade math, you get fourth-grade math.

The traditional approach to identifying giftedness is to use IQ scores, perhaps with 125 or 130 as a cutoff point.[114] Yet some students may be gifted in only one domain—say, in science or creative writing—and tests of general intelligence might not be especially helpful in identifying such students.[115] And for a variety of reasons, students from some minority-group backgrounds don't perform as well on intelligence tests as students raised in mainstream Western culture.[116] Students from some cultures may have had little experience with some of the tasks commonly used in intelligence tests, such as reasoning about self-contained logical problems or finding patterns in geometric figures (see the problems in the "Beings and Basketballs" exercise and Item 5 in the "Mock Intelligence Test" exercise on pp. 151 and 158, respectively.)[117] Other students, especially girls, may try to hide their talents, perhaps because they fear classmates' ridicule or perhaps because their cultures do not value high achievement in females.[118]

Observe Elena's desire for challenge in the "Motivation: Middle Childhood" video in the Additional Resources section in Chapter 5 of MyEducationLab.

It is critical, then, that school personnel not rely solely on intelligence tests to identify students who may be in need of a more challenging curriculum than their peers. The following are examples of traits teachers might look for:[119]

- More advanced vocabulary, language, and reading skills
- More general knowledge about the world
- Ability to learn more quickly, easily, and independently than peers
- More advanced and efficient cognitive processes and metacognitive skills
- Flexibility, originality, and resourcefulness in thinking and problem solving
- Ability to apply concepts and ideas to new, seemingly unrelated situations
- High standards for performance (sometimes to the point of unhealthy perfectionism)
- High motivation to accomplish challenging tasks; feelings of boredom about easy tasks
- Above-average social development and emotional adjustment (although a few extremely gifted students may have difficulties because they are so *very* different from their peers)

Researchers and expert teachers have found a variety of instructional strategies to be effective for students who are gifted. Common suggestions are presented and illustrated in the Classroom Strategies box "Working with Students Who Have Exceptional Abilities and Talents."

Consult with specialists if children show significant delays in development.

Whereas some children and adolescents show exceptionally advanced development, a few others show unusual *delays* in development. When delays appear only in a specific aspect of cognitive functioning, perhaps learners haven't had sufficient experience to develop it or perhaps a *learning disability* is present. In contrast, learners with **mental retardation** show

---

[112] K. R. Carter, 1991; Gallagher, 1991; Reis, 1989.

[113] Feldhusen, Van Winkel, & Ehle, 1996; Winner, 2000b.

[114] Keogh & MacMillan, 1996; J. T. Webb, Meckstroth, & Tolan, 1982.

[115] For example, see Moran & Gardner, 2006.

[116] McLoyd, 1998; Neisser, 1998a.

[117] Rogoff, 2003.

[118] Covington, 1992; G. A. Davis & Rimm, 1998; DeLisle, 1984.

[119] Candler-Lotven, Tallent-Runnels, Olivárez, & Hildreth, 1994; K. R. Carter & Ormrod, 1982; B. Clark, 1997; Cornell et al., 1990; Gottfried, Fleming, & Gottfried, 1994; Haywood & Lidz, 2007; Hoge & Renzulli, 1993; Janos & Robinson, 1985; Lupart, 1995; Maker & Schiever, 1989; Parker, 1997; Rabinowitz & Glaser, 1985; Steiner & Carr, 2003; Winner, 2000a, 2000b.

mental retardation Disability characterized by significantly below-average general intelligence and deficits in practical and social skills.

CLASSROOM STRATEGIES

Working with Students Who Have Exceptional Abilities and Talents

- **Individualize instruction in accordance with students' specific talents.**

    A middle school student with exceptional reading skills and an interest in Shakespeare is assigned several Shakespearean plays. After reading each play, he discusses it with his student teacher, who is an English major at a nearby university.

- **Form study groups of students with similar abilities and interests.**

    A music teacher forms and provides weekly instruction to a quartet of exceptionally talented music students.

- **Teach complex cognitive skills within the context of specific school topics rather than separately from the normal school curriculum.**

    A teacher has an advanced science study group conduct a series of experiments related to a single topic. To promote scientific reasoning and critical thinking, the teacher gives students several questions they should ask themselves as they conduct these experiments.

- **Provide opportunities for independent study.**

    A second-grade teacher finds educational software through which a mathematically gifted 8-year-old can study decimals, exponents, square roots, and other concepts that she appears to be ready to master.

- **Encourage students to set high goals for themselves.**

    A teacher encourages a student from a lower socioeconomic background to consider going to college and helps the student explore possible sources of financial assistance for higher education.

- **Seek outside resources to help students develop their exceptional talents.**

    A student with an exceptional aptitude for learning foreign language studies Russian at a local university.

Sources: Ambrose, Allen, & Huntley, 1994; Feldhusen, 1989; Fiedler, Lange, & Winebrenner, 1993; J. A. Kulik & Kulik, 1997; Lupart, 1995; Moon, Feldhusen, & Dillon, 1994; Patton, Blackbourn, & Fad, 1996; Piirto, 1999; Stanley, 1980.

developmental delays in most aspects of their academic and social functioning. More specifically, they exhibit *both* of the following characteristics:[120]

- **Significantly below-average general intelligence.** Intelligence test scores of children with mental retardation are quite low—usually no higher than 65 or 70, reflecting performance in the bottom 2 percent of their age-group.[121] These children show other signs of below-average intelligence as well. For instance, they learn slowly and perform quite poorly on school tasks in comparison with their age-mates. And they show consistently poor achievement across virtually all academic subject areas.

- **Deficits in adaptive behavior.** In addition to showing low intelligence and achievement, students with mental retardation typically behave in ways that we would expect of much younger children. Their deficits in *adaptive behavior* include limitations in practical intelligence—the ability to manage ordinary activities of daily living—and social intelligence—knowledge of appropriate conduct in social situations.

Mental retardation is often caused by genetic conditions. For example, it is common in children with Down syndrome, a condition marked by distinctive facial features, shorter-than-average arms and legs, and poor muscle tone. Other instances of mental retardation are due to biological but noninherited causes, such as severe malnutrition or excessive alcohol consumption during the mother's pregnancy or prolonged oxygen deprivation during a difficult birth.[122] In still other situations, environmental factors, such as parental neglect or an extremely impoverished and unstimulating home environment, may be at fault.[123] Although usually a long-term condition, mental retardation is not necessarily a lifelong disability, especially when the presumed cause is environmental rather than genetic.[124]

Severe instances of mental retardation are usually identified long before children begin kindergarten or first grade. Mild cases sometimes go undetected until school age, however. Teachers who suspect that a student has significant delays in cognitive development and

---

[120] Luckasson et al., 2002.
[121] Keogh & MacMillan, 1996; Turnbull, Turnbull, & Wehmeyer, 2007.
[122] Dorris, 1989; Keogh & MacMillan, 1996.

[123] Batshaw & Shapiro, 1997; A. A. Baumeister, 1989.
[124] Ormrod & McGuire, 2007; Landesman & Ramey, 1989.

CLASSROOM STRATEGIES

Working with Students Who Have Significant Delays in Cognitive Development

- **Introduce new material at a slower pace, and provide many opportunities for practice.**

  A teacher gives a student only two new addition facts a week because any more than two seems to overwhelm him. Every day the teacher has the student practice writing the new facts and review the facts learned in preceding weeks.

- **Explain tasks concretely and in very specific language.**

  An art teacher gives a student explicit training in the steps he needs to take at the end of each painting session: (a) Rinse the paintbrush out at the sink, (b) put the brush and watercolor paints on the shelf in the back room, and (c) put the painting on the counter by the window to dry. Initially the teacher needs to remind the student of every step in the process. However, with time and practice, the student eventually carries out the process independently.

- **Give students explicit guidance about how to study.**

  A teacher tells a student, "When you study a new spelling word, it helps if you repeat the letters out loud while you practice writing the word. Let's try it with *house*, the word you are learning this morning. Watch how I repeat the letters—H...O...U...S...E—as I write the word. Now you try doing what I just did."

- **Encourage independence.**

  A high school teacher teaches a student how to use her calculator to figure out what she needs to pay for lunch every day. The teacher also gives the student considerable practice in identifying the correct bills and coins to use when paying various amounts.

Sources: K. L. Fletcher & Bray, 1995; Patton et al., 1996; Turnbull et al., 2007.

---

adaptive behavior should definitely consult with specialists trained in identifying and working with children who have special educational needs.

Some students with mild mental retardation spend part or all of the school day in general education classrooms. They are apt to have poor reading and language skills, less general knowledge about the world, difficulty with abstract ideas, and little or no metacognitive awareness.[125] Nevertheless, they can make considerable academic progress when instruction is appropriately paced and provides a lot of guidance and support. The Classroom Strategies box "Working with Students Who Have Significant Delays in Cognitive Development" offers a few suggestions for working effectively with these students.

Fostering Cognitive Development

Vygotsky, Piaget, and contemporary researchers have offered numerous suggestions for fostering children's and adolescents' cognitive development. The following recommendations summarize many of their suggestions.

Encourage play activities.

Vygotsky suggested that play is hardly the frivolous activity it appears to be. Quite the contrary, play enables children to "stretch" their abilities in many ways.[126] For example, as a kindergartner, my son Jeff often played "restaurant" with his friend Scott. In a corner of our basement, the two boys created a restaurant "kitchen" with a toy sink and stove and stocked it with plastic dishes, cooking utensils, and "food" items. They created a separate dining area with child-sized tables and chairs and made menus for their customers. On one occasion they invited both sets of parents to "dine" at the restaurant, taking our orders, serving us our plastic "food," and eventually giving us our bills. Fortunately, they seemed quite happy with the few pennies we paid them for our "meals."

In their restaurant play, the two boys took on several adult roles (restaurant manager, waiter, cook) and practiced a variety of adult-like behaviors. In real life such a scenario would, of course, be impossible. Very few 5-year-old children have the cooking, reading, writing, mathematical, or organizational skills necessary to run a restaurant. Yet the element of make-believe brought these tasks within the boys' reach.

Furthermore, as children play, their behaviors must conform to certain standards or expectations. In the early elementary school years, children often act in accordance with how

---

[125] Beirne-Smith, Ittenbach, & Patton, 2002; Butterfield & Ferretti, 1987; Kail, 1990; Patton et al., 1996; Turnbull et al., 2007.

[126] Vygotsky, 1978.

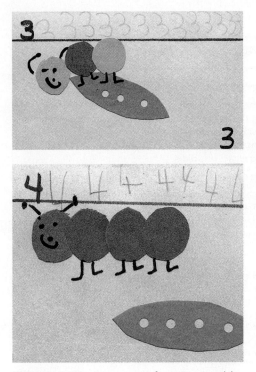

FIGURE 5.10 An excerpt from 5-year-old Luisa's "Caterpillar Number Book," in which she depicts the numbers 1 to 10 in three ways: as numerals, holes in a leaf, and segments of a caterpillar's body

a "daddy," "teacher," or "waiter" would behave. In the organized group games and sports that come later, children must follow a specific set of rules. By adhering to such restrictions on their behavior, children learn to plan ahead, to think before they act, and to engage in self-restraint—skills critical for successful participation in the adult world.

Play, then, is hardly a waste of time. Instead, it provides a valuable training ground for the adult world, and perhaps for this reason it is seen in virtually all cultures worldwide.

Share the wisdom of previous generations.

As we learned in Chapter 3, the culture of any social group ensures that each generation passes the group's accumulated wisdom down to the next generation. Some aspects of a culture are transmitted through informal conversations between adults and children, but many others are passed along through formal education in various academic disciplines. Each discipline includes numerous concepts, procedures, and other cognitive tools that can help students better understand and work effectively in their physical and social worlds.

Instruction in useful cognitive tools typically begins quite early. For example, in mainstream Western culture many children learn color and shape names, counting, and the alphabet in the preschool years. For those who don't, acquiring such basic tools must be a high priority in kindergarten or first grade. For example, Figure 5.10 shows an excerpt from one kindergartner's "Caterpillar Number Book," in which she practices representing the numbers 1 to 10.

Rely heavily on concrete objects and activities, especially in the early elementary grades.

As Piaget and many other researchers have discovered, children in the elementary grades have trouble thinking and reasoning about ideas that are abstract, hypothetical, or contrary to fact. It is important, then, that elementary school teachers make classroom subject matter concrete for students. In mathematics instruction, kindergarten and first-grade teachers might have students use concrete manipulatives (e.g., blocks, beads, pennies) to acquire conservation of number and understand basic addition and subtraction facts. In the middle elementary grades, paper and pencil may replace concrete objects to some extent, provided that mathematical concepts are still depicted in concrete terms—for instances, as pictures or diagrams.

Virtually any academic discipline has its share of abstract ideas, and elementary teachers should either translate those ideas into concrete terms or else, if possible, postpone discussion of them until the upper elementary grades at the earliest. For example, in history, the very idea of historical *time*—whether it be a particular year (e.g., 1492) or a certain lengthy time span (e.g., 100 years)—is far beyond children's immediate experience. Accordingly, elementary school teachers conducting history lessons should probably minimize the extent to which they talk about specific years before the recent past.[127] Instead, especially in the primary grades, teachers might focus on important events in their nation's history—for example, having children reenact the "first Thanksgiving" or showing photographs of covered wagons crossing the prairie—without much regard for the sequence of events over a long period. Such lessons may lead to a disjointed knowledge of history (recall Rita's understanding of Michigan's history in the opening case in Chapter 2), but they provide a concrete foundation on which more abstract and integrated history lessons can later build.

On some occasions teachers can have students engage in **discovery learning**, in which students derive new concepts and principles for themselves. Students sometimes remember and apply information more effectively if they discover it for themselves rather than simply reading or hearing about it.[128] The Classroom Strategies box "Facilitating Discovery Learning" offers several suggestions for conducting effective discovery learning sessions.

Probably the most important suggestion in the Classroom Strategies box is to *structure and guide* a discovery session to some extent. Occasionally students can learn from random explorations of their environment—for example, by experimenting with and thereby discovering the properties of dry sand, wet sand, and water.[129] By and large, however, students benefit more from carefully planned and structured activities that help them construct ap-

discovery learning Approach to instruction in which students develop an understanding of a topic through firsthand interaction with the environment.

[127] Barton & Levstik, 1996.

[128] de Jong & van Joolingen, 1998; M. A. McDaniel & Schlager, 1990; D. S. McNamara & Healy, 1995.

[129] Hutt, Tyler, Hutt, & Christopherson, 1989.

CLASSROOM STRATEGIES

Facilitating Discovery Learning

- Identify a concept or principle about which students can learn through interaction with their physical or social environment.

    A fifth-grade teacher realizes that rather than tell students how to calculate the area of a triangle, she can help them discover the procedure for themselves.

- Make sure students have the necessary prior knowledge for productively interpreting their discoveries.

    A first-grade teacher asks students what they already know about air (e.g., people breathe it, wind involves its movement). After determining that they have some intuitive awareness that it has physical substance and can affect other physical substances, she and her class conduct an experiment in which a glass containing a crumpled paper towel is turned upside-down and immersed in a bowl of water. The teacher eventually removes the glass from the water and asks students to explain why the paper towel didn't get wet. (A portion of this lesson is depicted in the "Properties of Air" video clip in Chapter 5 of MyEducationLab.)

- Show puzzling results to arouse curiosity.

    A middle school science teacher shows her class two glasses of water. In one glass an egg floats at the water's surface; in the other glass an egg rests on the bottom. The students give a simple and logical explanation for the difference: One egg has more air inside and so must be lighter. But then the teacher switches the eggs into opposite glasses. The egg that the students believe to be "heavier" now floats, and the "lighter" egg sinks to the bottom. The students are quite surprised and demand to know what is going on. (Ordinarily, water is less dense than an egg, so an egg placed in it will quickly sink. But in this situation, one glass contains saltwater—a mixture denser than an egg and so capable of keeping it afloat.)

- Structure and guide a discovery session so that students proceed logically toward discoveries you want them to make.

    A seventh-grade science teacher asks students to speculate about variables that might influence the rate at which a pendulum swings. His students offer three possibilities: length of the pendulum, weight of the object at the bottom, and angle at which the pendulum is initially dropped. The students work in small groups to test each of these hypotheses. When one group fails to separate and control variables, the teacher asks its members to look closely at their data: "What did you change between test one and test two? . . . Which caused the higher frequency [oscillation rate]? . . . Why can't you all come to a conclusion by looking at the numbers?" He continues to ask questions until the students realize they have simultaneously varied both length and weight in their experimentation. (This lesson is depicted in the "Designing Experiments" video clip in Chapter 5 of MyEducationLab.)

- Have students record their findings.

    A biology teacher has students make sketches of the specific organs they observe as they dissect an earthworm.

- Help students relate their findings to concepts and principles in the academic discipline they are studying.

    After students in a social studies class have collected data on average incomes and voting patterns in different counties within their state, their teacher asks, "How can we interpret these data given what we've learned about the relative wealth of members of the two major political parties?"

Sources: Bruner, 1966; de Jong & van Joolingen, 1998; N. Frederiksen, 1984a; Hardy, Jonen, Möller, & Stern, 2006; Hickey, 1997; Kirschner, Sweller, & Clark, 2006; R. E. Mayer, 2004; Minstrell & Stimpson, 1996; E. L. Palmer, 1965; B. Y. White & Frederiksen, 1998.

---

propriate interpretations.[130] The extent to which a discovery session should be structured depends partly on students' reasoning and problem-solving skills.[131] For example, some students may have trouble formulating and testing hypotheses or separating and controlling variables. Such students will gain more from their explorations if they are given specific, concrete problems and questions to address and considerable guidance about how to proceed.

Although discovery activities have considerable value, teachers should keep in mind their potential downside. In particular, students may "discover" evidence that supports their existing misconceptions and ignore evidence that contradicts those misconceptions, reflecting the *confirmation bias* I spoke of in Chapter 2.[132] The "Designing Experiments" video clip in MyEducationLab provides an example. Even though a group of seventh graders simultaneously varies both weight and length in experiments with a pendulum—thereby making a clear-cut conclusion impossible—at least two of the students erroneously conclude that *weight*, rather than length, affects a pendulum's oscillation rate.

Observe confirmation bias in discovery learning in the "Designing Experiments" video in the Additional Resources section in Chapter 5 of MyEducationLab.

Present abstract ideas more frequently in the middle school and high school grades, but tie them to concrete objects and events.

Many of the concepts, symbols, and other useful cognitive tools that previous generations have passed along to us are fairly abstract. Yet as we've seen, abstract thinking emerges only gradually over the course of childhood and adolescence. Accordingly, abstract ideas should

---

[130] Hardy et al., 2006; Hickey, 1997; R. E. Mayer, 2004; Minstrell & Stimpson, 1996; B. Y. White & Frederiksen, 1998, 2005.

[131] de Jong & van Joolingen, 1998; B. Y. White & Frederiksen, 1998.

[132] Hammer, 1997; Hynd, 1998b; Kirschner et al., 2006; Kuhn, Amsel, & O'Loughlin, 1988; Schauble, 1990.

Observe high school teachers making abstract ideas concrete in the "Scarlet Letter" and "Charles's Law" videos in the Additional Resources section in Chapter 5 of MyEducationLab.

be introduced slowly at first, especially in the upper elementary and middle school grades, and they should be accompanied by concrete activities and illustrations as often as possible.

Even in high school, actually *seeing* an abstract concept or principle in action can help students encode and remember it more effectively (recall our discussion of *visual imagery* in Chapter 2). For example, in the "Scarlet Letter" video clip in MyEducationLab, a high school English teacher has students find magazine photographs that suggest what the character Hester Prynne might have looked like. And in the "Charles's Law" video clip, a high school chemistry teacher brings Charles's law to life with balloons and beakers of water of varying temperatures.

Initially introduce sophisticated reasoning processes within the context of familiar situations and group work.

Piaget proposed, and other researchers have since confirmed, that sophisticated mathematical and scientific reasoning processes—proportional reasoning, formulating and testing hypotheses, testing and controlling variables, and so on—are abilities that don't fully emerge until adolescence. Such abilities are more likely to develop when they are actively nurtured rather than left to chance. Furthermore, as we discovered earlier, students are more likely to use them effectively in contexts they know well. For instance, a science teacher might initially ask students to separate and control variables related to a commonplace activity, perhaps fishing, growing sunflowers, or teaching new tricks to family pets. A social studies teacher might ask students to use proportional reasoning to compute distances on a local city map drawn to a particular scale. A physical education teacher might ask students to formulate and test various hypotheses about the most effective way to throw a football.

The importance of group work for nurturing advanced reasoning processes can be found in Vygotsky's concept of *internalization*. Many complex cognitive processes, Vygotsky reasoned, have their roots in social interactions, in that children gradually internalize—and so can eventually use independently—processes that they initially use in interactions with others. We see an example of this idea in **reciprocal teaching**, an approach to teaching reading and listening comprehension strategies in which students learn to ask one another questions about textbook passages and children's literature.[133] Several students and their teacher meet in a group to read a piece of text, occasionally stopping to discuss and process the text aloud. Initially, the teacher leads the discussion, asking questions about the text to promote four cognitive processes: summarizing, questioning, clarifying, and predicting. Gradually, he or she turns the role of "teacher" over to different students, who then take charge of the discussion and ask one another the kinds of questions their teacher has modeled. Eventually, students can read and discuss a text almost independently of their teacher. They work together to construct meaning and check one another for comprehension and possible misunderstandings, and they become increasingly flexible in how they apply their newly acquired strategies.

As an illustration, let's look at a reciprocal teaching session for a group of six first graders reading a passage about snowshoe rabbits. In this particular case the classroom teacher read the text in small segments (at higher grade levels, students take turns reading). After each segment, the teacher paused while students discussed and processed the segment. As you read the following dialogue, look for examples of summarizing, questioning, clarifying, and predicting (there is at least one instance of each):

> The children were reading about the snowshoe rabbit, and it was the 16th day of dialogue. The teacher had just read a segment of text describing the season in which baby rabbits are born and the ways in which the mother rabbit cares for her babies. A student named Kam is the dialogue leader.
>
> **Kam:** When was the babies born?
> **Teacher:** That's a good question to ask. Call on someone to answer that question.
> **Kam:** Robby? Milly?
> **Milly:** Summer.
> **Teacher:** What would happen if the babies were born in the winter? Let's think.

reciprocal teaching Approach to teaching reading and listening comprehension in which students take turns asking teacher-like questions of classmates.

---

[133] A. L. Brown & Palincsar, 1987; Palincsar & Brown, 1984, 1989; Palincsar & Herrenkohl, 1999.

Several children make a number of responses, including: "The baby would be very cold." "They would need food." "They don't have no fur when they are just born."

Kam: I have another question. How does she get the babies safe?

Kris: She hides them.

Kam: That's right but something else. . . .

Teacher: There is something very unusual about how she hides them that surprised me. I didn't know this.

Travis: They are all in a different place.

Teacher: Why do you think she does this?

Milly: Probably because I heard another story, and when they're babies they usually eat each other or fight with each other.

Teacher: That could be! And what about when that lynx comes?

Several children comment that that would be the end of all the babies.

Travis: If I was the mother, I would hide mine, I would keep them all together.

Kris: If the babies are hidden and the mom wants to go and look at them, how can she remember where they are?

Teacher: Good question. Because she does have to find them again. Why? What does she bring them?

Milly: She needs to bring food. She probably leaves a twig or something.

Teacher: Do you think she puts out a twig like we mark a trail?

Several children disagree and suggest that she uses her sense of smell. One child, recalling that the snowshoe rabbit is not all white in the winter, suggests that the mother might be able to tell her babies apart by their coloring.

Teacher: So we agree that the mother rabbit uses her senses to find her babies after she hides them. Kam, can you summarize for us now?

Kam: The babies are born in the summer. . . .

Teacher: The mother . . .

Kam: The mother hides the babies in different places.

Teacher: And she visits them . . .

Kam: To bring them food.

Travis: She keeps them safe.

Teacher: Any predictions?

Milly: What she teaches her babies . . . like how to hop.

Kris: They know how to hop already.

Teacher: Well, let's read and see.[134]

In this lesson the teacher modeled elaborative questions and connections to prior knowledge ("What would happen if the babies were born in the winter?" "Do you think she puts out a twig like we mark a trail?") and provided general guidance and occasional hints about how students should process the passage about snowshoe rabbits ("Kam, can you summarize for us now?" "And she visits them . . ."). Also notice in the dialogue how students support one another in their efforts to process what they are reading. Consider this exchange as an example:

Kam: I have another question. How does she get the babies safe?

Kris: She hides them.

Kam: That's right but something else. . . .

Reciprocal teaching has been used successfully with a wide variety of students, ranging from first graders to college students, to teach effective reading and listening comprehension skills.[135] In an early study of reciprocal teaching,[136] six seventh-grade students with a history of poor reading comprehension participated in 20 reciprocal teaching sessions, each lasting about 30 minutes. Despite this relatively short intervention, students showed remarkable improvement in their reading comprehension skills. They became increasingly

---

[134] Lesson courtesy of Annemarie Palincsar, University of Michigan.

[135] Alfassi, 1998; E. R. Hart & Speece, 1998; Johnson-Glenberg, 2000; K. D. McGee, Knight, & Boudah,

2001; Palincsar & Brown, 1989; Rosenshine & Meister, 1994.

[136] Palincsar & Brown, 1984.

able to process reading material in an effective manner and to do so independently of their classroom teacher. Furthermore, they generalized their new reading strategies to other classes, sometimes even surpassing the achievement of their classmates.[137]

Scaffold students' early efforts at challenging tasks and assignments.

Vygotsky proposed that growing children and adolescents gain the most from challenging tasks they can accomplish only with the guidance and support of others—that is, tasks within their zone of proximal development. The guidance and support that others provide is generally known as **scaffolding**.

To better understand this concept, let's first think about how scaffolding is used in the construction of a new building. The *scaffold* is an external structure that provides support for the workers (e.g., a place where they can stand) until the building itself is strong enough to support them. As the building gains stability, the scaffold becomes less necessary and so is gradually removed. In much the same way, an adult guiding a child through a new task may provide an initial scaffold to support the child's early efforts. As a child becomes capable of working without such support, the adult gradually removes it; this process is known as *fading*.

Scaffolding can take a variety of forms, including the following possibilities:[138]

Observe a teacher use questions to scaffold basic science inquiry techniques in the "Salamander Investigation" video in the Additional Resources section in Chapter 5 of MyEducationLab.

- Work with students to develop a plan for accomplishing a new task.
- Demonstrate the proper performance of the task in a way that students can easily imitate.
- Divide a complex task into several smaller, simpler tasks.
- Provide a structure or set of guidelines for how the task should be accomplished.
- Provide a calculator, computer software (word processing program, spreadsheet, etc.), or other technology that makes some aspects of the task easier.
- Ask questions that get students thinking in appropriate ways about the task.
- Keep students' attention focused on the relevant aspects of the task.
- Keep students motivated to complete the task.
- Remind students what their goal is in performing the task (e.g., what a problem solution should look like).
- Give frequent feedback about how students are progressing.

Scaffolding can come from other students as well as from teachers. In the opening case study, Lupita scaffolds two classmates' attempts at assembling puzzles. Furthermore, when several students work together on a difficult task, they may be able to accomplish something that none of them could accomplish on their own (recall our earlier discussions of *distributed cognition* and *distributed intelligence*). Cross-grade tutoring is yet another possibility, and students at both the giving and receiving ends of the instruction are likely to benefit. For instance, when older children tutor younger ones in such basic subjects as writing and math, the "teachers" gradually *internalize* the suggestions they give their "students" (e.g., "Make sure every sentence has a period," "Now carry that two to the tens column") and so are more likely to use those suggestions themselves.[139]

Through cross-age tutoring, older students can scaffold younger students' efforts to master school subject matter.

Involve students in age-appropriate ways in adult activities.

When you were a young child, did you sometimes help your mother, father, or an older sibling bake things in the kitchen? Did the cook let you pour, measure, and mix ingredients once you were old enough to do so? Did the cook also give you directions or suggestions as you performed these tasks?

Older family members often allow young children to perform household tasks (cooking, cleaning, painting, and so on) while providing guidance about how to do the tasks appropriately. Likewise, teachers should introduce students to common adult

---

scaffolding Support mechanism that helps a learner successfully perform a task within his or her zone of proximal development.

[137] A. L. Brown & Palincsar, 1987; Palincsar & Brown, 1984.
[138] A. Collins, 2006; Gallimore & Tharp, 1990; Good, McCaslin, & Reys, 1992; Lajoie & Derry, 1993; Merrill et al., 1996; Rogoff, 1990; Rosenshine & Meister, 1992; D. Wood, Bruner, & Ross, 1976.
[139] Biemiller, Shany, Inglis, & Meichenbaum, 1998.

activities within a structured and supportive context. For instance, students might take active roles (cashiers, waiters, etc.) in chili dinners, multifamily garage sales, or other school fund-raisers. They might assist with costume design and scenery construction for a school play. Or they might communicate with scientists or government officials through e-mail or teleconferences. When teachers get students actively involved in adult activities, they are engaging students in **guided participation** in the world of adults.[140]

In some instances adults work with children and adolescents in formal or informal **apprenticeships**, one-on-one relationships in which the adults teach the youngsters new skills, guide their initial efforts, and present increasingly difficult tasks as proficiency improves and the zone of proximal development changes.[141] Many cultures use apprenticeships as a way of gradually introducing children to particular skills and trades—perhaps playing a musical instrument, sewing, or weaving.[142]

Through an apprenticeship a student often learns not only how to perform a task but also how to *think about* a task. Such a situation is sometimes called a **cognitive apprenticeship**.[143] For instance, a student and a teacher might work together to accomplish a challenging task or solve a difficult problem (perhaps collecting data samples in biology fieldwork, solving a mathematical brainteaser, or translating a difficult passage from German to English). In the process of talking about various aspects of the task or problem, the teacher and student together analyze the situation and develop the best approach to take, and the teacher models effective ways of thinking about and mentally processing the situation.

Although apprenticeships differ widely from one context to another, they typically have many or all of these features:[144]

- **Modeling.** The teacher demonstrates the task and simultaneously thinks aloud about the process while the student observes and listens.
- **Coaching.** As the student performs the task, the teacher gives frequent suggestions, hints, and feedback.
- **Scaffolding.** The teacher provides various forms of support for the student, perhaps by simplifying the task, breaking it into smaller and more manageable components, or providing less complicated equipment.
- **Articulation.** The student explains what he or she is doing and why, allowing the teacher to examine the student's knowledge, reasoning, and problem-solving strategies.
- **Reflection.** The teacher asks the student to compare his or her performance with that of experts or perhaps with an ideal model of how the task should be done.
- **Increasing complexity and diversity of tasks.** As the student gains greater proficiency, the teacher presents more complex, challenging, and varied tasks to complete, often within real-world contexts.
- **Exploration.** The teacher encourages the student to frame questions and problems on his or her own and thereby expand and refine acquired skills.

Be optimistic that with appropriate guidance and support, all students can perform more intelligently.

Contemporary views of intelligence give us reason to be optimistic about what children and adolescents can accomplish, especially when teachers actively nurture and support their cognitive growth. If intelligence is as multifaceted as some psychologists believe, then scores from any single IQ test cannot possibly provide a complete picture of students' "intelligence."[145] In fact, teachers are likely to see intelligent behavior in many of their students—quite possibly in *all* of them—in one way or another. One student may show promise in mathematics, another may be an exceptionally gifted writer, and a third may show talent in art or music. Furthermore, intelligent behavior draws on a variety of cognitive processes

guided participation A child's performance, with guidance and support, of an activity in the adult world.

apprenticeship Mentorship in which a learner works intensively with an experienced adult to learn how to perform complex new skills.

cognitive apprenticeship Mentorship in which a teacher and a student work together on a challenging task and the teacher gives guidance about how to think about the task.

[140] Rogoff, 2003.
[141] A. Collins, 2006; Rogoff, 1990, 1991.
[142] D. J. Elliott, 1995; Lave & Wenger, 1991; Rogoff, 1990.
[143] A. Collins, 2006; J. S. Brown, Collins, & Duguid, 1989; John-Steiner, 1997; W. Roth & Bowen, 1995.
[144] A. Collins, 2006; A. Collins, Brown, & Newman, 1989; Hmelo-Silver, 2006.
[145] Neisser et al., 1996.

CLASSROOM STRATEGIES

Promoting Productive Styles and Dispositions

- When students consistently approach tasks in an impulsive, nonanalytical manner, focus their attention on accuracy rather than on speed, and teach them to talk themselves through detailed tasks.

    To help an impulsive third grader subtract two-digit numbers with regrouping ("borrowing"), his teacher instructs him to say these three phrases to himself as he solves each problem: (1) "Compare top and bottom numbers," (2) "If top number is smaller, borrow," and (3) "Subtract."

- Present important ideas both verbally and visually, ideally with each modality offering unique insights into the subject matter.

    As a high school history teacher describes key World War II battles, he presents maps and photographs of each battlefield and describes specific strategies that one side or the other used to outfox its opponent. To get his students to think analytically about both the visual and verbal information, he asks them questions such as "What challenges did the local topography present for the troops?" and "Why did the commanders choose the strategies they did?"

- Communicate your own eagerness to learn about new topics.

    A middle school science teacher asks her students, "Have you ever wondered why so many people are concerned about global climate change? I certainly have! I've brought in some magazine articles that can help us understand why they're worried."

- Model open-mindedness about diverse viewpoints and a willingness to suspend judgment until all the facts are in. Communicate that for some issues, a single "right" answer simply isn't possible.

    In a lesson about the novel *The Scarlet Letter*, a high school English teacher encourages students to describe their diverse views of the character Arthur Dimmesdale. Students hypothesize that "He's very unsure about himself" or "He's kind of a nerd-type guy." The teacher is receptive to both possibilities but also provokes students to consider why another character, Hester Prynne, would have found him so attractive. One student suggests, "Maybe he's got a good personality," and another speculates that he has a captivating physical feature: "It's his eyes. Yeah, the eyes." (You can observe this discussion in the "Scarlet Letter" video clip in Chapter 5 of MyEducationLab.)

that can definitely improve over time with experience and practice.[146] And the notion of distributed intelligence suggests that intelligent behavior should be relatively commonplace when students have the right tools, symbolic systems, and social groups with which to work.

Teachers must also remember that to the extent that intelligence is dependent on culture, intelligent behavior is apt to take different forms in students from different backgrounds.[147] In mainstream Western culture children's intelligence may be reflected in their ability to deal with complex problems and abstract ideas. Among students who have been raised in predominantly African American communities, it may be reflected in oral language, such as in colorful speech, creative storytelling, or humor.[148] In Native American cultures it may be reflected in interpersonal skills or exceptional craftsmanship.[149] Teachers must be careful not to limit their conception of intelligence only to students' ability to succeed at traditional academic tasks.

It is important, too, that teachers nurture the kinds of cognitive styles and dispositions that are likely to predispose students to think and act intelligently on a regular basis. Although researchers have not yet determined how best to promote productive cognitive styles and dispositions, we can reasonably assume that encouraging and modeling effective ways of thinking about classroom subject matter—for instance, paying close attention to critical details, asking students to evaluate the quality of scientific evidence, and consistently demonstrating open-mindedness about diverse perspectives—will get students off to a good start.[150] The Classroom Strategies box "Promoting Productive Styles and Dispositions" presents examples of what teachers might do.

Ultimately, intelligent behavior depends *both* on students' own thought processes and on the supportive contexts in which students work.[151] Rather than asking the question, "How intelligent are my students?" teachers should instead ask themselves, "How can I help my students think as intelligently as possible? What physical and cognitive tools and what social networks can I provide?"

[146] Sternberg et al., 2000.

[147] Gardner, 1995; Neisser et al., 1996; D. N. Perkins, 1995; Sternberg, 1985.

[148] Torrance, 1989.

[149] Kirschenbaum, 1989; Maker & Schiever, 1989.

[150] Halpern, 1998; Kuhn, 2001b; Messer, 1976; D. N. Perkins & Ritchhart, 2004.

[151] Salomon, 1993; Sfard, 1998.

SUMMARY

Children and adolescents reach various developmental milestones in a somewhat predictable sequence, although the ages at which they reach these milestones vary considerably from one youngster to the next. The course of development is often uneven, marked by dramatic changes or qualitative shifts at some points and by slower, more gradual changes at others. Both genetic and environmental factors influence development, but because they interact in their effects, and because children's own behaviors influence the development of various characteristics, the relative contributions of heredity and environment are often impossible to determine.

Although the brain changes in significant ways in the first few years of life, it continues to mature even after the teenage years. Developmental changes in the brain enable increasingly complex thought processes throughout childhood, adolescence, and early adulthood. The brain retains some plasticity throughout life, enabling people of all ages to acquire new knowledge and skills in most domains.

Young learners seem naturally inclined to learn about, organize, and adapt to their world, and they actively seek interactions both with their physical environment and with other people. Adults and other more advanced individuals foster children's cognitive development by providing labels for experiences, modeling procedures for tackling problems, and in other ways passing along culturally appropriate interpretations and behaviors. Social interaction has an additional benefit as well: Children gradually internalize the processes they initially use with others and so can eventually use those processes on their own. Ultimately, young learners benefit most from challenges, both those that call into question existing beliefs (those that create disequilibrium) and those that require use of newly emerging abilities (those that lie within learners' zones of proximal development).

Thanks in part to a growing and increasingly integrated knowledge base, thinking becomes more logical during the elementary school years and more abstract during the middle school and secondary school years. Young adolescents are most likely to use sophisticated reasoning processes—for instance, separating and controlling variables during a scientific investigation—with topics they know well. Advanced reasoning processes continue to develop during the high school years, especially if a learner's culture encourages them, but true expertise in any field comes only after many years of study and practice.

Although virtually all children and adolescents continue to gain new cognitive abilities and skills with age, youngsters in any particular age-group differ considerably in their overall ability levels. Most psychologists call this individual difference variable *intelligence*. Psychologists disagree, however, about the extent to which intelligence is a single entity that influences a wide variety of tasks, on the one hand, or a collection of relatively separate, unrelated abilities, on the other. Intelligence tests provide a general idea of how a child's general cognitive ability compares to that of his or her peer group, but they are imprecise measures at best and the IQ scores they yield may change somewhat over time. Furthermore, intelligent behavior depends on environmental factors, both those that may have nurtured or impeded a child's cognitive development in the past and those that may support or hinder a child's performance at present. Intelligent behavior also depends on cognitive styles and dispositions—analytical processing, critical thinking, open-mindedness, and so on—that predispose learners to think about new ideas and events in insightful and productive ways.

When considered within the context of other information, IQ scores can certainly help teachers get a general sense of students' current cognitive functioning. Equally helpful are problems and questions that reveal how students think and reason about various situations and topics. Through such information and through careful observation of students' day-to-day behaviors, teachers may discover that some students have exceptional abilities and talents begging to be nurtured and that other students have developmental delays requiring the attention of a specialist.

Not only must teachers ascertain where students are currently "at" in their thinking and reasoning, but they must also take active steps to help every student make reasonable advancements in cognitive abilities and skills. One important strategy is providing opportunities for pretend play, organized games and sports, and other play activities in which students practice adult-like skills and learn how to plan ahead and abide by certain rules for behavior. Another important (in fact, *essential*) strategy is to pass along the collective wisdom of the culture—the many concepts, procedures, and other cognitive tools that previous generations have found to be helpful in understanding and dealing with the world. Instruction should rely heavily on concrete objects and activities in the early years but should increasingly introduce abstract ideas and encourage sophisticated reasoning processes as students move through adolescence. Teachers should structure and guide—that is, *scaffold*—students' early attempts at challenging tasks, gradually removing such scaffolding as students gain proficiency. And as their abilities grow, students should participate in meaningful ways in adult activities.

PRACTICE FOR YOUR LICENSURE EXAM

Stones Lesson

Ms. Hennessey is conducting a demonstration in her first-grade class. She shows the children a large glass tank filled with water. She also shows them two stones. One stone, a piece of granite, is fairly small (about 2 cm in diameter). The other stone, a piece of pumice (i.e., cooled volcanic lava), is much bigger (about 10 cm in diameter). Ms. Hennessey does not allow the children to touch or hold the stones, and so they have no way of knowing that the pumice, which has many small air pockets in it, is much lighter than the granite. The demonstration proceeds as follows:

Ms. H.: Would anyone like to predict what he or she thinks will happen to these stones? Yes, Brianna.

Brianna: I think the . . . both stones will sink because I know stones sink. I've seen lots of stones sink and every time I throw a rock into the water, like it always sinks, yeah, it always does.

Ms. H.: You look like you want to say something else.

Brianna: Yeah the water can't hold up rocks like it holds up boats and I know they'll sink.

Ms. H.: You sound so sure, let me try another object.

Brianna: No you gotta throw it in, you gotta test my idea first. [Ms. H places the smaller stone in the tank; it sinks.] See, I told you I knew it would sink. [Ms. H. puts the larger, pumice stone down and picks up another object.] No you've gotta test the big one too because if the little one sunk the big one's gotta sunk (sic). [Ms. H places the pumice stone in the tank; it floats.] No! No! That's not right! That doesn't go with my mind [Brianna grabs hold of her head], it just doesn't go with my mind.[152]

1. Constructed-response question

Brianna is noticeably surprised, maybe even a little upset, when she sees the pumice stone float.

A. Use one or more concepts from Jean Piaget's theory of cognitive development to explain why Brianna reacts as strongly as she does to the floating pumice.

B. Again drawing on Piaget's theory, explain why Ms. Hennessey intentionally presents a phenomenon that will surprise the children.

2. Multiple-choice question

Imagine that you perform the same demonstration with high school students rather than first graders. If you were to follow Lev Vygotsky's theory of cognitive development, which one of the following approaches would you take in helping the students understand the floating pumice?

a. Before performing the demonstration, ask students to draw a picture of the tank and two stones.

b. Drop several light objects (e.g., a feather, a piece of paper, a small sponge) into the tank before dropping either stone into it.

c. Teach the concept of *density*, and explain that an object's average density relative to water determines whether it floats or sinks.

d. Praise students who correctly predict that the larger stone will float, even if they initially give an incorrect explanation about why it will float.

Once you have answered these questions, compare your responses with those presented in Appendix A.

FOR FURTHER READING

The following articles from the journal *Educational Leadership* are especially relevant to this chapter. You can find these articles in Chapter 5 of MyEducationLab for this text.

Bruer, J. T. (1998). Brain science, brain fiction. *Educational Leadership, 56*(3), 14–18.

Graves, M. F., Graves, B. B., & Braaten, S. (1996). Scaffolded reading experiences for inclusive classes. *Educational Leadership, 53*(5), 14–16.

Lent, R. (2006). In the company of critical thinkers. *Educational Leadership, 64*(2), 68–72.

MYEDUCATIONLAB

Now go to Chapter 5 of MyEducationLab at **www.myeducationlab.com**, where you can:

- Find instructional objectives for the chapter, along with focus questions that can help you zero in on important ideas in the chapter.
- Take a self-check quiz on concepts and principles you've just read about.
- Complete exercises and assignments that can help you more deeply understand the chapter content.
- Read supplementary material that can broaden your knowledge of one or more of the chapter's topics.
- Apply what you've learned to classroom contexts in Building Teaching Skills activities.

---

[152] Dialogue from M. G. Hennessey, 2003, pp. 120-121.

CHAPTER 6

Motivation and Affect

CASE STUDY   Passing Algebra

Fourteen-year-old Michael has been getting failing grades in his eighth-grade algebra class, prompting his family to ask graduate student Valerie Tucker to tutor him. In their initial tutoring session, Michael tells Ms. Tucker that he has no hope of passing algebra because he has little aptitude for math and his teacher doesn't teach the subject matter very well. In his mind, he is powerless to change either his own ability or his teacher's instructional strategies, making continuing failure inevitable.

As Ms. Tucker works with Michael over the next several weeks, she encourages him to think more about what *he* can do to master algebra and less about what his teacher may or may not be doing to help him. She points out that he did well in math in earlier years and so certainly has the ability to learn algebra if he puts his mind to it. She also teaches him a number of strategies for understanding and applying algebraic principles. Michael takes a giant step forward when he finally realizes that his own efforts play a role in his classroom success:

> [M]aybe I can try a little harder. . . . The teacher is still bad, but maybe some of this other stuff can work.[1]

When Michael sees gradual improvement on his algebra assignments and quizzes, he becomes increasingly aware that the specific *strategies* he uses are just as important as his effort:

> I learned that I need to understand information before I can hold it in my mind. . . . Now I do things in math step by step and listen to each step. I realize now that even if I don't like the teacher or don't think he is a good teacher, it is my responsibility to listen. I listen better now and ask questions more.[2]

As Michael's performance in algebra continues to improve in later weeks, he gains greater confidence that he *can* master algebra after all, and he comes to realize that his classroom success is ultimately up to him:

> [T]he teacher does most of his part, but it's no use to me unless I do my part. . . . [N]ow I try and comprehend, ask questions and figure out how he got the answer. . . . I used to just listen and not even take notes. I always told myself I would remember but I always seemed to forget. Now I take notes and I study at home every day except Friday, even if I don't have homework. Now I study so that I know that I have it. I don't just hope I'll remember.[3]

- On what factors does Michael initially blame his failure? What effects do his early beliefs appear to have on his classroom behavior and study habits?
- To what factors does Michael later attribute his success? How have his changing beliefs affected his learning strategies?
- Put yourself in Michael's shoes in this situation. How does Michael probably feel about his algebra class—and perhaps about algebra in general—when he is initially failing on his assignments and quizzes? How might he feel after he becomes more successful?

---

[1] Tucker & Anderman, 1999, p. 5.
[2] Tucker & Anderman, 1999, p. 5.
[3] Tucker & Anderman, 1999, p. 6.

Michael initially believes he is failing algebra because of two things he cannot control, his own low ability and his teacher's poor instruction. As a result, he doesn't listen very attentively or take notes in class. With Ms. Tucker's guidance, however, Michael acquires a better understanding of algebra and learns how to use it to solve mathematical problems. He also discovers that increased effort and better strategies (taking notes, asking questions when he doesn't understand, studying regularly, etc.) *do* affect his classroom performance. Suddenly Michael himself—not his teacher and not some genetically predetermined inability that lurks within him—is in control of the situation. As a result, his confidence skyrockets and he works hard to master algebra.

In our discussions of learning and development in previous chapters, we've focused primarily on the question "What can children and adolescents do and learn?" As we turn to motivation in this chapter, we focus on a very different question: "How *likely* are they to do what they're capable of doing and to learn what they're capable of learning?" Even when learners have the capabilities and prior experiences necessary to do something, their *motivation* will determine whether they actually do it. **Motivation** is an inner state that energizes, directs, and sustains behavior. It gets learners moving, points them in a particular direction, and keeps them going.

Psychologists' views about motivation have evolved and changed considerably over the years. Within the last two or three decades, their theories of motivation have focused largely on its cognitive elements—that is, on perceptions, interpretations, beliefs, and so on, that affect the choices learners make and the energy and persistence with which they pursue various activities. Table 6.1 describes two early perspectives of motivation, as well as several contemporary cognitive perspectives that will guide much of our discussion in this chapter. If you look closely at the descriptions in the table, you might notice that contemporary theories overlap to some extent. For example, the concepts of *competence* (self-determination theory), *self-worth* (self-worth theory), *expectancy* (expectancy-value theory), and *self-efficacy* (social cognitive theory) all reflect two general ideas: (a) People like to believe they can perform an activity competently, and (b) their self-confidence (or lack thereof) related to that activity affects their behavior. My approach in this chapter will be to synthesize, rather than identify differences among, current theories of motivation, and in doing so I will use some terms (e.g., *self-worth*, *self-efficacy*) more than others.

A close partner of motivation is **affect**, the feelings, emotions, and general moods that learners bring to bear on a task.[4] In the opening case study, Michael probably initially feels frustrated and doesn't like algebra very much. After learning effective strategies and improving his performance, however, he studies every day, "even if I don't have homework." At this point, we might suspect, Michael takes pride in his performance and perhaps even enjoys working on his algebra assignments.

In the upcoming pages we'll identify a variety of factors that influence motivation and affect—factors that we'll later translate into strategies for promoting motivation and positive affect in instructional settings. We'll begin by identifying several of human beings' most basic psychological needs.

BASIC HUMAN NEEDS

Occasionally I hear educators, policy makers, or the public at large talking about "unmotivated" students. In fact, virtually all human beings are motivated in one way or another. At school, for example, some students may be keenly interested in classroom subject matter and so may seek out challenging course work, participate actively in class discussions, and earn high marks on assigned projects. Other students may be more concerned with the social side of school, interacting with classmates frequently, attending extracurricular activities almost every day, and perhaps running for a student government office. Still others may be focused on excelling in physical education classes, playing or watching sports most

---

motivation Inner state that energizes, directs, and sustains behavior.

affect Feelings, emotions, and moods that a learner brings to bear on a task.

[4] Some psychologists use the terms *affect* and *emotion* interchangeably. But others suggest that we use *emotion* to refer only to short-term states and that we use *affect* in a broader sense to include both short-term emotions and longer-term moods and temperaments; for example, see Forgas, 2000; Linnenbrink & Pintrich, 2002; Rosenberg, 1998.

THEORETICAL PERSPECTIVES

TABLE 6.1 Theoretical Approaches to the Study of Motivation

Theoretical Perspective	General Description	Examples of Prominent Theorists	Where You Will See This Perspective in the Book
EARLY PERSPECTIVES			
Behaviorism	From a behaviorist perspective, motivation is often the result of *drives*, internal states caused by a lack of something necessary for optimal functioning. Consequences of behavior (reinforcement, punishment) are effective only to the extent that they either increase or decrease a learner's drive state. In recent years some behaviorists have added a *purposeful* element to the behaviorist perspective: They suggest that learners intentionally behave in order to achieve certain end results.	Clark Hull B. F. Skinner Dorothea Lerman Jack Michael *A supplementary reading on Skinner's theory appears in the Homework and Exercises section in Chapter 3 of MyEducationLab.*	We previously examined the effects of reinforcement and punishment in Chapter 3. In this chapter we draw on behaviorist ideas primarily in our discussions of extrinsic motivation. The purposeful element of behaviorism will be useful in our discussions of functional analysis and positive behavioral support in Chapter 9.
Humanism	Historically, humanists have objected to behaviorists' depiction of people's behaviors as being largely the result of external environmental factors. In the humanist view, people have within themselves a tremendous potential for psychological growth, and they continually strive to fulfill that potential. When given a caring and supportive environment, human beings strive to understand themselves, to enhance their abilities, and to behave in ways that benefit both themselves and others. Unfortunately, early humanist ideas were grounded more in philosophy than in research findings, so many contemporary motivation theorists have largely left them by the wayside. However, one contemporary perspective, positive psychology (see the final row of this table) has some roots in the humanist perspective.	Carl Rogers Abraham Maslow *A supplementary reading on Maslow's theory appears in the Homework and Exercises section in Chapter 6 of MyEducationLab.*	Because humanists conducted little research to substantiate their ideas, we don't specifically look at them in this book. However, the humanist focus on internal, growth-producing motives has clearly influenced the contemporary cognitive perspectives we *do* consider.
CONTEMPORARY PERSPECTIVES			
Self-determination theory	Self-determination theorists propose that human beings have three basic needs: a need to be effective in dealing with the environment (*competence*), a need to control the course of their lives (*autonomy*), and a need to have close, affectionate relationships with others (*relatedness*). Learners are more effectively motivated to learn school subject matter when these three needs are met.	Edward Deci Richard Ryan Johnmarshall Reeve	Self-determination theory guides much of our discussion of basic human needs early in the chapter, and recommendations related to these needs are presented in the chapter's final section. The discussion of internalized motivation is also based on self-determination theory.
Self-worth theory	Self-worth theorists believe that protecting one's own sense of competence—that is, one's sense of *self-worth*—is a high priority for human beings. One way to maintain and possibly enhance self-worth, of course, is to be successful in daily activities. But curiously, when learners suspect that they may fail at an activity, they sometimes do things (e.g., procrastinating until the last minute) that make failure even more likely. Although such *self-handicapping* decreases the probability of success, it also enables people to justify their failure, both to themselves and to others, and so enables them to maintain their self-worth.	Martin Covington	Self-worth theory is clearly evident in the chapter's discussion of basic human needs. Also, when we look at self-handicapping midway through the chapter, we identify a variety of counterproductive behaviors that help students maintain a sense of self-worth in the face of seemingly insurmountable challenges.
Expectancy-value theory	Expectancy-value theorists propose that motivation for performing a particular task is a function of two variables. First, learners must believe they can succeed. In other words, they must have a high expectation, or *expectancy*, for their task performance. Second, learners must believe that they will gain direct or indirect benefits for performing a task. In other words, they must place *value* on the task itself or on the outcomes that are likely to result.	Jacquelynne Eccles Allan Wigfield	Expectancy-value theorists' findings related to the effects of learners' values are presented midway through the chapter. Their findings related to the effects of learners' expectancies are incorporated into the discussion of self-efficacy.

(continued)

Theoretical Perspective	General Description	Examples of Prominent Theorists	Where You Will See This Perspective in the Book
Social cognitive theory	As noted in Table 2.1 in Chapter 2, social cognitive theory is a contemporary, cognitively oriented version of social learning theory. Social cognitive theorists emphasize the importance of *self-efficacy*—believing oneself capable of successfully performing certain behaviors or reaching certain goals—in motivation. Social cognitive theorists also point out that human behavior is typically goal directed, thereby providing a foundation for *goal theory* (described separately below).	Albert Bandura Dale Schunk Barry Zimmerman	As we see in this chapter, learners are more apt to initiate, exert effort in, and persist at activities for which they have high self-efficacy. To some degree high self-efficacy comes from past successes in an activity. Social factors (e.g., peer models who perform a task successfully, encouraging words from others) can also boost self-efficacy, at least for the short run.
Goal theory	Goal theorists focus on the kinds of outcomes (goals) toward which learners direct their behavior. Learners are apt to have goals in a variety of areas, including but not limited to academic performance, social relationships, careers, financial gain, and physical and psychological well-being. In recent years goal theorists have focused largely on students' goals in academic settings, which they refer to as *achievement goals*.	Carol Dweck Carol Ames Paul Pintrich Edwin Locke Gary Latham	The goal-directed nature of human motivation is evident early in the chapter. Later we look at the effects of various kinds of goals, with a particular focus on mastery goals (reflecting a desire to gain new knowledge and skills) and performance goals (reflecting a desire to look competent in the eyes of others).
Attribution theory	Attribution theorists look at learners' beliefs about why various things happen to them—for instance, about why they do well or poorly on academic tasks. These beliefs, known as *attributions*, influence learners' optimism about future success and about the actions they take (or perhaps don't take) to bring about such success. For instance, learners are more likely to work hard on classroom tasks if they believe that their ultimate success depends on something they themselves do—that is, if they attribute classroom success to internal and controllable factors.	Bernard Weiner Carol Dweck Sandra Graham	Midway through the chapter we look closely at the nature and effects of attributions. We also discover that over time, many learners acquire a general attributional style, either a realistically optimistic one (a mastery orientation) or an overly pessimistic one (learned helplessness).
Positive psychology	Positive psychology embraces early humanists' belief that people have many uniquely human qualities propelling them to engage in productive, worthwhile activities. But like other contemporary motivation theorists, it bases its views on research findings rather than philosophical speculations. As a distinct perspective of motivation, positive psychology emerged on the scene only in the late 1990s, and in its current form it is better characterized as a collection of ideas than as a full-fledged, well-integrated theory.	Martin Seligman Mihaly Csikszentmihalyi Christopher Peterson	The influence of positive psychology can best be seen in the discussions of flow (an intense form of intrinsic motivation), optimism (incorporated into sections on self-efficacy and attributions), and emotional self-regulation.

One early theorist, Abraham Maslow, suggested that people's various needs form a hierarchy, such that certain kinds of needs typically take precedence over others. Learn more about Maslow's hierarchy of needs in a supplementary reading in the Homework and Exercises section in Chapter 6 of MyEducationLab.

afternoons and weekends, and faithfully following a physical fitness regimen. And yet a few, perhaps because of undiagnosed learning disabilities, shy temperaments, or seemingly uncoordinated bodies, may be interested primarily in *avoiding* academics, social situations, or athletic activities.

Psychologists have speculated that people have a wide variety of needs. Some needs—for instance, for oxygen, food, water, and warmth—are related to physical well-being, and these needs undoubtedly take high priority when physical survival is in jeopardy.[5] Other needs are more closely related to *psychological* well-being—that is, to feeling comfortable and content in day-to-day activities. In the following principles, we explore four basic needs that can have a significant effect on people's motivation and psychological well-being.[6]

[5] Maslow, 1973, 1987.
[6] The second, third, and fourth principles are based loosely on Deci and Ryan's self-determination theory; for example, see Deci & Ryan, 1985, 1992; R. M. Ryan & Deci, 2000.

Learners have a basic need for arousal.

Several classic studies conducted in the 1950s and 1960s suggest that human beings have a basic need for stimulation—that is, a **need for arousal**.[7] As an example, try the following exercise.

SEE FOR YOURSELF

SEE FOR YOURSELF
Doing Nothing

For the next five minutes, you are going to be a student who has nothing to do. *Remain exactly where you are*, put your book aside, and *do nothing*. Time yourself so that you spend exactly five minutes on this "task." Let's see what happens.

What kinds of responses did you make during your five-minute break? Did you fidget a bit, perhaps wiggling tired body parts, scratching newly detected itches, or picking at your nails? Did you "interact" in some way with something or someone else, perhaps tapping loudly on a table, turning on a radio, or talking to another person in the room? Did you get out of your seat altogether—something I specifically asked you *not* to do? The exercise has, I hope, shown you that you tend to feel better when *something*, rather than nothing at all, is happening to you.

Some theorists have suggested that not only do people have a basic need for arousal but they also strive for a certain *optimal level* of arousal at which they feel best.[8] Too little stimulation is unpleasant, but so is too much. For example, you may enjoy watching a television game show or listening to music, but you would probably rather not have three television sets, five compact disk players, and a live rock band all blasting in your living room at once. Different people have different optimal levels, and they may prefer different kinds of stimulation. For instance, some children and adolescents are *sensation seekers* who thrive on physically thrilling and possibly dangerous experiences.[9] Others prefer a lot of cognitive stimulation—eagerly tackling challenging puzzles, reading about intriguing new ideas, arguing with peers about controversial issues, and so on—reflecting the *need for cognition* I spoke of in Chapter 5.[10]

The need for arousal explains some of the things students do in the classroom. For instance, it explains why many students happily pull out a favorite book and read if they finish in-class assignments before their classmates. But it also explains why students sometimes engage in off-task behaviors—for instance, by passing notes or playing practical jokes—during boring lessons. Obviously, students are most likely to stay *on* task when classroom activities keep them sufficiently aroused that they have little need to look elsewhere for stimulation.

Learners want to believe they are competent and have self-worth.

In Chapter 5 we learned that children are naturally inclined to make sense of and adapt to their environment. We also learned that events inconsistent with existing knowledge and beliefs can create disequilibrium and spur children to reexamine and possibly revise their current understandings. Underlying both of these principles may be a basic **need for competence**—a need for people to believe that they can deal effectively with their environment.[11] Some evidence indicates that *protecting* this sense of competence, which is sometimes known as **self-worth**, is one of people's highest priorities.[12]

Other people's judgments and approval play a key role in the development of a sense of competence and self-worth.[13] Regularly achieving success in new and challenging activities—as Michael eventually does in mathematics in the opening case study—is another

---

need for arousal Ongoing need for either physical or cognitive stimulation.

need for competence Basic need to believe that one can deal effectively with the overall environment.

self-worth Belief about the extent to which one is generally a good, capable individual.

---

[7] For example, see Berlyne, 1960; Heron, 1957; also see E. M. Anderman, Noar, Zimmerman, & Donohew, 2004, for a more contemporary discussion of this need.

[8] E. M. Anderman et al., 2004; Berlyne, 1960; Labouvie-Vief & González, 2004.

[9] Cleveland, Gibbons, Gerrard, Pomery, & Brody, 2005; V. F. Reyna & Farley, 2006.

[10] Cacioppo, Petty, Feinstein, & Jarvis, 1996; Raine, Reynolds, & Venables, 2002.

[11] Boggiano & Pittman, 1992; Connell & Wellborn, 1991; Reeve, Deci, & Ryan, 2004; R. White, 1959.

[12] Covington, 1992; Crocker & Knight, 2005.

[13] Harter, 1999; Rudolph, Caldwell, & Conley, 2005.

DOONESBURY   **BY GARRY TRUDEAU**

Accomplishing challenging tasks will help children and adolescents maintain a sense of self-worth, but easy "successes," such as those depicted here, are unlikely to do so.
Source: DOONESBURY © 1997 G. B. Trudeau. Reprinted with permission of UNIVERSAL PRESS SYNDICATE. All rights reserved.

important way of maintaining, perhaps even enhancing, self-worth. But consistent success isn't always possible, especially when learners must undertake especially difficult tasks. In the face of such tasks, an alternative way to maintain self-worth is to *avoid failure*, because failure gives the impression of low ability.[14] Failure avoidance manifests itself in a variety of ways. Learners might refuse to engage in a task, minimize the task's importance, or set exceedingly low expectations for their performance.[15] They might also hold tightly to their current beliefs despite considerable evidence to the contrary.[16] The need to protect self-worth, then, may be one reason why learners are reluctant to undergo conceptual change.

Learners want to determine the course of their lives to some degree.

Some theorists suggest that human beings not only want to feel competent but also want to have a sense of autonomy and self-direction regarding the things they do and the courses their lives take. In other words, human beings may have a basic **need for self-determination**.[17] For instance, when we think "I *want* to do this" or "I would *find it valuable* to do that," we have a high sense of self-determination. In contrast, when we think "I *have to*" or "I *should*," we are telling ourselves that someone or something else is making decisions for us. As an example of the latter situation, try the following exercise.

SEE FOR YOURSELF
Painting Between the Lines

Imagine that I give you a set of watercolor paints, a paintbrush, two sheets of paper (a fairly small one glued on top of a larger one), and some paper towels. I ask you to paint a picture of your house, apartment building, or dormitory and then give you the following instructions:

> Before you begin, I want to tell you some things you will have to do. They are rules that I have about painting. You have to keep the paints clean. You can paint only on this small sheet of paper, so don't spill any paint on the big sheet. And you must wash out your brush and wipe it with a paper towel before you switch to a new color of paint, so that you don't get the colors all mixed up. In general, I want you to be a good art student and not make a mess with the paints.[18]

- How much fun do you think your task would be? After reading my rules, how eager are you to begin painting?

My rules about painting are somewhat restrictive, aren't they? In fact, they are quite *controlling*. They make it clear that I am in charge of the situation and that you, as the artist, have little choice about how to go about your task. Chances are, you have little desire to paint

---

need for self-determination Basic need to believe that one has some autonomy and control regarding the course of one's life.

[14] Covington, 1992; Covington & Müeller, 2001; Urdan & Midgley, 2001.
[15] Covington, 1992; Harter, 1990; A. J. Martin, Marsh, & Debus, 2001.
[16] Sherman & Cohen, 2002.

[17] d'Ailly, 2003; deCharms, 1972; Kağitçibaşi, 2007; Reeve et al., 2004; R. M. Ryan & Deci, 2000.
[18] Based on Koestner, Ryan, Bernieri, & Holt, 1984, p. 239.

the picture I've asked you to make.[19] Furthermore, you would probably be less creative in your painting than if I hadn't been so controlling.[20]

Even kindergartners seem to prefer classroom activities of their own choosing, and their perceptions of autonomy versus control are often seen in their notions of "play" or "work."[21] The following conversation among several kindergarten students and their teacher illustrates this point:

Mary Ann: The boys don't like to work.
Teacher: They're making a huge train setup right now.
Mary Ann: That's not work. It's just playing.
Teacher: When do girls play?
Charlotte: In the doll corner.
Teacher: How about at the painting table?
Mary Ann: That's work. You could call it play sometimes, but it's really schoolwork.
Teacher: When is it work and when is it play?
Clarice: If you paint a real picture, it's work, but if you splatter or pour into an egg carton, then it's play.
Charlotte: It's mostly work, because that's where the teacher tells you how to do stuff.[22]

Learners want to feel connected to other people.

To some extent, we are all social creatures: We live, work, and play with our fellow human beings. It appears that most people of all ages have a fundamental need to feel socially connected and to secure the love and respect of others. In other words, they have a **need for relatedness**.[23]

At school the need for relatedness manifests itself in a variety of behaviors. Many children and adolescents place high priority on interacting with friends, often at the expense of getting their schoolwork done.[24] They may also be concerned about projecting a favorable public image—that is, by looking smart, popular, athletic, or cool. By looking good in the eyes of others, they not only satisfy their need for relatedness but also enhance their sense of self-worth.[25] Still another way to address the need for relatedness is to work for the betterment of others, for instance, by helping peers who are struggling with classroom assignments.[26]

The need for relatedness seems to be especially high in early adolescence.[27] (For example, see 11-year-old Ben's description of his class trip to Gettysburg in Figure 6.1.) Young adolescents tend to be quite concerned about what their classmates think of them, prefer to hang out in tight-knit groups, and are especially susceptible to peer influence (more on these points in Chapter 7).

As we proceed through the chapter, we'll discover that these basic needs affect learners' motives, classroom behavior, and learning in a variety of ways. But first, let's look at how motivation tends to influence human behavior and cognition in general.

HOW MOTIVATION AFFECTS BEHAVIOR AND COGNITION

Several general principles on the next three pages describe how motivation is apt to affect behavior, cognition, and learning.

My Trip to Gettysburg

"Honk!" sounded the bus. We had just left for one of the best times of my life. My friends, mom, teachers, and I were all going.

Last spring was my trip to Gettysburg. We had to wake up at 5:00 a.m. When we got there, I said "Hi!" to everyone in my group. We were at Gettysburg on time even though the bus was late.

When we got there, we went to the tour center and watched an informational video about Gettysburg. Now we were ready for a tour of the real battlefield the union and confederate soldiers fought on. Our guide tried to convince us that Lee was a great general. He told us the book and movie were a lie based on Longstreet's autobiography.

Then we went to the Wax Museum. It was cool! They looked so real. I liked the battlefield scene most.

We went to the Stonehenge for dinner. After that we went to the Jennie Wade house. While we where there we had a wax person talk to us. Finally we left. We watched three movies on the way home.

There were a lot of cool things I did at Gettysburg, but most of all I got closer to my friends because we spent all 18 hours together. We ate together, sat with each other on the bus, and went to every activity together. That's why I call it the best time of my life!!

FIGURE 6.1 In this personal narrative, 11-year-old Ben describes a school field trip to a Civil War battlefield. In the last paragraph he reveals what was, from his perspective, the most valuable part of the trip: the chance to be with his friends for the entire day.

---

[19] Deci, 1992; Koestner et al., 1984.
[20] Amabile & Hennessey, 1992; C. Peterson, 2006; Reeve, 2006.
[21] E. J. Langer, 1997; Paley, 1984.
[22] Dialogue from Paley, 1984, pp. 30–31.
[23] Connell & Wellborn, 1991; Kağitçibaşi, 2007; R. M. Ryan & Deci, 2000.
[24] Dowson & McInerney, 2001; W. Doyle, 1986a; Wigfield, Eccles, Mac Iver, Reuman, & Midgley, 1991.
[25] Harter, 1999; Juvonen, 2000; Rudolph et al., 2005.
[26] Dowson & McInerney, 2001; M. E. Ford, 1996.
[27] B. B. Brown, Eicher, & Petrie, 1986; Juvonen, 2000; A. M. Ryan & Patrick, 2001.

need for relatedness Basic need to feel socially connected to others and to secure others' love and respect.

Motivation directs behavior toward particular goals.

Many psychologists believe that human beings are purposeful by nature. That is, people set goals for themselves and initiate courses of action they think will help them achieve those goals. Such *goal-directed behavior* appears as early as 2 months of age.[28] For school-age children and adolescents, some goals (e.g., "I want to finish reading my dinosaur book") are short term and transitory. Others (e.g., "I want to be a paleontologist") are apt to be long term and relatively enduring.

Motivation determines the specific goals toward which learners strive.[29] Thus it affects the choices learners make—for instance, whether to enroll in physics or studio art, and whether to spend an evening playing video games with friends or, instead, completing a challenging homework assignment.

Motivation increases effort and persistence in activities.

Motivation increases the amount of effort and energy that learners expend in activities directly related to their needs and goals.[30] It determines whether they pursue a task enthusiastically and wholeheartedly, on the one hand, or apathetically and lackadaisically, on the other. Furthermore, motivated learners are more likely to continue a task until they've completed it, even if they are occasionally interrupted or frustrated in the process. In general, then, motivation increases learners' **time on task**, an important factor affecting their learning and achievement.[31]

Motivation affects cognitive processes.

Motivation affects what and how learners mentally process information.[32] For one thing, motivated learners are more likely to pay attention, and as we discovered in Chapter 2, attention is critical for getting information into working memory. Motivated learners also try to understand and elaborate on material—to learn it meaningfully—rather than simply "go through the motions" of learning in a superficial, rote manner.

We see this principle at work in the opening case study. As Michael's confidence and motivation increase, he begins to pay attention and take notes in class. He also asks questions when he doesn't understand a concept or procedure.

Motivation determines what consequences are reinforcing and punishing.

The more learners are motivated to achieve academic success, the more proud they will be of an A and the more upset they will be by an F or perhaps even a B (such feelings should remind you of the *self-imposed contingencies* we discussed in Chapter 4). The more learners want to be accepted and respected by their peers, the more meaningful the approval of the "in-group" will be and the more painful the ridicule of classmates will seem.[33] To a teenage boy uninterested in athletics, making or not making the school football team is no big deal, but to a teen whose life revolves around football, making or not making the team may be a consequence of monumental importance.

Motivation often leads to improved performance.

Because of the other effects just listed—goal-directed behavior, effort and energy, persistence, cognitive processing, and impact of consequences—motivation often leads to improved performance in the domain in question (see Figure 6.2). For instance, learners who are most motivated to learn and excel in classroom activities tend to be the highest achiev-

FIGURE 6.2 How motivation affects learning and performance

time on task Amount of time that students are actively engaged in a learning activity.

[28] Rovee-Collier, 1999.

[29] Locke & Latham, 2006; Maehr & Meyer, 1997; Pintrich, Marx, & Boyle, 1993; Vansteenkiste, Lens, & Deci, 2006.

[30] Csikszentmihalyi & Nakamura, 1989; Maehr, 1984; Pintrich et al., 1993.

[31] Brophy, 1988; G. A. Davis & Thomas, 1989; Larson, 2000; Maehr, 1984; Wigfield, 1994.

[32] Blumenfeld, Kempler, & Krajcik, 2006; Hidi & Renninger, 2006; Pintrich & Schunk, 2002; Voss & Schauble, 1992.

[33] Rudolph et al., 2005.

ers.[34] Conversely, learners who are least motivated to master academic subject matter are at high risk for dropping out before they graduate from high school.[35]

Intrinsic motivation is usually more beneficial than extrinsic motivation.

Not all forms of motivation have exactly the same effects on human learning and performance. Consider these two students in an advanced high school writing class:

- Sheryl doesn't enjoy writing and is taking the class for only one reason: Earning an A or B in the class will help her earn a scholarship at State University, where she desperately wants to go to college.
- Shannon has always liked to write. The class will help her get a scholarship at State University, but in addition, Shannon truly wants to become a better writer. She sees its usefulness for her future profession as a journalist. Besides, she's learning many new techniques for making her writing more vivid and engaging for readers.

Sheryl exhibits **extrinsic motivation**: She is motivated by factors external to herself and unrelated to the task she is performing. Learners who are extrinsically motivated may want the good grades, money, or recognition that particular activities and accomplishments bring. Essentially, they are motivated to perform a task as a means to an end, not as an end in and of itself. In contrast, Shannon exhibits **intrinsic motivation**: She is motivated by factors within herself or inherent in the task she is performing. Intrinsic motivation often results when learners engage in tasks that enable them to meet one or more of the basic psychological needs identified earlier.[36] Learners who are intrinsically motivated may engage in an activity because it intellectually stimulates them, helps them feel competent and self-determined, or provides an enjoyable vehicle for interacting with friends.

Learners are most likely to show motivation's beneficial effects (effort and energy, persistence, etc.) when they are *intrinsically* motivated to engage in classroom activities. Intrinsically motivated learners tackle assigned tasks willingly and are eager to learn classroom material, are more likely to process information in effective ways (e.g., by engaging in meaningful learning), and are more likely to achieve at high levels. Some learners with high levels of intrinsic motivation become so focused on and absorbed in an activity that they lose track of time and completely ignore other tasks—a phenomenon known as **flow**.[37] In contrast, extrinsically motivated learners may have to be enticed or prodded, may process information only superficially, and are often interested in performing only easy tasks and meeting minimal classroom requirements.[38]

In the second-grade class depicted in the "Author's Chair" video clip in MyEducationLab, we see numerous indications that the students are intrinsically motivated to learn and achieve. Several students are eager to read their stories to the class, and most others seem genuinely interested in listening. Furthermore, the story authors don't seem to mind having their work critiqued. Their willingness to hear constructive criticism reflects a *mastery goal*, a form of intrinsic motivation we'll examine later in the chapter.

Unfortunately, intrinsic motivation for learning school subject matter tends to decline during the school years.[39] This decline is probably the result of several factors. As learners get older, they are more frequently reminded of the importance of good grades (extrinsic motivators) for promotion, graduation, and college admission, and many begin to realize that they are not necessarily "at the top of the heap" in comparison with their peers.[40] Furthermore, they become more cognitively able to think about and strive for long-term goals, and they begin to evaluate school subjects in terms of their relevance to such goals, rather than

Observe numerous examples of intrinsic motivation in the "Author's Chair" video in the Additional Resources section in Chapter 6 of MyEducationLab.

extrinsic motivation Motivation resulting from factors external to the individual and unrelated to the task being performed.

intrinsic motivation Motivation resulting from personal characteristics or inherent in the task being performed.

flow Intense form of intrinsic motivation, involving complete absorption in and concentration on a challenging activity.

[34] Gottfried, 1990; Schiefele, Krapp, & Winteler, 1992; Walberg & Uguroglu, 1980.

[35] Hardré & Reeve, 2003; Hymel, Comfort, Schonert-Reichl, & McDougall, 1996; Vallerand, Fortier, & Guay, 1997.

[36] Cacioppo et al., 1996; Reeve, 2006; R. M. Ryan & Deci, 2000.

[37] Csikszentmihalyi, 1990, 1996.

[38] Larson, 2000; Reeve, 2006; Schiefele, 1991; Tobias, 1994; Voss & Schauble, 1992.

[39] Covington & Müeller, 2001; Harter, 1992; Lepper, Corpus, & Iyengar, 2005; J. M. T. Walker, 2001.

[40] Covington & Müeller, 2001; Harter, 1992; Wigfield, Byrnes, & Eccles, 2006.

in terms of any intrinsic appeal.[41] And they may grow increasingly impatient with the overly structured, repetitive, and boring activities that they often encounter at school.[42]

This is not to say, however, that extrinsic motivation is necessarily a bad thing. Oftentimes learners are motivated by both intrinsic and extrinsic factors simultaneously.[43] For example, although Shannon enjoys her writing course, she also knows that a good grade will help her get a scholarship at State U. Furthermore, good grades and other external rewards for high achievements may confirm for Shannon that she is, in fact, mastering school subject matter.[44] And over the course of time, extrinsic motivation may gradually move inward, as we'll discover in our discussion of *internalized motivation* later in the chapter. Thus the extrinsic–intrinsic distinction reflects a continuum rather than an either-or situation.

In some instances extrinsic motivation, perhaps in the form of extrinsic reinforcers for academic achievement or productive behavior, may be the *only* thing that can get learners on the road to successful classroom achievement and productivity. Yet intrinsic motivation is ultimately what will sustain them over the long run. It will encourage them to make sense of and apply what they are studying and will increase the odds that they continue to read and learn about writing, science, history, and other academic subject matter long after they have left their formal education behind.

Conditions in the learning environment influence intrinsic as well as extrinsic motivation.

A common misconception is that motivation is something people "carry around" inside of them—that some people are simply motivated to do something and others are not. In fact, learners' immediate environments can have dramatic effects on their motivation to learn and achieve. Such environment-dependent motivation is known as **situated motivation**.[45] Certainly extrinsic reinforcement and punishment steer learners toward certain activities and behaviors and away from others. Yet environmental factors play a significant role in *intrinsic* motivation as well. For instance, presenting an unexpected, puzzling phenomenon may pique learners' natural curiosity and interest in a topic. And providing scaffolding and guidance for challenging tasks may entice learners to tackle the tasks strictly for the pleasure and the sense of competence they bring. As we examine cognitive factors in motivation in the next section, we'll identify numerous environmental factors that are apt to affect learners' intrinsic motivation.

COGNITIVE FACTORS IN MOTIVATION

Earlier we noted that motivation affects cognitive processes: Motivated learners are likely to pay attention and engage in meaningful learning—processes that will help them understand and remember the topic at hand. But the reverse is true as well: *Cognitive processes affect motivation.* For example, in the opening case study Michael's initial beliefs about his math ability and his explanations for poor performance (low ability and poor instruction) contribute to a lackadaisical attitude: He simply *hopes* he'll remember (but usually forgets) his teacher's explanations. Later, when Michael's appraisal of the situation changes (when his self-confidence increases and he attributes success to effort and better strategies), he becomes a much more engaged and proactive learner.

The following principles describe a number of cognitive factors that influence learners' motivation, sometimes for the short run and sometimes for the long haul.

Learners find some topics inherently interesting.

When we say that people have **interest** in a particular topic or activity, we mean that they find the topic or activity intriguing and engaging. Interest, then, is a form of intrinsic mo-

---

situated motivation Motivation that emerges at least partly from conditions in a learner's immediate environment.

interest Feeling that a topic is intriguing or enticing.

[41] Lepper et al., 2005.
[42] Battistich, Solomon, Kim, Watson, & Schaps, 1995; Larson, 2000.
[43] Cameron, 2001; Covington, 2000; Hidi & Harackiewicz, 2000; Lepper et al., 2005.
[44] Hynd, 2003; Reeve, 2006.
[45] Paris & Turner, 1994; Rueda & Moll, 1994.

tivation. Engaging in interesting activities is, of course, one important way in which learners satisfy their general need for arousal.

Take a minute to consider your own interests in the following exercise.

SEE FOR YOURSELF
The Doctor's Office

You have just arrived at the doctor's office for your annual checkup. The receptionist tells you the doctor is running late and you will probably have to wait an hour before you can be seen. As you sit down in the waiting room, you notice six magazines on the table beside you: *Better Homes and Gardens*, *National Geographic*, *Newsweek*, *People*, *Popular Mechanics*, and *Sports Illustrated*.

1. Rate each of these magazines in terms of how *interesting* you think its articles would be to you:

	Not at All Interesting	Somewhat Interesting	Very Interesting
Better Homes and Gardens	_____	_____	_____
National Geographic	_____	_____	_____
Newsweek	_____	_____	_____
People	_____	_____	_____
Popular Mechanics	_____	_____	_____
Sports Illustrated	_____	_____	_____

2. Even though you think some of the magazines will be more interesting than others, you decide to spend 10 minutes reading each one. Estimate how much you think you might *remember* from what you read in each of the six magazines:

	Hardly Anything	A Moderate Amount	Quite a Bit
Better Homes and Gardens	_____	_____	_____
National Geographic	_____	_____	_____
Newsweek	_____	_____	_____
People	_____	_____	_____
Popular Mechanics	_____	_____	_____
Sports Illustrated	_____	_____	_____

Now compare your two sets of ratings. Chances are, the magazines you rated highest in interest to you are also the magazines from which you will learn and remember the most.

Learners who are interested in a particular topic devote more attention to it and become more cognitively engaged in it.[46] They are also apt to learn it in a more meaningful and elaborative fashion—for instance, by relating it to prior knowledge, interconnecting ideas, drawing inferences, forming visual images, generating examples, and identifying potential applications.[47] And unless they are emotionally attached to their current beliefs, interested learners are more likely to undergo conceptual change when they encounter information that contradicts their existing understandings.[48] As you might guess, then, learners who are interested in what they study show higher academic achievement and are more likely to remember the subject matter over the long run.[49]

Psychologists distinguish between two general types of interest. **Situational interest** is evoked by something in the immediate environment. Things that are new, different,

---

[46] Hidi & Renninger, 2006.
[47] Pintrich & Schrauben, 1992; Hidi & Renninger, 2006; Schraw & Lehman, 2001; Tobias, 1994.
[48] Andre & Windschitl, 2003; Linnenbrink & Pintrich, 2003.

[49] Garner, Brown, Sanders, & Menke, 1992; Hidi & Harackiewicz, 2000; Renninger, Hidi, & Krapp, 1992.

situational interest Interest evoked temporarily by something in the environment.

Observe high levels of situational interest in young children in the "Snail Investigation" video in the Additional Resources section in Chapter 6 of MyEducationLab.

unexpected, or especially vivid often generate situational interest, as do things that involve physical activity or intense emotions.[50] Learners also tend to be intrigued by topics related to people and culture (e.g., disease, violence, holidays), nature (e.g., dinosaurs, weather, the sea), and current events (e.g., television shows, popular music, substance abuse, gangs).[51] Works of fiction (novels, short stories, movies, and so on) are more interesting and engaging when they include themes and characters with which learners can personally identify.[52] And nonfiction is more interesting when it is easy to understand and relationships among ideas are clear.[53]

Other interests lie within: Learners tend to have personal preferences about the topics they pursue and the activities in which they engage. Because such **personal interests** are relatively stable over time, we see a consistent pattern in the choices learners make (e.g., see Figure 6.3). Some personal interests probably come from learners' prior experiences with various activities and topics. For example, events and subject matter that initially invoke situational interest may provide the seeds from which a personal interest eventually grows.[54] Often interest and knowledge perpetuate each other: Personal interest in a topic fuels a quest to learn more about the topic, and the increased knowledge gained, in turn, promotes greater interest.[55]

In the early grades, interests are mostly situational: Young children are readily attracted to novel, attention-getting events and stimuli. By the middle to upper elementary grades, however, many children acquire specific interests—perhaps in reptiles, ballet, or outer space—that persist over a period of time.[56] By and large, learners form interests in activities that they can do well in and that are stereotypically appropriate for their gender and socioeconomic group.[57] Personal interests are ultimately more beneficial than situational interests. Whereas the latter may temporarily capture a learner's attention, personal interest is the force that ultimately sustains involvement in an activity over the long run.[58]

To engage voluntarily in activities, learners want their chances of success to be reasonably good.

In our earlier discussion of self-worth, we discovered that human beings have a general need to feel competent in their environment. Yet people also realize that they have both strengths and weaknesses. In other words, their beliefs about their competence are somewhat specific to different tasks and activities. The following exercise illustrates this point.

SEE FOR YOURSELF

Self-Appraisal

Take a moment to answer the following questions:

1. Do you believe you'll be able to understand and apply educational psychology by reading this book and thinking carefully about its content? Or do you believe you're going to have trouble with the material regardless of how much you read and study it?
2. Do you think you could learn to execute a reasonable swan dive from a high diving board if you were shown how to do it and given time to practice? Or do you think you're such a klutz that no amount of training and practice would help?
3. Do you think you could walk barefoot over hot coals unscathed? Or do you think the soles of your feet would be burned to a crisp?

---

personal interest Long-term, relatively stable interest in a particular topic or activity.

[50] Hidi & Renninger, 2006; M. Mitchell, 1993; Renninger et al., 1992; Schank, 1979.
[51] Zahorik, 1994.
[52] Hidi & Harackiewicz, 2000; Schank, 1979; Wade, 1992.
[53] Schraw & Lehman, 2001; Wade, 1992.
[54] Hidi & Harackiewicz, 2000; Hidi & Renninger, 2006.

[55] P. A. Alexander, 1997; Hidi & McLaren, 1990; Tobias, 1994.
[56] Eccles, Wigfield, & Schiefele, 1998.
[57] L. S. Gottfredson, 1981; Hidi, Renninger, & Krapp, 2004; Nolen, 2007; Wigfield, 1994.
[58] P. A. Alexander, Kulikowich, & Schulze, 1994; Hidi & Renninger, 2006.

Soccer, the Pride and Passion

The sharp light blinds all onlookers from the reflection off the newly polished cast iron gauntlets of the twenty-two men of steel. Helms lowered, bodies bent in preparation for the battle Royal. Weapons drawn, shields raised, minds focused, focused on their enemy, their foe, their fellow competitor. Small colored flags wave in the stands, color coded with their respective prides and passions. Noises rumble through the stadium as random as the droplets of sweat flowing down the warriors' faces; teeth gritted, fists clenched, hearts pounding, pounding in anticipation of the things to come, the ultimate challenge of wills, the will to win for your fans, for your teammates, for yourself.

Fussebol, calcio, football, soccer; hundreds of names, one sport. Soccer is the most popular and most played game in the world, but that is not why I play the "Beautiful Game." Twenty-two players on a 120 by 90-yard battlefield scraping, fighting over one ball; that is not why I play it. Millions of players striving to be on their country s roster to play in the world's tournament that occurs only once every four years; that is not why I play it. The dream of playing in front of thousands of roaring fans and scoring the game-winning goal; that is not why I play it. For the emotion and passion of being able to walk out of my door every day to play the game I love, to give my all to the game, while taking everything I can from it, and not just progressing as a player, but a person; that is why I play it. That is why I play the "world's game." That is why I play soccer. . . .

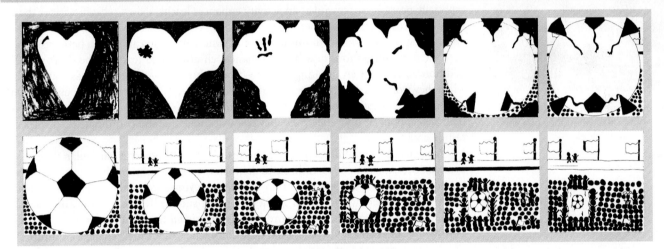

FIGURE 6.3 Many children and adolescents have personal interests that pervade much of what they do. Here we see two examples of Matt's passion for soccer in high school: (a) an excerpt from an essay assigned in writing class and (b) artwork created two years earlier for a language arts class portfolio. Matt's interest in soccer actually dates back to first grade. You will see evidence of his early interest in Figure 9.1 in Chapter 9.

Your responses say something about your self-efficacy for the tasks about which I asked you. In general, **self-efficacy** is a learner's self-constructed judgment about his or her ability to execute certain behaviors or reach certain goals; thus, it affects the learner's expectations for future performance. For example, I hope you believe that with careful thought about what you read, you will be able to understand and apply the ideas in this book. In other words, I hope you have high self-efficacy for learning educational psychology. You may or may not believe that with instruction and practice, you will eventually be able to perform a passable swan dive. That is, you may have high or low self-efficacy about learning to dive. You are probably quite skeptical that you could ever walk barefoot over hot coals, in which case you have low self-efficacy regarding this activity.

Learners are more likely to initiate and persist in tasks and activities for which they have high self-efficacy.[59] High self-efficacy also leads them to engage in effective cognitive and metacognitive processes (paying attention, organizing, elaborating, effectively managing study time, etc.) that help them learn and achieve at higher levels.[60]

To a considerable degree, self-efficacy for a particular task or activity arises out of past experience. Learners feel more confident that they can succeed at a task—that is, they have higher self-efficacy—when they have previously succeeded at that task or at similar ones.[61]

---

[59] Bandura, 1997, 2000, 2006; Schunk, 1989b; Wigfield & Eccles, 2002; Zimmerman, Bandura, & Martinez-Pons, 1992.

[60] Bandura, 1986; Bembenutty & Karabenick, 2004; Bong & Skaalvik, 2003; Klassen, 2002; Pajares, 2005.

[61] Bandura, 1986; Patrick, Anderman, & Ryan, 2002; Valentine, Cooper, Bettencourt, & DuBois, 2002.

self-efficacy Belief that one is capable of executing certain behaviors or reaching certain goals.

In the opening case study, Michael has been getting Fs in his algebra class, and so his expectations for passing the class are initially at rock-bottom. But as he sees himself improve with effort and new strategies, he gains confidence and begins to show signs of intrinsic motivation to master algebra. He starts listening carefully and taking notes in class, and he studies "every day except Friday, even if I don't have homework."[62]

Recall how Michael's initial pessimism about his math class is based not only on his self-assessment of his math ability but also on his teacher's poor instruction. When learners form expectations about the likelihood of future success, they consider not only their own past successes but other factors as well. The quality of instruction, the perceived difficulty of a task, the amount of effort that will be needed, and the availability of resources and support will all influence their predictions.[63] Under ideal circumstances, learners identify personal strengths on which they can depend, tried-and-true strategies they can use, and environmental support systems that can help them surmount any difficulties they may encounter—a combination that gives them hope and optimism about their chances for success.[64]

Social factors, too, play a role in the development of self-efficacy. Seeing other people, especially peers, be successful at an activity enhances learners' own self-efficacy for the activity.[65] Words of encouragement (e.g., "I bet Judy will play with you if you just ask her") and suggestions about how to improve (e.g., "I know that you can write a better essay, and here are some suggestions how") also enhance self-efficacy, at least for the short run.[66] In addition, learners often have higher self-efficacy about accomplishing a task successfully when they work in a group rather than alone. Such **collective self-efficacy** depends not only on learners' perceptions of their own and other group members' capabilities but also on their perceptions of how effectively they can work together and coordinate their roles and responsibilities.[67]

Once learners have developed a high sense of self-efficacy in a particular content domain, an occasional failure is unlikely to dampen their optimism much. In fact, when these learners encounter small setbacks on the way to achieving success, they learn that sustained effort and perseverance are key ingredients of that success. In other words, they develop **resilient self-efficacy**.[68] The key word here is *occasional* failure. If, in contrast, students *consistently* fail at an activity, they gain little confidence about their chances of future success. For instance, students with learning disabilities, who may have encountered failure after failure in classroom activities, often have low self-efficacy for mastering school subject matter.[69]

Most 4- to 6-year-olds are quite confident about their ability to perform various tasks. In fact, they often overestimate what they are capable of doing.[70] As they progress through the elementary grades, however, they can better recall their past successes and failures, and they become increasingly aware that their performance doesn't always compare favorably with that of their peers.[71] Presumably as a result of these changes, they become less confident, though usually more realistic, about their chances for success in specific academic domains.[72]

When learners think their chances of success are slim, they may behave in ways that make success even *less* likely.

Even with considerable persistence, learners cannot always be successful at certain tasks they are asked to perform. Repeated failures in a particular domain may lower not only their self-efficacy for the domain but also their general sense of competence and self-worth. When learners can't avoid tasks at which they think they will do poorly, they have alternative strategies at their disposal. Occasionally they make excuses that seemingly justify their poor performance.[73] They may also engage in **self-handicapping**, that is, doing things that actually

Students often have higher self-efficacy about challenging tasks when they can work with peers rather than alone.

collective self-efficacy Shared belief of members of a group that they can be successful when they work together on a task.

resilient self-efficacy Belief that one can perform a task successfully even after experiencing setbacks.

self-handicapping Behavior that undermines one's own success as a way of protecting self-worth during difficult tasks.

[62] Tucker & Anderman, 1999, p. 6.
[63] Dweck & Elliott, 1983; Wigfield & Eccles, 1992, 2000, 2002; Zimmerman et al., 1992.
[64] C. Peterson, 2006; Snyder, 1994, 2002.
[65] Schunk, 1983, 1989b.
[66] Parsons, Kaczala, & Meece, 1982; Pintrich & Schunk, 2002; Schunk, 1989a; Zeldin & Pajares, 2000.
[67] Bandura, 1997, 2000.

[68] Bandura, 1989; Dweck, 2000.
[69] Schunk, 1989b.
[70] R. Butler, 1990; Eccles et al., 1998; Nicholls, 1979.
[71] Eccles et al., 1998; Feld, Ruhland, & Gold, 1979.
[72] Bandura, 1986; Schunk & Zimmerman, 2006; Wigfield et al., 2006.
[73] Covington, 1992; Urdan & Midgley, 2001.

undermine their chances of success. Self-handicapping takes a variety of forms, including the following:[74]

- **Reducing effort:** Putting forth an obviously insufficient amount of effort to succeed
- **Misbehaving:** Engaging in off-task behaviors in class
- **Setting unattainably high goals:** Working toward goals that even the most capable individuals couldn't achieve
- **Taking on too much:** Assuming so many responsibilities that no one could possibly accomplish them all
- **Procrastinating:** Putting off a task until success is virtually impossible
- **Cheating:** Presenting others' work as one's own
- **Using alcohol or drugs:** Taking substances that will inevitably reduce performance

It might seem paradoxical that learners who want to be successful would actually try to undermine their own success. But if they believe they are unlikely to succeed no matter what they do—and especially if failure will reflect poorly on their intelligence and ability—they increase their chances of *justifying* the failure and thereby protecting their self-worth.[75] In the following interview, a student named Christine explains why she sometimes doesn't work very hard on her assignments:

> **Interviewer:** What if you don't do so well?
> **Christine:** Then you've got an excuse. . . . It's just easier to cope with if you think you haven't put as much work into it.
> **Interviewer:** What's easier to cope with?
> **Christine:** From feeling like a failure because you're not good at it. It's easier to say, "I failed because I didn't put enough work into it" than "I failed because I'm not good at it."[76]

Curiously, some learners are more likely to perform at their best, and less likely to display self-handicapping behaviors, when outside circumstances indicate that their chances of success are slim. In such cases failure doesn't indicate low ability and so doesn't threaten their sense of self-worth.[77]

Learners are more likely to devote time to activities that have value for them.

Another cognitive factor influencing motivation is **value:** Learners must believe there are direct or indirect benefits in performing a task. Their appraisal of the value of various tasks affects the subject matter and activities they pursue in their free time, the courses they choose in junior high and high school, and many other choices they make.[78]

Usually learners value activities that are intriguing and enjoyable—in other words, activities that are *interesting.*[79] Activities that are associated with desirable personal qualities—that is, activities viewed as *important*—also tend to be valued. For example, a boy who wants to be smart and thinks that smart people do well in school will place a premium on academic success. Still other activities have high value because they are seen as means to a desired goal; that is, they have *utility.* For example, much as my daughter Tina found mathematics confusing and frustrating, she struggled through four years of high school math classes simply because many colleges require that much math.

On the other hand, learners tend *not* to value activities that require more effort than they are worth—activities that essentially *cost* too much. For example, you could probably become an expert on some little-known topic (e.g., animal-eating plants of Borneo, the nature of rats' dreams), but I'm guessing that you have more important things to which to devote your time and energy right now. Other activities may be associated with too many bad

Knowing how to read clocks and tell time has *utility value* in mainstream Western culture.

---

[74] E. M. Anderman, Griesinger, & Westerfield, 1998; Covington, 1992; D. Y. Ford, 1996; E. E. Jones & Berglas, 1978; Riggs, 1992; Urdan, Ryan, Anderman, & Gheen, 2002.

[75] Covington, 1992; Riggs, 1992; Urdan et al., 2002.

[76] A. J. Martin, Marsh, Williamson, & Debus, 2003, p. 621.

[77] Covington, 1992.

[78] Durik, Vida, & Eccles, 2006; Jacobs, Davis-Kean, Bleeker, Eccles, & Malanchuk, 2005; Mac Iver, Stipek, & Daniels, 1991; Wigfield & Eccles, 2002.

[79] Eccles and Wigfield have suggested four possible reasons why value might be high or low: interest, importance, utility, and cost; see Eccles & Wigfield, 1985; Eccles (Parsons), 1983; Wigfield & Eccles, 1992, 2000.

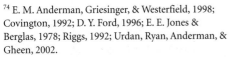

value Belief that an activity has direct or indirect benefits.

feelings. For example, if learners become frustrated often enough in their efforts to understand mathematics, they may eventually begin to steer clear of math whenever possible. And of course, anything likely to threaten a learner's sense of self-worth is a "must" to avoid.

In the early elementary years, children often pursue activities they find interesting and enjoyable, regardless of their expectations for success.[80] As they get older, however, they increasingly attach value to activities for which they have high expectations for success and to activities they think will help them meet long-term goals, and they begin to *de*value activities at which they expect to do poorly.[81]

Learners' social and cultural environments influence the things they value as well. As children grow older, they tend to adopt many of the priorities and values of the people around them. Such **internalized motivation** typically develops gradually over the course of childhood and adolescence. Initially, learners may engage in certain activities primarily because of the external consequences that result. For instance, students may do schoolwork to gain the approval of adults or to avoid being punished for poor grades. Gradually, however, they may internalize the "pressure" to perform the activities and begin to see the activities as important in their own right. Such internalization of values is most likely to take place if adults who espouse those values (parents, teachers, etc.) provide a warm, supportive, and structured environment yet also offer enough autonomy in decision making that learners have a sense of self-determination about their actions.[82] All too often, such conditions are *not* present when it comes to learning academic subject matter. Accordingly, the value students find in many school subjects (e.g., math, English, music, sports) declines markedly over the school years.[83]

The more learners have internalized the value of academic achievement, the more cognitively engaged they become in school subject matter and the better their overall learning is likely to be.[84] Appreciation of an activity's value also fosters self-regulated learning—a general work ethic in which learners spontaneously engage in activities that, although not always fun or immediately gratifying, are essential for reaching long-term goals.[85]

Some of my readers may think that internalized motivation is essentially the same as intrinsic motivation. Certainly both forms of motivation come from inside the learner rather than from outside factors in the immediate environment. But there's an important difference: Intrinsic motivation seems to arise spontaneously within the learner, and so it can increase or decrease somewhat unpredictably. In contrast, because internalized motivation is a product of ongoing social and cultural factors and eventually becomes an integral part of learners' sense of self—their beliefs about who they are as human beings—it remains fairly stable and dependable over time.[86]

Learners typically form goals related to their academic achievement; the specific nature of these goals influences learners' cognitive processes and behaviors.

As we learned early in the chapter, a great deal of human behavior is directed toward particular goals. For school-age children and adolescents, some of these goals are apt to relate to school learning and performance. Let's consider what three different boys might be thinking during the first day of a basketball unit in Mr. Wesolowski's physical education class:

Tim: This is my chance to show all the guys what a great basketball player I am. If I stay near the basket, Travis and Tony will keep passing to me, and I'll score a lot of points. I can really impress Wesolowski and my friends.

Travis: Boy, I hope I don't screw this up. If I shoot at the basket and miss, I'll look like a real jerk. Maybe I should just stay outside the three-point line and keep passing to Tim and Tony.

---

internalized motivation Adoption of others' priorities and values as one's own.

[80] Wigfield, 1994.
[81] Jacobs, Lanza, Osgood, Eccles, & Wigfield, 2002; Wigfield, 1994.
[82] Deci & Ryan, 1995; R. M. Ryan, Connell, & Grolnick, 1992; R. M. Ryan & Deci, 2000.
[83] Eccles et al., 1998; Jacobs et al., 2002; Watt, 2004; Wigfield, Eccles, Mac Iver, Reuman, & Midgley, 1991.

[84] Lens, 2001; Lens, Simons, & Dewitte, 2006; R. M. Ryan & Deci, 2000.
[85] Harter, 1992; McCombs, 1996; R. M. Ryan et al., 1992; Stipek, 1993.
[86] Otis, Grouzet, & Pelletier, 2005; Reeve et al., 2004; Walls & Little, 2005.

Tony: I'd really like to become a better basketball player. I can't figure out why I don't get more of my shots into the basket. I'll ask Wesolowski to give me feedback about how I can improve my game. Maybe some of my friends will have suggestions, too.

All three boys want to play basketball well. That is, they all have *achievement goals*. But they have different reasons for wanting to play well. Tim is concerned mostly about looking good in front of his teacher and classmates and so wants to maximize opportunities to demonstrate his skill on the court. Travis, too, is concerned about the impression he'll make, but he just wants to make sure he *doesn't look bad*. Unlike Tim and Travis, Tony isn't thinking about how his performance will appear to others. Instead, he is interested mainly in developing his basketball skills and doesn't expect immediate success. For Tony, making mistakes is an inevitable part of learning a new skill, not a source of embarrassment or humiliation.

Tony's approach to basketball illustrates a **mastery goal**, a desire to acquire additional knowledge or master new skills. Tim and Travis each have a **performance goal**, a desire to present themselves as competent in the eyes of others. More specifically, Tim has a **performance-approach goal**: He wants to look good and receive favorable judgments from others. In contrast, Travis has a **performance-avoidance goal**: He wants to avoid looking bad and receiving unfavorable judgments. Performance goals often have an element of social comparison, in that learners are concerned about how their accomplishments compare to those of their peers.[87]

Mastery goals, performance-approach goals, and performance-avoidance goals are not necessarily mutually exclusive. Learners may simultaneously have two kinds, or even all three.[88] For example, returning to our basketball example, we could imagine a fourth boy, Trey, who wants to improve his basketball skills *and* look good in front of his classmates *and* not come across as a klutz.

In most instances mastery goals are the optimal situation. As Table 6.2 reveals, learners with mastery goals tend to engage in the very activities that will help them learn. They pay attention in class, process information in ways that promote effective long-term memory storage, and learn from their mistakes. Furthermore, learners with mastery goals have a healthy perspective about learning, effort, and failure. They realize that learning is a process of trying hard and continuing to persevere even in the face of temporary setbacks. Consequently, these learners are the ones who are most likely to stay on task and who benefit the most from their classroom experiences.[89] In the "Portfolio" video clip in MyEducationLab, 8-year-old Keenan says several things that reflect mastery goals related to writing. She acknowledges her errors and doesn't seem embarrassed by them. And when she doesn't know how to spell a word, she is quite willing to ask a friend or teacher for help. Mastery goals are also evident in the "Author's Chair" clip, in which students willingly accept constructive suggestions from their classmates.

In contrast, learners with performance goals—especially those with performance-*avoidance* goals—may stay away from the challenging tasks that would do the most to help them master new skills. Furthermore, these learners tend to process information in a rote, relatively "thoughtless" manner. Performance-*approach* goals are a mixed bag. They sometimes have very positive effects, spurring learners on to achieve at high levels, especially in adolescence and especially in combination with mastery goals.[90] Yet by themselves, performance-approach goals may be less beneficial than mastery goals. To accomplish them, learners may exert only the minimal effort required, use relatively superficial learning strategies, and possibly cheat on classroom assessments.[91] Performance-approach goals appear to be most detrimental when learners are fairly young (e.g., in the elementary grades) and have low self-efficacy for classroom tasks.[92]

Observe mastery goals in the "Portfolio" and "Author's Chair" videos in the Additional Resources section in Chapter 6 of MyEducationLab.

mastery goal Desire to acquire additional knowledge or master new skills.

performance goal Desire to demonstrate high ability and make a good impression.

performance-approach goal Desire to look good and receive favorable judgments from others.

performance-avoidance goal Desire not to look bad or receive unfavorable judgments from others.

[87] Elliot & McGregor, 2000; Elliot & Thrash, 2001; Midgley et al., 1998.

[88] Covington & Müeller, 2001; Hidi & Harackiewicz, 2000; Meece & Holt, 1993.

[89] Gabriele & Montecinos, 2001; Kumar, Gheen, & Kaplan, 2002; Wentzel & Wigfield, 1998.

[90] Hidi & Harackiewicz, 2000; McNeil & Alibali, 2000; Linnenbrink, 2005; Rawsthorne & Elliot, 1999; Urdan, 1997.

[91] E. M. Anderman et al., 1998; Brophy, 1987; Midgley, Kaplan, & Middleton, 2001.

[92] Hidi & Harackiewicz, 2000; Kaplan, 1998; Kaplan & Midgley, 1997; Midgley et al., 2001.

TABLE 6.2   Characteristics of Learners with Mastery Goals Versus Performance Goals

Learners with Mastery Goals	Learners with Performance Goals (Especially Those with Performance-Avoidance Goals)
Are more likely to be actively engaged in classroom activities and intrinsically motivated to learn classroom subject matter	Are more likely to be extrinsically motivated (i.e., motivated by expectations of external reinforcement and punishment) and more likely to cheat to obtain good grades
Believe that competence develops over time through practice and effort	Believe that competence is a stable characteristic (people either have talent or they don't); think that competent people shouldn't have to try very hard
Exhibit more self-regulated learning and behavior	Exhibit less self-regulation
Use learning strategies that promote true comprehension and higher-level cognitive processes (e.g., elaboration, comprehension monitoring, transfer)	Use learning strategies that promote only rote learning (e.g., repetition, copying, word-for-word memorization); may procrastinate on assignments
Choose tasks that maximize opportunities for learning; seek out challenges	Choose tasks that maximize opportunities for demonstrating competence; avoid tasks and actions (e.g., asking for help) that make them look incompetent
Are more likely to undergo conceptual change when confronted with convincing evidence that contradicts current beliefs	Are less likely to undergo conceptual change, in part because they are less likely to notice the discrepancy between new information and existing beliefs
React to easy tasks with feelings of boredom or disappointment	React to success on easy tasks with feelings of pride or relief
Seek feedback that accurately describes their ability and helps them improve	Seek feedback that flatters them
Willingly collaborate with peers when doing so is likely to enhance learning	Collaborate with peers primarily when doing so can help them look competent or enhance social status
Evaluate their own performance in terms of the progress they make	Evaluate their own performance in terms of how they compare with others
Interpret failure as a sign that they need to exert more effort	Interpret failure as a sign of low ability and therefore predictive of future failures
View errors as a normal and useful part of the learning process; use errors to improve performance	View errors as a sign of failure and incompetence; engage in self-handicapping to provide apparent justification for errors and failures
Are satisfied with their performance if they try hard and make progress	Are satisfied with their performance only when they succeed; are apt to feel ashamed and depressed when they fail
View a teacher as a resource and guide to help them learn	View a teacher as a judge and as a rewarder or punisher
Remain relatively calm during tests and classroom assignments	Are often quite anxious about tests and other assessments
Are more likely to be enthusiastic about, and become actively involved in, school activities	Are more likely to distance themselves from the school environment

Sources: Ablard & Lipschultz, 1998; C. Ames & Archer, 1988; R. Ames, 1983; E. M. Anderman et al., 1998; E. M. Anderman & Maehr, 1994; Corpus, McClintic-Gilberg, & Hayenga, 2006; Dweck, 1986; Dweck & Elliott, 1983; Dweck, Mangels, & Good, 2004; Entwisle & Ramsden, 1983; L. S. Fuchs et al., 1997; Gabriele & Boody, 2001; Graham & Weiner, 1996; Hardré, Crowson, DeBacker, & White, 2007; Jagacinski & Nicholls, 1984, 1987; Kaplan, 1998; Kaplan & Midgley, 1999; Levy, Kaplan, & Patrick, 2000; Linnenbrink & Pintrich, 2002, 2003; Locke & Latham, 2006; McCombs, 1988; McGregor & Elliot, 2002; Meece, 1994; Middleton & Midgley, 1997; Murphy & Alexander, 2000; R. S. Newman & Schwager, 1995; Nolen, 1996; Pekrun, Elliot, & Maier, 2006; Pugh & Bergin, 2006; Rawsthorne & Elliot, 1999; A. M. Ryan, Pintrich, & Midgley, 2001; Schiefele, 1991, 1992; Shernoff & Hoogstra, 2001; Sideridis, 2005; Skaalvik, 1997; Southerland & Sinatra, 2003; Stipek, 1993; J. C. Turner, Thorpe, & Meyer, 1998; Urdan & Midgley, 2001; Urdan, Midgley, & Anderman, 1998.

Before children reach school age, they seem to focus primarily on mastery goals.[93] But when they begin elementary school at age 5 or 6, they are suddenly surrounded by peers with whom they can compare their own behavior, and so they begin to view success as doing as well as or better than classmates. In addition, they may have trouble evaluating their progress on the complex cognitive skills they are learning (reading, writing, mathematical

[93] Dweck & Elliott, 1983.

computations, etc.) and so must rely on others (e.g., teachers) to make judgments about their competence and progress. For such reasons, performance goals become increasingly prevalent as children progress through the elementary and secondary school grades.[94] Most high school students, if they are motivated to succeed in their schoolwork, are primarily concerned about getting good grades, and they prefer short, easy tasks to lengthier, more challenging ones. Performance goals are also common in team sports, where the focus is often more on winning and gaining public recognition than on developing new skills and seeing improvement over time.[95]

Learners must juggle their achievement goals with their many other goals.

Children and adolescents typically have a wide variety of goals.[96] Not only might they want to do well in school, but they also want to have a good time, be healthy and safe, earn money, and eventually embark on a rewarding career. Many of their goals are apt to be **social goals** that can help them meet their need for relatedness. For example, they may want to gain the approval of adults, be liked and respected by peers, belong to a supportive social group, and contribute to other people's welfare.[97] Among learners' many goals are certain **core goals** that drive much of what they do.[98] For instance, learners who attain high levels of academic achievement typically make classroom learning a high priority. Learners who achieve at lower levels are often more concerned with social relationships.[99]

Learners use several strategies to juggle their many goals.[100] Sometimes they find activities that allow them to address two or more goals simultaneously. For instance, they can address both achievement goals and social goals by forming a study group to prepare for a test. Sometimes they adjust their ideas of what it means to achieve particular goals. For instance, an ambitious high school student who initially hopes to earn all As in three advanced, time-consuming classes may eventually decide that earning Bs in two of them is more realistic. And sometimes learners entirely abandon one goal in order to satisfy another. For instance, they may find that the multiple demands of school coerce them into focusing on performance goals (e.g., getting good grades) rather than studying the subject matter as thoroughly as they'd like. In the following statement, a junior high school student expresses his concern about having to leave his mastery goals in the dust as he strives for performance goals:

> I sit here and I say, "Hey, I did this assignment in five minutes and I still got an A+ on it." I still have a feeling that I could do better, and it was kind of cheap that I didn't do my best and I still got this A. . . . I think probably it might lower my standards eventually, which I'm not looking forward to at all. . . . I'll always know, though, that I have it in me. It's just that I won't express it that much.[101]

Because most learners have a strong need for relatedness, their social goals often influence their classroom behavior and the priority they give to various achievement goals. If learners want to gain their teacher's attention and approval, they are apt to strive for good grades and in other ways shoot for performance goals.[102] If they seek friendly relationships with classmates or are concerned about others' welfare, they may eagerly engage in such activities as cooperative learning and peer tutoring.[103] A desire for close relationships with others may also lead them to ask peers for help, but if they are more interested in impressing peers with their

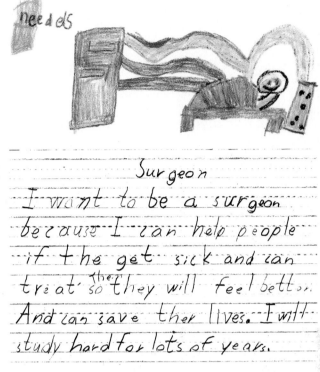

needed

Surgeon

I want to be a surgeon because I can help people if the get sick and can treat the so they will feel better. And can save ther lives. I will study hard for lots of years.

Career aspirations are often among learners' many goals. Here 7-year-old Ashton explains why he wants to be a surgeon. Notice how his career goal also has a social-goal component: "I can help people if [they] get sick."

[94] Blumenfeld, 1992; W. Doyle, 1986b; Dweck & Elliott, 1983; Elliot & McGregor, 2000; Harter, 1992.

[95] G. C. Roberts, Treasure, & Kavussanu, 1997.

[96] M. E. Ford, 1996; Schutz, 1994.

[97] H. A. Davis, 2003; Dowson & McInerney, 2001; M. E. Ford, 1996; Hinkley, McInerney, & Marsh, 2001; Patrick et al., 2002; Wentzel, Filisetti, & Looney, 2007.

[98] Boekaerts, de Koning, & Vedder, 2006; Schutz, 1994.

[99] Wentzel & Wigfield, 1998; Wigfield, Eccles, & Pintrich, 1996.

[100] Covington, 2000; Dodge, Asher, & Parkhurst, 1989; McCaslin & Good, 1996; Phelan, Yu, & Davidson, 1994; Urdan & Maehr, 1995.

[101] S. Thomas & Oldfather, 1997, p. 119.

[102] Corpus et al., 2006; Hinkley et al., 2001; Urdan & Mestas, 2006.

[103] L. H. Anderman & Anderman, 1999; Dowson & McInerney, 2001.

social goal Desire related to establishing or maintaining relationships with other people.

core goal Long-term goal that drives much of what a learner does.

high ability, they probably *won't* ask for help.[104] If they want to gain the approval of *low-achieving* peers, they may exert little effort in their studies and possibly even avoid classroom tasks altogether.[105]

Learners identify what are, in their minds, the likely causes of their successes and failures.

As we've seen in previous chapters, learners actively try to make sense of their experiences. Such sense-making sometimes involves identifying reasons for success or failure in particular situations. To gain insight into the kinds of explanations you yourself might identify, try the following exercise.

SEE FOR YOURSELF
Carberry and Seville

1. Professor Josiah S. Carberry has just returned the first set of exams, scored and graded, in your advanced psychoceramics class. You discover that you've gotten one of the few high test scores in the class, an A–. Why did you do so well when most of your classmates did poorly? Jot down several possible explanations as to why you might have received a high grade in Carberry's class.
2. An hour later, you get the results of the first test in Professor Barbara F. Seville's sociocosmetology class, and you learn that you *failed* it! Why did you do so poorly? Jot down several possible reasons for your F on Seville's test.

Here are some possible explanations for your A– in Carberry's class:

- You studied hard.
- You're smart.
- Psychoceramics just comes naturally to you.
- You were lucky. Carberry asked the right questions; if he'd asked different questions, you might not have done so well.
- Carberry likes you, so he gave you a good grade even though you didn't know what you were talking about.
- All those hours you spent in Carberry's office, asking questions about psychoceramics and requesting copies of the articles he's written (which you never actually read), really paid off.

In contrast, here are some possible reasons you failed the exam in Seville's class:

- You didn't study enough.
- You didn't study the right things.
- You didn't feel well when you took the test.
- The student next to you was sick, and the constant wheezing and coughing distracted you.
- You were unlucky. Seville asked the wrong questions; if she'd asked different questions, you would have done better.
- You're stupid.
- You've never been very good at sociocosmetology.
- It was a bad test: The questions were ambiguous and tested knowledge of trivial facts.
- Seville hates you and gave you a poor grade out of spite.

Learners' beliefs about what behaviors and other factors influence events in their lives are **attributions**. Learners form attributions for many events in their daily lives—why they do well or poorly on tests and assignments, why they are popular or unpopular with peers, why they are skilled athletes or total klutzes, and so on. Their attributions vary in three primary ways:[106]

---

attribution Personally constructed causal explanation for a success or failure.

[104] A. M. Ryan, Hicks, & Midgley, 1997.
[105] B. B. Brown, 1990; M. E. Ford & Nichols, 1991.

[106] Weiner, 1986, 2000.

- **Locus ("place"): Internal versus external.** Learners sometimes attribute the causes of events to *internal* things—to factors within themselves. Thinking that a good grade is due to your own hard work and believing that a poor grade is due to your lack of ability are examples of internal attributions. At other times learners attribute events to *external* things—to factors outside themselves. Concluding that you received a scholarship because you "lucked out" and interpreting a classmate's scowl as a sign of her bad mood (rather than something you might have deserved because of your behavior) are examples of external attributions.

- **Stability: Stable versus unstable.** Sometimes learners believe that events are due to *stable* factors—to things that probably won't change much in the near future. For example, if you believe that you do well in science because of your innate intelligence or that you have trouble making friends because you're overweight, then you are attributing events to stable, relatively long-term causes. But sometimes learners instead believe that events result from *unstable* factors—things that can change from one time to the next. Thinking that winning a tennis game was a lucky break and believing you got a bad test grade because you were tired when you took the test are examples of attributions involving unstable factors.

- **Controllability: Controllable versus uncontrollable.** On some occasions learners attribute events to *controllable* factors—to things they (or perhaps someone else) can influence and change. For example, if you think a classmate invited you to his birthday party because you always smile and say nice things to him, and if you think that you probably failed a test simply because you didn't study the right things, then you are attributing these events to controllable factors. On other occasions learners attribute events to *uncontrollable* factors—to things over which neither they nor others have influence. If you think that you were chosen for the lead in the school play only because you look "right" for the part or that you played a lousy game of basketball because you were sick, then you are attributing these events to uncontrollable factors.

Because attributions are self-constructed, they may or may not reflect the true state of affairs. For instance, a student may blame a low test grade on a "tricky" test or an "unfair" teacher when the cause was really the student's own lack of effort or poor study skills. Metacognition often enters into the picture here. In Chapter 4 we discovered that learners who don't carefully monitor their comprehension may have an *illusion of knowing*, thinking they have learned something they actually have *not* learned. When these learners do poorly on an exam, they cannot attribute their performance to internal, controllable factors because, in their minds, they studied hard and so "know" the material. Instead, they are apt to attribute the failure to such external factors as bad luck, exam difficulty, or teacher incompetence.[107]

In general, learners tend to attribute their successes to internal causes (e.g., high ability, hard work) and their failures to external causes (e.g., luck, other people's behaviors).[108] By patting themselves on the back for the things they do well and putting the blame elsewhere for poor performance, they are able to maintain their sense of self-worth.[109] Yet when learners *consistently* fail at tasks, and especially when they see their peers succeeding at those same tasks, they are apt to put the blame on a stable and uncontrollable internal factor: their own low ability.[110]

In the opening case study, Michael initially attributes his failure in algebra to two stable factors over which he himself has no control: low aptitude (an internal attribution) and poor instruction (an external attribution). But as his tutor helps him understand algebraic principles and procedures, and especially as he experiences success in class, he begins to attribute his performance to two unstable, internal factors he *can* control—effort and better strategies:

> I realize now that even if I don't like the teacher or don't think he is a good teacher, it is my responsibility to listen. . . . [T]he teacher does most of his part, but it's no use to me unless I do my part. . . . [N]ow I try and comprehend, ask questions and figure out how he got the answer.[111]

"And remember, kids: If you play to the best of your ability and still lose the game, just blame it all on the umpire."

By blaming the umpire for a loss, children can more easily maintain a sense of self-worth. However, such external attributions are counterproductive when the true causes for success and failure are actually internal and within children's control.

Source: IN THE BLEACHERS © 2002 Steve Moore. Reprinted with permission of UNIVERSAL PRESS SYNDICATE. All rights reserved.

---

[107] Horgan, 1990.

[108] Marsh, 1990; Whitley & Frieze, 1985.

[109] Clifford, 1990; Paris & Byrnes, 1989.

[110] Covington, 1987; Y. Hong, Chiu, & Dweck, 1995; Schunk, 1990; Weiner, 1984.

[111] Tucker & Anderman, 1999, pp. 5–6.

Learners' attributions for past successes and failures affect their future performance.

Let's return to those two fictional exams you considered in the earlier "Carberry and Seville" exercise—the psychoceramics exam (on which you got an A–) and the sociocosmetology exam (on which you got an F). Imagine that you will be taking second exams in both psychoceramics and sociocosmetology in about three weeks' time. How much will you study for each exam?

The amount of time you spend studying for your upcoming exams will depend somewhat on your attributions for your earlier performances. Let's first consider your A– on Professor Carberry's exam. If you think you did well because you studied hard, you will probably spend a lot of time studying for the second test as well. If you think you did well because you're smart or a natural whiz at psychoceramics, you may not study quite as much. If you believe that your success was a matter of luck, you may hardly study at all, but you might wear your lucky sweater when you take the next exam. And if you think the A– reflects how much Carberry likes you, you may decide that time spent buttering him up is more important than time spent with the textbook.

Now let's consider your failing grade on Professor Seville's exam. Once again, the reasons you identify for your failure will influence the ways in which you prepare for the second exam—if, in fact, you prepare at all. If you believe you didn't study enough or didn't study the right things, you may spend more time studying the next time. If you think your poor grade was due to a temporary situation—you were ill, the student sitting next to you distracted you, or Seville asked the wrong questions—then you may study in much the same way as you did before, hoping you'll do better the second time around. If you believe your failure was due to your low aptitude for sociocosmetology or, more generally, to low intelligence, you may study even less than you did the first time. (What good will it do to study when your poor test performance is beyond your control?) And if you are convinced that Seville dislikes you or writes lousy tests, not only will you not study, but you may also harbor an intense dislike for this capricious and incompetent professor.

Learners' attributions influence a number of factors that either directly or indirectly affect their future performance:

Learners are usually happy when they succeed at classroom tasks. But they also feel proud and satisfied if they attribute their successes to internal causes.

- **Emotional reactions to success and failure.** Naturally, learners are happy when they succeed. But they also have feelings of pride and satisfaction when they attribute their successes to internal causes—for instance, to something they themselves have done. When they instead credit their successes to the actions of another person or to some other external force, they are apt to feel grateful rather than proud. Along a similar vein, learners usually feel a certain amount of sadness after a failure. If they believe they are personally responsible for the failure, they may also feel guilty or ashamed, and such feelings may spur them to address their shortcomings. If they instead think that someone else was to blame, they are inclined to be angry, an emotion that's less likely to lead to productive follow-up behaviors.[112]

- **Expectations for future success or failure.** When learners attribute their successes and failures to stable factors, they expect their future performance to be similar to their current performance. In other words, successful learners anticipate that they will continue to succeed, and failing learners believe that they will always be failures. In contrast, when learners attribute their successes and failures to *un*stable factors (e.g., effort or luck), their current success rate will have less influence on their expectation for future success, and a few failures won't put much of a dent in their self-efficacy. The most optimistic learners—those with the highest expectations for future success—are the ones who attribute their successes to stable, dependable (and usually internal) factors such as innate ability and an enduring work ethic and attribute their failures to unstable factors such as lack of effort or inappropriate strategies.[113]

- **Future choices.** As you might expect, learners whose attributions lead them to expect success in a particular subject area are more likely to pursue that area—for example,

[112] Hareli & Weiner, 2002; Weiner, Russell, & Lerman, 1978.

[113] Dweck, 2000; Fennema, 1987; Pomerantz & Saxon, 2001; Schunk, 1990; Weiner, 1984, 1986.

by enrolling in more courses in the same discipline. Learners who believe that their chances for future success in an activity are slim will avoid the activity whenever they can.[114]

- **Effort and persistence.** When learners believe their failures result from their own lack of effort, they are apt to try harder and persist in the face of difficulty. But when they instead attribute failure to a lack of innate ability (they couldn't do it even if they tried), they give up easily and sometimes can't even perform tasks they have previously accomplished successfully.[115]
- **Learning strategies.** Learners who expect to succeed in the classroom and believe that academic success is a result of their own doing are more likely to apply effective learning and study strategies (especially when they are *taught* these strategies) and more likely to approach problem-solving tasks in a logical, systematic, and meaningful way. These learners are also more apt to be self-regulating learners and to seek help when they need it. In contrast, learners who expect failure and believe that their academic performance is largely out of their hands often reject effective learning and problem-solving strategies in favor of rote-learning approaches.[116]

Given all of these effects, it should not surprise you to learn that learners with internal, controllable attributions for classroom success (rather than external ones that they can't control) are more likely to achieve at high levels and graduate from high school.[117]

Let's consider how some of the factors just listed play out in the opening case study. Michael initially attributes his failure in algebra to both his own low ability and his teacher's poor instruction, and so he probably feels a combination of shame and anger. Because the perceived causes of his failure are both stable and out of his control, he expects future failure no matter what he does and thus has little reason to exert much effort (e.g., he doesn't take notes). As Michael acquires new study skills and gains a better understanding of algebraic concepts and procedures, he achieves greater success and realizes that his success is the direct result of his own hard work. His new internal and controllable attributions lead him to use more effective strategies and be a more self-regulating learner:

> Now I do things in math step by step and listen to each step. . . . I used to just listen and not even take notes. I always told myself I would remember but I always seemed to forget. Now I take notes and I study at home every day except Friday, even if I don't have homework. Now I study so that I know that I have it. I don't just hope I'll remember.[118]

With age, learners increasingly attribute their successes and failures to ability rather than to effort.

Preschool children don't have a clear understanding of the differences among the possible causes—effort, ability, luck, task difficulty, and so on—of their successes and failures.[119] Especially troublesome is the distinction between effort and ability, which they gradually get a better handle on over time. At about age 6, they start to realize that effort and ability are separate qualities but see them as positively correlated. In their minds, people who try hardest have the greatest ability, and effort is the primary determiner of success. Sometime around age 9, they begin to understand that effort and ability often compensate for one another and that people with less ability may need to exert greater effort. By age 13 or so, they make a clear distinction between effort and ability, realizing that people differ both in an underlying ability to perform a task and in the amount of effort exerted on a task. They also know that a lack of ability sometimes prevents success *regardless* of the amount of effort.[120]

With this growing appreciation of how effort and ability are different comes an increasing belief that successes and failures depend on ability rather than effort.[121] Children

[114] Eccles (Parsons), 1984; Stipek & Gralinski, 1990; Weiner, 1986.

[115] Blackwell, Trzesniewski, & Dweck, 2007; Dweck, 1978, 2000; Feather, 1982; Weiner, 1984.

[116] R. Ames, 1983; Dweck, Mangels, & Good, 2004; Mangels, 2004; D. J. Palmer & Goetz, 1988; Pressley, Borkowski, & Schneider, 1987; Tyler, 1958; Zimmerman, 1998.

[117] L. E. Davis, Ajzen, Saunders, & Williams, 2002; Dweck et al., 2004; Pintrich, 2003.

[118] Tucker & Anderman, 1999, pp. 5–6.

[119] Eccles et al., 1998; Nicholls, 1990.

[120] Nicholls, 1990.

[121] Covington, 1992; Dweck & Elliott, 1983; Nicholls, 1990.

in the early elementary grades tend to attribute their successes to hard work and practice and so are usually fairly optimistic about their chances for future success as long as they try hard. As they get older, however, many begin to attribute successes and failures to an inherited ability—that is, to "intelligence"—that they perceive to be fairly stable and beyond their control. If they are usually successful at school tasks, they will have high self-efficacy about such tasks. If failures are frequent, their self-efficacy may plummet.[122]

The degree to which intelligence is the result of heredity (and so stable and uncontrollable) or environment (and so able to improve with instruction and practice) is a matter of some controversy among psychologists (see Chapter 5). Even children and adolescents have differing opinions on the matter. Those with an **entity view** believe that intelligence is a "thing" that is fairly permanent and unchangeable. Those with an **incremental view** believe that intelligence can and does improve with effort and practice. As you might guess, learners who have an incremental view of intelligence and other abilities are more likely to attribute their failures to a temporary and unstable, rather than permanent, state of affairs. In contrast, learners with an entity view may continually try to assess their "natural" ability by comparing their own performance with that of others, and they are apt to adopt performance goals rather than mastery goals.[123]

Over time, learners acquire a general attributional style.

Consider these two girls, who have the *same* ability:

- Jane is an enthusiastic, energetic learner. She seems to enjoy working hard at school activities and takes obvious pleasure in doing well. She likes challenges and especially likes to solve the "brainteaser" problems her teacher assigns as extra-credit work each day. She can't always solve the problems, but she takes failure in stride and is eager for more problems the following day.
- Julie is an anxious, fidgety student. She doesn't seem to have much confidence in her ability to accomplish school tasks successfully. In fact, she is always underestimating what she can do: Even when she has succeeded, she doubts that she can do it again. She seems to prefer filling out drill-and-practice worksheets that help her practice skills she's already mastered, rather than attempting new tasks and problems. As for those daily brainteasers Jane likes so much, Julie sometimes takes a stab at them, but she gives up quickly if the answer isn't obvious.

Over time, some learners, like Jane, develop a general sense of optimism that they can master new tasks and succeed in a variety of endeavors. They attribute their accomplishments to their own ability and effort and have an *I can do it* attitude known as a **mastery orientation**. Other learners, like Julie, who are either unsure of their chances for success or else convinced that they *cannot* succeed, display a growing sense of futility about their chances for future success. They have an *I can't do it* attitude known as **learned helplessness**. You might think of this distinction between mastery orientation and learned helplessness—which really reflects a continuum rather than an either-or dichotomy—as a difference between *optimists* and *pessimists*.[124]

Even though learners with a mastery orientation and those with learned helplessness may have equal ability initially, those with a mastery orientation behave in ways that lead to higher achievement over the long run. In particular, they set ambitious goals, seek challenging situations, and persist in the face of failure. Learners with learned helplessness behave quite differently. Because they underestimate their ability, they set goals they can easily accomplish, avoid the challenges likely to maximize their learning and growth, and respond to failure in counterproductive ways (e.g., giving up quickly) that almost guarantee future failure.[125]

Even preschoolers can develop learned helplessness about a particular task if they consistently meet failure when attempting it.[126] By age 5 or 6, a few children begin to show a consistent tendency either to persist at a task and express confidence that they can master it,

entity view of intelligence Belief that intelligence is a "thing" that is relatively permanent and unchangeable.

incremental view of intelligence Belief that intelligence can improve with effort and practice.

mastery orientation General, fairly pervasive belief that one is capable of accomplishing challenging tasks.

learned helplessness General, fairly pervasive belief that one is incapable of accomplishing tasks and has little or no control over the environment.

[122] Dweck, 1986; Eccles (Parsons), 1983; Schunk, 1990.
[123] Blackwell et al., 2007; Dweck, 2000; Dweck et al., 2004; Dweck & Leggett, 1988; Weiner, 1994.
[124] C. Peterson, 1990, 2006; Scheier & Carver, 1992; Seligman, 1991.
[125] Dweck, 2000; Graham, 1989; C. Peterson, 1990, 2006; Seligman, 1991.
[126] Burhans & Dweck, 1995.

on the one hand, or to abandon a task quickly and say they don't have the ability to do it, on the other.[127] As a general rule, however, children younger than age 8 rarely exhibit extreme forms of learned helplessness, perhaps because they still believe that success is due largely to their own efforts.[128] By early adolescence, feelings of helplessness are more common. Some middle schoolers believe they cannot control the things that happen to them and are at a loss for strategies about how to avert future failures.[129] In the opening case study, Michael's initial pessimism about his chances of future success in his algebra class suggests some degree of learned helplessness, at least about mathematics.

Table 6.3 draws from developmental trends in attributions and other cognitive factors in motivation to describe the typical motivational characteristics of students in the elementary, middle, and high school grades.

Culture influences the cognitive factors underlying motivation.

Virtually all of the cognitive factors underlying motivation are influenced by learners' environments. Some of them—for instance, values, goals, and attributions—seem to be especially susceptible to cultural influence. The Cultural Considerations box "Cultural and Ethnic Differences in Motivation" (p. 210) describes numerous influences that culture is apt to have, not only on how learners prioritize various activities, form goals for themselves, and interpret consequences, but also on the specific ways in which learners satisfy their basic psychological needs.

Cognitive factors underlying sustained motivation build up over a period of time.

We've already discredited one common misconception about motivation: that it is something learners "carry around" inside of them. A second widely held misconception is that learners can turn their motivation "on" or "off" at will, much as one would flip a light switch. As should be evident from the preceding discussion, motivation—especially intrinsic motivation—is usually the result of many cognitive factors that develop gradually over time. In the opening case study, two things change for Michael during his tutoring sessions: His *self-efficacy* for mastering algebra increases, and his *attributions* for his performance begin to reflect controllable rather than uncontrollable factors. Neither of these factors changes overnight. Instead, they evolve slowly with time, better strategies, and a regular pattern of success experiences.

AFFECT AND ITS EFFECTS

In reflecting earlier on the opening case, we speculated that Michael might have varying emotions—frustration, dislike, pride, enjoyment—depending on whether he was failing or succeeding in his math class. Emotions, moods, and other forms of affect permeate many aspects of learners' lives, as reflected in the following principles.

Affect and motivation are interrelated.

How learners feel depends, to a considerable degree, on whether their needs are being met and their goals are being accomplished.[130] You can find numerous examples of this relationship in the three "Emotions" video clips in MyEducationLab. For example, 10-year-old Daniel explains that one common source of anger is "not getting what you want." For 13-year-old Crystal, people will be happy if they "have a boyfriend or girlfriend or if they get one." For 15-year-old Greg, friends and good grades are a source of happiness, and disrupted peer relationships can be a source of anger or sadness.

 Observe how affect and motivation are related in the three "Emotions" videos and in the "Motivation: Early Adolescence" video in the Additional Resources section in Chapter 6 of MyEducationLab.

Affect and motivation are interrelated in other ways as well. Learners pursuing a task they think is interesting experience considerable positive affect, such as pleasure, liking, and excitement, and such feelings can further enhance intrinsic motivation.[131] Positive affect

[127] Ziegert, Kistner, Castro, & Robertson, 2001.

[128] Eccles et al., 1998; Lockhart, Chang, & Story, 2002; Paris & Cunningham, 1996.

[129] Paris & Cunningham, 1996; C. Peterson, Maier, & Seligman, 1993.

[130] B. P. Ackerman, Izard, Kobak, Brown, & Smith, 2007; E. M. Anderman & Wolters, 2006.

[131] Hidi & Anderson, 1992; Hidi & Renninger, 2006; Pekrun, Goetz, Titz, & Perry, 2002; Schiefele, 1998.

DEVELOPMENTAL TRENDS

TABLE 6.3 Motivation at Different Grade Levels

Grade Level	Age-Typical Characteristics	Suggested Strategies
K–2	• Tendency to define teacher-chosen activities as "work" and self-chosen activities as "play" • Rapidly changing interests • Pursuit of interesting and enjoyable activities regardless of expectation for success • Emerging tendency to distinguish between effort and ability as causes for success and failure; belief that high effort is a sign of high ability • Tendency to attribute success to hard work and practice, leading to optimism about what can be accomplished	• Engage students' interest in important topics through hands-on, playlike activities. • Entice students into reading, writing, and other basic skills through high-interest books and subject matter (e.g., animals, superheroes, princes and princesses). • Show students how they've improved over time; point out how their effort and practice have contributed to their improvement.
3–5	• Emergence of fairly stable personal interests • Increasing tendency to observe peers' performance as a criterion for judging one's own performance, resulting in a gradual decline in self-efficacy for overall academic performance • Increasing focus on performance goals • Recognition that effort and ability compensate for each other, that people with lower ability must work harder to succeed • Increasing belief in innate ability as a significant and uncontrollable factor affecting learning and achievement	• Allow students to pursue personal interests in independent reading and writing tasks. • Teach students strategies for tracking their own progress over time. • Demonstrate your own fascination and enthusiasm about classroom topics; communicate that many topics are worth learning about for their own sake. • Identify strengths in every student; provide sufficient support to enable students to gain proficiency in areas of weakness.
6–8	• Increasing interest in activities that are stereotypically "gender appropriate"; decrease in activities considered to be "gender inappropriate" • Noticeable decline in self-efficacy and intrinsic motivation for mastering academic subject matter • Increasing tendency to value activities associated with long-term goals and high expectations for success • Decline in perceived value of many content domains (e.g., English, math, music, sports) • Increasing focus on social goals (e.g., interacting with peers, making a good impression) • Emerging realization that high effort cannot totally make up for low ability, that some tasks may be impossible regardless of effort	• Promote interest in classroom topics by presenting puzzling phenomena and building on students' personal interests. • Relate classroom subject matter to students' long-term goals (e.g., through authentic activities). • Provide opportunities for social interaction as students study and learn (e.g., through role-playing activities, classroom debates, cooperative learning projects). • Focus students' attention on their improvement; minimize opportunities for them to compare their own performance to that of classmates.
9–12	• Increasing integration of certain interests, values, and behaviors into one's *sense of self* (i.e., one's overall beliefs about who one is as a person; see Chapter 7) • Continuing decline in intrinsic motivation to master academic subject matter • Prevalence of performance goals (e.g., getting good grades), rather than mastery goals, for most students • Increase in cheating as a means of accomplishing performance goals • Increasing focus on postgraduation goals (e.g., college, careers); some students have insufficient self-regulation strategies to achieve these goals	• Provide opportunities to pursue interests and values through out-of-class projects and extracurricular activities (e.g., community service work). • Make it possible for students to attain high grades through reasonable effort and effective strategies (e.g., minimize competitive grading practices, such as grading on a curve). • Discourage cheating (e.g., by giving individualized assignments and monitoring behavior during in-class assessments), and impose appropriate consequences when it occurs. • Teach self-regulation strategies that can help students reach their long-term goals (see Chapter 4).

Sources: Blumenfeld et al., 2006; Cizek, 2003; Corpus et al., 2006; Covington, 1992; Dweck & Elliott, 1983; Eccles et al., 1998; Hidi et al., 2004; Jacobs et al., 2002, 2005; Lepper et al., 2005; Nicholls, 1990; Otis et al., 2005; Nolen, 2007; Paley, 1984; Patrick et al., 2002; Schunk & Zimmerman, 2006; Watt, 2004; Wigfield, 1994; Wigfield et al., 1991, 2006; Wigfield et al., 1991; B. L. Wilson & Corbett, 2001; Youniss & Yates, 1999.

comes with high self-efficacy as well. In the "Motivation: Early Adolescence" video clip in MyEducationLab, 12-year-old Claudia offers a simple yet powerful reason for liking math: "I'm good at it." Furthermore, learners' reactions to the outcomes of events will depend on how they *interpret* those outcomes—in particular, whether they hold themselves, other people, environmental circumstances, or something else responsible for what has happened (recall our earlier discussion of attributions).[132]

Affect is closely tied to learning and cognition.

Affect is often an integral part of learning and cognition.[133] For example, while learning how to perform a task, learners simultaneously learn whether or not they like doing it.[134] Problem solving is easier when learners enjoy what they're doing, and successful attempts at learning and problem solving often result in feelings of excitement, pleasure, and pride.[135] In contrast, learners may (like Michael in the opening case) feel frustrated and anxious when they must struggle to master new material, and they may develop a dislike for the subject matter.[136] An exchange between one of my educational psychology students (Brian) and his 16-year-old sister Megan illustrates the effects of mastery and nonmastery on learners' feelings for what they are studying:

Brian: How do you know when you have learned something?

Megan: I know that I have learned something when I get really excited about that topic while I am talking to a person about it. When I haven't learned something I tend to say that I hate it, because I don't understand it. When I am excited and can have a discussion about something is when I know that I fully understand and have studied enough on that topic.[137]

In addition, specific facts and ideas can occasionally evoke emotional reactions, as you'll discover in the following exercise.

SEE FOR YOURSELF
Flying High

As you read each of the following statements, decide whether it evokes positive feelings (e.g., happiness, excitement), negative feelings (e.g., sadness, anger), or no feelings whatsoever. Check the appropriate blank in each case.

	Positive Feelings	Negative Feelings	No Feelings
1. The city of Denver opened DIA, its new international airport, in 1995.	_____	_____	_____
2. In a recent commercial airline crash, ninety passengers and eight crew members lost their lives.	_____	_____	_____
3. A dozen people survived that crash, including a 3-month-old infant found in the rear of the plane.	_____	_____	_____
4. The area of an airplane in which food is prepared is called the *galley*.	_____	_____	_____
5. Several major airlines are offering $69 round-trip fares to Acapulco, Mexico.	_____	_____	_____
6. Those $69 fares apply only to flights leaving at 5:30 in the morning.	_____	_____	_____
7. Some flights between North America and Europe now include two full-course meals.	_____	_____	_____

You probably had little if any emotional reaction to Statements 1 (the opening of DIA) and 4 (the definition of *galley*). In contrast, you may have had pleasant feelings when you read

---

[132] Hareli & Weiner, 2002; Harter, 1999; J. E. Turner, Husman, & Schallert, 2002.

[133] Damasio, 1994; D. K. Meyer & Turner, 2002; Minsky, 2006; Ochsner & Lieberman, 2001.

[134] Zajonc, 1980.

[135] E. M. Anderman & Wolters, 2006; McLeod & Adams, 1989; Snow, Corno, & Jackson, 1996.

[136] C. S. Carver & Scheier, 1990; Stodolsky, Salk, & Glaessner, 1991.

[137] Interview courtesy of Brian Zottoli.

CULTURAL CONSIDERATIONS

Cultural and Ethnic Differences in Motivation

Virtually all children and adolescents have the basic needs we've identified in this chapter. However, the means by which they satisfy their needs, the particular goals they set for themselves, and the attributions they form for their successes and failures vary considerably depending, in part, on the behaviors and values that their culture and society model and encourage. Following are several areas in which researchers have found cultural and ethnic differences.

Achieving a sense of self-worth. In mainstream Western culture, achieving a sense of self-worth often involves *being good* at certain things and also *thinking* that one is good at these things. In such a context, learners are likely to engage in self-handicapping as a means of justifying poor performances. But not all cultures stress the importance of positive self-evaluations. For instance, many people in East Asian cultures (e.g., in Japan) place greater importance on how well other people view an individual as living up to society's high standards for behavior. In such cultures the focus is more likely to be on correcting existing weaknesses—that is, on *self-improvement*—than on demonstrating current strengths.[a]

Achieving a sense of self-determination. Children and adolescents around the world want some autonomy and self-determination, but the amount and forms that autonomy and self-determination take may differ considerably from group to group.[b] For example, adults in some Native American groups (e.g., those living in the Navajo Nation in the southwestern United States) give children more autonomy and control over decision making, and do so at an earlier age, than do many adults in mainstream Western culture.[c] (Recall the See for Yourself exercise "Jack" on p. 92 of Chapter 3.) In contrast, many African American adults who live in low-income neighborhoods give children *less* autonomy than other American adults, apparently as a way of ensuring children's safety in potentially hostile environments.[d]

Addressing the need for relatedness. Researchers have found several cultural differences in how children and adolescents address their need for relatedness. In comparison to other groups, Asian children tend to spend less time socializing with peers and place greater importance on gaining teachers' attention and approval.[e] Furthermore, whereas Asian students are likely to have friends who encourage academic achievement, some students from certain other ethnic groups (boys especially) may feel considerable peer pressure *not* to achieve at high levels, perhaps because high achievement reflects conformity to mainstream Western culture (more on this point in Chapter 7).

An additional factor in how learners address their need for relatedness is their family ties: Children and adolescents from many cultural and ethnic groups (e.g., those from many Native American, Hispanic, and Asian communities, as well as those in some rural European American communities) have especially strong loyalties to family and may have been raised to achieve for their respective communities, rather than just for themselves as individuals. Motivating statements such as "Think how proud your family will be!" and "If you go to college and get a good education, you can really help your community!" are likely to be especially effective for such learners.[f]

Information and events that evoke strong emotional reactions often remain vivid in memory for quite some time. In this reflection in her class journal, written more than a year after terrorists' attacks on the World Trade Center and Pentagon, 12-year-old Amaryth still has strong feelings about the attacks.

Statements 3 (the surviving infant) and 5 (the low fares to Acapulco) and unpleasant feelings when you read Statements 2 (the high number of deaths) and 6 (the dreadful departure time for those Acapulco flights). Your response to Statement 7 (the two full-course meals) may have been positive, negative, or neutral, depending on your previous experiences with airline cuisine.

As learners think about, learn, or retrieve something, their very thoughts and memories may become emotionally charged—a phenomenon known as **hot cognition**. For example, learners might get excited when they read about advances in science that could lead to effective treatments for spinal cord injuries, cancer, AIDS, or mental illness. They may feel sad when they read about living conditions in certain parts of the world. They will, we hope, get angry when they learn about the atrocities committed against African American slaves in the pre–Civil War days of the United States or against millions of Jewish people and members of other minority groups in Europe during World War II.

When information is emotionally charged, learners are more apt to pay attention to it, continue to think about it over a period of time, and repeatedly elaborate on it.[138]

---

[138] Bower, 1994; Heuer & Reisberg, 1992; Schacter, 1999.

The need for relatedness can sometimes be at odds with the need for self-determination. In particular, achieving relatedness can involve doing what *others* want one to do, whereas achieving self-determination involves doing what one *personally* wants to do. Many East Asians resolve this apparent conflict by willingly agreeing to adjust personal behaviors and goals to meet social demands and maintain overall group harmony.[g]

Values and goals.   Most cultural and ethnic groups place high value on getting a good education.[h] However, children and adolescents from some ethnic minority groups may be relatively pessimistic about their chances for future academic and professional success. To some extent, these low expectations may result from perceptions of low *teacher* expectations or from discriminative practices in society.[i] Learners from different ethnic backgrounds may also define academic success differently and so set different goals for themselves. For instance, Asian American students, on average, shoot for higher grades than students in other ethnic groups, in part because they believe their parents expect very high achievement and in part because they place high value on diligence and perseverance while studying.[j]

Even so, Asian American students—and African American students as well—may be more focused on mastery goals (i.e., on truly learning and understanding what they are studying) than European American students.[k] Students raised in cultures that value group achievement over individual achievement (e.g., many Asian, Native American, Mexican American, and Pacific Islander cultures) tend to focus their mastery goals not on how much they alone can improve, but instead on how much they *and their peers* can improve—or in some instances how much their own actions can contribute to the betterment of the larger social group or society.[l] And students from some ethnic backgrounds (e.g., those from some Native American and rural European American communities) may place higher priority on helping their families and communities than on graduating from high school.[m]

Attributions.   Learners' cultural and ethnic backgrounds influence their attributions as well. For instance, students from families with traditional Asian cultural beliefs are more likely to attribute classroom success and failure to unstable factors—effort in the case of academic achievement, and temporary situational factors in the case of appropriate or

inappropriate behaviors—than students brought up in mainstream Western culture.[n] Also, some studies indicate a greater tendency for African American students to develop a sense of learned helplessness about their ability to achieve academic success.[o] To some extent, racial prejudice may contribute to their learned helplessness: Students may begin to believe that because of the color of their skin, they have little chance of success no matter what they do.[p]

[a] Heine, 2007; Li, 2005.
[b] d'Ailly, 2003; Deyhle & LeCompte, 1999; Fiske & Fiske, 2007; Rogoff, 2003.
[c] Deyhle & LeCompte, 1999.
[d] Hale-Benson, 1986; McLoyd, 1998.
[e] Dien, 1998; L. Steinberg, 1996.
[f] Dien, 1998; Fiske & Fiske, 2007; Kağitçibaşi, 2007; Suina & Smolkin, 1994; Timm & Borman, 1997.
[g] Heine, 2007; Iyengar & Lepper, 1999; Kağitçibaşi, 2007; Li & Fischer, 2004.
[h] Fuligni & Hardway, 2004; Gallimore & Goldenberg, 2001; Okagaki, 2001; Spera, 2005.
[i] Eccles et al., 1998; Phalet, Andriessen, & Lens, 2004; Tenenbaum & Ruck, 2007.
[j] Li & Fischer, 2004; L. Steinberg, 1996.
[k] Freeman, Gutman, & Midgley, 2002; Qian & Pan, 2002.
[l] Li, 2005, 2006; Kağitçibaşi, 2007; Kaplan, 1998.
[m] Deyhle & Margonis, 1995; Timm & Borman, 1997.
[n] H. Grant & Dweck, 2001; R. D. Hess, Chih-Mei, & McDevitt, 1987; Li & Fischer, 2004; L. Steinberg, 1996.
[o] Graham, 1989; Holliday, 1985.
[p] S. Sue & Chin, 1983; van Laar, 2000.

And encountering information that conflicts with what they currently know or believe can cause learners considerable mental discomfort, something that Piaget called *disequilibrium* but that many contemporary theorists call **cognitive dissonance**. Such dissonance typically leads learners to try to resolve the inconsistency in some way, perhaps by undergoing conceptual change or perhaps by finding fault with the new information (recall our discussion of *confirmation bias* in Chapter 2).[139] Later on, learners can usually retrieve material with high emotional content more easily than they can recall relatively nonemotional information.[140] It appears that learners' affective reactions to classroom subject matter become integral parts of their network of associations in long-term memory.[141]

Observe a teacher creating cognitive dissonance in the "Properties of Air" video in the Additional Resources section in Chapter 6 of MyEducationLab.

Positive affect can trigger effective learning strategies.

In general, positive affect, such as enjoyment and excitement, leads learners to attend actively to the subject matter at hand, to work hard to make sense of it, and to think creatively

[139] Buehl & Alexander, 2001; Harmon-Jones, 2001; Sinatra & Pintrich, 2003b.
[140] Barkley, 1996; LaBar & Phelps, 1998; Reisberg & Heuer, 1992. Occasionally people may have trouble retrieving highly anxiety-arousing memories. This phenomenon, known as *repression*, is most likely to

occur with very traumatic personal events; for instance, see Erdelyi, 1985; Pezdek & Banks, 1996. It is unlikely to be a factor in the retrieval of academic subject matter.
[141] Bower & Forgas, 2001.

hot cognition Learning or cognitive processing that is emotionally charged.

cognitive dissonance Feeling of mental discomfort caused by new information that conflicts with current knowledge or beliefs.

and with an open mind about it. Positive affect also increases the likelihood that learners will engage in self-regulated learning strategies as they study.[142]

Affect can also trigger certain behaviors.

Learners' emotions often lead them to behave in certain ways. For example, feeling guilty or ashamed about something they've done can lead children and adolescents to make amends for their wrongdoings (more about this point in Chapter 7). Feeling frustrated when attempts to reach important goals are thwarted can lead them to lash out at others.[143] Feeling anxious about an upcoming event can be especially powerful in its influence on behavior, as the next principle reveals.

Some anxiety is helpful, but a lot is often a hindrance.

Imagine you are enrolled in Professor Josiah S. Carberry's course in advanced psychoceramics. Today is your day to give a half-hour presentation on the topic of psychoceramic califractions. You have read several books and numerous articles on your topic and undoubtedly know more about psychoceramic califractions than anyone else in the room. Furthermore, you have meticulously prepared a set of note cards to refer to during your presentation. As you sit in class waiting for your turn to speak, you should be feeling calm and confident. But instead you're a nervous wreck: Your heart is pounding wildly, your palms are sweaty, and your stomach is in a knot. When Professor Carberry calls you to the front of the room and you begin to speak, you have trouble remembering what you wanted to say, and you can't read your note cards because your hands are shaking so much.

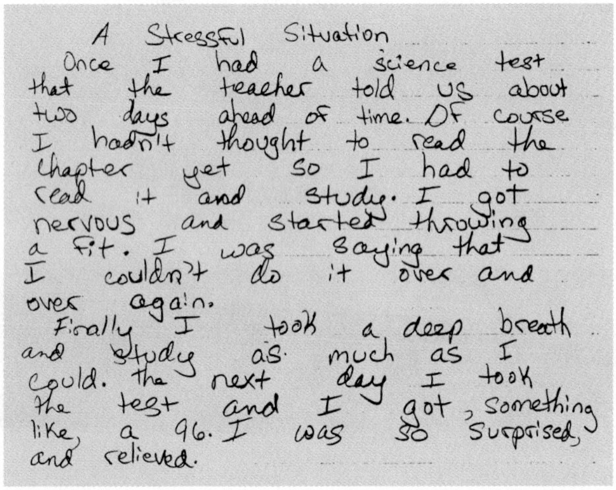

It's not as if you *want* to be nervous about speaking in front of your psychoceramics class. Furthermore, you can't think of a single reason why you *should* be nervous. After all, you're an expert on your topic, you're not having a "bad hair" day, and your classmates are not likely to giggle or throw rotten tomatoes if you make a mistake. So what's the big deal? What happened to the self-assured student who stood practicing in front of the mirror last night? You are a victim of **anxiety**: You have an uncontrollable feeling of uneasiness and apprehension about an event because you're not sure what its outcome will be. This feeling is accompanied by a variety of physiological symptoms, including a rapid heartbeat, increased perspiration, and muscular tension (e.g., a "knot" or "butterflies" in the stomach).

Just as learners have an optimal level of arousal, so, too, do they have an optimal level of anxiety. A small amount of anxiety often improves performance. When it does so, it is known as **facilitating anxiety**. A little anxiety spurs learners into action. For instance, it makes them go to class, read the textbook, do assignments, and study for exams (see Figure 6.4). It also leads learners to approach their classwork carefully and to reflect before making a response.[144] However, a great deal of anxiety usually interferes with effective performance. When it has this counterproductive effect, it is known as **debilitating anxiety**.

At what point does anxiety stop facilitating and begin debilitating performance? Very easy tasks—things that learners can do almost without thinking (e.g., running)—are typically facilitated by high levels of anxiety. But more difficult tasks—those that require considerable thought and mental effort—are best performed with only a small or moderate level of anxiety. A lot of anxiety in difficult situations can interfere with several processes critical for successful learning and performance:[145]

- Paying attention to what needs to be learned
- Processing information effectively (e.g., by organizing or elaborating on it)
- Retrieving and using information and skills that have previously been learned

Anxiety is especially likely to interfere with such processes when a task places heavy demands on working memory or long-term memory—for instance, when a task involves

A Stressful Situation
Once I had a science test that the teacher told us about two days ahead of time. Of course I hadn't thought to read the chapter yet so I had to read it and study. I got nervous and started throwing a fit. I was saying that I couldn't do it over and over again.
Finally I took a deep breath and study as much as I could. The next day I took the test and I got, something like, a 96. I was so surprised and relieved.

FIGURE 6.4 This writing sample, by 14-year-old Loretta, illustrates how anxiety can sometimes improve learning and achievement.

anxiety Feeling of uneasiness and apprehension concerning a situation with an uncertain outcome.

facilitating anxiety Level of anxiety (usually relatively low) that enhances performance.

debilitating anxiety Anxiety of sufficient intensity that it interferes with performance.

---

[142] Fredrickson, 2001; Linnenbrink & Pintrich, 2004; Pekrun et al., 2002.
[143] Berkowitz, 1989; Wisner Fries & Pollak, 2007.
[144] Shipman & Shipman, 1985.

[145] Ben-Zeev et al., 2005; Cassady, 2004; Covington, 1992; Eysenck, 1992; Hagtvet & Johnsen, 1992; I. G. Sarason, 1980.

problem solving or creativity. In such situations learners may be so preoccupied about doing poorly that they can't get their minds on what they need to accomplish.[146]

In general, learners are more likely to experience debilitating anxiety when they face a **threat**, a situation in which they believe they have little or no chance of succeeding. Facilitating anxiety is more common when learners face a **challenge**, a situation in which they believe they can probably achieve success with a significant yet reasonable amount of effort.[147]

Children and adolescents are apt to have some degree of anxiety, either facilitating or debilitating, about many of the following:[148]

- **A situation in which physical safety is at risk.** For example, they will understandably feel anxious if violence is common in their school or neighborhood.
- **A situation in which self-worth is threatened.** For example, they may feel anxious when someone makes unflattering remarks about their race or gender.
- **Physical appearance.** For example, they may be concerned about being too fat or thin or about reaching puberty either earlier or later than peers.
- **A new situation.** For example, they may experience uncertainty when moving to a new school district.
- **Judgment or evaluation by others.** For example, they may worry about receiving a low grade from a teacher or about being liked and accepted by peers.
- **Frustrating subject matter.** For example, they may have considerable anxiety about mathematics if they've had difficulty tackling mathematical concepts and problems in the past.
- **Excessive classroom demands.** For example, they are apt to feel anxious when teachers expect them to learn a great deal of material in a very short time.
- **Classroom tests.** For example, some students panic at the mere thought of having to take a test, and many students are exceedingly anxious about high-stakes tests that affect their chances for promotion or graduation.
- **The future.** For example, adolescents may worry about how they will make a living after they graduate from high school.

Learners' particular concerns change somewhat as they grow older. Table 6.4 describes developmental trends in anxiety, as well as in affect more generally, across childhood and adolescence.

Different cultures nurture different emotional responses.

Many human emotions—especially joy, sadness, fear, anger, disgust, and surprise—are seen even in young infants and so are undoubtedly part of our genetic heritage.[149] Nevertheless, different cultural groups have different views about what kinds of emotions and emotional reactions are appropriate, leading to differences in how they socialize growing children. The Cultural Considerations box "Cultural and Ethnic Differences in Affect" (p. 216) describes the kinds of cultural diversity researchers have observed. We turn our attention now to how one very important aspect of our own society and culture—*school*—can have positive influences on children's and adolescents' motivation and affect.

PROMOTING MOTIVATION AND POSITIVE AFFECT

As the concept of *situated motivation* reminds us, teachers' behaviors and the nature of classroom lessons and activities *do* make a difference in the extent to which students are motivated to learn and achieve at school.[150] Some instructional strategies stimulate intrinsic motivation

[146] Eysenck, 1992; Matthews, Zeidner, & Roberts, 2006; McLeod & Adams, 1989; Tobias, 1985; J. C. Turner, Thorpe, & Meyer, 1998.
[147] Combs, Richards, & Richards, 1976; Csikszentmihalyi & Nakamura, 1989; Deci & Ryan, 1992.
[148] Ashcraft, 2002; Cassady, 2004; Chabrán, 2003; Covington, 1992; DuBois, Burk-Braxton, Swenson, Tevendale, & Hardesty, 2002; Harter, 1992; Hembree, 1988; N. J. King & Ollendick, 1989; Phelan, Yu, & Davidson, 1994; I. G. Sarason, 1980; S. B. Sarason, 1972; Stipek, 1993; Stodolsky et al., 1991; Wigfield & Meece, 1988; K. M. Williams, 2001a.
[149] W. A. Collins, 2005.
[150] L. W. Anderson & Pellicer, 1998; J. T. Guthrie et al., 2004; Kumar et al., 2002; Legault, Green-Demers, & Pelletier, 2006; Murdock, 1999.

threat Situation in which a learner believes there is little or no chance of success.

challenge Situation in which a learner believes that success is possible with sufficient effort.

DEVELOPMENTAL TRENDS

TABLE 6.4   Anxiety and Other Forms of Affect at Different Grade Levels

Grade Level	Age-Typical Characteristics	Suggested Strategies
K–2	• Possible culture shock and intense anxiety upon beginning school, especially if students have had few or no preschool experiences • Possible separation anxiety when parents first leave the classroom (especially in the first few days of kindergarten) • Reduced anxiety when teachers and other adults are warm and supportive • Only limited control of overt emotional behaviors (e.g., may cry easily if distressed or act impulsively if frustrated)	• Ask parents about routines and procedures followed at home; when appropriate, incorporate them into classroom procedures. • If possible, provide an opportunity for students to meet you a few days or weeks before school begins. • Be warm, caring, and supportive with all students (but check school policies about hugs and other forms of physical affection). • Address inappropriate behaviors gently but firmly (see Chapter 9).
3–5	• Increasing control of overt emotional behaviors • Emergence of math anxiety for some students, especially if they are given little support or assistance with math tasks • Tendency for close friends (especially girls) to talk about and dwell on negative emotional events; continues into adolescence • Possible stress as a result of others' racist and sexist behaviors (e.g., racial slurs, unkind remarks about emerging sexual characteristics); continues into adolescence	• Monitor students' behaviors for subtle signs of serious anxiety or depression; talk with students privately if they are anxious or upset, and consult with the school counselor if necessary. • Ensure that students master basic concepts and procedures before proceeding to more complex material that depends on those concepts and procedures (especially important in teaching math, a subject area in which advanced knowledge and skills build on more basic concepts and skills). • Insist on respect for all class members' characteristics, feelings, and backgrounds; do not tolerate racist or sexist actions.
6–8	• General decline in positive emotions; extreme mood swings, partly as a result of hormonal changes accompanying puberty • Increased anxiety and potential depression accompanying the transition to middle school or junior high school • Decrease in enjoyment of school (especially for boys) • Increasing concern about how one appears to others (*imaginary audience*; see Chapter 7)	• Expect mood swings, but monitor students' behavior for signs of long-term depression. • Make a personal connection with every student; express confidence that students can succeed with effort, and offer support to facilitate success. • Design activities that capture students' interest in the subject matter; relate topics to students' personal lives and goals. • Provide opportunities for students to form friendships with classmates (e.g., cooperative group projects).
9–12	• Continuing emotional volatility (especially in grades 9 and 10) • Increasing ability to reflect on and control overt emotional reactions, due in part to ongoing brain maturation • Considerable anxiety if transition to a secondary school format has been delayed until high school • Susceptibility to serious depression in the face of significant stress • Increasing prevalence of debilitating anxiety regarding tests, especially high-stakes tests • Feelings of uncertainty about life after graduation	• Be especially supportive if students have just made the transition from an elementary school format (e.g., show personal interest in students' welfare, teach effective study skills). • Take seriously any signs that a student may be considering suicide (e.g., overt or veiled threats, such as "I won't be around much longer"; actions that indicate "putting one's affairs in order," such as giving away prized possessions). • Give frequent classroom assessments so that no single test score is a "fatal" one; help students prepare for high-stakes tests. • Present multiple options for postgraduation career paths.

Sources: Arnett, 1999; Ashcraft, 2002; Benes, 2007; Chabrán, 2003; DuBois et al., 2002; Eccles & Midgley, 1989; Elkind, 1981; Gentry, Gable, & Rizza, 2002; K. T. Hill & Sarason, 1966; Hine & Fraser, 2002; Kerns & Lieberman, 1993; Kuhl & Kraska, 1989; Lapsley, 1993; Larson & Brown, 2007; Larson, Moneta, Richards, & Wilson, 2002; Midgley, Middleton, Gheen, & Kumar, 2002; Roderick & Camburn, 1999; A. J. Rose, 2002; Rudolph, Lambert, Clark, & Kurlakowsky, 2001; Snow et al., 1996; Spear, 2000; Wiles & Bondi, 2001.

by addressing students' basic needs. Others lead students to think about classroom subject matter in ways that also foster intrinsic motivation. Still others generate feelings and emotions—affect—that enhance students' learning and classroom performance.

Fostering Intrinsic Motivation by Addressing Students' Basic Needs

As we've discovered, students are more likely to use effective learning strategies—and therefore more likely to understand and remember classroom subject matter, apply what they've

FIGURE 6.5 Examples of how teachers might generate situational interest in various content domains

Art: Have students make a mosaic from items they've found on a scavenger hunt around the school building.

Biology: Have class members debate the ethical implications of conducting medical research on animals.

Creative writing: Ask students to write newspaper-like restaurant reviews of the school cafeteria or neighborhood fast-food restaurants.

Geography: Present household objects not found locally, and ask students to guess where they might be from.

Health education: In a lesson about alcoholic beverages, have students role-play being at a party and being tempted to have a beer or wine cooler.

History: Have students read children's perspectives of historical events (e.g., Anne Frank's diary during World War II, Zlata Filipovic's diary during the Bosnian War).

Mathematics: Have students play computer games to improve their automaticity for number facts.

Music: In a unit on musical instruments, let students experiment with a variety of simple instruments.

Physical education: Incorporate steps from hip-hop, swing, or country line dancing into an aerobics workout.

Physical science: Have each student make several paper airplanes and then fly them to see which design travels farthest.

Reading: Turn a short story into a play, with each student taking a part.

Spelling: Occasionally depart from standard word lists, instead asking students to learn how to spell the names of favorite television shows or classmates' surnames.

Sources: Some ideas derived from Brophy, 1986; Lepper & Hodell, 1989; McCourt, 2005; Spalding, 1992; Stipek, 1993; Wlodkowski, 1978.

learned to new situations, and undergo appropriate conceptual change—if they are intrinsically rather than extrinsically motivated. Teachers are most likely to promote intrinsic motivation when classroom activities address one or more of students' basic psychological needs. Following are several strategies that are apt to address these needs.

Conduct stimulating lessons and activities.

One essential strategy for keeping students engaged and on task in the classroom is to conduct lessons that address students' basic need for arousal. Educational psychologists have identified numerous ways of provoking situational interest in classroom subject matter, and many of them work by satisfying students' need for either cognitive or physical stimulation. For instance, teachers can do the following:[151]

- Model their own excitement and enthusiasm about classroom topics.
- Occasionally incorporate novelty, variety, fantasy, and mystery into lessons and procedures.
- Encourage students to identify with historical figures or fictional characters and to imagine what these people might have been thinking or feeling.
- Provide opportunities for students to respond actively to the subject matter, perhaps by manipulating and experimenting with physical objects, creating new products, discussing controversial issues, or teaching something they've learned to peers.

In the "Motivation: Early Adolescence" video clip in MyEducationLab, 12-year-old Claudia explains how much she enjoys interacting with school subject matter:

>   **Adult:** What do you like best about school?
>   **Claudia:** I like to do projects. Like creative ones where you get to do, like, make models of things. And if you are in a group, then you get to get more ideas. Sometimes the teacher will start you out a little, but then you get to do most of it.
>   **Adult:** What kinds of things interest you in school?
>   **Claudia:** Um . . . like math and science. . . . You get to interact with them a little bit. That's always fun.

Figure 6.5 presents examples of how teachers might generate situational interest, and thereby promote intrinsic motivation, in a variety of content domains.

 Observe Claudia's eagerness for hands-on activities and social interaction in the "Motivation: Early Adolescence" video in the Additional Resources section in Chapter 6 of MyEducationLab.

---

[151] Andre & Windschitl, 2003; Brophy, 1987, 2004; Brophy & Alleman, 1991; Certo, Cauley, & Chafin, 2002; Chinn, 2006; Flum & Kaplan, 2006; Hidi & Renninger, 2006; Lepper & Hodell, 1989; Levstik, 1994; Zahorik, 1994.

CULTURAL CONSIDERATIONS

Cultural and Ethnic Differences in Affect

Researchers have seen consistent cultural differences in several aspects of affect: emotional expressiveness, views about appropriate emotions, extent to which cognitive dissonance occurs, and sources of anxiety.

Emotional expressiveness. On average, cultural groups differ in the degree to which they show their feelings in their behaviors and facial expressions. For example, whereas Americans and Mexicans are often quite expressive, people from East Asian cultures tend to be more reserved.[a] Considerable variability exists in any large society, of course. For instance, in one study with Americans, people of Irish ancestry were more apt to reveal their feelings in their facial expressions than were people of Scandinavian ancestry.[b]

The emotion for which cultural differences are most prevalent is anger. Mainstream Western culture encourages children to act and speak up if someone infringes on their rights and needs, and expressing anger in a nonviolent way is considered quite acceptable. In many southeast Asian cultures, however, any expression of anger is viewed as potentially undermining adults' authority or disrupting social harmony.[c]

Views about appropriate ways to feel. Children brought up in some cultural groups, including many Buddhist groups and certain Native American and Pacific Islander communities, are encouraged not even to *feel* anger.[d] As an illustration, if a child growing up in the Tamang culture of Nepal is unfairly embarrassed or accused, he or she might respond, "Tilda bomo khaba?" ("Why be angry?"). After all, the event has already occurred and being angry about it serves no purpose.[e]

Even seemingly "positive" emotions are not always viewed favorably. Some cultures that place high priority on social harmony discourage children from feeling pride about personal accomplishments, because such an emotion focuses attention on an individual rather than on the overall group.[f] And for some cultural groups, joy and happiness can often be too much of a good thing. For instance, many Chinese and Japanese advocate striving for contentment and serenity—relatively calm emotions—rather than joy.[g]

Cognitive dissonance as a motivator. For many learners, encountering two conflicting, seemingly opposite ideas causes what Piaget called *disequilibrium* and contemporary motivation theorists call *cognitive dissonance*—a form of mental discomfort that spurs learners to resolve the discrepancy in

Protect and enhance students' self-efficacy and overall sense of competence and self-worth.

Observe efficacy-enhancing feedback in the "Author's Chair" video in the Additional Resources section in Chapter 6 of MyEducationLab.

Simply telling students they are "good" or "smart" or "nice" is unlikely to boost a low sense of self-worth.[152] Furthermore, vague, abstract statements such as "You're special" have little meaning in the concrete realities of young children.[153] A more effective approach is to enhance students' self-efficacy for specific activities and tasks. As students become increasingly confident about their abilities in particular domains, they may also gain more confidence about their overall competence and worth.[154]

As we learned earlier, learners' own past successes in an activity enhance their self-efficacy for the activity. Their previous successes are most likely to increase their self-confidence when they realize that *they themselves* have been responsible for their successes—that is, when they attribute their performance to their own effort and ability.[155] Teachers can play a role here by drawing students' attention to their successes either in written form (e.g., see Figure 6.6) or by pointing out strengths in daily interactions. In the "Author's Chair" video clip in MyEducationLab, a second-grade teacher identifies particular strengths in a short story written by 8-year-old Liz. For instance, she says, "I could just *see* Liz hitting that pie thing in her face. Very well said."

But how do students acquire self-efficacy for a task they have never tried? As mentioned earlier, words of encouragement ("You can do it, I *know* you can!") can sometimes be helpful over the short run. But a more powerful approach is to show students that peers very

---

[152] Crocker & Knight, 2005; Katz, 1993; Marsh & Craven, 1997.
[153] McMillan, Singh, & Simonetta, 1994.
[154] Bong & Skaalvik, 2003; Harter, 1999; Swann, Chang-Schneider, & McClarty, 2007.
[155] Pintrich & Schunk, 2002.

some way. Not all cultural groups are bothered by logical conflicts, however. When I was in China a few years ago, I was struck by how often people described something as being both one thing and also its opposite. Researchers report that many East Asians are quite tolerant and accepting of logical contradictions.[h]

Sources of anxiety. Learners from different cultural backgrounds may have somewhat different sources of anxiety. For instance, some children and adolescents from Asian American families may feel so much family pressure to perform well in school that they often experience debilitating test anxiety.[i] And youngsters who are recent immigrants to a new country are frequently anxious about a variety of things: how to behave, how to interpret others' behaviors, how to make friends, and, more generally, how to make sense of the strange new culture in which they now find themselves (recall the discussion of *cultural mismatch* in Chapter 3).[j]

Anxiety may be at the root of a phenomenon known as **stereotype threat**, which can lead students from stereotypically low-achieving ethnic groups to perform more poorly on classroom assessments than they otherwise would perform simply because they are aware that their group traditionally *does* do poorly.[k] When students are aware of the unflattering stereotype, and especially when they believe that the task they are performing reflects their ability in an important domain, their heart rate and other physiological correlates of anxiety go up and their performance goes down.[l] We are more likely to see the negative effects of stereotype threat when students interpret their performance on a task as an evaluation of their competence or overall self-worth.[m] Furthermore, stereotype threat is more apt to occur when students have an entity view of ability—a belief that ability is relatively fixed and permanent—rather than an incremental view.[n]

[a] Camras, Chen, Bakeman, Norris, & Cain, 2006; P. M. Cole & Tan, 2007; Morelli & Rothbaum, 2007.
[b] Camras et al., 2006; P. M. Cole, Tamang, & Shrestha, 2006; Tsai & Chentsova-Dutton, 2003.
[c] Mesquita & Leu, 2007; Morelli & Rothbaum, 2007; Zahn-Waxler, Friedman, Cole, Mizuta, & Hiruma, 1996.
[d] P. M. Cole, Bruschi, & Tamang, 2002; P. M. Cole et al., 2006; Solomon, 1984.
[e] P. M. Cole et al., 2002, p. 992.
[f] Eid & Diener, 2001.
[g] P. M. Cole & Tan, 2007; Mesquita & Leu, 2007.
[h] Heine, 2007; Norenzayan, Choi, & Peng, 2007; Peng & Nisbett, 1999.
[i] Pang, 1995.
[j] P. M. Cole & Tan, 2007; Dien, 1998; Igoa, 1995.
[k] K. E. Ryan & Ryan, 2005; J. L. Smith, 2004; Steele, 1997.
[l] Aronson et al., 1999; McKown & Weinstein, 2003; Osborne & Simmons, 2002.
[m] Davies & Spencer, 2005; Huguet & Régner, 2007; McKown & Weinstein, 2003.
[n] Ben-Zeev et al., 2005; Dweck et al., 2004.

similar to themselves have successfully mastered the task at hand.[156] For example, in one research study,[157] elementary school children having trouble with subtraction were given 25 subtraction problems to complete. Children who had seen another student successfully complete the problems got an average of 19 correct, whereas those who saw a teacher complete the problems got only 13 correct, and those who saw no model at all solved only 8.

Ideally, learners should have a reasonably accurate sense of what they can and cannot accomplish, putting them in a good position to capitalize on their strengths, address their weaknesses, and set realistic goals.[158] Yet a tad of overconfidence can be beneficial, in that it entices learners to take on challenging activities that will help them develop new skills and abilities.[159] Within this context, it is often useful to distinguish between *self-efficacy for learning* ("I can learn this if I put my mind to it") and *self-efficacy for performance* ("I already know how to do this").[160] Self-efficacy for learning (for what one can *eventually* do with effort) should be on the optimistic side, whereas self-efficacy for performance should be more in line with current ability levels.

The Classroom Strategies box "Enhancing Self-Efficacy and Self-Worth" provides several examples of how teachers can boost students' self-efficacy for classroom subject matter and more general beliefs about their competence. Teachers should keep in mind, however, that academic achievement isn't necessarily the most important thing affecting students' sense of self-worth. For many children and adolescents, such factors as physical appearance, peer approval, and social success are more influential.[161] To the extent

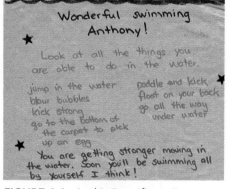

FIGURE 6.6 In this "certificate," a swimming teacher gives 5-year-old Anthony concrete feedback about skills he has mastered.

stereotype threat Awareness of a negative stereotype about one's own group and accompanying uneasiness that low performance will confirm the stereotype; leads (often unintentionally) to a reduction in performance.

[156] Schunk, 1983, 1989b.
[157] Schunk & Hanson, 1985.
[158] Försterling & Morgenstern, 2002; J. Wang & Lin, 2005.
[159] Assor & Connell, 1992; Lockhart et al., 2002; Pajares, 2005.
[160] Lodewyk & Winne, 2005; Schunk & Pajares, 2004.
[161] Eccles et al., 1998; Rudolph et al., 2005.

CLASSROOM STRATEGIES

Enhancing Self-Efficacy and Self-Worth

- **Teach basic knowledge and skills to mastery.**

  A high school biology teacher makes sure all students clearly understand the basic structure of DNA before moving to mitosis and meiosis, two topics that require a solid understanding of DNA's makeup.

- **Define success in terms of task accomplishment or improvement, not in terms of performance relative to others.**

  A second-grade teacher and one of her students meet to discuss items in the student's end-of-year portfolio. They identify several ways in which the student's writing has improved during the past year. (This example is depicted in the "Portfolio" video clip in the Additional Resources section in Chapter 6 of MyEducationLab.)

- **Assure students that they can be successful, and remind them that others like themselves have succeeded before them.**

  Students in beginning band express frustration about learning to play their instruments. Their teacher reminds them that students in last year's beginning band, like themselves, started out with little knowledge but eventually mastered their instruments.

- **Have students see successful peer models.**

  The students in beginning band class hear the school's advanced band (last year's beginning band class) play a medley from the musical *Cats*.

- **Assign large, complex tasks as small-group activities.**

  A middle school teacher has students work in groups of three or four to write research papers about early colonial life in North America. The teacher makes sure that the students in each group collectively have the skills in library research, writing, word processing, and art necessary to complete the task. She also makes sure that every student has unique skills to contribute to the group effort.

- **When negative feedback is necessary, present it in a way that communicates competence and the ability to improve.**

  A third-grade teacher tells a student, "I can see from the past few assignments that you're having trouble with long division. I think I know what the problem is. Here, let me show you what you need to do differently."

- **Promote mastery of challenging tasks—tasks at which students can succeed only with effort and perseverance.**

  A physical education teacher tells her students, "Today we've determined how far each of you can go in the broad jump. We will continue to practice the broad jump a little bit every week. Let's see if each one of you can jump at least two inches farther when I test you again at the end of the month."

Sources: Bandura, 1997, 2000; R. Butler, 1998a; Covington, 1992; Deci & Ryan, 1985; Graham & Golen, 1991; Pintrich & Schunk, 2002; Schunk, 1983.

A Book That canged me

The Book that canged me was At The Plat With Ken Jriffey Jr. This Book canged me because it was my first book that had over onehondred pagis after that I read On The Cort With Mikeol Jorden. I asow liked it because it was by Matt Crister the frist spotswiter for Kids.

FIGURE 6.7 In writing about "A Book That Changed Me," 8-year-old Anthony expresses pride in reading his first book of more than 100 pages. Also notice Anthony's personal interest in sports: One book (*At the Plate*) involves baseball; the other (*On the Court*) involves basketball.

 Observe Elena's and Greg's desire for challenge in the middle childhood and late adolescence "Motivation" videos in the Additional Resources section in Chapter 6 of MyEducationLab.

possible, then, teachers should help students achieve success in the nonacademic as well as academic aspects of their lives.

Present challenges that students can realistically accomplish.

Among the most effective strategies for promoting self-efficacy, self-worth, and, indirectly, intrinsic motivation is the final one listed in the Classroom Strategies box: *Promote mastery of challenging tasks.* Not only do challenges promote cognitive development (see Chapter 5), but in addition students who take on and master challenges experience considerable satisfaction and pride in their accomplishments.[162] The artifact in Figure 6.7 reveals 8-year-old Anthony's pride about finishing his first 100-page book.

Challenges have another advantage as well: They heighten students' interest in the subject matter.[163] The middle childhood and late adolescence "Motivation" video clips in MyEducationLab both reveal students' desire for challenge at school. For instance, when 15-year-old Greg is asked what things encourage him to do well at school, he says, "The challenge. If it's a really hard class, then I . . . I will usually try harder in harder classes." Once students are intrinsically motivated to learn about and master a topic, they are apt to pursue further challenges of their own accord. They also exhibit considerable persistence in the face of difficulty—in part because earlier successes have led to greater self-efficacy—and they continue to remain interested even when they make frequent errors.[164] As you can see, then,

---

[162] Clifford, 1990; Csikszentmihalyi & Nakamura, 1989; Deci & Ryan, 1992; Shernoff, Knauth, & Makris, 2000; J. C. Turner, 1995.

[163] Deci & Ryan, 1992; S. D. Miller & Meece, 1997; N. E. Perry, Turner, & Meyer, 2006; J. C. Turner, 1995.
[164] Covington, 1992; Deci, 1992; Harter, 1992.

challenges, self-efficacy, and intrinsic motivation mutually enhance one another, leading to a "vicious" cycle of the most desirable sort.

When are learners most likely to take on new and potentially risky challenges? Conditions such as the following appear to be optimal:[165]

- Standards for success are realistic for each individual.
- Scaffolding is sufficient to make success possible.
- There are few, if any, penalties for errors.
- The same rewards cannot be obtained by engaging in easier tasks, *or* rewards are greater for challenging tasks than they are for easy ones.
- Learners attribute their success to their own ability, efforts, and strategies.

Teachers should keep in mind, however, that the school day shouldn't necessarily be one challenge after another. Such a state of affairs would be absolutely exhausting and probably quite discouraging as well. Instead, teachers should strike a balance between relatively easy tasks, which will boost students' self-confidence over the short run, and the challenging tasks so critical for longer-term self-efficacy and self-worth.[166]

Give students control over some aspects of classroom life.

When students have some sense of autonomy about events at school—in other words, when they have a sense of self-determination—they are more likely to be intrinsically motivated to engage in academic and extracurricular activities, use skills acquired at school in out-of-school settings, and stay in school until graduation.[167] Naturally, teachers can't give students total freedom about what they can and cannot do in the classroom. Nevertheless, teachers can do several things to enhance students' sense of self-determination about school-related tasks and assignments. For one thing, they can let students make decisions, either individually or as a group, about some or all of the following:[168]

- Rules and procedures to make the class run more smoothly
- Specific topics for research or writing projects
- Specific works of literature to be read
- Due dates for some assignments
- The order in which specific tasks are done during the school day
- Ways of achieving mastery of a particular skill or of demonstrating that it has been mastered (e.g., see Figure 6.8)
- Criteria by which some assignments will be evaluated

To the extent that students can make choices about such matters, they are more likely to be interested in what they are doing, to work diligently and persistently, and to take pride in their work.[169] Furthermore, students who are given choices—even students with serious behavior problems—are less likely to misbehave in class.[170]

In some situations students' choices can be almost limitless. For example, in a unit on expository writing, a wide variety of student-selected research topics might be equally appropriate. In other situations teachers may need to impose certain limits on the choices students make. For example, if a teacher allows a class to

Choose One!

SCIENCE FICTION BOOK PROJECTS

_____ Write a "Dear Abby" letter from one of the main characters, in which he or she asks for advice on solving his or her main problem. Then answer the letter.

_____ Draw a time line of the main events of the book.

_____ Create a comic book or a comic strip page that features a major scene from the book in each box.

_____ Make a collage of objects and printed words from newspapers and magazines that give the viewer a feeling for the mood of the book.

_____ Your book probably takes place in an unusual or exotic setting, so illustrate and write a travel brochure describing that location.

_____ Imagine yourself as a scientist who has been asked to explain the unusual events in the book. Write up a report in scientific style.

_____ With other students who have read the same book, plan a bulletin board display. Write a plot summary; character and setting descriptions; discussions of special passages. Each group member must contribute one artistic piece—for example, new book cover, bookmark, poster, banner, some of the ideas listed above. Arrange the writing and artwork under a colorful heading announcing the book.

FIGURE 6.8 By offering several options for demonstrating understanding of a science fiction book, a sixth-grade language arts teacher enhances students' sense of self-determination.

[165] Brophy & Alleman, 1992; Clifford, 1990; Corno & Rohrkemper, 1985; Deci & Ryan, 1985; Dweck & Elliott, 1983; Stipek, 1993.

[166] Spaulding, 1992; Stipek, 1993, 1996.

[167] Hagger, Chatzisarantis, Barkoukis, Wang, & Baranowski, 2005; Hardré & Reeve, 2003; E. J. Langer, 1997; Reeve, Bolt, & Cai, 1999; Shernoff et al., 2000; Standage, Duda, & Ntoumanis, 2003.

[168] Kohn, 1993; Lane, Falk, & Wehby, 2006; Meece, 1994; Stipek, 1993.

[169] Deci & Ryan, 1992; Reeve, 2006; Ross, 1988; J. C. Turner, 1995.

[170] Dunlap et al., 1994; Lane et al., 2006; Powell & Nelson, 1997; B. J. Vaughn & Horner, 1997.

set its own due dates for certain assignments, it might be with the stipulation that the schedule evenly distributes the student and teacher workload over a reasonable time period.

Another way of enhancing students' sense of self-determination is to give them considerable autonomy within their organized extracurricular activities.[171] Ideally, students' extracurricular activities (clubs, theater groups, community service projects, etc.) can provide both the challenges that promote self-efficacy and the autonomy that enhances a sense of self-determination. A teacher who supervises such activities, then, can foster intrinsic motivation—plus the development of initiative and skills in planning and negotiation—by giving students considerable freedom and responsibility in determining the directions the activities take. At the same time, the teacher may need to provide the guidance students need to tackle challenges successfully—for instance, by helping them think through the likely outcomes of various courses of action.

Use extrinsic reinforcers when necessary, but do so in ways that preserve students' sense of self-determination.

Although intrinsic motivation is the optimal situation, extrinsic motivation is certainly better than *no* motivation to learn. Typically teachers encourage extrinsic motivation through praise, stickers, free time, good grades, and other extrinsic reinforcers. A potential problem with using extrinsic reinforcers is that they may undermine intrinsic motivation, especially if students perceive them to be limiting their choices, controlling their behavior, or in other ways undermining their sense of self-determination.[172] Extrinsic reinforcers may also communicate the message that classroom tasks are unpleasant "chores" (why else would a reinforcer be necessary?) rather than activities to be carried out and enjoyed for their own sake.[173]

Extrinsic reinforcers appear to have no adverse effects when they're unexpected (e.g., when students get special recognition for a public service project in the local community) or when they're not contingent on specific behaviors (e.g., when they're used simply to make an activity more enjoyable).[174] They can even be beneficial if used to encourage students not only to do something but also to do it *well*.[175] And if they communicate that students *have* done something well (as a high grade might) or have made considerable improvement, they can enhance students' sense of self-efficacy and competence and focus students' attention on mastering the subject matter.[176]

Sometimes students may initially find a new topic or skill boring or frustrating and therefore need external encouragement to continue.[177] So how can teachers use extrinsic reinforcers while preserving students' sense of self-determination? One strategy is to praise students in a manner that communicates information but does not show an intent to control behavior.[178] Consider these statements as examples:

- "Your description of the main character in your short story makes her come alive."
- "I think you have finally mastered the rolling *R* sound in Spanish."

Another strategy is to teach students to reinforce *themselves* for their accomplishments, a practice that clearly keeps control in students' hands (see the discussion of *self-imposed contingencies* in Chapter 4).

Evaluate students' performance in ways that communicate information rather than control.

In most classrooms teachers have the final word in evaluating students' performance. Unfortunately, such external evaluation can undermine students' sense of self-determination

---

[171] Larson, 2000.

[172] Deci, 1992; Lepper & Hodell, 1989; Reeve, 2006.

[173] B. A. Hennessey, 1995; Stipek, 1993.

[174] Cameron, 2001; Deci, Koestner, & Ryan, 2001; Reeve, 2006.

[175] Cameron, 2001.

[176] Cameron, 2001; Covington, 2000; Hynd, 2003.

[177] Cameron, 2001; Deci et al., 2001; Hidi & Harackiewicz, 2000.

[178] Deci, 1992; R. M. Ryan, Mims, & Koestner, 1983.

and intrinsic motivation, especially if communicated in a controlling manner.[179] Ideally, teachers should present evaluations of students' work not as "judgments" that remind students how they *should* perform but as information that can help them improve their knowledge and skills.[180] In the "Author's Chair" video clip in MyEducationLab, a second-grade teacher creates an environment in which evaluation is an important part of helping students improve. For example, in preparing her class for an activity in which some children will read their stories aloud, she tells the class, "As you listen to a friend, you may want to give them a compliment, or you may want to tell them something that will help them become a better writer."

Observe examples of noncontrolling evaluation in the "Author's Chair" video in the Additional Resources section in Chapter 6 of MyEducationLab.

Help students meet their need for relatedness.

Warm and caring interpersonal relationships are typically among students' highest priorities.[181] Students are more likely to be academically motivated and successful—and more likely to stay in school rather than drop out—when they believe that their teachers and peers like and respect them and when they feel that they truly "belong" in the classroom community.[182]

Teachers simply cannot ignore the high need for relatedness that many students bring to the classroom. In fact, when planning daily lessons and classroom activities, teachers should include opportunities for students to interact with one another—ideally identifying ways to help students learn academic subject matter *and* address their need for relatedness simultaneously.[183] Although some instructional goals can best be accomplished when students work independently, others can be accomplished just as easily (perhaps even more easily) when students work together. Group-based activities, such as discussions, debates, role playing, cooperative learning tasks, and competitions among two or more teams of equal ability, all provide the means through which students can satisfy their need for relatedness while simultaneously acquiring (and possibly co-constructing) new knowledge and skills.[184] Most effective are activities in which all students have something unique to contribute and so can in some way "shine" and gain the admiration of peers.

Interacting with peers—in this case, by passing a note during class—is a high priority for many students.

Virtually all students want good relationships with their teachers as well as their classmates. Thus teachers should show that they like their students, enjoy being with them, and are concerned about their well-being.[185] Teachers can communicate fondness for students in a variety of ways. For instance, teachers can express an interest in students' outside activities and accomplishments or provide extra assistance or a sympathetic ear when needed. Such "caring" messages may be especially important for students from culturally different backgrounds.[186]

The Classroom Strategies box "Addressing the Need for Relatedness" presents and illustrates several strategies for enhancing social relationships in the classroom.

Promoting "Motivating" Cognitions

Addressing the specific cognitive factors affecting motivation can also have a significant impact on students' learning and classroom performance. Following are several recommendations related to such factors.

Relate assignments to students' personal interests, values, and goals.

On some occasions teachers can foster intrinsic motivation by capitalizing on students' existing interests, values, and goals. For instance, teachers can have students apply new skills to authentic tasks that incorporate personal interests (e.g., see Figure 6.9). They can demonstrate how academic subject matter will help students address their present concerns and

[179] Deci & Ryan, 1992; Reeve et al., 2004; Stipek, 1996.
[180] Stipek, 1996.
[181] Dowson & McInerney, 2001; Geary, 1998; Juvonen, 2006.
[182] Goodenow, 1993; Furrer & Skinner, 2003; Hymel et al., 1996; A. M. Ryan & Patrick, 2001.
[183] Wentzel & Wigfield, 1998.
[184] Blumenfeld et al., 2006; Brophy, 1987; Linnenbrink, 2005; Urdan & Maehr, 1995.
[185] Juvonen, 2006; Patrick et al., 2002; Stipek, 1996.
[186] Meehan, Hughes, & Cavell, 2003; Milner, 2006; Phelan, Davidson, & Cao, 1991.

CLASSROOM STRATEGIES

Addressing the Need for Relatedness

- Have students work together on some learning tasks.

  A high school history teacher incorporates classroom debates, small-group discussions, and cooperative learning tasks into every month's activities.

- Continually communicate the message that you like and respect your students.

  A middle school teacher tells one of his students that he saw her dancing troupe's performance at the local mall over the weekend. "I had no idea you were so talented," he says. "How many years have you been studying dance?"

- Praise students privately when being a high achiever is not sanctioned by friends and classmates.

  While reading a stack of short stories his students have written, a high school English teacher discovers that one student—a young woman who, he knows, is quite concerned about looking cool in front of her peers—has written a particularly creative story. On the second page of her story (where the student's classmates won't be likely to see his comment), he writes, "This is great work, Brigitta! I think it's good enough to enter into the state writing contest. I'd like to meet with you before or after school some day this week to talk more about the contest."

- Create a classroom culture in which respect for *everyone's* needs and well-being is paramount.

  When a second-grade teacher overhears two boys making fun of a fellow student who stutters, she discretely pulls them aside, explains that the classmate is extremely self-conscious about his speech and is working hard to improve it, and gently reminds the boys that they, too, have imperfections as well as strengths.

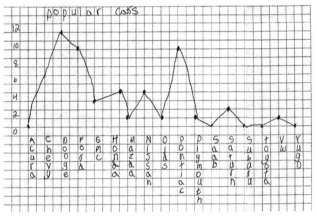

FIGURE 6.9 Teachers can capitalize on students' personal interests by allowing flexibility in the topics students explore as they work on basic skills. Twelve-year-old Connor gained practice in basic research and graphing skills by surveying fellow students about a favorite topic: cars. His findings are shown here.

long-term career goals. And in general, teachers can convey how classroom subject matter can help students make better sense of the world around them.[187]

Focus students' attention more on mastery goals than on performance goals.

To some degree, performance goals are inevitable in today's schools and in society at large.[188] Children and adolescents often use their peers' performance as a criterion for evaluating their own performance. Universities and colleges look for high grades and test scores when screening applicants. And many aspects of the adult world (seeking employment, working in private industry, playing professional sports, etc.) are inherently competitive in nature. Ultimately, however, mastery goals are the ones most likely to lead to effective learning and performance over the long run.[189]

Sometimes mastery goals come from within, especially when students have high interest in, and high self-efficacy for, learning something.[190] Yet classroom practices can also encourage mastery goals.[191] For instance, teachers can do the following:[192]

- Present subject matter that students find valuable in and of itself.
- Show how topics and skills are relevant to students' future personal and professional goals.
- Insist that students *understand*, rather than simply memorize, classroom material.
- Give specific suggestions about how students can improve.
- Encourage students to use their peers not as a reference point for their own progress, but rather as a source of ideas and help.

Focusing attention on mastery goals, especially when these goals relate to students' own lives, may especially benefit students from diverse ethnic backgrounds and students at risk for academic failure.[193]

[187] P. A. Alexander et al., 1994; C. Ames, 1992; Blumenfeld et al., 2006; Brophy & Alleman, 1991; Ferrari & Elik, 2003; Finke & Bettle, 1996.

[188] R. Butler, 1989; Elliot & McGregor, 2000.

[189] For example, see Elliot, Shell, Henry, & Maier, 2005; Gabriele, 2007; Vansteenkiste et al., 2006.

[190] Bandura, 1997; Murphy & Alexander, 2000; Schiefele, 1992.

[191] Church, Elliot, & Gable, 2001; R. S. Newman, 1998; Wentzel, 1999.

[192] C. Ames, 1992; E. M. Anderman & Maehr, 1994; Bong, 2001; Brophy, 2004; Graham & Weiner, 1996; Meece, 1994; Middleton & Midgley, 2002; J. C. Turner, Meyer, et al., 1998; Urdan et al., 2002.

[193] Alderman, 1990; Garcia, 1992; S. D. Miller & Meece, 1997; Wlodkowski & Ginsberg, 1995.

Ask students to set some personal goals for learning and performance.

Students typically work harder toward *self-chosen* goals than toward goals that others have chosen for them,[194] possibly because self-chosen goals help them maintain a sense of self-determination. Although teachers should certainly encourage students to develop long-term goals (e.g., going to college, becoming an environmental scientist), such goals are sometimes too general and abstract to guide immediate behavior.[195] (As an example, look once again at the interview in the Cultural Considerations box on p. 121 of Chapter 4.) Self-chosen goals are especially motivating when they are specific ("I want to learn how to do a cartwheel"), challenging ("Writing a limerick looks difficult, but I'm sure I can do it"), and short-term ("I'm going to learn to count to one hundred in French by the end of the month").[196] By setting and working for a series of short-term, concrete goals—sometimes called **proximal goals**—students get regular feedback about the progress they're making, develop a greater sense of self-efficacy that they can master school subject matter, and achieve at higher levels.[197] Such short-term goals, accompanied by regular *achievement* of these goals, may be especially important for students with a history of academic failure.[198] Students' goals should, of course, be compatible with their teachers' goals for student achievement—an issue we'll address in Chapter 8.

In the piece of writing shown in Figure 6.10, 12-year-old Kelvin reflects on goals he has previously set for himself and identifies a new set of goals. Kelvin's goals are mastery goals: improving his skills in reading, spelling, and writing. Unfortunately, his goals are so vague and general that they will be essentially useless in helping him direct his efforts and monitor his progress. For instance, how will he know when he is a "more advanced speller" or "a lot better at writing"? We cannot necessarily blame Kelvin for his imprecision because, as a sixth grader, he probably hasn't had much practice with either goal setting or self-monitoring. When asking students to set goals for their learning, then, teachers should initially scaffold their efforts, for instance, by providing examples of concrete criteria toward which to strive. As an illustration, rather than become "better at writing," Kelvin might work toward "greater variety in sentence structure." And rather than "more advanced speller," he might shoot for "a maximum of two misspellings per page."

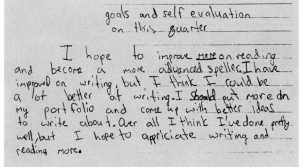

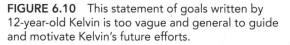

FIGURE 6.10 This statement of goals written by 12-year-old Kelvin is too vague and general to guide and motivate Kelvin's future efforts.

Form and communicate optimistic expectations and attributions.

Teachers typically draw conclusions about their students relatively early in the school year, forming opinions about each one's strengths, weaknesses, and potential for academic success. In many instances teachers size up their students fairly accurately. They know which ones need help with reading skills, which ones have short attention spans, which ones have trouble working together in a cooperative group, and so on, and they can adapt their instruction and assistance accordingly.[199]

Yet even the best teachers sometimes make errors in their judgments, perhaps underestimating students who are members of ethnic minority groups or come from low socioeconomic backgrounds.[200] Furthermore, many teachers have an entity view (rather than incremental view) of intelligence and so perceive students' ability levels to be relatively fixed and stable.[201] Their attributions regarding these "stable" abilities affect their expectations for students' performance, which in turn lead them to treat different students differently. When teachers have high expectations for students, they present more course material and more challenging topics, interact with students more frequently, provide more opportunities for students to respond, persist in their efforts to help students understand, and give more positive feedback. In contrast, when teachers have low expectations for certain students, they

[194] Wentzel, 1999.

[195] Bandura, 1997; Husman & Freeman, 1999.

[196] Alderman, 1990; Brophy, 2004; Locke & Latham, 2006.

[197] Bandura, 1997; Locke & Latham, 2002; Page-Voth & Graham, 1999; Schunk, 1996.

[198] E. S. Alexander, 2006.

[199] Goldenberg, 1992; Good & Brophy, 1994; Good & Nichols, 2001.

[200] Banks & Banks, 1995; McLoyd, 1998.

[201] Oakes & Guiton, 1995; C. Reyna, 2000.

proximal goal Concrete goal that can be accomplished within a short time period; may be a stepping stone toward a longer-term goal.

Teachers who hold high expectations for their students are more likely to give specific feedback about the strengths and weaknesses of students' responses.

Observe teacher messages about internal attributions in the "Author's Chair" video in the Homework and Exercises section in Chapter 6 of MyEducationLab.

present few if any challenging assignments, ask easier questions, offer fewer opportunities for speaking in class, and give less feedback about students' responses.[202]

Teachers' beliefs about students' abilities also affect their attributions for students' successes and failures.[203] Consider the following interpretations of a student's success:

- "You did it! You're so smart!"
- "That's wonderful. Your hard work has really paid off, hasn't it?"
- "You've done very well. It's clear that you really know how to study."
- "Terrific! This is certainly your lucky day!"

And now consider these interpretations of a student's failure:

- "Hmmm, maybe this just isn't something you're good at. Perhaps we should try a different activity."
- "Why don't you practice a little more and then try again?"
- "Let's see whether we can come up with some study strategies that might work better for you."
- "Maybe you're just having a bad day."

All of these comments are presumably intended to make a student feel good. But notice the different attributions they imply—in some cases to uncontrollable abilities (being smart or not "good at" something), in other cases to controllable and therefore changeable behaviors (hard work, lack of practice, effective or ineffective study strategies), and in still other cases to external, uncontrollable causes (a lucky break, a bad day). In the "Author's Chair" video clip in MyEducationLab, a second-grade teacher clearly communicates that acquiring good writing skills is within students' control. For instance, she tells her students, "Our job is to help [Lindsey] become a better writer. Give her, maybe, a compliment and something she can do to be a better writer."

Teachers communicate their attributions for students' performance not only through what they say but also through the emotions they convey.[204] As an example, let's return to the opening case study, in which Michael is initially doing poorly in his eighth-grade algebra class. Imagine that you are Michael's teacher. Imagine, too, that you believe Michael has low mathematical ability: He just doesn't have a "gift" for math. When you see him consistently get Ds and Fs on assignments and quizzes, you might reasonably conclude that his poor performance is beyond his control, and so you communicate pity and sympathy. But now imagine, instead, that you believe Michael has *high* math ability: He definitely has what it takes to do well in your class. When you see his poor marks on assignments and quizzes, you naturally assume he isn't trying very hard. In your eyes, Michael has complete control over the amount of effort he exerts, and so you might express anger or annoyance when he doesn't do well. Some teachers might even punish him for his poor performance.[205]

Most children and adolescents are well aware of their teachers' differing behaviors toward different students and use such behaviors to draw inferences about their own and others' abilities.[206] When they can't figure out why they are doing well or poorly, they may eagerly seek out information to help them explain their performance.[207] If teachers repeatedly give them low-ability messages, they may begin to see themselves as their teachers see them, and their behavior may mirror their self-perceptions.[208] In some cases, then, teachers' expectations and attributions may become **self-fulfilling prophecies**: What teachers expect students to achieve becomes what students actually *do* achieve.[209] Self-fulfilling prophecies

self-fulfilling prophecy Expectation for an outcome that either directly or indirectly leads to the expected result.

[202] Babad, 1993; Brophy, 2006; Good & Brophy, 1994; Graham, 1990; R. Rosenthal, 1994.
[203] Weiner, 2000.
[204] C. Reyna & Weiner, 2001; Weiner, 2000.
[205] C. Reyna & Weiner, 2001.
[206] R. Butler, 1994; Good & Nichols, 2001; Weinstein, 1993.
[207] Weiner, 2000.
[208] Marachi, Friedel, & Midgley, 2001; Murdock, 1999.
[209] For a classic study of the self-fulfilling prophecy, see R. Rosenthal & Jacobson, 1968.

CLASSROOM STRATEGIES

Forming Productive Expectations and Attributions for Student Achievement

- **Look for strengths in every student.**

  A 9-year-old boy who lives in a homeless shelter seems to have learned little about rules for punctuation and capitalization, and his spelling is more typical of a first grader than a fourth grader. Nonetheless, the stories he writes often have unusual plot twists and creative endings. His teacher suspects that his frequent moves from one school district to another have left big gaps in his knowledge of written language and so finds a parent volunteer who can work with him on his writing several times a week.

- **Communicate optimism about what students can accomplish.**

  In September a high school teacher tells his class, "Next spring I will ask you to write a fifteen-page research paper. Fifteen pages may seem like a lot now, but in the next few months we'll work on the various skills you will need to research and write your paper. By April, fifteen pages won't seem like a big deal at all!"

- **Be open to evidence that contradicts your initial assessments of students' abilities.**

  A kindergarten teacher initially has low expectations for the daughter of migrant workers, a girl named Lupita who has previously had little access to books, toys, or other educational resources. When a video camera captures Lupita's strong leadership ability and skill in assembling puzzles, the teacher realizes that Lupita has considerable potential and so works hard to help her acquire the math and literacy skills she will need to be successful in first grade. (See the opening case study "Hidden Treasure" in Chapter 5.)

- **Attribute students' successes to a combination of high ability and such controllable factors as effort and learning strategies.**

  In a unit on basketball, a middle school physical education teacher tells students, "From what I've seen so far, you all have the capability to play a good game of basketball. And it appears that many of you have been regularly practicing after school."

- **Attribute students' failures to factors that are controllable and easily changed.**

  A high school student seeks his teacher's advice about how he might improve his performance in her class. "I know you can do better than you have been, Frank," she replies. "I wonder if part of the problem might be that with your part-time job and all your extracurricular activities, you just don't have enough time to study. Let's sit down before school tomorrow and look at what and how much you're doing to prepare for class."

- **When students fail despite obvious effort, attribute their failures to a lack of effective strategies and then help them acquire such strategies.**

  A student in an advanced science class is having difficulty on the teacher's challenging weekly quizzes. The student works diligently on her science every night and attends the after-school help sessions her teacher offers on Thursdays, yet to no avail. The teacher observes that the student is trying to learn the material by rote—an ineffective strategy for answering the higher-level questions typically on quizzes—and so teaches her strategies that promote more meaningful learning.

- **Remember that teachers can definitely make a difference.**

  The teachers at a historically low-achieving middle school in a poor, inner-city neighborhood meet once a month to learn about teaching strategies that are especially effective with children from low-income families. They are encouraged by the many research studies indicating that children at all socioeconomic levels can achieve at high levels when instruction takes their existing skills into account and when teachers provide reasonable guidance and support. They experiment with various strategies in their own classrooms and share especially effective ones at their group meetings.

Sources: Some ideas based on Brophy, 2006; Carrasco, 1981; Curtis & Graham, 1991; J. A. Langer, 2000; Pressley et al., 1987; Weinstein, Madison, & Kuklinski, 1995.

---

occur most frequently when students are making a significant transition in their schooling (e.g., when they enter first grade or begin junior high school), and they are more common for girls and for students from ethnic minority groups.[210]

Teachers are most likely to facilitate students' learning and motivate them to achieve at high levels when they hold optimistic expectations for students' performance (within realistic limits, of course) and when they attribute students' successes and failures to things over which either students or teachers have control (*students'* effort, *teachers'* instructional methods, etc.). The Classroom Strategies box "Forming Productive Expectations and Attributions for Student Achievement" offers several strategies that can benefit teachers and students alike. The final strategy in the box—*Remember that teachers can definitely make a difference*—is probably the most important one. Teachers must keep in mind an important point about intelligence presented in Chapter 5: Ability can and does change over time, especially when environmental conditions are conducive to such change. For this reason, teachers should take an *incremental view* of students' abilities and continually reassess and modify their expectations and attributions for student achievement as new evidence presents itself.

---

[210] Graham, 1990; Jussim, Eccles, & Madon, 1996; Kuklinski & Weinstein, 2001; Raudenbush, 1984.

Minimize competition.

Competition is widespread in mainstream Western societies, not only in adult activities (e.g., in business and politics) but also in elementary and secondary schools.[211] Schools compare students in a variety of ways. When teachers post "best work" on a bulletin board, they indirectly communicate that other papers are not as good. When teachers grade "on the curve," their grades reflect how students stack up against one another, and only those at the top of the stack are identified as being successful. When students take college aptitude tests, their test scores reflect not what they know and can do but how their performance compares with that of their peers (more on this point in the discussion of *norm-referenced scores* in Chapter 10). Participation in school sports is also competitive, especially at the high school level, in that only students with the best athletic skills can join a team, and only the *best* of the best achieve starting-player status.

Students are apt to be motivated by competition *if* they believe they have a reasonable chance of winning.[212] (For example, earlier I recommended competitions among two or more teams of equal ability as a way of helping students meet their need for relatedness.) But competition can have several negative side effects of which you should be aware:[213]

- It promotes performance goals rather than mastery goals.
- It can lead to undesirable or counterproductive behaviors, such as cheating on quizzes or preventing classmates from getting needed resources for assignments.
- For students who expect to lose, it can lead to self-handicapping.
- For students who *actually* lose, it can promote low self-efficacy and self-worth.
- Because it makes differences among students more obvious, it encourages attributions to ability rather than to effort.

For such reasons, competition ultimately leads to lower achievement for most students. When classroom success is judged on the basis of how well students perform relative to one another rather than on the basis of how much improvement they make, most students earn lower grades, show less creativity, and develop more negative attitudes toward school.[214] Competitive classroom environments may be especially disadvantageous to female students and to students from ethnic minority groups.[215]

Generating Productive Affect

Students learn at high levels not only when they are intrinsically motivated to master classroom subject matter, but also when their emotional states are conducive to productive cognitive processes and behaviors. Here are three recommendations for generating productive affect in the classroom.

A teacher's enthusiasm about classroom topics can be contagious.

Get students emotionally involved in the subject matter.

Academic subject matter certainly doesn't need to be dry and emotionless. On the contrary, students will probably remember more if they have strong feelings about what they are studying, perhaps getting very excited about a scientific discovery or quite angry about social injustices. In addition to presenting subject matter that evokes emotional reactions, teachers can promote hot cognition by revealing their own feelings about a topic. For instance, they might bring in newspaper articles and other outside materials about which they are excited, present material in an enthusiastic or impassioned fashion, and share the particular questions and issues about which they themselves are concerned.[216] And although teachers don't necessarily want to give the impression that schoolwork is all fun and games, they can occasionally incorporate a few gamelike features into classroom tasks and activities.[217] For example, they might as-

[211] C. Ames, 1984.
[212] Deci & Ryan, 1992; Linnenbrink, 2005; Krampen, 1987; Stipek, 1996.
[213] C. Ames, 1984; C. Ames & Ames, 1981; Hagen, 1994; A. J. Martin et al., 2003; Nicholls, 1984; Spaulding, 1992; Stipek, 1993, 1996.

[214] Amabile & Hennessey, 1992; Covington, 1992; Graham & Golen, 1991; Krampen, 1987.
[215] Banks & Banks, 1995; Eccles, 1989; Inglehart, Brown, & Vida, 1994.
[216] Brophy, 2004; R. P. Perry, 1985.
[217] Brophy, 2004.

sign simple crossword puzzles to introduce new spelling words or use a television game show format for a class history review (the game show strategy also addresses students' need for relatedness).

Foster emotional self-regulation.

As the Cultural Considerations box on p. 216 indicates, various cultural groups differ in the extent to which they encourage emotional expressiveness or restraint. Even so, all children and adolescents function better at school when they engage in **emotional self-regulation**— that is, when they keep their emotional reactions, especially negative ones such as sadness and anger, within reasonable limits.[218] In the three "Emotions" video clips in MyEducationLab, 10-year-old Daniel, 13-year-old Crystal, and 15-year-old Greg describe several strategies— reading a book, playing a video game, venting frustrations on someone who will listen without being judgmental, or just sitting down for a while—that they might use to help themselves control their emotions when they get overly excited, angry, or sad.

Observe self-regulation strategies in the three "Emotions" videos in the Additional Resources section in Chapter 6 of MyEducationLab.

Certainly teachers should refer students with severe emotional difficulties to school counselors and other specially trained professionals. But a few simple strategies can help many students cope with the everyday disappointments and frustrations of life:[219]

- Help students identify strategies for minimizing the damage.
- Encourage students to find potential benefits in an unfortunate event—for instance, to treat it as a "wake-up call" or look for the "silver lining."
- Teach students strategies that can help them prevent similar unfortunate events in the future.

Through such coping strategies, students may learn that although they can't always control everything that happens to them, they can control how they *think* about what happens, enabling them to maintain at least some sense of self-determination.[220]

Keep anxiety at a low to moderate level.

As we learned earlier in the chapter, learners work most effectively and productively when they are a little bit anxious (enough to spur them into action) but not overly so. Teachers can address students' concerns about social matters—for instance, students' worries about peer acceptance and respect—by teaching social skills and planning activities that foster positive interactions with peers. Teachers can address students' concerns about their uncertain futures by teaching skills that will be marketable in the adult world and by providing assistance with college applications. But perhaps most importantly, teachers must take steps to ensure that students don't become overly anxious about classroom tasks and subject matter.

Because anxiety (like all emotions) is largely beyond students' immediate control, simply telling them to "Relax" or "Calm down" is unlikely to be effective. The key here is to prevent, rather than "cure," debilitating anxiety. Following are several strategies that should keep students' anxiety at a facilitative level:[221]

- Communicate clear, concrete, and realistic expectations for performance.
- Match instruction to students' cognitive levels and capabilities (e.g., use concrete materials to teach mathematics to students not yet capable of abstract thought).
- Provide supplementary sources of support for learning challenging topics and skills (e.g., additional practice, individual tutoring, a structure for taking notes) until mastery is attained.
- Teach strategies (e.g., effective study skills) that enhance learning and performance.
- Assess students' performance independently of how well their classmates are doing, and encourage students to assess their own performance in a similar manner.
- Provide feedback about specific behaviors, rather than global evaluations of classroom performance.
- Allow students to correct errors, so that no single mistake is ever a "fatal" one.

[218] Labouvie-Vief & González, 2004; Wisner Fries & Pollak, 2007.

[219] C. Peterson, 2006; N. C. Hall, Goetz, Haynes, Stupnisky, & Chipperfield, 2006; Richards, 2004.

[220] This phenomenon is known as *secondary control;* see Rothbaum, Weisz, & Snyder, 1982.

[221] Brophy, 1986; Hattie & Timperley, 2007; K. T. Hill & Wigfield, 1984; McCoy, 1990; I. G. Sarason, 1980; Stipek, 1993; Tryon, 1980; Zeidner, 1998.

emotional self-regulation Process of keeping one's affective states and resulting behaviors within productive, culturally desirable limits.

After students make the transition to middle school or high school, make an extra effort to minimize their anxiety and address their need for relatedness.

Elementary school classrooms are often very warm, nurturing ones in which teachers get to know 20 or 30 students very well. Students in elementary classrooms also get to know *one another* quite well: They often work together on academic tasks and may even see themselves as members of a classroom "family." But somewhere around fifth to seventh grade, many students move from elementary school to a middle school or junior high school. As they do so, they simultaneously encounter several changes in the nature of their schooling:[222]

- The school is larger and has more students.
- Students have several teachers at a time, and each teacher has many students. Teacher–student relationships are therefore more superficial and less personal than in elementary school, and teachers have less awareness of how well individual students are understanding and mastering classroom subject matter.
- There is more whole-class instruction, with less individualized instruction that takes into account each student's academic needs.
- Classes are less socially cohesive. Students may not know their classmates very well and may be reluctant to ask peers for assistance.
- Students have fewer opportunities to make choices about the topics they pursue and the tasks they complete. At the same time, they have more independence and responsibility regarding their learning. For example, they may have relatively unstructured assignments to be accomplished over a two- or three-week period, and they must take the initiative to seek help when they are struggling.
- Teachers place greater emphasis on demonstrating (rather than acquiring) competence. Thus mistakes are more costly for students. (This change reflects a shift from *mastery goals* to *performance goals*.)
- Standards for assigning grades are more rigorous, so students may earn lower grades than they did in elementary school. Grades are often assigned on a comparative and competitive basis, with only the highest-achieving students getting As and Bs.
- High-stakes tests—tests that affect promotion to the next grade level—become increasingly common.

Furthermore, previously formed friendships can be disrupted as students move to new (and perhaps differing) schools.[223] And, of course, students may find the physiological changes that accompany puberty and adolescence unsettling. This "multiple whammy" of changes often leads to decreased confidence, a lower sense of self-worth, less intrinsic motivation, and considerable anxiety. Focus on social relationships increases, academic achievement drops, and some students become emotionally disengaged from the school environment— a disengagement that may eventually result in dropping out of school.[224]

If students remain in an elementary school in early adolescence, rather than moving to a middle school or junior high environment, their attitudes and motivation are more likely to remain positive.[225] By the time they reach ninth grade, however, they almost inevitably make the transition to a secondary school format, where they will experience many of the changes that their peers in other school districts experienced a few grades earlier.[226] Students in lower-income, inner-city school districts are especially at risk for making a rough transition from an elementary to a secondary school format.[227] As an example, recall Anna's rocky start at her large city high school in the opening case study in Chapter 1.

---

[222] Bergamo & Evans, 2005; H. A. Davis, 2003; Eccles & Midgley, 1989; Harter, 1996; Hine & Fraser, 2002; Midgley et al., 2002; Wentzel & Wigfield, 1998; Wigfield et al., 2006.

[223] Pellegrini & Long, 2004; Wentzel, 1999.

[224] Eccles & Midgley, 1989; Gentry et al., 2002; Urdan & Maehr, 1995; Wigfield et al., 1996.

[225] Midgley et al., 2002; Rudolph, Lambert, Clark, & Kurlakowsky, 2001.

[226] Hine & Fraser, 2002; Midgley et al., 2002; Otis et al., 2005; Tomback, Williams, & Wentzel, 2005.

[227] Ogbu, 2003; Roderick & Camburn, 1999.

CLASSROOM STRATEGIES

Easing the Transition to Middle and Secondary School

- **Provide a means through which every student can feel part of a small, close-knit group.**

    During the first week of school, a ninth-grade math teacher establishes *base groups* of three or four students who provide support and assistance for one another throughout the school year. At the beginning or end of every class period, the teacher gives group members five minutes to help one another with questions and concerns about daily lessons and homework assignments.

- **Address students' personal and social needs as well as their academic needs.**

    Early in the school year, while his classes are working on a variety of cooperative learning activities, a middle school social studies teacher schedules individual appointments with each of his students. In these meetings he searches for common interests that he and his students share and encourages the students to seek him out whenever they need help with academic or personal problems. Throughout the semester he continues to touch base with individual students (often during lunch or before or after school) to see how they are doing.

- **Teach students the skills they need to be successful independent learners.**

    After discovering that few of her students know how to take effective notes in class, a high school science teacher distributes a daily "notes skeleton" that guides them through the note-taking process. The skeleton might include headings such as "Topic of the Lesson," "Definitions," "Important Ideas," and "Examples." As students' class notes improve over the course of the school year, she gradually reduces the amount of structure she provides.

- **Assign grades based on mastery (not on comparisons with peers), and provide reasonable opportunities for improvement.**

    A junior high school language arts teacher requires students to submit two drafts of every essay and short story he assigns; he gives students the option of submitting additional drafts as well. He judges the compositions on four criteria: cohesiveness, word usage, grammar, and spelling. He explains and illustrates each of these criteria and gives ample feedback on every draft that students turn in.

Students who make a smooth transition to secondary school are more likely to be academically successful and, as a result, more likely to graduate from high school.[228] The Classroom Strategies box "Easing the Transition to Middle and Secondary School" offers several strategies for teachers at the middle school and high school levels.

Up to this point, we have touched only briefly on those peer relationships that can make such a difference in students' successful transitions to middle schools and high schools. As we turn to personal and social development in the next chapter, we will look at such relationships more closely. We will also identify factors that help or hinder young people in their efforts to establish productive relationships with their age-mates.

SUMMARY

All human beings appear to share certain fundamental needs. In addition to basic needs for food, water, oxygen, and other substances essential for life, people seem to have a need for *arousal*—a need for some degree of physical and cognitive stimulation. They also seem to have needs for *competence, self-worth,* and *self-determination*—needs to believe that they can deal effectively with their environment; are generally good, capable individuals; and can direct the course of life events to some degree. Finally, they have a basic need for *relatedness*—that is, they want to feel socially connected to and gain the love and respect of other people.

Motivation supports learning and achievement in multiple ways. For example, effectively motivated learners pay attention, process information meaningfully, persist in the face of failure, use errors to help them improve their skills, and seek out ever more challenging tasks. Conversely, learning and achievement can foster the development of productive motivational patterns. For instance, when learners discover that they can usually accomplish academic tasks successfully, they bring a sense of self-confidence and a desire to learn into new lessons and activities. Thus motivation and learning go hand in hand, with each playing a crucial role in the development of the other.

Motivation and learning are also intertwined with *affect*, including both the emotions that learners bring to the learning situation and the feelings that instructional materials evoke. For instance, topics that evoke strong feelings (excitement, anger, etc.) tend to be more memorable, but situations that arouse considerable anxiety typically interfere with effective information processing and memory.

The best-case scenario is for a learner to be *intrinsically* motivated to learn and master classroom subject matter; in other words, the learner's motivation results from personal characteristics or is inherent in the task being performed. Yet motivation is not a "switch" that learners can turn on and off at will. Rather, it depends on several cognitive factors—including interests,

[228]Otis et al., 2005; Roderick & Camburn, 1999; Wigfield et al., 1996.

self-efficacy, values, goals, and attributions—that typically evolve only gradually over time.

Even so, teachers' instructional practices clearly do influence students' motivation in the classroom. Many motivational strategies can be summed up in six words: task, autonomy, recognition, grouping, evaluation, and time.[229] This multifaceted "TARGET" approach to motivation is presented in Table 6.5. If you look closely at the entries in the table, you'll find that they reflect many of the concepts we've addressed in this chapter, including the needs for arousal, competence and self-worth, self-determination, and relatedness; cognitive factors such as interests, self-efficacy, expectations, values, goals, and attributions; and affective variables such as hot cognition and anxiety.

TABLE 6.5   Six "TARGET" Principles of Motivation

Principle	Educational Implications	Example
Classroom **tasks** affect motivation.	• Present new topics through tasks that students find interesting, engaging, and perhaps emotionally charged. • Encourage meaningful rather than rote learning. • Relate activities to students' lives and goals. • Provide sufficient support to enable students to be successful.	Ask students to conduct a scientific investigation about an issue that concerns them.
The amount of **autonomy** students have affects motivation, especially intrinsic motivation.	• Give students some choice about what and how they learn. • Teach self-regulation strategies. • Solicit students' opinions about classroom practices and policies. • Have students take leadership roles in some activities.	Let students choose among several ways of accomplishing an instructional objective, being sure that each choice offers sufficient scaffolding to make success likely.
The amount and nature of the **recognition** students receive affect motivation.	• Acknowledge not only academic successes but also personal and social successes. • Commend students for improvement as well as for mastery. • Provide concrete reinforcers for achievement only when students are not intrinsically motivated to learn. • Show students how their own efforts and strategies are directly responsible for their successes.	Commend students for a successful community service project.
The **grouping** procedures in the classroom affect motivation.	• Provide frequent opportunities for students to interact (e.g., cooperative learning activities, peer tutoring). • Plan activities to which all students can make valuable contributions. • Teach the social skills that students need to interact effectively with peers. • Create an atmosphere of mutual caring, respect, and support.	Have students work in small groups to tackle a challenging issue or problem for which there is no single "right" answer.
The forms of **evaluation** in the classroom affect motivation.	• Make evaluation criteria clear; specify them in advance. • Minimize or eliminate competition for grades (e.g., don't grade "on a curve"). • Give specific feedback about what students are doing well. • Give concrete suggestions for how students can improve.	Give students concrete criteria with which they can evaluate the quality of their own writing.
How teachers schedule **time** affects motivation.	• Give students enough time to gain mastery of important topics and skills. • Let students' interests dictate some activities. • Include variety in the school day (e.g., intersperse high-energy activities among more sedentary ones).	After explaining a new concept, engage students in a hands-on activity that lets them see the concept in action.

Sources: J. L. Epstein, 1989; Maehr & Anderman, 1993.

PRACTICE FOR YOUR LICENSURE EXAM

Praising Students' Writing

Mrs. Gaskill's second graders are just beginning to learn how to write the letters of the alphabet in cursive. Every day Mrs. Gaskill introduces a new cursive letter and shows her students how to write it correctly. She also shows them some common errors in writing the letter—for instance, claiming that she's going to make the "perfect *f* " and then making it much too short and crossing the lines in the wrong place—and the children delight in finding her mistakes. After the class explores each letter's shape, Mrs. Gaskill asks her students to practice it, first by writing it in the air using large arm movements and then by writing it numerous times on lined paper.

[229] J. L. Epstein, 1989; Maehr & Anderman, 1993.

Meanwhile, Mrs. Gaskill has decided to compare the effects of two different kinds of praise on the children's performance. She has placed a small sticker on each child's desk, with one color indicating membership in one of two groups. When children in Group 1 write a letter with good form, she gives them a "happy face" token, says "Great" or "Perfect!," and either smiles at them or gives them a pat on the back. When children in Group 2 write a letter with good form at least once, she gives them a happy face token and says something along the lines of "You sure are working hard," "You can write beautifully in cursive," or "You are a natural at this." When children in either group fail to meet her standards for cursive writing, she gives them whatever corrective feedback they need.

Thus the only way in which Mrs. Gaskill treats the two groups differently is in what she says to them when they do well, either giving them fairly cryptic feedback (for Group 1) or telling them that they are trying hard or have high ability (for Group 2). Despite such a seemingly minor difference, Mrs. Gaskill finds that the children in Group 2 say they enjoy cursive writing more, and they use it more frequently in their spelling tests and other writing tasks. Curiously, too, the children in Group 1 often seem disappointed when they receive their "positive" feedback. For instance, on one occasion a girl who writes beautifully but has the misfortune of being in Group 1 asks, "Am *I* a natural at this?" Although the girl consistently gets a grade of "+" for her cursive writing, she never writes in cursive voluntarily throughout the three-week period in which Mrs. Gaskill conducts her experiment.[230]

1. **Constructed-response question**

   Mrs. Gaskill praises all of her students for their performance, yet some kinds of praise seem to be more effective than others.

   A. Identify two sources of evidence to support the claim that students who receive lengthy, specific feedback (Group 2) have more intrinsic motivation to write in cursive than students who receive brief, general feedback (Group 1).

   B. Explain why the praise given to Group 2 might be more motivating than the praise given to Group 1. Base your explanation on contemporary principles and theories of motivation.

2. **Multiple-choice question**

   Which one of the following teacher behaviors in the case is an example of an *attribution*?
   a. Commenting that "You sure are working hard"
   b. Awarding "happy face" tokens for good writing
   c. Giving students a pat on the back for good work
   d. Amusing the students by intentionally writing a letter incorrectly

   Once you have answered these questions, compare your responses with those presented in Appendix A.

FOR FURTHER READING

The following articles from the journal *Educational Leadership* are especially relevant to this chapter. You can find these articles in Chapter 6 of MyEducationLab for this text.

Cushman, K. (2006). Help us care enough to learn. *Educational Leadership, 63*(5), 34–37.

Darling-Hammond, L., & Ifill-Lynch, O. (2006). If they'd only do their work! *Educational Leadership, 63*(5), 8–13.

Koba, S. B. (1996). Narrowing the achievement gap in science. *Educational Leadership, 53*(8), 14–17.

Maierman, N. (1997). Reaching out to grieving students. *Educational Leadership, 55*(2), 62–65.

Ray, K. W. (2006). What are you thinking? *Educational Leadership, 64*(2), 58–62.

Reis, S. M., & Fogarty, E. A. (2006). Savoring reading, schoolwide. *Educational Leadership, 64*(2), 32–36.

Renard, L., & Rogers, S. (1999). Relationship-driven teaching. *Educational Leadership, 57*(1), 34–37.

Tatum, A. W. (2006). Engaging African American males in reading. *Educational Leadership, 63*(5), 44–49.

Vacca, R. T. (2006). They can because they think they can. *Educational Leadership, 63*(5), 56–59.

Vaughan, A. L. (2005). The self-paced student. *Educational Leadership, 62*(7), 69–73.

MYEDUCATIONLAB

Now go to Chapter 6 of MyEducationLab at **www.myeducationlab.com**, where you can:

- Find instructional objectives for the chapter, along with focus questions that can help you zero in on important ideas in the chapter.
- Take a self-check quiz on concepts and principles you've just read about.

- Complete exercises and assignments that can help you more deeply understand the chapter content.
- Read supplementary material that can broaden your knowledge of one or more of the chapter's topics.
- Apply what you've learned to classroom contexts in Building Teaching Skills activities.

---

[230] Study described by Gaskill, 2001.

CHAPTER 7

Personal and Social Development

CASE STUDY   The School Play

The eighth-grade class at Jefferson Middle School is an especially troublesome one. Students are sharply divided into two groups, the "popular" ones and the "unpopular" ones. The popular students have little time or tolerance for low-status peers, and a few of them frequently pick on a small, friendless boy named Peter.

When things get so bad that the faculty considers canceling the annual eighth-grade musical, music teacher Mr. Hughes suggests that "the show must go on" but perhaps not in the usual way. Rather than holding tryouts and selecting only a handful of students as cast members, he proposes that the school have the entire eighth-grade class participate in some way, either in the cast or in scenery construction, costume design, or lighting. "Maybe a group project will pull the class together," he explains. Many of the other teachers are skeptical, but everyone agrees to support Mr. Hughes's project.

Throughout March and April, all 92 members of the eighth-grade class and many teachers work on a production of the musical *You're a Good Man, Charlie Brown.* The sheer ambitiousness of the project and the fact that the class's efforts will be on public display on opening night instill a cohesiveness and class "spirit" that the faculty hasn't seen before. Peter, playing the dog Snoopy, surprises everyone with his talent, and on opening night his classmates give him rave reviews: "Did you see Peter? He was amazing." "I had no idea he was so good." "He was totally cool."[1]

- Middle school students often divide themselves into different social groups, with some groups having higher social status than others. Why might social groups be so important for young adolescents?
- What benefits might the all-class school play have? Why does it pull the class together?

---

[1] Case described by M. Thompson & Grace, 2001, pp. 93–94.

As we discovered in Chapter 6, early adolescence can, for many students, be a time of considerable anxiety. Students must grapple not only with the bodily changes of puberty, but also with disruptions of previous friendships, more superficial interactions with teachers, and higher expectations for academic performance. Self-worth often plummets, at least temporarily, and students are apt to look to their peers for emotional and moral support.[2] Being in a high-status, "popular" group can be a source of comfort, but students can have high status only if some of their peers have *low* status. With the all-class school play, everything changes. Suddenly the students have a common goal, and only by working cooperatively with *all* of their classmates can *any* of them look good.[3]

School is not just a place where children and adolescents acquire thinking skills and master academic subject matter. It is also a place where they acquire beliefs about themselves and strategies for getting along with other people. In other words, school is a place where young people grow personally and socially as well as academically.

As we consider personal and social development in this chapter, we'll discover that with age and experience, young learners construct increasingly sophisticated beliefs about themselves, other people, and society as a whole. Thus children's and adolescents' personal and social understandings are, like their understandings of the physical world, very much *self-constructions*. In our discussion we'll draw from all five of the theoretical perspectives of child and adolescent development we identified in Table 5.1 in Chapter 5 (p. 137).

PERSONALITY AND SENSE OF SELF

All of us have unique qualities that make us different from the people around us. Take a minute to reflect on the qualities that make *you* unique in the following exercise.

SEE FOR YOURSELF
Describing Yourself

On a sheet of paper, list at least 10 adjectives or phrases that describe the kind of person you think you are.

How did you describe yourself? Are you a good student? Are you physically attractive? Are you friendly? likable? moody? smart? funny? uncoordinated? open-minded? Your answers to these questions tell you something about your **sense of self**, your perceptions, beliefs, judgments, and feelings about who you are as a person. If you were able to be relatively objective, your answers also tell you something about your **personality**, your distinctive ways of behaving, thinking, and feeling.

Learners' personalities and sense of self have a significant influence on their adjustment at school and elsewhere. For example, at a typical middle school, students who are outgoing and self-assured may quickly converge to form an "in" crowd, whereas those who are shy and lack self-confidence may keep more to themselves. Students who have a flair for the dramatic, like Peter in the opening case study, may delight in performing for an audience, whereas those who are more reserved and reticent may prefer to stay out of the spotlight.

The following principles describe the nature, origins, and effects of a learner's personality and sense of self.

Heredity and environment interact to shape personality.

In Chapter 5, I introduced the concept of *temperament*, a general tendency to respond to environmental stimuli and events in particular ways. Children seem to have distinct temperaments almost from birth. Some are cheerful and easy to care for, whereas others are

---

sense of self Perceptions, beliefs, judgments, and feelings about oneself as a person.

personality Characteristic ways in which an individual behaves, thinks, and feels.

[2] D. A. Cole et al., 2001; Juvonen, 2006; Levitt, Guacci-Franco, & Levitt, 1993; Wigfield, Byrnes, & Eccles, 2006.   [3] M. Thompson & Grace, 2001.

fussy and demanding. Researchers have identified many temperamental styles that emerge early in life and are relatively enduring, including general activity level, adaptability, persistence, adventurousness, shyness, inhibitedness, irritability, and distractibility. Most psychologists agree that such temperamental differences are biologically based and have genetic origins.[4]

Genetic differences in temperament are only *predispositions* to behave in certain ways, however, and environmental conditions may point different children with the same predisposition in somewhat different directions.[5] One influential environmental factor is the parenting style that mothers, fathers, and other primary caregivers use in raising children. In mainstream Western culture the ideal situation seems to be **authoritative parenting**, which combines affection and respect for children with reasonable restrictions on behavior. Authoritative parents provide a loving and supportive home, hold high expectations and standards for performance, explain why behaviors are or are not acceptable, enforce household rules consistently, include children in decision making, and provide age-appropriate opportunities for autonomy. Children from authoritative homes tend to be happy, energetic, self-confident, and likeable. They make friends easily and show self-control and concern for the rights and needs of others. Children of authoritative parents appear well adjusted, in part, because their behavior fits well with the values espoused by mainstream Western culture. They listen respectfully to others, can follow rules by the time they reach school age, are relatively independent and self-regulating, and strive for academic achievement.[6]

Authoritative parenting is not universally "best," however. Certain other parenting styles may be better suited to particular cultures and environments. For instance, in **authoritarian parenting**, parents expect complete and immediate compliance; they neither negotiate expectations nor provide reasons for their requests. In many Asian American and Hispanic families, high demands for obedience are made within the context of close, supportive parent–child relationships. Underlying the "control" message is a more important message: "I love you and want you to do well, but it is equally important that you act for the good of the family and community."[7] Authoritarian parenting is also more common in impoverished economic environments. When families live in low-income, inner-city neighborhoods where danger potentially lurks around every corner, parents may better serve their children by being very strict and directive about activities.[8] In any case, keep in mind that parenting styles have, at most, only a *moderate* influence on children's personalities.[9] Many children and adolescents thrive despite their caregivers' diverse parenting styles, provided that those caregivers aren't severely neglectful or abusive.[10]

A child's cultural environment also influences personality development more directly by encouraging (i.e., *socializing*) certain kinds of behaviors.[11] For example, many children in China are raised to be shy, whereas many in Zambia and the United States are raised to smile and be outgoing.[12] And as we discovered in Chapter 6, cultures vary considerably in the extent to which they encourage children to show or hide their feelings.

Nature and nurture interact in numerous ways to shape children's personalities.[13] For instance, children who are temperamentally energetic and adventuresome will seek out a wider variety of experiences than those who are quiet and restrained (e.g., recall our discussion of *niche-picking* in Chapter 3). Children who are naturally vivacious and outgoing will have more opportunities than shy children to learn social skills and establish rewarding interpersonal relationships. When children have temperaments that clash with cultural norms or parental expectations, they are apt to evoke negative reactions in others and lead

Parenting practices probably influence children's personalities to some degree. But other environmental factors (e.g., the nature of peer relationships) and inherited factors (e.g., children's inborn temperaments) also affect personality development.

[4] Bates & Pettit, 2007; Caspi & Silva, 1995; Kagan & Snidman, 2007; M. Pfeifer, Goldsmith, Davidson, & Rickman, 2002; A. Thomas & Chess, 1977.

[5] Keogh, 2003; R. A. Thompson, 1998.

[6] Barber, Stolz, & Olsen, 2005; Baumrind, 1989, 1991; Gonzalez & Wolters, 2005; Gray & Steinberg, 1999; Maccoby & Martin, 1983; J. M. T. Walker & Hoover-Dempsey, 2006.

[7] Chao, 2000; Halgunseth, Ispa, & Rudy, 2006; Rothbaum & Trommsdorff, 2007.

[8] Hale-Benson, 1986; McLoyd, 1998.

[9] W. A. Collins, Maccoby, Steinberg, Hetherington, & Bornstein, 2000; Weiss & Schwarz, 1996.

[10] J. R. Harris, 1995, 1998; Lykken, 1997; Scarr, 1992.

[11] Mendoza-Denton & Mischel, 2007; Mischel & Shoda, 1995.

[12] X. Chen, Rubin, & Sun, 1992; Hale-Benson, 1986; D. Y. F. Ho, 1986, 1994; Huntsinger & Jose, 2006.

[13] Bates & Pettit, 2007; N. A. Fox, Henderson, Rubin, Calkins, & Schmidt, 2001; Keogh, 2003.

authoritative parenting Parenting style characterized by emotional warmth, high standards for behavior, explanation and consistent enforcement of rules, inclusion of children in decision making, and reasonable opportunities for autonomy.

authoritarian parenting Parenting style characterized by rigid rules and expectations for behavior that children are asked to obey without question.

parents to use a more controlling, authoritarian parenting style.[14] One psychologist has made this point by describing her experiences with her own two children:

> I . . . reared a pair of very different children. My older daughter hardly ever wanted to do anything that her father and I didn't want her to do. My younger daughter often did. Raising the first was easy; raising the second was, um, interesting. . . .
>
> How do you treat two children both the same when they *aren't* the same—when they do different things and say different things, have different abilities and different [temperaments]? . . . I would have been pegged as a permissive parent with my first child, a bossy one with my second. . . .
>
> My husband and I seldom had hard-and-fast rules with our first child; generally we didn't need them. With our second child we had all sorts of rules and none of them worked. Reason with her? Give me a break. Often we ended up taking the shut-your-mouth-and-do-what-you're-told route. That didn't work either. In the end we pretty much gave up. Somehow we all made it through her teens.[15]

As you can see, temperamentally lively or adventuresome children may sometimes call for more adult control than restrained, easygoing ones.[16]

As children grow older, they construct increasingly multifaceted understandings of who they are as people.

Some psychologists distinguish between two aspects of people's sense of self. One aspect is *self-concept*, which includes general assessments of one's own characteristics, strengths, and weaknesses (e.g., "I am a high achieving student," "My nose is a bit crooked"). The other aspect is *self-esteem*, which includes judgments and feelings about one's own value and worth (e.g., "I am *proud* of my academic record," "I *hate* my crooked nose!"). We've encountered related ideas before, albeit under different names. In Chapter 6 we noted that human beings seem to have a basic need to feel competent and worthy (recall our discussion of *self-worth*). We also noted that people realize they are more likely to be successful in—that is, they have higher *self-efficacy* for—some activities than others.

So how are these four terms—self-concept, self-esteem, self-worth, and self-efficacy—different from one another? In general, *self-concept* addresses the question "*Who* am I?" The terms *self-esteem* and *self-worth* both address the question "*How good am I* as a person?" I suggest you not agonize over subtle distinctions among these three terms, because their meanings overlap considerably, and so they are often used interchangeably.[17]

In contrast to the other three terms, *self-efficacy* addresses the question "*How well can I do* such-and-such?" In other words, it refers to people's beliefs about their competence, not in general, but in a specific domain or activity. To some extent, however, people's specific self-efficacies for various tasks and activities contribute to their more general sense of self.[18]

In their overall self-assessments, children in the early elementary grades tend to make distinctions between two general domains: how competent they are at day-to-day tasks and how well they are liked by family and friends. As they grow older, children make finer and finer distinctions. In the upper elementary grades, they realize that they may be more or less competent or "good" in their academic work, athletic activities, classroom behavior, acceptance by peers, and physical attractiveness. By adolescence, they also make general self-assessments about their ability to make friends, their competence at adult-like work tasks, and their romantic appeal.[19] Each of these domains may have a greater or lesser influence on learners' overall sense of self. For some, academic achievement may be the overriding factor, whereas for others physical attractiveness or popularity with peers may be more important.[20]

Tina drew this self-portrait in second grade. For children and adolescents alike, self-perceived physical attractiveness often plays a significant role in their overall sense of self. Tina, whose genetic heritage is Hispanic and Native American, is well aware that her skin tone and hair color are darker than those of many of her classmates, some of whom she has drawn in the background.

[14] N. Eisenberg & Fabes, 1994; Maccoby, 2007; Scarr, 1993; Stice & Barrera, 1995.
[15] J. R. Harris, 1998, pp. 26, 48.
[16] Clarke-Stewart, 1988; J. R. Harris, 1998; Stice & Barrera, 1995.

[17] Byrne, 2002; Harter, 1999; Pintrich & Schunk, 2002.
[18] Bong & Skaalvik, 2003.
[19] Davis-Kean & Sandler, 2001; Harter, 1999.
[20] Crocker & Knight, 2005; D. Hart, 1988; Harter, 1999.

With age, self-perceptions become more realistic, abstract, and stable.

In the preschool and early elementary school years, children tend to think of themselves in terms of concrete, easily observable characteristics and behaviors.[21] For example, notice the many concrete characteristics in my son Alex's self-description at age 9:

> I have brown hair, brown eyes. I like wearing short-sleeved shirts. My hair is curly. I was adopted. I was born in Denver. I like all sorts of critters. The major sport I like is baseball. I do fairly well in school. I have a lizard, and I'm going to get a second one.

Most young children have positive self-concepts and high self-esteem.[22] Often they believe they are more capable than they really *are* and that they can easily overcome initial failures. Such optimism is probably due to their tendency to base self-assessments on their continuing improvement in "big boy" and "big girl" tasks. But as children have more opportunities to compare themselves with peers in their elementary school classrooms, and as they become cognitively more able to make such comparisons, their self-assessments become more realistic.[23]

In the upper elementary grades, children begin to pull together their many self-observations into generalizations about the kinds of people they are—perhaps "friendly," "good at sports," "smart," or "dumb"—and, for good or for bad, such generalizations lead to increasingly stable self-concepts.[24] As children reach adolescence and gain greater capability for abstract thought, they are even more likely to think of themselves in terms of general, fairly stable traits. Consider my daughter Tina's self-description when she was in sixth grade:

> I'm cool. I'm awesome. I'm way cool. I'm twelve. I'm boy crazy. I go to Brentwood Middle School. I'm popular with my fans. I play viola. My best friend is Lindsay. I have a gerbil named Taj. I'm adopted. I'm beautiful.

Although Tina listed several concrete features about herself (her school, her best friend, her gerbil), she had clearly developed a fairly abstract self-perception. Tina's focus on coolness, popularity, and beauty, rather than on intelligence or academic achievement (or, I might add, modesty), is fairly typical: Social acceptance and physical appearance are far more important to most young adolescents than academic competence.[25] In girls especially, dissatisfaction with one's physical appearance can have a significant negative impact on self-esteem and occasionally leads to bouts of depression.[26]

Older adolescents increasingly reflect on their own characteristics and abilities and begin to struggle with seeming inconsistencies in their self-perceptions. One ninth grader explained it this way:

> I really don't understand how I can switch so fast from being cheerful with my friends, then coming home and feeling anxious, and then getting frustrated and sarcastic with my parents. Which one is the *real* me?[27]

Eventually (perhaps around 11th grade), they integrate their various self-perceptions into a complex, multifaceted self-concept that reconciles apparent contradictions. For instance, they may realize that diverse emotions mean they are "moody" and that their inconsistent behaviors on different occasions mean they are "flexible."[28]

As older adolescents pull the numerous "parts" of themselves together, many begin to form a general sense of **identity**: a self-constructed definition of who they are, what things they find important, and what goals they want to accomplish in life.[29] One researcher has observed four distinct patterns that characterize the status of different adolescents in the search for identity:[30]

- **Identity diffusion.** The adolescent has made no commitment to a particular career path or ideological belief system. Some haphazard experimentation with particular

As children get older, they increasingly include abstract qualities in their self-descriptions. In this self-description, 12-year-old Melinda identifies several abstract characteristics: musical, lovable, imaginative, noble, and animal-lover.

One early theorist, Erik Erikson, suggested that identity formation is a major preoccupation for adolescents. Learn more about Erikson's theory of psychosocial development in a supplementary reading in the Homework and Exercises section in Chapter 7 of MyEducationLab.

identity Self-constructed definition of who one thinks one is and what things are important in life.

---

[21] D. Hart, 1988; Harter, 1983.
[22] Harter, 1999; Lockhart, Chang, & Story, 2002; Paris & Cunningham, 1996; Robins & Trzesniewski, 2005.
[23] Chapman, Tunmer, & Prochnow, 2000; Harter, 1999.
[24] D. A. Cole, Martin, Peeke, Seroczynski, & Fier, 2001; Harter, 1999.
[25] D. Hart, 1988; Harter, 1999.

[26] C. G. Campbell, Parker, & Kollat, 2007; Stice, 2003; E. J. Wright, 2007.
[27] Harter, 1999, p. 67.
[28] Harter, 1999.
[29] Erikson, 1963, 1972; Wigfield, Eccles, & Pintrich, 1996.
[30] Marcia, 1980, 1991; also see Seaton, Scottham, & Sellers, 2006.

roles or beliefs may have taken place, but the individual has not yet embarked on a serious exploration of issues related to self-definition.

- **Foreclosure.** The adolescent has made a firm commitment to an occupation, a particular set of beliefs, or both. The choices have been based largely on what others (especially parents) have prescribed, without an earnest exploration of other possibilities.
- **Moratorium.** The adolescent has no strong commitment to a particular career or set of beliefs but is actively exploring and considering a variety of professions and ideologies. In essence, the individual is undergoing an identity crisis.
- **Identity achievement.** After going through a period of moratorium, the adolescent has emerged with a commitment to particular political or religious beliefs, a clear choice of occupation, or both.

For many adolescents, the ideal situation seems to be to proceed through a period of moratorium—an exploration that may continue into early adulthood—before finally settling on a clear identity.[31] Foreclosure—identity choice *without* prior exploration—rules out potentially more productive alternatives, and identity diffusion leaves young people without a clear sense of direction in life.

Even by the end of high school, however, only a small minority of teenagers in Western societies have begun to think seriously about their lifelong goals and the eventual role they will play in the adult world.[32] In the meantime, they may sometimes take on temporary "identities," aligning themselves strongly with a particular peer group, adhering rigidly to a single brand of clothing, or insisting on a certain hairstyle. Most adolescents need considerable time to explore various options related to careers, political beliefs, religious affiliations, and so on before they achieve a true sense of their adult identity.

As children reach puberty, they understand that they are unique individuals, but they often go overboard in this respect.

Young teenagers often believe themselves to be unlike anyone else—a phenomenon known as the **personal fable**.[33] They may think their own feelings are completely unique—those around them have never experienced such emotions—and so no one else, least of all parents and teachers, can possibly know how they feel. Furthermore, some have a sense of invulnerability and immortality, believing themselves immune to the normal dangers of life. Thus they may take foolish risks, such as experimenting with drugs and alcohol, having unprotected sexual intercourse, or driving at high speeds.[34] If admonished that they could overdose, create an unwanted pregnancy, or be in a serious automobile accident, they might respond, "It won't happen to me."

It is important to note, however, that young adolescents are apt to take risks even when they *don't* believe themselves to be invulnerable.[35] Several other factors also predispose young people to make foolish choices. Thanks, in part, to brains that have not yet fully matured, adolescents often have trouble planning ahead and controlling their impulses (see Chapter 5). In addition, adolescents tend to make choices based on their emotions ("This will be a lot of fun") rather than on logic ("There is a high probability of a bad outcome").[36] Thus, adolescent risk taking is especially common in social contexts, where having fun is typically a high priority and it's easy to get swept away by what peers are doing or suggesting.

The personal fable and risk taking both decline in the later adolescent years, but they don't entirely disappear.[37] Hence they are—and must be—a source of concern to parents and teachers of older adolescents as well as younger ones.

personal fable Belief that one is completely unlike anyone else and so cannot be understood by others.

[31] Berzonsky, 1988; Marcia, 1988.
[32] Archer, 1982; Durkin, 1995; Marcia, 1980, 1988; Seaton et al., 2006.
[33] Elkind, 1981; Lapsley, 1993.
[34] Arnett, 1995; DeRidder, 1993; Jacobs & Klaczynski, 2002; Nell, 2002; S. P. Thomas, Groër, & Droppleman, 1993.
[35] V. F. Reyna & Farley, 2006; L. Steinberg, 2007.
[36] Cleveland, Gibbons, Gerrard, Pomery, & Brody, 2005; V. F. Reyna & Farley, 2006; L. Steinberg, 2007.
[37] Frankenberger, 2000; Nell, 2002; V. F. Reyna & Farley, 2006.

Learners' self-perceptions influence their behaviors.

Learners tend to behave in ways that mirror their beliefs about themselves. Those who see themselves as "good students"—and especially those who have high self-efficacy in a particular academic domain—are more likely to pay attention, follow directions in class, use effective learning strategies, work independently and persistently to solve difficult problems, and enroll in challenging courses.[38] In contrast, those who believe they are "poor students" are apt to misbehave in class, study infrequently or not at all, ignore homework assignments, and avoid taking difficult subjects. Along a similar vein, learners who see themselves as friendly and likable are apt to seek the company of their classmates and perhaps run for student council, whereas those who believe they are disliked by classmates may keep to themselves or act with hostility and aggression toward their peers.[39] Learners with a high sense of physical competence will go out for extracurricular team sports, whereas those who see themselves as total klutzes probably will not.

When learners assess themselves fairly accurately, they are in a good position to choose age-appropriate activities and work toward realistic goals.[40] A slightly inflated self-assessment can be beneficial as well, in that it encourages learners to take on new challenges.[41] However, self-concepts that are *too* inflated may give some learners an unwarranted sense of superiority over classmates and lead them to bully or in other ways act aggressively toward peers.[42] And as you might guess, significant *under*estimates lead learners to avoid the many challenges that are apt to enhance their cognitive, social, and physical growth.[43]

In general, learners who have positive self-perceptions are more likely to succeed academically, socially, and physically, and such successes serve to maintain or enhance those positive self-perceptions.[44] But an interplay between self-perceptions and behavior exists for less flattering self-perceptions as well, creating a vicious cycle: A poor sense of self leads to less productive behavior, which leads to fewer successes, which perpetuates the poor sense of self.

Other people's behaviors affect learners' sense of self.

Not only do learners' past successes and failures influence their sense of self but so, too, do *other people* influence it, and in at least two ways. First, as mentioned earlier, how children evaluate themselves depends to some extent on how their own performance compares to that of other individuals, especially peers.[45] Adolescents in particular tend to judge themselves in comparison with peers. Those who see themselves achieving at higher levels than others in certain domains are apt to develop a more positive sense of self than those who consistently find themselves falling short.

Second, learners' self-perceptions are affected by how others behave *toward them*.[46] Adults and peers communicate their assessments of a person through a variety of behaviors. For example, parents and teachers foster more positive self-concepts when they have high expectations for children's performance and offer support and encouragement for the attainment of challenging goals.[47] Meanwhile, peers communicate information about children's social and athletic competence, perhaps by seeking out a child's companionship or ridiculing a child in front of others.[48] In the opening case study, when Peter initially has trouble making friends and the allegedly "popular" students pick on him, he may understandably have low self-esteem. Fortunately, the school play allows him to showcase his talent, and his classmates see him in a new light. Suddenly, he's "amazing" and "totally cool." Such comments from his classmates, if they continue for any length of time, should undoubtedly boost his self-esteem.

[38] Bandura, 2000; Marsh & Craven, 2006; Pintrich & Schunk, 2002; Roeser & Lau, 2002; Schunk, 1989b.
[39] M. S. Caldwell, Rudolph, Troop-Gordon, & Kim, 2004.
[40] R. F. Baumeister, Campbell, Krueger, & Vohs, 2003; Harter, 1999.
[41] Assor & Connell, 1992; Lockhart et al., 2002; Pajares, 2005.
[42] R. F. Baumeister et al., 2003; R. F. Baumeister, Smart, & Boden, 1996.
[43] Assor & Connell, 1992; D. Phillips & Zimmerman, 1990.
[44] M. S. Caldwell et al., 2004; Guay, Marsh, & Boivin, 2003; Ma & Kishor, 1997; Marsh & Craven, 2006; Valentine, Cooper, Bettencourt, & DuBois, 2002.
[45] Guay, Boivin, & Hodges, 1999; Marsh & Hau, 2003; Nicholls, 1984.
[46] Harter, 1996; Hartup, 1989; Rudolph, Caldwell, & Conley, 2005.
[47] Dweck, 2000; Eccles, Jacobs, Harold-Goldsmith, Jayaratne, & Yee, 1989; M. J. Harris & Rosenthal, 1985.
[48] Bukowski, Brendgan, & Vitaro, 2007; Harter, 1999.

DEVELOPMENTAL TRENDS

TABLE 7.1 Sense of Self at Different Grade Levels

Grade Level	Age-Typical Characteristics	Suggested Strategies
K–2	• Self-descriptions largely limited to concrete, easily observable characteristics • Tendency to overestimate abilities and chances of future success	• Encourage students to "stretch" themselves by tackling the challenging tasks they think they can accomplish. • Provide sufficient scaffolding to make success possible in various domains. • Praise students for the things they do well; be specific about the behaviors you are praising.
3–5	• Increasing awareness of, and differentiation among, particular strengths and weaknesses • Association of such emotions as pride and shame with various self-perceptions	• Focus students' attention on their improvement over time. • Encourage pride in individual and group achievements, but be aware that students from some ethnic groups may prefer that recognition be given only for group achievements. • Provide opportunities for students to look at one another's work only when *all* of them have something to be proud of.
6–8	• Increasingly abstract conceptions of oneself • For many, a decline in self-esteem after the transition to middle or junior high school • Excessive belief in one's own uniqueness (personal fable); may contribute to an increase in risk-taking behaviors • Heightened sensitivity to what others may think of oneself (imaginary audience)	• After students make the transition to middle school or junior high, be especially supportive and optimistic about their abilities and potential for success. • Show no tolerance for potentially dangerous behaviors on school grounds. • Be patient when students show exceptional self-consciousness; give them strategies for presenting themselves well to others.
9–12	• Search for the "real me" and an adult identity • Increasing integration of diverse self-perceptions into an overall, multifaceted sense of self • Gradual increase in self-esteem • Continuing risk-taking behavior, especially in males	• Give students opportunities to examine and try out a variety of adult-like roles. • When discussing the potential consequences of risky behaviors, present the facts but don't make students so anxious or upset that they can't effectively learn and remember the information (e.g., avoid scare tactics). • Encourage students to explore and take pride in their cultural and ethnic heritages.

Sources: Dweck, 2000; Elkind, 1981; Harter, 1999; Lockhart et al., 2002; Marcia, 1980, 1991; Nell, 2002; O'Mara, Marsh, Craven, & Debus, 2006; Robins & Trzesniewski, 2005; Seaton et al., 2006; Tatum, 1997.

In early adolescence youngsters seem to have a heightened concern about what others think of them. In fact, they may believe that in any social situation, everyone else's attention is focused squarely on them—a phenomenon known as the **imaginary audience**.[49] An eighth grader named Lindsay illustrates this phenomenon:

> In algebra I had to cough but I knew if I did everyone would stare at me and think I was stupid, hacking away. So I held my breath until I turned red and tears ran down my face and finally I coughed anyway and everyone *really* noticed then. It was horrible.[50]

Because they believe themselves to be the center of attention, young teenagers (girls especially) are often preoccupied with their physical appearance and can be quite self-critical. Concerned about how others may evaluate them and wanting desperately to fit in, they can be very conforming, rigidly imitating peers' choices in dress, music, slang, and behavior.[51]

Table 7.1 summarizes developmental trends in children's and adolescents' sense of self. It also offers ideas for how teachers can enhance students' sense of self at different grade levels.

---

imaginary audience Belief that one is the center of attention in any social situation.

[49] Elkind, 1981; Lapsley, 1993; R. M. Ryan & Kuczkowski, 1994.

[50] Orenstein, 1994, p. 47.
[51] Hartup, 1983; Owens, 1996.

Group memberships also affect learners' sense of self.

Membership in one or more groups (e.g., being in a "popular" group, as some students in the opening case study are) can also impact learners' sense of self.[52] If you think back to your own school years, perhaps you can recall taking pride in something your entire class accomplished, feeling good about a community service project completed through an extracurricular club, or reveling in the state championship earned by one of your school's athletic teams. In general, learners are more likely to have high self-esteem if they are members of a successful group.[53]

School groups are not the only important ones in learners' lives, however. For instance, in racially and culturally diverse communities, where different skin colors, languages, customs, and so on, are obvious, children's membership in a particular racial or ethnic group may be a significant aspect of their sense of self. We'll look at the importance of this *ethnic identity* more closely in a Cultural Considerations box later in the chapter.

For Better or For Worse®   **by Lynn Johnston**

Such an excessive concern about appearance illustrates a phenomenon known as the *imaginary audience*: Elizabeth believes she is the focus of everyone else's attention.

Source: For Better or For Worse © 1994 Lynn Johnston Productions. Dist. by Universal Press Syndicate. Reprinted with permission. All rights reserved.

Gender plays a significant role in most learners' sense of self.

As young children become increasingly aware of the typical characteristics and behaviors of boys, girls, men, and women, they begin to pull their knowledge together into self-constructed understandings, or **gender schemas**, of "what males are like" and "what females are like." These gender schemas, in turn, become part of their sense of self and provide guidance for how they themselves should behave—how they should dress, what toys they should play with, what interests and academic subject areas they should pursue, and so on.[54]

Because gender schemas are self-constructed, their contents may vary considerably from one individual to another.[55] In adolescence, for example, some girls incorporate into their "female" schema the unrealistic standards for beauty presented in popular media (films, fashion magazines, etc.). As they compare themselves to these standards, they almost invariably come up short and so their self-assessments of their physical attractiveness decline.[56] In an effort to achieve the super-thin body they believe to be ideal, they may fall victim to eating disorders.[57] Likewise, some teenage boys go out of their way to meet self-constructed "macho" standards for male behavior by putting on a tough-guy act at school and bragging (perhaps accurately, but more often not) about their many sexual conquests.[58]

Young adolescent girls are often preoccupied with thinness, fashion, and overall physical appearance, as this drawing by 11-year-old Marci illustrates.

Some researchers find gender differences in overall self-esteem in adolescence, with boys rating themselves more highly than girls. This gender difference appears to be partly due to boys' tendency to *over*estimate their abilities and possibly also to girls' tendency to *under*estimate theirs.[59] Most adolescent boys' and girls' self-perceptions tend to be consistent with stereotypes about what males and females are "good at." Even when actual ability levels are

---

[52] Brewer & Yuki, 2007; Phinney, 1989; Wigfield et al., 2006.

[53] Harter, 1999; Phinney, 1989; Wigfield et al., 1996.

[54] Bem, 1981; Leaper & Friedman, 2007; C. L. Martin & Ruble, 2004; Weisgram, Bigler, & Liben, 2007.

[55] Crouter, Whiteman, McHale, & Osgood, 2007; Liben & Bigler, 2002.

[56] Stice, 2003.

[57] Attie, Brooks-Gunn, & Petersen, 1990; Weichold, Silbereisen, & Schmitt-Rodermund, 2003.

[58] Pollack, 2006; K. M. Williams, 2001a.

[59] Bornholt, Goodnow, & Cooney, 1994; D. A. Cole et al., 1999; Harter, 1999; Pajares, 2005; Pajares & Valiante, 1999.

gender schema Self-constructed, organized body of beliefs about the traits and behaviors of males or females.

the same, on average boys rate themselves more highly in mathematics and sports, whereas girls rate themselves more highly in reading and literature.[60] On average, too, adolescent boys rate their physical appearance more positively than girls do.[61]

Despite the influence of others, learners define and socialize *themselves* to a considerable degree.

As we've seen, children's and adolescents' beliefs about themselves are, like their beliefs about the world, largely self-constructed. Young people get many messages—sometimes consistent, sometimes not—from parents, teachers, peers, and others about who they are, what they should think, and how they should behave. But rarely do they passively adopt others' ideas and opinions as their own.[62] Instead, they evaluate the information they get, choose some role models over others, weigh the pros and cons of "going along with the crowd," and gradually develop their own views about what their strengths and weaknesses are and which behaviors are and are not appropriate for themselves. Before long, much of the pressure to act "appropriately" comes from within rather than from outside (recall our discussion of self-regulation in Chapter 4). For example, when teachers actively encourage children to engage in non-gender-stereotypical activities (boys playing with dolls, girls playing with toy cars, etc.), the children may do so for a short time, but they soon revert to their earlier, more gender-typical ways.[63] This tendency for children and adolescents to conform to their own ideas about what behaviors are appropriate for themselves is known as **self-socialization.**[64]

The decisions that youngsters make about which individuals and sources of information to take seriously depend on their developmental levels and life experiences.[65] Parents are dominating forces in the lives of most children in the primary grades, and most parents continue to be influential, especially with respect to core beliefs and values, throughout their children's middle school and secondary school years. Nevertheless, growing children increasingly look to their peers for ideas about how to behave—how to dress, which music to listen to, how to spend leisure time, and so on. We turn to the nature of peer relationships now.

PEER RELATIONSHIPS

School is very much a social place. Students interact regularly with one another, and most of them actively seek out friendly relationships with classmates. In fact, for many students, interacting with and gaining the acceptance of peers are more important than classroom learning and achievement.[66] For example, in the "Motivation: Late Adolescence" video clip in MyEducationLab, when 15-year-old Greg is asked what he most likes about school, he quickly responds, "Lunch . . . all the social aspects . . . friends and cliques."

Several principles describe the nature and effects of peer relationships in childhood and adolescence.

Peer relationships promote personal and social development in ways that adult–child relationships often cannot.

Peer relationships, especially friendships, serve several unique functions in children's and adolescents' personal and social development. In the preschool and early elementary years, children see their age-mates primarily as sources of recreation and companionship (e.g., see Figure 7.1). As they grow older, they find that peers, and especially close friends, can also provide comfort, support, and safety—a group with whom to eat lunch, a "safe haven" from

Observe Greg's preference for the social aspects of school in the "Motivation: Late Adolescence" video in the Additional Resources section in Chapter 7 of MyEducationLab.

self-socialization Tendency to integrate personal observations and others' input into self-constructed standards for behavior and to choose actions consistent with those standards.

[60] D. A. Cole et al., 2001; Harter, 1999; Herbert & Stipek, 2005; Wigfield et al., 2006.

[61] D. A. Cole et al., 2001; Harter, 1999; R. M. Ryan & Kuczkowski, 1994; Stice, 2003.

[62] Markus & Hamedani, 2007.

[63] Lippa, 2002.

[64] B. B. Brown, 1990; Durkin, 1995; Leaper & Friedman, 2007; M. Lewis, 1991.

[65] Cauce, Mason, Gonzales, Hiraga, & Liu, 1994; Furman & Buhrmester, 1992; Neubauer, Mansel, Avrahami, & Nathan, 1994.

[66] B. B. Brown, 1993; Dowson & McInerney, 2001; W. Doyle, 1986a.

playground bullies, and so on.[67] (In the opening case study, Peter, who is initially picked on by other students, has no friends to come to his defense.) Once children reach puberty, they rely increasingly on their peers for emotional support, especially in times of confusion or trouble.[68] Although some adolescents adjust quite successfully on their own, as a general rule those who have the acceptance and support of peers have higher self-esteem, fewer emotional problems (e.g., depression), and higher school achievement.[69]

Many adolescents (especially girls) reveal their innermost thoughts and feelings to their friends.[70] Friends often understand a teenager's perspective—the preoccupation with physical appearance, the concerns about the opposite sex, and so on—when no one else seems to. By sharing their thoughts and feelings with one another, teens may discover that they aren't as unique as they once thought. Accordingly, the personal fable I mentioned earlier gradually fades from the scene.[71]

In addition, peer interactions provide an arena for learning and practicing social skills. Unlike in adult–child relationships, children participate as equal partners in most peer relationships. In doing so, they begin to develop skills in negotiation, persuasion, cooperation, compromise, emotional control, and conflict resolution.[72] Because friends have an emotional investment in their relationship, they work hard to look at a situation from one another's point of view and to resolve any disputes that threaten to separate them.[73]

The three "Friendships" video clips in MyEducationLab reveal how friends become more important as children get older. For 8-year-old Kate, having friends primarily means being nice, having companionship, and helping one another. But for 13-year-old Ryan and 17-year-old Paul, friends are also people they can trust, rely on, and confide in.

Peers help define "appropriate" ways of behaving.

Not only do peers provide social and emotional support, they can also be powerful socialization agents who encourage what are, at least in their own minds, appropriate ways of behaving.[74] Peers define options for leisure time, perhaps getting together in a study group or smoking cigarettes on the corner. They offer new ideas and perspectives, perhaps demonstrating how to do an "Ollie" on a skateboard or presenting arguments for becoming a vegetarian. They serve as role models and provide standards for acceptable behavior, showing what is possible, what is admirable, what is cool. They reinforce one another for acting in ways deemed appropriate for their age, gender, or ethnic group. And they sanction one another for stepping beyond acceptable bounds, perhaps through ridicule, gossip, or ostracism. Such **peer pressure** has its greatest effects during the junior high school years, and teenagers who have weak emotional bonds to their families seem to be especially vulnerable.[75]

Many peers encourage such desirable qualities as truthfulness, fairness, compassion, cooperation, and abstinence from drugs and alcohol.[76] Others, however, encourage aggression, criminal activity, and other dangerous and antisocial behaviors (recall our earlier discussion of adolescent risk taking).[77] Some peers encourage academic achievement, yet others convey the message that academic achievement is undesirable, perhaps by making fun of "brainy" students or by encouraging such behaviors as copying one another's homework, cutting class, and skipping school.[78]

FIGURE 7.1   In this writing sample, 7-year-old Andrew sees friends largely as companions and sources of entertainment (they're for "when you are lonely," "they play with you," "they tell stories"). Yet he also recognizes that friends can occasionally be a source of support ("they walk you to the nursce").

Observe developmental trends in the importance of friends in the three "Friendships" videos in the Additional Resources section in Chapter 7 of MyEducationLab.

[67] Berndt, 2002; Doll, Song, & Siemers, 2004; Laursen, Bukowski, Aunola, & Nurmi, 2007; Pellegrini & Bartini, 2000.

[68] Juvonen, 2006; Levitt et al., 1993; R. M. Ryan, Stiller, & Lynch, 1994.

[69] Berdan & Keane, 2005; Buhrmester, 1992; Guay et al., 1999; R. M. Ryan et al., 1994; Wentzel, 1999.

[70] Basinger, Gibbs, & Fuller, 1995; Levitt et al., 1993; A. J. Rose, 2002.

[71] Elkind, 1981.

[72] Asher & Parker, 1989; Erwin, 1993; Gauvain, 2001; Laursen et al., 2007; Pellegrini & Bohn, 2005.

[73] Basinger et al., 1995; DeVries, 1997; Newcomb & Bagwell, 1995.

[74] Erwin, 1993; Ginsburg, Gottman, & Parker, 1986; Laursen et al., 2007; A. M. Ryan, 2000.

[75] Berndt, Laychak, & Park, 1990; Erwin, 1993; R. M. Ryan & Lynch, 1989; Urdan & Maehr, 1995.

[76] Berndt & Keefe, 1996; McCallum & Bracken, 1993; Wentzel & Looney, 2007.

[77] Dodge, Dishion, & Lansford, 2006; W. E. Ellis & Zarbatany, 2007; Espelage, Holt, & Henkel, 2003; D. C. Gottfredson, 2001.

[78] Berndt, 1992; B. B. Brown, 1993; Kindermann, 2007; A. M. Ryan, 2001.

peer pressure Phenomenon whereby agemates strongly encourage some behaviors and discourage others.

Although peer pressure certainly is a factor affecting development, its effect on children's behaviors has probably been overrated.[79] Most children and adolescents acquire a strong set of values and behavioral standards from their families, and they do not necessarily discard these values and standards in the company of peers.[80] Furthermore, they tend to choose friends who are similar to themselves in motives, styles of behavior, academic achievement, and leisure-time activities.[81] In some cases youngsters lead "double lives" that enable them to attain academic success while maintaining peer acceptance. For example, although they attend class and do their homework faithfully, they may feign disinterest in scholarly activities, disrupt class with jokes or goofy behaviors, and express surprise at receiving high grades.[82] In the following reflection, a sixth grader explains how he successfully juggles his need to get good grades with his desire to maintain a cool image at school:

> You'd still have to have your bad attitude. You have to act—it's just like a movie. You have to act. And then at home you're a regular kind of guy, you don't act mean or nothing. But when you're around your friends you have to be sharp and stuff like that, like push everybody around.[83]

Boys and girls interact with peers in distinctly different ways.

Boys' and girls' playgroups and friendships are different in key ways that affect their personal and social development. Boys tend to hang out in relatively large groups that engage in rough-and-tumble play, organized group games, and physical risk-taking activities.[84] They enjoy competition and can be fairly assertive in their efforts to achieve individual and group goals.[85] Especially as they get older, they prefer keeping some personal space between themselves and their friends (for some boys, this appears to be a way of affirming their heterosexuality). And boys often try to hide their true emotions in social situations.[86] For instance, in the "Emotions: Late Adolescence" video clip in MyEducationLab, 15-year-old Greg responds to the question, "What are some things that kids do when they're sad?" by saying, "Cry . . . if you're a guy, you don't show it."

Whereas boys tend to be competitive, girls are more affiliative and cooperative. Girls seem to be more attuned to others' mental states and more sensitive to the subtle, nonverbal messages—the body language—that others communicate.[87] They spend much of their leisure time with one or two close friends, with whom they may share their innermost thoughts and feelings.[88] Although they can certainly be assertive at times, they also tend to be concerned about maintaining group harmony, and so they may occasionally subordinate their own wishes to those of others.[89] In the three "Friendships" video clips in MyEducationLab, notice how 8-year-old Kate talks about compromise and working out conflicts with friends, whereas 13-year-old Ryan and 17-year-old Paul are more apt to deal with conflict by "just forget[ting] about it." In fact, Paul specifically mentions a gender difference in conflict resolution strategies:

> Normally with, like, my guy friends, we just get over it. There's no working it out, you just sit . . . like, "Fine, whatever," you know? And we get over it. Girl friends, you gotta talk to them and work it out slowly. Apologize for doing whatever you did wrong. There's a whole process.

Social groups become increasingly important in adolescence.

Most children and adolescents frequently interact and enjoy being with peers besides their close friends. Over time, many form larger social groups that regularly get together.[90] Ini-

Observe gender differences in interpersonal behaviors and conflict resolution strategies in the "Emotions: Late Adolescence" video and three "Friendships" videos in the Additional Resources section in Chapter 7 of MyEducationLab.

[79] Berndt & Keefe, 1996.

[80] B. B. Brown, 1990; W. A. Collins et al., 2000; Galambos, Barker, & Almeida, 2003.

[81] Card & Ramos, 2005; W. A. Collins et al., 2000; Kindermann, McCollam, & Gibson, 1996; A. M. Ryan, 2001.

[82] B. B. Brown, 1993; Covington, 1992; Hemmings, 2004; Juvonen, 2006.

[83] Juvonen & Cadigan, 2002, p. 282.

[84] Maccoby, 2002; Pellegrini, Kato, Blatchford, & Baines, 2002.

[85] Benenson et al., 2002; N. Eisenberg, Martin, & Fabes, 1996; Leaper & Friedman, 2007; Maccoby, 2002.

[86] N. Eisenberg et al., 1996; Lippa, 2002; K. M. Williams, 2001a.

[87] Bosacki, 2000; Deaux, 1984.

[88] Block, 1983; N. Eisenberg et al., 1996; A. J. Rose, 2002.

[89] Benenson et al., 2002; Leaper & Friedman, 2007; Maccoby, 2002.

[90] N. Eisenberg et al., 1996; Gottman & Mettetal, 1986.

tially, such groups are usually composed of a single sex, but in adolescence they often include both boys and girls.[91]

Once children or adolescents gel as a group, they prefer other group members over non-members, and they develop feelings of loyalty to individuals within the group. In some cases they also develop feelings of hostility and rivalry toward members of other groups.[92] If you look back on your own adolescent years, you may recall that you and your friends attached names to members of different groups—not only the "popular" students mentioned in the opening case study but perhaps also "brains," "jocks," "druggies," or "geeks"—and you probably viewed some of the groups unfavorably.[93] As noted earlier, group memberships affect learners' sense of self, and associations with such unofficial groups as these are no exception. Even children in the primary grades know that social groups can vary considerably in social status.[94]

As youngsters reach puberty, larger groups become an especially prominent feature of their social worlds. Researchers have identified several distinct types of groups during the adolescent years: cliques, crowds, subcultures, and gangs. **Cliques** are moderately stable friendship groups of perhaps 3 to 10 individuals, and such groups provide the setting for most voluntary social interactions.[95] Clique boundaries tend to be fairly rigid and exclusive (some people are "in," others are "out"), and memberships in various cliques often affect social status.[96]

Crowds are considerably larger than cliques and may not have the tight-knit cohesiveness and carefully drawn boundaries of a clique. Their members tend to share common interests (e.g., "brains" study a lot, "jocks" are active in sports), attitudes about academic achievement, and (occasionally) ethnic background.[97] Sometimes a crowd takes the form of a **subculture**, a group that resists a powerful dominant culture by adopting a significantly different way of life.[98] Some subcultures are relatively benign; for example, the baggy-pants "skaters" with whom my son Alex affiliated spent much of their free time riding their skateboards and addressing almost everyone as "dude." Other subcultures are more worrisome, such as those that endorse racist and anti-Semitic behaviors (e.g., "skinheads") and those that practice Satanic worship and rituals. Adolescents are more likely to affiliate with troublesome subcultures when they feel alienated from the dominant culture (perhaps that of their school or that of society more generally) and want to distinguish themselves from it in some way.[99]

A **gang** is a cohesive social group characterized by initiation rites, distinctive colors and symbols, ownership of a specific "territory," and feuds with one or more rival groups. Typically, gangs are governed by strict rules for behavior, with stiff penalties for rule violations. Adolescents (and sometimes younger children as well) affiliate with gangs for a variety of reasons.[100] Some do so as a way of demonstrating loyalty to their family, friends, or neighborhood. Some seek the status and prestige that gang membership brings. Some have poor academic records and perceive the gang as an alternative arena in which they might gain recognition for their accomplishments. Many members of gangs have had troubled relationships with their families, or they have been consistently rejected by peers, and so they turn to gangs to get the emotional support they can find nowhere else.

In the upper secondary school grades, a greater capacity for abstract thought allows many adolescents to think of other people more as unique individuals and less as members of specific categories. They gain new awareness of the characteristics they share with people from diverse backgrounds. Perhaps as a result, ties to specific peer groups tend to dissipate, hostilities between groups soften, and young people become more flexible about the people with whom they associate.[101]

clique Moderately stable friendship group of perhaps 3 to 10 members.

crowd Large, loose-knit social group that shares common interests and attitudes.

subculture Group that resists the ways of the dominant culture and adopts its own norms for behavior.

gang Cohesive social group characterized by initiation rites, distinctive colors and symbols, territorial orientation, and feuds with rival groups.

[91] Gottman & Mettetal, 1986; J. R. Harris, 1995.
[92] Dunham, Baron, & Banaji, 2006; J. R. Harris, 1998; Nesdale, Maass, Durkin, & Griffiths, 2005.
[93] Eckert, 1989; J. R. Harris, 1995.
[94] Bigler, Brown, & Markell, 2001; Dunham et al., 2006; Nesdale et al., 2005.
[95] Crockett, Losoff, & Peterson, 1984; J. L. Epstein, 1986; Kindermann et al., 1996.
[96] Goodwin, 2006; Wigfield et al., 1996.
[97] L. Steinberg, 1996.
[98] J. S. Epstein, 1998.
[99] C. C. Clark, 1992; J. R. Harris, 1998.
[100] A. Campbell, 1984; C. C. Clark, 1992; Kodluboy, 2004; Parks, 1995; Simons, Whitbeck, Conger, & Conger, 1991.
[101] B. B. Brown, Eicher, & Petrie, 1986; Gavin & Fuhrman, 1989; Larkin, 1979; Shrum & Cheek, 1987.

Note Kate's interest in boys in the "Friendships: Middle Childhood" video in the Additional Resources section in Chapter 7 of MyEducationLab.

For many children, thoughts of romance emerge early. Here is just one of many notes 5-year-old Isabelle wrote about a classmate named Will.

Romantic relationships in adolescence provide valuable practice for the intimate relationships of adulthood.

Many children talk of love and romance even in kindergarten and the primary grades. For instance, they may claim to have "boyfriends" or "girlfriends." And the opposite sex is the subject of some curiosity throughout the elementary school years. For example, in the "Friendships: Middle Childhood" video clip in MyEducationLab, 8-year-old Kate mentions that she and her friends "try to catch boys."

With the onset of adolescence, the biological changes of puberty are accompanied by new, often unsettling feelings and sexual desires. Not surprisingly, then, romance is often on adolescents' minds and is a frequent topic of conversation at school.[102] From a developmental standpoint, romantic relationships have definite benefits: They can address young people's needs for companionship, affection, and security, and they provide an opportunity to experiment with new social skills and interpersonal behaviors.[103] At the same time, romance can wreak havoc with adolescents' emotions. Adolescents have more extreme mood swings than younger children or adults, and for many, this instability may be partly due to the excitement and frustrations of being romantically involved or *not* involved.[104]

Initially, "romances" often exist more in adolescents' minds than in reality.[105] Consider Sandy's recollection of her first foray into couplehood:

> In about fifth and sixth grade, all our little group that we had . . . was like, "OK," you know, "we're getting ready for junior high," you know, "it's time we all have to get a boyfriend." So I remember, it was funny, Carol, like, there were two guys who were just the heartthrobs of our class, you know . . . so, um, I guess it was Carol and Cindy really, they were, like, sort of the leaders of our group, you know, they were the, yeah, they were just the leaders, and they got Tim and Joe, each of those you know. Carol had Tim and Cindy had Joe. And then, you know, everyone else, then it kind of went down the line, everyone else found someone. I remember thinking, "Well, who am I gonna get? I don't even like anybody," you know. I remember, you know, all sitting around, we were saying, "OK, who can we find for Sandy?" you know, looking, so finally we decided, you know, we were trying to decide between Al and Dave and so finally I took Dave.[106]

For youngsters in the middle school grades, romantic thoughts may also involve crushes on people who are out of reach—perhaps favorite teachers, movie idols, or rock stars.[107]

Eventually, however, many adolescents begin to date, especially if their friends are also dating. Their early choices in dating partners are often based on physical attractiveness or social status, and dates may involve only limited and superficial interaction.[108] As adolescents move into the high school grades, some form more intense, affectionate, and long-term relationships with members of the opposite sex, and these relationships often (but by no means always) lead to some degree of sexual intimacy.[109] The age of first sexual intercourse has decreased steadily during the last few decades, perhaps in part because the media often communicate the message that sexual activity among unmarried partners is acceptable.[110] In the United States the average age of first sexual intercourse is now around age 16, and the majority of adolescents are sexually active by 18. However, the age varies considerably as a function of gender (boys begin earlier) and cultural background.[111]

As they reach high school (sometimes even earlier), some young people find themselves attracted to their own sex either instead of or in addition to the opposite sex. Adolescence can be a particularly confusing time for gay, lesbian, and bisexual individuals. Some actively try to ignore or stifle what they perceive to be deviant urges. Others accept their sexual yearnings yet struggle to form an identity while feeling different and isolated from peers.[112] Many describe feelings of anger and depression, some entertain thoughts of suicide, and a higher than average proportion drop out of school.[113]

[102] B. B. Brown, Feiring, & Furman, 1999.
[103] Furman & Simon, 1999; B. C. Miller & Benson, 1999.
[104] Arnett, 1999; Larson, Clore, & Wood, 1999.
[105] Gottman & Mettetal, 1986.
[106] Eckert, 1989, p. 84.
[107] B. B. Brown, 1999; B. C. Miller & Benson, 1999.

[108] Furman, Brown, & Feiring, 1999; Pellegrini, 2002.
[109] B. B. Brown, 1999; J. Connolly & Goldberg, 1999.
[110] Brooks-Gunn & Paikoff, 1993; Larson et al., 1999.
[111] Hofferth, 1990; Katchadourian, 1990; Lippa, 2002; D. S. Moore & Erickson, 1985.
[112] Morrow, 1997; C. J. Patterson, 1995.
[113] Elia, 1994; C. J. Patterson, 1995.

Teenagers often have mixed feelings about their early sexual experiences, and those around them—parents, teachers, peers—are often uncertain about how to handle the topic.[114] When parents and teachers do broach the topic of sexuality, they often raise it in conjunction with *problems*, such as irresponsible behavior, substance abuse, disease, and unwanted pregnancy. And they rarely raise the issue of gay, lesbian, and bisexual orientations except within the context of acquired immune deficiency syndrome (AIDS) and other risks.[115]

Truly popular children have good social skills.

When my daughter Tina was in junior high school, she sometimes told me, "No one likes the popular kids." Her remark was, of course, self-contradictory, and I usually told her so, but in fact it was consistent with research findings. When students are asked to identify their most "popular" classmates, they identify peers who have dominant social status at school (perhaps those who belong to a prestigious social group) but in many cases are aggressive or stuck-up. Truly **popular students**—those whom many classmates select as people they'd like to do things with—may or may not hold high-status positions, but they are kind and trustworthy.[116] Youngsters who are popular in this way typically have good social skills. For instance, they know how to initiate and sustain conversations, are sensitive to the subtle social and emotional cues that others give them, and adjust their behavior to changing circumstances. They also tend to show genuine concern for their peers. For instance, they are more likely to help, share, cooperate, and empathize with others.[117]

In contrast to popular students, **rejected students** are students who classmates select as being their *least* preferred social companions. Students with few social skills—for example, those who are impulsive or aggressive, and those who continually try to draw attention to themselves—typically experience peer rejection.[118] In addition, students from racial and ethnic minority groups often find themselves the targets of derogatory remarks and other forms of racism and discrimination, as do students from low-income families.[119] Especially when peer rejection and exclusion continue over a lengthy period, rejected students are at high risk for emotional problems, low school achievement, and poor school attendance.[120]

A third group, **controversial students**, are a mixed bag, in that some peers really like them and others really *dis*like them. These students can, like rejected students, be quite aggressive, but they also have good social skills that make them popular with at least some of their peers.[121]

Researchers have described another category as well.[122] **Neglected students** are those whom peers rarely identify as someone they would either most like or least like to do something with.[123] Neglected students tend to be quiet and keep to themselves. Some prefer to be alone, others may be very shy or may not know how to go about initiating interaction, and still others may be quite content with having only one or two close friends.[124] For some students, "neglected" status is a relatively temporary situation. Others are totally friendless for extended periods, and these students are at higher-than-average risk for depression.[125]

Underlying the social skills that affect popularity are certain ways of thinking about social relationships, as we shall see now.

Having at least one good friend seems to be important for children's and adolescents' emotional well-being.

[114] Alapack, 1991; Katchadourian, 1990.

[115] M. B. Harris, 1997.

[116] Cillessen & Rose, 2005; Parkhurst & Hopmeyer, 1998.

[117] Caprara, Barbaranelli, Pastorelli, Bandura, & Zimbardo, 2000; Crick & Dodge, 1994; Mostow, Izard, Fine, & Trantacosta, 2002; Wentzel & Asher, 1995.

[118] Bolger & Patterson, 2001; N. Eisenberg, Pidada, & Liew, 2001; Pedersen, Vitaro, Barker, & Borge, 2007; Pellegrini, Bartini, & Brooks, 1999.

[119] Banks & Banks, 1995; McBrien, 2005; Phelan, Yu, & Davidson, 1994.

[120] Buhs, Ladd, & Herald, 2006; Ladd, 2006.

[121] Bukowski et al., 2007; Newcomb, Bukowski, & Pattee, 1993.

[122] All together, researchers have identified five groups of students. The fifth group, *average students*, are liked by some peers and disliked by others, but without the intensity of feelings that is true for controversial students.

[123] Asher & Renshaw, 1981.

[124] Gazelle & Ladd, 2003; Guay et al., 1999; Rubin & Krasnor, 1986.

[125] Asher & Paquette, 2003; Gazelle & Ladd, 2003; Laursen et al., 2007.

popular student Student whom many peers like and perceive to be kind and trustworthy.

rejected student Student whom many peers identify as being an undesirable social partner.

controversial student Student whom some peers strongly like and other peers strongly dislike.

neglected student Student about whom most peers have no strong feelings, either positive or negative.

SOCIAL COGNITION

In Chapters 2, 4, and 5, we identified many ways in which children and adolescents become increasingly able to understand and think logically about the physical world and academic subject matter. Yet as they grow older, they also think in increasingly sophisticated ways about other people and social interactions. Such thinking about the nature of people and social events is known as **social cognition**.

At any particular age level, youngsters vary considerably in their interest in and awareness of other people's thoughts and feelings. Those who think regularly about such matters are more socially skillful, make friends more easily, and have better understandings of *themselves* as well.[126] You may occasionally see the term *emotional intelligence* in reference to such abilities.[127]

The following principles describe how social cognition influences children's and adolescents' interpersonal effectiveness.

As children get older, they become increasingly aware of other people's thoughts and emotions.

To truly understand and get along with others, people must be able to step into others' shoes—that is, to look at the world from other viewpoints. The following situation provides an example.

SEE FOR YOURSELF

Last Picked

Kenny and Mark are co-captains of the soccer team. They have one person left to choose for the team. Without saying anything, Mark winks at Kenny and looks at Tom, who is one of the remaining children left to be chosen for the team. Mark looks back at Kenny and smiles. Kenny nods and chooses Tom to be on their team. Tom sees Mark and Kenny winking and smiling at each other. Tom, who is usually one of the last to be picked for team sports, wonders why Kenny wants him to be on his team. . . .

- Why did Mark smile at Kenny?
- Why did Kenny nod?
- Why did Kenny choose Tom to be on the team? How do you know this?
- Do you think that Tom has any idea of why Kenny chose him to be on the team? How do you know this? . . .
- How do you think Tom feels?[128]

To answer these questions, you must look at the situation from the perspectives of three individuals: Kenny, Mark, and Tom. For instance, putting yourself in Tom's shoes for a moment, you might realize that as a child who has not yet been picked for the soccer team, Tom might initially feel embarrassed, upset, or demoralized. (Accordingly, asking some students to choose others for their teams, as might be done in a physical education class, is generally *not* recommended.) Such **perspective taking** helps people to make sense of actions that might otherwise be puzzling and to choose responses that are most likely to achieve desired results and maintain positive interpersonal relationships.

As we discovered in Chapter 4, metacognition improves with age: Children become increasingly aware of their own thought processes. In fact, as children learn more about their own thinking, they also become more adept at drawing inferences about what *other* people

Observe a discussion of perspective taking in a first-grade class in the "Promoting Perspective Taking" video in the Additional Resources section in Chapter 7 of MyEducationLab.

---

social cognition Process of thinking about how other people are likely to think, act, and react.

perspective taking Ability to look at a situation from someone's else viewpoint.

---

[126] Bosacki, 2000; Izard et al., 2001; P. L. Harris, 2006.
[127] Despite the prevalence of this concept in popular media, research to date has not conclusively validated it as a distinct ability separate from other aspects of people's intellectual and social functioning; for

example, see Brackett, Lopes, Ivcevic, Mayer, & Salovey, 2004; J. D. Mayer, 2001; J. D. Mayer & Cobb, 2000; Waterhouse, 2006; Zeidner, Roberts, & Matthews, 2002.
[128] Bosacki, 2000, p. 711, format adapted.

are thinking. More generally, children develop a **theory of mind** that encompasses increasingly complex understandings of human mental and psychological states—thoughts, beliefs, feelings, motives, and so on. Their theory of mind enables them to interpret and predict the behaviors of the important people in their lives and, as a result, to interact effectively with those individuals.[129]

Consistent with what we've learned about cognitive development, young children tend to think of other people in a fairly concrete fashion, with a focus on observable characteristics and behaviors (e.g., look once again at Andrew's essay about friends in Figure 7.1). However, they do have some awareness of other people's inner worlds. As early as age 4 or 5, they realize that what *they* know may be different from what *other people* know.[130] They also have some ability to draw inferences about other people's mental and emotional states—for instance, to deduce that people who behave in certain ways have certain intentions or feelings.[131]

As children progress through the elementary grades, they draw more sophisticated inferences about other people's mental states. For instance, they may realize that people's actions do not always reflect their thoughts and feelings (e.g., someone who appears happy may actually feel sad).[132] Children understand, too, that people *interpret* events—rather than simply "recording" events in an objective manner—and that others may therefore view a situation differently than they themselves do. In other words, children increasingly understand that thinking and learning are active, constructive processes.[133]

By early adolescence, youngsters realize that people can have ambivalent feelings about events and other individuals.[134] They also become aware that people can simultaneously have multiple, and possibly conflicting, intentions.[135] As an example, let's return to the "Last Picked" exercise you did earlier. You may have suspected that Tom has mixed feelings about being chosen for the team. He may think that he's a poor athlete (he's often one of the last picked) and so may wonder why Mark and Kenny have chosen him. He may also wonder what Mark's smile means. Perhaps it means that Mark is delighted to find a capable player still available to be picked, yet it might instead signal a malicious intention to make Tom look foolish on the soccer field. Despite misgivings, Tom may be happy to have a chance to play one of his favorite games. Young adolescents become increasingly thoughtful about such matters.[136]

Courtesy of their expanding cognitive abilities, memory capacity, and social awareness, young adolescents also become able to engage in **recursive thinking**.[137] That is, they can think about what other people might be thinking about them and eventually can reflect on other people's thoughts about themselves through multiple iterations (e.g., "You think that I think that you think . . ."). This is not to say that adolescents (or adults, for that matter) always use this capacity. In fact, thinking only about one's own perspective, without regard for the perspective of others, is a common phenomenon in the early adolescent years (recall our earlier discussion of the *imaginary audience*).[138]

In the high school years, teenagers can draw on a rich knowledge base derived from numerous social experiences, and so they become ever more skillful at drawing inferences about people's psychological characteristics, intentions, and needs.[139] In addition, they are more attuned to the complex dynamics—not only thoughts, feelings, and present circumstances but also past experiences—that influence behavior.[140] And they realize that other people are not always aware of why they act as they do.[141] What we see emerging in the high school years, then, is a budding psychologist: an individual who can be quite astute in deciphering and explaining the motives and actions of others.

As children get older, they become increasingly able to look at situations from another person's point of view. Such perspective taking helps them interact more effectively and prosocially with one another.

[129] Flavell, 2000; Gopnik & Meltzoff, 1997; Wellman & Gelman, 1998.

[130] P. L. Harris, 2006; Wellman, Cross, & Watson, 2001; Wimmer & Perner, 1983.

[131] Astington & Pelletier, 1996; Flavell, 2000; P. L. Harris, 2006; Schult, 2002; Wellman, Phillips, & Rodriguez, 2000.

[132] Flavell, Miller, & Miller, 2002; Gnepp, 1989; Selman, 1980.

[133] Chandler & Boyes, 1982; Flavell et al., 2002; Flavell, Green, & Flavell, 1995; Wellman, 1990.

[134] S. K. Donaldson & Westerman, 1986; Flavell & Miller, 1998; Harter & Whitesell, 1989.

[135] Chandler, 1987.

[136] Bosacki, 2000.

[137] Flavell et al., 2002; Oppenheimer, 1986; Perner & Wimmer, 1985.

[138] Tsethlikai & Greenhoot, 2006; Tsethlikai, Guthrie-Fulbright, & Loera, 2007.

[139] N. Eisenberg, Carlo, Murphy, & Van Court, 1995; Paget, Kritt, & Bergemann, 1984.

[140] Flanagan & Tucker, 1999; Selman, 1980.

[141] Selman, 1980.

theory of mind Self-constructed understanding of one's own and other people's mental and psychological states (thoughts, feelings, etc.).

recursive thinking Thinking about what other people may be thinking about oneself, possibly through multiple iterations.

DEVELOPMENTAL TRENDS

TABLE 7.2 Perspective Taking and Theory of Mind at Different Grade Levels

Grade Level	Age-Typical Characteristics	Suggested Strategies
K–2	<ul><li>Awareness that mental events are not physical entities</li><li>Awareness that others' knowledge and thoughts may be different from one's own</li><li>Ability to draw inferences about people's thoughts, feelings, and intentions from their behaviors, albeit in a simplistic manner (e.g., "She's sad"); nature of inferences dependent on own past experiences in social interactions</li></ul>	<ul><li>Talk frequently about people's thoughts, feelings, and motives; use words such as *think, remember, feel,* and *want.*</li><li>Ask questions about thoughts, feelings, and motives during storybook readings; encourage students to share and compare diverse perspectives and inferences.</li></ul>
3–5	<ul><li>Growing recognition that others interpret (rather than simply absorb) experiences and so may misconstrue events</li><li>Realization that other people's actions may hide their true feelings</li><li>Preoccupation with own feelings rather than others' feelings in conflict situations</li></ul>	<ul><li>As students read literature, ask them to consider why various characters might behave as they do.</li><li>Have students consider what people might have been thinking and feeling during events in history.</li><li>Help students resolve interpersonal conflicts by asking them to consider one another's perspectives and to develop a solution that addresses everyone's needs.</li></ul>
6–8	<ul><li>Increasing interest in other people's thoughts and feelings</li><li>Recognition that people may have multiple and possibly conflicting motives and emotions</li><li>Ability to think recursively about one's own and others' thoughts</li></ul>	<ul><li>Encourage students to look at historical and current events from the perspective of various historical figures and cultural groups.</li><li>In discussions of literature, talk about other people's complex (and sometimes conflicting) motives.</li></ul>
9–12	<ul><li>Recognition that people are products of their environment and that past events and present circumstances influence personality and behavior</li><li>Awareness that people are not always aware of why they act as they do</li></ul>	<ul><li>Explore the possible origins of people's perspectives and motives in discussions of real and fictional events.</li><li>Schedule debates in which students must present convincing arguments for perspectives opposite to their own.</li><li>Offer units or courses in psychology, with a focus on such "internal" activities as cognition, motivation, and emotion.</li></ul>

Sources: Astington & Pelletier, 1996; Bosacki, 2000; Brophy & Alleman, 1996; Brophy & VanSledright, 1997; N. Eisenberg et al., 1995; Flanagan & Tucker, 1999; Flavell, 2000; Flavell et al., 1995, 2002; Flavell & Miller, 1998; Greenhoot, Tsethlikai, & Wagoner, 2006; P. L. Harris, 2006; Harter & Whitesell, 1989; Perner & Wimmer, 1985; Ruffman, Slade, & Crowe, 2002; Schult, 2002; Selman, 1980; Shure & Aberson, 2006; Tsethlikai et al., 2007; Wainryb, Brehl, & Matwin, 2005; Wellman, 1990; Wellman et al., 2000, 2001; Woolfe, Want, & Siegal, 2002; Woolley, 1995.

Table 7.2 describes ways in which perspective taking and theory of mind tend to change over the course of childhood and adolescence. You can also observe the development of perspective taking in the three "Emotions" video clips in MyEducationLab. In the "Middle Childhood" clip, 10-year-old Daniel shows an understanding that people often (but not always) reveal their emotions in their facial expressions and body language—for instance, by smiling when happy, frowning when angry, or walking with drooping shoulders when sad. In the "Early Adolescence" and "Late Adolescence" clips, respectively, 13-year-old Crystal and 15-year-old Greg are aware of more subtle cues. For instance, people may get "hyper" or "won't stop talking" when they're happy, may "hide their face" or "don't talk" when sad, or "don't want you to be around them" when angry.

 Observe examples of social cognition in the three "Emotions" videos in the Additional Resources section in Chapter 7 of MyEducationLab.

Children's cognitive processes in social situations influence their behaviors toward others.

Children and adolescents have a lot to think about when they consider what other people are thinking, feeling, and doing. Such **social information processing**—the mental processes involved in understanding and responding to social events—is simply a more "social" ver-

social information processing Mental processes involved in understanding and responding to social events.

sion of the cognitive processes described in Chapter 2. Among other things, social information processing involves paying *attention* to certain behaviors in a social situation and trying to interpret and make sense of those behaviors through *elaboration*. For example, when children interact with peers, they might focus on certain remarks, facial expressions, and body language and try to figure out what a peer really means by, say, a thoughtless comment or sheepish grin. Children also consider one or more *goals* they hope to achieve during an interaction—perhaps preserving a friendship, on the one hand, or teaching somebody a "lesson," on the other. Then, taking into account both their interpretations and their goals, they draw on their previous knowledge and experiences to *retrieve* a number of possible responses and choose what is, in their eyes, a productive course of action.[142]

The behaviors youngsters attend to, the ways in which they interpret those behaviors, and the particular goals they have for their social interactions have a considerable impact on how effectively they interact with others. This point will become clear as we discuss the next principle.

Aggressive behavior is often the result of counterproductive cognitive processes.

Aggressive behavior is an action intentionally taken to harm another person either physically or psychologically. **Physical aggression**, an action that can potentially cause bodily injury (e.g., hitting, shoving), is more common in boys. **Relational aggression**, an action that can adversely affect friendships and other interpersonal relationships (e.g., ostracizing a peer, spreading unkind rumors), is more common in girls.[143] As a general rule, aggression declines over the course of childhood and adolescence, but it increases for a short time after children make the transition from elementary school to middle school or junior high.[144] For example, in the opening case study, a few of the allegedly "popular" (i.e., high-status) eighth graders regularly pick on Peter, perhaps by ridiculing him (relational aggression) and perhaps by occasionally poking or shoving him (physical aggression).

Researchers have identified two distinct groups of aggressive children.[145] Those who engage in **proactive aggression** deliberately initiate aggressive behaviors as a means of obtaining desired goals. Those who engage in **reactive aggression** act aggressively primarily in response to frustration or provocation. Of the two groups, children who exhibit proactive aggression are more likely to have difficulty maintaining friendships with others.[146] They may also direct considerable aggression toward particular peers, and those who do so are often known as **bullies**. Their hapless victims often are children who are immature, anxious, friendless, and lacking in self-esteem—some also have disabilities—and so are relatively defenseless.[147]

Some children and adolescents are genetically more predisposed to aggression than their peers, and others may exhibit heightened aggression as a result of neurological damage.[148] Yet several cognitive factors also play a role in aggressive behavior:

- **Poor perspective-taking ability.** Children who are highly aggressive tend to have limited ability to look at situations from other people's perspectives or to empathize with their victims.[149]
- **Misinterpretation of social cues.** Children who are either physically or relationally aggressive toward peers tend to interpret others' behaviors as reflecting hostile intentions, especially when such behaviors have ambiguous meanings. This **hostile attributional bias** is especially prevalent in children who are prone to *reactive* aggression.[150]

Boys' greater propensity for physical aggression often shows up in their fantasy play and fiction, as in this story by 7-year-old Grant. (His teacher has corrected some of his misspellings.)

aggressive behavior Action intentionally taken to harm another person either physically or psychologically.

physical aggression Action that can potentially cause bodily injury.

relational aggression Action that can adversely affect interpersonal relationships.

proactive aggression Deliberate aggression against another as a means of obtaining a desired goal.

reactive aggression Aggressive response to frustration or provocation.

bully Child or adolescent who frequently threatens, harasses, or causes injury to particular peers.

hostile attributional bias Tendency to interpret others' behaviors as reflecting hostile or aggressive intentions.

[142] Arsenio & Lemerise, 2004; Crick & Dodge, 1996; Dodge, 1986; E. R. Smith & Semin, 2007.

[143] Crick, Grotpeter, & Bigbee, 2002; French, Jansen, & Pidada, 2002; Goodwin, 2006; Pellegrini & Archer, 2005.

[144] Pellegrini, 2002; Pellegrini & Long, 2004.

[145] Crick & Dodge, 1996; Poulin & Boivin, 1999; Vitaro, Gendreau, Tremblay, & Oligny, 1998.

[146] Poulin & Boivin, 1999.

[147] Espelage & Swearer, 2004; Hyman et al., 2004; R. S. Newman & Murray, 2005.

[148] Brendgen et al., 2005; Raine & Scerbo, 1991; D. C. Rowe, Almeida, & Jacobson, 1999.

[149] Coie & Dodge, 1998; Damon & Hart, 1988; Marcus, 1980.

[150] Bukowski et al., 2007; E. Chen, Langer, Raphaelson, & Matthews, 2004; Crick et al., 2002; Dodge et al., 2003; Orobio de Castro, Veerman, Koops, Bosch, & Monshouwer, 2002.

- **Prevalence of self-serving goals.** For most young people, establishing and maintaining interpersonal relationships are a high priority. For aggressive children, however, more self-serving goals—perhaps maintaining an inflated self-image, seeking revenge, or gaining power and respect—often take precedence.[151]
- **Ineffective social problem-solving strategies.** Aggressive children often have little knowledge of how to persuade, negotiate, or compromise, and so they resort to hitting, shoving, barging into play activities, and other ineffective strategies.[152]
- **Beliefs about the appropriateness and effectiveness of aggression.** Many aggressive children believe that violence and other forms of aggression are acceptable ways of resolving conflicts and retaliating for others' misdeeds. Those who display high rates of *proactive* aggression are also apt to believe that aggressive action will yield positive results—for instance, that it will enhance their social status. Not surprisingly, aggressive children tend to associate with one another, thus confirming one another's beliefs that aggression is appropriate.[153]

Unless adults actively intervene, many aggressive children (especially those who exhibit proactive aggression) show a continuing pattern of aggression and violence as they grow older, almost guaranteeing long-term maladjustment and difficulties with peers.[154] The victims of aggression certainly suffer as well. Children who are frequent targets of bullying can become anxious, depressed, possibly even suicidal, and their classroom performance may deteriorate as a result.[155] Over time their self-esteem declines, and some begin to believe that they themselves are responsible for the harassment they endure.[156] They may fear retaliation if they alert adults to their plight and so have little optimism that things will improve.[157] One boy expressed this no-win situation as follows:

> Well I tell a teacher [when I get bullied] but that only gets me in more trouble from the bullies because they pick on me, they hit me, they call me names. Everybody except my friends in my class are bullies. They call me "stink bomb," "stinky," "dirty boy," and stuff like that.[158]

We'll consider strategies for addressing bullying and other forms of chronic aggression near the end of the chapter. In the meantime, we turn to the development of more general beliefs about right and wrong—in other words, to moral and prosocial development.

MORAL AND PROSOCIAL DEVELOPMENT

Some social behaviors, such as sharing, helping, and comforting, are aimed at benefiting others more than oneself. Such *prosocial behaviors*, plus such traits as honesty, fairness, and respect for other people's needs and rights, fall into the domain of **morality**.

Learners' beliefs about moral and immoral behavior—that is, their beliefs about right and wrong—affect their actions and achievement at school. For example, students are less likely to engage in theft or aggression when they respect the property and safety of their classmates. And their moral beliefs are likely to influence their cognitive and affective reactions to classroom subject matter—for instance, how they respond to descriptions of the Holocaust during World War II or to anti-Semitic dialogue in Shakespeare's *The Merchant of Venice*. By behaving and thinking morally and prosocially, students gain greater support from their teachers and classmates and thereby achieve greater academic and social success over the long run.[159]

Several principles describe the nature of moral and prosocial development over the course of childhood and adolescence.

morality One's general standards about right and wrong behavior.

[151] R. F. Baumeister et al., 1996; Bender, 2001; Crick & Dodge, 1996; Erdley & Asher, 1996; Gonsalves, Murawska, Blake, & Pope, 2007; Hemmings, 2004; Pellegrini, 2002.
[152] Lochman & Dodge, 1994; Neel, Jenkins, & Meadows, 1990; Schwartz et al., 1998; Shure & Spivack, 1980.
[153] Astor, 1994; Boldizar, Perry, & Perry, 1989; Dodge, Lochman, Harnish, Bates, & Pettit, 1997; Espelage & Swearer, 2004; Farmer et al., 2002; C. H. Hart, Ladd, & Burleson, 1990; Hemmings, 2004; Pellegrini & Bartini,
2000; Staub, 1995; Zelli, Dodge, Lochman, & Laird, 1999.
[154] Dodge et al., 2003; Kupersmidt & Coie, 1990; Ladd & Troop-Gordon, 2003.
[155] Buhs et al., 2006; Hyman et al., 2004; Schwartz, Gorman, Nakamoto, & Toblin, 2005.
[156] Troop-Gordon & Ladd, 2005.
[157] Holt & Keyes, 2004; R. S. Newman & Murray, 2005.
[158] Bergamo & Evans, 2005.
[159] Caprara et al., 2000.

Children begin using internal standards to evaluate behavior at an early age.

Even preschoolers have some understanding that behaviors causing physical or psychological harm are inappropriate. By age 4, most children understand that causing harm to another person is wrong regardless of what authority figures might tell them and regardless of what consequences certain behaviors may or may not bring.[160]

Children increasingly distinguish between moral and conventional transgressions.

Mainstream Western culture discourages some behaviors, known as **moral transgressions**, because they cause damage or harm, violate human rights, or run counter to basic principles of equality, freedom, or justice. It discourages other behaviors, known as **conventional transgressions**, that are not unethical but violate widely held understandings about how one should act (e.g., children shouldn't talk back to adults or burp at meals). Conventional transgressions are usually specific to a particular culture. For instance, although burping is frowned on in mainstream Western culture, people in some cultures burp as a compliment to the cook. In contrast, many moral transgressions are universal across cultures.

Even preschoolers realize that not all actions are wrong in the same way and that violations of moral standards are more serious than other transgressions.[161] Children's awareness of social conventions is minimal in early childhood but increases throughout the elementary school years.[162] However, children and adults do not always agree about which behaviors constitute moral transgressions, which ones fall into the conventional domain, and which ones are simply a matter of personal choice. For instance, whereas adults typically view use of illegal street drugs as a moral transgression, teenagers often think it is acceptable as long as it doesn't hurt other people.[163] And certain conventions occasionally take on moral overtones, as you can see in the Cultural Considerations box "Cultural and Ethnic Diversity in Personal and Social Development."

Children's capacity to respond emotionally to others' harm and distress increases throughout the school years.

How do you feel when you inadvertently cause inconvenience for someone else? when you hurt someone else's feelings? when a friend suddenly and unexpectedly loses a close family member? Perhaps such feelings as guilt, shame, and empathy come to mind. All of these emotions are associated with moral and prosocial development.[164]

Children begin to show signs of **guilt**, a feeling of discomfort when they know they have inflicted damage or caused distress, well before they reach school age.[165] By the time they reach the middle elementary grades, most of them also feel **shame**: They feel embarrassed or humiliated when they fail to meet the standards for moral behavior that adults have set for them.[166] Both guilt and shame, though unpleasant emotions, are good signs that children are developing a sense of right and wrong.

Guilt and shame emerge when children believe they have done something unacceptable. In contrast, **empathy**—experiencing the same feelings as someone in unfortunate circumstances—appears in the absence of wrongdoing. The ability to empathize continues to develop throughout the elementary school years and often into the high school years as well.[167] At the primary grade levels, children show empathy mostly for people they know, such as friends and classmates. But by the upper elementary school grades, they may also begin to feel empathy for people they *don't* know—perhaps for the poor, the homeless, or those in catastrophic circumstances (e.g., see Figure 7.2).[168]

hopes
goals
dreams
happiness
broken
destroyed
eliminated
exterminated
no steps forward
no evolution
no prosperity
no hope
But
maybe
perhaps
except
if we
help
together
we stand
a chance.

FIGURE 7.2 In this poem about the Holocaust, Matthew, a middle school student, expresses empathy for its victims.

moral transgression Action that causes harm or infringes on the needs or rights of others.

conventional transgression Action that violates a culture's general expectations regarding socially appropriate behavior.

guilt Feeling of discomfort when one knows one has caused someone else pain or distress.

shame Feeling of embarrassment or humiliation after failing to meet standards for moral behavior that adults have set.

empathy Experience of sharing the same feelings as someone in unfortunate circumstances.

[160] Helwig, Zelazo, & Wilson, 2001; J. M. Kim & Turiel, 1996; Laupa & Turiel, 1995; Smetana, 1981; Tisak, 1993.
[161] Nucci & Weber, 1995; Turiel, 1983; Yau & Smetana, 2003.
[162] Helwig & Jasiobedzka, 2001; Laupa & Turiel, 1995; Nucci, 2001; Nucci & Nucci, 1982; Turiel, 1983.
[163] Nucci, 2001.
[164] N. Eisenberg & Fabes, 1991; Hoffman, 1991; Kochanska, Gross, Lin, & Nichols, 2002; Turiel, 1998.
[165] Kochanska et al., 2002.
[166] Damon, 1988.
[167] N. Eisenberg, 1982; N. Eisenberg et al., 1995; N. Eisenberg, Lennon, & Pasternack, 1986.
[168] Damon, 1988; N. Eisenberg, 1982; Hoffman, 1991.

CULTURAL CONSIDERATIONS

Cultural and Ethnic Diversity in Personal and Social Development

As we discovered early in the chapter, children's personality traits (e.g., shyness versus outgoingness) are to some extent a product of the cultures in which they have been raised. Researchers have also found cultural and ethnic differences in children's sense of self, social skills and relationships, and morality and prosocial behavior. Here we look at examples of diversity in each of these areas.

Sense of self. As noted earlier in the chapter, learners' group memberships affect their sense of self. In fact, in some cultures—for instance, in many Middle Eastern and Far Eastern countries, as well as in many Native American communities—children see their group membership and connections with other individuals as central parts of who they are as human beings.[a] Such cultural groups encourage children to take pride in accomplishments that contribute to the greater good of the family or larger community as well as, or perhaps *instead of*, their own accomplishments.[b]

In addition, many young people are both aware and proud of their ethnic group and willingly adopt some of the group's behaviors. In other words, they have a strong **ethnic identity**.[c] Occasionally learners' ethnic identities can lead them to reject mainstream Western values. In some ethnic minority groups, peers may accuse high-achieving students of "acting white," a label that essentially means "you're not one of us."[d] We saw an example of this phenomenon in the opening case study in Chapter 3, when Sylvia, a high-achieving African American adolescent, encountered taunts from some of her neighborhood peers:

> Oh, here she come. Here come whitey. Hey, Doc, you scrape yourself an' you find that honky skin?[e]

For the most part, however, learners with a strong and positive ethnic identity do *well* in school both academically and socially.[f] Furthermore, pride in one's ethnic heritage can serve as an emotional "buffer" against the insults and discrimination that children and adolescents from minority groups sometimes encounter.[g] Consider this statement by Eva, an African American high school student, as an example:

> I'm proud to be black and everything. But, um, I'm aware of, you know, racist acts and racist things that are happening in the world, but I use that as no excuse, you know. I feel as though I can succeed. . . . I just know that I'm not gonna let [racism] stop me. . . . Being black is good. I'm proud to be black but you also gotta face reality. And what's going on, you know, black people are not really getting anywhere in life, but I know I will and I don't know—I just know I will.[h]

Not all young people from minority groups affiliate strongly with their cultural and ethnic groups. Some youngsters (especially those with multiple racial or cultural heritages) fluctuate in the strength of their ethnic identity depending on the context and situation.[i] In addition, older adolescents may experiment with varying forms of an ethnic identity. Some teens, for instance, may initially adopt a fairly intense, inflexible, and perhaps hostile ethnic identify before eventually retreating to a more relaxed, open-minded, and productive one.[j]

ethnic identity Awareness of one's membership in a particular ethnic or cultural group, and willingness to adopt behaviors characteristic of the group.

distributive justice Beliefs about what constitutes people's fair share of a desired commodity.

moral dilemma Situation in which two or more people's rights or needs may be at odds and the morally correct action is not clear-cut.

Children's understanding of fairness evolves throughout early and middle childhood.

The ability to share with others depends on children's sense of **distributive justice**, their beliefs about what constitutes a person's fair share of a desired commodity (e.g., food, toys, time on the classroom computer). Children's notions of distributive justice change with age. Preschoolers' beliefs about what's fair are based on their own needs and desires. In their minds, it would be perfectly "fair" to give themselves a large handful of candy and give others a smaller amount. In the early elementary grades, children base their judgments about fairness on strict equality: Everyone gets the same amount. Sometime around age 8, children begin to take merit and special needs into account. They reason, for instance, that people who contribute more to a group's efforts should reap a greater portion of the group's rewards or that people who are exceptionally poor might receive more resources than others.[169]

With age, reasoning about moral issues becomes increasingly abstract and flexible.

To probe people's reasoning about moral issues, researchers sometimes present **moral dilemmas**, situations in which two or more people's rights or needs may be at odds and for which there are no clear-cut right or wrong solutions. An example is presented in the following exercise.

---

[169] Damon, 1977, 1980; Nucci, 2001.

Social skills and relationships. Interpersonal skills and relationships may vary somewhat for students from different backgrounds. Some ethnic groups (e.g., African Americans living along the South Carolina coast and many Navajos in the American Southwest) place particular emphasis on maintaining group harmony and resolving interpersonal conflicts peacefully, and children from these groups may be especially adept at negotiation and peace making.[k] Although teasing and ridicule are discouraged in mainstream Western culture, such behaviors are common ways of teaching children to "keep their cool" and handle criticism in certain other cultures, such as in some communities in northern Canada and in the South Pacific.[l]

Children and adolescents of all cultures enjoy the company of age-mates, but the extent to which they actually spend time with their peers is partly a function of their cultural background. For instance, on average, Asian Americans spend less leisure time with friends, and are more likely to choose friends who value academic achievement, than young people from other groups.[m] Children who have recently immigrated from a non-English-speaking country may have relatively little interaction with peers because of their limited ability to communicate with other children in their neighborhoods and classrooms.[n]

Morality and prosocial behavior. Conceptions of moral and immoral behavior vary as a function of cultural background as well. Virtually all cultures espouse the importance of both individual rights and fairness (i.e., an *ethic of justice*) and compassion for others (i.e., an *ethic of caring*). However, different cultural groups tend to place greater emphasis on one than on the other.[o] For instance, in the United States, helping others (or not) is often considered to be a voluntary choice, but in some societies (e.g., in India) it is one's *duty* to help people in need. Such a sense of duty, which is often coupled with strong ties to family and the community, can lead to considerable prosocial behavior.[p]

Some variability is also seen in the behaviors that cultural groups view as moral transgressions versus those they see as conventional transgressions.[q] For instance, in mainstream Western culture, how one dresses is largely a matter of convention and personal choice. In some deeply religious groups, however, certain forms of dress (e.g., head coverings) are seen as moral imperatives that must be adhered to.

[a] Brewer & Yuki, 2007; Kağitçibaşi, 2007; Q. Wang, 2006; Whitesell, Mitchell, Kaufman, Spicer, & the Voices of Indian Teens Project Team, 2006.
[b] Banks & Banks, 1995; P. M. Cole & Tan, 2007.
[c] L. Allen & Aber, 2006; Y. Hong, Wan, No, & Chiu, 2007; Phinney, 1993; Sheets & Hollins, 1999.
[d] B. B. Brown, 1993; Cross, Strauss, & Fhagen-Smith, 1999; Graham, 1997; Ogbu, 2003; L. Steinberg, 1996.
[e] McCourt, 2005, p. 194.
[f] Altschul, Oyserman, & Bybee, 2006; Chavous et al., 2003; Spencer, Noll, Stoltzfus, & Harpalani, 2001.
[g] C. H. Caldwell, Zimmerman, Bernat, Sellers, & Notaro, 2002; Cross et al., 1999; DuBois, Burk-Braxton, Swenson, Tevendale, & Hardesty, 2002; Pahl & Way, 2006.
[h] Way, 1998, p. 257.
[i] Cross et al., 1999; Hitlin, Brown, & Elder, 2006; A. M. Lopez, 2003; Tatum, 1997; Yip & Fuligni, 2002.
[j] Cross et al., 1999; Seaton et al., 2006.
[k] P. Guthrie, 2001; Halgunseth et al., 2006; Witmer, 1996.
[l] Rogoff, 2003.
[m] L. Steinberg, 1996.
[n] Ahn, 2005; A. Doyle, 1982.
[o] J. G. Miller, 2007; Shweder, Mahapatra, & Miller, 1987; Snarey, 1995; Turiel, 2002.
[p] J. G. Miller, 2007; Greenfield, 1994; Markus & Kitayama, 1991; Triandis, 1995.
[q] Nucci, 2001.

SEE FOR YOURSELF

Heinz's Dilemma

Consider the following situation:

In Europe, a woman was near death from a rare form of cancer. There was one drug that the doctors thought might save her, a form of radium that a druggist in the same town had recently discovered. The druggist was charging $2,000, ten times what the drug cost him to make. The sick woman's husband, Heinz, went to everyone he knew to borrow the money, but he could only get together about half of what the drug cost. He told the druggist that his wife was dying and asked him to sell it cheaper or let him pay later. But the druggist said no. So Heinz got desperate and broke into the man's store to steal the drug for his wife.[170]

- Should Heinz have stolen the drug? What would *you* have done if you were Heinz? Which is worse, stealing something that belongs to someone else or letting another person die a preventable death? Why?

[170] Kohlberg, 1984, p. 186.

Following are three solutions to Heinz's dilemma offered by elementary and secondary school students. I have given the students fictitious names so that we can talk about them more easily.

James (a fifth grader): Maybe his wife is an important person and runs a store, and the man buys stuff from her and can't get it any other place. The police would blame the owner that he didn't save the wife. He didn't save an important person, and that's just like killing with a gun or a knife. You can get the electric chair for that.[171]

Jesse (a high school student): If he cares enough for her to steal for her, he should steal it. If not he should let her die. It's up to him.[172]

Jules (a high school student): In that particular situation Heinz was right to do it. In the eyes of the law he would not be doing the right thing, but in the eyes of the moral law he would. If he had exhausted every other alternative I think it would be worth it to save a life.[173]

Each boy offers a different reason to justify why Heinz should steal the lifesaving drug. James bases his decision on the needs of one person only—the "owner." It's not entirely clear who the owner is, but James certainly isn't concerned about Heinz's dying wife. Jesse, too, takes a self-serving view, proposing that the decision to either steal or not steal the drug depends on how much Heinz loves his wife. Only Jules considers the value of human life in justifying why Heinz should break the law.

After obtaining hundreds of responses to moral dilemmas, one groundbreaking cognitive-developmental psychologist, Lawrence Kohlberg, proposed that the development of moral reasoning is characterized by a sequence of six stages grouped into three general *levels* of morality: preconventional, conventional, and postconventional[174] (see Table 7.3). **Preconventional morality** is the earliest and least mature form of moral reasoning, in that a child has not yet adopted or internalized society's conventions regarding what is right or wrong—hence the label *preconventional*. James's response to the Heinz dilemma is a good example of preconventional, Stage 1 thinking, in that he considers the consequences of Heinz's actions for one particular individual, without regard for legal or moral standards for behavior. Kohlberg classified Jesse's response as a preconventional, Stage 2 response. Jesse is beginning to recognize the importance of saving someone else's life but believes Heinz's decision to do so ultimately depends on whether or not he loves his wife. In other words, Heinz's decision depends on *his* feelings alone.

Conventional morality is characterized by an acceptance of society's conventions concerning right and wrong. At this level of moral reasoning, an individual obeys rules and follows society's norms even when there are no consequences for obedience or disobedience. Adherence to rules and conventions is somewhat rigid, however, and a rule's appropriateness or fairness is seldom questioned. In contrast, people who exhibit **postconventional morality** view rules as useful but changeable mechanisms that maintain the general social order and protect human rights, rather than as absolute dictates that must be obeyed without question. They live by their own abstract principles about right and wrong—principles that typically include such basic human rights as life, liberty, and justice. They may disobey rules inconsistent with their principles, as we see in Jules's Stage 5 response to the Heinz dilemma: "In the eyes of the law he would not be doing the right thing, but in the eyes of the moral law he would."

The "Moral Reasoning" video clip in MyEducationLab shows four children's reasoning about a dilemma in which a boy named Steve cheats on a history test because work commitments have prevented him from studying. All four children conclude that Steve should not cheat on the test but give varying reasons. The first two (younger) children are concerned only with the negative consequences for Steve and so exhibit preconventional reasoning: "He'll get kicked out," "The teacher might find out." The last two (older) children are instead concerned with society's expectations for behavior and thus exhibit conventional reasoning: "He would be getting somebody else's grade instead of *his* grade," "He should have been paying attention earlier in the course."

Learn more about Kohlberg's theory of moral development in a supplementary reading in the Homework and Exercises section in Chapter 7 of MyEducationLab.

Observe examples of preconventional and conventional reasoning in the "Moral Reasoning" video in the Additional Resources section in Chapter 7 of MyEducationLab.

preconventional morality Lack of internalized standards about right and wrong; making decisions based solely on what is best for oneself.

conventional morality Uncritical acceptance of society's conventions regarding right and wrong.

postconventional morality Thinking in accordance with self-constructed, abstract principles regarding right and wrong.

[171] Kohlberg, 1981, pp. 265–266.
[172] Kohlberg, 1981, p. 132.
[173] Kohlberg, 1984, pp. 446–447.
[174] Colby et al., 1983; Kohlberg, 1963, 1976, 1984.

TABLE 7.3   Kohlberg's Three Levels and Six Stages of Moral Reasoning

Level	Proposed Age Range	Stage	Nature of Moral Reasoning
Level I: Preconventional morality	Seen in preschool children, most elementary school students, some junior high school students, and a few high school students	Stage 1: Punishment-avoidance and obedience	People make decisions based on what is best for themselves, without regard for others' needs or feelings. They obey rules only if established by more powerful individuals; they may disobey if they aren't likely to get caught. "Wrong" behaviors are those that will be punished.
		Stage 2: Exchange of favors	People recognize that others also have needs. They may try to satisfy others' needs if their own needs are also met ("You scratch my back and I'll scratch yours"). They continue to define right and wrong primarily in terms of consequences to themselves.
Level II: Conventional morality	Seen in a few older elementary school students, some junior high school students, and many high school students (Stage 4 typically does not appear before high school)	Stage 3: Good boy/ good girl	People make decisions based on what actions will please others, especially authority figures (e.g., teachers, popular peers). They are concerned about maintaining relationships through sharing, trust, and loyalty, and they take other people's perspectives and intentions into account when making decisions.
		Stage 4: Law and order	People look to society as a whole for guidelines about right or wrong. They know rules are necessary for keeping society running smoothly and believe it is their "duty" to obey them. However, they perceive rules to be inflexible; they don't necessarily recognize that as society's needs change, rules should change as well.
Level III: Postconventional morality	Rarely seen before college (Stage 6 is extremely rare even in adults)	Stage 5: Social contract	People recognize that rules represent agreements among many individuals about appropriate behavior. Rules are seen as useful mechanisms that maintain the general social order and protect individual rights, rather than as absolute dictates that must be obeyed simply because they are "the law." People also recognize the flexibility of rules; rules that no longer serve society's best interests can and should be changed.
		Stage 6: Universal ethical principle	Stage 6 is a hypothetical, "ideal" stage that few people ever reach. People in this stage adhere to a few abstract, universal principles (e.g., equality of all people, respect for human dignity, commitment to justice) that transcend specific norms and rules. They answer to a strong inner conscience and willingly disobey laws that violate their own ethical principles.

Sources: Colby & Kohlberg, 1984; Colby, Kohlberg, Gibbs, & Lieberman, 1983; Kohlberg, 1976, 1984, 1986; Reimer, Paolitto, & Hersh, 1983; Snarey, 1995.

A great deal of research on moral development has followed on the heels of Kohlberg's work. Some of it supports Kohlberg's sequence of moral reasoning: Generally speaking, children and adolescents seem to make advancements in the order that Kohlberg proposed.[175] Nevertheless, contemporary psychologists have identified several weaknesses in Kohlberg's theory. For one thing, Kohlberg included both moral issues (e.g., causing harm) and social conventions (e.g., having rules to help society run smoothly) into his views of morality, but as we have seen, children view these two domains differently. Furthermore, he largely overlooked one very important aspect of morality: that of *helping and showing compassion for* (as well as respecting the rights of) others.[176] Kohlberg also underestimated young children, who, as we discovered earlier, acquire some internal standards of right and wrong long before they begin kindergarten or first grade. Finally, Kohlberg overlooked motives, social benefits, and other situational factors that many children (older ones especially) consider when deciding what's morally right and wrong.[177] For example, children and adolescents are more apt to think of lying as immoral if it causes someone else harm than if it apparently has no adverse effect—that is, if it is just a "white lie" or if it enables them to escape from what they believe to be unreasonable restrictions on their behavior.[178]

[175] Boom, Brugman, & van der Heijden, 2001; Colby & Kohlberg, 1984; Snarey, 1995; Stewart & Pascual-Leone, 1992.
[176] Gilligan, 1982, 1987; J. G. Miller, 2007.

[177] Helwig et al., 2001; Piaget, 1932/1960; Thorkildsen, 1995; Turiel, 1998.
[178] S. A. Perkins & Turiel, 2007; Turiel, Smetana, & Killen, 1991.

Many contemporary developmental psychologists believe that moral reasoning involves general *trends* rather than distinct stages. It appears that children and adolescents gradually acquire several different standards that guide their moral reasoning and decision making in different situations. Such standards include the need to address one's own personal interests, a desire to abide by society's rules and conventions, and, eventually, an appreciation for abstract ideals regarding human rights and society's overall needs.[179] With age, youngsters increasingly apply more advanced standards, but occasionally a fairly primitive one—satisfying one's own needs without regard for others—may take priority.[180] Table 7.4 describes the forms that moral reasoning and other aspects of morality are apt to take at various grade levels. As you look at the suggested strategies in the right-hand column of the table, notice how several of them are consistent with the *authoritative parenting* style described earlier.

Challenges to moral reasoning promote advancement toward more sophisticated reasoning.

Kohlberg drew on Piaget's concept of *disequilibrium* to explain how learners progress to more advanced moral reasoning. (As you may recall from Chapter 6, some contemporary motivation theorists instead use the term *cognitive dissonance*.) In particular, learners occasionally encounter events and dilemmas that their existing moral beliefs cannot adequately address. With time and experience, they become increasingly aware of weaknesses in their usual ways of thinking about moral dilemmas, especially if their moral judgments are challenged by people who reason at one stage above their own. For example, a Stage 3 student who agrees to let a popular cheerleader copy his homework may begin to question his decision if a Stage 4 student argues that the cheerleader would learn more by doing her own homework. By struggling with such challenges, Kohlberg suggested, children and adolescents may begin to revise their own thoughts about morality and gradually move from one stage to the next.

Although most contemporary psychologists reject Kohlberg's idea of discrete stages, researchers have confirmed his view that disequilibrium spurs moral development. For instance, classroom discussions of controversial topics and moral issues appear to promote increased perspective taking and the transition to more advanced reasoning.[181] Implicit in this finding is a very important point: Children's moral reasoning does *not* result simply from adults handing down particular moral values and preachings.[182] Instead, it emerges out of children's own, personally constructed beliefs—beliefs they often revisit and revise over time.

Cognition, affect, and motivation all influence moral and prosocial behavior.

Most children behave more morally and prosocially—for instance, they become more generous—as they grow older.[183] Their increasingly moral behavior is due, in part, to more advanced moral reasoning.[184] For example, children and adolescents who, from Kohlberg's perspective, reason at higher stages are less likely to cheat or insult others, more likely to help people in need, and more likely to disobey orders that would cause someone harm.[185]

Yet the correlation between moral reasoning and moral behavior is not an especially strong one. Affective factors also enter into the picture. For instance, guilt can be an especially powerful motivator. When children feel guilty about damage or distress they have caused, they may work hard to repair the damage, soothe hurt feelings, and in other respects "make things right."[186] Guilt is limited to situations in which children themselves have caused harm, however. Truly prosocial children—those who help others even in the absence of their own wrongdoing—typically have a considerable capacity for perspective taking and

[179] Nucci, 2001; Rest, Narvaez, Bebeau, & Thoma, 1999.

[180] Rest et al., 1999; Turiel, 1998.

[181] DeVries & Zan, 1996; Power, Higgins, & Kohlberg, 1989; Schlaefli, Rest, & Thoma, 1985.

[182] Damon, 1988; Higgins, 1995; Turiel, 1998.

[183] N. Eisenberg, 1982; Rushton, 1980.

[184] Blasi, 1980; N. Eisenberg, Zhou, & Koller, 2001; Reimer et al., 1983.

[185] F. H. Davidson, 1976; Kohlberg, 1975; Kohlberg & Candee, 1984; P. A. Miller, Eisenberg, Fabes, & Shell, 1996; Turiel, 2002.

[186] N. Eisenberg, 1995; Harter, 1999.

DEVELOPMENTAL TRENDS

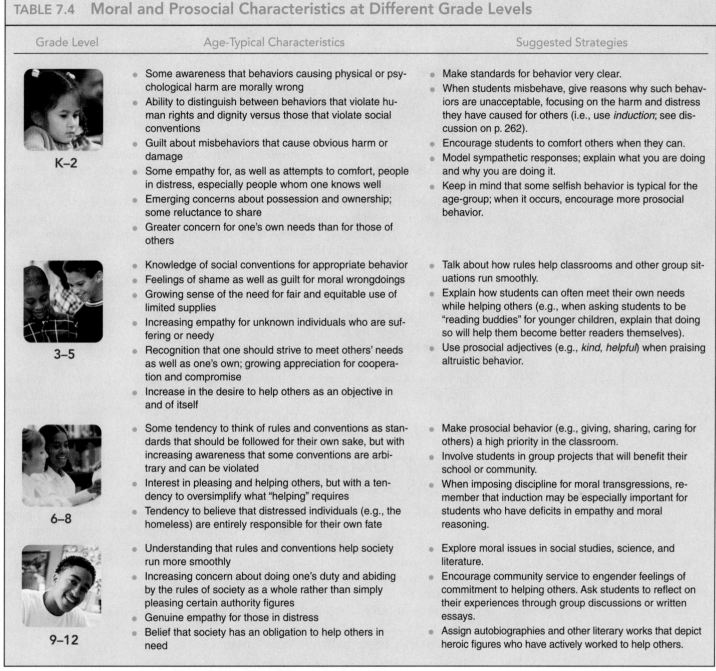

TABLE 7.4	Moral and Prosocial Characteristics at Different Grade Levels	
Grade Level	Age-Typical Characteristics	Suggested Strategies
K–2	• Some awareness that behaviors causing physical or psychological harm are morally wrong • Ability to distinguish between behaviors that violate human rights and dignity versus those that violate social conventions • Guilt about misbehaviors that cause obvious harm or damage • Some empathy for, as well as attempts to comfort, people in distress, especially people whom one knows well • Emerging concerns about possession and ownership; some reluctance to share • Greater concern for one's own needs than for those of others	• Make standards for behavior very clear. • When students misbehave, give reasons why such behaviors are unacceptable, focusing on the harm and distress they have caused for others (i.e., use *induction*; see discussion on p. 262). • Encourage students to comfort others when they can. • Model sympathetic responses; explain what you are doing and why you are doing it. • Keep in mind that some selfish behavior is typical for the age-group; when it occurs, encourage more prosocial behavior.
3–5	• Knowledge of social conventions for appropriate behavior • Feelings of shame as well as guilt for moral wrongdoings • Growing sense of the need for fair and equitable use of limited supplies • Increasing empathy for unknown individuals who are suffering or needy • Recognition that one should strive to meet others' needs as well as one's own; growing appreciation for cooperation and compromise • Increase in the desire to help others as an objective in and of itself	• Talk about how rules help classrooms and other group situations run smoothly. • Explain how students can often meet their own needs while helping others (e.g., when asking students to be "reading buddies" for younger children, explain that doing so will help them become better readers themselves). • Use prosocial adjectives (e.g., *kind, helpful*) when praising altruistic behavior.
6–8	• Some tendency to think of rules and conventions as standards that should be followed for their own sake, but with increasing awareness that some conventions are arbitrary and can be violated • Interest in pleasing and helping others, but with a tendency to oversimplify what "helping" requires • Tendency to believe that distressed individuals (e.g., the homeless) are entirely responsible for their own fate	• Make prosocial behavior (e.g., giving, sharing, caring for others) a high priority in the classroom. • Involve students in group projects that will benefit their school or community. • When imposing discipline for moral transgressions, remember that induction may be especially important for students who have deficits in empathy and moral reasoning.
9–12	• Understanding that rules and conventions help society run more smoothly • Increasing concern about doing one's duty and abiding by the rules of society as a whole rather than simply pleasing certain authority figures • Genuine empathy for those in distress • Belief that society has an obligation to help others in need	• Explore moral issues in social studies, science, and literature. • Encourage community service to engender feelings of commitment to helping others. Ask students to reflect on their experiences through group discussions or written essays. • Assign autobiographies and other literary works that depict heroic figures who have actively worked to help others.

Sources: Damon, 1988; N. Eisenberg, 1982; N. Eisenberg et al., 1986; N. Eisenberg & Fabes, 1998; Farver & Branstetter, 1994; Flanagan & Faison, 2001; Gibbs, 1995; D. Hart & Fegley, 1995; Helwig & Jasiobedzka, 2001; Helwig et al., 2001; Hoffman, 1975, 1991; Kohlberg, 1984; Krebs & Van Hesteren, 1994; Kurtines, Berman, Ittel, & Williamson, 1995; Laupa & Turiel, 1995; Nucci, 2001, 2006; Nucci & Weber, 1995; Rushton, 1980; Smetana & Braeges, 1990; Turiel, 1983, 1998; Wainryb et al., 2005; Yates & Youniss, 1996; Yau & Smetana, 2003; Youniss & Yates, 1999; Zahn-Waxler, Radke-Yarrow, Wagner, & Chapman, 1992.

empathy.[187] Empathy is especially likely to spur prosocial behavior when it leads to **sympathy**, whereby children not only assume another person's feelings but also have concerns for the individual's well-being.[188]

Even when children behave prosocially, their own needs and goals often come into play as well. For instance, although children may want to do the right thing, they may also be

---

[187] Damon, 1988; N. Eisenberg, Zhou, & Koller, 2001; Hoffman, 1991.

[188] Batson, 1991; N. Eisenberg & Fabes, 1998; Turiel, 1998.

sympathy Feeling of sorrow or concern for another person's problems or distress.

concerned about whether others will approve of their actions and about what positive or negative consequences might result. Children are more apt to behave in accordance with their moral standards if the benefits are high (e.g., they gain others' approval or respect) and the personal costs are low (e.g., an act of altruism involves little sacrifice).[189]

Moral values become an important part of some learners' sense of self.

In adolescence some young people begin to integrate a commitment to moral values into their overall sense of identity: They think of themselves as generally moral, caring individuals who are concerned about the rights and well-being of others.[190] Their acts of altruism and compassion are not limited to their friends and acquaintances but also extend to the community at large. For example, in one study[191] researchers conducted in-depth interviews with inner-city Hispanic and African American teenagers who showed an exceptional commitment to helping others (by volunteering many hours at Special Olympics, a neighborhood political organization, a nursing home, etc.). These teens did not necessarily display more advanced moral reasoning (as defined by Kohlberg's stages) than their peers, but they were more likely to describe themselves in terms of moral traits and goals (e.g., helping others) and to mention certain ideals toward which they were striving.

As you can see, then, morality and sense of self are interrelated. In fact, the various topics we've discussed in this chapter—personality, sense of self, peer relationships, social cognition, and moral and prosocial development—are all interconnected. For example, moral beliefs influence the interpersonal behaviors that learners believe are appropriate (social cognition). Those interpersonal behaviors influence the quality of peer relationships, which, in turn, influences learners' self-concepts and self-esteem. This ripple effect works in other directions as well. For instance, learners' sense of self is apt to influence their interpretations of other people's behaviors toward them (social cognition again) and so will also influence their responses and overall social effectiveness (e.g., recall our discussion of hostile attributional bias). And the general patterns we observe in learners' social and moral behaviors are all part of that general characteristic we call "personality."

PROMOTING PERSONAL AND SOCIAL DEVELOPMENT

The things we've learned about personal and social development have numerous implications for classroom practice. To organize our discussion, I've grouped them into three general categories—those that foster (a) personal development, (b) social cognition and interpersonal skills, and (c) moral reasoning and prosocial behavior. Keep in mind that various aspects of personal and social development are often closely intertwined. Thus, as you will often see in the upcoming sections, facilitating learners' development in one area is likely to enhance their development in other areas as well.

Fostering Personal Development

The personal characteristics students bring with them to school—their distinct temperaments and personality characteristics, their beliefs about who they are as individuals, and so on—are apt to have a significant influence on their performance in the classroom. The following strategies should enhance their academic and social success at school.

Accommodate students' diverse temperaments.

To some degree, students' ways of behaving in the classroom—their energy levels, their sociability, their impulse control, and so on—reflect temperamental differences that are not entirely within their control. Many temperamental variables affect how students engage in and

[189] Arsenio & Lemerise, 2004; Batson & Thompson, 2001; N. Eisenberg, 1987; Narváez & Rest, 1995.
[190] Arnold, 2000; Blasi, 1995; Hastings, Utendale, & Sullivan, 2007; Nucci, 2001; Youniss & Yates, 1999.
[191] D. Hart & Fegley, 1995.

CLASSROOM STRATEGIES

Accommodating Diverse Temperaments

- For students with high energy levels, minimize downtime between activities.

   A third-grade boy seems unable to sit still for more than a couple of minutes. As a way of letting him release pent-up energy throughout the school day, his teacher gives him small chores to do (erasing the board, sharpening pencils, cleaning art supplies, etc.) between activities and shows him how to complete the chores quietly so as not to disturb his classmates.

- Be especially warm and attentive with very shy students.

   Midway through the school year, a girl who's just moved to town from a distant state joins a ninth-grade science class. Over the next week or so, her teacher notices that she comes to class alone each day and doesn't join in conversations with peers before or after class. One day, the teacher also sees her eating lunch by herself in the cafeteria. He sits down beside her with his own lunch and engages her in conversation about her previous school and community. The following day in class, he assigns a small-group, cooperative learning project that students will work on periodically over the next two weeks. He forms cooperative groups of three or four students each, making sure that he partners the new girl with two students who he knows will be friendly and take her under their wings.

- When students have trouble adapting to new circumstances, give them advance notice of unusual activities and provide extra structure and reassurance.

   A kindergarten teacher has discovered that two children in his class do well when the school day is orderly and predictable, but they often become anxious or upset whenever the class departs from its usual routine. To prepare the children for a field trip to the fire station on Friday, he begins to talk about the trip at the beginning of the week, explaining what the class will do and see during the visit. He also recruits the father of one of the highly anxious children to serve as a parent assistant that day.

- If students seem overwhelmed by noisy or chaotic situations, find or create a more calm and peaceful environment for them.

   Several middle school students find the hustle and bustle of the school cafeteria unsettling. Their math teacher offers her classroom as a place where they can occasionally eat instead. On some days she eats with them. At other times she sits at her desk and grades papers, but they know that she will gladly stop to talk if they have a question or concern.

- Teach self-regulation strategies to students who act impulsively.

   A high school student often shouts out comments and opinions in her history class. The student's teacher takes her aside after school one day and gently explains that her lack of restraint is interfering with her classmates' ability to participate in discussions. To sensitize the student to the extent of the problem, the teacher asks her to keep a daily tally of how many times she talks without first raising her hand. A week later, the two meet again, and the teacher suggests a "self-talk" strategy that can help the student participate actively without dominating discussions.

Source: Some strategies based on suggestions by Keogh, 2003.

respond to classroom activities and so also affect students' learning and achievement. Yet there is no single "best" temperament that maximizes classroom success. Instead, children are more likely to succeed at school when their behaviors are a good fit, rather than a mismatch, with classroom expectations. For instance, highly energetic, outgoing children often shine—but quieter students might feel anxious or intimidated—when teachers want students to participate actively in group discussions and projects. Quieter children do better—and some energetic children may be viewed as disruptive—when teachers require a lot of independent seatwork.[192]

Teachers may be more tolerant of students' behavioral idiosyncrasies and more willing to adapt instruction and classroom management strategies to accommodate different behavioral styles when they realize that students' ways of responding to their environment are, in part, biologically "built in."[193] The Classroom Strategies box "Accommodating Diverse Temperaments" presents several examples of how teachers can effectively work with temperamental differences.

Help students get a handle on who they are as people.

Certainly, key components of a healthy sense of self are beliefs that one can successfully tackle certain challenging tasks (reflecting high self-efficacy) and that one is, overall, a good and capable individual (reflecting high self-worth). We identified several ways of enhancing students' sense of self-efficacy and self-worth in Chapter 6, and many additional ones are presented in the right-most column of Table 7.1 (p. 240). Undoubtedly the most important strategy is to *help students be successful*, not only at academic tasks but also in social situations.

Yet equally essential to the development of a sense of self is to gain an understanding of who one is as a person—one's strengths and weaknesses, likes and dislikes, hopes and fears,

---

[192] Keogh, 2003.   [193] Keogh, 2003.

and so on. Not all students can achieve at superior levels in the classroom, nor can they all be superstars on the playing field. Students are more likely to have a positive sense of self if they find an activity—perhaps singing, student government, or competitive jump-roping—in which they can shine.[194] And when students have long-standing difficulties in certain domains, discovering that their failures are due to a previously undiagnosed disability (e.g., dyslexia or attention-deficit hyperactivity disorder) can help repair some of the damage to self-esteem. Such a discovery helps children make sense of *why* they can't perform certain tasks as well as their peers. It can also spur students and their teachers to identify effective coping strategies. In the following reflection, one student reveals how, in coming to terms with his dyslexia, he's acquired a healthy sense of self despite his disability:

> Dyslexia is your brain's wired differently and there's brick walls for some things and you just have to work either around it or break it. I'm dyslexic at reading that means I need a little bit more help. If you have dyslexia the thing you have to find is how to get over the hump, the wall. Basically you either go around it and just don't read and get along in life without it or you break down the wall.[195]

Channel adolescents' risk-taking tendencies into safe activities.

Adolescents' propensity to engage in dangerous, high-risk behaviors must be of concern to all faculty members in middle schools and high schools. Yet scare tactics—perhaps talking about peers who've died from drug overdoses, contracted AIDS from unprotected sex, or been killed in high-speed chases—typically have little effect on teenagers' behavior. Nor do rational explanations of probabilities—such as the likelihood of getting pregnant in a single sexual encounter—make much of a difference. When adolescents get together in recreational activities, common sense and reason seem to go out the window. Teachers, administrators, parents, and other community members must all work together to keep adolescent risk taking in check. For instance, many communities now hold all-night after-prom parties in the school building or other supervised location as a way of keeping students from drinking and driving. Another strategy is to provide outlets for *reasonable* risk taking, such as climbing walls, skateboard parks, and small-group, supervised wilderness trips.[196]

Create a warm, supportive environment with clear standards for behavior and explanations of why some behaviors are unacceptable.

An *authoritative* environment—one that combines affection and respect for children with reasonable restrictions on their behavior—seems to be important not only in parenting but also in teaching.[197] Warm teacher–student relationships can help students meet their need for relatedness, and positive feedback about students' strengths and successes can enhance their sense of self. At the same time, teachers must let students know in no uncertain terms what behaviors are and are not acceptable in the classroom. Behaviors that jeopardize the rights, safety, or psychological well-being of others—stealing, aggression, remarks that ridicule a particular gender or ethnic group, and so on—must be immediately addressed and discouraged.

We'll look at specific strategies for establishing and maintaining good teacher–student relationships, as well as strategies for responding to inappropriate behaviors, in Chapter 9. But for now we should note that any disciplinary action for unacceptable behavior is most likely to foster students' long-term personal and social development when it is accompanied by **induction**—that is, by an explanation of *why* a behavior is unacceptable.[198] For example, a teacher might describe how a behavior harms another student either physically ("Having your hair pulled the way you just pulled Mai's can really be painful") or emotionally ("You hurt John's feelings when you call him names like that"). Alternatively, a teacher might explain how an action has caused someone else inconvenience ("Because you ruined Marie's jacket, her parents are making her work around the house to earn the money for a new one"). Still another approach is to explain someone else's perspective, intention, or motive

induction Explanation of why a certain behavior is unacceptable, often with a focus on the pain or distress that someone has caused another.

[194] Harter, 1999.
[195] Zambo, 2003, p. 10.
[196] Spear, 2007; L. Steinberg, 2005.
[197] For example, see J. M. T. Walker & Hoover-Dempsey, 2006.
[198] Hoffman, 1970, 1975.

("This science project you've just ridiculed may not be as fancy as yours, but I know that Camren spent many hours working on it and is quite proud of what he's done").

Induction is victim centered: It helps students focus on the distress of others and recognize that they themselves have been the cause.[199] The consistent use of induction in disciplining children, especially when accompanied by *mild* punishment for misbehavior, appears to promote cooperation with rules and facilitate the development of such prosocial characteristics as empathy, compassion, and altruism.[200]

Be especially supportive of students at risk.

Students who have a high probability of failing to acquire the minimum academic skills necessary for success in the adult world are known as **students at risk**. Many of them drop out before high school graduation, and many others graduate without basic skills in reading or mathematics.[201] Such individuals are often ill equipped to make productive contributions to their families, communities, or society at large. In the United States, the percentage of students who drop out before earning high school diplomas has risen considerably in the past few decades—for instance, from 24 percent in 1970 to 29 percent in 2000.[202]

Students at risk, especially those who eventually drop out, typically have some or all of the following characteristics:

- **A history of academic failure.** High school dropouts often have a history of poor academic achievement going back as far as third grade. On average, they have less effective reading and study skills, earn lower grades, obtain lower achievement test scores, and are more likely to have repeated a grade level than their classmates who graduate.[203]
- **Emotional and behavioral problems.** Potential dropouts tend to have lower self-esteem than their more successful classmates. They also are more apt to create discipline problems in class, to use drugs, and to engage in criminal activities.[204]
- **Increasing disinvolvement with school.** Dropping out is not necessarily an all-or-none thing. In fact, many high school dropouts show lesser forms of "dropping out" many years before they officially leave school. Future dropouts are absent from school more frequently than their peers. They are also more likely to be occasionally suspended from school or to show a long-term pattern of dropping out, returning to school, and dropping out again.[205]
- **Lack of psychological attachment to school.** Students at risk for academic failure are less likely to identify with their school or to perceive themselves as vital members of the school community. For example, they engage in fewer extracurricular activities than their classmates and may express dissatisfaction with school in general.[206]
- **Frequent interaction with low-achieving peers.** Students who drop out tend to associate with low-achieving, and in some cases antisocial, peers. Such peers may argue that school is not worthwhile, and they are likely to distract students' attention away from academic pursuits.[207]

A common assumption is that the reasons for dropping out lie largely within students themselves. In fact, characteristics of *schools* also play a significant role.[208] Perhaps academic subject matter is presented in such a way that students find it boring and irrelevant to their needs. Perhaps the school environment is overly controlling, on the one hand (recall our discussion of *self-determination* in Chapter 6), or violent and dangerous, on the other. Sadly,

Many students who drop out find the school curriculum boring and irrelevant to their needs.

[199] Hoffman, 1970.
[200] Baumrind, 1971; G. H. Brody & Shaffer, 1982; Hoffman, 1975; Maccoby & Martin, 1983; Rushton, 1980.
[201] Slavin, 1989.
[202] Carnoy, Elmore, & Siskin, 2003.
[203] K. L. Alexander, Entwisle, & Dauber, 1995; Battin-Pearson et al., 2000; Garnier, Stein, & Jacobs, 1997; Jozefowicz, Arbreton, Eccles, Barber, & Colarossi, 1994; Raber, 1990; L. Steinberg, Blinde, & Chan, 1984; Wilkinson & Frazer, 1990.

[204] Finn, 1991; Garnier et al., 1997; Jozefowicz et al., 1994; Rumberger, 1995; U.S. Dept. of Education, 1992.
[205] Finn, 1989; G. A. Hess, Lyons, & Corsino, 1990; Jozefowicz et al., 1994; Raber, 1990.
[206] Christenson & Thurlow, 2004; Hymel, Comfort, Schonert-Reichl, & McDougall, 1996; Rumberger, 1995.
[207] Battin-Pearson et al., 2000; Hymel et al., 1996.
[208] Hardré & Reeve, 2003; V. E. Lee & Burkam, 2003; Portes, 1996; Raber, 1990; Rumberger, 1995; U.S. Dept. of Education, 1992.

student at risk Student who has a high probability of failing to acquire the minimum academic skills necessary for success in the adult world.

teacher behaviors can enter into the picture as well, as the following dialogue between an interviewer (Ron) and two at-risk high school students (George and Rasheed) reveals:

Ron: Why do you think someone drops out of school?

George: I think people drop out of school cuz of the pressure that school brings them. Like, sometimes the teacher might get on the back of a student so much that the student doesn't want to do the work. . . . And then that passes and he says, "I'm gonna start doing good. . . ." Then he's not doing as good as he's supposed to and when he sees his grade, he's, "you mean I'm doin' all that for nothin'? I'd rather not come to school." . . .

Rasheed: I think kids drop out of school because they gettin' too old to be in high school. And I think they got, like, they think it's time to get a responsibility and to get a job and stuff. And, like George says, sometimes the teachers, you know, tell you to drop out, knowing that you might not graduate anyway.

Ron: How does a teacher tell you to drop out?

Rasheed: No, they recommend you take the GED program sometimes. Like, some kids just say, "Why don't you just take the GED. Just get it over with." Then, job or something. [Rasheed is referring to a general equivalency diploma, obtained by taking a series of achievement tests rather than completing the requirements for high school graduation.]

Ron: You talked about a kid being too old. Why is a kid too old?

Rasheed: Cuz he got left back too many times.[209]

Teachers may begin to see indicators of "dropping out," such as low school achievement and high absenteeism, as early as elementary school. Other signs, such as low self-esteem, disruptive behavior, and lack of involvement in school activities, often appear years before students officially withdraw from school. So it is quite possible to identify at-risk students early in their school careers and to take steps to prevent or remediate academic difficulties before they become insurmountable. Research indicates clearly that for students at risk, prevention, early intervention, and long-term support are more effective than later, short-term efforts.[210]

Students who are at risk for academic failure are a diverse group of individuals with a diverse set of needs, and there is probably no single strategy that can keep all of them in school until high school graduation.[211] Nevertheless, effective teaching practices go a long way toward helping these students stay on the road to academic success and high school graduation. For instance, teachers and schools that have high success rates with students at risk tend to be those that communicate a sense of caring, concern, and high regard for students.[212] The Classroom Strategies box "Encouraging and Supporting Students at Risk" presents additional suggestions that psychologists and educators have found to be effective.

Be on the lookout for exceptional challenges that students may face at home.

Ideally, families provide the guidance, encouragement, emotional support, and resources that students need to succeed at school and in the outside world. Unfortunately, not all families provide nurturing environments in which to grow. Some parents have such limited financial resources that they cannot afford adequate food, housing, or medical care. Others are so overwhelmed by crises in their own lives (e.g., marital conflict, loss of employment, or a life-threatening illness) that they have little time or energy to devote to their children. Still others suffer from mental illness or have serious substance abuse problems. And in some cases parents have learned only ineffective parenting strategies from their *own* parents.[213] Such challenges increase the likelihood that children will have emotional problems

[209] Farrell, 1990, p. 91.

[210] Brooks-Gunn, 2003; Christenson & Thurlow, 2004; McCall & Plemons, 2001; Paris, Morrison, & Miller, 2006; Ramey & Ramey, 1998.

[211] Finn, 1991; Janosz, LeBlanc, Boulerice, & Tremblay, 2000.

[212] L. W. Anderson & Pellicer, 1998; Christenson & Thurlow, 2004; Pianta, 1999.

[213] Cummings, Schermerhorn, Davies, Goeke-Morey, & Cummings, 2006; Hemmings, 2004; Serbin & Karp, 2003; R. A. Thompson & Wyatt, 1999; Werner & Smith, 1982.

CLASSROOM STRATEGIES

Encouraging and Supporting Students at Risk

- **Make the curriculum relevant to students' lives and needs.**

  A math class in an inner-city middle school expresses concern about the 13 liquor stores located within 1,000 feet of the school and about the shady customers and drug dealers the stores attract. The students use yardsticks and maps to calculate the distance of each store from the school, gather information about zoning restrictions and other city government regulations, identify potential violations, meet with a local newspaper editor (who publishes an editorial describing the situation), and eventually meet with state legislators and the city council. As a result of students' efforts, city police monitor the liquor stores more closely, major violations are identified (leading to the closing of two stores), and the city council makes it illegal to consume alcohol within 600 feet of the school.

- **Use students' strengths to promote high self-esteem.**

  A low-income, inner-city elementary school forms a singing group (the "Jazz Cats") for which students must try out. The group performs at a variety of community events, and the students enjoy considerable visibility for their talent. Group members exhibit increased self-esteem, improvement in other school subjects, and greater teamwork and leadership skills.

- **Provide extra support for academic success.**

  A middle school homework program meets every day after school in Room 103, where students find their homework assignments on a shelf. Students follow a particular sequence of steps to do each assignment (assembling materials, having someone check their work, etc.) and use a checklist to make sure no step is missed. Initially, a supervising teacher closely monitors what they do, but with time and practice the students are able to complete their homework with only minimal help and guidance.

- **Communicate optimism about students' chances for long-term personal and professional success.**

  A mathematics teacher at a low-income, inner-city high school recruits students to participate in an intensive math program. The teacher and students work on evenings, Saturdays, and vacations, and many of them eventually pass the Advanced Placement calculus exam.

- **Show students that they are personally responsible for their successes.**

  A teacher says to a student, "Your essay about recent hate crimes in the community is very powerful. You've given the topic considerable thought, and you've clearly mastered some of the techniques of persuasive writing that we've talked about this semester. I'd like you to think seriously about submitting your essay to the local paper for its editorial page. Can we spend some time during lunch tomorrow to fine-tune the grammar and spelling?"

- **Create peer support groups that enable students to provide mutual encouragement.**

  A high school holds regular meetings of its "Achievement Committee," a group of students from low-income backgrounds who are committed to earning high grades and in other ways achieving at high levels. Students share their strategies with one another: what study techniques they use, how they budget their time, how they say "no" to counterproductive peer pressure, and so on.

- **Get students involved in extracurricular activities.**

  A teacher encourages a student with a strong throwing arm to go out for the school baseball team and introduces the student to the baseball coach. The coach, in turn, expresses his enthusiasm for having the student join the team and asks several current team members to help make him feel at home during team practices.

- **Involve students in school policy and management decisions.**

  At an inner-city high school, students and teachers hold regular "town meetings" to discuss issues of fairness and justice and establish rules for appropriate behavior. Meetings are democratic, with students and teachers alike having one vote apiece, and the will of the majority is binding.

Sources: Alderman, 1990; L. W. Anderson & Pellicer, 1998; Belfiore & Hornyak, 1998 (homework program); Cosden, Morrison, Albanese, & Macias, 2001; Eilam, 2001; Feldman & Matjasko, 2005; Finn, 1989; Garcia, 1994; Garibaldi, 1993; Higgins, 1995 (town meeting example); Knapp, Turnbull, & Shields, 1990; Jenlink, 1994 (Jazz Cats example); Ladson-Billings, 1994a; Lee-Pearce, Plowman, & Touchstone, 1998; Menéndez, 1988 (story of high school math teacher Jaime Escalante, portrayed in the film *Stand and Deliver*); Ogbu, 2003 (Achievement Committee example); Ramey & Ramey, 1998; M. G. Sanders, 1996; Slavin, Karweit, & Madden, 1989; E. N. Walker, 2006.

(e.g., anxiety or depression) and ineffective social skills (e.g., aggression). The more challenges children face, the more vulnerable they are.[214]

Through newsletters, parent–teacher conferences, and parent discussion groups, teachers can serve as valuable resources to parents about possible strategies for promoting children's personal and social development (more about mechanisms for communicating with parents in Chapter 9). The important thing is to communicate information *without* pointing fingers or being judgmental about parenting styles. Let's revisit a point made early in the chapter: How parents treat their children is sometimes the *result*, rather than the cause, of how their children behave. If children are quick to comply with their parents' wishes, parents may have no reason to be overly strict disciplinarians. If children are hyperactive or hot tempered, parents may have to impose more restrictions on behavior and administer more severe consequences for misbehaviors. Teachers must be careful that they don't always place total credit or blame on parents for their parenting styles.

---

[214] Gerard & Buehler, 2004; H. C. Johnson & Friesen, 1993; Maughan & Cicchetti, 2002; G. R. Patterson, DeBaryshe, & Ramsey, 1989; Zahn-Waxler et al., 1988.

At the same time, teachers must be alert for signs of possible child maltreatment. In some cases parents and other primary caregivers neglect children: They fail to provide nutritious meals, adequate clothing, and other basic necessities of life. In other cases they abuse their children physically, sexually, or emotionally. Possible indicators of neglect or abuse are chronic hunger, lack of warm clothing in cold weather, untreated medical needs, frequent or serious physical injuries (e.g., bruises, burns, broken bones), and exceptional knowledge about sexual matters.[215]

Parental neglect and abuse have significant adverse effects on children's personal and social development.[216] On average, children who have been routinely neglected or abused have low self-esteem, poorly developed social skills, and low school achievement. Many are angry, aggressive, and defiant. Others can be depressed, anxious, socially withdrawn, and possibly suicidal. Teachers are both morally and legally obligated to report any cases of suspected child abuse or neglect to the proper authorities (e.g., the school principal or Child Protective Services). Two helpful resources are the National Child Abuse Hotline (1-800-4-A-CHILD, or 1-800-422-4453) and the Web site for Childhelp USA, www.childhelpusa.org.

Fortunately, many children and adolescents do well in school despite exceptional hardships on the home front.[217] Some are **resilient students** who acquire characteristics and coping skills that help them rise above their adverse circumstances. As a group, resilient students have likable personalities, positive self-concepts, and high yet realistic goals. They believe that success comes with hard work, and their bad experiences serve as constant reminders of the importance of getting a good education.[218]

Resilient students usually have one or more individuals in their lives whom they trust and can turn to in difficult times. Such individuals may be family members, neighbors, or school personnel. For example, resilient students often mention teachers who have taken a personal interest in them and been instrumental in their school success. Teachers are most likely to foster resilience in students by demonstrating true affection and respect for students, being available and willing to listen when students have concerns, holding high expectations for students' performance, and providing the encouragement and support students need to succeed both inside and outside the classroom.[219]

Encouraging Effective Social Cognition and Interpersonal Skills

Teachers are in an excellent position to foster productive ways of thinking about social situations. They are also in a good position to help students interact effectively with others. The following recommendations are based on research related to social cognition, social skills, and peer relationships.

Encourage perspective taking and empathy.

In any classroom, day-to-day events offer many opportunities for perspective taking and empathy. One strategy is to talk frequently and explicitly about the thoughts, feelings, and needs of various members of the classroom and school community (e.g., as is done in induction).[220] Another strategy is to ask students *themselves* to consider how others might feel in a particular situation. The following report from an elementary school teacher illustrates the value of having students reflect on how their actions might affect others:

> During gym lesson five of the boys misbehaved and were dismissed from class. They acted out their anger by insulting the gym teacher and the other staff greatly by answering back, shouting and even swearing, and throwing eggs at the school buildings. . . . When the boys came to my class they were very upset. . . . I told them I was not going to blame them at this point but I wanted them to write an essay at home about what had happened. . . . [The essays] were written sincerely in the sense that they described clearly what they had

---

resilient student Student who succeeds in school and in life despite exceptional hardships at home.

[215] Turnbull, Turnbull, & Wehmeyer, 2007.

[216] Bates & Pettit, 2007; J. Kim & Cicchetti, 2006; R. A. Thompson & Wyatt, 1999.

[217] S. Goldstein & Brooks, 2006; Schoon, 2006.

[218] S. Goldstein & Brooks, 2006; Masten & Coatsworth, 1998; Schoon, 2006; Werner & Smith, 2001.

[219] R. M. Clark, 1983; Masten & Coatsworth, 1998; McMillan & Reed, 1994; D. A. O'Donnell, Schwab-Stone, & Muyeed, 2002; Werner, 1995.

[220] Ruffman, Slade, & Crowe, 2002; Woolfe, Want, & Siegal, 2002.

done but to my surprise without any regret or tendency to see the staff members' point of view. Having read the essays I decided to discuss the event in class. . . . The children defined the problem and thought about the feelings of those involved. I spent a considerable time asking them to consider the staff members' feelings, whether they knew of somebody who worked in a place similar to the gym, which in fact they did, how that person felt, etc. Gradually, the boys' vehemence subsided. I never blamed them so that they wouldn't become defensive, because then I thought I might lose them. Instead, I tried to improve their understanding of the opinions and feelings of other people, which might differ from their own. . . . The boys improved their behavior in gym class, and this never happened again.[221]

Still another approach is to create or take advantage of opportunities in which students encounter multiple—and perhaps equally legitimate—perspectives and beliefs about a particular issue or conflict. An example of this approach is seen in **peer mediation**, in which students help one another solve interpersonal problems. More specifically, students learn how to mediate conflicts among classmates by asking opposing sides to express their differing points of view and then work together to devise a reasonable resolution.[222] In one study involving several second- through fifth-grade classrooms,[223] students were trained to help peers resolve interpersonal conflicts by asking the opposing sides to do the following:

1. Define the conflict (the problem).
2. Explain their own perspectives and needs.
3. Explain the *other* person's perspectives and needs.
4. Identify at least three possible solutions to the conflict.
5. Reach an agreement that addressed the needs of both parties.

Students took turns serving as mediator for their classmates, such that everyone had experience resolving the conflicts of others. As a result, the students more frequently resolved their *own* interpersonal conflicts in ways that addressed the needs of both parties, and they were less likely to ask for adult intervention, than students who had not had mediation training.

In peer mediation we see yet another example of Vygotsky's notion that effective cognitive processes often have their roots in social interactions. In a peer mediation session, students model effective conflict resolution skills for one another, and they may eventually internalize the skills they use in solving others' problems to solve their *own* problems. Peer mediation is most effective when students of diverse ethnic backgrounds, socioeconomic groups, and achievement levels all serve as mediators. Furthermore, it is typically most useful for relatively small, short-term interpersonal problems (hurt feelings, conflicts over use of limited academic resources, etc.). Even the most proficient of peer mediators may be ill prepared to handle conflicts that reflect deep-seated and emotionally charged attitudes and behaviors—for instance, conflicts that involve sexual harassment or homophobia.[224]

Opportunities for perspective taking and empathy arise not only in day-to-day classroom situations but also in lessons about academic subject matter. For instance, in discussions of current events (e.g., wars, famines, floods), teachers can expose students to circumstances in which other people's needs are far greater than their own. In history lessons, teachers can ask students to imagine how people must have felt during particularly traumatic and stressful times, or possibly even have students role-play such events.[225] Figure 7.3 shows two student artifacts created during history lessons about slavery in colonial America. The reaction paper on the left was written by 10-year-old Charmaine, whose fifth-grade class had been watching *Roots*, a miniseries about a young African man (Kunta Kinte) who is captured and brought to America to be a slave. The "diary" on the right side of Figure 7.3 was written by 14-year-old Craig, whose ninth-grade history teacher asked his class to write journal entries that might capture the life of a colonial plantation owner.

In her reaction paper, Charmaine certainly shows some perspective-taking ability: She talks about Kunta Kinte's "pain" and "fright" and about his parents' "hurt" at losing their firstborn son. She acknowledges that she cannot fully grasp Kunta Kinte's physical pain, as

Observe this process in action in the "Peer Mediation" video in the Additional Resources section in Chapter 7 of MyEducationLab.

[221] Adalbjarnardottir & Selman, 1997, pp. 423–424.
[222] Deutsch, 1993; D. W. Johnson & Johnson, 1996, 2006.
[223] D. W. Johnson, Johnson, Dudley, Ward, & Magnuson, 1995.
[224] Casella, 2001a; K. M. Williams, 2001b.
[225] Brophy & Alleman, 1996; Brophy & VanSledright, 1997.

peer mediation Approach to conflict resolution in which a student (mediator) asks peers in conflict to express their differing viewpoints and then work together to identify an appropriate compromise.

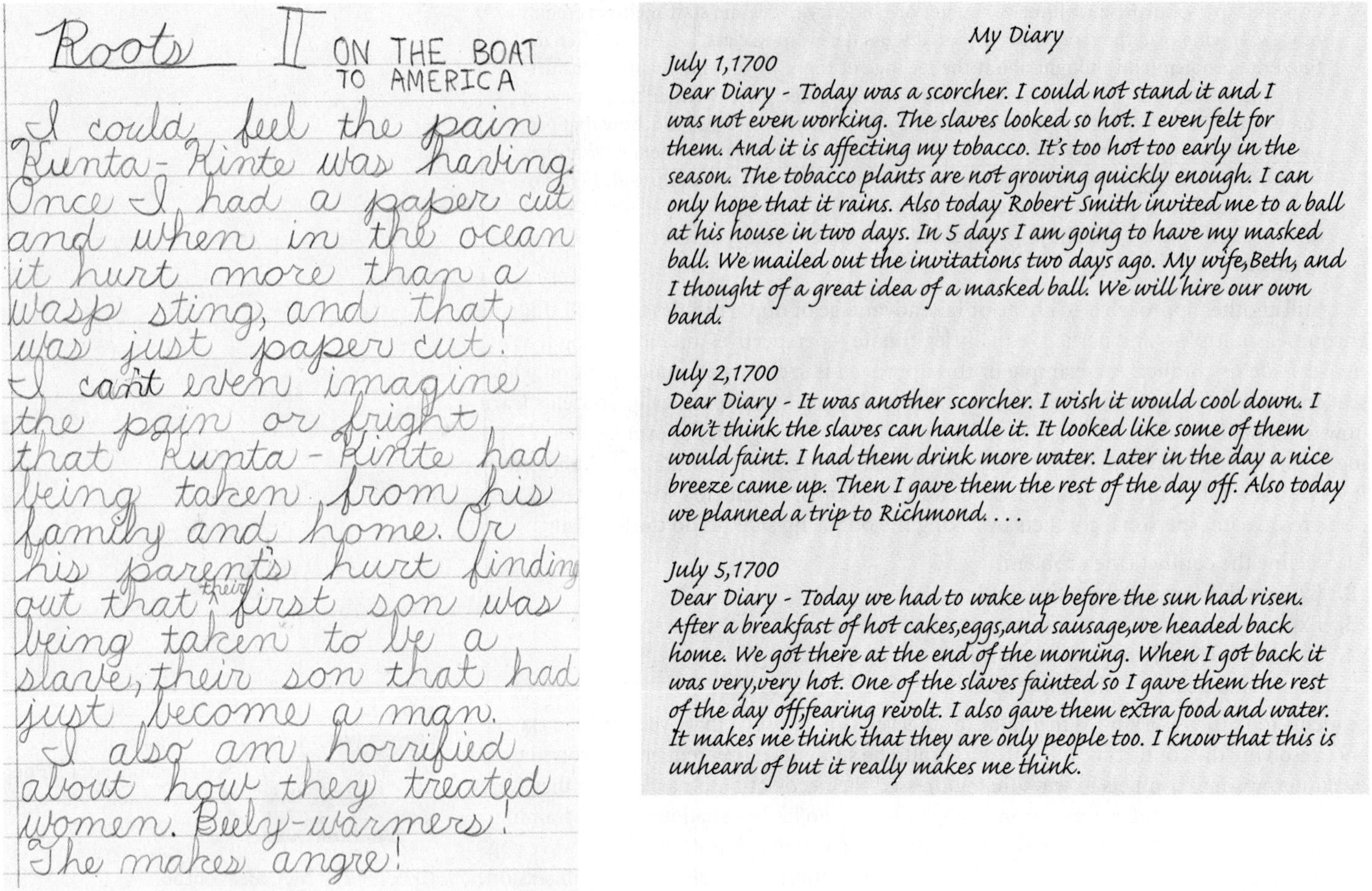

Roots II ON THE BOAT TO AMERICA

I could feel the pain Kunta-Kinte was having. Once I had a paper cut and when in the ocean it hurt more than a wasp sting, and that was just paper cut! I can't even imagine the pain or fright that Kunta-Kinte had being taken from his family and home. Or his parents hurt finding out that their first son was being taken to be a slave, their son that had just become a man. I also am horrified about how they treated women. Belly-warmers! The makes angry!

My Diary

July 1, 1700
Dear Diary - Today was a scorcher. I could not stand it and I was not even working. The slaves looked so hot. I even felt for them. And it is affecting my tobacco. It's too hot too early in the season. The tobacco plants are not growing quickly enough. I can only hope that it rains. Also today Robert Smith invited me to a ball at his house in two days. In 5 days I am going to have my masked ball. We mailed out the invitations two days ago. My wife, Beth, and I thought of a great idea of a masked ball. We will hire our own band.

July 2, 1700
Dear Diary - It was another scorcher. I wish it would cool down. I don't think the slaves can handle it. It looked like some of them would faint. I had them drink more water. Later in the day a nice breeze came up. Then I gave them the rest of the day off. Also today we planned a trip to Richmond. . . .

July 5, 1700
Dear Diary - Today we had to wake up before the sun had risen. After a breakfast of hot cakes, eggs, and sausage, we headed back home. We got there at the end of the morning. When I got back it was very, very hot. One of the slaves fainted so I gave them the rest of the day off, fearing revolt. I also gave them extra food and water. It makes me think that they are only people too. I know that this is unheard of but it really makes me think.

FIGURE 7.3 Two examples of perspective taking in history assignments

her own experience with pain has been limited to having a paper cut in saltwater. In recognizing that people's ability to take the perspective of another may be limited by the extent to which they've had similar experiences, Charmaine shows an understanding that people (herself included) are to some degree products of their past environments.

Craig, too, is able to put himself in another person's shoes. In fact, he tries to imagine someone else (a plantation owner) taking *other people's* perspectives (those of slaves). Such multilayered perspective taking is, in a way, similar to recursive thinking, but in this case it is a matter of thinking "I think that you think that someone else thinks. . . ." Like Charmaine, Craig realizes that people are products of their environment: The plantation owner struggles with the prevailing attitude during colonial times that slaves were not really human beings ("It makes me think that they are only people too. I know that this is unheard of but it really makes me think").

Teach effective social skills.

Because of their social isolation, rejected and neglected students have few opportunities to develop the social skills that many of them desperately need.[226] When they do interact with their peers, their behaviors may be counterproductive, leaving them more isolated than ever. Consider the plight of a seventh grader named Michelle:

Michelle is an extremely bright student, and her academic accomplishments have earned her much teacher praise over the years. But despite her many scholastic successes, Michelle has few friends. To draw attention to herself, she talks incessantly

---

[226] Bukowski et al., 2007; Coie & Cillessen, 1993.

about her academic achievements. Her classmates interpret such bragging as a sign of undeserved arrogance, and so they insult her frequently as a way of knocking her down a peg or two. In self-defense, Michelle begins hurling insults at her classmates as soon as she sees them—beating them to the punch, so to speak.

When students routinely offend or alienate others (as Michelle does), their peers seldom give them the constructive feedback that allows them to improve their behavior on future occasions, and so it may be up to teachers and other adults to give them that guidance.

Teachers and other school personnel can teach students appropriate ways of interacting with others both through explicit verbal instructions and through modeling desired behaviors. Such instruction is especially effective when students also have an opportunity to practice their newly learned social skills (perhaps through role playing) and get concrete feedback about how they are doing.[227]

Teaching social problem-solving skills is helpful as well. Some students lack productive ways of solving social problems. For example, if they want to use a dictionary that a classmate has been monopolizing, they may rudely snatch it away, or if they want to join a group of peers on the playground, they may simply barge into a game without asking. One effective approach in working with such students is to teach them a series of mental steps, as follows:[228]

1. Define the problem.
2. Identify several possible solutions.
3. Predict the likely consequences of each solution.
4. Choose the best solution.
5. Identify the steps required to carry out the solution.
6. Carry out the steps.
7. Evaluate the results.

Such steps—which you may recognize as involving *social cognition*—often help students who have interpersonal problems (e.g., students who are either socially withdrawn or overly aggressive) to develop more effective social skills.[229]

Provide numerous opportunities for social interaction and cooperation.

Children and adolescents gain considerable information about which social behaviors are and are not effective simply by interacting with one another. Because schools and classrooms present complex social situations, they provide an ideal context in which social skills can develop. For instance, students' play activities—whether the fantasy play of preschoolers and kindergartners or the rule-based games of older children and adolescents—can promote cooperation, sharing, perspective taking, and conflict resolution skills.[230] And assignments and activities that require students to cooperate with one another to achieve a common goal (as the school play does in the opening case study) teach help-giving skills and enhance students' views about the importance of justice and fairness among peers.[231]

Talk with students about the advantages and potential dangers of Internet communications.

For students who have easy access to computers, the Internet provides a variety of mechanisms for interacting with peers, both those in town and those in distant places. For instance, electronic mail (e-mail) offers a quick and easy way of asking classmates about homework assignments, making plans for weekend social activities, and seeking friends' advice and emotional support. Networking sites (e.g., facebook.com, myspace.com) provide a

[227] S. N. Elliott & Busse, 1991; Themann & Goldstein, 2001; S. Vaughn, 1991; Zirpoli & Melloy, 2001.
[228] S. N. Elliott & Busse, 1991; Meichenbaum, 1977; Shure & Aberson, 2006; Weissburg, 1985; Yell, Robinson, & Drasgow, 2001.
[229] K. R. Harris, 1982; Meichenbaum, 1977; Yell et al., 2001.
[230] Creasey, Jarvis, & Berk, 1998; Gottman, 1986; Pellegrini & Bohn, 2005; Rubin, 1982.
[231] Damon, 1988; Lickona, 1991; N. M. Webb & Farivar, 1994.

means of sharing personal information (e.g., news, interests, photos) and potentially finding like-minded age-mates. Internet-based chat rooms allow group discussions about virtually any topic. Judicious use of such mechanisms can enhance students' self-esteem, connectedness with peers, and general psychological well-being.[232]

Unfortunately, however, the Internet also provides a vehicle through which students can send demeaning messages or spread vicious rumors that adversely affect a peer's sense of self and social reputation.[233] Furthermore, unscrupulous individuals (usually adults) can misrepresent themselves in attempts (sometimes successful) to prey on unsuspecting children and adolescents.[234] To the extent that they have opportunities, then, teachers should talk with students about wise and socially appropriate uses of the Internet, and they must certainly monitor students' in-class use of computer technology.

Promote understanding, communication, and interaction among diverse groups.

Even though they are in the same building with a wide variety of peers, students frequently congregate in small groups or cliques with whom they spend most of their time (recall the division of the popular and unpopular students in the opening case study), and a few students remain socially isolated (recall Peter's isolation before taking the role as Snoopy in the school play). Immigrant students rarely interact with long-term residents, and newcomers to a school are often socially isolated. Many students with disabilities are neglected or rejected by their classmates.[235]

Often students divide themselves along ethnic lines when they eat lunch and interact in the school yard. In fact, ethnic segregation *increases* once students reach the middle school grades. As young adolescents from ethnic minority groups begin to look closely and introspectively at issues of racism and ethnic identity, they often find it helpful to compare experiences and perspectives with other group members.[236] Yet ethnic stereotypes and prejudices can also contribute to this self-imposed segregation.[237] And in some cases, students simply have little or no knowledge about a cultural group very different from their own. For example, thoughtless classmates might taunt a Muslim girl with names such as "Saddam's sister" or "Osama bin Laden's sister." Or if she wears a head scarf to school, they might ask, "Are you bald? Is there something wrong with your hair?"[238] Students who are frequent victims of such prejudice and misunderstandings are more likely than their peers to become ill or depressed.[239]

To promote intergroup interaction, then, a necessary first step is to help students understand the customs, perspectives, and needs of their classmates from diverse backgrounds. Especially as students get older and become cognitively capable of reflecting on their own and others' thoughts and feelings, they often benefit from heart-to-heart discussions about prejudice and racism in their own community and school. Some students from mainstream Western culture may initially feel uncomfortable talking about this topic with their minority-group peers, but once the ice is broken, greater cross-cultural understanding and communication are apt to result.[240] In addition, students are more likely to be accepting of classmates with disabilities if they understand the nature of those disabilities, *provided that* the students and their parents give permission to share what might otherwise be confidential information.

It is equally important that schools give students many opportunities to form productive cross-group relationships. Teachers and school administrators can take a variety of proactive steps to broaden the base of students' social interactions. Several possibilities are presented in the Classroom Strategies box "Encouraging Productive Interactions Among Diverse Groups," and additional strategies aimed specifically at reducing gang-related hostilities are presented in Chapter 9. When students from diverse groups interact regularly—and

Hear Crystal's concerns about racism in the "Emotions: Early Adolescence" video in the Additional Resources section in Chapter 7 of MyEducationLab.

[232] Ellison, Steinfield, & Lampe, 2007; Gross, Juvonen, & Gable, 2002; Valkenburg, Peter, & Schouten, 2006.

[233] Valkenburg et al., 2006; Willard, 2007.

[234] K. J. Mitchell, Wolak, & Finkelhor, 2005; Schofield, 2006.

[235] Hymel, 1986; Juvonen & Hiner, 1991; Olneck, 1995; Pérez, 1998; Schofield, 1995; Yuker, 1988.

[236] Schofield, 1995; Tatum, 1997.

[237] For instance, see Black-Gutman & Hickson, 1996.

[238] McBrien, 2005, p. 86.

[239] Allison, 1998; G. H. Brody et al., 2006; Tatum, 1997.

[240] Schultz, Buck, & Niesz, 2000; Tatum, 1997.

CLASSROOM STRATEGIES

Encouraging Productive Interactions Among Diverse Groups

- **Set up situations in which students can form new friendships.**

  A junior high school science teacher decides how students will be paired for weekly lab activities. She changes the pairings every month and frequently pairs students from different ethnic backgrounds.

- **Minimize or eliminate barriers to social interaction.**

  Students in a third-grade class learn basic words and phrases in American Sign Language so that they can work and play with a classmate who is deaf.

- **Conduct class discussions about the negative consequences of intergroup hostilities.**

  A high school English teacher in a low-income, inner-city school district uses a lesson on Shakespeare's *Romeo and Juliet* to start a discussion about an ongoing conflict between two rival ethnic-group gangs in the community. "Don't you think this family feud is stupid?" she asks her students, referring to Shakespeare's play. When they agree, she continues, "The Capulets are like the Latino gang, and the Montagues are like the Asian gang. . . . Don't you think it's stupid that the Latino gang and the Asian gang are killing each other?" The students immediately protest, but when she presses them to justify their thinking, they gradually begin to acknowledge the pointlessness of a long-standing rivalry whose origins they can't even recall.

- **Encourage and facilitate participation in extracurricular activities, and take steps to ensure that no single group** dominates in membership or leadership in any particular activity.

  When recruiting members for the scenery committee for the annual school play, the committee's teacher-adviser encourages both "popular" and "unpopular" students to participate. Later he divides the workload in such a way that students who don't know one another very well must work closely and cooperatively.

- **Develop nondisabled students' understanding of students with special educational needs.**

  In a widely publicized case, Ryan White, a boy who had contracted AIDS from a blood transfusion, met considerable resistance against his return to his neighborhood school because parents and students thought he might infect others. After Ryan's family moved to a different school district, school personnel actively educated the community about the fact that AIDS does not spread through typical day-to-day contact. Ryan's reception at his new school was overwhelmingly positive. Later Ryan described his first day at school: "When I walked into classrooms or the cafeteria, several kids called out at once, 'Hey, Ryan! Sit with me!'"

Sources: The Freedom Writers, 1999, p. 33 (Shakespeare example); Genova & Walberg, 1984; Mahoney, Cairns, & Farmer, 2003; Schofield, 1995; Schultz et al., 2000; Sleeter & Grant, 1999; Tatum, 1997; R. White & Cunningham, 1991, p. 149 (Ryan White quotation).

especially when they come together as equals, work toward a common goal, and see themselves as members of the same "team"—they are more apt to accept and possibly even *value* one another's differences.[241]

Explain what bullying is and why it cannot be tolerated.

Students often have misconceptions about bullying. For instance, they may think it involves only physical aggression, even though significant relational aggression constitutes bullying as well. An entry in one high school student's journal illustrates how bullying often involves psychological as well as physical tactics:

> One day in junior high, I was getting off the school bus from a seat in the back. . . . I heard people shouting, "Hey, Fatso!" "You big buffalo!" . . . I knew I had to face them before getting off. In order to leave the bus I had to walk through a long crowded aisle and face the obnoxious girls. As I stood up, the girls followed. They crowded together, and approached me as if they were ready to strike at me. . . . All of the [sic] sudden, the girls began to kick and sock me repeatedly. . . . They continued to hurt me as if there was nothing more important to them than to see me in pain. The last few kicks were the hardest; all I wanted to do was get off the bus alive. My friends were staring at me, hoping that I would do something to make the girls stop. . . . Finally, after what seemed like an eternity, I was able to release myself from their torture. I got off the bus alive. Imagining that the worst had already passed, I began to walk away from the bus and the girls stuck their heads out the window and spit on me. I could not believe it! They spit on my face! . . . While I was cleaning my face with a napkin, I could still hear the girls laughing.[242]

In some instances bullying involves *only* psychological abuse—taunts, name-calling, blatant exclusion from school social activities, and the like.[243]

---

[241] Dovidio & Gaertner, 1999; Oskamp, 2000; J. H. Pfeifer, Brown, & Juvonen, 2007; Ramsey, 1995.
[242] From THE FREEDOM WRITERS DIARY (pp. 37–38) by The Freedom Writers with Erin

Gruwell, copyright © 1999 by The Tolerance Education Foundation. Used by permission of Doubleday, a division of Random House, Inc.
[243] Doll et al., 2004; Goodwin, 2006; Graham, 2006.

Another common student misconception is that the victims of bullying somehow deserve what they get, perhaps because they display immature social and emotional behaviors or need to "toughen up" and learn to defend themselves. Thus many students condone bullying and may serve as a curious or supportive audience that encourages the perpetrators to persist.[244]

Certainly a recommendation offered earlier—*Encourage perspective taking and empathy*—can go part of the way toward discouraging bullying. But in addition, students must be told what bullying is—and also why it is unacceptable—in clear, concrete terms. One effective strategy is to use the mnemonic *PIC*, meaning that bullying is:

- **P**urposeful behavior ("He meant to do it")
- **I**mbalanced ("That's not fair, he's bigger")
- **C**ontinual ("I'm afraid to enter the classroom because she's always picking on me")[245]

As we'll discover in Chapter 9, mutual respect for one another's welfare is a key ingredient in the *sense of community* so important for students' school success.

Be alert for incidents of bullying and other forms of aggression, and take appropriate actions with both the victims and the perpetrators.

Teachers *must* intervene when some students victimize others, and they must keep a watchful eye for additional incidents of bullying down the road. The latter is easier said than done, because many incidents of bullying occur beyond the watchful eyes of school faculty members.[246] It is important, then, that students be encouraged to report (perhaps anonymously) any incidents of bullying they witness.

Regular victims of bullies need social and emotional support from both their teachers and their classmates. Some may also need one or more sessions with a school counselor, perhaps to address feelings of vulnerability and depression, or perhaps to learn the skills that will minimize future bullying incidents.[247]

Aggressive students must be given appropriate consequences for their actions, of course, but they should also be helped to behave more productively. Specific strategies should be tailored to the cognitive processes and motives that underlie their aggression. Such strategies as encouraging perspective taking, helping students interpret social situations more accurately, and teaching effective social problem-solving skills are all potentially useful in reducing aggression and other disruptive behaviors.[248] For example, in one research study involving third- through fifth-grade boys,[249] students attended a series of training sessions in which, through role playing, discussions of personal experiences, brainstorming, and similar activities, they practiced making inferences about other people's intentions and identifying appropriate courses of action. They also learned several guidelines to remind them of how to behave in various situations—for example, thinking to themselves, "When I don't have the information to tell what he meant, I should act as if it were an accident."[250] Following the training, the students were less likely to presume hostile intent or endorse aggressive retaliation in interpersonal situations.

Yet even when an aggressive student shows dramatic improvements in behavior, classmates may continue to steer clear, perhaps thinking "Once a bully, always a bully."[251] So when teachers and other adults work to improve the behaviors of aggressive students, they must work to improve the students' reputations as well. For example, teachers might encourage active involvement in extracurricular groups or conduct cooperative learning activities in which students can exhibit their newly developed social skills. Teachers should also demonstrate through words and actions that *they* like and appreciate every student, including formerly antisocial ones. When teachers do so, their attitudes are apt to be contagious.[252]

---

[244] Doll et al., 2004; Hyman et al., 2004.

[245] Horne, Orpinas, Newman-Carlson, & Bartolomucci, 2004, pp. 298–299.

[246] K. Carter & Doyle, 2006; Hyman et al., 2004.

[247] Espelage & Swearer, 2004; Yeung & Leadbeater, 2007.

[248] Crick & Dodge, 1996; Cunningham & Cunningham, 1998; Graham, 1997; Swearer, Grills, Haye, & Cary, 2004.

[249] Hudley & Graham, 1993.

[250] Hudley & Graham, 1993, p. 128.

[251] Bierman, Miller, & Stabb, 1987; Juvonen & Hiner, 1991; Juvonen & Weiner, 1993.

[252] Chang, 2003.

It is important to note, however, that interventions with individual students are likely to be effective only if their school is a relatively peaceful one. At some schools violence and aggression are commonplace, and students may believe that acting aggressively is the only way to ensure that they don't become victims of *someone else's* aggression. Unfortunately, they may be right: Putting on a tough, seemingly invulnerable appearance (sometimes known as "frontin' it") can be critical for their well-being.[253] Such a situation is, of course, hardly conducive to effective learning and academic achievement. We'll look at strategies for addressing schoolwide aggression and violence in Chapter 9.

Provide extra support and guidance for students who have disabilities that affect their social or personal functioning.

Many students have minor social, emotional, or behavioral difficulties at one time or another, particularly during times of unusual stress or major life changes. Often these problems are temporary, especially when students have the support of caring adults and peers. Yet some students show a pattern of behavior problems that consistently interfere with their classroom performance *regardless* of others' concern and compassion. Symptoms of such **emotional and behavioral disorders** typically fall into one of two broad categories. **Externalizing behaviors** have direct or indirect effects on other people; examples are aggression, defiance, lying, stealing, and general lack of self-control. **Internalizing behaviors** primarily affect the student with the disorder; examples are severe anxiety or depression, exaggerated mood swings, withdrawal from social interaction, and eating disorders. Some emotional and behavioral disorders result from environmental factors, such as stressful living conditions, inconsistent parenting practices, child maltreatment, or family alcohol or drug abuse. But biological causes, such as inherited predispositions, chemical imbalances, and brain injuries, may also be involved.[254]

Other disabilities that adversely affect students' social functioning—and sometimes their academic learning as well—are collectively known as **autism spectrum disorders**, which are probably caused by abnormalities in the brain. Common to all of them are marked impairments in social cognition (e.g., perspective taking), social skills, and social interaction. Students with autism spectrum disorders differ considerably in the severity of their condition (hence the term *spectrum*). For instance, in *Asperger syndrome*, a fairly mild form, students have normal language skills and average or above-average intelligence. In severe cases, which are often referred to simply as *autism*, children may have major delays in cognitive and linguistic development and exhibit certain bizarre behaviors—perhaps constantly rocking or waving fingers, continually repeating what someone else has said, or showing unusual fascination with certain objects (e.g., wristwatches).[255]

Professional intervention is called for whenever students are identified as having an emotional or behavior disorder or an autism spectrum disorder. Nevertheless, many students with these disabilities are in general education classrooms for much or all of the school day. Strategies for working effectively with them include the following:[256]

- Communicate a genuine interest in students' well-being.
- Teach and scaffold social cognition and effective interpersonal skills.
- Stick to a consistent and predictable weekly schedule (especially for students with autism spectrum disorders).
- Make classroom activities relevant to students' interests.
- Insist on appropriate classroom behavior.
- Expect gradual improvement rather than overnight success.

emotional and behavioral disorders Emotional states and behaviors that consistently and significantly disrupt academic learning and performance.

externalizing behavior Symptom of an emotional or behavioral disorder that has a direct effect on other people.

internalizing behavior Symptom of an emotional or behavioral disorder that primarily affects the student with the disorder but has little or no direct effect on others.

autism spectrum disorders Disorders marked by impaired social cognition, social skills, and social interaction, presumably due to a brain abnormality; extreme forms often associated with significant cognitive and linguistic delays and highly unusual behaviors.

[253] K. M. Williams, 2001a.

[254] Angold, Worthman, & Costello, 2003; D. Glaser, 2000; H. C. Johnson & Friesen, 1993; Koegel, 1995; Maughan & Cicchetti, 2002; G. R. Patterson, DeBaryshe, & Ramsey, 1989.

[255] American Psychiatric Association, 1994; Baron-Cohen, Tager-Flusberg, & Cohen, 1993; Hobson, 2004; Pelphrey & Carter, 2007; Théoret et al., 2005.

[256] Clarke et al., 1995; Dalrymple, 1995; S. C. Diamond, 1991; Evertson & Weinstein, 2006; Hudley & Graham, 1993; LeBlanc et al., 2003; McWhiter & Bloom, 1994; Nikopoulos & Keenan, 2004.

One final, essential strategy is to *be alert for signs that a student may be contemplating suicide.* Some seriously depressed students may think about taking their own lives. Warning signs include:[257]

- Sudden withdrawal from social relationships
- Increasing disregard for personal appearance
- Dramatic personality change (e.g., sudden elevation in mood)
- Preoccupation with death and morbid themes
- Overt or veiled threats (e.g., "I won't be around much longer")
- Actions that indicate "putting one's affairs in order" (e.g., giving away prized possessions)

Teachers must take any of these warning signs seriously and seek help from trained professionals, such as a school psychologist or counselor, *immediately.*

Promoting Moral Reasoning and Prosocial Behavior

Some of the suggestions we've already identified should promote moral and prosocial development as well as other aspects of personal and social development. For instance, as we've seen, the use of induction—explaining *why* certain behaviors will not be tolerated—can help students acquire more prosocial tendencies toward their classmates. And by encouraging perspective taking and empathy, teachers foster advancements in moral reasoning and altruistic behavior as well as in social skills. Following are three additional recommendations.

Model socially and morally appropriate behaviors.

Children and adolescents are more likely to exhibit moral and prosocial behavior when they see others behaving in moral rather than immoral ways. For instance, when youngsters see adults or peers being generous and showing concern for others, they tend to do likewise.[258] When they watch television programs that illustrate perspective taking and prosocial actions (e.g., *Sesame Street, Barney & Friends*), they are more inclined to exhibit such behaviors themselves.[259]

Powerful models can be found in literature as well. For example, in Harper Lee's *To Kill a Mockingbird*, set in the highly segregated and racially charged Alabama of the 1930s, a lawyer defends an obviously innocent African American man charged with raping a white woman. In doing so, he exemplifies a willingness to fight for high moral principles in the face of strong social pressure to let the man hang for the crime. In John Gunther's *Death Be Not Proud*, a young boy is generous and considerate despite his impending death from cancer.[260]

Engage students in discussions of social and moral issues.

As noted earlier, the disequilibrium (cognitive dissonance) that students experience when they wrestle with moral dilemmas can often promote more advanced moral reasoning. Social and moral dilemmas often arise within the school curriculum. Consider the following questions that might emerge in discussions related to history, social studies, science, or literature:

- Is military retaliation for acts of terrorism justified even when it may involve killing innocent people?
- How can a capitalistic society encourage free enterprise while at the same time protecting the rights of citizens and the ecology of the environment?
- Should laboratory rats be used to study the effects of cancer-producing agents?
- Was Hamlet justified in killing Claudius to avenge the murder of his father?

Students typically have a variety of opinions about social and moral issues, and they often get emotionally as well as cognitively involved in the subject matter (recall our discussion of *hot cognition* in Chapter 6). To facilitate productive discussions about such issues, teachers must create a trusting and nonthreatening classroom atmosphere in which stu-

---

[257] Kerns & Lieberman, 1993; Wiles & Bondi, 2001.

[258] Rushton, 1980; C. C. Wilson, Piazza, & Nagle, 1990.

[259] Dubow, Huesmann, & Greenwood, 2007; Hearold, 1986; Rushton, 1980; Singer & Singer, 1994.

[260] Ellenwood & Ryan, 1991; Nucci, 2001.

dents can express ideas without fear of censure or embarrassment. Teachers should also help students identify all aspects of a dilemma, including the needs and perspectives of the various individuals involved. The most fruitful discussions occur when teachers encourage students to explore their reasons for thinking as they do—that is, to clarify and reflect on the moral principles on which they are basing their judgments.[261]

Get students involved in community service.

As we have seen, adolescents are more likely to act in moral and prosocial ways when they have integrated a commitment to moral ideals into their overall sense of identity. Such integration is more probable when students become actively involved in service to others even before they reach puberty. Through ongoing community service activities—food and clothing drives, visits to homes for the elderly, community cleanup efforts, and so on—elementary and secondary students alike learn that they have the skills and the responsibility for helping those less fortunate than themselves and in other ways making the world a better place in which to live. In the process, they also begin to think of themselves as concerned, compassionate, and moral citizens.[262] And when high school students participate in community service projects, they gain a sense that their school activities can actually *make a difference* in other people's lives, increasing their desire to stay in school rather than drop out.[263]

Community service projects encourage students to integrate a commitment to helping others into their overall sense of identity.

SUMMARY

Children's and adolescents' personalities are the result of complex interactions between heredity (e.g., temperament) and environment (e.g., home environments, cultural expectations). As children grow older, they construct increasingly complex and abstract understandings of who they are. They derive their self-perceptions, collectively known as *sense of self*, not only from their own prior successes and failures but also from the behaviors of others and from the achievements of groups to which they belong. Despite the effects that others have, however, children and adolescents ultimately socialize *themselves* to a considerable degree, conforming to their own ideas about appropriate behavior.

Productive peer relationships are critical for optimal personal and social development. Peers provide a testing ground for emerging social skills, offer support and comfort in times of trouble or uncertainty, and are influential socialization agents. Furthermore, peers provide opportunities for young people to take others' perspectives, draw conclusions about others' motives and intentions, and develop workable solutions to interpersonal problems. In the middle school and high school years, many older children and adolescents become part of larger social groups (perhaps cliques, crowds, or gangs) and form romantic relationships. Yet some students are consistently rejected or neglected by their peers, and these students may especially need teachers' support and guidance.

Most children and adolescents actively try to make sense of their social world. With age, such *social cognition*—thinking about what other people might be thinking and feeling, and hypothesizing about how others might act and react in various situations—becomes increasingly complex and insightful, enabling effective interaction with adults and peers. But some young people have difficulty interpreting social cues correctly and may have few effective social skills. Such difficulties occasionally lead to aggressive and potentially dangerous actions toward others.

As children move through the grade levels, most acquire a definite sense of right and wrong, such that they behave in accordance with prosocial standards for behavior rather than acting solely out of self-interest. This developmental progression is the result of many things, including increasing capacities for abstract thought and empathy, an evolving appreciation for human rights and others' welfare, and ongoing encounters with moral dilemmas and problems. Even at the high school level, however, students do not always take the moral high road, because personal needs and self-interests almost invariably enter into their moral decision making.

Although teachers should certainly accommodate students' diverse temperaments and help students identify areas of particular talent, they must also communicate clear standards for behavior and explain why some behaviors are unacceptable. Teachers may frequently need to monitor and guide students' interactions with peers, and proactive steps may sometimes be necessary to promote communication and interaction among students with diverse backgrounds and characteristics.

---

[261] Nucci, 2001, 2006; Reimer et al., 1983.
[262] Celio, Durlak, Pachan, & Berger, 2007; Hastings et al., 2007; Nucci, 2001; Youniss & Yates, 1999.
[263] Eccles, 2007.

Furthermore, teachers can foster perspective taking, empathy, and more advanced moral reasoning by engaging students in regular discussions about social and moral issues. All students need ongoing teacher support and guidance, but such support and guidance are especially critical for students at risk for academic failure, students who face exceptional challenges at home, and students with disabilities that adversely affect their social behaviors and emotional well-being.

PRACTICE FOR YOUR LICENSURE EXAM

The Scarlet Letter

For the past several days, Ms. Southam's eleventh-grade English class has been reading Nathaniel Hawthorne's *The Scarlet Letter*. The novel, set in 17th-century Boston, focuses largely on two characters who have been carrying on an illicit love affair: Hester Prynne (a young woman who has not seen or heard from her husband for the past two years) and the Reverend Arthur Dimmesdale (a pious and well-respected local preacher). When Hester becomes pregnant, she is imprisoned for adultery and soon bears a child. The class is currently discussing Chapter 3, in which the governor and town leaders (including Dimmesdale) are urging Hester to name the baby's father. (You can observe the following interaction in the "Scarlet Letter" video clip in MyEducationLab.)

Ms. Southam: The father of the baby . . . how do you know it's Dimmesdale . . . the Reverend Arthur Dimmesdale? Why not the Reverend John Wilson or Governor Bellingham? . . . What are the clues in the text in Chapter 3? . . . Nicole?

Nicole: He acts very withdrawn. He doesn't even want to be involved with the situation. He wants the other guy to question her, because he doesn't want to look her in the face and ask her to name *him*.

Ms. Southam: OK. Anything else? . . .

Student: The baby.

Ms. Southam: What about the baby?

Student: She starts to cry, and her eyes follow him.

Ms. Southam: That is one of my absolutely favorite little Hawthornisms. . . . (Ms. Southam reads a paragraph in the novel that describes Dimmesdale's character.) In your logs, jot down some of the important characteristics of that description. What's the diction that strikes you as being essential to understanding Dimmesdale's character? How do you see him? If you were going to draw a portrait of him, what would you make sure he had? . . . Just write some things, or draw a picture if you'd like.

Ms. Southam walks around the room, monitoring what students are doing until they appear to have finished writing.

Ms. Southam: What pictures do you have in your minds of this man . . . if you were directing a film of *The Scarlet Letter*?

Mike: I don't have a person in mind, just characteristics. About five-foot-ten, short, well-groomed hair, well dressed. He looks really nervous and inexperienced. Guilty look on his face. Always nervous, shaking a lot.

Ms. Southam: He's got a guilty look on his face. His lips always trembling, always shaking.

Mike: He's very unsure about himself.

Matt: Sweating really bad. Always going like this. (He shows how Dimmesdale might be wiping his forehead.) He does . . . he has his hanky. . . .

Ms. Southam: Actually, we don't see him mopping his brow, but we do see him doing what? What's the action? Do you remember? If you go to the text, he's holding his hand over his heart, as though he's somehow suffering some pain.

Student: Wire-framed glasses. . . . I don't know why. He's like. . . .

Mike: He's kind of like a nerd-type guy. . . . Short pants. Michael J. Fox's dad. . . . (Mike is referring to a nerdish character in the film *Back to the Future*.)

Ms. Southam: With the short pants and everything.

Student: Yeah, George McFly. (Student identifies the nerdish character's name in the film.)

Ms. Southam: George McFly in his younger years. But at the same time . . . I don't know if it was somebody in this class or somebody in another class when we had all these pictures up here on the wall that characterize this woman. I guess it was one of the guys in fourth period. . . . He said, "Well, she was sure *worth* it." Worth risking your immortal soul for, you know? . . . Obviously she's sinned, but so has he, right? And if she was worth it, don't we also have to see him as somehow having been worthy of her risking *her* soul for this?

Student: Maybe he's got a good personality. . . .

Ms. Southam: He apparently is, you know, a spellbinding preacher. He really can grab the crowd.

Student: It's his eyes. Yeah, the eyes.

Ms. Southam: Those brown, melancholy eyes. Yeah, those brown, melancholy eyes. Absolutely.

1. **Constructed-response question**

   In this classroom dialogue Ms. Southam and her students speculate about what the characters in the novel, and especially Arthur Dimmesdale, might be thinking and feeling. In other words, they are engaging in social cognition.

   A. Identify two examples of student statements that show social cognition.

   B. For each example you identify, explain what it reveals about the speaker's social cognition.

2. **Multiple-choice question**

Ms. Southam does several things that are apt to enhance students' perspective-taking ability. Which one of the following is the best example?

a. She models enthusiasm for the novel ("That is one of my absolutely favorite little Hawthornisms").

b. She suggests that students draw a picture of Dimmesdale, one of the novel's central characters, in their class logs.

c. She points out that Dimmesdale is "holding his hand over his heart, as though he's somehow suffering some pain."

d. She reinforces Mike for drawing an analogy between Dimmesdale and a character in the film *Back to the Future*.

Once you have answered these questions, compare your responses with those presented in Appendix A.

FOR FURTHER READING

The following articles from the journal *Educational Leadership* are especially relevant to this chapter. You can find these articles in Chapter 7 of MyEducationLab for this text.

Barton, P. E. (2006). The dropout problem: Losing ground. *Educational Leadership, 63*(5), 14–18.

Benard, B. (1993). Fostering resiliency in kids. *Educational Leadership, 51*(3), 44–48.

Berreth, D., & Berman, S. (1997). The moral dimensions of schools. *Educational Leadership, 54*(8), 24–27.

Boston, B. O. (1998). If the water is nasty, fix it. *Educational Leadership, 56*(4), 66–69.

Collopy, R. B., & Green, T. (1995). Using motivation theory with at-risk children. *Educational Leadership, 53*(1), 37–40.

Froschl, M., & Gropper, N. (1999). Fostering friendships, curbing bullying. *Educational Leadership, 56*(8), 72–75.

Holden, G. (1997). Changing the way kids settle conflicts. *Educational Leadership, 54*(8), 74–76.

Johnson, D. W., Johnson, R., & Dudley, B. (1992). Teaching students to be peer mediators. *Educational Leadership, 50*(1), 10–13.

Krystal, S. (1998). The nurturing potential of service learning. *Educational Leadership, 56*(4), 58–61.

Lamperes, B. (1994). Empowering at-risk students to succeed. *Educational Leadership, 52*(3), 67–70.

Miller, M. (2006). Where they are: Working with marginalized students. *Educational Leadership, 63*(5), 50–54.

Olweus, D. (2003). A profile of bullying at school. *Educational Leadership, 60*(6), 12–17.

Price, L. F. (2005). The biology of risk taking. *Educational Leadership, 62*(7), 22–26.

Sapon-Shevin, M., with Dobbelaere, A., Corrigan, C., Goodman, K., & Mastin, M. (1998). Everyone here can play. *Educational Leadership, 56*(1), 42–45.

MYEDUCATIONLAB

Now go to Chapter 7 of MyEducationLab at **www. myeducationlab.com,** where you can:

- Find instructional objectives for the chapter, along with focus questions that can help you zero in on important ideas in the chapter.
- Take a self-check quiz on concepts and principles you've just read about.
- Complete exercises and assignments that can help you more deeply understand the chapter content.
- Read supplementary material that can broaden your knowledge of one or more of the chapter's topics.
- Apply what you've learned to classroom contexts in Building Teaching Skills activities.

CHAPTER 8

Instructional Strategies

CASE STUDY   The Oregon Trail

Fifth-grade teacher Michele Minichiello has recently begun a unit about American settlers traveling west on the Oregon Trail during the 1840s. Today's lesson focuses on how families prepared for the long, difficult trip.

"The covered wagons were about four feet by ten feet," Ms. Minichiello tells her class. She has students move their desks to clear the middle of the classroom and then instructs two students to mark a 4-foot by 10-foot rectangle on the carpet with masking tape. "These are the dimensions of a typical covered wagon. How much room would that give you for your family and supplies?" The students agree that the wagon is smaller than they had realized and that it would not provide room for many supplies.

"So they would have to be pretty choosy about what they brought on their trip," Ms. Minichiello observes. "Let's brainstorm some of the things the settlers might have packed." The students volunteer many possibilities—food, spare wagon parts, pots and pans, blankets, extra clothes, rifles, bullets, barrels of water, medicine—and Ms. Minichiello writes them on the chalkboard. She has the class get more specific about the list (e.g., what kinds of food? how much of each kind?) and then passes out reading materials that describe the supplies a typical family would actually pack for the journey. As the students read and discuss the materials in small groups, Ms. Minichiello circulates among them to show old photographs of how the inside of a covered wagon looked when occupied by a family and its possessions.

Once the students have finished their reading, Ms. Minichiello directs their attention to their own supply list on the chalkboard, and the following discussion ensues with the students and Ms. Berry, a special education teacher who is also in the room.

Ms. M: Do you think our list was accurate? Is there anything you want to change?
Lacy: We need much more flour.
Janie: (referring to an item listed in the reading materials) I don't think they should bring 100 pounds of coffee.
Curt: (also referring to the reading materials) I don't think they need 50 pounds of lard.
Ms. M: Does anyone know what lard is?
Tom: It's a kind of animal fat.
Ms. B: They used it for cooking, but they used it for lots of other things, too.
Ms. M: Do you think they used it for waterproofing?
Ms. B: Maybe so.
Ms. M: What were some of the things that pioneers had to be prepared for? (Here she is asking students to recall information they have just learned from the reading materials.)
Mark: Mountain travel.
René: Crossing rivers.
Ms. B: How about if you were going across the desert?
Lacy: You'd need a lot of water.
Tom: Food for the oxen.
Ms. M: If *you* were taking such a trip now—if you were moving far away from where you live now—what things would you bring with you?
Misha: Computer.
Lou: Cell phone.
Dana: Refrigerator.
Cerise: My dog.

Ms. M: Where would pioneers go now?

Curt: North or south pole.

Tom: Space.

Ms. M: Imagine that your family isn't doing well, and so you decide to travel to a distant planet. It's very expensive to travel there. You can only take *one* item, so pick the one item you would bring. Assume there will be food and a place to sleep. Take five minutes to pick one item, and explain why you would take it.

Ms. Minichiello distributes index cards on which the students can write their responses. She gives them a few minutes to do so and then asks, "Who found that it was hard to pick just one item?" Almost all of the students raise their hands. "What I wanted you to realize is that if you were a child back then, it would be really hard to leave most of your things behind."[1]

- Are the students engaged in the lesson? What evidence do you see to indicate that they are learning?
- What specific instructional strategies is Ms. Minichiello using to engage and motivate her students? What strategies is she using to help them understand the nature of travel in the mid-1800s?

The students in Ms. Minichiello's class are clearly engaged in the lesson (e.g., they are actively responding to her questions), and they have definitely learned some things (e.g., they notice differences between the two supply lists, and they can recall some of the difficulties the settlers faced). To engage and motivate her students, Ms. Minichiello arouses situational interest through a physical activity (students move their desks and make a "wagon" on the floor), creates cognitive dissonance (the list in the reading materials doesn't entirely match the one the class has generated), poses a challenging question ("You can only take *one* item. . . ."), and makes the lesson a very social, interactive one. Furthermore, Ms. Minichiello promotes learning and understanding by encouraging visual imagery and elaboration—for instance, by making the subject matter concrete and vivid (through the masking-tape wagon and the old photographs), having the class consider necessities and hazards that might justify items on the supply list ("What were some of the things that pioneers had to be prepared for?"), and asking students to relate the settlers' situation to a hypothetical one they themselves might face.

In the preceding chapters, we've learned a great deal about how children and adolescents think, learn, develop, and become motivated to engage actively and productively in classroom activities. In this chapter we'll build on what we've learned to identify a variety of ways in which teachers can effectively plan and carry out instruction. As you'll soon discover, planning and instruction are closely intertwined with two other essential aspects of teaching—creating an effective classroom environment and assessing students' progress and final achievements—topics we'll explore in depth in Chapters 9 and 10, respectively. Although we'll be switching our focus somewhat in these final three chapters, we must remember that student characteristics and behaviors should ultimately drive what teachers do in the classroom (see Figure 8.1). To repeat a point I made in Chapter 1, classroom practices should be *learner centered*.

The first step any teacher must take, of course, is *planning*—deciding in advance both what needs to be accomplished and how best to accomplish it. After examining various aspects of the planning process in this chapter, we'll look at two general approaches to instruction, teacher directed and learner directed.[2] In **teacher-directed instruction**, the teacher calls most of the shots, choosing what topics will be addressed, directing the course of the lesson, and so on. In **learner-directed instruction**, students have considerable say in the issues they address and how to address them. We're really talking about a *continuum*

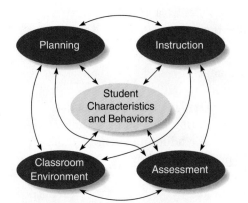

FIGURE 8.1 Planning, instruction, the classroom environment, classroom assessment practices, and student characteristics and behaviors are not independent. Each one influences the others.

teacher-directed instruction Approach to instruction in which the teacher is largely in control of the content and course of the lesson.

learner-directed instruction Approach to instruction in which students have considerable say in the issues they address and how to address them.

[1] I observed Michele's lesson when I was supervising her teaching internship at the end of her master's program, and she gave me permission to describe it here. The students' names are pseudonyms.

[2] Some theorists instead use the terms *teacher-centered* and *learner-centered* in reference to this distinction.

However, as I point out in Chapter 1 and illustrate in Figure 8.1, virtually all instructional strategies should focus (center) on what and how a student is learning. The essential difference here lies in who has control of the instructional activity.

here—not an either-or situation—because lessons can vary considerably in the degree to which teachers and their students control the course of events.

Traditionally, instruction in most elementary and secondary classrooms has been largely teacher directed. Yet educators are increasingly recognizing the value of learner-directed activities not only for fostering classroom learning and achievement but also for promoting the metacognitive and self-regulatory skills essential for lifelong success. Ultimately, teachers' decisions about whether to use teacher-directed or learner-directed strategies—or, more often, to combine the two approaches, as Ms. Minichiello does—should be based on their goals for instruction and on the knowledge and skills that their students bring to the situation. As you read the chapter, then, don't think about choosing a single "best" instructional strategy. Instead, think about how different strategies may be more or less suitable in different contexts.

PLANNING INSTRUCTION

Effective teaching begins long before students enter the classroom. Good teachers engage in considerable advance planning. They identify the knowledge and skills they want students to acquire, determine an appropriate sequence in which to teach such knowledge and skills, and develop classroom activities that will maximize learning and keep students continually motivated and on task. Ideally, teachers also coordinate their plans with one another—for example, by identifying common goals toward which they will all strive or by developing interdisciplinary units that involve two or more classes and subject areas.

Instructional planning typically involves the following strategies.

Identify the desired end results of instruction.

An essential part of planning instruction is identifying the specific things students should accomplish during a lesson or unit, as well as the things they should accomplish over the course of the semester or school year. Educators use a variety of terms for such end results, including *goals*, *objectives*, *outcomes*, *proficiencies*, *targets*, *benchmarks*, and *standards*. In this book I'll typically use the term **instructional goals** when referring to general, long-term outcomes of instruction. I'll use the term **instructional objectives** when referring to more specific outcomes of a particular lesson or unit.

Regardless of the terminology they use, experts agree that the desired end results of instruction should influence what teachers teach, how they teach it, and how they assess students' learning and achievement.[3] In fact, as a general rule, teachers should *begin* the planning process by determining what they ultimately want students to know and be able to do. One popular approach is a **backward design**, in which teachers proceed through this sequence:[4]

1. Identify the desired results in terms of knowledge and skills that students should ultimately attain.
2. Determine acceptable evidence—in the form of performance on various classroom assessment tasks—that students have achieved those results.
3. Plan learning experiences and instructional activities that enable students to demonstrate—through their performance on the assessment tasks—attainment of the desired results.

With such an approach, teachers essentially *begin at the end* and then choose assessment tasks and instructional strategies that are specifically related to that end. For example, if the objective for a unit on addition is *knowledge* of number facts, a teacher may want to use drill and practice (perhaps flash cards, perhaps gamelike computer software) to enhance students' automaticity for these facts and may want to use a timed test to measure students' ability to recall the facts quickly and easily. But if the objective is *application* of number facts, a teacher may instead want to focus instruction and assessment methods on word problems or on activities involving real objects and hands-on measurements.

instructional goal Desired long-term outcome of instruction.

instructional objective Desired outcome of a lesson or unit.

backward design Approach to instructional planning in which a teacher first determines the desired end result (i.e., what knowledge and skills students should acquire) and then identifies appropriate assessments and instructional strategies.

---

[3] For example, see Darling-Hammond & Bransford, 2005; Kuhn, 2007.

[4] Wiggins & McTighe, 1998.

Hear a teacher describe instructional objectives in the "Civil War" video in the Additional Resources section in Chapter 8 of MyEducationLab.

Students, too, benefit from knowing the desired final outcomes of instruction. When they know what they need to accomplish, they can make more informed decisions about how to focus their efforts and allocate their study time, and they can more effectively monitor their comprehension as they read and study.[5] For example, if their teacher tells them that they should be able to "apply science to everyday situations," they will probably think about and study science very differently than if they need to "know definitions by heart." In the "Civil War" video clip in MyEducationLab, the teacher tells students exactly what she hopes they will gain from the lesson. She also explains that the lesson will be only a first step toward gaining an understanding of the American Civil War:

> When this lesson is over, this is what I hope you will understand more about. The geography of the Civil War is our topic. I want you to understand better the meaning of these words, and you will. And I want you to have an understanding of the dynamics of the war—why it was fought, how it was fought, and why it ended the way it did. . . . I would like for you to have some good questions in your head that we don't answer today. This is like meeting somebody for the first time. You're going to meet the Civil War again in junior high and in high school and in college. So this is just a little introduction to the Civil War.

Teachers don't pull their goals and objectives out of the blue, of course. Usually they base their goals and objectives on guidelines that others have previously set. For example, in the United States many state departments of education—and some local school districts as well—have established comprehensive lists of content area **standards** that guide instruction and assessment from kindergarten or first grade through high school.[6] Such standards identify specific goals for different grade levels in reading, writing, mathematics, science, social studies, and sometimes also in domains such as art, music, foreign languages, and physical education. As an illustration, the middle column of Table 8.1 presents examples of Indiana's state standards for reading comprehension at grades 1, 4, 7, and 11. (California's state standards are almost identical to these.) In the rightmost column of the table I suggest teaching strategies that might address one or more of those standards. We'll revisit the same set of standards again in Chapter 10, when we consider how students' achievement of the standards might be assessed.

An additional source of guidance comes from standards created by national or international organizations that represent various academic disciplines. Numerous discipline-specific professional groups have established standards for their subject area that reflect the combined thinking of many experts in the field. Examples are presented in Table 8.2.

Existing standards are certainly useful in helping teachers focus instruction on important educational goals—including such higher-level thinking processes as transfer, problem solving, and critical thinking—in various content domains. If teachers rely on content area standards exclusively, however, they are apt to neglect other, equally important goals, such as helping students acquire effective learning strategies, self-regulation techniques, and social skills. In addition to considering existing local, state, national, and international standards, then, teachers should formulate some of their *own* goals and objectives. The Classroom Strategies box "Identifying the Goals and Objectives of Instruction" (p. 285) offers suggestions for developing useful ones.

One especially important suggestion in the Classroom Strategies box is to *include goals and objectives at varying levels of complexity and sophistication.* Notice how the standards presented in Table 8.1 focus largely on higher-level thinking skills, such as identifying main ideas, making predictions, and evaluating information. Such higher-level skills must, of course, be an important part of teacher-developed goals and objectives as well. One tool that can help teachers broaden their view of what students should learn and be able to do is **Bloom's taxonomy**, a list of six general cognitive processes that vary from simple to complex:[7]

1. **Remember**: Recognizing or recalling information learned at an earlier time and stored in long-term memory

standards General statements regarding the knowledge and skills that students should gain and the characteristics that their accomplishments should reflect.

Bloom's taxonomy Taxonomy of six cognitive processes, varying in complexity, that lessons might be designed to foster.

[5] Gronlund, 2004; McAshan, 1979.
[6] As I finish writing this book in January 2008, the Web site *Developing Educational Standards* (www.standards.org/Standards.html) provides links to standards in all 50 states and the District of Columbia.

[7] The original taxonomy was developed in 1956 by B. S. Bloom, Englehart, Furst, Hill, and Krathwohl. The taxonomy presented here is a revision developed in 2001 by L. W. Anderson et al.

DEVELOPMENTAL TRENDS

TABLE 8.1	**Examples of Indiana's State Standards for Reading Comprehension at Different Grade Levels**	

Grade Level	Examples of Grade-Specific Standards	Examples of Strategies That Address One or More Standards
Grade 1	• Respond to *who, what, when, where, why,* and *how* questions and discuss the main idea of what is read. • Follow one-step written instructions. • Use context (the meaning of the surrounding text) to understand word and sentence meanings. • Relate prior knowledge to what is read.	• Read high-interest stories, stopping frequently to ask questions that require students to go beyond the text itself (e.g., ask students to speculate about what a character might be feeling). • As students in a reading group read a story, occasionally ask them to summarize what has happened so far. • Include simple written directions on worksheets designed to promote basic skills (e.g., "Circle the word that rhymes with _____.").
Grade 4	• Use appropriate strategies when reading for different purposes. • Draw conclusions or make and confirm predictions about text by using prior knowledge and ideas presented in the text itself, including illustrations, titles, topic sentences, important words, foreshadowing clues (clues that indicate what might happen next), and direct quotations. • Evaluate new information and hypotheses (statements of theories or assumptions) by testing them against known information and ideas. • Distinguish between cause and effect and between fact and opinion in informational text.	• As students seek information in the school library, describe effective strategies for locating needed information in reference books. • As a reading group discusses an age-appropriate novel, ask students to speculate about how the plot might progress and to identify clues in the text that support their predictions. • As students read a passage in a history book, have them identify cause-and-effect relationships (stated or implied) among events.
Grade 7	• Understand and analyze the differences in structure and purpose between various categories of informational materials (such as textbooks, newspapers, and instructional or technical materials). • Identify and trace the development of an author's argument, point of view, or perspective in text. • Understand and explain the use of a simple mechanical device by following directions in a technical manual. • Assess the adequacy, accuracy, and appropriateness of the author's evidence to support claims and assertions, noting instances of bias and stereotyping.	• Have students identify ways in which they might use the headings and organizational structure of a textbook to help them organize and study its content. • Present examples of persuasive essays, and ask students to identify the main idea and supporting arguments. • After demonstrating how to use a microscope and prepare slides of water taken from a local frog pond, have students repeat the process by following a set of written instructions.
Grade 11	• Analyze the way in which clarity of meaning is affected by the patterns of organization, repetition of the main ideas, organization of language, and word choice in the text. • Verify and clarify facts presented in several types of expository texts by using a variety of consumer, workplace, and public documents. • Analyze an author's implicit and explicit assumptions and beliefs about a subject. • Critique the power, validity, and truthfulness of arguments set forth in public documents; their appeal to both friendly and hostile audiences; and the extent to which the arguments anticipate and address reader concerns and counterclaims.	• When studying poetry, have students find words and phrases with multiple possible meanings; ask them to consider how the poetic meter affects the mood a poem conveys. • Ask students to identify the unstated assumptions (e.g., that one group is "good" or "right" and another is "bad" or "wrong") underlying a history textbook's depiction of events. • Have students read several editorials on the same issue and evaluate the effectiveness of each author's persuasive strategies.

Source: Standards (middle column) are from a Web site maintained by the Indiana Department of Education. Retrieved October 11, 2007, from www.indianastandardsresources.org

2. **Understand**: Constructing meaning from instructional materials and messages (e.g., drawing inferences, identifying new examples, summarizing)
3. **Apply**: Using knowledge in a familiar or new situation
4. **Analyze**: Breaking information into its constituent parts, and perhaps identifying interrelationships among the parts

TABLE 8.2   Web Sites with Standards for Various Academic Disciplines

Content Domain	Organization	Internet Address	Once You Get There. . .[a]
Civics and government	Center for Civic Education	www.civiced.org	Go to *Publications* and then *Resource Materials*.
English and language arts	National Council of Teachers of English	www.ncte.org	Select *Standards* from the *Quick Links* menu.
Foreign language	American Council on the Teaching of Foreign Language	www.actfl.org	Select *Standards for Foreign Language Learning* from the *Publications* menu.
Geography	National Council for Geographic Education	www.ncge.org	Select *Geography Standards* from the *Geography* menu.
Health, physical education, and dance	National Association for Sport and Physical Education	www.aahperd.org/NASPE	Select *National Standards & Activity Guidelines* from the *Publications* menu.
History	National Center for History in the Schools	www.sscnet.ucla.edu/nchs	Click on *Standards* (*Online*).
Information literacy	American Association of School Librarians	www.ala.org/aasl	Click on *Issues & Advocacy* and then on *Information Literacy*.
Mathematics	National Council of Teachers of Mathematics	www.nctm.org	Click on *Standards and Focal Points*.
Music	National Association for Music Education	www.menc.org	Click on *National Standards*.
Science	National Academy of Sciences	www.nap.edu	Click on *Education* (under Topics) and then on *Testing, Assessments, and Standards* (under Subtopics).
Visual arts	National Art Education Association	www.naea-reston.org	Click on *Publications* and then on *Publications List*; scroll to the two-column table below the list of titles.

[a]These steps worked for me in January 2008. Given the dynamic nature of many Web sites, you may find that you have to do something different when you get to the site in question.

5. **Evaluate:** Making judgments about information using certain criteria or standards
6. **Create:** Putting together knowledge, procedures, or both to form a coherent, structured, and possibly original whole

This taxonomy is hardly an exhaustive list of what students should be able to do while learning classroom subject matter—for instance, it doesn't include motor skills, attitudes, or general dispositions—but it is a helpful reminder that there is much more to school learning and academic achievement than learning and recalling facts.

Ask students to identify some of their own objectives for instruction.

With this suggestion, we are simply revisiting a suggestion I made in Chapter 6: *Ask students to set some personal goals for learning and performance.* Naturally, student-chosen goals and objectives must be compatible with any mandated standards and with their teachers' goals and objectives. However, most school curricula do allow for some flexibility in what students focus on. For example, different students might choose different gymnastic skills to master, different art media to use, or different historical events to study in depth. By allowing students to identify some of their own goals and objectives, teachers encourage the *goal setting* that is an integral aspect of self-regulation (Chapter 4) and foster the sense of *self-determination* that is so important for intrinsic motivation (Chapter 6).

Break complex tasks and topics into smaller pieces, identify a logical sequence for the pieces, and decide how best to teach each one.

Consider these four teachers:

- Ms. Begay plans to teach her third graders how to solve arithmetic word problems. She also wants to help them learn more effectively from the things they read.

CLASSROOM STRATEGIES

Identifying the Goals and Objectives of Instruction

- **Identify both short-term objectives and long-term goals.**

  An elementary school teacher wants students to learn how to spell 10 new words each week. She also wants them to write a coherent and grammatically correct short story by the end of the school year.

- **In addition to goals related to specific topics and content areas, identify goals related to students' general long-term academic success.**

  A middle school social studies teacher realizes that early adolescence is an important time for developing the learning and study strategies that students will need in high school and college. Throughout the school year, then, he continually introduces new strategies for learning and remembering the subject matter—effective ways that students might organize their notes, mnemonic techniques they might use to help them remember specific facts, questions they might try to answer as they read a textbook chapter, and so on.

- **Include goals and objectives at varying levels of complexity and sophistication.**

  A high school physics teacher wants students not only to understand basic kinds of machines (e.g., levers, wedges) but also to recognize examples of these machines in their own lives and use them to solve real-world problems.

- **Consider physical, social, and affective outcomes as well as cognitive outcomes.**

  A physical education teacher wants his students to know the basic rules of basketball and to dribble and pass the ball appropriately. He also wants them to acquire a love of basketball, effective ways of working cooperatively with teammates, and a general desire to stay physically fit.

- **Describe goals and objectives not in terms of what the teacher will do during a lesson, but rather in terms of what *students* should be able to do at the *end* of instruction.**

  A Spanish teacher knows that students easily confuse the verbs *estar* and *ser* because both are translated in English as "to be." She identifies this objective for her students: "Students will correctly conjugate *estar* and *ser* in the present tense and use each one in appropriate contexts."

- **When formulating short-term objectives, identify specific behaviors that will reflect accomplishment of the objectives.**

  In a unit on the food pyramid, a health teacher identifies this objective for students: "Students will create menus for a breakfast, a lunch, and a dinner that, in combination, include all elements of the pyramid in appropriate proportions."

- **When formulating long-term goals that involve complex topics or skills, list a few abstract outcomes and then give examples of specific behaviors that reflect each one.**

  Faculty members at a junior high school identify this instructional goal for all students at their school: "Students will demonstrate effective classroom listening skills—for example, by taking complete and accurate notes, answering teacher questions correctly, and seeking clarification when they don't understand."

Sources: Some suggestions based on Brophy & Alleman, 1991; N. S. Cole, 1990; Gronlund, 2000, 2004; R. L. Linn & Miller, 2005; Popham, 1995.

- Mr. Marzano, a middle school physical education teacher, is beginning a unit on basketball. He wants his students to develop enough proficiency in the sport to feel comfortable playing both on organized school basketball teams and in less formal games with friends and neighbors.
- Mr. Wu, a junior high school music teacher, needs to teach his new trumpet students how to play a recognizable version of "Seventy-Six Trombones" in time for the New Year's Day parade.
- Ms. Flores, a high school social studies teacher, is going to introduce the intricacies of the federal judicial system to her classes.

All four teachers want to teach complex topics or skills. Accordingly, each of them should probably conduct a **task analysis**, a process of identifying the specific knowledge and behaviors necessary to master the subject matter in question. The task analysis can then guide them as they select the most appropriate methods and sequence in which to teach that subject matter.

A task analysis typically takes one of three forms:[8]

- **Behavioral analysis.** One way of analyzing a complex task is to identify the specific behaviors required to perform it. For example, Mr. Marzano can identify the specific physical movements involved in dribbling, passing, and shooting a basketball. Similarly, Mr. Wu can identify the behaviors that students must master to play a trumpet successfully: holding the instrument with the fingers placed appropriately on the valves, blowing correctly into the mouthpiece, and so on.
- **Subject matter analysis.** Another approach is to break down the subject matter into the specific topics, concepts, and principles it includes. For example, Ms. Flores can

task analysis Process of identifying the specific knowledge, behaviors, or cognitive processes necessary to master a particular subject area or skill.

---

[8] Jonassen, Hannum, & Tessmer, 1989.

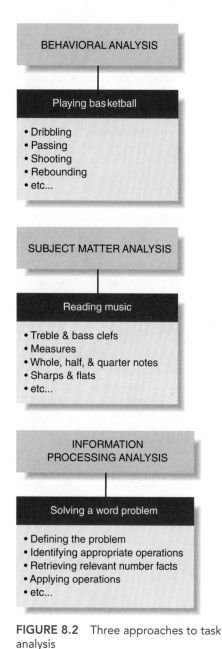

FIGURE 8.2 Three approaches to task analysis

identify various aspects of the judicial system (concepts such as *innocent until proven guilty* and *reasonable doubt*, the roles that judges and juries play, etc.) and their interrelationships. Mr. Wu, who needs to teach his new trumpet students how to read music as well as how to play the instrument, can identify the basic elements of written music that students must know to interpret such music: the difference between the treble and bass clefs, the number of beats associated with different kinds of notes, and so on.

- **Information processing analysis.** A third approach is to specify the cognitive processes involved in a task. To illustrate, Ms. Begay can identify the mental processes involved in successfully solving an arithmetic word problem, such as correct classification (encoding) of the problem (e.g., determining whether it requires addition, subtraction, etc.) and rapid retrieval of basic number facts. Similarly, she can identify specific cognitive strategies useful in reading comprehension, such as finding main ideas, elaborating, and summarizing.

Figure 8.2 illustrates the three approaches to task analysis just described.

To get a taste of what a task analysis involves, try the following exercise.

SEE FOR YOURSELF
Peanut Butter Sandwich

Conduct a task analysis for the process of making a peanut butter sandwich:

1. Decide whether your approach should be a behavioral analysis, a subject matter analysis, or an information processing analysis.
2. Now, using the approach you've selected, break the sandwich-making task into a number of small, "teachable" steps.
3. (Optional) If you're hungry and have the necessary materials close at hand, make an actual sandwich following the steps you've identified. Did your initial analysis omit any important steps?

Chances are, you chose a behavioral analysis. Making a peanut butter sandwich is largely a behavioral rather than mental task. For instance, you must know how to unscrew the peanut butter jar lid, get an appropriate amount of peanut butter on your knife, spread the peanut butter gently enough that you don't tear the bread, and so on.

Conducting task analyses for complex skills and topics has at least two advantages.[9] First, by identifying a task's specific components—whether those components are behaviors, concepts and ideas, or cognitive processes—a teacher gains a better sense of what things students need to learn and the order in which they can most effectively learn those things. For example, Mr. Wu must certainly teach his trumpet students how to blow into the mouthpiece before he can teach them how to play different notes.

A second advantage in conducting a task analysis is that it helps a teacher choose appropriate instructional strategies. Different tasks—and perhaps even different components of a single task—may require different approaches to instruction. For example, if one necessary component of solving arithmetic word problems is the rapid retrieval of math facts from memory, then repeated practice of these facts may be critical for developing automaticity. If another component of solving these problems is identifying the appropriate operation to apply in various situations, then promoting a true understanding of mathematical concepts and principles (perhaps by using concrete manipulatives or authentic activities) is essential.

Sometimes a task analysis may lead a teacher to conclude that he or she can most effectively teach a complex task by teaching some or all of its components separately from one another. For instance, Mr. Wu may initially ask his beginning trumpet students to practice blowing into the mouthpiece correctly without worrying about the specific notes they pro-

---

[9] Desberg & Taylor, 1986; Jonassen et al., 1989.

duce. On other occasions it may be more appropriate to teach the desired knowledge and behaviors entirely within the context of the overall task, in part because doing so makes the subject matter meaningful for students. For instance, Ms. Begay should almost certainly teach her students the processes involved in learning effectively from reading materials—elaborating, summarizing, and so on—primarily within the context of authentic reading tasks.

Develop a step-by-step lesson plan.

Once they have identified their goals for instruction, and perhaps conducted a task analysis as well, effective teachers develop a **lesson plan** to guide them during instruction. A lesson plan typically includes the following:

- The goal(s) or objective(s) of the lesson
- Instructional materials (e.g., textbooks, handouts) and equipment required
- Instructional strategies and the sequence in which they'll be used
- Assessment method(s) planned

Any lesson plan should, of course, take into account the students who will be learning—their developmental levels, prior knowledge, cultural backgrounds, and so on.

Many beginning teachers develop fairly detailed lesson plans that describe how they are going to help students learn the subject matter in question.[10] For instance, when I began teaching middle school geography, I spent many hours each week writing down the information, examples, questions, and student activities I wanted to use during the following week. But as teachers gain experience teaching certain topics, they learn which strategies work effectively and which do not, and they use some of the effective ones frequently enough that they can retrieve them quickly and easily from long-term memory. As time goes on, planning lessons becomes far less time consuming, and much of it becomes *mental* planning rather than planning on paper.

You should probably think of a lesson plan more as a guide than as a recipe—in other words, as a general plan of attack that can and should be adjusted as events unfold.[11] For instance, during the course of a lesson, a teacher may find that students have less prior knowledge than anticipated, and so the teacher may need to "back up" and teach material that he or she had mistakenly assumed students had already mastered. Or, if students express curiosity or have intriguing insights about a particular topic, a teacher may want to spend more time exploring the topic than originally planned.

As teachers proceed through the school year, their long-range plans will also change somewhat. For instance, they may find that their task analyses of desired knowledge and skills were overly simplistic. Or they may discover that their expectations for students' achievement, as reflected in previously identified instructional goals, are either unrealistically high or unnecessarily low. Teachers must continually revise their plans as instruction proceeds and as classroom assessments reveal how well students are learning and achieving.

CONDUCTING TEACHER-DIRECTED INSTRUCTION

In the opening case study, Ms. Minichiello directs the course of the lesson to a considerable degree. For instance, she instructs students to mark the dimensions of a covered wagon on the floor, has them brainstorm supplies that pioneers might have needed during their journey, and asks them to consider what single item they would want to take with them to a distant planet. And through questions such as "How much room would [a typical covered wagon] give you for your family and supplies?" "Do you think our list was accurate?" and "What were some of the things that pioneers had to be prepared for?" she nudges students toward the kinds of conclusions she wants them to draw about life on the Oregon Trail.

Some teacher-directed instruction takes the form of **expository instruction**, in which information is presented (*exposed*) in essentially the same form that students are expected

lesson plan Predetermined guide for a lesson that identifies instructional goals or objectives, necessary materials, instructional strategies, and one or more assessment methods.

expository instruction Approach to instruction in which information is presented in more or less the same form in which students are expected to learn it.

---

[10] Calderhead, 1996; Sternberg & Horvath, 1995.
[11] Calderhead, 1996.

to learn it.[12] Ms. Minichiello's lesson about the Oregon Trail has several elements of expository instruction. For instance, she presents the dimensions of a typical covered wagon, gives students reading materials about how the settlers packed for the long trip west, and shows photographs of pioneer families and their temporary covered-wagon "homes."

On some occasions expository instruction is exclusively one-way in nature, in that information goes only from teacher to learners. Examples are textbook reading assignments and educational films and videos. In each case a "teacher" (e.g., a textbook author or video narrator) presents information without any possibility of getting information from students in return. Other forms of expository instruction are more interactive, in that they incorporate some exchange of information between teacher (or perhaps a virtual "teacher," such as a computer) and students. For instance, effective classroom lectures typically include some opportunity for student input, perhaps in the form of answers to teacher questions, inquiries about ambiguous points, or reactions to certain ideas. In approaches such as *direct instruction* and *computer-based instruction*—both of which we'll consider shortly— student input is a frequent and essential ingredient despite the considerable control that the teacher or computer programmer has over the content and sequence of the lesson.

Strategies such as the following can enhance the effectiveness of teacher-directed instruction.

Begin with what students already know and believe.

Students are apt to engage in meaningful learning—to relate new material to things they already know—only if they have both the "new" and the "old" in working memory at the same time. Thus a strategy we first encountered in Chapter 2, *prior knowledge activation*, is an important first step in any teacher-directed instruction. In addition, asking students what they already know about a topic—or at least what they *think* they know about it—can uncover misconceptions that might wreak havoc with new learning and so must be vigorously addressed.

Promote effective cognitive processes.

The effectiveness of teacher-directed instruction ultimately depends on the particular cognitive processes that instruction enables and encourages.[13] To see this idea in action, try the following exercise.

SEE FOR YOURSELF

Finding Pedagogy in the Book

1. Look back at two or three of the preceding chapters. Find several places where specific things that I've done have helped you learn and remember the material more effectively. What specific techniques did I use to facilitate your cognitive processing?
2. In those same chapters, can you find places where you had difficulty processing the material presented? What might I have done differently in such instances?

I'm hoping that the See for Yourself exercises have helped you relate new topics to your own knowledge and experiences. I'm hoping, too, that the case studies and student and teacher artifacts have made abstract ideas more concrete and "real" for you. Perhaps some of the graphics, tables, and summaries have helped you organize concepts and principles. But if you've found certain parts of the books difficult to understand or in some other way troublesome, I encourage you to let me know.[14]

---

[12] Some theorists use the term *expository instruction* only in reference to lectures and textbooks. I am using the term more broadly to refer to any approach that centers around the *transmission* of information from expert (e.g., classroom teacher, textbook writer, computer software designer) to student.

[13] Ausubel, Novak, & Hanesian, 1978; R. E. Mayer, 2004; Moreno, 2006; Weinert & Helmke, 1995.
[14] As I complete this book in January 2008, my e-mail addresses are jormrod@comcast.net and jormrod@alumni.brown.edu.

TABLE 8.3   Enhancing Cognitive Processing in Teacher-Directed Instruction

Principle	Educational Implication	Example
An **advance organizer**—a verbal or graphic introduction that lays out the general organizational framework of upcoming material—helps students make meaningful connections among the things they learn.	Introduce a new unit by describing the major ideas and concepts to be discussed and showing how they are interrelated.	Introduce a unit on vertebrates by saying something like this: "Vertebrates all have backbones. We'll be talking about five phyla of vertebrates—mammals, birds, reptiles, amphibians, and fish—that differ from one another in several ways, including whether their members are warm blooded or cold blooded; whether they have hair, scales, or feathers; and whether they lay eggs or bear live young."
Ongoing **connections to prior knowledge** help students learn classroom material more meaningfully, provided that their existing understandings and beliefs are accurate.	Remind students of something they already know—that is, activate students' prior knowledge—and point out how a new idea is related. Also, address any erroneous beliefs students have about the topic (see the discussion of *conceptual change* in Chapter 2).	Draw an analogy between *peristalsis* (muscular contractions that push food through the digestive tract) and the process of squeezing ketchup from a packet: "You squeeze the packet near one corner and run your fingers along the length of the packet toward an opening at the other corner. When you do this, you push the ketchup through the packet, in one direction, ahead of your fingers, until it comes out of the opening."
An **organized presentation** of material helps students make appropriate interconnections among ideas.	Help students organize material in a particular way by presenting the information using that same organizational structure.	Use a *concept map* to depict the main concepts and ideas of a topic and their interrelationships (see the discussion of concept maps in Chapter 4).
Various **signals** built into a presentation (e.g., italicized print, interspersed questions) can draw students' attention to important points.	Stress important points—for instance, by writing them on the chalkboard, asking questions about them, or simply telling students what things are most important to learn.	When assigning a textbook chapter for homework, identify several questions that students should try to answer as they read the chapter.
Visual aids help students encode material visually as well as verbally.	Illustrate new material through pictures, photographs, diagrams, maps, physical models, and demonstrations.	When describing major battles of the American Civil War, present a map showing where each battle took place; point out that some battles were fought in especially strategic locations.
Appropriate **pacing** gives students adequate time to process information.	Pace a presentation slowly enough that students can draw inferences, form visual images, and in other ways engage in effective long-term memory storage processes.	Intersperse lengthy explanations with demonstrations or hands-on activities that illustrate some of the principles you are describing.
Summaries help students review and organize material and identify main ideas.	After a lecture or reading assignment, summarize the key points of the lesson.	At the end of a unit on Emily Dickinson, summarize her work by describing the characteristics that made her poetry so unique and influential.

Sources: Bulgren, Deshler, Schumaker, & Lenz, 2000; Carney & Levin, 2002; Corkill, 1992; Dansereau, 1995; Donnelly & McDaniel, 1993; E. L. Ferguson & Hegarty, 1995; R. H. Hall & O'Donnell, 1994; Hansen & Pearson, 1983; J. Hartley & Trueman, 1982; Krajcik, 1991; Levin & Mayer, 1993; M. C. Linn, Songer, & Eylon, 1996; Lorch, Lorch, & Inman, 1993; R. E. Mayer, 1989; R. E. Mayer & Gallini, 1990; M. A. McDaniel & Einstein, 1989; Moreno, 2006; Newby, Ertmer, & Stepich, 1994 (peristalsis example from p. 4); Pittman & Beth-Halachmy, 1997; R. E. Reynolds & Shirey, 1988; Sadoski & Paivio, 2001; Scevak, Moore, & Kirby, 1993; M. Y. Small, Lovett, & Scher, 1993; Tennyson & Cocchiarella, 1986; Verdi & Kulhavy, 2002; Wade, 1992; P. T. Wilson & Anderson, 1986; Winn, 1991; Zook, 1991; Zook & Di Vesta, 1991.

Researchers have identified several factors that improve the effectiveness of teacher-directed instruction through the cognitive processes they promote. Table 8.3 describes and illustrates these factors as general principles that teachers should keep in mind whenever they need to present information in a somewhat one-way fashion. You can see most of these principles in action in the "Civil War" video clip (a fifth-grade class) and "Charles's Law" video clip (a high school class) in MyEducationLab. Notice how much more abstract the Charles's law lecture is, consistent with high school students' greater capacity for abstract thought.

Observe effective expository instruction in the "Civil War" and "Charles's Law" videos in the Additional Resources section in Chapter 8 of MyEducationLab.

Intermingle explanations with examples and opportunities for practice.

By providing numerous examples of concepts and ideas, teachers make classroom topics more concrete for students and help them relate abstract subject matter to real-world objects and

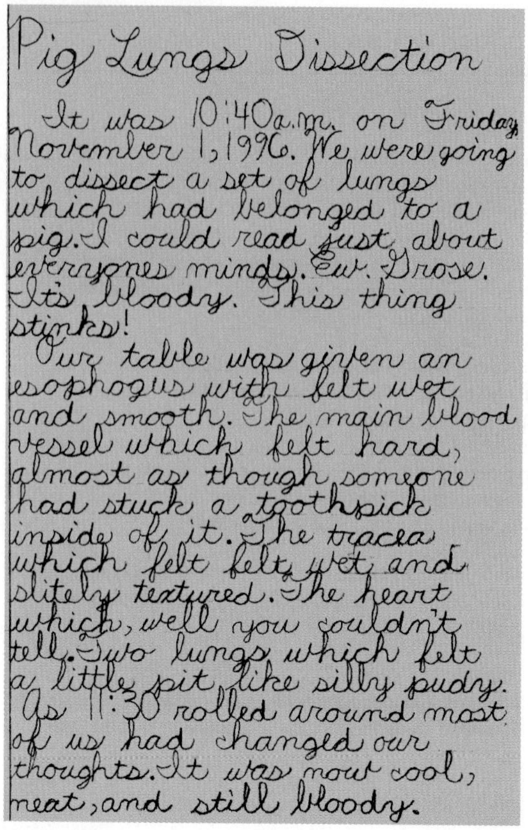

Pig Lungs Dissection

It was 10:40 a.m. on Friday November 1, 1996. We were going to dissect a set of lungs which had belonged to a pig. I could read just about everyones minds. Ew. Gross. Its bloody. This thing stinks!

Our table was given an esophogus with felt wet and smooth. The main blood vessel which felt hard, almost as though someone had stuck a toothpick inside of it. The tracea which felt felt wet and slitey textured. The heart which, well you couldn't tell. Two lungs which felt a little bit like silly pudy. As 11:30 rolled around most of us had changed our thoughts. It was now cool, neat, and still bloody.

FIGURE 8.3 In a unit on anatomy, 10-year-old Berlinda and her classmates gained firsthand experience with components of the respiratory and circulatory systems.

events (e.g., see Figure 8.3). And by providing many opportunities to practice new knowledge and skills, teachers foster automaticity and increase the likelihood that students will transfer what they've learned to real-world tasks and problems (see Chapters 2 and 4).

An approach known as **direct instruction** makes considerable use of examples and practice opportunities to keep students continually and actively engaged in learning and applying classroom subject matter.[15] This approach involves small and carefully sequenced steps, fast pacing, and a great deal of teacher–student interaction. Each lesson typically involves most or all of the following components:[16]

1. **Review of previously learned material.** The teacher reviews relevant content from previous lessons, checks homework assignments involving that content, and reteaches any information or skills that students have apparently not yet mastered.
2. **Statement of the objectives of the lesson.** The teacher describes one or more concepts or skills that students should master in the new lesson.
3. **Presentation of new material in small, logically sequenced steps.** The teacher presents a small amount of information or a specific skill, perhaps through a verbal explanation, modeling, and one or more examples. The teacher may also provide an advance organizer, ask questions, or in other ways scaffold students' efforts to process and remember the material.
4. **Guided student practice and assessment after each step.** Students have frequent opportunities to practice what they are learning, perhaps by answering questions, solving problems, or performing modeled procedures. The teacher gives hints during students' early responses, provides immediate feedback about their performance, makes suggestions about how to improve, and provides remedial instruction as needed.
5. **Assessment of mastery.** After students have completed guided practice, the teacher checks to be sure they have mastered the information or skill in question, perhaps by having them summarize what they've learned or answer a series of follow-up questions.
6. **Independent practice.** Once students have acquired some mastery (e.g., by correctly answering 80 percent of questions), they engage in further practice either independently or in small, cooperative groups. By doing so, they work toward achieving automaticity for the material in question.
7. **Frequent follow-up reviews.** The teacher provides many opportunities for students to review previously learned material over the course of the school year, perhaps through homework assignments, writing tasks, or paper-pencil quizzes.

The teacher moves back and forth among these steps as necessary to ensure that all students are truly mastering the subject matter.

Direct instruction is most suitable for teaching information and skills that are clear-cut and should be taught in a step-by-step sequence.[17] Because of the high degree of teacher–student interaction it involves, direct instruction is often implemented more easily with small groups than with an entire classroom. Under such circumstances, it can lead to substantial gains in achievement of both basic skills and higher-level thinking processes, high student interest and self-efficacy for the subject matter in question, and low rates of student misbehavior.[18] Using direct instruction *exclusively* may be too much of a good thing, however, especially if teachers don't vary instructional methods to maintain students' interest and engagement.[19] A teenager named Tommy shows obvious disgust about the rut one of his high school teachers has gotten into:

> [W]e just get one ditto after the next. My math teacher doesn't like the textbook, so he works up his own work sheets, and he gives us a million of them every day. If we get through all of them, we can pretty much get a good grade.[20]

direct instruction Approach to instruction that uses a variety of techniques (e.g., explanations, questions, guided and independent practice) in a fairly structured manner to promote learning of basic skills.

[15] As examples, see Englemann & Carnine, 1982; R. M. Gagné, 1985; Rosenshine & Stevens, 1986; Tarver, 1992; Weinert & Helmke, 1995.
[16] Rosenshine & Stevens, 1986.
[17] Rosenshine & Stevens, 1986.
[18] Rittle-Johnson, 2006; Rosenshine & Stevens, 1986; Tarver, 1992; Weinert & Helmke, 1995.
[19] Mac Iver, Reuman, & Main, 1995; Wasley, Hampel, & Clark, 1997.
[20] Wasley et al., 1997, p. 117.

Even in direct instruction, then, variety is the spice of—and an important source of motivation in—life.

Take advantage of well-designed educational software.

Many educational computer programs, collectively known as **computer-based instruction** (**CBI**), incorporate principles of learning and cognition we've considered in earlier chapters. For example, effective programs often take steps to capture and hold students' attention, activate students' prior knowledge about a topic, encourage meaningful learning and effective metacognitive processes, and present diverse examples and practice exercises that promote transfer. Students tend to remain physically and cognitively engaged with such programs, in large part because they must continually respond to questions and problems. In addition, working independently with a fairly structured computer program can be a good first step toward self-regulated learning. Some programs provide drill and practice of basic knowledge and skills (e.g., math facts, typing, fundamentals of music), helping students develop automaticity in these areas. Others serve as "intelligent tutors" that skillfully guide students through complex subject matter and can anticipate and address a wide variety of misconceptions and learning difficulties.[21]

Students taught with CBI often have higher academic achievement and better attitudes toward their schoolwork than do students taught with more traditional expository methods.[22] Furthermore, students studying academic subject matter on a computer may gain an increased sense that they can control their own learning, thereby developing more intrinsic motivation to learn.[23]

A downside of CBI is that it gives students few opportunities for social interaction and so does little to address their need for relatedness.[24] Yet it offers several advantages that are often not present with other approaches. For one thing, instructional programs can include animations, video clips, and spoken messages—components that are, of course, not possible with traditional printed materials. Second, a computer can record and maintain ongoing data for every student, including such information as how far students have progressed in a program, how quickly they respond to questions, and how often they are right and wrong. With such data, teachers can monitor each student's progress and identify students who appear to be struggling with the material. Finally, a computer can be used to provide instruction when flesh-and-blood teachers are not available. For example, CBI is often used in *distance learning*, a situation in which learners receive technology-based instruction at a location physically separate from that of their instructor.

At later points in the chapter, we will explore additional uses of computer technology. Keep in mind, however, that using a computer is not, *in and of itself*, necessarily the key to better instruction.[25] A computer can help students achieve at higher levels only when it provides instruction that teachers cannot offer as easily or effectively by other means. Little is gained when a student merely reads information on a computer screen rather than in a textbook.

Ask a lot of questions.

In the classroom lessons depicted in the video clips in MyEducationLab, the teachers ask many questions, and their questions serve a variety of purposes. Teacher questioning is a widely used teaching strategy. Some teacher questions are **lower-level questions** that ask students to retrieve information they've already acquired. Such questions have several benefits:[26]

- They give teachers a good idea of what prior knowledge and misconceptions students have about a topic.
- They help keep students' attention on the lesson in progress.

[21] Azevedo, 2005a; Graesser, McNamara, & VanLehn, 2005; Koedinger & Corbett, 2006; Merrill et al., 1996; Moreno, Mayer, Spires, & Lester, 2001; Snir, Smith, & Raz, 2003.
[22] Koedinger & Corbett, 2006; J. A. Kulik, Kulik, & Cohen, 1980; Lepper & Gurtner, 1989; Wise & Olson, 1998.
[23] Swan, Mitrani, Guerrero, Cheung, & Schoener, 1990.
[24] Winn, 2002.
[25] R. E. Clark, 1983; Moreno, 2006; Roblyer, 2003.
[26] Airasian, 1994; Brophy, 2006; F. W. Connolly & Eisenberg, 1990; P. W. Fox & LeCount, 1991; Wixson, 1984.

computer-based instruction (CBI) Instruction provided via computer technology.

lower-level question Question that requires students to express what they've learned in essentially the same form they learned it.

 Observe the wide variety of teacher questions, as well as the many purposes they serve, in the videos in the Additional Resources section in Chapter 8 of MyEducationLab.

- They help teachers assess whether students are learning class material successfully or are confused about particular points. (Even very experienced teachers sometimes overestimate what students are actually learning during expository instruction.)
- They give students the opportunity to monitor their *own* comprehension—to determine whether they understand the information being presented or, instead, should ask for help or clarification.
- When students are asked questions about material they've studied earlier, they must review that material, which should promote greater recall later on.

Following is an example of how one eighth-grade teacher promoted review of a lesson on ancient Egypt by asking questions:

Teacher: The Egyptians believed the body had to be preserved. What did they do to preserve the body in the earliest times?

Student: They dried them and stuffed them.

Teacher: I am talking about from the earliest times. What did they do? Carey.

Carey: They buried them in the hot sands.

Teacher: Right. They buried them in the hot sands. The sand was very dry, and the body was naturally preserved for many years. It would deteriorate more slowly, at least compared with here. What did they do later on after this time?

Student: They started taking out the vital organs.

Teacher: Right. What did they call the vital organs then?

Norm: Everything but the heart and brain.

Teacher: Right, the organs in the visceral cavity. The intestines, liver, and so on, which were the easiest parts to get at.

Teacher: Question?

Student: How far away from the Nile River was the burial of most kings?[27]

At the end of the dialogue, a *student* asks a question—one that requests information not previously presented. The student is apparently trying to elaborate on the material, perhaps speculating that only land a fair distance from the Nile would be dry enough to preserve bodies for a lengthy period. Teachers can encourage such elaboration, and therefore also encourage new knowledge construction, by asking **higher-level questions**, which require students to go beyond the information they have learned.[28] For instance, a higher-level question might ask students to think of their own examples of a concept, use a new principle to solve a problem, or speculate about possible explanations for a cause-and-effect relationship. As an illustration, consider these questions from a lesson on the telegraph:

> Was the need for a rapid communications system [in North America] greater during the first part of the nineteenth century than it had been during the latter part of the eighteenth century? Why do you think so?[29]

To answer these questions, students must recall what they know about the 18th and 19th centuries (including the increasing movement of settlers to distant western territories) and pull that knowledge together in a way they have possibly never done before.

Asking questions during a group lesson or as follow-up to an independent reading assignment often enhances students' learning.[30] This is especially true when teachers ask higher-level questions that call for inferences, applications, justifications, or solutions to problems. Yet teachers must give students adequate time to respond to their questions. Just as students need time to process new information, they also need time to consider questions and retrieve knowledge relevant to possible answers. As we discovered in our discussion of *wait time* in Chapter 2, when teachers allow at least three seconds to elapse after asking a question, a greater number of students volunteer answers, and their responses tend to be more sophisticated. Furthermore, as you will see in a Cultural Considerations box later in the chapter, students from some ethnic backgrounds are apt to wait for several seconds before answering a question as a way of showing courtesy and respect for the speaker.

higher-level question Question that requires students to do something new with something they've learned (i.e., to elaborate on it in some way).

---

[27] Aulls, 1998, p. 62.
[28] Brophy, 2006; Meece, 1994; Minstrell & Stimpson, 1996.
[29] Torrance & Myers, 1970, p. 214.
[30] Allington & Weber, 1993; Liu, 1990; Redfield & Rousseau, 1981.

CLASSROOM STRATEGIES

Asking Questions to Promote and Assess Learning

- Direct questions to the entire class, not just to a few who seem eager to respond.

  The girls in a high school science class rarely volunteer when their teacher asks questions. Although the teacher often calls on students who raise their hands, he occasionally calls on those who do not, and he makes sure that he calls on *every* student at least once a week.

- Have students "vote" when a question has only a few possible answers.

  When beginning a lesson on dividing one fraction by another, a middle school math teacher writes this problem on the chalkboard:

  $$\frac{3}{4} \div \frac{1}{2} = ?$$

She asks, "Before we talk about how we solve this problem, how many of you think the answer will be less than one? How many think it will be greater than one? How many think it will be *exactly* one?" She tallies the number of hands that go up after each question and then says, "Hmmm, most of you think the answer will be less than one. Let's look at how we solve a problem like this. Then each of you will know whether you were right or wrong."

- Ask follow-up questions to probe students' reasoning.

  In a geography lesson on Canada, a fourth-grade teacher points out the St. Lawrence River on a map. "Which way does the water flow, toward the ocean or away from it?" One student shouts out, "Away from it!" "Why do you think so?" the teacher asks. The student's explanation reveals a common misconception: that rivers can flow only from north to south, never vice versa.

The Classroom Strategies box "Asking Questions to Promote and Assess Learning" presents examples of how teachers might use questions to foster effective cognitive processes and enhance learning.

Extend the school day with age-appropriate homework assignments.

Students can accomplish only so much during class time, and homework provides a means through which teachers can, in essence, extend the school day. On some occasions teachers may want to use homework to give students extra practice with familiar information and procedures (perhaps as a way of promoting review and automaticity) or to introduce them to new yet simple material.[31] In other situations teachers might give homework assignments that ask students to apply classroom material to their outside lives.[32] For example, in a unit on lifestyle patterns, a teacher might ask second graders to:[33]

- Compare their own home or apartment with homes of different time periods (e.g., caves, stone huts, log cabins)
- Tour their homes (perhaps with a parent) and identify the modern conveniences that make their lives easier and more comfortable (e.g., sinks, electrical outlets, thermostats)
- Ask parents to explain why they made the choices they did about where they live (e.g., considering the trade-offs of renting versus purchasing a residence)

On still other occasions teachers might encourage students to bring items and ideas from home (e.g., a jar of tadpoles from a local pond, descriptions of events that occurred over the weekend) and use them as the basis for in-class activities.[34] When teachers ask students to make connections between classroom material and the outside world through homework assignments, they are, of course, promoting transfer.

Doing homework appears to have a small effect on achievement in the middle school and high school grades but little if any effect at the elementary level.[35] Although homework in the elementary grades may not enhance achievement very much, it can help students develop some of the study strategies and self-regulation skills they will need in later years.[36] Undoubtedly the *quality* of assignments (e.g., whether they encourage rote memorization or meaningful learning, whether students find them boring or engaging) makes an appreciable difference both in what and how much students learn and in what kinds of learning and self-regulation strategies they develop.[37]

[31] Cooper, 1989.

[32] Alleman & Brophy, 1998.

[33] Alleman & Brophy, 1998.

[34] Corno, 1996; C. Hill, 1994.

[35] Cooper, Robinson, & Patall, 2006.

[36] Cooper & Valentine, 2001; Zimmerman, 1998.

[37] Trautwein & Lüdtke, 2007; Trautwein, Lüdtke, Schnyder, & Niggli, 2006.

When assigning homework, teachers must remember that students differ considerably in the time and resources (reference books, computers, etc.) they have at home, in the amount and quality of assistance they can get from parents and other family members, and in the extent to which they have self-regulation strategies to keep themselves on task.[38] Furthermore, teachers should assign homework only to help students achieve important educational goals—*never* to punish students for misbehavior. Teachers can maximize the benefits of homework by following a few simple guidelines:[39]

- Use assignments primarily for instructional and diagnostic purposes; minimize the degree to which homework is used to assess learning and determine final class grades.
- Provide the information and structure students need to complete assignments with little or no assistance from others.
- Give a mixture of required and voluntary assignments (voluntary ones should help to give students a sense of self-determination and control, hence enhancing intrinsic motivation).
- When students have few if any self-regulation skills, establish supervised after-school homework programs that help students acquire such skills.

Students	**Lesson 1:** Concept of Fraction	**Lesson 2:** Reducing to Lowest Terms (Builds on Lesson 1)	**Lesson 3:** Adding Fractions with Same Denominators (Builds on Lesson 1)	**Lesson 4:** Adding Fractions & Reducing to Lowest Terms (Builds on Lessons 2 & 3)
Sarah	- - ->	- - ->	- - ->	- - ->
Laura	- - ->	- - ->	- - ->	- - ->
Jason K.	- - ->	- - ->	- - ->	- - ->
Jason M.	- - ->	- - ->	- - ->	- - ->
Alison	——>	- - ->	——>	- - ->
Reggie	——>	- - ->	——>	- - ->
Jason S.	——>	- - ->	——>	- - ->
Matt	——>	——>	- - ->	- - ->
Charlie	——>	——>	- - ->	- - ->
Maria F.	——>	——>	- - ->	- - ->
Maria W.	——>	——>	- - ->	- - ->
Paul	——>	——>	——>	- - ->
Arla	——>	——>	——>	- - ->
Karen	——>	——>	——>	- - ->
Kevin	——>	——>	——>	——>
Nori	——>	——>	——>	——>
Marcy	——>	——>	——>	——>
Janelle	——>	——>	——>	——>
Joyce	——>	——>	——>	——>
Ming Tang	——>	——>	——>	——>
Georgette	——>	——>	——>	——>
LaVeda	——>	——>	——>	——>
Mark	——>	——>	——>	——>
Seth	——>	——>	——>	——>
Joanne	——>	——>	——>	——>
Rita	——>	——>	——>	——>
Shauna	——>	——>	——>	——>

- - -> = nonmastery of subject matter
——> = mastery of subject matter

FIGURE 8.4 Sequential and hierarchical nature of knowledge about fractions

Shoot for mastery of basic knowledge and skills.

When teachers move through lessons without making sure that all students master the content of each one, they may lose more and more students as they go along. For example, imagine that a class of 27 students, listed in Figure 8.4, is beginning a unit on fractions. The class progresses through several lessons as follows:

- **Lesson 1:** The class studies the basic idea that a fraction represents parts of a whole: The denominator indicates the number of pieces into which the whole has been divided, and the numerator indicates how many of those pieces are present. By the end of the lesson, 23 children understand what a fraction is. But Sarah, Laura, Jason K., and Jason M. are either partly or totally confused.
- **Lesson 2:** The class studies the process of reducing fractions to lowest terms (e.g., $\frac{3}{4}$ can be reduced to $\frac{1}{2}$, $\frac{12}{20}$ can be reduced to $\frac{3}{5}$). By the end of the lesson, 20 children understand this process. But Alison, Reggie, and Jason S. haven't mastered the idea that they need to divide both the numerator and denominator by the same number. Sarah, Laura, and the other two Jasons still don't understand what fractions *are* and so have trouble with this lesson as well.
- **Lesson 3:** The class studies the process of adding two fractions, for now looking only at fractions with equal denominators (e.g., $\frac{2}{5} + \frac{2}{5} = \frac{4}{5}$, $\frac{1}{20} + \frac{11}{20} = \frac{12}{20}$). By the end of the lesson, 19 children can add fractions with the same denominator. Matt, Charlie, Maria F., and Maria W. keep adding the denominators together as well as the numerators (e.g., figuring that $\frac{2}{5} + \frac{2}{5} = \frac{4}{10}$). And Sarah, Laura, Jason K., and Jason M. still don't know what fractions actually are.
- **Lesson 4:** The class combines the processes of adding fractions and reducing fractions to lowest terms. They must first add two fractions together and then, if necessary, reduce the sum to its lowest terms (e.g., after adding $\frac{1}{20} + \frac{11}{20}$, they must reduce the sum of $\frac{12}{20}$ to $\frac{3}{5}$). Here we lose Paul, Arla, and Karen because they keep forgetting to reduce the sum to lowest terms. And of course, we've already lost Sarah, Laura, Alison, Reggie, Matt, Charlie, the two Marias, and the three Jasons on prerequisite skills. *We now have only 13 of our original 27 students understanding what they are doing—less than half the class!* (See the rightmost column of Figure 8.4.)

Mastery learning, in which students demonstrate mastery of one topic before proceeding to the next, minimizes the likelihood that some students are left in the dust as a class proceeds to increasingly challenging material.[40] This approach is based on three underlying assumptions:

mastery learning Approach to instruction in which students learn one topic thoroughly before moving to a subsequent one.

[38] Eilam, 2001; Garbe & Guy, 2006; Hoover-Dempsey et al., 2001.
[39] Belfiore & Hornyak, 1998; Cooper, 1989; Cosden, Morrison, Albanese, & Macias, 2001; Garbe & Guy, 2006.
[40] For example, see B. S. Bloom, 1981; L. S. Fuchs et al., 2005; Guskey, 1985; M. Hunter, 1982; J. F. Lee & Pruitt, 1984.

- Almost every student can learn a particular topic to mastery.
- Some students need more time to master a topic than others.
- Some students need more assistance than others.

As you can see, mastery learning represents a very optimistic approach to instruction. It assumes that most learners *can* learn school subject matter if they are given sufficient time and instruction to do so. Furthermore, truly mastering a classroom topic increases the odds that students will be able to transfer what they've learned to new situations and problems and to think critically and creatively about it (recall our discussion of *less is more* in Chapter 4).

A mastery learning approach to instruction looks a lot like direct instruction, in that the subject matter is broken into a series of small and logically sequenced steps, numerous opportunities for practice are provided, and learning is assessed after each step. But in addition, students move to the next step only after demonstrating mastery of the preceding one. Mastery is defined in specific, concrete terms—perhaps answering at least 90 percent of quiz items correctly. Students engaged in mastery learning often proceed through instructional units at their own speed, and so different students may be studying different units at any given time.

Mastery learning has several advantages over nonmastery approaches to instruction.[41] In particular, students tend to learn more, and they maintain better study habits—for instance, studying regularly rather than procrastinating and cramming. In addition, they enjoy their classes and teachers more, and they have greater interest in the subject matter and higher self-efficacy about their ability to learn it. Mastery learning is most appropriate when the subject matter is *hierarchical* in nature—that is, when certain concepts and skills provide the foundation for future learning and conceptual understanding. When instructional goals deal with such basics as word recognition, rules of grammar, arithmetic, or key scientific concepts, instruction designed to promote mastery learning may be in order. Nevertheless, the very notion of mastery may be *in*appropriate for some long-term instructional goals. For example, skills such as critical thinking, scientific reasoning, and creative writing may continue to improve throughout childhood and adolescence without ever being completely mastered.

CONDUCTING LEARNER-DIRECTED INSTRUCTION

At one point in the opening case study, students convene in small groups to discuss reading materials about the Oregon Trail. As we discovered in Chapter 3, discussions with peers can enhance learning in numerous ways. For instance, when learners talk about and exchange ideas, they must organize and elaborate on their thoughts, may find gaps and inconsistencies in their existing understandings, may discover that others have different yet equally valid perspectives about an issue, and may encounter explanations that are more accurate and useful than their own. Not only can a group of learners engage in such *co-construction* of meaning, but they can also *scaffold* one another's learning efforts (see Chapter 5). Clearly, then, learners have a great deal to gain from interacting frequently not only with their teachers but also with one another.

Learner-directed instruction, in which students have considerable control over what and how they learn, often—although not always—involves interaction with classmates. The following strategies can enhance the effectiveness of learner-directed lessons.

Have students discuss issues that lend themselves to multiple perspectives, explanations, or approaches.

Discussions of multifaceted and possibly controversial topics appear to have several benefits. Students are more likely to voice their opinions if they know there are multiple "right" answers. They may, of their own accord, seek out new information that resolves seemingly

---

[41] Block & Burns, 1976; Born & Davis, 1974; C. C. Kulik, Kulik, & Bangert-Drowns, 1990; J. A. Kulik, Kulik, & Cohen, 1979; Shuell, 1996.

contradictory data—in other words, they may be intrinsically motivated to resolve inconsistencies. They may reexamine and possibly revise their positions on issues. And they are more apt to develop a meaningful and well-integrated understanding of the subject matter they are studying.[42]

Student discussions can be fruitful in virtually any academic discipline. For example, students might discuss various interpretations of classic works of literature, addressing questions that have no easy answers.[43] In history classes, students can read and discuss various documents related to a single historical event and so begin to recognize that history is not necessarily as cut-and-dried as traditional textbooks portray it.[44] (Recall our discussion of *epistemological beliefs* in Chapter 4.) In science, discussions of various and conflicting explanations of observed phenomena can enhance scientific reasoning skills, promote conceptual change, and help students begin to understand that science is not a collection of facts as much as it is a dynamic and continually evolving set of understandings.[45] (This point, too, has implications for students' epistemological beliefs.) And in mathematics, discussions that focus on alternative approaches to solving the same problem can promote more complete understanding and better transfer to new situations and problems.[46] You can find examples of whole-class or small-group discussions in each of these domains—literature, history, science, and math—in several video clips in MyEducationLab.

Students gain more from a class discussion when they participate actively in it.[47] And they are often more willing to speak openly when their audience is only two or three peers rather than the class as a whole, with the difference being especially noticeable for girls and for students with disabilities.[48] On some occasions, then, teachers may want to have students discuss an issue in small groups first—thereby giving them the chance to test and possibly gain support for their ideas in a relatively private context—before bringing them together for a whole-class discussion.[49]

Observe examples of whole-class and small-group discussions in several content domains in the "Scarlet Letter," "Civil War," "Designing Experiments," "Properties of Air," "Group Work," and "Cooperative Learning" videos in the Additional Resources section in Chapter 8 of MyEducationLab.

Create a classroom atmosphere conducive to open debate and the constructive evaluation of ideas.

Students are more likely to share their ideas and opinions if their teacher is supportive of multiple viewpoints and if disagreeing with classmates is socially acceptable.[50] To promote such an atmosphere, a teacher might do the following:[51]

- Communicate the message that understanding a topic at the end of a discussion is more important than having the "correct" answer at the beginning of the discussion.
- Communicate the beliefs that asking questions reflects curiosity, that differing perspectives on a controversial topic are both inevitable and healthy, and that changing one's opinion on a topic is a sign of thoughtful reflection.
- Ask students to explain their reasoning and to try to understand one another's explanations.
- Help clarify a student's line of reasoning for other group members.
- Suggest that students build on one another's ideas whenever possible.
- Encourage students to be open in their agreement or disagreement with their classmates—that is, to "agree to disagree."
- Depersonalize challenges to a student's line of reasoning by framing questions in a third-person voice—for example, by saying, "What if someone were to respond to your claim by saying . . . ?"

[42] L. M. Anderson, 1993; Cohen, 1994; E. H. Hiebert & Raphael, 1996; D. W. Johnson & Johnson, 1985; Kuhn, Shaw, & Felton, 1997; Lampert, 1990; K. Smith, Johnson, & Johnson, 1981.

[43] Eeds & Wells, 1989; E. H. Hiebert & Raphael, 1996; L. M. McGee, 1992; P. K. Murphy, 2007.

[44] Leinhardt, 1994; vanSledright & Limón, 2006.

[45] Andriessen, 2006; Bell & Linn, 2002; K. Hogan, Nastasi, & Pressley, 2000; Schwarz, Neuman, & Biezuner, 2000.

[46] Cobb et al., 1991; J. Hiebert & Wearne, 1996; Lampert, 1990.

[47] Lotan, 2006; A. M. O'Donnell, 1999; N. M. Webb, 1989.

[48] A.-M. Clark et al., 2003; Théberge, 1994.

[49] Minstrell & Stimpson, 1996; Onosko, 1996.

[50] A.-M. Clark et al., 2003; Cobb & Yackel, 1996; Lampert, Rittenhouse, & Crumbaugh, 1996.

[51] Cobb & Yackel, 1996; Hadjioannou, 2007; Hatano & Inagaki, 1993, 2003; Herrenkohl & Guerra, 1998; K. Hogan et al., 2000; Horowitz, Darling-Hammond, & Bransford, 2005; Lampert et al., 1996; Staples, 2007; van Drie, van Boxtel, & van der Linden, 2006.

- Occasionally ask students to defend a position that is in direct opposition to what they actually believe.
- Require students to develop compromise solutions that take into account opposing perspectives.

Such strategies can not only promote more productive classroom discussions but also help to create a *sense of community* among students. We'll look at this concept more closely in Chapter 9.

When students become comfortable with disagreeing in a congenial way, they often find their interactions highly motivating, especially if they are emotionally involved in the topic under discussion (recall the concept of *hot cognition*, described in Chapter 6).[52] One fourth grader, whose class regularly engaged in small-group discussions, put it this way:

> I like it when we get to argue, because I have a big mouth sometimes, and I like to talk out in class, and I get really tired of holding my hand up in the air. Besides, we only get to talk to each other when we go outside at recess, and this gives us a chance to argue in a nice way.[53]

Furthermore, students often acquire effective social skills during classroom discussions about academic subject matter. For example, when students meet in small, self-directed groups to discuss children's literature, they may develop and model for one another such skills as expressing agreement ("I agree with Kordell because . . ."), disagreeing tactfully ("Yeah, but they could see the fox sneak in"), justifying an opinion ("I think it shouldn't be allowed, because if he got to be king, who knows what he would do to the kingdom"), and seeking everyone's participation ("Ssshhh! Be quiet! Let Zeke talk!").[54]

Conduct activities in which students must depend on one another for their learning.

In the opening case study of Chapter 7, we saw a situation in which students' success depended on their ability to work together on the annual eighth-grade class play. Cooperation with peers can enhance students' learning and achievement on smaller tasks as well. As an example, try the following exercise.

SEE FOR YOURSELF
Purple Satin

Imagine yourself as a student in each of the three classrooms described here. How would you behave in each situation?

1. Mr. Alexander tells your class, "Let's find out which students can learn the most in this week's unit on the human digestive system. The three students getting the highest scores on Friday's test will get free tickets to the Purple Satin concert." Purple Satin is a popular musical group. You would give your eyeteeth to hear them perform, but the concert has been sold out for months.
2. Ms. Bernstein introduces her lesson this way: "Let's see whether each of you can learn all about the digestive system this week. If you can get a score of at least 90 percent on this Friday's test, I'll give you a free ticket to the Purple Satin concert."
3. Mr. Camacho begins the same lesson like this: "Today we begin studying the human digestive system. Let's see how many students can get scores of 90 percent or better on Friday's test. I want you to work in groups of three to help one another learn the material. If all three members of a group score at least 90 percent on the test, then that group will get free tickets to the Purple Satin concert."

In which class(es) are you likely to work hard to get free tickets to Purple Satin? How might you work *differently* in the different situations?

---

[52] A.-M. Clark et al., 2003; Hadjioannou, 2007.

[53] A.-M. Clark et al., 2003, p. 194.

[54] R. C. Anderson et al., 2001, pp. 16, 25.

The first classroom (Mr. Alexander's) is obviously a very competitive one: Only the three best students are getting tickets to the concert. Will you try to earn one of those tickets? It all depends on what you think your chances are of being a top scorer on Friday's test. If you've been doing well on tests all year, you will undoubtedly study harder than ever during this week's unit. If, instead, you've been doing poorly in class despite your best efforts, you probably won't work for something you're unlikely to get. But in either case, will you help your fellow students learn about the digestive system? Not if you want to go to the concert yourself!

In Ms. Bernstein's classroom there's no competition for concert tickets. As long as you get a score of 90 percent or higher on the test, you get a ticket. Even if you think half the students in class are smarter than you are, you know you have a good chance of going to the concert, and so you will probably study diligently for Friday's test. But will you help your classmates understand what the pancreas does or learn the difference between the large and small intestines? Maybe . . . *if* you have the time and are in a good mood.

Cooperative learning has personal and social benefits as well as academic ones. For instance, it often promotes self-efficacy, social skills, and cross-cultural friendships.

Now consider Mr. Camacho's classroom. Whether or not you get a concert ticket depends on how well you *and two other students* score on Friday's test. Are you going to help those two students learn about salivation and digestive enzymes? And can you expect them, in turn, to help you understand where the liver fits into the whole system? Absolutely!

In **cooperative learning**,[55] students work in small groups to achieve a common goal. Unlike an individualistic classroom such as Ms. Bernstein's (where one student's success is unrelated to peers' achievement) or a competitive classroom such as Mr. Alexander's (where one student's success actually depends on the *failure* of others), students in a cooperative learning environment such as Mr. Camacho's work together to achieve joint successes. Cooperative learning yields the same advantages that emerge from class discussions, including greater comprehension and integration of the subject matter, recognition of inadequacies or misconceptions in understanding, and increased perspective taking. Furthermore, when students help one another learn, they provide scaffolding for one another's efforts and so tend to have higher self-efficacy for accomplishing challenging tasks.[56]

Numerous research studies indicate that cooperative learning activities, when designed and structured appropriately, are effective in many ways. Students of all ability levels show higher academic achievement, with females, members of ethnic minority groups, and students at risk for academic failure being especially likely to benefit.[57] Cooperative learning activities may also promote higher-level cognitive processes. Students essentially "think aloud," modeling various learning and problem-solving strategies for one another and developing greater metacognitive awareness as a result.[58] Furthermore, students are more likely to believe they are liked and accepted by their classmates, and friendships across racial and ethnic groups and between students with and without disabilities are apt to form.[59]

Cooperative learning has several potential pitfalls, however. Some students may be more interested in meeting social and performance goals (e.g., making friends, creating a good impression, getting the right answer quickly) than they are in mastering the material, and so their willingness to assist one another or ask for help may be compromised.[60] Stu-

cooperative learning Approach to instruction in which students work with a small group of peers to achieve a common goal and help one another learn.

[55] Some theorists distinguish between *cooperative* learning and *collaborative* learning, although different theorists draw the line somewhat differently; for example, see Palincsar & Herrenkohl, 1999; B. L. Smith & MacGregor, 1992; Teasley & Roschelle, 1993. Part of their reasoning, I suspect, is that the term *cooperative learning* has historically been associated with certain theorists who advocate particular instructional strategies. Here I am using *cooperative learning* more broadly to refer to any instructional method in which students work together in a somewhat structured format to achieve a shared learning goal.
[56] Good, McCaslin, & Reys, 1992; Hatano & Inagaki, 1991; A. M. O'Donnell & O'Kelly, 1994; N. M. Webb & Palincsar, 1996.

[57] Ginsburg-Block, Rohrbeck, & Fantuzzo, 2006; Lou, Abrami, & d'Apollonia, 2001; Lou et al., 1996; Nichols, 1996; Qin, Johnson, & Johnson, 1995; Rohrbeck, Ginsburg-Block, Fantuzzo, & Miller, 2003.
[58] Good et al., 1992; A. King, 1999; Paris & Winograd, 1990.
[59] Lou et al., 1996, 2001; Marsh & Craven, 1997; Nichols, 1996; Slavin, 1990; Stevens & Slavin, 1995; N. M. Webb & Palincsar, 1996.
[60] Levy, Kaplan, & Patrick, 2000; M. C. Linn et al., 1996; Moje & Shepardson, 1998.

dents who do most of the work and most of the talking are likely to learn more than other group members.[61] Students may occasionally agree to use an incorrect strategy or method that a particular group member has suggested, or they may share misconceptions about the topic they are studying.[62] In some cases students may simply not have the skills to cooperate and help one another learn.[63] (For example, see 12-year-old Amaryth's concerns—"not really focused," "yelling a lot," etc.—in Figure 8.5.) Clearly, then, teachers must keep a close eye on cooperative group discussions, providing additional structure and guidance when necessary to promote maximal learning and achievement.

As you can see, cooperative learning is not simply a process of putting students in groups and setting them loose to work on an assignment together. Oftentimes students are more accustomed to competitive and individualistic classroom situations than they are to working cooperatively with their peers. For a cooperative learning activity to be successful, teachers must structure the activity in such a way that cooperation is not only helpful for academic success but is actually necessary for it.[64] The Classroom Strategies box "Enhancing the Effectiveness of Cooperative Learning" presents and illustrates several strategies that experts recommend for conducting effective cooperative group activities.

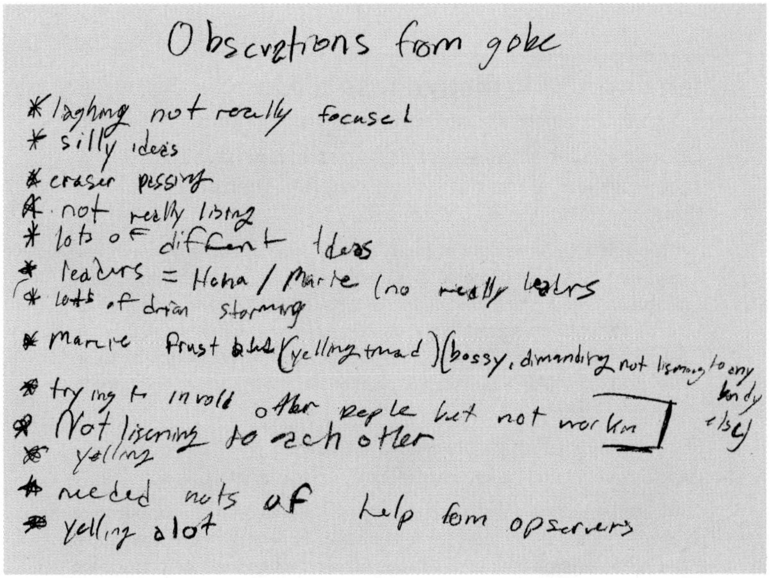
Obscvrations from gobe
*laghing not really focusel
* silly ideas
*eraser passing
* not really lising
* lots of diffent Ideas
* leaders = Hana / Marie (no really leaders
* lots of brian storming
* Marie frust (yelling mad)(bossy, dimanding not lisening to any body else)
* trying to invold other peple but not workin
* Not lisening to each other
* yelling
* needed nots of help from opservers
* yelling alot

FIGURE 8.5 In an entry in her class journal, 12-year-old Amaryth reflects on the effectiveness of a cooperative group (she misspells *group* as "gobe").

Have students conduct their own research.

In Chapter 1 my use of the term *research* referred to planned, systematic inquiry designed to acquire new knowledge for humankind in general. Here I mean it in a much looser sense: to find new information for *oneself* rather than having it spoon-fed. In some instances such research may take the form of *discovery learning* (e.g., see the Classroom Strategies box "Facilitating Discovery Learning" on p. 173 of Chapter 5). But in many other cases it involves finding information already available in books, magazines, newspapers, encyclopedias, electronic databases, Internet Web sites, and elsewhere.

As our collective knowledge about the world grows by leaps and bounds every year, it is becoming increasingly important that students acquire **information literacy**—knowledge and skills that help them find, use, evaluate, organize, and present information about a particular topic. Information literacy includes a number of skills, all of which require nurturance throughout the school years. To a large degree, these skills are *metacognitive*, in that they involve reflecting on the nature of knowledge in general as well as on specific pieces of information. One widely used approach, known as the Big6 ("big six"), involves teaching the following skills and subskills:[65]

1. Task definition
   - Defining the problem to be solved, identifying the questions to be answered
   - Identifying the information needed to solve the problem and answer the questions
2. Information-seeking strategies
   - Brainstorming all possible sources
   - Evaluating the sources and choosing the best options
3. Location and access
   - Finding the selected sources
   - Finding the needed information within those sources
4. Use of information
   - Engaging with (e.g., reading, hearing, or touching) the information
   - Extracting relevant information

information literacy Knowledge and skills that help a learner find, use, evaluate, organize, and present information about a particular topic.

[61] Blumenfeld, 1992; Gayford, 1992; N. M. Webb, 1989.
[62] Good et al., 1992; Stacey, 1992.
[63] D. M. Hogan & Tudge, 1999; A. M. O'Donnell & O'Kelly, 1994.
[64] D. W. Johnson & Johnson, 1991; van Drie et al., 2006.
[65] M. B. Eisenberg & Berkowitz, 2000.

CLASSROOM STRATEGIES

Enhancing the Effectiveness of Cooperative Learning

- **Choose challenging tasks that students may have difficulty accomplishing alone but *can* accomplish when several of them coordinate their efforts.**

  Although they have not yet been taught how to divide by fractions, students in a fourth-grade class are asked to solve the following problem: *Mom makes small apple tarts, using three-quarters of an apple for each small tart. She has 20 apples. How many small apple tarts can she make?* They work in small cooperative groups to solve the problem. (An example of one group's discussion appears in Chapter 3; see p. 69.)

- **Form groups of students who are likely to work together productively and have unique knowledge and skills to offer.**

  An elementary school teacher divides his class into cooperative groups of three or four students each. He makes sure that each group includes students of various ethnic backgrounds and students who will be able to contribute different skills to the task at hand. He also makes sure that students who don't work well together (e.g., close friends who get off task when they're together) are in different groups.

- **Provide clear goals toward which groups should work.**

  Students in a high school Spanish class work in small groups to create an episode of a soap opera (*telenovela*) spoken entirely in Spanish. Over the course of a three-week period, each cooperative group writes a short screenplay, collects the necessary props and costumes, and videotapes the episode.

- **Structure tasks so that group members are dependent on one another for success.**

  A high school biology teacher asks cooperative groups to prepare for an upcoming class debate on the pros and cons of mosquito control in the community. She gives each group member a unique function. One student acts as *reader* of information about the issue, another acts as *recorder* of group members' arguments, a third acts as *checker* to determine whether all group members agree with each argument, and so on.

- **Provide clear guidelines about how to behave.**

  A seventh-grade math teacher forms cooperative groups in which students will work on a series of math problems. Before the students begin the task, the teacher has them brainstorm ground rules for working effectively in their groups. Students volunteer such ideas as "Talk so you don't disturb the other groups," "Help someone who is having trouble," and "Be patient." (You can observe this brainstorming session in the "Cooperative Learning" video clip in Chapter 8 of MyEducationLab.)

- **Monitor group interactions.**

  A middle school social studies teacher asks cooperative groups to identify a possible plan for helping homeless people secure suitable housing. When he hears one student disparaging another because of a difference of opinion, he reminds the group that students should criticize ideas rather than people.

- **Provide critical information and insights when (but only when) a group is unlikely or unable to provide such information and insights for itself.**

  The same social studies teacher tells a group, "The solution you have developed assumes that most taxpayers would be willing to pay much higher taxes than they do now. Is that realistic?"

- **Make students individually accountable for their achievement.**

  An elementary school teacher has incorporated cooperative learning into a unit on calculating perimeters of squares, rectangles, and triangles. Later she gives all students a quiz to assess their individual mastery of perimeters.

- **Reinforce group success.**

  A seventh-grade math teacher awards bonus points to students whose entire group performs at or above a certain quiz score. (You can observe this strategy in the "Cooperative Learning" video clip in Chapter 8 of MyEducationLab.)

- **Ask students to evaluate their effectiveness in working as a group.**

  After cooperative groups have completed their assigned tasks, a teacher asks the groups to answer questions such as these: "Did all group members actively participate?" "Did they ask questions when they didn't understand one another?" "Did they criticize ideas rather than people?"

Sources: Blumenfeld, Marx, Soloway, & Krajcik, 1996; Cohen, 1994; Crook, 1995; Deutsch, 1993; Finn, Pannozzo, & Achilles, 2003; Gillies & Ashman, 1998; Ginsburg-Block et al., 2006; J. Hiebert et al., 1997 (apple tarts problem from p. 118); D. W. Johnson & Johnson, 1991; Karau & Williams, 1995; Lotan, 2006; Lou et al., 1996; A. M. O'Donnell & O'Kelly, 1994; Stevens & Slavin, 1995; van Drie et al., 2006; N. M. Webb & Farivar, 1999; N. M. Webb & Palincsar, 1996.

---

5. Synthesis
   - Organizing information from the selected sources
   - Creating a product or performance, presenting the results
6. Evaluation
   - Judging the product or performance (in terms of its effectiveness)
   - Judging the process undertaken (in terms of its efficiency)

Learners who effectively find and use information typically apply all of these skills, in some instances taking them in a sequential order and in other instances moving flexibly back and forth among them.[66] Information literacy skills are probably most effectively taught when teachers and school librarians collaborate to plan and teach lessons within the context of authentic learning tasks.[67]

---

[66] M. B. Eisenberg, 2004.   [67] Grover, 1996.

One invaluable resource in information gathering is, of course, computer technology. For instance, most computer-based encyclopedias now take the form of **hypermedia**, collections of both visual and auditory material (printed materials, diagrams, photographs, spoken messages, videos, etc.) about a wide variety of topics. Often students begin by reading a short, introductory passage about a topic and then proceed to more specific information that addresses their specific interests and needs. For example, a student looking for information about airplanes might find a general description of airplanes with links to such topics as aerodynamics, the history of air travel, and military aircraft.

Students' access to new information through computer technology is hardly limited to computer resources at their own school. Through telephone and cable lines, students at many schools have access to the Internet and World Wide Web, a network of computers, software programs, and computer databases that can be accessed from any microcomputer with the appropriate hardware and software. For example, my middle school geography students and I once used the U.S. Geological Survey Web site to track the path of a hurricane as it made its way through the Caribbean and up the Atlantic coast. A wide variety of government offices, public institutions, private associations, and individual educators provide information, lesson plans, and links to other relevant Web sites. Following are just a few of the almost limitless possibilities:

U.S. Geological Survey: www.usgs.gov
U.S. Census Bureau: www.census.gov
National Aeronautic and Space Administration: www.nasa.gov
National Museum of Natural History: www.mnh.si.edu
The Knowledge Loom: www.knowledgeloom.org
Discovery Channel: http://school.discovery.com

In addition, Internet *search engines*, such as Google (www.google.com) and Yahoo (www.yahoo.com) allow students and teachers to find Web sites on virtually any topic.

The use of hypermedia and the Internet for instructional purposes is based on the assumption that students benefit from imposing their own organization on a subject area and selecting topics that are most personally relevant.[68] Teachers should keep in mind, however, that not all students can make wise choices about what to study and in what sequence to study it. They may be overwhelmed by the many directions in which they can go, may have trouble identifying important information, or may lack the self-regulation skills to use a program effectively and determine when they have mastered the material.[69] Furthermore, the Internet has no good quality-control mechanism to ensure that information is accurate, especially when posted by individuals rather than by government agencies or professional organizations. And some students may venture into unproductive domains, perhaps finding prewritten research papers they can pass off as their own (plagiarism) or perhaps stumbling on sites that preach racist attitudes or offer pornographic images.[70]

Clearly, then, students may need considerable scaffolding as they conduct their own research on a topic, and their journeys into cyberspace should be closely monitored.[71] Elementary school librarian Carol Lincoln gives students precise, step-by-step directions on how to use Searchasaurus, a search engine available to libraries that is geared specifically for young students (more information can be found at the EBSCO Information Service Web site, www.epnet.com/school/search.asp). She tells them what icons to click on, what words to type in a search box, and so on. When students reach the Web site she has in mind, she provides specific questions that guide their learning (e.g., see Figure 8.6). Her approach is fairly teacher directed, but this may be necessary for students who have limited information literacy skills. As students become more proficient, they can proceed with greater independence, perhaps working in small cooperative groups to research particular topics in depth.

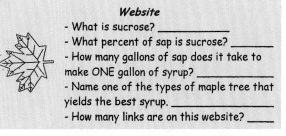

Website
- What is sucrose? _____
- What percent of sap is sucrose? _____
- How many gallons of sap does it take to make ONE gallon of syrup? _____
- Name one of the types of maple tree that yields the best syrup. _____
- How many links are on this website? _____

FIGURE 8.6 Students may need some scaffolding—for instance, specific questions to answer as they look at a Web site about maple sugaring—to develop basic information literacy skills.

hypermedia Collection of multimedia, computer-based instructional materials (e.g., text, pictures, sound, animations) that students can examine in a sequence of their own choosing.

---

[68] Jonassen, 1996; R. V. Small & Grabowski, 1992.
[69] K. Hartley & Bendixen, 2001; Kuiper, Volman, & Terwel, 2005; Lanza & Roselli, 1991; E. R. Steinberg, 1989.
[70] Nixon, 2005; Schofield, 2006.
[71] Azevedo, 2005b; Schofield, 2006.

Have students teach one another.

Having some students provide instruction to other students—**peer tutoring**—is often an effective learner-directed approach to teaching fundamental knowledge and skills. For example, a teacher might have students within a single class tutor one another. Alternatively, two or more collaborating teachers might have older students teach younger ones—for instance, having fourth or fifth graders teach students in kindergarten or first grade.[72]

In some cases peer tutoring leads to greater academic gains than either mastery learning or more traditional whole-class instruction.[73] One possible reason for its effectiveness is that it provides a context in which struggling students may be more comfortable asking questions when they don't understand something. In one study[74] students asked 240 times as many questions during peer tutoring as they did during whole-class instruction!

Peer tutoring typically benefits tutors as well as those being tutored.[75] When students study material with the expectation that they will be teaching it to someone else, they are more intrinsically motivated to learn it, find it more interesting, study it more meaningfully, and remember it longer.[76] Furthermore, in the process of directing and guiding other students' learning and problem solving, tutors may internalize these processes (recall our discussion of *internalization* in Chapter 5) and so become better able to direct and guide their *own* learning and problem solving. In other words, peer tutoring can foster greater self-regulation.[77] Peer tutoring has nonacademic benefits as well. Cooperation and other social skills improve, behavior problems diminish, and friendships form among students of different ethnic groups and between students with and without disabilities.[78]

Students don't always have the knowledge and skills that will enable them to become effective tutors, however, especially in the elementary grades.[79] In most cases, then, tutoring sessions should be limited to subject matter that the tutors know well (we'll see an exception in just a moment). Training in effective tutoring skills is also helpful. For example, a teacher might show tutors how to establish a good relationship with the students they are tutoring, how to break a task into simple steps, how and when to give feedback, and so on.[80]

Providing a structure for tutoring sessions often helps students tutor others more effectively.[81] In one approach students are given "starters" that help them form questions that encourage elaboration, critical thinking, and other effective cognitive processes as they work in pairs to study academic reading material.[82] Here are some examples of such starters:

- Describe . . . in your own words.
- What is the difference between . . . and . . . ?
- What do you think would happen to . . . if . . . happened?
- How did you figure that out?[83]

When students have guidance in formulating and asking one another good questions, highly effective tutoring sessions can result. Following is an example in which two seventh graders are following a prescribed questioning procedure as they work together to learn more about muscles, a topic that neither of them previously knew much about:

Jon: How does the muscular system work, Kyle?
Kyle: Well . . . it retracts and contracts when you move.
Jon: Can you tell me more?
Kyle: Um . . . well . . .

[72] Inglis & Biemiller, 1997; Kermani & Moallem, 1997; D. R. Robinson, Schofield, & Steers-Wentzell, 2005; J. R. Sullivan & Conoley, 2004.

[73] D. Fuchs, Fuchs, Mathes, & Simmons, 1997; Greenwood, Carta, & Hall, 1988; D. R. Robinson et al., 2005.

[74] Graesser & Person, 1994.

[75] Cushing & Kennedy, 1997; D. Fuchs et al., 1997; Inglis & Biemiller, 1997; A. M. O'Donnell, 2006; J. R. Sullivan & Conoley, 2004.

[76] Benware & Deci, 1984; A. M. O'Donnell, 2006; Semb, Ellis, & Araujo, 1993.

[77] Biemiller, Shany, Inglis, & Meichenbaum, 1998.

[78] Cushing & Kennedy, 1997; DuPaul, Ervin, Hook, & McGoey, 1998; Greenwood et al., 1988; D. R. Robinson et al., 2005; J. R. Sullivan & Conoley, 2004.

[79] Greenwood et al., 1988; Kermani & Moallem, 1997; D. Wood, Wood, Ainsworth, & O'Malley, 1995.

[80] Fueyo & Bushell, 1998; Inglis & Biemiller, 1997; Kermani & Moallem, 1997; D. R. Robinson et al., 2005.

[81] Fantuzzo, King, & Heller, 1992; L. S. Fuchs et al., 1996; Mathes, Torgesen, & Allor, 2001.

[82] A. King, 1997, 1999.

[83] A. King, 1997, pp. 229–231.

peer tutoring Approach to instruction in which one student provides instruction to help another student master a classroom topic.

Jon: Um, why are muscles important, Kyle?

Kyle: They are important because if we didn't have them we couldn't move around.

Jon: But . . . how do muscles work? Explain it more.

Kyle: Um, muscles have tendons. Some muscles are called skeletal muscles. They are in the muscles that—like—in your arms—that have tendons that hold your muscles to your bones—to make them move and go back and forth. So you can walk and stuff.

Jon: Good. All right! How are the skeletal muscles and the cardiac muscles the same?

Kyle: Uhh—the cardiac and the smooth muscles?

Jon: The cardiac and the skeletal.

Kyle: Well, they're both a muscle. And they're both pretty strong. And they hold things. I don't really think they have much in common.

Jon: Okay. Why don't you think they have much in common?

Kyle: Because the smooth muscle is—I mean the skeletal muscle is voluntary and the cardiac muscle is involuntary. Okay, I'll ask now. What do you think would happen if we didn't have smooth muscles?

Jon: We would have to be chewing harder. And so it would take a long time to digest food. We would have to think about digesting because the smooth muscles—like the intestines and stomach—are *in*voluntary.

Kyle: Have you really thought about it?

Jon: Yeah.

Kyle: Yeah, well—um—but, do you think it would *hurt* you if you didn't have smooth muscles?

Jon: Well, yeah—because you wouldn't have muscles to push the food along—in the stomach and intestines—you'd get plugged up! Maybe you'd hafta drink liquid—just liquid stuff. Yuk.[84]

Notice how the boys ask each other questions that encourage elaboration (e.g., "How are the skeletal muscles and the cardiac muscles the same?" "Do you think it would hurt you if you didn't have smooth muscles?"). They also ask questions that encourage self-reflection and may promote metacognition (e.g., "Why don't you think they have much in common?" "Have you really thought about it?"). Through such structured interactions, students at the same grade and ability levels can provide valuable scaffolding for one another's learning efforts.[85]

Ideally, *all* students should have an opportunity to tutor others at one time or another.[86] This is often easier said than done, as a few students may consistently achieve at a lower level than most of their peers. One strategy is to ask low-achieving students to tutor classmates who have cognitive or physical disabilities.[87] Another possibility is to teach the students specific tasks or procedures that they can share with their higher-achieving, but in this case uninformed, classmates.[88]

Assign authentic real-world tasks, perhaps as group activities.

In Chapter 4 we noted the importance of *authentic activities*—activities similar to ones that students are apt to encounter in the outside world—as a means of promoting transfer of classroom subject matter to real-world situations. Complex tasks in the outside world must often be handled with little if any explicit guidance from others, and so growing children can best prepare for them by making many of their own decisions while completing similar tasks in the classroom. Most authentic activities, then, should be more learner directed than teacher directed.

Some real-world tasks are easy to carry out within school walls. For example, students can, in a school setting, bake a cake, write a newspaper article, or calculate the amount of carpet needed for an irregularly shaped room. Other tasks can be accomplished only in the outside community. For instance, in **service learning**, students work on meaningful community service projects that are closely related to the classroom curriculum. To illustrate, children in the primary grades might regularly monitor the quantity of house pet "droppings" in an environmentally sensitive city park, and middle school students might gather

service learning Activity that promotes learning and development through participation in a meaningful community service project.

[84] A. King, Staffieri, & Adelgais, 1998, p. 141.
[85] A. King, 1998.
[86] Greenwood, 1991; J. R. Sullivan & Conoley, 2004.
[87] Cushing & Kennedy, 1997.
[88] Cohen, Lockheed, & Lohman, 1976; N. M. Webb & Palincsar, 1996.

The popular software program *Where in the World Is Carmen Sandiego?* promotes knowledge of geography and higher-level thinking skills by asking students to act as detectives in international mysteries.

Carmen Sandiego screen shot used with permission. © 2005 Riverdeep Interactive Learning Limited, and its licensors. All rights reserved.

information about liquor stores and possible zoning violations near school grounds (the latter example is described more fully in the Classroom Strategies box on p. 265 of Chapter 7).[89] In addition to the social, moral, and motivational benefits of community service projects (see Chapter 7), those that are closely tied to important instructional goals also appear to enhance classroom learning.[90]

Yet not all real-world tasks are possible and practical to complete either in or outside of school, and in such instances *simulations* offer a reasonable alternative. For example, students might conduct a mock trial of a historical figure (e.g., Adolf Hitler, Saddam Hussein) or test the aerodynamic effectiveness of variously shaped paper airplanes. In addition, many computer programs offer simulations of such events as running a lemonade stand, dissecting a frog, growing plants under varying environmental conditions, or exploring the effects of various business practices. Other computer programs, such as the popular geography program *Where in the World Is Carmen Sandiego?* and the Jasper Woodbury series described in Chapter 4, simulate real-world, problem-solving tasks. Classroom simulations are often both motivating and challenging (thereby keeping students on task for extended periods) and can significantly enhance students' problem-solving and scientific reasoning skills.[91] In many cases the tasks involved are sufficiently complex and challenging that students must work on them in small groups rather than as individuals—a situation that many students find especially appealing.[92]

Use technology to enhance communication and collaboration.

Effective student interactions don't necessarily have to be face to face. Through such mechanisms as electronic mail (e-mail), Web-based chat rooms, and electronic bulletin boards, computer technology enables students to communicate with peers (either in their own classroom or elsewhere), exchange perspectives, and build on one another's ideas.[93] Technology also allows subject matter experts to be pulled occasionally into the conversation.[94]

As an example, researchers at the University of Toronto have developed software that allows students to communicate regularly using a classwide database and essentially creates a computer-based community of learners.[95] Using the database, students share their questions, ideas, notes, writing products, and graphic constructions. Their classmates (and sometimes a subject matter expert as well) respond regularly, perhaps by giving feedback, building on ideas, offering alternative perspectives, or synthesizing what has been learned. In an anthropology unit on "Prehistory of the New World" in a fifth- and sixth-grade classroom, students worked in groups of three or four to study particular topics and then shared their findings through their computer database.[96] One group, which studied various theories about how human beings first migrated from Asia to the Americas, reported the following:

> **What We Have Learned:** We know that we have learned lots on this project, but the more that we learn the more we get confused about which is fact and which is fiction. The problem within this problem is that there isn't any real proof to say when they came or how. The theory that is most believed is the Bering Strait theory in which people from Asia walked over a land bridge. Another theory is they kayaked the distance between the two continents. We have also unfortunately found racist theories done by people who hate people unlike

[89] Pickens, 2006; Tate, 1995.

[90] Celio, Durlak, Pachan, & Berger, 2007; Dymond, Renzaglia, & Chun, 2007.

[91] Cognition and Technology Group at Vanderbilt, 1996; de Jong & van Joolingen, 1998; Vye et al., 1998; B. Y. White & Frederiksen, 1998.

[92] Lou et al., 2001.

[93] Fabos & Young, 1999; Hewitt & Scardamalia, 1996; Noss & Hoyles, 2006; Stahl, Koschmann, & Suthers, 2006.

[94] A. L. Brown & Campione, 1996; Winn, 2002.

[95] For example, see Hewitt & Scardamalia, 1996, 1998; Lamon, Chan, Scardamalia, Burtis, & Brett, 1993; Scardamalia & Bereiter, 2006. An early version of this software was known as Computer Supported Intentional Learning Environment, or CSILE (pronounced like the name *Cecil*). A second generation of CSILE, called Knowledge Forum (available commercially from Learning in Motion, Inc.), allows collaboration across schools and other institutions (e.g., see www.Knowledgeforum.com).

[96] Hewitt, Brett, Scardamalia, Frecker, & Webb, 1995.

their own saying that the people of the New World are these people because of human sacrifices and only this race of people would do that.

We have made are [our] own theories using information we found and trying to make sense of it. We have heard some people say they come from outer space but this theory is pretty much out of the question. I don't think the Native peoples or the Inuit would like to hear that theory either. How they came isn't easily answered for some of the theories but it does make since [sense] with the Bering Strait theory.[97]

Studies of the interactive software's effects have been encouraging. Students are concerned about truly understanding classroom subject matter rather than simply "getting things done" (i.e., they adopt mastery goals rather than performance goals), actively try to relate new material to what they already know (i.e., they engage in meaningful learning), and can better remember and apply classroom subject matter. Furthermore, as the preceding "What We Have Learned" passage illustrates, the ongoing student dialogue can often foster more sophisticated epistemological beliefs about the subject matter in question.[98]

Provide sufficient scaffolding to ensure successful accomplishment of assigned tasks.

Regardless of the tasks that learner-directed instruction involves, students are apt to need some structure and guidance. As an example of how important structure can be, try the following exercise.

SEE FOR YOURSELF
Take Five

Grab a blank sheet of paper and a pen or pencil, and complete these two tasks:

Task A: Using single words or short phrases, list six characteristics of an effective teacher.

Task B: Explain the general effects of school attendance on children's lives.

Don't continue reading until you've spent a total of at least *five minutes* on these tasks.

Once you have completed the two tasks, answer either "Task A" or "Task B" to each of the following questions:

1. For which task did you have a better understanding of what you were being asked to do?
2. During which task did your mind more frequently wander to irrelevant topics?
3. During which task did you engage in more off-task behaviors (e.g., looking around the room, doodling, getting out of your seat)?

I am guessing that you found the first task relatively straightforward, whereas the second wasn't at all clear-cut. Did Task B's ambiguity lead to more irrelevant thoughts and off-task behaviors for you?

Off-task behavior in the classroom occurs more frequently when activities are so loosely structured that students don't have a clear sense of what they are supposed to do. Effective teachers tend to give assignments with some degree of structure. They also give clear directions about how to proceed with a task and a great deal of feedback about appropriate responses, especially during the first few weeks of class.[99]

Yet teachers need to strike a happy medium here. They certainly don't want to structure classroom tasks to the point where students never make their own decisions about how to proceed or to the point where only lower-level thinking skills are required. Ultimately, teachers want students to develop and use higher-level processes—for example, to think analytically, critically, and creatively—and they must have classroom assignments and activities that promote such processes.[100]

---

[97] Hewitt et al., 1995, p. 7.

[98] Bereiter & Scardamalia, 2006; Lamon et al., 1993; Scardamalia & Bereiter, 2006.

[99] W. Doyle, 1990; Evertson & Emmer, 1982; Gettinger & Kohler, 2006; Weinert & Helmke, 1995.

[100] W. Doyle, 1986a; Weinert & Helmke, 1995.

The concept of *scaffolding* is helpful in this context: Teachers can provide a great deal of structure for tasks early in the school year, gradually removing it as students become better able to structure tasks for themselves. For example, when introducing students to cooperative learning, a teacher might structure initial group meetings by breaking down each group task into several subtasks, giving clear directions about how to carry out each subtask, and assigning every group member a particular role to serve in the group. As the school year progresses and students become more adept at learning cooperatively with their classmates, their teacher can gradually become less directive about how group tasks are accomplished.

We have already seen examples of structure and scaffolding in our earlier discussions of cooperative learning, Internet research (see the questions about maple sugaring in Figure 8.6), and peer tutoring (recall the "starter" questions). Following are additional examples:

- Students with learning disabilities use the spell-check and grammar-check functions in word processing software to help them proofread and revise their writing (e.g., see Figure 8.7).
- Before students conduct an experiment, their teacher asks them to make predictions about what will happen and to explain and defend their predictions. Later, after students have observed the outcome of the experiment, the teacher asks them to explain what happened and why.[101]
- A teacher has students meet in four-member groups to discuss a controversial social issue. Each group proceeds through five steps:[102]

1. The group subdivides into two pairs.
2. Each pair studies a particular position on the issue and presents its position to the other pair.
3. The group has an open discussion of the issue, with each group member having an opportunity to argue persuasively for his or her own position.
4. Each pair presents the perspective of the *opposing* side as sincerely and persuasively as possible.
5. The group strives for consensus on a position that incorporates all the evidence presented.

The amount of structure and scaffolding teachers provide should depend on how much students need in order to be productive. For example, when monitoring small-group discussions, teachers should be more directive with a group that seems to be unfocused and floundering than with one in which students are effectively articulating, critiquing, and building on one another's ideas.[103]

GENERAL INSTRUCTIONAL STRATEGIES

In planning and conducting lessons—whether they involve teacher-directed instruction, learner-directed instruction, or some combination of the two—many of the strategies we've identified in previous chapters are, of course, relevant. In my own mind, some of the most critical ones are these:

- Regularly assess students' understandings. (Chapter 2)
- Encourage and support self-regulated behavior and learning. (Chapter 4)
- Pursue topics in depth rather than superficially. (Chapter 4)
- Conduct stimulating lessons and activities. (Chapter 6)
- Present challenges that students can realistically accomplish. (Chapter 6)

The following three strategies also apply across the board.

Take group differences into account.

Some instructional strategies will be a better fit with students' cultural backgrounds than others. Recent immigrants from some Asian countries may be more accustomed to teacher-

When I was young it was almost impossible to read. One of my teachers told me I could learn to read if I worked hard. Learning to read was like climbing Mount Rushmore. It took a very long time but I finally got it. My Mom said she was vary proud. Reading was hard for me. It took five years for me to learn to read. Every day I would go to the learning center to learn my 400 site words. It was hard for me to learn these words but I did it. Reading is one of the most important things I have learned so far in my life.

FIGURE 8.7 Daniel, a fifth grader who struggles with reading and writing, wrote this very cohesive paragraph with the help of a word processing program. A spell checker enabled him to spell most, but not all, of the words correctly (he meant to use the words *very* and *sight*, not *vary* and *site*).

---

[101] Hatano & Inagaki, 1991; B. Y. White & Frederiksen, 1998.

[102] Deutsch, 1993.

[103] K. Hogan et al., 2000.

directed instruction than to learner-directed classroom activities.[104] In contrast, students from cultures that place a high premium on interpersonal cooperation (e.g., as is true in many Hispanic and Native American communities) are apt to achieve at higher levels in classrooms with many interactive and collaborative activities.[105] Culture-specific patterns of verbal interaction may also come into play, affecting the nature and amount of students' participation in whole-class discussions and question-answer sessions (see the Cultural Considerations box "Cultural and Ethnic Differences in Verbal Interaction").

Gender differences, too, must be taken into account. Although many boys thrive on competition, girls tend to do better when instructional activities are interactive and cooperative. Girls can be intimidated by whole-class discussions, however, and are more likely to participate when discussions and activities take place in small groups.[106] Because boys sometimes take charge of small-group activities, teachers may occasionally want to form all-female groups. By doing so, they are likely to increase girls' participation and encourage them to take leadership roles.[107]

Teachers' choices of instructional strategies may be especially critical in schools in low-income neighborhoods. Students in such schools often have more than their share of drill-and-practice work in basic skills—work that is hardly conducive to fostering excitement about academic subject matter.[108] Mastering basic knowledge and skills is essential, to be sure, but teachers can often incorporate them into engaging lessons that ask students to apply what they're learning to personal interests and real-world contexts.[109] For example, in a curriculum called "Kids Voting USA," students in kindergarten through grade 12 have age-appropriate lessons about voting, political parties, and political issues, and they relate what they learn to local election campaigns.[110] Depending on the grade level, they might conduct their own mock elections, analyze candidates' attacks on opponents, or give speeches about particular propositions on the ballot. Students who participate in the program are more likely to attend regularly to media reports about an election, initiate discussions about the election with friends and family members, and be knowledgeable about candidates and election results. In fact, their knowledge and excitement about politics is contagious, because even their *parents* begin to pay more attention to the news, talk more frequently about politics, and gain greater knowledge about candidates and political issues.

Take developmental levels and special educational needs into account.

Instructional strategies must to some extent depend on students' ages and developmental levels. Strategies that involve teaching well-defined topics in a structured manner and giving students a lot of guidance and feedback (e.g., direct instruction, mastery learning, computer-based instruction) are often more appropriate for younger students than for older ones.[111] Lectures (which are often somewhat abstract) and lengthy homework assignments tend to be more effective for older students.[112]

The knowledge and skills that students bring to a lesson must also be a consideration.[113] Structured, teacher-directed approaches are usually most appropriate when students know little or nothing about the subject matter. But when students have mastered basic knowledge and skills, and particularly when they are self-regulating learners, they should begin directing some of their own learning, perhaps in group discussions, authentic activities, or independent research through hypermedia and the Internet.

Even when working with a single age-group, teachers must often modify their instructional goals and strategies for students who have exceptional cognitive abilities or disabilities, a practice known as **differentiated instruction**. For example, to ensure that all students are working within their specific *zone of proximal development* (see Chapter 5), teachers may need to identify more basic goals for some students (e.g., those with mental retardation) and

[104] Igoa, 1995.

[105] Garcia, 1994, 1995; McAlpine & Taylor, 1993; N. M. Webb & Palincsar, 1996.

[106] Théberge, 1994.

[107] Fennema, 1987; MacLean, Sasse, Keating, Steward, & Miller, 1995.

[108] Duke, 2000; R. Ferguson, 1998; Portes, 1996.

[109] Lee-Pearce, Plowman, & Touchstone, 1998; M. McDevitt & Chaffee, 1998.

[110] M. McDevitt & Chaffee, 1998.

[111] Rosenshine & Stevens, 1986.

[112] Ausubel et al., 1978; Cooper et al., 2006.

[113] Gustafsson & Undheim, 1996; Kalyuga & Sweller, 2004; Rosenshine & Stevens, 1986.

differentiated instruction Practice of individualizing instructional methods, and possibly also individualizing specific content and instructional goals, to align with each student's existing knowledge, skills, and needs.

CULTURAL CONSIDERATIONS

Cultural and Ethnic Differences in Verbal Interaction

If you've grown up in mainstream Western culture, you've learned that there are certain ways of conversing with others that are socially acceptable and certain other ways that are definitely *not* acceptable. For instance, if you are having lunch with a friend, the two of you will probably try to keep a conversation going throughout the meal. And if someone else is speaking—especially if that someone else is an authority figure—you probably know not to interrupt until the speaker has finished what he or she is saying. Once the speaker *is* finished, however, you can ask a question if you are confused about the message or need further information.

Such social conventions are by no means universal. Here we look at cultural and ethnic differences in several aspects of verbal interaction: dialect, talking versus remaining silent, asking and answering questions, and waiting versus interrupting.

Dialect. Even if children speak English at home, they may use a form of English different from the Standard English that is typically considered acceptable at school. More specifically, they may speak in a different dialect, a form of English (or, more generally, a form of any language) that includes some unique pronunciations, idioms, and grammatical structures. Dialects tend to be associated either with particular geographical regions or particular ethnic and cultural groups. Perhaps the most widely studied ethnic dialect is African American English (you may also see the terms *Black English*, *Black English vernacular*, and *Ebonics*). This dialect, which is actually a group of similar dialects, is used in many African American communities throughout the United States and is characterized by certain ways of speaking that are distinctly different from those of Standard English (e.g., "He got ten dollar," "Momma she mad," "I be going to

dance tonight").[a] At one time researchers believed that an African American dialect represented a less complex form of speech than Standard English, and they urged educators to teach students to speak "properly" as quickly as possible. But researchers now realize that African American dialects are, in fact, very complex languages that have their own predictable idioms and grammatical rules and that these dialects promote communication and complex thought as readily as Standard English.[b]

When a local dialect is the language preferred by residents of a community, it is often the means through which people can most effectively connect with one another in day-to-day interactions. Furthermore, many children and adolescents view their native dialect as an integral part of their ethnic identity.[c]

Nevertheless, many people in mainstream Western culture associate higher social status with people who speak Standard English, and they perceive speakers of other dialects in a lesser light.[d] In addition, children who are familiar with Standard English have an easier time learning to read than those who are not.[e] For such reasons, most experts recommend that all students develop proficiency in Standard English because success in mainstream adult society will be difficult to achieve without it.[f] To function most effectively, students should ideally be encouraged to use both their local dialect and Standard English in appropriate contexts. For example, although teachers may wish to encourage Standard English in most written work or in formal oral presentations, they might find other dialects quite appropriate in creative writing or informal classroom discussions.[g]

Talking versus remaining silent. In comparison to some other cultures, mainstream

Western culture is a chatty one. People often say things to one another even when they have very little to communicate, making small talk as a way of maintaining interpersonal relationships and filling awkward silences.[h] In some African American communities as well, people speak frequently—for instance, spontaneously shouting out during church services.[i]

In certain other cultures, however, silence is golden. Brazilians and Peruvians often greet their guests silently, Arabs stop talking to indicate a desire for privacy, and many Native American communities value silence in general.[j] Many Chinese believe that effective learning is best accomplished through attentive listening rather than through speaking.[k] And as noted in Chapter 5, some cultures (e.g., many Japanese and Canadian Inuits) interpret talking a lot as a sign of a person's immaturity or low intelligence.[l]

Asking questions. Different cultural and ethnic groups also have diverse views about when it is appropriate for children to speak to adults. In most Western communities the expectation is that children will speak up whenever they have comments or questions. Yet in many parts of the world, and especially in developing nations, children are expected to learn primarily by close, quiet observation of adults, rather than by asking questions or otherwise interrupting what adults are doing.[m] And in some cultures (e.g., in many Mexican American and Southeast Asian communities, and in some African American communities) children learn very early that they should engage in conversation with adults only when their participation has been directly solicited.[n] In fact, children from some backgrounds, including many Puerto Ricans, Mexican Americans, and Native Americans, have been

Standard English Form of English generally considered acceptable at school, as reflected in textbooks and grammar instruction.

dialect Form of a language that has certain unique pronunciations, idioms, and grammatical structures and is characteristic of a particular region or ethnic group.

African American English Dialect of some African American communities characterized by certain pronunciations, idioms, and grammatical constructions different from those of Standard English.

taught that speaking directly and assertively to adults is rude, perhaps even rebellious.[o]

Answering questions. A common interaction pattern in mainstream Western classrooms is the **IRE cycle**: A teacher *initiates* an interaction by asking a question, a student *responds* to the question, and the teacher *evaluates* the response.[p] Similar interactions are often found in parent–child interactions in middle-class European American homes. For instance, when my own children were toddlers and preschoolers, I often asked them questions such as "How old are you?" and "What does a cow say?" and praised them when they answered correctly. But children raised in other environments—for instance, many of those raised in lower-income homes, as well as those raised in some Central American, Native American, and Hawaiian communities—are unfamiliar with such question-and-answer sessions when they first come to school.[q] Furthermore, some children may be quite puzzled when a teacher asks questions to which he or she already knows the answers.[r]

It's not that children are unaccustomed to questions, it's only that they have little experience with certain *kinds* of questions. For example, parents in African American communities in parts of the southeastern United States are more likely to ask questions involving comparisons and analogies. Rather than asking "What's that?" they may instead ask "What's that like?"[s] In addition, children in these communities are specifically taught *not* to answer questions from strangers about personal and home life—questions such as "What's your name?" and "Where do you live?" The complaints of parents in these communities illustrate how much of a cultural mismatch there can be between the children and their European American teachers:

* "My kid, he too scared to talk, 'cause nobody play by the rules he know. At home I can't shut him up."

* "Miss Davis, she complain 'bout Ned not answerin' back. He says she asks dumb questions she already know about."[t]

Teachers' comments about these children reflect their own lack of understanding about the culture from which the children come:

* "I would almost think some of them have a hearing problem; it is as though they don't hear me ask a question. I get blank stares to my questions. Yet when I am making statements or telling stories which interest them, they always seem to hear me."

* "The simplest questions are the ones they can't answer in the classroom; yet on the playground, they can explain a rule for a ballgame or describe a particular kind of bait with no problem. Therefore, I know they can't be as dumb as they seem in my class."[u]

Waiting versus interrupting. After asking students a question, many teachers wait a second or less for them to respond (see Chapter 2). Not only does such a short wait time give many students insufficient time to retrieve relevant information and formulate an answer, but it is also incompatible with the interactional styles of some cultural groups. People from some cultures leave lengthy pauses before responding as a way of indicating respect, as this statement by a Northern Cheyenne illustrates:

Even if I had a quick answer to your question, I would never answer immediately. That would be saying that your question was not worth thinking about.[v]

Students from such cultures are more likely to participate in class and answer questions when given several seconds to respond.[w] An extended wait time both allows students to show respect and gives those with limited English proficiency some mental "translation" time.

Rather than pausing as a way to show respect, children from certain other backgrounds may interrupt adults or peers who haven't finished speaking—behavior that many from mainstream Western culture might interpret as rudeness. For instance, in some African American, Puerto Rican, and Jewish families, adults and children alike sometimes speak spontaneously and simultaneously. In such settings, waiting for one's turn may mean being excluded from the conversation altogether.[x] And in some Hawaiian communities, an interruption is taken as a sign of personal involvement in the conversation.[y]

[a] Owens, 1995, p. A-8.
[b] DeLain, Pearson, & Anderson, 1985; Fairchild & Edwards-Evans, 1990; Owens, 1996.
[c] McAlpine, 1992; Ogbu, 1999, 2003; Tatum, 1997.
[d] Gollnick & Chinn, 2002; Purcell-Gates, 1995; H. L. Smith, 1998.
[e] Charity, Scarborough, & Griffin, 2004.
[f] Casanova, 1987; Craft, 1984; Ogbu, 1999.
[g] Gollnick & Chinn, 2002; Ogbu, 1999; Smitherman, 1994; Warren & McCloskey, 1993.
[h] Irujo, 1988; Trawick-Smith, 2003.
[i] Lein, 1975.
[j] Basso, 1972; Menyuk & Menyuk, 1988; Trawick-Smith, 2003.
[k] Li, 2005; Li & Fischer, 2004.
[l] Crago, 1988; Minami & McCabe, 1996.
[m] Correa-Chávez, Rogoff, & Mejía Arauz, 2005; Garcia, 1994; Gutiérrez & Rogoff, 2003; Kağitçibaşi, 2007.
[n] Delgado-Gaitan, 1994; C. A. Grant & Gomez, 2001; Ochs, 1982.
[o] Banks & Banks, 1995; Delgado-Gaitan, 1994.
[p] Mehan, 1979.
[q] Losey, 1995; Rogoff, 2003.
[r] Crago, Annahatak, & Ningiuruvik, 1993; Heath, 1989; Rogoff, 2003.
[s] Heath, 1980, 1989.
[t] Heath, 1980, p. 107.
[u] Heath, 1980, pp. 107–108.
[v] Gilliland, 1988, p. 27.
[w] Gilliland, 1988; C. A. Grant & Gomez, 2001; Mohatt & Erickson, 1981; Tharp, 1989.
[x] Condon & Yousef, 1975; Farber, Mindel, & Lazerwitz, 1988; Hale-Benson, 1986; Slonim, 1991.
[y] Tharp, 1989.

IRE cycle Adult–child interaction marked by adult initiation (e.g., a question), child response, and adult evaluation.

raise the bar for others (e.g., those who are gifted). Strictly expository instruction (e.g., a lecture or textbook chapter) can provide a quick and efficient means of presenting new ideas to students who process information quickly and abstractly, yet it may very well be incomprehensible and overwhelming to students with low cognitive ability. In contrast, direct instruction and mastery learning have been shown to be effective with students who have learning difficulties (including many students with identified cognitive disabilities), yet may prevent rapid learners from progressing at a rate commensurate with their potential.[114]

Combine several instructional approaches into a single lesson.

Historically, many educators have looked for—and in some cases decided that they've found—the single "best" way to teach children and adolescents. The result has been a series of movements in which educators advocate a particular instructional approach and then, a few years later, advocate a very different approach.[115] I've often wondered why the field of education is characterized by such "pendulum swings," and I've developed several hypotheses. Perhaps some people are looking for an *algorithm* for teaching—a specific procedure they can follow to guarantee high achievement. Perhaps they confuse theory with fact, thinking that the latest theoretical fad must inevitably be the "correct" explanation of how children learn or develop, and so conclude that the teaching implications they derive from the theory must also be correct. Or maybe they just have an overly simplistic view of what the goals of our educational system should be.

As should be clear by now, *there is no single best approach to classroom instruction.* Every instructional strategy has its merits, and each is useful in different situations and for different students. The choice of an instructional strategy must depend on at least three things: the objective of the lesson, the nature of the subject matter that the lesson involves, and the characteristics and abilities of students. Table 8.4 presents general conditions and specific examples in which different instructional methods might be most appropriate. In general, however, *all* students should have experience with a wide variety of instructional approaches, often within the context of a single lesson. For instance, although some students may need to spend considerable time on basic skills, too much time in structured, teacher-directed activities may minimize opportunities to choose what and how to study and learn and, as a result, may prevent students from developing a sense of self-determination.[116] In addition, authentic activities, though often unstructured and complex, give students of all levels a greater appreciation for the relevance and meaningfulness of classroom subject matter than may be possible with more traditional classroom tasks. A successful classroom—one in which students are acquiring and using school subject matter in truly meaningful ways—is undoubtedly a classroom in which a variety of approaches to instruction can be found.

TABLE 8.4   Choosing an Instructional Strategy

You Might Use . . .	When . . .	For Example, You Might . . .
Expository instruction (e.g., lectures, textbook readings)	• The *objective* is to acquire new information. • The *lesson* involves information best learned within a specific organizational structure. • *Students* have some capacity for abstract thought, have knowledge to which they can relate new material, and have effective learning strategies for the medium in question (e.g., note-taking skills for lectures, comprehension monitoring skills for reading assignments).	• Describe critical battles of World War I to advanced history students. • Demonstrate several defensive strategies to a junior high school soccer team.
Direct instruction	• The *objective* is to learn a well-defined body of knowledge and skills. • The *lesson* provides critical information or skills for later instructional units. • *Students* need considerable guidance and practice in order to learn successfully.	• Explain how to add fractions with different denominators, and give students practice in adding such fractions both in class and through homework. • Demonstrate how to use a jigsaw, and watch carefully as students use the tool to cut irregularly shaped pieces of wood. *(continued)*

---

[114] Arlin, 1984; J. L. Fletcher, Lyon, Fuchs, & Barnes, 2007; Leinhardt & Pallay, 1982; Rosenshine & Stevens, 1986.   [115] K. R. Harris & Alexander, 1998; Sfard, 1998.   [116] Battistich, Solomon, Kim, Watson, & Schaps, 1995.

You Might Use . . .	When . . .	For Example, You Might . . .
Computer-based instruction	• The *objective* is to acquire basic knowledge and skills. • The *lesson* involves information that students can learn from reading text or from watching and listening to multimedia presentations. • *Students* have some familiarity with computers and can work with only minimal guidance from their teacher.	• Use a typing-skills tutorial that helps students develop automaticity in keyboarding. • Use educational software designed to teach the basics of musical notation. After students have mastered the basics, follow up with *music editor* software that allows them to experiment with different notes, keys, instrumental sounds, and time signatures.
Teacher questions	• The *objective* is to understand and elaborate on a topic in greater depth. • The *lesson* involves complex material, such that frequent monitoring of students' learning is essential, mental elaboration of ideas is beneficial, or both. • *Students* are unlikely to elaborate spontaneously or to monitor their own comprehension effectively.	• Ask questions that promote recall and review of the previous day's lesson. • Ask students for examples of how nonrenewable resources are recycled in their own community.
Homework	• The *objective* is to learn new yet simple material, gain additional practice with familiar information and procedures, or relate classroom subject matter to the outside world. • The *lesson* involves a task that students can complete with little or no help from others. • *Students* have sufficient self-regulation skills to complete the task independently.	• Have students read the next chapter in their health book and answer several questions about its content. • For a unit on migration, have students find out what state, province, or country their parents and grandparents were born in.
Mastery learning	• The *objective* is to learn knowledge or skills very well (perhaps to automaticity). • The *lesson* provides critical information or skills for later instructional units. • *Students* vary in the time they need to achieve mastery.	• Have each student in instrumental music practice the C major scale until he or she can do so perfectly. • Have students practice 100 single-digit addition facts until they can answer all of the facts correctly within a five-minute period.
Class discussion	• The *objective* is to achieve greater conceptual understanding, acquire a multisided perspective of a topic, or both. • The *lesson* involves complex and possibly controversial issues. • *Students* have sufficient knowledge about the topic to offer informed ideas and opinions.	• Ask students to discuss the ethical implications of Harry Truman's decision to drop an atomic bomb on Hiroshima. • Ask groups of four or five students to prepare arguments for an upcoming debate on the pros and cons of increasing the minimum wage.
Cooperative learning	• The *objective* is to develop the ability to work cooperatively with others on academic tasks. • The *lesson* involves tasks that are too large or difficult for a single student to accomplish independently. • *Students'* cultural backgrounds emphasize cooperation rather than competition.	• Have groups of two or three students work together on complex, multifaceted mathematical problems. • Have students in a Spanish class work in small groups to write and videotape a soap opera episode spoken entirely in Spanish.
Discovery learning	• The *objective* is to gain firsthand experience with a phenomenon. • The *lesson* involves information that can be correctly deduced from experimentation or other personal experience. • *Students* have enough knowledge to interpret findings correctly but may have trouble learning from strictly abstract material.	• Ask students to find out what happens when two primary colors of paint (red and yellow, red and blue, or yellow and blue) are mixed together. • Conduct a simulation activity in which students discover firsthand how it feels to experience "taxation without representation."
Computer-based research	• The *objective* is to gain information literacy skills, especially in use of the World Wide Web. • The *lesson* requires information not readily available in the classroom. • *Students* have some familiarity with computers, Internet software (e.g., Web browsers), and search engines.	• Ask students to identify demographic differences among various regions of the United States using data from the U.S. Census Bureau. • Have students learn about current events by visiting the Web sites of national news bureaus and newsmagazines.
Peer tutoring	• The *objective* is to learn basic knowledge or skills. • The *lesson* contains material that can effectively be taught by students. • *Students* vary in their mastery of the material, yet even the most advanced can gain increased understanding by teaching it to someone else.	• Have students work in pairs to test each other on their conjugations of irregular French verbs. • Have some students help others work through simple mathematical word problems.
Authentic activities	• The *objective* is to apply class material to real-world situations. • The *lesson* involves synthesizing and applying a variety of knowledge and skills. • *Students* have mastered the prerequisite knowledge and skills necessary to perform the task.	• Have students construct maps of their local community, using appropriate symbols to convey direction, scale, and natural and man-made features. • Have students write a résumé using a word processing program.

SUMMARY

Effective teachers engage in considerable advance planning. They identify the general instructional goals and more specific instructional objectives that they would like students to accomplish. They conduct task analyses to break complex tasks into smaller and simpler components. They develop lesson plans that spell out the activities they will use on a daily basis. And they continually evaluate and modify their plans as the school year progresses.

Some forms of instruction are *teacher directed* to a considerable degree, in that the teacher chooses the specific topics the class will address and controls the course of a lesson. Often such instruction is expository in nature, presenting information in essentially the same form that students are expected to learn it. In some cases (e.g., in lectures and textbook reading assignments), teacher-directed instruction is "one-way," with information going primarily from the teacher or some other expert (e.g., a textbook author) to students. In other cases it is more "two-way," with information flowing regularly back and forth between the teacher (or perhaps a virtual "teacher," such as a computer) and students. For instance, direct instruction, computer-based instruction, and mastery learning all involve many opportunities for student practice and teacher feedback. Teacher-directed instruction is, like all instruction, most effective when it promotes effective cognitive processes—for instance, when it captures students' attention and encourages students to elaborate on what they're learning.

Other forms of instruction are more *learner directed*, in that students have a good deal of control over the issues they address and how to address them. For instance, in class discussions, cooperative learning activities, independent research, peer tutoring, and authentic activities, students largely control the flow of events. Learner-directed instruction is most useful when topics and tasks lend themselves to multiple perspectives and approaches and when students have some ability to regulate their own learning and behavior. Even so, students may need some structure and guidance to help them accomplish assigned tasks successfully.

Different instructional strategies are appropriate for different objectives and for different students. For instance, direct instruction or mastery learning is often advisable when students must learn basic skills to automaticity, whereas authentic activities are more appropriate when the goal is for students to apply those skills to real-world situations and problems. Interactive and cooperative instructional strategies may be especially effective for females, as well as for students whose cultural backgrounds have emphasized cooperation rather than competition. Abstract lectures tend to be more useful with high-achieving adolescents, whereas more concrete approaches (e.g., direct instruction) are often preferable for younger students, students who have a history of low academic achievement, and students who have little prior knowledge about the topic or skill in question. Ultimately, there is no single "best" instructional strategy.

PRACTICE FOR YOUR LICENSURE EXAM

Cooperative Learning Project

Ms. Mihara is beginning the unit "Customs in Other Lands" in her fourth-grade class. Having heard about the benefits of cooperative learning, she asks students to form groups of four that will work together throughout the unit. On Monday she assigns each group a particular country: Australia, Colombia, Ireland, Greece, Japan, or South Africa. She then instructs the groups: "Today we will go to the school library, where you can find information on the customs of your country and check out materials you think will be useful. Over the next two weeks, you will have time every day to work as a group. You should learn all you can about the customs of your country. A week from Friday, each group will give an oral report to the rest of the class."

During the next few class sessions, Ms. Mihara runs into many more problems than she anticipated. For example, when the students form their groups, she notices that high achievers have gotten together to form two groups and that many socially oriented, "popular" students have flocked to two others. The remaining two groups are comprised of whichever students are left over. Some groups immediately get to work on their task, others spend their group time sharing gossip and planning upcoming social events, and still others are neither academically nor socially productive.

As the unit progresses, Ms. Mihara hears more and more complaints from students about their task ("Janet and I are doing all the work; Karen and Mary Kay aren't helping at all," "Eugene thinks he can boss the rest of us around because

we're studying Ireland and he's Irish," "We're spending all this time but just can't seem to get anywhere!"). And the group reports at the end of the unit differ markedly in quality: Some are carefully planned and informative, whereas others are disorganized and lack substantive information.

"So much for this cooperative learning stuff," Ms. Mihara mumbles to herself. "If I want students to learn something, I'll just have to teach it to them myself."

1. **Constructed-response question**

   Ms. Mihara's cooperative learning groups are not as productive as she had hoped.

   A. Describe two things you might do to improve Ms. Mihara's cooperative learning activity.
   B. Justify your improvements based on either research findings regarding effective cooperative learning strategies or on contemporary principles and theories of learning, cognition, or development.

2. **Multiple-choice question**

   Ms. Mihara never identifies an instructional objective for her unit on "Customs in Other Lands." Which one of the following objectives reflects recommended guidelines regarding how instructional objectives should be formulated?

   a. "The teacher should expose students to many differences in behaviors and beliefs (e.g., eating habits, ceremonial practices, religious beliefs, moral values) that exist in diverse cultures."

b. "The teacher should use a variety of instructional practices, including (but not limited to) lectures, direct instruction, textbook readings, cooperative learning activities, and computer-based instruction."

c. "Students should study a variety of cultural behaviors and beliefs, including those of countries in diverse parts of the world."

d. "Students should demonstrate knowledge of diverse cultural practices, for example by describing three different ways in which another culture is different from their own."

Once you have answered these questions, compare your responses with those presented in Appendix A.

FOR FURTHER READING

The following articles from the journal *Educational Leadership* are especially relevant to this chapter. You can find these articles in Chapter 8 of MyEducationLab for this text.

Allington, R. L. (2002). You can't learn much from books you can't read. *Educational Leadership, 60*(3), 16–19.

Aukerman, M. (2006). Who's afraid of the big "bad answer"? *Educational Leadership, 64*(2), 37–41.

Cohen, E. G. (1998). Making cooperative learning equitable. *Educational Leadership, 56*(1), 18–21.

Copen, P. (1995). Connecting classrooms through telecommunications. *Educational Leadership, 53*(2), 44–47.

Engelmann, S. (1999). The benefits of direct instruction: Affirmative action for at-risk students. *Educational Leadership, 57*(1), 77, 79.

Lotan, R. A. (2003). Group-worthy tasks. *Educational Leadership, 60*(6), 72–75.

McKeown, M. G., & Beck, I. L. (1999). Getting the discussion started. *Educational Leadership, 57*(3), 25–28.

Pettig, K. L. (2000). On the road to differentiated practice. *Educational Leadership, 58*(1), 14–18.

Schniedewind, N., & Davidson, E. (2000). Differentiating cooperative learning. *Educational Leadership, 58*(1), 24–27.

Strong, R. W., Silver, H. F., & Perini, M. J. (2001). Making students as important as standards. *Educational Leadership, 59*(3), 56–61.

Teicher, J. (1999). An action plan for smart Internet use. *Educational Leadership, 56*(5), 70–74.

Tomlinson, C. A. (1999). Mapping a route toward differentiated instruction. *Educational Leadership, 57*(1), 12–16.

MYEDUCATIONLAB

Now go to Chapter 8 of MyEducationLab at **www. myeducationlab.com,** where you can:

- Find instructional objectives for the chapter, along with focus questions that can help you zero in on important ideas in the chapter.
- Take a self-check quiz on concepts and principles you've just read about.
- Complete exercises and assignments that can help you more deeply understand the chapter content.
- Apply what you've learned to classroom contexts in Building Teaching Skills activities.

CHAPTER 9

Strategies for Creating an Effective Classroom Environment

CASE STUDY A Contagious Situation

Ms. Cornell received her teaching certificate in May. Soon after, she accepted a position as a fifth-grade teacher at Twin Pines Elementary School. She spent the summer planning her classroom curriculum, identifying her instructional goals for the year, and developing numerous activities to help students achieve those goals. She now feels well prepared for her first year in the classroom.

After the long, hot summer, most of Ms. Cornell's students seem happy to be back at school. On the first day of school, Ms. Cornell jumps headlong into the curriculum she has planned. But three problems quickly present themselves—problems in the form of Eli, Jake, and Vanessa.

These three students seem determined to disrupt the class at every possible opportunity. They move about the room without permission, making a point of annoying others as they walk to the pencil sharpener or wastebasket. They talk out of turn, sometimes being rude and disrespectful to their teacher and classmates and at other times belittling the activities Ms. Cornell has so carefully planned. They rarely complete in-class assignments, preferring instead to engage in horseplay or practical jokes. They seem especially prone to misbehavior during downtimes in the daily schedule—for example, at the beginning and end of the school day, before and after recess and lunch, and on occasions when Ms. Cornell is preoccupied with other students.

Ms. Cornell continues to follow her daily lesson plans, ignoring her problem students and hoping they will begin to shape up. Yet with the three of them egging one another on, the disruptive behavior continues. Furthermore, it begins to spread to other students. By the middle of October, Ms. Cornell's classroom is a three-ring circus, and instructional objectives are rarely accomplished. The few students who still seem intent on learning something are having a difficult time doing so.

- In what ways has Ms. Cornell planned for her classroom in advance? In what ways has she *not* planned?
- Why are Eli, Jake, and Vanessa so disruptive right from the start? Can you think of possible reasons related to how Ms. Cornell has begun the school year? Can you think of possible reasons related to the activities Ms. Cornell has planned? Can you think of possible reasons related to our discussions of learning and motivation in previous chapters?
- Why does the misbehavior of the three problem students continue? Why does it spread to other students in the classroom? Why is it especially common during downtimes in the school day? Can you answer these questions using principles presented in earlier chapters?

A well-managed classroom is one in which students are consistently engaged in learning. It is not necessarily one in which everyone is quiet.

As a first-year teacher, Ms. Cornell is well prepared in some respects but not at all prepared in others. She has carefully identified her instructional goals and planned relevant lessons. But she has neglected to think about how she might keep students on task or how she might adjust her lessons based on how students are progressing. And she has not considered how she might nip behavior problems in the bud, before they begin to interfere with students' learning. In the absence of such planning, no curriculum—not even one grounded firmly in sound principles of learning, development, and motivation—can be very effective.

As we proceed through the chapter, we'll occasionally return to the opening case to identify reasons why Eli, Jake, and Vanessa are so disruptive and why their misbehaviors spread to other students. But I must make one point clear at the very beginning: The problem in Ms. Cornell's classroom is *not* one of too much noise and activity. Effective **classroom management**— creating and maintaining a classroom environment conducive to learning and achievement—has little to do with noise or activity level. A well-managed classroom is one in which students are consistently engaged in productive learning activities and in which students' behaviors rarely interfere with their own or others' achievement of instructional goals.[1]

Creating and maintaining an environment in which students are continually engaged in productive activities can be a challenging task indeed.[2] Teachers must tend to the unique needs of many different students, must sometimes coordinate several activities occurring at the same time, and must often make quick decisions about how to respond to unanticipated events. Furthermore, teachers must vary their classroom management techniques considerably depending on the particular instructional strategies (e.g., direct instruction, class discussions, or cooperative activities) in progress. So it is not surprising that many beginning teachers mention classroom management as their number one concern.[3]

A good general model of effective classroom management is *authoritative parenting*, a parenting style I introduced in Chapter 7.[4] As you may recall, authoritative parents:

- Provide a loving and supportive home environment.
- Hold high expectations and standards for children's behavior.
- Explain why some behaviors are acceptable and others are not.
- Consistently enforce household rules.
- Include children in decision making.
- Provide age-appropriate opportunities for independence.

As we explore classroom management strategies in the following sections, we'll often see one or more of these characteristics of authoritative parenting at work. We'll begin our discussion by looking at proactive, *preventive* strategies—those designed to establish a productive learning environment right from the start. Later we'll turn to strategies for addressing the unproductive behaviors that sometimes occur even in the best-managed classrooms.

CREATING AN ENVIRONMENT CONDUCIVE TO LEARNING

Think back on your many years as a student. Can you recall a class in which you were afraid of being ridiculed if you asked a "stupid" question? Can you recall one in which you and your classmates spent more time goofing off than getting your work done because no one had much reason to take the class seriously? Can you recall one in which you never knew what to expect because your instructor was continually changing expectations and giving last-minute assignments without warning?

When we talk about the classroom environment, we are to some extent talking about the actual physical setup—the arrangement of tables and chairs, the availability of tools and

---

classroom management Establishment and maintenance of a classroom environment conducive to learning and achievement.

[1] Brophy, 2006; W. Doyle, 1990; Emmer & Evertson, 1981.

[2] W. Doyle, 1986a; Emmer & Stough, 2001.

[3] Evertson & Weinstein, 2006; V. Jones, 2006.

[4] For a good discussion of this point, see J. M. T. Walker & Hoover-Dempsey, 2006.

resources (painting supplies, dictionaries, computer-based encyclopedias, etc.), the use of bulletin boards and other displays to present information and engage students' interest, and so on. But even more important is the psychological environment, or **classroom climate**.[5] The ideal classroom is one in which students feel safe and secure, make learning a high priority, and are willing to take the risks and make the mistakes so critical for long-term academic success. Such characteristics are especially important for students at risk for academic failure and dropping out of school.[6] The "Author's Chair" and "Scarlet Letter" video clips in MyEducationLab present two examples of supportive classroom climates (one each at the elementary and secondary levels) that facilitate learning and encourage risk taking.

Researchers and experienced educators have identified many strategies for creating and maintaining an environment conducive to students' learning and academic achievement. These strategies can be summed up by the following general suggestions.

Observe the supportive classroom climates in the "Author's Chair" and "Scarlet Letter" videos in the Additional Resources section in Chapter 9 of MyEducationLab.

Arrange the classroom to maximize attention and minimize disruptions.

Good management begins well before the first day of class. As teachers arrange classroom furniture, decide where to put instructional materials and equipment, and think about where each student might sit, they should consider the effects that various arrangements are likely to have on students' behavior. Here are several widely recommended strategies:[7]

- Arrange desks, tables, and chairs so that you and your students can easily interact and so that you can regularly survey the entire classroom for possible signs of confusion, frustration, or boredom.
- Establish traffic patterns that allow students to move around the classroom without disturbing one another.
- Keep intriguing materials out of sight and reach until they need to be used.
- Split up friends who easily get off task when they are together (e.g., put them on opposite sides of the room).
- Place chronically misbehaving or uninvolved students close at hand.

Hear three experienced teachers offer their suggestions in the "Arranging the Classroom" video in the Additional Resources section in Chapter 9 of MyEducationLab.

Communicate acceptance, caring, and respect for every student.

As you should recall from Chapter 6, human beings seem to have a fundamental need to feel socially connected with others. In the classroom this *need for relatedness* may reveal itself in a variety of ways. For instance, some students might eagerly seek their teacher's approval for something they've done well. Other students might actually misbehave to gain their teacher's attention (this might be the case for Eli, Jake, and Vanessa in the opening case study). But in my own experiences as a teacher and school psychologist, I've never met a child or adolescent who, deep down, didn't want positive, productive relationships with school faculty members.

To some extent, teachers can help meet students' need for relatedness by demonstrating, through the many little things they do, that they care about and respect students as people.[8] A smile and warm greeting at the beginning of the day, a compliment about a new hairstyle, and a concerned inquiry when a student comes to school angry or upset—all of these behaviors communicate caring and respect. One high school student described caring teachers this way:

> They show it. You might see them in the hallway and they ask how you're doing, how was your last report card, is there anything you need. Or, maybe one day you're looking a little upset. They'll pull you to the side and ask you what's wrong, is there anything I can do.[9]

One effective strategy is to have students create two-way *dialogue journals* in which they regularly express their thoughts and feelings, ask questions, and request assistance. At least once a week—preferably more often—their teacher reads and responds to their entries. For

---

[5] Hamre & Pianta, 2005; Hardré, Crowson, DeBacker, & White, 2007; Patrick, Ryan, & Kaplan, 2007.

[6] Hamre & Pianta, 2005; V. E. Lee & Burkam, 2003.

[7] K. Carter & Doyle, 2006; W. Doyle, 1986a; Emmer, Evertson, & Worsham, 2000; Gettinger & Kohler, 2006; Sabers, Cushing, & Berliner, 1991; Woolfolk & Brooks, 1985.

[8] Allday & Pakurar, 2007; Certo, Cauley, & Chafin, 2002.

[9] Certo et al., 2002, p. 15.

classroom climate Overall psychological atmosphere of the classroom.

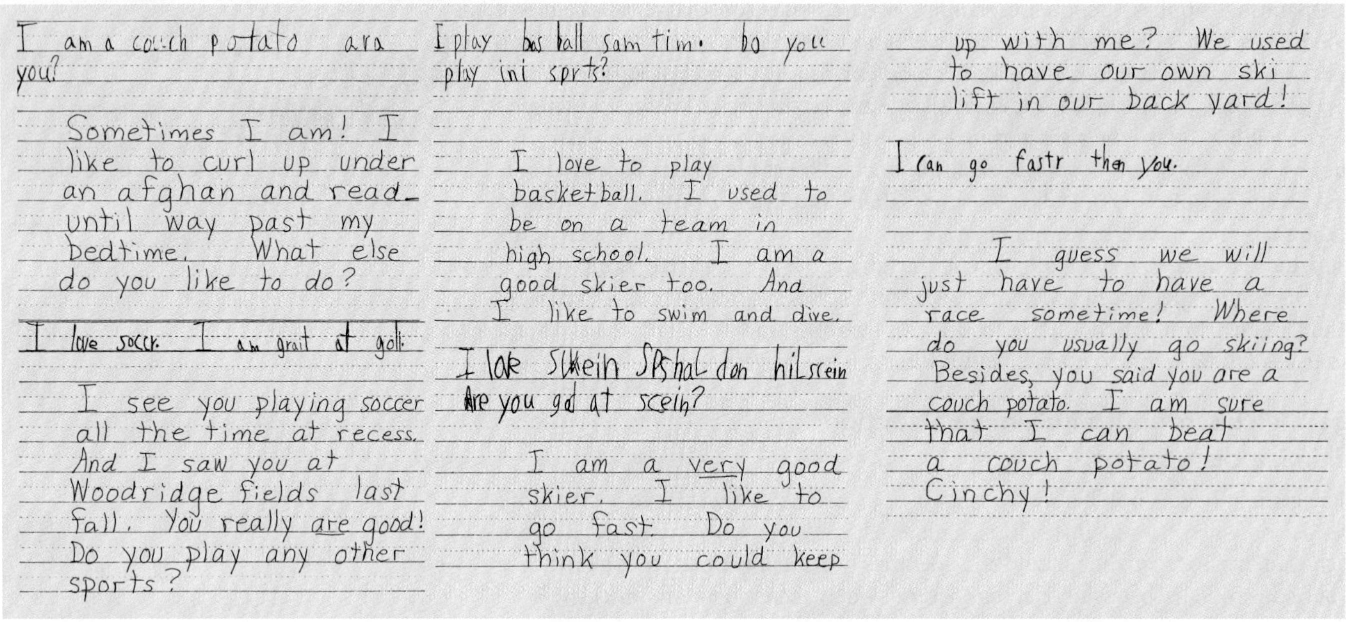

I am a couch potato ara you?

> Sometimes I am! I like to curl up under an afghan and read until way past my bedtime. What else do you like to do?

I love soccr. I am grait at gol!

> I see you playing soccer all the time at recess. And I saw you at Woodridge fields last fall. You really are good! Do you play any other sports?

I play bas ball sam tim. Do you play ini sprts?

> I love to play basketball. I used to be on a team in high school. I am a good skier too. And I like to swim and dive.

I lok Skein Skshal don hilscein Are you god at sceih?

> I am a very good skier. I like to go fast Do you think you could keep

up with me? We used to have our own ski lift in our back yard!

I can go fastr than you.

> I guess we will just have to have a race sometime! Where do you usually go skiing? Besides, you said you are a couch potato. I am sure that I can beat a couch potato! Cinchy!

FIGURE 9.1 Six-year-old Matt and his first-grade teacher communicate regularly through a two-way dialogue journal.

example, Figure 9.1 shows several entries in 6-year-old Matt's journal. After each of Matt's entries is a response (indented) from his first-grade teacher. The teacher communicates caring by telling him that she often watches him playing soccer at recess and by complimenting him on his soccer skills. Through the journal the two also discover a common interest: skiing. (Matt's fourth entry is his attempt to write, "I love skiing, especially downhill skiing. Are you good at skiing?") Obviously, Matt feels comfortable enough with his teacher to engage in some one-upmanship ("I can go fastr then you"), and she is sufficiently confident about their relationship that she can tease him a bit ("I can beat a couch potato! Cinchy!"). Notice that the teacher does *not* correct Matt's misspellings. Her primary purposes are to encourage him to write and to keep open the lines of communication, and negative feedback about spelling might interfere with both of these goals. Instead, she simply models correct spelling in her own entries.

Yet it is not enough simply to be "warm and fuzzy" with students. To show genuine caring and respect for them, teachers must also do the following:[10]

- Be well prepared for class and in other ways demonstrate that they enjoy teaching and take their teaching responsibilities seriously.
- Convey high (yet realistic) expectations for student performance and provide the support students need to meet those expectations.
- Include students in decision making and in evaluations of their schoolwork.
- Acknowledge that students can occasionally have an "off" day and not hold it against them.

The quality of teacher–student relationships is one of the most influential factors affecting students' emotional well-being, motivation, and achievement at school. When students have positive, supportive relationships with teachers, they have higher self-efficacy and more intrinsic motivation to learn, engage in more self-regulated learning, are more likely to ask for help when they need it, are less apt to cheat on classroom assignments, and achieve at higher levels.[11]

Teacher affection, respect, and support are especially important for students who face exceptional hardships (poverty, uninvolved or abusive parents, violent neighborhoods, etc.)

[10] L. H. Anderman, Patrick, Hruda, & Linnenbrink, 2002, p. 274; Certo et al., 2002; H. A. Davis, 2003; H. A. Davis, Schutz, & Chambless, 2001; J. M. T. Walker & Hoover-Dempsey, 2006.

[11] Hamre & Pianta, 2005; Marchand & Skinner, 2007; Marzano, 2003; Midgley, Middleton, Gheen, & Kumar, 2002; Murdock, Miller, & Kohlhardt, 2004; Pianta, 1999; A. M. Ryan & Patrick, 2001.

at home. When such students have one or more caring, trustworthy adults in their lives—and when they regularly come to a classroom that is warm, predictable, and dependable—they are more likely to have a strong sense of self-worth and to rise above their many challenges to succeed both in the classroom and in the outside world (recall our discussion of *resilient students* in Chapter 7).[12]

Work hard to improve relationships that have gotten off to a bad start.

Occasionally students come to school with an apparent chip on the shoulder, distrusting their teachers from day one because of previous hurtful relationships with parents or other adults. At other times teachers get relationships with certain students off to a bad start through their own actions—perhaps because they incorrectly attribute a student's low achievement to lack of effort rather than lack of skill or perhaps because they accuse a temperamentally high-energy child of being intentionally disobedient. Oftentimes students who have the poorest relationships with teachers are the ones most in need of *good* ones.[13]

Regardless of the causes of poor teacher–student relationships, teachers must work hard to turn them into productive ones. The first step, of course, is to *identify* poor relationships using such signs as these:[14]

- A teacher has hostile feelings (e.g., dislike, anger) toward a student.
- A teacher rarely interacts with a student.
- A teacher's messages to a student usually involve criticism or faultfinding.
- A teacher has a sense of learned helplessness about his or her ability to work effectively with a student.

Several strategies can help teachers repair these relationships. One is to think actively—perhaps in a brainstorming session with one or more colleagues—about alternative hypotheses for why the student behaves as he or she does, being sure that the list of hypotheses offers potential solutions. Another is to meet one-on-one with the student to talk openly about the problem and possible ways to fix it (more on this point later in the chapter). Still another strategy, especially effective when working with young children, is simply to spend some time with the student in a noninstructional, noncontrolling, "fun" context that might allow more positive feelings to emerge.[15]

Create a sense of community and belongingness.

In Chapter 3 we considered the nature of a *community of learners*, a classroom in which teacher and students consistently work together to help one another learn. Ultimately, teachers should also create a **sense of community** in the classroom—a sense that they and their students have shared goals, are mutually respectful and supportive of one another's efforts, and believe that everyone makes an important contribution to classroom learning.[16] Creating a sense of community engenders feelings of **belongingness**: Students see themselves as important and valued members of the classroom.[17] In the following interview, a middle school student named Barnie describes how it feels *not* to belong at school:

Adult: Are there times when you feel you are really different from your classmates?
Barnie: Yeah, all the time. . . . Because they all answer the questions, when I raise my hand I always get it wrong. Last week I was in a group, a smart group and I am not that smart. And I mostly get all the wrong answers and they yell at me.
Adult: What do they say?
Barnie: "You're dumb! You're stupid!"

[12] Becker & Luthar, 2002; Juvonen, 2006; Masten, 2001; O'Connor & McCartney, 2007; D. A. O'Donnell, Schwab-Stone, & Muyeed, 2002; Pomeroy, 1999; Werner & Smith, 2001.
[13] Darch & Kame'enui, 2004; H. A. Davis, 2003; Hanish, Kochenderfer-Ladd, Fabes, Martin, & Denning, 2004; Keogh, 2003; Pianta, 1999; Silverberg, 2003.
[14] Pianta, 1999; Sutherland & Morgan, 2003.
[15] Pianta, 1999, 2006; Silverberg, 2003; Sutton & Wheatley, 2003.
[16] Hom & Battistich, 1995; D. Kim, Solomon, & Roberts, 1995; Osterman, 2000.
[17] E. M. Anderman, 2002.

sense of community Shared belief that teacher and students have common goals, are mutually respectful and supportive, and all make important contributions to classroom learning.

belongingness General sense that one is an important and valued member of the classroom.

Adult: What do you tell them?

Barnie: That's the way I am.

Adult: Can you tell me about any other times when you felt different?

Barnie: When I am in the gym, I cannot run as fast as everybody and they all laugh at me. . . . It feels like I am the worst student ever.[18]

Numerous strategies can create a sense of classroom community and enhance students' feelings of belongingness:[19]

Students achieve at higher levels in the classroom when they have a *sense of community*—that is, when they have shared goals and are respectful and supportive of one another's efforts.

- Convey the general message that *all* students deserve the respect of their classmates and are important members of the classroom community.
- Make frequent use of interactive and collaborative teaching strategies (class discussions, cooperative learning activities, peer tutoring, etc.).
- Solicit students' ideas and opinions, and incorporate them into classroom discussions and activities.
- Create mechanisms through which students can help make the classroom run smoothly and efficiently (e.g., assign various "helper" roles on a rotating basis).
- Provide opportunities for students to help one another (e.g., by asking, "Who has a problem that someone else might be able to help you solve?").
- Give public recognition to students' contributions to the overall success of the classroom.
- Institute a "no exclusion" policy in group activities (e.g., by insisting that any student who wants to be involved in a play activity *can* be involved).
- Encourage students to be on the lookout for classmates on the periphery of ongoing activities (perhaps students with disabilities) and to ask these children to join in.
- Work on social skills with students whose interpersonal behaviors may alienate others.
- Be vigilant for incidents of bullying and other forms of peer harassment, and administer appropriate consequences to the perpetrators.

When students share a sense of community, they are more likely to exhibit prosocial behavior, stay on task, express enthusiasm about classroom activities, and achieve at high levels. Furthermore, a sense of classroom community is associated with lower rates of emotional distress, disruptive classroom behavior, truancy, violence, drug use, and dropping out.[20]

Create a goal-oriented, businesslike (but nonthreatening) atmosphere.

Although caring relationships with students are essential, teachers and students alike must recognize that they are at school to get certain things accomplished. Accordingly, a relatively businesslike atmosphere should prevail in the classroom most of the time. This is not to say that classroom activities must be boring and tedious. On the contrary, they should be interesting and engaging, and they can sometimes even be exciting. Entertainment and excitement should not be thought of as goals in and of themselves, however. Rather, they are means to a more important goal: mastering academic subject matter.[21]

Despite this emphasis on "business," the classroom atmosphere should never be uncomfortable or threatening. As noted in Chapter 6, students who are excessively anxious are unlikely to perform at their best. How can teachers be businesslike without being threatening? They can hold students accountable for achieving instructional objectives yet not place

---

[18] Dialogue from Kumar, Gheen, & Kaplan, 2002, p. 161.

[19] Emmer et al., 2000; D. Kim et al., 1995; Lickona, 1991; Osterman, 2000; A. M. Ryan & Patrick, 2001; Sapon-Shevin, Dobbelaere, Corrigan, Goodman, & Mastin, 1998.

[20] D. C. Gottfredson, 2001; Hom & Battistich, 1995; Juvonen, 2006; D. Kim et al., 1995; Osterman, 2000; M. D. Resnick et al., 1997.

[21] Brophy, 2006; G. A. Davis & Thomas, 1989; Gettinger & Kohler, 2006.

FIGURE 9.2   Beginning the school year with a few rules

Effective teachers typically begin the school year with a few rules that will help classroom activities run smoothly. Such rules often include variations on the following:

Bring all needed materials to class. (Students should have books, homework assignments, permission slips, and any needed supplies for planned activities.)

Be in your seat and ready to work when the bell rings. (Students should be at their desks, have paper out and pencils sharpened, and be physically and mentally ready to work.)

Respect and be polite to all people. (Students should listen attentively when someone else is speaking, behave appropriately for a substitute teacher, and refrain from insults, fighting, and other disrespectful or hostile behavior.)

Respect other people's property. (Students should keep the classroom clean and neat, refrain from defacing school property, ask for permission to borrow another's possessions, and return those possessions in a timely fashion.)

Obey all school rules. (Students must obey the rules of the school building as well as the rules of the classroom.)

Sources: Based on Emmer et al., 2000, pp. 22–23; Evertson, Emmer, & Worsham, 2000, p. 23.

students under continual surveillance. They can point out mistakes yet not make students feel like failures. And they can admonish students for misbehavior yet not hold grudges against them from one day to the next.[22]

Establish reasonable rules and procedures.

In the opening case study, Ms. Cornell failed to provide guidelines about how students should behave, which she should have done the first week of school. A class without guidelines for appropriate behavior is apt to be chaotic and unproductive. And students must learn that certain behaviors—especially those that cause injury, damage school property, or interfere with others' learning and performance—will simply not be tolerated. Setting reasonable limits on classroom behavior not only promotes a more productive learning environment but also helps prepare students to become productive members of adult society and culture (recall our discussion of *socialization* in Chapter 3).

Effective classroom managers establish and communicate certain rules and procedures right from the start.[23] They identify acceptable and unacceptable behaviors (e.g., see Figure 9.2). They develop consistent procedures and routines for such things as completing seatwork, asking for help, and turning in assignments. And they have procedures in place for nonroutine events such as school assemblies, field trips, and fire drills. Teachers should communicate such rules and procedures clearly and explicitly and describe the consequences of noncompliance. Taking time to clarify rules and procedures seems to be especially important in the early elementary grades, when students may not be very familiar with "how things are done" at school.[24]

Ideally, students should understand that rules and procedures are not merely the result of a teacher's personal whims but are designed to help the classroom run smoothly and efficiently. And despite restrictions on their behavior, students should have some sense of *self-determination* in the classroom (see Chapter 6). One strategy is to include students in decision making about the rules and procedures by which the class will operate.[25] When students have a say in classroom rules, their sense of "ownership" of the rules increases the likelihood that they will abide by them.

Another strategy for preserving students' sense of self-determination is to present rules and requirements as *information*—for instance, as conditions that can help students accomplish classroom objectives—rather than as mechanisms of *control* over students.[26] Examples of informational versus controlling messages are presented in Figure 9.3. Notice how all of the informational messages provide reasons for imposing certain restrictions.

 Observe two class discussions of appropriate student behaviors in the "Classroom Rules" and "Preparing for a Field Trip" videos in the Additional Resources section in Chapter 9 of MyEducationLab.

[22] C. R. Rogers, 1983; Spaulding, 1992.

[23] Borko & Putnam, 1996; W. Doyle, 1990; Gettinger & Kohler, 2006.

[24] K. Carter & Doyle, 2006; Evertson & Emmer, 1982; Gettinger & Kohler, 2006.

[25] G. A. Davis & Thomas, 1989; M. L. Fuller, 2001; Lickona, 1991.

[26] Deci, 1992; Koestner, Ryan, Bernieri, & Holt, 1984.

FIGURE 9.3 Presenting classroom rules and procedures as information

A teacher might say this (information):	. . . rather than this (control):
"You'll get your independent assignments done more quickly if you get right to work."	"Please be quiet and do your own work."
"As we practice for our fire drill, it is important to line up quickly and be quiet so that we can hear the instructions we are given and will know what to do."	"When the fire alarm sounds, line up quickly and quietly, and then wait for further instructions."
"This assignment is designed to help you develop the writing skills you will need after you graduate. It is unfair to other authors to copy their work word for word, so we will practice putting ideas into our own words and giving credit to authors whose ideas we borrow. Passing off another's writing and ideas as your own can lead to suspension in college or a lawsuit in the business world."	"Cheating and plagiarism are not acceptable in this classroom."
"It's important that others can read your writing. If your words are illegible and your cross-outs are confusing, I may not be able to give you as high a grade as you deserve on an assignment."	"Use good penmanship on all assignments, and erase any errors carefully and completely. Points will be deducted for sloppy writing."

The following scenario provides a simple illustration of how giving a reason can make all the difference in the world:

> Gerard is a boy with little tolerance for frustration. Whenever he asks Ms. Donnelly for assistance, he wants it *now*. If she is unable to help him immediately, he screams, "You're no good!" or "You don't care!" and shoves other students' desks as he walks angrily back to his seat.
>
> At one point during the school year, the class has a unit on interpersonal skills. One lesson in the unit addresses *timing*—the most appropriate and effective time to ask for another person's assistance with a problem.
>
> A week later, Gerard approaches Ms. Donnelly for help with a math problem. She is working with another student, but she turns briefly to Gerard and says, "Timing."
>
> Ms. Donnelly waits expectantly for Gerard's usual screaming. Instead, he responds, "Hey, Ms. D., I get it! I can ask you at another time!" He returns to his seat with a smile on his face.[27]

Observe the teacher in the "Classroom Rules" and "Reading Group" videos in the Additional Resources section in Chapter 9 of MyEducationLab. Would you characterize this teacher as "informational" or "controlling"?

Whether rules and instructions are presented in an informational or controlling manner is sometimes in the eye of the beholder, however. For example, when I have shown my own classes the "Classroom Rules" and "Reading Group" video clips in MyEducationLab, some students perceive the teacher to be providing helpful information and guidance about classroom behavior, whereas others find her a bit controlling.

Keep in mind that rules and procedures are easier to remember and therefore easier to follow if they are relatively simple and few in number.[28] Effective classroom managers tend to stress only the most important rules and procedures at the beginning of the school year. They introduce other rules and procedures later on as needed.[29] Also keep in mind that although some order and predictability are essential for student productivity, *too much* order may make a classroom a rather boring, routine place—one without an element of fun and spontaneity. Classrooms don't necessarily need rules and procedures for everything!

Enforce rules consistently and equitably.

Classroom rules are apt to be effective only if they're consistently enforced. Imposing no adverse consequence for inappropriate behavior, especially when such a consequence has been

---

[27] Based on Sullivan-DeCarlo, DeFalco, & Roberts, 1998, p. 81.

[28] G. A. Davis & Thomas, 1989; Emmer & Gerwels, 2006.

[29] W. Doyle, 1986a.

spelled out in advance, can actually be a form of reinforcement. As we discovered in Chapter 3, learners form expectations about the kinds of consequences to which various actions are likely to lead. Such expectations are based not only on what teachers tell them will happen but also on what actually *does* happen. In the opening case study, Ms. Cornell imposes no consequences when her three troublesome students misbehave. Not only do *their* antics continue, but other students—realizing that "anything goes" in Ms. Cornell's classroom—follow suit.

I'll offer guidelines for administering punishment later in the chapter, but for now we should note that consistency in enforcing classroom rules should apply not only across occasions but also across *students*. If you think back to your years in elementary and secondary school, you can probably recall at least one student who was "teacher's pet"—someone who was clearly a favorite and had special privileges. You might also recall a few students who were continually blamed for misdeeds, sometimes even when they weren't the true culprits. Teachers tend to like some students more than others (e.g., they're apt to prefer high achievers), but they must keep their preferences to themselves. Students can be quite resentful of teachers who grant special favors to, and perhaps overlook rule infractions of, a few "pet" students.[30] And students who are unfairly accused or punished are, of course, even more resentful, as one high school student explains:

> Because like if you had a past record or whatever like in middle school if you got in trouble like at all, they would think that you're a slight trouble maker and if you got in trouble again, they would always . . . if you were anywhere that something bad happened or something against the rules or whatever, they pick you first because they think that you have a past. So they wouldn't like pick the kids that had never done anything.[31]

Thus consistency and equitable treatment for all students—or lack thereof—is likely to have a significant effect on teacher–student relationships and overall classroom climate.[32]

Keep students productively engaged in worthwhile tasks.

As effective teachers plan lessons and classroom activities, they also plan specific ways of keeping students on task (something Ms. Cornell neglected to do in the opening case study). One strategy, of course, is to make the subject matter interesting and relevant to students' values and goals (see Chapter 6). Another is to incorporate variety into lessons, perhaps by using colorful audiovisual aids, conducting novel activities (e.g., small-group discussions, class debates), or occasionally moving to a different location (e.g., the computer lab or school yard).[33] But above all else, effective teachers make sure students have something to do at all times. Thanks to their basic need for arousal, human beings have a hard time doing *nothing at all* for any length of time (again see Chapter 6). Students often misbehave when they have nothing to do or are bored with what they *are* doing.[34]

Effective classroom managers make sure there is little "empty" time in which nothing is going on. Following are several strategies for keeping students productively engaged:[35]

- Have something specific for students to do each day, even on the first day of class.
- Have materials organized and equipment set up before class.
- Conduct activities that ensure *all* students' involvement and participation.
- Maintain a brisk pace throughout each lesson (but not so fast that students can't keep up).
- Ensure that students' comments are relevant and helpful but not excessively long winded (perhaps by taking any chronic time-monopolizers aside for a private discussion about giving classmates a chance to speak).
- Spend only short periods of time assisting individual students during class unless other students are capable of working independently and productively in the meantime.

[30] Babad, 1995; Babad, Avni-Babad, & Rosenthal, 2003; J. Baker, 1999.

[31] Certo et al., 2002, p. 25.

[32] Babad et al., 2003; J. Baker, 1999; Certo et al., 2002.

[33] G. A. Davis & Thomas, 1989; Munn, Johnstone, & Chalmers, 1990.

[34] Gettinger & Kohler, 2006; J. Hunter & Csikszentmihalyi, 2003; Shernoff, Csikszentmihalyi, Schneider, & Shernoff, 2003.

[35] G. A. Davis & Thomas, 1989; W. Doyle, 1986a; Emmer et al., 2000; Evertson & Harris, 1992; Gettinger, 1988; Munn et al., 1990.

Students who are actively engaged in classroom activities rarely exhibit problem behaviors.

- Have a system in place that ensures that students who finish an assigned task quickly have something else to do (perhaps writing in a class journal or reading a book).

Plan for transitions.

In the opening case study, Eli, Jake, and Vanessa often misbehave at the beginning and end of the school day, as well as before and after recess and lunch. Misbehaviors most frequently occur during transition times—as students end one activity and begin a second, or as they move from one classroom to another. Effective classroom managers take steps to ensure that transitions proceed quickly and without a loss of momentum.[36] For example, they establish procedures for moving from one activity to the next. They also ensure that there is little between-activity slack time in which students have nothing to do. For instance, at the secondary level, where students change classes every hour or so, effective classroom managers typically have a task for students to complete as soon as they enter the classroom.

How might a teacher plan for the various transitions that occur throughout the school day? Here are some examples:

- A physical education teacher has students begin each class session with five minutes of stretching exercises.
- An elementary school teacher has students follow the same procedure each day as lunchtime approaches. Students must (a) place completed assignments in a basket on the teacher's desk, (b) put away supplies they have been using, (c) get their lunches from the coatroom, and (d) line up quietly by the door.
- A middle school mathematics teacher has students copy the evening's homework assignment as soon as they come to class.
- A high school English composition teacher writes a topic or question (e.g., "My biggest pet peeve," "Whatever happened to hula hoops?") on the chalkboard at the beginning of each class period. Students know that when they come to class, they should immediately begin to write on the topic or question of the day.

All of these strategies, though very different in nature, share the common goal of keeping students focused on productive activities.

Keep in mind that some students may have difficulty moving from one activity to another, especially if they are deeply engaged in what they are doing. Accordingly, it is often helpful to give students advance warning that a transition is coming, describe what the subsequent activity will be, and remind students of the usual procedures for switching from one task to another.[37]

Take individual and developmental differences into account.

Earlier I mentioned the importance of consistency and equity in enforcing classroom rules. Yet when it comes to *preventing* off-task behavior, optimal strategies may differ considerably from one student to the next. For instance, during independent seatwork assignments, some students may work quite well with classmates close by, whereas others may be easily distracted unless they can work in a quiet spot, perhaps near a teacher's desk. During small-group work, some groups may function quite effectively on their own, whereas others may need considerable guidance and supervision.

One important source of individual differences affecting classroom behavior is *temperament*—the extent to which a student is energetic, adaptable, irritable, impulsive, and so on. In Chapter 7 we examined the nature of temperament and its implications for classroom management (to refresh your memory, revisit the "Personality and Sense of Self" section and the Classroom Strategies box titled "Accommodating Diverse Temperaments"). To be truly effective classroom managers, teachers must realize that students' vastly different classroom behaviors may be due, in part, to biological predispositions that are not entirely controllable. Such a realization will influence teachers' beliefs about why students act as they

[36] W. Doyle, 1984, 2006; Gettinger & Kohler, 2006. A phenomenon known as *behavioral momentum* is relevant here; for instance, see Ardoin, Martens, &

Wolfe, 1999; Belfiore, Lee, Vargas, & Skinner, 1997; Mace et al., 1988; Nevin, Mandell, & Atak, 1983.
[37] K. Carter & Doyle, 2006; Emmer & Gerwels, 2006.

do—that is, it will influence teachers' *attributions*—and these beliefs will, in turn, affect teachers' willingness to adapt classroom strategies to foster productive classroom behavior.[38] Notice what happened to one fourth grader (now a successful college professor) when his teacher took his temperament into consideration:

> One day when I was especially restless . . . I could see Miss Rickenbrood circling to the back of the room. I wasn't aware of having done anything in particular, but I knew her eyes were on me. After a few minutes she leaned over and whispered in my ear, "Tom, would you like to go outside and run?"
>
> I was stunned. To go outside and run? On my own? When it wasn't recess? What could have possessed this woman to ignore all school rules and allow me to run? I said yes and quietly went to put on my coat. As I recall, I didn't actually run in the playground (people would be watching from inside the building), but stood outside in the doorway, in the cold, marveling at my freedom. I returned to class after about ten minutes, settled for the rest of the day.[39]

Another individual difference variable that influences classroom behavior is ability level. Students are more likely to get involved in their classwork, rather than in off-task behavior, when they have tasks and assignments appropriate for their current knowledge and skills. They are apt to misbehave when they are asked to do things that are probably too difficult for them—in other words, when they are incapable of completing assigned tasks successfully.[40] (Such may have been the case for Eli, Jake, and Vanessa in the opening case study.) This is not to suggest that teachers should plan activities so easy that students are not challenged and learn nothing new in doing them (recall the concept of *zone of proximal development* introduced in Chapter 5). One workable strategy is to *begin* the school year with relatively easy tasks that students can readily complete. Such early tasks enable students to practice normal classroom routines and procedures and give them a sense that they can enjoy and be successful in classroom activities. Once a supportive classroom climate has been established and students are comfortable with classroom procedures, teachers can gradually introduce more difficult and challenging assignments.[41] A similar approach is useful when introducing new instructional strategies. For instance, when first asking students to engage in cooperative activities, a teacher might have them work with relatively familiar content so that they can focus on mastering effective group interaction skills (asking for help, giving explanations, etc.) without being distracted by difficult subject matter.[42]

Developmental differences, too, must dictate classroom management strategies to some extent. Many children in the early elementary grades haven't had enough experience with formal education to know all the unspoken "rules" that govern classroom interactions—for instance, that students should remain silent when a teacher or other adult is talking, that only the student who is called on should answer a question, and so on.[43] Children just beginning kindergarten or first grade may find their new school environment to be unsettling and anxiety arousing, as will many adolescents making the transition to middle school or high school (see Chapter 6). And, of course, children gain better social skills as they grow older, impacting their ability to interact effectively with their teacher and classmates (see Chapter 7). Table 9.1 presents these and other developmental differences, along with examples of how teachers might accommodate them in classroom practice.

Continually monitor what students are doing.

Effective teachers communicate something called **withitness**: They know—and their students *know* that they know—what students are doing at all times. They regularly scan the classroom, often move from one spot to another, and make frequent eye contact with

---

[38] W. Johnson, McGue, & Iacono, 2005; Keogh, 2003; A. Miller, 2006.
[39] Newkirk, 2002, pp. 25–26.
[40] Mac Iver, Reuman, & Main, 1995; J. W. Moore & Edwards, 2003; S. L. Robinson & Griesemer, 2006.
[41] W. Doyle, 1990; Evertson & Emmer, 1982; Evertson, Emmer, & Worsham, 2000.
[42] N. M. Webb & Farivar, 1999.
[43] Mehan, 1979.

withitness Classroom management strategy in which a teacher gives the impression of knowing what all students are doing at all times.

DEVELOPMENTAL TRENDS

TABLE 9.1 Effective Classroom Management at Different Grade Levels

Grade Level	Age-Typical Characteristics	Suggested Strategies
K–2	• Lack of familiarity with unspoken rules about appropriate classroom behavior • Anxiety about being in school, especially in the first few weeks and especially for students without preschool experience • Short attention span and distractibility • Little self-regulation • Desire for teacher affection and approval • Considerable individual differences in social skills	• Invite students and their parents to visit the classroom before the school year begins. • Especially during the first few weeks of school, place high priority on establishing a warm, supportive relationship with every student. • Keep assignments relatively short and focused. • Create a gathering place (e.g., a carpet) where students can sit close at hand for whole-class discussions. • Create areas where students can work independently on tasks of their choosing (e.g., a reading center where students can listen to storybooks on tape). • Be explicit about acceptable classroom behavior; correct inappropriate behavior gently but consistently.
3–5	• Continuing desire for teacher approval, but with increasing concern about peer approval as well • Greater attentiveness to teachers who are emotionally expressive (e.g., teachers who often smile and show obvious concern in times of distress) • Increasing self-regulation skills • Gradually improving ability to reflect on one's own and others' thoughts and motives (i.e., increasing social cognition) • Increasing disengagement from school if students have consistently encountered academic and social failures	• Use two-way journals to communicate regularly with students about academic, social, and emotional issues. • In your words and actions, consistently show students that you are concerned about their academic progress and emotional well-being. • Provide increasing opportunities for independent work, but with enough structure to guide students' efforts. • In times of disagreement or conflict among classmates, ask students to reflect on one another's thoughts and feelings. • Make an extra effort to establish close, supportive relationships with students who seem to be "unmotivated" and socially disengaged.
6–8	• Considerable anxiety about the transition to middle school, due in part to less close and less supportive relationships with teachers • Decrease in intrinsic motivation to learn academic subject matter • Increase in cheating behaviors; cheating less common if students think teachers respect them and are committed to helping them learn • Heightened concern about ability to "fit in" and be accepted by peers • Increase in bullying behaviors	• Find occasions to see students outside of class (e.g., chaperone dances, attend sporting events). • Plan lessons that are engaging and relevant to students' lives and needs. • Provide sufficient academic support that students have no reason to cheat; nevertheless, be on the lookout for possible cheating. • Do not tolerate bullying and other forms of aggression; address their underlying causes (see the discussion of aggression in Chapter 7). • Reach out to students who seem socially unconnected (e.g., invite them to join you for lunch in your classroom).
9–12	• Anxiety about the transition to high school, especially if seventh and eighth grades were part of elementary school (as in some small school districts) • Social and romantic relationships often a source of distraction • Considerable self-regulation skills in some but not all students • High incidence of cheating, in part because peers communicate that it's acceptable • Disdain for classmates who work too hard for teacher approval (i.e., "brownnosers") • Tendency for some adolescents to think that classroom misbehavior will gain the admiration of peers • Increase in violent behaviors, especially at schools in low-income neighborhoods	• Remember that even in the high school grades, students achieve at higher levels when they have close, supportive relationships with teachers. • Regularly plan activities that involve social interaction; if possible, move desks and chairs to allow students to interact more easily. • Provide guidance and support for students who have few self-regulating skills to keep them on task. • Describe what cheating is and why it's unacceptable. • Communicate approval privately rather than publicly. • Proactively address violence (see the section "Addressing Aggression and Violence at School" later in the chapter).

Sources: Some characteristics and suggestions based on Blugental, Lyon, Lin, McGrath, & Bimbela, 1999; K. Carter & Doyle, 2006; Cizek, 2003; Emmer & Gerwels, 2006; Fingerhut & Christoffel, 2002; Hamre & Pianta, 2005; Mehan, 1979; Murdock, Hale, & Weber, 2001; O'Connor & McCartney, 2007; Pellegrini, 2002; many other ideas derived from discussions in earlier chapters.

individual students. They know what misbehaviors are occurring *when* those misbehaviors occur, and they know who the perpetrators are.[44] Consider the following classroom as an example:

> In one second-grade classroom, an hour and a half of each morning is devoted to reading. Students spend part of this time with their teacher in small reading groups. They spend the remainder of the time working on independent assignments tailored to their individual reading skills. As the teacher works with each reading group at the front of the classroom, she situates herself with her back to the wall so that she can simultaneously keep an eye on students working independently at their seats. She sends a quick and subtle signal—perhaps a stern expression, a finger to the lips, or a call of a student's name—to any student who gets off task.

Observe this classroom in action in the "Reading Group" video in the Additional Resources section in Chapter 9 of MyEducationLab.

When teachers demonstrate such withitness, especially at the beginning of the school year, students are more likely to behave appropriately, stay on task, and achieve at high levels.[45]

EXPANDING THE SENSE OF COMMUNITY BEYOND THE CLASSROOM

Students' learning and development depend not only on what happens inside a particular classroom but also on what happens in other parts of the school building, in the neighborhood and community, and at home. Thus, effective teachers coordinate their efforts with other influential individuals in students' lives—with fellow school faculty members, with professionals at community agencies, and especially with students' parents or other primary caregivers. Ideally, teachers should think of such joint efforts as *partnerships* in which everyone is working together to promote students' long-term development and learning.[46] Following are several recommendations.

Collaborate with colleagues to create an overall sense of school community.

Although teachers spend much of the school day working in individual classrooms, they are far more effective if they coordinate their efforts with other faculty members.[47] Important components of such coordination include the following strategies:[48]

- Communicate and collaborate regularly with other classroom teachers and with specialists (e.g., librarians, special education teachers, counselors).
- Form common goals regarding what students should learn and achieve.
- Work together to identify obstacles to students' academic achievement and to develop strategies for overcoming the obstacles.
- Establish a shared set of strategies for encouraging productive student behaviors.
- Make a group commitment to promote equality and multicultural sensitivity throughout the school community.

Thus, effective teachers not only create a sense of community within their individual classrooms but also create an overall **sense of school community**.[49] Students should get the same messages from every faculty member: that teachers are working together to help them become informed, successful, and productive citizens, and that students can and should help one another as well. One critical element of a sense of school community is a commitment to *respect* for people with diverse backgrounds and needs—a commitment that translates into prohibitions against malicious teasing, derogatory rumor spreading, bullying, and

---

[44] Gettinger & Kohler, 2006; T. Hogan, Rabinowitz, & Craven, 2003; Kounin, 1970.

[45] W. Doyle, 1986a; Gettinger & Kohler, 2006; Woolfolk & Brooks, 1985.

[46] For instance, see Hidalgo, Siu, Bright, Swap, & Epstein, 1995.

[47] Battistich, Solomon, Watson, & Schaps, 1997; Hoy, Tarter, & Woolfolk Hoy, 2006; Levine & Lezotte, 1995; M. Watson & Battistich, 2006.

[48] Battistich et al., 1997; Levine & Lezotte, 1995; T. J. Lewis, Newcomer, Trussell, & Richter, 2006.

[49] Battistich, Solomon, Kim, Watson, & Schaps, 1995; Battistich et al., 1997.

sense of school community Shared belief that all faculty and students within a school are working together to help everyone learn and succeed.

other forms of peer harassment.[50] Fernando Arias, a high school vocational education teacher, has described such respectfulness this way:

> In our school, our philosophy is that we treat everybody the way we'd like to be treated.... Our school is a unique situation where we have pregnant young ladies who go to our school. We have special education children. We have the regular kids, and we have the drop-out recovery program . . . we're all equal. We all have an equal chance. And we have members of every gang at our school, and we hardly have any fights, and there are close to about 300 gangs in our city. We all get along. It's one big family unit it seems like.[51]

When teachers and students share an overall sense of school community, students have more positive attitudes toward school, are more motivated to achieve at high levels, exhibit more prosocial behavior, and are more likely to interact with peers from diverse backgrounds. Furthermore, teachers have higher expectations for students' achievement and a greater sense of self-efficacy about their teaching effectiveness.[52] In fact, when teachers collaborate in their efforts, they often have high *collective self-efficacy* about their ability to help students learn and achieve (recall our discussion of this concept in Chapter 6), and their self-confidence is indeed related to students' performance.[53]

Such a "team spirit" has an additional advantage for beginning teachers: It provides the support structure (scaffolding) they may need, especially when working with students who are at risk for school failure. New teachers report greater confidence in their ability to help their students learn and achieve when they collaborate regularly with their colleagues.[54]

Work cooperatively with other agencies that play key roles in students' lives.

Students almost always have regular contact with other institutions besides their schools—possibly with community recreation centers, social services, churches, hospitals, mental health clinics, or local judicial systems. Teachers are most effective if they think of themselves as part of a larger community team that promotes growing children's long-term development. Thus, they should keep in contact with other people and institutions that play major roles in students' lives, coordinating efforts whenever possible.[55] Keep in mind, however, that school–agency cooperation regarding *individual* students—especially if it involves sharing potentially sensitive information—can typically occur only with the written permission of students' parents.

Communicate regularly with parents and other primary caregivers.

Without a doubt, productive parent–teacher relationships enhance students' learning and achievement in the classroom, and ongoing communication between school and home is critical for these relationships.[56] At a minimum, teachers must stay in regular contact with students' parents and other caregivers about the progress students are making. Regular communication also provides a means through which families can give *teachers* information (for instance, about current circumstances at home or about effective motivational strategies). Following are several common mechanisms for enhancing school–family communication:

- **Parent–teacher conferences.** In most school districts, formal parent–teacher conferences are scheduled one or more times a year. Teachers sometimes include students in conferences (essentially making them parent–teacher–student conferences). Inviting other family members who share caregiving responsibilities (e.g., grandparents) can also be helpful.
- **Written communication.** Written communication can take a variety of forms, including (a) homework slips explaining each night's assignments, (b) informal notes acknowledging significant accomplishments, (c) teacher-constructed checklists that

[50] Espelage & Swearer, 2004; Langdon, in press.
[51] Quoted in Turnbull, Pereira, & Blue-Banning, 2000, p. 67.
[52] Battistich et al., 1995, 1997; M. Watson & Battistich, 2006.
[53] Bandura, 2000; Goddard, Hoy, & Woolfolk Hoy, 2000; Hoy et al., 2006.
[54] Chester & Beaudin, 1996.
[55] J. L. Epstein, 1996.
[56] Gutman & McLoyd, 2000; J. Hughes & Kwok, 2007.

9/14/01

Dear Parents,

I have been lucky so far and have not had to go back for jury duty. I have two more weeks to go [in terms of possibly being summoned for duty] and hope I will continue to be in the classroom.

We have been trying to keep the routine pretty regular, despite one or two testing sessions per day. The children have been pretty focused, although it is difficult when they are unfamiliar with the format and look to us for help. I don't like telling them that they are on their own! We are done, thank goodness. I believe you will receive results in the mail.

Homework and spelling will resume next week. I could also use my regular volunteers to help get through the spelling assessments. The times you have been coming are still fine. Call or e-mail me if you need the available times for helping.

We finished our unit on germs and sanitation, although we did not get into any discussions about Anthrax. It seems that you are keeping the children protected at home from details of the scary news, as we are at school. We kept our discussions to common illnesses that they are aware of and how they can avoid them with proper sanitation.

A few classrooms are doing activities to raise money for many of the children involved in the tragedy. Sarah [the teacher intern] and I decided not to work with our children on a fundraiser because we don't want to get into anxiety-producing discussions. It is hard to help young children understand that they are safe where they are and that it is unlikely that they will be involved in such things.

Next week, we will be starting a Nutrition Unit and beginning to read some Halloween stories. We will continue working to become automatic with math facts, along with our regular routine of phonics lessons, DOL [daily oral language], reading, writing, spelling, etc.

We are running out of Kleenex and could use some donations. We would also like some boxes of baby wipes to use in cleaning hands and desks when there is not time for the entire class to wash. Someone mentioned to me that there is a homemade recipe for baby wipes out there somewhere. Is there a parent who knows and would be willing to share?

Have a great weekend.

Ann

FIGURE 9.4   Example of a teacher newsletter. This one was written on September 14, 2001, three days after the terrorist attacks on the World Trade Center and Pentagon and during a week when students were taking a districtwide standardized test.

describe academic progress, and (d) general newsletters describing ongoing classroom activities. Figure 9.4 shows an example of the newsletters that one second-grade teacher sends home with her students each Friday.

- **Telephone conversations.** Telephone calls are useful when issues require immediate attention—for instance, when a student has won a prestigious award or, alternatively, has shown a sudden decline in performance for no apparent reason. In addition, telephone calls are a useful way of introducing oneself as a child's elementary school teacher for the coming school year.[57]
- **E-mail messages.** In the newsletter in Figure 9.4, the teacher encourages parents to contact her by e-mail, a strategy that is quite appropriate in her middle-socioeconomic school district. Suggesting the use of e-mail would, of course, be inappropriate in communities where many families cannot afford computers or where parents have limited knowledge of English.

In their communications with students' families, teachers don't necessarily have to limit themselves to what's going on in the classroom. Many parents welcome teachers' suggestions about how best to help their children at home. For instance, parents are often grateful for suggestions about how to assist with homework or how to foster their children's development more generally. And they appreciate knowing what kinds of behaviors are and are not normal for a particular age-group.[58]

See a teacher and father effectively discuss how they might coordinate their efforts in the "Parent–Teacher Conference" video in the Additional Resources section in Chapter 9 of MyEducationLab.

Invite families to participate in the academic and social life of the school.

In general, effective schools are *welcoming* schools that encourage not only students but also family members to participate in school activities.[59] Some parents are available during the day and are happy to assist with occasional field trips and class parties or to provide one-on-one

[57] Striepling-Goldstein, 2004.

[58] C. Davis & Yang, 2005; J. M. T. Walker & Hoover-Dempsey, 2006.

[59] J. L. Epstein, 1996; N. E. Hill et al., 2004; G. R. López, 2001; Serpell, Baker, & Sonnenschein, 2005.

Schoolwide projects and fund-raisers, such as this pancake breakfast, provide one means of getting parents actively involved in their children's schooling and fostering productive parent–teacher relationships.

tutoring once or twice a week. Most others are available in the evenings and can attend school open houses, school plays, band and choir performances, and fund-raising dinners. Some teachers have successfully used parent *coffee nights* during which they explain a new instructional strategy or *author teas* during which students read the poetry or short stories they have written.

In some instances teachers or other faculty members might assemble a group of parents to discuss issues of mutual interest.[60] For example, they might use such a group as a sounding board when selecting topics to include in the classroom curriculum or thinking about assigning potentially controversial works of literature. Alternatively, teachers can use a discussion group as a mechanism through which teachers and parents alike can share ideas about how best to promote students' academic, personal, and social development on the home front.

Make an extra effort with seemingly "reluctant" parents.

Despite many opportunities, some parents are apt to remain uninvolved in their children's education; for example, they may rarely if ever attend scheduled parent–teacher conferences. Rather than jumping to the conclusion that these parents are also *uninterested* in their children's education, teachers must recognize several possible reasons that parents may fail to make contact with their children's schools. Some of them may have an exhausting work schedule or lack adequate child care. A few may have debilitating physical or mental illnesses that greatly restrict their activities. Other parents may have difficulty communicating in English or finding their way through the school system to the people they most need to talk with. Still others may believe that it's inappropriate to bother teachers with questions about their children's progress or to offer information and suggestions. And a handful may simply have had bad experiences with school when they themselves were children.[61]

In such cases a personal invitation can sometimes make a difference, as this parent's statement illustrates:

> The thing of it is, had someone not walked up to me and asked me specifically, I would not hold out my hand and say, "I'll do it." ... You get parents here all the time, Black parents that are willing, but maybe a little on the shy side and wouldn't say I really want to serve on this subject. You may send me the form, I may never fill the form out. Or I'll think about it and not send it back. But you know if that principal, that teacher, my son's math teacher called and asked if I would. . . .[62]

Experienced educators have offered additional recommendations for getting seemingly reluctant parents more involved in their children's schooling:[63]

- Make an extra effort to establish parents' trust and confidence—for instance, by demonstrating that their input is valued and helpful and that faculty members would never try to make them appear foolish.
- Encourage parents to be assertive when they have questions or concerns.
- Give parents suggestions about learning activities they can easily do with their children at home.
- Find out what parents do exceptionally well (e.g., carpentry, cooking), and ask them to share their talents with the students.
- Provide opportunities for parents to volunteer for jobs that don't require them to leave home (e.g., to be someone whom students can call when unsure of homework assignments).

[60] J. L. Epstein, 1996; Fosnot, 1996; Rudman, 1993.
[61] Brooks-Gunn, 2003; Heymann & Earle, 2000; H.-Z. Ho, Hinckley, Fox, Brown, & Dixon, 2001; J.-S. Lee & Bowen, 2006; Mistry, Vandewater, Huston, & McLoyd, 2002; Pérez, 1998; Petterson & Albers, 2001.
[62] A. A. Carr, 1997, p. 2.

[63] J. L. Epstein, 1996; Finders & Lewis, 1994; Hidalgo et al., 1995; H.-Z. Ho et al., 2001; Howe, 1994; G. R. López, 2001; Salend & Taylor, 1993; M. G. Sanders, 1996; Striepling-Goldstein, 2004; J. M. T. Walker & Hoover-Dempsey, 2006.

- Identify specific individuals (e.g., bilingual parents) who can translate for those who speak little or no English.
- Conduct parent–teacher conferences or parent discussions at times and locations more convenient for families; make use of home visits *if* such visits are welcomed.
- Offer resources for parents at the school building (e.g., a parent resource room with easy chairs and reading materials on a variety of topics; contacts with social and health services; classes in English, literacy, home repairs, arts and crafts).

Still another potentially effective strategy is to reinforce *parents* as well as students when the students do well at school. One administrator at a school with a large population of immigrant students put it this way:

> One of the things we do . . . is that we identify those students that had perfect attendance, those students that passed all areas of the [statewide achievement tests] and were successful. We don't honor the student, we honor the parents. We give parents a certificate. Because, we tell them, "through your efforts, and through your hard work, your child was able to accomplish this."[64]

A few parents will resist all efforts to get them involved, and a subset of them may truly have little interest in helping their children do well. In such circumstances, teachers must never penalize students for their parents' actions or inactions. Teachers must also realize that *they themselves* are apt to be among the most important academic and emotional resources in these students' lives.

REDUCING UNPRODUCTIVE BEHAVIORS

Despite teachers' best efforts, students sometimes behave in ways that significantly disrupt classroom activities and interfere with learning. Effective teachers not only plan and structure a classroom that minimizes potential behavior problems but also deal with the misbehaviors that do occur.

For purposes of our discussion, we'll define a **misbehavior** as any action that disrupts classroom learning and planned classroom activities, puts one or more students' physical safety or psychological well-being in jeopardy, or violates basic moral and ethical standards. Some classroom misbehaviors are relatively minor ones that have little long-term impact on students' well-being and achievement. Such behaviors as talking out of turn, writing brief notes to classmates during a lecture, and submitting homework assignments after their due date—especially if such behaviors occur infrequently—generally fall in this category. Other misbehaviors are far more serious, in that they definitely interfere with the learning or well-being of one or more students. For example, when students scream at their teachers, hit their classmates, or habitually refuse to participate in classroom activities, then classroom learning—certainly the learning of the "guilty party" and often the learning of other students as well—and the overall classroom climate can be adversely affected.

As is true in the opening case study, it is often just a handful of students who are responsible for the great majority of misbehaviors in a classroom.[65] Such students are apt to be among teachers' greatest challenges, and it can be all too tempting to write them off as lost causes. Yet teachers must work vigorously to point these students in more productive directions. Without active interventions by teachers and other caring adults, students who are consistently disruptive or in other ways off-task in the early grades often continue to show behavior problems in the later years as well.[66]

Teachers should plan ahead about how to respond to the variety of misbehaviors they may see in the classroom. Although they must certainly be consistent in the consequences they impose for blatant rule infractions, different strategies for reducing disruptive behavior over the long run may be useful and appropriate under different circumstances. Following are a number of possibilities.

misbehavior Action that disrupts learning and planned classroom activities, puts students' physical safety or psychological well-being in jeopardy, or violates basic moral standards.

[64] G. R. López, 2001, p. 273.
[65] W. Doyle, 2006.
[66] Emmer & Gerwels, 2006; Vitaro, Brendgen, Larose, & Tremblay, 2005.

Consider whether instructional strategies or classroom assignments might be partly to blame for off-task behaviors.

Principles of effective classroom management go hand in hand with principles of learning and motivation. When students are learning and achieving successfully and when they clearly want to pursue the classroom's instructional goals, they are apt to be busily engaged in productive activities for most of the school day.[67] In contrast, when they have difficulty understanding classroom subject matter or little interest in learning it, they are likely to exhibit the nonproductive or counterproductive classroom behaviors that result from frustration or boredom.

When students misbehave, beginning teachers often think about what the students are doing wrong. In contrast, experienced, "expert" teachers are more likely to think about what *they themselves* can do differently to keep students on task, and they modify their plans accordingly.[68] Here are several self-questions that can help a beginning teacher start thinking like an expert:

- How can I change my instructional strategies to stimulate interest in and excitement about a topic?
- Are instructional materials so difficult or unstructured that students are becoming frustrated? Or are they so easy or routine that students are bored?
- What are students really concerned about? For example, are they more concerned about interacting with their classmates than in gaining new knowledge and skills?
- How can I address students' motives and goals (e.g., their desire to affiliate with peers) while simultaneously helping them achieve classroom objectives?

Addressing such questions can help a teacher focus his or her efforts on the ultimate purpose of schooling: to help students *learn*.

Occasionally current events on the international, national, or local scene (e.g., a terrorist attack, a natural disaster, or a tragic car accident involving classmates) may take priority. When students' minds are justifiably preoccupied with something other than the topic of instruction, they will have difficulty paying attention to a preplanned lesson and are likely to learn little from it. In such extenuating circumstances, teachers may want to abandon their lesson plans altogether, at least for a short while.

When students are frequently off task, expert teachers think about what *they themselves* might do differently to keep them engaged in classroom activities.

Consider whether cultural background might influence students' classroom behaviors.

As teachers determine which behaviors are truly unacceptable in their classrooms, they must keep in mind that some behaviors that their own culture deems inappropriate may be quite appropriate in another culture.[69] In the following exercise, we look at some examples.

SEE FOR YOURSELF
Identifying Misbehaviors

Read each of the three scenarios on the following page and consider

- Whether you would classify it as a misbehavior
- What group(s) might find the behavior appropriate
- How you might deal with the behavior

---

[67] W. Doyle, 1990; Gettinger & Kohler, 2006.
[68] Emmer & Stough, 2001; Sabers et al., 1991; H. L. Swanson, O'Connor, & Cooney, 1990.

[69] For example, see Gay, 2006.

1. A student is frequently late for school, sometimes arriving more than an hour after the school bell has rung.
2. Two students are sharing answers as they take a quiz.
3. Several students are exchanging insults that become increasingly more derogatory.

Tardiness (Example 1) interferes with learning, in that the student loses valuable instructional time. A student who is chronically late for school may live in a family or community that does not observe strict timelines, a pattern common in some Hispanic and Native American groups (see the Cultural Considerations box in Chapter 3). Furthermore, arrival time may not be entirely within the student's control. For instance, perhaps the student has household responsibilities or transportation issues that make punctuality difficult. A private conversation with the student, perhaps followed up by a conference with family members, would be the most effective way to determine the root of the problem and identify potential solutions (more about such strategies shortly).

Sharing answers during a quiz (Example 2) is a misbehavior *if* students have been specifically instructed to do their own work. Because a quiz helps a teacher determine what students have and have not learned, inaccurate quiz scores affect the teacher's instructional planning and so indirectly affect future learning. (Cheating lowers the *validity* of the quiz scores; we'll discuss this concept in Chapter 10.) Although the behavior represents cheating to many people, it may reflect the cooperative spirit and emphasis on group achievement evident in the cultures of some Native American, Mexican American, and Southeast Asian students (again see the Cultural Considerations box in Chapter 3). *If* a teacher has previously explained what cheating is in a way that students understand and *if* the teacher has clearly described situations in which collaboration is and is not appropriate—in other words, if students know full well that their behavior violates classroom policy—then an adverse consequence is called for. A teacher who has *not* laid such groundwork must certainly do so in order to prevent such behavior from occurring again.

An exchange of insults (Example 3) might be psychologically harmful for the students involved and adversely affect the overall classroom climate. Alternatively, however, it might simply be an instance of *playing the dozens*, a playful verbal interaction common in some African American communities (see the "Ruckus in the Lunchroom" exercise in Chapter 3). How a teacher handles the situation must depend on the spirit in which students seem to view the exchange. Their body language—whether they are smiling or scowling, whether they seem relaxed or tense—can reveal a great deal. If the insults truly signal escalating hostilities, an immediate intervention is in order. If, instead, the insults reflect creative verbal play, a teacher may simply need to establish reasonable boundaries (e.g., "indoor" voices should be used, racial or ethnic slurs are unacceptable).

Ignore misbehaviors that are temporary, minor, and unlikely to be repeated or copied.

On some occasions the best course of action is *no* action, at least nothing of a disciplinary nature.[70] For example, consider these situations:

- Dimitra rarely breaks classroom rules. But on one occasion, after you have just instructed students to work quietly and independently at their seats, you see her briefly whisper to the girl beside her. None of the other students seems to notice that Dimitra has disobeyed your instructions.
- Herb is careless in chemistry lab and accidentally knocks over a small container of liquid (a harmless one, fortunately). He quickly apologizes and cleans up the mess.

Will these behaviors interfere with Dimitra's or Herb's academic achievement? Are they "contagious" behaviors that will spread to other students, as the horseplay did in Ms. Cornell's class? The answer to both questions is "Probably not."

Whenever a teacher stops an instructional activity to deal with a misbehavior, even for a few seconds, the teacher runs the risk of disrupting the momentum of the activity and

[70] G. A. Davis & Thomas, 1989; W. Doyle, 2006.

drawing students' attention to their misbehaving classmates.[71] Furthermore, by drawing class attention to a particular student's behavior, the teacher may actually be reinforcing it rather than discouraging it.

Following are some general circumstances in which *ignoring* an unproductive behavior may be the wisest course of action:[72]

- When the behavior is a rare occurrence and probably won't be repeated
- When the behavior is unlikely to spread to other students
- When unusual circumstances (e.g., the last day of school before a holiday or an unsettling event in a student's personal life) elicit inappropriate behavior only temporarily
- When the behavior is typical for a particular age-group (e.g., when kindergartners become restless after sitting for an extended time, when sixth-grade boys and girls resist holding one another's hands during dance instruction)
- When the behavior's result (its natural consequence) is unpleasant enough to deter a student from repeating the behavior
- When the behavior is not seriously affecting classroom learning

Dimitra's behavior—whispering briefly to a classmate during independent seatwork—is unlikely to spread to her classmates (they didn't see her do it) and is probably not an instance of cheating (it occurred before she began working on the assignment). Herb's behavior—knocking over a container of liquid in chemistry lab—has, in and of itself, resulted in an unpleasant consequence: He must clean up the mess. In both situations, then, ignoring the misbehavior is probably the best thing to do.

Give signals and reminders about what is and is not appropriate.

In some situations off-task behaviors, though not serious in nature, *do* interfere with classroom learning and must be discouraged. Consider these misbehaviors as examples:

- As you're explaining a difficult concept, Marjorie is busily writing. At first you think she's taking notes, but then you see her pass the paper across the aisle to Kang. A few minutes later, you see Kang pass the same sheet back to Marjorie. It appears that the two students are writing personal notes to each other and possibly not hearing a word you're saying.
- You have separated your class into small groups for a cooperative learning exercise. One group seems to be more interested in discussing an upcoming school dance than in accomplishing assigned work. The group is not making the progress that other groups are making and probably won't complete the assignment if its members don't get down to business soon.

Effective classroom managers handle such minor behavior problems as unobtrusively as possible. They don't stop the lesson, distract other students, or call unnecessary attention to the behavior they're trying to stop.[73] In many cases they use *cueing*, a strategy I introduced in Chapter 3. That is, they let students know, through a signal of one kind or another, that they are aware of the misbehavior and would like it to stop.

Cueing takes a variety of forms. For instance, a teacher might use *body language*, perhaps making eye contact, raising an eyebrow, or frowning. When body language doesn't get the attention of a misbehaving student, a more obvious cue is *physical proximity*: moving close to the student and standing there until the problem behavior stops. When such subtle signals don't work, a brief *verbal cue*—stating a student's name, reminding students of correct behavior, or (if necessary) pointing out an inappropriate behavior—may be in order. Ideally, a verbal cue should focus students' attention

Simple body language can often lead to more productive and on-task behavior. While this teacher is temporarily preoccupied, her hand on a student's shoulder provides a subtle reminder that he should be attending to his schoolwork.

[71] W. Doyle, 1986a.

[72] G. A. Davis & Thomas, 1989; W. Doyle, 1986a, 2006; Munn et al., 1990; Silberman & Wheelan, 1980; Wynne, 1990.

[73] K. Carter & Doyle, 2006; W. Doyle, 1990; Emmer, 1987.

on what *should* be done rather than on what *isn't* being done.[74] Indirect requests are often effective for older students (e.g., "I see some art supplies that still need to be put away"). More explicit ones may be necessary for young children (e.g., "Table 3 needs to clean up its art supplies before it can go to lunch"). In the "Reading Group" video clip in MyEducationLab, a second-grade teacher cues one student first indirectly, and then more directly, to get her to join her reading group: "I called the Tigers. Someone wasn't listening. Sema, the Tigers were called."

Observe indirect and then more explicit cueing in the "Reading Group" video in the Additional Resources section in Chapter 9 of MyEducationLab.

Get students' perspectives about their behaviors.

Sometimes in-class signals are insufficient to change a student's misbehavior. Consider these misbehaviors:

- Alonzo is almost always several minutes late to your third-period algebra class. When he finally arrives, he takes an additional two or three minutes to pull his textbook and other class materials out of his backpack. You have often reminded him about the importance of coming to class on time, yet the tardiness continues.
- Trudy rarely completes classroom assignments. In fact, she often doesn't even *begin* them. On many occasions you have tried unsuccessfully to get her on task with explicit verbal cues (e.g., "Your book should be open to page 27," "Your cooperative group is brainstorming possible solutions to a difficult problem, and they could really use your ideas"). A few times, when you have looked Trudy in the eye and asked her point-blank to get to work, she has defiantly responded, "I'm not going to do it. You can't make me!"

In such situations talking privately with the student is the next logical step. The discussion should be a *private* one for several reasons.[75] First, as noted earlier, calling peers' attention to a problem behavior may actually reinforce the behavior rather than discourage it. Or, instead, the attention of classmates may cause a student to feel excessively embarrassed or humiliated—feelings that may make the student anxious and uncomfortable in the classroom. Finally, when a teacher spends too much class time dealing with a single misbehaving student, other students are apt to get off task.

Conversations with individual students give a teacher a chance to explain why certain behaviors are unacceptable and must stop. (Recall our discussion of *induction* in Chapter 7.) Furthermore, teacher–student conversations give students a chance to explain why they behave as they do. For instance, Alonzo might explain his chronic tardiness by revealing that he has diabetes and must check his blood sugar level between his second- and third-period classes. He can perform the procedure himself, but it takes a few minutes, and he would prefer to do it in the privacy of the nurse's office at the other end of the building. Meanwhile, Trudy might explain her refusals to do assigned work as the result of her frustration about not being able to read or understand the subject matter as well as her classmates do.

Students' explanations can sometimes provide clues about how best to deal with their behavior over the long run. For example, given his diabetes, Alonzo's continued tardiness to class may be inevitable. Instead, his teacher might reassign him to a seat by the door so he can join class unobtrusively when he arrives. Trudy's frustration with her schoolwork suggests that she needs additional scaffolding to help her succeed. It also hints at a possible undiagnosed learning disability that may warrant a referral to the school psychologist or other diagnostician. In some cases conversations with students may reveal maladaptive interpretations of social situations. For instance, a chronically aggressive student may express the inaccurate belief that classmates "are always trying to pick a fight" (recall our discussion of *hostile attributional bias* in Chapter 7). In this instance a teacher might consult with the school counselor about how to help the student interpret social interactions more productively.

Yet students won't always provide explanations that lead to such straightforward solutions. For example, it may be that Alonzo is late to class simply because he wants to spend a few extra minutes hanging out with his friends in the hall. Or perhaps Trudy says she doesn't

If cueing a misbehaving student is ineffective, a private conversation might be the best next step. From a motivational standpoint, how might private discussions with students be helpful?

[74] Emmer et al., 2000; Good & Brophy, 1994.

[75] W. Doyle, 2006; Emmer & Gerwels, 2006; Scott & Bushell, 1974.

want to do her assignments because she's "sick and tired" of other people telling her what to do all the time. In such circumstances it is essential that teachers not get in a power struggle— a situation where one person "wins" by dominating over the other in some way.[76] Several strategies can minimize the likelihood of a power struggle:[77]

- Speak in a calm, matter-of-fact manner, describing the problem as you see it. ("You haven't turned in a single assignment in the past three weeks. You and I would both like for you to do well in my class, but that can't happen unless we *both* work to make it happen.")
- Listen empathetically to what the student has to say, being openly accepting of the student's feelings and opinions. ("I get the impression that you don't enjoy classroom activities very much; I'd really like to hear what your concerns are.")
- Summarize what you think the student has told you, and seek clarification if necessary. ("It sounds as if you'd rather not let your classmates know how much trouble you're having with your schoolwork. Is that the problem, or is it something else?")
- Describe the effects of the problem behavior, including your own reactions to it. ("When you come to class late each day, I worry that you're getting further and further behind. Sometimes I even feel a little hurt that you don't seem to value your time in my classroom.")
- Give the student a choice from among two or more acceptable options. ("Would you rather try to work quietly at your group's table, or would it be easier if you sat somewhere by yourself to complete your work?")
- Especially when working with an adolescent, try to identify a solution that enables the student to maintain credibility in the eyes of peers. ("I suspect you might be worrying that your friends will think less of you if you comply with my request. What might we do to address this problem?")

Ultimately, a teacher must communicate interest in the student's long-term school achievement, concern that the misbehavior is interfering with that achievement, and commitment to working cooperatively with the student to resolve the problem.

Teach self-regulation strategies.

When students express their *own* concern about their problem behaviors, teaching self-regulation strategies can be helpful. Consider the following situations as examples:

- Bradley doesn't seem to be making much progress in his academic work. For instance, his performance on assignments and tests is usually rather low. As Bradley's teacher, you know he's capable of better work, because he occasionally turns in an assignment or test paper of exceptionally high quality. The root of Bradley's problem seems to be that he is off task most of the time. When he should be paying attention to a lesson or doing an assignment, he is instead sketching pictures of sports cars and airplanes, fiddling with whatever objects he has found on the floor, or daydreaming. Bradley would really like to improve his academic performance but doesn't seem to know how to do it.
- Georgia often talks without permission. She blurts out answers to your questions, preventing anyone else from answering them first. She rudely interrupts other students' comments with her own point of view. And she initiates conversations with classmates at the most inopportune times. On several occasions you speak with Georgia, and she always vows to exercise more self-control in the future. Her behavior improves for a day or so, but after that her mouth is off and running once again.

Bradley's off-task behavior interferes with his own learning, and Georgia's excessive chattiness interferes with the learning of her classmates. Cueing and private discussions haven't led to any improvement. But both Bradley and Georgia have something going for them: They *want* to change their behavior.

---

[76] S. C. Diamond, 1991; Emmer et al., 2000.
[77] Colvin, Ainge, & Nelson, 1997; Emmer et al., 2000; Keller & Tapasak, 2004; Lane, Falk, & Wehby, 2006.

In Chapter 4 we examined a variety of strategies for promoting self-regulated learning and behavior, and some of them might be valuable for Bradley and Georgia. *Self-monitoring* is especially useful when students need a reality check about the severity of a problem. For instance, Bradley may think he's on task far more often than he really is. To help him get a sense of how frequently he's *off* task, his teacher might give him a timer set to beep every 10 minutes and ask him to write down whether he has been on task each time he hears a beep. (Figure 9.5 shows the kind of recording sheet he might use.) Similarly, Georgia may not realize how frequently she prevents her classmates from speaking. To alert her to the extent of the problem, her teacher might ask her to make a check mark on a tally sheet every time she talks without permission. When students genuinely want to improve their behavior, problems such as Bradley's and Georgia's can often be successfully addressed through self-monitoring alone.[78]

If, by itself, self-monitoring doesn't do the trick, *self-instructions* might help Georgia gain some self-restraint in classroom discussions:

1. *Button* my lips (by holding them tightly together).
2. *Raise* my hand.
3. *Wait* until I'm called on.

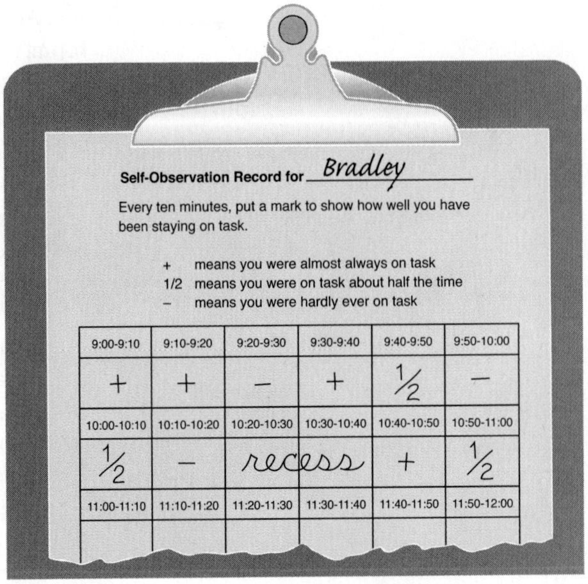

In addition, both students might use *self-imposed contingencies* to give themselves a motivational boost. For example, Bradley might award himself a point for each 10-minute period he's been on task. Georgia might give herself five points at the beginning of each school day and then *subtract* a point each time she speaks out of turn. By accumulating a certain number of points, the students could earn opportunities to engage in favorite activities.

Self-regulatory strategies have several advantages. They help teachers avoid power struggles with students about who's "in charge." They increase students' sense of self-determination and thus also increase students' intrinsic motivation to behave in productive ways in the classroom. Furthermore, self-regulation techniques benefit students over the long run, promoting productive behaviors that are apt to continue long after students have moved on from a particular classroom or school. And when students learn how to monitor and modify their own behavior, rather than depending on adults to do it for them, their teachers become free to do other things—for instance, to teach!

FIGURE 9.5 Example of a self-monitoring sheet for staying on task.

When administering punishment, use only those consequences that have been shown to be effective in reducing problem behaviors.

In a well-managed classroom, reinforcement for productive behavior occurs far more often than punishment for inappropriate behavior. But consider the following situations:

- Bonnie doesn't handle frustration very well. Whenever she encounters an obstacle she cannot immediately overcome, she responds by hitting, punching, or kicking something. On one occasion, during a class Valentine's Day party, she accidentally drops her cupcake upside-down on the floor. When she discovers that the cupcake is no longer edible, she throws her carton of milk across the room, hitting another child on the side of the head.
- Two days before a high school football game against a cross-town rival, several members of the football team are caught spray-painting obscene words on the bleachers of the rival school's stadium.

Some misbehaviors interfere significantly with classroom learning or reflect total disregard for other people's rights and welfare. These actions require an immediate remedy, and teachers or administrators must impose consequences sufficiently unpleasant to discourage them. In other words, educators must occasionally use *punishment*. Punishment is especially useful when students appear to have little motivation to change their behavior.

---

[78] Broden, Hall, & Mitts, 1971; DuPaul & Hoff, 1998; K. R. Harris, 1986; Mace, Belfiore, & Shea, 1989; Mace & Kratochwill, 1988.

As a general rule, teachers should use relatively mild forms of punishment in the classroom.[79] Severe punishment—for instance, something that lasts for several weeks or months, or something that seriously undermines students' sense of self-worth—can lead to such unwanted side effects as resentment, hostility, or truancy. Several forms of mild punishment are often effective in reducing undesirable classroom behaviors:

- **Verbal reprimands.** Although some students seem to thrive on teacher scolding because of the attention it brings, most students, especially if they are scolded only infrequently, find verbal reprimands to be unpleasant and punishing. In general, reprimands are more effective when they are immediate, brief, and unemotional. They also work better when they are given in a soft voice and in close proximity to the student, perhaps because they are less likely to be noticed and so less likely to draw the attention of classmates. Reprimands should be given in private whenever possible. When scolded in front of peers, some students may relish the attention it brings them, and others (e.g., many Native American and Hispanic students) may feel totally humiliated.[80]

- **Response cost.** The loss either of a previously earned reinforcer or of an opportunity to obtain reinforcement is known as **response cost**. A form of *removal punishment*, response cost is especially effective when used in combination with reinforcement of appropriate behavior.[81] For instance, when dealing with students who exhibit chronic behavior problems, teachers sometimes incorporate response cost into a point system or *token economy*, awarding points, check marks, plastic chips, or the like for good behavior (reinforcement) and taking away these things for inappropriate behavior (response cost). Students who accumulate a sufficient number of points or tokens can use them to "buy" objects, privileges, or enjoyable activities that are otherwise not available. (You may want to revisit the discussions of removal punishment and token economy in Chapter 3.)

- **Logical consequences.** Something that follows naturally or logically from a student's misbehavior, a **logical consequence** is a punishment that fits the crime. For example, if a student destroys a classmate's possession, a reasonable consequence is for the student to replace it or pay for a new one. If two close friends talk so much that they aren't completing assignments, a reasonable consequence is for them to be separated. If a student intentionally makes a mess in the cafeteria, an appropriate consequence is to clean it up.[82]

- **Time-out.** A misbehaving student given a **time-out** is placed in a dull, boring (but not scary) situation—perhaps a separate room designed especially for time-outs, a little-used office, or a remote corner of the classroom. A student in time-out has no opportunity to interact with classmates and no opportunity to obtain reinforcement. The length of the time-out is typically quite short (perhaps 2 to 10 minutes, depending on the student's age), but the student is not released until inappropriate behavior (e.g., swearing, kicking) has stopped. Keep in mind, however, that a time-out is apt to be effective only if ongoing classroom activities are a source of pleasure and reinforcement for a student. If, instead, it allows a student to escape difficult tasks or an overwhelming amount of noise and stimulation, it might actually be reinforcing and so *increase* undesirable behavior.[83]

- **In-school suspension.** Like time-out, **in-school suspension** involves placing a student in a quiet, boring room within the school building. However, it often lasts one or more school days and involves close adult supervision. Students receiving in-school suspension spend the day working on the same assignments that their nonsuspended peers do, enabling them to keep up with their schoolwork. But they have no opportunity for interaction with peers—an aspect of school that is

Some mild forms of punishment, such as brief time-outs, can reduce inappropriate behaviors, but teachers must monitor their effectiveness for different students.

response cost Loss either of a previously earned reinforcer or of an opportunity to obtain reinforcement.

logical consequence Unpleasant consequence that follows naturally or logically from a student's misbehavior.

time-out Form of punishment in which a student is placed in a dull, boring situation with no opportunity for reinforcement or social interaction.

in-school suspension Form of punishment in which a student is placed in a quiet, boring room within the school building, typically to do schoolwork under close adult supervision.

[79] Landrum & Kauffman, 2006.
[80] M. L. Fuller, 2001; Landrum & Kauffman, 2006; O'Leary, Kaufman, Kass, & Drabman, 1970; Pfiffner & O'Leary, 1993; Van Houten, Nau, MacKenzie-Keating, Sameoto, & Colavecchia, 1982.
[81] Conyers et al., 2004; Iwata & Bailey, 1974; Lentz, 1988; Rapport, Murphy, & Bailey, 1982.

[82] Dreikurs, 1998; Nucci, 2001; L. S. Wright, 1982.
[83] Alberto & Troutman, 2003; McClowry, 1998; Pfiffner & Barkley, 1998; Rortvedt & Miltenberger, 1994; A. G. White & Bailey, 1990.

reinforcing to most students. In-school suspension programs tend to be most effective when part of the suspension session is devoted to teaching appropriate behaviors and tutoring academic skills and when the supervising teacher acts as a supportive resource rather than as a punisher.[84]

Several other forms of punishment are typically *not* recommended. *Physical punishment* can, of course, lead to physical harm, and even mild forms (e.g., slapping a hand with a ruler) can lead to such undesirable behaviors as resentment of the teacher, inattention to school tasks, lying, aggression, vandalism, avoidance of school tasks, and truancy.[85] Any consequence that seriously threatens a student's sense of self-worth—*psychological punishment*—can lead to some of the same side effects as physical punishment (e.g., resentment of the teacher, inattention to school tasks, truancy from school) and may possibly inflict long-term psychological harm.[86] *Assigning extra classwork* beyond that required for other students is inappropriate if done simply to punish a student's wrongdoing, in that it communicates the message that "schoolwork is unpleasant."[87] Finally, *out-of-school suspension* is rarely an effective means of changing a student's behavior. For one thing, suspension from school may be exactly what a student wants, in which case inappropriate behaviors are being reinforced rather than punished. Second, because many students with chronic behavior problems also tend to do poorly in their schoolwork, suspension involves a loss of valuable instructional time and interferes with any psychological "attachment" to school, thereby decreasing even further the students' chances for academic and social success.[88]

Two additional forms of punishment get mixed reviews regarding their effectiveness. In some situations *missing recess* may be a logical consequence for students who fail to complete their schoolwork during regular class time due to off-task behavior. Yet research indicates that, especially at the elementary level, students can more effectively concentrate on school tasks if they have frequent breaks and opportunities to release pent-up energy.[89] And although *after-school detentions* are common practice at many schools, some students simply cannot stay after school hours, perhaps because they have transportation issues, must take care of younger siblings until parents get home from work, or are justifiably afraid to walk through certain neighborhoods after dark.[90]

A frequent criticism of punishment is that it is "inhumane," or somehow cruel and barbaric. Indeed, certain forms of punishment, such as physical abuse or public humiliation, do constitute inhumane treatment.[91] Furthermore, physical punishment is *illegal* in many states. Teachers must be *extremely careful* in their use of punishment in the classroom. But when administered judiciously—and especially when administered within the context of a warm, supportive teacher–student relationship—some consequences can lead to a rapid reduction in misbehavior without causing physical or psychological harm.[92] And when teachers can decrease counterproductive classroom behaviors quickly and effectively—especially when those behaviors are harmful to self or others—then punishment may, in fact, be one of the most humane approaches they can take.[93] The Classroom Strategies box "Using Punishment Humanely and Effectively" offers several guidelines for administering punishment in ways that will yield more productive student behavior over the long run.

Consult with parents.

Teachers may sometimes need to consult with students' parents or other primary caregivers about a behavior problem. Consider these situations:

- You give your students short homework assignments almost every night. Over the past three months, Carolyn has turned in only about a third of them. You're pretty

[84] Gootman, 1998; Huff, 1988; Pfiffner & Barkley, 1998; J. S. Sullivan, 1989.

[85] W. Doyle, 1990; Landrum & Kauffman, 2006; Nucci, 2006.

[86] Brendgen, Wanner, Vitaro, Bukowski, & Tremblay, 2007; G. A. Davis & Thomas, 1989; Hyman et al., 2004.

[87] Cooper, 1989; Corno, 1996.

[88] Fenning & Bohanon, 2006; Moles, 1990; Skiba & Rausch, 2006.

[89] Maxmell, Jarrett, & Dickerson, 1998; Pellegrini & Bohn, 2005; Pellegrini, Huberty, & Jones, 1995.

[90] Nichols, Ludwin, & Iadicola, 1999.

[91] For a good discussion of this point, see Hyman et al., 2004.

[92] Landrum & Kauffman, 2006; Nucci, 2001.

[93] Lerman & Vorndran, 2002.

CLASSROOM STRATEGIES

Using Punishment Humanely and Effectively

- **Inform students ahead of time that certain behaviors are unacceptable, and explain how those behaviors will be punished.**

  A third-grade teacher makes one rule for recess perfectly clear: *Students must not do anything that may hurt someone else.* He gives his class several concrete examples: throwing rocks, pulling hair, pushing someone off the slide, and so on. "If you do anything that might hurt another child," he says, "you will spend the next three recesses sitting on the bench outside the classroom door."

- **Help students understand why the punished behavior is unacceptable.**

  When several members of a high school football team are caught spray-painting obscenities on a rival school's bleachers, three consequences are imposed: (a) The students will not be able to play in the upcoming game against the rival school, (b) they must visit the rival school's principal to make a formal apology and acknowledge that their actions showed poor sportsmanship and disregard for other people's property, and (c) they must repaint the affected areas of the bleachers, purchasing the necessary paint with their own money.

- **Emphasize that it is the behavior—*not* the student—that is undesirable.**

  When a kindergartner angrily throws her carton of milk at a classmate, her teacher puts her in the "time-out corner" at the back of the room. "I like you a lot, Bonnie," the teacher tells her, "but I simply cannot have you doing something that might hurt Susan. I like her just as much as I like you, and I want both of you to feel safe in my classroom."

- **Administer punishment privately, especially when other students are not aware of the transgression.**

  As a junior high school teacher walks down the hall, she overhears a student tell two friends a "knock-knock" joke that includes an insulting racial slur, and the friends laugh uproariously. The teachers pulls the three students aside and explains that she heard the joke and found it quite offensive. "Whether you told the joke or merely laughed at it," she says, "you were all showing disrespect for certain teachers and students at this school. Not only does your disrespect undermine our overall sense of school community, but it also violates school policy. The consequence of such behavior is one day of in-school suspension. I'll notify the principal's office that you'll be reporting for in-school suspension tomorrow. Be sure to bring your textbooks and class assignments so that you won't get behind in your schoolwork."

- **Simultaneously teach and reinforce desirable alternative behaviors.**

  In small-group discussions and cooperative learning activities, a middle school student often belittles other students' ideas. Her teacher takes her aside and reprimands her but also teaches her productive strategies for disagreeing with classmates. "One strategy," he suggests, "is to say something *good* about another person's idea but then to suggest an alternative that the group might consider. For example, you might say, 'I like how carefully you've thought about the problem, Jerry. Here's a different perspective I'd like the group to think about as well. . . .'" Later, when the teacher hears the student using the strategy during a small-group project, he catches her eye and gives her a "thumbs-up" sign.

Sources: Landrum & Kauffman, 2006; Lerman & Vorndran, 2002; Moles, 1990; Nucci, 2001; Parke, 1974; D. G. Perry & Perry, 1983; Ruef, Higgins, Glaeser, & Patnode, 1998.

sure she's capable of doing the work, and you know from previous parent–teacher conferences that her parents give her the time and support she needs to get her assignments done. You've spoken with Carolyn about the situation on several occasions, but she shrugs you off as if she doesn't really care whether or not she does well in your class.

- Students have frequently found things missing from their tote trays or desks after Roger has been in the vicinity. A few students have told you they've seen Roger taking things that belong to others. Many of the missing objects have later turned up in Roger's possession. When you confront him about your suspicion that he's been stealing from classmates, he adamantly denies it. He says he has no idea how Cami's mittens or Marvin's baseball trading cards ended up in his desk.

Conferring with parents is especially important when students' behavior problems show a pattern over time and have serious implications for students' long-term academic or social success. In some cases a simple telephone call may be sufficient. For example, Carolyn's parents may be unaware that she hasn't been doing her homework (she's been telling them she doesn't have any) and may be able to take the steps necessary to ensure it gets done. In other instances a school conference may be more productive. For example, a teacher might want to discuss Roger's stealing habits with both Roger and his parent(s) together—something the teacher can do more effectively when everyone sits face-to-face in the same room.

Some ways of talking with parents are far more effective than others. Put yourself in a parent's shoes in the following exercise.

Putting Yourself in a Parent's Shoes

Imagine you're the parent of a seventh grader named Tommy. As you and Tommy are eating dinner one evening, the telephone rings. You get up to answer the phone.

You: Hello?

Ms. J.: Hi. This is Ms. Johnson, Tommy's teacher. May I talk with you for a few minutes?

You: Of course. What can I do for you?

Ms. J.: Well, I'm afraid I've been having some trouble with your son, and I thought you ought to know about it.

You: Really? What's the problem?

Ms. J.: Tommy hardly ever gets to class on time. When he does arrive, he spends most of his time talking with friends rather than paying attention to what I'm saying. It seems as if I have to speak to him three or four times every day about his behavior.

You: How long has all this been going on?

Ms. J.: For several weeks now. And the problem is getting worse rather than better. I'd really appreciate it if you'd talk with Tommy about the situation.

You: Well, thank you for letting me know about this, Ms. Johnson.

Ms. J.: You're most welcome. Good night.

You: Good night, Ms. Johnson.

Take a few minutes to jot down some of the things that, as a parent, you might be thinking after this telephone conversation.

You may have had a variety of reactions to your conversation with Ms. Johnson. Here are some possibilities:

- Why isn't Tommy taking his schoolwork more seriously?
- Isn't Tommy doing anything *right*?
- Has Ms. Johnson tried anything else besides reprimanding Tommy for his behavior? Or is she laying all of this on *my* shoulders?
- Tommy's a good kid. I should know, because I raised him. For some reason, Ms. Johnson doesn't like him, and so she'll find fault with *anything* he does.

Only the first of these four reactions is likely to lead to a productive response on your part.

Notice how Ms. Johnson focused strictly on the negative aspects of Tommy's classroom performance. As a result, you (as Tommy's parent) may possibly have felt anger toward your son or guilt about your ineffective parenting skills. Alternatively, you may have maintained your confidence in your son's scholastic abilities and in your own ability as a parent. If so, you may have begun to wonder about Ms. Johnson's ability to teach and motivate seventh graders. Sadly, too many teachers reach out to parents only to talk about students' weaknesses—never their strengths—as the following interview with Jamal illustrates:

Adult: Has your grandpa [Jamal's primary caregiver] come to school?

Jamal: Yup, when the teachers call him.

Adult: What did they call him for?

Jamal: The only time they call him is when I am being bad, the teacher will call him, he will come up here and have a meeting with the teacher.

Adult: If you are being good do the teachers call?

Jamal: No.[94]

Ideally, teacher–parent discussions about problem behaviors are initiated within the context of an ongoing relationship characterized by mutual trust and respect and a shared concern for students' learning and well-being. For instance, a phone call to parents is most likely to yield productive results if teacher and parents already have a good working relationship and

---

[94] Dialogue from Kumar et al., 2002, p. 164.

CLASSROOM STRATEGIES

Talking with Parents About Students' Misbehaviors

- **Consult with parents if a collaborative effort might bring about a behavior change.**

    At a parent–teacher conference, a high school math teacher expresses his concern that a student is not turning in her homework assignments. Her parents are surprised to hear this, saying, "Carolyn usually tells us that she doesn't *have* any homework." Together they work out a strategy for communicating about what assignments have been given and when they are due.

- **Tell parents about children's many strengths, even when communicating information about their shortcomings.**

    A teacher talks on the telephone with the father of one of her students. She describes several areas in which the student has made considerable progress and then asks for advice about strategies for helping him stay on task and be more conscientious about his work.

- **Don't place blame; instead, acknowledge that raising children is rarely easy.**

    When talking with the mother of a middle school student, a teacher mentions that the student seems to be more interested in talking with her friends than in getting her schoolwork done. The mother says she has encountered a similar problem at home: "Marnie's always been a much more social girl than I ever was. It's like pulling teeth just getting her off the telephone to do her homework, and then we end up having a shouting match that gets us nowhere!" The teacher sympathetically responds, "Students seem to become especially concerned about social matters once they reach adolescence. How about if you, Marnie, and I meet some day after school to talk about the problem? Perhaps by working together the three of us can find a way to solve it."

- **Ask for information, and be a good listener.**

    When a teacher finds that a student has regularly been taking items from classmates' tote trays, she sets up an appointment to meet with the student and his grandmother (the student's primary caregiver). "I like Roger a lot," she says. "He has a great sense of humor, and his smile often lights up my day. I can't understand why he might want to 'borrow' items from other children without asking them first. His actions have cost him several friendships. Do either of you have any ideas about how we might tackle the problem? I'd like to do whatever I can to help Roger repair his reputation in the eyes of his classmates."

- **Agree on a strategy.**

    While reviewing a student's academic progress at a parent–teacher conference, an elementary teacher says, "Mark has a tendency to fiddle with things at his desk—for example, twisting paperclips, playing with rubber bands, or making paper airplanes—when he should be getting his work done. As a result, he often doesn't complete his assignments." "I've noticed the same thing when he works on his homework," the student's father replies, "but I bring a lot of paperwork home from the office every night and don't have time to constantly hound him to stay on task." The teacher and father talk more about the problem and agree that reinforcement for completed assignments might be helpful. Mark will earn points for high scores that will help him "buy" the new bicycle he's been asking his father for.

Sources: Christenson & Sheridan, 2001; Emmer et al., 2000; Evertson et al., 2000.

if the teacher is confident that parents won't overreact with harsh, excessive punishment of their child. Furthermore, when communicating with parents, teachers' overall messages about students should be positive and optimistic. For instance, a teacher might couch negative aspects of a student's classroom performance within the context of the many things the student does *well*. (Rather than starting out by complaining about Tommy's behavior, Ms. Johnson might have begun by saying that Tommy is a bright and capable young man with many friends and a good sense of humor.) And teachers must be clear about their commitment to working *together* with parents to help a student succeed in the classroom. The Classroom Strategies box "Talking with Parents About Students' Misbehaviors" presents several strategies for working effectively with parents and other primary caregivers.

Teachers must recognize, too, that different cultures have different perspectives on how best to address behavior problems (see the Cultural Considerations box "Cultural Differences in Parental Discipline"). Ultimately, teachers and parents must try to find common ground on which to develop strategies for helping children and adolescents thrive at school.[95] At the same time, teachers must tactfully and sensitively help parents understand that certain consequences—for instance, severe physical and psychological punishments—are unlikely to be productive over the long run.

To address a chronic problem, plan and carry out a systematic intervention.

Sometimes problem behaviors are so disruptive and persistent that they require a systematic effort to change them. Consider these situations:

- Tucker is out of his chair so often that at times you have to wonder whether he knows where his chair *is*. He finds many reasons to roam about the room—he "has to"

---

[95] Good & Nichols, 2001; Salend & Taylor, 1993.

sharpen a pencil, "has to" get his homework out of his backpack, "has to" get a drink of water, and so on. Naturally, Tucker gets very little work done, and his classmates are continually distracted by his perpetual motion.
- Janet's verbal abusiveness is getting out of hand. She regularly insults her classmates by using sexually explicit language, and she frequently likens you to an X-rated body part. You have tried praising her on occasions when she's pleasant to others, and she seems to appreciate your doing so, yet her abusive remarks continue.

Imagine that both Tucker and Janet are in your class. You've already spoken with each of them about their unacceptable behavior, yet you've seen no improvement. You've suggested methods of self-regulation, but neither student seems interested in changing for the better. You've tried putting them in time-out for their actions, but Janet seems to appreciate the time away from her schoolwork, and Tucker sometimes has a valid reason for getting out of his seat. Although both students' parents are aware of and concerned about their children's classroom behaviors, their efforts at home haven't had an impact. And after all, these are largely *school* problems rather than home problems. So what do you do now?

When a serious misbehavior persists despite ongoing efforts to curtail it, a more intensive intervention is in order. Some interventions, known by such labels as **applied behavior analysis**, *behavior therapy*, or *contingency management*, focus on changing stimulus conditions and response-consequence contingencies in a student's environment.[96] These approaches are based largely on principles presented in Chapter 3:

- Some stimuli tend to elicit certain kinds of behaviors.
- Learners are more likely to acquire behaviors that lead to desired consequences.
- Learners tend to steer clear of behaviors that lead to unpleasant consequences.

With these principles in mind, effective teachers change the classroom environment to elicit more productive behaviors and establish more beneficial response-consequence contingencies. Thus they are apt to use strategies such as these:

- Identify problem behaviors and desired behaviors in explicit (and ideally measurable) terms. Often the desired behaviors identified are incompatible with problem behaviors.
- Identify reinforcers, punishments, or both that are truly effective for the student.
- Develop a specific intervention plan. The plan may involve reinforcement of desired behaviors, shaping, extinction, reinforcement of incompatible behaviors, punishment, or some combination of these.
- Modify the classroom environment to minimize conditions that might trigger inappropriate behaviors.
- Collect data on the frequency of problem behaviors and desired behaviors both before and during the intervention.
- Monitor the program's effectiveness by observing how various behaviors change over time, and modify the program if necessary.
- Take steps to promote transfer of newly acquired behaviors (e.g., by having the student practice the behaviors in a variety of realistic situations).
- Gradually phase out the intervention (e.g., through intermittent reinforcement) after the desired behaviors are acquired.

Often the strategies just listed are more effective when cognitive and motivational factors affecting students' behavior are also addressed—an approach known as *cognitive behavioral therapy*. For example, teachers might also use one or more of the following strategies:

- Teach self-regulation skills.
- Teach effective social skills.
- Encourage better perspective taking and other aspects of social cognition.
- Make adaptations in the curriculum, instructional methods, or both to maximize the likelihood of academic success and self-efficacy.

---

[96] For examples of such strategies, see Alberto & Troutman, 2003; S. N. Elliott & Busse, 1991; E. McNamara, 1987; O'Leary & O'Leary, 1972; Ormrod, 2008.

applied behavior analysis (ABA) Systematic application of stimulus–response principles to address a chronic behavior problem.

CULTURAL CONSIDERATIONS

Cultural Differences in Parental Discipline

The vast majority of parents want what's best for their children and recognize the value of a good education for children's long-term success.[a] Yet parents from different cultural and ethnic groups sometimes have radically different ideas about what behaviors are problematic. As an example, let's return to the See for Yourself exercise titled "Jack" in Chapter 3 (p. 92). Jack, a Native American seventh grader, had been absent from school for an entire week. Not only were his parents seemingly unconcerned, but they didn't even go looking for him until they needed him at home to help with the family farm. Their attitudes and actions make sense only when we understand that they knew their son was probably safe with neighbors and believed that, as a young adolescent, Jack was essentially an adult and responsible for his own decisions.[b] In contrast, many parents from Asian cultures expect children to defer to and obey adult authority figures (e.g., parents and teachers) and think that Western teachers are much too lenient with students.[c]

Disciplinary strategies also differ from culture to culture. In mainstream Western culture, praise is widely used as a strategy for encouraging good behavior, and reprimands and denial of privileges (e.g., "grounding") are often the consequences for unacceptable behavior. But such practices are hardly universal. Children in some cultures may be unaccustomed to direct praise for appropriate behavior and personal successes, perhaps because appropriate behavior is a social obligation (and so not praiseworthy) or perhaps because adults express approval in other ways—for instance, by telling other people how skillful a child is.[d] And in other cultures (e.g., in Haiti), reprimands are often used to com-

How might a teacher use some of the preceding strategies to improve Tucker's classroom behavior? One approach would be to identify one or more effective reinforcers (given Tucker's constant fidgeting, opportunities for physical activity might be reinforcing) and then gradually shape more sedentary behavior. Because some out-of-seat responses (e.g., getting a reference book from the bookshelf, delivering a completed assignment to the teacher's "In" basket) are quite appropriate, the teacher might also give Tucker a reasonable allotment of out-of-seat "tickets" he can use during the day. In addition, Tucker can probably benefit from instruction and scaffolding regarding general organizational skills—in particular, assembling necessary supplies (notebooks, sharpened pencils, completed homework, etc.) before lessons begin.

A systematic intervention may be helpful with Janet as well. In this case we might suspect that Janet has learned few social skills with which she can interact effectively with others. Her teacher or a school counselor might therefore need to begin by teaching her such skills through modeling, role playing, and so on (see Chapter 7). After Janet acquires effective interpersonal skills, her teacher can begin to reinforce her for using those skills. (Praise might be an effective reinforcer, as she has responded positively to praise in the past.) Meanwhile, the teacher should also punish (perhaps with a time-out) any relapses into old, abusive behavior patterns.

Determine whether certain undesirable behaviors might serve particular purposes for students.

Sometimes a student's misbehaviors, although maladaptive from a teacher's perspective, in one way or another help the student preserve a sense of well-being. As an example, consider 9-year-old Samantha:

> Samantha has been identified as having a mild form of autism and moderate speech disabilities. Consistent with the Individuals with Disabilities Education Act (IDEA) described in Chapter 3, she is a full-fledged member of a third-grade class. However, she frequently runs out of the classroom, damaging school property and classmates' belongings in her flight. When a teacher or other adult tries to intervene, she fights back by biting, hitting, kicking, or pulling hair. On such occasions school personnel often call her parents and ask that they come to take her home.

municate concern and affection.[e] For example, on one occasion a Haitian teacher was reprimanding her students for proceeding across a parking lot without her. The following conversation ensued:

Teacher: Did I tell you to go?
Children: No.
Teacher: Can you cross this parking lot by yourselves?
Children: No.
Teacher: That's right. There are cars here. They're dangerous. I don't want you to go alone. Why do I want you to wait for me, do you know?
Child: Yes . . . because you like us.[f]

In certain other cultures (including some Native American and Asian groups), ostracism is a common disciplinary strategy. If a child's misbehaviors are seen as bringing shame on the family or community, the child is ignored for an extended time period.[g]

It is important to note that some cultural groups believe physical punishment to be necessary for behavioral transgressions. When physical punishment is a common form of discipline in one's culture, children are more likely to accept *mild* physical punishment as appropriate and deserved. Even in such contexts, however, physical punishment is apt to have adverse effects on children's psychological well-being.[h] Accordingly, teachers should

dissuade parents from using it, ideally by suggesting alternative consequences that can effectively reduce problem behaviors without causing harm.

[a] Gallimore & Goldenberg, 2001; Hidalgo, Siu, Bright, Swap, & Epstein, 1995; Okagaki, 2001; Spera, 2005.
[b] Deyhle & LeCompte, 1999.
[c] Chao, 1994; Dien, 1998; Hidalgo et al., 1995; Kağitçibaşi, 2007; Tudge et al., 1999.
[d] Greenfield et al., 2006; Kitayama, Duffy, & Uchida, 2007; Rogoff, 2003.
[e] Ballenger, 1992, 1999.
[f] Ballenger, 1992, p. 205.
[g] Pang, 1995; Salend & Taylor, 1993.
[h] Lansford et al., 2005; Lansford, Deater-Decker, & Dodge, Bates, & Pettit, 2003.

A multidisciplinary team of teachers and specialists, which has been working with Samantha and systematically observing her classroom performance, discovers that her aggressive and destructive behaviors typically occur when she is given a difficult assignment or is expecting such an assignment. Noisy or chaotic events, departures from the routine schedule, and the absences of favorite teachers further increase the probability of inappropriate behaviors.

The team hypothesizes that Samantha's undesirable behaviors serve two purposes: They (a) help her avoid overwhelming situations or unpleasant tasks and (b) enable her to gain the attention of valued adults. The team suspects, too, that Samantha feels as if she has little or no control over classroom activities and that she yearns for more social interaction with her teachers and classmates.[97]

In trying to determine why Samantha misbehaves as she does, the multidisciplinary team is taking an approach known as **functional analysis**. That is, the team identifies the specific stimulus conditions that exist both before and after Samantha makes inappropriate responses—the antecedents and consequences of particular behaviors—like so:

Antecedent → Behavior → Consequence

The team soon realizes that Samantha's behaviors are the result of *both* antecedent events (challenging tasks and changes in routine) and desirable consequences (getting attention, going home). In other words, Samantha's behaviors are serving certain *functions* for her: They get her attention from others (positive reinforcement) and enable her to escape things she doesn't want to do and places she doesn't want to be (such escape is negative reinforcement). Like Samantha, students with chronic behavior problems often misbehave when they are asked to do difficult or unpleasant tasks and when their misbehavior either helps them avoid those tasks or gains the attention of their teacher or peers.[98]

Once a functional analysis has been completed, an approach known as **positive behavioral support (PBS)** takes the process a step further. In particular, PBS builds on knowledge

functional analysis Examination of inappropriate behavior and its antecedents and consequences to determine one or more purposes (functions) that the behavior might serve for the learner.

positive behavioral support (PBS) Systematic intervention that addresses chronic misbehaviors by (a) identifying the purposes those behaviors might serve for a student and (b) providing more appropriate ways for a student to achieve the same ends.

[97] DeVault, Krug, & Fake, 1996.
[98] K. M. Jones, Drew, & Weber, 2000; McComas, Thompson, & Johnson, 2003; McKerchar & Thompson, 2004; K. A. Meyer, 1999; Van Camp et al., 2000.

Misbehaviors often help students satisfy certain needs or achieve certain goals. In such situations a teacher may want to identify and encourage alternative behaviors that will enable students to accomplish the same ends.

about the functions of misbehaviors to encourage more productive behaviors. Following are typical strategies:[99]

- Teach behaviors that can serve the same purpose as—and can therefore replace—inappropriate behaviors.
- Modify the classroom environment to minimize conditions that might trigger inappropriate behaviors.
- Establish a predictable daily routine as a way of minimizing anxiety and making the student feel more comfortable and secure.
- Give the student opportunities to make choices; in this way, the student can often gain desired outcomes without having to resort to inappropriate behavior.
- Make adaptations in the curriculum, instruction, or both to maximize the likelihood of academic success (e.g., build on the student's interests, present material at a slower pace, or intersperse challenging tasks among easier and more enjoyable ones).
- Monitor the frequency of various behaviors to determine whether the intervention is working or, instead, requires modification.

For instance, after Samantha's multidisciplinary team has formed reasonable hypotheses regarding the roots of her inappropriate behaviors, it takes several steps to help her acquire more productive ones:[100]

- Samantha is given a consistent and predictable daily schedule that includes frequent breaks from potentially challenging academic tasks and numerous opportunities to interact with others.
- Samantha is given "goal sheets" from which she can choose the academic tasks she will work on, the length of time she will work on them, and a reward she will receive for achieving each goal.
- Samantha is taught how to ask for assistance when she needs it—a strategy she can use instead of fleeing from the classroom in the face of a challenging task.
- When Samantha feels she needs a break from academic tasks, she can ask to spend time in the "relaxation room," a quiet and private space where she can sit in a beanbag chair and listen to soothing audiotapes.
- If Samantha tries to leave the classroom, an adult places her immediately in the relaxation room, where she can calm down without a great deal of adult attention.
- Samantha is given explicit instruction in how to interact appropriately with classmates. Initially, she earns points for appropriate social behaviors and can trade them for special treats (e.g., a family trip to Dairy Queen or a video store). Eventually, her new social skills lead to natural consequences—friendly interactions with peers—that make extrinsic reinforcers unnecessary.

Samantha's teachers and parents communicate regularly to coordinate their efforts. Samantha's problem behaviors don't disappear overnight, but they show a dramatic decline over the next several months. By the time Samantha is 12 years old and in sixth grade, her grades consistently earn her a place on the honor roll, and she has a group of friends with whom she participates in several extracurricular activities. Her teachers describe her as sociable, inquisitive, and creative. Her principal calls her a "model student."[101]

Let's return once again to Ms. Cornell's difficulties with Eli, Jake, and Vanessa in the opening case study. Here, too, a planned, systematic intervention, possibly including functional analysis and positive behavioral support, may be in order. Reinforcing appropriate behaviors (if necessary, shaping such behaviors over a period of time) and punishing inappropriate behaviors are two obvious strategies. Furthermore, Ms. Cornell should make response-consequence contingencies clear, perhaps by using contingency contracts (see Chapter 3). Ms. Cornell might also determine the purpose(s) that the students' misbehaviors serve (e.g., perhaps the three students crave attention, or perhaps they misbehave to avoid doing assignments for which they do not have adequate reading skills) and then either (a) identify more pro-

[99] Crone & Horner, 2003; Koegel et al., 1996; Ruef, Higgins, Glaeser, & Patnode, 1998.

[100] DeVault et al., 1996.

[101] DeVault et al., 1996

ductive behaviors that can serve the same purpose(s) or (b) address academic or social problems that may be directly or indirectly contributing to the students' unproductive behaviors.

Occasionally chronic behavior problems involve not just a handful of students but an entire *school*, or at least a large subpopulation of a school's students (recall the opening case study "The School Play" in Chapter 7). Perhaps most troubling is the prevalence of aggression and violence at some schools. Teachers play a key role in—and can also be highly effective in—addressing widespread aggression and violence. In the final section of the chapter, we look at some strategies for doing so.

ADDRESSING AGGRESSION AND VIOLENCE AT SCHOOL

In recent years the news media have focused considerable attention on violent school crime, and especially on school shootings, leading many people to believe that aggression in schools is on the rise. In reality, *violent* aggression involving serious injury or death is relatively rare on school grounds and, in the United States at least, has *declined* over the past 10 to 15 years.[102] Most aggression at school involves psychological harm, minor physical injury, or destruction of property. For instance, it might involve sexual or racial harassment, bullying, or vandalizing of student lockers.[103]

If we consider only violent aggression (that which causes serious injury or death), then school is probably the safest place that young people can be.[104] But if we consider *all* forms of aggression (mild as well as severe), then aggression among children and adolescents occurs more frequently at school—especially in areas where adult supervision is minimal (e.g., hallways, restrooms, parking lots)—than at any other location in youngster's daily lives.[105] The relative prevalence of aggression at school is almost certainly due to two factors. First, youngsters spend a great deal of time at school, more so than in any other place except home. Second, the sheer number of students attending even the smallest of schools makes some interpersonal conflict almost inevitable.

The roots of school aggression and violence are many and diverse. As we discovered in Chapter 7, a variety of cognitive factors (lack of perspective-taking, misinterpretation of social cues, poor social problem-solving skills, etc.) predispose some students to aggressive behavior. Furthermore, perhaps because of the home or neighborhood environment in which they live, some students believe that aggression is an appropriate and effective way to resolve conflicts. Developmental factors come into play as well. For instance, many young children and a few adolescents have poor impulse control. And during the unsettling transition to middle school, students who worry about fitting in may bully weaker age-mates as a way of maintaining or gaining social status.[106] The school culture is also involved. For instance, at some high schools it is acceptable practice to threaten or fight with a peer who tries to steal one's boyfriend or girlfriend.[107] Finally, aggression is a common reaction to frustration, and some students are repeatedly frustrated in their efforts to be academically and socially successful at school.[108]

Regardless of the roots of the behavior, educators must obviously not tolerate *any* form of aggression or violence on school grounds. Students can learn and achieve at optimal levels only if they know they are both physically and psychologically safe at school. Furthermore, if they *don't* feel safe, they're at increased risk for dropping out before high school graduation.[109] To be truly effective in combating aggression and violence, teachers and other school faculty members must attack it on three levels, depicted graphically in Figure 9.6.[110] The first three of the following

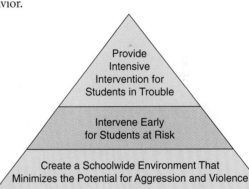

FIGURE 9.6 A three-level approach to preventing aggression and violence in schools

Based on a figure in *Safeguarding Our Children: An Action Guide* (p. 3), by K. Dwyer and D. Osher, 2000, Washington, DC: U.S. Departments of Education and Justice, American Institutes for Research.

[102] DeVoe et al., 2003; DeVoe, Peter, Noonan, Snyder, & Baum, 2005.

[103] Bender, 2001; Casella, 2001b; Pellegrini, 2002.

[104] Burstyn & Stevens, 2001; DeVoe et al., 2003; Garbarino, Bradshaw, & Vorrasi, 2002.

[105] Astor, Meyer, & Behre, 1999; Casella, 2001b; Finkelhor & Ormrod, 2000.

[106] Bronson, 2000; Espelage, Holt, & Henkel, 2003; Pellegrini, 2002.

[107] K. M. Williams, 2001a, 2001b.

[108] Bender, 2001; Casella, 2001b; Miles & Stipek, 2006.

[109] Rumberger, 1995.

[110] Dwyer & Osher, 2000; Hyman et al., 2004; T. J. Lewis et al., 2006; H. M. Walker et al., 1996. For a more in-depth discussion of the three levels, I urge you to read Dwyer and Osher's (2000) monograph *Safeguarding Our Children: An Action Guide*. This monograph is in the public domain and thus available for widespread use and duplication. You can download a copy through a variety of Internet Web pages, such as www.ed.gov/admins/lead/safety/actguide/index.html or www.air.org/cecp/guide/actionguide.htm

four recommendations reflect these three levels; the final one specifically addresses aggression that can result from hostilities among rival gangs on school grounds.

Make the creation of a nonviolent school environment a long-term effort.

One-shot "antiviolence" campaigns have little lasting effect on school aggression and violence.[111] Instead, creating a peaceful, nonviolent school environment must be a long-term effort that includes the following:[112]

- Schoolwide commitment to supporting *all* students' academic and social success
- A challenging and engaging curriculum
- Caring, trusting faculty–student relationships
- Genuine and equal respect—among students as well as faculty—for students of diverse backgrounds, races, and ethnicities
- Emphasis on prosocial behaviors (e.g., sharing, helping, cooperation)
- Schoolwide policies and practices that foster appropriate behavior (e.g., clear guidelines for behavior, consistently applied consequences for infractions, instruction in effective social interaction and problem-solving skills)
- Close working relationships with community agencies and families
- Student participation in school decision making
- Mechanisms through which students can communicate their concerns openly and without fear of reprisal
- Open discussion of safety issues

Most of these strategies should look familiar, because they've surfaced at various places throughout the book. The final strategy—an open discussion of safety issues—encompasses a number of more specific strategies. For example, teachers should explain what bullying is and why it is unacceptable (see Chapter 7). Faculty members might also solicit students' input on potentially unsafe areas (perhaps an infrequently used restroom or back stairwell) that require more adult supervision. And a willingness to listen to students' complaints about troublesome classmates can provide important clues about which children and adolescents are most in need of assistance and intervention.

Intervene early for students at risk.

In our earlier discussion of students at risk in Chapter 7, we focused largely on students at risk for *academic* failure. Yet students can be at risk for *social* failure as well. For instance, they may have few if any friends, be overtly bullied or rejected by many of their peers, or in other ways find themselves excluded from the overall social life of the school.[113]

Perhaps 10 to 15 percent of students will need some sort of intervention to help them interact effectively with peers, establish good working relationships with teachers, and become bona fide members of the school community.[114] Such intervention cannot be a one-size-fits-all approach but must instead be tailored to students' particular strengths and needs. For some students it might take the form of social skills training. In other cases it might mean getting students actively involved in school clubs or extracurricular activities. In still others it may require ongoing, systematic efforts to encourage and reinforce productive behaviors, perhaps through functional analysis and positive behavioral support. But regardless of their nature, interventions are more effective when they occur *early* in the game—before students go too far down the path of antisocial behavior—and when they are developed by a multidisciplinary team of teachers and other professionals who bring various areas of expertise to the planning table.[115]

---

[111] Burstyn & Stevens, 2001.

[112] Burstyn & Stevens, 2001; Dwyer & Osher, 2000; Dwyer, Osher, & Warger, 1998; Learning First Alliance, 2001; Meehan, Hughes, & Cavell, 2003; G. M. Morrison, Furlong, D'Incau, & Morrison, 2004; Pellegrini, 2002.

[113] For instance, see Bender, 2001.

[114] Dwyer & Osher, 2000; H. M. Walker et al., 1996.

[115] Dryfoos, 1997; Dwyer & Osher, 2000.

FIGURE 9.7   Early warning signs of violent behavior

Experts have identified numerous warning signs that a student may possibly be contemplating violent actions against others. Any one of them alone is unlikely to signal a violent attack, but several of them *in combination* should lead a teacher to consult with school administrators and specially trained professionals about the student(s) of concern.

Social withdrawal. Over time, a student interacts less and less frequently with teachers and with all or most peers.

Excessive feelings of isolation, rejection, or persecution. A student may directly or indirectly express the belief that he or she is friendless, disliked, or unfairly "picked on."

Rapid decline in academic performance. A student shows a dramatic change in academic performance and seems unconcerned about doing well. Cognitive and physical factors (e.g., learning disabilities, ineffective study skills, brain injury) have been ruled out as the cause of the decline.

Poor coping skills. A student has little ability to deal effectively with frustration, takes the smallest affront personally, and has trouble "bouncing back" after minor disappointments.

Lack of anger control. A student frequently responds with uncontrolled anger to even the slightest injustice and may misdirect anger at innocent bystanders.

Sense of superiority, self-centeredness, and lack of empathy. A student depicts himself or herself as "smarter" or in some way better than peers, is preoccupied with his or her own needs, and has little regard for the needs of others.

Lengthy grudges. A student is unforgiving of others' transgressions, even after considerable time has elapsed.

Violent themes in drawings and written work. Violence predominates in a student's artwork, stories, and journal entries, and perhaps certain individuals (e.g., a parent or particular classmate) are regularly targeted in these fantasies. (Keep in mind that *occasional* violence in writing and art is not unusual, especially for boys.)

Intolerance of individual and group differences. A student shows intense disdain and prejudice toward people of a certain race, ethnicity, gender, sexual orientation, religion, or disability.

History of violence, aggression, and other discipline problems. A student has a long record of seriously inappropriate behavior extending over several years.

Association with violent peers. A student associates regularly with a gang or other antisocial peer group.

Inappropriate role models. A student may speak with admiration about Satan, Hitler, Osama bin Laden, or some other malevolent figure.

Excessive alcohol or drug use. A student who abuses alcohol or drugs may have reduced self-control. In some cases substance abuse signals significant mental illness.

Inappropriate access to firearms. A student has easy access to guns and ammunition and may regularly practice using them.

Threats of violence. A student has openly expressed an intent to harm someone else. *This warning sign alone requires immediate action.*

Sources: Dwyer et al., 1998; O'Toole, 2000; M. W. Watson, Andreas, Fischer, & Smith, 2005.

Provide intensive intervention for students in trouble.

For a variety of reasons, minor interventions are not always sufficient when students are predisposed to be aggressive and violent. For instance, some students have serious mental illnesses that interfere with their ability to think rationally, cope appropriately with every-day frustrations, and control impulses. Typically, schools must work closely and collaboratively with other community agencies—perhaps mental health clinics, police and probation departments, and social services—to help students at high risk for aggression and violence.[116] Teachers are a vital component of this collaborative effort, offering insights about students' strengths and weaknesses, communicating with students' families about available services, and working with specialists to develop appropriate intervention strategies.

Teachers' frequent interactions with students also put them in an ideal position to identify those children and adolescents most in need of intensive intervention to get them back on track for academic and social success. Especially after working with a particular age-group for a period of time, teachers acquire a good sense of what characteristics are and are not normal for that age level. Teachers should also be on the lookout for the early warning signs of violence presented in Figure 9.7.

Although teachers must be ever vigilant about indicators that a student may be planning to cause harm to others, it is essential that they keep several points in mind. First, as I mentioned earlier, extreme violence is *very rare* in schools. Unreasonable paranoia about potential school violence will prevent a teacher from working effectively with students.

---

[116] Dwyer & Osher, 2000; Greenberg et al., 2003; Hyman et al., 2004.

Second, the great majority of students who exhibit one or a few of the warning signs in Figure 9.7 will *not* become violent. And most importantly, a teacher must *never* use the warning signs as a reason to unfairly accuse, isolate, or punish a student.[117] These signs provide a means of getting students the help they may need, not of excluding them from the education that all children and adolescents deserve.

Take additional measures to address gang violence.

A frequent source of aggression at some schools is gang-related hostilities. Although gangs are more prevalent in low-income, inner-city schools, they are sometimes found in suburban and rural schools as well.[118]

The three-level approach to combating school aggression and violence just described can go a long way toward suppressing violent gang activities, but school personnel often need to take additional measures as well. Recommended strategies include the following:[119]

- Develop, communicate, and enforce clear-cut policies regarding potential threats to school safety.
- Identify the specific nature and scope of gang activity in the student population.
- Forbid clothing, jewelry, and behaviors that signify membership in a particular gang (e.g., bandanas, shoelaces in gang colors, certain hand signs).[120]
- Actively mediate between-gang and within-gang disputes.

A case study at one middle school[121] illustrates just how effective the last of these strategies—mediation—can sometimes be in addressing gang-related aggression. Many students belonged to one of several gangs that seemed to "rule the school." Fights among rival gangs were common, and nongang members were frequent victims of harassment. Dress codes, counseling, and suspensions of chronic trouble makers had little impact on students' behavior. In desperation, two school counselors suggested that the school implement a peer mediation program, beginning with three large gangs that were responsible for most of the trouble. Interpersonal problems involving two or more gangs would be brought to a mediation team, comprised of five school faculty members and three representatives from each of the three gangs. Team members had to abide by the following rules:

1. Really try to solve the problem.
2. No name-calling or put-downs.
3. No interrupting.
4. Be as honest as possible.
5. No weapons or acts of intimidation.
6. All sessions to be confidential until an agreement is reached or mediation is called off.[122]

To lay the groundwork for productive discussions, faculty members of the mediation team met separately with each of the three gangs to establish feelings of rapport and trust, explain how the mediation process would work, and gain students' cooperation with the plan.

In the first mediation session, common grievances were aired. Students agreed that they didn't like being put down or intimated, that they worried about their physical safety, and that they all wanted one another's respect. In several additional meetings during the next two weeks, the team reached agreement that a number of behaviors would be unacceptable at school: There would be no put-downs, name calling, hateful stares, threats, shoving, or gang graffiti. After the final meeting, each gang was separately called into the conference

---

[117] Dwyer et al., 1998.

[118] Howell & Lynch, 2000; Kodluboy, 2004.

[119] Kodluboy, 2004.

[120] A potential problem with this strategy is that it may violate students' civil liberties. For guidance on how to walk the line between ensuring students' safety and giving them reasonable freedom of expression, see Kodluboy, 2004; Rozalski & Yell, 2004.

[121] Sanchez & Anderson, 1990.

[122] Sanchez & Anderson, 1990, p. 54.

room. Its representatives on the mediation team explained the agreement, and other members of the gang were asked to sign it. Despite some skepticism, most members of all three gangs signed the agreement.

A month later, it was clear that the process had been successful. Members of rival gangs nodded pleasantly to one another or gave one another a "high five" sign as they passed in the hall. Gang members no longer felt compelled to hang out in groups for safety's sake. Members of two of the gangs were seen playing soccer together one afternoon. And there had been no gang-related fights all month.

As should be apparent from our discussion in this chapter, helping growing children and adolescents develop into successful, productive adults can occasionally be quite a challenge. But in my own experience, discovering that you actually *can* make a difference in students' lives—including the lives of some who are at risk for academic or social failure—is one of the most rewarding aspects of being a teacher.

SUMMARY

Effective teachers create a classroom in which students are consistently engaged in planned tasks and activities and in which few student behaviors interfere with those tasks and activities. The physical arrangement of the classroom makes a difference, but more important is a psychological environment, or *classroom climate*, in which students feel safe and secure, make learning a high priority, and are willing to take risks and make mistakes. Central to such a climate are (a) teacher–student relationships that communicate genuine caring and concern for every student and (b) an overall sense of community in the classroom—a sense that teachers and students have shared goals, are mutually respectful and supportive of one another's efforts, and believe that everyone makes an important contribution to classroom learning. At the same time, teachers must "take charge" to some extent, establishing rules and planning age-appropriate activities to ensure that students are continually working toward instructional goals and objectives.

Effective teachers work cooperatively with other faculty members, other institutions, and parents to promote students' learning, development, and achievement. It is especially important that teachers stay in regular contact with parents, sharing information in both directions about the progress that students are making and coordinating efforts at school with those on the home front. Teachers may need to make an extra effort to establish productive working relationships with those parents who, on the surface, seem reluctant to become involved in their children's education.

Despite teachers' best efforts, children and adolescents sometimes engage in behaviors that disrupt classroom learning, put one or more students' physical safety or psychological well-being in jeopardy, or violate basic moral and ethical standards. Some minor misbehaviors are usually best ignored, including those that probably won't be repeated, those that are unlikely to be imitated by other students, and those that occur only temporarily and within the context of unusual circumstances. Other minor infractions can be dealt with simply and quickly by cueing students or by talking with them privately about their counterproductive behaviors. More serious and chronic behavior problems may require instruction in self-regulation strategies, punishment, consultation with parents, or intensive interventions that combine a variety of strategies in a planned, systematic manner. Table 9.2 (p. 352) summarizes these various strategies for addressing student misbehavior.

When some students' behaviors seriously threaten others' sense of safety and well-being, and especially when aggression and violence are prevalent throughout the school, a three-tiered approach may be necessary. First, faculty members must coordinate their efforts in creating a schoolwide environment that makes aggression and violence unlikely—for instance, by establishing trusting teacher–student relationships, fostering a sense of caring and respect among students from diverse backgrounds, and providing mechanisms through which students can communicate their concerns without fear of reprisal. Second, faculty members must intervene early for the 10 to 15 percent of students at risk for academic or social failure, providing them with the cognitive and social skills they need to be successful at school. Third, the faculty must seek intensive intervention for students who are especially prone to violence, show signs of significant mental illness, or in some other way are seriously troubled. Additional measures are sometimes needed to address incidents of aggression associated with intergang hostilities.

TABLE 9.2   Strategies for Dealing with Student Misbehavior

Strategy	Situations in Which It's Appropriate	Possible Examples
Ignoring the behavior	• The misbehavior is unlikely to be repeated. • The misbehavior is unlikely to spread to other students. • Unusual circumstances elicit the misbehavior temporarily. • The misbehavior does not seriously interfere with learning.	• One student discreetly passes a note to another student just before the end of class. • A student accidentally drops her books, startling other students and temporarily distracting them from their work. • An entire class is hyperactive on the last afternoon before spring break.
Cueing the student	• The misbehavior is a minor infraction yet interferes with students' learning. • The behavior is likely to change with a subtle reminder.	• A student forgets to close his notebook at the beginning of a test. • Members of a cooperative learning group are talking so loudly that they distract other groups. • Several students are exchanging jokes during an independent seatwork assignment.
Discussing the problem with the student	• Cueing has been ineffective in changing the behavior. • The reasons for the misbehavior, if made clear, might suggest possible strategies for addressing it.	• A student is frequently late to class. • A student refuses to do certain kinds of assignments. • A student shows a sudden drop in motivation for no apparent reason.
Promoting self-regulation	• The student has a strong desire to improve his or her behavior.	• A student doesn't realize how frequently she interrupts her classmates. • A student seeks help in learning to control his anger. • A student acknowledges that her inability to stay on task is adversely affecting the good grades she wants to get.
Punishment	• A behavior significantly interferes with classroom learning or reflects blatant disregard for others' rights and welfare. • The student has little or no understanding or concern that the behavior is unacceptable.	• A student punches a classmate who inadvertently brushes past him. • A student tells a joke that insults people of a particular ethnic group. • A student vandalizes other students' lockers.
Consulting with parents	• The source of the problem may lie outside school walls. • Parents are likely to work collaboratively with school personnel to bring about a behavior change.	• A student does well in class but rarely turns in required homework assignments. • A student falls asleep in class almost every day. • A student is caught stealing classmates' lunches.
Conducting a planned, systematic intervention (e.g., applied behavior analysis, positive behavioral support)	• The misbehavior has continued over a period of time and significantly interferes with student learning and achievement. • Other, less intensive approaches (e.g., cueing, teacher-student discussions, mild punishment) have been ineffective. • The student seems unwilling or unable to use self-regulation techniques. • The misbehavior may in some way enable a student to achieve desired outcomes.	• A student has unusual difficulty sitting still for age-appropriate periods of time. • A member of the soccer team displays bursts of anger and aggression that are potentially dangerous to other players. • A student engages in disruptive behavior every time a difficult task is assigned.

PRACTICE FOR YOUR LICENSURE EXAM

The Good Buddy

Mr. Schulak has wanted to be a teacher for as long as he can remember. In his many volunteer activities over the years—coaching a girls' basketball team, assisting in a Boy Scout troop, teaching Sunday school—he has discovered how much he enjoys working with children. Children obviously enjoy working with him as well. Many occasionally call or stop by his home to shoot baskets, talk over old times, or just say hello. Some of them even call him by his first name.

Now that he has completed his college degree and obtained his teaching certificate, Mr. Schulak is a first-year teacher at his hometown's junior high school. He is delighted to find that he already knows many of his students—he has coached them, taught them, or gone to school with their older brothers and sisters—and so he spends the first few days of class renewing his friendships with them. But by the end of the week, he realizes that he and his students have accomplished little of an academic nature.

The following Monday Mr. Schulak vows to get down to business. He begins each of his six class sessions by describing his instructional goals for the weeks to come; he then begins the first lesson. He is surprised to discover that many of his students—students with whom he has such a good rapport— are resistant to settling down and getting to work. They want to move from one seat to another, talk with their friends, toss wadded-up paper "baseballs" across the room, and, in fact, do anything *except* the academic tasks Mr. Schulak has in mind. In his second week as a new teacher, Mr. Schulak has already lost total control of his classroom.

1. **Constructed-response question**

   Mr. Schulak is having a great deal of difficulty bringing his class to order.

   A. Identify two critical things that Mr. Schulak has *not* done to get the school year off to a good start.
   B. Describe two strategies that Mr. Schulak might now use to remedy the situation.

2. **Multiple-choice question**

   Mr. Schulak is undoubtedly aware that good teachers show that they care about and respect their students. Which one of the following statements describes the kind of teacher–student relationship that is most likely to foster students' learning and achievement?

   a. The teacher communicates optimism about a student's potential for success and offers the support necessary for that success.
   b. The teacher spends a lot of time engaging in recreational activities with students after school and on weekends.
   c. The teacher focuses almost exclusively on what students do well and ignores or downplays what students do poorly.
   d. The teacher listens empathetically to students' concerns but reminds students that he or she must ultimately be the one to decide what transpires in the classroom.

   Once you have answered these questions, compare your responses with those presented in Appendix A.

FOR FURTHER READING

The following articles from the journal *Educational Leadership* are especially relevant to this chapter. You can find these articles in Chapter 9 of MyEducationLab for this text.

Corbett, D., & Wilson, B. (2002). What urban students say about good teaching. *Educational Leadership, 60*(1), 18–22.

Davern, L. (1996). Listening to parents of children with disabilities. *Educational Leadership, 53*(7), 52–54.

Dowd, J. (1997). Refusing to play the blame game. *Educational Leadership, 54*(8), 67–69.

Gootman, M. E. (1998). Effective in-house suspension. *Educational Leadership, 56*(1), 39–41.

Hansen, J. M., & Childs, J. (1998). Creating a school where people like to be. *Educational Leadership, 56*(1), 14–17.

Marzano, R. J., & Marzano, J. S. (2003). The key to classroom management. *Educational Leadership, 61*(1), 6–13.

McCloud, S. (2005). From chaos to consistency. *Educational Leadership, 62*(5), 46–49.

Quiroz, B., Greenfield, P. M., & Altcheck, M. (1999). Bridging cultures with a parent–teacher conference. *Educational Leadership, 56*(7), 68–70.

Remboldt, C. (1998). Making violence unacceptable. *Educational Leadership, 56*(1), 32–38.

Stewart, J. (2001). Preventing violent behavior. *Educational Leadership, 58*(5), 78–79.

Taylor, J. A., & Baker, R. A., Jr. (2001). Discipline and the special education student. *Educational Leadership, 59*(4), 28–30.

Wolk, S. (2003). Hearts and minds. *Educational Leadership, 61*(1), 14–18.

MYEDUCATIONLAB

Now go to Chapter 9 of MyEducationLab at **www.myeducationlab.com**, where you can:

- Find instructional objectives for the chapter, along with focus questions that can help you zero in on important ideas in the chapter.
- Take a self-check quiz on concepts and principles you've just read about.
- Complete exercises and assignments that can help you more deeply understand the chapter content.
- Apply what you've learned to classroom contexts in Building Teaching Skills activities.

CHAPTER 10

Assessment Strategies

CASE STUDY Akeem

Midway through the school year, 9-year-old Akeem joined Susan Gordon's third-grade class at the Bronx New School in New York City. The school records that accompanied him showed a history of failure at his previous school: His scores on citywide achievement tests in reading and math were extremely low, and his teachers had given him "unsatisfactory" ratings in many areas.

Ms. Gordon quickly discovered that there were two sides to Akeem. On some occasions he was constantly moving, perhaps running and jumping on the playground or fidgeting and tapping objects in the classroom. On other occasions he was quiet, subdued, and seemingly quite sad. Ms. Gordon soon learned, too, that Akeem had trouble with even the simplest reading, writing, and arithmetic tasks. When asked to engage in such activities, he would often respond with angry, disruptive behaviors, in some instances overturning chairs or throwing objects across the room.

Each day's class schedule included several lengthy time periods in which students could pursue their individual interests—reading, playing math games, working with clay, and so on—and the classroom shelves were stocked with a variety of materials with which students could work. Determined to work effectively with Akeem, Ms. Gordon began to look for things he enjoyed and could do *well* during these times. Ms. Gordon observed that Akeem spent much of his time drawing and building things. She nurtured this interest by providing drawing paper, wooden blocks, Legos, and other construction materials and by frequently talking with him about what he was doing.

Given the time to engage in areas of strength and interest, Akeem's classroom behavior improved dramatically. Be-fore the school year was out, he had completed several complex projects, including (a) a set of airplanes and other flying vehicles, along with an illustrated book depicting the history of flight; (b) drawings and Lego constructions showing some of the city's most notable architecture; and (c) a detailed, 28-page action-figures catalog entitled "Man after Man." A typical page in this catalog appears below.

Although Akeem's projects enabled him to practice and strengthen his emerging literacy skills, his scores on districtwide multiple-choice achievement tests remained quite low, not only that year but in the fourth and fifth grades as well. Fortunately, Akeem and Ms. Gordon compiled a portfolio that revealed his ongoing progress in reading and writing, his exceptional talents in drawing and sculpture, and his persistence and attention to detail in activities about which he was passionate. Several years later, in eighth grade, Akeem was still doing well in school, as Linda Darling-Hammond and her colleagues reported in their book *Authentic Assessment in Action*:

> While academics are still not easy for him, his effort and regular attendance are reflected by his record of practically all A's on his spring report card. He continues to draw and design on his own, is connected to his

strengths and to his interests. These understandings appear to serve him well as he makes plans to attend a high school oriented toward art and design. He hopes to become an architect or an engineer.[1]

- Students' abilities can be assessed in a variety of ways. What particular forms of assessment do you see in this case study? What purpose might each of these assessments have served?
- Why might Akeem's performance on districtwide tests have remained low even though his reading and writing skills were improving?

[1] Reprinted by permission of the Publisher. From Linda Darling-Hammond, Jacqueline Ancess, and Beverly Falk, *Authentic Assessment in Action: Studies of Schools and Students at Work*, New York: Teachers College Press, © 1995 by Teachers College, Columbia University. All rights reserved.

You probably identified the citywide tests and previous teachers' "unsatisfactory" ratings as assessments of Akeem's achievement. Did you also identify Ms. Gordon's ongoing observations of Akeem's behavior as being instances of assessment? And did you include Akeem's portfolio on your list? In this chapter we see that assessment can—and *should*—come in many different forms. The following definition sums up assessment's major features:

> **Assessment** is a process of observing a sample of a student's behavior and drawing inferences about the student's knowledge and abilities.

Several parts of this definition are important to note. First, assessment is an observation of students' *behavior*. It's impossible to look inside students' heads and see what knowledge and skills lurk there. Teachers can see only how students actually perform in particular situations. Second, an assessment typically involves just a *sample* of behavior. Teachers certainly can't observe and keep track of everything their students do during the school day. Finally, assessment involves drawing *inferences* from observed behaviors to make judgments about students' overall classroom achievement—a tricky business at best, and one that requires considerable thought about which behaviors can provide a reasonably accurate estimate of what students know and can do.

Some assessments reflect **informal assessment**, in that they involve spontaneous, day-to-day observations of what students say and do in the classroom. For instance, Ms. Gordon is conducting informal assessment when she notices that Akeem is most likely to engage in disruptive behaviors when he's given assignments that require reading, writing, or math. (Her detective work here should remind you of our discussion of *functional analysis* in Chapter 9.) Observing that certain topics and activities readily engage Akeem's interest and persistence also constitutes informal assessment.

Other assessments reflect **formal assessment**, in that they are planned in advance and used for a specific purpose—perhaps to determine what students have learned from an instructional unit or whether they can apply what they've learned to real-world problems. Formal assessment is "formal" in the sense that a particular time is set aside for it, students can prepare for it in advance, and it is intended to yield information about particular instructional objectives or content area standards. The citywide achievement tests that Akeem took throughout the elementary grades were examples of formal assessment. So, too, was the portfolio that Akeem and his teacher created to showcase his talents and academic progress.

Classroom assessment practices are intertwined with virtually every other aspect of classroom functioning (look once again at Figure 8.1 in Chapter 8). Teachers' instructional goals determine—or at least *should* determine—not only the content of classroom lessons

assessment Process of observing a sample of a student's behavior and drawing inferences about the student's knowledge and abilities.

informal assessment Assessment that results from a teacher's spontaneous, day-to-day observations of how students behave and perform in class.

formal assessment Preplanned, systematic attempt to ascertain what students have learned.

but also the nature of tests, assignments, and other measures of student learning.[2] Conversely, how students perform on ongoing assessments influences teachers' future planning, instructional methods, and classroom management strategies. For example, Akeem's classroom behavior improved considerably during his third-grade year, thanks in large part to Ms. Gordon's keen observations of the things that turned him "on" and "off" and her flexibility in allowing him to pursue the "on" things.

The citywide achievement tests that Akeem took were undoubtedly intended to track students' progress in basic skills. In Akeem's case, however, the results were less useful than they might have been, in part because of his occasional hyperactivity (which would make it hard to keep his attention focused on lengthy paper-pencil tests) and in part because of his limited reading and writing skills (which would affect his performance not only on literacy tests but on measures of other content domains as well). Good classroom assessment practices must take into account students' existing characteristics and behaviors—their attention spans, vocabulary levels, reading and writing skills, and so on[3] (reflecting the interplay of student characteristics and assessment practices depicted in Figure 8.1). Later in the chapter, when we learn how scores on standardized achievement tests are typically determined, we'll discover an additional reason for Akeem's consistently low scores despite noticeable progress in basic skills.

Both informal and formal classroom assessments are *tools* that can help teachers make informed decisions about how best to help students learn and achieve and how best to sum up what students have accomplished during the school year. The usefulness of these tools depends on how well suited they are to the circumstances in which they are being used. In this final chapter of the book, we explore the various purposes for which classroom assessments might be used. We also identify characteristics and strategies that maximize their usefulness.

USING ASSESSMENT FOR DIFFERENT PURPOSES

As noted in our earlier definition, assessment involves drawing inferences, and such inferences often have an evaluative component. Educators distinguish between two general forms of evaluation.[4] On some occasions teachers engage in **formative evaluation**, assessing what students know and can do *before or during instruction*, perhaps to identify students' existing strengths and interests (as Ms. Gordon does), perhaps to determine what students already know and believe about the topic of a new unit (e.g., see Figure 10.1), or perhaps to assess students' progress in mastering challenging subject matter. At other times teachers and other school personnel engage in **summative evaluation**, conducting an assessment *after instruction* to make final judgments about what students have achieved. Summative evaluations are used to determine whether students have mastered the content of a lesson or unit, what final grades to assign, which students are ready for more advanced classes, and the like.

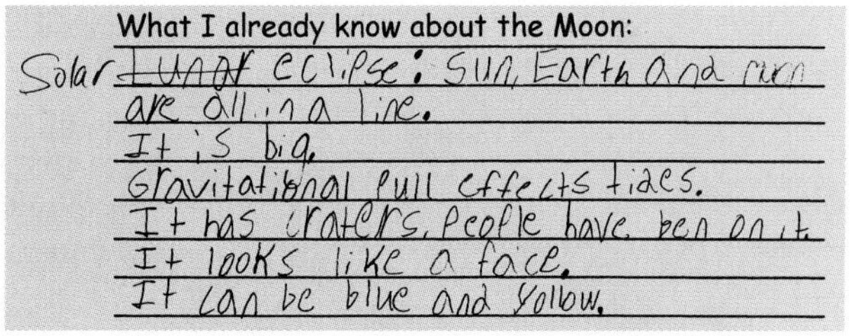

With these two basic kinds of evaluation in mind, let's consider the roles that educational assessments can play in (a) guiding instructional decision making, (b) diagnosing learning and performance problems, (c) determining what students have learned at the end of instruction, (d) evaluating the quality of instruction, and most important, (e) helping students learn *better*.

Guiding Instructional Decision Making

Both summative and formative evaluations can guide instructional decision making. Any future summative evaluations—annual citywide or statewide tests of basic skills, for instance—must inevitably guide teachers somewhat as they prioritize topics and skills on which to focus. After appropriate priorities have been identified, a formative evaluation can help a teacher

What I already know about the Moon:

Solar ~~LUAN~~ eclipse: Sun, Earth and run are all in a line.
It is big.
Gravitational pull effects tides.
It has craters. People have ben on it.
It looks like a face.
It can be blue and yellow.

FIGURE 10.1 Some assessments reflect *formative evaluation*, in that they provide helpful information before or during instruction. Here 8-year-old Richard reveals his current knowledge and beliefs before a unit about the moon.

formative evaluation Evaluation conducted before or during instruction to facilitate instructional planning and enhance students' learning.

summative evaluation Evaluation conducted after instruction to assess students' final achievement.

---

[2] For a good discussion of this point, see Bransford, Derry, Berliner, & Hammerness, 2005.
[3] S. M Carver, 2006.

[4] For example, see Shepard, Hammerness, Darling-Hammond, & Rust, 2005.

determine a suitable point at which to begin instruction. Furthermore, conducting formative evaluations throughout a lesson or unit can provide ongoing information about the appropriateness of current instructional goals and the effectiveness of current instructional strategies. For instance, after finding that almost all students are completing assignments quickly and easily, a teacher might set instructional goals a bit higher. Alternatively, if many students are struggling with material already presented in class lectures, a teacher might revisit that material using a different instructional approach—perhaps a more concrete, hands-on one.

Diagnosing Learning and Performance Problems

Why is Akeem having trouble learning to read? Why is Gretel misbehaving in class? Why does Martin seem excessively anxious during exams? Teachers ask such questions when they suspect that certain students might learn differently from their classmates and could in some instances benefit from special educational services. Some assessment instruments are specifically designed to identify any special academic, social, and emotional needs that students may have. Most of these instruments require explicit training in their use and so are often administered and interpreted by specialists (school psychologists, counselors, speech and language pathologists, etc.). Yet teachers' classroom assessments can provide considerable diagnostic information as well, especially when they suggest where students are going wrong and why. In other words, classroom assessments can, and ideally they *should*, yield information teachers can use to help students improve.[5]

Determining What Students Have Learned from Instruction

Teachers typically need to use formal assessments to determine whether students have achieved instructional goals or met certain content area standards. Such information is essential when using a mastery-learning approach to instruction; it is also important for assigning final grades. School counselors and administrators, too, may use assessment results for making placement decisions, such as deciding which students are most likely to do well in advanced classes, which might need additional coursework in basic skills, and so on.

Evaluating the Quality of Instruction

Final measures of student achievement are useful not only in assessing students' achievement but also in evaluating the quality of instruction. When most students perform poorly after an instructional unit, teachers should reflect not only on what students might have done differently but also on what *they themselves* might have done differently.[6] For instance, perhaps a teacher moved too quickly through material or provided insufficient opportunities to practice critical skills. In any event, consistently low assessment results for many or all students indicate that some modification of instruction is in order.

Promoting Learning

Whenever teachers conduct formative evaluations to help them develop or modify lesson plans, they are obviously using assessment to facilitate students' learning. Yet summative evaluation can influence learning as well. It is likely to do so in the following ways.

Assessments encourage review.

As we discovered in Chapter 2, long-term memory is not necessarily "forever." For a variety of reasons, human beings tend to forget things as time goes on. Students have a better chance of remembering classroom subject matter over the long run if they review it at a later time. Studying for formal assessments provides one way of reviewing material related to important instructional goals.[7]

---

[5] Baek, 1994; Baxter, Elder, & Glaser, 1996; Covington, 1992; Shepard et al., 2005.

[6] Shepard et al., 2005.

[7] Dempster, 1991; Kiewra, 1989; Roediger & Karpicke, 2006.

Assessments influence motivation.

On average, students study class material more and learn it better when they are told they will be tested on it or in some other way held accountable for it, rather than when they are simply told to learn it.[8] Yet *how* students are assessed is as important as *whether* they're assessed. Assessments are especially effective as motivators when students are challenged to do their very best and their performance is judged on the basis of how well they've accomplished instructional goals.[9] Students' self-efficacy and attributions affect their perceptions of the "challenge," of course. Students must believe that success on an assessment task is possible if they exert reasonable effort and use appropriate strategies.

Although regular classroom assessments can be highly motivating, they are, in and of themselves, usually *extrinsic* motivators. Thus they may direct students' attention to performance goals and undermine intrinsic motivation to learn. Assessments are especially likely to encourage performance goals when students perceive them to be an evaluation of their performance rather than a mechanism for facilitating future learning.[10]

Assessments influence students' cognitive processes as they study.

Students draw inferences about important instructional goals partly from the ways their teachers assess their learning. Thus different assessment tasks can lead them to study and learn quite differently.[11] For instance, students typically spend more time studying the things they think will be addressed on an assessment than the things they think the assessment won't cover. Their expectations about the kinds of tasks they will need to perform and the questions they will need to answer also influence whether they memorize isolated facts, on the one hand, or construct a meaningful, integrated body of knowledge, on the other. Unfortunately, many students believe (incorrectly) that trying to learn information meaningfully—that is, trying to understand and make sense of what they study—interferes with their ability to do well on classroom assessments that emphasize knowledge of isolated facts.[12]

A sixth-grade teacher used the geology test shown in Figure 10.2 to assess students' knowledge and understanding of basic principles of rock formation. Part A (identifying rocks shown at the front of the room) may be assessing either basic knowledge or transfer, depending on whether the students have seen those particular rocks before. The

A. Write whether each of the rocks shown at the front of the room is a sedimentary, igneous, or metamorphic rock.
1. _____
2. _____
3. _____

B. The following are various stages of the rock cycle. Number them from 1 to 9 to indicate the order in which they occur.
_____ Heat and pressure
_____ Crystallization and cooling
_____ Igneous rock forms
_____ Magma
_____ Weathering and erosion into sediments
_____ Melting
_____ Sedimentary rock forms
_____ Pressure and cementing
_____ Metamorphic rock forms

C. Write the letter for the correct definition of each rock group.
1. ____ Igneous   a. Formed when particles of eroded rock are deposited together and become cemented.
2. ____ Sedimentary b. Produced by extreme pressures or high temperatures below the earth's surface.
3. ____ Metamorphic c. Formed by the cooling of molten rock material from within the earth.

D. Fill in the blanks in each sentence.
1. The process of breaking down rock by the action of water, ice, plants, animals, and chemical changes is called _____ .
2. All rocks are made of _____ .
3. The hardness of rocks can be determined by a _____ .
4. Continued weathering of rock will eventually produce _____ .
5. Every rock has a _____ .

[The test continues with several additional fill-in-the-blank and short-answer items.]

FIGURE 10.2 Much of this sixth-grade geology test focuses on knowledge of specific facts and may encourage students to memorize, rather than understand, information about rocks.

[8] Dempster, 1991; N. Frederiksen, 1984b; Halpin & Halpin, 1982.
[9] Mac Iver, Reuman, & Main, 1995; Maehr & Anderman, 1993; Natriello & Dornbusch, 1984.
[10] Grolnick & Ryan, 1987; Paris & Turner, 1994; Spaulding, 1992.

[11] N. Frederiksen, 1984b; Lundeberg & Fox, 1991; Shepard, 2000; Shepard et al., 2005.
[12] Crooks, 1988.

What and how students study is, in part, a function of how they expect their learning to be assessed.

rest of the test clearly focuses on memorized facts—stages of the rock cycle, definitions of terms, and so on—and is likely to encourage students to engage in rote learning as they study for future tests. For instance, consider the last item, "Every rock has a _____." Students can answer this item correctly *only* if they have learned the material verbatim: The missing word here is "story."

Classroom assessments can also affect students' views about the nature of various academic disciplines—that is, students' *epistemological beliefs*. For example, if their teacher gives quizzes that assess knowledge of specific facts (as most of the test items in Figure 10.2 do), students are apt to conclude that a discipline is just that: a collection of undisputed facts. If a teacher instead asks students to take a position on a controversial issue and justify that position with evidence and logic, they get a very different message: that the discipline involves an integrated set of understandings that must be supported with reasoning and are subject to change over time.

Assessments can be learning experiences in and of themselves.

You can probably recall classroom assessments that actually taught you something. Perhaps an essay question asked you to compare two things you hadn't compared before and so helped you discover similarities you hadn't noticed earlier. Or perhaps a test problem asked you to apply a scientific principle to a situation you hadn't realized was related to that principle. Such tasks not only assessed what you learned, they also *helped* you learn.

In general, the very process of completing an assessment on class material helps students learn the material better, especially if the assessment tasks ask students to elaborate on the material in some way.[13] But two qualifications are important to note here. First, an assessment helps students learn only the material it specifically addresses. Second, when teachers present *incorrect* information on an assessment (as they often do in true–false and multiple-choice questions), students may eventually remember that misinformation as being true rather than false.[14] Fortunately, such misinformation does not appear to have a *major* impact on students' later understandings.[15]

Assessments can provide feedback about learning progress.

Regular classroom assessments can give students valuable feedback about which things they have and have not mastered. But simply knowing one's final score on a test or assignment (e.g., knowing the percentage of items correctly answered) is not terribly helpful. To facilitate students' learning—and ultimately to enhance their self-efficacy for mastering the subject matter—assessment results must include concrete information about where students have succeeded, where they've had difficulty, and how they might improve.[16]

Assessments can encourage intrinsic motivation and self-regulation if students play an active role in the assessment process.

As noted earlier, classroom assessments are typically extrinsic motivators that provide only an externally imposed reason for learning school subject matter. Yet students learn more effectively when they are *in*trinsically motivated, and they are more likely to be intrinsically motivated if they have some sense of self-determination about classroom activities (see Chapter 6). Furthermore, if students are to become self-regulating learners, they must acquire skills in self-monitoring and self-evaluation (see Chapter 4). For such reasons, students should be regular and active participants in the assessment of their learning and performance. Ultimately, teachers should think of assessment as something they do *with* students rather than *to* them.[17]

Students become increasingly skillful in self-assessment as they grow older,[18] but even students in the elementary grades have some ability to evaluate their own perfor-

---

[13] Dempster, 1997; Fall, Webb, & Chudowsky, 2000; Foos & Fisher, 1988; Roediger & Karpicke, 2006.

[14] A. S. Brown, Schilling, & Hockensmith, 1999; N. Frederiksen, 1984b; Roediger & Marsh, 2005.

[15] Roediger & Karpicke, 2006.

[16] Baron, 1987; Krampen, 1987; Pintrich & Schunk, 2002.

[17] For example, see Covington, 1992; Paris & Ayres, 1994; Vye et al., 1998.

[18] van Kraayenoord & Paris, 1997.

CLASSROOM STRATEGIES

Using Classroom Assessments to Promote Learning and Achievement

- Give a formal or informal pretest to determine where to begin instruction.

  When beginning a new unit on cultural geography, a teacher gives a pretest designed to identify misconceptions that students may have about various cultural groups. He can then address the misconceptions during the unit.

- Choose or develop an assessment instrument that reflects the actual knowledge and skills you want students to achieve.

  While planning how to assess his students' achievement, a teacher initially decides to use questions from the set of test items (i.e., the *test bank*) that accompanies his textbook. When he looks more closely at these test items, however, he discovers that they measure only knowledge of isolated facts. Instead, he develops several assessment tasks that involve higher-level thinking and better reflect his primary instructional goal: for students to be able to apply what they've learned to real-world problems.

- Construct assessment instruments that reflect how you want students to think about and cognitively process information as they study.

  A teacher tells her students, "As you study for next week's vocabulary test, remember that the test questions will ask you to put defi-

nitions in your own words and give your own examples to show what each word means."

- Use an assessment task as a learning experience in and of itself.

  A high school science teacher has students collect samples of the local drinking water and test them for bacterial content. She is assessing her students' ability to use procedures she has taught them, but she also hopes they will discover the importance of protecting the community's natural resources.

- Use an assessment to give students specific feedback about what they have and have not mastered.

  As he grades students' persuasive essays, a teacher writes numerous notes in the margins of the papers to indicate places where students have analyzed a situation logically or illogically, identified a relevant or irrelevant example, proposed an appropriate or inappropriate solution, and so on.

- Provide criteria that students can use to evaluate their own performance.

  The teacher of a Foods and Nutrition class gives her students a checklist of qualities to look for in the pies they have baked.

---

mance if they have the encouragement and guidance to do so. Later in the chapter we'll identify strategies for helping students acquire self-monitoring skills through classroom assessments.

The Classroom Strategies box "Using Classroom Assessments to Promote Learning and Achievement" presents several examples of how teachers might use classroom assessments to encourage effective cognitive processes, foster self-regulation skills, and enhance students' learning and motivation.

Observe 8-year-old Keenan and her teacher reflect on Keenan's writing progress in the "Portfolio" video in the Additional Resources section in Chapter 10 of MyEducationLab.

IMPORTANT QUALITIES OF GOOD ASSESSMENT

As a student, have you ever been assessed in a way you thought was unfair? If so, *why* was it unfair? For example:

1. Did the teacher evaluate students' responses inconsistently?
2. Were some students assessed under more favorable conditions than others?
3. Was the assessment a poor measure of what you had learned?
4. Was the assessment so time consuming that, after a while, you no longer cared how well you performed?

In light of your experiences, what characteristics seem to be essential for a good classroom assessment instrument?

My four numbered questions reflect, respectively, four *RSVP* characteristics of good classroom assessment: *r*eliability, *s*tandardization, *v*alidity, and *p*racticality. The following principles reflect these characteristics.

A good assessment is reliable.

The **reliability** of an assessment instrument or procedure is the extent to which it yields consistent information about the knowledge, skills, or characteristics being assessed. To get a feel for what reliability involves, try the following exercise.

reliability Extent to which an assessment instrument yields consistent information about the knowledge, skills, or characteristics being assessed.

Fowl Play

Here is a sequence of events in the life of biology teacher Ms. Fowler:

- **Monday.** After a unit on the bone structures of both birds and dinosaurs, Ms. Fowler asks her students to write an essay explaining why many scientists believe that birds are descended from dinosaurs. After school she tosses the pile of essays on the back seat of her cluttered, '57 Chevy.
- **Tuesday.** Ms. Fowler looks high and low for the essays both at home and in her classroom, but she can't find them anywhere.
- **Wednesday.** Because Ms. Fowler wants to use the essay to determine what her students have learned, she asks the class to write the same essay a second time.
- **Thursday.** Ms. Fowler discovers Monday's essays on the back seat of her Chevy.
- **Friday.** Ms. Fowler grades both sets of essays. She is surprised to find little consistency between them. Students who wrote the best essays on Monday did not necessarily do well on Wednesday, and some of Monday's poorest performers did quite well on Wednesday.

- Which results should Ms. Fowler use, Monday's or Wednesday's?

When teachers assess learning and achievement, they must be confident that their assessment results will be essentially the same regardless of whether they give the assessment Monday or Wednesday, whether the weather is sunny or rainy, and whether they evaluate students' responses while in a good mood or a foul frame of mind. Ms. Fowler's assessment instrument has poor reliability, because the results it yields are completely different from one day to another. So which day's results should she use? I've asked you a trick question, because we have no way of knowing which set is more accurate.

Any single assessment instrument will rarely yield *exactly* the same results for the same student on two different occasions, even if the knowledge or ability being assessed remains the same. Many temporary conditions unrelated to the knowledge or ability being measured are apt to affect students' performance and almost inevitably lead to some fluctuation in assessment results. For instance, the inconsistencies in Ms. Fowler's students' essays might have been due to temporary factors such as these:

- **Day-to-day changes in students**—for example, changes in health, motivation, mood, and energy level
  The 24-hour Netherlands flu was making the rounds in Ms. Fowler's classroom.
- **Variations in the physical environment**—for example, variations in room temperature, noise level, and outside distractions
  On Monday, students who sat by the window in Ms. Fowler's classroom enjoyed peace and quiet. On Wednesday, those who sat by the window worked while noisy construction machinery tore up the pavement outside.
- **Variations in administration of the assessment**—for example, variations in instructions, timing, and the teacher's responses to students' questions
  On Monday, a few students wrote the essay after school because they had attended a dress rehearsal for the school play during class time. Ms. Fowler explained the task more clearly for them than she had during class, and she gave them as much time as they needed to finish. On Wednesday, a different group of students had to write the essay after school because of an across-town band concert during class time. Ms. Fowler explained the task very hurriedly and collected the essays before students had finished.
- **Characteristics of the assessment instrument**—for example, the length, clarity, and difficulty of tasks (e.g., ambiguous and very difficult tasks increase students' tendency to guess randomly)
  The essay topic, "Explain why many scientists believe that birds are descended from dinosaurs," was a vague one that students interpreted differently from one day to the next.

Informal observations of student performance can yield valuable information about how students are progressing. But teachers should draw firm conclusions about students' achievement only when they know their assessment methods are *reliable*, yielding consistent results about particular students time after time.

- **Subjectivity in scoring**—for example, judgments made when the teacher must determine the "rightness" or "wrongness" of responses and when responses are scored on the basis of vague, imprecise criteria

  Ms. Fowler graded both sets of essays while she watched "Chainsaw Murders at Central High" on television Friday night. She gave higher scores during kissing scenes, lower scores during stalking scenes.

When drawing conclusions about students' learning and achievement, teachers must be confident that the information on which they're basing their conclusions has not been overly distorted by temporary, irrelevant factors. Several strategies can increase the likelihood that an assessment instrument will yield reliable results:

- Include several tasks in the instrument, and look for consistency in students' performance from one task to another.
- Define each task clearly enough that students know exactly what they are being asked to do.
- Identify specific, concrete criteria with which to evaluate students' performance.
- Try not to let expectations for students' performance influence judgments.
- Avoid evaluating students when they are tired, ill, or in some other way not in the best frame of mind.
- Administer the assessment in similar ways and under similar conditions for all students.

The last of these recommendations suggests that assessment procedures be *standardized*—the second of the RSVP characteristics.

A good assessment is standardized for most students.

A second important characteristic of good assessment is **standardization**, the extent to which the assessment involves similar content and format and is administered and scored in the same way for everyone. In most situations students should all get the same instructions, perform identical or similar tasks, have the same time limits, and work under the same constraints. Furthermore, all students' responses should be scored using the same criteria. For example, unless there are extenuating circumstances, a teacher shouldn't use tougher standards for one student than for another.

Many tests constructed and published by large-scale testing companies are called *standardized tests*. This label indicates that the tests have explicit procedures for administration and scoring that are consistently applied wherever the tests are used. (We'll look at standardized tests more closely later in the chapter.) Yet standardization is important in teachers' self-constructed classroom assessments as well. Standardization reduces the chance of error in assessment results, especially error due to variation in test administration or subjectivity in scoring.

Equity is an additional consideration. Under most circumstances, it is only fair to ask all students to be evaluated under similar conditions. We find an exception in the assessment of students with special educational needs. In the United States the Individuals with Disabilities Education Act (IDEA) mandates that schools make appropriate accommodations for students with physical, mental, social, or emotional disabilities. This mandate applies not only to instructional practices but to assessment practices as well. Specific modifications to assessment instruments and procedures must, of course, be tailored to students' particular disabilities. Following are examples:[19]

- Read paper-pencil test questions to students with limited reading skills (e.g., to students with dyslexia).
- Divide a lengthy assessment task into several shorter tasks for students with a limited attention span (e.g., for students with ADHD).
- Administer an assessment in a quiet room with few distractions (e.g., for students with learning disabilities or ADHD).
- Give more time or frequent breaks during the assessment (e.g., for students who tire easily due to a chronic illness or traumatic brain injury).

[19] American Educational Research Association, American Psychological Association, & National Council on Measurement in Education, 1999; Sireci, Scarpati, & Li, 2005.

standardization Extent to which assessments involve similar content and format and are administered and scored similarly for everyone.

• Construct individualized assessment instruments when instructional goals differ for some students (e.g., as may often be the case for students with mental retardation).

A good assessment has validity for its purpose.

Earlier you learned about *reliability*. Let's see whether you can apply (transfer) your understanding of reliability to the following exercise.

I have developed a new test called the FTOI: the Fathead Test of Intelligence. It consists of only a tape measure and a *table of norms* that shows how children and adults of various ages typically perform on the test. Administration of the FTOI is quick and easy. You simply measure a person's head circumference just above the eyebrows (firmly but not too tightly) and compare your measure against the average head circumference for the person's age-group. People with large heads (comparatively speaking) are given high IQ scores. People with smaller heads get low scores.

• Does the FTOI have high reliability? Answer the question before you read further.

No matter how often you measure a person's head circumference, you are going to get a similar score. Fatheads will continue to be fatheads, and pinheads will always be pinheads. So the answer to my question is *yes*: The FTOI has high reliability because it yields consistent results. If you answered *no*, you were probably thinking that the FTOI isn't a very good measure of intelligence. But that's a problem with the instrument's *validity*, not with its reliability.

The **validity** of an assessment instrument is the extent to which it measures what it is intended to measure and allows us to draw appropriate inferences about the characteristic or ability in question. Does the FTOI measure intelligence? Are scores on a standardized, multiple-choice achievement test a good indication of whether students have mastered basic skills in reading and writing? Does students' performance at a school concert reflect what they have achieved in their instrumental music class? When assessments don't fulfill their purposes—when they are poor measures of students' knowledge and abilities—then we have a validity problem.

As noted earlier, numerous irrelevant factors are apt to influence how well students perform in assessment situations. Some of these—students' health, classroom distractions, errors in scoring, and so on—are temporary conditions that lead to fluctuations in assessment results and therefore lower reliability. But other irrelevant factors—perhaps reading ability or low self-efficacy about academic tasks—are more stable, and so their effects on assessment results may be relatively constant. For example, if Akeem has poor reading skills, he may get consistently low scores on paper-pencil, multiple-choice achievement tests regardless of how much he has actually achieved in science, math, or social studies. When assessment results continue to be affected by the same irrelevant variables, the *validity* of the assessments is in doubt.

Psychologists distinguish among different kinds of validity, which are important in different situations. In some cases we might be interested in *predictive validity*. That is, we might want to know how well scores on an assessment instrument predict performance in some future activity—for example, how well IQ scores predict students' future classroom performance. At other times we might be interested in *construct validity*. That is, we might want to know whether an assessment instrument measures a particular human trait or characteristic—for example, whether my FTOI test actually measures intelligence, or whether an alleged measure of a personality trait actually measures personality. In general, however, classroom teachers should be most concerned about **content validity**. That is, they need to be sure their assessment questions and tasks are a representative sample of the overall body of knowledge and skills—the *content domain*—they are assessing.

As an illustration, Table 10.1 revisits the Indiana state standards for reading comprehension presented in Chapter 8. The table's right-hand column offers examples of assessment strategies that might address those standards. Some of the examples in the table—for

validity Extent to which an assessment instrument actually measures what it is intended to measure and allows appropriate inferences about the characteristic or ability in question.

content validity Extent to which an assessment includes a representative sample of tasks within the domain being assessed.

DEVELOPMENTAL TRENDS

TABLE 10.1   Matching Assessment Tasks to the Indiana State Standards for Reading Comprehension at Different Grade Levels

Grade Level	Examples of Grade-Specific Standards	Examples of Assessment Tasks That Address One or More Standards
Grade 1	• Respond to *who*, *what*, *when*, *where*, *why*, and *how* questions and discuss the main idea of what is read. • Follow one-step written instructions. • Use context (the meaning of the surrounding text) to understand word and sentence meanings. • Relate prior knowledge to what is read.	• Ask specific questions about a story's characters, setting, and plot. • Ask students to draw inferences about characters' thoughts and feelings based on their own experiences in similar situations. • Have students describe what they've just learned from a book about animal camouflage. • Have students act out a story they've recently read.
Grade 4	• Use appropriate strategies when reading for different purposes. • Draw conclusions or make and confirm predictions about text by using prior knowledge and ideas presented in the text itself, including illustrations, titles, topic sentences, important words, foreshadowing clues (clues that indicate what might happen next), and direct quotations. • Evaluate new information and hypotheses (statements of theories or assumptions) by testing them against known information and ideas. • Distinguish between cause and effect and between fact and opinion in informational text.	• Ask students to use a book's index to quickly locate information about a particular topic. • Ask students to use the headings and subheadings in their science textbook to identify specific questions that each section might answer. • Modify a text passage so that it includes several inconsistent statements; ask students to identify the inconsistencies. • Present a paragraph from an age-appropriate persuasive essay, and ask students to underline facts with a red pencil and opinions with a green pencil.
Grade 7	• Understand and analyze the differences in structure and purpose between various categories of informational materials (such as textbooks, newspapers, and instructional or technical materials). • Identify and trace the development of an author's argument, point of view, or perspective in text. • Understand and explain the use of a simple mechanical device by following directions in a technical manual. • Assess the adequacy, accuracy, and appropriateness of the author's evidence to support claims and assertions, noting instances of bias and stereotyping.	• Have students identify similarities and differences between two descriptions of the same historical event: (a) a newspaper article written during or immediately after the event and (b) a description of the event in a history textbook. • Present an opinion piece from *Reader's Digest*, and have students identify the author's main point and supporting arguments. • Ask students to follow written directions to construct an electromagnet. • Give students an advertisement for a self-improvement product (e.g., a diet pill or exercise equipment); ask them to evaluate any evidence of the product's effectiveness presented in the ad.
Grade 11	• Analyze the way in which clarity of meaning is affected by the patterns of organization, repetition of the main ideas, organization of language, and word choice in the text. • Verify and clarify facts presented in several types of expository texts by using a variety of consumer, workplace, and public documents. • Analyze an author's implicit and explicit assumptions and beliefs about a subject. • Critique the power, validity, and truthfulness of arguments set forth in public documents; their appeal to both friendly and hostile audiences; and the extent to which the arguments anticipate and address reader concerns and counterclaims.	• Ask students to find examples of a particular theme (e.g., ethnic stereotyping) in the dialogue of a Shakespearean play. • Search the Internet for a corporate or personal Web site that presents information about a topic of general interest (e.g., air pollution or use of vitamin supplements); ask students to search the library for sources that either verify or discredit the author's claims. • Present a history book's description of the Battle of the Alamo, and ask students to identify the author's assumptions and biases in writing it. • Give students an editorial from the local newspaper and ask them to describe (a) what kinds of people are apt to agree with the piece and (b) what kinds of people are apt to disagree with it, and for what reasons.

Source: Standards (middle column) are from a Web site maintained by the Indiana Department of Education. Retrieved October 11, 2007, from www.indianastandardsresources.org

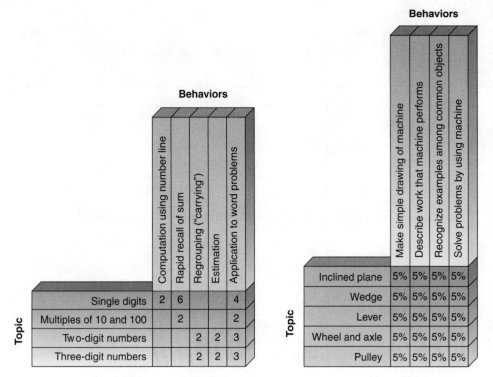

FIGURE 10.3   Two examples of a table of specifications. The table on the left provides specifications for a 30-item paper-pencil test on addition. It assigns different weights (different numbers of items) to different topic–behavior combinations, with some combinations intentionally not being assessed at all. The table on the right provides specifications for a combination paper-pencil and performance assessment on simple machines. It assigns equal importance (the same percentage of points) to each topic–behavior combination.

instance, distinguishing between facts and opinions in an essay and identifying themes in a Shakespearean play—can easily be paper-pencil tasks. In **paper-pencil assessment**, teachers present questions to answer, topics to address, or problems to solve, and students respond on paper. But other examples—for instance, acting out a story and using written directions to make an electromagnet—reflect **performance assessment**. That is, students show what they have learned by actively *doing* something rather than simply writing about it. As we will discover later, paper-pencil and performance assessment tasks tend to be useful in different situations.

In an assessment instrument with high content validity, questions and tasks reflect all parts of the content domain in appropriate proportions and require the particular behaviors and skills identified in instructional goals or objectives. How can a teacher make sure that a test or assignment is truly *representative* of the content domain being assessed? The most widely recommended strategy is to construct a blueprint that identifies the specific things a teacher wants to assess and the proportion of questions or tasks that should address each one. This blueprint frequently takes the form of a **table of specifications**, a two-way grid that indicates both what topics should be covered and what students should be able to *do* with each topic. Each cell of the grid indicates the relative importance of each topic–behavior combination, perhaps as a particular number or percentage of tasks or test items to be included in the overall assessment. Figure 10.3 shows two examples, one for a paper-pencil test on addition and a second for a combined paper-pencil and performance assessment on simple machines. After creating a table of specifications, a teacher can develop paper-pencil items or performance tasks that reflect both the topics and the behaviors that need to be assessed and have some confidence that the assessment instrument has content validity for the domain it is intended to represent.

High content validity is *essential* whenever teachers give a test or assignment for summative evaluation purposes—that is, to determine what students have ultimately learned from instruction. A teacher maximizes content validity when the tasks students are asked to perform are as similar as possible to the things they should ultimately be able to do. In other words, any assessment used in summative evaluation should reflect instructional goals and objectives.

A good assessment is practical.

The last of the four RSVP characteristics is **practicality**, the extent to which assessment instruments and procedures are relatively easy to use.[20] Practicality encompasses issues such as these:

- How much time will it take to develop the instrument?
- How easily can the assessment be administered to many students at once?
- Are expensive materials involved?

paper-pencil assessment Assessment in which students provide written responses to written items.

performance assessment Assessment in which students demonstrate their knowledge and skills in a nonwritten fashion.

table of specifications Two-way grid indicating the topics to be covered in an assessment and the things students should be able to do with those topics.

practicality Extent to which an assessment instrument or procedure is inexpensive and easy to use and takes only a small amount of time to administer and score.

---

[20] Many psychologists use the term *usability*, but I think *practicality* better communicates the idea.

TABLE 10.2 The RSVP Characteristics of Good Assessment

Characteristic	Definition	Questions to Consider
Reliability	The extent to which an assessment instrument or procedure yields consistent results for each student	• How much are students' scores affected by temporary conditions unrelated to the characteristic being measured? • Do different people score students' performances similarly? • Do different parts of a single assessment instrument lead to similar conclusions about a student's achievement?
Standardization	The extent to which assessment instruments and procedures are similar for all students	• Are all students assessed on identical or similar content? • Do all students have the same types of tasks to perform? • Are instructions the same for everyone? • Do all students have similar time constraints? • Is everyone's performance evaluated using the same criteria?
Validity	The extent to which an assessment instrument or procedure measures what it is intended to measure and allows appropriate inferences	• Does the assessment tap into a representative sample of the content domain being assessed (*content validity*)? • Do students' scores predict their later success in a domain (*predictive validity*)? • Does the instrument accurately measure a particular characteristic or trait (*construct validity*)?
Practicality	The extent to which an assessment instrument or procedure is easy and inexpensive to use	• How much class time does the assessment take? • How quickly and easily can students' responses be scored? • Is special training required to administer or score the assessment? • Does the assessment require specialized materials that must be purchased?

- How much time will the assessment take away from instructional activities?
- How quickly and easily can students' performance be evaluated?

There is often a trade-off between practicality and such other characteristics as validity and reliability. For example, a true–false test for a unit on tennis would be easy to construct and administer, but a performance assessment in which students actually demonstrate their tennis skills—even though it takes more time and energy—undoubtedly would be a more valid measure of how well students have mastered the game.

The four RSVP characteristics are summarized in Table 10.2. Of these characteristics, *validity is the most important.* Teachers must use assessment techniques that validly assess students' accomplishment of instructional goals and objectives. It is important to note, however, that *reliability is a necessary condition for validity.* Assessments can yield valid results only when they also yield consistent results—results that are only minimally affected by variations in administration, subjectivity in scoring, and so on. Reliability does not guarantee validity, however, as the FTOI exercise you completed earlier illustrates. Standardization enhances the reliability of assessment results. Practicality should be a consideration only when validity, reliability, and standardization are not seriously jeopardized.

Now that we've examined desirable characteristics of any classroom assessment, we're in a good position to explore both informal and formal classroom assessment strategies. As we go along, we'll consider the goals and objectives for which various assessment strategies might be most appropriate and the RSVP characteristics of different approaches.

CONDUCTING INFORMAL ASSESSMENTS

Informal assessments—observing the many "little things" students say and do over the course of the school day—are helpful in several ways.[21] First and foremost, they provide continuing feedback about the effectiveness of current instructional tasks and activities. Second, they are easily adjusted at a moment's notice. For example, when students express

---

[21] Airasian, 1994; Stiggins, 2001.

Group Participation and Work Habits

☺ **Demonstrates attentiveness as a listener through body language or facial expressions-** Meghan is still developing this skill. Sometimes it is difficult for her to listen when she is sitting near her friends.

☺ **Follows directions.**

☺ **Enters ongoing discussion on the subject.** -Sometimes needs to be encouraged to share her ideas.

☺ **Makes relevant contributions to ongoing activities.**

☺ **Completes assigned activities.** -Meghan is very responsible about her assignments.

☺ **Shows courtesy in conversations and discussions by waiting for turn to speak.**

Meghan enjoys lunch with her friends.

FIGURE 10.4 This page from 6-year-old Meghan's kindergarten portfolio shows her teacher's assessment of her work habits and social skills.

misconceptions about a particular topic, their teacher can ask follow-up questions that probe their beliefs and reasoning processes. Third, informal assessments provide information that may either support or call into question the results obtained from more formal assessment tasks. Finally, ongoing observations of students' behaviors provide clues about social, emotional, and motivational factors affecting their classroom performance and may often be the only practical means of assessing such instructional goals as "shows courtesy" or "enjoys reading." In the portfolio excerpt shown in Figure 10.4, a kindergarten teacher describes 6-year-old Meghan's progress in social skills and work habits—areas that the teacher can probably assess only through informal observation.

Several general strategies enhance the usefulness of informal assessments.

Observe both verbal and nonverbal behaviors.

Teachers can learn a lot from what students say during the school day. For instance, a teacher might

- Ask questions during a lesson (e.g., see the Classroom Strategies box "Asking Questions to Promote and Assess Learning" on p. 293 of Chapter 8)
- Make note of the kinds of questions students ask
- Listen to what and how much students contribute to whole-class and small-group discussions
- Observe students' interactions with peers in class, at lunch, and on the playground
- Have students write daily or weekly entries in personal journals (e.g., see Figure 9.1, the two-way dialogue journal presented in Chapter 9)
- Hold brief conferences with individual students

Nonverbal behaviors can also be quite informative. For example, a teacher might

- Observe how well students perform physical tasks
- Look at the relative frequency of on-task and off-task behaviors
- Identify the kinds of activities in which students engage voluntarily (as Ms. Gordon did in the opening case study)
- Watch the "body language" that might reflect students' emotional reactions to classroom tasks

By looking at both verbal and nonverbal behaviors, teachers can acquire a lot of information not only about students' knowledge and misconceptions but also about students' study strategies, self-regulation skills, sense of self, interests and priorities, feelings about classroom subject matter, and attributions for success and failure.

Ask yourself whether your existing beliefs and expectations might be biasing your judgments.

Let's return to a principle we identified in our discussion of knowledge construction in Chapter 2: *Prior knowledge and beliefs affect new learning.* This principle applies to teachers as well as to students. Like all human beings, teachers impose meanings on the things they see and hear, and those meanings are influenced by the things they already know or believe to be true. Teachers' existing beliefs about particular students, as well as their expectations for students' performance, inevitably affect teachers' assessments of students' behaviors.[22]

One common source of bias in teachers' informal assessments of student performance is their existing beliefs about students of different ethnic groups, genders, and socioeconomic groups. An experiment with college students[23] provides an example. Students were told that they were participating in a study on teacher evaluation methods and were asked to view a videotape of a fourth grader named Hannah. Two versions of the videotape gave differing im-

---

[22] Farwell & Weiner, 1996; Ritts, Patterson, & Tubbs, 1992; Stiggins, 2001.

[23] Darley & Gross, 1983.

pressions about Hannah's socioeconomic status. Her clothing, the kind of playground on which she played, and information about her parents' occupations indirectly conveyed to some students that she was from a high socioeconomic background and to others that she was from a low socioeconomic background. All students watched Hannah taking an oral achievement test (one on which she performed at grade level) and were asked to rate Hannah on several characteristics. Students who had been led to believe that Hannah came from wealthy surroundings rated her ability well above grade level, whereas students believing that she came from a poor family evaluated her as being below grade level. The two groups of students also rated Hannah's work habits, motivation, social skills, and general maturity differently.

Keep a written record of your observations.

Let's revisit another principle we identified in Chapter 2: *Long-term memory isn't necessarily forever.* Teachers' memories of students' classroom behaviors can probably never be totally accurate and dependable records of what students have actually said and done. As normal human beings, teachers are apt to remember some behaviors but not others. When teachers must depend heavily on informal in-class observations of students' performance—and this will often be the case when working with young children who have limited reading and writing skills—they should keep ongoing, written records of what they see students do and what they hear students say.[24]

Don't take any single observation too seriously; instead, look for a pattern over time.

The greatest strength of informal assessment is its practicality. It typically involves little if any teacher time either beforehand or after the fact (except when teachers keep written records of their observations). Furthermore, it is flexible, in that teachers can adapt their assessment procedures on the spur of the moment, altering them as events in the classroom change.

Despite the practicality of informal assessment, its other RSVP characteristics are often questionable. For one thing, children and adolescents can behave inconsistently from one day to the next, or even within a single day or class period. Such inconsistency calls the reliability of informal assessments into question. A teacher who sees Naomi off task during an activity may happen to look at her during the *only* time she is off task. A teacher who asks Muhammed a question in class may happen to ask him one of the few questions for which he doesn't know the answer. Furthermore, informal assessments are rarely, if ever, standardized for all students. Teachers ask different questions of different students, and they are apt to observe each student's behavior in different contexts. Hence such assessments will definitely *not* yield the same kinds of information for all students.

Even when teachers see consistency in students' behavior over time, they do not always get accurate information about what students have learned. In other words, validity may be a problem.[25] For instance, Tom may intentionally answer questions incorrectly so that he doesn't look "smart" in front of his friends. Margot may be reluctant to say anything in class because she tends to stutter when she speaks in front of others. In general, when teachers use in-class questions to assess students' learning, they must be aware that some students (especially females and students from ethnic minority groups) will be less eager to respond than others.[26]

When teachers use informal assessment to draw conclusions about what students know and can do, then, they should base their conclusions on many observations over a long period.[27] Furthermore, they should treat any conclusions only as *hypotheses* that they

Many social and emotional factors affecting students' classroom learning—for instance, how comfortable students appear to be in public speaking activities—can best be assessed through informal observations. Rather than drawing conclusions from a single event, however, teachers should look for consistent patterns over time.

---

[24] R. L. Linn & Miller, 2005; Stiggins, 2001.
[25] Airasian, 1994; Stiggins, 2001.
[26] Altermatt, Jovanovic, & Perry, 1998; Sadker & Sadker, 1994; also see the Cultural Considerations box

"Cultural and Ethnic Differences in Verbal Interaction" in Chapter 8.
[27] Airasian, 1994.

must either confirm or disconfirm through other means. In the end, most teachers rely more heavily on formal assessment techniques to determine whether students have achieved instructional goals and objectives.

DESIGNING AND GIVING FORMAL ASSESSMENTS

As we've seen, classroom assessments not only assess students' learning but also *influence* students' learning. Furthermore, the conclusions teachers draw from assessment results—conclusions that affect final grades and decisions about promotion and graduation—can have a significant effect on students' future educational and career plans. Accordingly, teachers must take their formal assessments *very* seriously, planning and designing them carefully, administering them under optimal conditions for student performance, and scoring them reliably and equitably.

Following are several suggestions that should increase the RSVP characteristics of formal classroom assessments.

Get as much information as possible within reasonable time limits.

On average, longer assessment instruments have greater validity and reliability. To see why this might be so, try the next exercise.

SEE FOR YOURSELF

SEE FOR YOURSELF
Quick Quiz

You have presumably already read the discussion of motivation in Chapter 6. The following multiple-choice quiz assesses what you learned in that chapter. No peeking at the answers until you've responded to both items!

1. Which one of the following situations best illustrates *situated motivation*?
   a. Alexander has been interested in air travel and aerodynamics since he was a toddler, and he can often be seen sketching airplanes during his free time in class.
   b. When Barbara gets a lower grade on an assignment than she had anticipated, she complains to her friends, "I deserved a much higher grade. Mr. Smith obviously doesn't like me very much."
   c. Colby is confident he'll do well on an upcoming history test because he's done well on other history tests throughout the semester.
   d. Although Donna has never been terribly interested in being physically fit, she eagerly learns an aerobic exercise routine that her teacher has set to some of her favorite rap music.
2. Which one of the following is the best example of *cognitive dissonance*?
   a. Alicia says to herself, "I don't really like math very much, but I'm taking it because it's important for getting into a good college."
   b. Bob is certain that metal always sinks, and so he is puzzled when he sees a large metal battleship floating in the harbor.
   c. Carly gets so anxious during an important test that she can hardly concentrate on the test items.
   d. David gets really angry when he reads about the mass murders and other atrocities that Saddam Hussein committed against Iraqi citizens.

Now score your quiz. The correct answers are *d* and *b* for Items 1 and 2, respectively. If you answered both questions correctly, you earned an A (100%) on the quiz. If you answered only one question correctly, you earned an F (50%). And, of course, answering neither question correctly also means an F on the quiz.

Unfortunately, the length of my quiz is problematic. First, I assessed only two concepts (situated motivation and cognitive dissonance) out of the many concepts presented in

Chapter 6. Two concepts are hardly a representative sample of what you've learned about motivation, and so the quiz has questionable validity. Second, if you interpreted one of the items differently than I intended for you to interpret it, you might have answered an item incorrectly despite having the knowledge to answer it correctly. For example, in Item 2, if you assumed that David's previous impressions of Saddam Hussein were positive, then you might reasonably have selected *d* as an example of cognitive dissonance. With this one slip-up you would have gone from an A to an F. When a single misinterpretation moves a student from a very good grade to a very poor one—a misinterpretation that might happen on one occasion but not another—the reliability of the assessment is in doubt.

To some degree, then, longer is better when it comes to formal assessments. Ideally, a classroom assessment should include enough questions and tasks that (a) it adequately represents the content domain being assessed and (b) one or two errors due to irrelevant factors (e.g., misinterpretation of items) do not have a significant effect on the final result. Teachers shouldn't go overboard, however. Students become very tired—and teachers have little time left over for instruction—when tests and other assessment tasks take a great deal of time to complete.

When practical, use authentic tasks.

Historically, most educational assessment instruments have focused on measuring basic knowledge and skills in relative isolation from tasks typically found in the outside world. Spelling quizzes, mathematics word problems, and physical fitness tests are examples of such traditional assessments. Yet ultimately students must be able to transfer their knowledge and skills to complex tasks outside the classroom. The notion of **authentic assessment**—assessing students' knowledge and skills in an authentic, "real-life" context—is gaining increasing prominence in today's schools.[28]

In some situations an authentic assessment can involve paper and pencil. For example, a teacher might ask students to write a letter to a friend or develop a school newspaper. And in the opening case study, Akeem creates an action-figures catalog and a book about the history of flight. At other times it involves performance tasks. For example, a teacher might ask students to converse in a foreign language, design and build a bookshelf, or successfully maneuver a car into a parallel parking space.[29]

Whether they be paper-pencil or performance based, assessment tasks might be authentic to varying degrees. For instance, they might ask students to apply new skills to imagined or hypothetical—rather than truly real-world—situations. As an illustration, one seventh-grade social studies teacher gave her students this "semi-authentic" assignment in a unit on mapping elevation and topography:

Island Map Assignment

1. Using a contour interval of 15 feet and a scale of one inch to one mile, construct a contour map of an island that:
    a. Is 6 miles from east to west and 4 miles from north to south
    b. Has a maximum elevation of 124 feet, but rises to at least 105 feet
    c. Is steepest on the east side
    a. Has a stream running into the ocean on the west shore, with its source at an elevation of 90 feet
2. Draw two profile maps of your island, one showing the island from west to east and the other showing it from north to south.

Figure 10.5 shows 12-year-old Francisco's response to this assignment.

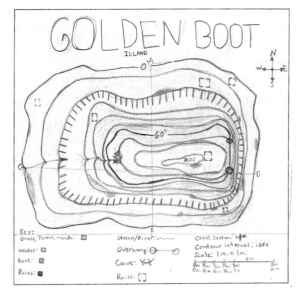

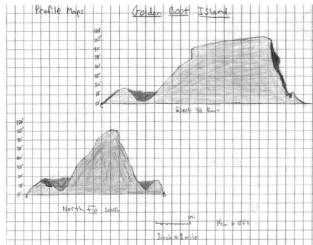

FIGURE 10.5   In his aerial and side-view drawings of "Golden Boot Island," 12-year-old Francisco demonstrates what he's learned about depicting elevation and topography.

---

[28] For example, see Darling-Hammond et al., 1995; DiMartino & Castaneda, 2007; Lester, Lambdin, & Preston, 1997; Paris & Paris, 2001; Valencia, Hiebert, & Afflerbach, 1994.

[29] Educators are not in complete agreement in their use of the terms *performance assessment* and *authentic*

assessment, and many treat the terms more or less as synonyms. I find it useful to consider separately whether an assessment involves *performance* (rather than paper and pencil) and whether it involves a complex, real-world (*authentic*) task. In the discussion here, then, I do *not* use the two terms interchangeably.

authentic assessment Assessment of students' knowledge and skills in a "real-life" context.

Use paper-pencil measures when they are consistent with instructional goals.

In some situations, such as when the desired outcome is simple recall of facts, a teacher might ask students to respond to multiple-choice or short-answer questions on a paper-pencil test. In other situations—for instance, when the objective is for students to critique a literary work or to explain everyday phenomena by using principles of physics—essay tasks that require students to follow a logical line of reasoning are appropriate. *If* a teacher can truly assess knowledge of a domain by having students respond in writing, then a paper-pencil assessment is a good choice.

Paper-pencil assessment is typically easier and faster, and so has greater practicality, than performance assessment. Usually a paper-pencil task can be administered to everyone in the classroom at the same time and under the same conditions, so it is easily standardized. To the extent that a paper-pencil assessment has a large number of items that can be objectively scored—as is true for true–false and multiple-choice tests—then it is also apt to be fairly reliable.

The RSVP characteristic of most concern in a paper-pencil assessment is its validity. When teachers ask questions that require only short, simple responses (e.g., true–false, multiple-choice, and matching questions), they can sample students' knowledge about many topics within a relatively short time period. In this sense, then, such questions can yield high content validity. Yet in some situations these types of items may not accurately reflect instructional goals. To assess students' ability to apply what they've learned to new situations, solve complex real-world problems, or engage in other higher-level thinking processes, teachers may sometimes need to be satisfied with a few tasks requiring lengthy responses.[30]

Unfortunately, many paper-pencil assessment instruments—especially teacher-created tests—focus primarily on lower-level skills.[31] (As an example, look once again at the geology test in Figure 10.2.) But with a little ingenuity, teachers can develop a wide variety of assessment tasks that require higher-level skills. The map interpretation task presented in Figure 4.10 (Chapter 4) and the map construction task illustrated in Figure 10.5 are two examples. The following essay task is another:

> You are to play the role of an advisor to President Nixon after his election to office in 1968. As his advisor, you are to make a recommendation about the United States' involvement in Vietnam.
>
> Your paper is to be organized around three main parts: An introduction that shows an understanding of the Vietnam War up to this point by explaining who is involved in the war and what their objectives are; also in the Introduction, you are to state a recommendation in one or two sentences to make the advice clear.
>
> The body of the paper should be written to convince the President to follow your advice by discussing: (a) the pros of the advice, including statistics, dates, examples, and general information . . . ; (b) the cons of the advice, letting the President know that the advisor is aware of how others might disagree. Anticipate one or two recommendations that others might give, and explain why they are not the best advice.
>
> The conclusion makes a final appeal for the recommendation and sells the President on the advice.[32]

Teachers can also assess higher-level skills with carefully constructed multiple-choice questions. In the "Quick Quiz" exercise you did earlier, you saw two multiple-choice questions that required you to transfer what you learned about motivation to new situations. The last two items in the Classroom Strategies box "Constructing Multiple-Choice Items" are additional examples.

Use performance assessments when necessary to ensure validity.

Because paper-pencil assessment is so practical, it should generally be the method of choice *if* it can yield a valid measure of what students know and can do. But in situations

---

[30] J. R. Frederiksen & Collins, 1989; Popham, 1995; Stiggins, 2001.

[31] Bransford et al., 2006; J. R. Frederiksen & Collins, 1989; Nickerson, 1989; Poole, 1994; Shepard et al., 2005.

[32] Newmann, 1997, p. 368.

CLASSROOM STRATEGIES

Constructing Multiple-Choice Items

- When assessing basic knowledge, rephrase ideas presented in class or in the textbook.

  A middle school language arts teacher uses short multiple-choice quizzes to assess students' understanding of each week's new vocabulary words. The items never include the specific definitions students have been given. For instance, for the word *manacle*, students have been given this definition: "Device used to restrain a person's hands or wrists." But the item on the quiz is this one:

  > Which one of the following words or phrases is closest in meaning to the word *manacle*?
  >
  > a. Insane
  > b. Handcuffs
  > c. Out of control
  > d. Saltwater creature that clings to hard surfaces
  > (*The correct answer is* b.)

- Present incorrect alternatives that are clearly wrong to students who know the material but plausible to students who haven't mastered it.

  After a unit on the seasons, a middle school science teacher asks this question:

  > What is the *main* reason that it is colder in winter than in summer?
  >
  > a. Because the earth is in the part of its orbit farthest away from the sun
  > b. Because wind is more likely to come from the north than from the south
  > c. Because the sun's rays hit our part of the earth at more of an angle
  > d. Because the snow on the ground reflects rather than absorbs the sun's heat
  > (*The correct answer is* c.)

- To assess higher-level thinking skills, ask students to apply what they've learned to new situations.

  A high school physics teacher includes the following question on a quiz designed to assess what students have learned about simple machines:

  > An inventor has just designed a new device for cutting paper. Without knowing anything else about his invention, we can predict that it is probably which type of machine?

  > a. A lever
  > b. A movable pulley
  > c. An inclined plane
  > d. A wedge
  > (*The correct answer is* d.)

- Occasionally incorporate visual materials.

  A high school geography teacher includes maps in some of his questions. Following is an example:

  > Using the map below, choose the most logical explanation of why the languages of the Far East are so distinctly different from those of the Middle East.
  >
  > a. Because people in the Far East had little contact with those who lived in the Middle East
  > b. Because people who lived by the ocean had very different lifestyles than people who lived in the mountains
  > c. Because people who lived in southern climates had very different lifestyles than people who lived in northern climates
  > d. Because people in the two regions were constantly fighting over desirable farmland
  > (*The correct answer is* a.)

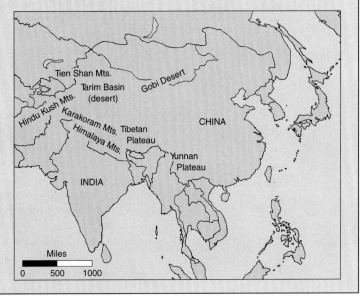

where paper-pencil tasks are clearly not a good reflection of what students have learned, teachers may need to sacrifice such practicality to gain the greater validity that a performance assessment provides.

A wide variety of performance tasks can be used to assess students' mastery of classroom subject matter. Here are just a few of the many possibilities:[33]

- Playing a musical instrument
- Conversing in a foreign language
- Identifying an unknown chemical substance
- Engaging in a debate about social issues
- Fixing a malfunctioning machine

---

[33] DiMartino & Castaneda, 2007; Gronlund, 1993; C. Hill & Larsen, 1992; D. B. Swanson, Norman, & Linn, 1995.

- Role-playing a job interview
- Performing a workplace routine
- Creating a computer simulation of a real-world activity
- Presenting research findings to a gathering of teachers, peers, and community members

Performance assessment lends itself especially well to the assessment of complex achievements, such as those that involve simultaneous use of multiple skills. It may also be quite helpful in assessing such higher-level thinking skills as problem solving, creativity, and critical thinking. Furthermore, performance tasks are often more meaningful, thought provoking, and authentic for students—and so often more motivating—than paper-pencil tasks.[34]

Some performance assessments focus on tangible *products* that students create—perhaps a sculpture, scientific invention, or poster display. In situations with no tangible product, teachers must instead look at the specific *processes and behaviors* that students exhibit—perhaps how they give an oral presentation, execute a forward roll, or play an instrumental solo. When teachers look at processes rather than products, they may in some instances probe students' *thinking processes*. For example, a teacher who wants to determine whether students have developed some of the concrete operational or formal operational abilities that Piaget described (e.g., conservation, multiple classification, separation and control of variables) might present tasks similar to those Piaget used and ask students to explain their reasoning (see Chapter 5). And a teacher can often learn a great deal about how students reason about scientific phenomena by asking them to manipulate physical objects (e.g., chemicals in a chemistry lab, electrical circuit boards in a physics class), make predictions about what will happen under varying circumstances, and then explain their results.[35] The Classroom Strategies box "Developing Performance Assessments" presents and illustrates several suggestions for using performance assessments for different age levels and content domains.

One form of performance assessment gaining popularity is **dynamic assessment**.[36] In this approach, rather than find out what students have already learned, a teacher assesses students' *ability to learn something new*, perhaps with the assistance of the teacher, a teacher aide, or parent volunteer. Such an approach reflects Vygotsky's *zone of proximal development* and can reveal what students are likely to be able to accomplish with appropriate structure and guidance. Hence it is most appropriate for formative (rather than summative) evaluation.

As previously noted, performance assessment tasks sometimes provide more valid indicators of what students have accomplished relative to instructional goals. However, students' responses to a *single* performance assessment task are frequently *not* a good indication of their overall achievement.[37] Content validity is at stake here. If time constraints allow students to perform only one or two complex tasks, those tasks may not be a representative sample of what students have learned and can do. In addition, teachers may have difficulty standardizing assessment conditions for everyone and scoring students' performance consistently—problems that adversely affect reliability.[38] And performance assessments are often less practical than more traditional paper-pencil assessments.[39] Conducting an assessment can be quite time consuming, especially when a teacher must observe students one by one or when a task requires students to spend considerable time in the outside community.

As you can see, then, informal assessment, formal paper-pencil assessment, and formal performance assessment all have their strengths and weaknesses. Table 10.3 summarizes their RSVP characteristics and offers relevant suggestions. In the end, teachers may find that they can best assess students' achievement with a combination of paper-pencil and performance tasks and supplement their findings with informal observations of students' typical classroom behavior.[40]

---

dynamic assessment Systematic examination of how easily a student can acquire new knowledge or skills, perhaps with an adult's assistance.

[34] Darling-Hammond et al., 1995; Khattri & Sweet, 1996; Paris & Paris, 2001; D. P. Resnick & Resnick, 1996.
[35] De Corte, Greer, & Verschaffel, 1996; Magnusson, Boyle, & Templin, 1994; Quellmalz & Hoskyn, 1997.
[36] For example, see Feuerstein, Feuerstein, & Gross, 1997; Hamers & Ruijssenaars, 1997; Haywood & Lidz, 2007; Shepard, 2000; H. L. Swanson & Lussier, 2001; Tzuriel, 2000.

[37] Koretz, Stecher, Klein, & McCaffrey, 1994; R. L. Linn, 1994; Shavelson, Baxter, & Pine, 1992; D. B. Swanson et al., 1995.
[38] S. Burger & Burger, 1994; R. L. Linn, 1994; Shavelson et al., 1992; D. B. Swanson et al., 1995.
[39] L. M. Carey, 1994; Hambleton, 1996; Popham, 1995.
[40] Messick, 1994a; Stiggins, 2001; D. B. Swanson et al., 1995.

CLASSROOM STRATEGIES

Developing Performance Assessments

- **Have students create products that reflect what they have learned.**

    A middle school science teacher asks students to make posters that summarize their projects for the school science fair. The teacher tells the students that the posters should include (a) a research question or hypothesis, (b) the method used to address the question or hypothesis, (c) results obtained, and (d) one or more conclusions.

- **When the assigned task doesn't yield a tangible product, observe students' behaviors and, if appropriate, probe their thinking processes.**

    After a unit on major and minor scales in an instrumental band class, a music teacher assesses students' understanding of natural minor scales by having them play three different ones on their instruments. If a student plays a scale incorrectly, the teacher asks the student to describe the structure of a minor scale (whole-step, half-step, whole-step, whole-step, half-step, whole-step, whole-step) and explain why the scale might not have sounded right.

- **Consider assigning complex, lengthy tasks as group projects.**

    In a unit on urban geography, a high school social studies teacher assigns this authentic assessment task as a cooperative group project:

    First, select one of the neighborhoods marked on the city map. Second, identify its current features by doing an inventory of its buildings, businesses, housing, and public facilities. Also, identify current transportation patterns and traffic flow. From the information made available, identify any special problems this neighborhood has, such as dilapidated housing, traffic congestion, or a high crime rate. Third, as a group, consider various plans for changing and improving your neighborhood.

    In evaluating students' performance, the teacher considers each group's overall accomplishments plus individual students' contributions to the group effort.

- **Consider incorporating the assessment into normal instructional activities.**

    To assess students' understanding of simple graphs, a first-grade teacher distributes a table that lists the 12 months of the year. She asks her students to circulate around the room, gathering each class member's signature in a box beside his or her birthday month. In this way, students create graphs showing how many class members were born in each month. The graphs indicate that some but not all students have a general understanding of graphs. In the example below, many students (e.g., Cam, Sara, Kelsey, Adrienne, Spencer) have all written their names inside a single box in the table. However, a few students (Kristen, Jesse, Kristah, and Cameron) have used two cells to write their names, perhaps because they (a) haven't mastered the idea that one person equals one box in the table or (b) can't write small enough to fit their names inside a box and don't know how to solve this problem. The graph also shows that one child (Meg, who has a March birthday) has not yet learned to write words, including her name, in the traditional left-to-right manner.

Birthday Graph

January	CANK/ISEN M			
February	SARA			
March	KELSEY	EGM		
April	JESSE P			TON
May	W WT			
June	ADRIENNE			
July	Allison	Kristah		
August	AJ	MAGGIE		
September	3PAB	casey	BenB.	
October	Mrs. O'Byrne	Margaret	VICKY	
November	Ben D	Ms. Gray	CAMERON	
December	SPENCER	May		

Sources: Baxter, Elder, & Glaser, 1996; Boschee & Baron, 1993; DiMartino & Castaneda, 2007; Kennedy, 1992; Lester et al., 1997; Newmann, 1997 ("neighborhoods" task from p. 369); Shavelson & Baxter, 1992; Stiggins, 2001.

Define tasks clearly, and give students some structure to guide their responses.

Contrary to what some teachers believe, there is usually little to be gained from assigning ambiguous tasks to assess students' learning and achievement. Whether or not students know how to respond to assessment tasks, they should at least understand what they are being asked to do.

As an illustration, consider this essay question in an American history class:
List the causes of the American Revolution.

What does the teacher actually want students to do? One student might take the word *list* literally and simply write "Stamp Act, Boston Massacre, Quartering Act." Yet another student might write several pages describing Britain's increasing restriction of navigation, the colonists' resentment of taxation without representation, and King George III's apparent lack of concern about the colonists' welfare. Responses to unstructured tasks may go in so many different directions that scoring them consistently and reliably is virtually impossible. Especially in situations where a great deal of material is potentially relevant, students need some guidance about the length and completeness of desired responses and

TABLE 10.3 Evaluating RSVP Characteristics of Different Kinds of Assessments

Kind of Assessment	Reliability	Standardization	Validity	Practicality
Informal assessment	A single, brief assessment is not a reliable indicator of achievement. Teachers must look for consistency in a student's performance across time and in different contexts.	Informal observations are rarely, if ever, standardized. Thus teachers should not compare one student to another on the basis of informal assessments alone.	Students' "public" behavior in the classroom is not always a valid indicator of their achievement (e.g., some may try to hide high achievement from peers, others may come from cultures that encourage listening more than talking).	Informal assessment is definitely practical. It is flexible and can occur spontaneously during instruction.
Formal paper-pencil assessment	Objectively scorable items are highly reliable. Teachers can enhance the reliability of subjectively scorable items by specifying scoring criteria in concrete terms.	In most instances paper-pencil instruments are easily standardized for all students. Giving students choices (e.g., regarding topics to write about or questions to answer) may increase motivation, but it reduces standardization.	Using numerous questions that require short, simple responses can make an assessment a more representative sample of the content domain. But tasks requiring lengthier responses may sometimes more closely match instructional goals.	Paper-pencil assessment is usually practical. All students can be assessed at once, and no special materials are required.
Formal performance assessment	It is often difficult to score performance assessment tasks reliably. Teachers can enhance reliability by specifying scoring criteria in concrete terms.	Some performance assessment tasks are easily standardized, whereas others are not.	Performance tasks may sometimes be more consistent with instructional goals than paper-pencil tasks. A single performance task may not provide a representative sample of the content domain; several tasks may be necessary to ensure content validity.	Performance assessment is typically less practical than other approaches. It may involve special materials, and it can take a fair amount of class time, especially if students must be assessed one at a time.

about the things they should specifically address. For example, to assess what students have learned about causes of the American Revolution, a teacher might present this task:

> Identify three policies or events during the 1760s and/or 1770s that contributed to the outbreak of the American Revolution. For each of the three things you identify, explain in three to five sentences how it increased tension between England and the American colonies.

Performance assessment tasks, too, require a certain amount of structure, especially if they are used for summative (rather than formative) evaluation. For instance, students should have detailed directions about what they should accomplish, what materials and equipment they can use, and how much time they have to get the job done.[41] Such structure helps to standardize the assessment and so enables a teacher to evaluate students' performance more reliably. A *lot* of structure can decrease a performance task's validity, however. Especially when giving authentic assessments, teachers want assigned tasks to be similar to those in the outside world, and real-world tasks don't always have a lot of structure. Teachers must often seek a happy medium, providing enough structure to guide students in the right direction but not so much that students make few if any decisions for themselves about how to proceed.

Carefully scrutinize items and tasks to be sure they are free from cultural bias.

An assessment instrument has **cultural bias** if any of its items either offend or unfairly penalize some students on the basis of their ethnicity, gender, or socioeconomic status.[42] There are two important points to note about this definition. First, cultural bias includes biases related to gender and socioeconomic status as well as to culture and ethnicity. Second, an as-

cultural bias Extent to which assessment tasks either offend or unfairly penalize some students because of their ethnicity, gender, or socioeconomic status.

---

[41] Gronlund, 1993; E. H. Hiebert, Valencia, & Afflerbach, 1994; Shepard et al., 2005; Stiggins, 2001.

[42] This definition is based on one suggested by Popham, 1995.

sessment is biased if it either penalizes or *offends* a particular group. For example, imagine a test question that implies that boys are more competent than girls, and imagine another question that includes a picture in which members of a particular racial group are engaging in criminal behavior. Such questions have cultural bias because some groups of students (girls in the first situation and members of the depicted racial group in the second) are likely to be offended by the questions and thus distracted from doing their best on the test.

Historically, educators have been most concerned about eliminating cultural bias in large-scale standardized tests used for assessing intelligence and overall school achievement. Yet teachers should also screen their self-constructed classroom assessment instruments for possible biases that may put some groups of students at a disadvantage. The Cultural Considerations box "Potential Sources of Cultural Bias" gives examples of things teachers might look for.

Identify evaluation criteria in advance.

Some paper-pencil tasks, such as multiple-choice questions and many mathematics word problems, have clear-cut right and wrong answers. Some performance assessment tasks, too, are objectively scorable. A teacher can easily count the errors on a typing test or time students' performance in a 100-meter dash. But whenever a variety of student responses might be appropriate, and especially whenever students' responses might have varying degrees of quality, then teachers need to specify the criteria by which responses will be evaluated—not only for themselves but also for *students*.

Evaluating the quality as well as the quantity of what students produce is almost always in students' long-term best interest. For example, if a teacher gives full credit for completing an assignment without regard to the quality of what students produce, students may focus more on "getting the work done" than on acquiring a conceptual understanding of what they are studying.[43] At the same time, evaluation criteria must be realistic. Overly ambitious criteria for acceptable performance are apt to discourage students from taking risks and making errors—risks and errors that are inevitable when students tackle the challenges that can best promote their cognitive development.

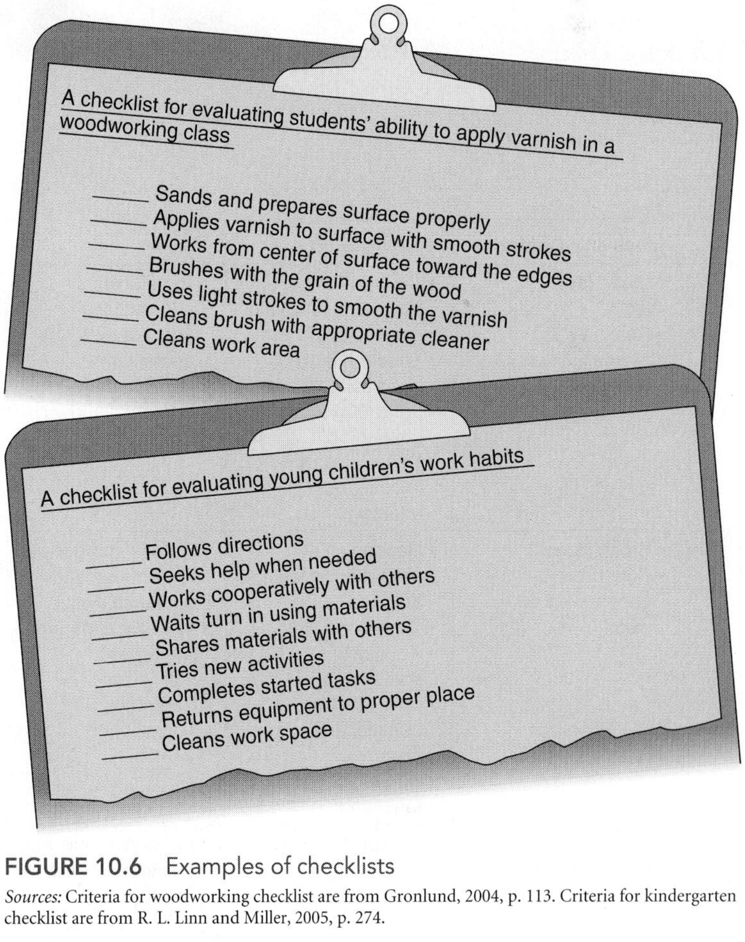

Teachers should typically determine the nature of good responses at the same time they develop their assessment instruments. Whenever an assessment task involves subjective evaluation of a complex performance—for instance, when it involves scoring lengthy essays, science fair posters, or art projects—teachers should list components that a good response should include or characteristics that will be considered in the evaluation. Such a list is known as a **rubric**. Some rubrics take the form of *checklists*, lists of behaviors or qualities that either are or are not present in a student's performance. Figure 10.6 presents examples of checklists for evaluating varnishing in a high school woodworking class and work habits in a kindergarten class. Other rubrics take the form of *rating scales*, which allow teachers to rate aspects of a student's performance on one or more continua. For example, Figure 10.7 presents a rating-scale rubric that teachers at Littleton High School in Colorado have used to evaluate students' writing. Notice how the rubric addresses six distinct aspects of a writing sample that a teacher should look for: ideas and content, organization, voice, word choice, sentence fluency, and use of conventions. It also provides guidance on criteria to use in assigning high, middle, or low scores.

Teachers and students alike benefit when scoring criteria are explicit. Teachers can evaluate students' responses more consistently, reliably, and (often) quickly, and their judgments are less likely to be influenced by their prior expectations

A checklist for evaluating students' ability to apply varnish in a woodworking class

_____ Sands and prepares surface properly
_____ Applies varnish to surface with smooth strokes
_____ Works from center of surface toward the edges
_____ Brushes with the grain of the wood
_____ Uses light strokes to smooth the varnish
_____ Cleans brush with appropriate cleaner
_____ Cleans work area

A checklist for evaluating young children's work habits

_____ Follows directions
_____ Seeks help when needed
_____ Works cooperatively with others
_____ Waits turn in using materials
_____ Shares materials with others
_____ Tries new activities
_____ Completes started tasks
_____ Returns equipment to proper place
_____ Cleans work space

FIGURE 10.6 Examples of checklists

Sources: Criteria for woodworking checklist are from Gronlund, 2004, p. 113. Criteria for kindergarten checklist are from R. L. Linn and Miller, 2005, p. 274.

---

[43] W. Doyle, 1983.

rubric List of components that a student's performance on an assessment task should ideally include.

CULTURAL CONSIDERATIONS

Potential Sources of Cultural Bias

Consider these two assessment tasks:

Task 1: Would you rather swim in the ocean, a lake, or a swimming pool? Write a two-page persuasive essay defending your choice.

Task 2: Mary is making a patchwork quilt from 36 separate squares of fabric, as shown at right. Each square of fabric has a perimeter of 20 inches. Mary sews the squares together, using a half-inch seam allowance. She then 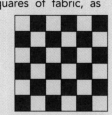 sews the assembled set of squares to a large piece of cotton that will serve as the flip side of the quilt, again using a half-inch seam allowance. How long is the perimeter of the finished quilt?

Task 1 would obviously be difficult for students who haven't been swimming in all three environments and would be even more difficult for students who have never swum at all. Students from low-income, inner-city families might easily fall into one of these two categories. Task 2 assumes a fair amount of knowledge about sewing (e.g., what a *seam allowance* is). This is knowledge that some students (especially girls) are more likely to have than others. Such tasks have cultural bias because some students will perform better than others because of differences in their background experiences, *not* because of differences in what they have learned in the classroom. The "Building a Treehouse" exercise in Chapter 3 (p. 73) has cultural bias as well, in that boys are more likely than girls—and children in rural areas are more likely than children in urban areas—to have had treehouse-building experience.

In considering possible sources of bias in classroom assessments, teachers must look

	Ideas and Content	Organization	Voice	Word Choice	Sentence Fluency	Conventions
5	• Clear, focused topic. • Relevant and accurate supporting details.	• Clear intro and body and satisfying conclusion. • Thoughtful transitions clearly show how ideas are connected. • Sequencing is logical and effective.	• Tone furthers purpose and appeals to audience. • Appropriately individual and expressive.	• Words are specific and accurate. • Language and phrasing is natural, effective, and appropriate.	• Sentence construction produces natural flow and rhythm.	• Grammar and usage are correct and contribute to clarity and style.
3	• Broad topic. • Support is generalized or insufficient.	• Recognizable beginning, middle, and end. • Transitions often work well; sometimes connections between ideas are fuzzy. • Sequencing is functional.	• Tone is appropriate for purpose and audience. • Not fully engaged or involved.	• Words are adequate and support the meaning. • Language is general but functional.	• Sentences are constructed correctly.	• Grammar and usage mistakes do not impede meaning.
1	• Unclear topic. • Lacking or irrelevant support.	• No apparent organization. • Lack of transitions. • Sequencing is illogical.	• Not concerned with audience or fails to match purpose. • Indifferent or inappropriate.	• Improper word choice/usage makes writing difficult to understand. • Language is vague or redundant.	• Sentences are choppy, incomplete, or unnatural.	• Grammar and mistakes distract the reader or impede meaning.

FIGURE 10.7 Example of a rating-scale rubric for evaluating the quality of high school students' writing

Source: From *Breaking Ranks II: Strategies for Leading High School Reform* by the National Association of Secondary School Principals (NASSP), p. 103. Copyright 2004, National Association of Secondary School Principals, Reston, VA. Reprinted with permission.

not only at the content of their assessment tasks but also at how the tasks are being administered. For instance, students who have recently immigrated and only begun to learn English—even those students with strong math skills—may do poorly on mathematics word problems because such problems require a good command of written English.[a] In such instances a teacher might restate the problems in simpler language and perhaps draw pictures to help students understand the problem-solving tasks. And let's return to a point made in Chapter 3: Children from some cultural groups (e.g., those from some Native American communities) prefer to practice a skill privately until they attain reasonable mastery.[b] In such

cases a teacher might let students practice new skills away from the limelight and demonstrate their progress in private, one-on-one sessions.

An assessment instrument isn't necessarily biased just because one group of students gets higher scores than another group. It is biased only if the groups' scores are different when the knowledge and skills a teacher is trying to assess *aren't* different. In some cases different groups have different backgrounds that affect their classroom learning as well as their performance on assessments. For example, the fact that boys tend to have more "mathematical" toys and experiences than girls may give them an advantage that affects both their ability to

learn certain mathematical concepts and processes *and* their ability to perform well on tasks assessing mastery of those concepts and processes.[c] Similarly, if students from low-income families have had few opportunities to venture beyond their immediate neighborhoods (fewer museum trips, less travel, etc.), their more limited exposure to diverse environments is likely to impact *both* their classroom achievement and their performance on assessments measuring that achievement.

[a] Garcia, 2005.
[b] Garcia, 1994; S. Sanders, 1987; Suina & Smolkin, 1994.
[c] Jacobs, Davis-Kean, Bleeker, Eccles, & Malanchuk, 2005; Leaper & Friedman, 2007.

for particular students' performances. Meanwhile, students have clear targets toward which to shoot as they study and practice. And, of course, a rubric helps teachers provide concrete, constructive feedback to help students improve.[44]

When giving tests, encourage students to do their best, but don't arouse a lot of anxiety.

Most students get a little bit anxious about tests and other important assessments, and as we discovered in Chapter 6, a small amount of anxiety may actually enhance performance. But some students become extremely anxious in test-taking situations—that is, they have **test anxiety**—to the point where they get scores that significantly underestimate what they've learned.[45] Such students appear to be concerned primarily about the *evaluative* aspect of tests, in that they are terribly concerned that someone else (e.g., their teacher) will make negative judgments about them.[46] Test anxiety interferes not only with retrieval at the time of the test but also with encoding and storage when learners are studying for the test.[47] Thus highly test-anxious students don't just *test* poorly, they also *learn* poorly.

Test anxiety is rare in the early grades but increases throughout the elementary school years.[48] Many secondary and upper elementary students have test anxiety that significantly interferes with their test performance. Debilitating test anxiety is especially common in students from some ethnic minority groups, students with disabilities, and students with a history of academic failure.[49]

Table 10.4 distinguishes between classroom assessment practices that are likely to lead to facilitating anxiety and those that may elicit debilitating anxiety.

[44] Meltzer, Pollica, & Barzillai, 2007; Shepard et al., 2005.
[45] Cassady & Johnson, 2002; Hembree, 1988; K. T. Hill, 1984; E. Hong, O'Neil, & Feldon, 2005.
[46] Harter, Whitesell, & Kowalski, 1992; B. N. Phillips, Pitcher, Worsham, & Miller, 1980; Wine, 1980.
[47] Cassady & Johnson, 2002.
[48] Kirkland, 1971; S. B. Sarason, 1972.
[49] Kirkland, 1971; Pang, 1995; B. N. Phillips et al., 1980.

test anxiety Excessive anxiety about a particular test or about assessment in general.

TABLE 10.4   Keeping Students' Anxiety at a Facilitative Level During Classroom Assessments

What to Do	What *Not* to Do
Point out the value of the assessment as a feedback mechanism to improve learning.	Stress the fact that students' competence is being evaluated.
Administer a practice assessment or pretest that gives students an idea of what the final assessment will be like.	Keep the nature of the assessment a secret until the day it is administered.
Encourage students to do their best.	Remind students that failing will have dire consequences.
Provide or allow the use of memory aids (e.g., a list of formulas or a single note card containing key facts) when instructional goals do not require students to commit information to memory.	Insist that students commit even trivial facts to memory.
Eliminate time limits unless speed is an important part of the skill being measured.	Give more questions or tasks than students can possibly respond to in the allotted time.
Continually survey the room, and be available to answer students' questions.	Hover over students, watching them closely as they respond.
Use unannounced ("pop") quizzes only for formative evaluation (e.g., to determine an appropriate starting point for instruction).	Give occasional pop quizzes to motivate students to study regularly and to punish those who do not.
Use the results of several assessments to make decisions (e.g., to assign grades).	Evaluate students on the basis of a single assessment.

Sources: Brophy, 1986, 2004; Cizek, 2003; Gaudry & Bradshaw, 1971; K. T. Hill, 1984; K. T. Hill & Wigfield, 1984; Popham, 1990; Sax, 1989; Sieber, Kameya, & Paulson, 1970; Spaulding, 1992; Stipek, 1993.

Establish conditions that enable students to maximize their performance.

Teachers' concerns about maximizing the validity of a classroom assessment must not end once they've determined how they're going to assess students' learning and achievement. Teachers must also keep validity in mind while administering the assessment. For example, students are more likely to perform at their best when they complete an assessment in a comfortable environment with acceptable room temperature, adequate lighting, reasonable workspace, and minimal distractions. This comfort factor may be especially important for students who are easily distracted, unaccustomed to formal assessments, or unmotivated to exert much effort—for instance, it's an important consideration for students at risk.[50]

In addition, students should be able to ask questions when assigned tasks are not clear. Despite good intentions, a teacher may present a task or question that is unclear, ambiguous, or even misleading. (Even with more than 30 years' experience developing assignments and exams, I still have students occasionally interpreting them in ways I didn't anticipate.) To increase the likelihood that students will respond in desired ways, a teacher should encourage them to ask for clarification whenever they are uncertain about a task. Such encouragement is especially important for students from ethnic minority groups, many of whom may be reluctant to ask questions during a formal assessment situation.[51]

Take reasonable steps to discourage cheating.

The prevalence of cheating increases as students get older, and by high school the great majority of students are apt to cheat on assessments at one time or another. In fact, in the high school grades, many students think that occasional cheating is "no big deal" and report that some of their teachers seem unconcerned when it occurs. In fact, cheating *is* a big deal, and its occurrence should concern teachers quite a bit. Not only does cheating render assessment

---

[50] Popham, 1990.

[51] L. R. Cheng, 1987; C. A. Grant & Gomez, 2001.

results invalid, but it also can be habit forming when students discover that it enables them to get good grades with minimal effort.[52]

Students cheat for a number of reasons. For instance, they may be more interested in doing well on an assessment than in actually learning the subject matter (i.e., performance goals predominate over mastery goals). Students may believe that teachers' or parents' expectations for their performance are so high as to be unattainable and that success is out of reach unless they *do* cheat. They may perceive certain assessments (tests especially) to be poorly constructed, arbitrarily graded, or in some other way a poor reflection of what they have learned. Furthermore, their peers may communicate that cheating is common and justifiable.[53]

The best approach is prevention—making sure students don't cheat in the first place. For instance, teachers can take the following precautions:

In the weeks or days before the assessment:

- Focus students' attention on mastery rather than performance goals.
- Make success without cheating a realistic possibility.
- Construct assessment instruments with obvious validity for important instructional goals.
- Explain exactly what cheating is and why it is unacceptable (e.g., explain that cheating includes plagiarism, such as copying material word for word from the Internet without giving appropriate credit).[54]
- Explain what the consequence for cheating will be.

During the assessment (especially during a test or quiz):

- Use two or more assessment instruments that are equivalent in form and content but have different answers. For example, use one form in class and another for make-ups, or use different forms for different class periods.
- Have teacher-chosen assigned seats during any assessments that require individual (rather than group) work.
- Seat students as far away from one another as possible.
- Remain attentive to what students are doing throughout an assessment session, but without hovering over or in some other way focusing on particular students.

If, despite reasonable precautions, cheating does occur, a teacher must administer the consequence he or she has previously described. This consequence should be severe enough to discourage a student from cheating again, yet not so severe that the student's motivation and chances for academic success are significantly diminished over the long run. For instance, what I have typically done is to require a student to redo the task, often for less credit than he or she would have earned otherwise.

EVALUATING STUDENTS' PERFORMANCE ON FORMAL ASSESSMENTS

As teachers evaluate students' performance on an assessment task, they must continue to be concerned about the four RSVP characteristics. Furthermore, they must keep in mind that their most important role is not to evaluate performance, but rather to help students learn. And for both pedagogical and legal reasons, they must preserve students' general sense of well-being and right to privacy. Each of the following strategies is valuable in achieving one or more of these ends.

After students have completed an assessment, review evaluation criteria to be sure they can adequately guide scoring.

Even the most experienced teachers can't anticipate the many possible directions in which students might go in responding to classroom assessment tasks. As a general rule, teachers

[52] Cizek, 2003.
[53] E. M. Anderman, Griesinger, & Westerfield, 1998; Cizek, 2003; E. D. Evans & Craig, 1990; Murdock & Anderman, 2006; Murdock, Miller, & Kohlhardt, 2004.

[54] One recent study found that many middle school students erroneously believe copying material verbatim from the Internet to be appropriate and acceptable (Nixon, 2005).

should use the criteria they have told students they would use. However, they may occasionally need to adjust (or perhaps add or eliminate) one or more criteria to accommodate unexpected responses and improve their ability to score the responses consistently, fairly, and reliably. Any adjustments should be made *before* a teacher begins scoring, rather than midway through a stack of papers. For example, when grading written assessments, it is often helpful to skim a sample of students' papers first, looking for unusual responses and revising the criteria as needed.

Be as objective as possible.

A scoring rubric can certainly help teachers apply evaluation criteria objectively and consistently for all students, thereby increasing standardization and, indirectly, reliability. In addition, when assessments involve multiple tasks (e.g., several essay questions, or lab reports with several discrete sections), teachers can often score students' responses more reliably by grading everyone's response to the first task, then everyone's response to the second task, and so on. And covering students' names with small, self-stick notes can help teachers keep their existing beliefs and expectations about particular students from influencing their judgments of the students' work.

Make note of any significant aspects of a student's performance that a rubric doesn't address.

Scoring rubrics are rarely perfect. Whenever teachers break down students' performance on a complex task into discrete behaviors, they can lose valuable information in the process.[55] When teachers use rubrics in scoring, then, they may occasionally want to jot down other noteworthy characteristics of students' performance. This aspect of the scoring process will be neither standardized nor reliable, of course, but it can sometimes be useful in identifying students' unique strengths and needs and can therefore be helpful in future instructional planning.

Ask students to evaluate their performance as well.

As noted early in the chapter, playing an active role in their own assessments—in other words, engaging in *self-assessment*—can help students develop proficiency in such self-regulation skills as self-monitoring and self-evaluation. Following are several strategies for helping students develop self-regulation skills by including them in the assessment process:[56]

- Provide examples of "good" and "poor" products, and ask students to compare them on the basis of several criteria.
- Solicit students' ideas about evaluation criteria and rubric design.
- Have students identify their most common errors and create personalized checklists that enable them to double-check their work for these errors.
- Have students compare self-ratings with teacher ratings (e.g., note the "Self" and "Teacher" columns in the word problem rubric in Figure 10.8).
- Have students chart their progress over time.
- Have students reflect on their work in daily or weekly journal entries, where they can keep track of knowledge and skills they have and have not mastered, as well as learning strategies that have and have not been effective.
- Ask students to write practice questions similar to those they expect to see on upcoming quizzes and tests.
- Ask students to lead parent conferences.

An additional strategy is having students compile portfolios of their work. We'll look at portfolios more closely later in the chapter.

Elements	Possible Points	Points Earned	
		Self	Teacher
1. You highlighted the question(s) to solve.	2	____	____
2. You picked an appropriate strategy.	2	____	____
3. Work is neat and organized.	2	____	____
4. Calculations are accurate.	2	____	____
5. Question(s) answered.	2	____	____
6. You have explained in words how you solved the problem.	5	____	____
Total	____	____	____

FIGURE 10.8 In this rubric for scoring solutions to mathematics word problems in a fourth-grade class, both teacher and student evaluate various aspects of the student's performance.

[55] Delandshere & Petrosky, 1998.
[56] A. L. Brown & Campione, 1996; R. L. Linn & Miller, 2005; Meltzer et al., 2007; Paris & Ayres, 1994; Shepard, 2000; Stiggins, 2001; Valencia et al., 1994.

When determining overall scores, don't compare students to one another unless there is a compelling reason to do so.

For all intents and purposes, scores on tests and other assessments take one of three forms. Most commonly used on teacher-constructed assessments is a **raw score**, which is based solely on the number or percentage of points earned or items answered correctly. For example, a student who correctly answers 15 items on a 20-item multiple-choice test might get a score of 75 percent. A student who gets 3 points, 8 points, and 5 points on three essay questions, respectively, might get an overall score of 16. Raw scores are easy to calculate, and they appear to be easy to understand. But in fact, we sometimes have trouble knowing what raw scores really mean. Are scores of 75 percent and 16 good scores or bad ones? Without knowing what kinds of tasks an assessment includes, we have no easy way of interpreting a raw score.

A **criterion-referenced score** indicates what students have achieved in relation to specific instructional objectives or standards. Some criterion-referenced scores are "either-or" scores indicating that a student has passed or failed a unit, mastered or not mastered a skill, or met or not met an objective. As an example, Figure 10.9 illustrates the use of this approach in a beginning swimming class. Other criterion-referenced scores indicate various levels of competence or achievement. For instance, the rubric presented in Figure 10.7 enables teachers to assign six specific, criterion-referenced scores, each on a 1-to-5 scale, to students' written work.

Both raw scores and criterion-referenced scores are determined solely by looking at an individual student's performance. In contrast, a **norm-referenced score** is determined by comparing a student's performance with the performance of others. For teacher-constructed classroom assessments, these "others" are typically other students in the same class. In the case of published standardized tests, the comparison group is typically a large group of peers in a nationwide *norm group*. A norm-referenced score tells us little about what a student specifically knows and can do. Instead, it tells us whether a student's performance is typical or unusual for the age or grade level.

Norm-referenced scores—in everyday lingo, those that result from "grading on the curve"—are often used in standardized tests (more about this point later). They are far less common in teacher-constructed classroom assessments. They may occasionally be necessary when designating "first chair" in an instrumental music class or choosing the best entries for a regional science fair. Teachers may also need to resort to a norm-referenced approach when assessing complex skills (e.g., poetry writing, advanced athletic skills, or critical analysis of literature) that are difficult to describe as "mastered." Teachers should probably *not* use norm-referenced scores on a regular basis, however. Such scores create a competitive situation in which students do well only if their performance surpasses that of their classmates. Thus norm-referenced scores focus students' attention primarily on performance goals rather than mastery goals and may possibly encourage them to cheat on assessment tasks.[57] Furthermore, the competitive atmosphere that norm-referenced scores create is inconsistent with the *sense of community* described in Chapter 9.

Criterion-referenced scores communicate what teachers and students alike most need to know: whether instructional goals and objectives have been achieved. In doing so, they focus attention on mastery goals and, by showing improvement over time, can enhance students' self-efficacy for learning academic subject matter. When criterion-referenced scores are difficult to determine—perhaps because a single assessment addresses too many objectives simultaneously—raw scores are usually the second best choice, at least on teacher-assigned classroom assessment tasks.

Give detailed and constructive feedback.

As teachers score students' performance on classroom assessments, they should remember that virtually *any* classroom assessment can promote future learning as well as determine current achievement levels. Accordingly, teachers should provide detailed comments that tell students what they did well, where their weaknesses lie, and how they can improve.[58]

---

[57] E. M. Anderman et al., 1998; Mac Iver et al., 1995.
[58] Bangert-Drowns, Kulik, Kulik, & Morgan, 1991; Krampen, 1987; Shepard et al., 2005.

Springside Parks and Recreation Department Beginner Swimmer Class

Students must demonstrate proficiency in each of the following:

☐ Jump into chest-deep water
☐ Hold breath under water for 8 seconds
☐ Float in prone position for 10 seconds
☐ Glide in prone position with flutter kick
☐ Float on back for 10 seconds
☐ Glide on back with flutter kick
☐ Demonstrate crawl stroke and rhythmic breathing while standing in chest-deep water
☐ Show knowledge of basic water safety rules

FIGURE 10.9 In this swimming class, students' performance is reported in a criterion-referenced fashion.

raw score Assessment score based solely on the number or point value of correctly answered items.

criterion-referenced score Assessment score that specifically indicates what a student knows or can do.

norm-referenced score Assessment score that indicates how a student's performance on an assessment compares with the average performance of others.

Make allowances for risk taking and the occasional "bad day."

Students should feel comfortable enough about the assessment process that they feel free to take risks and make mistakes. Only under these circumstances will they tackle the challenging tasks that can maximize their learning and cognitive development. Certainly they are unlikely to take risks if they strive for perfection in everything they do, as some high-achieving gifted students are apt to do.[59] Teachers encourage risk taking—and also decrease debilitating anxiety—not only when they communicate that mistakes are a normal part of learning but also when classroom assessment practices give students some leeway to be wrong without penalty.[60]

One strategy for encouraging risk taking is to *give frequent assessments*. Students who are assessed frequently are more likely to take occasional risks, and they will have less test anxiety, because they know that no single assessment will be "sudden death" if they earn low scores. Frequent assessment has other benefits as well. It provides ongoing information to both students and teachers about the progress students are making and about areas of weakness that need attention. It motivates students, especially those with lower ability, to study regularly; and with the pressure off to perform well on every single test and assignment, students are less likely to cheat to obtain good grades. The bottom line is that students who are assessed frequently learn and achieve at higher levels than students who are assessed infrequently.[61]

Another strategy is to *give students a chance to correct errors*. Especially when an assessment includes most or all of the content domain in question, students often benefit from correcting their errors on an assessment task. For example, when performance on a math quiz makes it clear that students haven't mastered a particular procedure, high school math teacher Dan Wagner has them complete an assignment that includes the following:

1. **Identification of the error.** Students describe in a short paragraph exactly what it is that they do not yet know how to do.
2. **Statement of the process.** Students explain, in words rather than mathematical symbols, the steps involved in the procedure they are trying to master.
3. **Practice.** Students demonstrate their mastery of the procedure with three new problems similar to the problem(s) they previously solved incorrectly.
4. **Statement of mastery.** Students state in a sentence or two that they have now mastered the procedure.[62]

By completing these four steps, students can replace a grade on a previous assessment with the new, higher one. The approach has a more general, long-term benefit as well. Dan tells me that many of his students eventually incorporate the four steps into their regular, internalized learning strategies.

Still another strategy is to *give retakes* when students perform poorly the first time around. As noted in the discussion of mastery learning in Chapter 8, some students need more time to master a topic than others and may therefore need to be assessed on the same material more than once. However, students who are allowed to redo the *same* test or assignment may work on the specific things the assessment covers without studying equally important but nonassessed material. (Remember, most assessment tasks can only represent small samples of the content in question.) Thus a teacher might construct two assessment instruments for the same content domain, using one as the initial assessment and the other for retakes. If this approach is too time consuming to be practical, a teacher might allow students to redo the same assessment a second time but then average the two scores earned.

Respect students' right to privacy.

How would you feel if one of your instructors

- Returned test papers in the order of students' test scores, so that those with highest scores were handed out first, and you received yours *last*?

To encourage risk taking and reduce anxiety about classroom assessments, assess students' learning frequently and provide opportunities for students to correct errors. Here a teacher uses a student's errors on a paper-pencil assessment to guide her future studying efforts.

[59] Parker, 1997.

[60] Clifford, 1990; N. E. Perry & Winne, 2004; Shepard et al., 2005.

[61] Crooks, 1988; E. D. Evans & Craig, 1990; Gaynor & Millham, 1976; Glover, 1989; Roediger & Karpicke, 2006; Sax, 1989.

[62] I thank Dan Wagner at the University Schools in Greeley, Colorado, for giving me permission to describe his approach.

- Told your other instructors how poorly you had done on a test so that they could be on the lookout for other stupid things you might do?
- Looked through your school records and discovered that you scored 92 on an "IQ" test you took last year and furthermore that a personality test revealed some unusual sexual fantasies?

You would probably be outraged that your instructor would do any of these things. Students' performance on assessment instruments should be somewhat confidential. But exactly *how* confidential? When should people know the results of students' assessments, and who should know them?

In the United States we get legal guidance on these questions from the **Family Educational Rights and Privacy Act (FERPA)**, passed by the U.S. Congress in 1974. This legislation limits normal school testing practices primarily to the assessment of achievement and scholastic aptitude, two things that are clearly within the school's domain. Furthermore, it restricts access to students' assessment results to the few individuals who really need to know them: the students who earn them, their parents, and school personnel directly involved with students' education and well-being. Assessment results can be shared with other individuals, such as a family doctor or a psychologist in private practice, *only* if parents or students give written permission (students must be at least 18 years old to grant permission themselves).

This legislative mandate for confidentiality has several implications for school assessment practices. For example, teachers *cannot*

- Ask students to reveal their political affiliation, sexual behavior or attitudes, illegal or antisocial behavior, potentially embarrassing mental or psychological problems, or family income. (An exception: Questions about income are appropriate when used to determine eligibility for financial assistance.)
- Post test scores in ways that allow students to learn one another's scores. For example, teachers cannot post scores according to birthdays, Social Security numbers, or code numbers reflecting the alphabetical order of students' names.
- Distribute papers in any way that allows students to observe one another's scores. For example, teachers cannot let students search through a stack of scored papers to find their own.

Keeping students' assessment scores confidential makes educational as well as legal sense. Students getting low scores may feel embarrassed or ashamed if classmates know their scores, and they may become more anxious about their future performance than they would be otherwise. Students with high scores may also suffer from having their scores made public. In many classrooms it isn't cool to be smart, and high achievers may perform at lower levels to avoid risking the rejection of peers. And, of course, publicizing students' assessment results focuses students' attention on performance goals—how they appear to others—rather than on mastering the subject matter.

Many educators initially interpreted FERPA as forbidding teachers to have students grade one another's test papers. In 2002, however, the U.S. Supreme Court ruled that this practice does not violate FERPA because the test scores obtained are not yet a part of students' permanent school records.[63] Nevertheless, having students grade one another's classroom assessments—and thereby revealing some students' exceptionally high or low performance—can have adverse effects on students' sense of psychological well-being in the classroom. For this reason, I strongly urge teachers *not* to have students swap and grade one another's papers.

SUMMARIZING STUDENTS' ACHIEVEMENT WITH GRADES AND PORTFOLIOS

Teachers summarize student achievement in a variety of ways. Some preschool and early elementary teachers use checklists to indicate specific accomplishments, and others compose three- to four-paragraph summaries describing students' strengths and weaknesses.

---

[63] *Owasso Independent School District v. Falvo*, 534 U.S. 426; for a more detailed explanation of this ruling, see Underwood and Webb, 2006.

Family Educational Rights and Privacy Act (FERPA) U.S. legislation passed in 1974 mandating that teachers and other school personnel (a) restrict access to students' test results and school records only to students, their parents, and school employees directly involved in the students' education; and (b) upon request, make test scores and other information in students' records available to students and parents, with appropriate assistance in interpreting this information.

Our focus here will be on the two most commonly used methods of summarizing achievement: grades and portfolios. Following are several recommendations for using them.

Base final grades largely on achievement and hard data.

Tempting as it might be to reward well-behaved, cooperative students with good grades and to punish chronic misbehavers with Ds or Fs, grades should ultimately reflect how much students have *learned.* Awarding good grades simply for good behavior or exceptional effort may mislead students and their parents into believing that students are making better progress than they actually are. Awarding low grades as punishment for disruptive behavior leads students to conclude (perhaps with good reason) that their teacher's grading system is arbitrary and meaningless.[64]

By and large, teachers should use hard data, such as the results of formal paper-pencil and performance assessments, when arriving at final conclusions about what students have achieved. For reasons we've previously identified, subjective teacher judgments—forming opinions based on casual observations and general impressions—tend to be unreliable and sometimes have little validity. Although teachers can generally judge the achievement of high-ability students with some accuracy, they are less accurate when they subjectively assess the achievement of low-ability students. Teachers are especially likely to underestimate the achievement of students from ethnic minority groups and those from low socioeconomic backgrounds.[65]

Use many assessments to determine final grades.

Earlier I listed several advantages of assessing students' learning and achievement frequently. Using multiple assessments to determine final grades can also help compensate for the imperfect reliability and validity of any single assessment. At the same time, teachers probably don't want to consider *everything* students do. For instance, they may not want to include students' early efforts at new tasks, which are likely to involve considerable trial and error. And many assessments may be more appropriately used for formative evaluation purposes—to help students learn—than for summative evaluation.[66]

Share grading criteria with students, and keep students continually apprised of their progress.

To give students a sense that they themselves have control over their grades and other summaries of achievement (recall our discussion of *internal attributions* in Chapter 6), their teachers must tell them early in the semester or school year what the grading criteria will be. In addition, by providing concrete information about how grades will be assigned, teachers avoid unpleasant surprises when students actually receive their grades. If a teacher discovers that initial grading criteria are overly stringent, he or she may need to "lighten up" in some way, perhaps by adjusting cutoffs or allowing retakes of critical assessments. But a teacher must never change criteria midstream in a way that unfairly penalizes some students or imposes additional, unanticipated requirements.

Keep in mind that many students, younger ones especially, have limited self-monitoring skills. Furthermore, given the undependable nature of long-term memory (see Chapter 2), they may not have an accurate recollection of their various assessment scores over a period of several weeks or months. Thus it is often helpful to give students ongoing progress reports (e.g., see Figure 10.10) or show them how to keep their own records (e.g., look once again at Figure 4.7 in Chapter 4).

Keep parents in the loop as well.

Certainly parents don't need to be apprised of every score their child gets on a classroom assessment. But they, too, have a right to know how their children are

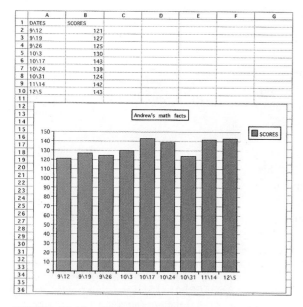

FIGURE 10.10   Computer software can often help teachers and students keep track of students' performance on classroom assessments. Here we see 10-year-old Andrew's performance on regular quizzes of math facts. Each quiz is worth 150 points.

---

[64] Brookhart, 2004; Cizek, 2003; Shepard et al., 2005.

[65] Brookhart, 2004; Gaines & Davis, 1990; Hoge & Coladarci, 1989; R. L. Linn & Miller, 2005.

[66] Brookhart, 2004; Frisbie & Waltman, 1992; Shepard et al., 2005.

progressing. In fact, in the United States, an additional provision of FERPA is that parents have the right to review any test scores and other school records. Furthermore, school personnel must present and interpret this information in a way that parents can understand.

In Chapter 9 we identified several ways of keeping the lines of communication open with parents, and some of them—parent–teacher conferences, brief notes and checklists sent home, and e-mail messages—are obviously suitable for transmitting information about students' assessment results and ongoing academic progress. For instance, the computer printout presented in Figure 10.10 can be informative to parents as well as to students.

What teachers must certainly *not* do is use their communications with parents as punishment for what they perceive to be insufficient effort on students' part. As an example, let's look in on Ms. Ford's middle school math class. Ms. Ford has just handed back test papers with disappointing results, and the following class discussion ensues:

> **Ms. Ford:** When I corrected these papers, I was really, really shocked at some of the scores. And I think you will be too. I thought there were some that were so-so, and there were some that were devastating, in my opinion.
>
> **Student:** [Noise increasing.] Can we take them over?
>
> **Ms. Ford:** I am going to give them back to you. This is what I would like you to do: Every single math problem that you got wrong, for homework tonight and tomorrow, it is your responsibility to correct these problems and turn them in. In fact, I will say this, I want this sheet back to me by Wednesday at least. All our math problems that we got wrong I want returned to me with the correct answer.
>
> **Student:** Did anybody get 100?
>
> **Ms. Ford:** No.
>
> **Student:** Nobody got 100? [Groans]
>
> **Ms. Ford:** OK, boys and girls, shhh. I would say, on this test in particular, boys and girls, if you received a grade below 75 you definitely have to work on it. I do expect this quiz to be returned with Mom or Dad's signature on it. I want Mom and Dad to be aware of how we're doing.
>
> **Student:** No!
>
> **Student:** Do we have to show our parents? Is it a requirement to pass the class?
>
> **Ms. Ford:** If you do not return it with a signature, I will call home.[67]

Ms. Ford obviously wants parents to know that their children are not doing well in her math class. However, there are several drawbacks to her approach. First, many students may find it easier to forge an adult-like signature than to deliver bad news to their parents. Second, parents who do see their children's test papers won't have much information to help them interpret the results (are the low scores due to low effort? to poor study strategies? to an undiagnosed learning disability? to poor instruction?). Finally, Ms. Ford focuses entirely on the problem— low achievement—without offering any concrete suggestions for *solving* the problem.

Ultimately, teachers must think of themselves as working in cooperation with students and parents for something that everyone wants: students' academic success. Teachers' primary goal in communicating assessment results is to share information that will foster achievement of that end—something Ms. Ford neglects to do. Furthermore, because virtually all of her students have done poorly on the test, Ms. Ford should consider whether something *she* has done—or not done—might account for the low scores. For instance, perhaps she allocated insufficient class time to certain concepts and skills, used ineffective strategies in teaching them, or constructed an exceptionally difficult test.

Accompany grades with descriptions of what the grades reflect.

As a general rule, final grades should reflect mastery of classroom subject matter and instructional goals. In other words, they should be criterion referenced.[68] When setting up a

[67] J. C. Turner, Meyer, et al., 1998, pp. 740–741.

[68] For example, see Stiggins, 2001; Shepard et al., 2005; Terwilliger, 1989. Over the past several decades, teachers have gradually moved from norm-referenced grading (i.e., grading on the curve) to criterion-referenced grading. This focus on mastery of instructional goals and objectives, rather than on comparing students with one another, partly accounts for the increasing grade point averages ("grade inflation") about which some public figures complain.

criterion-referenced grading system, teachers should determine as concretely as possible what they want each grade to communicate about students' achievement. For example, when assigning traditional letter grades, a teacher might use descriptors such as the following:

Grade	Criteria
A	The student has a firm command of both basic and advanced knowledge and skills in the content domain. He or she is well prepared for future learning tasks.
B	The student has mastered all basic knowledge and skills. Mastery at a more advanced level is evident in some, but not all, areas. In most respects, he or she is ready for future learning tasks.
C	The student has mastered basic knowledge and skills but has difficulty with more advanced aspects of the subject matter. He or she lacks a few of the prerequisites critical for future learning tasks.
D	The student has mastered some but not all of the basics in the content domain. He or she lacks many prerequisites for future learning tasks.
F	The student shows little if any mastery of instructional objectives and cannot demonstrate the most elementary knowledge and skills. He or she lacks most of the prerequisites essential for success in future learning tasks.[69]

It is especially important to specify grading criteria when different students in the same class are working toward different instructional goals. For example, in the United States the IDEA legislation stipulates that teachers and other school personnel identify appropriate instructional goals for individual children and adolescents who have special educational needs. Final evaluations of achievement, including final grades, should be based on students' accomplishment of those goals.[70]

Accompany grades with additional qualitative information about students' performance.

Even when final grades are accompanied by descriptions of what they reflect, they are at best only general indicators of the "quantity" of what students have learned. It is often helpful to also provide additional, more qualitative information—for instance, information about students' particular academic strengths, work habits, attitudes, social skills, unique contributions to the classroom community, and so on. Students and parents alike often find such qualitative feedback quite informative and helpful. Comments should be fairly explicit, however. Feedback such as "a pleasure to have in class" communicates little if any information.[71]

Use portfolios to show complex skills or improvements over time.

In the opening case study Akeem's portfolio showed his exceptional talents in drawing and sculpture and his ongoing progress in literacy skills. In general, a **portfolio** is a collection of a student's work systematically collected over a lengthy time period. It might include writing samples, student-constructed objects (e.g., sculptures, inventions), photographs, audiotapes, videotapes, or a combination of these. Some portfolios are *developmental* in nature, in that various products are included to show how a student has improved over time. Other portfolios include only a student's best work as a reflection of his or her final achievement.[72] Figure 10.4, which appears earlier in the chapter, presents a page from 6-year-old Meghan's portfolio that focuses on her social skills and work habits. Figure 10.11 presents another page from Meghan's portfolio, this one using photographs to show her emerging math skills. The portfolio definitely has a developmental bent, in that it's designed to document and communicate Meghan's progress in basic skills.

Portfolios have several advantages.[73] First, they capture the complex nature of students' achievement, often over a prolonged period, in ways that single-letter grades can't

Meghan makes arrangements of six in math.

Meghan displays her collection of 100.

FIGURE 10.11 In a kindergarten portfolio, Meghan and her teacher included these two digital photographs to illustrate Meghan's developing math skills.

portfolio Collection of a student's work systematically compiled over a lengthy time period.

---

[69] Based on criteria described by Frisbie & Waltman, 1992.
[70] Brookhart, 2004; Mac Iver, Stipek, & Daniels, 1991; Mastropieri & Scruggs, 2000; Venn, 2000.
[71] Brookhart, 2004, p. 183.

[72] Spandel, 1997; Winograd & Jones, 1992.
[73] Darling-Hammond et al., 1995; DiMartino & Castaneda, 2007; Koretz et al., 1994; Paris & Paris, 2001; Paulson, Paulson, & Meyer, 1991; Spandel, 1997.

SELF-EVALUATION

The three pieces of writing in my portfolio that best represent who I am are: 1) "Author Ben Hoff," which is a story in the language of Ben Hoff; 2) "Quotes from The Tao of Pooh"; and 3) "Discrimination."

What "Author Ben Hoff" shows about me as a learner or a writer is that I am able to analyze and absorb the types and styles of an author and then transfer what I learn onto paper in a good final understandable piece of writing. This piece has good description, a good plot line, gets the point across, has a basic setting, and is understandable. I did not change too much of this piece from one draft to the next except punctuation, grammar and spelling. I did, however, add a quote from The Tao of Pooh.

"Quotes from The Tao of Pooh" shows that I am able to pull out good and significant quotes from a book, understand them, and put them into my own words. Then I can make them understandable to other people. This piece gets the point across well and is easy to understand. I really only corrected spelling and punctuation from one draft to the next.

"Discrimination" shows me that I am learning more about discrimination and how it might feel (even though I have never experienced really bad discrimination). I found I can get my ideas across through realistic writing. This piece has good description and was well written for the assignment. Besides correcting some punctuation and spelling, I changed some wording to make the story a little more clear.

For all three pieces, the mechanics of my writing tend to be fairly poor on my first draft, but that is because I am writing as thoughts come into my mind rather than focusing on details of grammar. Then my final drafts get better as I get comments and can turn my attention to details of writing.

The four most important things that I'm able to do as a writer are to: 1) get thoughts pulled into a story; 2) have that story understandable and the reader get something from it; 3) have the reader remember it was a good piece of writing; and 4) like the piece myself.

FIGURE 10.12 In this self-reflection 14-year-old Kurt explains why he has chosen certain pieces to include in his eighth-grade language arts portfolio.

possibly do. Second, portfolios provide a mechanism through which teachers can easily intertwine assessment with instruction, because students often include products that teachers may have assigned primarily for instructional purposes. Third, the process of constructing a portfolio encourages students to reflect on and evaluate their accomplishments. Finally, portfolios sometimes influence the very nature of the instruction that takes place. Because the focus of portfolios is usually on complex skills, teachers are more likely to *teach* those skills.

Creating a portfolio requires a teacher–student partnership.[74] Typically the teacher identifies a specific purpose for which the portfolio will be used—perhaps to demonstrate a student's progress over time or to reveal the multifaceted nature of a student's final achievements. The teacher also identifies criteria (sometimes in collaboration with the student) to guide the selection of items to include in the portfolio. In most cases, however, it is the *student* who ultimately decides which products to include in a portfolio.

In addition to examples of students' work, many portfolios include documentation that describes each product and the student's reason for including it. For example, in Figure 10.12, 14-year-old Kurt describes and evaluates the writing samples he has included in a portfolio for his eighth-grade language arts class (note that his portfolio includes two or more drafts of each piece of writing). Such documentation encourages students to reflect on and judge their own work in ways that teachers typically do.[75] Thus, it is likely to promote the self-evaluation skills so essential for self-regulated learning.

RSVP characteristics can be a source of concern when teachers use portfolios, however, especially if the portfolios are used to *evaluate*, rather than simply communicate, students' learning and achievement.[76] When portfolios must be scored in some way, scoring is often unreliable, with different teachers rating them differently. By their very nature, portfolios are not standardized, because their contents vary from one student to another. Validity may or may not be a problem: Some portfolios may include enough work samples to adequately represent what students have accomplished relative to instructional goals, but others may be unrepresentative. And because portfolios are apt to take a great deal of teacher time, they are less practical than other methods of summarizing achievement. All this is *not* to say that

[74] Paulson et al., 1991; Popham, 1995; Spandel, 1997; Stiggins, 2001.
[75] Airasian, 1994; Arter & Spandel, 1992; Popham, 1995.
[76] Airasian, 1994; Arter & Spandel, 1992; Koretz et al., 1994; Popham, 1995.

teachers should shy away from using portfolios. But they should be sure the potential benefits outweigh the disadvantages when asking students to compile them. And they should identify explicit criteria for evaluating portfolios when using them as summative reflections of what students have accomplished.[77]

ASSESSING STUDENTS' ACHIEVEMENT WITH STANDARDIZED TESTS

Final grades and portfolios are both derived directly from things students do in the classroom. A very different approach to summarizing what students know and can do is the **standardized test**, a test developed by test construction experts and published for use in many different schools and classrooms. The test is *standardized* in several ways: All students are given the same instructions and time limits, respond to the same (or very similar) questions or tasks, and have their responses evaluated in accordance with the same criteria. A test manual describes the instructions to give students, the time limits to impose, and the specific scoring criteria to use. Often the manual also provides information about test reliability for different populations and age-groups, as well as information from which teachers and school administrators can draw inferences about test validity for their own situation and purposes.

Four kinds of standardized tests that school districts use frequently—achievement tests, general scholastic aptitude tests, specific aptitude tests, and school readiness tests—are described in Table 10.5.[78] Most of these tests yield norm-referenced scores. For instance, if you look once again at the explanation of IQ scores in Chapter 5 (p. 158), you will realize that IQ scores indicate *only* how children stack up against one another and so are norm referenced. Common forms of norm-referenced scores used in standardized testing, including IQ scores, are described in depth in Appendix B.

Consistent with our emphasis on assessing students' learning and achievement in this chapter, our focus in the upcoming pages will be on standardized *achievement* tests. Such tests are useful in at least two ways.[79] First, they enable teachers and school administrators to compare their own students' general achievement with the achievement of students elsewhere and to get a rough idea of the effectiveness of their instructional programs. Second, standardized achievement tests provide a means of tracking students' general progress over time and raising red flags about potential trouble spots. For example, if Lucas has been getting average test scores over the years, then suddenly performs well below average in eighth grade (even though the test and norm group are the same as in previous years), we have a signal that Lucas may possibly not be learning and performing at a level commensurate with his ability. At this point, his teachers would want to ascertain whether the low performance was a fluke (perhaps due to illness on the test day or to some other temporary condition) or whether the relative decline in performance was due to other, longer-term issues that require attention.

With the preceding information in mind, let's return one final time to the opening case study. Despite Akeem's improvement in reading and writing as he moved through the grade levels, his performance on districtwide achievement tests remained low. Quite possibly those tests yielded norm-referenced scores—that is, they compared Akeem's performance to that of his age-mates around the city. He was improving, certainly, but so was almost everyone else improving. Thus, his performance *relative to his peers* continued to be near the bottom of the heap. Fortunately, his elementary and middle school teachers consistently recognized and fostered his strengths in other areas, encouraging him to stay in school and set his sights on a rewarding career.

High-Stakes Tests and Accountability

In recent years a great deal of emphasis—entirely too much emphasis, in my opinion—has been placed on students' performance on standardized achievement tests. Within the past two or

---

standardized test Test developed by test construction experts and published for use in many different schools and classrooms.

[77] Darling-Hammond et al., 1995, present several examples of criteria that schools have successfully used.
[78] You can find descriptions of several widely used standardized tests at www.ctb.com (for CTB and

McGraw-Hill), www.riverpub.com (for Riverside Publishing), and www.harcourt.com (for Harcourt Assessment and Psychological Corporation).
[79] Ansley, 1997.

TABLE 10.5	Commonly Used Standardized Tests		
Kind of Test	Purpose	General Description	Special Considerations
Achievement tests	To assess how much students have learned from what they have specifically been taught	Test items are written to reflect the curriculum common to many schools. Test scores indicate achievement only in a very broad and (usually) norm-referenced sense: They estimate a student's general level of knowledge and skills in a particular domain relative to other students across the country.	• These tests are usually more appropriate for measuring general levels of achievement than for determining specific information and skills that students have and have not acquired.
General scholastic aptitude and intelligence tests	To assess students' general capability to learn; to predict their general academic success over the short run	Test items typically focus on what and how much students have learned and deduced from their general, everyday experiences. For example, the tests may include items that ask students to define words, draw logical deductions, recognize analogies between seemingly unrelated topics, analyze geometric figures, or solve problems.	• Test scores should not be construed as an indication of learning potential over the long run. • Individually administered tests (in which the tester works one-on-one with a particular student) are preferable when students' verbal skills are limited or when exceptional giftedness or a significant disability is suspected.
Specific aptitude and ability tests	To predict how well students are likely to perform in a specific content domain	Test items are similar to those in general scholastic aptitude tests, except that they focus on a specific domain (e.g., verbal skills, mathematical reasoning). Some aptitude tests, called *multiple aptitude batteries*, yield subscores for a variety of domains simultaneously.	• Test scores should not be construed as an indication of learning potential over the long run. • Tests tend to have only limited ability to predict students' success in a particular domain and so should be used only in combination with other information about students.
School readiness tests	To determine whether young children have the prerequisite cognitive skills to be successful in a typical kindergarten or first-grade curriculum	Test items focus on basic knowledge and skills—for instance, recognition of colors and shapes, knowledge of numbers and letters, and ability to remember and follow directions.	• Test scores should be interpreted cautiously. Young children have shorter attention spans and less motivation to perform testlike tasks than older children do, leading to lower reliability and validity of test scores. • Tests should be used primarily for instructional planning purposes, *not* for deciding whether students are ready to begin formal schooling.[a]

[a]School readiness tests have become increasingly controversial in recent years. For various perspectives on these tests, see La Paro & Pianta, 2000; Lidz, 1991; Pellegrini, 1998; C. E. Sanders, 1997; Stipek, 2002.

three decades, many politicians, business leaders, and other public figures have lamented what appear to be low achievement levels among students and have called for major overhauls of the public schools.[80] Some of these reform-minded individuals equate high achievement with high scores on standardized tests and, conversely, low achievement with low test scores. Policy makers have put considerable pressure on teachers and educational administrators to get the test scores up, and some threaten serious consequences (reduced funding, restrictions on salary, etc.) for those schools and faculty members who do *not* get the scores up. Here we are talking about both **high-stakes testing**—making major decisions on the basis of single assessments— and **accountability**—a mandated obligation of teachers, administrators, and other school personnel to accept responsibility for students' performance on those assessments.

In the United States the **No Child Left Behind Act** of 2001—sometimes known simply as **NCLB**—now mandates both high-stakes testing and accountability in all public elementary and secondary schools. It also mandates that all states establish

challenging academic content standards in academic subjects that —
(I) specify what children are expected to know and be able to do;
(II) contain coherent and rigorous content; and
(III) encourage the teaching of advanced skills[81]

high-stakes testing Practice of using students' performance on a single assessment instrument to make major decisions about students or school personnel.

accountability Mandated obligation of teachers and other school personnel to accept responsibility for students' performance on high-stakes assessments.

No Child Left Behind Act (NCLB) U.S. legislation passed in 2001 that mandates regular assessments of basic skills to determine whether students are making adequate yearly progress in relation to state-determined standards in reading, math, and science.

[80] In the United States a report entitled *A Nation at Risk*, published by the National Commission on Excellence in Education in 1983, has been especially influential.

[81] P.L. 107-110, Sec. 1111.

School districts must annually assess students in grades 3 through 8 and at least once during grades 10 through 12 to determine whether students are making *adequate yearly progress* in meeting state-determined standards in reading, math, and (beginning with the 2007–2008 school year) science. The nature of this progress is defined by the state (and so differs from state to state), but assessment results must clearly show that all students, including those from diverse racial and socioeconomic groups, are making significant gains in knowledge and skills. (Students with significant cognitive disabilities may be given alternative assessments, but they must show improvement commensurate with their ability levels.) Schools that demonstrate progress receive rewards, such as teacher bonuses or increased budgets. Schools that do not are subject to sanctions and corrective actions (e.g., bad publicity, administrative restructuring, dismissal of staff members), and students have the option of attending a better public school at the school district's expense.[82]

Sometimes individual students, too, are held accountable for their performance on statewide or schoolwide assessments. Some school districts have used students' performance on tests or other assessments as a basis for promotion to the next grade level or for awarding high school diplomas.[83] Typically, school personnel begin by identifying certain content area standards (they sometimes use the word *competencies*) that students' final achievement should reflect. They then assess students' performance levels (sometimes known as *outcomes*) at the end of instruction, and only those students whose performance meets the predetermined standards and competencies move forward. Such practice, of course, requires criterion-referenced rather than norm-referenced scores. For instance, one school district developed four possible scores for students' performance on its districtwide writing assessment, three of which reflected some degree of mastery:

In progress: Is an underdeveloped and/or unfocused message.

Essential: Is a series of related ideas. The pattern of organization and the descriptive or supporting details are adequate and appropriate.

Proficient: Meets Essential Level criteria and contains a logical progression of ideas. The pattern of organization and the transition of ideas flow. Word choice enhances the writing.

Advanced: Meets Proficient Level criteria and contains examples of one or more of the following: insight, creativity, fluency, critical thinking, or style.[84]

In the United States, legislation in more than 20 states now requires that promotion or high school graduation be contingent on passing statewide or school district assessments.[85] Such efforts to monitor schools' instructional effectiveness and students' academic progress are certainly well intentioned. Ideally, they can help schools determine whether instructional methods need revision and whether teachers need retooling, and they can help teachers identify students who are not acquiring the basic skills necessary for successful participation in the adult world. The current emphasis on boosting students' test scores is fraught with difficulties in implementation, however. For example, teachers often spend a great deal of time teaching to the tests—a serious problem if the tests reflect only a few of the many instructional goals toward which students should be striving. And recall the teacher's dilemma in the opening case study ("Taking Over") in Chapter 4. In order to "cover" all the material on the ninth-grade math competency exam, Ms. Gaunt eventually abandons her efforts to help students master basic concepts and procedures, essentially throwing the *less is more* principle out the window.[86]

---

[82] You can learn more about the No Child Left Behind Act at the U.S. Department of Education's Web site at www.ed.gov. You can also find a good summary in R. M. Thomas, 2005.

[83] Such approaches go by a variety of names; *outcomes-based education* and *minimum competency testing* are two common ones.

[84] Criteria adapted from "District 6 Writing Assessment, Narrative and Persuasive Modes, Scoring Criteria, Intermediate Level" (Working Copy) by School District 6 (Greeley/Evans, CO), 1993; adapted by permission.

[85] Jacob, 2003.

[86] For various perspectives on the problems associated with high-stakes testing and the No Child Left Behind Act, see W. Au, 2007; Carnoy, Elmore, & Siskin, 2003; Firestone & Mayrowetz, 2000; B. Fuller, Wright, Gesicki, & Kang, 2007; S. Kelly & Monczunski, 2007; J. Lee & Wong, 2004; R. L. Linn, 2000; Shepard et al., 2005; Stringfield & Yakimowski-Srebnick, 2005; R. M. Thomas, 2005; W. E. Wright, 2006.

Using Standardized Achievement Tests Judiciously

In my final set of recommendations, I offer several suggestions for using standardized and high-stakes achievement tests in ways that maximize their usefulness.

When you have a choice in the test you use, choose a test that has high validity for your curriculum and students.

Content validity is just as much a concern for standardized achievement tests as it is for teacher-constructed classroom assessments. Teachers and school administrators can best determine the content validity of a standardized achievement test by comparing a table of specifications for the test[87] to their own curriculum. School faculty members should also scrutinize the actual test items to see whether they emphasize lower- or higher-level thinking skills. (Some commonly used achievement tests focus predominantly on lower-level skills.[88]) A test has high content validity for a particular school and classroom only if the topics and thinking skills emphasized in test items match local instructional goals and content area standards.

Teach to the test if, but only if, it reflects important instructional goals.

When teachers are held accountable for their students' performance on a particular test, many of them understandably devote many class hours to the knowledge and skills that the test assesses, and students may focus their studying efforts accordingly.[89] The result is often that students perform at higher levels on a high-stakes test *without* improving their achievement and abilities more generally.[90] If a test truly measures the things that are most important for students to learn—including such higher-level skills as transfer, problem solving, and critical thinking—then focusing on those things is quite appropriate. If the test primarily assesses rote knowledge and lower-level skills, however, then such emphasis may undermine the improvements teachers *really* want to see in students' achievement.[91]

Make sure students are adequately prepared to take the test.

Teachers should typically prepare students ahead of time for a standardized test. For instance, teachers can do the following:[92]

- Explain the general nature of the test and the tasks it involves (e.g., if applicable, mention that students aren't necessarily expected to know all the answers and that many students won't have enough time to respond to every item).
- Encourage students to do their best, but without describing the test as a life-or-death matter.
- Give students practice with the item types and format of a test (e.g., show them how to answer multiple-choice questions and fill in computer-scored answer sheets).
- Encourage students to get a full night's sleep and eat a good breakfast.

To some degree, teachers can also help students prepare for standardized achievement tests by teaching them useful test-taking strategies, such as temporarily skipping difficult items, double-checking to be sure answers are marked in the correct spots, and so on. Teachers should keep in mind, however, that having effective test-taking skills—**testwiseness**—typically makes only a small difference in students' test scores.[93] Furthermore, test-taking skills

[87] Test publishers typically construct such a table and either include it in the test manual or make it available upon request. If a table is *not* available, school personnel can construct one by tallying up the number of items that tap into various topics and thinking skills.

[88] Alleman & Brophy, 1997; Bransford et al., 2006; Marzano & Costa, 1988.

[89] Jacob, 2003; R. L. Linn, 2000; Pianta, Belsky, Houts, & Morrison, 2007; L. B. Resnick & Resnick, 1992; R. M. Thomas, 2005.

[90] Amrein & Berliner, 2002a, 2002b, 2002c; Jacob, 2003; Shepard et al., 2005.

[91] Amrein & Berliner, 2002b; Kumar, Gheen, & Kaplan, 2002; R. M. Ryan, 2005; W. Au, 2007.

[92] Kirkland, 1971; Popham, 1990; Sax, 1989.

[93] Bangert-Drowns, Kulik, & Kulik, 1983; Hembree, 1987; A. J. Reynolds & Oberman, 1987; Scruggs & Lifson, 1985.

testwiseness Test-taking know-how that enhances test performance.

Some standardized tests are administered one-on-one. Such tests minimize the importance of testwiseness, and they enable the examiner to observe a student's attention span, motivation, and other factors that may affect the student's performance. For these reasons, individually administered tests are typically used when identifying students who have special educational needs.

Speed Tests!

Speed Tests make everyone a nervous reck before I tasted Speed Test I I would barle eat and had troble sleeping. Now, this very day I find out I passed Speed Test II and maybe I passed Speed Test III! Oh God please, oh please let me passe Speed Test III. Effen if I never passe Speed Test 15 ten I want you to know I tried my hardest.

FIGURE 10.13 Eight-year-old Connie describes how overwhelming test anxiety can be.

and student achievement are positively correlated: Students with many test-taking strategies tend to be higher achievers than students with few strategies. In other words, very few students get low test scores *only* because they are poor test takers.[94] In most cases teachers better serve their students by teaching them the knowledge and skills that tests are designed to assess rather than spending an inordinate amount of time teaching them how to take tests.[95]

When administering the test, follow the directions closely and report any unusual circumstances.

Once the testing session begins, teachers should follow the test administration procedures to the letter, distributing test booklets as directed, asking students to complete any practice items provided, keeping time faithfully, and responding to students' questions in the prescribed manner. Remember, students in the test's norm group have taken the test under certain standardized conditions, and teachers must replicate those conditions as closely as possible. Occasionally teachers will encounter events (a noisy construction project nearby, an unexpected power failure, etc.) that are beyond their control. When such events significantly alter the conditions under which students are taking the test, they jeopardize the validity of the test results and so must be reported. Teachers should also make note of any individual students who are behaving in ways unlikely to lead to maximum performance—students who appear exceptionally nervous, stare out the window for long periods, seem to be marking answers haphazardly, and so on.[96]

Take students' age and developmental level into account when interpreting test results.

Virtually any test score will be influenced by a variety of irrelevant factors—language skills, motivation, mood, energy level, general health, and so on—that will impact the score's reliability and validity. Such factors are especially likely to influence the test results of young children, many of whom may have limited verbal skills, short attention spans, little motivation to do their best, and low tolerance for frustration.[97] Furthermore, young children's erratic behaviors may make it difficult to maintain standardized testing conditions.[98]

In adolescence other variables can affect the validity of scores on standardized tests. Although students may get a bit nervous about tests in the elementary grades (e.g., see Figure 10.13), test anxiety increases in the middle school and high school grades, sometimes to the point of interfering with students' concentration during a test. Furthermore, especially in high school, some students become quite cynical about the validity and usefulness of standardized paper-pencil tests.[99] When students see little point to taking a test, they may read test items superficially if at all, and a few may complete answer sheets simply by following a certain pattern (e.g., alternating between A and B) or making "pictures" as they fill in the bubbles.[100] At *any* grade level, then, teachers and educational administrators must be careful not to place too much stock in the specific scores that tests yield.

Never use a single test score to make important decisions about students.

What I've seen and heard in the media leads me to think that many politicians and other policy makers overestimate how much high-stakes and other standardized achievement tests can tell us: They assume that such instruments are highly accurate and comprehensive measures of students' overall academic achievement. True, these tests are often developed by experts with considerable training in test construction, but no test is completely reliable, and its validity will vary considerably depending on the context in which it is being used. Every test is fallible, and students may do poorly on a test for a variety of reasons. Thus teachers, school administrators, parents, and others should never—and I do mean *never*—use a single assessment instrument or single test score to make important decisions about

---

[94] Scruggs & Lifson, 1985.
[95] J. R. Frederiksen & Collins, 1989.
[96] R. L. Linn & Miller, 2005.
[97] Bracken & Walker, 1997; Fleege, Charlesworth, & Burts, 1992; Messick, 1983.

[98] Wodtke, Harper, & Schommer, 1989.
[99] Paris, Lawton, Turner, & Roth, 1991.
[100] Paris et al., 1991; W. E. Wright, 2006.

individual students. Nor should they use the results of a single test to make important decisions about large groups of students or about the teachers who teach them. It behooves everyone who has a personal or professional stake in children's education to be aware of the limitations of standardized tests and enlighten their fellow citizens accordingly.

Regardless of how students' learning and achievement are assessed, we must continually keep one point in mind: *Tests and other educational assessments are useful but imperfect tools.* Standardized tests, teacher quizzes, classroom assignments, performance tasks, portfolios—all of these can tell us something about what students know and can do and what students still need to learn and master. The usefulness of any assessment strategy depends on how well matched it is to the situation in which it will be used and how reliable and valid it is for that situation. As a general rule, we should think of any educational assessment as a tool that, in combination with the other tools at teachers' disposal, can help improve classroom instruction and maximize students' learning and achievement over the long run.

SUMMARY

Assessment is a process of observing a sample of a student's behavior and drawing inferences about the student's knowledge and abilities. Some classroom assessments are used for formative evaluation, to guide future instruction. Others are used for summative evaluation, to determine what students know and can do at the end of instruction. Regardless of a teacher's purpose in assessing students' knowledge and skills, the nature of the teacher's assessment instruments gives students messages about what things are most important to learn and about how students should study and think about classroom subject matter. Not only is assessment closely interconnected with instruction, but in a very real sense it *is* instruction.

Teachers should keep four "RSVP" characteristics in mind when identifying assessment strategies and developing assessment instruments. First, an assessment should be *reliable*, yielding consistent results regardless of the circumstances in which a teacher administers and scores it. Second, it should be *standardized*, in that it has similar content and is administered and evaluated in a similar manner for everyone (some students with disabilities may be exceptions). Third, it should be *valid*, being an accurate reflection of the knowledge and skills the teacher is trying to assess. Finally, it should be *practical*, staying within reasonable costs and time constraints.

Teachers sometimes assess achievement informally, perhaps by simply observing what students do and listening to what they say in everyday classroom activities. Informal assessment is flexible and practical and requires little or no advance planning. Unfortunately, it usually doesn't provide a representative sample of what students know and can do, and teachers' judgments are often biased by their beliefs and expectations about different students.

When drawing firm conclusions about what students have and have not achieved—for instance, when assigning final grades—teachers should base their conclusions largely on preplanned, formal assessments. Paper-pencil assessment tasks are usually more practical, and so they are often preferable *if* they truly reflect instructional goals. Performance assessment tasks are often more appropriate for assessing complex achievements that require the integration of numerous skills, and accomplishment of some instructional objectives can be assessed *only* through direct observation of what students can do. Paper-pencil and performance assessments alike usually yield more useful information when tasks have some structure and when explicit, concrete scoring criteria are identified ahead of time.

Although teachers must be the final judges of students' performance on classroom assessments, involving students in the assessment process—for instance, soliciting students' input about evaluation criteria and asking them to rate their own performance—can encourage intrinsic motivation and foster self-regulation skills. Furthermore, classroom assessment practices should allow leeway for students to take the risks so essential for the pursuit of challenging tasks. No single failure should ever be a fatal one that seriously impacts a student's long-term academic success.

Most teachers eventually need to boil down the results of classroom assessments into more general indicators of what students have learned. The most common procedure is to assign final grades that summarize what students have achieved over the course of the term or school year. In most instances final grades should reflect actual achievement and be based on hard data. The problem with grades, of course, is that they communicate very little about what a student specifically has learned and can do. Student portfolios, which can represent the multifaceted, complex nature of students' achievements, can often be an effective alternative or supplement to overall class grades.

Standardized achievement tests provide a means of tracking students' general progress over time and getting a rough idea of how students at a particular school compare to their peers elsewhere. In recent years, we have seen increasing use of standardized achievement tests to make important decisions about students and to hold school personnel accountable for students' achievement. Such *high-stakes testing* is here to stay (at least for the short run), and teachers must become vocal advocates for reasonable and valid approaches to assessing students' overall progress and achievement.

For both legal and educational reasons, teachers must keep students' assessment results confidential, communicating students' test scores, grades, and other information only to the students themselves, to their parents, and to school personnel directly involved in the students' education and well-being. Teachers must also remember that the ultimate purpose of *any* assessment is not to pass judgment, but rather to help students learn and achieve more effectively.

PRACTICE FOR YOUR LICENSURE EXAM

Two Science Quizzes

Knowing that frequent review of class material leads to higher achievement and that a paper-pencil test is one way of providing such review, Mr. Bloskas tells his ninth-grade science students that they will have a quiz every Friday. As a first-year teacher, he has had little experience developing test questions, so he decides to use the questions in the test bank that accompanies the class textbook. The night before the first quiz, Mr. Bloskas types 30 multiple-choice and true–false items from the test bank, making sure they cover the specific topics that he has addressed in class.

His students complain that the questions are "picky." As he looks carefully at his quiz, he realizes that the students are right: The quiz measures nothing more than memorization of trivial details. So when he prepares the second quiz, Mr. Bloskas casts the test bank aside and writes two essay questions asking students to apply scientific principles they have studied to real-life situations. He's proud of his efforts, because his quiz clearly assesses higher-level thinking skills.

The following Friday, his students complain even more loudly about the second quiz than they had about the first. "This is too hard!" a couple shout out. Others follow with "We never studied this stuff!" and "I liked the first quiz better!" Later, as Mr. Bloskas scores the essays, he is appalled to discover how poorly his students have performed.

1. Constructed-response question

When identifying classroom assessment tasks, teachers must be sure that the tasks have validity, especially *content validity*.

  A. Compare the content validity of Mr. Bloskas's two quizzes.

  B. Describe a reasonable approach Mr. Bloskas might use to create quizzes that have good content validity for his classes.

2. Multiple-choice question

The following alternatives present four possible explanations for why Mr. Bloskas's students react as negatively as they do to the second quiz. Drawing on contemporary theories of learning and motivation, choose the most likely explanation.

  a. Multiple-choice and true–false items are more likely than essay questions to enhance students' sense of self-determination.

  b. Learners behave and study in ways that they expect will lead to reinforcement.

  c. Multiple-choice and true–false items are apt to foster learning goals, whereas essay questions are more likely to foster performance goals.

  d. Multiple-choice and true–false items assess information in short-term memory, whereas essay questions usually assess information in long-term memory.

Once you have answered these questions, compare your responses with those presented in Appendix A.

FOR FURTHER READING

The following articles from the journal *Educational Leadership* are especially relevant to this chapter. You can find these articles in Chapter 10 of MyEducationLab for this text.

Andrade, H. G. (2000). Using rubrics to promote thinking and learning. *Educational Leadership, 57*(5), 13–18.

Baker, E. L. (1994). Making performance assessment work: The road ahead. *Educational Leadership, 51*(6), 58–62.

Colby, S. A. (1999). Grading in a standards-based system. *Educational Leadership, 56*(6), 52–55.

Khattri, N., Kane, M. B., & Reeve, A. L. (1995). How performance assessments affect teaching and learning. *Educational Leadership, 53*(3), 80–83.

Leahy, S. (2005). Classroom assessment: Minute by minute, day by day. *Educational Leadership, 63*(3), 19–24.

McTighe, J., & O'Connor, K. (2005). Seven practices for effective learning. *Educational Leadership, 63*(3), 10–17.

Munk, D. D. (2003). Grading students with disabilities. *Educational Leadership, 61*(2), 38–43.

Munk, D. D., & Bursuck, W. D. (1997). Can grades be helpful and fair? *Educational Leadership, 55*(4), 44–47.

Schnitzer, S. (1993). Designing an authentic assessment. *Educational Leadership, 50*(7), 32–35.

Seeley, M. M. (1994). The mismatch between assessment and grading. *Educational Leadership, 52*(2), 4–6.

Shepard, L. A. (1995). Using assessment to improve learning. *Educational Leadership, 52*(5), 38–43.

Simmons, R. (1994). The horse before the cart: Assessing for understanding. *Educational Leadership, 51*(5), 22–23.

MYEDUCATIONLAB

Now go to Chapter 10 of MyEducationLab at **www.myeducationlab.com,** where you can:

- Find instructional objectives for the chapter, along with focus questions that can help you zero in on important ideas in the chapter.
- Take a self-check quiz on concepts and principles you've just read about.

- Complete exercises and assignments that can help you more deeply understand the chapter content.
- Read supplementary material that can broaden your knowledge of one or more of the chapter's topics.
- Apply what you've learned to classroom contexts in Building Teaching Skills activities.

Answers to "Practice for Your Licensure Exam" Exercises

CHAPTER 1: NEW SOFTWARE (pp. 13–14)

1. We can draw conclusions about cause-and-effect relationships—for instance, that computer software helps or hinders learning in mathematics—only from an *experimental study*, in which the researcher systematically manipulates one variable while holding other potentially influential variables constant. The researcher then measures the effect of the manipulated variable on another (dependent) variable. Mr. Gualtieri has instead conducted a *correlational study*, in which he simply looked at the relationship between two variables (software use and math achievement) as they occurred naturally in his classroom. We cannot conclude that the software is the cause of students' difficulty because Mr. Gualtieri did not eliminate other possible explanations for the differing math achievement of computer users and noncomputer users.

   A number of factors probably influenced students' decisions to use or not use the computer lab—their involvement in other after-school activities, their access to transportation home in the late afternoon, and so on—and thus the two groups of students are probably different in a variety of ways. One likely explanation for the computer users' lower scores is that students who chose to use the new software did so because they were having trouble understanding class material, whereas many of the nonusers were mastering the material on their own.

2. d—Because students are randomly assigned to the Problem-Excel and Write-Away software programs, the two groups should be roughly equivalent (on average) with respect to other factors (intelligence, motivation, involvement in extracurricular activities, etc.) that might influence their math achievement. The two groups in alternatives *a* and *b* are not necessarily equal with respect to other factors. The improvement observed in alternative *c* could be due to other mathematics learning experiences during the three-month interval, increased neurological (brain) maturation, or other factors that came into play between September and December.

CHAPTER 2: VISION UNIT (pp. 53–54)

1. Some students may not have been paying attention to the lesson; if this was the case, they have never stored the information in working memory, let alone in long-term memory. But even if students were paying attention, their prior knowledge and beliefs probably influenced their learning. This process of *meaningful learning*—interpreting new information within the context of what is already "known"—is usually beneficial, but it can be counterproductive if students relate new material to existing misconceptions. In fact, many students have a *confirmation bias*, in that they look for and accept information that is consistent with their existing beliefs and reject information that contradicts those beliefs.

To increase students' understanding of how human vision actually works—that is, to promote conceptual change—you might use the following strategies (your response should include at least two of these):

- At the beginning of the lesson, ask students to describe how they think vision works.
- Point out how the new information explicitly contradicts students' existing beliefs about vision.
- Ask questions that encourage students to reflect on and identify problems with their existing beliefs about vision.
- Show students how the scientifically accepted explanation (light travels *to* rather than *from*) the eye is more plausible than their existing beliefs.
- Give corrective feedback when students' explanations reflect misunderstanding.
- Build on aspects of students' understandings that *are* correct (e.g., acknowledge that students are correct when they say that the retina of the eye is sensitive to light).
- Engage students in a discussion of the pros and cons of different views of how vision works.
- Ask students to apply the correct explanation to new situations.

By using such strategies, you activate students' prior beliefs about vision—that is, you encourage them to "put" these beliefs in working memory, where they can critically examine them—and you make it less likely that students will distort (i.e., elaborate on) the new information in such a way that it confirms what they already believe. Asking students to apply the correct explanation to new situations increases the likelihood that they will connect this explanation to a variety of other topics in long-term memory, thus increasing the likelihood that they will retrieve it in future situations.

2. c—Conceptual change is a process of revising one's understanding of a topic in response to new information about the topic. In contrast, a script (alternative *a*) is knowledge about a common event that typically occurs in a predictable sequence. Automaticity (alternative *b*) is the ability to respond quickly and efficiently when thinking about or physically performing a task. Procedural knowledge (alternative *d*) is knowledge about how to perform a particular task (e.g., how to ride a bicycle or write a persuasive essay).

CHAPTER 3: ADAM (p. 97)

1. From an operant conditioning standpoint, factors that may possibly be contributing to Adam's problem behaviors include the following (your response should include at least two of these):

- Attention from teacher, peers, or both may be a reinforcer for Adam. If he behaves appropriately, he may "blend in" too well with his classmates and be virtually ignored. Inappropriate behaviors are more likely to bring him the attention he craves.
- Some of Adam's peers may actually be praising, and thus reinforcing, Adam's misbehaviors.
- If Adam's misbehaviors enable him to avoid or escape unpleasant tasks, then those behaviors are being negatively reinforced.
- If Adam comes to school hungry (perhaps because his family doesn't provide breakfast, give him lunch money, or send him to school with a lunch), stealing other students' lunches may be the only way he gets anything to eat. In this case, the consequence of his misbehavior is food, a primary reinforcer.
- Even if Adam is not currently being reinforced for his misbehaviors, he may have been reinforced for these behaviors in the past. Especially if the behaviors continue to yield reinforcement for him once in a while, they will be unlikely to undergo extinction.

Principles of reinforcement can also work in Adam's favor, however. Following are examples of things you might do to help Adam acquire more productive behaviors (your response should include two of these or similar ideas):

- Work closely with Adam on academic tasks, giving him any extra help and support he might need to be successful at them. In this way, engaging in classroom assignments will lead to success (reinforcement) rather than failure.
- If Adam truly finds teacher attention reinforcing, make your attention contingent on his behaving appropriately rather than inappropriately.
- If possible, ignore inappropriate behaviors—and encourage other students to ignore them as well—as a way of extinguishing those behaviors.
- If attention is *not* an effective reinforcer for Adam, observe him closely to determine what kinds of consequences he does enjoy and is likely to work for.
- Gradually shape more productive behaviors over time.
- Do not let inappropriate behaviors enable Adam to escape unpleasant tasks.
- Meet with Adam in private to develop a contingency contract in which the two of you agree to (a) the behaviors that Adam will exhibit and (b) the desirable consequences he can obtain when he does so.
- If Adam is coming to school hungry, arrange for him to get free or low-cost breakfasts and lunches at school so that stealing other students' lunches is neither necessary nor likely to be reinforced.

2. b—In reciprocal causation, environment, behavior, and person variables *mutually influence* one another. Alternative *b* depicts the mutual influences of two of these factors: Adam's behavior affects his environment (his teacher's instruction), which in turn affects Adam's behavior. Alternative *a* depicts a person variable (low expectations) affecting behavior. Alternative *c* depicts an environmental variable (for the classmate, this is Adam's behavior) having an impact on a classmate's behavior. Alternative *d* depicts an environmental variable (Adam's classroom behavior) influencing parents' behavior. In none of the three incorrect alternatives are two variables *mutually influencing each other*.

CHAPTER 4: INTERVIEW WITH EMILY (pp. 132–133)

1. Your response should include at least three of the following strategies:

- Solving practice problems (for math)
- Taking and reviewing notes
- Making flash cards and repeating what's on them
- Self-checking for memory of material after a break (i.e., comprehension monitoring)
- Attempting to identify important information (e.g., phrases in boldface print)
- Outlining a reading assignment (rarely)

Evaluation of your three chosen strategies should include three or more of the following concepts: *encoding, attention, working memory, long-term memory, rote learning* (or *rehearsal*), *meaningful learning, elaboration, organization, comprehension monitoring* (or *self-monitoring*), *automaticity, transfer*. Following are examples of points that your response might include:

- Practice in solving math problems should help Emily master, and perhaps gain automaticity for, mathematical problem-solving procedures. If the practice problems are fairly authentic in nature, they should help Emily transfer what she's learning to real-world situations.
- Taking and reviewing notes and creating outlines ensure that Emily pays attention to and encodes the material in some way, and reviewing her notes at a later time

will enhance her memory for the material. However, the quantity and quality of her notes and outlines—for instance, the extent to which they involve organizing and elaborating on the material—will have a significant impact on how much she remembers and how well she can apply (transfer) it.

- Repeated use of flash cards should foster automaticity for specific facts. However, Emily's heavy reliance on flash cards and rehearsal and her view that "phrases in bold print are important" indicate that she engages primarily in rote learning and reads her textbooks only superficially. Material she studies in this fashion is unlikely to stay with her for any length of time.
- One effective strategy is Emily's comprehension monitoring after a break, because at this point the material is definitely in long-term memory rather than only in working memory. However, the material may not be easily retrievable over the long run if Emily emphasizes rote learning rather than meaningful learning.

2. d—Students' views about the nature of knowledge and its acquisition—for instance, that knowledge consists of many isolated facts, on the one hand, or of an integrated body of concepts and their interrelationships, on the other—are known as *epistemological beliefs*.

CHAPTER 5: STONES LESSON   (pp. 179–180)

1. Brianna's *scheme* for rocks includes the fact that they are heavy and sink in water, and her prediction that the pumice will sink reflects *assimilation* to that scheme. Ms. Hennessey presumably knows that the floating pumice will create a mildly uncomfortable state of *disequilibrium*, which should motivate the children to learn more about rocks (and in particular, about pumice). The disequilibrium should prompt *accommodation*, in which the children either modify their "rock" schemes or form a new scheme for pumice. In Piaget's view, the process of going from equilibrium to disequilibrium and then (through accommodation) back to equilibrium again—a process known as *equilibration*—should promote children's cognitive development.

2. c—*Density* is a culturally derived concept (i.e., a *cognitive tool*) that can help students make better sense of the phenomenon they've seen. By providing a scientific explanation for the floating pumice, you are essentially *mediating* the students' learning experience. Density is an abstract idea, however; although an explanation of the concept would be effective with high school students, a first grader such as Brianna would be unlikely to benefit from it. None of the other three alternatives is apt to help students make sense of the puzzling phenomenon, and in fact alternative *d* may be counterproductive, in that it might reinforce students' misconceptions.

CHAPTER 6: PRAISING STUDENTS' WRITING   (pp. 230–231)

1. The students in Group 2 are more likely to say that they enjoy writing in cursive. They also use cursive writing more frequently in tasks where cursive is not required. Both of these behaviors reflect intrinsic motivation, which comes from within the learner rather than being elicited by an outside source (such as an extrinsic reinforcer).

Comments such as "You sure are working hard" and "You can write beautifully in cursive" reflect *internal attributions* that place the credit for students' good performance on their own abilities or efforts. Thus such comments are also likely to enhance students' *self-efficacy* about writing and their more general sense of *self-worth*. Feedback such as "Great!" and "Perfect!", while positive, does not specifically communicate that students themselves are responsible for their successes.

If you have already read Chapter 3, you might also have pointed out that Group 1 students hear the kinds of feedback that their Group 2 classmates receive. Hearing this flattering feedback may lead to expectations that they, too, will receive such feedback. When they get less specific feedback, their expectations are not met—something that can actually be a form of punishment. (To refresh your memory on these points, see the discussion related to the principle *By seeing what happens to themselves and others, learners form expectations about the probable outcomes of various behaviors* in Chapter 3.)

2. a—With this comment, Mrs. Gaskill attributes a student's performance to effort, an internal, unstable, and controllable cause. Alternatives *b* and *c* are examples of extrinsic reinforcers. Alternative *d* is likely to be an effective strategy for capturing students' interest in, and thus their attention to, the lesson.

CHAPTER 7: *THE SCARLET LETTER* (pp. 276–277)

1. Your response should refer to at least two of the following:

- Nicole says, "He acts very withdrawn. He doesn't even want to be involved with the situation. He wants the other guy to question her, because he doesn't want to look her in the face and ask her to name *him*." Here Nicole reveals an understanding that Dimmesdale's reluctance to question Hester about her sin reveals considerable discomfort that might be the result of guilt over fathering an illegitimate child.
- A student mentions that the baby (Dimmesdale's daughter) "starts to cry, and her eyes follow him." The student appears to be speculating that the baby has strong feelings (either positive or negative) for Dimmesdale—feelings that a child might have for a parent.
- Mike describes Dimmesdale as looking "really nervous and inexperienced. Guilty look on his face. Always nervous, shaking a lot . . . very unsure about himself." Here Mike shows his understanding that people's feelings are often reflected in certain kinds of behaviors.
- Matt describes Dimmesdale as "Sweating really bad. Always going like this" (Matt dabs his brow to demonstrate). Matt, too, shows his understanding that certain behaviors are associated with certain feelings.
- The students who remark that "Maybe he's got a good personality" and "It's his eyes" are speculating about why Hester might find Dimmesdale so attractive.

2. c—All four alternatives show effective teaching strategies, but only in alternative *c* does Ms. Southam ask students to reflect on how someone else might be feeling. Alternative *a* is a strategy that is apt to promote situational interest (see Chapter 6). Alternatives *b* and *d* are apt to promote effective long-term memory storage processes, such as visual imagery and elaboration (see Chapter 2).

CHAPTER 8: COOPERATIVE LEARNING PROJECT   (pp. 312–313)

1. As fourth graders, most of Ms. Mihara's students are only 9 or 10 years old and so may have little if any experience and skill in working cooperatively with their classmates on a complex task. With this point in mind, your response should include two of the following improvements:

- Give students a more specific, concrete goal than simply to "find information on the customs of your country" and "give an oral report to the rest of the class." For example, you might give them a handout that instructs them to (a) find information on typical dress and diet, national holidays, and common religious beliefs; (b) prepare a map that shows where their country is located; (c) make an outline they will use to organize their report; and (d) practice their oral report at least once before presenting it to the class.
- Rather than letting students form the groups, form groups on the basis of which student combinations are likely to work productively. Ideally, every member of a group should have unique knowledge or skills to contribute to the group effort (e.g., one might have good word processing skills, another might be a good artist who can provide colorful illustrations).

- Give students a specific structure within which to work, perhaps in the form of different roles that different group members should play. For example, you might create one or more unique roles for each group member (e.g., researcher, secretary, presenter, coordinator, and the like), so that each student's involvement is essential for overall group success.
- Give students guidelines about how to behave in their groups (e.g., "Stay focused on the assignment," "Make sure every group member contributes ideas").
- Teach students effective information literacy skills (e.g., how to locate books on a particular topic on the library shelves, how to use a child-friendly search engine). As fourth graders, many of the students are apt to have little prior experience locating needed information in the library or on the Internet.
- Hold all students individually accountable for learning about customs in their assigned country. For example, after the oral reports have been completed, you might ask students to write one or two paragraphs describing what they have learned about their assigned country.
- Reinforce group success. For example, one measure of success would be that students' classmates learn something from each oral report. You might ask groups to give their classmates a short quiz on the country they've reported on. If their classmates do well on the quiz (i.e., if their average score is, say, 80 percent or higher), group members earn 30 minutes of free time on Friday afternoon.

2. d—Instructional goals and objectives should focus on what the student should be able to do at the end of instruction. Sometimes they can identify specific behaviors. At other times they can be stated as relatively abstract outcomes, but they should include examples of specific behaviors that reflect those outcomes. Alternatives *a* and *b* focus on what the teacher, rather than the student, should do. Alternative *c* focuses on what the student should do *during* (rather than at the end of) instruction; furthermore, the word *study* does not communicate a specific, easily observable behavior.

CHAPTER 9: THE GOOD BUDDY (pp. 352–353)

1. Rather than establish a goal-oriented, businesslike atmosphere (in which the primary goal is mastering classroom subject matter), Mr. Schulak has instead communicated the message that his class will be mostly fun and games. Furthermore, he has not set any limits for behavior—something he should have done in the first week of class.

   Possible strategies at this point include the following (your response should mention at least two of them):

- Emphasize that there are instructional goals students must achieve this year and that it is time to get down to business.
- Identify a set of rules and procedures by which the class will operate in order to achieve instructional goals, *or* involve students in a discussion of reasonable rules and procedures. (The latter strategy should be motivating for students, in that it will enhance their sense of self-determination and give them ownership of the rules and procedures by which the class will operate.)
- Identify reasonable consequences for disregarding the rules and procedures.
- Enforce the new rules and procedures consistently and equitably.
- Create engaging lessons that elicit intrinsic motivation and draw students into the subject matter.

After his rocky start, Mr. Schulak should not expect overnight success. It may take a while for students to become focused on their schoolwork, and he will have to be consistent about enforcing the new rules and procedures.

2. a—Teachers are most effective when they have realistically high expectations for students and provide the guidance and scaffolding that students need to meet those expectations. In doing so, teachers enhance students' self-efficacy for mastering school subject matter and so indirectly also enhance their general sense of self-worth. Spend-

ing some time in recreational activities (alternative *b*) can sometimes be productive, but not to the point where students think of their teachers primarily as "playmates." Providing only positive feedback (alternative *c*) is a disservice, in that it decreases the likelihood that students will address and improve on their weaknesses. Giving students no choice about classroom events (alternative *d*) may undermine their sense of self-determination and so also undermine their intrinsic motivation to learn (see Chapter 6).

CHAPTER 10: TWO SCIENCE QUIZZES (p. 396)

1. In constructing the first quiz, Mr. Bloskas does not match his questions to his instructional goals, which presumably go beyond rote memorization of trivial details. In constructing the second quiz, Mr. Bloskas gives only two essay questions, which may not provide an adequate sample of the content domain. Both quizzes, then, may have questionable content validity—the first because it does not focus on desired behaviors, and the second because it is too restricted in the topics that it covers.

   Mr. Bloskas would be wise to construct a table of specifications for the knowledge and skills he is trying to assess. He should then either find or construct quiz items that assess both the key ideas of the week's material and the specific behaviors he wants students to demonstrate with regard to those ideas. He may want to include both (a) multiple-choice or short-answer items (which can tap into a representative sample of the content domain), and (b) one or two essays, performance tasks, or other complex tasks (which can more easily assess higher-level thinking skills) in a single quiz.

2. b—Mr. Bloskas has neglected to consider the effects that classroom assessment practices have on students' future studying and learning. Wanting to get a good grade on the second quiz and expecting it to be similar to the first, his students probably studied for it by memorizing trivial details rather than thinking about ways to apply what they had learned. They expected their studying behavior to lead to reinforcement. Students should know what to expect on a classroom assessment instrument so that they can prepare accordingly. Any radical changes in the nature of assessment from one time to the next should be clearly described ahead of time; for example, a teacher might show students a few questions similar to those that will be on an upcoming quiz.

APPENDIX B

Interpreting Standardized Test Scores

Students' performance on standardized tests is often reported in terms of one or more *norm-referenced* scores—in particular, as scores that show a student's performance relative to others in a nationwide *norm group*. In some cases the scores are derived by comparing a student's performance with the performance of students at a variety of grade or age levels; such comparisons give us grade- or age-equivalent scores. In other cases the scores are based on comparisons only with students of the *same* age or grade; these comparisons give us either percentile ranks or standard scores.

GRADE-EQUIVALENT AND AGE-EQUIVALENT SCORES

Imagine that Shawn takes a standardized test, the Reading Achievement Test (RAT). He gets 46 of the 60 test items correct; thus 46 is his raw score. We turn to the norms reported in the test manual and find the average raw scores for students at different grade and age levels, shown in Figure B.1. Shawn's raw score of 46 is the same as the average score of 11th graders in the norm group, so he has a **grade-equivalent score** of 11. His score is halfway between the average score of 16-year-old and 17-year-old students, so he has an **age-equivalent score** of about 16½. Shawn is 13 years old and in eighth grade, so he has obviously done well on the RAT.

More generally, grade- and age-equivalent scores are determined by matching a student's raw score to a particular grade or age level in the norm group. A student who performs as well as the average second grader on a reading test will get a grade-equivalent score of 2, regardless of the student's actual grade level. A student who gets the same raw score as the average 10-year-old on a physical fitness test will get an age-equivalent score of 10, regardless of whether that student is 5, 10, or 15 years old.

Grade- and age-equivalent scores are frequently used because they seem so simple and straightforward. But they have a serious drawback: They give us no idea of the typical *range* of performance for students at a particular grade or age level. For example, a raw score of 34 on the RAT gives us a grade-equivalent score of 8, but obviously not all eighth graders will get raw scores of exactly 34. It is possible, and in fact quite likely, that many "normal" eighth graders will get raw scores several points above or below 34, thus getting grade-equivalent scores of 9 or 7 (perhaps even 10 or higher, or 6 or lower). Yet grade-equivalent scores are often used inappropriately as a standard for performance: Parents, school personnel, government officials, and the public at large may believe that *all* students should perform at grade level on an achievement test. Given the normal variability within most classrooms, this goal is probably impossible to meet.

Norms for Grade Levels		Norms for Age Levels	
Grade	Average Raw Score	Age	Average Raw Score
5	19	10	18
6	25	11	24
7	30	12	28
8	34	13	33
9	39	14	37
10	43	15	41
11	46	16	44
12	50	17	48

FIGURE B.1 Hypothetical norm-group data for the Reading Achievement Test (RAT)

PERCENTILE RANKS

A different approach is to compare students only with others at the same age or grade level. One way of making such a peer-based comparison is to use a **percentile rank**: the percentage of people getting a raw score less than or equal to the student's raw score. (Such a score is sometimes known simply as a *percentile*.) To illustrate, let's once again consider Shawn's performance on the RAT. Because Shawn is in eighth grade, we would turn to the eighth-grade norms in the RAT test manual. Perhaps we discover that a raw score of 46 is at the 98th

grade-equivalent score Test score indicating the grade level of students to whom a test taker performed most similarly.

age-equivalent score Test score indicating the age level of students to whom a test taker performed most similarly.

percentile rank (percentile) Test score indicating the percentage of people in the norm group getting a raw score less than or equal to a particular student's raw score.

percentile for eighth graders. This means that Shawn has done as well as or better than 98 percent of eighth graders in the norm group. Similarly, a student getting a percentile rank of 25 has performed better than 25 percent of the norm group, and a student getting a score at the 60th percentile has done better than 60 percent. It is important to note that percentile ranks refer to a percentage of *people*, not to the percentage of correct items—a common misconception among teacher education students. [1]

Because percentile ranks are relatively simple to understand, they are used frequently in reporting test results. But they have a major weakness: They distort actual differences among students. As an illustration, consider the percentile ranks of these four boys on the RAT:

Student	Percentile Rank
Ernest	45
Frank	55
Giorgio	89
Wayne	99

In *actual achievement* (as measured by the RAT), Ernest and Frank are probably very similar to one another even though their percentile ranks are 10 points apart. Yet a 10-point difference at the upper end of the scale probably reflects a substantial difference in achievement: Giorgio's percentile rank of 89 tells us that he knows quite a bit, but Wayne's percentile rank of 99 tells us that he knows an exceptional amount. In general, percentiles tend to *over*estimate differences in the middle range of the characteristic being measured: Scores a few points apart reflect similar achievement or ability. Meanwhile, they *under*estimate differences at the lower and upper extremes: Scores only a few points apart often reflect significant differences in achievement or ability. We avoid this problem when we use standard scores.

STANDARD SCORES

The school nurse measures the heights of all 25 students in Ms. Oppenheimer's third-grade class. The students' heights are presented on the left side of Figure B.2. The nurse then makes a graph of the children's heights, as you can see on the right side of Figure B.2. Notice that the graph is high in the middle and low on both ends. This shape tells us that most of Ms. Oppenheimer's students are more or less average in height, with only a handful of very short students (e.g., Pat, Amy, and Wil) and just a few very tall ones (e.g., Hal, Roy, and Jan).

Many psychologists believe that educational and psychological characteristics (including academic achievement and abilities) typically follow the same pattern we see for height: Most people are close to average, with fewer and fewer people as we move farther from this average. This theoretical pattern of educational and psychological characteristics, known as the **normal distribution** (or **normal curve**), is shown to the left. Standard scores reflect this normal distribution: Many students get scores in the middle range, and only a few get very high or very low scores.

Before we examine standard scores in more detail, we need to understand two numbers used to derive these scores—the mean and standard deviation. The **mean (M)** is the average of a set of scores: We add all of the scores together and divide by the total number of scores (or people). For example, if we add the heights of all 25 students in Ms. Oppenheimer's class

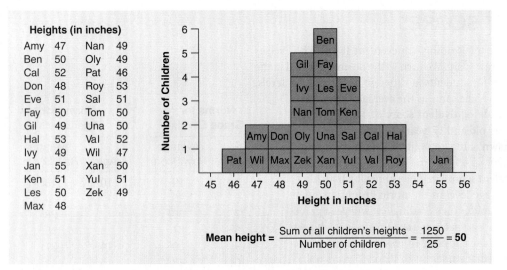

Heights (in inches)

Amy	47	Nan	49
Ben	50	Oly	49
Cal	52	Pat	46
Don	48	Roy	53
Eve	51	Sal	51
Fay	50	Tom	50
Gil	49	Una	50
Hal	53	Val	52
Ivy	49	Wil	47
Jan	55	Xan	50
Ken	51	Yul	51
Les	50	Zek	49
Max	48		

$$\text{Mean height} = \frac{\text{Sum of all children's heights}}{\text{Number of children}} = \frac{1250}{25} = 50$$

FIGURE B.2   Heights of children in Ms. Oppenheimer's third-grade class

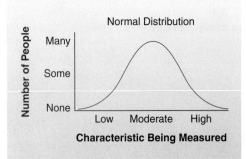

normal distribution (normal curve)
Theoretical pattern of educational and psychological characteristics in which most individuals lie somewhere in the middle range and only a few lie at either extreme.

mean (M) Mathematical average of a set of scores.

---

[1] Lennon, Ormrod, Burger, & Warren, 1990.

and then divide by 25, we get a mean height of 50 inches (see the calculation at the bottom of Figure B.2).

The **standard deviation (SD)** indicates the *variability* of a set of scores. A small number tells us that, generally speaking, the scores are close together, and a large number tells us that they are spread far apart. For example, third graders tend to be more similar in height than eighth graders (some eighth graders are less than five feet tall, whereas others may be almost six feet tall). The standard deviation for the heights of third graders is therefore smaller than the standard deviation for the heights of eighth graders. The procedure for computing a standard deviation is more complex than that for computing a mean (you can find the procedure in the supplementary reading "Calculating Standard Deviations" in MyEducationLab). Fortunately, no complex calculation is needed simply to *interpret* standardized test scores. The standard deviation for any particular standard test is typically provided in the test manual.

The mean and standard deviation can be used to divide the normal distribution into several parts, as shown in Figure B.3. The vertical line at the middle of the curve shows the mean; for a normal distribution, it is at the midpoint and highest point of the curve. The thinner lines to either side reflect the standard deviation: We count out a standard deviation's worth higher and lower than the mean and mark those spots with two lines, and then count another standard deviation to either side and draw two more lines. When we divide the normal distribution in this way, the percentages of students getting scores in each part are always the same. Approximately two-thirds (68%) get scores within one standard deviation of the mean (34% in each direction). As we go farther away from the mean, we find fewer and fewer students, with 28 percent lying between one and two standard deviations away (14% on each side) and only 4 percent being more than two standard deviations away (2% at each end).

Now that we better understand the normal distribution and two statistics that describe it, let's look at standard scores. A **standard score** reflects a student's position in the normal distribution: It tells us how far the student's performance is from the mean with respect to standard deviation units. Unfortunately, not all standard scores use the same scale: Scores used for various tests have different means and standard deviations. Four commonly used standard scores, depicted graphically in Figure B.4, are the following:

- **IQ scores.** IQ scores are frequently used to report students' performance on intelligence tests. They have a *mean of 100* and, for most tests, a *standard deviation of 15*. (If you look back at Figure 5.7 in Chapter 5, you'll see that I've broken that curve up by thirds of a standard deviation unit. The lines for 85 and 115 reflect one standard deviation from the mean score of 100. The lines for 70 and 130 reflect two SDs from the mean.)
- **ETS scores.** ETS scores are used on tests published by the Educational Testing Service, such as the SAT and the Graduate Record Examination (GRE). They have a *mean of 500* and a *standard deviation of 100*. However, no scores fall below 200 or above 800.
- **Stanines.** Stanines (short for *standard nines*) are often used to report standardized achievement test results. They have a *mean of 5* and a *standard deviation of 2*. Because they are always reported as whole numbers, each score reflects a *range* of test performance (reflected by the shaded and unshaded portions of the upper right-hand curve in Figure B.4).
- **z-scores.** Standard scores known as *z*-scores are often used by statisticians. They have a *mean of 0* and a *standard deviation of 1*.

INTERPRETING TEST SCORES: AN EXAMPLE

Figure B.5 presents a computer printout of 12-year-old Ingrid's scores on various subtests of a national achievement test. Ingrid's percentiles and stanines have been computed by comparing her raw scores with those of a national norm group. On the basis of her test scores, Ingrid appears to have achieved at average or below-average levels in spelling and math computation, at an average or above-average level in math concepts,

Learn how to calculate standard deviations in a supplementary reading in the Homework and Exercises section in Chapter 10 of MyEducationLab.

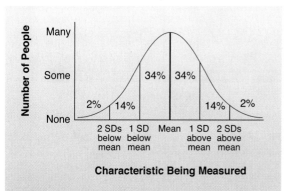

FIGURE B.3 Normal distribution divided by the mean and standard deviation

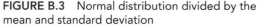

standard deviation (SD) Statistic that reflects how close together or far apart a set of scores are and thereby indicates the variability of the scores.

standard score Test score indicating how far a student's performance is from the mean with respect to standard deviation units.

IQ score Score on an intelligence test, determined by comparing a student's performance on the test with the performance of others in the same age-group. For most tests, it is a standard score with a mean of 100 and a standard deviation of 15.

ETS score Standard score with a mean of 500 and a standard deviation of 100.

stanine Standard score with a mean of 5 and a standard deviation of 2; it is always reported as a whole number.

z-score Standard score with a mean of 0 and a standard deviation of 1.

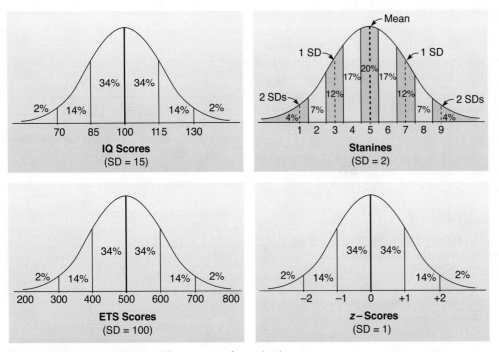

FIGURE B.4 Distributions of four types of standard scores

and at well-above-average levels in reading comprehension, science, and social studies.

The "national percentile bands" (i.e., rows of Xs) in Figure B.5 are **confidence intervals** that reflect the amount of error (due to imperfect reliability) that is apt to be in Ingrid's percentile scores. Ingrid's confidence intervals for spelling and math overlap, so even though she has gotten somewhat higher scores in math concepts than in spelling or math computation, the scores are not different *enough* to say that she is better at math concepts than in the other two areas. The confidence intervals for reading comprehension, science, and social studies overlap as well, so she performed similarly in these three areas. The confidence intervals for her three highest scores do *not* overlap with those for her lowest three scores. We can say, then, that Ingrid's relative strengths are in reading comprehension, science, and social studies, and that she has achieved at lower levels in spelling and math.

confidence interval Range around a test score that reflects the amount of error likely to be affecting the score's accuracy.

Notice that the numbers for the percentile confidence intervals (the numbers on the bottom line) are unevenly spaced. Remember, percentile ranks tend to overestimate differences near the mean and underestimate differences at the extremes. The uneven spacing is the test publisher's way of showing this fact: It squishes the middle percentile scores close together and spreads high and low percentile scores farther apart. In this way, it tries to give students and parents an idea about where students' test scores fall on a normal curve.

```
                                          NATIONAL PERCENTILE BANDS

                                         :          BELOW  :        : ABOVE  :
                                         : WELL BELOW AVERAGE : AVERAGE : AVERAGE : AVERAGE :   WELL ABOVE AVERAGE      :
                                         :                    :         :         :         :                          :
                        STANINE  PERCENTILE : 1    5     10   20  30   40  50  60  70  80   90        95        99      :
READING COMPREHENSION      8        92    :                                              XXXXXXXXXXXXX               :
SPELLING                   4        39    :                            XXXXXXXXXXXX                                  :
MATH COMPUTATION           4        37    :                           XXXXXXXXXXX                                    :
MATH CONCEPTS              5        57    :                                 XXXXXXXXXXXX                             :
SCIENCE                    8        90    :                                              XXXXXXXXXXXXXX              :
SOCIAL STUDIES             7        84    :                                         XXXXXXXX                        :
                                         : 1    5     10   20  30   40  50  60  70  80   90        95        99      :
```

FIGURE B.5 Computer printout showing 12-year-old Ingrid's performance on a standardized achievement test

GLOSSARY

accommodation Responding to a new object or event by either modifying an existing scheme or forming a new one.

accountability Mandated obligation of teachers and other school personnel to accept responsibility for students' performance on high-stakes assessments.

advance organizer Introduction to a lesson that provides an overall organizational scheme for the lesson.

affect Feelings, emotions, and moods that a learner brings to bear on a task.

African American English Dialect of some African American communities characterized by certain pronunciations, idioms, and grammatical constructions different from those of Standard English.

age-equivalent score Test score indicating the age level of students to whom a test taker performed most similarly.

aggressive behavior Action intentionally taken to harm another person either physically or psychologically.

algorithm Prescribed sequence of steps that guarantees a correct problem solution.

antecedent stimulus Stimulus that increases the likelihood that a particular response will follow.

anxiety Feeling of uneasiness and apprehension concerning a situation with an uncertain outcome.

APA style Rules and guidelines on referencing, editorial style, and manuscript format prescribed by the American Psychological Association.

applied behavior analysis (ABA) Systematic application of stimulus–response principles to address a chronic behavior problem.

apprenticeship Mentorship in which a learner works intensively with an experienced adult to learn how to perform complex new skills.

arousal See *need for arousal.*

assessment Process of observing a sample of a student's behavior and drawing inferences about the student's knowledge and abilities.

assimilation Responding to and possibly interpreting a new event in a way that is consistent with an existing scheme.

attention Focusing of mental processes on particular stimuli.

attention-deficit hyperactivity disorder (ADHD) Disorder marked by inattention, inability to inhibit inappropriate thoughts and behaviors, or both.

attribution Personally constructed causal explanation for a success or failure.

attribution theory Theoretical perspective focusing on people's explanations (*attributions*) concerning the causes of events that befall them, as well as on the behaviors that result from such explanations.

authentic activity Approach to instruction similar to one students might encounter in the outside world.

authentic assessment Assessment of students' knowledge and skills in a "real-life" context.

authoritarian parenting Parenting style characterized by rigid rules and expectations for behavior that children are asked to obey without question.

authoritative parenting Parenting style characterized by emotional warmth, high standards for behavior, explanation and consistent enforcement of rules, inclusion of children in decision making, and reasonable opportunities for autonomy.

autism spectrum disorders Disorders marked by impaired social cognition, social skills, and social interaction, presumably due to a brain abnormality; extreme forms often associated with significant cognitive and linguistic delays and highly unusual behaviors.

automaticity Ability to respond quickly and efficiently while mentally processing or physically performing a task.

backward design Approach to instructional planning in which a teacher first determines the desired end result (i.e., what knowledge and skills students should acquire) and then identifies appropriate assessments and instructional strategies.

behaviorism Theoretical perspective in which learning and behavior are described and explained in terms of stimulus-response relationships, and motivation is often the result of deficit-based drives. Adherents to this perspective are called **behaviorists**.

belongingness General sense that one is an important and valued member of the classroom.

Bloom's taxonomy Taxonomy of six cognitive processes, varying in complexity, that lessons might be designed to foster.

bully Child or adolescent who frequently threatens, harasses, or causes injury to particular peers.

central executive Component of the human information processing system that oversees the flow of information throughout the system.

challenge Situation in which a learner believes that success is possible with sufficient effort.

classroom climate Overall psychological atmosphere of the classroom.

classroom management Establishment and maintenance of a classroom environment conducive to learning and achievement.

clinical method Procedure in which an adult probes a child's reasoning about a task or problem, tailoring follow-up questions to the child's earlier responses.

clique Moderately stable friendship group of perhaps 3 to 10 members.

cognition Various ways of thinking about information and events.

cognitive apprenticeship Mentorship in which a teacher and a student work together on a challenging task and the teacher gives guidance about how to think about the task.

cognitive-developmental theory Theoretical perspective that focuses on qualitative, stagelike changes in children's characteristics and abilities, with a particular emphasis on how children's active, constructive thinking processes contribute to such changes.

cognitive dissonance Feeling of mental discomfort caused by new information that conflicts with current knowledge or beliefs.

cognitive process Particular way of mentally responding to or thinking about information or an event.

cognitive style Characteristic way in which a learner tends to think about a task and process new information; typically comes into play automatically rather than by choice.

cognitive tool Concept, symbol, strategy, procedure, or other culturally constructed mechanism that helps people think about and respond to situations more effectively.

collective self-efficacy Shared belief of members of a group that they can be successful when they work together on a task.

community of learners Class in which teacher and students actively and collaboratively work to create a body of knowledge and help one another learn.

competence See *need for competence.*

comprehension monitoring Process of checking oneself to be sure one understands and remembers newly acquired information.

computer-based instruction (CBI) Instruction provided via computer technology.

concept Mental grouping of objects or events that have something in common.

concept map Diagram of concepts and their interrelationships; used to enhance learning and memory of a topic.

conceptual change Revision of one's understanding of a topic in response to new information.

conceptual understanding Knowledge about a topic acquired in an integrated and meaningful fashion.

concrete operations stage Piaget's third stage of cognitive development, in which adult-like logic appears but is limited to concrete reality.

confidence interval Range around a test score that reflects the amount of error likely to be affecting the score's accuracy.

confirmation bias Tendency to seek information that confirms rather than discredits current beliefs.

conservation Realization that if nothing is added or taken away, amount stays the same regardless of alterations in shape or arrangement.

constructivism Theoretical perspective proposing that learners construct (rather than absorb) a body of knowledge from their experiences—knowledge that may or may not be an accurate representation of external reality. Adherents to this perspective are called **constructivists**.

content validity Extent to which an assessment includes a representative sample of tasks within the domain being assessed.

contingency Situation in which one event (e.g., reinforcement) happens only after another event (e.g., a specific response) has already occurred (one event is *contingent* on the other's occurrence).

contingency contract Formal agreement between teacher and student that identifies behaviors the student will exhibit and the reinforcers that will follow.

control group Group of people in a research study who are given either no treatment or a treatment that is unlikely to have an effect on the dependent variable.

controversial student Student whom some peers strongly like and other peers strongly dislike.

conventional morality Uncritical acceptance of society's conventions regarding right and wrong.

conventional transgression Action that violates a culture's general expectations regarding socially appropriate behavior.

convergent thinking Process of pulling several pieces of information together to draw a conclusion or solve a problem.

cooperative learning Approach to instruction in which students work with a small group of peers to achieve a common goal and help one another learn.

core goal Long-term goal that drives much of what a learner does.

co-regulated learning Process through which an adult and child share responsibility for directing various aspects of the child's learning.

correlation Extent to which two variables are associated, such that when one variable increases, the other either increases or decreases somewhat predictably.

correlational study Research study that explores possible relationships among variables. Such a study enables researchers to predict one variable on the basis of their knowledge of another but not to draw a conclusion about a cause-effect relationship.

cortex Upper and outer parts of the human brain, which are largely responsible for conscious and higher-level human thought processes.

covert strategy Learning strategy that is strictly mental (rather than behavioral) in nature and so cannot be observed by others.

creativity New and original behavior that yields a productive and culturally appropriate result.

criterion-referenced score Assessment score that specifically indicates what a student knows or can do.

critical thinking Process of evaluating the accuracy and worth of information and lines of reasoning.

crowd Large, loose-knit social group that shares common interests and attitudes.

cueing Use of simple signals to indicate that a certain behavior is desired or that a certain behavior should stop.

cultural bias Extent to which assessment tasks either offend or unfairly penalize some students because of their ethnicity, gender, or socioeconomic status.

cultural mismatch Situation in which a child's home culture and the school culture hold conflicting expectations for the child's behavior.

culture Behaviors and belief systems that members of a long-standing social group share and pass along to successive generations.

culture shock Sense of confusion when a student encounters a culture with behavioral expectations very different from those previously learned.

debilitating anxiety Anxiety of sufficient intensity that it interferes with performance.

decay Weakening over time of information stored in long-term memory, especially if the information is used infrequently.

declarative knowledge Knowledge related to "what is"—that is, to the nature of how things are, were, or will be.

delay of gratification Ability to forego small, immediate reinforcers to obtain larger ones later on.

descriptive study Research study that enables researchers to draw conclusions about the current state of affairs but not about correlational or cause-and-effect relationships.

developmental milestone Appearance of a new, developmentally more advanced behavior.

dialect Form of a language that has certain unique pronunciations, idioms, and grammatical structures and is characteristic of a particular region or ethnic group.

differentiated instruction Practice of individualizing instructional methods, and possibly also individualizing specific content and instructional goals, to align with each student's existing knowledge, skills, and needs.

direct instruction Approach to instruction that uses a variety of techniques (e.g., explanations, questions, guided and independent practice) in a fairly structured manner to promote learning of basic skills.

discovery learning Approach to instruction in which students develop an understanding of a topic through firsthand interaction with the environment.

disequilibrium Inability to explain new events with existing schemes; tends to be accompanied by a sense of discomfort.

disposition General inclination to approach and think about learning and problem-solving tasks in a particular way; typically has a motivational component in addition to cognitive components.

distributed cognition Process in which two or more learners each contribute knowledge and ideas as they work collaboratively on an issue or problem.

distributed intelligence Idea that people act more "intelligently" when they have physical, symbolic, or social assistance.

distributive justice Beliefs about what constitutes people's fair share of a desired commodity.

divergent thinking Process of mentally moving in a variety of directions from a single idea.

dynamic assessment Systematic examination of how easily a student can acquire new knowledge or skills, perhaps with an adult's assistance.

educational psychology Academic discipline that studies and applies concepts and theories of psychology relevant to instructional practice.

elaboration Cognitive process in which learners embellish on new information based on what they already know.

emotional and behavioral disorders Emotional states and behaviors that consistently and significantly disrupt academic learning and performance.

emotional self-regulation Process of keeping one's affective states and resulting behaviors within productive, culturally desirable limits.

empathy Experience of sharing the same feelings as someone in unfortunate circumstances.

encoding Changing the format of information being stored in memory in order to remember it more easily.

entity view of intelligence Belief that intelligence is a "thing" that is relatively permanent and unchangeable.

epistemological belief Belief about the nature of knowledge or knowledge acquisition.

equilibration Movement from equilibrium to disequilibrium and back to equilibrium, a process that promotes development of more complex thought and understandings.

equilibrium State of being able to explain new events with existing schemes.

ethnic group People who have common historical roots, values, beliefs, and behaviors and who share a sense of interdependence.

ethnic identity Awareness of one's membership in a particular ethnic or cultural group, and willingness to adopt behaviors characteristic of the group.

ETS score Standard score with a mean of 500 and a standard deviation of 100.

expectancy-value theory Theoretical perspective proposing that human motivation is a function of two beliefs: that one can succeed in an activity (*expectancy*) and that there are direct or indirect benefits in performing the activity (*value*).

experimental study (experiment) Research study that involves the manipulation of one variable to determine its possible effect on another variable.

expertise Extensive and well-integrated knowledge of a topic that comes from many years of study and practice.

expository instruction Approach to instruction in which information is presented in more or less the same form in which students are expected to learn it.

externalizing behavior Symptom of an emotional or behavioral disorder that has a direct effect on other people.

extinction Gradual disappearance of an acquired response; in the case of a response acquired through operant conditioning, it results from repeated lack of reinforcement for the response.

extrinsic motivation Motivation resulting from factors external to the individual and unrelated to the task being performed.

extrinsic reinforcer Reinforcer that comes from the outside environment, rather than from within the learner.

facilitating anxiety Level of anxiety (usually relatively low) that enhances performance.

Family Educational Rights and Privacy Act (FERPA) U.S. legislation passed in 1974 mandating that teachers and other school personnel (a) restrict access to students' test results and school records only to students, their parents, and school employees directly involved in the students' education; and (b) upon request, make test scores and other information in students' records available to students and parents, with appropriate assistance in interpreting this information.

flow Intense form of intrinsic motivation, involving complete absorption in and concentration on a challenging activity.

formal assessment Preplanned, systematic attempt to ascertain what students have learned.

formal operations stage Piaget's fourth and final stage of cognitive development, in which logical reasoning processes are applied to abstract ideas as well as to concrete objects, and more sophisticated scientific and mathematical reasoning processes emerge.

formative evaluation Evaluation conducted before or during instruction to facilitate instructional planning and enhance students' learning.

functional analysis Examination of inappropriate behavior and its antecedents and consequences to determine one or more purposes (functions) that the behavior might serve for the learner.

g Theoretical general factor in intelligence that influences one's ability to learn in a wide variety of contexts.

gang Cohesive social group characterized by initiation rites, distinctive colors and symbols, territorial orientation, and feuds with rival groups.

gender schema Self-constructed, organized body of beliefs about the traits and behaviors of males or females.

general transfer Instance of transfer in which the original learning task and the transfer task are different in content.

giftedness Unusually high ability in one or more areas, to the point where students require special educational services to help them meet their full potential.

goal theory Theoretical perspective that portrays human motivation as being directed toward particular goals; the nature of these goals determines the specific ways in which people think and behave.

grade-equivalent score Test score indicating the grade level of students to whom a test taker performed most similarly.

guided participation A child's performance, with guidance and support, of an activity in the adult world.

guilt Feeling of discomfort when one knows one has caused someone else pain or distress.

heuristic General strategy that facilitates problem solving or creativity but does not always yield a successful outcome.

higher-level cognitive process Cognitive process that involves going well beyond information specifically learned (e.g., by analyzing, applying, or evaluating it).

higher-level question Question that requires students to do something new with something they've learned (i.e., to elaborate on it in some way).

high-stakes testing Practice of using students' performance on a single assessment instrument to make major decisions about students or school personnel.

hostile attributional bias Tendency to interpret others' behaviors as reflecting hostile or aggressive intentions.

hot cognition Learning or cognitive processing that is emotionally charged.

humanism Philosophical perspective in which people are seen as having tremendous potential for psychological growth and as continually striving to fulfill that potential. Adherents to this perspective are called **humanists**.

hypermedia Collection of multimedia, computer-based instructional materials (e.g., text, pictures, sound, animations) that students can examine in a sequence of their own choosing.

identity Self-constructed definition of who one thinks one is and what things are important in life.

illusion of knowing Thinking that one knows something that one actually does *not* know.

imaginary audience Belief that one is the center of attention in any social situation.

incentive Hoped-for, but not guaranteed, future consequence of behavior.

inclusion The practice of educating all students, including those with severe and multiple disabilities, in neighborhood schools and general education classrooms.

incompatible behaviors Two or more behaviors that cannot be performed simultaneously.

incremental view of intelligence Belief that intelligence can improve with effort and practice.

individual constructivism Theoretical perspective that focuses on how people, as individuals, construct meaning from the events around them.

Individuals with Disabilities Education Act (IDEA) U.S. legislation granting educational rights to people with cognitive, emotional, or physical disabilities from birth until age 21; initially passed in 1975, it has been amended and reauthorized several times.

induction Explanation of why a certain behavior is unacceptable, often with a focus on the pain or distress that someone has caused another.

informal assessment Assessment that results from a teacher's spontaneous, day-to-day observations of how students behave and perform in class.

information literacy Knowledge and skills that help a learner find, use, evaluate, organize, and present information about a particular topic.

information processing theory Theoretical perspective that focuses on how learners mentally think about (process) new information and events and how such processes change with development.

inner speech Process of "talking" to oneself mentally (usually to guide oneself through a task) rather than aloud.

in-school suspension Form of punishment in which a student is placed in a quiet, boring room within the school building, typically to do schoolwork under close adult supervision.

instructional goal Desired long-term outcome of instruction.

instructional objective Desired outcome of a lesson or unit.

intelligence Ability to modify and adjust behaviors to accomplish new tasks successfully; involves many different mental processes and may vary in nature depending on one's culture.

intelligence test General measure of current cognitive functioning, used primarily to predict academic achievement over the short run.

interest Feeling that a topic is intriguing or enticing.

internalization Process through which a learner gradually incorporates socially based activities into his or her internal cognitive processes.

internalized motivation Adoption of others' priorities and values as one's own.

internalizing behavior Symptom of an emotional or behavioral disorder that primarily affects the student with the disorder but has little or no direct effect on others.

intrinsic motivation Motivation resulting from personal characteristics or inherent in the task being performed.

intrinsic reinforcer Reinforcer provided by oneself or inherent in a task being performed.

IQ score Score on an intelligence test, determined by comparing a student's performance on the test with the performance of others in the same age-group. For most tests, it is a standard score with a mean of 100 and a standard deviation of 15.

IRE cycle Adult–child interaction marked by adult initiation (e.g., a question), child response, and adult evaluation.

keyword method Mnemonic technique in which an association is made between two ideas by forming a visual image of one or more concrete objects (*keywords*) that either sound similar to, or symbolically represent, those ideas.

knowledge base One's existing knowledge about specific topics and the world in general.

learned helplessness General, fairly pervasive belief that one is incapable of accomplishing tasks and has little or no control over the environment.

learner-centered instruction Approach to teaching in which instructional strategies are chosen largely on the basis of students' existing abilities, predispositions, and needs.

learner-directed instruction Approach to instruction in which students have considerable say in the issues they address and how to address them.

learning Long-term change in mental representations or associations due to experience.

learning disability Deficiency in one or more specific cognitive processes despite relatively normal cognitive functioning in other areas.

learning strategy Intentional use of one or more cognitive processes for a particular learning task.

lesson plan Predetermined guide for a lesson that identifies instructional goals or objectives, necessary materials, instructional strategies, and one or more assessment methods.

live model Individual whose behavior is directly observed in one's immediate environment.

logical consequence Unpleasant consequence that follows naturally or logically from a student's misbehavior.

long-term memory Component of memory that holds knowledge and skills for a relatively long time.

lower-level question Question that requires students to express what they've learned in essentially the same form they learned it.

mastery goal Desire to acquire additional knowledge or master new skills.

mastery learning Approach to instruction in which students learn one topic thoroughly before moving to a subsequent one.

mastery orientation General, fairly pervasive belief that one is capable of accomplishing challenging tasks.

maturation Unfolding of genetically controlled changes as a child develops.

mean (M) Mathematical average of a set of scores. It is calculated by adding all the scores obtained (counting each score every time it occurs) and then dividing by the total number of people who have obtained those scores.

meaningful learning Cognitive process in which learners relate new information to things they already know.

mediated learning experience Social interaction in which an adult helps a child interpret a phenomenon or event in particular (usually culturally appropriate) ways.

memory Ability to save something (mentally) that has been previously learned; also, the mental "location" where such information is saved.

mental retardation Disability characterized by significantly below-average general intelligence and deficits in practical and social skills.

mental set Inclination to encode a problem or situation in a way that excludes potential solutions.

metacognition Knowledge and beliefs about one's own cognitive processes, as well as conscious attempts to engage in behaviors and thought processes that increase learning and memory.

misbehavior Action that disrupts learning and planned classroom activities, puts students' physical safety or psychological well-being in jeopardy, or violates basic moral standards.

mnemonic Memory aid or trick designed to help students learn and remember a specific piece of information.

model Person who demonstrates a behavior for someone else.

modeling Demonstrating a behavior for another; also, observing and imitating another's behavior.

moral dilemma Situation in which two or more people's rights or needs may be at odds and the morally correct action is not clear-cut.

moral transgression Action that causes harm or infringes on the needs or rights of others.

morality One's general standards about right and wrong behavior.

motivation Inner state that energizes, directs, and sustains behavior.

multicultural education Instruction that integrates perspectives and experiences of numerous cultural groups throughout the curriculum.

myelination Growth of a fatty coating (myelin) around neurons, enabling faster transmission of messages.

nativism Theoretical perspective that proposes that certain characteristics, behaviors, knowledge, and predispositions are biologically built in.

need for arousal Ongoing need for either physical or cognitive stimulation.

need for competence Basic need to believe that one can deal effectively with the overall environment.

need for relatedness Basic need to feel socially connected to others and to secure others' love and respect.

need for self-determination Basic need to believe that one has some autonomy and control regarding the course of one's life.

negative reinforcement Phenomenon in which a response increases as a result of the removal (rather than presentation) of a stimulus.

negative transfer Phenomenon in which something learned at one time interferes with learning or performance at a later time.

neglected student Student about whom most peers have no strong feelings, either positive or negative.

neuron Cell in the brain or another part of the nervous system that transmits information to other cells.

neurotransmitter Chemical substance with which one neuron sends a message to another.

niche-picking Tendency for a learner to seek out environmental conditions that are a good match with his or her existing characteristics and behaviors.

No Child Left Behind Act (NCLB) U.S. legislation passed in 2001 that mandates regular assessments of basic skills to determine whether students are making adequate yearly progress in relation to state-determined standards in reading, math, and science.

normal distribution (normal curve) Theoretical pattern of educational and psychological characteristics in which most individuals lie somewhere in the middle range and only a few lie at either extreme.

norm-referenced score Assessment score that indicates how a student's performance on an assessment compares with the average performance of others.

operant conditioning Form of learning in which a response increases in frequency as a result of its being followed by reinforcement.

organization Cognitive process in which learners find connections (e.g., by forming categories, identifying hierarchies, determining cause-and-effect relationships) among various pieces of information they need to learn.

overt strategy Learning strategy that is at least partially evident in the learner's behavior (e.g., taking notes during a lecture).

paper-pencil assessment Assessment in which students provide written responses to written items.

peer mediation Approach to conflict resolution in which a student (mediator) asks peers in conflict to express their differing viewpoints and then work together to identify an appropriate compromise.

peer pressure Phenomenon whereby age-mates strongly encourage some behaviors and discourage others.

peer tutoring Approach to instruction in which one student provides instruction to help another student master a classroom topic.

percentile rank (percentile) Test score indicating the percentage of people in the norm group getting a raw score less than or equal to a particular student's raw score.

performance-approach goal Desire to look good and receive favorable judgments from others.

performance assessment Assessment in which students demonstrate their knowledge and skills in a nonwritten fashion.

performance-avoidance goal Desire not to look bad or receive unfavorable judgments from others.

performance goal Desire to demonstrate high ability and make a good impression.

personal fable Belief that one is completely unlike anyone else and so cannot be understood by others.

personal interest Long-term, relatively stable interest in a particular topic or activity.

personal space Personally or culturally preferred distance between two people during social interaction.

personality Characteristic ways in which an individual behaves, thinks, and feels.

perspective taking Ability to look at a situation from someone's else viewpoint.

physical aggression Action that can potentially cause bodily injury.

plasticity Capacity for the brain to learn and adapt to new circumstances.

popular student Student whom many peers like and perceive to be kind and trustworthy.

portfolio Collection of a student's work systematically compiled over a lengthy time period.

positive behavioral support (PBS) Systematic intervention that addresses chronic misbehaviors by (a) identifying the purposes those behaviors might serve for a student and (b) providing more appropriate ways for a student to achieve the same ends.

positive psychology Theoretical perspective that portrays people as having many unique qualities that propel them to engage in productive, worthwhile activities; it shares early humanists' belief that people strive to fulfill their potential but also shares contemporary psychologists' belief that theories of motivation must be research-based.

positive reinforcement Phenomenon in which a response increases as a result of the presentation (rather than removal) of a stimulus.

positive transfer Phenomenon in which something learned at one time facilitates learning or performance at a later time.

postconventional morality Thinking in accordance with self-constructed, abstract principles regarding right and wrong.

practicality Extent to which an assessment instrument or procedure is inexpensive and easy to use and takes only a small amount of time to administer and score.

preconventional morality Lack of internalized standards about right and wrong; making decisions based solely on what is best for oneself.

preoperational stage Piaget's second stage of cognitive development, in which children can think about objects beyond their immediate view but do not yet reason in logical, adult-like ways.

presentation punishment Punishment involving presentation of a new stimulus, presumably one a learner finds unpleasant.

primary reinforcer Consequence that satisfies a biologically built-in need.

prior knowledge activation Process of reminding learners of things they have already learned relative to a new topic.

proactive aggression Deliberate aggression against another as a means of obtaining a desired goal.

problem-based learning Classroom activity in which students acquire new knowledge and skills while working on a complex problem similar to those in the outside world.

problem solving Using existing knowledge or skills to address an unanswered question or troubling situation.

procedural knowledge Knowledge concerning how to do something (e.g., a skill).

project-based learning Classroom activity in which students acquire new knowledge and skills while working on a complex, multifaceted project that yields a concrete end product.

prosocial behavior Behavior directed toward promoting the well-being of another.

proximal goal Concrete goal that can be accomplished within a short time period; may be a stepping stone toward a longer-term goal.

psychodynamic theory Theoretical perspective proposing that a person's development is greatly affected by the person's early experiences, including experiences that are unavailable for conscious recall and reflection.

punishment Consequence that decreases the frequency of the response it follows.

raw score Assessment score based solely on the number or point value of correctly answered items.

reactive aggression Aggressive response to frustration or provocation.

reciprocal causation Mutual cause-and-effect relationships among environment, behavior, and personal variables as these three factors influence learning and development.

reciprocal teaching Approach to teaching reading and listening comprehension in which students take turns asking teacher-like questions of classmates.

reconstruction error Construction of a logical but incorrect "memory" by using information retrieved from long-term memory in combination with general knowledge and beliefs about the world.

recursive thinking Thinking about what other people may be thinking about oneself, possibly through multiple iterations.

rehearsal Cognitive process in which information is repeated over and over as a possible way of learning and remembering it.

reinforcement Act of following a response with a reinforcer.

reinforcer Consequence of a response that leads to increased frequency of the response.

rejected student Student whom many peers identify as being an undesirable social partner.

relatedness See *need for relatedness*.

relational aggression Action that can adversely affect interpersonal relationships.

reliability Extent to which an assessment instrument yields consistent information about the knowledge, skills, or characteristics being assessed.

removal punishment Punishment involving removal of an existing stimulus, presumably one a learner finds desirable and doesn't want to lose.

resilient self-efficacy Belief that one can perform a task successfully even after experiencing setbacks.

resilient student Student who succeeds in school and in life despite exceptional hardships at home.

response Specific behavior that an individual exhibits.

response cost Loss either of a previously earned reinforcer or of an opportunity to obtain reinforcement.

retrieval Process of "finding" information previously stored in memory.

retrieval cue Stimulus that provides guidance about where to "look" for a piece of information in long-term memory.

retrieval failure Inability to locate information that currently exists in long-term memory.

rote learning Learning information in a relatively uninterpreted form, without making sense of it or attaching much meaning to it.

rubric List of components that a student's performance on an assessment task should ideally include.

scaffolding Support mechanism that helps a learner successfully perform a task within his or her zone of proximal development.

schema General understanding of what an object or event is typically like.

scheme In Piaget's theory, organized group of similar actions or thoughts that are used repeatedly in response to the environment.

script Schema that involves a predictable sequence of events related to a common activity.

secondary reinforcer Consequence that becomes reinforcing over time through its association with another reinforcer.

self-determination theory Theoretical perspective proposing that human beings have a basic need for autonomy (*self-determination*) about the courses that their lives take; it further proposes that humans also have basic needs to feel competent and to have close, affectionate relationships with others. Also see *need for self-determination*.

self-efficacy Belief that one is capable of executing certain behaviors or reaching certain goals.

self-evaluation Judgment of one's own performance or behavior.

self-fulfilling prophecy Expectation for an outcome that either directly or indirectly leads to the expected result.

self-handicapping Behavior that undermines one's own success as a way of protecting self-worth during difficult tasks.

self-imposed contingency Self-reinforcement or self-punishment that follows a particular behavior.

self-instructions Instructions that one gives oneself while executing a complex task.

self-monitoring Observing and recording one's own behavior to check progress toward a goal.

self-regulation Process of taking control of and evaluating one's own learning and behavior.

self-socialization Tendency to integrate personal observations and others' input into self-constructed standards for behavior and to choose actions consistent with those standards.

self-talk Process of talking to oneself as a way of guiding oneself through a task.

self-worth Belief about the extent to which one is generally a good, capable individual.

self-worth theory Theoretical perspective proposing that protecting one's own sense of competence (one's sense of *self-worth*) is a high priority for human beings.

sense of community Shared belief that teacher and students have common goals, are mutually respectful and supportive, and all make important contributions to classroom learning.

sense of school community Shared belief that all faculty and students within a school are working together to help everyone learn and succeed.

sense of self Perceptions, beliefs, judgments, and feelings about oneself as a person.

sensitive period Genetically determined age range during which a certain aspect of a child's development is especially susceptible to environmental conditions.

sensorimotor stage Piaget's first stage of cognitive development, in which schemes are based largely on behaviors and perceptions.

sensory register Component of memory that holds incoming information in an unanalyzed form for a very brief time (perhaps one to two seconds).

service learning Activity that promotes learning and development through participation in a meaningful community service project.

shame Feeling of embarrassment or humiliation after failing to meet standards for moral behavior that adults have set.

shaping Process of reinforcing successively closer and closer approximations to a desired behavior.

situated learning and cognition Knowledge, behaviors, and thinking skills acquired and used primarily within certain contexts, with limited if any use in other contexts.

situated motivation Motivation that emerges at least partly from conditions in a learner's immediate environment.

situational interest Interest evoked temporarily by something in the environment.

social cognition Process of thinking about how other people are likely to think, act, and react.

social cognitive theory See *social learning theory*.

social constructivism Theoretical perspective that focuses on people's collective efforts to impose meaning on the world.

social goal Desire related to establishing or maintaining relationships with other people.

social information processing Mental processes involved in understanding and responding to social events.

social learning theory Theoretical perspective in which learning by observing others is the focus of study. Initially, this perspective focused largely on stimulus-response relationships. More recently, it has come to incorporate cognitive processes as well, hence its alternative name **social cognitive theory**.

socialization Process of molding a child's behavior and beliefs to be appropriate for the cultural group.

society Large, enduring social group that is socially and economically organized and has collective institutions and activities.

sociocultural theory Theoretical perspective that emphasizes the importance of society and culture for promoting learning and cognitive development.

socioeconomic status (SES) One's general social and economic standing in society (encompasses family income, educational level, occupational status, and related factors).

specific transfer Instance of transfer in which the original learning task and the transfer task overlap in content.

stage theory Theory that depicts development as a series of relatively discrete periods (*stages*).

standard deviation (SD) Statistic that reflects how close together or far apart a set of scores are and thereby indicates the variability of the scores.

Standard English Form of English generally considered acceptable at school, as reflected in textbooks and grammar instruction.

standard score Test score indicating how far a student's performance is from the mean with respect to standard deviation units.

standardization Extent to which assessments involve similar content and format and are administered and scored similarly for everyone.

standardized test Test developed by test construction experts and published for use in many different schools and classrooms.

standards General statements regarding the knowledge and skills that students should gain and the characteristics that their accomplishments should reflect.

stanine Standard score with a mean of 5 and a standard deviation of 2; it is always reported as a whole number.

stereotype threat Awareness of a negative stereotype about one's own group and accompanying uneasiness that low performance will confirm the stereotype; leads (often unintentionally) to a reduction in performance.

stimulus (pl. stimuli) Specific object or event that influences an individual's learning or behavior.

storage Process of "putting" new information into memory.

student at risk Student who has a high probability of failing to acquire the minimum academic skills necessary for success in the adult world.

student with special needs Student who is different enough from peers that he or she requires specially adapted instructional materials and practices.

subculture Group that resists the ways of the dominant culture and adopts its own norms for behavior.

summative evaluation Evaluation conducted after instruction to assess students' final achievement.

superimposed meaningful structure Familiar shape, word, sentence, poem, or story imposed on information in order to facilitate recall.

symbolic model Real or fictional character portrayed in the media that influences an observer's behavior.

sympathy Feeling of sorrow or concern for another person's problems or distress.

synapse Tiny space across which one neuron regularly communicates with another; reflects an ongoing but modifiable connection between the two neurons.

synaptic pruning Universal process in brain development in which many previously formed synapses wither away.

synaptogenesis Universal process in early brain development in which many new synapses form spontaneously.

table of specifications Two-way grid indicating the topics to be covered in an assessment and the things students should be able to do with those topics.

task analysis Process of identifying the specific knowledge, behaviors, or cognitive processes necessary to master a particular subject area or skill.

teacher-directed instruction Approach to instruction in which the teacher is largely in control of the content and course of the lesson.

temperament Genetic predisposition to respond in particular ways to one's physical and social environments.

test anxiety Excessive anxiety about a particular test or about assessment in general.

testwiseness Test-taking know-how that enhances test performance.

theory Integrated set of concepts and principles developed to explain a particular phenomenon; may be constructed jointly by researchers over time (see Chapter 1) or individually by a single learner (see Chapter 2).

theory of mind Self-constructed understanding of one's own and other people's mental and psychological states (thoughts, feelings, etc.).

threat Situation in which a learner believes there is little or no chance of success.

time on task Amount of time that students are actively engaged in a learning activity.

time-out Form of punishment in which a student is placed in a dull, boring situation with no opportunity for reinforcement or social interaction.

token economy Classroom strategy in which desired behaviors are reinforced by tokens that the learner can use to "purchase" a variety of other, backup reinforcers.

transfer Phenomenon in which something a person has learned at one time affects how the person learns or performs in a later situation.

treatment group Group of people in a research study who are given a particular experimental treatment (e.g., a particular method of instruction).

universal (in development) Similar pattern in how children change and progress over time regardless of their specific environment.

validity Extent to which an assessment instrument actually measures what it is intended to measure and allows appropriate inferences about the characteristic or ability in question.

value Belief that an activity has direct or indirect benefits.

verbal mediator Word or phrase that forms a logical connection or "bridge" between two pieces of information.

vicarious punishment Phenomenon in which a response decreases in frequency when another (observed) person is punished for that response.

vicarious reinforcement Phenomenon in which a response increases in frequency when another (observed) person is reinforced for that response.

visual imagery Process of forming mental pictures of objects or ideas.

wait time Length of time a teacher pauses, after either asking a question or hearing a student's comment, before saying something.

withitness Classroom management strategy in which a teacher gives the impression of knowing what all students are doing at all times.

working memory Component of memory that holds and actively thinks about and processes a limited amount of information.

worldview General, culturally based set of assumptions about reality that influence understandings of a wide variety of phenomena.

zone of proximal development (ZPD) Range of tasks that a child can perform with the help and guidance of others but cannot yet perform independently.

z-score Standard score with a mean of 0 and a standard deviation of 1.

REFERENCES

Ablard, K. E., & Lipschultz, R. E. (1998). Self-regulated learning in high-achieving students: Relations to advanced reasoning, achievement goals, and gender. *Journal of Educational Psychology, 90,* 94–101.

Achenbach, T. M. (1974). *Developmental psychopathology.* New York: Ronald Press.

Ackerman, B. P., Izard, C. E., Kobak, R., Brown, E. D., & Smith, C. (2007). Relation between reading problems and internalizing behavior in school for preadolescent children from economically disadvantaged families. *Child Development, 78,* 581–596.

Ackerman, P. L., & Lohman, D. F. (2006). Individual differences in cognitive functions. In P. A. Alexander & P. H. Winne (Eds.), *Handbook of educational psychology* (2nd ed., pp. 139–161). Mahwah, NJ: Erlbaum.

Adalbjarnardottir, S., & Selman, R. L. (1997). "I feel I have received a new vision": An analysis of teachers' professional development as they work with students on interpersonal issues. *Teaching and Teacher Education, 13,* 409–428.

Ahn, J. (2005, April). *Young immigrant children's cultural transition and self-transformation.* Paper presented at the annual meeting of the American Educational Research Association, Montreal.

Airasian, P. W. (1994). *Classroom assessment* (2nd ed.). New York: McGraw-Hill.

Alapack, R. (1991). The adolescent first kiss. *Humanistic Psychologist, 19,* 48–67.

Alberto, P. A., & Troutman, A. C. (2003). *Applied behavior analysis for teachers* (6th ed.). Upper Saddle River, NJ: Merrill/Prentice Hall.

Alderman, M. K. (1990). Motivation for at-risk students. *Educational Leadership, 48*(1), 27–30.

Alexander, E. S. (2006, April). *Beyond S.M.A.R.T.? Integrating hopeful thinking into goal setting for adolescents at-risk of dropping out of high school.* Paper presented at the annual meeting of the American Educational Research Association, San Francisco.

Alexander, J. M., Johnson, K. E., Albano, J., Freygang, T., & Scott, B. (2006). Relations between intelligence and the development of metaconceptual knowledge. *Metacognition and Learning, 1,* 51–67.

Alexander, J. M., Johnson, K. E., Scott, B., & Meyer, R. D. (2008). Stegosaurus and spoonbills: Mechanisms for transfer across biological domains. In M. F. Shaughnessy, M. V. E. Vennemann, & C. K. Kennedy (Eds.), *Metacognition: A recent review of research, theory, and perspectives.* Happauge, NY: Nova Publications.

Alexander, K. L., Entwisle, D. R., & Dauber, S. L. (1995). *On the success of failure.* New York: Cambridge University Press.

Alexander, P. A. (1997). Mapping the multidimensional nature of domain learning: The interplay of cognitive, motivational, and strategic forces. In P. R. Pintrich & M. L. Maehr (Eds.), *Advances in motivation and achievement* (Vol. 10). Greenwich, CT: JAI Press.

Alexander, P. A. (1998). Positioning conceptual change within a model of domain literacy. In B. Guzzetti & C. Hynd (Eds.), *Perspectives on conceptual change: Multiple ways to understand knowing and learning in a complex world* (pp. 55–76). Mahwah, NJ: Erlbaum.

Alexander, P. A. (2004). A model of domain learning: Reinterpreting expertise as a multidimensional, multistage process. In D. Y. Dai & R. J. Sternberg (Eds.), *Motivation, emotion, and cognition: Integrative perspectives on intellectual functioning and development* (pp. 273–298). Mahwah, NJ: Erlbaum.

Alexander, P. A., & Judy, J. E. (1988). The interaction of domain-specific and strategic knowledge in academic performance. *Review of Educational Research, 58,* 375–404.

Alexander, P. A., Kulikowich, J. M., & Schulze, S. K. (1994). How subject-matter knowledge affects recall and interest. *American Educational Research Journal, 31,* 313–337.

Alfassi, M. (1998). Reading for meaning: The efficacy of reciprocal teaching in fostering reading comprehension in high school students in remedial reading classes. *American Educational Research Journal, 35,* 309–332.

Allday, R. A., & Pakurar, K. (2007). Effects of teacher greetings on student on-task behavior. *Journal of Applied Behavior Analysis, 40,* 317–320.

Alleman, J., & Brophy, J. (1997). Elementary social studies: Instruments, activities, and standards. In G. D. Phye (Ed.), *Handbook of classroom assessment: Learning, achievement, and adjustment.* San Diego, CA: Academic Press.

Alleman, J., & Brophy, J. (1998). Strategic learning opportunities during out-of-school hours. *Social Studies and the Young Learner, 10*(4), 10–13.

Allen, K. D. (1998). The use of an enhanced simplified habit-reversal procedure to reduce disruptive outbursts during athletic performance. *Journal of Applied Behavior Analysis, 31,* 489–492.

Allen, L., & Aber, J. L. (2006). The development of ethnic identity during adolescence. *Developmental Psychology, 42,* 1–10.

Allington, R. L., & Weber, R. (1993). Questioning questions in teaching and learning from texts. In B. K. Britton, A. Woodward, & M. Binkley (Eds.), *Learning from textbooks: Theory and practice.* Mahwah, NJ: Erlbaum.

Allison, K. W. (1998). Stress and oppressed social category membership. In J. Swim & C. Stangor (Eds.), *Prejudice: The target's perspective* (pp. 149–170). San Diego, CA: Academic Press.

Altermatt, E. R., Jovanovic, J., & Perry, M. (1998). Bias or responsivity? Sex and achievement-level effects on teachers' classroom questioning practices. *Journal of Educational Psychology, 90,* 516–527.

Altmann, E. M., & Gray, W. D. (2002). Forgetting to remember: The functional relationship of decay and interference. *Psychological Science, 13,* 27–33.

Altschul, I., Oyserman, D., & Bybee, D. (2006). Racial-ethnic identity in mid-adolescence: Content and change as predictors of academic achievement. *Child Development, 77,* 1155–1169.

Amabile, T. M., & Hennessey, B. A. (1992). The motivation for creativity in children. In A. K. Boggiano & T. S. Pittman (Eds.), *Achievement and motivation: A social-developmental perspective.* Cambridge, England: Cambridge University Press.

Ambrose, D., Allen, J., & Huntley, S. B. (1994). Mentorship of the highly creative. *Roeper Review, 17,* 131–133.

American Educational Research Association, American Psychological Association, & National Council on Measurement in Education. (1999). *Standards for educational and psychological testing* (2nd ed.). Washington, DC: American Educational Research Association.

American Psychiatric Association. (1994). *Diagnostic and statistical manual of mental disorders* (4th ed.). Washington, DC: Author.

American Psychological Association. (2001). *Publication manual of the American Psychological Association* (5th ed.). Washington, DC: Author.

Ames, C. (1984). Competitive, cooperative, and individualistic goal structures: A cognitive-motivational analysis. In R. Ames & C. Ames (Eds.), *Research on motivation in education: Vol. 1. Student motivation.* San Diego, CA: Academic Press.

Ames, C. (1992). Classrooms: Goals, structures, and student motivation. *Journal of Educational Psychology, 84,* 261–271.

Ames, C., & Ames, R. (1981). Competitive versus individualistic goal structures: The salience of past performance information for causal attributions and affect. *Journal of Educational Psychology, 73,* 411–418.

Ames, C., & Archer, J. (1988). Achievement goals in the classroom: Students' learning strategies and motivation processes. *Journal of Educational Psychology, 80,* 260–267.

Ames, R. (1983). Help-seeking and achievement orientation: Perspectives from attribution theory. In A. Nadler, J. Fisher, & B. DePaulo (Eds.), *New directions in helping* (Vol. 2). New York: Academic Press.

Amrein, A. L., & Berliner, D. C. (2002a, December). *An analysis of some unintended and negative consequences of high-stakes testing* (Report EPSL-0211-125-EPRU). Educational Policy Study Laboratory Web site: Retrieved April 28, 2003, from Arizona State University, http://www.asu.edu/educ/epsl/EPRU/epru_2002_Research_Writing.htm

Amrein, A. L., & Berliner, D. C. (2002b, March). High-stakes testing, uncertainty, and student learning. *Education Policy Analysis Archives, 10*(18). Retrieved April 9, 2002, from http://epaa.asu.edu/epaa/v10n18/

Amrein, A. L., & Berliner, D. C. (2002c). The impact of high-stakes tests on student academic performance: An analysis of NAEP results in states with high-stakes tests and ACT, SAT, and AP test results in states with high school graduation exams. Retrieved April 28, 2003, from Arizona State University, Education Policy Studies Laboratory Web site: http://www.asu.edu/educ/epsl/EPRU/epru_2002_Research_Writing.htm

Amsterlaw, J. (2006). Children's beliefs about everyday reasoning. *Child Development, 77,* 443–464.

Anderman, E. M. (2002). School effects on psychological outcomes during adolescence. *Journal of Educational Psychology, 94,* 795–809.

Anderman, E. M., Griesinger, T., & Westerfield, G. (1998). Motivation and cheating during early adolescence. *Journal of Educational Psychology, 90,* 84–93.

Anderman, E. M., & Maehr, M. L. (1994). Motivation and schooling in the middle grades. *Review of Educational Research, 64,* 287–309.

Anderman, E. M., Noar, S., Zimmerman, R. S., & Donohew, L. (2004). The need for sensation as a prerequisite for motivation to engage in academic tasks. In M. L. Maehr & P. Pintrich (Eds.), *Advances in motivation and achievement: Motivating students, improving schools: The legacy of Carol Midgley* (Vol. 13). Greenwich, JAI Press.

Anderman, E. M., & Wolters, C. A. (2006). Goals, values, and affect: Influences on student motivation. In P. A. Alexander & P. H. Winne (Eds.), *Handbook of educational psychology* (2nd ed., pp. 369–389). Mahwah, NJ: Erlbaum.

Anderman, L. H., & Anderman, E. M. (1999). Social predictors of changes in students' achievement goal orientation. *Contemporary Educational Psychology, 25,* 21–37.

Anderman, L. H., Patrick, H., Hruda, L. Z., & Linnenbrink, E. A. (2002). Observing classroom goal structures to clarify and expand goal theory. In C. Midgley (Ed.), *Goals, goal structures, and patterns of adaptive learning* (pp. 243–278). Mahwah, NJ: Erlbaum.

Anderson, C. A., Berkowitz, L., Donnerstein, E., Huesmann, L. R., Johnson, J. D., Linz, D., et al. (2003). The influence of media violence on youth. *Psychological Science in the Public Interest, 4*, 81–110.

Anderson, J. R. (1983). *The architecture of cognition.* Cambridge, MA: Harvard University Press.

Anderson, J. R. (1987). Skill acquisition: Compilation of weak-method problem solutions. *Psychological Review, 94*, 192–210.

Anderson, J. R. (1990). *Cognitive psychology and its implications* (3rd ed.). New York: Freeman.

Anderson, J. R. (1995). *Learning and memory: An integrated approach.* New York: Wiley.

Anderson, J. R., Greeno, J. G., Reder, L. M., & Simon, H. A. (2000). Perspectives on learning, thinking, and activity. *Educational Researcher, 29*(4), 11–13.

Anderson, J. R., Reder, L. M., & Simon, H. A. (1996). Situated learning and education. *Educational Researcher, 25*(4), 5–11.

Anderson, J. R., & Schooler, L. J. (1991). Reflections of the environment in memory. *Psychological Science, 2*, 396–408.

Anderson, L. H. (1999). *Speak.* New York: Puffin Books.

Anderson, L. M. (1993). Auxiliary materials that accompany textbooks: Can they promote "higher-order" learning? In B. K. Britton, A. Woodward, & M. Binkley (Eds.), *Learning from textbooks: Theory and practice.* Mahwah, NJ: Erlbaum.

Anderson, L. W., Krathwohl, D. R., Airasian, P. W., Cruikshank, K. A., Mayer, R. E., Pintrich, P. R., et al. (Eds.). (2001). *A taxonomy for learning, teaching, and assessing: A revision of Bloom's taxonomy of educational objectives.* New York: Longman.

Anderson, L. W., & Pellicer, L. O. (1998). Toward an understanding of unusually successful programs for economically disadvantaged students. *Journal of Education for Students Placed at Risk, 3*, 237–263.

Anderson, R. C., Nguyen-Jahiel, K., McNurlen, B., Archodidou, A., Kim, S.-Y., Reznitskaya, A., et al. (2001). The snowball phenomenon: Spread of ways of talking and ways of thinking across groups of children. *Cognition and Instruction, 19*, 1–46.

Anderson, R. C., Reynolds, R. E., Schallert, D. L., & Goetz, E. T. (1977). Frameworks for comprehending discourse. *American Educational Research Journal, 14*, 367–381.

Andre, T., & Windschitl, M. (2003). Interest, epistemological belief, and intentional conceptual change. In G. M. Sinatra & P. R. Pintrich (Eds.), *Intentional conceptual change* (pp. 173–197). Mahwah, NJ: Erlbaum.

Andriessen, J. (2006). Arguing to learn. In R. K. Sawyer (Ed.), *The Cambridge handbook of the learning sciences* (pp. 443–459). Cambridge, England: Cambridge University Press.

Angold, A., Worthman, C., & Costello, E. J. (2003). Puberty and depression. In C. Hayward (Ed.), *Gender differences at puberty* (pp. 137–164). Cambridge, England: Cambridge University Press.

Ansley, T. (1997). The role of standardized achievement tests in grades K–12. In G. D. Phye (Ed.), *Handbook of classroom assessment: Learning, achievement, and adjustment.* San Diego, CA: Academic Press.

Archer, S. L. (1982). The lower age boundaries of identity development. *Child Development, 53*, 1551–1556.

Ardoin, S. P., Martens, B. K., & Wolfe, L. A. (1999). Using high-probability instructional sequences with fading to increase student compliance during transitions. *Journal of Applied Behavior Analysis, 32*, 339–351.

Arlin, M. (1979). Teacher transitions can disrupt time flow in classrooms. *American Educational Research Journal, 16*, 42–56.

Arnett, J. (1995). The young and the reckless: Adolescent reckless behavior. *Current Directions in Psychological Science, 4*, 67–71.

Arnett, J. (1999). Adolescent storm and stress, reconsidered. *American Psychologist, 54*, 317–326.

Arnold, M. L. (2000). Stage, sequence, and sequels: Changing conceptions of morality, post-Kohlberg. *Educational Psychology Review, 12*, 365–383.

Aronson, J., Lustina, M. J., Good, C., Keough, K., Steele, C. M., & Brown, J. (1999). When white men can't do math: Necessary and sufficient factors in stereotype threat. *Journal of Experimental Social Psychology, 35*, 29–46.

Arsenio, W. F., & Lemerise, E. A. (2004). Aggression and moral development: Integrating social information processing and moral domain models. *Child Development, 75*, 987–1002.

Arter, J. A., & Spandel, V. (1992). Using portfolios of student work in instruction and assessment. *Educational Measurement: Issues and Practice, 11*(1), 36–44.

Ash, D. (2002). Negotiations of thematic conversations about biology. In G. Leinhardt, K. Crowley, & K. Knutson (Eds.), *Learning conversations in museums* (pp. 357–400). Mahwah, NJ: Erlbaum.

Ashcraft, M. H. (2002). Math anxiety: Personal, educational, and cognitive consequences. *Current Directions in Psychological Science, 11*, 181–184.

Asher, S. R., & Paquette, J. A. (2003). Loneliness and peer relations in childhood. *Current Directions in Psychological Science, 12*, 75–78.

Asher, S. R., & Parker, J. G. (1989). Significance of peer relationship problems in childhood. In B. H. Schneider, G. Attili, J. Nadel, & R. P. Weissberg (Eds.), *Social competence in developmental perspective.* Dordrecht, Netherlands: Kluwer.

Asher, S. R., & Renshaw, P. D. (1981). Children without friends: Social knowledge and social skill training. In S. R. Asher & J. M. Gottman (Eds.), *The development of children's friendships.* New York: Cambridge University Press.

Assor, A., & Connell, J. P. (1992). The validity of students' self-reports as measures of performance affecting self-appraisals. In D. H. Schunk & J. L. Meece (Eds.), *Student perceptions in the classroom.* Mahwah, NJ: Erlbaum.

Astington, J. W., & Pelletier, J. (1996). The language of mind: Its role in teaching and learning. In D. R. Olson & N. Torrance (Eds.), *The handbook of education and human development: New models of learning, teaching, and schooling.* Cambridge, MA: Blackwell.

Astor, R. A. (1994). Children's moral reasoning about family and peer violence: The role of provocation and retribution. *Child Development, 65*, 1054–1067.

Astor, R. A., Meyer, H. A., & Behre, W. J. (1999). Unowned places and times: Maps and interviews about violence in high schools. *American Educational Research Journal, 36*, 3–42.

Astuti, R., Solomon, G. E. A., & Carey, S. (2004). Constraints on conceptual development. *Monographs of the Society for Research in Child Development, 69*(3, Serial No. 277).

Atance, C. M., & Meltzoff, A. N. (2006). Preschoolers' current desires warp their choices for the future. *Psychological Science, 17*, 583–587.

Atkinson, R. C., & Shiffrin, R. M. (1968). Human memory: A proposed system and its control processes. In K. W. Spence & J. T. Spence (Eds.), *The psychology of learning and motivation: Advances in research and theory* (Vol. 2). San Diego, CA: Academic Press.

Atkinson, R. K., Levin, J. R., Kiewra, K. A., Meyers, T., Kim, S., Atkinson, L. A., et al. (1999). Matrix and mnemonic text-processing adjuncts: Comparing and combining their components. *Journal of Educational Psychology, 91*, 342–357.

Atran, S., Medin, D. L., & Ross, N. O. (2005). The cultural mind: Environmental decision making and cultural modeling within and across populations. *Psychological Review, 112*, 744–776.

Attie, I., Brooks-Gunn, J., & Petersen, A. (1990). A developmental perspective on eating disorders and eating problems. In M. Lewis & S. M. Miller (Eds.), *Handbook of developmental psychopathology* (pp. 409–420). New York: Plenum Press.

Au, K. H. (1980). Participation structures in a reading lesson with Hawaiian children: Analysis of a culturally appropriate instructional event. *Anthropology and Education Quarterly, 11*, 91–115.

Au, W. (2007). High-stakes testing and curricular control: A qualitative metasynthesis. *Educational Researcher, 36*(5), 258–267.

Aulls, M. W. (1998). Contributions of classroom discourse to what content students learn during curriculum enactment. *Journal of Educational Psychology, 90*, 56–69.

Ausubel, D. P. (1968). *Educational psychology: A cognitive view.* New York: Holt, Rinehart & Winston.

Ausubel, D. P., Novak, J. D., & Hanesian, H. (1978). *Educational psychology: A cognitive view* (2nd ed.). New York: Holt, Rinehart & Winston.

Awh, E., Barton, B., & Vogel, E. D. (2007). Visual working memory represents a fixed number of items regardless of complexity. *Psychological Science, 18*, 622–628.

Azevedo, R. (2005a). Computer environments as metacognitive tools for enhancing learning. *Educational Psychologist, 40*, 193–197.

Azevedo, R. (2005b). Using hypermedia as a metacognitive tool for enhancing student learning? The role of self-regulated learning. *Educational Psychologist, 40*, 199–209.

Babad, E. (1993). Teachers' differential behavior. *Educational Psychology Review, 5*, 347–376.

Babad, E. (1995). The "teacher's pet phenomenon," students' perceptions of teachers' differential behavior, and students' morale. *Journal of Educational Psychology, 87*, 361–374.

Babad, E., Avni-Babad, D., & Rosenthal, R. (2003). Teachers' brief nonverbal behaviors in defined instructional situations can predict students' evaluations. *Journal of Educational Psychology, 95*, 553–562.

Baddeley, A. D. (2001). Is working memory still working? *American Psychologist, 56*, 851–864.

Baek, S. (1994). Implications of cognitive psychology for educational testing. *Educational Psychology Review, 6*, 373–389.

Bagley, C., & Mallick, K. (1998). Field independence, cultural context and academic achievement: A commentary. *British Journal of Educational Psychology, 68*, 581–587.

Baillargeon, R. (1994). How do infants learn about the physical world? *Current Directions in Psychological Science, 3*, 133–140.

Baker, J. (1999). Teacher-student interaction in urban at-risk classrooms: Differential behavior, relationship quality, and student satisfaction with school. *The Elementary School Journal, 100*, 57–70.

Baker, L. (1989). Metacognition, comprehension monitoring, and the adult reader. *Educational Psychology Review, 1*, 3–38.

Baker, L., & Brown, A. L. (1984). Metacognitive skills of reading. In D. Pearson (Ed.), *Handbook of reading research.* White Plains, NY: Longman.

Ballenger, C. (1992). Because you like us: The language of control. *Harvard Educational Review, 62*, 199–208.

Ballenger, C. (1999). *Teaching other people's children: Literacy and learning in a bilingual classroom.* New York: Teachers College Press.

Bandura, A. (1977). *Social learning theory.* Upper Saddle River, NJ: Prentice Hall.

Bandura, A. (1986). *Social foundations of thought and action: A social cognitive theory.* Upper Saddle River, NJ: Prentice Hall.

Bandura, A. (1989). Human agency in social cognitive theory. *American Psychologist, 44*, 1175–1184.

Bandura, A. (1997). *Self-efficacy: The exercise of control.* New York: Freeman.

Bandura, A. (2000). Exercise of human agency through collective efficacy. *Current Directions in Psychological Science, 9*, 75–78.

Bandura, A. (2006). Toward a psychology of human agency. *Perspectives on Psychological Science, 1*, 164–180.

Bangert-Drowns, R. L., Kulik, J. A., & Kulik, C.-L. C. (1983). Effects of coaching programs on achievement test performance. *Review of Educational Research, 53*, 571–585.

Bangert-Drowns, R. L., Kulik, C. C., Kulik, J. A., & Morgan, M. (1991). The instructional effect of feedback in test-like events. *Review of Educational Research, 61*, 213–238.

Banks, J. A. (1991). Multicultural literacy and curriculum reform. *Educational Horizons, 69*(3), 135–140.

Banks, J. A. (1994). *An introduction to multicultural education.* Needham Heights, MA: Allyn & Bacon.

Banks, J. A. (1995). Multicultural education: Historical development, dimensions, and practice. In J. A. Banks & C. A. M. Banks (Eds.), *Handbook of research on multicultural education.* New York: Macmillan.

Banks, J. A., & Banks, C. A. M. (Eds.). (1995). *Handbook of research on multicultural education.* New York: Macmillan.

Barab, S. A., & Plucker, J. A. (2002). Smart people or smart contexts? Cognition, ability, and talent development in an age of situated approaches to knowing and learning. *Educational Psychologist, 37,* 165–182.

Barber, B. K., Stolz, H. E., & Olsen, J. A. (2005). Parental support, psychological control, and behavioral control: Assessing relevance across time, culture, and method. *Monographs of the Society for Research in Child Development, 70* (4; Serial No. 282).

Barchfeld, P., Sodian, B., Thoermer, C., & Bullock, M. (2005, April). *The development of experiment generation abilities from primary school to late adolescence.* Poster presented at the biennial meeting of the Society for Research in Child Development, Atlanta.

Barkley, R. A. (1996). Linkages between attention and executive functions. In G. R. Lyon & N. A. Krasnegor (Eds.), *Attention, memory, and executive function.* Baltimore: Brookes.

Barkley, R. A. (1998). *Attention-deficit hyperactivity disorder: A handbook for diagnosis and treatment* (2nd ed.). New York: Guilford Press.

Barnes, D. (1976). *From communication to curriculum.* London: Penguin.

Barnet, S. M., & Ceci, S. J. (2002). When and where do we apply what we learn? A taxonomy of far transfer. *Psychological Bulletin, 128,* 612–637.

Barnett, J. E. (2001, April). *Study strategies and preparing for exams: A survey of middle and high school students.* Paper presented at the annual meeting of the American Educational Research Association, Seattle, WA.

Baron, J. B. (1987). Evaluating thinking skills in the classroom. In J. B. Baron & R. J. Sternberg (Eds.), *Teaching thinking skills: Theory and practice.* New York: Freeman.

Baron-Cohen, S., Tager-Flusberg, H., & Cohen, D. J. (1993). *Understanding other minds: Perspectives from autism.* Oxford, England: Oxford University Press.

Bartholomew, D. J. (2004). *Measuring intelligence: Facts and fallacies.* Cambridge, England: Cambridge University Press.

Bartlett, F. C. (1932). *Remembering: A study in experimental and social psychology.* Cambridge, England: Cambridge University Press.

Barton, K. C., & Levstik, L. S. (1996). "Back when God was around and everything": Elementary children's understanding of historical time. *American Educational Research Journal, 33,* 419–454.

Basinger, K. S., Gibbs, J. C., & Fuller, D. (1995). Context and the measurement of moral judgment. *International Journal of Behavioral Development, 18,* 537–556.

Basso, K. (1972). To give up on words: Silence in western Apache culture. In P. Giglioli (Ed.), *Language and social context.* New York: Penguin Books.

Bassok, M. (1990). Transfer of domain-specific problem-solving procedures. *Journal of Experimental Psychology: Learning, Memory, and Cognition, 16,* 522–533.

Bassok, M., & Holyoak, K. (1990, April). *Transfer of solution procedures between quantitative domains.* Paper presented at the annual meeting of the American Educational Research Association, Boston.

Bassok, M., & Holyoak, K. J. (1993). Pragmatic knowledge and conceptual structure: Determinants of transfer between quantitative domains. In D. K. Detterman & R. J. Sternberg (Eds.), *Transfer on trial: Intelligence, cognition, and instruction.* Norwood, NJ: Ablex.

Bates, J. E., & Pettit, G. S. (2007). Temperament, parenting, and socialization. In J. E. Grusec & P. D. Hastings (Eds.), *Handbook of socialization: Theory and research* (pp. 153–177). New York: Guilford Press.

Batshaw, M. L., & Shapiro, B. K. (1997). Mental retardation. In M. L. Batshaw (Ed.), *Children with disabilities* (4th ed.). Baltimore: Brookes.

Batson, C. D. (1991). *The altruism question: Toward a social-psychological answer.* Hillsdale, NJ: Erlbaum.

Batson, C. D., & Thompson, E. R. (2001). Why don't moral people act morally? Motivational considerations. *Current Directions in Psychological Science, 10,* 54–57.

Battin-Pearson, S., Newcomb, M. D., Abbott, R. D., Hill, K. G., Catalano, R. F., & Hawkins, J. D. (2000). Predictors of early high school dropout: A test of five theories. *Journal of Educational Psychology, 92,* 568–582.

Battistich, V., Solomon, D., Kim, D., Watson, M., & Schaps, E. (1995). Schools as communities, poverty levels of student populations, and students' attitudes, motives, and performance: A multilevel analysis. *American Educational Research Journal, 32,* 627–658.

Battistich, V., Solomon, D., Watson, M., & Schaps, E. (1997). Caring school communities. *Educational Psychologist, 32,* 137–151.

Bauer, P. J. (2002). Long-term recall memory: Behavioral and neuro-developmental changes in the first 2 years of life. *Current Directions in Psychological Science, 11,* 137–141.

Bauer, P. J., DeBoer, T., & Lukowski, A. F. (2007). In the language of multiple memory systems: Defining and describing developments in long-term declarative memory. In L. M. Oakes & P. J. Bauer (Eds.), *Short- and long-term memory in infancy and early childhood: Taking the first steps toward remembering* (pp. 240–270). New York: Oxford University Press.

Baumeister, A. A. (1989). Mental retardation. In C. G. Lask & M. Hersen (Eds.), *Handbook of child psychiatric diagnosis.* New York: Wiley.

Baumeister, R. F., Campbell, J. D., Krueger, J. I., & Vohs, K. D. (2003). Does high self-esteem cause better performance, interpersonal success, happiness, or healthier lifestyles? *Psychological Science in the Public Interest, 4,* 1–44.

Baumeister, R. F., Smart, L., & Boden, J. M. (1996). Relation of threatened egotism to violence and aggression: The dark side of high self-esteem. *Psychological Review, 103,* 5–33.

Baumrind, D. (1971). Current patterns of parental authority. *Developmental Psychology Monograph, 4*(1, Pt. 2).

Baumrind, D. (1989). Rearing competent children. In W. Damon (Ed.), *Child development today and tomorrow.* San Francisco: Jossey-Bass.

Baumrind, D. (1991). Parenting styles and adolescent development. In R. M. Lerner, A. C. Petersen, & J. Brooks-Gunn (Eds.), *Encyclopedia of adolescence.* New York: Garland.

Baxter, G. P., Elder, A. D., & Glaser, R. (1996). Knowledge-based cognition and performance assessment in the science classroom. *Educational Psychologist, 31,* 133–140.

Bay-Hinitz, A. K., Peterson, R. F., & Quilitch, H. R. (1994). Cooperative games: A way to modify aggressive and cooperative behaviors in young children. *Journal of Applied Behavior Analysis, 27,* 435–446.

Bebko, J. M., Burke, L., Craven, J., & Sarlo, N. (1992). The importance of motor activity in sensorimotor development: A perspective from children with physical handicaps. *Human Development, 35,* 226–240.

Beck, S. R., Robinson, E. J., Carroll, D. J., & Apperly, I. A. (2006). Children's thinking about counterfactuals and future hypotheticals as possibilities. *Child Development, 77,* 413–426.

Becker, B. E., & Luthar, S. S. (2002). Social-emotional factors affecting achievement outcomes among disadvantaged students: Closing the achievement gap. *Educational Psychologist, 37,* 197–214.

Bédard, J., & Chi, M. T. H. (1992). Expertise. *Current Directions in Psychological Science, 1,* 135–139.

Behl-Chadha, G. (1996). Basic-level and superordinate-like categorical representations in early infancy. *Cognition, 60,* 105–141.

Behrmann, M. (2000). The mind's eye mapped onto the brain's matter. *Current Directions in Psychological Science, 9,* 50–54.

Beilock, S. L., & Carr, T. H. (2003). From novice to expert performance: Memory, attention, and the control of complex sensorimotor skills. In A. M. Williams, N. J. Hodges, M. A. Scott, & M. L. J. Court (Eds.), *Skill acquisition in sport: Research, theory, and practice.* New York: Routledge.

Beirne-Smith, M., Ittenbach, R. F., & Patton, J. R. (2002). *Mental retardation* (6th ed.). Upper Saddle River, NJ: Merrill/Prentice Hall.

Belfiore, P. J., & Hornyak, R. S. (1998). Operant theory and application to self-monitoring in adolescents. In D. H. Schunk & B. J. Zimmerman (Eds.), *Self-regulated learning: From teaching to self-reflective practice.* New York: Guilford Press.

Belfiore, P. J., Lee, D. L., Vargas, A. U., & Skinner, C. H. (1997). Effects of high-preference single-digit mathematics problem completion on multiple-digit mathematics problem performance. *Journal of Applied Behavior Analysis, 30,* 327–330.

Belfiore, P. J., Skinner, C. H., & Ferkis, M. A. (1995). Effects of response and trial repetition on sight-word training for students with learning disabilities. *Journal of Applied Behavior Analysis, 28,* 347–348.

Bell, P., & Linn, M. C. (2002). Beliefs about science: How does science instruction contribute? In B. K. Hofer & P. R. Pintrich (Eds.), *Personal epistemology: The psychology of beliefs about knowledge and knowing* (pp. 321–346). Mahwah, NJ: Erlbaum.

Bem, S. L. (1981). Gender schema theory: A cognitive account of sex typing. *Psychological Review, 88,* 354–364.

Bembenutty, H., & Karabenick, S. A. (2004). Inherent association between academic delay of gratification, future time perspective, and self-regulated learning. *Educational Psychology Review, 16,* 35–57.

Bender, G. (2001). Resisting dominance? The study of a marginalized masculinity and its construction within high school walls. In J. N. Burstyn, G. Bender, R. Casella, H. W. Gordon, D. P. Guerra, K. V. Luschen, et al., *Preventing violence in schools: A challenge to American democracy* (pp. 61–77). Mahwah, NJ: Erlbaum.

Benenson, J. F., Maiese, R., Dolenszky, E., Dolensky, N., Sinclair, N., & Simpson, A. (2002). Group size regulates self-assertive versus self-deprecating responses to interpersonal competition. *Child Development, 73,* 1818–1829.

Benes, F. M. (2007). Corticolimbic circuitry and psychopathology: Development of the corticolimbic system. In D. Coch, G. Dawson, & K. W. Fischer (Eds.), *Human behavior, learning, and the developing brain: Atypical development* (pp. 331–361). New York: Guilford Press.

Benware, C., & Deci, E. L. (1984). Quality of learning with an active versus passive motivational set. *American Educational Research Journal, 21,* 755–765.

Ben-Yehudah, G., & Fiez, J. A. (2007). Development of verbal working memory. In D. Coch, K. W. Fischer, & G. Dawson (Eds.), *Human behavior, learning, and the developing brain: Typical development* (pp. 301–328). New York: Guilford Press.

Ben-Zeev, T., Carrasquillo, C. M., Ching, A. M. L., Kliengklom, T. J., McDonald, K. L., Newhall, D. C., et al. (2005). "Math is hard!" (Barbie™, 1994): Responses of threat vs. challenge-mediated arousal to stereotypes alleging intellectual inferiority. In A. M. Gallagher & J. C. Kaufman (Eds.), *Gender differences in mathematics: An integrative psychological approach* (pp. 189–206). Cambridge, England: Cambridge University Press.

Berdan, L. E., & Keane, S. P. (2005, April). *The protective effects of peer-rated and self-perceived acceptance.* Poster presented at the biennial meeting of the Society for Research in Child Development, Atlanta.

Bereiter, C. (1995). A dispositional view of transfer. In A. McKeough, J. Lupart, & A. Marini (Eds.), *Teaching for transfer: Fostering generalization in learning.* Mahwah, NJ: Erlbaum.

Bereiter, C., & Scardamalia, M. (2006). Education for the Knowledge Age: Design-centered models of teaching and instruction. In P. A. Alexander & P. H. Winne (Eds.), *Handbook of educational psychology* (2nd ed., pp. 695–713). Mahwah, NJ: Erlbaum.

Bergamo, M., & Evans, M. A. (2005, April). *Rules of surviving peer relationships: Advice from middle school students.* Poster presented at the annual meeting of the American Educational Research Association, Montreal.

Berk, L. E. (1994). Why children talk to themselves. *Scientific American, 271*, 78–83.

Berk, L. E. (2003). *Child development* (6th ed.). Boston: Allyn & Bacon.

Berkowitz, L. (1989). Frustration-aggression hypothesis: Examination and reformulation. *Psychological Bulletin, 106*, 59–73.

Berlyne, D. E. (1960). *Conflict, arousal, and curiosity.* New York: McGraw-Hill.

Berndt, T. J. (1992). Friendship and friends' influence in adolescence. *Current Directions in Psychological Science, 1*, 156–159.

Berndt, T. J. (2002). Friendship quality and social development. *Current Directions in Psychological Science, 11*, 7–10.

Berndt, T. J., & Keefe, K. (1996). Friends' influence on school adjustment: A motivational analysis. In J. Juvonen & K. R. Wentzel (Eds.), *Social motivation: Understanding children's school adjustment* (pp. 248–278). Cambridge, England: Cambridge University Press.

Berndt, T. J., Laychak, A. E., & Park, K. (1990). Friends' influence on adolescents' academic achievement motivation: An experimental study. *Journal of Educational Psychology, 82*, 664–670.

Berzonsky, M. D. (1988). Self-theorists, identity status, and social cognition. In D. K. Lapsley & F. C. Power (Eds.), *Self, ego, and identity: Integrative approaches* (pp. 243–261). New York: Springer-Verlag.

Beyer, B. K. (1985). Critical thinking: What is it? *Social Education, 49*, 270–276.

Bialystok, E. (1994). Representation and ways of knowing: Three issues in second language acquisition. In N. C. Ellis (Ed.), *Implicit and explicit learning of languages.* London: Academic Press.

Bielaczyc, K., & Collins, A. (2006). Fostering knowledge-creating communities. In A. M. O'Donnell, C. E. Hmelo-Silver, & G. Erkens (Eds.), *Collaborative learning, reasoning, and technology* (pp. 37–60). Mahwah, NJ: Erlbaum.

Biemiller, A., Shany, M., Inglis, A., & Meichenbaum, D. (1998). Factors influencing children's acquisition and demonstration of self-regulation on academic tasks. In D. H. Schunk & B. J. Zimmerman (Eds.), *Self-regulated learning: From teaching to self-reflective practice* (pp. 203–224). New York: Guilford Press.

Bierman, K. L., Miller, C. L., & Stabb, S. D. (1987). Improving the social behavior and peer acceptance of rejected boys: Effect of social skill training with instructions and prohibitions. *Journal of Consulting and Clinical Psychology, 55*, 194–200.

Bigler, R. S., Brown, C. S., & Markell, M. (2001). When groups are not created equal: Effects of group status on the formation of intergroup attitudes in children. *Child Development, 72*, 1151–1162.

Birch, S. A. J., & Bloom, P. (2002). Preschoolers are sensitive to the speaker's knowledge when learning proper names. *Child Development, 73*, 434–444.

Bivens, J. A., & Berk, L. E. (1990). A longitudinal study of the development of elementary school children's private speech. *Merrill-Palmer Quarterly, 36*, 443–463.

Bjorklund, D. F. (1987). How age changes in knowledge base contribute to the development of children's memory: An interpretive review. *Developmental Review, 7*, 93–130.

Bjorklund, D. F., & Coyle, T. R. (1995). Utilization deficiencies in the development of memory strategies. In F. E. Weinert & W. Schneider (Eds.), *Research on memory development: State of the art and future directions.* Mahwah, NJ: Erlbaum.

Bjorklund, D. F., & Jacobs, J. W. (1985). Associative and categorical processes in children's memory: The role of automaticity in the development of organization in free recall. *Journal of Experimental Child Psychology, 39*, 599–617.

Bjorklund, D. F., Schneider, W., Cassel, W. S., & Ashley, E. (1994). Training and extension of a memory strategy: Evidence for utilization deficiencies in high- and low-IQ children. *Child Development, 65*, 951–965.

Black-Gutman, D., & Hickson, F. (1996). The relationship between racial attitudes and social-cognitive development in children: An Australian study. *Developmental Psychology, 32*, 448–456.

Blackwell, L. S., Trzesniewski, K. H., & Dweck, C. S. (2007). Implicit theories of intelligence predict achievement across an adolescent transition: A longitudinal study and an intervention. *Child Development, 78*, 246–263.

Blair, C. (2002). School readiness: Integrating cognition and emotion in a neurobiological conceptualization of children's functioning at school entry. *American Psychologist, 57*, 111–127.

Blake, S. B., & Clark, R. E. (1990, April). *The effects of metacognitive selection on far transfer in analogical problem-solving tasks.* Paper presented at the annual meeting of the American Educational Research Association, Boston.

Blasi, A. (1980). Bridging moral cognition and moral action: A critical review of the literature. *Psychological Bulletin, 88*, 593–637.

Blasi, A. (1995). Moral understanding and the moral personality: The process of moral integration. In W. M. Kurtines & J. L. Gewirtz (Eds.), *Moral development: An introduction.* Boston: Allyn & Bacon.

Block, J. H. (1983). Differential premises arising from differential socialization of the sexes: Some conjectures. *Child Development, 54*, 1335–1354.

Block, J. H., & Burns, R. B. (1976). Mastery learning. In L. Shulman (Ed.), *Review of research in education* (Vol. 4). Itasca, IL: Peacock.

Bloom, B. S. (1981). *All our children learning.* New York: McGraw-Hill.

Bloom, B. S., Englehart, M. D., Furst, E. J., Hill, W. H., & Krathwohl, D. R. (1956). *Taxonomy of educational objectives. The classification of educational goals: Handbook I. Cognitive domain.* New York: David McKay.

Bloom, L., & Tinker, E. (2001). The intentionality model and language acquisition. *Monographs of the Society for Research in Child Development, 66*(4, Serial No. 267).

Blugental, D. B., Lyon, J. E., Lin, E. K., McGrath, E. P., & Bimbela, A. (1999). Children "tune out" to the ambiguous communication style of powerless adults. *Child Development, 70*, 214–230.

Blumenfeld, P. C. (1992). The task and the teacher: Enhancing student thoughtfulness in science. In J. Brophy (Ed.), *Advances in research on teaching: Vol. 3. Planning and managing learning tasks and activities.* Greenwich, CT: JAI Press.

Blumenfeld, P. C., Kempler, T. M., & Krajcik, J. S. (2006). Motivation and cognitive engagement in learning environments. In R. K. Sawyer (Ed.), *The Cambridge handbook of the learning sciences* (pp. 475–488). Cambridge, England: Cambridge University Press.

Blumenfeld, P. C., Marx, R. W., Soloway, E., & Krajcik, J. (1996). Learning with peers: From small group cooperation to collaborative communities. *Educational Researcher, 25*(8), 37–40.

Boekaerts, M., de Koning, E., & Vedder, P. (2006). Goal-directed behavior and contextual factors in the classroom: An innovative approach to the study of multiple goals. *Educational Psychologist, 41*, 33–51.

Boggiano, A. K., & Pittman, T. S. (Eds.). (1992). *Achievement and motivation: A social-developmental perspective.* Cambridge, England: Cambridge University Press.

Boldizar, J. P., Perry, D. G., & Perry, L. C. (1989). Outcome values and aggression. *Child Development, 60*, 571–579.

Bolger, K. E., & Patterson, C. J. (2001). Developmental pathways from child maltreatment to peer rejection. *Child Development, 72*, 549–568.

Bong, M. (2001). Between- and within-domain relations of academic motivation among middle and high school students: Self-efficacy, task-value, and achievement goals. *Journal of Educational Psychology, 93*, 23–34.

Bong, M., & Skaalvik, E. M. (2003). Academic self-concept and self-efficacy: How different are they really? *Educational Psychology Review, 15*, 1–40.

Boom, J., Brugman, D., & van der Heijden, P. G. M. (2001). Hierarchical structure of moral stages assessed by a sorting task. *Child Development, 72*, 535–548.

Borko, H., & Putnam, R. T. (1996). Learning to teach. In D. C. Berliner & R. C. Calfee (Eds.), *Handbook of educational psychology.* New York: Macmillan.

Born, D. G., & Davis, M. L. (1974). Amount and distribution of study in a personalized instruction course and in a lecture course. *Journal of Applied Behavior Analysis, 7*, 365–375.

Bornholt, L. J., Goodnow, J. J., & Cooney, G. H. (1994). Influences of gender stereotypes on adolescents' perceptions of their own achievement. *American Educational Research Journal, 31*, 675–692.

Bornstein, M. H., Hahn, C.-S., Bell, C., Haynes, O. M., Slater, A., Golding, J., et al. (2006). Stability in cognition across early childhood: A developmental cascade. *Psychological Science, 17*, 151–158.

Bortfeld, H., & Whitehurst, G. J. (2001). Sensitive periods in first language acquisition. In D. B. Bailey, Jr., J. T. Bruer, F. J. Symons, & J. W. Lichtman (Eds.), *Critical thinking about critical periods* (pp. 173–192). Baltimore: Brookes.

Bosacki, S. L. (2000). Theory of mind and self-concept in preadolescents: Links with gender and language. *Journal of Educational Psychology, 92*, 709–717.

Boschee, F., & Baron, M. A. (1993). *Outcome-based education: Developing programs through strategic planning.* Lancaster, PA: Technomic.

Bouchard, T. J., Jr. (1997). IQ similarity in twins reared apart: Findings and responses to critics. In R. J. Sternberg & E. L. Grigorenko (Eds.), *Intelligence, heredity, and environment* (pp. 126–160). Cambridge, England: Cambridge University Press.

Bower, G. H. (1994). Some relations between emotions and memory. In P. Ekman & R. J. Davidson (Eds.), *The nature of emotion: Fundamental questions.* New York: Oxford University Press.

Bower, G. H., Black, J. B., & Turner, T. J. (1979). Scripts in memory for text. *Cognitive Psychology, 11*, 177–220.

Bower, G. H., & Clark, M. C. (1969). Narrative stories as mediators for serial learning. *Psychonomic Science, 14*, 181–182.

Bower, G. H., Clark, M. C., Lesgold, A. M., & Winzenz, D. (1969). Hierarchical retrieval schemes in recall of categorized word lists. *Journal of Verbal Learning and Verbal Behavior, 8*, 323–343.

Bower, G. H., & Forgas, J. P. (2001). Mood and social memory. In J. P. Forgas (Ed.), *Handbook of affect and social cognition* (pp. 95–120). Mahwah, NJ: Erlbaum.

Bower, G. H., Karlin, M. B., & Dueck, A. (1975). Comprehension and memory for pictures. *Memory and Cognition, 3*, 216–220.

Bowman, L. G., Piazza, C. C., Fisher, W. W., Hagopian, L. P., & Kogan, J. S. (1997). Assessment of preference for varied versus constant reinforcers. *Journal of Applied Behavior Analysis, 30*, 451–458.

Braaksma, M. A. H., Rijlaarsdam, G., & van den Bergh, H. (2002). Observational learning and the effects of model-observer similarity. *Journal of Educational Psychology, 94*, 405–415.

Bracken, B. A., McCallum, R. S., & Shaughnessy, M. F. (1999). An interview with Bruce A. Bracken and R. Steve McCallum, authors of the Universal Nonverbal Intelligence Test (UNIT). *North American Journal of Psychology, 1*, 277–288.

Bracken, B. A., & Walker, K. C. (1997). The utility of intelligence tests for preschool children. In D. P. Flanagan, J. L. Genshaft, & P. L. Harrison (Eds.), *Contemporary intellectual assessment: Theories, tests, and issues* (pp. 484–502). New York: Guilford Press.

Brackett, M. A., Lopes, P. N., Ivcevic, Z., Mayer, J. D., & Salovey, P. (2004). Integrating emotion and cognition: The role of emotional intelligence. In D. Y. Dai & R. J. Sternberg (Eds.), *Motivation, emotion, and cognition: Integrative perspectives on intellectual functioning and development* (pp. 175–194). Mahwah, NJ: Erlbaum.

Brainerd, C. J. (2003). Jean Piaget, learning research, and American education. In B. J. Zimmerman & D. H. Schunk (Eds.), *Educational psychology: A century of contributions* (pp. 251–287). Mahwah, NJ: Erlbaum.

Bransford, J., Derry, S., Berliner, D., & Hammerness, K. (with Beckett, K. L.). (2005). Theories of learning and their roles in teaching. In L. Darling-Hammond & J. Bransford (Eds.), *Preparing teachers for a changing world: What teachers should learn and be able to do* (pp. 40–87). San Francisco: Jossey-Bass/Wiley.

Bransford, J. D., & Johnson, M. K. (1972). Contextual prerequisites for understanding: Some investigations of comprehension and recall. *Journal of Verbal Learning and Verbal Behavior, 11*, 717–726.

Bransford, J., Stevens, R., Schwartz, D., Meltzoff, A., Pea, R., Reschelle, J., et al. (2006). Learning theories and education: Toward a decade of synergy. In P. A. Alexander & P. H. Winne (Eds.), *Handbook of educational psychology* (2nd ed., pp. 209–244). Mahwah, NJ: Erlbaum.

Braun, L. J. (1998). *The cat who saw stars.* New York: G. P. Putnam's Sons.

Brendgen, M., Dionne, G., Girard, A., Boivin, M., Vitaro, F., & Pérusse, D. (2005). Examining genetic and environmental effects on social aggression: A study of 6-year-old twins. *Child Development, 76*, 930–946.

Brendgen, M., Wanner, G., Vitaro, F., Bukowski, W. M., & Tremblay, R. E. (2007). Verbal abuse by the teacher during childhood and academic, behavioral, and emotional adjustment in young adulthood. *Journal of Educational Psychology, 99*, 26–38.

Brenner, M. E., Mayer, R. E., Moseley, B., Brar, T., Durán, R., Reed, B. S., et al. (1997). Learning by understanding: The role of multiple representations in learning algebra. *American Educational Research Journal, 34*, 663–689.

Bressler, S. L. (2002). Understanding cognition through large-scale cortical networks. *Current Directions in Psychological Science, 11*, 58–61.

Brewer, M. B., & Yuki, M. (2007). Culture and social identity. In S. Kitayama & D. Cohen (Eds.), *Handbook of cultural psychology* (pp. 307–322). New York: Guilford Press.

Brigham, F. J., & Scruggs, T. E. (1995). Elaborative maps for enhanced learning of historical information: Uniting spatial, verbal, and imaginal information. *Journal of Special Education, 28*, 440.

Broden, M., Hall, R. V., & Mitts, B. (1971). The effect of self-recording on the classroom behavior of two eighth-grade students. *Journal of Applied Behavior Analysis, 4*, 191–199.

Brody, G. H., Chen, Y.-F., Murry, V. M., Ge, X., Simons, R. L., Gibbons, F. X., et al. (2006). Perceived discrimination and the adjustment of African American youths: A five-year longitudinal analysis with contextual moderation effects. *Child Development, 77*, 1170–1189.

Brody, G. H., & Shaffer, D. R. (1982). Contributions of parents and peers to children's moral socialization. *Developmental Review, 2*, 31–75.

Brody, N. (1992). *Intelligence* (2nd ed.). San Diego, CA: Academic Press.

Brody, N. (1997). Intelligence, schooling, and society. *American Psychologist, 52*, 1046–1050.

Bronfenbrenner, U. (1989). Ecological systems theory. In R. Vasta (Ed.), *Annals of child development* (Vol. 6, pp. 187–251). Greenwich, CT: JAI Press.

Bronfenbrenner, U. (2005). *Making human beings human: Bioecological perspectives on human development.* Thousand Oaks, CA: Sage.

Bronfenbrenner, U., & Morris, P. A. (1998). The ecology of developmental processes. In W. Damon (Series Ed.) & R. M. Lerner (Vol. Ed.), *Handbook of child psychology: Vol. 1. Theoretical models of human development* (5th ed., pp. 993–1028). New York: Wiley.

Bronson, M. B. (2000). *Self-regulation in early childhood: Nature and nurture.* New York: Guilford Press.

Brooke, R. R., & Ruthren, A. J. (1984). The effects of contingency contracting on student performance in a PSI class. *Teaching of Psychology, 11*, 87–89.

Brookhart, S. M. (2004). *Grading.* Upper Saddle River, NJ: Merrill/Prentice Hall.

Brooks, L. W., & Dansereau, D. F. (1987). Transfer of information: An instructional perspective. In S. M. Cormier & J. D. Hagman (Eds.), *Transfer of learning: Contemporary research and applications.* San Diego, CA: Academic Press.

Brooks-Gunn, J. (2003). Do you believe in magic?: What we can expect from early childhood intervention programs. *Social Policy Report of the Society for Research in Child Development, 17*(1), 3–14.

Brooks-Gunn, J., Klebanov, P. K., & Duncan, G. J. (1996). Ethnic differences in children's intelligence test scores: Role of economic deprivation, home environment, and maternal characteristics. *Child Development, 67*, 396–408.

Brooks-Gunn, J., & Paikoff, R. L. (1993). "Sex is a gamble, kissing is a game": Adolescent sexuality and health promotion. In S. G. Millstein, A. C. Petersen, & E. O. Nightingale (Eds.), *Promoting the health of adolescents: New directions for the twenty-first century* (pp. 180–208). New York: Oxford University Press.

Brophy, J. E. (1986). *On motivating students* (Occasional Paper No. 101). East Lansing: Michigan State University, Institute for Research on Teaching.

Brophy, J. E. (1987). Synthesis of research on strategies for motivating students to learn. *Educational Leadership, 45*(2), 40–48.

Brophy, J. E. (1988). Research linking teacher behavior to student achievement: Potential implications for instruction of Chapter 1 students. *Educational Psychologist, 23*, 235–286.

Brophy, J. E. (1992). Probing the subtleties of subject-matter teaching. *Educational Leadership, 49*(7), 4–8.

Brophy, J. E. (2004). *Motivating students to learn* (2nd ed.). Mahwah, NJ: Erlbaum.

Brophy, J. E. (2006). Observational research on generic aspects of classroom teaching. In P. A. Alexander & P. H. Winne (Eds.), *Handbook of educational psychology* (2nd ed., pp. 755–780). Mahwah, NJ: Erlbaum.

Brophy, J. E., & Alleman, J. (1991). Activities as instructional tools: A framework for analysis and evaluation. *Educational Researcher, 20*(4), 9–23.

Brophy, J. E., & Alleman, J. (1992). Planning and managing learning activities: Basic principles. In J. Brophy (Ed.), *Advances in research on teaching: Vol. 3. Planning and managing learning tasks and activities.* Greenwich, CT: JAI Press.

Brophy, J. E., & Alleman, J. (1996). *Powerful social studies for elementary students.* Fort Worth, TX: Harcourt, Brace.

Brophy, J. E., & VanSledright, B. (1997). *Teaching and learning history in elementary schools.* New York: Teachers College Press.

Brown, A. L., & Campione, J. C. (1994). Guided discovery in a community of learners. In K. McGilly (Ed.), *Classroom lessons: Integrating cognitive theory and classroom practice.* Cambridge, MA: MIT Press.

Brown, A. L., & Campione, J. C. (1996). Psychological theory and the design of innovative learning environments: On procedures, principles, and systems. In L. Schauble & R. Glaser (Eds.), *Innovations in learning: New environments for education.* Mahwah, NJ: Erlbaum.

Brown, A. L., Campione, J., & Day, J. (1981). Learning to learn: On training students to learn from texts. *Educational Researcher, 10*(2), 14–21.

Brown, A. L., & Palincsar, A. S. (1987). Reciprocal teaching of comprehension strategies: A natural history of one program for enhancing learning. In J. Borkowski & J. D. Day (Eds.), *Cognition in special education: Comparative approaches to retardation, learning disabilities, and giftedness.* Norwood, NJ: Ablex.

Brown, A. L., Smiley, S. S., Day, J. D., Townsend, M. A. R., & Lawton, S. C. (1977). Intrusion of a thematic idea in children's comprehension and retention of stories. *Child Development, 48*, 1454–1466.

Brown, A. S., Schilling, H. E. H., & Hockensmith, M. L. (1999). The negative suggestion effect: Pondering incorrect alternatives may be hazardous to your knowledge. *Journal of Educational Psychology, 91*, 756–764.

Brown, B. B. (1990). Peer groups. In S. Feldman & G. Elliott (Eds.), *At the threshold: The developing adolescent* (pp. 171–196). Cambridge, MA: Harvard University Press.

Brown, B. B. (1993). School culture, social politics, and the academic motivation of U.S. students. In T. M. Tomlinson (Ed.), *Motivating students to learn: Overcoming barriers to high achievement.* Berkeley, CA: McCutchan.

Brown, B. B. (1999). "You're going out with *who*?" Peer group influences on adolescent romantic relationships. In W. Furman, B. B. Brown, & C. Feiring (Eds.), *The development of romantic relationships in adolescence* (pp. 291–329). Cambridge, England: Cambridge University Press.

Brown, B. B., Eicher, S. A., & Petrie, S. (1986). The importance of peer group ("crowd") affiliation in adolescence. *Journal of Adolescence, 9*, 73–96.

Brown, B. B., Feiring, C., & Furman, W. (1999). Missing the love boat: Why researchers have shied away from adolescent romance. In W. Furman, B. B. Brown, & C. Feiring (Eds.), *The development of romantic relationships in adolescence* (pp. 1–16). Cambridge, England: Cambridge University Press.

Brown, J. S., Collins, A., & Duguid, P. (1989). Situated cognition and the culture of learning. *Educational Researcher, 18*(1), 32–42.

Brown, R. D., & Bjorklund, D. F. (1998). The biologizing of cognition, development, and education: Approach with cautious enthusiasm. *Educational Psychology Review, 10*, 355–373.

Brown, W. H., Fox, J. J., & Brady, M. P. (1987). Effects of spatial density on 3- and 4-year-old children's socially directed behavior during freeplay: An investigation of a setting factor. *Education and Treatment of Children, 10*, 247–258.

Bruer, J. T. (1997). Education and the brain: A bridge too far. *Educational Researcher, 26*(8), 4–16.

Bruer, J. T. (1999). *The myth of the first three years: A new understanding of early brain development and lifelong learning.* New York: Free Press.

Bruer, J. T., & Greenough, W. T. (2001). The subtle science of how experience affects the brain. In D. B. Bailey, Jr., J. T. Bruer, F. J. Symons, & J. W. Lichtman (Eds.), *Critical thinking about critical periods* (pp. 209–232). Baltimore: Brookes.

Bruner, J. S. (1966). *Toward a theory of instruction.* Cambridge, MA: Harvard University Press.

Bryan, J. H. (1975). Children's cooperation and helping behaviors. In E. M. Hetherington (Ed.), *Review of child development research* (Vol. 5). Chicago: University of Chicago Press.

Buehl, M. M., & Alexander, P. A. (2001). Beliefs about academic knowledge. *Educational Psychology Review, 13*, 385–418.

Buehl, M. M., & Alexander, P. A. (2006). Examining the dual nature of epistemological beliefs. *International Journal of Educational Research, 45*, 28–42.

Buhrmester, D. (1992). The developmental courses of sibling and peer relationships. In F. Boer and J. Dunn (Eds.), *Children's sibling relationships: Developmental and clinical issues.* Mahwah, NJ: Erlbaum.

Buhs, E. S., Ladd, G. W., & Herald, S. L. (2006). Peer exclusion and victimization: Processes that mediate the relation between peer group rejection and children's classroom engagement and achievement? *Journal of Educational Psychology, 98*, 1–13.

Bukowski, W. M., Brendgan, M., & Vitaro, F. (2007). Peers and socialization: Effects on externalizing and internalizing problems. In J. E. Grusec & P. D. Hastings (Eds.), *Handbook of socialization: Theory and research* (pp. 355–381). New York: Guilford Press.

Bulgren, J. A., Deshler, D. D., Schumaker, J. B., & Lenz, B. K. (2000). The use and effectiveness of analogical instruction in diverse secondary content classrooms. *Journal of Educational Psychology, 92*, 426–441.

Bulgren, J. A., Schumaker, J. B., & Deshler, D. D. (1994). The effects of a recall enhancement routine on the test performance of secondary students with and without learning disabilities. *Learning Disabilities Research and Practice, 9*, 2–11.

Burger, H. G. (1973). Cultural pluralism and the schools. In C. S. Brembeck & W. H. Hill (Eds.), *Cultural challenges to education: The influence of cultural factors in school learning.* Lexington, MA: Heath.

Burger, S., & Burger, D. (1994). Determining the validity of performance-based assessment. *Educational Measurement: Issues and Practice, 13*(1), 9–15.

Burhans, K. K., & Dweck, C. S. (1995). Helplessness in early childhood: The role of contingent worth. *Child Development, 66*, 1719–1738.

Burstyn, J. N., & Stevens, R. (2001). Involving the whole school in violence prevention. In J. N. Burstyn, G. Bender, R. Casella, H. W. Gordon, D. P. Guerra, K. V. Luschen et al., *Preventing violence in schools: A challenge to American democracy* (pp. 139–158). Mahwah, NJ: Erlbaum.

Butler, D. L., & Winne, P. H. (1995). Feedback and self-regulated learning: A theoretical synthesis. *Review of Educational Research, 65,* 245–281.

Butler, R. (1989). Mastery versus ability appraisal: A developmental study of children's observations of peers' work. *Child Development, 60,* 1350–1361.

Butler, R. (1990). The effects of mastery and competitive conditions on self-assessment at different ages. *Child Development, 61,* 201–210.

Butler, R. (1994). Teacher communication and student interpretations: Effects of teacher responses to failing students on attributional inferences in two age groups. *British Journal of Educational Psychology, 64,* 277–294.

Butler, R. (1998a). Age trends in the use of social and temporal comparison for self-evaluation: Examination of a novel developmental hypothesis. *Child Development, 69,* 1054–1073.

Butler, R. (1998b). Determinants of help seeking: Relations between perceived reasons for classroom help-avoidance and help-seeking behaviors in an experimental context. *Journal of Educational Psychology, 90,* 630–644.

Butterfield, E. C., & Ferretti, R. P. (1987). Toward a theoretical integration of cognitive hypotheses about intellectual differences among children. In J. G. Borkowski & J. D. Day (Eds.), *Cognition in special children: Approaches to retardation, learning disabilities, and giftedness.* Norwood, NJ: Ablex.

Byrne, B. M. (2002). Validating the measurement and structure of self-concept: Snapshots of past, present, and future research. *American Psychologist, 57,* 897–909.

Byrnes, J. P. (1988). Formal operations: A systematic reformulation. *Developmental Review, 8,* 66–87.

Byrnes, J. P. (2001). *Minds, brains, and learning: Understanding the psychological and educational relevance of neuroscientific research.* New York: Guilford Press.

Byrnes, J. P. (2003). Factors predictive of mathematics achievement in White, Black, and Hispanic 12th graders. *Journal of Educational Psychology, 95,* 316–326.

Byrnes, J. P. (2007). Some ways in which neuroscientific research can be relevant to education. In D. Coch, K. W. Fischer, & G. Dawson (Eds.), *Human behavior, learning, and the developing brain: Typical development* (pp. 30–49). New York: Guilford Press.

Byrnes, J. P., & Fox, N. A. (1998). The educational relevance of research in cognitive neuroscience. *Educational Psychology Review, 10,* 297–342.

Cacioppo, J. T., Petty, R. E., Feinstein, J. A., & Jarvis, W. B. G. (1996). Dispositional differences in cognitive motivation: The life and times of individuals varying in need for cognition. *Psychological Bulletin, 119,* 197–253.

Calderhead, J. (1996). Teachers: Beliefs and knowledge. In D. C. Berliner & R. C. Calfee (Eds.), *Handbook of educational psychology.* New York: Macmillan.

Caldwell, C. H., Zimmerman, M. A., Bernat, D. H., Sellers, R. M., & Notaro, P. C. (2002). Racial identity, maternal support, and psychological distress among African American adolescents. *Child Development, 73,* 1322–1336.

Caldwell, M. S., Rudolph, K. D., Troop-Gordon, W., & Kim, D. (2004). Reciprocal influences among relational self-views, social disengagement, and peer stress during early adolescence. *Child Development, 75,* 1140–1154.

Calfee, R. (1981). Cognitive psychology and educational practice. In D. C. Berliner (Ed.), *Review of research in education* (Vol. 9). Washington, DC: American Educational Research Association.

Cameron, J. (2001). Negative effects of reward on intrinsic motivation—a limited phenomenon: Comment on Deci, Koestner, and Ryan (2001). *Review of Educational Research, 71,* 29–42.

Campbell, A. (1984). *The girls in the gang: A report from New York City.* New York: Blackwell.

Campbell, C. G., Parker, J. G., & Kollat, S. H. (2007, March). *The influence of contingent self-esteem and appearance.* Paper presented at the biennial meeting of the Society for Research in Child Development, Boston.

Campione, J. C., Shapiro, A. M., & Brown, A. L. (1995). Forms of transfer in a community of learners: Flexible learning and understanding. In A. McKeough, J. Lupart, & A. Marini (Eds.), *Teaching for transfer: Fostering generalization in learning.* Mahwah, NJ: Erlbaum.

Camras, L. A., Chen, Y., Bakeman, R., Norris, K., & Cain, T. R. (2006). Culture, ethnicity, and children's facial expressions: A study of European American, Mainland Chinese, Chinese American, and adopted Chinese girls. *Emotion, 6,* 103–114.

Candler-Lotven, A., Tallent-Runnels, M. K., Olivárez, A., & Hildreth, B. (1994, April). *A comparison of learning and study strategies of gifted, average-ability, and learning-disabled ninth-grade students.* Paper presented at the annual meeting of the American Educational Research Association, New Orleans, LA.

Caprara, G. V., Barbaranelli, C., Pastorelli, C., Bandura, A., & Zimbardo, P. G. (2000). Prosocial foundations of children's academic achievement. *Psychological Science, 11,* 302–306.

Capron, C., & Duyme, M. (1989). Assessment of effects of socio-economic status on IQ in a full cross-fostering study. *Nature, 340,* 552–554.

Card, N. A., & Ramos, J. F. (2005, April). *Friends' similarity on academic characteristics: A meta-analytic review.* Paper presented at the annual meeting of the American Educational Research Association, Montreal.

Carey, L. M. (1994). *Measuring and evaluating school learning* (2nd ed.). Needham Heights, MA: Allyn & Bacon.

Carey, S. (1978). The child as word learner. In M. Halle, J. Bresnan, & G. A. Miller (Eds.), *Linguistic theory and psychological reality.* Cambridge, MA: MIT Press.

Carey, S. (1985). *Conceptual change in childhood.* Cambridge, MA: MIT Press.

Carey, S. (1986). Cognitive science and science education. *American Psychologist, 41,* 1123–1130.

Carlson, R., Chandler, P., & Sweller, J. (2003). Learning and understanding science instructional material. *Journal of Educational Psychology, 95,* 629–640.

Carney, R. N., & Levin, J. R. (2002). Pictorial illustrations *still* improve students' learning from text. *Educational Psychology Review, 14,* 5–26.

Carnoy, M., Elmore, R., & Siskin, L. S. (Eds.). (2003). *The new accountability: High schools and high-stakes testing.* New York: RoutledgeFalmer.

Carr, A. A. (1997, March). *The participation "race": Kentucky's site based decision teams.* Paper presented at the annual meeting of the American Educational Research Association, Chicago.

Carr, M., & Biddlecomb, B. (1998). Metacognition in mathematics from a constructivist perspective. In D. J. Hacker, J. Dunlosky, & A. C. Graesser (Eds.), *Metacognition in educational theory and practice* (pp. 69–91). Mahwah, NJ: Erlbaum.

Carrasco, R. L. (1981). Expanded awareness of student performance: A case study in applied ethnographic monitoring in a bilingual classroom. In H. T. Trueba, G. P. Guthrie, & K. H. Au (Eds.), *Culture and the bilingual classroom: Studies in classroom ethnography.* Rowley, MA: Newbury House.

Carroll, J. B. (2003). The higher stratum structure of cognitive abilities: Current evidence supports g and about ten broad factors. In H. Nyborg (Ed.), *The scientific study of general intelligence.* New York: Pergamon.

Carter, K., & Doyle, W. (2006). Classroom management in early childhood and elementary classrooms. In C. M. Evertson & C. S. Weinstein (Eds.), *Handbook of classroom management: Research, practice, and contemporary issues* (pp. 373–406). Mahwah, NJ: Erlbaum.

Carter, K. R. (1991). Evaluation of gifted programs. In N. Buchanan & J. Feldhusen (Eds.), *Conducting research and evaluation in gifted education: A handbook of methods and applications.* New York: Teachers College Press.

Carter, K. R., & Ormrod, J. E. (1982). Acquisition of formal operations by intellectually gifted children. *Gifted Child Quarterly, 26,* 110–115.

Carver, C. S., & Scheier, M. F. (1990). Origins and functions of positive and negative affect: A control-process view. *Psychological Review, 97,* 19–35.

Carver, S. M. (2006). Assessing for deep understanding. In R. K. Sawyer (Ed.), *The Cambridge handbook of the learning sciences* (pp. 205–221). Cambridge, England: Cambridge University Press.

Casanova, U. (1987). Ethnic and cultural differences. In V. Richardson-Koehler (Ed.), *Educator's handbook: A research perspective.* White Plains, NY: Longman.

Case, R., & Okamoto, Y., in collaboration with Griffin, S., McKeough, A., Bleiker, C., Henderson, B., & Stephenson, K. M. (1996). The role of central conceptual structures in the development of children's thought. *Monographs of the Society for Research in Child Development, 61*(1, Serial No. 246).

Casella, R. (2001a). The cultural foundations of peer mediation: Beyond a behaviorist model of urban school conflict. In J. N. Burstyn, G. Bender, R. Casella, H. W. Gordon, D. P. Guerra, K. V. Luschen, et al., *Preventing violence in schools: A challenge to American democracy* (pp. 159–179). Mahwah, NJ: Erlbaum.

Casella, R. (2001b). What is violent about "school violence"? The nature of violence in a city high school. In J. N. Burstyn, G. Bender, R. Casella, H. W. Gordon, D. P. Guerra, K. V. Luschen, et al., *Preventing violence in schools: A challenge to American democracy* (pp. 15–46). Mahwah, NJ: Erlbaum.

Caspi, A., & Silva, P. A. (1995). Temperamental qualities at age three predict personality traits in young adulthood: Longitudinal evidence from a birth cohort. *Child Development, 66,* 486–498.

Caspi, A., Taylor, A., Moffitt, T. E., & Plomin, R. (2000). Neighborhood deprivation affects children's mental health: Environmental risks identified in a genetic design. *Psychological Science, 11,* 338–342.

Cassady, J. C. (2004). The influence of cognitive test anxiety across the learning-testing cycle. *Learning and Instruction, 14,* 569–592.

Cassady, J. C., & Johnson, R. E. (2002). Cognitive test anxiety and academic performance. *Contemporary Educational Psychology, 27,* 270–295.

Cauce, A. M., Mason, C., Gonzales, N., Hiraga, Y., & Liu, G. (1994). Social support during adolescence: Methodological and theoretical considerations. In F. Nestemann & K. Hurrelmann (Eds.), *Social networks and social support in childhood and adolescence.* Berlin, Germany: Aldine de Gruyter.

Ceci, S. J. (2003). Cast in six ponds and you'll reel in something: Looking back on 25 years of research. *American Psychologist, 58,* 855–864.

Celio, C. I., Durlak, J. A., Pachan, M. K., & Berger, S. R. (2007, March). *Helping others and helping oneself: A meta-analysis of service-learning programs.* Paper presented at the biennial meeting of the Society for Research in Child Development, Boston.

Certo, J., Cauley, K. M., & Chafin, C. (2002, April). *Students' perspectives on their high school experience.* Paper presented at the annual meeting of the American Educational Research Association, New Orleans, LA.

Chabrán, M. (2003). Listening to talk from and about students on accountability. In M. Carnoy, R. Elmore, & L. S. Siskin (Eds.), *The new accountability: High schools and high-stakes testing* (pp. 129–145). New York: RoutledgeFalmer.

Chall, J. S. (1996). *Stages of reading development* (2nd ed.). Fort Worth, TX: Harcourt Brace.

Chalmers, D. J. (1996). *The conscious mind: In search of a fundamental theory.* New York: Oxford University Press.

Chambliss, M. J. (1994). Why do readers fail to change their beliefs after reading persuasive text? In R. Garner & P. A. Alexander (Eds.), *Beliefs about text and instruction with text.* Mahwah, NJ: Erlbaum.

Chan, C., Burtis, J., & Bereiter, C. (1997). Knowledge building as a mediator of conflict in conceptual change. *Cognition and Instruction, 15,* 1–40.

Chandler, M. (1987). The Othello effect: Essay on the emergence and eclipse of skeptical doubt. *Human Development, 30,* 137–159.

Chandler, M., & Boyes, M. (1982). Social-cognitive development. In B. Wolman (Ed.), *Handbook of developmental psychology.* Upper Saddle River, NJ: Prentice Hall.

Chandler, M., Hallett, D., & Sokol, B. W. (2002). Competing claims about competing knowledge claims. In B. K. Hofer & P. R. Pintrich (Eds.), *Personal epistemology: The psychology of beliefs about knowledge and knowing* (pp. 145–168). Mahwah, NJ: Erlbaum.

Chang, L. (2003). Variable effects of children's aggression, social withdrawal, and prosocial leadership as functions of teacher beliefs and behaviors. *Child Development, 74*, 535–548.

Chao, R. K. (1994). Beyond parental control and authoritarian parenting style: Understanding Chinese parenting through the cultural notion of training. *Child Development, 65*, 1111–1119.

Chao, R. K. (2000). Cultural explanations for the role of parenting in the school success of Asian-American children. In R. Taylor & M. Wang (Eds.), *Resilience across contexts: Family, work, culture, and community* (pp. 333–363). Mahwah, NJ: Erlbaum.

Chapman, J. W., Tunmer, W. E., & Prochnow, J. E. (2000). Early reading-related skills and performance, reading self-concept, and the development of academic self-concept: A longitudinal study. *Journal of Educational Psychology, 92*, 703–708.

Charity, A. H., Scarborough, H. S., & Griffin, D. M. (2004). Familiarity with school English in African American children and its relation to early reading achievement. *Child Development, 75*, 1340–1356.

Chavous, T. M., Bernat, D. H., Schmeelk-Cone, K., Caldwell, C. H., Kohn-Wood, L., & Zimmerman, M. A. (2003). Racial identity and academic attainment among African American adolescents. *Child Development, 74*, 1076–1090.

Chen, E., Langer, D. A., Raphaelson, Y. E., & Matthews, K. A. (2004). Socioeconomic status and health in adolescents: The role of stress interpretations. *Child Development, 75*, 1039–1052.

Chen, X., Rubin, K. H., & Sun, Y. (1992). Social reputation and peer relationships in Chinese and Canadian children: A cross-cultural study. *Child Development, 63*, 1336–1343.

Cheng, L. R. (1987). *Assessing Asian language performance.* Rockville, MD: Aspen.

Cheng, P. W. (1985). Restructuring versus automaticity: Alternative accounts of skill acquisition. *Psychological Review, 92*, 414–423.

Chester, M. D., & Beaudin, B. Q. (1996). Efficacy beliefs of newly hired teachers in urban schools. *American Educational Research Journal, 33*, 233–257.

Chi, M. T. H. (1978). Knowledge structures and memory development. In R. S. Siegler (Ed.), *Children's thinking: What develops?* Mahwah, NJ: Erlbaum.

Chi, M. T. H., Feltovich, P., & Glaser, R. (1981). Categorization and representation of physics problems by experts and novices. *Cognitive Science, 5*, 121–152.

Chi, M. T. H., Glaser, R., & Rees, E. (1982). Expertise in problem solving. In R. J. Sternberg (Ed.), *Advances in the psychology of human intelligence.* Hillsdale, NJ: Erlbaum.

Chinn, C. A. (2006). Learning to argue. In A. M. O'Donnell, C. E. Hmelo-Silver, & G. Erkens (Eds.), *Collaborative learning, reasoning, and technology* (pp. 355–383). Mahwah, NJ: Erlbaum.

Chinn, C. A., & Brewer, W. F. (1993). The role of anomalous data in knowledge acquisition: A theoretical framework and implications for science instruction. *Review of Educational Research, 63*, 1–49.

Chisholm, J. S. (1996). Learning "respect for everything": Navajo images of development. In C. P. Hwant, M. E. Lamb, & I. E. Sigel (Eds.), *Images of childhood* (pp. 167–183). Mahwah, NJ: Erlbaum.

Christenson, S. L., & Sheridan, S. M. (2001). *Schools and families: Creating essential connections for learning.* New York: Guilford Press.

Christenson, S. L., & Thurlow, M. L. (2004). School dropouts: Prevention, considerations, interventions, and challenges. *Current Directions in Psychological Science, 13*, 36–39.

Church, M. A., Elliot, A. J., & Gable, S. L. (2001). Perceptions of classroom environment, achievement goals, and achievement outcomes. *Journal of Educational Psychology, 93*, 43–54.

Cillessen, A. H. N., & Rose, A. J. (2005). Understanding popularity in the peer system. *Current Directions in Psychological Science, 14*, 102–105.

Cizek, G. J. (2003). *Detecting and preventing classroom cheating: Promoting integrity in assessment.* Thousand Oaks, CA: Corwin.

Clark, A.-M., Anderson, R. C., Kuo, L., Kim, I., Archodidou, A., & Nguyen-Jahiel, K. (2003). Collaborative reasoning: Expanding ways for children to talk and think in school. *Educational Psychology Review, 15*, 181–198.

Clark, B. (1997). *Growing up gifted* (5th ed.). Upper Saddle River, NJ: Merrill/Prentice Hall.

Clark, C. C. (1992). Deviant adolescent subcultures: Assessment strategies and clinical interventions. *Adolescence, 27*(106), 283–293.

Clark, D. B. (2006). Longitudinal conceptual change in students' understanding of thermal equilibrium: An examination of the process of conceptual restructuring. *Cognition and Instruction, 24*, 467–563.

Clark, J. M., & Paivio, A. (1991). Dual coding theory and education. *Educational Psychology Review, 3*, 149–210.

Clark, R. E. (1983). Reconsidering research on learning from media. *Review of Educational Research, 53*, 445–459.

Clark, R. M. (1983). *Family life and school achievement: Why poor black children succeed or fail.* Chicago: University of Chicago Press.

Clarke, S., Dunlap, G., Foster-Johnson, L., Childs, K. E., Wilson, D., White, R., & Vera, A. (1995). Improving the conduct of students with behavioral disorders by incorporating student interests into curricular areas. *Behavioral Disorders, 20*, 221–237.

Clarke-Stewart, K. A. (1988). Parents' effects on children's development: A decade of progress? *Journal of Applied Developmental Psychology, 9*, 41–84.

Cleveland, M. J., Gibbons, F. X., Gerrard, M., Pomery, E. A., & Brody, G. H. (2005). The impact of parenting on risk cognitions and risk behavior: A study of mediation and moderation in a panel of African American adolescents. *Child Development, 76*, 900–916.

Clifford, M. M. (1990). Students need challenge, not easy success. *Educational Leadership, 48*(1), 22–26.

Cobb, P., Wood, T., Yackel, E., Nicholls, J., Wheatley, G., Trigatti, B., et al. (1991). Assessment of a problem centered second-grade mathematics project. *Journal for Research in Mathematics Education, 22*, 3–29.

Cobb, P., & Yackel, E. (1996). Constructivist, emergent, and sociocultural perspectives in the context of developmental research. *Educational Psychologist, 31*, 175–190.

Coch, D., Dawson, G., & Fischer, K. W. (Eds.). (2007). *Human behavior, learning, and the developing brain: Atypical development.* New York: Guilford Press.

Cognition and Technology Group at Vanderbilt. (1990). Anchored instruction and its relationship to situated cognition. *Educational Researcher, 19*(6), 2–10.

Cognition and Technology Group at Vanderbilt. (1993). Anchored instruction and situated cognition revisited. *Educational Technology, 33*(3), 52–70.

Cognition and Technology Group at Vanderbilt. (1996). Looking at technology in context: A framework for understanding technology and education research. In D. C. Berliner & R. C. Calfee (Eds.), *Handbook of educational psychology* (pp. 807–840). New York: Macmillan.

Cognition and Technology Group at Vanderbilt. (1997). *The Jasper project: Lessons in curriculum, instruction, assessment, and professional development.* Mahwah, NJ: Erlbaum.

Cohen, E. G. (1994). Restructuring the classroom: Conditions for productive small groups. *Review of Educational Research, 64*, 1–35.

Cohen, E. G., Lockheed, M. E., & Lohman, M. R. (1976). The center for interracial cooperation: A field experiment. *Sociology of Education, 59*, 47–58.

Coie, J. D., & Cillessen, A. H. N. (1993). Peer rejection: Origins and effects on children's development. *Current Directions in Psychological Science, 2*, 89–92.

Coie, J. D., & Dodge, K. A. (1998). Aggression and antisocial behavior. In W. Damon (Series Ed.) & N. Eisenberg (Vol. Ed.), *Handbook of child psychology: Vol. 3. Social, emotional, and personality development* (5th ed., pp. 779–862). New York: Wiley.

Colby, A., & Kohlberg, L. (1984). Invariant sequence and internal consistency in moral judgment stages. In W. M. Kurtines & J. L. Gewirtz (Eds.), *Morality, moral behavior, and moral development.* New York: Wiley.

Colby, A., Kohlberg, L., Gibbs, J., & Lieberman, M. (1983). A longitudinal study of moral judgment. *Monographs of the Society for Research in Child Development, 48*(1–2, Serial No. 200).

Cole, A. S., & Ibarra, R. A. (2005). Examining gender-related differential item functioning using insights from psychometric and multicontext theory. In A. M. Gallagher & J. C. Kaufman (Eds.), *Gender differences in mathematics: An integrative psychological approach* (pp. 143–171). Cambridge, England: Cambridge University Press.

Cole, D. A., Martin, J. M., Peeke, L. A., Seroczynski, A. D., & Fier, J. (1999). Children's over- and underestimation of academic competence: A longitudinal study of gender differences, depression, and anxiety. *Child Development, 70*, 459–473.

Cole, D. A., Maxwell, S. E., Martin, J. M., Peeke, L. G., Seroczynski, A. D., Tram, et al. (2001). The development of multiple domains of child and adolescent self-concept: A cohort sequential longitudinal design. *Child Development, 72*, 1723–1746.

Cole, M. (1990). Cognitive development and formal schooling: The evidence from cross-cultural research. In L. C. Moll (Ed.), *Vygotsky and education* (pp. 89–110). New York: Cambridge University Press.

Cole, M. (2006). Culture and cognitive development in phylogenetic, historical and ontogenetic perspective. In W. Damon & R. M. Lerner (Series Eds.), D. Kuhn & R. Siegler (Vol. Eds.), *Handbook of child psychology: Vol. 2. Cognition, perception, and language* (6th ed.). New York: Wiley.

Cole, N. S. (1990). Conceptions of educational achievement. *Educational Researcher, 19*(3), 2–7.

Cole, P. M., Bruschi, C. J., & Tamang, B. L. (2002). Cultural differences in children's emotional reactions to difficult situations. *Child Development, 73*, 983–996.

Cole, P. M., Tamang, B. L., & Shrestha, S. (2006). Cultural variations in the socialization of young children's anger and shame. *Child Development, 77*, 1237–1251.

Cole, P. M., & Tan, P. Z. (2007). Emotion socialization from a cultural perspective. In J. E. Grusec & P. D. Hastings (Eds.), *Handbook of socialization: Theory and research* (pp. 516–542). New York: Guilford Press.

Collins, A. (2006). Cognitive apprenticeship. In R. K. Sawyer (Ed.), *The Cambridge handbook of the learning sciences* (pp. 47–60). Cambridge, England: Cambridge University Press.

Collins, A., Brown, J. S., & Newman, S. E. (1989). Cognitive apprenticeship: Teaching the crafts of reading, writing, and mathematics. In L. B. Resnick (Ed.), *Knowing, learning, and instruction: Essays in honor of Robert Glaser.* Mahwah, NJ: Erlbaum.

Collins, W. A. (2005, April). *A "new look" in social development? Re-framing and extending the canon.* Invited address at the Developmental Science Teaching Institute at the biennial meeting of the Society for Research in Child Development, Atlanta.

Collins, W. A., Maccoby, E. E., Steinberg, L., Hetherington, E. M., & Bornstein, M. H. (2000). Contemporary research on parenting: The case for nature and nurture. *American Psychologist, 55*, 218–232.

Colvin, G., Ainge, D., & Nelson, R. (1997). How to defuse defiance, threats, challenges, confrontations. *Teaching Exceptional Children, 29*(6), 47–51.

Combs, A. W., Richards, A. C., & Richards, F. (1976). *Perceptual psychology.* New York: Harper & Row.

Condon, J. C., & Yousef, F. S. (1975). *An introduction to intercultural communication.* Indianapolis, IN: Bobbs-Merrill.

Connell, J. P., & Wellborn, J. G. (1991). Competence, autonomy, and relatedness: A motivational analysis of self-system processes. In M. R. Gunnar & L. A. Sroufe (Eds.), *Self processes and development: The Minnesota Symposia on Child Psychology* (Vol. 23). Mahwah, NJ: Erlbaum.

Connolly, F. W., & Eisenberg, T. E. (1990). The feedback classroom: Teaching's silent friend. *T.H.E. Journal, 17*(5), 75–77.

Connolly, J., & Goldberg, A. (1999). Romantic relationships in adolescence: The role of friends and peers in their emergence and development. In W. Furman, B. B. Brown, & C. Feiring (Eds.), *The development of romantic relationships in adolescence* (pp. 266–290). Cambridge, England: Cambridge University Press.

Conyers, C., Miltenberger, R., Maki, A., Barenz, R., Jurgens, M., Sailer, A., et al. (2004). A comparison of response cost and differential reinforcement of other behavior to reduce disruptive behavior in a preschool classroom. *Journal of Applied Behavior Analysis, 37,* 411–415.

Cook, T. D., Herman, M. R., Phillips, M., & Settersten, R. A., Jr. (2002). Some ways in which neighborhoods, nuclear families, friendship groups, and schools jointly affect changes in early adolescent development. *Child Development, 73,* 1283–1309.

Cooney, C. (1997). *Wanted.* New York: Scholastic.

Cooper, H. (1989). Synthesis of research on homework. *Educational Leadership, 47*(3), 85–91.

Cooper, H., Robinson, J. C., & Patall, E. A. (2006). Does homework improve academic achievement? A synthesis of research, 1987–2003. *Review of Educational Research, 76,* 1–62.

Cooper, H., & Valentine, J. C. (2001). Using research to answer practical questions about homework. *Educational Psychologist, 36,* 143–153.

Corkill, A. J. (1992). Advance organizers: Facilitators of recall. *Educational Psychology Review, 4,* 33–67.

Cormier, S. M. (1987). The structural processes underlying transfer of training. In S. M. Cormier & J. D. Hagman (Eds.), *Transfer of learning: Contemporary research and applications.* San Diego, CA: Academic Press.

Cornell, D. G., Pelton, G. M., Bassin, L. E., Landrum, M., Ramsay, S. G., Cooley, M. R., et al. (1990). Self-concept and peer status among gifted program youth. *Journal of Educational Psychology, 82,* 456–463.

Corno, L. (1993). The best-laid plans: Modern conceptions of volition and educational research. *Educational Researcher, 22*(2), 14–22.

Corno, L. (1996). Homework is a complicated thing. *Educational Researcher, 25*(8), 27–30.

Corno, L., Cronbach, L. J., Kupermintz, H., Lohman, D. F., Mandinach, E. B., Porteus, A. W., et al. (2002). *Remaking the concept of aptitude: Extending the legacy of Richard E. Snow.* Mahwah, NJ: Erlbaum.

Corno, L., & Rohrkemper, M. M. (1985). The intrinsic motivation to learn in classrooms. In C. Ames & R. Ames (Eds.), *Research on motivation in education: Vol. 2. The classroom milieu.* San Diego, CA: Academic Press.

Corpus, J. H., McClintic-Gilberg, M. S., & Hayenga, A. O. (2006, April). *Understanding intrinsic and extrinsic motivation: Age differences and links to children's beliefs and goals.* Paper presented at the annual meeting of the American Educational Research Association, San Francisco, CA.

Correa-Chávez, M., Rogoff, B., & Mejía Arauz, R. (2005). Cultural patterns in attending to two events at once. *Child Development, 76,* 664–678.

Cosden, M., Morrison, G., Albanese, A. L., & Macias, S. (2001). When homework is not home work: After-school programs for homework assistance. *Educational Psychologist, 36,* 211–221.

Covington, M. V. (1987). Achievement motivation, self-attributions, and the exceptional learner. In J. D. Day & J. G. Borkowski (Eds.), *Intelligence and exceptionality.* Norwood, NJ: Ablex.

Covington, M. V. (1992). *Making the grade: A self-worth perspective on motivation and school reform.* Cambridge, England: Cambridge University Press.

Covington, M. V. (2000). Intrinsic versus extrinsic motivation in schools: A reconciliation. *Current Directions in Psychological Science, 9,* 22–25.

Covington, M. V., & Müeller, K. J. (2001). Intrinsic versus extrinsic motivation: An approach/avoidance reformulation. *Educational Psychology Review, 13,* 157–176.

Cowan, N. (1995). *Attention and memory: An integrated framework.* New York: Oxford University Press.

Cowan, N. (2007). What infants can tell us about working memory development. In L. M. Oakes & P. J. Bauer (Eds.), *Short- and long-term memory in infancy and early childhood: Taking the first steps toward remembering* (pp. 126–150). New York: Oxford University Press.

Cowan, N., Chen, Z., & Rouder, J. N. (2004). Constant capacity in an immediate serial-recall task: A logical sequel to Miller (1956). *Psychological Science, 15,* 634–640.

Cowan, N., Saults, J. S., & Morey, C. C. (2006). Development of working memory for verbal-spatial associations. *Journal of Memory and Language, 55,* 274–289.

Cox, B. D. (1997). The rediscovery of the active learner in adaptive contexts: A developmental-historical analysis of transfer of training. *Educational Psychologist, 32,* 41–55.

Craft, M. (1984). Education for diversity. In M. Craft (Ed.), *Educational and cultural pluralism.* London: Falmer Press.

Crago, M. B. (1988). *Cultural context in the communicative interaction of young Inuit children.* Unpublished doctoral dissertation, McGill University, Montreal, Canada.

Crago, M. B., Annahatak, B., & Ningiuruvik, L. (1993). Changing patterns of language socialization in Inuit homes. *Anthropology and Education Quarterly, 24,* 205–223.

Craik, F. I. M., & Watkins, M. J. (1973). The role of rehearsal in short-term memory. *Journal of Verbal Learning and Verbal Behavior, 12,* 599–607.

Creasey, G. L., Jarvis, P. A., & Berk, L. E. (1998). Play and social competence. In O. N. Saracho & B. Spodek (Eds.), *Multiple perspectives on play in early childhood education.* Albany: State University of New York Press.

Crick, N. R., & Dodge, K. A. (1994). A review and reformulation of social information-processing mechanisms in children's social adjustment. *Psychological Bulletin, 115,* 74–101.

Crick, N. R., & Dodge, K. A. (1996). Social information-processing mechanisms in reactive and proactive aggression. *Child Development, 67,* 993–1002.

Crick, N. R., Grotpeter, J. K., & Bigbee, M. A. (2002). Relationally and physically aggressive children's intent attributions and feelings of distress for relational and instrumental peer provocation. *Child Development, 73,* 1134–1142.

Crocker, J., & Knight, K. M. (2005). Contingencies of self-worth. *Current Directions in Psychological Science, 14,* 200–203.

Crockett, L., Losoff, M., & Peterson, A. C. (1984). Perceptions of the peer group and friendship in early adolescence. *Journal of Early Adolescence, 4,* 155–181.

Cromley, J. G., & Azevedo, R. (2007). Testing and refining the direct and inferential mediation model of reading comprehension. *Journal of Educational Psychology, 99,* 311–325.

Crone, D. A., & Horner, R. H. (2003). *Building positive behavior support systems in schools: Functional behavioral assessment.* New York: Guilford Press.

Crook, C. (1995). On resourcing a concern for collaboration within peer interactions. *Cognition and Instruction, 13,* 541–547.

Crooks, T. J. (1988). The impact of classroom evaluation practices on students. *Review of Educational Research, 58,* 438–481.

Cross, W. E., Jr., Strauss, L., & Fhagen-Smith, P. (1999). African American identity development across the life span: Educational implications. In R. H. Sheets & E. R. Hollins (Eds.), *Racial and ethnic identity in school practices: Aspects of human development* (pp. 29–47). Mahwah, NJ: Erlbaum.

Crouter, A. C., Whiteman, S. D., McHale, S. M., & Osgood, D. W. (2007). Development of gender attitude traditionality across middle childhood and adolescence. *Child Development, 78,* 911–926.

Csikszentmihalyi, M. (1990). *Flow: The psychology of optimal experience.* New York: HarperPerennial.

Csikszentmihalyi, M. (1996). *Creativity: Flow and the psychology of discovery and invention.* New York: HarperCollins.

Csikszentmihalyi, M., & Nakamura, J. (1989). The dynamics of intrinsic motivation: A study of adolescents. In C. Ames & R. Ames (Eds.), *Research on motivation in education: Vol. 3. Goals and cognitions.* San Diego, CA: Academic Press.

Cummings, E. M., Schermerhorn, A. C., Davies, P. T., Goeke-Morey, M. C., & Cummings, J. S. (2006). Interparental discord and child adjustment: Prospective investigations of emotional security as an explanatory mechanism. *Child Development, 77,* 132–152.

Cunningham, C. E., & Cunningham, L. J. (1998). Student-mediated conflict resolution programs. In R. A. Barkley, *Attention-deficit hyperactivity disorder: A handbook for diagnosis and treatment* (2nd ed., pp. 491–509). New York: Guilford Press.

Curry, L. (1990). A critique of the research on learning styles. *Educational Leadership, 47*(2), 50–56.

Curtis, K. A., & Graham, S. (1991, April). *Altering beliefs about the importance of strategy: An attributional intervention.* Paper presented at the annual meeting of the American Educational Research Association, Chicago.

Cushing, L. S., & Kennedy, C. H. (1997). Academic effects of providing peer support in general education classrooms on students without disabilities. *Journal of Applied Behavior Analysis, 30,* 139–151.

Dahlin, B., & Watkins, D. (2000). The role of repetition in the processes of memorizing and understanding: A comparison of the views of Western and Chinese secondary students in Hong Kong. *British Journal of Educational Psychology, 70,* 65–84.

Dai, D. Y. (2002, April). *Effects of need for cognition and reader beliefs on the comprehension of narrative text.* Paper presented at the annual meeting of the American Educational Research Association, New Orleans.

Dai, D. Y., & Sternberg, R. J. (2004). Beyond cognitivism: Toward an integrated understanding of intellectual functioning and development. In D. Y. Dai & R. J. Sternberg (Eds.), *Motivation, emotion, and cognition: Integrative perspectives on intellectual functioning and development* (pp. 3–38). Mahwah, NJ: Erlbaum.

d'Ailly, H. (2003). Children's autonomy and perceived control in learning: A model of motivation and achievement in Taiwan. *Journal of Educational Psychology, 95,* 84–96.

Daley, T. C., Whaley, S. E., Sigman, M. D., Espinosa, M. P., & Neumann, C. (2003). IQ on the rise: The Flynn effect in rural Kenyan children. *Psychological Science, 14,* 215–219.

Dalrymple, N. J. (1995). Environmental supports to develop flexibility and independence. In K. A. Quill (Ed.), *Teaching children with autism: Strategies to enhance communication and socialization.* New York: Delmar.

Damasio, A. R. (1994). *Descartes' error: Emotion, reason, and the human brain.* New York: Avon Books.

D'Amato, R. C., Chittooran, M. M., & Whitten, J. D. (1992). Neuropsychological consequences of malnutrition. In D. I. Templer, L. C. Hartlage, & W. G. Cannon (Eds.), *Preventable brain damage: Brain vulnerability and brain health.* New York: Springer.

Damon, W. (1977). *The social world of the child.* San Francisco: Jossey-Bass.

Damon, W. (1988). *The moral child: Nurturing children's natural moral growth.* New York: Free Press.

Damon, W., & Hart, D. (1988). *Self-understanding from childhood and adolescence.* New York: Cambridge University Press.

Danner, F. W., & Day, M. C. (1977). Eliciting formal operations. *Child Development, 48,* 1600–1606.

Dansereau, D. F. (1995). Derived structural schemas and the transfer of knowledge. In A. McKeough, J. Lupart, & A. Marini (Eds.), *Teaching for transfer: Fostering generalization in learning.* Mahwah, NJ: Erlbaum.

Darch, C. B., & Kame'enui, E. J. (2004). *Instructional classroom management: A proactive approach to behavior management* (2nd ed.). Upper Saddle River, NJ: Merrill/Prentice Hall.

Darley, J. M., & Gross, P. H. (1983). A hypothesis-confirming bias in labeling effects. *Journal of Personality and Social Psychology, 44,* 20–33.

Darling-Hammond, L., Ancess, J., & Falk, B. (1995). *Authentic assessment in action: Studies of schools and students at work.* New York: Teachers College Press.

Darling-Hammond, L., & Bransford, J. (Eds.). (2005). *Preparing teachers for a changing world: What teachers should learn and be able to do.* San Francisco: Jossey-Bass/Wiley.

Darwin, C. J., Turvey, M. T., & Crowder, R. G. (1972). An auditory analogue of the Sperling partial report procedure: Evidence for brief auditory storage. *Cognitive Psychology, 3*, 255–267.

Davidson, F. H. (1976). Ability to respect persons compared to ethnic prejudice in childhood. *Journal of Personality and Social Psychology, 34*, 1256–1267.

Davidson, J. E., & Sternberg, R. J. (1998). Smart problem solving: How metacognition helps. In D. J. Hacker, J. Dunlosky, & A. C. Graesser (Eds.), *Metacognition in educational theory and practice* (pp. 47–68). Mahwah, NJ: Erlbaum.

Davidson, J. E., & Sternberg, R. J. (Eds.). (2003). *The psychology of problem solving.* Cambridge, England: Cambridge University Press.

Davies, P. G., & Spencer, S. J. (2005). The gender-gap artifact: Women's underperformance in quantitative domains through the lens of stereotype threat. In A. M. Gallagher & J. C. Kaufman (Eds.), *Gender differences in mathematics: An integrative psychological approach* (pp. 172–188). Cambridge, England: Cambridge University Press.

Davis, C., & Yang, A. (2005). *Parents and teachers working together.* Turners Falls, MA: Northeast Foundation for Children.

Davis, G. A., & Rimm, S. B. (1998). *Education of the gifted and talented* (4th ed.). Boston: Allyn & Bacon.

Davis, G. A., & Thomas, M. A. (1989). *Effective schools and effective teachers.* Needham Heights, MA: Allyn & Bacon.

Davis, H. A. (2003). Conceptualizing the role and influence of student-teacher relationships on children's social and cognitive development. *Educational Psychologist, 38*, 207–234.

Davis, H. A., Schutz, P. A., & Chambless, C. B. (2001, April). *Uncovering the impact of social relationships in the classroom: Viewing relationships with teachers from different lenses.* Paper presented at the annual meeting of the American Educational Research Association, Seattle, WA.

Davis, L. E., Ajzen, I., Saunders, J., & Williams, T. (2002). The decision of African American students to complete high school: An application of the theory of planned behavior. *Journal of Educational Psychology, 94*, 810–819.

Davis-Kean, P. E., & Sandler, H. M. (2001). A meta-analysis of measures of self-esteem for young children: A framework for future measures. *Child Development, 72*, 887–906.

Deaux, K. (1984). From individual differences to social categories: Analysis of a decade's research on gender. *American Psychologist, 39*, 105–116.

deCharms, R. (1972). Personal causation training in the schools. *Journal of Applied Social Psychology, 2*, 95–113.

Deci, E. L. (1992). The relation of interest to the motivation of behavior: A self-determination theory perspective. In K. A. Renninger, S. Hidi, & A. Krapp (Eds.), *The role of interest in learning and development.* Mahwah, NJ: Erlbaum.

Deci, E. L., Koestner, R., & Ryan, R. M. (2001). Extrinsic rewards and intrinsic motivation in education: Reconsidered once again. *Review of Educational Research, 71*, 1–27.

Deci, E. L., & Ryan, R. M. (1985). *Intrinsic motivation and self-determination in human behavior.* New York: Plenum Press.

Deci, E. L., & Ryan, R. M. (1992). The initiation and regulation of intrinsically motivated learning and achievement. In A. K. Boggiano & T. S. Pittman (Eds.), *Achievement and motivation: A social-developmental perspective.* Cambridge, England: Cambridge University Press.

Deci, E. L., & Ryan, R. M. (1995). Human autonomy: The basis for true self-esteem. In M. H. Kernis (Ed.), *Efficacy, agency, and self-esteem.* New York: Plenum Press.

De Corte, E. (2003). Transfer as the productive use of acquired knowledge, skills, and motivations. *Current Directions in Psychological Science, 12*, 142–146.

De Corte, E., Greer, B., & Verschaffel, L. (1996). Mathematics teaching and learning. In D. C. Berliner & R. C. Calfee (Eds.), *Handbook of educational psychology.* New York: Macmillan.

Dee-Lucas, D., & Larkin, J. H. (1991). Equations in scientific proofs: Effects on comprehension. *American Educational Research Journal, 28*, 661–682.

de Jong, T., & van Joolingen, W. R. (1998). Scientific discovery learning with computer simulations of conceptual domains. *Review of Educational Research, 68*, 179–201.

DeLain, M. T., Pearson, P. D., & Anderson, R. C. (1985). Reading comprehension and creativity in black language use: You stand to gain by playing the sounding game! *American Educational Research Journal, 22*, 155–173.

Delandshere, G., & Petrosky, A. R. (1998). Assessment of complex performances: Limitations of key measurement assumptions. *Educational Researcher, 27*(2), 14–24.

De La Paz, S. (2005). Effects of historical reasoning instruction and writing strategy mastery in culturally and academically diverse middle school classrooms. *Journal of Educational Psychology, 97*, 139–156.

deLeeuw, N., & Chi, M. T. H. (2003). Self-explanation: Enriching a situation model or repairing a domain model? In G. M. Sinatra & P. R. Pintrich (Eds.), *Intentional conceptual change* (pp. 55–78). Mahwah, NJ: Erlbaum.

Delgado-Gaitan, C. (1994). Socializing young children in Mexican-American families: An intergenerational perspective. In P. M. Greenfield & R. R. Cocking (Eds.), *Cross-cultural roots of minority child development.* Mahwah, NJ: Erlbaum.

De Lisi, R., & Golbeck, S. L. (1999). Implications of Piagetian theory for peer learning. In A. M. O'Donnell & A. King (Eds.), *Cognitive perspectives on peer learning* (pp. 3–37). Mahwah, NJ: Erlbaum.

DeLisle, J. R. (1984). *Gifted children speak out.* New York: Walker.

DeLoache, J. S., & Todd, C. M. (1988). Young children's use of spatial categorization as a mnemonic strategy. *Journal of Experimental Child Psychology, 46*, 1–20.

Demetriou, A., Christou, C., Spanoudis, G., & Platsidou, M. (2002). The development of mental processing: Efficiency, working memory, and thinking. *Monographs of the Society for Research in Child Development, 67*(1, Serial No. 268).

Dempster, F. N. (1991). Synthesis of research on reviews and tests. *Educational Leadership, 48*(7), 71–76.

Dempster, F. N. (1992). The rise and fall of the inhibitory mechanism: Toward a unified theory of cognitive development and aging. *Developmental Review, 12*, 45–75.

Dempster, F. N. (1997). Using tests to promote classroom learning. In R. F. Dillon (Ed.), *Handbook on testing* (pp. 332–346). Westport, CT: Greenwood Press.

DeRidder, L. M. (1993). Teenage pregnancy: Etiology and educational interventions. *Educational Psychology Review, 5*, 87–107.

Derry, S. J. (1996). Cognitive schema theory in the constructivist debate. *Educational Psychologist, 31*, 163–174.

Derry, S. J., Levin, J. R., Osana, H. P., & Jones, M. S. (1998). Developing middle school students' statistical reasoning abilities through simulation gaming. In S. P. Lajoie (Ed.), *Reflections on statistics: Learning, teaching, and assessment in grades K–12* (pp. 175–195). Mahwah, NJ: Erlbaum.

Desberg, P., & Taylor, J. H. (1986). *Essentials of task analysis.* Lanham, MD: University Press of America.

Deutsch, M. (1993). Educating for a peaceful world. *American Psychologist, 48*, 510–517.

DeVault, G., Krug, C., & Fake, S. (1996, September). Why does Samantha act that way: Positive behavioral support leads to successful inclusion. *Exceptional Parent*, 43–47.

DeVoe, J. F., Peter, K., Kaufman, P., Ruddy, S. A., Miller, A. K., Planty, M., et al. (2003). *Indicators of school crime and safety: 2003* (NCES 2004-004/NCJ 201257). Washington, DC: U.S. Departments of Education and Justice. Retrieved February 27, 2004, from http://nces.ed.gov/

DeVoe, J. F., Peter, K., Noonan, M., Snyder, T. D., & Baum, K. (2005). *Indicators of school crime and safety: 2005* (NCES 2006–001/NCJ 210697). Washington, DC: U.S. Departments of Education and Justice. Retrieved February 6, 2007, from http://ojp.usdoj.gov/bjs/abstract/iscs05.htm

DeVries, R. (1997). Piaget's social theory. *Educational Researcher, 26*(2), 4–17.

DeVries, R., & Zan, B. (1996). A constructivist perspective on the role of the sociomoral atmosphere in promoting children's development. In C. T. Fosnot (Ed.), *Constructivism: Theory, perspectives, and practice.* New York: Teachers College Press.

Dewhurst, S. A., & Conway, M. A. (1994). Pictures, images, and recollective experience. *Journal of Experimental Psychology: Learning, Memory, and Cognition, 20*, 1088–1098.

Deyhle, D., & LeCompte, M. (1999). Cultural differences in child development: Navajo adolescents in middle schools. In R. H. Sheets & E. R. Hollins (Eds.), *Racial and ethnic identity in school practices: Aspects of human development* (pp. 123–139). Mahwah, NJ: Erlbaum.

Deyhle, D., & Margonis, F. (1995). Navajo mothers and daughters: Schools, jobs, and the family. *Anthropology and Education Quarterly, 26*, 135–167.

Diamond, M., & Hopson, J. (1998). *Magic trees of the mind.* New York: Dutton.

Diamond, S. C. (1991). What to do when you can't do anything: Working with disturbed adolescents. *Clearing House, 64*, 232–234.

Dickens, W. T., & Flynn, J. R. (2006). Black Americans reduce the racial IQ gap: Evidence from standardization samples. *Psychological Science, 17*, 913–920.

Dien, T. (1998). Language and literacy in Vietnamese American communities. In B. Pérez (Ed.), *Sociocultural contexts of language and literacy.* Mahwah, NJ: Erlbaum.

Dilworth, J. E., & Moore, C. F. (2006). Mercy mercy me: Social injustice and the prevention of environmental pollutant exposures among ethnic minority and poor children. *Child Development, 77*, 247–265.

DiMartino, J., & Castaneda, A. (2007). Assessing applied skills. *Educational Leadership, 64*, 38–42.

Dirks, J. (1982). The effect of a commercial game on children's Block Design scores on the WISC-R test. *Intelligence, 6*, 109–123.

diSessa, A. A. (2006). A history of conceptual change research. In R. K. Sawyer (Ed.), *The Cambridge handbook of the learning sciences* (pp. 265–281). Cambridge, England: Cambridge University Press.

Di Vesta, F. J., & Gray, S. G. (1972). Listening and notetaking. *Journal of Educational Psychology, 63*, 8–14.

Di Vesta, F. J., & Peverly, S. T. (1984). The effects of encoding variability, processing activity and rule example sequences on the transfer of conceptual rules. *Journal of Educational Psychology, 76*, 108–119.

Dodge, K. A. (1986). A social information processing model of social competence in children. In M. Perlmutter (Ed.), *Minnesota Symposia on Child Psychology: Vol. 18. Cognitive perspectives in children's social and behavioral development.* Mahwah, NJ: Erlbaum.

Dodge, K. A., Asher, S. R., & Parkhurst, J. T. (1989). Social life as a goal-coordination task. In C. Ames & R. Ames (Eds.), *Research on motivation in education: Vol. 3. Goals and cognitions.* San Diego, CA: Academic Press.

Dodge, K. A., Dishion, T. J., & Lansford, J. E. (2006). Deviant peer influences in intervention and public policy for youth. *Social Policy Report, 20*(1), 3–19.

Dodge, K. A., Lansford, J. E., Burks, V. S., Bates, J. E., Pettit, G. S., Fontaine, R., et al. (2003). Peer rejection and social information-processing factors in the development of aggressive behavior problems in children. *Child Development, 74*, 374–393.

Dodge, K. A., Lochman, J. E., Harnish, J. D., Bates, J. E., & Pettit, G. S. (1997). Reactive and proactive aggression in school children and psychiatrically impaired chronically assaultive youth. *Journal of Abnormal Psychology, 106*, 37–51.

Dole, J. A., Duffy, G. G., Roehler, L. R., & Pearson, P. D. (1991). Moving from the old to the new: Research on reading comprehension instruction. *Review of Educational Research, 61*, 239–264.

Doll, B., Song, S., & Siemers, E. (2004). Classroom ecologies that support or discourage bullying. In D. L. Espelage & S. M. Swearer (Eds.), *Bullying in American* schools: A social-ecological perspective on prevention and intervention (pp. 161–183). Mahwah, NJ: Erlbaum.

Dominowski, R. L. (1998). Verbalization and problem solving. In D. J. Hacker, J. Dunlosky, & A. C. Graesser (Eds.), Metacognition in educational theory and practice (pp. 25–45). Mahwah, NJ: Erlbaum.

Donaldson, M. (1978). Children's minds. New York: Norton.

Donaldson, S. K., & Westerman, M. A. (1986). Development of children's understanding of ambivalence and causal theories of emotion. Developmental Psychology, 22, 655–662.

Donnelly, C. M., & McDaniel, M. A. (1993). Use of analogy in learning scientific concepts. Journal of Experimental Psychology: Learning, Memory, and Cognition, 19, 975–987.

Dorris, M. (1989). The broken cord. New York: Harper & Row.

Dougherty, T. M., & Haith, M. M. (1997). Infant expectations and reaction time as predictors of childhood speed of processing and IQ. Developmental Psychology, 33, 146–155.

Dovidio, J. F., & Gaertner, S. L. (1999). Reducing prejudice: Combating intergroup biases. Current Directions in Psychological Science, 8, 101–105.

Dowson, M., & McInerney, D. M. (2001). Psychological parameters of students' social and work avoidance goals: A qualitative investigation. Journal of Educational Psychology, 93, 35–42.

Doyle, A. (1982). Friends, acquaintances, and strangers: The influence of familiarity and ethnolinguistic backgrounds on social interaction. In K. Rubin & H. Ross (Eds.), Peer relationships and social skills in childhood. New York: Springer-Verlag.

Doyle, W. (1983). Academic work. Review of Educational Research, 53, 159–199.

Doyle, W. (1984). How order is achieved in classrooms: An interim report. Journal of Curriculum Studies, 16, 259–277.

Doyle, W. (1986a). Classroom organization and management. In M. C. Wittrock (Ed.), Handbook of research on teaching (3rd ed.). New York: Macmillan.

Doyle, W. (1986b). Content representation in teachers' definitions of academic work. Journal of Curriculum Studies, 18, 365–379.

Doyle, W. (1990). Classroom management techniques. In O. C. Moles (Ed.), Student discipline strategies: Research and practice. Albany: State University of New York Press.

Doyle, W. (2006). Ecological approaches to classroom management. In C. M. Evertson & C. S. Weinstein (Eds.), Handbook of classroom management: Research, practice, and contemporary issues (pp. 97–125). Mahwah, NJ: Erlbaum.

Dreikurs, R. (1998). Maintaining sanity in the classroom: Classroom management techniques (2nd ed.). Bristol, PA: Hemisphere.

Dryfoos, J. G. (1997). The prevalence of problem behaviors: Implications for programs. In R. P. Weissberg, T. P. Gullotta, R. L. Hampton, B. A. Ryan, & G. R. Adams (Eds.), Enhancing children's wellness (Vol. 8, pp. 17–46). Thousand Oaks, CA: Sage.

DuBois, D. L., Burk-Braxton, C., Swenson, L. P., Tevendale, H. D., & Hardesty, J. L. (2002). Race and gender influences on adjustment in early adolescence: Investigation of an integrative model. Child Development, 73, 1573–1592.

Dubow, E. F., Huesmann, L. R., & Greenwood, D. (2007). Media and youth socialization: Underlying processes and moderators of effects. In J. E. Grusec & P. D. Hastings (Eds.), Handbook of socialization: Theory and research (pp. 404–430). New York: Guilford Press.

Duckworth, A. L., & Seligman, M. E. P. (2005). Self-discipline outdoes IQ in predicting academic performance of adolescents. Psychological Science, 16, 939–944.

Duke, N. K. (2000). For the rich it's richer: Print experiences and environments offered to children in very low- and very high-socioeconomic status first-grade classrooms. American Educational Research Journal, 37, 441–478.

Duncan, G. J., & Magnuson, K. A. (2005). Can family socioeconomic resources account for racial and ethnic test score gaps? The Future of Children, 15(1), 35–54.

Duncker, K. (1945). On problem solving. Psychological Monographs, 58 (Whole No. 270).

Dunham, Y., Baron, A. S., & Banaji, M. R. (2006). From American city to Japanese village: A cross-cultural investigation of implicit race attitudes. Child Development, 77, 1268–1281.

Dunlap, G., dePerczel, M., Clarke, S., Wilson, D., Wright, S., White, R., et al. (1994). Choice making to promote adaptive behavior for students with emotional and behavioral challenges. Journal of Applied Behavior Analysis, 27, 505–518.

Dunning, D., Heath, C., & Suls, J. M. (2004). Flawed self-assessment: Implications for health, education, and the workplace. Psychological Science in the Public Interest, 5, 69–106.

DuPaul, G. J., Ervin, R. A., Hook, C. L., & McGoey, K. E. (1998). Peer tutoring for children with attention deficit hyperactivity disorder: Effects on classroom behavior and academic performance. Journal of Applied Behavior Analysis, 31, 579–592.

DuPaul, G., & Hoff, K. (1998). Reducing disruptive behavior in general education classrooms: The use of self-management strategies. School Psychology Review, 27, 290–304.

Duran, B. J., & Weffer, R. E. (1992). Immigrants' aspirations, high school process, and academic outcomes. American Educational Research Journal, 29, 163–181.

Durik, A. M., Vida, M., & Eccles, J. S. (2006). Task values and ability beliefs as predictors of high school literacy choices: A developmental analysis. Journal of Educational Psychology, 98, 382–393.

Durkin, K. (1995). Developmental social psychology: From infancy to old age. Cambridge, MA: Blackwell.

Dweck, C. S. (1978). Achievement. In M. E. Lamb (Ed.), Social and personality development. New York: Holt, Rinehart & Winston.

Dweck, C. S. (1986). Motivational processes affecting learning. American Psychologist, 41, 1040–1048.

Dweck, C. S. (2000). Self-theories: Their role in motivation, personality, and development. Philadelphia: Psychology Press.

Dweck, C. S., & Elliott, E. S. (1983). Achievement motivation. In E. M. Hetherington (Ed.), Handbook of child psychology: Vol. 4. Socialization, personality, and social development (4th ed., pp. 643–691). New York: Wiley.

Dweck, C. S., & Leggett, E. L. (1988). A social-cognitive approach to motivation and personality. Psychological Review, 95, 256–273.

Dweck, C. S., Mangels, J. A., & Good, C. (2004). Motivational effects on attention, cognition, and performance. In D. Y. Dai & R. J. Sternberg (Eds.), Motivation, emotion, and cognition: Integrative perspectives on intellectual functioning and development (pp. 41–55). Mahwah, NJ: Erlbaum.

Dwyer, K., & Osher, D. (2000). Safeguarding our children: An action guide. Washington, DC: U.S. Departments of Education and Justice, American Institutes for Research. Retrieved February 26, 2004, from http://www.ed.gov/pubs/edpubs.html

Dwyer, K., Osher, D., & Warger, C. (1998). Early warning, timely response: A guide to safe schools. Washington, DC: U.S. Department of Education. Retrieved February 26, 2004, from http://www.ed.gov/offices/OSERS/OSEP/earlywrn.html

Dymond, S. K., Renzaglia, A., & Chun, E. (2007). Elements of effective high school service learning programs that include students with and without disabilities. Remedial and Special Education, 28, 227–243.

Eacott, M. J. (1999). Memory for the events of early childhood. Current Directions in Psychological Science, 8, 46–49.

Eaton, J. F., Anderson, C. W., & Smith, E. L. (1984). Students' misconceptions interfere with science learning: Case studies of fifth-grade students. Elementary School Journal, 84, 365–379.

Eccles, J. S. (1989). Bringing young women to math and science. In M. Crawford & M. Gentry (Eds.), Gender and thought: Psychological perspectives. New York: Springer-Verlag.

Eccles, J. S. (2007). Families, schools, and developing achievement-related motivations and engagement. In J. E. Grusec & P. D. Hastings (Eds.), Handbook of socialization: Theory and research (pp. 665–691). New York: Guilford Press.

Eccles, J. S., Jacobs, J., Harold-Goldsmith, R., Jayaratne, T., & Yee, D. (1989, April). The relations between parents' category-based and target-based beliefs: Gender roles and biological influences. Paper presented at the Society for Research in Child Development, Kansas City, MO.

Eccles, J. S., & Midgley, C. (1989). Stage-environment fit: Developmentally appropriate classrooms for young adolescents. In C. Ames & R. Ames (Eds.), Research on motivation in education: Vol. 3. Goals and cognitions. San Diego, CA: Academic Press.

Eccles, J. S., & Wigfield, A. (1985). Teacher expectations and student motivation. In J. B. Dusek (Ed.), Teacher expectancies. Mahwah, NJ: Erlbaum.

Eccles, J. S., Wigfield, A., & Schiefele, U. (1998). Motivation to succeed. In W. Damon (Series Ed.) & N. Eisenberg (Vol. Ed.), Handbook of child psychology: Vol. 3. Social, emotional, and personality development (5th ed., pp. 1017–1095). New York: Wiley.

Eccles (Parsons), J. S. (1983). Expectancies, values, and academic behaviors. In J. T. Spence (Ed.), Achievement and achievement motivation. San Francisco: Freeman.

Eccles (Parsons), J. S. (1984). Sex differences in mathematics participation. In M. Steinkamp & M. Maehr (Eds.), Women in science. Greenwich, CT: JAI Press.

Eckert, P. (1989). Jocks and burnouts: Social categories and identity in the high school. New York: Teachers College Press.

Edens, K. M., & Potter, E. F. (2001). Promoting conceptual understanding through pictorial representation. Studies in Art Education, 42, 214–233.

Eeds, M., & Wells, D. (1989). Grand conversations: An explanation of meaning construction in literature study groups. Research in the Teaching of English, 23, 4–29.

Eid, M., & Diener, E. (2001). Norms for experiencing emotions in different cultures: Inter- and intranational differences. Journal of Personality and Social Psychology, 81, 869–885.

Eilam, B. (2001). Primary strategies for promoting homework performance. American Educational Research Journal, 38, 691–725.

Eimas, P. D., & Quinn, P. C. (1994). Studies on the formation of perceptually based basic-level categories in young infants. Child Development, 65, 903–917.

Eisenberg, M. B. (2004). A Big6™ skills overview. Retrieved April 23, 2004, from http://big6.com/showarticle/php?id=16.

Eisenberg, M. B., & Berkowitz, R. E. (2000). Teaching information and technology skills: The Big6 in elementary schools. Worthington, OH: Linworth.

Eisenberg, N. (1982). The development of reasoning regarding prosocial behavior. In N. Eisenberg (Ed.), The development of prosocial behavior. San Diego, CA: Academic Press.

Eisenberg, N. (1987). The relation of altruism and other moral behaviors to moral cognition: Methodological and conceptual issues. In N. Eisenberg (Ed.), Contemporary topics in developmental psychology (pp. 165–189). New York: Wiley.

Eisenberg, N. (1995). Prosocial development: A multifaceted model. In W. M. Kurtines & J. L. Gewirtz (Eds.), Moral development: An introduction. Boston: Allyn & Bacon.

Eisenberg, N., Carlo, G., Murphy, B., & Van Court, N. (1995). Prosocial development in late adolescence: A longitudinal study. Child Development, 66, 1179–1197.

Eisenberg, N., & Fabes, R. A. (1991). Prosocial behavior: A multimethod developmental perspective. In M. S. Clark (Ed.), Review of personality and social psychology (Vol. 2, pp. 34–61). Newbury Park, CA: Sage.

Eisenberg, N., & Fabes, R. A. (1994). Mothers' reactions to children's negative emotions: Relations to children's temperament and anger behavior. Merrill-Palmer Quarterly, 40, 138–156.

Eisenberg, N., & Fabes, R. A. (1998). Prosocial development. In W. Damon (Series Ed.) & N. Eisenberg (Vol. Ed.), *Handbook of child psychology: Vol. 3. Social, emotional, and personality development* (5th ed., pp. 701–778). New York: Wiley.

Eisenberg, N., Lennon, R., & Pasternack, J. F. (1986). Altruistic values and moral judgment. In N. Eisenberg (Ed.), *Altruistic emotion, cognition, and behavior.* Mahwah, NJ: Erlbaum.

Eisenberg, N., Martin, C. L., & Fabes, R. A. (1996). Gender development and gender effects. In D. C. Berliner & R. C. Calfee (Eds.), *Handbook of educational psychology.* New York: Macmillan.

Eisenberg, N., Pidada, S., & Liew, J. (2001). The relations of regulation and negative emotionality to Indonesian children's social functioning. *Child Development, 72,* 1747–1763.

Eisenberg, N., Zhou, Q., & Koller, S. (2001). Brazilian adolescents' prosocial moral judgment and behavior: Relations to sympathy, perspective taking, gender-role orientation, and demographic characteristics. *Child Development, 72,* 518–534.

Elder, A. D. (2002). Characterizing fifth grade students' epistemological beliefs in science. In B. K. Hofer & P. R. Pintrich (Eds.), *Personal epistemology: The psychology of beliefs about knowledge and knowing* (pp. 347–363). Mahwah, NJ: Erlbaum.

Elia, J. P. (1994). Homophobia in the high school: A problem in need of a resolution. *Journal of Homosexuality, 77*(1), 177–185.

Elkind, D. (1981). *Children and adolescents: Interpretive essays on Jean Piaget* (3rd ed.). New York: Oxford University Press.

Ellenwood, S., & Ryan, K. (1991). Literature and morality: An experimental curriculum. In W. M. Kurtines & J. L. Gewirtz (Eds.), *Moral behavior and development: Vol. 3. Application.* Mahwah, NJ: Erlbaum.

Elliot, A. J., & McGregor, H. A. (2000, April). Approach and avoidance goals and autonomous-controlled regulation: Empirical and conceptual relations. In A. Assor (Chair), *Self-determination theory and achievement goal theory: Convergences, divergences, and educational implications.* Symposium conducted at the annual meeting of the American Educational Research Association, New Orleans, LA.

Elliot, A. J., Shell, M. M., Henry, K. B., & Maier, M. A. (2005). Achievement goals, performance contingencies, and performance attainment: An experimental test. *Journal of Educational Psychology, 97,* 630–640.

Elliot, A. J., & Thrash, T. M. (2001). Achievement goals and the hierarchical model of achievement motivation. *Educational Psychology Review, 13,* 139–156.

Elliott, D. J. (1995). *Music matters: A new philosophy of music education.* New York: Oxford University Press.

Elliott, S. N., & Busse, R. T. (1991). Social skills assessment and intervention with children and adolescents. *School Psychology International, 12,* 63–83.

Ellis, E. S., & Friend, P. (1991). Adolescents with learning disabilities. In B. Y. L. Wong (Ed.), *Learning about learning disabilities.* San Diego, CA: Academic Press.

Ellis, W. E., & Zarbatany, L. (2007). Peer group status as a moderator of group influence on children's deviant, aggressive, and prosocial behavior. *Child Development, 78,* 1240–1254.

Ellison, N. B., Steinfield, C., & Lampe, C. (2007). The benefits of *Facebook* "friends": Social capital and college students' use of online social network sites. *Journal of Computer-Mediated Communication, 12,* 1143–1168.

Emmer, E. T. (1987). Classroom management and discipline. In V. Richardson-Koehler (Ed.), *Educators' handbook: A research perspective.* White Plains, NY: Longman.

Emmer, E. T. (1994, April). *Teacher emotions and classroom management.* Paper presented at the annual meeting of the American Educational Research Association, New Orleans, LA.

Emmer, E. T., & Evertson, C. M. (1981). Synthesis of research on classroom management. *Educational Leadership, 38*(4), 342–347.

Emmer, E. T., Evertson, C. M., & Worsham, M. E. (2000). *Classroom management for secondary teachers* (5th ed.). Boston: Allyn & Bacon.

Emmer, E. T., & Gerwels, M. C. (2006). Classroom management in middle and high school classrooms. In C. M. Evertson & C. S. Weinstein (Eds.), *Handbook of classroom management: Research, practice, and contemporary issues* (pp. 407–437). Mahwah, NJ: Erlbaum.

Emmer, E. T., & Stough, L. M. (2001). Classroom management: A critical part of educational psychology, with implications for teacher education. *Educational Psychologist, 36,* 103–112.

Empson, S. B. (1999). Equal sharing and shared meaning: The development of fraction concepts in a first-grade classroom. *Cognition and Instruction, 17,* 283–342.

Engle, R. A. (2006). Framing interactions to foster generative learning: A situative explanation of transfer in a community of learners classroom. *Journal of the Learning Sciences, 15,* 451–498.

Englemann, S., & Carnine, D. (1982). *Theory of instruction: Principles and applications.* New York: Irvington.

Entwisle, N. J., & Ramsden, P. (1983). *Understanding student learning.* London: Croom Helm.

Epstein, J. L. (1986). Friendship selection: Developmental and environmental influences. In E. Mueller & C. Cooper (Eds.), *Process and outcome in peer relationships* (pp. 129–160). New York: Academic Press.

Epstein, J. L. (1989). Family structures and student motivation. In R. E. Ames & C. Ames (Eds.), *Research on motivation in education: Vol. 3. Goals and cognitions* (pp. 259–295). New York: Academic Press.

Epstein, J. L. (1996). Perspectives and previews on research and policy for school, family, and community partnerships. In A. Booth & J. F. Dunn (Eds.), *Family-school links: How do they affect educational outcomes?* Mahwah, NJ: Erlbaum.

Epstein, J. S. (1998). Introduction: Generation X, youth culture, and identity. In J. S. Epstein (Ed.), *Youth culture: Identity in a postmodern world.* Malden, MA: Blackwell.

Epstein, T. (2000). Adolescents' perspectives on racial diversity in U.S. history: Case studies from an urban classroom. *American Educational Research Journal, 37,* 185–214.

Erdelyi, M. H. (1985). *Psychoanalysis: Freud's cognitive psychology.* New York: Freeman.

Erdley, C. A., & Asher, S. R. (1996). Children's social goals and self-efficacy perceptions as influences on their responses to ambiguous provocation. *Child Development, 67,* 1329–1344.

Ericsson, K. A. (2003). The acquisition of expert performance as problem solving. In J. E. Davidson & R. J. Sternberg (Eds.), *The psychology of problem solving* (pp. 31–83). Cambridge, England: Cambridge University Press.

Ericsson, K. A., & Chalmers, N. (1994). Expert performance: Its structure and acquisition. *American Psychologist, 49,* 725–747.

Eriks-Brophy, A., & Crago, M. B. (1994). Transforming classroom discourse: An Inuit example. *Language and Education, 8*(3), 105–122.

Erikson, E. H. (1963). *Childhood and society* (2nd ed.). New York: Norton.

Erikson, E. H. (1972). *Eight ages of man.* In C. S. Lavatelli & F. Stendler (Eds.), *Readings in child behavior and child development.* San Diego, CA: Harcourt Brace Jovanovich.

Eron, L. D. (1980). Prescription for reduction of aggression. *American Psychologist, 35,* 244–252.

Erwin, P. (1993). *Friendship and peer relations in children.* Chichester, England: Wiley.

Espelage, D. L., Holt, M. K., & Henkel, R. R. (2003). Examination of peer-group contextual effects on aggression during early adolescence. *Child Development, 74,* 205–220.

Espelage, D. L., & Swearer, S. M. (Eds.). (2004). *Bullying in American schools: A social-ecological perspective on prevention and intervention.* Mahwah, NJ: Erlbaum.

Evans, E. D., & Craig, D. (1990). Teacher and student perceptions of academic cheating in middle and senior high schools. *Journal of Educational Research, 84*(1), 44–52.

Evans, E. M. (2001). Cognitive and contextual factors in the emergence of diverse belief systems: Creation versus evolution. *Cognitive Psychology, 42,* 217–266.

Evertson, C. M., & Emmer, E. T. (1982). Effective management at the beginning of the year in junior high classes. *Journal of Educational Psychology, 74,* 485–498.

Evertson, C. M., Emmer, E. T., & Worsham, M. E. (2000). *Classroom management for elementary teachers* (5th ed.). Boston: Allyn & Bacon.

Evertson, C. M., & Harris, A. H. (1992). What we know about managing classrooms. *Educational Leadership, 49*(7), 74–78.

Evertson, C. M., & Weinstein, C. S. (Eds.). (2006). *Handbook of classroom management: Research, practice, and contemporary issues.* Mahwah, NJ: Erlbaum.

Eysenck, M. W. (1992). *Anxiety: The cognitive perspective.* Hove, England: Erlbaum.

Fabos, B., & Young, M. D. (1999). Telecommunication in the classroom: Rhetoric versus reality. *Review of Educational Research, 69,* 217–259.

Facione, P. A., Facione, N. C., & Giancarlo, C. A. (2000). The disposition toward critical thinking: Its character, measurement, and relationship to critical thinking skill. *Informal Logic, 20,* 61–84.

Fahrmeier, E. D. (1978). The development of concrete operations among the Hausa. *Journal of Cross-Cultural Psychology, 9,* 23–44.

Fairchild, H. H., & Edwards-Evans, S. (1990). African American dialects and schooling: A review. In A. M. Padilla, H. H. Fairchild, & C. M. Valadez (Eds.), *Bilingual education: Issues and strategies.* Newbury Park, CA: Sage.

Fall, R., Webb, N. M., & Chudowsky, N. (2000). Group discussion and large-scale language arts assessment: Effects on students' comprehension. *American Educational Research Journal, 37,* 911–941.

Fantuzzo, J. W., King, J., & Heller, L. R. (1992). Effects of reciprocal peer tutoring on mathematics and school adjustment: A component analysis. *Journal of Educational Psychology, 84,* 331–339.

Farber, B., Mindel, C. H., & Lazerwitz, B. (1988). The Jewish American family. In C. H. Mindel, R. W. Habenstein, & R. Wright (Eds.), *Ethnic families in America: Patterns and variations.* New York: Elsevier.

Farmer, T. W., Leung, M.-C., Pearl, R., Rodkin, P. C., Cadwallader, T. W., & Van Acker, R. (2002). Deviant or diverse peer groups? The peer affiliations of aggressive elementary students. *Journal of Educational Psychology, 94,* 611–620.

Farrell, E. (1990). *Hanging in and dropping out: Voices of at-risk high school students.* New York: Teachers College Press.

Farver, J. A. M., & Branstetter, W. H. (1994). Preschoolers' prosocial responses to their peers' distress. *Developmental Psychology, 30,* 334–341.

Farwell, L., & Weiner, B. (1996). Self-perception of fairness in individual and group contexts. *Personality and Social Psychology Bulletin, 22,* 867–881.

Feather, N. T. (1982). *Expectations and actions: Expectancy-value models in psychology.* Mahwah, NJ: Erlbaum.

Feld, S., Ruhland, D., & Gold, M. (1979). Developmental changes in achievement motivation. *Merrill-Palmer Quarterly, 25,* 43–60.

Feldhusen, J. F. (1989). Synthesis of research on gifted youth. *Educational Leadership, 26*(1), 6–11.

Feldhusen, J. F., & Treffinger, D. J. (1980). *Creative thinking and problem solving in gifted education.* Dubuque, IA: Kendall/Hunt.

Feldhusen, J. F., Treffinger, D. J., & Bahlke, S. J. (1970). Developing creative thinking: The Purdue Creativity Program. *Journal of Creative Behavior, 4,* 85–90.

Feldhusen, J. F., Van Winkle, L., & Ehle, D. A. (1996). Is it acceleration or simply appropriate instruction for precocious youth? *Teaching Exceptional Children, 28*(3), 48–51.

Feldman, A. F., & Matjasko, J. L. (2005). The role of school-based extracurricular activities in adolescent development: A comprehensive review and future directions. *Review of Educational Research, 75,* 159–210.

Feltz, D. L., Chase, M. A., Moritz, S. E., & Sullivan, P. J. (1999). A conceptual model of coaching efficacy: Preliminary investigation and instrument development. *Journal of Educational Psychology, 91,* 765–776.

Fennema, E. (1987). Sex-related differences in education: Myths, realities, and interventions. In V. Richardson-Koehler (Ed.), *Educators' handbook: A research perspective.* White Plains, NY: Longman.

Fenning, P. A., & Bohanon, H. (2006). Schoolwide discipline policies: An analysis of discipline codes of conduct. In C. M. Evertson & C. S. Weinstein (Eds.), *Handbook of classroom management: Research, practice, and contemporary issues* (pp. 1021–1039). Mahwah, NJ: Erlbaum.

Ferguson, E. L., & Hegarty, M. (1995). Learning with real machines or diagrams: Application of knowledge to real-world problems. *Cognition and Instruction, 13,* 129–160.

Ferguson, R. (1998). Can schools narrow the Black-White test score gap? In C. Jencks & M. Phillips (Eds.), *The Black-White test score gap* (pp. 318–374). Washington, DC: Brookings Institute.

Ferrari, M., & Elik, N. (2003). Influences on intentional conceptual change. In G. M. Sinatra & P. R. Pintrich (Eds.), *Intentional conceptual change* (pp. 21–54). Mahwah, NJ: Erlbaum.

Feuerstein, R. (1990). The theory of structural cognitive modifiability. In B. Z. Presseisen (Ed.), *Learning and thinking styles: Classroom interaction.* Washington, DC: National Education Association.

Feuerstein, R., Feuerstein, R., & Gross, S. (1997). The Learning Potential Assessment Device. In D. P. Flanagan, J. L. Genshaft, & P. L. Harrison (Eds.), *Contemporary intellectual assessment: Theories, tests, and issues* (pp. 297–313). New York: Guilford Press.

Feuerstein, R., Klein, P. R., & Tannenbaum, A. (Eds.). (1991). *Mediated learning experience: Theoretical, psychosocial, and learning implications.* London: Freund.

Fiedler, E. D., Lange, R. E., & Winebrenner, S. (1993). In search of reality: Unraveling the myths about tracking, ability grouping and the gifted. *Roeper Review, 16*(1), 4–7.

Field, D. (1987). A review of preschool conservation training: An analysis of analyses. *Developmental Review, 7,* 210–251.

Finders, M., & Lewis, C. (1994). Why some parents don't come to school. *Educational Leadership, 51*(8), 50–54.

Fingerhut, L. A., & Christoffel, K. K. (2002). Firearm-related death and injury among children and adolescents. *The Future of Children, 12*(2), 25–37.

Finke, R. A., & Bettle, J. (1996). *Chaotic cognition: Principles and applications.* Mahwah, NJ: Erlbaum.

Finkelhor, D., & Ormrod, R. (2000, December). *Juvenile victims of property crimes.* Washington, DC: U.S. Department of Justice, Office of Justice Programs, Office of Juvenile Justice and Delinquency Prevention.

Finn, J. D. (1989). Withdrawing from school. *Review of Educational Research, 59,* 117–142.

Finn, J. D. (1991). How to make the dropout problem go away. *Educational Researcher, 20*(1), 28–30.

Finn, J. D., Pannozzo, G. M., & Achilles, C. M. (2003). The "why's" of class size: Student behavior in small classes. *Review of Educational Research, 73,* 321–368.

Firestone, W. A., & Mayrowetz, D. (2000). Rethinking "high stakes": Lessons from the United States and England and Wales. *Teachers College Record, 102,* 724–749.

Fischer, K. W., & Daley, S. G. (2007). Connecting cognitive science and neuroscience to education: Potentials and pitfalls in inferring executive processes. In L. Meltzer (Ed.), *Executive function in education: From theory to practice* (pp. 55–72). New York: Guilford Press.

Fischer, K. W., & Immordino-Yang, M. H. (2006). Cognitive development and education: From dynamic general structure to specific learning and teaching. In W. Damon & R. M. Lerner (Series Eds.), D. Kuhn & R. Siegler (Vol. Eds.), *Handbook of child psychology: Vol. 1. Cognition, perception, and language* (6th ed.). New York: Wiley.

Fischer, K. W., Knight, C. C., & Van Parys, M. (1993). Analyzing diversity in developmental pathways: Methods and concepts. In R. Case & W. Edelstein (Eds.), *The new structuralism in cognitive development: Theory and research on individual pathways.* Basel, Switzerland: Karger.

Fisher, W. W., & Mazur, J. E. (1997). Basic and applied research on choice responding. *Journal of Applied Behavior Analysis, 30,* 387–410.

Fiske, A. P., & Fiske, S. T. (2007). Social relationships in our species and cultures. In S. Kitayama & D. Cohen (Eds.), *Handbook of cultural psychology* (pp. 283–306). New York: Guilford Press.

Fivush, R., Haden, C., & Adam, S. (1995). Structure and coherence of preschoolers' personal narratives over time: Implications for childhood amnesia. *Journal of Experimental Child Psychology, 60,* 32–56.

Flanagan, C. A., & Faison, N. (2001). Youth civic development: Implications of research for social policy and programs. *Social Policy Report of the Society for Research in Child Development, 15*(1), 1–14.

Flanagan, C. A., & Tucker, C. J. (1999). Adolescents' explanations for political issues: Concordance with their views of self and society. *Developmental Psychology, 35,* 1198–1209.

Flavell, J. H. (1963). *The developmental psychology of Jean Piaget.* New York: Van Nostrand Reinhold.

Flavell, J. H. (1994). Cognitive development: Past, present, and future. In R. D. Parke, P. A. Ornstein, J. J. Rieser, & C. Zahn-Waxler (Eds.), *A century of developmental psychology.* Washington, DC: American Psychological Association.

Flavell, J. H. (2000). Development of children's knowledge about the mental world. *International Journal of Behavioral Development, 24*(1), 15–23.

Flavell, J. H., Friedrichs, A. G., & Hoyt, J. D. (1970). Developmental changes in memorization processes. *Cognitive Psychology, 1,* 324–340.

Flavell, J. H., Green, F. L., & Flavell, E. R. (1995). Young children's knowledge about thinking. *Monographs of the Society for Research in Child Development, 60*(1, Serial No. 243).

Flavell, J. H., & Miller, P. H. (1998). Social cognition. In W. Damon (Series Ed.), D. Kuhn & R. S. Siegler (Vol. Eds.), *Handbook of child psychology: Vol. 2. Cognition, perception, and language* (5th ed.). New York: Wiley.

Flavell, J. H., Miller, P. H., & Miller, S. A. (2002). *Cognitive development* (4th ed.). Upper Saddle River, NJ: Prentice Hall.

Fleege, P. O., Charlesworth, R., & Burts, D. C. (1992). Stress begins in kindergarten: A look at behavior during standardized testing. *Journal of Research in Childhood Education, 7*(1), 20–26.

Fletcher, J. M., Lyon, G. R., Fuchs, L. S., & Barnes, M. A. (2007). *Learning disabilities: From identification to intervention.* New York: Guilford Press.

Fletcher, K. L., & Bray, N. W. (1995). External and verbal strategies in children with and without mild mental retardation. *American Journal on Mental Retardation, 99,* 363–475.

Flieller, A. (1999). Comparison of the development of formal thought in adolescent cohorts aged 10 to 15 years (1967–1996 and 1972–1993). *Developmental Psychology, 35,* 1048–1058.

Flood, W. A., Wilder, D. A., Flood, A. L., & Masuda, A. (2002). Peer-mediated reinforcement plus prompting as treatment for off-task behavior in children with attention deficit hyperactivity disorder. *Journal of Applied Behavior Analysis, 35,* 199–204.

Flum, H., & Kaplan, A. (2006). Exploratory orientation as an educational goal. *Educational Psychologist, 41,* 99–110.

Flynn, J. R. (1987). Massive IQ gains in 14 nations: What IQ tests really measure. *Psychological Bulletin, 101,* 171–191.

Flynn, J. R. (2003). Movies about intelligence: The limitations of *g. Current Directions in Psychological Science, 12,* 95–99.

Foos, P. W., & Fisher, R. P. (1988). Using tests as learning opportunities. *Journal of Educational Psychology, 80,* 179–183.

Ford, D. Y. (1996). *Reversing underachievement among gifted black students.* New York: Teachers College Press.

Ford, M. E. (1996). Motivational opportunities and obstacles associated with social responsibility and caring behavior in school contexts. In J. Juvonen & K. R. Wentzel (Eds.), *Social motivation: Understanding children's school adjustment* (pp. 126–153). Cambridge, England: Cambridge University Press.

Ford, M. E., & Nichols, C. W. (1991). Using goal assessments to identify motivational patterns and facilitate behavioral regulation and achievement. In M. Maehr & P. R. Pintrich (Eds.), *Advances in motivation and achievement: Vol. 7. Goals and self-regulatory processes.* Greenwich, CT: JAI Press.

Forgas, J. P. (2000). The role of affect in social cognition. In J. Forgas (Ed.), *Feeling and thinking: The role of affect in social cognition* (pp. 1–28). New York: Cambridge University Press.

Försterling, F., & Morgenstern, M. (2002). Accuracy of self-assessment and task performance: Does it pay to know the truth? *Journal of Educational Psychology, 94,* 576–585.

Fosnot, C. T. (1996). Constructivism: A psychological theory of learning. In C. T. Fosnot (Ed.), *Constructivism: Theory, perspectives, and practice.* New York: Teachers College Press.

Fowler, S. A., & Baer, D. M. (1981). "Do I have to be good all day?" The timing of delayed reinforcement as a factor in generalization. *Journal of Applied Behavior Analysis, 14,* 13–24.

Fox, N. A., Henderson, H. A., Rubin, K. H., Calkins, S. D., & Schmidt, L. A. (2001). Continuity and discontinuity of behavioral inhibition and exuberance: Psychophysical and behavioral influences across the first four years of life. *Child Development, 72,* 1–21.

Fox, P. W., & LeCount, J. (1991, April). *When more is less: Faculty misestimation of student learning.* Paper presented at the annual meeting of the American Educational Research Association, Chicago.

Frankenberger, K. D. (2000). Adolescent egocentrism: A comparison among adolescents and adults. *Journal of Adolescence, 23,* 343–354.

Frederiksen, J. R., & Collins, A. (1989). A systems approach to educational testing. *Educational Researcher, 18*(9), 27–32.

Frederiksen, N. (1984a). Implications of cognitive theory for instruction in problem-solving. *Review of Educational Research, 54,* 363–407.

Frederiksen, N. (1984b). The real test bias: Influences of testing on teaching and learning. *American Psychologist, 39,* 193–202.

Fredrickson, B. L. (2001). The role of positive emotions in positive psychology: The broaden-and-build theory of positive emotions. *American Psychologist, 56,* 218–226.

The Freedom Writers (with Gruwell, E.). (1999). *The Freedom Writers diary: How a teacher and 150 teens used writing to change themselves and the world around them.* New York: Broadway Books.

Freeman, K. E., Gutman, L. M., & Midgley, C. (2002). Can achievement goal theory enhance our understanding of the motivation and performance of African American young adolescents? In C. Midgley (Ed.), *Goals, goal structures, and patterns of adaptive learning* (pp. 175–204). Mahwah, NJ: Erlbaum.

French, D. C., Jansen, E. A., & Pidada, S. (2002). United States and Indonesian children's and adolescents' reports of relational aggression by disliked peers. *Child Development, 73,* 1143–1150.

Frisbie, D. A., & Waltman, K. K. (1992). Developing a personal grading plan. *Educational Measurement: Issues and Practice, 11*(3), 35–42. Reprinted in K. M. Cauley, F. Linder, & J. H. McMillan (Eds.), 1994, *Educational psychology 94/95.* Guilford, CT: Dushkin.

Frost, J. L., Shin, D., & Jacobs, P. J. (1998). Physical environments and children's play. In O. N. Saracho & B. Spodek (Eds.), *Multiple perspectives on play in early childhood education.* Albany: State University of New York Press.

Fry, A. F., & Hale, S. (1996). Processing speed, working memory, and fluid intelligence. *Psychological Science, 7,* 237–241.

Fuchs, D., Fuchs, L. S., Mathes, P. G., & Simmons, D. C. (1997). Peer-assisted learning strategies: Making classrooms more responsive to diversity. *American Educational Research Journal, 34,* 174–206.

Fuchs, L. S., Compton, D. L., Fuchs, D., Paulsen, K., Bryant, J. D., & Hamlett, C. L. (2005). The prevention, identification, and cognitive determinants of math difficulty. *Journal of Educational Psychology, 97,* 493–513.

Fuchs, L. S., Fuchs, D., Karns, K., Hamlett, C. L., Dutka, S., & Katzaroff, M. (1996). The relation between student ability and the quality and effectiveness of explanations. *American Educational Research Journal, 33,* 631–664.

Fuchs, L. S., Fuchs, D., Karns, K., Hamlett, C. L., Katzaroff, M., & Dutka, S. (1997). Effects of task-focused goals on low-achieving students with and without learning disabilities. *American Educational Research Journal, 34,* 513–543.

Fueyo, V., & Bushell, D., Jr. (1998). Using number line procedures and peer tutoring to improve the mathematics computation of low-performing first graders. *Journal of Applied Behavior Analysis, 31,* 417–430.

Fujimura, N. (2001). Facilitating children's proportional reasoning: A model of reasoning processes and effects of intervention on strategy change. *Journal of Educational Psychology, 93,* 589–603.

Fuligni, A. J. (1998). The adjustment of children from immigrant families. *Current Directions in Psychological Science, 7,* 99–103.

Fuligni, A. J., & Hardway, C. (2004). Preparing diverse adolescents for the transition to adulthood. *The Future of Children, 14*(2), 99–119.

Fuller, B., Wright, J., Gesicki, K., & Kang, E. (2007). Gauging growth: How to judge No Child Left Behind. *Educational Researcher, 36*(5), 268–278.

Fuller, M. L. (2001). Multicultural concerns and classroom management. In C. A. Grant & M. L. Gomez, *Campus and classroom: Making schooling multicultural* (2nd ed., pp. 109–134). Upper Saddle River, NJ: Merrill/Prentice Hall.

Furman, W., Brown, B. B., & Feiring, C. (Eds.). (1999). *The development of romantic relationships in adolescence.* Cambridge, England: Cambridge University Press.

Furman, W., & Buhrmester, D. (1992). Age and sex differences in perceptions of networks and personal relationships. *Child Development, 63,* 103–115.

Furman, W., & Simon, V. A. (1999). Cognitive representations of adolescent romantic relationships. In W. Furman, B. B. Brown, & C. Feiring (Eds.), *The development of romantic relationships in adolescence* (pp. 75–98). Cambridge, England: Cambridge University Press.

Furrer, C., & Skinner, E. (2003). Sense of relatedness as a factor in children's academic engagement and performance. *Journal of Educational Psychology, 95,* 148–162.

Gabriele, A. J. (2007). The influence of achievement goals on the constructive activity of low achievers during collaborative problem solving. *British Journal of Educational Psychology, 77,* 121–141.

Gabriele, A. J., & Boody, R. M. (2001, April). *The influence of achievement goals on the constructive activity of low achievers during collaborative problem solving.* Paper presented at the annual meeting of the American Educational Research Association, Seattle, WA.

Gabriele, A. J., & Montecinos, C. (2001). Collaborating with a skilled peer: The influence of achievement goals and perceptions of partner's competence on the participation and learning of low-achieving students. *Journal of Experimental Education, 69,* 152–178.

Gage, N. L. (1991). The obviousness of social and educational research results. *Educational Researcher, 20*(1), 10–16.

Gagné, E. D. (1985). *The cognitive psychology of school learning.* Boston: Little, Brown.

Gagné, R. M. (1985). *The conditions of learning and theory of instruction* (4th ed.). New York: Holt, Rinehart & Winston.

Gaines, M. L., & Davis, M. (1990, April). *Accuracy of teacher prediction of elementary student achievement.* Paper presented at the annual meeting of the American Educational Research Association, Boston.

Galambos, N. L., Barker, E. T., & Almeida, D. M. (2003). Parents *do* matter: Trajectories of change in externalizing and internalizing problems in early adolescence. *Child Development, 74,* 578–594.

Gallagher, J. J. (1991). Personal patterns of underachievement. *Journal for the Education of the Gifted, 14,* 221–233.

Gallimore, R., & Goldenberg, C. (2001). Analyzing cultural models and settings to connect minority achievement and school improvement research. *Educational Psychologist, 36,* 45–56.

Gallimore, R., & Tharp, R. (1990). Teaching mind in society: Teaching, schooling, and literate discourse. In L. C. Moll (Ed.), *Vygotsky and education: Instructional implications and applications of sociohistorical psychology.* Cambridge, England: Cambridge University Press.

Garbarino, J., Bradshaw, C. P., & Vorrasi, J. A. (2002). Mitigating the effects of gun violence on children and youth. *The Future of Children, 12*(2), 73–85.

Garbe, G., & Guy, D. (2006, Summer). No homework left behind. *Educational Leadership* (online issue). Retrieved May 23, 2007, from the Association for Supervision and Curriculum Development Web site: http://www.ascd.org/portal/site/ascd/menuitem.459dee008f99653fb85516f762108a0c

Garcia, E. E. (1992). "Hispanic" children: Theoretical, empirical, and related policy issues. *Educational Psychology Review, 4,* 69–93.

Garcia, E. E. (1994). *Understanding and meeting the challenge of student cultural diversity.* Boston: Houghton Mifflin.

García, E. E. (1995). Educating Mexican American students: Past treatment and recent developments in theory, research, policy, and practice. In J. A. Banks & C. A. M. Banks (Eds.), *Handbook of research on multicultural education.* New York: Macmillan.

Garcia, E. E. (2005, April). *Any test in English is a test of English: Implications for high stakes testing.* Paper presented at the annual meeting of the American Educational Research Association, Montreal.

Gardner, H. (1983). *Frames of mind: The theory of multiple intelligences.* New York: Basic Books.

Gardner, H. (1995). Reflections on multiple intelligences: Myths and messages. *Phi Delta Kappan, 77,* 200–209.

Gardner, H. (1998, April). *Where to draw the line: The perils of new paradigms.* Paper presented at the annual meeting of the American Educational Research Association, San Diego, CA.

Gardner, H. (1999). *Intelligence reframed: Multiple intelligences for the 21st century.* New York: Basic Books.

Gardner, H. (2000a). A case against spiritual intelligence. *International Journal for the Psychology of Religion, 10*(1), 27–34.

Gardner, H. (2000b). *The disciplined mind: Beyond facts and standardized tests, the K–12 education that every child deserves.* New York: Penguin Books.

Gardner, H. (2003, April). *Multiple intelligences after twenty years.* Paper presented at the annual meeting of the American Educational Research Association, Chicago.

Garibaldi, A. M. (1993). Creating prescriptions for success in urban schools: Turning the corner on pathological explanations for academic failure. In T. M. Tomlinson (Ed.), *Motivating students to learn: Overcoming barriers to high achievement.* Berkeley, CA: McCutchan.

Garner, R., Alexander, P. A., Gillingham, M. G., Kulikowich, J. M., & Brown, R. (1991). Interest and learning from text. *American Educational Research Journal, 28,* 643–659.

Garner, R., Brown, R., Sanders, S., & Menke, D. J. (1992). "Seductive details" and learning from text. In K. A. Renninger, S. Hidi, & A. Krapp (Eds.), *The role of interest in learning and development.* Mahwah, NJ: Erlbaum.

Garnier, H. E., Stein, J. A., & Jacobs, J. K. (1997). The process of dropping out of high school: A 19-year perspective. *American Educational Research Journal, 34,* 395–419.

Garrison, L. (1989). Programming for the gifted American Indian student. In C. J. Maker & S. W. Schiever (Eds.), *Critical issues in gifted education: Vol. 2. Defensible programs for cultural and ethnic minorities.* Austin, TX: Pro-Ed.

Gaskill, P. J. (2001, April). *Differential effects of reinforcement feedback and attributional feedback on second-graders' self-efficacy.* Paper presented at the annual meeting of the American Educational Research Association, Seattle, WA.

Gaskins, I. W., & Pressley, M. (2007). Teaching metacognitive strategies that address executive function processes within a schoolwide curriculum. In L. Meltzer (Ed.), *Executive function in education: From theory to practice* (pp. 261–286). New York: Guilford Press.

Gaskins, I. W., Satlow, E., & Pressley, M. (2007). Executive control of reading comprehension in the elementary school. In L. Meltzer (Ed.), *Executive function in education: From theory to practice* (pp. 194–215). New York: Guilford Press.

Gathercole, S. E., & Hitch, G. J. (1993). Developmental changes in short-term memory: A revised working memory perspective. In A. F. Collins, S. E. Gathercole, M. A. Conway, & P. E. Morris (Eds.), *Theories of memory.* Hove, England: Erlbaum.

Gaudry, E., & Bradshaw, G. D. (1971). The differential effect of anxiety on performance in progressive and terminal school examinations. In E. Gaudry & C. D. Spielberger (Eds.), *Anxiety and educational achievement.* Sydney, Australia: Wiley.

Gauvain, M. (2001). *The social context of cognitive development.* New York: Guilford Press.

Gavin, L. A., & Fuhrman, W. (1989). Age differences in adolescents' perceptions of their peer groups. *Developmental Psychology, 25,* 827–834.

Gay, G. (2006). Connections between classroom management and culturally responsive teaching. In C. M. Evertson & C. S. Weinstein (Eds.), *Handbook of classroom management: Research, practice, and contemporary issues* (pp. 343–370). Mahwah, NJ: Erlbaum.

Gayford, C. (1992). Patterns of group behavior in open-ended problem solving in science classes of 15-year-old students in England. *International Journal of Science Education, 14,* 41–49.

Gaynor, J., & Millham, J. (1976). Student performance and evaluation under variant teaching and testing methods in a large college course. *Journal of Educational Psychology, 68,* 312–317.

Gazelle, H., & Ladd, G. W. (2003). Anxious solitude and peer exclusion: A diathesis-stress model of internalizing trajectories in childhood. *Child Development, 74,* 257–278.

Geary, D. C. (1998). What is the function of mind and brain? *Educational Psychology Review, 10,* 377–387.

Geary, D. C. (2005). Folk knowledge and academic learning. In B. J. Ellis & D. F. Bjorklund (Eds.), *Origins of the social mind: Evolutionary psychology and child development* (pp. 493–519). New York: Guilford Press.

Gelman, S. A. (2003). *The essential child: Origins of essentialism in everyday thought.* New York: Oxford University Press.

Gelman, S. A., & Kalish, C. W. (2006). Conceptual development. In W. Damon & R. M. Lerner (Series Eds.), D. Kuhn & R. Siegler (Vol. Eds.), *Handbook of child psychology: Vol. 1. Cognition, perception, and language* (6th ed.). New York: Wiley.

Genova, W. J., & Walberg, H. J. (1984). Enhancing integration in urban high schools. In D. E. Bartz & M. L. Maehr (Eds.), *Advances in motivation and achievement: Vol. 1. The effects of school desegregation on motivation and achievement.* Greenwich, CT: JAI Press.

Gentry, M., Gable, R. K., & Rizza, M. G. (2002). Students' perceptions of classroom activities: Are there grade-level and gender differences? *Journal of Educational Psychology, 94,* 539–544.

Gerard, J. M., & Buehler, C. (2004). Cumulative environmental risk and youth maladjustment: The role of youth attributes. *Child Development, 75,* 1832–1849.

Gerst, M. S. (1971). Symbolic coding processes in observational learning. *Journal of Personality and Social Psychology, 19,* 7–17.

Gettinger, M. (1988). Methods of proactive classroom management. *School Psychology Review, 17,* 227–242.

Gettinger, M., & Kohler, K. M. (2006). Process-outcome approaches to classroom management and effective teaching. In C. M. Evertson & C. S. Weinstein (Eds.), *Handbook of classroom management: Research, practice, and contemporary issues* (pp. 73–95). Mahwah, NJ: Erlbaum.

Giaconia, R. M. (1988). Teacher questioning and wait-time (Doctoral dissertation, Stanford University, 1988). *Dissertation Abstracts International, 49*, 462A.

Gibbs, J. C. (1995). The cognitive developmental perspective. In W. M. Kurtines & J. L. Gewirtz (Eds.), *Moral development: An introduction.* Boston: Allyn & Bacon.

Gick, M. L., & Holyoak, K. J. (1987). The cognitive basis of knowledge transfer. In S. M. Cormier & J. D. Hagman (Eds.), *Transfer of learning: Contemporary research and applications.* San Diego, CA: Academic Press.

Giedd, J. N., Blumenthal, J., Jeffries, N. O., Castellanos, F. X., Liu, H., Zijdenbos, A., et al. (1999). Brain development during childhood and adolescence: A longitudinal MRI study. *Nature Neuroscience, 2*, 861–863.

Gillies, R. M., & Ashman, A. D. (1998). Behavior and interactions of children in cooperative groups in lower and middle elementary grades. *Journal of Educational Psychology, 90*, 746–757.

Gilligan, C. F. (1982). *In a different voice.* Cambridge, MA: Harvard University Press.

Gilligan, C. F. (1987). Moral orientation and moral development. In E. F. Kittay & D. T. Meyers (Eds.), *Women and moral theory.* Totowa, NJ: Rowman & Littlefield.

Gilliland, H. (1988). Discovering and emphasizing the positive aspects of the culture. In H. Gilliland & J. Reyhner (Eds.), *Teaching the Native American.* Dubuque, IA: Kendall/Hunt.

Ginsberg, D., Gottman, J. M., & Parker, J. G. (1986). The importance of friendship. In J. M. Gottman & J. G. Parker (Eds.), *Conversations of friends: Speculations on affective development* (pp. 3–48). Cambridge, England: Cambridge University Press.

Ginsburg-Block, M. D., Rohrbeck, C. A., & Fantuzzo, J. W. (2006). A meta-analytic review of social, self-concept, and behavioral outcomes of peer-assisted learning. *Journal of Educational Psychology, 98*, 732–749.

Girotto, V., & Light, P. (1993). The pragmatic bases of children's reasoning. In P. Light & G. Butterworth (Eds.), *Context and cognition: Ways of learning and knowing.* Mahwah, NJ: Erlbaum.

Glaser, D. (2000). Child abuse and neglect and the brain: A review. *Journal of Child Psychology and Psychiatry and Allied Disciplines, 41*, 97–116.

Glover, J. A. (1989). The "testing" phenomenon: Not gone but nearly forgotten. *Journal of Educational Psychology, 81*, 392–399.

Glover, J. A., Ronning, R. R., & Reynolds, C. R. (Eds.). (1989). *Handbook of creativity.* New York: Plenum Press.

Gnepp, J. (1989). Children's use of personal information to understand other people's feelings. In C. Saarni & P. L. Harris (Eds.), *Children's understanding of emotion.* Cambridge, England: Cambridge University Press.

Goddard, R. D., Hoy, W. K., & Woolfolk Hoy, A. (2000). Collective teacher efficacy: Its meaning, measure, and impact on student achievement. *American Educational Research Journal, 37*, 479–507.

Goldenberg, C. (1992). The limits of expectations: A case for case knowledge about teacher expectancy effects. *American Educational Research Journal, 29*, 517–544.

Goldenberg, C. (2001). Making schools work for low-income families in the 21st century. In S. B. Neuman & D. K. Dickinson (Eds.), *Handbook of early literacy research* (pp. 211–231). New York: Guilford Press.

Goldenberg, C., Gallimore, R., Reese, L., & Garnier, H. (2001). Cause or effect? A longitudinal study of immigrant Latino parents' aspirations and expectations, and their children's school performance. *American Educational Research Journal, 38*, 547–582.

Goldstein, L. S., & Lake, V. E. (2000). "Love, love, and more love for children": Exploring preservice teachers' understanding of caring. *Teaching and Teacher Education, 16*, 861–872.

Goldstein, N. E., Arnold, D. H., Rosenberg, J. L., Stowe, R. M., & Ortiz, C. (2001). Contagion of aggression in day care classrooms as a function of peer and teacher responses. *Journal of Educational Psychology, 93*, 708–719.

Goldstein, S., & Brooks, R. B. (Eds.). (2006). *Handbook of resilience in children.* New York: Springer.

Gollnick, D. M., & Chinn, P. C. (2002). *Multicultural education in a pluralistic society* (6th ed.). Upper Saddle River, NJ: Merrill/Prentice Hall.

Gonsalves, L., Murawska, M., Blake, F., & Pope, A. W. (2007, March). *Roles of overt aggression and social preference in determining children's social goals in peer conflict situations.* Paper presented at the biennial meeting of the Society for Research in Child Development, Boston.

Gonzalez, A.-L., & Wolters, C. A. (2005, April). *The relations between perceived parenting practices and adolescent motivation.* Paper presented at the annual meeting of the American Educational Research Association, Montreal.

Good, T. L., & Brophy, J. E. (1994). *Looking in classrooms* (6th ed.). New York: HarperCollins.

Good, T. L., McCaslin, M. M., & Reys, B. J. (1992). Investigating work groups to promote problem solving in mathematics. In J. Brophy (Ed.), *Advances in research on teaching: Vol. 3. Planning and managing learning tasks and activities.* Greenwich, CT: JAI Press.

Good, T. L., & Nichols, S. L. (2001). Expectancy effects in the classroom: A special focus on improving the reading performance of minority students in first-grade classrooms. *Educational Psychologist, 36*, 113–126.

Goodenow, C. (1993). Classroom belonging among early adolescent students: Relationships to motivation and achievement. *Journal of Early Adolescence, 13*, 21–43.

Goodman, C. S., & Tessier-Lavigne, M. (1997). Molecular mechanisms of axon guidance and target recognition. In W. M. Cowan, T. M. Jessell, & S. L. Zipursky (Eds.), *Molecular and cellular approaches to neural development* (pp. 108–137). New York: Oxford University Press.

Goodwin, M. H. (2006). *The hidden life of girls: Games of stance, status, and exclusion.* Malden, MA: Blackwell.

Gootman, M. E. (1998). Effective in-house suspension. *Educational Leadership, 56*(1), 39–41.

Gopnik, A., & Meltzoff, A. N. (1997). *Words, thoughts, and theories.* Cambridge, MA: MIT Press.

Gottfredson, D. C. (2001). *Schools and delinquency.* Cambridge, England: Cambridge University Press.

Gottfredson, L. S. (1981). Circumscription and compromise: A developmental theory of occupational aspirations. *Journal of Counseling Psychology Monograph, 28*, 545–579.

Gottfried, A. E. (1990). Academic intrinsic motivation in young elementary school children. *Journal of Educational Psychology, 82*, 525–538.

Gottfried, A. E., Fleming, J. S., & Gottfried, A. W. (1994). Role of parental motivational practices in children's academic intrinsic motivation and achievement. *Journal of Educational Psychology, 86*, 104–113.

Gottlieb, G. (2000). Environmental and behavioral influences on gene activity. *Current Directions in Psychological Science, 9*, 93–97.

Gottman, J. M. (1983). How children become friends. *Monographs of the Society for Research in Child Development, 48*(3, Serial No. 201).

Gottman, J. M. (1986). The world of coordinated play: Same- and cross-sex friendship in young children. In J. M. Gottman & J. G. Parker (Eds.), *Conversations of friends: Speculations on affective development* (pp. 139–191). Cambridge, England: Cambridge University Press.

Gottman, J. M., & Mettetal, G. (1986). Speculations about social and affective development: Friendship and acquaintanceship through adolescence. In J. M. Gottman & J. G. Parker (Eds.), *Conversations of friends: Speculations on affective development* (pp. 192–237). Cambridge, England: Cambridge University Press.

Gould, E., Beylin, A., Tanapat, P., Reeves, A., & Shors, T. J. (1999). Learning enhances adult neurogenesis in the hippocampal formation. *Nature Neuroscience, 2*, 260–265.

Graesser, A. C., McNamara, D. S., & VanLehn, K. (2005). Scaffolding deep comprehension strategies through Point&Query, AutoTutor, and iSTART. *Educational Psychologist, 40*, 225–234.

Graesser, A., & Person, N. K. (1994). Question asking during tutoring. *American Educational Research Journal, 31*, 104–137.

Graham, S. (1989). Motivation in Afro-Americans. In G. L. Berry & J. K. Asamen (Eds.), *Black students: Psychosocial issues and academic achievement.* Newbury Park, CA: Sage.

Graham, S. (1990). Communicating low ability in the classroom: Bad things good teachers sometimes do. In S. Graham & V. S. Folkes (Eds.), *Attribution theory: Applications to achievement, mental health, and interpersonal conflict.* Mahwah, NJ: Erlbaum.

Graham, S. (1997). Using attribution theory to understand social and academic motivation in African American youth. *Educational Psychologist, 32*, 21–34.

Graham, S. (2006). Peer victimization in school: Exploring the ethnic context. *Current Directions in Psychological Science, 15*, 317–321.

Graham, S., & Golen, S. (1991). Motivational influences on cognition: Task involvement, ego involvement, and depth of information processing. *Journal of Educational Psychology, 83*, 187–194.

Graham, S., & Harris, K. R. (1996). Addressing problems in attention, memory, and executive functioning. In G. R. Lyon & N. A. Krasnegor (Eds.), *Attention, memory, and executive function* (pp. 349–365). Baltimore: Brookes.

Graham, S., Harris, K. R., & Fink, B. (2000). Is handwriting causally related to learning to write? Treatment of handwriting problems in beginning writers. *Journal of Educational Psychology, 92*, 620–633.

Graham, S., & Weiner, B. (1996). Theories and principles of motivation. In D. C. Berliner & R. C. Calfee (Eds.), *Handbook of educational psychology.* New York: Macmillan.

Grant, C. A., & Gomez, M. L. (2001). *Campus and classroom: Making schooling multicultural* (2nd ed.). Upper Saddle River, NJ: Merrill/Prentice Hall.

Grant, H., & Dweck, C. (2001). Cross-cultural response to failure: Considering outcome attributions with different goals. In F. Salili & C. Chiu (Eds.), *Student motivation: The culture and context of learning* (pp. 203–219). Dordrecht, The Netherlands: Kluwer Academic.

Gray, M. R., & Steinberg, L. (1999). Unpacking authoritative parenting: Reassessing a multidimensional concept. *Journal of Marriage and the Family, 61*, 574–587.

Gray, W. D., & Orasanu, J. M. (1987). Transfer of cognitive skills. In S. M. Cormier & J. D. Hagman (Eds.), *Transfer of learning: Contemporary research and applications.* San Diego, CA: Academic Press.

Green, L., Fry, A. F., & Myerson, J. (1994). Discounting of delayed rewards: A life-span comparison. *Psychological Science, 5*, 33–36.

Greenberg, M. T., Weissberg, R. P., O'Brien, M. U., Zins, J. E., Fredericks, L., Resnik, H., et al. (2003). Enhancing school-based prevention and youth development through coordinated social, emotional, and academic learning. *American Psychologist, 58*, 466–474.

Greenfield, P. M. (1994). Independence and interdependence as developmental scripts: Implications for theory, research, and practice. In P. M. Greenfield & R. R. Cocking (Eds.), *Cross-cultural roots of minority child development.* Mahwah, NJ: Erlbaum.

Greenfield, P. M., Trumbull, E., Keller, H., Rothstein-Fisch, C., Suzuki, L. K., & Quiroz, B. (2006). Cultural conceptions of learning and development. In P. A. Alexander & P. H. Winne (Eds.), *Handbook of educational psychology* (2nd ed., pp. 675–692). Mahwah, NJ: Erlbaum.

Greenhoot, A. F., Tsethlikai, M., & Wagoner, B. J. (2006). The relations between children's past experiences, social knowledge, and memories for social situations. *Journal of Cognition and Development, 7*, 313–340.

Greeno, J. G., Collins, A. M., & Resnick, L. B. (1996). Cognition and learning. In D. C. Berliner & R. C. Calfee (Eds.), *Handbook of educational psychology.* New York: Macmillan.

Greenough, W. T., Black, J. E., & Wallace, C. S. (1987). Experience and brain development. *Child Development, 58*, 539–559.

Greenwood, C. R. (1991). Classwide peer tutoring: Longitudinal effects on the reading, language, and mathematics achievement of at-risk students. *Journal of Reading, Writing, and Learning Disabilities International, 7*(2), 105–123.

Greenwood, C. R., Carta, J. J., & Hall, R. V. (1988). The use of peer tutoring strategies in classroom management and educational instruction. *School Psychology Review, 17*, 258–275.

Gregg, M., & Leinhardt, G. (1994, April). *Constructing geography.* Paper presented at the annual meeting of the American Educational Research Association, New Orleans, LA.

Gregoire, M. (2003). Is it a challenge or a threat? A dual-process model of teachers' cognition and appraisal processes during conceptual change. *Educational Psychology Review, 15*, 147–179.

Greif, M. L., Kemler Nelson, D. G., Keil, F. C., & Gutierrez, F. (2006). What do children want to know about animals and artifacts? Domain-specific requests for information. *Psychological Science, 17*, 455–459.

Griffin, M. M., & Griffin, B. W. (1994, April). *Some can get there from here: Situated learning, cognitive style, and map skills.* Paper presented at the annual meeting of the American Educational Research Association, New Orleans, LA.

Griffin, S. A., Case, R., & Capodilupo, A. (1995). Teaching for understanding: The importance of the central conceptual structures in the elementary mathematics curriculum. In A. McKeough, J. Lupart, & A. Marini (Eds.), *Teaching for transfer: Fostering generalization in learning.* Mahwah, NJ: Erlbaum.

Grissmer, D. W., Williamson, S., Kirby, S. N., & Berends, M. (1998). Exploring the rapid rise in Black achievement scores in the United States (1970–1990). In U. Neisser (Ed.), *The rising curve: Long-term gains in IQ and related measures* (pp. 251–285). Washington, DC: American Psychological Association.

Grolnick, W. S., & Ryan, R. M. (1987). Autonomy in children's learning: An experimental and individual difference investigation. *Journal of Personality and Social Psychology, 52*, 890–898.

Gronlund, N. E. (1993). *How to make achievement tests and assessments* (5th ed.). Needham Heights, MA: Allyn & Bacon.

Gronlund, N. E. (2000). *How to write and use instructional objectives* (6th ed.). Upper Saddle River, NJ: Merrill/Prentice Hall.

Gronlund, N. E. (2004). *Writing instructional objectives for teaching and assessment* (7th ed.). Upper Saddle River, NJ: Merrill/Prentice Hall.

Gross, E. F., Juvonen, J., & Gable, S. L. (2002). Internet use and well-being in adolescence. *Journal of Social Issues, 58*, 75–90.

Grover, R. (Ed.). (1996). *Collaboration: Lessons learned series.* Chicago: American Library Association.

Guay, F., Boivin, M., & Hodges, E. V. E. (1999). Social comparison processes and academic achievement: The dependence of the development of self-evaluations on friends' performance. *Journal of Educational Psychology, 91*, 564–568.

Guay, F., Marsh, H. W. & Boivin, M. (2003). Academic self-concept and academic achievement: Developmental perspectives on their causal ordering. *Journal of Educational Psychology, 95*, 124–136.

Guerra, N. G., Huesmann, L. R., & Spindler, A. (2003). Community violence exposure, social cognition, and aggression among urban elementary school children. *Child Development, 74*, 1561–1576.

Gunstone, R. F. (1994). The importance of specific science content in the enhancement of metacognition. In P. J. Fensham, R. F. Gunstone, & R. T. White (Eds.), *The content of science: A constructivist approach to its teaching and learning.* London: Falmer Press.

Gunstone, R. F., & White, R. T. (1981). Understanding of gravity. *Science Education, 65*, 291–299.

Guskey, T. R. (1985). *Implementing mastery learning.* Belmont, CA: Wadsworth.

Gustafsson, J., & Undheim, J. O. (1996). Individual differences in cognitive functions. In D. C. Berliner & R. C. Calfee (Eds.), *Handbook of educational psychology.* New York: Macmillan.

Guthrie, J. T., Wigfield, A., Barbosa, P., Perencevich, K. C., Taboada, A., Davis, M. H., Scafiddi, N. T., & Tonks, S. (2004). Increasing reading comprehension and engagement through concept-oriented reading instruction. *Journal of Educational Psychology, 96*, 403–423.

Guthrie, P. (2001). "Catching sense" and the meaning of belonging on a South Carolina Sea island. In S. S. Walker (Ed.), *African roots/American cultures: Africa in the creation of the Americas* (pp. 275–283). Lanham, MD: Rowman & Littlefield.

Gutiérrez, K. D., & Rogoff, B. (2003). Cultural ways of learning: Individual traits or repertoires of practice. *Educational Researcher, 32*(5), 19–25.

Gutman, L. M., & McLoyd, V. C. (2000). Parents' management of their children's education within the home, at school, and in the community: An examination of African-American families living in poverty. *Urban Review, 32*(1), 2000.

Hacker, D. J. (1998). Self-regulated comprehension during normal reading. In D. J. Hacker, J. Dunlosky, & A. C. Graesser (Eds.), *Metacognition in educational theory and practice* (pp. 165–191). Mahwah, NJ: Erlbaum.

Hacker, D. J., Bol, L., Horgan, D. D., & Rakow, E. A. (2000). Test prediction and performance in a classroom context. *Journal of Educational Psychology, 92*, 160–170.

Haden, C. A., Ornstein, P. A., Eckerman, C. O., & Didow, S. M. (2001). Mother-child conversational interactions as events unfold: Linkages to subsequent remembering. *Child Development, 72*, 1016–1031.

Hadjioannou, X. (2007). Bringing the background to the foreground: What do classroom environments that support authentic discussions look like? *American Educational Research Journal, 44*, 370–399.

Hagen, A. S. (1994, April). *Achievement motivation processes and the role of classroom context.* Paper presented at the annual meeting of the American Educational Research Association, New Orleans, LA.

Hagger, M. S., Chatzisarantis, N. L. D., Barkoukis, V., Wang, C. K. J., & Baranowski, J. (2005). Perceived autonomy support in physical education and leisure-time physical activity: A cross-cultural evaluation of the trans-contextual model. *Journal of Educational Psychology, 97*, 376–390.

Hagtvet, K. A., & Johnsen, T. B. (Eds.). (1992). *Advances in test anxiety research* (Vol. 7). Amsterdam: Swets & Zeitlinger.

Haier, R. J. (2001). PET studies of learning and individual differences. In J. L. McClelland & R. S. Siegler (Eds.), *Mechanisms of cognitive development: Behavioral and neural perspectives* (pp. 123–145). Mahwah, NJ: Erlbaum.

Haier, R. J. (2003). Positron emission tomography studies of intelligence: From psychometrics to neurobiology. In H. Nyborg (Ed.), *The scientific study of general intelligence.* New York: Pergamon.

Hale-Benson, J. E. (1986). *Black children: Their roots, culture, and learning styles.* Baltimore: Johns Hopkins University Press.

Halford, G. S. (1989). Cognitive processing capacity and learning ability: An integration of two areas. *Learning and Individual Differences, 1*, 125–153.

Halford, G. S., & Andrews, G. (2006). Reasoning and problem solving. In W. Damon & R. M. Lerner (Series Eds.), D. Kuhn & R. Siegler (Vol. Eds.), *Handbook of child psychology: Vol. 2. Cognition, perception, and language* (6th ed.). New York: Wiley.

Halgunseth, L. C., Ispa, J. M., & Rudy, D. (2006). Parental control in Latino families: An integrated review of the literature. *Child Development, 77*, 1282–1297.

Hall, N. C., Goetz, T., Haynes, T. L., Stupnisky, R. H., & Chipperfield, J. G. (2006, April). *Self-regulation of primary and secondary control: Optimizing control striving in an academic achievement setting.* Paper presented at the annual meeting of the American Educational Research Association, San Francisco, CA.

Hall, R. H., & O'Donnell, A. (1994, April). *Alternative materials for learning: Cognitive and affective outcomes of learning from knowledge maps.* Paper presented at the annual meeting of the American Educational Research Association, New Orleans, LA.

Hall, R. V., Axelrod, S., Foundopoulos, M., Shellman, J., Campbell, R. A., & Cranston, S. S. (1971). The effective use of punishment to modify behavior in the classroom. *Educational Technology, 11*(4), 24–26. Reprinted in K. D. O'Leary & S. O'Leary (Eds.), 1972, *Classroom management: The successful use of behavior modification.* New York: Pergamon.

Haller, E. P., Child, D. A., & Walberg, H. J. (1988). Can comprehension be taught? A quantitative synthesis of "metacognitive" studies. *Educational Researcher, 17*(9), 5–8.

Halpern, D. F. (1997). *Critical thinking across the curriculum: A brief edition of thought and knowledge.* Mahwah, NJ: Erlbaum.

Halpern, D. F. (1998). Teaching critical thinking for transfer across domains. *American Psychologist, 53*, 449–455.

Halpern, D. F. (2006). Assessing gender gaps in learning and academic achievement. In P. A. Alexander & P. H. Winne (Eds.), *Handbook of educational psychology* (2nd ed., pp. 635–653). Mahwah, NJ: Erlbaum.

Halpern, D. F., & LaMay, M. L. (2000). The smarter sex: A critical review of sex differences in intelligence. *Educational Psychology Review, 12*, 229–246.

Halpin, G., & Halpin, G. (1982). Experimental investigations of the effects of study and testing on student learning, retention, and ratings of instruction. *Journal of Educational Psychology, 74*, 32–38.

Halvorsen, A. T., & Sailor, W. (1990). Integration of students with severe and profound disabilities: A review of research. In R. Gaylord-Ross (Ed.), *Issues and research in special education* (Vol. 1, pp. 110–172). New York: Teachers College Press.

Hambleton, R. K. (1996). Advances in assessment models, methods, and practices. In D. C. Berliner & R. C. Calfee (Eds.), *Handbook of educational psychology.* New York: Macmillan.

Hambrick, D. Z., & Engle, R. W. (2003). The role of working memory in problem solving. In J. E. Davidson & R. J. Sternberg (Eds.), *The psychology of problem solving* (pp. 176–206). Cambridge, England: Cambridge University Press.

Hamers, J. H. M., & Ruijssenaars, A. J. J. M. (1997). Assessing classroom learning potential. In G. D. Phye (Ed.), *Handbook of academic learning: Construction of knowledge.* San Diego, CA: Academic Press.

Hammer, D. (1997). Discovery learning and discovery teaching. *Cognition and Instruction, 15*, 485–529.

Hamre, B. K., & Pianta, R. C. (2005). Can instructional and emotional support in the first-grade classroom make a difference for children at risk of school failure? *Child Development, 76*, 949–967.

Hanish, L. D., Kochenderfer-Ladd, B., Fabes, R. A., Martin, C. L., & Denning, D. (2004). Bullying among young children: The influence of peers and teachers. In D. L. Espelage & S. M. Swearer (Eds.), *Bullying in American schools: A social-ecological perspective on prevention and intervention* (pp. 141–159). Mahwah, NJ: Erlbaum.

Hansen, J., & Pearson, P. D. (1983). An instructional study: Improving the inferential comprehension of good and poor fourth-grade readers. *Journal of Educational Psychology, 75*, 821–829.

Hardré, P. L., & Reeve, J. (2003). A motivational model of rural students' intentions to persist in, versus drop out of, high school. *Journal of Educational Psychology, 95*, 347–356.

Hardré, P. L., Crowson, H. M., DeBacker, T. K., & White, D. (2007). Predicting the motivation of rural high school students. *Journal of Experimental Education, 75*, 247–269.

Hardy, I., Jonen, A., Möller, K., & Stern, E. (2006). Effects of instructional support within constructivist learning environments for elementary school students' understanding of "floating and sinking." *Journal of Educational Psychology, 98*, 307–326.

Hareli, S., & Weiner, B. (2002). Social emotions and personality inferences: A scaffold for a new direction in the study of achievement motivation. *Educational Psychologist, 37*, 183–193.

Harlow, H. F., & Zimmerman, R. R. (1959). Affectional responses in the infant monkey. *Science, 130*, 421–432.

Harmon-Jones, E. (2001). The role of affect in cognitive-dissonance processes. In J. P. Forgas (Ed.), *Handbook of affect and social cognition* (pp. 237–255). Mahwah, NJ: Erlbaum.

Harnishfeger, K. K. (1995). The development of cognitive inhibition: Theories, definitions, and research evidence. In F. N. Dempster & C. J. Brainerd (Eds.), *Interference and inhibition in cognition.* San Diego, CA: Academic Press.

Harris, A. C. (1986). *Child development.* St. Paul, MN: West.

Harris, C. R. (1991). Identifying and serving the gifted new immigrant. *Teaching Exceptional Children, 23*(4), 26–30.

Harris, J. R. (1995). Where is the child's environment? A group socialization theory of development. *Psychological Review, 102*, 458–489.

Harris, J. R. (1998). *The nurture assumption: Why children turn out the way they do.* New York: Free Press.

Harris, K. R. (1982). Cognitive-behavior modification: Application with exceptional students. *Focus on Exceptional Children, 15*, 1–16.

Harris, K. R. (1986). Self-monitoring of attentional behavior versus self-monitoring of productivity: Effects of on-task behavior and academic response rate among learning disabled children. *Journal of Applied Behavior Analysis, 19*, 417–423.

Harris, K. R., & Alexander, P. A. (1998). Integrated, constructivist education: Challenge and reality. *Educational Psychology Review, 10*, 115–127.

Harris, M. B. (1997). Preface: Images of the invisible minority. In M. B. Harris (Ed.), *School experiences of gay and lesbian youth: The invisible minority* (pp. xiv–xxii). Binghamton, NY: Harrington Park Press.

Harris, M. J., & Rosenthal, R. (1985). Mediation of interpersonal expectancy effects: 31 meta-analyses. *Psychological Bulletin, 97*, 363–386.

Harris, P. L. (2006). Social cognition. In W. Damon & R. M. Lerner (Series Eds.), D. Kuhn & R. Siegler (Vol. Eds.), *Handbook of child psychology: Vol. 2. Cognition, perception, and language* (6th ed.). New York: Wiley.

Harris, R. J. (1977). Comprehension of pragmatic implications in advertising. *Journal of Applied Psychology, 62*, 603–608.

Hart, C. H., Ladd, G. W., & Burleson, B. (1990). Children's expectations of the outcomes of social strategies: Relations with sociometric status and maternal disciplinary styles. *Child Development, 61*, 127–137.

Hart, D. (1988). The adolescent self-concept in social context. In D. K. Lapsley & F. C. Power (Eds.), *Self, ego, and identity: Integrative approaches* (pp. 71–90). New York: Springer-Verlag.

Hart, D., & Fegley, S. (1995). Prosocial behavior and caring in adolescence: Relations to self-understanding and social judgment. *Child Development, 66*, 1346–1359.

Hart, E. R., & Speece, D. L. (1998). Reciprocal teaching goes to college: Effects for postsecondary students at risk for academic failure. *Journal of Educational Psychology, 90*, 670–681.

Harter, S. (1983). Children's understanding of multiple emotions: A cognitive-developmental approach. In W. F. Overton (Ed.), *The relationship between social and cognitive development.* Mahwah, NJ: Erlbaum.

Harter, S. (1990). Causes, correlates, and the functional role of global self-worth: A life-span perspective. In R. J. Sternberg & J. Kolligian, Jr. (Eds.), *Competence considered.* New Haven, CT: Yale University Press.

Harter, S. (1992). The relationship between perceived competence, affect, and motivational orientation within the classroom: Processes and patterns of change. In A. K. Boggiano & T. S. Pittman (Eds.), *Achievement and motivation: A social-developmental perspective.* Cambridge, England: Cambridge University Press.

Harter, S. (1996). Teacher and classmate influences on scholastic motivation, self-esteem, and level of voice in adolescents. In J. Juvonen & K. Wentzel (Eds.), *Social motivation: Understanding children's school adjustment.* New York: Cambridge University Press.

Harter, S. (1999). *The construction of the self: A developmental perspective.* New York: Guilford Press.

Harter, S., & Whitesell, N. R. (1989). Developmental changes in children's understanding of single, multiple, and blended emotion concepts. In C. Saarni & P. Harris (Eds.), *Children's understanding of emotion* (pp. 81–116). Cambridge, England: Cambridge University Press.

Harter, S., Whitesell, N. R., & Kowalski, P. (1992). Individual differences in the effects of educational transitions on young adolescents' perceptions of competence and motivational orientation. *American Educational Research Journal, 29*, 777–807.

Hartley, J., & Trueman, M. (1982). The effects of summaries on the recall of information from prose: Five experimental studies. *Human Learning, 1*, 63–82.

Hartley, K., & Bendixen, L. D. (2001). Educational research in the Internet age: Examining the role of individual characteristics. *Educational Researcher, 30*(9), 22–26.

Hartup, W. W. (1983). Peer relations. In E. M. Hetherington (Ed.), *Handbook of child psychology: Vol. 4. Socialization, personality, and social development* (4th ed., pp. 103–196). New York: Wiley.

Hartup, W. W. (1989). Social relationships and their developmental significance. *American Psychologist, 44*, 120–126.

Haskell, R. E. (2001). *Transfer of learning: Cognition, instruction, and reasoning.* San Diego, CA: Academic Press.

Hastings, P. D., Utendale, W. T., & Sullivan, C. (2007). The socialization of prosocial development. In J. E. Grusec & P. D. Hastings (Eds.), *Handbook of socialization: Theory and research* (pp. 638–664). New York: Guilford Press.

Hatano, G., & Inagaki, K. (1991). Sharing cognition through collective comprehension activity. In L. B. Resnick, J. M. Levine, & S. D. Teasley (Eds.), *Perspectives on socially shared cognition.* Washington, DC: American Psychological Association.

Hatano, G., & Inagaki, K. (1993). Desituating cognition through the construction of conceptual knowledge. In P. Light & G. Butterworth (Eds.), *Context and cognition: Ways of learning and knowing.* Mahwah, NJ: Erlbaum.

Hatano, G., & Inagaki, K. (2003). When is conceptual change intended? A cognitive-sociocultural view. In G. M. Sinatra & P. R. Pintrich (Eds.), *Intentional conceptual change* (pp. 407–427). Mahwah, NJ: Erlbaum.

Hattie, J., Biggs, J., & Purdie, N. (1996). Effects of learning skills interventions on student learning: A meta-analysis. *Review of Educational Research, 66*, 99–136.

Hattie, J., & Timperley, H. (2007). The power of feedback. *Review of Educational Research, 77*, 81–112.

Hauser-Cram, P., Sirin, S. R., & Stipek, D. (2003). When teachers' and parents' values differ: Teachers' ratings of academic competence in children from low-income families. *Journal of Educational Psychology, 95*, 813–820.

Hayslip, B., Jr. (1994). Stability of intelligence. In R. J. Sternberg (Ed.), *Encyclopedia of human intelligence* (Vol. 2). New York: Macmillan.

Haywood, H. C., & Lidz, C. S. (2007). *Dynamic assessment in practice: Clinical and educational applications.* Cambridge, England: Cambridge University Press.

Hearold, S. (1986). A synthesis of 1,043 effects of television on social behavior. In G. Comstock (Ed.), *Public communication and behavior* (Vol. 1). New York: Academic Press.

Heath, S. B. (1980). Questioning at home and at school: A comparative study. In G. Spindler (Ed.), *The ethnography of schooling: Educational anthropology in action.* New York: Holt, Rinehart & Winston.

Heath, S. B. (1989). Oral and literate traditions among black Americans living in poverty. *American Psychologist, 44*, 367–373.

Heatherton, T. F., Macrae, C. N., & Kelley, W. M. (2004). What the social brain sciences can tell us about the self. *Current Directions in Psychological Science, 13*, 190–193.

Heine, S. J. (2007). Culture and motivation: What motivates people to act in the ways that they do? In S. Kitayama & D. Cohen (Eds.), *Handbook of cultural psychology* (pp. 714–733). New York: Guilford Press.

Heller, J. I., & Hungate, H. N. (1985). Implications for mathematics instruction of research on scientific problem solving. In E. A. Silver (Ed.), *Teaching and learning mathematical problem solving: Multiple research perspectives.* Mahwah, NJ: Erlbaum.

Helton, G. B., & Oakland, T. D. (1977). Teachers' attitudinal responses to differing characteristics of elementary school students. *Journal of Educational Psychology, 69*, 261–266.

Helwig, C. C., & Jasiobedzka, U. (2001). The relation between law and morality: Children's reasoning about socially beneficial and unjust laws. *Child Development, 72*, 1382–1393.

Helwig, C. C., Zelazo, P. D., & Wilson, M. (2001). Children's judgments of psychological harm in normal and noncanonical situations. *Child Development, 72*, 66–81.

Hembree, R. (1987). Effects of noncontent variables on mathematics test performance. *Journal for Research in Mathematics Education, 18*, 197–214.

Hembree, R. (1988). Correlates, causes, effects, and treatment of test anxiety. *Review of Educational Research, 58*, 47–77.

Hemmings, A. B. (2004). *Coming of age in U.S. high schools: Economic, kinship, religious, and political cross-currents.* Mahwah, NJ: Erlbaum.

Hemphill, L., & Snow, C. (1996). Language and literacy development: Discontinuities and differences. In D. R. Olson & N. Torrance (Eds.), *The handbook of education and human development: New models of learning, teaching, and schooling.* Cambridge, MA: Blackwell.

Hennessey, B. A. (1995). Social, environmental, and developmental issues and creativity. *Educational Psychology Review, 7*, 163–183.

Hennessey, B. A., & Amabile, T. M. (1987). *Creativity and learning.* Washington, DC: National Education Association.

Hennessey, M. G. (2003). Metacognitive aspects of students' reflective discourse: Implications for intentional conceptual change teaching and learning. In G. M. Sinatra & P. R. Pintrich (Eds.), *Intentional conceptual change* (pp. 103–132). Mahwah, NJ: Erlbaum.

Herbert, J., & Stipek, D. (2005). The emergence of gender differences in children's perceptions of their academic competence. *Journal of Applied Developmental Psychology, 26*, 276–295.

Heron, W. (1957). The pathology of boredom. *Scientific American, 196*(1), 52–56.

Herrenkohl, L. R., & Guerra, M. R. (1998). Participant structures, scientific discourse, and student engagement in fourth grade. *Cognition and Instruction, 16*, 431–473.

Hess, G. A., Jr., Lyons, A., & Corsino, L. (1990, April). *Against the odds: The early identification of dropouts.* Paper presented at the annual meeting of the American Educational Research Association, Boston.

Hess, R. D., Chih-Mei, C., & McDevitt, T. M. (1987). Cultural variations in family beliefs about children's performance in mathematics: Comparisons among People's Republic of China, Chinese-American, and Caucasian-American families. *Journal of Educational Psychology, 79*, 179–188.

Hess, R. D., & Holloway, S. D. (1984). Family and school as educational institutions. In R. D. Parke, R. N. Emde, H. P. McAdoo, & G. P. Sackett (Eds.), *Review of child development research* (Vol. 7). Chicago: University of Chicago Press.

Heuer, F., & Reisberg, D. (1992). Emotion, arousal, and memory for detail. In S. Christianson (Ed.), *Handbook of emotion and memory.* Hillsdale, NJ: Erlbaum.

Hewitt, J., Brett, C., Scardamalia, M., Frecker, K., & Webb, J. (1995, April). *Schools for thought: Transforming classrooms into learning communities.* Paper presented at the annual meeting of the American Educational Research Association, San Francisco.

Hewitt, J., & Scardamalia, M. (1996, April). *Design principles for the support of distributed processes.* Paper presented at the annual meeting of the American Educational Research Association, New York.

Hewitt, J., & Scardamalia, M. (1998). Design principles for distributed knowledge building processes. *Educational Psychology Review, 10,* 75–96.

Heymann, S. J., & Earle, A. (2000). Low-income parents: How do working conditions affect their opportunity to help school-age children at risk? *American Educational Research Journal, 37,* 833–848.

Hickey, D. T. (1997). Motivation and contemporary socio-constructivist instructional perspectives. *Educational Psychologist, 32,* 175–193.

Hickey, D. T., Moore, A. L., & Pellegrino, J. W. (2001). The motivational and academic consequences of elementary mathematics environments: Do constructivist innovations and reforms make a difference? *American Educational Research Journal, 38,* 611–652.

Hidalgo, N. M., Siu, S., Bright, J. A., Swap, S. M., & Epstein, J. L. (1995). Research on families, schools, and communities: A multicultural perspective. In J. A. Banks & C. A. M. Banks (Eds.), *Handbook of research on multicultural education.* New York: Macmillan.

Hidi, S., & Anderson, V. (1986). Producing written summaries: Task demands, cognitive operations, and implications for instruction. *Review of Educational Research, 86,* 473–493.

Hidi, S., & Anderson, V. (1992). Situational interest and its impact on reading and expository writing. In K. A. Renninger, S. Hidi, & A. Krapp (Eds.), *The role of interest in learning and development.* Mahwah, NJ: Erlbaum.

Hidi, S., & Harackiewicz, J. M. (2000). Motivating the academically unmotivated: A critical issue for the 21st century. *Review of Educational Research, 70,* 151–179.

Hidi, S., & McLaren, J. (1990). The effect of topic and theme interestingness on the production of school expositions. In H. Mandl, E. De Corte, N. Bennett, & H. F. Friedrich (Eds.), *Learning and instruction in an international context.* Oxford, England: Pergamon Press.

Hidi, S., & Renninger, K. A. (2006). The four-phase model of interest development. *Educational Psychologist, 41,* 111–127.

Hidi, S., Renninger, K. A., & Krapp, A. (2004). Interest, a motivational variable that combines affecting and cognitive functioning. In D. Y. Dai & R. J. Sternberg (Eds.), *Motivation, emotion, and cognition: Integrative perspectives on intellectual functioning and development* (pp. 89–115). Mahwah, NJ: Erlbaum.

Hiebert, E. H., & Fisher, C. W. (1992). The tasks of school literacy: Trends and issues. In J. Brophy (Ed.), *Advances in research on teaching: Vol. 3. Planning and managing learning tasks and activities.* Greenwich, CT: JAI Press.

Hiebert, E. H., & Raphael, T. E. (1996). Psychological perspectives on literacy and extensions to educational practice. In D. C. Berliner & R. C. Calfee (Eds.), *Handbook of educational psychology.* New York: Macmillan.

Hiebert, E. H., Valencia, S. W., & Afflerbach, P. P. (1994). Definitions and perspectives. In S. W. Valencia, E. H. Hiebert, & P. P. Afflerbach (Eds.), *Authentic reading assessment: Practices and possibilities.* Newark, DE: International Reading Association.

Hiebert, J., Carpenter, T. P., Fennema, E., Fuson, K. C., Wearne, D., Murray, H., et al. (1997). *Making sense: Teaching and learning mathematics with understanding.* Portsmouth, NH: Heinemann.

Hiebert, J., & Lefevre, P. (1986). Conceptual and procedural knowledge in mathematics: An introductory analysis. In J. Hiebert (Ed.), *Conceptual and procedural knowledge: The case of mathematics.* Mahwah, NJ: Erlbaum.

Hiebert, J., & Wearne, D. (1996). Instruction, understanding, and skill in multidigit addition and subtraction. *Cognition and Instruction, 14,* 251–283.

Higgins, A. (1995). Educating for justice and community: Lawrence Kohlberg's vision of moral education.

In W. M. Kurtines & J. L. Gewirtz (Eds.), *Moral development: An introduction.* Boston: Allyn & Bacon.

Hill, C. (1994). Testing and assessment: An applied linguistic perspective. *Educational Assessment, 2*(3), 179–212.

Hill, C., & Larsen, E. (1992). *Testing and assessment in secondary education: A critical review of emerging practices.* Berkeley: University of California, National Center for Research in Vocational Education.

Hill, K. T. (1984). Debilitating motivation and testing: A major educational problem, possible solutions, and policy applications. In R. Ames & C. Ames (Eds.), *Research on motivation in education: Vol. 1. Student motivation.* San Diego, CA: Academic Press.

Hill, K. T., & Sarason, S. B. (1966). The relation of test anxiety and defensiveness to test and school performance over the elementary school years: A further longitudinal study. *Monographs for the Society of Research in Child Development, 31*(2, Serial No. 104).

Hill, K. T., & Wigfield, A. (1984). Test anxiety: A major educational problem and what can be done about it. *Elementary School Journal, 85,* 105–126.

Hill, N. E., Bush, K. R., & Roosa, M. W. (2003). Parenting and family socialization strategies and children's mental health: Low-income Mexican-American and Euro-American mothers and children. *Child Development, 74,* 189–204.

Hill, N. E., Castellino, D. R., Lansford, J. E., Nowlin, P., Dodge, K. A., Bates, J. E., & Pettit, G. S. (2004). Parent academic involvement as related to school behavior, achievement, and aspirations: Demographic variations across adolescence. *Child Development, 75,* 1491–1509.

Hine, P., & Fraser, B. J. (2002, April). *Combining qualitative and quantitative methods in a study of Australian students' transition from elementary to high school.* Paper presented at the annual meeting of the American Educational Research Association, New Orleans, LA.

Hinkley, J. W., McInerney, D. M., & Marsh, H. W. (2001, April). *The multi-faceted structure of school achievement motivation: A case for social goals.* Paper presented at the annual meeting of the American Educational Research Association, Seattle, WA.

Hitlin, S., Brown, J. S., & Elder, G. H., Jr. (2006). Racial self-categorization in adolescence: Multiracial development and social pathways. *Child Development, 77,* 1298–1308.

Hmelo-Silver, C. E. (2004). Problem-based learning: What and how do students learn? *Educational Psychology Review, 16,* 235–266.

Hmelo-Silver, C. E. (2006). Design principles for scaffolding technology-based inquiry. In A. M. O'Donnell, C. E. Hmelo-Silver, & G. Erkens (Eds.), *Collaborative learning, reasoning, and technology* (pp. 147–170). Mahwah, NJ: Erlbaum.

Hmelo-Silver, C. E., Duncan, R. G., & Chinn, C. A. (2007). Scaffolding and achievement in problem-based and inquiry learning: A response to Kirschner, Sweller, and Clark (2006). *Educational Psychologist, 42,* 99–107.

Ho, D. Y. F. (1986). Chinese pattern of socialization: A critical review. In M. H. Bond (Ed.), *The psychology of Chinese people.* Oxford, England: Oxford University Press.

Ho, D. Y. F. (1994). Cognitive socialization in Confucian heritage cultures. In P. M. Greenfield & R. R. Cocking (Eds.), *Cross-cultural roots of minority child development.* Mahwah, NJ: Erlbaum.

Ho, H.-Z., Hinckley, H. S., Fox, K. R., Brown, J. H., & Dixon, C. N. (2001, April). *Family literacy: Promoting parent support strategies for student success.* Paper presented at the annual meeting of the American Educational Research Association, Seattle, WA.

Hobson, P. (2004). *The cradle of thought: Exploring the origins of thinking.* Oxford, England: Oxford University Press.

Hofer, B. K., & Pintrich, P. R. (1997). The development of epistemological theories: Beliefs about knowledge and knowing and their relation to learning. *Review of Educational Research, 67,* 88–140.

Hofer, B. K., & Pintrich, P. R. (Eds.). (2002). *Personal epistemology: The psychology of beliefs about knowledge and knowing.* Mahwah, NJ: Erlbaum.

Hofferth, S. L. (1990). Trends in adolescent sexual activity, contraception, and pregnancy in the United States. In J. Bancroft & J. M. Reinisch (Eds.), *Adolescence and puberty* (pp. 217–233). New York: Oxford University Press.

Hoffman, M. L. (1970). Moral development. In P. H. Mussen (Ed.), *Carmichael's manual of child psychology* (Vol. 2). New York: Wiley.

Hoffman, M. L. (1975). Altruistic behavior and the parent-child relationship. *Journal of Personality and Social Psychology, 31,* 937–943.

Hoffman, M. L. (1991). Empathy, social cognition, and moral action. In W. M. Kurtines & J. L. Gewirtz (Eds.), *Moral behavior and development: Vol. 1. Theory* (pp. 275–301). Mahwah, NJ: Erlbaum.

Hogan, D. M., & Tudge, J. R. H. (1999). Implications of Vygotsky's theory for peer learning. In A. M. O'Donnell & A. King (Eds.), *Cognitive perspectives on peer learning* (pp. 39–65). Mahwah, NJ: Erlbaum.

Hogan, K., Nastasi, B. K., & Pressley, M. (2000). Discourse patterns and collaborative scientific reasoning in peer and teacher-guided discussions. *Cognition and Instruction, 17,* 379–432.

Hogan, T., Rabinowitz, M., & Craven, J. A., III. (2003). Representation in teaching: Inferences from research of expert and novice teachers. *Educational Psychologist, 38,* 235–247.

Hoge, R. D., & Coladarci, T. (1989). Teacher-based judgments of academic achievement: A review of literature. *Review of Educational Research, 59,* 297–313.

Hoge, R. D., & Renzulli, J. S. (1993). Exploring the link between giftedness and self-concept. *Review of Educational Research, 63,* 449–465.

Holley, C. D., & Dansereau, D. F. (1984). *Spatial learning strategies: Techniques, applications, and related issues.* San Diego, CA: Academic Press.

Holliday, B. G. (1985). Towards a model of teacher-child transactional processes affecting black children's academic achievement. In M. B. Spencer, G. K. Brookins, & W. R. Allen (Eds.), *Beginnings: The social and affective development of black children.* Mahwah, NJ: Erlbaum.

Hollins, E. R. (1996). *Culture in school learning: Revealing the deep meaning.* Mahwah, NJ: Erlbaum.

Hollon, R. E., Roth, K. J., & Anderson, C. W. (1991). Science teachers' conceptions of teaching and learning. In J. Brophy (Ed.), *Advances in research on teaching: Vol. 2. Teachers' knowledge of subject matter as it relates to their teaching practice.* Greenwich, CT: JAI Press.

Holt, M. K., & Keyes, M. A. (2004). Teachers' attitudes toward bullying. In D. L. Espelage & S. M. Swearer (Eds.), *Bullying in American schools: A social-ecological perspective on prevention and intervention* (pp. 121–139). Mahwah, NJ: Erlbaum.

Holt-Reynolds, D. (1992). Personal history-based beliefs as relevant prior knowledge in course work. *American Educational Research Journal, 29,* 325–349.

Hom, A., & Battistich, V. (1995, April). *Students' sense of school community as a factor in reducing drug use and delinquency.* Paper presented at the annual meeting of the American Educational Research Association, San Francisco.

Homme, L. E., deBaca, P. C., Devine, J. V., Steinhorst, R., & Rickert, E. J. (1963). Use of the Premack principle in controlling the behavior of nursery school children. *Journal of the Experimental Analysis of Behavior, 6,* 544.

Hong, E., O'Neil, H. F., & Feldon, D. (2005). Gender effects on mathematics achievement: Mediating role of state and trait self-regulation. In A. M. Gallagher & J. C. Kaufman (Eds.), *Gender differences in mathematics: An integrative psychological approach* (pp. 264–293). Cambridge, England: Cambridge University Press.

Hong, Y., Chiu, C., & Dweck, C. S. (1995). Implicit theories of intelligence: Reconsidering the role of confidence in achievement motivation. In M. H. Kernis (Ed.), *Efficacy, agency, and self-esteem.* New York: Plenum Press.

Hong, Y., Morris, M. W., Chiu, C., & Benet-Martínez, V. (2000). Multicultural minds: A dynamic constructivist approach to culture and cognition. *American Psychologist, 55,* 709–720.

Hong, Y., Wan, C., No, S., & Chiu, C.-Y. (2007). Multicultural identities. In S. Kitayama & D. Cohen (Eds.), *Handbook of cultural psychology* (pp. 323–345). New York: Guilford Press.

Hoover-Dempsey, K. V., Battiato, A. C., Walker, J. M. T., Reed, R. P., DeJong, J. M., & Jones, K. P. (2001). Parental involvement in homework. *Educational Psychologist, 36*, 195–209.

Horgan, D. (1990, April). *Students' predictions of test grades: Calibration and metacognition.* Paper presented at the annual meeting of the American Educational Research Association, Boston.

Horgan, D. D., Hacker, D., & Huffman, S. (1997, May). *How students predict their exam performance.* Paper presented at the annual meeting of the Southern Society for Philosophy and Psychology, Atlanta, GA.

Horne, A. M., Orpinas, P., Newman-Carlson, D., & Bartolomucci, C. L. (2004). Elementary school Bully Busters Program: Understanding why children bully and what to do about it. In D. L. Espelage & S. M. Swearer (Eds.), *Bullying in American schools: A social-ecological perspective on prevention and intervention* (pp. 297–325). Mahwah, NJ: Erlbaum.

Horowitz, F. D., Darling-Hammond, L., & Bransford, J. (with Comer, J., Rosebrock, K., Austin, K., & Rust, F.). (2005). Educating teachers for developmentally appropriate practice. In L. Darling-Hammond & J. Bransford (Eds.), *Preparing teachers for a changing world: What teachers should learn and be able to do* (pp. 88–125). San Francisco: Jossey-Bass/Wiley.

Hossler, D., & Stage, F. K. (1992). Family and high school experience influences on the postsecondary educational plans of ninth-grade students. *American Educational Research Journal, 29*, 425–451.

Houtz, J. C. (1990). Environments that support creative thinking. In C. Hedley, J. Houtz, & A. Baratta (Eds.), *Cognition, curriculum, and literacy.* Norwood, NJ: Ablex.

Howe, C. K. (1994). Improving the achievement of Hispanic students. *Educational Leadership, 51*(8), 42–44.

Howell, J. C., & Lynch, J. P. (2000, August). Youth gangs in schools. *Juvenile Justice Bulletin* (OJJDP Publication NCJ-183015). Washington, DC: U.S. Department of Justice, Office of Juvenile Justice and Delinquency Prevention.

Hoy, W. K., Tarter, C. J., & Woolfolk Hoy, A. (2006). Academic optimism of schools: A force for student achievement. *American Educational Research Journal, 43*, 425–446.

Hubbs-Tait, L., Nation, J. R., Krebs, N. F., & Bellinger, D. C. (2005). Neurotoxicants, micronutrients, and social environments: Individual and combined effects on children's development. *Psychological Science in the Public Interest, 6*, 57–121.

Hudley, C., & Graham, S. (1993). An attributional intervention to reduce peer-directed aggression among African American boys. *Child Development, 64*, 124–138.

Huey, E. D., Krueger, F., & Grafman, J. (2006). Representations in the human prefrontal cortex. *Current Directions in Psychological Science, 15*, 167–171.

Huff, J. A. (1988). Personalized behavior modification: An in-school suspension program that teaches students how to change. *School Counselor, 35*, 210–214.

Hughes, J., & Kwok, O. (2007). Influence of student-teacher and parent-teacher relationships on lower achieving readers' engagement and achievement in the primary grades. *Journal of Educational Psychology, 99*, 39–51.

Huguet, P., & Régner, I. (2007). Stereotype threat among schoolgirls in quasi-ordinary classroom circumstances. *Journal of Educational Psychology, 99*, 545–560.

Hunt, P., & Goetz, L. (1997). Research on inclusive educational programs, practices, and outcomes for students with severe disabilities. *Journal of Special Education, 31*, 3–29.

Hunter, J., & Csikszentmihalyi, M. (2003). The positive psychology of interested adolescents. *Journal of Youth and Adolescence, 32*, 27–35.

Hunter, M. (1982). *Mastery teaching.* El Segundo, CA: TIP.

Huntsinger, C. S., & Jose, P. E. (2006). A longitudinal investigation of personality and social adjustment among Chinese American and European American adolescents. *Child Development, 77*, 1309–1324.

Husman, J., & Freeman, B. (1999, April). *The effect of perceptions of instrumentality on intrinsic motivation.* Paper presented at the annual meeting of the American Educational Research Association, Montreal, Canada.

Hutt, S. J., Tyler, S., Hutt, C., & Christopherson, H. (1989). *Play, exploration, and learning: A natural history of the pre-school.* London: Routledge.

Huttenlocher, P. R., & Dabholkar, A. S. (1997). Regional differences in synaptogenesis in human cerebral cortex. *Journal of Comparative Neurology, 387*, 167–178.

Hyman, I., Mahon, M., Cohen, I., Snook, P., Britton, G., & Lurkis, L. (2004). Student alienation syndrome: The other side of school violence. In J. C. Conoley & A. P. Goldstein (Eds.), *School violence intervention* (2nd ed., pp. 483–506). New York: Guilford Press.

Hymel, S. (1986). Interpretations of peer behavior: Affective bias in childhood and adolescence. *Child Development, 57*, 431–445.

Hymel, S., Comfort, C., Schonert-Reichl, K., & McDougall, P. (1996). Academic failure and school dropout: The influence of peers. In J. Juvonen & K. R. Wentzel (Eds.), *Social motivation: Understanding children's school adjustment* (pp. 313–345). Cambridge, England: Cambridge University Press.

Hynd, C. (1998a). Conceptual change in a high school physics class. In B. Guzzetti & C. Hynd (Eds.), *Perspectives on conceptual change: Multiple ways to understand knowing and learning in a complex world* (pp. 27–36). Mahwah, NJ: Erlbaum.

Hynd, C. (1998b). Observing learning from different perspectives: What does it mean for Barry and his understanding of gravity? In B. Guzzetti & C. Hynd (Eds.), *Perspectives on conceptual change: Multiple ways to understand knowing and learning in a complex world* (pp. 235–244). Mahwah, NJ: Erlbaum.

Hynd, C. (2003). Conceptual change in response to persuasive messages. In G. M. Sinatra & P. R. Pintrich (Eds.), *Intentional conceptual change* (pp. 291–315). Mahwah, NJ: Erlbaum.

Igoa, C. (1995). *The inner world of the immigrant child.* Mahwah, NJ: Erlbaum.

Inagaki, K., & Hatano, G. (2006). Young children's conception of the biological world. *Current Directions in Psychological Science, 15*, 177–181.

Inglehart, M., Brown, D. R., & Vida, M. (1994). Competition, achievement, and gender: A stress theoretical analysis. In P. R. Pintrich, D. R. Brown, & C. E. Weinstein (Eds.), *Student motivation, cognition, and learning: Essays in honor of Wilbert J. McKeachie.* Mahwah, NJ: Erlbaum.

Inglis, A., & Biemiller, A. (1997, March). *Fostering self-direction in mathematics: A cross-age tutoring program that enhances math problem solving.* Paper presented at the annual meeting of the American Educational Research Association, Chicago.

Inhelder, B., & Piaget, J. (1958). *The growth of logical thinking from childhood to adolescence* (A. Parsons & S. Milgram, Trans.). New York: Basic Books.

Irujo, S. (1988). An introduction to intercultural differences and similarities in nonverbal communication. In J. S. Wurzel (Ed.), *Toward multiculturalism: A reader in multicultural education.* Yarmouth, ME: Intercultural Press.

Irvine, J. J., & York, D. E. (1995). Learning styles and culturally diverse students: A literature review. In J. A. Banks & C. A. M. Banks (Eds.), *Handbook of research on multicultural education.* New York: Macmillan.

Iwata, B. A., & Bailey, J. S. (1974). Reward versus cost token systems: An analysis of the effects on students and teacher. *Journal of Applied Behavior Analysis, 7*, 567–576.

Iyengar, S. S., & Lepper, M. R. (1999). Rethinking the value of choice: A cultural perspective on intrinsic motivation. *Journal of Personality and Social Psychology, 76*, 349–366.

Izard, C., Fine, S., Schultz, D., Mostow, A., Ackerman, B., & Youngstrom, E. (2001). Emotion knowledge as a predictor of social behavior and academic competence in children at risk. *Psychological Science, 12*, 18–23.

Jacob, B. A. (2003). Accountability, incentives, and behavior: The impact of high-stakes testing in the Chicago Public Schools. *Education Next, 3*(1). Retrieved March 10, 2004, from http://www.educationnext.org/unabridged/20031/jacob.pdf

Jacobs, J. E., Davis-Kean, P., Bleeker, M., Eccles, J. S., & Malanchuk, O. (2005). "I can, but I don't want to": The impact of parents, interests, and activities on gender differences in math. In A. M. Gallagher & J. C. Kaufman (Eds.), *Gender differences in mathematics: An integrative psychological approach* (pp. 246–263). Cambridge, England: Cambridge University Press.

Jacobs, J. E., & Klaczynski, P. A. (2002). The development of judgment and decision making during childhood and adolescence. *Current Directions in Psychological Science, 11*, 145–149.

Jacobs, J. E., Lanza, S., Osgood, D. W., Eccles, J. S., & Wigfield, A. (2002). Changes in children's self-competence and values: Gender and domain differences across grades one through twelve. *Child Development, 73*, 509–527.

Jagacinski, C. M., & Nicholls, J. G. (1984). Conceptions of ability and related affects in task involvement and ego involvement. *Journal of Educational Psychology, 76*, 909–919.

Jagacinski, C. M., & Nicholls, J. G. (1987). Competence and affect in task involvement and ego involvement: The impact of social comparison information. *Journal of Educational Psychology, 79*, 107–114.

Janos, P. M., & Robinson, N. M. (1985). Psychosocial development in intellectually gifted children. In F. D. Horowitz & M. O'Brien (Eds.), *The gifted and talented: Developmental perspectives.* Washington, DC: American Psychological Association.

Janosz, M., LeBlanc, M., Boulerice, B., & Tremblay R. E. (1997). Disentangling the weight of school dropout predictors: A test on two longitudinal samples. *Journal of Youth and Adolescence, 26*, 733–762.

Jenlink, C. L. (1994, April). *Music: A lifeline for the self-esteem of at-risk students.* Paper presented at the annual meeting of the American Educational Research Association, New Orleans, LA.

Jimerson, S., Egeland, B., & Teo, A. (1999). A longitudinal study of achievement trajectories: Factors associated with change. *Journal of Educational Psychology, 91*, 116–126.

Johanning, D. I., D'Agostino, J. V., Steele, D. F., & Shumow, L. (1999, April). *Student writing, post-writing group collaboration, and learning in pre-algebra.* Paper presented at the annual meeting of the American Educational Research Association, Montreal, Canada.

Johnson, D. W., & Johnson, R. T. (1985). Classroom conflict: Controversy versus debate in learning groups. *American Educational Research Journal, 22*, 237–256.

Johnson, D. W., & Johnson, R. T. (1991). *Learning together and alone: Cooperative, competitive, and individualistic learning* (3rd ed.). Upper Saddle River, NJ: Prentice Hall.

Johnson, D. W., & Johnson, R. T. (1996). Conflict resolution and peer mediation programs in elementary and secondary schools: A review of the research. *Review of Educational Research, 66*, 459–506.

Johnson, D. W., & Johnson, R. T. (2006). Conflict resolution, peer mediation, and peacemaking. In C. M. Evertson & C. S. Weinstein (Eds.), *Handbook of classroom management: Research, practice, and contemporary issues* (pp. 803–832). Mahwah, NJ: Erlbaum.

Johnson, D. W., Johnson, R., Dudley, B., Ward, M., & Magnuson, D. (1995). The impact of peer mediation training on the management of school and home conflicts. *American Educational Research Journal, 32*, 829–844.

Johnson, H. C., & Friesen, B. (1993). Etiologies of mental and emotional disorders in children. In H. Johnson (Ed.), *Child mental health in the 1990s: Curricula for graduate and undergraduate.* Washington, DC: U.S. Department of Health and Human Services.

Johnson, M. H., & de Haan, M. (2001). Developing cortical specialization for visual-cognitive function: The case of face recognition. In J. L. McClelland & R. S. Siegler (Eds.), *Mechanisms of cognitive development: Behavioral and neural perspectives* (pp. 253–270). Mahwah, NJ: Erlbaum.

Johnson, W., McGue, M., & Iacono, W. G. (2005). Disruptive behavior and school grades: Genetic and environmental relations in 11-year-olds. *Journal of Educational Psychology, 97*, 391–405.

Johnson-Glenberg, M. C. (2000). Training reading comprehension in adequate decoders/poor comprehenders: Verbal versus visual strategies. *Journal of Educational Psychology, 92*, 772–782.

John-Steiner, V. (1997). *Notebooks of the mind: Explorations of thinking* (Rev. ed.). New York: Oxford University Press.

John-Steiner, V., & Mahn, H. (1996). Sociocultural approaches to learning and development: A Vygotskian framework. *Educational Psychologist, 31*, 191–206.

Johnstone, A. H., & El-Banna, H. (1986). Capacities, demands and processes—a predictive model for science education. *Education in Chemistry, 23*, 80–84.

Jonassen, D. H. (1996). *Computers in the classroom: Mindtools for critical thinking.* Upper Saddle River, NJ: Merrill/Prentice Hall.

Jonassen, D. H., & Grabowski, B. L. (1993). *Handbook of individual differences: Learning and instruction.* Mahwah, NJ: Erlbaum.

Jonassen, D. H., Hannum, W. H., & Tessmer, M. (1989). *Handbook of task analysis procedures.* New York: Praeger.

Jones, D., & Christensen, C. A. (1999). Relationship between automaticity in handwriting and students' ability to generate written text. *Journal of Educational Psychology, 91*, 44–49.

Jones, E. E., & Berglas, S. (1978). Control of attributions about the self through self-handicapping strategies: The appeal of alcohol and the role of underachievement. *Personality and Social Psychology Bulletin, 4*, 200–206.

Jones, K. M., Drew, H. A., & Weber, N. L. (2000). Noncontingent peer attention as treatment for disruptive classroom behavior. *Journal of Applied Behavior Analysis, 33*, 343–346.

Jones, M. S., Levin, M. E., Levin, J. R., & Beitzel, B. D. (2000). Can vocabulary-learning strategies and pair-learning formats be profitably combined? *Journal of Educational Psychology, 92*, 256–262.

Jones, V. (2006). How do teachers learn to be effective classroom managers. In C. M. Evertson & C. S. Weinstein (Eds.), *Handbook of classroom management: Research, practice, and contemporary issues* (pp. 887–907). Mahwah, NJ: Erlbaum.

Jozefowicz, D. M., Arbreton, A. J., Eccles, J. S., Barber, B. L., & Colarossi, L. (1994, April). *Seventh grade student, parent, and teacher factors associated with later school dropout or movement into alternative educational settings.* Paper presented at the annual meeting of the American Educational Research Association, New Orleans, LA.

Jussim, L., Eccles, J., & Madon, S. (1996). Social perception, social stereotypes, and teacher expectations: Accuracy and the quest for the powerful self-fulfilling prophecy. In L. Berkowitz (Ed.), *Advances in experimental social psychology.* New York: Academic Press.

Juvonen, J. (2000). The social functions of attributional face-saving tactics among early adolescents. *Educational Psychology Review, 12*, 15–32.

Juvonen, J. (2006). Sense of belonging, social bonds, and school functioning. In P. A. Alexander & P. H. Winne (Eds.), *Handbook of educational psychology* (2nd ed., pp. 655–674). Mahwah, NJ: Erlbaum.

Juvonen, J., & Cadigan, R. J. (2002). Social determinants of public behavior of middle school youth: Perceived peer norms and need to be accepted. In F. Pajares & T. Urdan (Eds.), *Adolescence and education, Vol. 2: Academic motivation of adolescents* (pp. 277–297). Greenwich, CT: Information Age.

Juvonen, J., & Hiner, M. (1991, April). *Perceived responsibility and annoyance as mediators of negative peer reactions.* Paper presented at the annual meeting of the American Educational Research Association, Chicago.

Juvonen, J., & Weiner, B. (1993). An attributional analysis of students' interactions: The social consequences of perceived responsibility. *Educational Psychology Review, 5*, 325–345.

Kagan, J. (1998). Biology and the child. In W. Damon (Series Ed.) & N. Eisenberg (Vol. Ed.), *Handbook of child psychology: Vol. 3. Social, emotional, and personality development* (5th ed., pp. 177–235). New York: Wiley.

Kagan, J., & Snidman, N. (2007). Temperament and biology. In D. Coch, K. W. Fischer, & G. Dawson (Eds.), *Human behavior, learning, and the developing brain: Typical development* (pp. 219–246). New York: Guilford Press.

Kağitçibaşi, Ç. (2007). *Family, self, and human development across cultures: Theory and applications* (2nd ed.). Mahwah, NJ: Erlbaum.

Kahl, B., & Woloshyn, V. E. (1994). Using elaborative interrogation to facilitate acquisition of factual information in cooperative learning settings: One good strategy deserves another. *Applied Cognitive Psychology, 8*, 465–478.

Kail, R. V. (1990). *The development of memory in children* (3rd ed.). New York: Freeman.

Kail, R. V. (1998). *Children and their development.* Upper Saddle River, NJ: Prentice Hall.

Kail, R. V. (2007). Longitudinal evidence that increases in processing speed and working memory enhance children's reasoning. *Psychological Science, 18*, 312–313.

Kalyuga, S., & Sweller, J. (2004). Measuring knowledge to optimize cognitive load factors during instruction. *Journal of Educational Psychology, 96*, 558–568.

Kaplan, A. (1998, April). *Task goal orientation and adaptive social interaction among students of diverse cultural backgrounds.* Paper presented at the annual meeting of the American Educational Research Association, San Diego, CA.

Kaplan, A., & Midgley, C. (1997). The effect of achievement goals: Does level of perceived academic competence make a difference? *Contemporary Educational Psychology, 22*, 415–435.

Kaplan, A., & Midgley, C. (1999). The relationship between perceptions of the classroom goal structure and early adolescents' affect in school: The mediating role of coping strategies. *Learning and Individual Differences, 11*, 187–212.

Karau, S. J., & Williams, K. D. (1995). Social loafing: Research findings, implications, and future directions. *Current Directions in Psychological Science, 4*, 134–140.

Kardash, C. A. M., & Amlund, J. T. (1991). Self-reported learning strategies and learning from expository text. *Contemporary Educational Psychology, 16*, 117–138.

Kardash, C. A. M., & Howell, K. L. (2000). Effects of epistemological beliefs and topic-specific beliefs on undergraduates' cognitive and strategic processing of dual-positional text. *Journal of Educational Psychology, 92*, 524–535.

Kardash, C. A. M., & Scholes, R. J. (1996). Effects of preexisting beliefs, epistemological beliefs, and need for cognition on interpretation of controversial issues. *Journal of Educational Psychology, 88*, 260–271.

Karplus, R., Pulos, S., & Stage, E. K. (1983). Proportional reasoning of early adolescents. In R. Lesh & M. Landau (Eds.), *Acquisition of mathematics concepts and processes.* San Diego, CA: Academic Press.

Karpov, Y. V., & Haywood, H. C. (1998). Two ways to elaborate Vygotsky's concept of mediation: Implications for instruction. *American Psychologist, 53*, 27–36.

Katayama, A. D., & Robinson, D. H. (2000). Getting students "partially" involved in note-taking using graphic organizers. *Journal of Experimental Education, 68*, 119–133.

Katchadourian, H. (1990). Sexuality. In S. S. Feldman & G. R. Elliott (Eds.), *At the threshold: The developing adolescent* (pp. 330–351). Cambridge, MA: Harvard University Press.

Katz, L. (1993). All about me: Are we developing our children's self-esteem or their narcissism? *American Educator, 17*(2), 18–23.

Kavsek, M. (2004). Predicting later IQ from infant visual habituation and dishabituation: A meta-analysis. *Applied Developmental Psychology, 25*, 369–393.

Keefer, M. W., Zeitz, C. M., & Resnick, L. B. (2000). Judging the quality of peer-led student dialogues. *Cognition and Instruction, 18*, 53–81.

Keil, F. C. (1986). The acquisition of natural kind and artifact terms. In W. Demopolous & A. Marras (Eds.), *Language learning and concept acquisition.* Norwood, NJ: Ablex.

Keil, F. C. (1987). Conceptual development and category structure. In U. Neisser (Ed.), *Concepts and conceptual development: Ecological and intellectual factors in categorization.* Cambridge, England: Cambridge University Press.

Keil, F. C. (1989). *Concepts, kinds, and cognitive development.* Cambridge, MA: MIT Press.

Keil, F. C. (1994). The birth and nurturance of concepts by domains: The origins of concepts of living things. In L. A. Hirschfeld & S. A. Gelman (Eds.), *Mapping the mind: Domain specificity in cognition and culture.* New York: Cambridge University Press.

Keil, F. C., & Silberstein, C. S. (1996). Schooling and the acquisition of theoretical knowledge. In D. R. Olson & N. Torrance (Eds.), *The handbook of education and human development: New models of learning, teaching, and schooling.* Cambridge, MA: Blackwell.

Kelemen, D. (2004). Are children "intuitive theists"?: Reasoning about purpose and design in nature. *Psychological Science, 15*, 295–301.

Keller, H. R., & Tapasak, R. C. (2004). Classroom-based approaches. In J. C. Conoley & A. P. Goldstein (Eds.), *School violence intervention* (2nd ed., pp. 103–130). New York: Guilford Press.

Kelley, M. L., & Carper, L. B. (1988). Home-based reinforcement procedures. In J. C. Witt, S. N. Elliott, & F. M. Gresham (Eds.), *Handbook of behavior therapy in education.* New York: Plenum Press.

Kelly, S., & Monczunski, L. (2007). Overcoming the volatility in school-level gain scores: A new approach to identifying value added with cross-sectional data. *Educational Researcher, 36*(5), 279–287.

Kelly, S. W., Burton, A. M., Kato, T., & Akamatsu, S. (2001). Incidental learning of real-world regularities. *Psychological Science, 12*, 86–89.

Kennedy, R. (1992). What is performance assessment? *New Directions for Education Reform, 1*(2), 21–27.

Keogh, B. K. (2003). *Temperament in the classroom.* Baltimore: Brookes.

Keogh, B. K., & MacMillan, D. L. (1996). Exceptionality. In D. C. Berliner & R. C. Calfee (Eds.), *Handbook of educational psychology.* New York: Macmillan.

Kermani, H., & Moallem, M. (1997, March). *Cross-age tutoring: Exploring features and processes of peer-mediated learning.* Paper presented at the annual meeting of the American Educational Research Association, Chicago.

Kerns, L. L., & Lieberman, A. B. (1993). *Helping your depressed child.* Rocklin, CA: Prima.

Khattri, N., & Sweet, D. (1996). Assessment reform: Promises and challenges. In M. B. Kane & R. Mitchell (Eds.), *Implementing performance assessment: Promises, problems, and challenges* (pp. 1–21). Mahwah, NJ: Erlbaum.

Kiewra, K. A. (1985). Investigating notetaking and review: A depth of processing alternative. *Educational Psychologist, 20*, 23–32.

Kiewra, K. A. (1989). A review of note-taking: The encoding-storage paradigm and beyond. *Educational Psychology Review, 1*, 147–172.

Killeen, P. R. (2001). The four causes of behavior. *Current Directions in Psychological Science, 10*, 136–140.

Kim, D., Solomon, D., & Roberts, W. (1995, April). *Classroom practices that enhance students' sense of community.* Paper presented at the annual meeting of the American Educational Research Association, San Francisco.

Kim, J., & Cicchetti, D. (2006). Longitudinal trajectories of self-system processes and depressive symptoms among maltreated and nonmaltreated children. *Child Development, 77*, 624–639.

Kim, J. M., & Turiel, E. (1996). Korean and American children's concepts of adult and peer authority. *Social Development, 5*, 310–329.

Kindermann, T. A. (2007). Effects of naturally existing peer groups on changes in academic engagement in a cohort of sixth graders. *Child Development, 78*, 1186–1203.

Kindermann, T. A., McCollam, T., & Gibson, E. (1996). Peer networks and students' classroom engagement during childhood and adolescence. In J. Juvonen & K. Wentzel (Eds.), *Social motivation: Understanding children's school adjustment.* Cambridge, England: Cambridge University Press.

King, A. (1992). Comparison of self-questioning, summarizing, and notetaking-review as strategies for learning from lectures. *American Educational Research Journal, 29,* 303–323.

King, A. (1994). Guiding knowledge construction in the classroom: Effects of teaching children how to question and how to explain. *American Educational Research Journal, 31,* 338–368.

King, A. (1997). ASK to THINK—TEL WHY®©: A model of transactive peer tutoring for scaffolding higher level complex learning. *Educational Psychologist, 32,* 221–235.

King, A. (1998). Transactive peer tutoring: Distributing cognition and metacognition. *Educational Psychology Review, 10,* 57–74

King, A. (1999). Discourse patterns for mediating peer learning. In A. M. O'Donnell & A. King (Eds.), *Cognitive perspectives on peer learning* (pp. 87–115). Mahwah, NJ: Erlbaum.

King, A., Staffieri, A., & Adelgais, A. (1998). Mutual peer tutoring: Effects of structuring tutorial interaction to scaffold peer learning. *Journal of Educational Psychology, 90,* 134–152.

King, N. J., & Ollendick, T. H. (1989). Children's anxiety and phobic disorders in school settings: Classification, assessment, and intervention issues. *Review of Educational Research, 59,* 431–470.

King, P. M., & Kitchener, K. S. (2002). The reflective judgment model: Twenty years of research on epistemic cognition. In B. K. Hofer & P. R. Pintrich (Eds.), *Personal epistemology: The psychology of beliefs about knowledge and knowing* (pp. 37–61). Mahwah, NJ: Erlbaum.

Kirkland, M. C. (1971). The effect of tests on students and schools. *Review of Educational Research, 41,* 303–350.

Kirschenbaum, R. J. (1989). Identification of the gifted and talented American Indian student. In C. J. Maker & S. W. Schiever (Eds.), *Critical issues in gifted education: Vol. 2. Defensible programs for cultural and ethnic minorities.* Austin, TX: Pro-Ed.

Kirschner, P. A., Sweller, J., & Clark, R. E. (2006). Why minimal guidance during instruction does not work: An analysis of the failure of constructivist, discovery, problem-based, experiential, and inquiry-based teaching. *Educational Psychologist, 41,* 75–86.

Kitayama, S., Duffy, S., & Uchida, Y. (2007). Self as cultural mode of being. In S. Kitayama & D. Cohen (Eds.), *Handbook of cultural psychology* (pp. 136–174). New York: Guilford Press.

Klaczynski, P. A. (2001). Analytic and heuristic processing influences on adolescent reasoning and decision-making. *Child Development, 72,* 844–861.

Klahr, D., & Nigam, M. (2004). The equivalence of learning paths in early science instruction: Effects of direct instruction and discovery learning. *Psychological Science, 15,* 661–667.

Klassen, R. (2002). Writing in early adolescence: A review of the role of self-efficacy beliefs. *Educational Psychology Review, 14,* 173–203.

Klibanoff, R. S., Levine, S. C., Huttenlocher, J., Vasilyeva, M., & Hedges, L. V. (2006). Preschool children's mathematical knowledge: The effect of teacher "math talk." *Developmental Psychology, 42,* 59–69.

Knapp, M. S., Turnbull, B. J., & Shields, P. M. (1990). New directions for educating the children of poverty. *Educational Leadership, 48*(1), 4–9.

Knutson, D. J., & Mantzicopoulos, P. Y. (1999, April). *Contextual factors of geographic mobility and their relation to the achievement and adjustment of children.* Paper presented at the annual meeting of the American Educational Research Association, Montreal, Canada.

Kochanska, G., Gross, J. N., Lin, M.-H., & Nichols, K. E. (2002). Guilt in young children: Development, determinants, and relations with a broader system of standards. *Child Development, 73,* 461–482.

Kodluboy, D. W. (2004). Gang-oriented interventions. In J. C. Conoley & A. P. Goldstein (Eds.), *School violence*

intervention (2nd ed., pp. 194–232). New York: Guilford Press.

Koedinger, K. R., & Corbett, A. (2006). Cognitive tutors: Technology bringing learning sciences to the classroom. In R. K. Sawyer (Ed.), *The Cambridge handbook of the learning sciences* (pp. 61–77). Cambridge, England: Cambridge University Press.

Koegel, L. K. (1995). Communication and language intervention. In R. L. Koegel & L. K. Koegel (Eds.), *Strategies for initiating positive interactions and improving learning opportunities.* Baltimore: Brookes.

Koegel, L. K., Koegel, R. L., & Dunlap, G. (Eds.). (1996). *Positive behavioral support: Including people with difficult behavior in the community.* Baltimore: Brookes.

Koeppel, J., & Mulrooney, M. (1992). The Sister Schools Program: A way for children to learn about cultural diversity—when there isn't any in their school. *Young Children, 48*(1), 44–47.

Koestner, R., Ryan, R. M., Bernieri, F., & Holt, K. (1984). Setting limits in children's behavior: The differential effects of controlling versus informational styles on intrinsic motivation and creativity. *Journal of Personality, 52,* 233–248.

Koger, S. M., Schettler, T., & Weiss, B. (2005). Environmental toxins and developmental disabilities: A challenge for psychologists. *American Psychologist, 60,* 243–255.

Kohlberg, L. (1963). Moral development and identification. In H. W. Stevenson (Ed.), *Child psychology: 62nd yearbook of the National Society for the Study of Education* (pp. 277–332). Chicago: University of Chicago Press.

Kohlberg, L. (1975). The cognitive-developmental approach to moral education. *Phi Delta Kappan, 57,* 670–677.

Kohlberg, L. (1976). Moral stages and moralization: The cognitive-developmental approach. In T. Lickona (Ed.), *Moral development and behavior: Theory, research, and social issues.* New York: Holt, Rinehart & Winston.

Kohlberg, L. (1981). *The philosophy of moral development: Moral stages and the idea of justice.* San Francisco: Harper & Row.

Kohlberg, L. (1984). *The psychology of moral development: The nature and validity of moral stages.* San Francisco: Harper & Row.

Kohlberg, L. (1986). A current statement on some theoretical issues. In S. Modgil & C. Modgil (Eds.), *Lawrence Kohlberg: Consensus and controversy.* Philadelphia: Falmer Press.

Kohlberg, L., & Candee, D. (1984). The relationship of moral judgment to moral action. In W. M. Kurtines & J. L. Gewirtz (Eds.), *Morality, moral behavior, and moral development.* New York: Wiley.

Kohn, A. (1993). Choices for children: Why and how to let students decide. *Phi Delta Kappan, 75*(1), 8–20.

Kolb, B., Gibb, R., & Robinson, T. E. (2003). Brain plasticity and behavior. *Current Directions in Psychological Science, 12,* 1–5.

Kolb, B., & Whishaw, I. Q. (1990). *Fundamentals of human neuropsychology* (3rd ed.). New York: Freeman.

Kolodner, J. (1985). Memory for experience. In G. H. Bower (Ed.), *The psychology of learning and motivation: Advances in research and theory* (Vol. 19). San Diego, CA: Academic Press.

Koltko-Rivera, M. E. (2004). The psychology of worldviews. *Review of General Psychology, 8,* 3–58.

Koretz, D., Stecher, B., Klein, S., & McCaffrey, D. (1994). The Vermont portfolio assessment program: Findings and implications. *Educational Measurement: Issues and Practice, 13*(3), 5–16.

Kosslyn, S. M. (1985). Mental imagery ability. In R. J. Sternberg (Ed.), *Human abilities: An information-processing approach.* New York: Freeman.

Kosslyn, S. M., Margolis, J. A., Barrett, A. M., Goldknopf, E. J., & Daly, P. F. (1990). Age differences in imagery ability. *Child Development, 61,* 995–1010.

Kounin, J. S. (1970). *Discipline and group management in classrooms.* New York: Holt, Rinehart & Winston.

Kovas, Y., Petrill, S. A., & Plomin, R. (2007). The origins of diverse domains of mathematics: Generalist genes

but specialist environments. *Journal of Educational Psychology, 99,* 128–139.

Krajcik, J. S. (1991). Developing students' understanding of chemical concepts. In S. M. Glynn, R. H. Yeany, & B. K. Britton (Eds.), *The psychology of learning science.* Mahwah, NJ: Erlbaum.

Krajcik, J. S., & Blumenfeld, P. C. (2006). Project-based learning. In R. K. Sawyer (Ed.), *The Cambridge handbook of the learning sciences* (pp. 317–333). Cambridge, England: Cambridge University Press.

Kramarski, B., & Mevarech, Z. R. (2003). Enhancing mathematical reasoning in the classroom: The effects of cooperative learning and metacognitive training. *American Educational Research Journal, 40,* 281–310.

Krampen, G. (1987). Differential effects of teacher comments. *Journal of Educational Psychology, 79,* 137–146.

Krätzig, G. P., & Arbuthnott, K. D. (2006). Perceptual learning style and learning proficiency: A test of the hypothesis. *Journal of Educational Psychology, 98,* 238–246.

Krebs, D. L., & Van Hesteren, F. (1994). The development of altruism: Toward an integrative model. *Developmental Review, 14,* 103–158.

Krumboltz, J. D., & Krumboltz, H. B. (1972). *Changing children's behavior.* Upper Saddle River, NJ: Prentice Hall.

Kuhl, J. (1985). Volitional mediators of cognition-behavior consistency: Self-regulatory processes and actions versus state orientation. In J. Kuhl & J. Beckmann (Eds.), *Action control: From cognition to behavior.* Berlin, Germany: Springer-Verlag.

Kuhl, J., & Kraska, K. (1989). Self-regulation and meta-motivation: Computational mechanisms, development, and assessment. In R. Kanfer, P. L. Ackerman, & R. Cudeck (Eds.), *Abilities, motivation, and methodology: The Minnesota Symposium on Learning and Individual Differences* (pp. 343–374). Mahwah, NJ: Erlbaum.

Kuhn, D. (2001a). How do people know? *Psychological Science, 12,* 1–8.

Kuhn, D. (2001b). Why development does (and does not) occur: Evidence from the domain of inductive reasoning. In J. L. McClelland & R. S. Siegler (Eds.), *Mechanisms of cognitive development: Behavioral and neural perspectives* (pp. 221–249). Mahwah, NJ: Erlbaum.

Kuhn, D. (2006). Do cognitive changes accompany developments in the adolescent brain? *Perspectives on Psychological Science, 1,* 59–67.

Kuhn, D. (2007). Is direct instruction an answer to the right question? *Educational Psychologist, 42,* 109–113.

Kuhn, D., Amsel, E., & O'Loughlin, M. (1988). *The development of scientific thinking skills.* San Diego, CA: Academic Press.

Kuhn, D., Daniels, S., & Krishnan, A. (2003, April). *Epistemology and intellectual values as core metacognitive constructs.* Paper presented at the annual meeting of the American Educational Research Association, Chicago.

Kuhn, D., & Dean, D., Jr. (2005). Is developing scientific thinking all about learning to control variables? *Psychological Science, 16,* 866–870.

Kuhn, D., & Franklin, S. (2006). The second decade: What develops (and how)? In W. Damon & R. M. Lerner (Series Eds.), D. Kuhn & R. Siegler (Vol. Eds.), *Handbook of child psychology: Vol. 1. Cognition, perception, and language* (6th ed.). New York: Wiley.

Kuhn, D., Garcia-Mila, M., Zohar, A., & Andersen, C. (1995). Strategies of knowledge acquisition. *Monographs of the Society for Research in Child Development, 60* (Whole No. 245).

Kuhn, D., & Park, S.-H. (2005). Epistemological understanding and the development of intellectual values. *International Journal of Educational Research, 43,* 111–124.

Kuhn, D., Shaw, V., & Felton, M. (1997). Effects of dyadic interaction on argumentative reasoning. *Cognition and Instruction, 15,* 287–315.

Kuhn, D., & Weinstock, M. (2002). What is epistemological thinking and why does it matter? In B. K. Hofer & P. R. Pintrich (Eds.), *Personal epistemology: The psy-*

chology of beliefs about knowledge and knowing (pp. 121–144). Mahwah, NJ: Erlbaum.

Kuiper, E., Volman, M., & Terwel, J. (2005). The Web as an information resource in K–12 education: Strategies for supporting students in searching and processing information. Review of Educational Research, 75, 285–328.

Kuklinski, M. R., & Weinstein, R. S. (2001). Classroom and developmental differences in a path model of teacher expectancy effects. Child Development, 72, 1554–1578.

Kulhavy, R. W., Lee, J. B., & Caterino, L. C. (1985). Conjoint retention of maps and related discourse. Contemporary Educational Psychology, 10, 28–37.

Kulik, C. C., Kulik, J. A., & Bangert-Drowns, R. L. (1990). Effectiveness of mastery learning programs: A meta-analysis. Review of Educational Research, 60, 265–299.

Kulik, J. A., & Kulik, C. C. (1997). Ability grouping. In N. Colangelo & G. Davis (Eds.), Handbook of gifted education (2nd ed., pp. 230–242). Boston: Allyn & Bacon.

Kulik, J. A., Kulik, C. C., & Cohen, P. A. (1979). A meta-analysis of outcome studies of Keller's Personalized System of Instruction. American Psychologist, 34, 307–318.

Kulik, J. A., Kulik, C. C., & Cohen, P. A. (1980). Effectiveness of computer-based college teaching: A meta-analysis of findings. Review of Educational Research, 50, 525–544.

Kumar, R., Gheen, M. H., & Kaplan, A. (2002). Goal structures in the learning environment and students' disaffection from learning and schooling. In C. Midgley (Ed.), Goals, goal structures, and patterns of adaptive learning (pp. 143–173). Mahwah, NJ: Erlbaum.

Kunzinger, E. L., III (1985). A short-term longitudinal study of memorial development during early grade school. Developmental Psychology, 21, 642–646.

Kupersmidt, J. B., & Coie, J. D. (1990). Preadolescent peer status, aggression, and school adjustment as predictors of externalizing problems in adolescence. Child Development, 61, 1350–1362.

Kurtines, W. M., Berman, S. L., Ittel, A., & Williamson, S. (1995). Moral development: A co-constructivist perspective. In W. M. Kurtines & J. L. Gewirtz (Eds.), Moral development: An introduction. Boston: Allyn & Bacon.

Kyle, W. C., & Shymansky, J. A. (1989, April). Enhancing learning through conceptual change teaching. NARST News, 31, 7–8.

LaBar, K. S., & Phelps, E. A. (1998). Arousal-mediated memory consolidation: Role of the medial temporal lobe in humans. Psychological Science, 9, 490–493.

Labouvie-Vief, G., & González, M. M. (2004). Dynamic integration: Affect optimization and differentiation in development. In D. Y. Dai & R. J. Sternberg (Eds.), Motivation, emotion, and cognition: Integrative perspectives on intellectual functioning and development (pp. 237–272). Mahwah, NJ: Erlbaum.

Ladd, G. W. (2006). Peer rejection, aggressive or withdrawn behavior, and psychological maladjustment from ages 5 to 12: An examination of four predictive models. Child Development, 77, 822–846.

Ladd, G. W., & Troop-Gordon, W. (2003). The role of chronic peer difficulties in the development of children's psychological adjustment problems. Child Development, 74, 1344–1367.

Ladson-Billings, G. (1994a). The dreamkeepers: Successful teachers of African American children. San Francisco: Jossey-Bass.

Ladson-Billings, G. (1994b). What we can learn from multicultural education research. Educational Leadership, 51(8), 22–26.

Ladson-Billings, G. (1995). Toward a theory of culturally relevant pedagogy. American Educational Research Journal, 32, 465–491.

LaFromboise, T., Coleman, H. L. K., & Gerton, J. (1993). Psychological impact of biculturalism: Evidence and theory. Psychological Bulletin, 114, 395–412.

Lajoie, S. P., & Derry, S. J. (Eds.). (1993). Computers as cognitive tools. Mahwah, NJ: Erlbaum.

Lamon, M., Chan, C., Scardamalia, M., Burtis, P. J., & Brett, C. (1993, April). Beliefs about learning and constructive processes in reading: Effects of a computer supported intentional learning environment (CSILE). Paper presented at the annual meeting of the American Educational Research Association, Atlanta, GA.

Lampert, M. (1990). When the problem is not the question and the solution is not the answer: Mathematical knowing and teaching. American Educational Research Journal, 27, 29–63.

Lampert, M., Rittenhouse, P., & Crumbaugh, C. (1996). Agreeing to disagree: Developing sociable mathematical discourse. In D. R. Olson & N. Torrance (Eds.), The handbook of education and human development: New models of learning, teaching, and schooling. Cambridge, MA: Blackwell.

Landesman, S., & Ramey, C. (1989). Developmental psychology and mental retardation: Integrating scientific principles with treatment practices. American Psychologist, 44, 409–415.

Landrum, T. J., & Kauffman, J. M. (2006). Behavioral approaches to classroom management. In C. M. Evertson & C. S. Weinstein (Eds.), Handbook of classroom management: Research, practice, and contemporary issues (pp. 47–71). Mahwah, NJ: Erlbaum.

Lane, K., Falk, K., & Wehby, J. (2006). Classroom management in special education classrooms and resource rooms. In C. M. Evertson & C. S. Weinstein (Eds.), Handbook of classroom management: Research, practice, and contemporary issues (pp. 439–460). Mahwah, NJ: Erlbaum.

Langdon, S. (in press). Respect and school climate: "My respect is unconditional unless. . . ." Journal of Psychology.

Langer, E. J. (1997). The power of mindful learning. Reading, MA: Addison-Wesley.

Langer, E. J. (2000). Mindful learning. Current Directions in Psychological Science, 9, 220–223.

Langer, J. A. (2000). Excellence in English in middle and high school: How teachers' professional lives support student achievement. American Educational Research Journal, 37, 397–439.

Lansford, J. E., Chang, L., Dodge, K. A., Malone, P. S., Oburu, P., Palmérus, K., et al. (2005). Physical discipline and children's adjustment: Cultural normativeness as a moderator. Child Development, 76, 1234–1246.

Lansford, J. E., Deater-Decker, K., Dodge, K. A., Bates, J. E., & Pettit, G. S. (2003). Ethnic differences in the link between physical discipline and later adolescent externalizing behaviors. Journal of Child Psychology and Psychiatry, 44, 1–13.

Lanza, A., & Roselli, T. (1991). Effect of the hyper-textual approach versus the structured approach on students' achievement. Journal of Computer-Based Instruction, 18(2), 48–50.

La Paro, K. M., & Pianta, R. C. (2000). Predicting children's competence in the early school years: A meta-analytic review. Review of Educational Research, 70, 443–484.

Lapsley, D. K. (1993). Toward an integrated theory of adolescent ego development: The "new look" at adolescent egocentrism. American Journal of Orthopsychiatry, 63, 562–571.

Larkin, R. W. (1979). Suburban youth in cultural crisis. New York: Oxford University Press.

Larson, R. W. (2000). Toward a psychology of positive youth development. American Psychologist, 55, 170–183.

Larson, R. W., & Brown, J. R. (2007). Emotional development in adolescence: What can be learned from a high school theater program? Child Development, 78, 1083–1099.

Larson, R. W., Clore, G. L., & Wood, G. A. (1999). The emotions of romantic relationships: Do they wreak havoc on adolescents? In W. Furman, B. B. Brown, & C. Feiring (Eds.), The development of romantic relationships in adolescence (pp. 19–49). Cambridge, England: Cambridge University Press.

Larson, R. W., Moneta, G., Richards, M. H., & Wilson, S. (2002). Continuity, stability, and change in daily emotional experience across adolescence. Child Development, 73, 1151–1165.

Laupa, M., & Turiel, E. (1995). Social domain theory. In W. M. Kurtines & J. L. Gewirtz (Eds.), Moral development: An introduction. Boston: Allyn & Bacon.

Laursen, B., Bukowski, W. M., Aunola, K., & Nurmi, J.-E. (2007). Friendship moderates prospective associations between social isolation and adjustment problems in young children. Child Development, 78, 1395–1404.

Lave, J., & Wenger, E. (1991). Situated learning: Legitimate peripheral participation. Cambridge, England: Cambridge University Press.

Leaper, C., & Friedman, C. K. (2007). The socialization of gender. In J. E. Grusec & P. D. Hastings (Eds.), Handbook of socialization: Theory and research (pp. 561–587). New York: Guilford Press.

Learning First Alliance. (2001). Every child learning: Safe and supportive schools. Washington, DC: Association for Supervision and Curriculum Development.

Learning Technology Center, Vanderbilt University. (1996). Jasper in the classroom (videodisc). Mahwah, NJ: Erlbaum.

LeBlanc, L. A., Coates, A. M., Daneshvar, S., Charlop-Christy, M. H., Morris, C., & Lancaster, B. M. (2003). Using video modeling and reinforcement to teach perspective-taking skills to children with autism. Journal of Applied Behavior Analysis, 36, 253–257.

Lee, C. D., & Slaughter-Defoe, D. T. (1995). Historical and sociocultural influences on African and American education. In J. A. Banks & C. A. M. Banks (Eds.), Handbook of research on multicultural education. New York: Macmillan.

Lee, J., & Wong, K. K. (2004). The impact of accountability on racial and socioeconomic equity: Considering both school resources and achievement outcomes. American Educational Research Journal, 41, 797–832.

Lee, J. F., Jr., & Pruitt, K. W. (1984). Providing for individual differences in student learning: A mastery learning approach. Springfield, IL: Charles C. Thomas.

Lee, J.-S., & Bowen, N. K. (2006). Parent involvement, cultural capital, and the achievement gap among elementary school children. American Educational Research Journal, 43, 193–218.

Lee, O. (1999). Science knowledge, world views, and information sources in social and cultural contexts: Making sense after a natural disaster. American Educational Research Journal, 36, 187–219.

Lee, S. (1985). Children's acquisition of conditional logic structure: Teachable? Contemporary Educational Psychology, 10, 14–27.

Lee, V. E., & Burkam, D. T. (2003). Dropping out of high school: The role of school organization and structure. American Educational Research Journal, 40, 353–393.

Lee-Pearce, M. L., Plowman, T. S., & Touchstone, D. (1998). Starbase-Atlantis, a school without walls: A comparative study of an innovative science program for at-risk urban elementary students. Journal of Education for Students Placed at Risk, 3, 223–235.

LeFevre, J., Bisanz, J., & Mrkonjic, J. (1988). Cognitive arithmetic: Evidence for obligatory activation of arithmetic facts. Memory and Cognition, 16, 45–53.

Legault, L., Green-Demers, I., & Pelletier, L. (2006). Why do high school students lack motivation in the classroom? Toward an understanding of academic amotivation and the role of social support. Journal of Educational Psychology, 98, 567–582.

Lehmann, M., & Hasselhorn, M. (2007). Variable memory strategy use in children's adaptive intratask learning behavior: Developmental changes and working memory influences in free recall. Child Development, 78, 1068–1082.

Leichtman, M. D., & Ceci, S. J. (1995). The effects of stereotypes and suggestions on preschoolers' reports. Developmental Psychology, 31, 568–578.

Lein, L. (1975). Black American immigrant children: Their speech at home and school. Council on Anthropology and Education Quarterly, 6, 1–11.

Leinhardt, G. (1994). History: A time to be mindful. In G. Leinhardt, I. L. Beck, & C. Stainton (Eds.), Teaching and learning in history. Mahwah, NJ: Erlbaum.

Leinhardt, G., & Pallay, A. (1982). Restrictive educational settings: Exile or haven? Review of Educational Research, 52, 557–578.

Lejuez, C. W., Schaal, D. W., & O'Donnell, J. (1998). Behavioral pharmacology and the treatment of substance abuse. In J. J. Plaud & G. H. Eifert (Eds.), *From behavior theory to behavior therapy* (pp. 116–135). Needham Heights, MA: Allyn & Bacon.

Lennon, R., Ormrod, J. E., Burger, S. F., & Warren, E. (1990, October). *Belief systems of teacher education majors and their possible influences on future classroom performance.* Paper presented at the Northern Rocky Mountain Educational Research Association, Greeley, CO.

Lenroot, R. K., & Giedd, J. N. (2007). The structural development of the human brain as measured longitudinally with magnetic resonance imaging. In D. Coch, K. W. Fischer, & G. Dawson (Eds.), *Human behavior, learning, and the developing brain: Typical development* (pp. 50–73). New York: Guilford Press.

Lens, W. (2001). How to combine intrinsic task motivation with the motivational effects of the instrumentality of present tasks for future goals. In A. Efklides, J. Kuhl, & R. Sorrentino, (Eds.), *Trends and prospects in motivation research* (pp. 37–52). Dordrecht, the Netherlands: Kluwer.

Lens, W., Simons, J., & Dewitte, S. (2006). From duty to desire: The role of students' future time perspective and instrumentality perceptions for study motivation and self-regulation. In F. Pajares & T. Urdan (Eds.), *Adolescence and education: Vol. 2. Academic motivation of adolescents.* Greenwich, CT: Information Age.

Lentz, F. E. (1988). Reductive procedures. In J. C. Witt, S. N. Elliott, & F. M. Gresham (Eds.), *Handbook of behavior therapy in education.* New York: Plenum Press.

Lepper, M. R., Corpus, J. H., & Iyengar, S. S. (2005). Intrinsic and extrinsic motivational orientations in the classroom: Age differences and academic correlates. *Journal of Educational Psychology, 97,* 184–196.

Lepper, M. R., & Gurtner, J. (1989). Children and computers: Approaching the twenty-first century. *American Psychologist, 44,* 170–178.

Lepper, M. R., & Hodell, M. (1989). Intrinsic motivation in the classroom. In C. Ames & R. Ames (Eds.), *Research on motivation in education: Vol. 3. Goals and cognitions.* San Diego, CA: Academic Press.

Lerman, D. C., & Vorndran, C. M. (2002). On the status of knowledge for using punishment: Implications for treating behavior disorders. *Journal of Applied Behavior Analysis, 35,* 431–464.

Lerner, R. M. (2002). *Adolescence: Development, diversity, context, and application.* Upper Saddle River, NJ: Prentice Hall.

Lester, F. K., Jr., Lambdin, D. V., & Preston, R. V. (1997). A new vision of the nature and purposes of assessment in the mathematics classroom. In G. D. Phye (Ed.), *Handbook of classroom assessment: Learning, achievement, and adjustment.* San Diego, CA: Academic Press.

Leventhal, T., & Brooks-Gunn, J. (2000). The neighborhoods they live in: The effects of neighborhood residence upon child and adolescent outcomes. *Psychological Bulletin, 126,* 309–337.

Levin, J. R., & Mayer, R. E. (1993). Understanding illustrations in text. In B. K. Britton, A. Woodward, & M. Binkley (Eds.), *Learning from textbooks: Theory and practice.* Mahwah, NJ: Erlbaum.

Levine, D. U., & Lezotte, L. W. (1995). Effective schools research. In J. A. Banks & C. A. M. Banks (Eds.), *Handbook of research on multicultural education.* New York: Macmillan.

Levitt, M. J., Guacci-Franco, N., & Levitt, J. L. (1993). Convoys of social support in childhood and early adolescence: Structure and function. *Developmental Psychology, 29,* 811–818.

Levstik, L. S. (1994). Building a sense of history in a first-grade classroom. In J. Brophy (Ed.), *Advances in research on teaching: Vol. 4. Case studies of teaching and learning in social studies.* Greenwich, CT: JAI Press.

Levy, I., Kaplan, A., & Patrick, H. (2000, April). *Early adolescents' achievement goals, intergroup processes, and attitudes towards collaboration.* Paper presented at the annual meeting of the American Educational Research Association, New Orleans, LA.

Lewis, M. (1991). Self-knowledge and social influence. In M. Lewis & S. Feinman (Eds.), *Social influences and socialization in infancy: Vol. 6. Genesis of behavior* (pp. 111–134). New York: Plenum Press.

Lewis, T. J., Newcomer, L. L., Trussell, R., & Richter, M. (2006). Schoolwide positive behavior support: Building systems to develop and maintain appropriate social behavior. In C. M. Evertson & C. S. Weinstein (Eds.), *Handbook of classroom management: Research, practice, and contemporary issues* (pp. 833–854). Mahwah, NJ: Erlbaum.

Li, J. (2004). High abilities and excellence: A cultural perspective. In L. V. Shavinina & M. Ferrari (Eds.), *Beyond knowledge: Extracognitive aspects of developing high ability* (pp. 187–208). Mahwah, NJ: Erlbaum.

Li, J. (2005). Mind or virtue: Western and Chinese beliefs about learning. *Current Directions in Psychological Science, 14,* 190–194.

Li, J. (2006). Self in learning: Chinese adolescents' goals and sense of agency. *Child Development, 77,* 482–501.

Li, J., & Fischer, K. W. (2004). Thought and affect in American and Chinese learners' beliefs about learning. In D. Y. Dai & R. J. Sternberg (Eds.), *Motivation, emotion, and cognition: Integrative perspectives on intellectual functioning and development* (pp. 385–418). Mahwah, NJ: Erlbaum.

Liben, L. S., & Bigler, R. S. (2002). The developmental course of gender differentiation: Conceptualizing, measuring, and evaluating constructs and pathways. *Monographs of the Society for Research in Child Development, 67*(2, Serial No. 269).

Liben, L. S., & Downs, R. M. (1989). Understanding maps as symbols: The development of map concepts in children. In H. W. Reese (Ed.), *Advances in child development and behavior* (Vol. 22). San Diego, CA: Harcourt Brace Jovanovich.

Lichtman, J. W. (2001). Developmental neurobiology overview: Synapses, circuits, and plasticity. In D. B. Bailey, Jr., J. T. Bruer, F. J. Symons, & J. W. Lichtman (Eds.), *Critical thinking about critical periods* (pp. 27–42). Baltimore: Brookes.

Lickona, T. (1991). Moral development in the elementary school classroom. In W. M. Kurtines & J. L. Gewirtz (Eds.), *Moral behavior and development: Vol. 3. Application.* Mahwah, NJ: Erlbaum.

Lidz, C. S. (1991). Issues in the assessment of preschool children. In B. A. Bracken (Ed.), *The psychoeducational assessment of preschool children* (2nd ed., pp. 18–31). Boston: Allyn & Bacon.

Light, P., & Butterworth, G. (Eds.). (1993). *Context and cognition: Ways of learning and knowing.* Mahwah, NJ: Erlbaum.

Linderholm, T., Gustafson, M., van den Broek, P., & Lorch, R. F., Jr. (1997, March). *Effects of reading goals on inference generation.* Paper presented at the annual meeting of the American Educational Research Association, Chicago.

Linn, M. C., Clement, C., Pulos, S., & Sullivan, P. (1989). Scientific reasoning during adolescence: The influence of instruction in science knowledge and reasoning strategies. *Journal of Research in Science Teaching, 26,* 171–187.

Linn, M. C., Songer, N. B., & Eylon, B. (1996). Shifts and convergences in science learning and instruction. In D. C. Berliner & R. C. Calfee (Eds.), *Handbook of educational psychology.* New York: Macmillan.

Linn, R. L. (1994). Performance assessment: Policy promises and technical measurement standards. *Educational Researcher, 23*(9), 4–14.

Linn, R. L. (2000). Assessments and accountability. *Educational Researcher, 29*(2), 4–16.

Linn, R. L., & Miller, M. D. (2005). *Measurement and assessment in teaching* (9th ed.). Upper Saddle River, NJ: Merrill/Prentice Hall.

Linnenbrink, E. A. (2005). The dilemma of performance-approach goals: The use of multiple goal contexts to promote students' motivation and learning. *Journal of Educational Psychology, 97,* 197–213.

Linnenbrink, E. A., & Pintrich, P. R. (2002). Achievement goal theory and affect: An asymmetrical bidirectional model. *Educational Psychologist, 37,* 69–78.

Linnenbrink, E. A., & Pintrich, P. R. (2003). Achievement goals and intentional conceptual change. In G. M. Sinatra & P. R. Pintrich (Eds.), *Intentional conceptual change* (pp. 347–374). Mahwah, NJ: Erlbaum.

Linnenbrink, E. A., & Pintrich, P. R. (2004). Role of affect in cognitive processing in academic contexts. In D. Y. Dai & R. J. Sternberg (Eds.), *Motivation, emotion, and cognition: Integrative perspectives on intellectual functioning and development* (pp. 57–87). Mahwah, NJ: Erlbaum.

Linton, M. (1986). Ways of searching and the contents of memory. In D. C. Rubin (Ed.), *Autobiographical memory.* Cambridge, England: Cambridge University Press.

Lippa, R. A. (2002). *Gender, nature, and nurture.* Mahwah, NJ: Erlbaum.

Lipson, M. Y. (1983). The influence of religious affiliation on children's memory for text information. *Reading Research Quarterly, 18,* 448–457.

Liu, L. G. (1990, April). *The use of causal questioning to promote narrative comprehension and memory.* Paper presented at the annual meeting of the American Educational Research Association, Boston.

Lochman, J. E., & Dodge, K. A. (1994). Social-cognitive processes of severely violent, moderately aggressive, and nonaggressive boys. *Journal of Consulting and Clinical Psychology, 62,* 366–374.

Locke, E. A., & Latham, G. P. (1990). *A theory of goal setting and task performance.* Upper Saddle River, NJ: Prentice Hall.

Locke, E. A., & Latham, G. P. (2002). Building a practically useful theory of goal setting and task motivation: A 35-year odyssey. *American Psychologist, 57,* 705–717.

Locke, E. A., & Latham, G. P. (2006). New directions in goal-setting theory. *Current Directions in Psychological Science, 15,* 265–268.

Lockhart, K. L., Chang, B., & Story, T. (2002). Young children's beliefs about the stability of traits: Protective optimism? *Child Development, 73,* 1408–1430.

Lodewyk, K. R., & Winne, P. H. (2005). Relations among the structure of learning tasks, achievement, and changes in self-efficacy in secondary students. *Journal of Educational Psychology, 97,* 3–12.

Lodico, M. G., Ghatala, E. S., Levin, J. R., Pressley, M., & Bell, J. A. (1983). The effects of strategy monitoring training on children's selection of effective memory strategies. *Journal of Experimental Child Psychology, 35,* 273–277.

Loftus, E. F. (1991). Made in memory: Distortions in recollection after misleading information. In G. H. Bower (Ed.), *The psychology of learning and motivation: Advances in research and theory* (Vol. 27). San Diego, CA: Academic Press.

Loftus, E. F., & Loftus, G. R. (1980). On the permanence of stored information in the human brain. *American Psychologist, 35,* 409–420.

Lomawaima, K. T. (1995). Educating Native Americans. In J. A. Banks & C. A. M. Banks (Eds.), *Handbook of research on multicultural education.* New York: Macmillan.

Lopez, A. M. (2003). Mixed-race school-age children: A summary of census 2000 data. *Educational Researcher, 32*(6), 25–37.

López, G. R. (2001). Redefining parental involvement: Lessons from high-performing migrant-impacted schools. *American Educational Research Journal, 38,* 253–288.

Loranger, A. L. (1994). The study strategies of successful and unsuccessful high school students. *Journal of Reading Behavior, 26,* 347–360.

Lorch, R. F., Jr., Lorch, E. P., & Inman, W. E. (1993). Effects of signaling topic structure on text recall. *Journal of Educational Psychology, 85,* 281–290.

Losey, K. M. (1995). Mexican American students and classroom interaction: An overview and critique. *Review of Educational Research, 65,* 283–318.

Losh, S. C. (2003). On the application of social cognition and social location to creating causal explanatory structures. *Educational Research Quarterly, 26*(3), 17–33.

Lotan, R. A. (2006). Managing groupwork in heterogeneous classrooms. In C. M. Evertson & C. S. Weinstein (Eds.), *Handbook of classroom management: Research, practice, and contemporary issues* (pp. 525–539). Mahwah, NJ: Erlbaum.

Lou, Y., Abrami, P. C., & d'Apollonia, S. (2001). Small group and individual learning with technology: A meta-analysis. *Review of Educational Research, 71*, 449–521.

Lou, Y., Abrami, P. C., Spence, J. C., Poulsen, C., Chambers, B., & d'Apollonia, S. (1996). Within-class grouping: A meta-analysis. *Review of Educational Research, 66*, 423–458.

Lovell, K. (1979). Intellectual growth and the school curriculum. In F. B. Murray (Ed.), *The impact of Piagetian theory: On education, philosophy, psychiatry, and psychology.* Baltimore: University Park Press.

Lovett, S. B., & Flavell, J. H. (1990). Understanding and remembering: Children's knowledge about the differential effects of strategy and task variables on comprehension and memorization. *Child Development, 61*, 1842–1858.

Lubart, T. I., & Mouchiroud, C. (2003). Creativity: A source of difficulty in problem solving. In J. E. Davidson & R. J. Sternberg (Eds.), *The psychology of problem solving* (pp. 127–148). Cambridge, England: Cambridge University Press.

Lucariello, J., Kyratzis, A., & Nelson, K. (1992). Taxonomic knowledge: What kind and when? *Child Development, 63*, 978–998.

Luchins, A. S. (1942). Mechanization in problem solving: The effect of Einstellung. *Psychological Monographs, 54* (Whole No. 248).

Luciana, M., Conklin, H. M., Hooper, C. J., & Yarger, R. S. (2005). The development of nonverbal working memory and executive control processes in adolescents. *Child Development, 76*, 697–712.

Luckasson, R., Borthwick-Duffy, S., Buntinx, W. H. E., Coulter, D. L., Craig, E. M., Reeve, A., et al. (Eds.). (2002). *Mental retardation: Definition, classification, and systems of supports* (10th ed.). Washington, DC: American Association on Mental Retardation.

Luna, B., Garver, K. E., Urban, T. A., Lazar, N. A., & Sweeney, J. A. (2004). Maturation of cognitive processes from late childhood to adulthood. *Child Development, 75*, 1357–1372.

Lundeberg, M. A., & Fox, P. W. (1991). Do laboratory findings on test expectancy generalize to classroom outcomes? *Review of Educational Research, 61*, 94–106.

Lupart, J. L. (1995). Exceptional learners and teaching for transfer. In A. McKeough, J. Lupart, & A. Marini (Eds.), *Teaching for transfer: Fostering generalization in learning.* Mahwah, NJ: Erlbaum.

Lykken, D. T. (1997). The American crime factory. *Psychological Inquiry, 8*, 261–270.

Ma, X., & Kishor, N. (1997). Attitude toward self, social factors, and achievement in mathematics: A meta-analytic review. *Educational Psychology Review, 9*, 89–120.

Maccoby, E. E. (2002). Gender and group process: A developmental perspective. *Current Directions in Psychological Science, 11*, 54–58.

Maccoby, E. E. (2007). Historical overview of socialization research and theory. In J. E. Grusec & P. D. Hastings (Eds.), *Handbook of socialization: Theory and research* (pp. 13–41). New York: Guilford Press.

Maccoby, E. E., & Martin, J. A. (1983). Socialization in the context of the family: Parent-child interaction. In E. M. Hetherington (Ed.), *Handbook of child psychology: Vol. 4. Socialization, personality, and social development* (4th ed.). New York: Wiley.

MacDonald, S., Uesiliana, K., & Hayne, H. (2000). Cross-cultural and gender differences in childhood amnesia. *Memory, 8*, 365–376.

Mace, F. C., Belfiore, P. J., & Shea, M. C. (1989). Operant theory and research on self-regulation. In B. J. Zimmerman & D. H. Schunk (Eds.), *Self-regulated learning and academic achievement: Theory, research, and practice.* New York: Springer-Verlag.

Mace, F. C., Hock, M. L., Lalli, J. S., West, B. J., Belfiore, P., Pinter, E., et al. (1988). Behavioral momentum in the treatment of noncompliance. *Journal of Applied Behavior Analysis, 21*, 123–141.

Mace, F. C., & Kratochwill, T. R. (1988). Self-monitoring. In J. C. Witt, S. N. Elliott, & F. M. Gresham (Eds.), *Handbook of behavior therapy in education.* New York: Plenum Press.

Mac Iver, D. J., Reuman, D. A., & Main, S. R. (1995). Social structuring of the school: Studying what is, illuminating what could be. In J. T. Spence, J. M. Darley, & D. J. Foss (Eds.), *Annual review of psychology* (Vol. 46, pp. 375–400). Palo Alto, CA: Annual Review.

Mac Iver, D. J., Stipek, D. J., & Daniels, D. H. (1991). Explaining within-semester changes in student effort in junior high school and senior high school courses. *Journal of Educational Psychology, 83*, 201–211.

MacLean, D. J., Sasse, D. K., Keating, D. P., Stewart, B. E., & Miller, F. K. (1995, April). *All-girls' mathematics and science instruction in early adolescence: Longitudinal effects.* Paper presented at the annual meeting of the American Educational Research Association, San Francisco.

Maehr, M. L. (1984). Meaning and motivation: Toward a theory of personal investment. In R. Ames & C. Ames (Eds.), *Research on motivation in education: Vol. 1. Student motivation.* San Diego, CA: Academic Press.

Maehr, M. L., & Anderman, E. M. (1993). Reinventing schools for early adolescents: Emphasizing task goals. *Elementary School Journal, 93*, 593–610.

Maehr, M. L., & Meyer, H. A. (1997). Understanding motivation and schooling: Where we've been, where we are, and where we need to go. *Educational Psychology Review, 9*, 371–409.

Magnusson, S. J., Boyle, R. A., & Templin, M. (1994, April). *Conceptual development: Re-examining knowledge construction in science.* Paper presented at the annual meeting of the American Educational Research Association, New Orleans, LA.

Mahoney, J. L., Cairns, B. D., & Farmer, T. W. (2003). Promoting interpersonal competence and educational success through extracurricular activity participation. *Journal of Educational Psychology, 95*, 409–418.

Maker, C. J., & Schiever, S. W. (Eds.). (1989). *Critical issues in gifted education: Vol. 2. Defensible programs for cultural and ethnic minorities.* Austin, TX: Pro-Ed.

Mandler, G., & Pearlstone, Z. (1966). Free and constrained concept learning and subsequent recall. *Journal of Verbal Learning and Verbal Behavior, 5*, 126–131.

Mangels, J. (2004, May). *The influence of intelligence beliefs on attention and learning: A neurophysiological approach.* Invited address presented at the annual meeting of the American Psychological Society, Chicago.

Marachi, R., Friedel, J., & Midgley, C. (2001, April). *"I sometimes annoy my teacher during math": Relations between student perceptions of the teacher and disruptive behavior in the classroom.* Paper presented at the annual meeting of the American Educational Research Association, Seattle, WA.

Marchand, G., & Skinner, E. A. (2007). Motivational dynamics of children's academic help-seeking and concealment. *Journal of Educational Psychology, 99*, 65–82.

Marcia, J. E. (1980). Identity in adolescence. In J. Adelson (Ed.), *Handbook of adolescent psychology.* New York: Wiley.

Marcia, J. E. (1988). Common processes underlying ego identity, cognitive/moral development, and individuation. In D. K. Lapsley & F. C. Power (Eds.), *Self, ego, and identity: Integrative approaches* (pp. 211–225). New York: Springer-Verlag.

Marcia, J. (1991). Identity and self-development. In R. M. Lerner, A. C. Petersen, & J. Brooks-Gunn (Eds.), *Encyclopedia of adolescence* (Vol. 1, pp. 529–533). New York: Garland.

Marcus, R. F. (1980). Empathy and popularity of preschool children. *Child Study Journal, 10*, 133–145.

Mareschal, D., Johnson, M. H., Sirois, S., Spratling, M. W., Thomas, M. S. C., & Westermann, G. (2007). *Neuroconstructivism: Vol. 1. How the brain constructs cognition.* Oxford, England: Oxford University Press.

Maria, K. (1998). Self-confidence and the process of conceptual change. In B. Guzzetti & C. Hynd (Eds.), *Perspectives on conceptual change: Multiple ways to understand knowing and learning in a complex world* (pp. 7–16). Mahwah, NJ: Erlbaum.

Markman, E. M. (1977). Realizing that you don't understand: A preliminary investigation. *Child Development, 48*, 986–992.

Markman, E. M. (1979). Realizing that you don't understand: Elementary school children's awareness of inconsistencies. *Child Development, 50*, 643–655.

Markus, H. R., & Hamedani, M. G. (2007). Sociocultural psychology: The dynamic interdependence among self systems and social systems. In S. Kitayama & D. Cohen (Eds.), *Handbook of cultural psychology* (pp. 3–39). New York: Guilford Press.

Markus, H. R., & Kitayama, S. (1991). Culture and the self: Implications for cognition, emotion, and motivation. *Psychological Review, 98*, 224–253.

Marsh, H. W. (1990). Causal ordering of academic self-concept and academic achievement: A multiwave, longitudinal panel analysis. *Journal of Educational Psychology, 82*, 646–656.

Marsh, H. W., & Craven, R. (1997). Academic self-concept: Beyond the dustbowl. In G. D. Phye (Ed.), *Handbook of classroom assessment: Learning, achievement, and adjustment.* San Diego, CA: Academic Press.

Marsh, H. W., & Craven, R. G. (2006). Reciprocal effects of self-concept and performance from a multidimensional perspective: Beyond seductive pleasure and unidimensional perspectives. *Perspectives on Psychological Science, 1*, 133–163.

Marsh, H. W., & Hau, K.-T. (2003). Big-fish–little-pond effect on academic self-concept: A cross-cultural (26-country) test of the negative effects of academically selective schools. *American Psychologist, 58*, 364–376.

Marshall, H. H. (1992). *Redefining student learning: Roots of educational change.* Norwood, NJ: Ablex.

Martin, A. J., Marsh, H. W., & Debus, R. L. (2001). A quadripolar need achievement representation of self-handicapping and defensive pessimism. *American Educational Research Journal, 38*, 583–610.

Martin, A. J., Marsh, H. W., Williamson, A., & Debus, R. L. (2003). Self-handicapping, defensive pessimism, and goal orientation: A qualitative study of university students. *Journal of Educational Psychology, 95*, 617–628.

Martin, C. L., & Ruble, D. (2004). Children's search for gender cues: Cognitive perspectives on gender development. *Current Directions in Psychological Science, 13*, 67–70.

Martin, S. S., Brady, M. P., & Williams, R. E. (1991). Effects of toys on the social behavior of preschool children in integrated and nonintegrated groups: Investigation of a setting event. *Journal of Early Intervention, 15*, 153–161.

Martin, V. L., & Pressley, M. (1991). Elaborative-interrogation effects depend on the nature of the question. *Journal of Educational Psychology, 83*, 113–119.

Marzano, R. J. (with Marzano, J. S., & Pickering, D. J.). (2003). *Classroom management that works: Research-based strategies for every teacher.* Alexandria, VA: Association for Supervision and Curriculum Development.

Marzano, R. J., & Costa, A. L. (1988). Question: Do standardized tests measure general cognitive skills? Answer: No. *Educational Leadership, 45*(8), 66–71.

Maslow, A. H. (1973). Theory of human motivation. In R. J. Lowry (Ed.), *Dominance, self-esteem, self-actualization: Germinal papers of A. H. Maslow.* Monterey, CA: Brooks/Cole.

Maslow, A. H. (1987). *Motivation and personality* (3rd ed.). New York: Harper & Row.

Massialas, B. G., & Zevin, J. (1983). *Teaching creatively: Learning through discovery.* Malabar, FL: Krieger.

Masten, A. S. (2001). Ordinary magic: Resilience processes in development. *American Psychologist, 56*, 227–238.

Masten, A. S., & Coatsworth, J. D. (1998). The development of competence in favorable and unfavorable environments. *American Psychologist, 53*, 205–220.

Mastropieri, M. A., & Scruggs, T. E. (2000). *The inclusive classroom: Strategies for effective instruction.* Upper Saddle River, NJ: Merrill/Prentice Hall.

Mathes, P. G., Torgesen, J. K., & Allor, J. H. (2001). The effects of peer-assisted literacy strategies for first-grade readers with and without additional computer-assisted instruction. *American Educational Research Journal, 38*, 371–410.

Matthews, G., Zeidner, M., & Roberts, R. D. (2006). Models of personality and affect for education: A review and synthesis. In P. A. Alexander & P. H. Winne (Eds.), *Handbook of educational psychology* (2nd ed., pp. 163–186). Mahwah, NJ: Erlbaum.

Maughan, A., & Cicchetti, D. (2002). Impact of child maltreatment and interadult violence on children's emotion regulation abilities and socioemotional adjustment. *Child Development, 73,* 1525–1542.

Maxmell, D., Jarrett, O. S., & Dickerson, C. (1998, April). *Are we forgetting the children's needs? Recess through the children's eyes.* Paper presented at the annual meeting of the American Educational Research Association, San Diego, CA.

Mayer, J. D. (2001). Emotion, intelligence, and emotional intelligence. In J. P. Forgas (Ed.), *Handbook of affect and social cognition* (pp. 410–431). Mahwah, NJ: Erlbaum.

Mayer, J. D., & Cobb, C. D. (2000). Educational policy on emotional intelligence. *Educational Psychology Review, 12,* 163–183.

Mayer, R. E. (1989). Models for understanding. *Review of Educational Research, 59,* 43–64.

Mayer, R. E. (1996). Learning strategies for making sense out of expository text: The SOI model for guiding three cognitive processes in knowledge construction. *Educational Psychology Review, 8,* 357–371.

Mayer, R. E. (1998). Does the brain have a place in educational psychology? *Educational Psychology Review, 10,* 389–396.

Mayer, R. E. (2004). Should there be a three-strikes rule against pure discovery learning? *American Psychologist, 59,* 14–19.

Mayer, R. E., & Gallini, J. (1990). When is an illustration worth ten thousand words? *Journal of Educational Psychology, 82,* 715–726.

Mayer, R. E., & Massa, L. J. (2003). Three facets of visual and verbal learners: Cognitive ability, cognitive style, and learning preference. *Journal of Educational Psychology, 95,* 833–846.

Mayer, R. E., & Wittrock, M. C. (1996). Problem-solving transfer. In D. C. Berliner & R. C. Calfee (Eds.), *Handbook of educational psychology.* New York: Macmillan.

Mayer, R. E., & Wittrock, M. C. (2006). Problem solving. In P. A. Alexander & P. H. Winne (Eds.), *Handbook of educational psychology* (2nd ed., pp. 287–303). Mahwah, NJ: Erlbaum.

Mayfield, K. H., & Chase, P. N. (2002). The effects of cumulative practice on mathematics problem solving. *Journal of Applied Behavior Analysis, 35,* 105–123.

McAlpine, L. (1992). Language, literacy and education: Case studies of Cree, Inuit and Mohawk communities. *Canadian Children, 17*(1), 17–30.

McAlpine, L., & Taylor, D. M. (1993). Instructional preferences of Cree, Inuit, and Mohawk teachers. *Journal of American Indian Education, 33*(1), 1–20.

McAshan, H. H. (1979). *Competency-based education and behavioral objectives.* Englewood Cliffs, NJ: Educational Technology.

McBrien, J. L. (2005). *Discrimination and academic motivation in adolescent refugee girls.* Unpublished doctoral dissertation, Emory University, Atlanta, GA.

McCall, R. B., & Mash, C. W. (1995). Infant cognition and its relation to mature intelligence. *Annals of Child Development, 4,* 27–56.

McCall, R. B., & Plemons, B. W. (2001). The concept of critical periods and their implications for early childhood services. In D. B. Bailey, Jr., J. T. Bruer, F. J. Symons, & J. W. Lichtman (Eds.), *Critical thinking about critical periods* (pp. 267–287). Baltimore: Brookes.

McCallum, R. S., & Bracken, B. A. (1993). Interpersonal relations between school children and their peers, parents, and teachers. *Educational Psychology Review, 5,* 155–176.

McCarty, T. L., & Watahomigie, L. J. (1998). Language and literacy in American Indian and Alaska Native communities. In B. Pérez (Ed.), *Sociocultural contexts of language and literacy.* Mahwah, NJ: Erlbaum.

McCaslin, M., & Good, T. L. (1996). The informal curriculum. In D. C. Berliner & R. C. Calfee (Eds.), *Handbook of educational psychology.* New York: Macmillan.

McClowry, S. G. (1998). The science and art of using temperament as the basis for intervention. *School Psychology Review, 27,* 551–563.

McComas, J. J., Thompson, A., & Johnson, L. (2003). The effects of presession attention on problem behavior maintained by different reinforcers. *Journal of Applied Behavior Analysis, 36,* 297–307.

McCombs, B. L. (1988). Motivational skills training: Combining metacognitive, cognitive, and affective learning strategies. In C. E. Weinstein, E. T. Goetz, & P. A. Alexander (Eds.), *Learning and study strategies: Issues in assessment, instruction, and evaluation.* San Diego, CA: Harcourt Brace Jovanovich.

McCombs, B. L. (1996). Alternative perspectives for motivation. In L. Baker, P. Afflerbach, & D. Reinking (Eds.), *Developing engaged readers in school and home communities.* Hillsdale, NJ: Erlbaum.

McCombs, B. L. (Ed.). (2005). *Learner-centered principles: A framework for teaching.* Mahwah, NJ: Erlbaum.

McCourt, F. (2005). *Teacher man: A memoir.* New York: Scribner.

McCoy, L. P. (1990, April). *Correlates of mathematics anxiety.* Paper presented at the annual meeting of the American Educational Research Association, Boston.

McCutchen, D. (1996). A capacity theory of writing: Working memory in composition. *Educational Psychology Review, 8,* 299–325.

McDaniel, L. (1997). *For better, for worse, forever.* New York: Bantam.

McDaniel, M. A., & Einstein, G. O. (1989). Material-appropriate processing: A contextualist approach to reading and studying strategies. *Educational Psychology Review, 1,* 113–145.

McDaniel, M. A., & Schlager, M. S. (1990). Discovery learning and transfer of problem-solving skills. *Cognition and Instruction, 7,* 129–159.

McDevitt, M., & Chaffee, S. H. (1998). Second chance political socialization: "Trickle-up" effects of children on parents. In T. J. Johnson, C. E. Hays, & S. P. Hays (Eds.), *Engaging the public: How government and the media can reinvigorate American democracy* (pp. 57–66). Lanham, MD: Rowman & Littlefield.

McDevitt, T. M., & Ormrod, J. E. (2007). *Child development and education* (3rd ed.). Upper Saddle River, NJ: Merrill/Prentice Hall.

McGee, K. D., Knight, S. L., & Boudah, D. J. (2001, April). *Using reciprocal teaching in secondary inclusive English classroom instruction.* Paper presented at the annual meeting of the American Educational Research Association, Seattle, WA.

McGee, L. M. (1992). An exploration of meaning construction in first graders' grand conversations. In C. K. Kinzer & D. J. Leu (Eds.), *Literacy research, theory, and practice: Views from many perspectives.* Chicago: National Reading Conference.

McGregor, H. A., & Elliot, A. J. (2002). Achievement goals as predictors of achievement-relevant processes prior to task engagement. *Journal of Educational Psychology, 94,* 381–395.

McGrew, K. S., Flanagan, D. P., Zeith, T. Z., & Vanderwood, M. (1997). Beyond *g*: The impact of *Gf-Gc* specific cognitive abilities research on the future use and interpretation of intelligence tests in the schools. *School Psychology Review, 26,* 189–210.

McKerchar, P. M., & Thompson, R. H. (2004). A descriptive analysis of potential reinforcement contingencies in the preschool classroom. *Journal of Applied Behavior Analysis, 37,* 431–444.

McKown, C., & Weinstein, R. S. (2003). The development and consequences of stereotype consciousness in middle childhood. *Child Development, 74,* 498–515.

McLeod, D. B., & Adams, V. M. (Eds.). (1989). *Affect and mathematical problem solving: A new perspective.* New York: Springer-Verlag.

McLoyd, V. C. (1998). Socioeconomic disadvantage and child development. *American Psychologist, 53,* 185–204.

McMillan, J. H., & Reed, D. F. (1994). At-risk students and resiliency: Factors contributing to academic success. *Clearing House, 67*(3), 137–140.

McMillan, J. H., Singh, J., & Simonetta, L. G. (1994). The tyranny of self-oriented self-esteem. *Educational Horizons, 72*(3), 141–145.

McNamara, D. S., & Healy, A. F. (1995). A generation advantage for multiplication skill training and nonword vocabulary acquisition. In A. F. Healy & L. E. Bourne, Jr. (Eds.), *Learning and memory of knowledge and skills: Durability and specificity.* Thousand Oaks, CA: Sage.

McNamara, E. (1987). Behavioural approaches in the secondary school. In K. Wheldall (Ed.), *The behaviourist in the classroom.* London: Allen & Unwin.

McNeil, N. M., & Alibali, M. W. (2000). Learning mathematics from procedural instruction: Externally imposed goals influence what is learned. *Journal of Educational Psychology, 92,* 734–744.

McRobbie, C., & Tobin, K. (1995). Restraints to reform: The congruence of teacher and student actions in a chemistry classroom. *Journal of Research in Science Teaching, 32,* 373–385.

McWhiter, C. C., & Bloom, L. A. (1994). The effects of a student-operated business curriculum on the on-task behavior of students with behavioral disorders. *Behavioral Disorders, 19,* 136–141.

Medin, D. L. (2005, August). *Role of culture and expertise in cognition.* Invited address presented at the annual meeting of the American Psychological Association, Washington, DC.

Meece, J. L. (1994). The role of motivation in self-regulated learning. In D. H. Schunk & B. J. Zimmerman (Eds.), *Self-regulation of learning and performance: Issues and educational applications.* Mahwah, NJ: Erlbaum.

Meece, J. L., & Holt, K. (1993). A pattern analysis of students' achievement goals. *Journal of Educational Psychology, 85,* 582–590.

Meehan, B. T., Hughes, J. N., & Cavell, T. A. (2003). Teacher-student relationships as compensatory resources for aggressive children. *Child Development, 74,* 1145–1157.

Mehan, H. (1979). *Social organization in the classroom.* Cambridge, MA: Harvard University Press.

Meichenbaum, D. (1977). *Cognitive-behavior modification: An integrative approach.* New York: Plenum Press.

Meichenbaum, D., & Goodman, J. (1971). Training impulsive children to talk to themselves: A means of developing self-control. *Journal of Abnormal Psychology, 77,* 115–126.

Mejía-Arauz, R., Rogoff, B., Dexter, A., & Najafi, B. (2007). Cultural variation in children's social organization. *Child Development, 78,* 1001–1014.

Meltzer, L. (Ed.). (2007). *Executive function in education: From theory to practice.* New York: Guilford Press.

Meltzer, L., & Krishnan, K. (2007). Executive function difficulties and learning disabilities: Understandings and misunderstandings. In L. Meltzer (Ed.), *Executive function in education: From theory to practice* (pp. 77–105). New York: Guilford Press.

Meltzer, L., Pollica, L. S., & Barzillai, M. (2007). Executive function in the classroom: Embedding strategy instruction into daily teaching practices. In L. Meltzer (Ed.), *Executive function in education: From theory to practice* (pp. 165–193). New York: Guilford Press.

Mendoza-Denton, R., & Mischel, W. (2007). Integrating system approaches to culture and personality: The cultural cognitive-affective processing system. In S. Kitayama & D. Cohen (Eds.), *Handbook of cultural psychology* (pp. 175–195). New York: Guilford Press.

Menéndez, R. (Director). (1988). *Stand and deliver* [Motion picture]. United States: Warner Studios.

Menyuk, P., & Menyuk, D. (1988). Communicative competence: A historical and cultural perspective. In J. S. Wurzel (Ed.), *Toward multiculturalism: A reader in multicultural education.* Yarmouth, ME: Intercultural Press.

Mergendoller, J. R., Markham, T., Ravitz, J., & Larmer, J. (2006). Pervasive management of project based learning: Teachers as guides and facilitators. In C. M. Evertson & C. S. Weinstein (Eds.), *Handbook of classroom management: Research, practice, and contemporary issues* (pp. 583–615). Mahwah, NJ: Erlbaum.

Merrill, P. F., Hammons, K., Vincent, B. R., Reynolds, P. L., Christensen, L., & Tolman, M. N. (1996).

Computers in education (3rd ed.). Needham Heights, MA: Allyn & Bacon.

Merzenich, M. M. (2001). Cortical plasticity contributing to child development. In J. L. McClelland & R. S. Siegler (Eds.), *Mechanisms of cognitive development: Behavioral and neural perspectives* (pp. 67–95). Mahwah, NJ: Erlbaum.

Mesquita, B., & Leu, J. (2007). The cultural psychology of emotion. In S. Kitayama & D. Cohen (Eds.), *Handbook of cultural psychology* (pp. 734–759). New York: Guilford Press.

Messer, S. B. (1976). Reflection-impulsivity: A review. *Psychological Bulletin, 83,* 1026–1052.

Messick, S. (1983). Assessment of children. In W. Kessen (Ed.), *Handbook of child psychology* (Vol. 1). New York: Wiley.

Messick, S. (1994a). The interplay of evidence and consequences in the validation of performance assessments. *Educational Researcher, 23*(2), 13–23.

Messick, S. (1994b). The matter of style: Manifestations of personality in cognition, learning, and testing. *Educational Psychologist, 29,* 121–136.

Metz, K. E. (1995). Reassessment of developmental constraints on children's science instruction. *Review of Educational Research, 65,* 93–127.

Meyer, D. K., & Turner, J. C. (2002). Discovering emotion in classroom motivation research. *Educational Psychologist, 37,* 107–114.

Meyer, K. A. (1999). Functional analysis and treatment of problem behavior exhibited by elementary school children. *Journal of Applied Behavior Analysis, 32,* 229–232.

Middleton, M. J., & Midgley, C. (1997). Avoiding the demonstration of lack of ability: An under-explored aspect of goal theory. *Journal of Educational Psychology, 89,* 710–718.

Middleton, M. J., & Midgley, C. (2002). Beyond motivation: Middle school students' perceptions of press for understanding in math. *Contemporary Educational Psychology, 27,* 373–391.

Midgley, C., Kaplan, A., & Middleton, M. (2001). Performance-approach goals: Good for what, for whom, under what circumstances, and at what cost? *Journal of Educational Psychology, 93,* 77–86.

Midgley, C., Kaplan, A., Middleton, M., Maehr, M., Urdan, T., Anderman, L., et al. (1998). The development and validation of scales assessing students' achievement goal orientations. *Contemporary Educational Psychology, 23,* 113–131.

Midgley, C., Middleton, M. J., Gheen, M. H., & Kumar, R. (2002). Stage-environment fit revisited: A goal theory approach to examining school transitions. In C. Midgley (Ed.), *Goals, goal structures, and patterns of adaptive learning* (pp. 109–142). Mahwah, NJ: Erlbaum.

Mikaelsen, B. (1996). *Countdown.* New York: Hyperion Books for Children.

Miles, S. B., & Stipek, D. (2006). Contemporaneous and longitudinal associations between social behavior and literacy achievement in a sample of low-income elementary school children. *Child Development, 77,* 103–117.

Miller, A. (1987). Cognitive styles: An integrated model. *Educational Psychology, 7,* 251–268.

Miller, A. (2006). Contexts and attributions for difficult behavior in English classrooms. In C. M. Evertson & C. S. Weinstein (Eds.), *Handbook of classroom management: Research, practice, and contemporary issues* (pp. 1093–1120). Mahwah, NJ: Erlbaum.

Miller, B. C., & Benson, B. (1999). Romantic and sexual relationship development during adolescence. In W. Furman, B. B. Brown, & C. Feiring (Eds.), *The development of romantic relationships in adolescence* (pp. 99–121). Cambridge, England: Cambridge University Press.

Miller, D. L., & Kelley, M. L. (1994). The use of goal setting and contingency contracting for improving children's homework performance. *Journal of Applied Behavior Analysis, 27,* 73–84.

Miller, G. A. (1956). The magical number seven, plus or minus two: Some limits on our capacity for processing information. *Psychological Review, 63,* 81–97.

Miller, G. A., & Gildea, P. M. (1987). How children learn words. *Scientific American, 257,* 94–99.

Miller, J. G. (1997). A cultural-psychology perspective on intelligence. In R. J. Sternberg & E. L. Grigorenko (Eds.), *Intelligence, heredity, and environment* (pp. 269–302). Cambridge, England: Cambridge University Press.

Miller, J. G. (2007). Cultural psychology of moral development. In S. Kitayama & D. Cohen (Eds.), *Handbook of cultural psychology* (pp. 477–499). New York: Guilford Press.

Miller, L. S. (1995). *An American imperative: Accelerating minority educational advancement.* New Haven, CT: Yale University Press.

Miller, P. A., Eisenberg, N., Fabes, R. A., & Shell, R. (1996). Relations of moral reasoning and vicarious emotion to young children's prosocial behavior toward peers and adults. *Developmental Psychology, 32,* 210–219.

Miller, R. B., & Brickman, S. J. (2004). A model of future-oriented motivation and self-regulation. *Educational Psychology Review, 16,* 9–33.

Miller, S. D., Heafner, T., Massey, D., & Strahan, D. B. (2003, April). *Students' reactions to teachers' attempts to create the necessary conditions to promote the acquisition of self-regulation skills.* Paper presented at the annual meeting of the American Educational Research Association, Chicago.

Miller, S. D., & Meece, J. L. (1997). Enhancing elementary students' motivation to read and write: A classroom intervention study. *Journal of Educational Research, 90,* 286–300.

Milner, H. R. (2006). Classroom management in urban classrooms. In C. M. Evertson & C. S. Weinstein (Eds.), *Handbook of classroom management: Research, practice, and contemporary issues* (pp. 491–522). Mahwah, NJ: Erlbaum.

Minami, M., & McCabe, A. (1996). Compressed collections of experiences: Some Asian American traditions. In A. McCabe (Ed.), *Chameleon readers: Some problems cultural differences in narrative structure pose for multicultural literacy programs* (pp. 72–97). New York: McGraw-Hill.

Minsky, M. (2006). *The emotion machine: Commonsense thinking, artificial intelligence, and the future of the human mind.* New York: Simon and Schuster.

Minstrell, J., & Stimpson, V. (1996). A classroom environment for learning: Guiding students' reconstruction of understanding and reasoning. In L. Schauble & R. Glaser (Eds.), *Innovations in learning: New environments for education.* Mahwah, NJ: Erlbaum.

Mintzes, J. J., Wandersee, J. H., & Novak, J. D. (1997). Meaningful learning in science: The human constructivist perspective. In G. D. Phye (Ed.), *Handbook of academic learning: Construction of knowledge.* San Diego, CA: Academic Press.

Mischel, W., & Shoda, Y. (1995). A cognitive-affective system theory of personality: Reconceptualizing situations, dispositions, dynamics, and invariance in personality structure. *Psychological Review, 102,* 246–268.

Mistry, R. S., Vandewater, E. A., Huston, A. C., & McLoyd, V. C. (2002). Economic well-being and children's social adjustment: The role of family process in an ethnically diverse low-income sample. *Child Development, 73,* 935–951.

Mitchell, D. B. (2006). Nonconscious priming after 17 years: Invulnerable implicit memory? *Psychological Science 17,* 925–929.

Mitchell, K. J., Wolak, J., & Finkelhor, D. (2005). Internet sex crimes against minors. In K. A. Kendall-Tackett & S. M. Giacomoni (Eds.), *Child victimization: Maltreatment, bullying and dating violence, prevention and intervention.* Kingston, NJ: Civic Research Institute.

Mitchell, M. (1993). Situational interest: Its multifaceted structure in the secondary school mathematics classroom. *Journal of Educational Psychology, 85,* 424–436.

Mohatt, G., & Erickson, F. (1981). Cultural differences in teaching styles in an Odawa school: A sociolinguistic approach. In H. T. Trueba, G. P. Guthrie, & K. H. Au (Eds.), *Culture and the bilingual classroom: Studies in classroom ethnography.* Rowley, MA: Newbury House.

Moje, E. B., & Shepardson, D. P. (1998). Social interactions and children's changing understanding of electric circuits: Exploring unequal power relations in "peer"-learning groups. In B. Guzzetti & C. Hynd (Eds.), *Perspectives on conceptual change: Multiple ways to understand knowing and learning in a complex world* (pp. 225–234). Mahwah, NJ: Erlbaum.

Moles, O. C. (Ed.). (1990). *Student discipline strategies: Research and practice.* Albany: State University of New York Press.

Moon, S. M., Feldhusen, J. F., & Dillon, D. R. (1994). Long-term effects of an enrichment program based on the Purdue Three-Stage Model. *Gifted Child Quarterly, 38,* 38–48.

Mooney, C. M. (1957). Age in the development of closure ability in children. *Canadian Journal of Psychology, 11,* 219–226.

Moore, D. S., & Erickson, P. I. (1985). Age, gender, and ethnic differences in sexual and contraceptive knowledge, attitudes, and behavior. *Family and Community Health, 8,* 38–51.

Moore, J. W., & Edwards, R. P. (2003). An analysis of aversive stimuli in classroom demand contexts. *Journal of Applied Behavior Analysis, 36,* 339–348.

Moran, S., & Gardner, H. (2006). Extraordinary achievements: A developmental and systems analysis. In W. Damon & R. M. Lerner (Series Eds.), D. Kuhn & R. Siegler (Vol. Eds.), *Handbook of child psychology: Vol. 2. Cognition, perception, and language* (6th ed.). New York: Wiley.

Morelli, G. A., & Rothbaum, F. (2007). Situating the child in context: Attachment relationships and self-regulation in different cultures. In S. Kitayama & D. Cohen (Eds.), *Handbook of cultural psychology* (pp. 500–527). New York: Guilford Press.

Moreno, R. (2006). Learning in high-tech and multimedia environments. *Current Directions in Psychological Science, 15,* 63–67.

Moreno, R., Mayer, R. E., Spires, H. A., & Lester, J. C. (2001). The case for social agency in computer-based teaching: Do students learn more deeply when they interact with animated pedagogical agents? *Cognition and Instruction, 19,* 177–213.

Morgan, M. (1985). Self-monitoring of attained subgoals in private study. *Journal of Educational Psychology, 77,* 623–630.

Morrison, G. M., Furlong, M. J., D'Incau, B., & Morrison, R. L. (2004). The safe school: Integrating the school reform agenda to prevent disruption and violence at school. In J. C. Conoley & A. P. Goldstein (Eds.), *School violence intervention* (2nd ed., pp. 256–296). New York: Guilford Press.

Morrow, S. L. (1997). Career development of lesbian and gay youth: Effects of sexual orientation, coming out, and homophobia. In M. B. Harris (Ed.), *School experiences of gay and lesbian youth: The invisible minority* (pp. 1–15). Binghamton, NY: Harrington Park Press.

Mostow, A. J., Izard, C. E., Fine, S., & Trantacosta, C. J. (2002). Modeling emotional, cognitive, and behavioral predictors. *Child Development, 73,* 1775–1787.

Muis, K. R. (2004). Personal epistemology and mathematics: A critical review and synthesis of research. *Review of Educational Research, 74,* 317–377.

Muis, K. R., Bendixen, L. D., & Haerle, F. C. (2006). Domain-generality and domain-specificity in personal epistemology research: Philosophical and empirical reflections in the development of a theoretical framework. *Educational Psychology Review, 18,* 3–54.

Munn, P., Johnstone, M., & Chalmers, V. (1990, April). *How do teachers talk about maintaining effective discipline in their classrooms?* Paper presented at the annual meeting of the American Educational Research Association, Boston.

Murdock, T. B. (1999). The social context of risk: Status and motivational predictors of alienation in middle school. *Journal of Educational Psychology, 91,* 62–75.

Murdock, T. B. (2000). Incorporating economic context into educational psychology: Methodological and conceptual challenges. *Educational Psychologist, 35,* 113–124.

Murdock, T. B., & Anderman, E. M. (2006). Motivational perspectives on student cheating: Toward an integrated model of academic dishonesty. *Educational Psychologist, 41*, 129–145.

Murdock, T. B., Hale, N. M., & Weber, M. J. (2001). Predictors of cheating among early adolescents: Academic and social motivations. *Contemporary Educational Psychology, 26*, 96–115.

Murdock, T. B., Miller, A., & Kohlhardt, J. (2004). Effects of classroom context variables on high school students' judgments of the acceptability and likelihood of cheating. *Journal of Educational Psychology, 96*, 765–777.

Murphy, P. K. (2007). The eye of the beholder: The interplay of social and cognitive components in change. *Educational Psychologist, 42*, 41–53.

Murphy, P. K., & Alexander, P. A. (2000). A motivated exploration of motivation terminology. *Contemporary Educational Psychology, 25*, 3–53.

Murphy, P. K., & Alexander, P. A. (in press). Examining the influence of knowledge, beliefs, and motivation in conceptual change. In S. Vosniadou (Ed.), *Handbook of research on conceptual change*. Mahwah, NJ: Erlbaum.

Murphy, P. K., & Mason, L. (2006). Changing knowledge and beliefs. In P. A. Alexander & P. H. Winne (Eds.), *Handbook of educational psychology* (2nd ed., pp. 305–324). Mahwah, NJ: Erlbaum.

Murray, F. B. (1978). Teaching strategies and conservation training. In A. M. Lesgold, J. W. Pellegrino, S. D. Fokkema, & R. Glaser (Eds.), *Cognitive psychology and instruction*. New York: Plenum Press.

Narváez, D., & Rest, J. (1995). The four components of acting morally. In W. M. Kurtines & J. L. Gewirtz (Eds.), *Moral development: An introduction*. Boston: Allyn & Bacon.

National Association of Secondary School Principals. (2004). *Breaking ranks II: Strategies for leading high school reform*. Reston, VA: Author.

National Commission on Excellence in Education. (1983). *A nation at risk: The imperative for educational reform*. Washington, DC: U.S. Government Printing Office.

National Research Council. (2000). *How people learn: Brain, mind, experience, and school* (expanded ed.). Washington, DC: National Academies Press.

Natriello, G., & Dornbusch, S. M. (1984). *Teacher evaluative standards and student effort*. White Plains, NY: Longman.

NCSS Task Force on Ethnic Studies Curriculum Guidelines. (1992). Curriculum guidelines for multicultural education. *Social Education, 56*, 274–294.

Neel, R. S., Jenkins, Z. N., & Meadows, N. (1990). Social problem-solving behaviors and aggression in young children: A descriptive observational study. *Behavioral Disorders, 16*, 39–51.

Neisser, U. (1998a). Introduction: Rising test scores and what they mean. In U. Neisser (Ed.), *The rising curve: Long-term gains in IQ and related measures* (pp. 3–22). Washington, DC: American Psychological Association.

Neisser, U. (Ed.). (1998b). *The rising curve: Long-term gains in IQ and related measures*. Washington, DC: American Psychological Association.

Neisser, U., Boodoo, G., Bouchard, T. J., Boykin, A. W., Brody, N., Ceci, S. J., et al. (1996). Intelligence: Knowns and unknowns. *American Psychologist, 51*, 77–101.

Nell, V. (2002). Why young men drive dangerously: Implications for injury prevention. *Current Directions in Psychological Science, 11*, 75–79.

Nelson, C. A., III, Thomas, K. M., & de Haan, M. (2006). Neural bases of cognitive development. In D. Kuhn, R. Siegler (Vol. Eds.), W. Damon, & R. M. Lerner (Series Eds.), *Handbook of child psychology. Vol. 2: Cognition, perception, and language* (6th ed., pp. 3–57).

Nelson, K. (1993). The psychological and social origins of autobiographical memory. *Psychological Science, 4*, 7–14.

Nelson, K. (1996). *Language in cognitive development: The emergence of the mediated mind*. Cambridge, England: Cambridge University Press.

Nelson, K., & Fivush, R. (2004). The emergence of autobiographical memory: A social cultural developmental theory. *Psychological Review, 111*, 486–511.

Nelson, T. O., & Dunlosky, J. (1991). When people's judgments of learning (JOLs) are extremely accurate at predicting subsequent recall: The "delayed-JOL effect." *Psychological Science, 2*, 267–270.

Nesbit, J. C., & Adesope, O. O. (2006). Learning with concept and knowledge maps: A meta-analysis. *Review of Educational Research, 76*, 413–448.

Nesdale, D., Maass, A., Durkin, K., & Griffiths, J. (2005). Group norms, threat, and children's racial prejudice. *Child Development, 76*, 652–663.

Neubauer, G., Mansel, J., Avrahami, A., & Nathan, M. (1994). Family and peer support of Israeli and German adolescents. In F. Nestemann & K. Hurrelmann (Eds.), *Social networks and social support in childhood and adolescence*. Berlin, Germany: Aldine de Gruyter.

Nevin, J. A., Mandell, C., & Atak, J. R. (1983). The analysis of behavioral momentum. *Journal of the Experimental Analysis of Behavior, 39*, 49–59.

Newby, T. J., Ertmer, P. A., & Stepich, D. A. (1994, April). *Instructional analogies and the learning of concepts*. Paper presented at the annual meeting of the American Educational Research Association, New Orleans, LA.

Newcomb, A. F., & Bagwell, C. L. (1995). Children's friendship relations: A meta-analysis review. *Psychological Bulletin, 117*, 306–347.

Newcomb, A. F., Bukowski, W. M., & Pattee, L. (1993). Children's peer relations: A meta-analytic review of popular, rejected, neglected, controversial, and average sociometric status. *Psychological Bulletin, 113*, 99–128.

Newcombe, N., & Huttenlocher, J. (1992). Children's early ability to solve perspective-taking problems. *Developmental Psychology, 28*, 635–643.

Newkirk, T. (2002). *Misreading masculinity: Boys, literacy, and popular culture*. Portsmouth, NH: Heinemann.

Newman, L. S. (1990). Intentional and unintentional memory in young children: Remembering vs. playing. *Journal of Experimental Child Psychology, 50*, 243–258.

Newman, R. S. (1998). Students' help seeking during problem solving: Influences of personal and contextual achievement goals. *Journal of Educational Psychology, 90*, 644–658.

Newman, R. S., & Murray, B. J. (2005). How students and teachers view the seriousness of peer harassment: When is it appropriate to seek help? *Journal of Educational Psychology, 97*, 347–365.

Newman, R. S., & Schwager, M. T. (1995). Students' help seeking during problem solving: Effects of grade, goal, and prior achievement. *American Educational Research Journal, 32*, 352–376.

Newmann, F. M. (1997). Authentic assessment in social studies: Standards and examples. In G. D. Phye (Ed.), *Handbook of classroom assessment: Learning, achievement, and adjustment*. San Diego, CA: Academic Press.

Ni, Y., & Zhou, Y.-D. (2005). Teaching and learning fraction and rational numbers: The origins and implications of whole number bias. *Educational Psychologist, 40*, 27–52.

Nicholls, J. G. (1979). Development of perception of own attainment and causal attributions for success and failure in reading. *Journal of Educational Psychology, 71*, 94–99.

Nicholls, J. G. (1984). Conceptions of ability and achievement motivation. In R. Ames & C. Ames (Eds.), *Research on motivation in education: Vol. 1. Student motivation*. San Diego, CA: Academic Press.

Nicholls, J. G. (1990). What is ability and why are we mindful of it? A developmental perspective. In R. J. Sternberg & J. Kolligian (Eds.), *Competence considered*. New Haven, CT: Yale University Press.

Nichols, J. D. (1996). The effects of cooperative learning on student achievement and motivation in a high school geometry class. *Contemporary Educational Psychology, 21*, 467–476.

Nichols, J. D., Ludwin, W. G., & Iadicola, P. (1999). A darker shade of gray: A year-end analysis of discipline and suspension data. *Equity and Excellence in Education, 32*(1), 43–55.

Nickerson, R. S. (1989). New directions in educational assessment. *Educational Researcher, 18*(9), 3–7.

Nikopoulos, C. K., & Keenan, M. (2004). Effects of video modeling on social initiations by children with autism. *Journal of Applied Behavior Analysis, 37*, 93–96.

Nippold, M. A. (1988). The literate lexicon. In M. A. Nippold (Ed.), *Later language development: Ages nine through nineteen*. Boston: Little, Brown.

Nist, S. L., Simpson, M. L., Olejnik, S., & Mealey, D. L. (1991). The relation between self-selected study processes and test performance. *American Educational Research Journal, 28*, 849–874.

Nixon, A. S. (2005, April). *Moral reasoning in the digital age: How students, teachers, and parents judge appropriate computer uses*. Paper presented at the annual meeting of the American Educational Research Association, Montreal.

Nolen, S. B. (1996). Why study? How reasons for learning influence strategy selection. *Educational Psychology Review, 8*, 335–355.

Nolen, S. B. (2007). Young children's motivation to read and write: Development in social contexts. *Cognition and Instruction, 25*, 219–270.

Norenzayan, A., Choi, I., & Peng, K. (2007). Perception and cognition. In S. Kitayama & D. Cohen (Eds.), *Handbook of cultural psychology* (pp. 569–594). New York: Guilford Press.

Northup, J. (2000). Further evaluation of the accuracy of reinforcer surveys: A systematic replication. *Journal of Applied Behavior Analysis, 33*, 335–338.

Noss, R., & Hoyles, C. (2006). Exploring mathematics through construction and collaboration. In R. K. Sawyer (Ed.), *The Cambridge handbook of the learning sciences* (pp. 389–405). Cambridge, England: Cambridge University Press.

Novak, J. D. (1998). *Learning, creating, and using knowledge: Concept maps as facilitative tools in schools and corporations*. Mahwah, NJ: Erlbaum.

Novak, J. D., & Gowin, D. B. (1984). *Learning how to learn*. Cambridge, England: Cambridge University Press.

Nucci, L. P. (2001). *Education in the moral domain*. Cambridge, England: Cambridge University Press.

Nucci, L. (2006). Classroom management for moral and social development. In C. M. Evertson & C. S. Weinstein (Eds.), *Handbook of classroom management: Research, practice, and contemporary issues* (pp. 711–731). Mahwah, NJ: Erlbaum.

Nucci, L. P., & Nucci, M. S. (1982). Children's social interactions in the context of moral and conventional transgressions. *Child Development, 53*, 403–412.

Nucci, L. P., & Weber, E. K. (1995). Social interactions in the home and the development of young children's conceptions of the personal. *Child Development, 66*, 1438–1452.

Nussbaum, J. (1985). The earth as a cosmic body. In R. Driver (Ed.), *Children's ideas of science*. Philadelphia: Open University Press.

Oakes, J., & Guiton, G. (1995). Matchmaking: The dynamics of high school tracking decisions. *American Educational Research Journal, 32*, 3–33.

Ochs, E. (1982). Talking to children in western Samoa. *Language and Society, 11*, 77–104.

Ochsner, K. N., & Lieberman, M. D. (2001). The emergence of social cognitive neuroscience. *American Psychologist, 56*, 717–734.

O'Connor, E., & McCartney, K. (2007). Examining teacher-child relationships and achievement as part of an ecological model of development. *American Educational Research Journal, 44*, 340–369.

O'Donnell, A. M. (1999). Structuring dyadic interaction through scripted cooperation. In A. M. O'Donnell & A. King (Eds.), *Cognitive perspectives on peer learning* (pp. 179–196). Mahwah, NJ: Erlbaum.

O'Donnell, A. M. (2006). The role of peers and group learning. In P. A. Alexander & P. H. Winne (Eds.), *Handbook of educational psychology* (2nd ed., pp. 781–802). Mahwah, NJ: Erlbaum.

O'Donnell, A. M., Hmelo-Silver, C. E., & Erkens, G. (Eds.). (2006). *Collaborative learning, reasoning, and technology*. Mahwah, NJ: Erlbaum.

O'Donnell, A. M., & O'Kelly, J. (1994). Learning from peers: Beyond the rhetoric of positive results. *Educational Psychology Review, 6*, 321–349.

O'Donnell, D. A., Schwab-Stone, M. E., & Muyeed, A. Z. (2002). Multidimensional resilience in urban children exposed to community violence. *Child Development, 73,* 1265–1282.

Ogbu, J. U. (1992). Understanding cultural diversity and learning. *Educational Researcher, 21*(8), 5–14, 24.

Ogbu, J. U. (1994). From cultural differences to differences in cultural frame of reference. In P. M. Greenfield & R. R. Cocking (Eds.), *Cross-cultural roots of minority child development.* Mahwah, NJ: Erlbaum.

Ogbu, J. U. (1999). Beyond language: Ebonics, proper English, and identity in a Black-American speech community. *American Educational Research Journal, 36,* 147–184.

Ogbu, J. U. (2003). *Black American students in an affluent suburb: A study of academic disengagement.* Mahwah, NJ: Erlbaum.

Okagaki, L. (2001). Triarchic model of minority children's school achievement. *Educational Psychologist, 36,* 9–20.

Okagaki, L. (2006). Ethnicity and learning. In P. A. Alexander & P. H. Winne (Eds.), *Handbook of educational psychology* (2nd ed., pp. 615–634). Mahwah, NJ: Erlbaum.

O'Leary, K. D., Kaufman, K. F., Kass, R. E., & Drabman, R. S. (1970). The effects of loud and soft reprimands on the behavior of disruptive students. *Exceptional Children, 37,* 145–155.

O'Leary, K. D., & O'Leary, S. G. (Eds.). (1972). *Classroom management: The successful use of behavior modification.* New York: Pergamon Press.

Olneck, M. R. (1995). Immigrants and education. In J. A. Banks & C. A. M. Banks (Eds.), *Handbook of research on multicultural education.* New York: Macmillan.

O'Mara, A. J., Marsh, H. W., Craven, R. G., & Debus, R. L. (2006). Do self-concept interventions make a difference? A synergistic blend of construct validation and meta-analysis. *Educational Psychologist, 41,* 181–206.

Onosko, J. J. (1989). Comparing teachers' thinking about promoting students' thinking. *Theory and Research in Social Education, 17,* 174–195.

Onosko, J. J. (1996). Exploring issues with students despite the barriers. *Social Education, 60*(1), 22–27.

Onosko, J. J., & Newmann, F. M. (1994). Creating more thoughtful learning environments. In J. N. Mangieri & C. C. Block (Eds.), *Advanced educational psychology: Enhancing mindfulness.* Fort Worth, TX: Harcourt Brace Jovanovich.

Oppenheimer, L. (1986). Development of recursive thinking: Procedural variations. *International Journal of Behavioral Development, 9,* 401–411.

Orenstein, P. (1994). *Schoolgirls: Young women, self-esteem, and the confidence gap.* New York: Doubleday.

Ormrod, J. E. (2008). *Human learning* (5th ed.). Upper Saddle River, NJ: Merrill/Prentice Hall.

Ormrod, J. E., & McGuire, D. J. (2007). *Case studies: Applying educational psychology* (2nd ed.). Upper Saddle River, NJ: Merrill/Prentice Hall.

Ornstein, R. (1997). *The right mind: Making sense of the hemispheres.* San Diego, CA: Harcourt Brace.

Orobio de Castro, B., Veerman, J. W., Koops, W., Bosch, J. D., & Monshouwer, H. J. (2002). Hostile attribution of intent and aggressive behavior: A meta-analysis. *Child Development, 73,* 916–934.

Osborne, J. W., & Simmons, C. M. (2002, April). *Girls, math, stereotype threat, and anxiety: Physiological evidence.* Paper presented at the annual meeting of the American Educational Research Association, New Orleans, LA.

Oskamp, S. (Ed.). (2000). *Reducing prejudice and discrimination.* Mahwah, NJ: Erlbaum.

Osterman, K. F. (2000). Students' need for belonging in the school community. *Review of Educational Research, 70,* 323–367.

Otis, N., Grouzet, F. M. E., & Pelletier, L. G. (2005). Latent motivational change in an academic setting: A 3-year longitudinal study. *Journal of Educational Psychology, 97,* 170–183.

O'Toole, M. E. (2000). *The school shooter: A threat assessment perspective.* Quantico, VA: Federal Bureau of Investigation. Retrieved February 26, 2004, from http://www.fbi.gov/publications/school/school2.pdf

Owens, R. E., Jr. (1995). *Language disorders: A functional approach to assessment and intervention* (2nd ed.). Boston: Allyn & Bacon.

Owens, R. E., Jr. (1996). *Language development* (4th ed.). Boston: Allyn & Bacon.

Padilla, A. M. (1994). Bicultural development: A theoretical and empirical examination. In R. G. Malgady & O. Rodriguez (Eds.), *Theoretical and conceptual issues in Hispanic mental health* (pp. 20–51). Malabar, FL: Krieger.

Paget, K. F., Kritt, D., & Bergemann, L. (1984). Understanding strategic interactions in television commercials: A developmental study. *Journal of Applied Developmental Psychology, 5,* 145–161.

Page-Voth, V., & Graham, S. (1999). Effects of goal setting and strategy use on the writing performance and self-efficacy of students with writing and learning problems. *Journal of Educational Psychology, 91,* 230–240.

Pahl, K., & Way, N. (2006). Longitudinal trajectories of ethnic identity among urban Black and Latino adolescents. *Child Development, 77,* 1403–1415.

Pajares, F. (2005). Gender differences in mathematics self-efficacy beliefs. In A. M. Gallagher & J. C. Kaufman (Eds.), *Gender differences in mathematics: An integrative psychological approach* (pp. 294–315). Cambridge, England: Cambridge University Press.

Pajares, F., & Valiante, G. (1999). *Writing self-efficacy of middle school students: Relation to motivation constructs, achievement, gender, and gender orientation.* Paper presented at the annual meeting of the American Educational Research Association, Montreal, Canada.

Paley, V. G. (1984). *Boys and girls: Superheroes in the doll corner.* Chicago: University of Chicago Press.

Palincsar, A. S., & Brown, A. L. (1984). Reciprocal teaching of comprehension-fostering and comprehension-monitoring activities. *Cognition and Instruction, 1,* 117–175.

Palincsar, A. S., & Brown, A. L. (1989). Classroom dialogues to promote self-regulated comprehension. In J. Brophy (Ed.), *Advances in research on teaching* (Vol. 1). Greenwich, CT: JAI Press.

Palincsar, A. S., & Herrenkohl, L. R. (1999). Designing collaborative contexts: Lessons from three research programs. In A. M. O'Donnell & A. King (Eds.), *Cognitive perspectives on peer learning* (pp. 151–177). Mahwah, NJ: Erlbaum.

Palmer, D. J., & Goetz, E. T. (1988). Selection and use of study strategies: The role of the studier's beliefs about self and strategies. In C. E. Weinstein, E. T. Goetz, & P. A. Alexander (Eds.), *Learning and study strategies: Issues in assessment, instruction, and evaluation.* San Diego, CA: Academic Press.

Palmer, E. L. (1965). Accelerating the child's cognitive attainments through the inducement of cognitive conflict: An interpretation of the Piagetian position. *Journal of Research in Science Teaching, 3,* 324.

Pang, V. O. (1995). Asian Pacific American students: A diverse and complex population. In J. A. Banks & C. A. M. Banks (Eds.), *Handbook of research on multicultural education.* New York: Macmillan.

Paris, S. G. (1988). Models and metaphors of learning strategies. In C. E. Weinstein, E. T. Goetz, & P. A. Alexander (Eds.), *Learning and study strategies: Issues in assessment, instruction, and evaluation.* San Diego, CA: Academic Press.

Paris, S. G., & Ayres, L. R. (1994). *Becoming reflective students and teachers with portfolios and authentic assessment.* Washington, DC: American Psychological Association.

Paris, S. G., & Byrnes, J. P. (1989). The constructivist approach to self-regulation and learning in the classroom. In B. J. Zimmerman & D. H. Schunk (Eds.), *Self-regulated learning and academic achievement: Theory, research, and practice.* New York: Springer-Verlag.

Paris, S. G., & Cunningham, A. E. (1996). Children becoming students. In D. C. Berliner & R. C. Calfee (Eds.), *Handbook of educational psychology.* New York: Macmillan.

Paris, S. G., Lawton, T. A., Turner, J. C., & Roth, J. L. (1991). A developmental perspective on standardized achievement testing. *Educational Researcher, 20*(5), 12–20, 40.

Paris, S. G., Morrison, F. J., & Miller, K. F. (2006). Academic pathways from preschool through elementary school. In P. A. Alexander & P. H. Winne (Eds.), *Handbook of educational psychology* (2nd ed., pp. 61–85). Mahwah, NJ: Erlbaum.

Paris, S. G., & Paris, A. H. (2001). Classroom applications of research on self-regulated learning. *Educational Psychologist, 36,* 89–101.

Paris, S. G., & Turner, J. C. (1994). Situated motivation. In P. R. Pintrich, D. R. Brown, & C. E. Weinstein (Eds.), *Student motivation, cognition, and learning: Essays in honor of Wilbert J. McKeachie.* Mahwah, NJ: Erlbaum.

Paris, S. G., & Winograd, P. (1990). How metacognition can promote academic learning and instruction. In B. F. Jones & L. Idol (Eds.), *Dimensions of thinking and cognitive instruction.* Mahwah, NJ: Erlbaum.

Parke, R. D. (1974). Rules, roles, and resistance to deviation: Explorations in punishment, discipline, and self-control. In A. Pick (Ed.), *Minnesota Symposia on Child Psychology* (Vol. 8). Minneapolis: University of Minnesota Press.

Parker, W. D. (1997). An empirical typology of perfectionism in academically talented children. *American Educational Research Journal, 34,* 545–562.

Parkhurst, J. T., & Hopmeyer, A. (1998). Sociometric popularity and peer-perceived popularity: Two distinct dimensions of peer status. *Journal of Early Adolescence, 18,* 125–144.

Parks, C. P. (1995). Gang behavior in the schools: Reality or myth? *Educational Psychology Review, 7,* 41–68.

Parsons, J. E., Kaczala, C. M., & Meece, J. L. (1982). Socialization of achievement attitudes and beliefs: Classroom influences. *Child Development, 53,* 322–339.

Patrick, H., Anderman, L. H., & Ryan, A. M. (2002). Social motivation and the classroom social environment. In C. Midgley (Ed.), *Goals, goal structures, and patterns of adaptive learning* (pp. 85–108). Mahwah, NJ: Erlbaum.

Patrick, H., & Pintrich, P. R. (2001). Conceptual change in teachers' intuitive conceptions of learning, motivation, and instruction: The role of motivational and epistemological beliefs. In B. Torff & R. J. Sternberg (Eds.), *Understanding and teaching the intuitive mind: Student and teacher learning* (pp. 117–143). Mahwah, NJ: Erlbaum.

Patrick, H., Ryan, A. M., & Kaplan, A. M. (2007). Early adolescents' perceptions of the classroom social environment, motivational beliefs, and engagement. *Journal of Educational Psychology, 99,* 83–98.

Patterson, C. J. (1995). Sexual orientation and human development: An overview. *Developmental Psychology, 31,* 3–11.

Patterson, G. R., DeBaryshe, B. D., & Ramsey, E. (1989). A developmental perspective on antisocial behavior. *American Psychologist, 44,* 329–335.

Patton, J. R., Blackbourn, J. M., & Fad, K. S. (1996). *Exceptional individuals in focus* (6th ed.). Upper Saddle River, NJ: Merrill/Prentice Hall.

Paulson, F. L., Paulson, P. R., & Meyer, C. A. (1991). What makes a portfolio a portfolio? *Educational Leadership, 49*(5), 60–63.

Paus, T., Zijdenbos, A., Worsley, K., Collins, D. L., Blumenthal, J., Giedd, J. N., et al. (1999). Structural maturation of neural pathways in children and adolescents: In vivo study. *Science, 283,* 1908–1911.

Paxton, R. J. (1999). A deafening silence: History textbooks and the students who read them. *Review of Educational Research, 69,* 315–339.

Pea, R. D. (1987). Socializing the knowledge transfer problem. *International Journal of Educational Research, 11,* 639–663.

Pea, R. D. (1993). Practices of distributed intelligence and designs for education. In G. Salomon (Ed.), *Distributed cognitions: Psychological and educational considerations.* Cambridge, England: Cambridge University Press.

Pearce, R. R. (2006). Effects of cultural and social structural factors on the achievement of White and Chinese American students at school transition points. *American Educational Research Journal, 43,* 75–101.

Pedersen, S., Vitaro, F., Barker, E. D., & Borge, A. I. H. (2007). The timing of middle-childhood peer rejection and friendship: Linking early behavior to early-adolescent adjustment. *Child Development, 78,* 1037–1051.

Pekrun, R., Elliot, A., & Maier, M. A. (2006). Achievement goals and discrete achievement emotions: A theoretical model and prospective test. *Journal of Educational Psychology, 98,* 583–597.

Pekrun, R., Goetz, T., Titz, W., & Perry, R. P. (2002). Academic emotions in students' self-regulated learning and achievement: A program of qualitative and quantitative research. *Educational Psychologist, 37,* 91–105.

Pellegrini, A. D. (1998). Play and the assessment of young children. In O. N. Saracho & B. Spodek (Eds.), *Multiple perspectives on play in early childhood education.* Albany: State University of New York Press.

Pellegrini, A. D. (2002). Bullying, victimization, and sexual harassment during the transition to middle school. *Educational Psychologist, 37,* 151–163.

Pellegrini, A. D., & Archer, J. (2005). Sex differences in competitive and aggressive behavior. In B. J. Ellis & D. F. Bjorklund (Eds.), *Origins of the social mind: Evolutionary psychology and child development* (pp. 219–244). New York: Guilford Press.

Pellegrini, A. D., & Bartini, M. (2000). A longitudinal study of bullying, victimization, and peer affiliation during the transition from primary school to middle school. *American Educational Research Journal, 37,* 699–725.

Pellegrini, A. D., Bartini, M., & Brooks, F. (1999). School bullies, victims, and aggressive victims: Factors relating to group affiliation and victimization in early adolescence. *Journal of Educational Psychology, 91,* 216–224.

Pellegrini, A. D., & Bohn, C. M. (2005). The role of recess in children's cognitive performance and school adjustment. *Educational Researcher, 34*(1), 13–19.

Pellegrini, A. D., Huberty, P. D., & Jones, I. (1995). The effects of recess timing on children's playground and classroom behaviors. *American Educational Research Journal, 32,* 845–864.

Pellegrini, A. D., Kato, K., Blatchford, P., & Baines, E. (2002). A short-term longitudinal study of children's playground games across the first year of school: Implications for social competence and adjustment to school. *American Educational Research Journal, 39,* 991–1015.

Pellegrini, A. D., & Long, J. D. (2004). Part of the solution and part of the problem: The role of peers in bullying, dominance, and victimization during the transition from primary school through secondary school. In D. L. Espelage & S. M. Swearer (Eds.), *Bullying in American schools: A social-ecological perspective on prevention and intervention* (pp. 107–117). Mahwah, NJ: Erlbaum.

Pelphrey, K. A., & Carter, E. J. (2007). Brain mechanisms underlying social perception deficits in autism. In D. Coch, G. Dawson, & K. W. Fischer (Eds.), *Human behavior, learning, and the developing brain: Atypical development* (pp. 56–86). New York: Guilford Press.

Peng, K., & Nisbett, R. E. (1999). Culture, dialecticism, and reasoning about contradiction. *American Psychologist, 54,* 741–754.

Pérez, B. (1998). *Sociocultural contexts of language and literacy.* Mahwah, NJ: Erlbaum.

Perfetti, C. A. (1983). Reading, vocabulary, and writing: Implications for computer-based instruction. In A. C. Wilkinson (Ed.), *Classroom computers and cognitive science.* New York: Academic Press.

Perkins, D. N. (1990). The nature and nurture of creativity. In B. F. Jones & L. Idol (Eds.), *Dimensions of thinking and cognitive instruction.* Mahwah, NJ: Erlbaum.

Perkins, D. N. (1992). *Smart schools: From training memories to educating minds.* New York: Free Press/Macmillan.

Perkins, D. N. (1995). *Outsmarting IQ: The emerging science of learnable intelligence.* New York: Free Press.

Perkins, D., & Ritchhart, R. (2004). When is good thinking? In D. Y. Dai & R. J. Sternberg (Eds.), *Motivation, emotion, and cognition: Integrative perspectives on in-tellectual functioning and development* (pp. 351–384). Mahwah, NJ: Erlbaum.

Perkins, D. N., & Salomon, G. (1987). Transfer and teaching thinking. In D. N. Perkins, J. Lochhead, & J. Bishop (Eds.), *Thinking: The second international conference.* Mahwah, NJ: Erlbaum.

Perkins, D. N., & Salomon, G. (1989). Are cognitive skills context-bound? *Educational Researcher, 18*(1), 16–25.

Perkins, D. N., Tishman, S., Ritchhart, R., Donis, K., & Andrade, A. (2000). Intelligence in the wild: A dispositional view of intellectual traits. *Educational Psychology Review, 12,* 269–293.

Perkins, S. A., & Turiel, E. (2007). To lie or not to lie: To whom and under what circumstances. *Child Development, 78,* 609–621.

Perner, J., & Wimmer, H. (1985). "John *thinks* that Mary *thinks* that . . ." Attribution of second-order beliefs by 5- to 10-year-old children. *Journal of Experimental Child Psychology, 39,* 437–471.

Perry, D. G., & Perry, L. C. (1983). Social learning, causal attribution, and moral internalization. In J. Bisanz, G. L. Bisanz, & R. Kail (Eds.), *Learning in children: Progress in cognitive development research.* New York: Springer-Verlag.

Perry, N. E. (1998). Young children's self-regulated learning and contexts that support it. *Journal of Educational Psychology, 90,* 715–729.

Perry, N. E., Turner, J. C., & Meyer, D. K. (2006). Classrooms as contexts for motivating learning. In P. A. Alexander & P. H. Winne (Eds.), *Handbook of educational psychology* (2nd ed., pp. 327–348). Mahwah, NJ: Erlbaum.

Perry, N. E., VandeKamp, K. O., Mercer, L. K., & Nordby, C. J. (2002). Investigating teacher-student interactions that foster self-regulated learning. *Educational Psychologist, 37,* 5–15.

Perry, N. E., & Winne, P. H. (2004). Motivational messages from home and school: How do they influence young children's engagement in learning? In D. M. McInerney & S. Van Etten (Eds.), *Big theories revisited* (pp. 199–222). Greenwich, CT: Information Age.

Perry, R. P. (1985). Instructor expressiveness: Implications for improving teaching. In J. G. Donald & A. M. Sullivan (Eds.), *Using research to improve teaching* (pp. 35–49). San Francisco: Jossey-Bass.

Peterson, C. (1990). Explanatory style in the classroom and on the playing field. In S. Graham & V. S. Folkes (Eds.), *Attribution theory: Applications to achievement, mental health, and interpersonal conflict.* Mahwah, NJ: Erlbaum.

Peterson, C. (2006). *A primer in positive psychology.* New York: Oxford University Press.

Peterson, C., Maier, S., & Seligman, M. (1993). *Learned helplessness: A theory for the age of personal control.* New York: Oxford University Press.

Peterson, L. R., & Peterson, M. J. (1959). Short-term retention of individual items. *Journal of Experimental Psychology, 58,* 193–198.

Petrill, S. A., & Wilkerson, B. (2000). Intelligence and achievement: A behavioral genetic perspective. *Educational Psychology Review, 12,* 185–199.

Petterson, S. M., & Albers, A. B. (2001). Effects of poverty and maternal depression on early child development. *Child Development, 72,* 1794–1813.

Pettito, A. L. (1985). Division of labor: Procedural learning in teacher-led small groups. *Cognition and Instruction, 2,* 233–270.

Peverly, S. T., Brobst, K. E., Graham, M., & Shaw, R. (2003). College adults are not good at self-regulation: A study on the relationship of self-regulation, note taking, and test taking. *Journal of Educational Psychology, 95,* 335–346.

Pezdek, K., & Banks, W. P. (Eds.). (1996). *The recovered memory/false memory debate.* San Diego, CA: Academic Press.

Pfeifer, J. H., Brown, C. S., & Juvonen, J. (2007). Teaching tolerance in schools: Lessons learned since Brown v. Board of Education about the development and reduction of children's prejudice. *Social Policy Report, 21*(2), 3–13, 16–17, 20–23. Ann Arbor, MI: Society for Research in Child Development.

Pfeifer, M., Goldsmith, H. H., Davidson, R. J., & Rickman, M. (2002). Continuity and change in inhibited and uninhibited children. *Child Development, 73,* 1474–1485.

Pfiffner, L. J., & Barkley, R. A. (1998). Treatment of ADHD in school settings. In R. A. Barkley, *Attention-deficit hyperactivity disorder: A handbook for diagnosis and treatment* (2nd ed., pp. 458–490). New York: Guilford Press.

Pfiffner, L. J., & O'Leary, S. G. (1993). School-based psychological treatments. In J. L. Matson (Ed.), *Handbook of hyperactivity in children* (pp. 234–255). Boston: Allyn & Bacon.

Phalet, K., Andriessen, I., & Lens, W. (2004). How future goals enhance motivation and learning in multicultural classrooms. *Educational Psychology Review, 16,* 59–89.

Phelan, P., Davidson, A. L., & Cao, H. T. (1991). Students' multiple worlds: Negotiating the boundaries of family, peer, and school cultures. *Anthropology and Education Quarterly, 22,* 224–250.

Phelan, P., Yu, H. C., & Davidson, A. L. (1994). Navigating the psychosocial pressures of adolescence: The voices and experiences of high school youth. *American Educational Research Journal, 31,* 415–447.

Phillips, B. N., Pitcher, G. D., Worsham, M. E., & Miller, S. C. (1980). Test anxiety and the school environment. In I. G. Sarason (Ed.), *Test anxiety: Theory, research, and applications.* Mahwah, NJ: Erlbaum.

Phillips, D., & Zimmerman, M. (1990). The developmental course of perceived competence and incompetence among competent children. In R. Sternberg & J. Kolligian (Eds.), *Competence considered* (pp. 41–66). New Haven, CT: Yale University Press.

Phillips, G., McNaughton, S., & MacDonald, S. (2004). Managing the mismatch: Enhancing early literacy progress for children with diverse language and cultural identities in mainstream urban schools in New Zealand. *Journal of Educational Psychology, 96,* 309–323.

Phinney, J. S. (1989). Stages of ethnic identity development in minority group adolescents. *Journal of Early Adolescence, 9,* 34–39.

Phinney, J. (1993). A three-stage model of ethnic identity development in adolescence. In M. E. Bernal & G. P. Knight (Eds.), *Ethnic identity: Formation and transmission among Hispanics and other minorities* (pp. 61–79). Albany: State University of New York Press.

Piaget, J. (1928). *Judgment and reasoning in the child* (M. Warden, Trans.). New York: Harcourt, Brace.

Piaget, J. (1952a). *The child's conception of number* (C. Gattegno & F. M. Hodgson, Trans.). London: Routledge & Kegan Paul.

Piaget, J. (1952b). *The origins of intelligence in children* (M. Cook, Trans.). New York: Norton.

Piaget, J. (1959). *The language and thought of the child* (3rd ed.; M. Gabain, Trans.). London: Routledge & Kegan Paul.

Piaget, J. (1960). *The moral judgment of the child* (M. Gabain, Trans.). Glencoe, IL: Free Press. (First published in 1932)

Piaget, J. (1970). Piaget's theory. In P. H. Mussen (Ed.), *Carmichael's manual of psychology.* New York: Wiley.

Piaget, J. (1980). *Adaptation and intelligence: Organic selection and phenocopy* (S. Eames, Trans.). Chicago: University of Chicago Press.

Pianta, R. C. (1999). *Enhancing relationships between children and teachers.* Washington, DC: American Psychological Association.

Pianta, R. C. (2006). Classroom management and relationships between children and teachers: Implications for research and practice. In C. M. Evertson & C. S. Weinstein (Eds.), *Handbook of classroom management: Research, practice, and contemporary issues* (pp. 685–709). Mahwah, NJ: Erlbaum.

Pianta, R. C., Belsky, J., Houts, R., & Morrison, F. (2007). Opportunities to learn in America's elementary classrooms. *Science, 315*(5820), 1795–1796.

Pickens, J. (2006, Winter). "Poop study" engages primary students. *Volunteer Monitor* (National Newsletter of Volunteer Watershed Monitoring), *18*(1), 13, 21.

Piirto, J. (1999). *Talented children and adults: Their development and education* (2nd ed.). Upper Saddle River, NJ: Merrill/Prentice Hall.

Pillow, B. H. (2002). Children's and adults' evaluation of the certainty of deductive inferences, inductive inferences, and guesses. *Child Development, 73*, 779–792.

Pine, K. J., & Messer, D. J. (2000). The effect of explaining another's actions on children's implicit theories of balance. *Cognition and Instruction, 18*, 35–51.

Pintrich, P. R. (2003). Motivation and classroom learning. In W. M. Reynolds, G. E. Miller (Vol. Eds.), & I. B. Weiner (Editor-in-Chief), *Handbook of psychology: Vol. 7. Educational psychology* (pp. 103–122). New York: Wiley.

Pintrich, P. R., & De Groot, E. V. (1990). Motivational and self-regulated learning components of classroom academic performance. *Journal of Educational Psychology, 82*, 33–40.

Pintrich, P. R., Marx, R. W., & Boyle, R. A. (1993). Beyond cold conceptual change: The role of motivational beliefs and classroom contextual factors in the process of conceptual change. *Review of Educational Research, 63*, 167–199.

Pintrich, P. R., & Schrauben, B. (1992). Students' motivational beliefs and their cognitive engagement in academic tasks. In D. Schunk & J. Meece (Eds.), *Students' perceptions in the classroom: Causes and consequences.* Mahwah, NJ: Erlbaum.

Pintrich, P. R., & Schunk, D. H. (2002). *Motivation in education: Theory, research, and applications* (2nd ed.). Upper Saddle River, NJ: Merrill/Prentice Hall.

Pittman, K., & Beth-Halachmy, S. (1997, March). *The role of prior knowledge in analogy use.* Paper presented at the annual meeting of the American Educational Research Association, Chicago.

Plomin, R. (1994). *Genetics and experience: The interplay between nature and nurture.* Thousand Oaks, CA: Sage.

Plomin, R., & Spinath, F. M. (2004). Intelligence: Genetics, genes, and genomics. *Journal of Personality and Social Psychology, 86*, 112–129.

Plucker, J. A., Beghetto, R. A., & Dow, G. T. (2004). Why isn't creativity more important to educational psychologists? Potentials, pitfalls, and future directions in creativity research. *Educational Psychologist, 39*, 83–96.

Plumert, J. M. (1994). Flexibility in children's use of spatial and categorical organizational strategies in recall. *Developmental Psychology, 30*, 738–747.

Pollack, W. S. (2006). Sustaining and reframing vulnerability and connection: Creating genuine resilience in boys and young males. In S. Goldstein & R. B. Brooks (Eds.), *Handbook of resilience in children* (pp. 65–77). New York: Springer.

Polman, J. L. (2004). Dialogic activity structures for project-based learning environments. *Cognition and Instruction, 22*, 431–466.

Pomerantz, E. M., & Saxon, J. L. (2001). Conceptions of ability as stable and self-evaluative processes: A longitudinal examination. *Child Development, 72*, 152–173.

Pomeroy, E. (1999). The teacher-student relationship in secondary school: Insights from excluded students. *British Journal of Sociology of Education, 20*, 465–482.

Poole, D. (1994). Routine testing practices and the linguistic construction of knowledge. *Cognition and Instruction, 12*, 125–150.

Popham, W. J. (1990). *Modern educational measurement: A practitioner's perspective* (2nd ed.). Upper Saddle River, NJ: Prentice Hall.

Popham, W. J. (1995). *Classroom assessment: What teachers need to know.* Needham Heights, MA: Allyn & Bacon.

Porat, D. A. (2004). *It's not written here, but this is what happened:* Students' cultural comprehension of textbook narratives on the Israeli-Arab conflict. *American Educational Research Journal, 41*, 963–996.

Porath, M. (1988, April). *Cognitive development of gifted children: A neo-Piagetian perspective.* Paper presented at the annual meeting of the American Educational Research Association, New Orleans, LA.

Porter, A. C. (1989). A curriculum out of balance: The case of elementary school mathematics. *Educational Researcher, 18*(5), 9–15.

Portes, P. R. (1996). Ethnicity and culture in educational psychology. In D. C. Berliner & R. C. Calfee (Eds.), *Handbook of educational psychology.* New York: Macmillan.

Posner, G. J., Strike, K. A., Hewson, P. W., & Gertzog, W. A. (1982). Accommodation of a scientific conception: Toward a theory of conceptual change. *Science Education, 66*, 211–227.

Poulin, F., & Boivin, M. (1999). Proactive and reactive aggression and boys' friendship quality in mainstream classrooms. *Journal of Emotional and Behavioral Disorders, 7*, 168–177.

Powell, S., & Nelson, B. (1997). Effects of choosing academic assignments on a student with attention deficit hyperactivity disorder. *Journal of Applied Behavior Analysis, 30*, 181–183.

Power, F. C., Higgins, A., & Kohlberg, L. (1989). *Lawrence Kohlberg's approach to moral education.* New York: Columbia University Press.

Powers, L. E., Sowers, J. A., & Stevens, T. (1995). An exploratory, randomized study of the impact of mentoring on the self-efficacy and community-based knowledge of adolescents with severe physical challenges. *Journal of Rehabilitation, 61*(1), 33–41.

Prawat, R. S. (1989). Promoting access to knowledge, strategy, and disposition in students: A research synthesis. *Review of Educational Research, 59*, 1–41.

Prawat, R. S. (1992). From individual differences to learning communities: Our changing focus. *Educational Leadership, 49*(7), 9–13.

Prawat, R. S. (1993). The value of ideas: Problems versus possibilities in learning. *Educational Researcher, 22*(6), 5–16.

Premack, D. (1959). Toward empirical behavior laws: I. Positive reinforcement. *Psychological Review, 66*, 219–233.

Premack, D. (1963). Rate differential reinforcement in monkey manipulation. *Journal of Experimental Analysis of Behavior, 6*, 81–89.

Presseisen, B. Z., & Beyer, F. S. (1994, April). *Facing history and ourselves: An instructional tool for constructivist theory.* Paper presented at the annual meeting of the American Educational Research Association, New Orleans, LA.

Pressley, M. (1982). Elaboration and memory development. *Child Development, 53*, 296–309.

Pressley, M., Borkowski, J. G., & Schneider, W. (1987). Cognitive strategies: Good strategy users coordinate metacognition and knowledge. In R. Vasta (Ed.), *Annals of child development* (Vol. 4). Greenwich, CT: JAI Press.

Pressley, M., El-Dinary, P. B., Marks, M. B., Brown, R., & Stein, S. (1992). Good strategy instruction is motivating and interesting. In K. A. Renninger, S. Hidi, & A. Krapp (Eds.), *The role of interest in learning and development.* Mahwah, NJ: Erlbaum.

Pressley, M., Harris, K. R., & Marks, M. B. (1992). But good strategy instructors are constructivists! *Educational Psychology Review, 4*, 3–31.

Pressley, M., & Hilden, K. (2006). Cognitive strategies: Production deficiencies and successful strategy instruction everywhere. In W. Damon & R. M. Lerner (Series Eds.), D. Kuhn & R. Siegler (Vol. Eds.), *Handbook of child psychology: Vol. 2. Cognition, perception, and language* (6th ed.). New York: Wiley.

Pressley, M., Levin, J. R., & Delaney, H. D. (1982). The mnemonic keyword method. *Review of Educational Research, 52*, 61–91.

Pribram, K. H. (1997). The work in working memory: Implications for development. In N. A. Krasnegor, G. R. Lyon, & P. S. Goldman-Rakic (Eds.), *Development of the prefrontal cortex: Evolution, neurobiology, and behavior* (pp. 359–378). Baltimore: Brookes.

Price-Williams, D. R., Gordon, W., & Ramirez, M. (1969). Skill and conservation. *Developmental Psychology, 1*, 769.

Proctor, R. W., & Dutta, A. (1995). *Skill acquisition and human performance.* Thousand Oaks, CA: Sage.

Pruitt, R. P. (1989). Fostering creativity: The innovative classroom environment. *Educational Horizons, 68*(1), 51–54.

Pugh, K. J., & Bergin, D. A. (2006). Motivational influences on transfer. *Educational Psychologist, 41*, 147–160.

Pugh, K. J., Bergin, D. A., & Rocks, J. (2003, April). *Motivation and transfer: A critical review.* Paper presented at the annual meeting of the American Educational Research Association, Chicago.

Pulos, S., & Linn, M. C. (1981). Generality of the controlling variables scheme in early adolescence. *Journal of Early Adolescence, 1*, 26–37.

Purcell-Gates, V. (1995). *Other people's words: The cycle of low literacy.* Cambridge, MA: Harvard University Press.

Purdie, N., & Hattie, J. (1996). Cultural differences in the use of strategies for self-regulated learning. *American Educational Research Journal, 33*, 845–871.

Purdie, N., Hattie, J., & Carroll, A. (2002). A review of the research on interventions for attention deficit hyperactivity disorder: What works best? *Review of Educational Research, 72*, 61–99.

Purdie, N., Hattie, J., & Douglas, G. (1996). Student conceptions of learning and their use of self-regulated learning strategies: A cross-cultural comparison. *Journal of Educational Psychology, 88*, 87–100.

Putnam, R. T. (1992). Thinking and authority in elementary-school mathematics tasks. In J. Brophy (Ed.), *Advances in research on teaching: Vol. 3. Planning and managing learning tasks and activities.* Greenwich, CT: JAI Press.

Qian, G., & Pan, J. (2002). A comparison of epistemological beliefs and learning from science text between American and Chinese high school students. In B. K. Hofer & P. R. Pintrich (Eds.), *Personal epistemology: The psychology of beliefs about knowledge and knowing* (pp. 365–385). Mahwah, NJ: Erlbaum.

Qin, Z., Johnson, D. W., & Johnson, R. T. (1995). Cooperative versus competitive efforts and problem solving. *Review of Educational Research, 65*, 129–143.

Quellmalz, E., & Hoskyn, J. (1997). Classroom assessment of reading strategies. In G. D. Phye (Ed.), *Handbook of classroom assessment: Learning, achievement, and adjustment.* San Diego, CA: Academic Press.

Quinn, P. C. (2002). Category representation in young infants. *Current Directions in Psychological Science, 11*, 66–70.

Quinn, P. C. (2003). Concepts are not just for objects: Categorization of spatial relation information by young infants. In D. H. Rakison & L. M. Oakes (Eds.), *Early category and concept development: Making sense of the blooming, buzzing confusion.* Oxford, England: Oxford University Press.

Quinn, P. C., Bhatt, R. S., Brush, D., Grimes, A., & Sharpnack, H. (2002). Development of form similarity as a Gestalt grouping principle in infancy. *Psychological Science, 13*, 320–328.

Quintana, C., Zhang, M., & Krajcik, J. (2005). A framework for supporting metacognitive aspects of online inquiry through software-based scaffolding. *Educational Psychologist, 40*, 235–244.

Quintana, S. M., Aboud, F. E., Chao, R. K., Contreras-Grau, J., Cross, W. E., Jr., Hudley, C., et al. (2006). Race, ethnicity, and culture in child development: Contemporary research and future directions. *Child Development, 77*, 1129–1141.

Raber, S. M. (1990, April). *A school system's look at its dropouts: Why they left school and what has happened to them.* Paper presented at the annual meeting of the American Educational Research Association, Boston.

Rabinowitz, M., & Glaser, R. (1985). Cognitive structure and process in highly competent performance. In F. D. Horowitz & M. O'Brien (Eds.), *The gifted and the talented: Developmental perspectives.* Washington, DC: American Psychological Association.

Radziszewska, B., & Rogoff, B. (1988). Influence of adult and peer collaborators on children's planning skills. *Developmental Psychology, 24*, 840–848.

Raikes, H., Pan, B. A., Luze, G., Tamis-LeMonda, C. S., Brooks-Gunn, J., Constantine, J., et al. (2006). Mother-child book reading in low-income families: Correlates and outcomes during the first three years of life. *Child Development, 77*, 924–953.

Raine, A., Reynolds, C., & Venables, P. H. (2002). Stimulation seeking and intelligence: A prospective longitudinal study. *Journal of Personality and Social Psychology, 82,* 663–674.

Raine, A., & Scerbo, A. (1991). Biological theories of violence. In J. S. Milner (Ed.), *Neuropsychology of aggression* (pp. 1–25). Boston: Kluwer.

Ramey, C. T. (1992). High-risk children and IQ: Altering intergenerational patterns. *Intelligence, 16,* 239–256.

Ramey, C. T., & Ramey, S. L. (1998). Early intervention and early experience. *American Psychologist, 53,* 109–120.

Ramsey, P. G. (1987). *Teaching and learning in a diverse world: Multicultural education for young children.* New York: Teachers College Press.

Ramsey, P. G. (1995). Growing up with the contradictions of race and class. *Young Children, 50,* 18–22.

Rapport, M. D., Murphy, H. A., & Bailey, J. S. (1982). Ritalin vs. response cost in the control of hyperactive children: A within-subject comparison. *Journal of Applied Behavior Analysis, 15,* 205–216.

Raudenbush, S. W. (1984). Magnitude of teacher expectancy effects on pupil IQ as a function of credibility induction: A synthesis of findings from 18 experiments. *Journal of Educational Psychology, 76,* 85–97.

Rawson, K. A., & Kintsch, W. (2005). Rereading effects depend on time of test. *Journal of Educational Psychology, 97,* 70–80.

Rawsthorne, L. J., & Elliot, A. J. (1999). Achievement goals and intrinsic motivation: A meta-analytic review. *Personality and Social Psychology Review, 3,* 326–344.

Rayner, K., Foorman, B. R., Perfetti, C. A., Pesetsky, D., & Seidenberg, M. S. (2001). How psychological science informs the teaching of reading. *Psychological Science in the Public Interest, 2,* 31–74.

Reber, A. S. (1993). *Implicit learning and tacit knowledge: An essay on the cognitive unconscious.* New York: Oxford University Press.

Redfield, D. L., & Rousseau, E. W. (1981). A meta-analysis of experimental research on teacher questioning behavior. *Review of Educational Research, 51,* 237–245.

Reese, E., & Fivush, R. (1993). Parental styles of talking about the past. *Developmental Psychology, 29,* 596–606.

Reeve, J. (2006). Extrinsic rewards and inner motivation. In C. M. Evertson & C. S. Weinstein (Eds.), *Handbook of classroom management: Research, practice, and contemporary issues* (pp. 645–664.). Mahwah, NJ: Erlbaum.

Reeve, J., Bolt, E., & Cai, Y. (1999). Autonomy-supportive teachers: How they teach and motivate students. *Journal of Educational Psychology, 91,* 537–548.

Reeve, J., Deci, E. L., & Ryan, R. M. (2004). Self-determination theory: A dialectical framework for understanding sociocultural influences on student motivation. In D. M. McInerney & S. Van Etten (Eds.), *Big theories revisited* (pp. 31–60). Greenwich, CT: Information Age.

Reid, N. (1989). Contemporary Polynesian conceptions of giftedness. *Gifted Education International, 6*(1), 30–38.

Reimann, P., & Schult, T. J. (1996). Turning examples into cases: Acquiring knowledge structures for analogical problem solving. *Educational Psychologist, 31,* 123–132.

Reimer, J., Paolitto, D. P., & Hersh, R. H. (1983). *Promoting moral growth: From Piaget to Kohlberg* (2nd ed.). White Plains, NY: Longman.

Reiner, M., Slotta, J. D., Chi, M. T. H., & Resnick, L. B. (2000). Naive physics reasoning: A commitment to substance-based conceptions. *Cognition and Instruction, 18,* 1–34.

Reis, S. M. (1989). Reflections on policy affecting the education of gifted and talented students: Past and future perspectives. *American Psychologist, 44,* 399–408.

Reisberg, D. (1997). *Cognition: Exploring the science of the mind.* New York: Norton.

Reisberg, D., & Heuer, F. (1992). Remembering the details of emotional events. In E. Winograd & U. Neisser (Eds.), *Affect and accuracy in recall: Studies of "flashbulb" memories.* Cambridge, England: Cambridge University Press.

Reiter, S. N. (1994). Teaching dialogically: Its relationship to critical thinking in college students. In P. R. Pin-trich, D. R. Brown, & C. E. Weinstein (Eds.), *Student motivation, cognition, and learning: Essays in honor of Wilbert J. McKeachie.* Mahwah, NJ: Erlbaum.

Renninger, K. A., Hidi, S., & Krapp, A. (Eds.). (1992). *The role of interest in learning and development.* Mahwah, NJ: Erlbaum.

Renzulli, J. S. (2002). Emerging conceptions of giftedness: Building a bridge to the new century. *Exceptionality, 10*(2), 67–75.

Resnick, D. P., & Resnick, L. B. (1996). Performance assessment and the multiple functions of educational measurement. In M. B. Kane & R. Mitchell (Eds.), *Implementing performance assessment: Promises, problems, and challenges* (pp. 23–38). Mahwah, NJ: Erlbaum.

Resnick, L. B. (1989). Developing mathematical knowledge. *American Psychologist, 44,* 162–169.

Resnick, L. B., & Resnick, D. P. (1992). Assessing the thinking curriculum: New tools for educational reform. In B. G. Gifford & M. C. O'Connor (Eds.), *Changing assessments: Alternative views of aptitude, achievement and instruction* (pp. 37–75). Boston: Kluwer Academic.

Resnick, M. D., Bearman, P. S., Blum, R. W., Bauman, K. E., Harris, K. M., Jones, J., et al. (1997). Protecting adolescents from harm: Findings from the National Longitudinal Study on Adolescent Health. *Journal of the American Medical Association, 278,* 823–832.

Rest, J., Narvaez, D., Bebeau, M., & Thoma, S. (1999). A neo-Kohlbergian approach: The DIT and schema theory. *Educational Psychology Review, 11,* 291–324.

Reusser, K. (1990, April). *Understanding word arithmetic problems: Linguistic and situational factors.* Paper presented at the annual meeting of the American Educational Research Association, Boston.

Reyna, C. (2000). Lazy, dumb, or industrious: When stereotypes convey attribution information in the classroom. *Educational Psychology Review, 12,* 85–110.

Reyna, C., & Weiner, B. (2001). Justice and utility in the classroom: An attributional analysis of the goals of teachers' punishment and intervention strategies. *Journal of Educational Psychology, 93,* 309–319.

Reyna, V. F., & Farley, F. (2006). Risk and rationality in adolescent decision making: Implications for theory, practice, and public policy. *Psychological Science in the Public Interest, 7*(1), 1–44.

Reynolds, A. J., & Oberman, G. L. (1987, April). *An analysis of a PSAT preparation program for urban gifted students.* Paper presented at the annual meeting of the American Educational Research Association, Washington, DC.

Reynolds, R. E., & Shirey, L. L. (1988). The role of attention in studying and learning. In C. E. Weinstein, E. T. Goetz, & P. A. Alexander (Eds.), *Learning and study strategies: Issues in assessment, instruction, and evaluation.* San Diego, CA: Academic Press.

Reynolds, R. E., Taylor, M. A., Steffensen, M. S., Shirey, L. L., & Anderson, R. C. (1982). Cultural schemata and reading comprehension. *Reading Research Quarterly, 17,* 353–366.

Ricciuti, H. N. (1993). Nutrition and mental development. *Current Directions in Psychological Science, 2,* 43–46.

Richards, J. M. (2004). The cognitive consequences of concealing feelings. *Current Directions in Psychological Science, 13,* 131–134.

Riding, R. J., & Cheema, I. (1991). Cognitive styles—an overview and integration. *Educational Psychology, 11,* 193–215.

Riggs, J. M. (1992). Self-handicapping and achievement. In A. K. Boggiano & T. S. Pittman (Eds.), *Achievement and motivation: A social-developmental perspective.* Cambridge, England: Cambridge University Press.

Rimm, D. C., & Masters, J. C. (1974). *Behavior therapy: Techniques and empirical findings.* San Diego, CA: Academic Press.

Ripple, R. E. (1989). Ordinary creativity. *Contemporary Educational Psychology, 14,* 189–202.

Rittle-Johnson, B. (2006). Promoting transfer: Effects of self-explanation and direct instruction. *Child Development, 77,* 1–15.

Rittle-Johnson, B., Siegler, R. S., & Alibali, M. W. (2001). Developing conceptual understanding and procedural skill in mathematics: An iterative process. *Journal of Educational Psychology, 93,* 346–362.

Ritts, V., Patterson, M. L., & Tubbs, M. E. (1992). Expectations, impressions, and judgments of physically attractive students: A review. *Review of Educational Research, 62,* 413–426.

Roberts, G. C., Treasure, D. C., & Kavussanu, M. (1997). Motivation in physical activity contexts: An achievement goal perspective. *Advances in Motivation and Achievement, 10,* 413–447.

Roberts, T., & Kraft, R. (1987). Reading comprehension performance and laterality: Evidence for concurrent validity of dichotic, haptic, and EEG laterality measures. *Neuropsychologia, 25,* 817–828.

Robins, R. W., & Trzesniewski, K. H. (2005). Self-esteem development across the lifespan. *Current Directions in Psychological Science, 14,* 158–162.

Robinson, C. W., & Sloutsky, V. M. (2004). Auditory dominance and its change in the course of development. *Child Development, 75,* 1387–1401.

Robinson, D. R., Schofield, J. W., & Steers-Wentzell, K. L. (2005). Peer and cross-age tutoring in math: Outcomes and their design implications. *Educational Psychology Review, 17,* 327–362.

Robinson, S. L., & Griesemer, S. M. R. (2006). Helping individual students with problem behavior. In C. M. Evertson & C. S. Weinstein (Eds.), *Handbook of classroom management: Research, practice, and contemporary issues* (pp. 787–802). Mahwah, NJ: Erlbaum.

Roblyer, M. D. (2003). *Integrating educational technology into teaching* (3rd ed.). Upper Saddle River, NJ: Merrill/Prentice Hall.

Roderick, M., & Camburn, E. (1999). Risk and recovery from course failure in the early years of high school. *American Educational Research Journal, 36,* 303–343.

Roediger, H. L., III, & Karpicke, J. D. (2006). The power of testing memory: Basic research and implications for educational practice. *Perspectives on Psychological Science, 1,* 181–210.

Roediger, H. L., III, & Marsh, E. J. (2005). The positive and negative consequences of multiple-choice testing. *Journal of Experimental Psychology: Learning, Memory, and Cognition, 31,* 1155–1159.

Roediger, H. L., III, & McDermott, K. B. (2000). Tricks of memory. *Current Directions in Psychological Science, 9,* 123–127.

Roeser, R. W., & Lau, S. (2002). On academic identity formation in middle school settings during early adolescence. In T. M. Brinthaupt & R. P. Lipka (Eds.), *Understanding early adolescent self and identity: Applications and interventions* (pp. 91–131). Albany: State University of New York Press.

Rogers, C. R. (1983). *Freedom to learn for the 80's.* Upper Saddle River, NJ: Merrill/Prentice Hall.

Rogers, T. B., Kuiper, N. A., & Kirker, W. S. (1977). Self-reference and the encoding of personal information. *Journal of Personality and Social Psychology, 35,* 677–688.

Rogoff, B. (1990). *Apprenticeship in thinking: Cognitive development in social context.* New York: Oxford University Press.

Rogoff, B. (1991). Social interaction as apprenticeship in thinking: Guidance and participation in spatial planning. In L. B. Resnick, J. M. Levine, & S. D. Teasley (Eds.), *Perspectives on socially shared cognition.* Washington, DC: American Psychological Association.

Rogoff, B. (1994, April). *Developing understanding of the idea of communities of learners.* Paper presented at the annual meeting of the American Educational Research Association, New Orleans, LA.

Rogoff, B. (2003). *The cultural nature of human development.* Oxford, England: Oxford University Press.

Rogoff, B., Matusov, E., & White, C. (1996). Models of teaching and learning: Participation in a community of learners. In D. R. Olson & N. Torrance (Eds.), *The handbook of education and human development: New models of learning, teaching, and schooling.* Cambridge, MA: Blackwell.

Rogoff, B., Moore, L., Najafi, B., Dexter, A., Correa-Chávez, M., & Solís, J. (2007). Children's development of cultural repertoires through participation in everyday routines and practices. In J. E. Grusec & P. D. Hastings (Eds.), *Handbook of socialization: Theory and research* (pp. 490–515). New York: Guilford Press.

Rohrbeck, C. A., Ginsburg-Block, M. D., Fantuzzo, J. W., & Miller, T. R. (2003). Peer-assisted learning interventions with elementary school students: A meta-analytic review. *Journal of Educational Psychology, 95,* 240–257.

Roid, G. (2003). *Stanford-Binet Intelligence Scales* (5th ed.). Itasca, IL: Riverside.

Root, M. P. P. (1999). The biracial baby boom: Understanding ecological constructions of racial identity in the 21st century. In R. H. Sheets & E. R. Hollins (Eds.), *Racial and ethnic identity in school practices: Aspects of human development* (pp. 67–89). Mahwah, NJ: Erlbaum.

Rortvedt, A. K., & Miltenberger, R. G. (1994). Analysis of a high-probability instructional sequence and time-out in the treatment of child noncompliance. *Journal of Applied Behavior Analysis, 27,* 327–330.

Rose, A. J. (2002). Co-rumination in the friendship of girls and boys. *Child Development, 73,* 1830–1843.

Rose, R. J., Viken, R. J., Dick, D. M., Bates, J. E., Pulkkinen, L., & Kaprio, J. (2003). It *does* take a village: Nonfamiliar environments and children's behavior. *Psychological Science, 14,* 273–277.

Rose, S. A., & Feldman, J. F. (1995). Prediction of IQ and specific cognitive abilities at 11 years from infancy measures. *Developmental Psychology, 31,* 685–696.

Rosenberg, E. L. (1998). Levels of analysis and the organization of affect. *Review of General Psychology, 2,* 247–270.

Rosenshine, B., & Meister, C. (1992). The use of scaffolds for teaching higher-level cognitive strategies. *Educational Leadership, 49*(7), 26–33.

Rosenshine, B., & Meister, C. (1994). Reciprocal teaching: A review of the research. *Review of Educational Research, 64,* 479–530.

Rosenshine, B., Meister, C., & Chapman, S. (1996). Teaching students to generate questions: A review of the intervention studies. *Review of Educational Research, 66,* 181–221.

Rosenshine, B., & Stevens, R. (1986). Teaching functions. In M. C. Wittrock (Ed.), *Handbook of research on teaching* (3rd ed.). New York: Macmillan.

Rosenthal, R. (1994). Interpersonal expectancy effects: A 30-year perspective. *Current Directions in Psychological Science, 3,* 176–179.

Rosenthal, R., & Jacobson, L. (1968). *Pygmalion in the classroom: Teacher expectation and pupils' intellectual development.* New York: Holt, Rinehart & Winston.

Rosenthal, T. L., Alford, G. S., & Rasp, L. M. (1972). Concept attainment, generalization, and retention through observation and verbal coding. *Journal of Experimental Child Psychology, 13,* 183–194.

Ross, J. A. (1988). Controlling variables: A meta-analysis of training studies. *Review of Educational Research, 58,* 405–437.

Rosser, R. (1994). *Cognitive development: Psychological and biological perspectives.* Needham Heights, MA: Allyn & Bacon.

Rotenberg, K. J., & Mayer, E. V. (1990). Delay of gratification in Native and White children: A cross-cultural comparison. *International Journal of Behavioral Development, 13,* 23–30.

Roth, K. J. (1990). Developing meaningful conceptual understanding in science. In B. F. Jones & L. Idol (Eds.), *Dimensions of thinking and cognitive instruction.* Mahwah, NJ: Erlbaum.

Roth, K. J., & Anderson, C. (1988). Promoting conceptual change learning from science textbooks. In P. Ramsden (Ed.), *Improving learning: New perspectives.* London: Kogan Page.

Roth, W., & Bowen, G. M. (1995). Knowing and interacting: A study of culture, practices, and resources in a grade 8 open-inquiry science classroom guided by a cognitive apprenticeship metaphor. *Cognition and Instruction, 13,* 73–128.

Rothbaum, F., & Trommsdorff, G. (2007). Do roots and wings complement or oppose one another? The so-cialization of relatedness and autonomy in cultural context. In J. E. Grusec & P. D. Hastings (Eds.), *Handbook of socialization: Theory and research* (pp. 461–489). New York: Guilford Press.

Rothbaum, F., Weisz, J., Pott, M., Miyake, K., & Morelli, G. (2000). Attachment and culture: Security in the United States and Japan. *American Psychologist, 55,* 1093–1104.

Rothbaum, F., Weisz, J. R., & Snyder, S. S. (1982). Changing the world and changing the self: A two-process model of perceived control. *Journal of Personality and Social Psychology, 42,* 5–37.

Rovee-Collier, C. (1993). The capacity for long-term memory in infancy. *Current Directions in Psychological Science, 2,* 130–135.

Rovee-Collier, C. (1999). The development of infant memory. *Current Directions in Psychological Science, 8,* 80–85.

Rowe, D. C., Almeida, D. M., & Jacobson, K. C. (1999). School context and genetic influences on aggression in adolescence. *Psychological Science, 10,* 277–280.

Rowe, M. B. (1974). Wait-time and rewards as instructional variables, their influence on language, logic, and fate control: Part one—wait time. *Journal of Research in Science Teaching, 11,* 81–94.

Rowe, M. B. (1987). Wait-time: Slowing down may be a way of speeding up. *American Educator, 11,* 38–43, 47.

Rozalski, M. E., & Yell, M. L. (2004). Law and school safety. In J. C. Conoley & A. P. Goldstein (Eds.), *School violence intervention* (2nd ed., pp. 507–523). New York: Guilford Press.

Rubin, K. H. (1982). Nonsocial play in preschoolers: Necessarily evil? *Child Development, 53,* 651–657.

Rubin, K. H., & Krasnor, L. R. (1986). Social-cognitive and social behavioral perspectives on problem solving. In M. Perlmutter (Ed.), *Minnesota Symposia on Child Psychology: Vol. 18. Cognitive perspectives on children's social and behavioral development.* Mahwah, NJ: Erlbaum.

Rudman, M. K. (1993). Multicultural children's literature: The search for universals. In M. K. Rudman (Ed.), *Children's literature: Resource for the classroom* (2nd ed.). Norwood, MA: Christopher-Gordon.

Rudolph, K. D., Caldwell, M. S., & Conley, C. S. (2005). Need for approval and children's well-being. *Child Development, 76,* 309–323.

Rudolph, K. D., Lambert, S. F., Clark, A. G., & Kurlakowsky, K. D. (2001). Negotiating the transition to middle school: The role of self-regulatory processes. *Child Development, 72,* 929–946.

Rueda, R., & Moll, L. C. (1994). A sociocultural perspective on motivation. In H. F. O'Neil, Jr., & M. Drillings (Eds.), *Motivation: Theory and research.* Mahwah, NJ: Erlbaum.

Ruef, M. B., Higgins, C., Glaeser, B., & Patnode, M. (1998). Positive behavioral support: Strategies for teachers. *Intervention in School and Clinic, 34*(1), 21–32.

Rueger, D. B., & Liberman, R. P. (1984). Behavioral family therapy for delinquent substance-abusing adolescents. *Journal of Drug Abuse, 14,* 403–418.

Ruffman, T., Slade, L., & Crowe, E. (2002). The relation between children's and mothers' mental state language and theory-of-mind understanding. *Child Development, 73,* 734–751.

Rumberger, R. W. (1995). Dropping out of middle school: A multilevel analysis of students and schools. *American Educational Research Journal, 32,* 583–625.

Rumelhart, D. E., & Ortony, A. (1977). The representation of knowledge in memory. In R. C. Anderson, R. J. Spiro, & W. E. Montague (Eds.), *Schooling and the acquisition of knowledge.* Mahwah, NJ: Erlbaum.

Runco, M. A. (2004). Creativity as an extracognitive phenomenon. In L. V. Shavinina & M. Ferrari (Eds.), *Beyond knowledge: Extracognitive aspects of developing high ability* (pp. 17–25). Mahwah, NJ: Erlbaum.

Runco, M. A., & Chand, I. (1995). Cognition and creativity. *Educational Psychology Review, 7,* 243–267.

Rushton, J. P. (1980). *Altruism, socialization, and society.* Upper Saddle River, NJ: Prentice Hall.

Ryan, A. M. (2000). Peer groups as a context for the socialization of adolescents' motivation, engagement, and achievement in school. *Educational Psychologist, 35,* 101–111.

Ryan, A. M. (2001). The peer group as a context for the development of young adolescent motivation and achievement. *Child Development, 72,* 1135–1150.

Ryan, A. M., Hicks, L., & Midgley, C. (1997). Social goals, academic goals, and avoiding help seeking in the classroom. *Journal of Early Adolescence, 17,* 152–171.

Ryan, A. M., & Patrick, H. (2001). The classroom social environment and changes in adolescents' motivation and engagement during middle school. *American Educational Research Journal, 38,* 437–460.

Ryan, A. M., Pintrich, P. R., & Midgley, C. (2001). Avoiding seeking help in the classroom: Who and why? *Educational Psychology Review, 13,* 93–114.

Ryan, K. E., & Ryan, A. M. (2005). Psychological processes underlying stereotype threat and standardized math test performance. *Educational Psychologist, 40,* 53–63.

Ryan, R. M. (2005, April). *Legislating competence: High stakes testing, school reform, and motivation from a self-determination theory viewpoint.* Paper presented at the annual meeting of the American Educational Research Association, Montreal.

Ryan, R. M., Connell, J. P., & Grolnick, W. S. (1992). When achievement is *not* intrinsically motivated: A theory of internalization and self-regulation in school. In A. K. Boggiano & T. S. Pittman (Eds.), *Achievement and motivation: A social-developmental perspective.* Cambridge, England: Cambridge University Press.

Ryan, R. M., & Deci, E. L. (2000). Self-determination theory and the facilitation of intrinsic motivation, social development, and well-being. *American Psychologist, 55,* 68–78.

Ryan, R. M., & Kuczkowski, R. (1994). The imaginary audience, self-consciousness, and public individuation in adolescence. *Journal of Personality, 62,* 219–237.

Ryan, R. M., & Lynch, J. H. (1989). Emotional autonomy versus detachment: Revisiting the vicissitudes of adolescence and young adulthood. *Child Development, 60,* 340–356.

Ryan, R. M., Mims, V., & Koestner, R. (1983). Relation of reward contingency and interpersonal context to intrinsic motivation: A review and test using cognitive evaluation theory. *Journal of Personality and Social Psychology, 45,* 736–750.

Ryan, R. M., Stiller, J. D., & Lynch, J. H. (1994). Representations of relationships to teachers, parents, and friends as predictors of academic motivation and self-esteem. *Journal of Early Adolescence, 14,* 226–249.

Sabers, D. S., Cushing, K. S., & Berliner, D. C. (1991). Differences among teachers in a task characterized by simultaneity, multidimensionality, and immediacy. *American Educational Research Journal, 28,* 63–88.

Sadker, M. P., & Sadker, D. (1994). *Failing at fairness: How our schools cheat girls.* New York: Touchstone.

Sadoski, M., Goetz, E. T., & Fritz, J. B. (1993). Impact of concreteness on comprehensibility, interest, and memory for text: Implications for dual coding theory and text design. *Journal of Educational Psychology, 85,* 291–304.

Sadoski, M., & Paivio, A. (2001). *Imagery and text: A dual coding theory of reading and writing.* Mahwah, NJ: Erlbaum.

Salend, S. J., & Taylor, L. (1993). Working with families: A cross-cultural perspective. *Remedial and Special Education, 14*(5), 25–32, 39.

Säljö, R., & Wyndhamn, J. (1992). Solving everyday problems in the formal setting: An empirical study of the school as context for thought. In S. Chaiklin & J. Lave (Eds.), *Understanding practice.* New York: Cambridge University Press.

Salomon, G. (1993). No distribution without individuals' cognition: A dynamic interactional view. In G. Salomon (Ed.), *Distributed cognitions: Psychological and educational considerations* (pp. 111–138). Cambridge, England: Cambridge University Press.

Sanchez, F., & Anderson, M. L. (1990). Gang mediation: A process that works. *Principal, 69*(4), 54–56.

Sanders, C. E. (1997). Assessment during the preschool years. In G. D. Phye (Ed.), *Handbook of classroom assessment: Learning, achievement, and adjustment.* San Diego, CA: Academic Press.

Sanders, M. G. (1996). Action teams in action: Interviews and observations in three schools in the Baltimore School–Family–Community Partnership Program. *Journal of Education for Students Placed at Risk, 1,* 249–262.

Sanders, S. (1987). Cultural conflicts: An important factor in academic failures of American Indian students. *Journal of Multicultural Counseling and Development, 15*(2), 81–90.

Sapolsky, R. M. (1999). Glucocorticoids, stress, and their adverse neurological effects: Relevance to aging. *Experimental Gerontology, 34,* 721–732.

Sapon-Shevin, M., Dobbelaere, A., Corrigan, C., Goodman, K., & Mastin, M. (1998). Everyone here can play. *Educational Leadership, 56*(1), 42–45.

Sarason, I. G. (Ed.). (1980). *Test anxiety: Theory, research, and applications.* Mahwah, NJ: Erlbaum.

Sarason, S. B. (1972). What research says about test anxiety in elementary school children. In A. R. Binter & S. H. Frey (Eds.), *The psychology of the elementary school child.* Chicago: Rand McNally.

Sasso, G. M., & Rude, H. A. (1987). Unprogrammed effects of training high-status peers to interact with severely handicapped children. *Journal of Applied Behavior Analysis, 20,* 35–44.

Sattler, J. M. (2001). *Assessment of children: Cognitive applications* (4th ed.). San Diego, CA: Author.

Sawyer, R. J., Graham, S., & Harris, K. R. (1992). Direct teaching, strategy instruction, and strategy instruction with explicit self-regulation: Effects on the composition skills and self-efficacy of students with learning disabilities. *Journal of Educational Psychology, 84,* 340–352.

Sawyer, R. K. (2003). Emergence in creativity and development. In R. K. Sawyer, V. John-Steiner, S. Moran, R. J. Sternberg, D. H. Feldman, J. Nakamura, & M. Csikszentmihalyi, *Creativity and development* (pp. 12–60). Oxford, England: Oxford University Press.

Sax, G. (1989). *Principles of educational and psychological measurement and evaluation* (3rd ed.). Belmont, CA: Wadsworth.

Scardamalia, M., & Bereiter, C. (2006). Knowledge building: Theory, pedagogy, and technology. In R. K. Sawyer (Ed.), *The Cambridge handbook of the learning sciences* (pp. 97–115). Cambridge, England: Cambridge University Press.

Scarr, S. (1992). Developmental theories for the 1990s: Development and individual differences. *Child Development, 63,* 1–19.

Scarr, S. (1993). Biological and cultural diversity: The legacy of Darwin for development. *Child Development, 64,* 1333–1353.

Scarr, S., & McCartney, K. (1983). How people make their own environments: A theory of genotype environment effects. *Child Development, 54,* 424–435.

Scarr, S., & Weinberg, R. A. (1976). IQ test performance of black children adopted by white families. *American Psychologist, 31,* 726–739.

Scevak, J. J., Moore, P. J., & Kirby, J. R. (1993). Training students to use maps to increase text recall. *Contemporary Educational Psychology, 18,* 401–413.

Schacter, D. L. (1999). The seven sins of memory: Insights from psychology and neuroscience. *American Psychologist, 54,* 182–203.

Schank, R. C. (1979). Interestingness: Controlling inferences. *Artificial Intelligence, 12,* 273–297.

Schank, R. C., & Abelson, R. P. (1995). Knowledge and memory: The real story. In R. S. Wyer, Jr. (Ed.), *Advances in social cognition: Vol. 8. Knowledge and memory: The real story.* Mahwah, NJ: Erlbaum.

Schauble, L. (1990). Belief revision in children: The role of prior knowledge and strategies for generating evidence. *Journal of Experimental Child Psychology, 49,* 31–57.

Scheier, M. F., & Carver, C. S. (1992). Effects of optimism on psychological and physical well-being: Theoretical overview and empirical update. *Cognitive Therapy and Research, 16,* 201–228.

Schiefele, U. (1991). Interest, learning, and motivation. *Educational Psychologist, 26,* 299–323.

Schiefele, U. (1992). Topic interest and levels of text comprehension. In K. A. Renninger, S. Hidi, & A. Krapp (Eds.), *The role of interest in learning and development.* Mahwah, NJ: Erlbaum.

Schiefele, U. (1998). Individual interest and learning: What we know and what we don't know. In L. Hoffman, A. Krapp, K. Renninger, & J. Baumert (Eds.), *Interest and learning: Proceedings of the Seeon Conference on Interest and Gender* (pp. 91–104). Kiel, Germany: IPN.

Schiefele, U., Krapp, A., & Winteler, A. (1992). Interest as a predictor of academic achievement: A meta-analysis of research. In K. A. Renninger, S. Hidi, & A. Krapp (Eds.), *The role of interest in learning and development.* Mahwah, NJ: Erlbaum.

Schimmoeller, M. A. (1998, April). *Influence of private speech on the writing behaviors of young children: Four case studies.* Paper presented at the annual meeting of the American Educational Research Association, San Diego, CA.

Schlaefli, A., Rest, J. R., & Thoma, S. J. (1985). Does moral education improve moral judgment? A meta-analysis of intervention studies using the defining issues test. *Review of Educational Research, 55,* 319–352.

Schliemann, A. D., & Carraher, D. W. (1993). Proportional reasoning in and out of school. In P. Light & G. Butterworth (Eds.), *Context and cognition: Ways of learning and knowing.* Mahwah, NJ: Erlbaum.

Schmidt, R. A., & Bjork, R. A. (1992). New conceptualizations of practice: Common principles in three paradigms suggest new concepts for training. *Psychological Science, 3,* 207–217.

Schneider, W. (1993). Domain-specific knowledge and memory performance in children. *Educational Psychology Review, 5,* 257–273.

Schneider, W., & Pressley, M. (1989). *Memory development between 2 and 20.* New York: Springer-Verlag.

Schneider, W., & Shiffrin, R. M. (1977). Controlled and automatic human information processing: I. Detection, search, and attention. *Psychological Review, 84,* 1–66.

Schoenfeld, A. H., & Hermann, D. J. (1982). Problem perception and knowledge structure in expert and novice mathematical problem solvers. *Journal of Experimental Psychology: Learning, Memory, and Cognition, 8,* 484–494.

Schofield, J. W. (1995). Improving intergroup relations among students. In J. A. Banks & C. A. M. Banks (Eds.), *Handbook of research on multicultural education.* New York: Macmillan.

Schofield, J. W. (2006). Internet use in schools: Promise and problems. In R. K. Sawyer (Ed.), *The Cambridge handbook of the learning sciences* (pp. 521–534). Cambridge, England: Cambridge University Press.

Schommer, M. (1990). Effects of beliefs about the nature of knowledge on comprehension. *Journal of Educational Psychology, 82,* 498–504.

Schommer, M. (1994a). An emerging conceptualization of epistemological beliefs and their role in learning. In R. Garner & P. A. Alexander (Eds.), *Beliefs about text and instruction with text.* Mahwah, NJ: Erlbaum.

Schommer, M. (1994b). Synthesizing epistemological belief research: Tentative understandings and provocative confusions. *Educational Psychology Review, 6,* 293–319.

Schommer, M. (1997). The development of epistemological beliefs among secondary students: A longitudinal study. *Journal of Educational Psychology, 89,* 37–40.

Schommer-Aikins, M. (2001). An evolving theoretical framework for an epistemological belief system. In B. K. Hofer & P. R. Pintrich (Eds.), *Personal epistemology: The psychology of beliefs about knowledge and knowing.* Mahwah, NJ: Erlbaum.

Schoon, I. (2006). *Risk and resilience: Adaptations in changing times.* Cambridge, England: Cambridge University Press.

Schraw, G., & Lehman, S. (2001). Situational interest: A review of the literature and directions for future research. *Educational Psychology Review, 13,* 23–52.

Schraw, G., & Moshman, D. (1995). Metacognitive theories. *Educational Psychology Review, 7,* 351–371.

Schraw, G., Potenza, M. T., & Nebelsick-Gullet, L. (1993). Constraints on the calibration of performance. *Contemporary Educational Psychology, 18,* 455–463.

Schraw, G., Wade, S. E., & Kardash, C. A. M. (1993). Interactive effects of text-based and task-based importance on learning from text. *Journal of Educational Psychology, 85,* 652–661.

Schroth, M. L. (1992). The effects of delay of feedback on a delayed concept formation transfer task. *Contemporary Educational Psychology, 17,* 78–82.

Schult, C. A. (2002). Children's understanding of the distinction between intentions and desires. *Child Development, 73,* 1727–1747.

Schultz, K., Buck, P., & Niesz, T. (2000). Democratizing conversations: Racialized talk in a post-desegregated middle school. *American Educational Research Journal, 37,* 33–65.

Schunk, D. H. (1981). Modeling and attributional effects on children's achievement: A self-efficacy analysis. *Journal of Educational Psychology, 73,* 93–105.

Schunk, D. H. (1983). Developing children's self-efficacy and skills: The roles of social comparative information and goal setting. *Contemporary Educational Psychology, 8,* 76–86.

Schunk, D. H. (1987). Peer models and children's behavioral change. *Review of Educational Research, 57,* 149–174.

Schunk, D. H. (1989a). Self-efficacy and achievement behaviors. *Educational Psychology Review, 1,* 173–208.

Schunk, D. H. (1989b). Social cognitive theory and self-regulated learning. In B. J. Zimmerman & D. H. Schunk (Eds.), *Self-regulated learning and academic achievement: Theory, research, and practice.* New York: Springer-Verlag.

Schunk, D. H. (1990, April). *Socialization and the development of self-regulated learning: The role of attributions.* Paper presented at the annual meeting of the American Educational Research Association, Boston.

Schunk, D. H. (1996). Goal and self-evaluative influences during children's cognitive skill learning. *American Educational Research Journal, 33,* 359–382.

Schunk, D. H. (1998). Teaching elementary students to self-regulate practice of mathematical skills with modeling. In D. H. Schunk & B. J. Zimmerman (Eds.), *Self-regulated learning: From teaching to self-reflective practice* (pp. 137–159). New York: Guilford Press.

Schunk, D. H., & Hanson, A. R. (1985). Peer models: Influence on children's self-efficacy and achievement. *Journal of Educational Psychology, 77,* 313–322.

Schunk, D. H., & Pajares, F. (2004). Self-efficacy in education revisited: Empirical and applied evidence. In D. M. McInerney & S. Van Etten (Eds.), *Big theories revisited* (pp. 115–138). Greenwich, CT: Information Age.

Schunk, D. H., & Swartz, C. W. (1993). Goals and progress feedback: Effects on self-efficacy and writing achievement. *Contemporary Educational Psychology, 18,* 337–354.

Schunk, D. H., & Zimmerman, B. J. (Eds.). (1998). *Self-regulated learning: From teaching to self-reflective practice.* New York: Guilford Press.

Schunk, D. H., & Zimmerman, B. J. (2006). Competence and control beliefs: Distinguishing the means and ends. In P. A. Alexander & P. H. Winne (Eds.), *Handbook of educational psychology* (2nd ed., pp. 349–367). Mahwah, NJ: Erlbaum.

Schutz, P. A. (1994). Goals as the transactive point between motivation and cognition. In P. R. Pintrich, D. R. Brown, & C. E. Weinstein (Eds.), *Student motivation, cognition, and learning: Essays in honor of Wilbert J. McKeachie.* Mahwah, NJ: Erlbaum.

Schwartz, D., Dodge, K. A., Coie, J. D., Hubbard, J. A., Cillesen, A. H., Lemerise, E. A., et al. (1998). Social-cognitive and behavioral correlates of aggression and victimization in boys' play groups. *Journal of Abnormal Child Psychology, 26,* 431–440.

Schwartz, D., Gorman, A. H., Nakamoto, J., & Toblin, R. L. (2005). Victimization in the peer group and children's academic functioning. *Journal of Educational Psychology, 97,* 425–435.

Schwarz, B. B., Neuman, Y., & Biezuner, S. (2000). Two wrongs may make a right . . . if they argue together! *Cognition and Instruction, 18,* 461–494.

Scott, J., & Bushell, D. (1974). The length of teacher contacts and students' off-task behavior. *Journal of Applied Behavior Analysis, 7,* 39–44.

Scruggs, T. E., & Lifson, S. A. (1985). Current conceptions of test-wiseness: Myths and realities. *School Psychology Review, 14,* 339–350.

Scruggs, T. E., & Mastropieri, M. A. (1989). Mnemonic instruction of learning disabled students: A field-based evaluation. *Learning Disabilities Quarterly, 12,* 119–125.

Scruggs, T. E., & Mastropieri, M. A. (1994). Successful mainstreaming in elementary science classes: A qualitative study of three reputational cases. *American Educational Research Journal, 31,* 785–811.

Seaton, E. K., Scottham, K. M., & Sellers, R. M. (2006). The status model of racial identity development in African American adolescents: Evidence of structure, trajectories, and well-being. *Child Development, 77,* 1416–1426.

Segalowitz, S. J. (2007). The role of neuroscience in historical and contemporary theories of human development. In D. Coch, K. W. Fischer, & G. Dawson (Eds.), *Human behavior, learning, and the developing brain: Typical development* (pp. 3–29). New York: Guilford Press.

Seligman, M. E. P. (1991). *Learned optimism.* New York: Knopf.

Selman, R. L. (1980). *The growth of interpersonal understanding.* San Diego, CA: Academic Press.

Semb, G. B., & Ellis, J. A. (1994). Knowledge taught in school: What is remembered? *Review of Educational Research, 64,* 253–286.

Semb, G. B., Ellis, J. A., & Araujo, J. (1993). Long-term memory for knowledge learned in school. *Journal of Educational Psychology, 85,* 305–316.

Serbin, L., & Karp, J. (2003). Intergenerational studies of parenting and the transfer of risk from parent to child. *Current Directions in Psychological Science, 12,* 138–142.

Serpell, R., Baker, L., & Sonnenschein, S. (2005). *Becoming literate in the city: The Baltimore Early Childhood Project.* Cambridge, England: Cambridge University Press.

Sfard, A. (1998). On two metaphors for learning and the dangers of choosing just one. *Educational Researcher, 27*(2), 4–13.

Shapiro, A. M. (2004). How including prior knowledge as a subject variable may change outcomes of learning research. *American Educational Research Journal, 41,* 159–189.

Shavelson, R. J., & Baxter, G. P. (1992). What we've learned about assessing hands-on science. *Educational Leadership, 49*(8), 20–25.

Shavelson, R. J., Baxter, G. P., & Pine, J. (1992). Performance assessments: Political rhetoric and measurement reality. *Educational Researcher, 21*(4), 22–27.

Shaw, P., Greenstein, D., Lerch, J., Clasen, L., Lenroot, R., Gogtay, N., et al. (2006). Intellectual ability and cortical development in children and adolescents. *Nature, 440,* 676–679.

Shaywitz, S. E., Mody, M., & Shaywitz, B. A. (2006). Neural mechanisms in dyslexia. *Current Directions in Psychological Science, 15,* 278–281.

Sheets, R. H., & Hollins, E. R. (Eds.). (1999). *Racial and ethnic identity in school practices: Aspects of human development.* Mahwah, NJ: Erlbaum.

Shepard, L. A. (2000). The role of assessment in a learning culture. *Educational Researcher, 29*(7), 4–14.

Shepard, L., Hammerness, K., Darling-Hammond, L., & Rust, F. (with Snowden, J. B., Gordon, E., Gutierrez, C., & Pacheco, A.). (2005). Assessment. In L. Darling-Hammond & J. Bransford (Eds.), *Preparing teachers for a changing world: What teachers should learn and be able to do* (pp. 275–326). San Francisco: Jossey-Bass/ Wiley.

Sherman, D. K., & Cohen, G. L. (2002). Accepting threatening information: Self-affirmation and the reduction of defensive biases. *Current Directions in Psychological Science, 11,* 119–123.

Shernoff, D., Csikszentmihalyi, M., Schneider, B., & Shernoff, E. (2003). Student engagement in high school classrooms from the perspective of flow theory. *School Psychology Quarterly, 18,* 158–176.

Shernoff, D. J., & Hoogstra, L. A. (2001). Continuing motivation beyond the high school classroom. In M. Michaelson & J. Nakamura (Eds.), *Supportive frameworks for youth engagement* (pp. 73–87). San Francisco: Jossey-Bass.

Shernoff, D. J., Knauth, S., & Makris, E. (2000). The quality of classroom experiences. In M. Csikszentmihalyi & B. Schneider, *Becoming adult: How teenagers prepare for the world of work.* New York: Basic Books.

Shipman, S., & Shipman, V. C. (1985). Cognitive styles: Some conceptual, methodological, and applied issues. In E. W. Gordon (Ed.), *Review of research in education* (Vol. 12). Washington, DC: American Educational Research Association.

Short, E. J., Schatschneider, C. W., & Friebert, S. E. (1993). Relationship between memory and metamemory performance: A comparison of specific and general strategy knowledge. *Journal of Educational Psychology, 85,* 412–423.

Shrum, W., & Cheek, N. H. (1987). Social structure during the school years: Onset of the degrouping process. *American Sociological Review, 52,* 218–223.

Shuell, T. J. (1996). Teaching and learning in a classroom context. In D. C. Berliner & R. C. Calfee (Eds.), *Handbook of educational psychology.* New York: Macmillan.

Shure, M. B., & Aberson, B. (2006). Enhancing the process of resilience through effective thinking. In. S. Goldstein & R. B. Brooks (Eds.), *Handbook of resilience in children* (pp. 373–394). New York: Springer.

Shure, M. B., & Spivack, G. (1980). Interpersonal problem-solving as a mediator of behavioral adjustment in preschool and kindergarten children. *Journal of Applied Developmental Psychology, 1,* 29–44.

Shweder, R. A., Goodnow, J., Hatano, G., Levine, R. A., Marcus, H., & Miller, P. (1998). The cultural psychology of development: One mind, many mentalities. In W. Damon (Editor-in-Chief) & R. M. Lerner (Vol. Ed.), *Handbook of child psychology: Vol. 1. Theoretical models of human development* (5th ed., pp. 865–937). New York: Wiley.

Shweder, R. A., Mahapatra, M., & Miller, J. G. (1987). Culture and moral development. In J. Kagan & S. Lamb (Eds.), *The emergence of morality in young children* (pp. 1–83). Chicago: University of Chicago Press.

Sidel, R. (1996). *Keeping women and children last: America's war on the poor.* New York: Penguin Books.

Sideridis, G. D. (2005). Goal orientation, academic achievement, and depression: Evidence in favor of a revised goal theory framework. *Journal of Educational Psychology, 97,* 366–375.

Sieber, J. E., Kameya, L. I., & Paulson, F. L. (1970). Effect of memory support on the problem-solving ability of test-anxious children. *Journal of Educational Psychology, 61,* 159–168.

Siegler, R. S., & Alibali, M. W. (2005). *Children's thinking* (4th ed.). Upper Saddle River, NJ: Prentice Hall.

Siegler, R. S., & Svetina, M. (2006). What leads children to adopt new strategies? A microgenetic/cross-sectional study of class inclusion. *Child Development, 77,* 997–1015.

Sigman, M., & Whaley, S. E. (1998). The role of nutrition in the development of intelligence. In U. Neisser (Ed.), *The rising curve: Long-term gains in IQ and related measures* (pp. 155–182). Washington, DC: American Psychological Association.

Silberman, M. L., & Wheelan, S. A. (1980). *How to discipline without feeling guilty: Assertive relationships with children.* Champaign, IL: Research Press.

Silverberg, R. P. (2003, April). *Developing relational space: Teachers who came to understand themselves and their students as learners.* Paper presented at the annual meeting of the American Educational Research Association, Chicago.

Silveri, M. M., Rohan, M. L., Pimentel, P. J., Gruber, S. A., Rosso, I. M., & Yurgelun-Todd, D. A. (2006). Sex differences in the relationship between white matter microstructure and impulsivity in adolescents. *Magnetic Resonance Imaging, 24,* 833–841.

Simon, H. A. (1974). How big is a chunk? *Science, 183,* 482–488.

Simons, R. L., Whitbeck, L. B., Conger, R. D., & Conger, K. J. (1991). Parenting factors, social skills, and value commitments as precursors to school failure, involvement with deviant peers, and delinquent behavior. *Journal of Youth and Adolescence, 20,* 645–664.

Simonton, D. K. (2000). Creativity: Cognitive, personal, developmental, and social aspects. *American Psychologist, 55,* 151–158.

Simonton, D. K. (2001). Talent development as a multidimensional, multiplicative, and dynamic process. *Current Directions in Psychological Science, 10,* 39–42.

Sinatra, G. M., & Pintrich, P. R. (Eds.). (2003a). *Intentional conceptual change.* Mahwah, NJ: Erlbaum.

Sinatra, G. M., & Pintrich, P. R. (2003b). The role of intentions in conceptual change learning. In G. M. Sinatra & P. R. Pintrich (Eds.), *Intentional conceptual change* (pp. 1–18). Mahwah, NJ: Erlbaum.

Singer, D. G., & Singer, J. L. (1994). *Barney & Friends as education and entertainment: Phase 3. A national study: Can preschoolers learn through exposure to Barney & Friends?* New Haven, CT: Yale University Family Television Research and Consultation Center.

Sireci, S. G., Scarpati, S. E., & Li, S. (2005). Test accommodations for students with disabilities: An analysis of the interaction hypothesis. *Review of Educational Research, 75,* 457–490.

Sirin, S. R. (2005). Socioeconomic status and academic achievement: A meta-analytic review of research. *Review of Educational Research, 75,* 417–453.

Sizer, T. R. (1992). *Horace's school: Redesigning the American high school.* Boston: Houghton Mifflin.

Skaalvik, E. (1997). Self-enhancing and self-defeating ego orientation: Relations with task avoidance orientation, achievement, self-perceptions, and anxiety. *Journal of Educational Psychology, 89,* 71–81.

Skiba, R. J., & Rausch, M. K. (2006). Zero tolerance, suspension, and expulsion: Questions of equity and effectiveness. In C. M. Evertson & C. S. Weinstein (Eds.), *Handbook of classroom management: Research, practice, and contemporary issues* (pp. 1063–1089). Mahwah, NJ: Erlbaum.

Skinner, B. F. (1953). *Science and human behavior.* New York: Macmillan.

Skinner, B. F. (1954). The science of learning and the art of teaching. *Harvard Educational Review, 24,* 86–97.

Skinner, B. F. (1968). *The technology of teaching.* New York: Appleton-Century-Crofts.

Slavin, R. E. (1987). Ability grouping and student achievement in elementary schools: A best-evidence synthesis. *Review of Educational Research, 57,* 293–336.

Slavin, R. E. (1989). Students at risk of school failure: The problem and its dimensions. In R. E. Slavin, N. L. Karweit, & N. A. Madden (Eds.), *Effective programs for students at risk.* Needham Heights, MA: Allyn & Bacon.

Slavin, R. E. (1990). *Cooperative learning: Theory, research, and practice.* Upper Saddle River, NJ: Prentice Hall.

Slavin, R. E., Karweit, N. L., & Madden, N. A. (Eds.). (1989). *Effective programs for students at risk.* Needham Heights, MA: Allyn & Bacon.

Sleeter, C. E., & Grant, C. A. (1999). *Making choices for multicultural education: Five approaches to race, class, and gender* (3rd ed.). Upper Saddle River, NJ: Merrill/Prentice Hall.

Slonim, M. B. (1991). *Children, culture, ethnicity: Evaluating and understanding the impact.* New York: Garland.

Slusher, M. P., & Anderson, C. A. (1996). Using causal persuasive arguments to change beliefs and teach new information: The mediating role of explanation availability and evaluation bias in the acceptance of knowledge. *Journal of Educational Psychology, 88,* 110–122.

Small, M. Y., Lovett, S. B., & Scher, M. S. (1993). Pictures facilitate children's recall of unillustrated expository prose. *Journal of Educational Psychology, 85,* 520–528.

Small, R. V., & Grabowski, B. L. (1992). An exploratory study of information-seeking behaviors and learning with hypermedia information systems. *Journal of Educational Multimedia and Hypermedia, 1,* 445–464.

Smedley, A., & Smedley, B. D. (2005). Race as biology is fiction, racism as a social problem is real: Anthropological and historical perspectives on the social construction of race. *American Psychologist, 60,* 16–26.

Smetana, J. G. (1981). Preschool children's conceptions of moral and social rules. *Child Development, 52,* 1333–1336.

Smetana, J. G., & Braeges, J. L. (1990). The development of toddlers' moral and conventional judgments. *Merrill-Palmer Quarterly, 36,* 329–346.

Smith, B. L., & MacGregor, J. T. (1992). What is collaborative learning? In A. Goodsell, M. Maher, & V. Tinto (Eds.), *Collaborative learning: A sourcebook for higher education.* University Park: National Center on Postsecondary Teaching, Learning, and Assessment, The Pennsylvania State University.

Smith, C. L., Maclin, D., Grosslight, L., & Davis, H. (1997). Teaching for understanding: A study of students' preinstruction theories of matter and a comparison of the effectiveness of two approaches to teaching about matter and density. *Cognition and Instruction, 15,* 317–393.

Smith, C. L., Maclin, D., Houghton, C., & Hennessey, M. G. (2000). Sixth-grade students' epistemologies of science: The impact of school science experiences on epistemological development. *Cognition and Instruction, 18,* 349–422.

Smith, E. E. (2000). Neural bases of human working memory. *Current Directions in Psychological Science, 9,* 45–49.

Smith, E. R., & Semin, G. R. (2007). Situated social cognition. *Current Directions in Psychological Science, 16,* 132–135.

Smith, H. L. (1998). Literacy and instruction in African American communities: Shall we overcome? In B. Pérez (Ed.), *Sociocultural contexts of language and literacy.* Mahwah, NJ: Erlbaum.

Smith, J. L. (2004). Understanding the process of stereotype threat: A review of mediational variables and new performance goal directions. *Educational Psychology Review, 16,* 177–206.

Smith, K., Johnson, D. W., & Johnson, R. T. (1981). Can conflict be constructive? Controversy versus concurrence seeking in learning groups. *Journal of Educational Psychology, 73,* 651–663.

Smitherman, G. (1994). "The blacker the berry the sweeter the juice": African American student writers. In A. H. Dyson & C. Genishi (Eds.), *The need for story: Cultural diversity in classroom and community.* Urbana, IL: National Council of Teachers of English.

Snarey, J. (1995). In a communitarian voice: The sociological expansion of Kohlbergian theory, research, and practice. In W. M. Kurtines & J. L. Gewirtz (Eds.), *Moral development: An introduction.* Boston: Allyn & Bacon.

Sneider, C., & Pulos, S. (1983). Children's cosmographies: Understanding the earth's shape and gravity. *Science Education, 67,* 205–221.

Snider, V. E. (1990). What we know about learning styles from research in special education. *Educational Leadership, 48*(2), 53.

Snir, J., Smith, C. L., & Raz, G. (2003). Linking phenomena with competing underlying models: A software tool for introducing students to the particulate model of matter. *Science Education, 87,* 794–830.

Snow, R. E., Corno, L., & Jackson, D., III (1996). Individual differences in affective and conative functions. In D. C. Berliner & R. C. Calfee (Eds.), *Handbook of educational psychology.* New York: Macmillan.

Snyder, C. R. (1994). *The psychology of hope: You can get there from here.* New York: Free Press.

Snyder, C. R. (2002). Hope theory: Rainbows in the mind. *Psychological Inquiry, 13,* 249–275.

Solomon, R. C. (1984). Getting angry: The Jamesian theory of emotion in anthropology. In R. Shweder & R. A. Levine (Eds.), *Culture theory: Essays on mind, self, and emotion* (pp. 238–256). Cambridge, England: Cambridge University Press.

Sosniak, L. A., & Stodolsky, S. S. (1994). Making connections: Social studies education in an urban fourth-grade classroom. In J. Brophy (Ed.), *Advances in research on teaching: Vol. 4. Case studies of teaching and learning in social studies.* Greenwich, CT: JAI Press.

Southerland, S. A., & Sinatra, G. M. (2003). Learning about biological evolution: A special case of intentional conceptual change. In G. M. Sinatra & P. R. Pintrich (Eds.), *Intentional conceptual change* (pp. 317–345). Mahwah, NJ: Erlbaum.

Sowell, E. R., & Jernigan, T. L. (1998). Further MRI evidence of late brain maturation: Limbic volume increases and changing asymmetries during childhood and adolescence. *Developmental Neuropsychology, 14,* 599–617.

Sowell, E. R., Thompson, P. M., Holmes, C. J., Jernigan, T. L., & Toga, A. W. (1999). *In vivo* evidence for postadolescent brain maturation in frontal and striatal regions. *Nature Neuroscience, 2,* 859–861.

Spandel, V. (1997). Reflections on portfolios. In G. D. Phye (Ed.), *Handbook of academic learning: Construction of knowledge.* San Diego, CA: Academic Press.

Spaulding, C. L. (1992). *Motivation in the classroom.* New York: McGraw-Hill.

Spear, L. P. (2000). Neurobehavioral changes in adolescence. *Current Directions in Psychological Science, 9,* 11–114.

Spear, L. P. (2007). Brain development and adolescent behavior. In D. Coch, K. W. Fischer, & G. Dawson (Eds.), *Human behavior, learning, and the developing brain: Typical development* (pp. 362–396). New York: Guilford Press.

Spearman, C. (1904). General intelligence, objectively determined and measured. *American Journal of Psychology, 15,* 201–293.

Spearman, C. (1927). *The abilities of man: Their nature and measurement.* New York: Macmillan.

Spelke, E. S. (1994). Initial knowledge: Six suggestions. *Cognition, 50,* 431–445.

Spencer, M. B., Noll, E., Stoltzfus, J., & Harpalani, V. (2001). Identity and school adjustment: Revisiting the "acting White" phenomenon. *Educational Psychologist, 36,* 21–30.

Spera, C. (2005). A review of the relationship among parenting practices, parenting styles, and adolescent school achievement. *Educational Psychology Review, 17,* 125–146.

Sperling, G. (1960). The information available in brief visual presentations. *Psychological Monographs, 74* (Whole No. 498).

Squire, L. R., & Alvarez, P. (1998). Retrograde amnesia and memory consolidation: A neurobiological perspective. In L. R. Squire & S. M. Kosslyn (Eds.), *Findings and current opinion in cognitive neuroscience* (pp. 75–84). Cambridge, MA: MIT Press.

Sroufe, L. A., Cooper, R. G., DeHart, G., & Bronfenbrenner, U. (1992). *Child development: Its nature and course* (2nd ed.). New York: McGraw-Hill.

Stacey, K. (1992). Mathematical problem solving in groups: Are two heads better than one? *Journal of Mathematical Behavior, 11,* 261–275.

Stack, C. B., & Burton, L. M. (1993). Kinscripts. *Journal of Comparative Family Studies, 24,* 157–170.

Stahl, G., Koschmann, T., & Suthers, D. D. (2006). Computer-supported collaborative learning. In R. K. Sawyer (Ed.), *The Cambridge handbook of the learning sciences* (pp. 409–425). Cambridge, England: Cambridge University Press.

Stainback, S., & Stainback, W. (1992). Schools as inclusive communities. In W. Stainback & S. Stainback (Eds.), *Controversial issues confronting special education: Divergent perspectives.* Boston: Allyn & Bacon.

Standage, M., Duda, J. L., & Ntoumanis, N. (2003). A model of contextual motivation in physical education: Using constructs from self-determination and achievement goal theories to predict physical activity intentions. *Journal of Educational Psychology, 95,* 97–110.

Stanley, J. C. (1980). On educating the gifted. *Educational Researcher, 9*(3), 8–12.

Stanovich, K. E. (1999). *Who is rational? Studies of individual differences in reasoning.* Mahwah, NJ: Erlbaum.

Stanovich, K. E. (2000). *Progress in understanding reading: Scientific foundations and new frontiers.* New York: Guilford Press.

Staples, M. (2007). Supporting whole-class collaborative inquiry in a secondary mathematics classroom. *Cognition and Instruction, 25,* 161–217.

Staub, E. (1995). The roots of prosocial and antisocial behavior in persons and groups: Environmental influence, personality, culture, and socialization. In W. M. Kurtines & J. L. Gewirtz (Eds.), *Moral development: An introduction.* Boston: Allyn & Bacon.

Steele, C. M. (1997). A threat in the air: How stereotypes shape intellectual identity and performance. *American Psychologist, 52,* 613–629.

Steffensen, M. S., Joag-Dev, C., & Anderson, R. C. (1979). A cross-cultural perspective on reading comprehension. *Reading Research Quarterly, 15,* 10–29.

Stein, B. S. (1989). Memory and creativity. In J. A. Glover, R. R. Ronning, & C. R. Reynolds (Eds.), *Handbook of creativity.* New York: Plenum Press.

Steinberg, E. R. (1989). Cognition and learner control: A literature review, 1977–1988. *Journal of Computer-Based Instruction, 16*(4), 117–121.

Steinberg, L. (1996). *Beyond the classroom: Why school reform has failed and what parents need to do.* New York: Touchstone.

Steinberg, L. (2005). Cognitive and affective development in adolescence. *Trends in Cognitive Sciences, 9*(2), 69–74.

Steinberg, L. (2007). Risk taking in adolescence. *Current Directions in Psychological Science, 16,* 55–59.

Steinberg, L., Blinde, P. L., & Chan, K. S. (1984). Dropping out among language minority youth. *Review of Educational Research, 54,* 113–132.

Steiner, H. H., & Carr, M. (2003). Cognitive development in gifted children: Toward a more precise understanding of emerging differences in intelligence. *Educational Psychology Review, 15,* 215–246.

Stepans, J. (1991). Developmental patterns in students' understanding of physics concepts. In S. M. Glynn, R. H. Yeany, & B. K. Britton (Eds.), *The psychology of learning science.* Mahwah, NJ: Erlbaum.

Sternberg, R. J. (1984). Toward a triarchic theory of human intelligence. *Behavioral and Brain Sciences, 7,* 269–287.

Sternberg, R. J. (1985). *Beyond IQ: A triarchic theory of human intelligence.* Cambridge, England: Cambridge University Press.

Sternberg, R. J. (1996). Myths, countermyths, and truths about intelligence. *Educational Researcher, 25*(2), 11–16.

Sternberg, R. J. (1997). The concept of intelligence and its role in lifelong learning and success. *American Psychologist, 52,* 1030–1037.

Sternberg, R. J. (1998). Applying the triarchic theory of human intelligence in the classroom. In R. J. Sternberg & W. M. Williams (Eds.), *Intelligence, instruction, and assessment: Theory into practice.* Mahwah, NJ: Erlbaum.

Sternberg, R. J. (2003). *Wisdom, intelligence, and creativity synthesized.* Cambridge, England: Cambridge University Press.

Sternberg, R. J. (2004). Culture and intelligence. *American Psychologist, 59,* 325–338.

Sternberg, R. J. (2007). Intelligence and culture. In S. Kitayama & D. Cohen (Eds.), *Handbook of cultural psychology* (pp. 547–568). New York: Guilford Press.

Sternberg, R. J., & Detterman, D. K. (Eds.). (1986). *What is intelligence? Contemporary views on its nature and definition.* Norwood, NJ: Ablex.

Sternberg, R. J., Forsythe, G. B., Hedlund, J., Horvath, J. A., Wagner, R. K., Williams, W. M., et al. (2000). *Practical intelligence in everyday life.* Cambridge, England: Cambridge University Press.

Sternberg, R. J., & Frensch, P. A. (1993). Mechanisms of transfer. In D. K. Detterman & R. J. Sternberg (Eds.), *Transfer on trial: Intelligence, cognition, and instruction.* Norwood, NJ: Ablex.

Sternberg, R. J., & Horvath, J. A. (1995). A prototype view of expert teaching. *Educational Researcher, 24*(6), 9–17.

Sternberg, R. J., & Wagner, R. K. (Eds.). (1994). *Mind in context: Interactionist perspectives on human intelligence.* Cambridge, England: Cambridge University Press.

Stevens, R. J., & Slavin, R. E. (1995). The cooperative elementary school: Effects of students' achievement, attitudes, and social relations. *American Educational Research Journal, 32,* 321–351.

Stevenson, H. W., Chen, C., & Uttal, D. H. (1990). Beliefs and achievement: A study of black, white, and Hispanic children. *Child Development, 61,* 508–523.

Stewart, L., & Pascual-Leone, J. (1992). Mental capacity constraints and the development of moral reasoning. *Journal of Experimental Child Psychology, 54,* 251–287.

Stice, E. (2003). Puberty and body image. In C. Hayward (Ed.), *Gender differences at puberty* (pp. 61–76). Cambridge, England: Cambridge University Press.

Stice, E., & Barrera, M., Jr. (1995). A longitudinal examination of the reciprocal relations between perceived parenting and adolescents' substance use and externalizing behaviors. *Developmental Psychology, 31,* 322–334.

Stiggins, R. J. (2001). *Student-involved classroom assessment* (3rd ed.). Upper Saddle River, NJ: Merrill/Prentice Hall.

Stipek, D. J. (1993). *Motivation to learn: From theory to practice* (2nd ed.). Boston: Allyn & Bacon.

Stipek, D. J. (1996). Motivation and instruction. In D. C. Berliner & R. C. Calfee (Eds.), *Handbook of educational psychology.* New York: Macmillan.

Stipek, D. (2002). At what age should children enter kindergarten? A question for policy makers and parents. *Social Policy Report of the Society for Research in Child Development, 16*(2), 3–16.

Stipek, D. J., & Gralinski, H. (1990, April). *Gender differences in children's achievement-related beliefs and emotional responses to success and failure in math.* Paper presented at the annual meeting of the American Educational Research Association, Boston.

Stodolsky, S. S., Salk, S., & Glaessner, B. (1991). Student views about learning math and social studies. *American Educational Research Journal, 28,* 89–116.

Stone, N. J. (2000). Exploring the relationship between calibration and self-regulated learning. *Educational Psychology Review, 12,* 437–475.

Striepling-Goldstein, S. H. (2004). The low-aggression classroom: A teacher's view. In J. C. Conoley & A. P. Goldstein (Eds.), *School violence intervention* (2nd ed., pp. 23–53). New York: Guilford Press.

Stright, A. D., Neitzel, C., Sears, K. G., & Hoke-Sinex, L. (2001). Instruction begins in the home: Relations between parental instruction and children's self-regulation in the classroom. *Journal of Educational Psychology, 93,* 456–466.

Strike, K. A., & Posner, G. J. (1992). A revisionist theory of conceptual change. In R. A. Duschl & R. J. Hamilton (Eds.), *Philosophy of science, cognitive psychology, and educational theory and practice.* New York: State University of New York Press.

Stringfield, S. C., & Yakimowski-Srebnick, M. E. (2005). Promise, progress, problems, and paradoxes of three phases of accountability: A longitudinal case study of the Baltimore City Public Schools. *American Educational Research Journal, 42,* 43–75.

Sue, D. W. (1990). Culture-specific strategies in counseling: A conceptual framework. *Professional Psychology: Research and Practice, 21,* 424–433.

Sue, S., & Chin, R. (1983). The mental health of Chinese-American children: Stressors and resources. In G. J. Powell (Ed.), *The psychosocial development of minority children.* New York: Brunner/Mazel.

Suina, J. H., & Smolkin, L. B. (1994). From natal culture to school culture to dominant society culture: Supporting transitions for Pueblo Indian students. In P. M. Greenfield & R. R. Cocking (Eds.), *Cross-cultural roots of minority child development.* Mahwah, NJ: Erlbaum.

Sullivan, J. R., & Conoley, J. C. (2004). Academic and instructional interventions with aggressive students. In J. C. Conoley & A. P. Goldstein (Eds.), *School violence intervention* (2nd ed., pp. 235–255). New York: Guilford Press.

Sullivan, J. S. (1989). Planning, implementing, and maintaining an effective in-school suspension program. *Clearing House, 62,* 409–410.

Sullivan-DeCarlo, C., DeFalco, K., & Roberts, V. (1998). Helping students avoid risky behavior. *Educational Leadership, 56*(1), 80–82.

Sund, R. B. (1976). *Piaget for educators.* Upper Saddle River, NJ: Merrill/Prentice Hall.

Sutherland, K. S., & Morgan, P. L. (2003). Implications of transactional processes in classrooms for students with emotional/behavioral disorders. *Preventing School Failure, 48*(6), 32–45.

Sutton, R. E., & Wheatley, K. F. (2003). Teachers' emotions and teaching: A review of the literature and directions for future research. *Educational Psychology Review, 15,* 327–358.

Swan, K., Mitrani, M., Guerrero, F., Cheung, M., & Schoener, J. (1990, April). *Perceived locus of control and computer-based instruction.* Paper presented at the annual meeting of the American Educational Research Association, Boston.

Swann, W. B., Jr., Chang-Schneider, C., & McClarty, K. L. (2007). Do people's self-views matter? Self-concept and self-esteem in everyday life. *American Psychologist, 62,* 84–94.

Swanson, D. B., Norman, G. R., & Linn, R. L. (1995). Performance-based assessment: Lessons from the health professions. *Educational Researcher, 24*(5), 5–11, 35.

Swanson, H. L. (2006). Cross-sectional and incremental changes in working memory and mathematical problem solving. *Journal of Educational Psychology, 98,* 265–281.

Swanson, H. L., & Lussier, C. M. (2001). A selective synthesis of the experimental literature on dynamic assessment. *Review of Educational Research, 71,* 321–363.

Swanson, H. L., O'Connor, J. E., & Cooney, J. B. (1990). An information processing analysis of expert and novice teachers' problem solving. *American Educational Research Journal, 27,* 533–556.

Swearer, S. M., Grills, A. E., Haye, K. M., & Cary, P. T. (2004). Internalizing problems in students involved in bullying and victimization: Implications for intervention. In D. L. Espelage & S. M. Swearer (Eds.), *Bullying in American schools: A social-ecological perspective on prevention and intervention* (pp. 63–83). Mahwah, NJ: Erlbaum.

Sweller, J. (1994). Cognitive load theory, learning difficulty, and instructional design. *Learning and Instruction, 4,* 295–312.

Tamburrini, J. (1982). Some educational implications of Piaget's theory. In S. Modgil & C. Modgil (Eds.), *Jean Piaget: Consensus and controversy.* New York: Praeger.

Tanner, J. M., & Inhelder, B. (Eds.). (1960). *Discussions of child development: A consideration of the biological, psychological, and cultural approaches to the understanding of human development and behavior: Vol. 4. The proceedings of the fourth meeting of the World Health Organization Study Group on the Psychobiological Development of the Child, Geneva, 1956.* New York: International Universities Press.

Tarver, S. G. (1992). Direct Instruction. In W. Stainback & S. Stainback (Eds.), *Controversial issues confronting special education.* Boston: Allyn & Bacon.

Tate, W. F. (1995). Returning to the root: A culturally relevant approach to mathematics pedagogy. *Theory into Practice, 34,* 166–173.

Tatum, B. D. (1997). *"Why are all the black kids sitting together in the cafeteria?" and other conversations about race.* New York: Basic Books.

Teasley, S. D., & Roschelle, J. (1993). Constructing a joint problem space: The computer as a tool for sharing information. In S. P. Lajoie & S. J. Derry (Eds.), *Computers as cognitive tools* (pp. 229–258). Hillsdale, NJ: Erlbaum.

Tenenbaum, H. R., & Ruck, M. D. (2007). Are teachers' expectations different for racial minority than for European American students? A meta-analysis. *Journal of Educational Psychology, 99,* 253–273.

Tennyson, R. D., & Cocchiarella, M. J. (1986). An empirically based instructional design theory for teaching concepts. *Review of Educational Research, 56,* 40–71.

Terman, L. M., & Merrill, M. A. (1972). *Stanford-Binet Intelligence Scale* (3rd ed.). Boston: Houghton Mifflin.

Terwilliger, J. S. (1989). Classroom standard setting and grading practices. *Educational Measurement: Issues and Practice, 8*(2), 15–19.

Tessler, M., & Nelson, K. (1994). Making memories: The influence of joint encoding on later recall by young children. *Consciousness and Cognition, 3,* 307–326.

Tharp, R. G. (1989). Psychocultural variables and constants: Effects on teaching and learning in schools. *American Psychologist, 44,* 349–359.

Tharp, R. G. (1994). Intergroup differences among Native Americans in socialization and child cognition: An ethnogenetic analysis. In P. M. Greenfield & R. R. Cocking (Eds.), *Cross-cultural roots of minority child development.* Mahwah, NJ: Erlbaum.

Théberge, C. L. (1994, April). *Small-group vs. whole-class discussion: Gaining the floor in science lessons.* Paper presented at the annual meeting of the American Educational Research Association, New Orleans, LA.

Thelen, E., & Smith, L. B. (1998). Dynamic systems theories. In W. Damon (Series Ed.) & R. M. Lerner (Vol. Ed.), *Handbook of child psychology: Vol. 1. Theoretical models of human development.* New York: Wiley.

Themann, K. S., & Goldstein, H. (2001). Social stories, written text cues, and video feedback: Effects on social communication of children with autism. *Journal of Applied Behavior Analysis, 34,* 425–446.

Théoret, H., Halligan, E., Kobayashi, M., Fregni, F., Tager-Flusberg, H., & Pascual-Leone, A. (2005). Impaired motor facilitation during action observation in individuals with autism spectrum disorder. *Current Biology, 15,* 84–85.

Thomas, A., & Chess, S. (1977). *Temperament and development.* New York: Brunner/Mazel.

Thomas, J. W. (1993). Expectations and effort: Course demands, students' study practices, and academic achievement. In T. M. Tomlinson (Ed.), *Motivating students to learn: Overcoming barriers to high achievement.* Berkeley, CA: McCutchan.

Thomas, R. M. (2005). *High-stakes testing: Coping with collateral damage.* Mahwah, NJ: Erlbaum.

Thomas, S., & Oldfather, P. (1997). Intrinsic motivations, literacy, and assessment practices: "That's my grade. That's me." *Educational Psychologist, 32,* 107–123.

Thomas, S. P., Groër, M., & Droppleman, P. (1993). Physical health of today's school children. *Educational Psychology Review, 5,* 5–33.

Thompson, M., & Grace, C. O. (with Cohen, L. J.). (2001). *Best friends, worst enemies: Understanding the social lives of children.* New York: Ballantine.

Thompson, R. A. (1998). Early sociopersonality development. In W. Damon (Series Ed.) & N. Eisenberg (Vol. Ed.), *Handbook of child psychology: Vol. 3: Social, emotional, and personality development* (5th ed.). New York: Wiley.

Thompson, R. A., & Nelson, C. A. (2001). Developmental science and the media: Early brain development. *American Psychologist, 56,* 5–15.

Thompson, R. A., & Wyatt, J. M. (1999). Current research on child maltreatment: Implications for educators. *Educational Psychology Review, 11,* 173–201.

Thorkildsen, T. A. (1995). Conceptions of social justice. In W. M. Kurtines & J. L. Gewirtz (Eds.), *Moral development: An introduction.* Boston: Allyn & Bacon.

Thorndike, R., Hagen, E., & Sattler, J. (1986). *Stanford-Binet Intelligence Scale* (4th ed.). Itasca, IL: Riverside.

Thurstone, L. L. (1938). *Primary mental abilities.* Chicago: University of Chicago Press.

Timm, P., & Borman, K. (1997). The soup pot don't stretch that far no more: Intergenerational patterns of school leaving in an urban Appalachian neighborhood. In M. Sellter & L. Weis (Eds.), *Beyond black and white: New faces and voices in U.S. schools.* Albany: State University of New York Press.

Tirosh, D., & Graeber, A. O. (1990). Evoking cognitive conflict to explore preservice teachers' thinking about division. *Journal for Research in Mathematics Education, 21,* 98–108.

Tisak, M. (1993). Preschool children's judgments of moral and personal events involving physical harm and property damage. *Merrill-Palmer Quarterly, 39,* 375–390.

Tobias, S. (1985). Test anxiety: Interference, defective skills, and cognitive capacity. *Educational Psychologist, 20,* 135–142.

Tobias, S. (1994). Interest, prior knowledge, and learning. *Review of Educational Research, 64,* 37–54.

Tobin, K. (1987). The role of wait time in higher cognitive level learning. *Review of Educational Research, 57,* 69–95.

Tomback, R. M., Williams, A. Y., & Wentzel, K. R. (2005, April). *Young adolescents' concerns about the transition to high school.* Poster presented at the annual meeting of the American Educational Research Association, Montreal.

Torney-Purta, J. (1994). Dimensions of adolescents' reasoning about political and historical issues: Ontological switches, developmental processes, and situated learning. In M. Carretero & J. F. Voss (Eds.), *Cognitive and instructional processes in history and the social sciences* (pp. 103–122). Mahwah, NJ: Erlbaum.

Torrance, E. P. (1970). *Encouraging creativity in the classroom.* Dubuque, IA: Wm. C. Brown.

Torrance, E. P. (1989). A reaction to "Gifted black students: Curriculum and teaching strategies." In C. J. Maker & S. W. Schiever (Eds.), *Critical issues in gifted education: Vol. 2. Defensible programs for cultural and ethnic minorities.* Austin, TX: Pro-Ed.

Torrance, E. P. (1995). Insights about creativity: Questioned, rejected, ridiculed, ignored. *Educational Psychology Review, 7,* 313–322.

Torrance, E. P., & Myers, R. E. (1970). *Creative learning and teaching.* New York: Dodd, Mead.

Torres-Guzmán, M. E. (1998). Language, culture, and literacy in Puerto Rican communities. In B. Pérez (Ed.), *Sociocultural contexts of language and literacy.* Mahwah, NJ: Erlbaum.

Tourniaire, F., & Pulos, S. (1985). Proportional reasoning: A review of the literature. *Educational Studies in Mathematics, 16,* 181–204.

Trautwein, U., & Lüdtke, O. (2007). Students' self-reported effort and time on homework in six school subjects: Between-student differences and within-student variation. *Journal of Educational Psychology, 99,* 432–444.

Trautwein, L., Lüdtke, O., Schnyder, I., & Niggli, A. (2006). Predicting homework effort: Support for a domain-specific, multilevel homework model. *Journal of Educational Psychology, 98,* 438–456.

Trawick-Smith, J. (2003). *Early childhood development: A multicultural perspective* (3rd ed.). Upper Saddle River, NJ: Merrill/Prentice Hall.

Treffinger, D. J. (1995). Creative problem solving: Overview and educational implications. *Educational Psychology Review, 7,* 301–312.

Triandis, H. C. (1995). *Individualism and collectivism.* Boulder, CO: Westview Press.

Troop-Gordon, W., & Ladd, G. W. (2005). Trajectories of peer victimization and perceptions of the self and schoolmates: Precursors to internalizing and externalizing problems. *Child Development, 76,* 1072–1091.

Tryon, G. S. (1980). The measurement and treatment of anxiety. *Review of Educational Research, 50,* 343–372.

Tsai, J. L., & Chentsova-Dutton, Y. (2003). Variation among European Americans in emotional facial expression. *Journal of Cross Cultural Psychology, 34,* 650–657.

Tsethlikai, M., & Greenhoot, A. F. (2006). The influence of another's perspective on children's recall of previously misconstrued events. *Developmental Psychology, 42,* 732–745.

Tsethlikai, M., Guthrie-Fulbright, Y., & Loera, S. (2007, March). *Social perspective coordination ability and children's recall of mutual conflict.* Paper presented at the biennial meeting of the Society for Research in Child Development, Boston.

Tucker, V. G., & Anderman, L. H. (1999, April). *Cycles of learning: Demonstrating the interplay between motivation, self-regulation, and cognition.* Paper presented at the annual meeting of the American Educational Research Association, Montreal, Canada.

Tudge, J., Hogan, D., Lee, S., Tammeveski, P., Meltsas, M., Kulakova, N., et al. (1999). Cultural heterogeneity: Parental values and beliefs and their preschoolers' activities in the United States, South Korea, Russia, and Estonia. In A. Göncü (Ed.), *Children's engagement in the world: Sociocultural perspectives* (pp. 62–96). Cambridge, England: Cambridge University Press.

Tulving, E. (1962). Subjective organization in free recall of "unrelated" words. *Psychological Review, 69,* 344–354.

Tulving, E. (1983). *Elements of episodic memory.* Oxford, England: Oxford University Press.

Tulving, E., & Thomson, D. M. (1973). Encoding specificity and retrieval processes in episodic memory. *Psychological Review, 80,* 352–373.

Turiel, E. (1983). *The development of social knowledge: Morality and convention.* Cambridge, England: Cambridge University Press.

Turiel, E. (1998). The development of morality. In W. Damon (Series Ed.) & N. Eisenberg (Vol. Ed.), *Handbook of child psychology: Vol. 3. Social, emotional, and personality development* (5th ed., pp. 863–932). New York: Wiley.

Turiel, E. (2002). *The culture of morality: Social development, context, and conflict.* Cambridge, England: Cambridge University Press.

Turiel, E., Smetana, J. G., & Killen, M. (1991). Social contexts in social cognitive development. In W. M. Kurtines & J. L. Gewirtz (Eds.), *Moral behavior and development: Vol. 2. Research.* Mahwah, NJ: Erlbaum.

Turnbull, A. P., Pereira, L., & Blue-Banning, M. (2000). Teachers as friendship facilitators. *Teaching Exceptional Children, 32*(5), 66–70.

Turnbull, A. P., Turnbull, R., & Wehmeyer, M. L. (2007). *Exceptional lives: Special education in today's schools* (5th ed.). Upper Saddle River, NJ: Merrill/Prentice Hall.

Turner, J. C. (1995). The influence of classroom contexts on young children's motivation for literacy. *Reading Research Quarterly, 30,* 410–441.

Turner, J. C., Meyer, D. K., Cox, K. E., Logan, C., DiCintio, M., & Thomas, C. T. (1998). Creating contexts for involvement in mathematics. *Journal of Educational Psychology, 90,* 730–745.

Turner, J. C., Thorpe, P. K., & Meyer, D. K. (1998). Students' reports of motivation and negative affect: A theoretical and empirical analysis. *Journal of Educational Psychology, 90,* 758–771.

Turner, J. E., Husman, J., & Schallert, D. L. (2002). The importance of students' goals in their emotional experience of academic failure: Investigating the precursors and consequences of shame. *Educational Psychologist, 37,* 79–89.

Tyler, B. (1958). Expectancy for eventual success as a factor in problem solving behavior. *Journal of Educational Psychology, 49,* 166–172.

Tzuriel, D. (2000). Dynamic assessment of young children: Educational and intervention perspectives. *Educational Psychology Review, 12,* 385–435.

Ulichny, P. (1996). Cultures in conflict. *Anthropology and Education Quarterly, 27,* 331–364.

Underwood, J., & Webb, L. D. (2006). *School law for teachers: Concepts and applications.* Upper Saddle River, NJ: Merrill/Prentice Hall.

Urdan, T. C. (1997). Achievement goal theory: Past results, future directions. In M. L. Maehr & P. R. Pintrich (Eds.), *Advances in motivation and achievement* (Vol. 10, pp. 99–141). Greenwich, CT: JAI Press.

Urdan, T. C., & Maehr, M. L. (1995). Beyond a two-goal theory of motivation and achievement: A case for social goals. *Review of Educational Research, 65,* 213–243.

Urdan, T., & Mestas, M. (2006). The goals behind performance goals. *Journal of Educational Psychology, 98,* 354–365.

Urdan, T., & Midgley, C. (2001). Academic self-handicapping: What we know, what more there is to learn. *Educational Psychology Review, 13,* 115–138.

Urdan, T. C., Midgley, C., & Anderman, E. M. (1998). The role of classroom goal structure in students' use of self-handicapping strategies. *American Educational Research Journal, 35,* 101–122.

Urdan, T., Ryan, A. M., Anderman, E. M., & Gheen, M. H. (2002). Goals, goal structures, and avoidance behaviors. In C. Midgley (Ed.), *Goals, goal structures, and patterns of adaptive learning* (pp. 55–83). Mahwah, NJ: Erlbaum.

U.S. Department of Education. (1992). *To assure the free appropriate public education of all children with disabilities: Fourteenth annual report to Congress on the implementation of the Individuals with Disabilities Education Act.* Washington, DC: Author.

Valencia, S. W., Hiebert, E. H., & Afflerbach, P. P. (1994). Realizing the possibilities of authentic assessment: Current trends and future issues. In S. W. Valencia, E. H. Hiebert, & P. P. Afflerbach (Eds.), *Authentic reading assessment: Practices and possibilities.* Newark, DE: International Reading Association.

Valentine, J. C., Cooper, H., Bettencourt, B. A., & DuBois, D. L. (2002). Out-of-school activities and academic achievement: The mediating role of self-beliefs. *Educational Psychologist, 37,* 245–256.

Valkenburg, P. M., Peter, J., & Schouten, A. P. (2006). Friend networking sites and their relationship to adolescents' well-being and social self-esteem. *CyberPsychology & Behavior, 9,* 584–590.

Vallerand, R. J., Fortier, M. S., & Guay, F. (1997). Self-determination and persistence in a real-life setting: Toward a motivational model of high school dropout. *Journal of Personality and Social Psychology, 72,* 1161–1176.

Van Camp, C. M., Lerman, D. C., Kelley, M. E., Roane, H. S., Contrucci, S. A., & Vorndran, C. M. (2000). Further analysis of idiosyncratic antecedent influences during the assessment and treatment of problem behavior. *Journal of Applied Behavior Analysis, 33,* 207–221.

Van Dooren, W., De Bock, D., Hessels, A., Janssens, D., & Verschaffel, L. (2005). Not everything is proportional: Effects of age and problem type on propensities for overgeneralization. *Cognition and Instruction, 23,* 57–86.

van Drie, J., van Boxtel, C., & van der Linden, J. (2006). Historical reasoning in a computer-supported collaborative learning environment. In A. M. O'Donnell, C. E. Hmelo-Silver, & G. Erkens (Eds.), *Collaborative learning, reasoning, and technology* (pp. 265–296). Mahwah, NJ: Erlbaum.

Van Houten, R., Nau, P., MacKenzie-Keating, S., Sameoto, D., & Colavecchia, B. (1982). An analysis of some variables influencing the effectiveness of reprimands. *Journal of Applied Behavior Analysis, 15,* 65–83.

van IJzendoorn, M. H., & Juffer, F. (2005). Adoption is a successful natural intervention enhancing adopted children's IQ and school performance. *Current Directions in Psychological Science, 14,* 326–330.

van Kraayenoord, C. E., & Paris, S. G. (1997). Australian students' self-appraisal of their work samples and academic progress. *Elementary School Journal, 97,* 523–537.

van Laar, C. (2000). The paradox of low academic achievement but high self-esteem in African American students: An attributional account. *Educational Psychology Review, 12,* 33–61.

Van Leijenhorst, L., Crone, E. A., & Van der Molen, M. W. (2007). Developmental trends for object and spatial working memory: A psychophysiological analysis. *Child Development, 78,* 987–1000.

Van Meter, P. (2001). Drawing construction as a strategy for learning from text. *Journal of Educational Psychology, 93,* 129–140.

Van Meter, P., & Garner, J. (2005). The promise and practice of learner-generated drawing: Literature review and synthesis. *Educational Psychology Review, 17,* 285–325.

VanSledright, B., & Brophy, J. (1992). Storytelling, imagination, and fanciful elaboration in children's historical reconstructions. *American Educational Research Journal, 29,* 837–859.

VanSledright, B., & Limón, M. (2006). Learning and teaching social studies: A review of cognitive research in history and geography. In P. A. Alexander & P. H. Winne (Eds.), *Handbook of educational psychology* (2nd ed., pp. 545–570). Mahwah, NJ: Erlbaum.

Vansteenkiste, M., Lens, W., & Deci, E. L. (2006). Intrinsic versus extrinsic goal contents in self-determination theory: Another look at the quality of academic motivation. *Educational Psychologist, 41*, 19–31.

Vasquez, J. A. (1988). Contexts of learning for minority students. *Educational Forum, 6*, 243–253.

Vaughn, B. J., & Horner, R. H. (1997). Identifying instructional tasks that occasion problem behaviors and assessing the effects of student versus teacher choice among these tasks. *Journal of Applied Behavior Analysis, 30*, 299–312.

Vaughn, S. (1991). Social skills enhancement in students with learning disabilities. In B. Y. L. Wong (Ed.), *Learning about learning disabilities*. San Diego, CA: Academic Press.

Venn, J. J. (2000). *Assessing students with special needs* (2nd ed.). Upper Saddle River, NJ: Merrill/Prentice Hall.

Verdi, M. P., & Kulhavy, R. W. (2002). Learning with maps and texts: An overview. *Educational Psychology Review, 14*, 27–46.

Verdi, M. P., Kulhavy, R. W., Stock, W. A., Rittschof, K. A., & Johnson, J. T. (1996). Text learning using scientific diagrams: Implications for classroom use. *Contemporary Educational Psychology, 21*, 487–499.

Vernon, P. A. (1993). Intelligence and neural efficiency. In D. K. Detterman (Ed.), *Current topics in human intelligence* (Vol. 3). Norwood, NJ: Ablex.

Vintere, P., Hemmes, N. S., Brown, B. L., & Poulson, C. L. (2004). Gross-motor skill acquisition by preschool dance students under self-instruction procedures. *Journal of Applied Behavior Analysis, 37*, 305–322.

Vitaro, F., Brendgen, M., Larose, S., & Tremblay, R. E. (2005). Kindergarten disruptive behaviors, protective factors, and educational achievement by early adulthood. *Journal of Educational Psychology, 97*, 617–629.

Vitaro, F., Gendreau, P. L., Tremblay, R. E., & Oligny, P. (1998). Reactive and proactive aggression differentially predict later conduct problems. *Journal of Child Psychology and Psychiatry and Allied Disciplines, 39*, 377–385.

Volet, S. (1999). Learning across cultures: Appropriateness of knowledge transfer. *International Journal of Educational Research, 31*, 625–643.

Vollmer, T. R., & Hackenberg, T. D. (2001). Reinforcement contingencies and social reinforcement: Some reciprocal relations between basic and applied research. *Journal of Applied Behavior Analysis, 34*, 241–253.

Vosniadou, S. (1991). Conceptual development in astronomy. In S. M. Glynn, R. H. Yeany, & B. K. Britton (Eds.), *The psychology of learning science*. Hillsdale, NJ: Erlbaum.

Vosniadou, S. (1994). Universal and culture-specific properties of children's mental models of the earth. In L. A. Hirschfeld & S. A. Gelman (Eds.), *Mapping the mind: Domain specificity in cognition and culture*. Cambridge, England: Cambridge University Press.

Vosniadou, S., & Brewer, W. F. (1987). Theories of knowledge restructuring in development. *Review of Educational Research, 57*, 51–67.

Voss, J. F. (1987). Learning and transfer in subject-matter learning: A problem-solving model. *International Journal of Educational Research, 11*, 607–622.

Voss, J. F., Greene, T. R., Post, T. A., & Penner, B. D. (1983). Problem-solving skill in the social sciences. In G. H. Bower (Ed.), *The psychology of learning and motivation* (Vol. 17). San Diego, CA: Academic Press.

Voss, J. F., & Schauble, L. (1992). Is interest educationally interesting? An interest-related model of learning. In K. A. Renninger, S. Hidi, & A. Krapp (Eds.), *The role of interest in learning and development*. Mahwah, NJ: Erlbaum.

Vye, N. J., Schwartz, D. L., Bransford, J. D., Barron, B. J., Zech, L., & The Cognition and Technology Group at Vanderbilt. (1998). SMART environments that support monitoring, reflection, and revision. In D. J. Hacker, J. Dunlosky, & A. C. Graesser (Eds.), *Metacognition in educational theory and practice* (pp. 305–346). Mahwah, NJ: Erlbaum.

Vygotsky, L. S. (1962). *Thought and language* (E. Haufmann & G. Vakar, Eds. and Trans.). Cambridge, MA: MIT Press.

Vygotsky, L. S. (1978). *Mind in society: The development of higher psychological processes*. Cambridge, MA: Harvard University Press.

Vygotsky, L. S. (1987). *The collected works of L. S. Vygotsky* (Vol. 3; R. W. Rieber & A. S. Carton, Eds.). New York: Plenum Press.

Vygotsky, L. S. (1997). *Educational psychology* (R. Silverman, Trans.). Boca Raton, FL: St. Lucie Press.

Wade, S. E. (1992). How interest affects learning from text. In K. A. Renninger, S. Hidi, & A. Krapp (Eds.), *The role of interest in learning and development*. Mahwah, NJ: Erlbaum.

Wade-Stein, D., & Kintsch, E. (2004). Summary Street: Interactive computer support for writing. *Cognition and Instruction, 22*, 333–362

Wainryb, C., Brehl, B. A., & Matwin, S. (2005). Being hurt and hurting others: Children's narrative accounts and moral judgments of their own interpersonal conflicts. *Monographs of the Society for Research in Child Development, 70* (3; Serial No. 281).

Walberg, H. J., & Uguroglu, M. (1980). Motivation and educational productivity: Theories, results, and implications. In L. J. Fyans, Jr. (Ed.), *Achievement motivation: Recent trends in theory and research*. New York: Plenum Press.

Walker, E. F. (2002). Adolescent neurodevelopment and psychopathology. *Current Directions in Psychological Science, 11*, 24–28.

Walker, E. N. (2006). Urban high school students' academic communities and their effects on mathematics success. *American Educational Research Journal, 43*, 43–73.

Walker, H. M., Horner, R. H., Sugai, G., Bullis, M., Sprague, J. R., Bricker, D., et al. (1996). Integrated approaches to preventing antisocial behavior patterns among school-age children and youth. *Journal of Emotional and Behavioral Disorders, 4*, 194–209.

Walker, J. M. T. (2001, April). *A cross-sectional study of student motivation, strategy knowledge and strategy use during homework: Implications for research on self-regulated learning*. Paper presented at the annual meeting of the American Educational Research Association, Seattle, WA.

Walker, J. M. T., & Hoover-Dempsey, K. V. (2006). Why research on parental involvement is important to classroom management. In C. M. Evertson & C. S. Weinstein (Eds.), *Handbook of classroom management: Research, practice, and contemporary issues* (pp. 665–684). Mahwah, NJ: Erlbaum.

Walls, T. A., & Little, T. D. (2005). Relations among personal agency, motivation, and school adjustment in early adolescence. *Journal of Educational Psychology, 97*, 23–31.

Walters, G. C., & Grusec, J. E. (1977). *Punishment*. San Francisco: Freeman.

Wang, J., & Lin, E. (2005). Comparative studies on U.S. and Chinese mathematics learning and the implications for standards-based mathematics teaching reform. *Educational Researcher, 34*(5), 3–13.

Wang, Q. (2006). Culture and the development of self-knowledge. *Current Directions in Psychological Science, 15*, 182–187.

Wang, Q., & Ross, M. (2007). Culture and memory. In S. Kitayama & D. Cohen (Eds.), *Handbook of cultural psychology* (pp. 645–667). New York: Guilford Press.

Warren, A. R., & McCloskey, L. A. (1993). Pragmatics: Language in social contexts. In J. Berko Gleason (Ed.), *The development of language* (3rd ed.). New York: Macmillan.

Wasik, B. A., Karweit, N., Burns, L., & Brodsky, E. (1998, April). *Once upon a time: The role of rereading and retelling in storybook reading*. Paper presented at the annual meeting of the American Educational Research Association, San Diego, CA.

Wasley, P. A., Hampel, R. L., & Clark, R. W. (1997). *Kids and school reform*. San Francisco: Jossey-Bass.

Waterhouse, L. (2006). Multiple intelligences, the Mozart effect, and emotional intelligence: A critical review. *Educational Psychologist, 41*, 207–225.

Watson, M., & Battistich, V. (2006). Building and sustaining caring communities. In C. M. Evertson & C. S. Weinstein (Eds.), *Handbook of classroom management: Research, practice, and contemporary issues* (pp. 253–279). Mahwah, NJ: Erlbaum.

Watson, M. W., Andreas, J. B., Fischer, K. W., & Smith, K. (2005). Patterns of risk factors leading to victimization and aggression in children and adolescents. In K. A. Kendall-Tackett & S. M. Giacomoni (Eds.), *Child victimization: Maltreatment, bullying and dating violence, prevention and intervention*. Kingston, NJ: Civic Research Institute.

Watt, H. M. G. (2004). Development of adolescents' self-perceptions, values, and task perceptions according to gender and domain in 7th- through 11th-grade Australian students. *Child Development, 75*, 1556–1574.

Way, N. (1998). *Everyday courage: The lives and stories of urban teenagers*. New York: New York University Press.

Weatherford, J. (1988). *Indian givers: How the Indians of the Americas transformed the world*. New York: Crown.

Weaver, C. A., III, & Kelemen, W. L. (1997). Judgments of learning at delays: Shifts in response patterns or increased metamemory accuracy? *Psychological Science, 8*, 318–321.

Webb, J. T., Meckstroth, E. A., & Tolan, S. S. (1982). *Guiding the gifted child: A practical source for parents and teachers*. Dayton: Ohio Psychology Press.

Webb, N. M. (1989). Peer interaction and learning in small groups. *International Journal of Educational Research, 13*, 21–39.

Webb, N. M., & Farivar, S. (1994). Promoting helping behavior in cooperative small groups in middle school mathematics. *American Educational Research Journal, 31*, 369–395.

Webb, N. M., & Farivar, S. (1999). Developing productive group interaction in middle school mathematics. In A. M. O'Donnell & A. King (Eds.), *Cognitive perspectives on peer learning* (pp. 117–149). Mahwah, NJ: Erlbaum.

Webb, N. M., & Palincsar, A. S. (1996). Group processes in the classroom. In D. C. Berliner & R. C. Calfee (Eds.), *Handbook of educational psychology*. New York: Macmillan.

Webber, J., Scheuermann, B., McCall, C., & Coleman, M. (1993). Research on self-monitoring as a behavior management technique in special education classrooms: A descriptive review. *Remedial and Special Education, 14*(2), 38–56.

Wechsler, D. (2003). *Wechsler Intelligence Scale for Children* (4th ed.). San Antonio, TX: Psychological Corporation.

Weichold, K., Silbereisen, R. K., & Schmitt-Rodermund, E. (2003). Short-term and long-term consequences of early versus late physical maturation in adolescents. In C. Hayward (Ed.), *Gender differences at puberty* (pp. 241–276). Cambridge, England: Cambridge University Press.

Weiner, B. (1984). Principles for a theory of student motivation and their application within an attributional framework. In R. Ames & C. Ames (Eds.), *Research on motivation in education: Vol. 1. Student motivation*. San Diego, CA: Academic Press.

Weiner, B. (1986). *An attributional theory of motivation and emotion*. New York: Springer-Verlag.

Weiner, B. (1994). Ability versus effort revisited: The moral determinants of achievement evaluation and achievement as a moral system. *Educational Psychologist, 29*, 163–172.

Weiner, B. (2000). Intrapersonal and interpersonal theories of motivation from an attributional perspective. *Educational Psychology Review, 12*, 1–14.

Weiner, B., Russell, D., & Lerman, D. (1978). Affective consequences of causal ascriptions. In J. Harvey, W. Ickes, & R. Kidd (Eds.), *New directions in attribution research* (Vol. 2). Mahwah, NJ: Erlbaum.

Weinert, F. E., & Helmke, A. (1995). Learning from wise Mother Nature or Big Brother Instructor: The wrong choice as seen from an educational perspective. *Educational Psychologist, 30*, 135–142.

Weinstein, R. S. (1993). Children's knowledge of differential treatment in school: Implications for motivation. In T. M. Tomlinson (Ed.), *Motivating students to learn: Overcoming barriers to high achievement*. Berkeley, CA: McCutchan.

Weinstein, R. S., Madison, S. M., & Kuklinski, M. R. (1995). Raising expectations in schooling: Obstacles and opportunities for change. *American Educational Research Journal, 32,* 121–159.

Weisgram, E. S., Bigler, R. S., & Liben, L. S. (2007, March). *Altruism, money, power, and family: How values and gender shape occupational judgments and aspirations.* Paper presented at the biennial meeting of the Society for Research in Child Development, Boston.

Weiss, L. H., & Schwarz, J. C. (1996). The relationship between parenting types and older adolescents' personality, academic achievement, adjustment, and substance use. *Child Development, 67,* 2101–2114.

Weissberg, R. P. (1985). Designing effective social problem-solving programs for the classroom. In B. H. Schneider, K. H. Rubin, & J. E. Ledingham (Eds.), *Children's peer relations: Issues in assessment and intervention.* New York: Springer-Verlag.

Welch, G. J. (1985). Contingency contracting with a delinquent and his family. *Journal of Behavior Therapy and Experimental Psychiatry, 16,* 253–259.

Wellman, H. M. (1985). The child's theory of mind: The development of conceptions of cognition. In S. R. Yussen (Ed.), *The growth of reflection in children.* San Diego, CA: Academic Press.

Wellman, H. M. (1990). *The child's theory of mind.* Cambridge, MA: MIT Press.

Wellman, H. M., Cross, D., & Watson, J. (2001). Meta-analysis of theory-of-mind development: The truth about false belief. *Child Development, 72,* 655–684.

Wellman, H. M., & Gelman, S. A. (1998). Acquisition of knowledge. In W. Damon (Series Ed.), D. Kuhn & R. S. Siegler (Vol. Eds.), *Handbook of child psychology: Vol. 2. Cognition, perception, and language* (5th ed.). New York: Wiley.

Wellman, H. M., Phillips, A. T., & Rodriguez, T. (2000). Young children's understanding of perception, desire, and emotion. *Child Development, 71,* 895–912.

Wentzel, K. R. (1999). Social-motivational processes and interpersonal relationships: Implications for understanding motivation at school. *Journal of Educational Psychology, 91,* 76–97.

Wentzel, K. R., & Asher, S. R. (1995). The academic lives of neglected, rejected, popular, and controversial children. *Child Development, 66,* 754–763.

Wentzel, K. R., Filisetti, L., & Looney, L. (2007). Adolescent prosocial behavior: The role of self-processes and contextual cues. *Child Development, 78,* 895–910.

Wentzel, K. R., & Looney, L. (2007). Socialization in school settings. In J. E. Grusec & P. D. Hastings (Eds.), *Handbook of socialization: Theory and research* (pp. 382–403). New York: Guilford Press.

Wentzel, K. R., & Wigfield, A. (1998). Academic and social motivational influences on students' academic performance. *Educational Psychology Review, 10,* 155–175.

Werner, E. E. (1995). Resilience in development. *Current Directions in Psychological Science, 4,* 81–85.

Werner, E. E., & Smith, R. S. (1982). *Vulnerable but invincible: A longitudinal study of resilient children.* New York: McGraw-Hill.

Werner, E. E., & Smith, R. S. (2001). *Journeys from childhood to midlife: Risk, resilience, and recovery.* Ithaca, NY: Cornell University Press.

West, R. F., & Stanovich, K. E. (1991). The incidental acquisition of information from reading. *Psychological Science, 2,* 325–329.

White, A. G., & Bailey, J. S. (1990). Reducing disruptive behaviors of elementary physical education students with sit and watch. *Journal of Applied Behavior Analysis, 23,* 353–359.

White, B. Y., & Frederiksen, J. R. (1998). Inquiry, modeling, and metacognition: Making science accessible to all students. *Cognition and Instruction, 16,* 3–118.

White, B. Y., & Frederiksen, J. (2005). A theoretical framework and approach for fostering metacognitive development. *Educational Psychologist, 40,* 211–223.

White, J. J., & Rumsey, S. (1994). Teaching for understanding in a third-grade geography lesson. In J. Brophy (Ed.), *Advances in research on teaching: Vol. 4. Case studies of teaching and learning in social studies.* Greenwich, CT: JAI Press.

White, R. (1959). Motivation reconsidered: The concept of competence. *Psychological Review, 66,* 297–333.

White, R., & Cunningham, A. M. (1991). *Ryan White: My own story.* New York: Signet.

Whitesell, N. R., Mitchell, C. M., Kaufman, C. E., Spicer, P., & the Voices of Indian Teens Project Team. (2006). Developmental trajectories of personal and collective self-concept among American Indian adolescents. *Child Development, 77,* 1487–1503.

Whitley, B. E., Jr., & Frieze, I. H. (1985). Children's causal attributions for success and failure in achievement settings: A meta-analysis. *Journal of Educational Psychology, 77,* 608–616.

Wideen, M., Mayer-Smith, J., & Moon, B. (1998). A critical analysis of the research on learning to teach: Making the case for an ecological perspective on inquiry. *Review of Educational Research, 68,* 130–178.

Wigfield, A. (1994). Expectancy-value theory of achievement motivation: A developmental perspective. *Educational Psychology Review, 6,* 49–78.

Wigfield, A., Byrnes, J. P., & Eccles, J. S. (2006). Development during early and middle adolescence. In P. A. Alexander & P. H. Winne (Eds.), *Handbook of educational psychology* (2nd ed., pp. 87–113). Mahwah, NJ: Erlbaum.

Wigfield, A., & Eccles, J. (1992). The development of achievement task values: A theoretical analysis. *Developmental Review, 12,* 265–310.

Wigfield, A., & Eccles, J. (2000). Expectancy-value theory of achievement motivation. *Contemporary Educational Psychology, 25,* 68–81.

Wigfield, A., & Eccles, J. (2002). The development of competence beliefs, expectancies for success, and achievement values from childhood to adolescence. In A. Wigfield & J. Eccles (Eds.), *Development of achievement motivation* (pp. 91–120). San Diego, CA: Academic Press.

Wigfield, A., Eccles, J., Mac Iver, D., Reuman, D., & Midgley, C. (1991). Transitions at early adolescence: Changes in children's domain-specific self-perceptions and general self-esteem across the transition to junior high school. *Developmental Psychology, 27,* 552–565.

Wigfield, A., Eccles, J. S., & Pintrich, P. R. (1996). Development between the ages of 11 and 25. In D. C. Berliner & R. C. Calfee (Eds.), *Handbook of educational psychology.* New York: Macmillan.

Wigfield, A., & Meece, J. L. (1988). Math anxiety in elementary and secondary school students. *Journal of Educational Psychology, 80,* 210–216.

Wiggins, G., & McTighe, J. (1998). *Understanding by design.* Alexandria, VA: Association for Supervision and Curriculum Development.

Wilder, A. A., & Williams, J. P. (2001). Students with severe learning disabilities can learn higher order comprehension skills. *Journal of Educational Psychology, 93,* 268–278.

Wiles, J., & Bondi, J. (2001). *The new American middle school: Educating preadolescents in an era of change.* Upper Saddle River, NJ: Merrill/Prentice Hall.

Wiley, J., & Bailey, J. (2006). Effects of collaboration and argumentation on learning from Web pages. In A. M. O'Donnell, C. E. Hmelo-Silver, & G. Erkens (Eds.), *Collaborative learning, reasoning, and technology* (pp. 297–321). Mahwah, NJ: Erlbaum.

Wilkinson, L. D., & Frazer, L. H. (1990, April). *Fine-tuning dropout prediction through discriminant analysis: The ethnic factor.* Paper presented at the annual meeting of the American Educational Research Association, Boston.

Willard, N. E. (2007). *Cyberbullying and cyberthreats: Responding to the challenge of online social aggression, threats, and distress.* Champaign, IL: Research Press.

Williams, K. M. (2001a). "Frontin' it": Schooling, violence, and relationships in the 'hood. In J. N. Burstyn, G. Bender, R. Casella, H. W. Gordon, D. P. Guerra, K. V. Luschen, et al., *Preventing violence in schools: A challenge to American democracy* (pp. 95–108). Mahwah, NJ: Erlbaum.

Williams, K. M. (2001b). What derails peer mediation? In J. N. Burstyn, G. Bender, R. Casella, H. W. Gordon, D. P. Guerra, K. V. Luschen, et al., *Preventing violence in schools: A challenge to American democracy* (pp. 199–208). Mahwah, NJ: Erlbaum.

Willingham, D. T. (2004). *Cognition: The thinking animal* (2nd ed.). Upper Saddle River, NJ: Prentice Hall.

Wilson, B. L., & Corbett, H. D. (2001). *Listening to urban kids: School reform and the teachers they want.* Albany: State University of New York Press.

Wilson, C. C., Piazza, C. C., & Nagle, R. (1990). Investigation of the effect of consistent and inconsistent behavioral examples upon children's donation behaviors. *Journal of Genetic Psychology, 151,* 361–376.

Wilson, P. T., & Anderson, R. C. (1986). What they don't know will hurt them: The role of prior knowledge in comprehension. In J. Orasanu (Ed.), *Reading comprehension: From research to practice.* Mahwah, NJ: Erlbaum.

Wimmer, H., & Perner, J. (1983). Beliefs about beliefs: Representation and constraining function of wrong beliefs in young children's understanding of deception. *Cognition, 13,* 103–128.

Wine, J. D. (1980). Cognitive-attentional theory of test anxiety. In I. G. Sarason (Ed.), *Test anxiety: Theory, research, and applications.* Mahwah, NJ: Erlbaum.

Winn, W. (1991). Learning from maps and diagrams. *Educational Psychology Review, 3,* 211–247.

Winn, W. (2002). Current trends in educational technology research: The study of learning environments. *Educational Psychology Review, 14,* 331–351.

Winne, P. H. (1995a). Inherent details in self-regulated learning. *Educational Psychologist, 30,* 173–187.

Winne, P. H. (1995b). Self-regulation is ubiquitous but its forms vary with knowledge. *Educational Psychologist, 30,* 223–228.

Winne, P. H., & Hadwin, A. F. (1998). Studying as self-regulated learning. In D. J. Hacker, J. Dunlosky, & A. C. Graesser (Eds.), *Metacognition in educational theory and practice* (pp. 277–304). Mahwah, NJ: Erlbaum.

Winner, E. (1988). *The point of words.* Cambridge, MA: Harvard University Press.

Winner, E. (2000a). Giftedness: Current theory and research. *Current Directions in Psychological Science, 9,* 153–156.

Winner, E. (2000b). The origins and ends of giftedness. *American Psychologist, 55,* 159–169.

Winograd, P., & Jones, D. L. (1992). The use of portfolios in performance assessment. *New Directions for Education Reform, 1*(2), 37–50.

Winsler, A., & Naglieri, J. (2003). Overt and covert verbal problem-solving strategies: Developmental trends in use, awareness, and relations with task performance in children aged 5 to 17. *Child Development, 74,* 659–678.

Wise, B. W., & Olson, R. K. (1998). Studies of computer-aided remediation for reading disabilities. In C. Hulme & R. M. Joshi (Eds.), *Reading and spelling: Development and disorders.* Mahwah, NJ: Erlbaum.

Wisner Fries, A. B., & Pollak, S. D. (2007). Emotion processing and the developing brain. In D. Coch, K. W. Fischer, & G. Dawson (Eds.), *Human behavior, learning, and the developing brain: Typical development* (pp. 329–361). New York: Guilford Press.

Witmer, S. (1996). Making peace, the Navajo way. *Tribal College Journal, 8,* 24–27.

Wittrock, M. C. (1994). Generative science teaching. In P. J. Fensham, R. F. Gunstone, & R. T. White (Eds.), *The content of science: A constructivist approach to its teaching and learning.* London: Falmer Press.

Wixson, K. K. (1984). Level of importance of post-questions and children's learning from text. *American Educational Research Journal, 21,* 419–433.

Wixted, J. T. (2005). A theory about why we forget what we once knew. *Current Directions in Psychological Science, 14,* 6–9.

Wlodkowski, R. J. (1978). *Motivation and teaching: A practical guide.* Washington, DC: National Education Association.

Wlodkowski, R. J., & Ginsberg, M. B. (1995). *Diversity and motivation: Culturally responsive teaching.* San Francisco: Jossey-Bass.

Wodtke, K. H., Harper, F., & Schommer, M. (1989). How standardized is school testing? An exploratory observational study of standardized group testing in kindergarten. *Educational Evaluation and Policy Analysis, 11,* 223–235.

Woloshyn, V. E., Pressley, M., & Schneider, W. (1992). Elaborative-interrogation and prior-knowledge effects on learning of facts. *Journal of Educational Psychology, 84,* 115–124.

Wolters, C. A. (1998). Self-regulated learning and college students' regulation of motivation. *Journal of Educational Psychology, 90,* 224–235.

Wolters, C. A. (2003). Regulation of motivation: Evaluating an underemphasized aspect of self-regulated learning. *Educational Psychologist, 38,* 189–205.

Wolters, C. A., & Rosenthal, H. (2000). The relation between students' motivational beliefs and their use of motivational regulation strategies. *International Journal of Educational Research, 33,* 801–820.

Wong, B. Y. L. (1985). Self-questioning instructional research: A review. *Review of Educational Research, 55,* 227–268.

Wood, D., Bruner, J. S., & Ross, G. (1976). The role of tutoring in problem-solving. *Journal of Child Psychology and Psychiatry, 17,* 89–100.

Wood, D., Wood, H., Ainsworth, S., & O'Malley, C. (1995). On becoming a tutor: Toward an ontogenetic model. *Cognition and Instruction, 13,* 565–581.

Wood, E., Willoughby, T., McDermott, C., Motz, M., Kaspar, V., & Ducharme, M. J. (1999). Developmental differences in study behavior. *Journal of Educational Psychology, 91,* 527–536.

Woolfe, T., Want, S. C., & Siegal, M. (2002). Signposts to development: Theory of mind in deaf children. *Child Development, 73,* 768–778.

Woolfolk, A. E., & Brooks, D. M. (1985). The influence of teachers' nonverbal behaviors on students' perceptions and performances. *Elementary School Journal, 85,* 513–528.

Woolfolk Hoy, A., Davis, H., & Pape, S. J. (2006). Teacher knowledge and beliefs. In P. A. Alexander & P. H. Winne (Eds.), *Handbook of educational psychology* (2nd ed., pp. 715–737). Mahwah, NJ: Erlbaum.

Woolley, J. D. (1995). The fictional mind: Young children's understanding of pretense, imagination, and dreams. *Developmental Review, 15,* 172–211.

Wright, E. J. (2007, March). *The negative self-focus trap: Emerging self-focused emotion regulation and increased depression risk.* Paper presented at the biennial meeting of the Society for Research in Child Development, Boston.

Wright, L. S. (1982). The use of logical consequences in counseling children. *School Counselor, 30,* 37–49.

Wright, W. E. (2006). A catch-22 for language learners. *Educational Leadership, 64*(3), 22–27.

Wynne, E. A. (1990). Improving pupil discipline and character. In O. C. Moles (Ed.), *Student discipline strategies: Research and practice.* Albany: State University of New York Press.

Yates, M., & Youniss, J. (1996). A developmental perspective on community service in adolescence. *Social Development, 5,* 85–111.

Yau, J., & Smetana, J. G. (2003). Conceptions of moral, social-conventional, and personal events among Chinese preschoolers in Hong Kong. *Child Development, 74,* 647–658.

Yell, M. L., Robinson, T. R., & Drasgow, E. (2001). Cognitive behavior modification. In T. J. Zirpoli & K. J. Melloy, *Behavior management: Applications for teachers* (3rd ed., pp. 200–246). Upper Saddle River, NJ: Merrill/Prentice Hall.

Yeung, R. S., & Leadbeater, B. J. (2007, March). *Peer victimization and emotional and behavioral problems in adolescence: The moderating effect of adult emotional support.* Paper presented at the biennial meeting of the Society for Research in Child Development, Boston.

Yip, T., & Fuligni, A. J. (2002). Daily variation in ethnic identity, ethnic behaviors, and psychological well-being among American adolescents of Chinese descent. *Child Development, 73,* 1557–1572.

Youniss, J., & Yates, M. (1999). Youth service and moral-civic identity: A case for everyday morality. *Educational Psychology Review, 11,* 361–376.

Yuker, H. E. (Ed.). (1988). *Attitudes toward persons with disabilities.* New York: Springer.

Zahn-Waxler, C., Friedman, R. J., Cole, P., Mizuta, I., & Hiruma, N. (1996). Japanese and United States preschool children's responses to conflict and distress. *Child Development, 67,* 2462–2477.

Zahn-Waxler, C., Mayfield, A., Radke-Yarrow, M., McKnew, D. H., Cytryn, L., & Davenport, Y. B. (1988). A follow-up investigation of offspring of parents with bipolar disorder. *American Journal of Psychiatry, 145,* 506–509.

Zahn-Waxler, C., Radke-Yarrow, M., Wagner, E., & Chapman, M. (1992). Development of concern for others. *Developmental Psychology, 28,* 126–136.

Zahorik, J. A. (1994, April). *Making things interesting.* Paper presented at the annual meeting of the American Educational Research Association, New Orleans, LA.

Zajonc, R. B. (1980). Feeling and thinking: Preferences need no inferences. *American Psychologist, 35,* 151–175.

Zambo, D. (2003, April). *Thinking about reading: Talking to children with learning disabilities.* Paper presented at the annual meeting of the American Educational Research Association, Chicago.

Zambo, D., & Brem, S. K. (2004). Emotion and cognition in students who struggle to read: New insights and ideas. *Reading Psychology, 25,* 1–16.

Zeidner, M. (1998). *Test anxiety: The state of the art.* New York: Plenum Press.

Zeidner, M., Roberts, R. D., & Matthews, G. (2002). Can emotional intelligence be schooled? A critical review. *Educational Psychologist, 37,* 215–231.

Zeitz, C. M. (1994). Expert-novice differences in memory, abstraction, and reasoning in the domain of literature. *Cognition and Instruction, 12,* 277–312.

Zelazo, P. D., Müller, U., Frye, D., & Marcovitch, S. (2003). The development of executive function in early childhood. *Monographs of the Society for Research in Child Development, 68*(3), Serial No. 274.

Zeldin, A. L., & Pajares, F. (2000). Against the odds: Self-efficacy beliefs of women in mathematical, scientific, and technological careers. *American Educational Research Journal, 37,* 215–246.

Zelli, A., Dodge, K. A., Lochman, J. E., & Laird, R. D. (1999). The distinction between beliefs legitimizing aggression and deviant processing of social cues: Testing measurement validity and the hypothesis that biased processing mediates the effects of beliefs on aggression. *Journal of Personality and Social Psychology, 77,* 150–166.

Zhang, L.-F., & Sternberg, R. J. (2006). *The nature of intellectual styles.* Mahwah, NJ: Erlbaum.

Ziegert, D. I., Kistner, J. A., Castro, R., & Robertson, B. (2001). Longitudinal study of young children's responses to challenging achievement situations. *Child Development, 72,* 609 624.

Zigler, E. F., & Finn-Stevenson, M. (1992). Applied developmental psychology. In M. H. Bornstein & M. E. Lamb (Eds.), *Developmental psychology: An advanced textbook.* Mahwah, NJ: Erlbaum.

Zigler, E. F., & Seitz, V. (1982). Social policy and intelligence. In R. J. Sternberg (Ed.), *Handbook of human intelligence* (pp. 586–641). Cambridge, England: Cambridge University Press.

Zimmerman, B. J. (1998). Developing self-fulfilling cycles of academic regulation: An analysis of exemplary instructional models. In D. H. Schunk & B. J. Zimmerman (Eds.), *Self-regulated learning: From teaching to self-reflective practice* (pp. 1–19). New York: Guilford Press.

Zimmerman, B. J., Bandura, A., & Martinez-Pons, M. (1992). Self-motivation for academic attainment: The role of self-efficacy beliefs and personal goal setting. *American Educational Research Journal, 29,* 663–676.

Zimmerman, B. J., & Campillo, M. (2003). Motivating self-regulated problem solvers. In J. E. Davidson & R. J. Sternberg (Eds.), *The psychology of problem solving* (pp. 233–262). Cambridge, England: Cambridge University Press.

Zimmerman, B. J., & Risemberg, R. (1997). Self-regulatory dimensions of academic learning and motivation. In G. D. Phye (Ed.), *Handbook of academic learning: Construction of knowledge.* San Diego, CA: Academic Press.

Zimmerman, B. J., & Schunk, D. H. (2004). Self-regulating intellectual processes and outcomes: A social cognitive perspective. In D. Y. Dai & R. J. Sternberg (Eds.), *Motivation, emotion, and cognition: Integrative perspectives on intellectual functioning and development* (pp. 323–349). Mahwah, NJ: Erlbaum.

Zirpoli, T. J., & Melloy, K. J. (2001). *Behavior management: Applications for teachers.* Upper Saddle River, NJ: Merrill/Prentice Hall.

Zook, K. B. (1991). Effects of analogical processes on learning and misrepresentation. *Educational Psychology Review, 3,* 41–72.

Zook, K. B., & Di Vesta, F. J. (1991). Instructional analogies and conceptual misrepresentations. *Journal of Educational Psychology, 83,* 246–252.

SUBJECT INDEX

Treatment groups, defined, 10
Triarchic model of intelligence, 160–161, 161n
Tutoring. *See* Peer tutoring

Universals (in development), defined, 138

Validity
   of assessment, 364, 366, 367
   content validity, 364, 366, 372, 374, 393
   defined, 364
   of informal assessment, 369, 376
   of paper-pencil assessment, 372, 376
   of performance assessment, 372–374, 376
   of portfolios, 389
   of standardized achievement tests, 393
Values
   cultural factors and, 211
   defined, 197
   expectancy-value theory, 185
   mainstream Western culture and, 71
   modeling and, 72
   moral values, 157, 260
   motivation and, 197–198, 221–222
Variables
   experimental studies and, 10
   person variables, 80
   separating and controlling, 10, 11,
      152–153, 154, 157, 166–167, 174
Verbal behaviors, 85–86, 368

Verbal cues, 334–335
Verbal interactions, 157, 307, 308–309, 325
Verbal mediators, defined, 48
Verbal reasoning, 119
Verbal reprimands, 338
Verbal versus visual learning, 164
Vicarious punishment, defined, 66
Vicarious reinforcement
   defined, 66
   effects of, 67
Violence. *See also* Aggression
   approaches to, 347–351
   beliefs about, 252
   early warning signs of violent
      behavior, 349
   modeling and, 65
   socioeconomic status and, 80
Visual aids, 289
Visual imagery
   defined, 32
   information processing theory and, 19
   as meaningful learning, 31, 32–33
   promoting effective cognitive processes
      and, 20, 21, 46
   study strategies and, 101
Visual versus verbal learning, 164
Vygotsky, Lev
   cognitive development and, 136
   internalization and, 144, 174

language development and, 143
   play activities and, 171
   scaffolding and, 176
   social interaction and, 143–144, 267
   sociocultural theory and, 20, 136, 137
   zone of proximal development, 146, 374

Waiting versus interrupting, 309
Wait time
   cultural factors and, 292, 309
   defined, 46
   promoting effective cognitive processes
      with, 46
   questions and, 46, 292
Web sites
   information gathering and, 301
   standards and, 284
Weiner, Bernard, 186
Where in the World is Carmen Sandiego?, 304
Wigfield, Allan, 185
Withitness
   classroom environment and, 325, 327
   defined, 325
Working memory
   anxiety and, 212–213
   attention and, 26, 44
   capacity of, 27, 39, 41–42, 47, 115, 147
   central executive and, 105

as component of memory, 25, 27
   components of, 27n
   defined, 27
   duration of, 27, 40–41
   information processing theory and, 19
   rehearsal and, 27
Worldviews
   accommodating cultural differences in, 94
   defined, 75
   formal operational reasoning skills
      and, 157
World Wide Web, 301
Written communication, parent
   communication, 328–329

Yahoo, 301

Zimmerman, Barry, 19, 186
Zone of proximal development (ZPD)
   defined, 146
   diversity of learners and, 168
   dynamic assessment and, 374
   instructional strategies and, 307
   on-task behavior and, 325
z-scores, defined, 409